HMH | into Literature™

TEACHER'S EDITION

GRADE 10

Program Consultants:
Kylene Beers
Martha Hougen
Elena Izquierdo
Carol Jago
Erik Palmer
Robert E. Probst

Front Cover Photo Credits: (outer ring): ©Roman Voloshyn/Shutterstock, (inner ring): ©Javier Martin/Shutterstock, (c) ©Carrie Garcia/Houghton Mifflin Harcourt, (c overlay): ©Eyewire/Getty Images, (bc overlay): ©elenamiv/Shutterstock

Back Cover Photo Credits: (Units 1-6): ©Paul Bradbury/Caiaimage/Getty Images; ©Eclipse Images/iStock/Getty Images Plus/Getty Images; ©Krzysztof Wiktor/Adobe Stock; ©Tonktiti/Shutterstock; ©Tayfun Cokun/Anadolu Agency/Getty Images; ©Anthony J Hall/iStock/Getty Images Plus/Getty Images

Printed in the U.S.A.

ISBN 978-1-328-47488-9

2 3 4 5 6 7 8 9 10 0690 27 26 25 24 23 22 21 20 19

4500752975   B C D E F G

Teacher's Edition Table of Contents

PROGRAM CONSULTANTS

Kylene Beers

Nationally known lecturer and author on reading and literacy; coauthor with Robert Probst of *Disrupting Thinking, Notice & Note: Strategies for Close Reading,* and *Reading Nonfiction*; former president of the National Council of Teachers of English. Dr. Beers is the author of *When Kids Can't Read: What Teachers Can Do* and coeditor of *Adolescent Literacy: Turning Promise into Practice*, as well as articles in the *Journal of Adolescent and Adult Literacy*. Former editor of *Voices from the Middle,* she is the 2001 recipient of NCTE's Richard W. Halle Award, given for outstanding contributions to middle school literacy. She recently served as Senior Reading Researcher at the Comer School Development Program at Yale University as well as Senior Reading Advisor to Secondary Schools for the Reading and Writing Project at Teachers College.

Martha Hougen

National consultant, presenter, researcher, and author. Areas of expertise include differentiating instruction for students with learning difficulties, including those with learning disabilities and dyslexia; and teacher and leader preparation improvement. Dr. Hougen has taught at the middle school through graduate levels. In addition to peer-reviewed articles, curricular documents, and presentations, Dr. Hougen has published two college textbooks: *The Fundamentals of Literacy Instruction and Assessment Pre-K–6* (2012) and *The Fundamentals of Literacy Instruction and Assessment 6–12* (2014). Dr. Hougen has supported Educator Preparation Program reforms while working at the Meadows Center for Preventing Educational Risk at The University of Texas at Austin and at the CEEDAR Center, University of Florida.

Elena Izquierdo

Nationally recognized teacher educator and advocate for English language learners. Dr. Izquierdo is a linguist by training, with a Ph.D. in Applied Linguistics and Bilingual Education from Georgetown University. She has served on various state and national boards working to close the achievement gaps for bilingual students and English language learners. Dr. Izquierdo is a member of the Hispanic Leadership Council, which supports Hispanic students and educators at both the state and federal levels. She served as Vice President on the Executive Board of the National Association of Bilingual Education and as Publications and Professional Development Chair.

Carol Jago

Teacher of English with 32 years of experience at Santa Monica High School in California; author and nationally known lecturer; former president of the National Council of Teachers of English. Ms. Jago currently serves as Associate Director of the California Reading and Literature Project at UCLA. With expertise in standards assessment and secondary education, Ms. Jago is the author of numerous books on education, including *With Rigor for All* and *Papers, Papers, Papers*, and is active with the California Association of Teachers of English, editing its scholarly journal *California English* since 1996. Ms. Jago also served on the planning committee for the 2009 NAEP Reading Framework and the 2011 NAEP Writing Framework.

Erik Palmer

Veteran teacher and education consultant based in Denver, Colorado. Author of *Well Spoken: Teaching Speaking to All Students* and *Digitally Speaking: How to Improve Student Presentations with Technology*. His areas of focus include improving oral communication, promoting technology in classroom presentations, and updating instruction through the use of digital tools. He holds a bachelor's degree from Oberlin College and a master's degree in curriculum and instruction from the University of Colorado.

Robert E. Probst

Nationally respected authority on the teaching of literature; Professor Emeritus of English Education at Georgia State University. Dr. Probst's publications include numerous articles in *English Journal* and *Voices from the Middle*, as well as professional texts including (as coeditor) *Adolescent Literacy: Turning Promise into Practice* and (as coauthor with Kylene Beers) *Disrupting Thinking, Notice & Note: Strategies for Close Reading*, and *Reading Nonfiction*. He regularly speaks at national and international conventions including those of the International Literacy Association, the National Council of Teachers of English, the Association for Supervision and Curriculum Development, and the National Association of Secondary School Principals. He has served NCTE in various leadership roles, including the Conference on English Leadership Board of Directors, the Commission on Reading, and column editor of the NCTE journal *Voices from the Middle*. He is also the 2004 recipient of the CEL Exemplary Leader Award.

Lead and Learn

Students who communicate...

- **Listen** actively
- **Present** effectively
- **Expand** vocabulary
- **Question** appropriately
- **Engage** constructively

SPEAKING AND
LISTENING TASK

Create a Podcast

You will now adapt your research report as a podcast that your classmates can listen and respond to. You also will listen to their podcasts, ask questions to better understand their ideas, and help them improve their work.

Go to **Using Media in a Presentation** in the **Listening and Speaking Studio** for help planning and crafting your presentation.

1 Adapt Your Report as a Podcast

Review your research report, and use the chart below to guide you as you adapt your report and follow instructions for creating a script and effects for your podcast. Ensure that the vocabulary, language, and tone of your podcast are appropriate for your audience. Also, make sure to link your ideas clearly using connecting words to transition smoothly from one idea to the next.

Podcast Planning Chart

Title and Introduction	How will you revise your title and introduction to capture the listener's attention? Is there a catchier way to state your thesis? Consider putting your thesis in the form of a question that you can then answer.
Audience	Who is your audience? What information will your audience already know? What information can you exclude? What should you add?
Effective Language and Organization	Which parts of your report should be simplified? What can you change to strike a more informal voice and tone? Make sure you use standard language conventions so your ideas are clear to listeners.
Sound	Think about whether you want to begin your podcast with music or sound effects. What kind of music is appropriate to the topic? Are there sound effects you ca[...] that will help you create [...]

SPEAKING AND LISTENING STUDIO

What Makes a Dynamic Presentation?

This Speaker was assigned to give an informal demonstration of the verbal and noverbal elements of speech delivery. View each segment of her presentation and respond to the questions.

Question and Respond

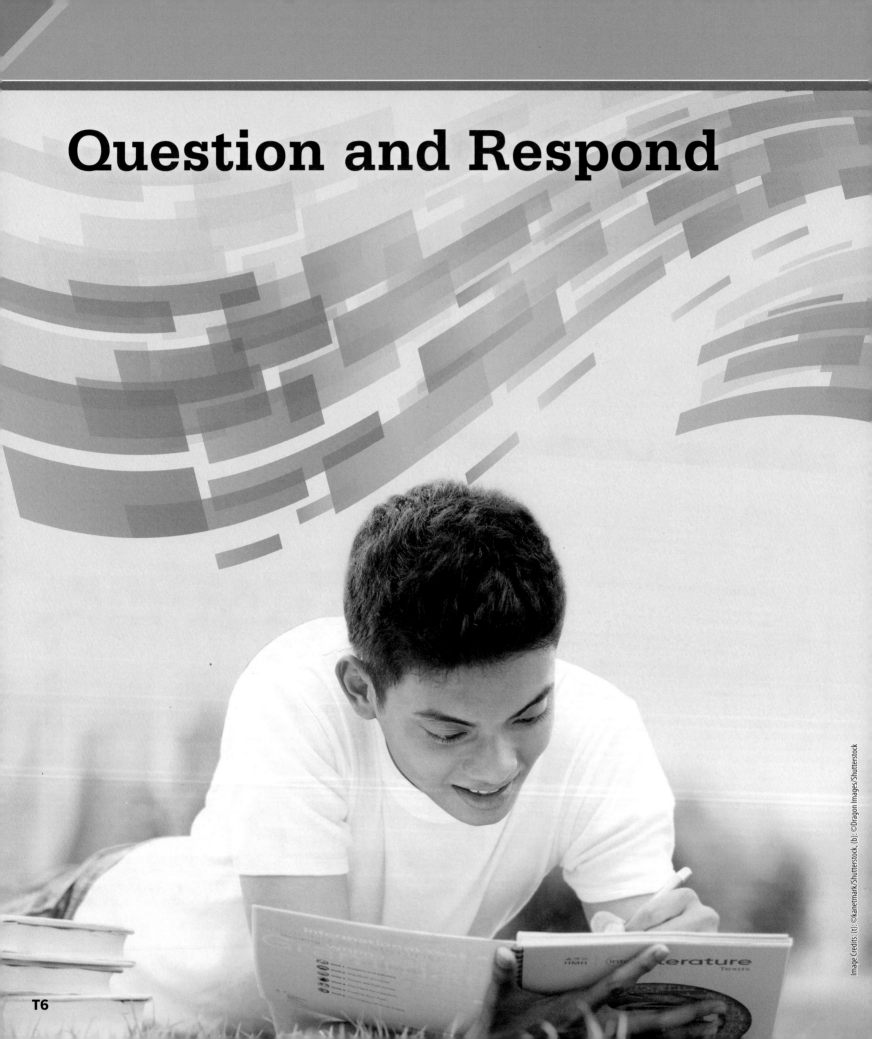

Students who read...

- **Acquire** fluency
- **Choose** independently
- **Monitor** understanding
- **Annotate** and use evidence
- **Write** and discuss within and across texts

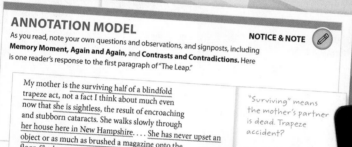

ANNOTATION MODEL

NOTICE & NOTE

As you read, note your own questions and observations, and signposts, including
Memory Moment, Again and Again, and **Contrasts and Contradictions.** Here
is one reader's response to the first paragraph of "The Leap."

My mother is the surviving half of a blindfold
trapeze act, not a fact I think about much even
now that she is sightless, the result of encroaching
and stubborn cataracts. She walks slowly through
her house here in New Hampshire.... She has never upset an
object or as much as brushed a magazine onto the
floor. She has never lost her balance or bumped
into a closet door left carelessly open.

"Surviving" means
the mother's partner
is dead. Trapeze
accident?

"The mother is
blind, but has never
bumped into anything"
Contradiction?

HMH DIGITAL LIBRARY

The Time Machine

An Invention

H. G. Wells

UNIT 2

THE STRUGGLE FOR FREEDOM

? ESSENTIAL QUESTION:

How do people
find freedom
in the midst of
oppression?

> If there is no struggle, there is no progress.
>
> Frederick Douglass

ACADEMIC VOCABULARY

Academic Vocabulary words are words you use when you discuss and write about texts. In this
unit you will practice and learn five words.

☑ decline   ☐ enable   ☐ impose   ☐ integrate   ☐ reveal

Study the Word Network to learn more about the word decline.

SYNONYMS
sink, weaken

DEFINITION
to fall apart or
deteriorate slowly

ANTONYMS
grow, strengthen

decline
(dĭ-klīn´)
v.

CLARIFYING EXAMPLE
Feudalism declined as more
peasants took paying jobs
as soldiers.

WORD ROOT
Comes from the Latin word
declinare, meaning "to turn
away"

RELATED WORDS
declension, descent

Write and Discuss Discuss the completed Word Network with a partner, making sure to
talk through all of the boxes until you both understand the word, its synonyms, antonyms,
and related forms. Then, fill out a Word Network for each of the four remaining words. Use a
dictionary or online resource to help you complete the activity.

Go online to access the Word Networks.

RESPOND TO THE ESSENTIAL QUESTION

In this unit, you will explore the universal desire for freedom. As you
read, you will revisit the **Essential Question** and gather your ideas
about it in the **Response Log.** At the end of the unit, you will have the
opportunity to write a **research report** about the difficulties people
have as they struggle for freedom. Filling out the Response Log will
help you prepare for this writing task.

You can also go online to access the Response Log.

82   Unit 2

The Struggle For Freedom   83

Connect
Reading and Writing

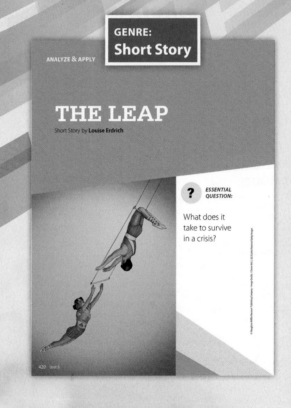

ANALYZE & APPLY

GENRE:
Short Story

THE LEAP

Short Story by **Louise Erdrich**

? ESSENTIAL QUESTION:

What does it take to survive in a crisis?

420   Unit 5

ANALYZE & APPLY

GENRE:
History Writing

from
HIDDEN FIGURES

History Writing by **Margot Lee Shetterly**

? ESSENTIAL QUESTION:

How do people find freedom in the midst of oppression?

Students who explore genre…

- **Analyze** features

- **Understand** effects of authors' choices

- **Emulate** craft

- **Use** mentor texts

- **Synthesize** ideas

QUICK START

What do you know about opportunities that were once closed to African Americans, women, or other minorities? Name some jobs a woman or an African American might not have been able to apply for in the past.

ANALYZE TEXT STRUCTURE

Authors use a variety of **text structures.** These include thesis or main idea and details; cause and effect; problem and solution; and chronology, or time order. Most historical texts are a combination of chronology, main idea, and cause and effect. Sometimes these organizational designs are intertwined.

As you read, keep track of the important events, the order in which they happen, any causal relationships, and key ideas.

TEXT STRUCTURES	EXAMPLE FROM *HIDDEN FIGURES*
Narration of an Event	By 1943, the American aircraft industry was the largest, most productive, and most sophisticated in the world, making three times more planes than the Germans, who were fighting on the other side of the war.
Cause and Effect	But in the spring of 1943, with World War II in full swing and many men off serving in the military . . . employers were beginning to hire women to do jobs that had once belonged only to men.
Thesis/Important Ideas	The NACA's mission was . . . to help the United States develop the most powerful and efficient airplanes in the world. . . . World leaders felt that the country that ruled the skies would win the war.

MAKE PREDICTIONS

To read historical text effectively, it is important to **make predictions** as you read. A prediction is an informed guess about what the author is about to say.

- Before you read, use text features such as the title, headings, and background information to make initial predictions about the text.

- As you read, use text structure as well as genre characteristics to correct your initial predictions and to predict what you will read about next.

- After you read, confirm your predictions. They may not always be correct. If the author surprises you, your predictions will help you evaluate and remember the unexpected information.

Use a chart like this one to help you make and evaluate your predictions:

WHAT I KNOW	MY PREDICTION	WAS IT CORRECT?

Hidden Figures 105

GET R

GENRE ELEMENTS: HISTORY WRITING

- uses chronological order

- is a form of informational text

- includes evidence to support ideas

- contains text features to help the reader absorb and retain information

GENRE ELEMENTS: HISTORY WRITING

- uses chronological order
- is a form of informational text
- includes evidence to support ideas
- contains text features to help the reader absorb and retain information

WRITING STUDIO

Ways to Organize Reasons and Evidence

Every argument must include reasons and evidence to support a claim. There are several effective ways you can organize that support. Check out some of those ways here.

Read the following techniques that will help you achieve cohesion, or coherence, in your writing.

Order of Importance

Least to most important

Claim: Homewood must switch from a volunteer fire department to a full-time fire department

COLLABORATE & COMPARE

**GENRE:
Poem**

POEM

THE JOURNEY

by **Mary Oliver**
pages 555–557

COMPARE THEME AND MAIN IDEA

Now that you've read the excerpt from *The Cruelest Journey: 600 Miles to Timbuktu*, read "The Journey" and consider how this poem explores some of the same ideas. As you read, think about how "The Journey" relates to the idea of a journey or quest as well to your own experiences. After you are finished, you will collaborate with a small group on a final project that involves an analysis of both texts.

? ESSENTIAL QUESTION:

What drives us to take on a challenge?

TRAVEL WRITING

from

THE CRUELEST JOURNEY: 600 MILES TO TIMBUKTU

by **Kira Salak**
pages 539–547

552 Unit 6

Craft and Communicate

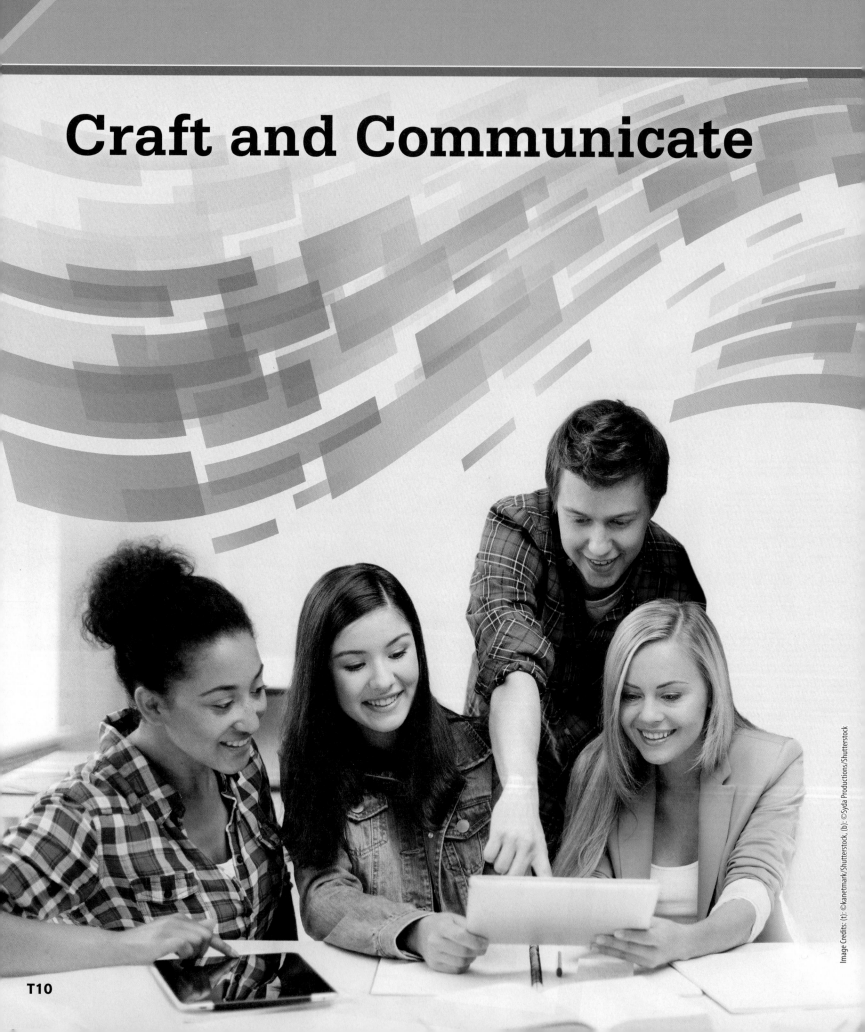

Students who compose...

- **Inform,** argue, and connect
- **Create** in a literary genre
- **Imitate** mentor texts
- **Apply** conventions
- **Use** process and partners

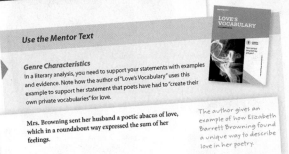

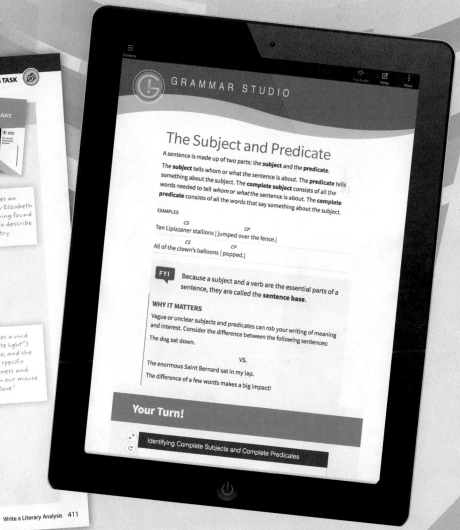

Explore and Research

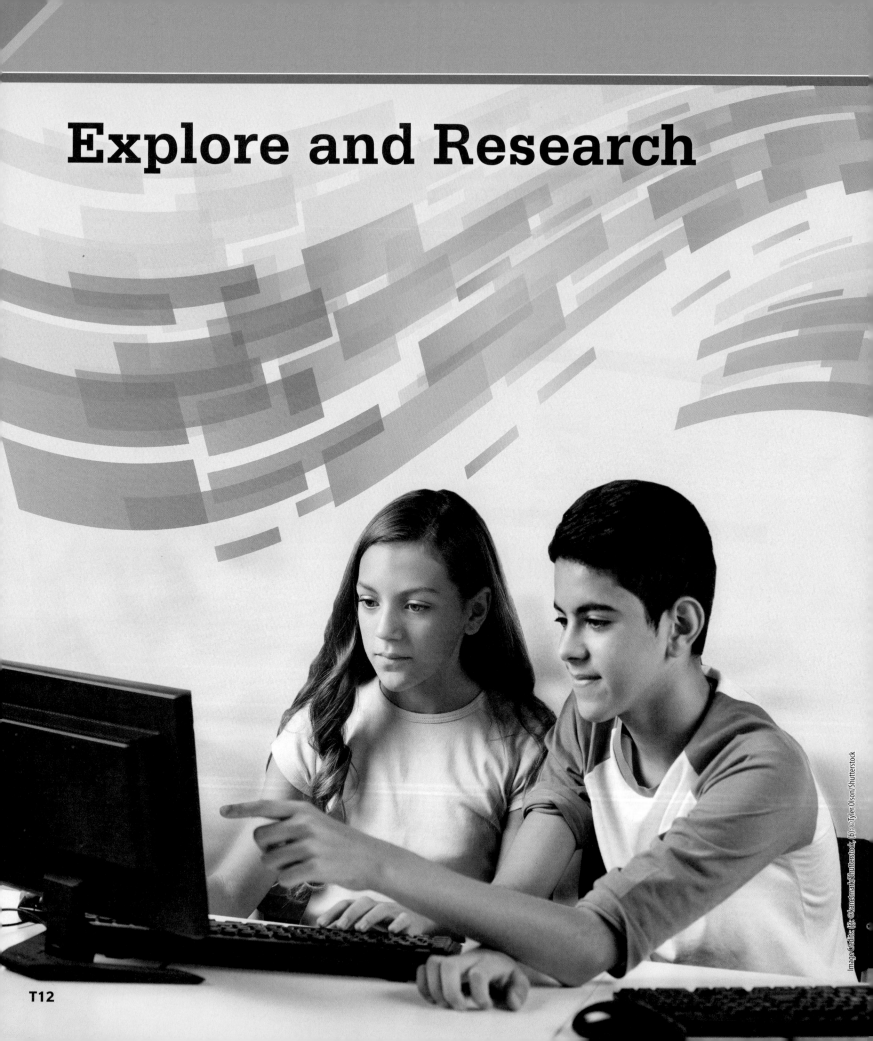

Students who inquire...

- **Generate** questions
- **Plan** and revise
- **Synthesize** information
- **Cite** sources
- **Deliver** results

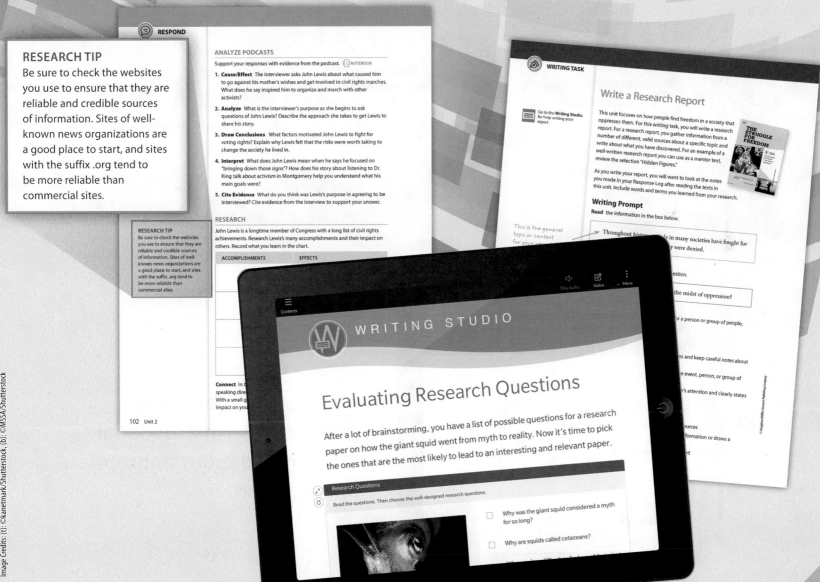

RESEARCH TIP
Be sure to check the websites you use to ensure that they are reliable and credible sources of information. Sites of well-known news organizations are a good place to start, and sites with the suffix .org tend to be more reliable than commercial sites.

RESPOND

ANALYZE PODCASTS
Support your responses with evidence from the podcast. NOTEBOOK

1. **Cause/Effect** The interviewer asks John Lewis about what caused him to go against his mother's wishes and get involved in civil rights marches. What does he say inspired him to organize and march with other activists?

2. **Analyze** What is the interviewer's purpose as she begins to ask questions of John Lewis? Describe the approach she takes to get Lewis to share his story.

3. **Draw Conclusions** What factors motivated John Lewis to fight for voting rights? Explain why Lewis felt that the risks were worth taking to change the society he lived in.

4. **Interpret** What does John Lewis mean when he says he was focused on "bringing down those signs"? How does his story about listening to Dr. King talk about activism in Montgomery help you understand what his main goals were?

5. **Cite Evidence** What do you think was Lewis's purpose in agreeing to be interviewed? Cite evidence from the interview to support your answer.

RESEARCH
John Lewis is a longtime member of Congress with a long list of civil rights achievements. Research Lewis's many accomplishments and their impact on others. Record what you learn in the chart.

RESEARCH TIP
Be sure to check the websites you use to ensure that they are reliable and credible sources of information. Sites of well-known news organizations are a good place to start, and sites with the suffix .org tend to be more reliable than commercial sites.

ACCOMPLISHMENTS	EFFECTS

Connect In t...
speaking dire...
With a small g...
impact on you...

102   Unit 2

WRITING TASK

Go to the **Writing Studio** for help writing your report.

Write a Research Report

This unit focuses on how people find freedom in a society that oppresses them. For this writing task, you will write a research report. For a research report, you gather information from a number of different, valid sources about a specific topic and write about what you have discovered. For an example of a well-written research report you can use as a mentor text, review the selection "Hidden Figures."

As you write your report, you will want to look at the notes you made in your Response Log after reading the texts in this unit. Include words and terms you learned from your research.

Writing Prompt
Read the information in the box below.

This is the general topic or context for your...

Throughout histor... in many societies have fought for... y were denied.

...estion.

...the midst of oppression?

...r a person or group of people.

...es and keep careful notes about

...e event, person, or group of

...r's attention and clearly states

...urces

...formation or draws a

WRITING STUDIO

Evaluating Research Questions

After a lot of brainstorming, you have a list of possible questions for a research paper on how the giant squid went from myth to reality. Now it's time to pick the ones that are the most likely to lead to an interesting and relevant paper.

Research Questions
Read the questions. Then choose the well-designed research questions.

☐ Why was the giant squid considered a myth for so long?

☐ Why are squids called cetaceans?

Maximize Growth through Data-Driven Differentiation and Assessment

Ongoing assessment and data reporting provide critical feedback loops to teachers and students, so that each experience encourages self-assessment and reflection, and drives positive learning outcomes for all students.

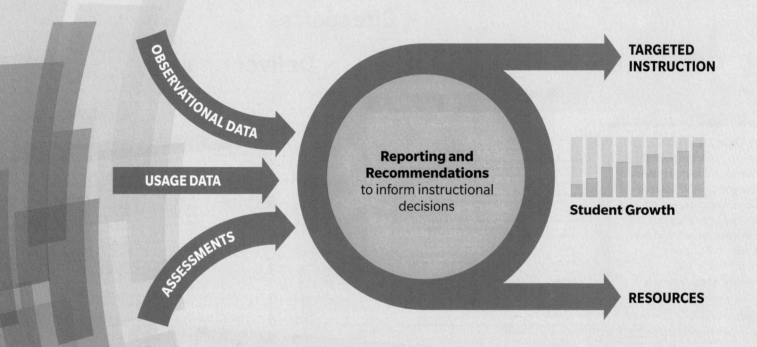

OBSERVATIONAL DATA

USAGE DATA

ASSESSMENTS

Reporting and Recommendations to inform instructional decisions

TARGETED INSTRUCTION

Student Growth

RESOURCES

Actionable reports drive grouping and instructional recommendations appropriate for each learner.

Program Assessments

Adaptive Growth Measure

3 times per year

Adaptive Growth Measure allows teachers to gain an understanding of where students are on the learning continuum and identify students in need of intervention or enrichment.

Unit Assessments

6 times per year

Unit Assessments identify mastery of skills covered during the course of the unit across all literacy strands.

Ongoing Feedback from Daily Classroom Activities

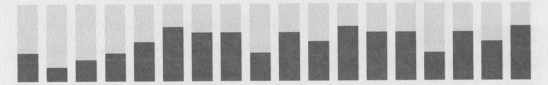

Formative Assessment data is collected across a variety of student activities to help teachers make informed instructional decisions based on data.

- Check Your Understanding
- Selection Tests
- Writing Tasks
- Independent Reading

- Usage Data
- Online Essay Scoring
- Teacher Observations
- Research Projects

Assessments

HMH Into Literature has a comprehensive suite of assessments to help you determine what students already know and how they are progressing through the program lessons.

Diagnostic Assessment for Reading is an informal, criterion-referenced assessment designed to diagnose the specific reading comprehension skills that need attention.

Skills-based Diagnostic Assessments will help you quickly gauge a student's mastery of common, grade-level appropriate skills.

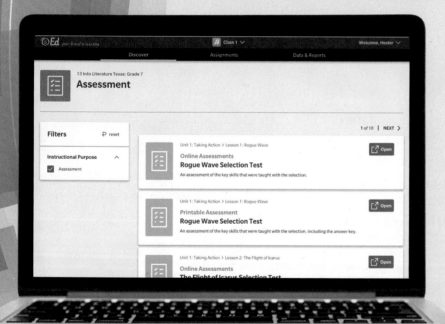

Every selection in the Into Literature program has a corresponding **Selection Test,** focusing on the skills taught in each lesson.

- Analyze & Apply
- Collaborate & Compare, and
- Independent Reading

A **Unit Test** assesses mastery of the skills taught in the entire Unit using new readings aligned with the Unit topic.

The **Diagnostic Screening Test** for Grammar, Usage, and Mechanics provides an assessment of strengths and weaknesses in the conventions of written English.

Each Module in the Grammar Studio has a **Diagnostic Assessment** and a **Summative Assessment,** for before and after instruction.

Foster a Learning Culture

As you encourage a culture of responsibility and collaboration, essential for students' success in the world of work, you will find learning activities that are social, active, and student owned.

Collaborate & Compare Designed to support individual accountability as well as team aptitude, this section requires students to read and annotate texts and compare their responses in small groups.

Peer Review is a critical part of students' creative process. Tools like Checklists for writing and listening and speaking tasks and the Revision Guide with questions, tips, and techniques offer practical support for peer interaction.

Learning Mindset notes and strategies in your Teacher's Edition are designed to help students acquire the attitude of perseverance needed to successfully negotiate learning obstacles. Other resources such as ongoing formative assessments, peer evaluation, and Reflect on the Unit questions encourage students to monitor their progress and develop metacognitive ability.

LEARNING MINDSET

Persistence Remind students that learning requires taking on challenges. Point out that taking on a challenge requires working hard and putting forth real effort. You might use a sports analogy to make your point. Ask students what their favorite football, basketball, or soccer teams do when they are losing early in a game. Discuss how persistence and confidence—a sense that "I can do this"—propel athletes and sports teams to victory. Remind students that academic subjects, like sports, require that same level of confidence and persistence and a commitment to work hard. Just as athletes put in many hours of practice to hone their skills, completing homework and other assignments is, in essence, how students practice and improve upon their academic skills.

Build a Culture of Professional Growth

Embedded and on-going Professional Learning empowers you to develop high-impact learning experiences that provide all students with opportunities for reading and writing success.

Build agency with purposeful, embedded teacher support and high-impact strategies

- Notice & Note Strategies for Close Reading
- Classroom Videos
- On-Demand Professional Learning Modules

A QUILT OF A COUNTRY

You are about to read the argument "A Quilt of a Country." In it, you will encounter notice and note signposts that will give you clues about the essay's claims and evidence. Here are three key signposts to look for as you read this essay and other informative writing.

For more information on these and other signposts to Notice & Note, visit the **Reading Studio**.

When you see phrases like these, pause to see if it's a **Big Questions** signpost:
- "Everyone has heard of..."
- "It goes without saying that..."
- "There was a time when..."
- "Most people know that..."

Big Questions Even in a simple conversation between two friends, there are frequent references to information that both speakers already know. Even though they may be exchanging new information, two people communicate better if they understand each other in a variety of ways. Authors count on their readers to understand certain information, such as:

- historical and current events
- shared opinions or ideas
- common words, terms, or concepts

If you're reading a text and feel lost, stop and ask yourself: **What does the author think I already know?** Read this part of "Quilt of a Country" to see one student's annotation of Big Questions.

1. That's because it was built of bits and pieces that seem discordant, like the crazy quilts that were one of its great folk-art forms, velvet and calico and checks and brocades. Out of many, one. That is the ideal.

2. The reality is often quite different, a great national striving consisting frequently of failure. Many of the oft-told stories of the most pluralistic nation on earth are stories not of tolerance, but of bigotry. Slavery and sweatshops, the burning of crosses and the ostracism of the other. Children learn in social-studies class and in the news of the lynching of blacks, the denial of rights to women, the murders of gay men.

What does the author assume her audience understands about America?	Qvindlen has an understanding of America as a melting pot, a mosaic, or a "crazy quilt."
Which historical or social events does the author assume her audience is familiar with?	The author expects that her audience knows about the historical mistreatment of African Americans and other minorities, and the struggle of women for equality.

2   Unit 1

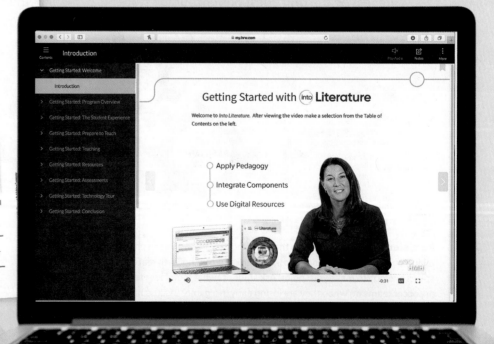

Grow Your Practice with Personalized Blended Professional Learning

- **Getting Started Course and Professional Learning Guide:** Learn the program components, pedagogy, and digital resources to successfully teach with *Into Literature*.

- **Follow-Up:** Choose from relevant instructional topics to create a personalized in-person or online Follow-Up experience to deepen program mastery and enhance teaching practices.

- **Coaching and Modeling:** Experience just-in-time support to ensure continuous professional learning that is student-centered and grounded in data.

- **askHMH:** Get on-demand access to program experts who will answer questions and provide personalized conferencing and digital demonstrations to support implementation.

- **Technical Services:** Plan, prepare, implement, and operate technology with ease.

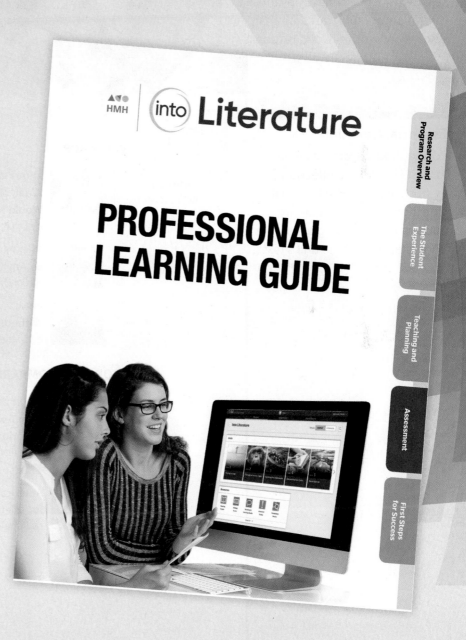

Annotated Student Edition Table of Contents

UNIT 1

OURSELVES AND OTHERS

PAGE 1

Topical Focus
Each unit reflects a topic linking selections, an Essential Question, a quotation, and unit tasks for analysis, discussion, synthesis, and response.

Essential Question
Posing thought-provoking ideas for discussion and reflection as students read, the Essential Question stimulates analysis and synthesis, leading to a richer understanding of the unit's texts.

? **ESSENTIAL QUESTION:**

How do we engage with others while staying true to ourselves?

INDEPENDENT READING 62

These selections can be accessed through the digital edition.

MEMOIR
from **The Pleasure of Reading**
by Kamila Shamsie

POEM
Magic Island
by Cathy Song

SHORT STORY
The Wife's Story
by Ursula K. Le Guin

ARGUMENT
America: The Multinational Society
by Ishmael Reed

Suggested Novel Connection

NOVEL
Frankenstein
by Mary Shelley

Additional Novel Connections

• **The Lord of the Flies**
by William Golding

• **In the Time of Butterflies**
by Julia Alvarez

Key Learning Objectives

In abbreviated form, each unit's main instructional goals are listed for planning and quick reference.

Key Learning Objectives

• Analyze literary devices
• Analyze author's purpose
• Make inferences
• Evaluate evidence
• Evaluate an argument
• Analyze rhetoric

 Visit the Interactive Student Edition for:

• Unit and Selection Videos
• Media Selections
• Selection Audio Recordings
• Enhanced Digital Instruction

Annotated Student Edition Table of Contents

UNIT **2**

HOW WE SEE THINGS
PAGE 72

? **ESSENTIAL
QUESTION:**

How does our point of
view shape what we
think we know?

Analyze & Apply

This section of the Table of Contents
groups a variety of selections for
analysis, annotation, and application
of the Notice & Note protocol, as
well as standards instruction.

ANALYZE & APPLY

Collaborate & Compare

This section of the Table of Contents
provides a comparative analysis
of two selections linked by topic
but different in genre, craft, or
focus. Standards instruction and
annotation are also applied.

COLLABORATE & COMPARE

© Houghton Mifflin Harcourt Publishing Company • Image Credits (t to b): ©eclipse_images/iStock/Getty Images Plus/Getty Images • ©Ryan Herron/iStockPhoto.com • ©chris-mueller/iStock/Getty Images Plus/Getty Images • ©StudioThreeDots/iStock/Getty Images Plus/Getty Images • ©Megapress/Alamy • ©Rawpixel.com/Shutterstock

UNIT 2

 INDEPENDENT READING 130
These selections can be accessed through the digital edition.

POEM
Before I got my eye put out
by Emily Dickinson

ESSAY
What Our Telescopes Couldn't See
by Pippa Goldschmidt

INFORMATIONAL TEXT
from **Big Bang: The Origin of the Universe**
by Simon Singh

SHORT STORY
By the Waters of Babylon
by Stephen Vincent Benét

Suggested Novel Connection

NOVEL
Brave New World
by Aldous Huxley

Independent Reading
Interactive digital texts linked to the unit topic and in a wide range of genres and Lexile levels provide additional resources for students' independent reading, expanding student choice and experience.

Additional Connections

- **Our Town**
  by Thorton Wilder (drama)

- **The Turn of the Screw**
  by Henry James (novel)

 Unit 2 **Tasks**

Key Learning Objectives
- Analyze development of ideas
- Analyze tone
- Analyze plot structure
- Analyze speaker
- Analyze figurative language
- Interpret graphics
- Analyze poetic structure
- Compare details

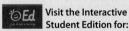 **Visit the Interactive Student Edition for:**
- Unit and Selection Videos
- Media Selections
- Selection Audio Recordings
- Enhanced Digital Instruction

© Houghton Mifflin Harcourt Publishing Company • Image Credits (t to b): ©Ivy Reynolds/The Image Bank/Getty Images • ©Paulo Afonso/Shutterstock • ©Millkovasa/Shutterstock • ©victor zastol'skiy/Adobe Stock • ©Nick Koudis/Photodisc/Getty Images

Contents   FM9

Annotated Student Edition Table of Contents

UNIT (3)

THE NATURAL WORLD
PAGE 142

**? ESSENTIAL
QUESTION:**

What effect do we have
on nature, and how
does nature affect us?

Notice & Note Reading Model

Using a gradual release model to teach
the signposts referred to as Notice & Note,
the Reading Model describes two to three
signposts and illustrates them in a selection.

ANALYZE & APPLY

NOTICE & NOTE
READING MODEL

MENTOR TEXT

COLLABORATE & COMPARE

COMPARE THEMES

Mentor Text

This selection exemplifies genre
characteristics and craft choices that
will be used in end-of-unit writing
tasks as models for students.

INDEPENDENT READING 206

These selections can be accessed through the digital edition.

ARGUMENT
from **Hope for Animals and Their World**
by Jane Goodall

ESSAY
Sea Stars
by Barbara Hurd

POEM
Starfish
by Lorna Dee Cervantes

SHORT STORY
Wolves
by José Luis Zárate

Suggested Novel Connection

NOVEL
Life of Pi
by Yann Martel

Unit 3 **Tasks**

Additional Connections

• **Into the Wild**
by Jon Krakauer (biography)

• **The Old Man and the Sea**
by Ernest Hemingway (novel)

Key Learning Objectives

• Analyze structure in fiction and nonfiction
• Analyze language and style
• Analyze media techniques
• Analyze purpose
• Analyze symbol and theme
• Analyze plot
• Analyze free verse

 Visit the Interactive Student Edition for:

• Unit and Selection Videos
• Media Selections
• Selection Audio Recordings
• Enhanced Digital Instruction

UNIT **4**

**Instructional Overview
and Resources** 218A

UNIT **4**

HARD-WON LIBERTY

PAGE 218

? **ESSENTIAL
QUESTION:**

What do we need in
order to feel free?

Variety of Genres

Each unit is comprised of different kinds of
texts or genres. Essential characteristics of
each genre are identified and illustrated.
Students then apply those characteristics
to their own writing.

ANALYZE & APPLY

COLLABORATE & COMPARE

INDEPENDENT READING 304

These selections can be accessed through the digital edition.

 SPEECH
from **Speech at the March on Washington**
by Josephine Baker

 SHORT STORY
The Book of the Dead
by Edwidge Danticat

 POEM
Cloudy Day
by Jimmy Santiago Baca

 HISTORY WRITING
from **Crispus Attucks**
by Kareem Abdul-Jabbar

Suggested Nonfiction Connection

 NONFICTION
Why We Can't Wait
by Martin Luther King Jr.

> **Tasks**
> Each unit concludes with one or two culminating tasks that demonstrate essential understandings, synthesizing ideas and text references in oral and written responses.

 Unit **4** Tasks

Additional Connections

- **A Wreath for Emmett Till**
  by Marilyn Nelson
  (narrative poem)

- **The Autobiography of Malcolm X**
  by Malcolm X

Key Learning Objectives
- Analyze argument
- Analyze rhetorical devices
- Analyze poetic structure
- Analyze diction and syntax
- Analyze character and theme
- Analyze media techniques

Ed Visit the Interactive Student Edition for:

- Unit and Selection Videos
- Media Selections
- Selection Audio Recordings
- Enhanced Digital Instruction

Contents FM13

Annotated Student Edition Table of Contents

UNIT 5

RESPONSES TO CHANGE
PAGE 316

? ***ESSENTIAL
QUESTION:***

How do changes
around us reveal who
we are?

Cultural Diversity

Each unit includes a rich
array of selections that
represent multicultural
authors and experiences.

ANALYZE & APPLY

COLLABORATE & COMPARE

INDEPENDENT READING 382

These selections can be accessed through the digital edition.

 SHORT STORY
The Norwegian Rat
by Naguib Mahfouz

 MEMOIR
After the Storm
by Orhan Pamuk

 SCIENCE WRITING
from **Simplexity**
by Jeffrey Kluger

 NOVELLA
from **The Metamorphosis**
by Franz Kafka

Suggested Novel Connection

NOVEL
A Separate Peace
by John Knowles

> **Suggested Novel Connection**
> One extended text is recommended for its topical and thematic connection to other texts in the unit.

Unit 5 **Task**

Additional Connections

• **A Raisin in the Sun**
  by Lorraine Hansberry (drama)

• **The Grapes of Wrath**
  by John Steinbeck (novel)

© Houghton Mifflin Harcourt Publishing Company • Image Credits: (t to b): ©Matthijs Kuijpers/Alamy • ©Enrique Diaz/Moment/Getty Images • ©Daniel Shanken/AP Images • Louis C. Kramer/Library of Congress Prints & Photographs Division • ©145/Donovan Reese/Ocean/Corbis

Key Learning Objectives

• Analyze literary nonfiction
• Analyze style
• Analyze text structure
• Analyze purpose and audience

• Analyze plot and setting
• Analyze word choice
• Analyze media techniques
• Analyze purpose and theme

Ed **Visit the Interactive Student Edition for:**

• Unit and Selection Videos
• Media Selections
• Selection Audio Recordings
• Enhanced Digital Instruction

Contents **FM15**

Annotated Student Edition Table of Contents

UNIT ⑥
ABSOLUTE POWER
PAGE 392

? **ESSENTIAL
QUESTION:**

What are the sources of
true power?

ANALYZE & APPLY

COLLABORATE & COMPARE

INDEPENDENT READING 526

These selections can be accessed through the digital edition.

HISTORY WRITING
from Holinshed's Chronicles
by Raphael Holinshed

ARGUMENT
Why Read Shakespeare?
by Michael Mack

POEM
Ozymandias
by Percy Bysshe Shelley

DRAMA
Julius Caesar, Act III, Scene 2
by William Shakespeare

Suggested Novel Connection

NOVEL
Animal Farm
by George Orwell

Additional Connections

• **Julius Caesar**
  by William Shakespeare (drama)

• **The Prince**
  by Niccolo Machiavelli (treatise)

Reflection
Students may pause and reflect on their process and understanding of the selections and the themes in each unit.

Key Learning Objectives
• Analyze drama
• Analyze character and theme
• Analyze media representations
• Analyze satire
• Analyze visual elements
• Analyze evidence

 Visit the Interactive Student Edition for:

• Unit and Selection Videos
• Media Selections
• Selection Audio Recordings
• Enhanced Digital Instruction

© Houghton Mifflin Harcourt Publishing Company • Image Credits (t to b): ©Lebrecht Music and Arts Photo Library/Alamy • ©Lana Isabella/Flickr Open/Getty Images • ©Tom Hanley/Alamy • ©Geraint Lewis/Alamy • ©Digital Vision/Getty Images

SELECTIONS BY GENRE

© Houghton Mifflin Publishing Company

HMH
Into Literature Dashboard

Easy to use and personalized for your learning.

Monitor your progress in the course.

Review your assignments and check your progress.

Quickly access content and search program resources.

Online
Explore Online to Experience the Power of HMH *Into Literature*

All in One Place
Readings and assignments are supported by a variety of resources to bring literature to life and give you the tools you need to succeed.

Supporting 21st-Century Skills
Whether you're working alone or collaborating with others, it takes effort to analyze the complex texts and competing ideas that bombard us in this fast-paced world. What will help you succeed? Staying engaged and organized. The digital tools in this program will help you take charge of your learning.

FM20   Grade 10

Ignite Your Investigation

You learn best when you're engaged. The **Stream to Start** videos at the beginning of every unit are designed to spark your interest before you read. Get curious and start reading!

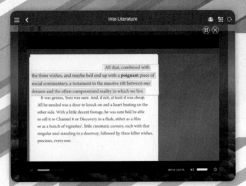

Learn How to Close Read

Close reading effectively is all about examining the details. See how it's done by watching the **Close Read Screencasts** in your eBook. Hear modeled conversations on targeted passages.

Personalized Annotations

My Notes encourages you to take notes as you read and allows you to mark the text in your own customized way. You can easily access annotations to review later as you prepare for exams.

Interactive Graphic Organizers

Graphic organizers help you process, summarize, and keep track of your learning and prepare for end-of-unit writing tasks. **Word Networks** help you learn academic vocabulary, and **Response Logs** help you explore and deepen your understanding of the **Essential Question** in each unit.

No Wi-Fi? No problem!

With HMH *Into Literature,* you always have access: download when you're online and access what you need when you're offline. Work offline and then upload when you're back online.

Communicate "Raise a Hand" to ask or answer questions without having to be in the same room as your teacher.

Collaborate Collaborate with your teacher via chat and work with a classmate to improve your writing.

FM21

HMH
Into Literature
STUDIOS

All the help you need to be successful in your literature class is one click away with the Studios. These digital-only lessons are here to tap into the skills that you already use and help you sharpen those skills for the future.

WRITING STUDIO

Ways to Organize Reasons and Evidence

Every argument must include reasons and evidence to support a claim. There are several effective ways you can organize that support. Check out some of those ways here.

Read the following techniques that will help you achieve cohesion, or coherence, in your writing.

Order of Importance

Least to most important

Claim: Homewood must switch from a volunteer fire department to a full-time fire department.

- Reason 1: The town is growing and getting more calls during they day when volunteers are at their full-time jobs

- Reason 2: Full-time firefighters can train daily instead of once a month, giving them more time to improve firefighting skills.

Easy-to-find resources, organized in five separate STUDIOS. On demand and on ED!

Look for links in each lesson to take you to the appropriate Studio.

READING STUDIO

Go beyond the book with the Reading Studio. With over 100 full-length down-loadable titles to choose from, find the right story to continue your journey.

WRITING STUDIO

Being able to write clearly and effectively is a skill that will help you throughout life. The Writing Studio will help you become an expert communicator—in print or online.

SPEAKING & LISTENING STUDIO

Communication is more than just writing. The Speaking & Listening Studio will help you become an effective speaker and a focused listener.

GRAMMAR STUDIO

Go beyond traditional worksheets with the Grammar Studio. These engaging, interactive lessons will sharpen your grammar skills.

VOCABULARY STUDIO

Learn the skills you need to expand your vocabulary. The interactive lessons in the Vocabulary Studio will grow your vocabulary to improve your reading.

FM23

THE PERSPICACIOUS READER (And **yes**, you want to be one)

YOUR TEACHER AGREES!

Dr. Kylene Beers and Dr. Robert E. Probst

From Dr. Beers:

When Dr. Probst said he wanted to call this essay "The Perspicacious Reader," I had to ask him what that word meant. Did we want kids in high school to be perspicacious? Is that a good thing? Dr. Probst—who knows more words than anyone I know—said, "Of course it is good to be a perspicacious reader," and then he made me look it up. Yes, he's one of those folks who believes looking up words you don't know is good for you. So, off I went, to look it up . . .

I discovered that if you were to be a perspicacious reader, it would be a very good thing. It would mean that you were able to think deeply about what you are reading and make smart inferences. It would mean that you notice a lot as you are reading. And since we wrote a book for teachers titled **Notice and Note**, we like the idea that being a perspicacious reader means you would notice a lot as you read!

From **Both** of Us

We both think reading is one of the most important skills you will ever learn. We know that every day you read. Take a moment and think of all you read each day. Here is our combined list.

Text messages
Emails
Tweets
FB posts
Newspaper/magazine articles
How-to info for texting/using our technology
Novels we choose to read for fun
Articles for work – some we have to read and some we choose to read
Bills we get that have to be paid
Food magazines (Who do you think reads these?)
Books about teaching
Articles about technology (And who do you think reads these?)
Crossword puzzles

And then there are some things we occasionally read:

Party/wedding invitations
Birth announcements
Jokes or cartoons
Job applications
Report cards
School test results
Income tax information
Reports from doctors
Sympathy cards when someone
    has died
Information about world events

No matter what you read, we want you to read well. We want you to know what to do when you get confused because we all get confused from time to time as we read. We want you to know what to do when you come to a word you might not know (such as *perspicacious*). We want you to be able to figure out the author's theme if you are reading fiction or the author's purpose and main idea if you are reading nonfiction. We don't want you to have to wait around for someone else to tell you what the text means, which would make you dependent on that person.

We suspect, now that you're in high school, the last thing you want is to depend on others all the time. So, we want you to read smart, read critically, read closely, and always read wondering just what else there is you need to know.

But Sometimes I **Hate** to Read

We don't doubt that. You've got a lot going on in your life. Friends. Sports. Music. Jobs, maybe. Homework. Worrying about who likes whom and who is invited to what and if your grades are good and how things are going at home and who you'll sit with at lunch, stand with in the hall, go to the party with — even if you'll get invited to the party. First, it will all work out. How do we know? We've been your age. It will all work out.

What's important—along with the many other things that are important in your life right now—is to remember that you want to end up getting smarter about a lot of things each year, and the best way—yes THE BEST WAY—to do that is to make sure you become a better reader each year. So, sometimes this year your teacher may ask you to read a text that makes you say, "Really? Seriously?" We want you to dig in deep and do it because we promise there's a reason, and the reason is about making sure you, the young adult you're becoming, are prepared to deal with all the texts that get thrown your way.

Because here's what most people won't tell you: not all the texts will be honest. Right. That online ad about the used car might not mention everything you need to know. The social media post about your favorite presidential candidate just might be fake news. That Instagram photo showing everyone looking so

© Houghton Mifflin Harcourt Publishing Company

Ask students to list at least two examples of what Beers and Probst mean by "reading well." Discuss their examples. Ask students to add additional examples.

FM25

Note that Beers and Probst ask students to always read with these three questions in mind:

What surprised me?

What did the author think I already knew?

What changed or confirmed what I already knew?

Ask students to circle these and draw an arrow from them to the margin.

Discuss these three questions.

Beers and Probst introduce the concept of **signposts** which will be used throughout *Into Literature*. Ask students to underline this definition in their book.

perfect, so very happy? Chances are it was posed, shot, reshot, put through several filters, and touched up. The newspaper story about why your school district should or shouldn't build a new school might only offer one perspective. You—not a teacher, not a parent, not your best buddy—you have an obligation to yourself and to the community you live in to always ask yourself if you are reading closely enough to know when you should agree and when you shouldn't. So, we want you to always read with these three questions in mind:

If you'll do that, then we know you'll be on your way to becoming a smarter reader.

AND (Of course there is an AND) . . .

. . . we also want you to learn to read being aware of something we call

signposts.

A signpost is simply a cue an author gives you as you read that can help you figure out the theme (if reading fiction) or author's purpose (if reading nonfiction). In the same way that drivers pay attention (we hope!) to signs as they drive, we want you paying attention to signposts as you read.

So I'm Supposed to Read Just to Look for Signposts?

No, of course not! No one should ever set out to read an article, a chapter in a book, an online essay, a play, or a novel just to hunt for signposts. That would be like taking a drive to your favorite destination just so you can count the stop signs you see on your way there. **No!** You drive to that favorite place to see it and to enjoy the scenery along the way. But if you don't notice the stop signs or one-way signs or curve ahead signs while driving there, you might not ever get there. The signs help you make the journey safely, but noticing the signs isn't the point of the journey.

The same is true of reading. You read to enjoy the journey, to learn some things along the way, and to get to the end of the text with new insights and understandings. Understanding those insights means also noticing the signposts so that you are better able to understand what the author has in mind.

The End!

IN CONCLUSION

We are always reading. We may not always be reading books, poems, articles, newspapers, webpages, or texts of any kind, but we are always reading. We read the weather, the teacher's mood, the expression on our friend's face, the demeanor of a group of strangers we encounter on the street, the unusual silence—or noise—in the hallway. We observe and listen, we try to make sense of what we have noticed, and then we act accordingly. We can't get through the day without reading.

And the essence of all of this reading—of both texts and the world around us—is simply paying attention. If we don't see the storm on the horizon, if we don't see the expression on our friend's face, if we don't see the teacher's devious grin, then we won't be able to react intelligently. Noticing is the first step.

So it is with the reading of texts. If you aren't paying attention, if you aren't noticing, then you may as well not be staring at the page at all. If you look out the window and don't notice the storm clouds forming, then you'll be drenched in the afternoon. Looking out the window without seeing what is there—noticing—does you little good.

This is a signpost showing that we are about to wrap this up!

© Houghton Mifflin Harcourt Publishing Company

FM27

Ask students why the term *signpost*, which is used in other contexts, is also a good one for reading. ***Possible answer:*** *Writers give us direction, clues, and insight with their words just as drivers are given vital information with stop signs, yield signs, and school zone warnings.*

The authors state that there is much more to the process of reading than just "noticing."

Ask students to answer the following question in writing in the margin of their book:

Explain how reading is more than noticing.

Then ask students to get into groups of three and share their written responses and discuss. Ask for volunteers to share responses. Discuss.

And then you must do more. You must take note of what you have noticed. If you do notice the clouds but fail to ask yourself what they might mean, fail to recognize that they forewarn you of the approaching storm, you'll still get soaked. Noticing alone isn't enough; you have to take note of it and ask what it means.

Again, so it is with reading. If you notice what the character has said, what the author has emphasized or ignored, what the setting is like, and you don't bother asking what all that you have noticed tells you, then you may as well not have noticed it in the first place. Looking out the window and noticing the clouds—without thinking about what they mean—does you little good.

NOW WHAT?

Finally, after noticing and noting, you must do something. You must ask yourself, "So what? Now what do I need to do (or think, or feel, or say)?" If you don't reach that third step, the first two have been little more than an exercise.

Again, so it is with reading texts. If you notice what the text offers, think about it, and simply lay it aside without considering how you might change your own thinking or your own actions, then you will have missed an opportunity to grow and change. The effort of reading will have been wasted. If you notice the clouds forming, take note of that and realize that it warns you of the approaching storm, and still walk out the door without your raincoat or your umbrella, you will *still* get drenched. Reading—of the sky or of the book —should enable us to deal with life more effectively.

That's because the pages of a book allow you to explore places you've never been, meet people and characters who are far different from you, and discover through all this that reading— more than anything else— is what gives you the opportunity to reflect and in that reflection perhaps change something about yourself. Reading is a changemaker. We hope this is your year for growing and changing as a reader. We hope this is the year when, as you read, you learn to notice and note.

NOTICE & NOTE SIGNPOSTS

Signpost	Definition	Anchor Question(s)
FICTION		
Contrasts and Contradictions	A sharp contrast between what we would expect and what we observe the character doing; behavior that contradicts previous behavior or well-established patterns	Why would the character act (feel) this way?
Aha Moment	A character's realization of something that shifts his actions or understanding of himself, others, or the world around him	How might this change things?
Tough Questions	Questions a character raises that reveal his or her inner struggles	What does this question make me wonder about?
Words of the Wiser	The advice or insight about life that a wiser character, who is usually older, offers to the main character	What is the life lesson, and how might this affect the character?
Again and Again	Events, images, or particular words that recur over a portion of the story	Why might the author bring this up again and again?
Memory Moment	A recollection by a character that interrupts the forward progress of the story	Why might this memory be important?
NONFICTION		
Contrasts and Contradictions	A sharp contrast between what we would expect and what we observe happening. A difference between two or more elements in the text.	What is the difference, and why does it matter?
Extreme or Absolute Language	Language that leaves no doubt about a situation or an event, allows no compromise, or seems to exaggerate or overstate a case.	Why did the author use this language?
Numbers and Stats	Specific quantities or comparisons to depict the amount, size, or scale. Or, the writer is vague and imprecise about numbers when we would expect more precision.	Why did the author use these numbers or amounts?
Quoted Words	Opinions or conclusions of someone who is an expert on the subject, or someone who might be a participant in or a witness to an event. Or, the author might cite other people to provide support for a point.	Why was this person quoted or cited, and what did this add?
Word Gaps	Vocabulary that is unfamiliar to the reader—for example, a word with multiple meanings, a rare or technical word, a discipline-specific word, or one with a far-removed antecedent.	Do I know this word from someplace else? Does it seem like technical talk for this topic? Can I find clues in the sentence to help me understand the word?

FM29

Ask students to mark this page for future reference.

Read the chart on this page noting that it is divided into **Fiction** and **Nonfiction** signposts and includes a definition and an anchor question for each. An **anchor question** helps students identify the signposts as they read by "questioning" the text.

The essay by program consultant Carol Jago is an accessible explanation of **genre** and its importance. Genre has an elevated role in the new standards—both in reading and writing.

Ask students to read the first and second paragraphs and then to write their own definition of genre in the margin of their book.

If your students need an analogy to better understand **genre**, explain that genre refers to different categories or kinds of texts we read. This is similar to vehicles that we use for transportation. Vehicles transport people and goods but may be trucks, vans, sedans or sports cars—different categories for vehicles—different genres for texts.

Ask students to turn to a partner and provide examples of their favorite genre.

READING AND WRITING ACROSS GENRES

by Carol Jago

Reading is a first-class ticket around the world. Not only can you explore other lands and cultures, but you can also travel to the past and future. That journey is sometimes a wild ride. Other books can feel like comfort food, enveloping you in an imaginative landscape full of friends and good times. Making time for reading is making time for life.

Genre

One of the first things readers do when we pick up something to read is notice its genre. You might not think of it exactly in those terms, but consider how you approach a word problem in math class compared to how you read a science fiction story. Readers go to different kinds of text for different purposes. When you need to know how to do or make something, you want a reliable, trusted source of information. When you're in the mood to spend some time in a world of fantasy, you happily suspend your normal disbelief in dragons.

In every unit of *Into Literature,* you'll find a diverse mix of genres all connected by a common theme, allowing you to explore a topic from many different angles.

Writer's Craft

Learning how writers use genre to inform, to explain, to entertain, or to surprise readers will help you better understand—as well as enjoy—your reading. Imitating how professional writers employ the tools of their craft—descriptive language, repetition, sensory images, sentence structure, and a variety of other features—will give you many ideas for making your own writing more lively.

Into Literature provides you with the tools you need to understand the elements of all the critical genres and advice on how to learn from professional texts to improve your own writing in those genres.

GENRE ELEMENTS: SHORT STORY
- is a work of short fiction that centers on a single idea and can be read in one sitting
- usually includes one main conflict that involves the characters and keeps [...] moving
- includes the basic ele[...] of fiction—plot, chara[...] setting, and theme
- may be based on real [...] and historical events

GENRE ELEMENTS: INFORMATIONAL TEXT
- provides factual information
- includes evidence to support ideas
- contains text features
- includes many forms, such as news articles and essays

GENRE ELEMENTS: LITERARY NONFICTION
- shares factual information, ideas, or experiences
- develops a key insight about the topic that goes beyond the facts
- uses literary tech[...] as figurative lang[...] narration
- reflects a person[...] involvement in t[...]

GENRE ELEMENTS: POETRY
- may use figurative language, including personification
- often includes imagery that appeals to the five senses
- expresses a theme, or a "big idea" message about life

Reading with Independence

Finding a good book can sometimes be a challenge. Like every other reader, you have probably experienced "book desert" when nothing you pick up seems to have what you are looking for (not that it's easy to explain exactly what you are looking for, but whatever it is, "this" isn't it). If you find yourself in this kind of reading funk, bored by everything you pick up, give yourself permission to range more widely, exploring graphic novels, contemporary biographies, books of poetry, historical fiction. And remember that long doesn't necessarily mean boring. My favorite kind of book is one that I never want to end.

Frankenstein
Or, The Modern Prometheus
Mary Shelley

The Turn of the Screw
Henry James

Take control over your own reading with *Into Literature's* Reader's Choice selections and the HMH Digital Library. And don't forget: your teacher, librarian, and friends can offer you many more suggestions.

SHORT STORY
The Wife's Story
Ursula K. Le Guin
Is the narrator's husband, who has begun acting strangely, really one of the group, or has he become something else?

POEM
Starfish
Lorna Dee Cervantes
This poem explores the human fascination with starfish: their life cycle, beauty, and ocean habitat.

HISTORY
Crispus Attucks
Kareem Abdul-Jabbar
Learn the story of Crispus Attucks, an African American remembered as the first American to die in the Revolutionary War.

Direct students to read the paragraph under the heading "Writer's Craft." Ask students to write their own definition of *writer's craft* in the margin of *Into Literature*. Discuss, asking students to cite examples.

Encourage students to find the Genre Elements feature with each selection in *Into Literature*.

Call students' attention to the **Reader's Choice** selections listed at the end of each unit and show students how to find the **HMH Digital Library** in the **Reading Studio.**

FM31

TEACHER'S EDITION

GRADE 10

Program Consultants:

Kylene Beers

Martha Hougen

Elena Izquierdo

Carol Jago

Erik Palmer

Robert E. Probst

Instructional Overview and Resources

		Instructional Focus	Online Ed Resources

Unit Introduction
Ourselves and Others

Instructional Focus
Unit 1 Essential Question
Unit 1 Academic Vocabulary

Resources
Stream to Start: Ourselves and Others
Unit 1 Response Log

ANALYZE & APPLY

"What, of this Goldfish, Would You Wish?"
Short Story by Etgar Keret
Lexile 900L

NOTICE & NOTE READING MODEL

Signposts
• Tough Questions
• Memory Moment
• Words of the Wiser

Reading
• Analyze Archetypes
• Analyze Literary Devices

Writing: Write a Fable

Speaking and Listening: Present a Fable

Vocabulary: Context Clues

Language Conventions: Tone

 Audio

Close Read Screencasts: Modeled Discussions

Reading Studio: Notice & Note

Level Up Tutorial: Making Inferences

Writing Studio: Writing Narratives

Speaking and Listening Studio: Giving a Presentation

Vocabulary Studio: Context Clues

Mentor Text
"By Any Other Name"
Memoir by Santha Rama Rau
Lexile 1120L

Reading
• Analyze Historical Context
• Analyze Author's Purpose

Writing: Write a Poem

Speaking and Listening: Discuss with a Small Group

Vocabulary: Foreign Words Used in English

Language Conventions: Appropriate Verb Tense

Audio

Reading Studio: Notice & Note

Level Up Tutorial: Historical and Cultural Context

Speaking and Listening Studio: Participating in Collaborative Discussions

Vocabulary Studio: Foreign Words Used in English

Grammar Studio: Module 7: Lesson 3: Verb Tense

"Without Title"
Poem by Diane Glancy

Reading
• Analyze Setting
• Make Inferences About Theme

Writing: Write a Narrative

Speaking and Listening: Present a Narrative

Audio

Reading Studio: Notice & Note

Level Up Tutorial: Setting

Writing Studio: Writing Narratives

Speaking and Listening Studio: Delivering Your Presentation

SUGGESTED PACING: 30 DAYS

Unit Introduction	What, of this Goldfish, Would You Wish?	By Any Other Name	Without Title
1	2 3 4 5 6	7 8 9 10 11 12	13 14 15 16

English Learner Support		Differentiated Instruction	Assessment
• Learn New Expressions • Use Strategies			
• Text X-Ray • Recognize Irony • Understand Sarcasm • Use Cognates • Listen for Intonation • Identify Motifs • Analyze Idioms • Distinguish Formal and Informal Language	• Understand Informal Language • Understand Connotation • Connect Synonyms • Confirm Understanding • Oral Assessment • Present a Fable • Vocabulary Strategy • Analyze Slang and Idioms	**When Students Struggle** • Use Strategies • Analyze Shifts in Focus • Support Comprehension	**Selection Test**
• Text X-Ray • Contrast Verb Forms • Use Cognates • Use Various Grammatical Structures • Identify Adverbs • Discuss Verb Forms • Discuss Idioms	• React to the Language of Imagery • Oral Assessment • Discuss with a Small Group • Articulate Foreign Words • Use Appropriate Verb Tense	**When Students Struggle** • Relate Context to Conflict **To Challenge Students** • Consider Another Perspective	**Selection Test**
• Text X-Ray • Share Connections • Learn Plural Nouns	• Elaborate Using Comparisons • Oral Assessment • Present a Narrative	**When Students Struggle** • Describe Settings	**Selection Test**

from **Texas v. Johnson Majority Opinion/**
American Flag Stands for Tolerance

Independent Reading

End of Unit

17 ⟩ 18 ⟩ 19 ⟩ 20 ⟩ 21 ⟩ 22 ⟩ 23 ⟩ 24 ⟩ 25 ⟩ 26 ⟩ 27 ⟩ 28 ⟩ 29 ⟩ 30 ⟩

UNIT 1 Continued

	Instructional Focus	Online **Resources**

COLLABORATE & COMPARE

from *Texas v. Johnson Majority Opinion*
Court Opinion by William J. Brennan
Lexile 1420L

Reading
• Monitor Comprehension
• Evaluate Evidence

Writing: Write a Comparison

Speaking and Listening: Create a Multimedia Presentation

Vocabulary: Words from Latin

Language Conventions: Commas to Set Off Phrases and Clauses

 Audio

Close Read Screencasts: Modeled Discussions

Reading Studio: Notice & Note

Writing Studio: Using Textual Evidence

Speaking and Listening Studio: Using Media in a Presentation

Vocabulary Studio: Words from Latin

Grammar Studio: Module 11: Lesson 4: Punctuating Independent Clauses

---

"American Flag Stands for Tolerance"
Argument by Ronald J. Allen
Lexile 1170L

Reading
• Evaluate an Argument
• Analyze Rhetoric

Writing: Write a Letter to the Editor

Speaking and Listening: Debate the Issue

Vocabulary: Connotations

Language Conventions: Dashes

 Audio

Close Read Screencasts: Modeled Discussions

Reading Studio: Notice & Note

Level Up Tutorial: Analyzing Arguments

Writing Studio: Using Formal Style

Speaking and Listening Studio: Listening and Responding Constructively

Vocabulary Studio: Connotations

Grammar Studio: Module 12: Lesson 6: Dashes and Parentheses

Collaborate and Compare

Reading: Compare Arguments

Speaking and Listening: Research and Discuss

Online

INDEPENDENT READING

The Independent Reading selections are only available in the eBook.

 Go to the Reading Studio for more information on Notice & Note.

 from *The Pleasure of Reading*
Memoir by Kamila Shamsie
Lexile 1270L

 "Magic Island"
Poem by Cathy Song

END OF UNIT

Writing Task: Write a Personal Essay

Reflect on the Unit

Writing: Write a Personal Essay

Language Conventions: Appropriate Verb Tenses

Unit 1 Response Log

Mentor Text: "By Any Other Name"

Reading Studio: Notice & Note

Writing Studio: Writing as a Process

Grammar Studio: Module 7: Lesson 3: Verb Tense

English Learner Support	Differentiated Instruction	**Online** Ed **Assessment**
• Text X-Ray • Use Cognates • Identify Formal English • Oral Assessment • Use Basic Language • Vocabulary Strategy • Use Commas in Sentences	**When Students Struggle** • Aid Comprehension	**Selection Test**
• Text X-Ray • Understand Directionality • Use Cognates • Review Multiple Meanings • Oral Assessment • Write a Letter to the Editor • Vocabulary Strategy • Language and Style	**When Students Struggle** • Reteaching: Evaluate an Argument	**Selection Test**
• Ask Questions	**To Challenge Students** • Report on Debate Moderators	

"The Wife's Story"
Short Story by Ursula K. Le Guin
Lexile 880L

"America: The Multinational Society"
Argument by Ishmael Reed
Lexile 1440L

Selection Tests

English Learner Support	Differentiated Instruction	Assessment
• Language X-Ray • Complete a Brainstorming Chart • Create a Narrative • Use the Mentor Text • Use Sensory Details	**When Students Struggle** • Use Partner Brainstorming • Use Drafting Strategies • Present, Past, and Past Perfect Tenses	**Unit Test**

OURSELVES AND OTHERS

 Connect to the
ESSENTIAL QUESTION

Ask a volunteer to read aloud the Essential Question. Have volunteers explain what "staying true to ourselves" might mean. Ask: Is it important to stay true to yourself? Prompt students to think of real-life instances in which they interacted with others and may not have been "true" to themselves. Then have them consider one way they could have responded to the situation differently in order to stay "true." Would it have changed the encounter completely?

■ English Learner Support

Learn New Expressions Make sure students understand the Essential Question. If necessary, explain the following idiomatic expressions:

- *Engage with others* means "get to know, talk with, or work with other people."

- *Staying true to ourselves* means "doing what you believe in and what you think is right."

Help students restate the question in simpler language: How can we be with others and still do what we think is right?
ALL LEVELS

DISCUSS THE QUOTATION

Tell students that Barbara Jordan (1936–1996) was a leader of the Civil Rights movement, who later became the first African American elected to the Texas Senate (post-Reconstruction) and the first Southern African American woman elected to the U.S. House of Representatives. Ask students to read the quotation and pause for a moment to reflect on it. Then have students discuss specific ways to follow Jordan's suggestion. Ask them to consider whether enacting the examples they came up with would enable students to stay true to themselves and why.

 ESSENTIAL QUESTION:

How do we engage with others while staying true to ourselves?

" We, as human beings, must be willing to accept people who are different from ourselves. "

Barbara Jordan

⚙ LEARNING MINDSET

Growth Mindset Explain that students who believe they can improve their skills will be more successful than students who believe they're "just not good at" certain subjects or skills. Emphasize that learning takes effort and, though it may be challenging, to "grow" their brain they must continue to work hard. Tell students that mistakes are natural when learning something new; they help people learn. Then share a mistake you've made, and model how you reflected on the mistake and learned from it.

ACADEMIC VOCABULARY

Academic Vocabulary words are words you use when you discuss and write about texts. In this unit you will practice and learn five words.

☑ discriminate   ☐ diverse   ☐ inhibit   ☐ intervene   ☐ rational

Study the Word Network to learn more about the word **discriminate**.

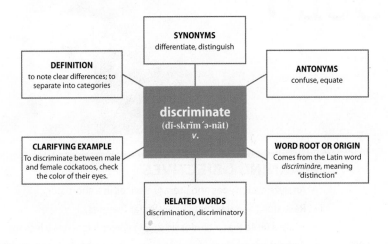

SYNONYMS
differentiate, distinguish

DEFINITION
to note clear differences; to separate into categories

ANTONYMS
confuse, equate

discriminate
(dĭ-skrĭm´ə-nāt)
v.

CLARIFYING EXAMPLE
To discriminate between male and female cockatoos, check the color of their eyes.

WORD ROOT OR ORIGIN
Comes from the Latin word *discrīmināre*, meaning "distinction"

RELATED WORDS
discrimination, discriminatory

Write and Discuss Discuss the completed Word Network with a partner, making sure to talk through all of the boxes until you both understand the word, its synonyms, antonyms, and related forms. Then, fill out Word Networks for the remaining four words. Use a dictionary or online resource to help you complete the activity.

 Go online to access the Word Networks.

RESPOND TO THE ESSENTIAL QUESTION

In this unit, you will explore how people interact with others who agree or disagree with their ideas, yet stay true to themselves. As you read, you will revisit the **Essential Question** and gather your ideas about it in the **Response Log** that appears on page R1. At the end of the unit, you will have the opportunity to write a **personal essay** in which you will reflect on a significant event in your life. Filling out the Response Log will help you prepare for this writing task.

 You can also go online to access the Response Log.

ACADEMIC VOCABULARY

As students complete Word Networks for the remaining four vocabulary words, encourage them to include all the categories shown in the completed network if possible, but point out that some words do not have clear synonyms or antonyms.

discriminate (dĭ-skrĭm´ə-nāt´) *v.* To note clear differences; to separate into categories. (Spanish cognate: *discriminar*)

diverse (dĭ-vûrs´) *adj.* Made up of elements that are different from each other. (Spanish cognate: *diverso*)

inhibit (ĭn-hĭb´ĭt) *v.* To hold back or prevent from acting. (Spanish cognate: *inhibir*)

intervene (ĭn´tər-vēn´) *v.* To come between two things, persons, or events. (Spanish cognate: *intervenir*)

rational (răsh´ə-nəl) *adj.* Based on logic or sound reasoning. (Spanish cognate: *racional*)

RESPOND TO THE ESSENTIAL QUESTION

Direct students to the Unit 1 Response Log. Explain that students will use it to record ideas and details from the selections that help answer the Essential Question. When they work on the writing task at the end of the unit, their Response Logs will help them think about what they have read and make connections between the texts.

 ENGLISH LEARNER SUPPORT

Use Strategies Use this strategy to help students learn how to analyze new sayings and expressions they come across in this unit:

- Before reading a selection, tell students to look for phrases that may be in italics, parentheses, or quotation marks, or set as footnotes (with a number after them and the explanation at the bottom of the page). Explain that these can be clues to sayings and expressions that are new to them.

- When they encounter a saying or expression they don't know, have them circle or highlight it in their books. Suggest they try to figure out its meaning by using context clues and write down what they think it means. Then, suggest they compare their ideas with another student.

- After reading the selection, list the new sayings and expressions students identified as a whole group and then review them in the context of the selection to ensure that everyone understands their meanings. **ALL LEVELS**

READING MODEL

WHAT, OF THIS GOLDFISH, WOULD YOU WISH?

**Short Story by Etgar Keret
translated by Nathan Englander**

GENRE ELEMENTS
SHORT STORY

Remind students that a **short story** usually includes the basic elements of fiction—setting, characters, plot, conflict, and resolution; however, due to its shorter length, a short story typically focuses on a small number of characters and a single theme, specific event, or moment in time. Fiction writers may be inspired by real people, places, and events, but the **narrative**, or the telling of the story, is unique to each writer's imagination and style.

LEARNING OBJECTIVES

- Analyze archetypes and literary devices in a short story.
- Research folk tales that share similar features.
- Write a fable that includes an archetype and teaches a lesson.
- Present a fable, incorporating expression, gestures, and visuals.
- Use context clues to define unfamiliar words and phrases.
- Adjust writing for audience and purpose.
- **Language** Show comprehension of a short story through basic reading skills such as rereading and retelling.

TEXT COMPLEXITY

Quantitative Measures	What, of This Goldfish, Would You Wish?	Lexile: 900L
Qualitative Measures	**Ideas Presented** Single level of complex meaning with some need for inference; use of motif and irony.	
	Structures Used Presents more than one point of view; deviates from sequential order.	
	Language Used Includes some unfamiliar language; some domain-specific words.	
	Knowledge Required Explores moderately complex ideas; includes historical and cultural references.	

RESOURCES

Online **Ed**

- Unit 1 Response Log

- 🔊 Selection Audio

- ▶ Close Read Screencasts: Modeled Discussions

- 📖 Reading Studio: Notice & Note

- LEVEL UP Level Up Tutorial: Making Inferences

- Writing Studio: Writing Narratives

- 💬 Speaking and Listening Studio: Giving a Presentation

- Vocabulary Studio: Context Clues

- ✓ "What, of This Goldfish, Would You Wish?" Selection Test

SUMMARIES

English

A young man named Yoni (Yonatan) decides to film a documentary in which he asks people what they would wish for if a magic goldfish gave them three wishes. One day, he meets Sergei, an older Russian man who actually has a magic goldfish. Fearing that Yoni wants to steal the fish, Sergei hits Yoni and kills him. Sergei previously used two wishes but has saved one for a long time. As the goldfish and Sergei talk, Sergei grapples with losing the goldfish to save the boy but ultimately decides to save Yoni.

Spanish

Un joven llamado Yoni (Yonatan) decide filmar un documental en el que le pregunta a la gente qué desearían si un pez dorado mágico les concediera tres deseos. Un día, conoce a Sergei, un viejo Ruso, quien de hecho tiene un pez dorado mágico. Temiendo que Yoni quiera robarle el pez, Sergei golpea a Yoni y lo mata. Sergei había utilizado previamente dos deseos, pero había guardado uno por largo tiempo. Mientras el pez dorado y Sergei hablan, Sergei lucha con la idea de perder a su pez dorado para salvar al chico pero finalmente decide salvar a Yoni.

SMALL-GROUP OPTIONS

Have students work in small groups to read and discuss the selection.

Pinwheel Discussion

- Form groups of 8 (or 6) with students who are facing out paired with students who are facing in.

- Provide a question for discussion by all pairs and allow a prescribed amount of time. (Possible questions: Why did Yonatan hope to find an Arab man for his documentary? How do archetypes help to show conflict in the story? What role does flashback play in the story?)

- Call on random pairs to summarize their discussion for the class and answer any clarifying questions.

- Have outer students rotate one spot to the right to form a new pair. Repeat the process so that all students work with all others.

Think-Pair-Share

- After students have read and analyzed "What, of This Goldfish, Would You Wish?" remind students that a theme is an important idea about life or human nature expressed through a story's characters and events. Then pose this question: What theme does this story convey? What details support your answer?

- Have students think about the question individually and take notes.

- Then have pairs discuss their ideas about the question.

- Finally, ask pairs to share their responses with the class.

Text X-Ray: English Learner Support
for "What, of This Goldfish, Would You Wish?"

Use the Text X-Ray and the supports and scaffolds in the Teacher's Edition to help guide students at different proficiency levels through the selection.

INTRODUCE THE SELECTION
DISCUSS CULTURAL BACKGROUND

Explain to students that the author includes characters from different cultural backgrounds and that these differences are a source of conflict in the story. To help students understand:

- Read aloud the Background information on Student Edition page 7. Have students summarize what they know about the backgrounds of people living in this region.

- Discuss what *cultural background* means. For example, it can refer to a shared identity among people who have certain things in common, such as history, language, and religion.

- Brainstorm to develop a definition of the term *cultural background*. Have students write this definition in their notebooks.

As students read the story, encourage them to consider how each character's cultural background influences his behavior and actions.

CULTURAL REFERENCES

The following words or phrases may be unfamiliar to students:

- *documentary* (paragraph 1): a nonfiction film
- *camera crew* (paragraph 1): the people who operate the film camera
- *clips* (paragraph 2): short parts of a film
- *footage* (paragraph 3): film material that has not been edited
- *lens* (paragraph 5): the part of the camera that makes images
- *shooting schedule* (paragraph 7): the plan for filming a movie
- *promo* (paragraph 40): short for promotion, which means publicity

LISTENING

Interpret Tone

Draw students' attention to paragraphs 3–5. Before reading the paragraphs aloud, ask students to listen for unfamiliar words or phrases. Remind students that a writer may use certain language, including slang or idioms, to create an informal tone.

Have students listen as you read aloud paragraphs 3–5. Then, use the following supports with students at varying proficiency levels:

- Point out the phrase "killer wishes" in paragraph 3. Tell students that this is an example of slang. Explain that here, *killer* means "impressive" or "having a strong impact." **SUBSTANTIAL**

- Ask students if they can spot any examples of slang or idioms in paragraph 4. *(cash out)* Ask: How would you say this using more formal language? Have students repeat the sentence aloud using the more formal language. **MODERATE**

- Have students work in pairs to identify slang or idioms in paragraph 5. *(shave off, lady-killer)* Ask students to define the terms in the context of the story. **LIGHT**

SPEAKING

Present a Fable

Work with students as they adapt their fable for presentation to their classmates on Student Edition page 15.

Use the following supports with students at varying proficiency levels:

- Have students present their fable as a series of labeled drawings. Tell them to work with partners to correctly pronounce the vowels, silent letters, and consonant clusters in the labels. **SUBSTANTIAL**
- Encourage students to use drawings or words from their home language to explain part of the fable. **MODERATE**
- Have students create notecards summarizing key parts of the fable. Instead of reading the entire fable, tell them to use the notecards during their presentation. **LIGHT**

READING

Demonstrate Comprehension

Tell students that understanding the plot of a short story can require using several strategies.

Use the following supports with students at varying proficiency levels:

- Read aloud paragraphs 39–42 as students follow along. Guide students to identify the time shift between paragraphs 39 and 40. Ask: Did Sergei use his last wish? *(yes)* Did Sergei use his wish to save Yonatan's life? *(yes)* **SUBSTANTIAL**
- In pairs, reread paragraphs 39–40. Tell pairs to work together to explain what has just happened. **MODERATE**
- In small groups, ask students to reread paragraphs 39–42 and discuss their answers to these questions: What does Sergei do in response to the goldfish's question? Which lines of the story give you the clues to his response? **LIGHT**

WRITING

Write a Fable

Work with students to complete the writing assignment on Student Edition page 15.

Use the following supports with students at varying proficiency levels:

- Have students create a fable as a series of labeled pictures. In their labels, they should use their knowledge of sound/symbol relationships to spell correctly. **SUBSTANTIAL**
- Provide sentence frames that students can use as they create their fable: *The setting of this fable is _____. The main character in this fable is _____. The main problem is that _____.* **MODERATE**
- Remind students that language and sentence structure can affect tone. As students write, encourage them to decide whether their fable should have an informal or formal tone. Have them identify wording or sentence structures in their writing that help set this tone. **LIGHT**

EXPLAIN THE SIGNPOSTS

Explain that **NOTICE & NOTE Signposts** are significant moments in the text that help readers understand and analyze works of fiction or nonfiction. Use the instruction on these pages to introduce students to the signposts **Tough Questions**, **Memory Moment**, and **Words of the Wiser**. Then use the selection that follows to have students apply the signposts to a text.

For a full list of the fiction and nonfiction signposts, see p. 62.

▶ TOUGH QUESTIONS

Explain that **Tough Questions** seem to not have clear or right answers. When characters ask themselves or other characters tough questions, it helps readers gain insight into their **internal conflicts**, or personal struggles. Such conflicts may include the character's worries, fears, or hopes. The way a character responds to a tough question can reveal a story's **theme**, or message. Tough questions also help readers make connections to a text as they consider possible outcomes of various choices as well as how they or others might answer the questions themselves.

Read aloud the example passage. Then ask volunteers to suggest reasons why Yonatan thinks asking different people what they would wish for in a documentary is a "brilliant idea." Guide students to recognize that Yonatan's question is a Tough Question signpost due to the wide range of responses it would elicit.

Tell students that when they spot a Tough Question, they should pause, mark it in their consumable text, and ask themselves the anchor question: *What does this question make me wonder about?*

READING MODEL

For more information on these and other signposts to Notice & Note, visit the **Reading Studio**.

WHAT, OF THIS GOLDFISH, WOULD YOU WISH?

You are about to read the short story "What, of This Goldfish, Would You Wish?" You will notice and note signposts that will give you clues about the story's characters and themes. Here are three key signposts to look for as you read this story and other works of fiction.

Some **Tough Questions** are easy to spot. Others are signaled by phrases that express doubt or confusion:

"How could I…?"

"What could I possibly do…?"

"I can't imagine how I could cope with…"

"But what if…?"

"Never had I been so confused about…"

▶ **Tough Questions**   Would you rather be stuck at a party where you don't know anyone or stuck in a car with a relative who never stops talking? The "Would You Rather . . .?" game requires you to choose between two equally bad or good options. The way you respond can be funny, but it can also reveal something about your personality or what matters to you.

Likewise, when an author confronts a character with a tough question, the answer usually reveals something important. Paying attention to a **Tough Question** and its answer can:

- tell you something deeply personal about the character
- reveal a character's internal conflict or motivation
- provide insight into the story's message about life

The paragraph below illustrates a student's annotation within "What, of This Goldfish, Would You Wish?" and a response to a Notice and Note signpost.

Anchor Question
When you notice this signpost, ask: What does this question make me wonder about?

1   Yonatan had a brilliant idea for a documentary. He'd knock on doors. Just him. No camera crew, no nonsense. Just Yonatan, on his own, a small camera in hand, asking, "If you found a talking goldfish that granted you three wishes, what would you wish for?"

What's the tough question?	If you had three wishes, what would you wish for?
What does the question make you wonder about?	What's the catch? Can the fish be trusted? Can I wish for more wishes?

© Houghton Mifflin Harcourt Publishing Company

Memory Moment Have you ever noticed a landmark that triggers a long-ago memory? A memory can change the way you experience something in the present. When an author pauses to revisit a character's memory, it also has a strong effect. Paying attention to a **Memory Moment** can:

- explain or provide insight into the current situation
- show what motivates or drives a character's actions
- hint at the theme or a lesson of the story

Here is how a student might mark a Memory Moment in this story:

> 8   Sergei Goralick doesn't much like strangers banging on his door. Especially when those strangers are asking him questions. <u>In Russia, when Sergei was young, it happened plenty. The KGB felt right at home knocking on his door. His father had been a Zionist,</u> which was pretty much an invitation for them to drop by any old time.

When you read and encounter a phrase like these, pause to see if it's a Memory Moment signpost:

"I remembered when . . ."

"That reminded me of . . ."

"Grandma used to tell a story about . . ."

"A local legend said that . . ."

Anchor Question
When you notice this signpost, ask: Why might this memory be important?

What memory is introduced?	When Sergei was young, the KGB, or secret police, often showed up knocking on the door to question his father.
Why do you think this memory is important to the story?	Yonatan is knocking on Sergei's door. Is something bad about to happen?

Words of the Wiser In movies, an older character often offers sage advice to the main character. In any story, a wise character's advice may provide an insight about life or help the main character with a problem or decision.

In this example, a student marked some Words of the Wiser from the story:

> 20   "Nonsense," the fish says. "He was only here to make a little something for TV."
> 21   "But he said . . ."
> 22   "He said," says the fish, interrupting, "exactly what he was doing. <u>But you didn't get it.</u> Honestly, your Hebrew, it's terrible."

Anchor Question
When you notice this signpost, ask: What is the life lesson, and how might it affect the character?

What insight does the wiser character provide?	Sergei misunderstood what Yonatan wanted to do.
How might this affect the character?	Sergei will understand that he made a mistake and might make a different choice.

Notice & Note   3

WHEN STUDENTS STRUGGLE . . .

Use Strategies If students are struggling to identify the signposts, have them use the Somebody Wanted But So strategy to summarize the story's essential elements. Have students divide a sheet of paper into four columns and label the columns *Somebody*, *Wanted*, *But*, and *So*. As they read, have them take notes on *somebody* important to the story, what that person *wanted*, *but* then what happens to that person, and *so* what happens as a result. Tell students to record paragraph numbers in their notes. When students are finished, have them reread passages referenced in their notes with these questions in mind to help them identify Tough Questions, Memory Moments, and Words of the Wiser.

MEMORY MOMENT

Explain that **Memory Moments** often interrupt the flow of a narrative to give readers information needed to understand a character's present situation. Authors may use Memory Moments to add **suspense,** or explain a character's motivations.

Read aloud the example passage. Draw students' attention to the annotated portion of the passage. Explain that the KGB was an intelligence and security agency of the Soviet Union that used surveillance, imprisonment, and force in an effort to suppress opposing political and religious ideas, including Zionism (the movement to support the state of Israel as a Jewish homeland). Discuss with students how Sergei may have felt when the KGB knocked on the door of his family home and how these past feelings may connect to his current situation. (*Sergei may have felt threatened and afraid, which hints at how he might respond to Yonatan.*)

Tell students that when they spot a Memory Moment, they should pause, mark it in their consumable text, and ask themselves the anchor question: *Why might this memory be important?*

WORDS OF THE WISER

Tell students that **Words of the Wiser** are often offered by another character to help a main character with a problem or decision. The wiser character is usually older, and the words of advice or insight are often shared in a quiet, serious moment of the story. In addition to helping the main character resolve a present **conflict,** Words of the Wiser may also suggest a **theme** that could be helpful throughout life.

Read aloud the example passage. Then ask: What character flaw does the fish's words emphasize? What might Sergei learn from these words? (*The fish points out Sergei's irrational behavior, which Sergei might learn to correct.*)

Tell students that when they spot Words of the Wiser, they should pause, mark them in their consumable text, and ask themselves the anchor question: *What is the life lesson, and how might it affect the character?*

APPLY THE SIGNPOSTS

Have students use the selection that follows as a model text to apply the signposts. As students encounter signposts, prompt them to stop, reread, and ask themselves the anchor questions that will help them understand the story's themes and characters.

Tell students to continue to look for these and other signposts as they read the other selections in the unit.

Connect to the
ESSENTIAL QUESTION

Yoni, the character whom author Etgar Keret introduces at the start of "What, of This Goldfish, Would You Wish?" is eager to engage with others as part of an interview project—but how eager are they to engage with him? Yoni is true to his mission, but then he meets up with an especially reluctant subject. By focusing on the interaction of these two characters, students are invited to consider what may happen when there is a marked difference between the "truths" by which people live.

ANALYZE & APPLY

WHAT, OF THIS GOLDFISH, WOULD YOU WISH?

Short Story by **Etgar Keret**
translated by Nathan Englander

? ESSENTIAL QUESTION:

How do we engage with others while staying true to ourselves?

4   Unit 1

LEARNING MINDSET

Setting Goals Encourage students to consider how setting goals and working toward achieving them differs from simply dreaming or wishing for something to happen. For example, point out that dreams and wishes ("*I hope I get a B in math*") are not the same thing as goals ("*My goal is to study math for an hour every night so that I get a B on the math test*"). As a group, talk about the process of setting goals that are challenging yet achievable and then making a plan for achieving them. Ask students to share goals they would like to reach this week and then to describe specific steps they plan to take to achieve these goals.

QUICK START

If you were granted three wishes, what would you wish for? Would you use your wishes right away or save them? Discuss your answers with a partner.

ANALYZE ARCHETYPES

A character who grants three wishes sounds familiar, right? That's because it's an **archetype**—a character or situation that shows up in many works from different cultures.

Brainstorm examples of archetypal characters from stories, movies, or shows.

ARCHETYPE	EXAMPLE CHARACTER / WORK
The Hero	
The Mentor	
The Villain	
The Sidekick	

ANALYZE LITERARY DEVICES

A **literary device** is a technique used to convey meaning or create interest.

- When a writer uses **irony**, the opposite of what is expected happens. For example, a character getting a speeding ticket the day he earns an A+ in Driver's Education would be ironic.
- **Sarcasm** is the taunting use of praise to mean its opposite. For example, *"I heard zombies only eat brains, so you should be fine."*
- A **motif** is an image or idea that occurs many times in a work of literature. This repetition may create a particular tone, reveal the meaning of a symbol, or point toward a theme, or message, of the story.

As you read the story, note examples of irony, sarcasm, and motif.

DEVICE	WHAT HAPPENS?
Irony	*Yoni goes out to ask the "magic goldfish" question and meets a guy who actually owns such a goldfish.*
Sarcasm	*The goldfish is sarcastic with Sergei*
Motif	*The motif of wishes and dreams fills this story.*

GENRE ELEMENTS: SHORT STORY

- includes the basic elements of fiction—setting, characters, plot, conflict, resolution, and theme
- centers on one particular moment or event in life
- can be read in one sitting

What, of This Goldfish, Would You Wish?   5

© Houghton Mifflin Harcourt Publishing Company

EL ENGLISH LEARNER SUPPORT

Recognize Irony To help students spot irony, make sure they understand that a writer uses irony—something meaning the opposite of what it seems—to be funny or get the reader to see a point. Tell students that paragraphs 3 and 4 contain instances of irony.

- Ask students if they think the author is being funny or making a point in the first sentence of paragraph 3 and all of paragraph 4. Why do they think so? **SUBSTANTIAL**
- Ask students to work in pairs and find the irony in these paragraphs. What is the author using irony for in these examples? **MODERATE**

QUICK START

As partners discuss their responses to the Quick Start question, ask them to create a list of wishes that students might make right away. Invite partners to share their responses and to tell how having a wish come true immediately would change their lives and the lives of others. Would getting their wish make them happier? How would it affect people around them, or even people they have never met? Have partners and then the class also discuss why they might want to save one, two, or maybe even all three wishes. What might be the positive and negative results of that decision?

ANALYZE ARCHETYPES

Define and pronounce *archetype*. Point out that the word comes from two ancient Greek words meaning "beginning model." It may help students to think of a particular archetype as a "model" hero, mentor, and so on.

If students are having difficulty naming examples of the character archetypes listed, encourage them to think about traits that may commonly be associated with each character. (For example, a hero may be portrayed as fearless or strong.) Then ask students to think of a fictional character who demonstrates these traits.

ANALYZE LITERARY DEVICES

Make sure students understand the examples of irony and sarcasm; you may wish to give weather conditions as examples of motif. Tell students that three types of irony often appear in literary works: verbal irony (when what a character says is the opposite of what he or she means), situational irony (when something other than what is expected happens, as in the example in the text), and dramatic irony (when a character and the reader have a different understanding of a situation or event).

■ English Learner Support

Understand Sarcasm Explain that sarcasm is typically expressed through dialogue. Since readers cannot hear a character's tone, sarcastic comments may sometimes be misinterpreted and taken literally. To demonstrate, read aloud a sentence plainly and then read it again using a sarcastic tone of voice. **MODERATE**

CRITICAL VOCABULARY

Encourage students to read all the sentences before deciding which word best completes each one. Remind them to look for context clues that match the precise meaning of each word.

Answers:

1. *fluent*

2. *beleaguered*

3. *poignant*

4. *wizened*

■ English Learner Support

Use Cognates Tell students that the Critical Vocabulary word *fluent* and the Spanish word *fluido* are cognates.
ALL LEVELS

LANGUAGE CONVENTIONS

Read aloud the example of an informal tone. Explain that it shows the casual storytelling style of the narrator whom the author has created. Then read aloud the example of a formal tone. Invite students to share their reactions to the sentences. Point out that an author's tone reflects, in part, the audience whom the author is trying to reach.

✎ ANNOTATION MODEL

Students can review the Reading Model introduction if they have questions about any of the signposts. Suggest that they underline important phrases or circle key words that help them identify signposts. They may want to color-code their annotations by using a different color highlighter for each signpost. Point out that they may follow this suggestion or use their own system for marking up the selections in their write-in texts.

◎ **GET READY**

CRITICAL VOCABULARY

poignant	wizened	beleaguered	fluent

Practice and Apply Complete the sentences to see how many Critical Vocabulary words you already know.

1. Before visiting Mexico, I want to be _____ in Spanish so I can easily speak to the people I meet.

2. Gabriella felt _____ by the demands of school and her job.

3. My eyes welled with tears as the _____ music ended the movie.

4. The older apples turned _____ and rotten.

LANGUAGE CONVENTIONS

Tone An author's word choices and sentence structures express a particular tone, or attitude, toward characters and events. The tone may also reflect the personality of one or more characters.

An **informal tone** resembles how you might speak to friends. It may include short or incomplete sentences and slang, as in this example from the story:

> **Until one day some kid with a ring in his ear . . . comes knocking. Hard like that—rapping at his door. Just the way Sergei doesn't like.**

A **formal tone** includes proper grammar and complex sentences. This is the tone you would use for formal writing, such as a business letter. For example:

> **Until one day, a young man knocked on his door, hard. It was the kind of knock that Sergei did not like.**

ANNOTATION MODEL   **NOTICE & NOTE**

As you read, notice and note signposts, including **Tough Questions, Memory Moments,** and **Words of the Wiser.** Here is an example of how one reader marked the opening paragraphs of the text.

> It was genius, Yoni was sure. And, if not, at least it was cheap. All he needed was a door to knock on and a heart beating on the other side. With a little decent footage, he was sure he'd be able to sell it to Channel 8 or Discovery in a flash, either as a film or a bunch of vignettes, little <u>cinematic</u> corners, . . . <u>precious</u>, every one.
>
> Even better, maybe he'd <u>cash out</u>, <u>package</u> it with a <u>slogan</u> and sell it to a bank or cellular phone company. Maybe <u>tag</u> it with something like, "Different dreams, different wishes, one bank." Or "The bank that makes dreams come true."

The contrast between "genius" and "cheap" is ironic.

He wants to make something artistic.

Here, though, he thinks it's "even better" to be commercial, and he sounds sarcastic.

BACKGROUND

The Jewish people were expelled from their homeland in the first century CE. In the late 1800s, Jews from Europe, Asia, Africa, and the Americas began returning to the region; World War II and the Holocaust drastically increased this immigration. Israel became an independent nation in 1948, but tensions with its Arab neighbors and its Arab citizens have led to conflict. With the collapse of the Soviet Union in 1991, many Russian Jews were able to move to Israel and make their own mark on the nation's culture. In this story, Israeli writer **Etgar Keret** *(b. 1967) explores the hopes and dreams of people in this diverse society.*

WHAT, OF THIS GOLDFISH, WOULD YOU WISH?

Short Story by Etgar Keret
translated by Nathan Englander

SETTING A PURPOSE

After reading the title, what questions do you have about the topic of this story? As you read, add questions you have about the text. After reading, reread or discuss with a partner to clear up any remaining questions you have.

Notice & Note
You can use the side margins to notice and note signposts in the text.

1 Yonatan had a brilliant idea for a documentary. He'd knock on doors. Just him. No camera crew, no nonsense. Just Yonatan, on his own, a small camera in hand, asking, "If you found a talking goldfish that granted you three wishes, what would you wish for?"

2 Folks would give their answers, and Yoni would edit them down and make clips of the more surprising responses. Before every set of answers, you'd see the person standing stock-still in the entrance to his house. Onto this shot he'd superimpose[1] the subject's name, family situation, monthly income, and maybe even the party he'd voted for in the last election. All that, combined with the three wishes, and maybe he'd end up with a **poignant** piece of social commentary, a testament to the massive

[Close Read]

poignant
(poin´yənt) *adj.* emotionally moving or stimulating.

[1] **superimpose:** place one thing on top of another so that both remain visible.

BACKGROUND

Read the Background note aloud, pausing after each sentence to clarify information or answer questions relating to the time period described. Tell students that various groups still clash over what the internal boundaries of Israel are and which government controls which portions of land. In the story, Yoni (Yonatan) would have had no trouble visiting cities located outside of the contested West Bank area, such as Tel Aviv and Ashdod. Within that area, however, which is surrounded by a protective wall, he would have had more difficulty interviewing people living in Palestinian-controlled cities.

You also may wish to direct students to the question that forms the story's title—a question whose structure may sound odd to students. Tell students that the story was originally written in Hebrew and that they will be reading a translation, including a translation of the title. Explain that in Hebrew, there are various ways to ask a question and that the word order usually puts the more important details early in the question. In this case, that means that a goldfish is likely to be very important to this story.

SETTING A PURPOSE

Direct students to use the Setting a Purpose prompt to focus their reading.

(EL) ENGLISH LEARNER SUPPORT

Listen for Intonation Read aloud the last sentence of paragraph 1. Point out that when you ask a question, your voice rises at the end. Then say several questions and statements. Have students listen carefully to your intonation and identify which are questions.
SUBSTANTIAL

CRITICAL VOCABULARY

poignant: Yoni plans to create a documentary that moves viewers' emotions by contrasting images and facts about each person's life with information about his or her wishes.

ASK STUDENTS why the film Yoni plans to create might be poignant. *(Hearing about what people wish for while seeing what their lives actually are like could be very emotional for viewers.)*

CLOSE READ SCREENCAST

Modeled Discussion In their eBook, have students view the Close Read Screencast, in which readers discuss and annotate the key passage that describes how Yoni envisions his project (paragraph 2, sentence 4–paragraph 3).

As a class, view and discuss this video. Then have students pair up to do an independent close read of an additional passage—the exchange that fleshes out the relationship and conflict between Sergei and the goldfish (paragraphs 19–25). Students can record their answers on the Close Read Practice PDF.

[Close Read] **Close Read Practice PDF**

TEACH

ANALYZE LITERARY DEVICES

Remind students that a **motif** is a type of literary device that a writer uses to add meaning or create interest. The repetition of an image or idea may create a particular tone, develop a symbol, or point toward a story's **theme** (main message or lesson). (**Answer:** *Students may say that doors or doorways might represent a passage into other people's lives.*)

■ English Learner Support

Identify Motifs To make sure students understand what a **motif** is, identify some examples of motifs used in popular movies, TV shows, advertisements, or songs. Discuss how the repetition of a particular symbol or image (for example, a storm, a sunrise, a particular color, some kind of travel) might help convey the message of a work.
LIGHT

For **listening support** for students at varying proficiency levels, see the **Text X-Ray** on page 2C.

CRITICAL VOCABULARY

wizened: The old woman Yoni interviews shows the signs of a hard life as well as of her age. She wishes for a child she can no longer have because of her age.

ASK STUDENTS why the old lady is described as *wizened*. (*Her skin is probably saggy and wrinkled.*)

beleaguered: Yoni imagines getting into Hebron and meeting an Arab man whose life has been plagued by problems.

ASK STUDENTS why the Arab man might wish for peace. (*Peace would be a blessing after the challenges he has faced as an Arab living in Israel.*)

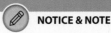

rift between our dreams and the often compromised reality in which we live.

3   It was genius, Yoni was sure. And, if not, at least it was cheap. All he needed was a door to knock on and a heart beating on the other side. With a little decent footage, he was sure he'd be able to sell it to Channel 8 or Discovery in a flash, either as a film or as a bunch of vignettes,[2] little cinematic corners, each with that singular soul standing in a doorway, followed by three killer wishes, precious, every one.

4   Even better, maybe he'd cash out, package it with a slogan and sell it to a bank or cellular phone company. Maybe tag it with something like "Different dreams, different wishes, one bank." Or "The bank that makes dreams come true."

5   No prep, no plotting, natural as can be, Yoni grabbed his camera and went out knocking on doors. In the first neighborhood he went to, the kindly folk that took part generally requested the foreseeable things: health, money, bigger apartments, either to shave off a couple of years or a couple of pounds. But there were also powerful moments. One drawn, **wizened** old lady asked simply for a child. A Holocaust survivor with a number on his arm asked very slowly, in a quiet voice—as if he'd been waiting for Yoni to come, as if it wasn't an exercise at all—he'd been wondering (if this fish didn't mind), would it be possible for all the Nazis left living in the world to be held accountable for their crimes? A cocky, broadshouldered lady-killer put out his cigarette and, as if the camera wasn't there, wished he were a girl. "Just for a night," he added, holding a single finger right up to the lens.

6   And these were wishes from just one short block in one small, sleepy suburb of Tel Aviv. Yonatan could hardly imagine what people were dreaming of in the development towns and the collectives[3] along the northern border, in the West Bank settlements and Arab villages, the immigrant absorption centers full of broken trailers and tired people left to broil out in the desert sun.

7   Yonatan knew that if the project was going to have any weight, he'd have to get to everyone, to the unemployed, to the ultrareligious, to the Arabs and Ethiopians and American expats.[4] He began to plan a shooting schedule for the coming days: Jaffa, Dimona, Ashdod, Sderot, Taibe, Talpiot. Maybe Hebron, even. If he could sneak past the wall, Hebron would be great. Maybe somewhere in that city some **beleaguered** Arab man would stand in his doorway and, looking through Yonatan and his camera, looking out into nothingness, just pause for a minute, nod his head, and wish for peace—that would be something to see.

---

[2] **vignettes:** small scenes or images.
[3] **collectives:** here, communal settlements.
[4] **expats:** expatriates, people living in a foreign country.

ANALYZE LITERARY DEVICES

Annotate: Mark references to doors and doorways up to this point in the story.

Analyze: What might a door or doorway symbolize? Why do you think the author uses this motif?

wizened
(wĭz´ənd) *adj.* shrunken and wrinkled.

beleaguered
(bĭ-lē´gərd) *adj.* troubled with many problems.

ENGLISH LEARNER SUPPORT

Analyze Idioms Using a whiteboard, project paragraph 4. Underline the phrase "cash out." Explain that this phrase is an idiom—a phrase with a meaning that is different from the literal meaning of the individual words. Note that students can use context clues in the sentences to help them figure out an idiom's meaning. Coach students in responding to the following questions to confirm understanding: What does the phrase *cash out* mean here? (*to take what money you can get for something*) How does this idiom contribute to the passage? (*It shows that Yoni is just as tempted to make money from his film as he is to create a work of art.*)
ALL LEVELS

8   Sergei Goralick doesn't much like strangers banging on his door. Especially when those strangers are asking him questions. In Russia, when Sergei was young, it happened plenty. The KGB felt right at home knocking on his door. His father had been a Zionist,[5] which was pretty much an invitation for them to drop by any old time.

9   When Sergei got to Israel and then moved to Jaffa, his family couldn't wrap their heads around it. They'd ask him, What are you looking to find in a place like that? There's no one there but addicts and Arabs and pensioners.[6] But what is most excellent about addicts and Arabs and pensioners is that they don't come around knocking on Sergei's door. That way Sergei can get his sleep, and get up when it's still dark. He can take his little boat out into the sea and fish until he's done fishing. By himself. In silence. The way it should be. The way it was.

---

[5] **Zionist:** supporter of a separate state for Jewish people.
[6] **pensioners:** people living on modest retirement payments.

What, of This Goldfish, Would You Wish?   9

ENGLISH LEARNER SUPPORT

Analyze Idioms Remind students that an **idiom** is a phrase with a meaning that is different from the literal meaning of the words that form it. Then ask a volunteer to read aloud the first three sentences of paragraph 9. Ask if students note any idioms in the passage. Once students correctly identify the idiom *wrap their heads around it*, guide them to use context clues to help them figure out the idiom's meaning. Ask: Who can't "wrap their heads around it"? *(Sergei's family)* What is the "it"? *(Sergei's decision to live in Jaffa)* What do the family members do because they can't "wrap their heads around it"? *(They ask him what he hopes to find in Jaffa and make a cruel comment about the people who live there.)* Why do you think they ask the question? *(They are trying to figure out his reason.)* So, what does the phrase "wrap their heads around it" mean here? *(to understand something that seems confusing)* How does this idiom contribute to the passage? *(It suggests that Sergei's family does not approve of where he lives and that he is an outsider in this place.)*

SUBSTANTIAL/MODERATE

WHEN STUDENTS STRUGGLE . . .

Analyze Shifts in Focus In paragraph 8, the focus of the story shifts. The narrator introduces a new character: Sergei, who becomes the main character in the rest of the story. Some students may find this shift abrupt or confusing. As a class, discuss the following questions and continue to explore them as the story unfolds:

1. Why do you think the author shifts from Yoni to Sergei? *(With this shift, the author can present different cultural backgrounds and ways of looking at the world.)*

2. How do Yoni's personality and attitude contrast with Sergei's? *(Yoni is upbeat, easygoing, and interested in people; Sergei is serious, seems unhappy, and wants to be left alone.)*

LANGUAGE CONVENTIONS

Remind students that, earlier, in paragraphs 8 and 9, the author uses a series of sentence fragments and short sentences to show that Sergei does not like people coming to his door and prefers to be alone (*By himself. In silence. The way it should be. The way it was.*). Explain that the author uses an informal style—for example, by using repetition, incomplete sentences, and slang—to convey what Sergei is thinking and how he is feeling now that Yoni has come to his door. **(Answer:** *The author's choices make it sound as if we are listening to the thoughts quickly going through Sergei's mind. The situation is moving too quickly for him to make good decisions.)*

■ English Learner Support

Distinguish Formal and Informal Language Make two columns on the board and label them "Formal" and "Informal." Work with students to list characteristics of formal and informal language such as these:

- Formal language typically uses longer, more sophisticated sentence structures. Informal language might use shorter and even incomplete sentence structures.

- Formal language uses standard grammar and spelling; it generally avoids grammatical errors such as sentence fragments and run-on sentences. Informal language may not follow such standards.

- Informal language uses idioms, contractions, and exclamation points far more often than formal language does. In addition, informal language may start sentences with conjunctions such as *and* or *but*, which formal language usually does not.

MODERATE/LIGHT

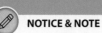 **NOTICE & NOTE**

LANGUAGE CONVENTIONS

Annotate: Mark unusual or informal word choices and sentence structures in paragraphs 10 and 11.

Analyze: How do these choices develop Sergei's character?

10   Until one day some kid with a ring in his ear . . . comes knocking. Hard like that—rapping at his door. Just the way Sergei doesn't like. And he says, this kid, that he has some questions he wants to put on the TV.

11   Sergei tells the boy, tells him in what he thinks is a straightforward manner, that he doesn't want it. Not interested. Sergei gives the camera a shove, to help make it clear. But the earring boy is stubborn. He says all kinds of things, fast things. And it's hard for Sergei to follow; his Hebrew isn't so good.

12   The boy slows down, tells Sergei he has a strong face, a nice face, and that he simply has to have him for this movie picture. Sergei can also slow down, he can also make clear. He tells the kid to shove off. But the kid is slippery, and somehow between saying no and pushing the door closed, Sergei finds that the kid is in his house. He's already making his movie, running his camera without any permission, and from behind the camera he's still telling Sergei about his face, that it's full of feeling, that it's tender. Suddenly the kid spots Sergei's goldfish flitting around in its big glass jar in his kitchen.

13   The kid with the earring starts screaming, "Goldfish, goldfish," he's so excited. And this, this really pressures Sergei, who tells the kid, it's nothing, just a regular goldfish, stop filming it. Just a goldfish, Sergei tells him, just something he found flapping around in the net, a deep-sea goldfish. But the boy isn't listening. He's still filming and getting closer and saying something about talking and fish and a magic wish.

14   Sergei doesn't like this, doesn't like that the boy is almost at it, already reaching for the jar. In this instant Sergei understands the boy didn't come for television, what he came for, specifically, is to snatch Sergei's fish, to steal it away. Before the mind of Sergei Goralick really understands what it is his body has done, he seems to have taken the burner off the stove and hit the boy in the head. The boy falls. The camera falls with him. The camera breaks open on the floor, along with the boy's skull. There's a lot of blood coming out of the head, and Sergei really doesn't know what to do.

APPLYING ACADEMIC VOCABULARY

❑ **discriminate**   ☑ **diverse**   ❑ **inhibit**   ❑ **intervene**   ☑ **rational**

Write and Discuss Have students turn to a partner to discuss the following questions. Guide students to include the academic vocabulary words *diverse* and *rational* in their responses. Ask volunteers to share their responses with the class.

- Why do you think the author introduces characters who live in Israel but come from **diverse** backgrounds?

- How **rational** is Sergei's reaction to Yoni's appearance at his door? In what ways does Sergei's cultural background and history influence his behavior?

15   That is, he knows exactly what to do, but it really would complicate things. Because if he takes this kid to the hospital, people are going to ask what happened, and it would take things in a direction Sergei doesn't want to go.

16   "No reason to take him to the hospital anyway," <u>says the goldfish, in Russian.</u> "That one's already dead."

17   "He can't be dead," Sergei says, with a moan. "I barely touched him. It's only a burner. Only a little thing." Sergei holds it up to the fish, taps it against his own skull to prove it. "It's not even that hard."

18   "Maybe not," says the fish. "But, apparently, it's harder than that kid's head."

19   "He wanted to take you from me," Sergei says, almost crying.

20   "Nonsense," the fish says. "He was only here to make a little something for TV."

21   "But he said . . . "

22   "He said," says the fish, interrupting, "exactly what he was doing. But you didn't get it. Honestly, your Hebrew, it's terrible."

23   "Yours is better?" Sergei says. "Yours is so great?"

24   "Yes. Mine's supergreat," the goldfish says, sounding impatient. "I'm a magic fish. I'm **fluent** in everything." All the while the puddle of blood from the earring kid's head is getting bigger and bigger and Sergei is on his toes, up against the kitchen wall, desperate not to step in it, not to get blood on his feet.

25   "You do have one wish left," the fish reminds Sergei. He says it easy like that, as if Sergei doesn't know—as if either of them ever loses count.

26   "No," Sergei says. He's shaking his head from side to side. "I can't," he says. "I've been saving it. Saving it for something."

27   "For what?" the fish says.

28   But Sergei won't answer.

29   <u>That first wish, Sergei used up when they discovered a cancer in his sister.</u> A lung cancer, the kind you don't get better from. The fish undid it in an instant—the words barely out of Sergei's mouth. <u>The second wish Sergei used up five years ago, on Sveta's boy.</u> The kid was still small then, barely three, but the doctors already knew something in her son's head wasn't right. He was going to grow big but not in the brain. Three was about as smart as he'd get. Sveta cried to Sergei in bed all night. Sergei walked home along the beach when the sun came up, and he called to the fish, asked the goldfish to fix it as soon as he'd crossed through the door. He never told Sveta. And a few months later she left him for some cop, a Moroccan with a shiny Honda. In his heart, Sergei kept telling himself it wasn't for Sveta that he'd done it, that he'd wished his wish purely for the boy. In his mind, he was less sure, and all kinds of thoughts about other things he could have done with that wish continued to gnaw at him, half driving him mad. The third wish, Sergei hadn't yet wished for.

ANALYZE ARCHETYPES

Annotate: What do we learn about the goldfish in paragraph 16? Mark the words that communicate this fact.

Evaluate: What is ironic about this archetypal character appearing in the story?

fluent
(floo͞′ənt) *adj.* able to express oneself clearly and easily.

WORDS OF THE WISER

Notice & Note: Mark the advice that the goldfish gives Sergei in this conversation.

Analyze: What do the goldfish's words tell you about the relationship between him and Sergei?

MEMORY MOMENT

Notice & Note: In paragraph 29, mark the memories that flow through Sergei's mind.

Analyze: How do you think these memories will affect what Sergei will do next?

What, of This Goldfish, Would You Wish?   11

✎ ANALYZE ARCHETYPES

Briefly discuss how learning that the goldfish is magic changes readers' understanding of Sergei's actions up to this point. (**Answer**: *It's ironic that Yoni bases his interview question on the archetype of a magical, wish-granting fish and then winds up at the home of someone who actually has such a fish—a move that causes his death.*)

▶ WORDS OF THE WISER

Remind students that this signpost encourages them to think about a lesson a **character** needs to learn. Discuss why the goldfish reminds Sergei about his wish and how Sergei feels about being reminded. (**Answer**: *The goldfish and Sergei know each other very well. The goldfish is encouraging Sergei to do the right thing. Sergei seems upset because he does not want to spend his last wish.*)

■ English Learner Support

Understand Informal Language Point out the informal sentence that begins, "He says it easy like that" in paragraph 25. Ask students what they think the author is trying to suggest. (*The goldfish may find it easy to talk about the wish, but it is a difficult topic for Sergei.*) **ALL LEVELS**

▶ MEMORY MOMENT

Have students identify the previous two wishes. Elicit that both were used to restore health to someone; in other words, Sergei did not use either wish to help himself. (**Answer**: *Sergei might weigh this situation against the two times he chose to use a wish to see whether this is a worthy moment for the final wish.*)

■ English Learner Support

Understand Connotation Point out that Sergei "used up" the two earlier wishes. Explain that the expression "used up" has a negative connotation, or feeling, which suggests that Sergei may regret those wishes. **ALL LEVELS**

CRITICAL VOCABULARY

fluent: The goldfish is *fluent* in all languages because he is magic.

ASK STUDENTS how being fluent in Hebrew makes the goldfish's reaction to Yoni different from Sergei's reaction. (*Unlike Sergei, the goldfish understands exactly what Yoni wants to do.*)

IMPROVE READING FLUENCY

Targeted Passage Use paired oral reading to help students use appropriate intonation (the rise and fall in the sound of one's voice when speaking) and expression (the way in which one's voice shows emotion) in reading text that includes dialogue. Begin by reading aloud paragraphs 16–21, emphasizing intonation and expression. Next, have student pairs take turns reading paragraphs 22–28 so that one student reads Sergei's dialogue and the other reads the goldfish's dialogue. Finally, have students switch roles and reread the passage.

   Go to the **Reading Studio** for additional support in developing fluency.

TOUGH QUESTIONS

Tell students that the goldfish's question marks a pivotal point in the story—a moment in which Sergei's true **character** will be revealed. Remind students that Sergei must give up something in order to save Yoni. As a group, discuss whether the goldfish is being ironic by using the verb "waste" in reference to using the wish to save someone's life. (**Answer:** *It is possible that Sergei thinks that the second wish, in particular, was wasted because Sveta left him. However, he seems to have made the wishes selflessly, to help his sister and the boy.*)

■ English Learner Support

Connect Synonyms Remind students that according to paragraph 29, Sergei "used up" the two earlier wishes. Encourage students to see the connection between the synonyms *used up* and *wasted*. **ALL LEVELS**

ENGLISH LEARNER SUPPORT

Confirm Understanding Use the following support of the word *superphotogenic* with students at varying proficiency levels.

- Write *superphotogenic* on the board and read the definition from the footnote. Draw lines to separate the word into three parts—*super/photo/genic*. Pronounce the word a few times, emphasizing the three parts. Ask students to name the word the slang term is based on. (*photogenic*) **SUBSTANTIAL**

- Have students reread paragraph 40, including the definition of *superphotogenic* from the footnote. Ask students to identify context clues that help them understand the meaning of the term. (*a handsome man, perfect, his promo for sure*) **MODERATE**

- Remind students that Etgar Keret uses tone to suggest the personalities of the characters. Read aloud paragraph 40, using the footnoted definition in place of *superphotogenic*. Ask students what the use of the slang term and informal language in the paragraph says about Yoni. (*He is youthful, very enthusiastic and excited about his documentary.*) **LIGHT**

 For **reading support** for students at varying proficiency levels, see the **Text X-Ray** on page 2D.

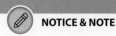
NOTICE & NOTE

30 "I can restore him," says the goldfish. "I can bring him back to life."

31 "No one's asking," Sergei says.

32 "I can bring him back to the moment before," the goldfish says. "To before he knocks on your door. I can put him back to right there. I can do it. All you need to do is ask."

33 "To wish my wish," Sergei says. "My last."

34 The fish swishes his fish tail back and forth in the water, the way he does, Sergei knows, when he's truly excited. The goldfish can already taste freedom. Sergei can see it on him.

35 After the last wish, Sergei won't have a choice. He'll have to let the goldfish go. His magic goldfish. His friend.

36 "Fixable," Sergei says. "I'll just mop up the blood. A good sponge and it'll be like it never was."

37 That tail just goes back and forth, the fish's head steady.

38 Sergei takes a deep breath. He steps out into the middle of the kitchen, out into the puddle. "When I'm fishing, while it's dark and the world's asleep," he says, half to himself and half to the fish, "I'll tie the kid to a rock and dump him in the sea. Not a chance, not in a million years, will anyone ever find him."

39 "You killed him, Sergei," the goldfish says. "You murdered someone—but you're not a murderer." The goldfish stops swishing his tail. "If, on this, you won't waste a wish, then tell me, Sergei, what is it good for?"

40 It was in Bethlehem, actually, that Yonatan found his Arab, a handsome man who used his first wish for peace. His name was Munir; he was fat with a big white mustache. Superphotogenic.[7] It was moving, the way he said it. Perfect, the way in which Munir wished his wish. Yoni knew even as he was filming that this guy would be his promo for sure.

41 Either him or that Russian. The one with the faded tattoos that Yoni had met in Jaffa. The one that looked straight into the camera and said, if he ever found a talking goldfish he wouldn't ask of it a single thing. He'd just stick it on a shelf in a big glass jar and talk to him all day, it didn't matter about what. Maybe sports, maybe politics, whatever a goldfish was interested in chatting about.

42 Anything, the Russian said, not to be alone.

---

[7] **superphotogenic:** looking extremely good in photos or on film.

TOUGH QUESTIONS

Notice & Note: In paragraphs 38–40, mark an example of a tough question.

Make Connections: Think about Sergei's two earlier wishes. Do you think he considers them wasted wishes?

WHEN STUDENTS STRUGGLE . . .

Support Comprehension To guide students' comprehension of the final events of the story, have students work in pairs to fill out a sequence chain. Instruct students to fill in the first oval in the chain with a note about what happens in paragraphs 38–39 and the third oval with a note about what happens in paragraph 40. Finally, have students infer and describe what must have taken place between these two events. (*Sergei must have used the third wish to save Yoni.*)

 For additional support, go to the **Reading Studio** and assign the following **Level Up Tutorial: Making Inferences.**

CHECK YOUR UNDERSTANDING

Answer these questions before moving on to the **Analyze the Text** section on the following page.

1 Why does Yonatan come to Sergei's door?

 A He has gone to the wrong apartment by accident.

 B He is with the KGB and has tracked Sergei from Russia.

 C He wants to interview Sergei for a documentary film.

 D He has come to thank Sergei for his kindness.

2 What misunderstanding causes the story's main problem?

 F The fish lies to Sergei about why Yonatan is there.

 G Sergei thinks that Yonatan wants to take the goldfish.

 H Sergei and Yonatan understand nothing of each other's language.

 J Yonatan feels threatened by Sergei, who means him no harm.

3 Sergei does not want to use his last wish because —

 A the fish is his only friend

 B Yonatan was a genuine threat

 C he plans to use it to get rich

 D he is saving it for a true emergency

CHECK YOUR UNDERSTANDING

Have students answer the questions independently.

Answers:

 1. *C*

 2. *G*

 3. *A*

If they answer any questions incorrectly, have them reread the text to confirm their understanding. Then they may proceed to ANALYZE THE TEXT on page 14.

 ## ENGLISH LEARNER SUPPORT

Oral Assessment Use the following questions to assess students' comprehension and speaking skills.

 1. Why does Yonatan come to Sergei's door? (*He wants to interview Sergei for a documentary film.*)

 2. What does Sergei mistakenly think? (*Sergei thinks that Yonatan wants to take the goldfish.*)

 3. Why does Sergei not want to use his last wish? (*The fish is his only friend but will go away when all the wishes are spent.*)

SUBSTANTIAL/MODERATE

ANALYZE THE TEXT

Possible answers:

1. **DOK 4:** *Sergei's response seems reasonable given his history. He's Jewish and from Russia, and he grew up having the KGB knock on his door because his father was a Zionist. He is accustomed to being at least wary, if not afraid, of a knock at the door.*

2. **DOK 2:** *Sergei is a genuinely kind and generous person. He uses both of the first two wishes helping other people, and he never tells his girlfriend what he did for her.*

3. **DOK 3:** *Yoni wishes for success; Sergei wishes for unconditional companionship; and the goldfish wishes for freedom. Yoni pursues his wish without really thinking it through. Sergei seems to have tried in the past to achieve his wish but now is mostly isolated. The goldfish understands its situation well and is able to achieve its wish through persuasion.*

4. **DOK 4:** *The flash forward is an effective structure because it makes the reader think about how Sergei made his decision. Going into the details just would have slowed down the story. The last paragraph shows that Yoni was correct to think that Sergei was a good person.*

5. **DOK 4:** *The goldfish is trying to help Sergei understand that most people present themselves in an honest and straightforward way that is worth believing. Sergei has learned in the past that he can't trust people, but the fish is teaching him that he should give everyone a chance before shutting them out. One theme is that people need to trust others in order to be happy.*

RESEARCH

Urge students to consider more than one key phrase as they search for traditional tales that include talking animals and/ or the rule of three. Once students have identified several tales, divide them into small groups and assign each one of the identified tales. Have each group take notes to compare their tale with Etgar Keret's.

Extend Tell students that their summaries should include key details from their research in addition to their conclusions about the similarities between the tales.

 RESPOND

ANALYZE THE TEXT

Support your responses with evidence from the text.   NOTEBOOK

1. **Analyze** Consider how Sergei reacts when Yoni comes to his door. Does his response seem reasonable? How does Sergei's cultural experience help explain his reaction?

2. **Infer** When you **infer**, you use details in a text to draw a conclusion about something that the author does not state directly. What can you infer about Sergei's character based on the way he used his first two wishes?

3. **Draw Conclusions** How does the motif of wishing apply to each of the story's major characters: Yoni, Sergei, and the goldfish? What is similar and different about their wishes?

4. **Evaluate** The last section of the story is a flash forward. Readers must infer what happens in the time between Sergei's conversation with the fish and Yoni's final report on his video. Is this structure effective, or would it have been better to know the details about Sergei's decision? Explain.

5. **Notice & Note** Reread what the goldfish tells Sergei in paragraph 22. What lesson is this archetypal wise character trying to convey? How does this lesson reveal a theme of the story?

RESEARCH TIP
To begin your research, type the key words "rule of three and traditional tales" into your web browser. Take notes from each story so you can use the details to synthesize, or come to a new understanding, of the information.

RESEARCH

This story provides a modern twist on two features of many folk tales: talking animals and the rule of three. Work with a small group to research traditional tales that include one or both of these elements. Then, synthesize the story ideas your group has gathered to make a comparison between these stories and Etgar Keret's story. In what ways are the talking animals similar and different? What kinds of events, characters, or details appear in groups of three?

	KERET'S STORY	OTHER STORIES
Talking Animals	*Students' research notes should identify similarities between Keret's story and other traditional tales.*	
Rule of Three		

Extend Write a summary of your group's conclusions about Keret's story in comparison with the traditional tales you researched.

 LEARNING MINDSET

Belonging Remind students that they are all valuable members of the class and that they should support each other as learners. When researching folk tales, encourage students to share stories that may reflect their family or cultural background. If other students are not familiar with these stories, suggest that they conduct further research and consider how these stories may be similar to or different from stories they already know.

CREATE AND PRESENT

Write a Fable Write a fable to teach a lesson about life, using an archetypal character.

❏ Begin with details that introduce the archetypical character(s) and establish the conflict. Include dialogue and details that make the tale colorful and entertaining.

❏ Then, describe events that build the conflict toward a turning point. That buildup may mean that the same basic sequence of events plays out a second time. The repetition builds tension.

❏ Resolve the conflict and draw your fable to a logical conclusion.

Present a Fable Adapt your fable for presentation to your classmates.

❏ Practice reading the fable, adjusting your pace and expression to emphasize the content. For example, change your voice when different characters are speaking.

❏ Consider memorizing key parts of your fable so you can recite them without reading from a script. This frees you to make eye contact with listeners. It's fine to paraphrase parts that are mostly narration.

❏ Use visuals and gestures to bring your story to life for your audience.

 Go to the **Writing Studio** for more on writing a narrative.

 Go to the **Speaking and Listening Studio** for more on giving a presentation.

RESPOND TO THE ESSENTIAL QUESTION

 ? How do we engage with others while staying true to ourselves?

Gather Information Review your annotations and notes on "What, of This Goldfish, Would You Wish?" Then, add relevant information to your Response Log. As you determine which information to include, think about:

• what makes people happy
• how people who have been hurt by others tend to respond
• internal conflict created by that response

At the end of the unit, you will use your notes to help you write a personal essay.

ACADEMIC VOCABULARY
As you write and discuss what you learned from the short story, be sure to use the Academic Vocabulary words. Check off each of the words that you use.

❏ **discriminate**
❏ **diverse**
❏ **inhibit**
❏ **intervene**
❏ **rational**

CREATE AND PRESENT

Write a Fable Explain that a fable is a short story that has a clear (and often a clearly stated) lesson about how people should act and that often includes talking animals. Then discuss the steps for writing a fable. Note that fables include the same basic elements as other stories:

• characters and setting (who, where, when)
• beginning (introduction of a problem or conflict)
• middle (sequence of events, building to a climax)
• end (resolution)

For **writing support** for students at varying proficiency levels, see the **Text X-Ray** on page 2D.

Present a Fable Pair students and have them practice reading aloud their fables to each other. Encourage students to offer each other tips for improving their pace and expression and to suggest visuals or gestures that may make the presentation more interesting. If students are anxious about reading to the class, you can allow student pairs to work together in presenting the fables. For example, one student can narrate events while the second student reads the characters' dialogue.

For **speaking support** for students at varying proficiency levels, see the **Text X-Ray** on page 2D.

RESPOND TO THE ESSENTIAL QUESTION

Allow time for students to add details from "What, of This Goldfish, Would You Wish?" to their Unit 1 Response Logs.

 ENGLISH LEARNER SUPPORT

Present a Fable Use the following supports with students at varying proficiency levels:

• Help students identify two or three key events or ideas in their fables. Then have them create visuals or practice gestures that illustrate those events or ideas. **SUBSTANTIAL**

• Pair up students to practice reading their fables. Ask students to reread key sections, changing their pace and expression. Have students discuss whether these changes improve or take away from the content. **MODERATE**

• Ask students to read their fables to a small group. See if the group can state the lesson of the fable and receive help as needed from the author to identify it. **LIGHT**

APPLY

CRITICAL VOCABULARY

Possible answers:

1. *I probably will remember a poignant post because it has moved me emotionally.*

2. *I might put wizened flowers in fresh water or maybe the refrigerator to see if they perk up. If not, I would throw them away because they have dried up and no longer look attractive.*

3. *Maria almost certainly would not look confident, for a beleaguered person would feel overwhelmed by problems.*

4. *No; if Doug is fluent in French, he can speak the language with ease and probably doesn't need a French dictionary.*

VOCABULARY STRATEGY:
Context Clues

Explain that there are many types of context clues, including synonym and antonym clues. Sometimes the clue is obvious; at other times, students must consider text details and then make an inference about the meaning of the unfamiliar word. Students may check their definitions against a print or digital dictionary, but even an inferred definition is better than simply glossing over the unfamiliar word. If needed, review with students the definitions of *part of speech, noun, verb, adjective,* and *adverb* before having them work on the chart.

 RESPOND

WORD BANK
poignant
wizened
beleaguered
fluent

For more on using context clues, visit the **Vocabulary Studio.**

CRITICAL VOCABULARY

Practice and Apply Answer these questions to demonstrate your understanding of each Critical Vocabulary word.

1. You have just read a **poignant** blog post. Will you still be thinking about it tomorrow, or will you forget it immediately? Explain.

2. The flowers you received last week appear **wizened**. What will you do with them? Why?

3. Maria feels **beleaguered** on the first day of school. Does her facial expression show that she is confident or that she is overwhelmed? Why?

4. Doug is **fluent** in French. Does he need to pack a French dictionary when he travels to France? Explain.

VOCABULARY STRATEGY:
Context Clues

If you come across an unfamiliar word while reading, you can use **context clues,** or information within a sentence or in the surrounding text, to figure out the word's meaning. For example, the word *fluent* appears in the context of a conversation about Sergei's poor understanding of the Hebrew language. The goldfish says, "Mine's supergreat . . . I'm fluent in everything. "The contrast between Sergei's poor Hebrew and the fish's fluent Hebrew helps you guess that *fluent* means "able to express oneself clearly and easily."

Practice and Apply Find the following words in the story: *testament* (paragraph 2), *foreseeable* (paragraph 5), *accountable* (paragraph 5), *promo* (paragraph 40). Working with a partner, complete the chart, using context clues to determine each word's meaning as it is used in the story.

TERM	PART OF SPEECH	CONTEXT CLUES	MY DEFINITION
testament	*noun*	*"a testament to the massive rift between our dreams and... reality." Yoni wants people to make statements about what they want out of life.*	*I think a testament is a statement about what a person wants or believes.*
foreseeable	*adjective*	*"foreseeable things . . . But there were also powerful moments." There's a contrast between powerful moments typical answers.*	*I think foreseeable means predictable or expected.*
accountable	*adjective*	*The Holocaust survivor wishes "for all the Nazis...to be held accountable for their crimes." The survivor would want to see justice done.*	*I think accountable means responsible.*
promo	*noun*	*Yoni thinks "this guy would be his promo for sure." I think it's short for promotional.*	*I think a promo is probably an ad of some kind.*

© Houghton Mifflin Harcourt Publishing Company

EL ENGLISH LEARNER SUPPORT

Vocabulary Strategy Help students internalize new vocabulary words by creating a set of vocabulary cards. For each word, students should make a card showing the word, part of speech, definition written in their first language, and an example sentence. Next, have students use a dictionary or other classroom or online resource to include synonyms and antonyms for each vocabulary word. As a class, discuss the synonyms and antonyms that students have identified. **SUBSTANTIAL/MODERATE**

LANGUAGE CONVENTIONS:
Tone

An author might use word choice and sentence structure to express a particular **tone**, or attitude, toward characters and events. The tone may also reflect the personality of one or more characters. Etgar Keret uses techniques such as slang and incomplete sentences to create an informal tone. Read this passage from the story:

> **Yonatan had a brilliant idea for a documentary. He'd knock on doors. Just him. No camera crew, no nonsense. Just Yonatan, on his own, a small camera in hand, asking, "If you found a talking goldfish that granted you three wishes, what would you wish for?"**

The author could have used more formal language, such as this:

> **Yonatan had a brilliantly simple idea for a documentary. He would do all the filming himself, without a camera crew. Knocking on people's doors with a small hand-held camera, he would inquire of each person, "If you found a talking goldfish that granted you three wishes, what would you wish for?"**

The informal language that Etgar Keret chose sets a tone that is better suited to Yoni's youthful enthusiasm and his spirit of adventure.

Here are some other examples of language from the story and how they contribute to the informal tone.

EXAMPLE FROM TEXT	HOW IT AFFECTS TONE
three killer wishes	*Killer* is slang for "excellent." Slang is the language of casual, everyday speech.
When Sergei got to Israel and then moved to Jaffa, his family couldn't wrap their heads around it.	The expression *wrap their heads around* (meaning "understand") is an idiom that people use in conversation but not in formal writing or speech.
But the earring boy is stubborn.	Calling Yoni "the earring boy" reflects Sergei's private thoughts. The humor in this mild insult fits the informal tone of the story.

Practice and Apply Write two versions of a paragraph describing an experience you have had. Choose words, phrases, and sentence structures that create a formal tone in the first version and an informal tone in the second. Identify which version best fits the event your writing describes.

LANGUAGE CONVENTIONS:
Tone

Read aloud, or call on volunteers to read aloud, the first passage from the story. Help students identify an example of slang (*no nonsense*) and incomplete sentences (*Just him. No camera crew, no nonsense.*). As you go on to discuss the formal version, point out that the two incomplete sentences have been combined into a single complete sentence and that the slang has been dropped altogether. However, the fact that the wording of the interview question does not change indicates that Yoni always intended to address his interview subjects in a formal, polite way. Invite students to rephrase the three additional examples of language from the story using more formal language. Discuss the effect such changes might have on the overall tone of that part of the story.

Practice and Apply Have students work in pairs to compare the two versions of their paragraphs. Instruct partners to identify specific instances where informal or formal language is used (for example, by underlining or circling words or phrases). Have students discuss whether an informal or formal tone is better suited for their paragraph, considering both the event described and the audience for whom the paragraph is intended.

 ENGLISH LEARNER SUPPORT

Analyze Slang and Idioms Remind students that informal language often uses slang (the language of informal, everyday speech) and idioms (expressions with meanings that are different from the literal meaning of their individual words). Divide students into small groups and instruct them to reread the text to identify examples of slang and idioms. Using a graphic organizer, have students write down the word or phrase and then work together to define it. Ask groups to share the examples they found and the definitions they chose. (For example, students may note *shave off* in paragraph 5, *lady-killer* in paragraph 5, *ultrareligious* in paragraph 7, or *supergreat* in paragraph 24.) Conclude by briefly reviewing how the use of slang and idioms affects the story. **ALL LEVELS**

MENTOR TEXT

BY ANY OTHER NAME

Memoir by Santha Rama Rau

This memoir serves as a **mentor text**, a model for students to follow when they come to the Unit 1 Writing Task: Writing a Personal Essay.

GENRE ELEMENTS
MEMOIR

Remind students that the purpose of a **memoir** is to tell about an experience or a set of related experiences from the writer's past. Explain that memoirs and autobiographies both use a first-person point of view. However, autobiographies tend to be much longer and more comprehensive. In addition, the writer of a memoir tends to reflect more upon the meaning of the experience(s) and to present details and insights that point to a particular theme.

LEARNING OBJECTIVES

- Analyze how a text's historical and cultural context is related to the author's perspective and purpose for writing.
- Conduct research about a person who has changed his or her name.
- Write a poem about the importance of their own name.
- Discuss why names matter.
- Use foreign words that have entered the English language.
- Analyze and use verb tenses.
- **Language** Discuss with a partner cultural differences in the memoir.

TEXT COMPLEXITY

Quantitative Measures	By Any Other Name	Lexile: 1120L
Qualitative Measures	**Ideas Presented** Mostly explicit, but moves to some implied meaning.	
	Structures Used Text is somewhat complex, with a dual perspective and some variations from a strictly chronological order.	
	Language Used Mostly Tier I and Tier II words; some setting-specific terms are used.	
	Knowledge Required Most of the text deals with easily imagined experiences, but students also need to take into account historical/cultural references.	

Online

RESOURCES

- Unit 1 Response Log

- 🔊 Selection Audio

- 📖 Reading Studio: Notice & Note

- **LEVEL UP** Level Up Tutorial: Historical and Cultural Context

- 💬 Speaking and Listening Studio: Participating in Collaborative Discussions

- ⚙️ Vocabulary Studio: Foreign Words Used in English

- ❗ Grammar Studio: Module 7: Lesson 3: Verb Tense

- ☑️ "By Any Other Name" Selection Test

SUMMARIES

English

At the age of five, and a half, Santha Rama Rau and Premila, her eight-year-old sister, are sent to an Anglo-Indian school. There, their names are changed to "Cynthia" and "Pamela." As Indians, they are looked down upon and are expected to adopt British cultural norms. When Premila is told that Indian children cheat on tests, she takes herself and Santha out of school. Santha is not upset, however, for she has separated herself from "Cynthia" from the start.

Spanish

A los cinco años y medio, Santha Rama Rau y Premila, su hermana de ocho años, son enviadas a una escuela anglo-hindú. Ahí, les cambian los nombres a "Cynthia" y "Pamela". Como hindúes, son despreciadas y se espera que se adapten a las normas culturales británicas. Cuando le dicen a Premila que los niños hindúes hacen trampa en los exámenes, ella se retira con Santha de la escuela. Sin embargo, Santha no está molesta, puesto que se ha separado a sí misma de "Cynthia" desde el principio.

 ## SMALL-GROUP OPTIONS

Have students work in small groups to read and discuss the selection.

Three-Minute Review

- As students read "By Any Other Name," have them pause periodically.

- Set a timer for three minutes. During that time, students should skim or reread the text and review notes that they have made while reading.

- When the timer sounds, ask one or more of these questions and briefly discuss students' responses:

  — What did you notice as you reviewed this text?

  — What questions do you have about the text?

  — What in this text seems especially important?

  — What do you think will happen next?

Cubing

- Use card stock to create a cube for each group of students, each face showing one of these question words: *Who, What, Where, When, Why,* and *How.*

- After students have read "By Any Other Name," divide them into groups and give each group one cube.

- Instruct group members to roll the cube and then identify a detail from the memoir that answers the question. Several responses are possible for each question word. *(for example: Who—Premila, Santha, their mother and father, the headmistress, the teacher, the other girls at school)*

- Note: You can use a set of six index cards per group instead of a cube.

Text X-Ray: English Learner Support
for "By Any Other Name"

Use the Text X-Ray and the supports and scaffolds in the Teacher's Edition to help guide students at different proficiency levels through the selection.

INTRODUCE THE SELECTION
DISCUSS A CULTURE CLASH

In this lesson, students will need to be able to discuss the challenges involved in requiring people from one culture to act like people from another. Read paragraph 1 with students and offer these explanations:

- The girls start to attend an *Anglo-Indian day school*, where Indian children mix with children of British immigrants.
- On the first day, the girls are *renamed*.
- The *headmistress* is in charge. She can help make the girls' school experience pleasant or miserable.

Have volunteers use the terms to complete these sentence frames: *The girls meet the _____ when they arrive at the _____. She decides to _____ them.*

CULTURAL REFERENCES

The following words or phrases may be unfamiliar to students:

- *an officer of the civil service* (paragraph 5): a person who works for the government in a job related to the public good, but not as part of the armed forces
- *examinations* (paragraph 6): formal tests administered in the British educational system and required in order to apply for certain jobs
- *veranda* (paragraph 7): a porch, usually with a roof, that is attached to and extends along the ground floor of a building's exterior

LISTENING

Understand Spoken Language in Context

Have students listen as you read aloud paragraph 3. Explain that the headmistress's use of the word *jolly* means "pleasing" or "enjoyable" in this context.

Use the following supports with students at varying proficiency levels:

- Ask: Would most children think it is pleasing to have to change their names at a new school? *(no)* Does the headmistress want the girls to accept their school names? *(yes)* **SUBSTANTIAL**
- Have students respond to questions about the paragraph. For example, ask: Why do you think the headmistress says it would be "jolly" to give the girls "pretty English names"? *(She wants them to accept their school names.)* **MODERATE**
- After listening to the paragraph, have partners discuss the headmistress's reasons for using the words *jolly, pretty,* and *nice* in her explanation of the girls' new names. **LIGHT**

SPEAKING

Discuss Character Interactions

Have students discuss cultural differences in the text and the way that young Santha's classmates respond to her. Circulate around the room to answer questions and keep the discussion moving.

Use the following supports with students at varying proficiency levels:

- Read aloud paragraphs 9–14. Ask students to say, "same" when they hear a detail that connects Santha to her Indian classmates and" different" when they hear a detail that shows a contrast between the Indian and British children. Then have students complete this sentence frame orally: _____ *children have black around their eyes.* **SUBSTANTIAL**
- Ask students to read aloud paragraphs 9–14 and then complete these sentence frames orally: *When Santha doesn't know what to say, the British children* _____. *The Indian girl with braids shows sympathy for Santha by* _____. **MODERATE**
- Have small groups read aloud sentences from paragraphs 9–14, pausing after each sentence to discuss how well young Santha seems to be fitting in. **LIGHT**

READING

Analyze Perspective

As students read paragraphs 3–7, tell them to look for details that show the author's perspective and her feelings about the subject she writes about.

Use the following supports with students at varying proficiency levels:

- Point out Santha's description in paragraph 4 of how she thanked the headmistress "in a very tiny voice." Then guide students to complete this frame: *This shows that Santha felt* _____. *(scared, shy)* **SUBSTANTIAL**
- Tell students to listen for Santha's reaction to her new name as you read aloud paragraph 4. Ask, how is Santha's sister feeling here? *(angry)* How is Santha feeling here? *(scared, shy)* **MODERATE**
- Ask: How does Santha feel about her new name? Have students cite evidence from the text that supports their answer. **LIGHT**

WRITING

Write a Poem

Work with students as they complete the writing assignment on Student Edition page 29.

Review the characteristics of free-verse poetry. Then use the following supports with students at varying proficiency levels:

- Help students begin to generate ideas by inviting them to complete sentences such as: *I (like/do not like) my name. My name makes me feel* _____. **SUBSTANTIAL**
- Give students a concept map graphic organizer and tell them to write their name in the center. Encourage them to populate the rest of the graphic organizer with details that they might include in the poem. **MODERATE**
- Remind students of the value of vivid word choices. Guide them in the use of a print or digital thesaurus as they consider the words (especially verbs and adjectives) that best express their feelings. **LIGHT**

Connect to the
ESSENTIAL QUESTION

"By Any Other Name" presents the real-life experiences of two children in colonial India, told in a memoir by Santha Rama Rau. When entering classes at a British-run school, she and her sister are pushed to adopt the culture of their teacher and most of their classmates. Must the sisters sacrifice their home culture in order to be accepted and to succeed in school? As Rama Rau shows, there comes a point at which standing up for yourself overshadows other considerations.

MENTOR TEXT

At the end of the unit, students will be asked to write a personal essay. "By Any Other Name" provides a model for how a writer can not only relate the details of an event in which he or she participated but also reflect upon and share insights about the significance of that event.

ANALYZE & APPLY

BY ANY OTHER NAME

Memoir by **Santha Rama Rau**

18   Unit 1

? ESSENTIAL QUESTION:

How do we engage with others while staying true to ourselves?

© Houghton Mifflin Harcourt Publishing Company • ©The Print Collector/Alamy

LEARNING MINDSET

Setting Goals Explain to students that setting goals can help them accomplish a task efficiently and evaluate their progress while doing so. When students approach a new text, setting goals means choosing a focus for their reading and identifying the steps they will take to understand that focus. Remind students that people learn at different speeds and that their goals should be realistic. Suggest that students base their goals for this selection upon the lesson skills—analyzing historical context and the author's purpose—but also encourage them to stretch beyond those. Suggest, for example, that understanding the sisters' actions and motives is also a worthy goal and may be a good starting place.

QUICK START

The title of this piece comes from Shakespeare's *Romeo and Juliet*. Because their families are enemies, Juliet wishes that Romeo had a different surname. "What's in a name?" Juliet asks. "That which we call a rose / By any other name would smell as sweet."

How important is a person's name? How would you react if someone took your name away and assigned you a new one? Turn to a partner and share your thoughts.

ANALYZE HISTORICAL CONTEXT

At the time of this account (around 1928), India was a colony of Great Britain. Educated Indians were expected to learn English in addition to their native languages. (Many languages are spoken in India.) The headmistress, or principal, of Santha Rama Rau's school was British, as were most of the students, who were the children of British civil servants sent to India as colonial rulers. Great Britain ruled the Indian subcontinent from 1858 to 1947.

To analyze the point of view that Santha Rama Rau brings to her experiences at school, identify details of history and culture that help to define India in the 1920s. Then, make inferences about Rama Rau's perspective on these details.

TEXT EXCERPT	INFERENCE
Up to then, my mother had refused to send Premila to school in the British-run establishments of that time . . .	Rama Rau notices her parents have mixed feelings about the British.
I had never really grasped the system of competitive games. . . . it was not for years that I really learned the spirit of the thing.	Rama Rau finds the competitive atmosphere of the British school different from the caring atmosphere at home.

ANALYZE AUTHOR'S PURPOSE

An **author's purpose** is the reason the author writes a particular piece, whether to inform, persuade, or entertain the audience. As you read this piece, analyze Rama Rau's authorial choices. What historical and cultural details does she share with readers? Based on her choices, what can you infer about her purpose for writing?

- As you read, mark details about history and culture. The details may relate to food, dress, customs, language, class, or ways of interacting. They may also relate to the people Rama Rau comes into contact with.

- Think about why Rama Rau shares these details. What do the details reveal about her purpose for writing?

GENRE ELEMENTS: MEMOIR

- a true story told as a memory, usually in the past tense

- the author is the narrator, who uses a first-person point of view

- does not retell the author's entire life

- a selected memory or memories reflect a message or lesson

QUICK START

Help students paraphrase the quotation from *Romeo and Juliet* (for example, "A rose smells sweet, no matter what you call it"). Then have them read the Quick Start questions and think about the importance of a person's name—in particular, their own name. As partners talk, have them focus on the scenario of having to answer to a new name. Encourage them to consider why this change might be required, how they would feel about it, and whether they would try to do anything about it. Invite partners to share responses with the class.

ANALYZE HISTORICAL CONTEXT

Relate the concept of *context* to what students already know about context clues in vocabulary development: Just as the text that surrounds a word can help students understand the meaning of that word, so the historical and cultural information that "surrounds" (exists as a background setting for) a narrative can help students understand some details about characters and events. Discuss the chart, noting that historical context can inform even minor text details. Point out, however, that when it comes to major events and themes in "By Any Other Name," students should keep in mind the potential for conflict between India's home cultures and the culture of Great Britain.

ANALYZE AUTHOR'S PURPOSE

Explain that when we speak of an author's purpose in a text, we are talking about the overall purpose. For example, the author of a persuasive text may include information and even some entertaining details, but the purpose of the text as a whole is to encourage readers to agree with the author's opinion. As students read "By Any Other Name," have them look for ways in which young Santha and her sister Premila attempt to navigate the culture clash they face at school. How do they become aware of the cultural differences, and how do their reactions point to an overall purpose for the writing of this memoir?

ENGLISH LEARNER SUPPORT

Contrast Verb Forms Point out to students that in this memoir they will see the verb *had* used in two ways: to show ownership in the past ("that steamy little provincial town, where he *had* his headquarters at that time," paragraph 5) and to work with one or more other verbs to show that some actions happened earlier than other past actions did ("she was not able to continue the lessons she *had* been giving us every morning," paragraph 6). Work with students to create a few sentences modeled after these examples. As students read "By Any Other Name," suggest that they pause when they come to an appearance of *had* and check their understanding of its use. **SUBSTANTIAL**

TEACH

CRITICAL VOCABULARY

Encourage students to read all the sentences before deciding which word best completes each one. Remind them to look for context clues that match the precise meaning of each word.

Answers:

1. *tepid*

2. *precarious*

3. *sedately*

4. *insular*

■ English Learner Support

Use Cognates Tell students that two of the Critical Vocabulary words have Spanish cognates (*precarious/ precario* and *insular/insular*) and that another comes from the same Latin root (*tepidus*) as its Spanish counterpart (*tepid/ tibio*). **ALL LEVELS**

LANGUAGE CONVENTIONS

Review the information about verb tenses. (You may wish to relate it to the English Learner Support note on Teacher Edition page 19.) Emphasize that a memoir usually is written in the past tense but that other tenses can place events on a timeline that students may visualize as they read.

Read aloud the example sentence. Have students identify the verb in the past tense (*met*) and then the verb in the past perfect tense (*had talked*). Invite students to visualize these events on a timeline and then to express the relationship between the events in their own words. (*I met Tara in person. Before that meeting, however, I had talked to her on the phone three times.*)

ANNOTATION MODEL

Discuss annotation ideas such as underlining details in the text that catch students' attention, circling unfamiliar words, and bracketing key details. Explain that students may follow these suggestions or use their own system for marking up the selection in their write-in text. They may want to color-code their annotations using highlighters. Their notes in the margin may include questions about ideas that are unclear, insights into the text, or topics they want to learn more about.

CRITICAL VOCABULARY

precarious	insular	sedately	tepid

To see how many Critical Vocabulary words you already know, use them to complete the sentences.

1. My former best friend greeted me with a(n) _____ half-hug.

2. The painter balanced atop a very old and _____ three-story ladder.

3. No longer an over-excited pup, our Max responds _____ to the sight of another dog.

4. She found the experience of living in a tiny cabin miles from the nearest neighbor _____.

LANGUAGE CONVENTIONS

Appropriate Verb Tense In this lesson, you will learn about how the author of a memoir uses verb tense to orient the reader. The author describes a central episode in her life but also alludes to events that came before it. She also describes her present-day feelings about the events.

Notice how one writer uses the past perfect tense to indicate an action completed before something else happened:

I had talked to Tara on the phone three times before we met in person.

As you read "By Any Other Name," note the author's use of verb tenses to make the order of events clear.

ANNOTATION MODEL   NOTICE & NOTE

As you read, note passages that interest you and any questions or observations you have. In the model, you can see one reader's notes about the opening of "By Any Other Name."

> At the Anglo-Indian day school in Zorinabad to which my sister and I were sent when she was eight and I was five and a half, they changed our names. On the first day of school, a hot, windless morning of a north Indian September, we stood in the headmistress's study, and she said, "Now you're the *new* girls. What are your names?"

author and her sister were very young

changing names is dramatic detail

"headmistress" shows that the school was run on a British model

BACKGROUND

Santha Rama Rau *(1923–2009) was born into one of India's most influential families but spent most of her life in other lands. After living for some time in England, Rama Rau returned to India, making a conscious effort to reorient herself to her homeland and her extended family. She recorded her impressions in her first book,* Home to India *(1944). Rama Rau published numerous travel books, several novels, and an autobiography.*

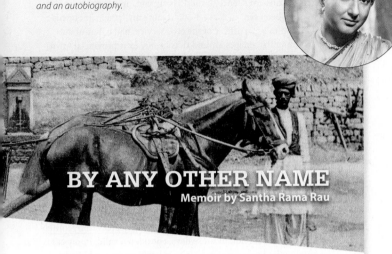

BY ANY OTHER NAME
Memoir by Santha Rama Rau

SETTING A PURPOSE

As you read, think about how the author's experiences remind you of your own experiences or other experiences you have heard or read about.

1 At the Anglo-Indian[1] day school in Zorinabad to which my sister and I were sent when she was eight and I was five and a half, they changed our names. On the first day of school, a hot, windless morning of a north Indian September, we stood in the headmistress's study, and she said, "Now you're the *new* girls. What are your names?"

2 My sister answered for us. "I am Premila, and she"—nodding in my direction—"is Santha."

3 The headmistress had been in India, I suppose, fifteen years or so, but she still smiled her helpless inability to cope with Indian names. Her rimless half-glasses glittered, and the **precarious** bun on the top of her head trembled as she shook her head. "Oh, my dears, those are much too hard for me. Suppose

---
[1] **Anglo-Indian:** English and Indian; also refers to the British colonists living in India.

Notice & Note

You can use the side margins to notice and note signposts in the text.

---

precarious
(prĭ-kâr´ē-əs) *adj.* dangerously insecure.

NOTICE & NOTE

By Any Other Name 21

APPLYING ACADEMIC VOCABULARY

☑ **discriminate**   ☐ **diverse**   ☑ **inhibit**   ☐ **intervene**   ☐ **rational**

Write and Discuss Have students turn to a partner to discuss the following questions. Guide students to include the academic vocabulary words *discriminate* and *inhibit* in their responses. Ask volunteers to share their responses with the class.

- How might changing someone's name be a way to **discriminate** against that person?
- The headmistress emphasizes *new* when she says, "Now you're the *new* girls." Do you think that her comment will **inhibit** the sisters' behavior? Why or why not?

TEACH

BACKGROUND

Have students read the Background note about Santha Rama Rau. You may wish to note that at the outbreak of World War II in 1939, Lady Rama Rau, her mother, moved her and her sister Premila from England to India for safety. In 1947, after the war, Rama Rau witnessed the turmoil of India's independence from Great Britain. Her continued travels in later years provided material for many of her works, including *East of Home* (1950) and *My Russian Journey* (1959). At the same time, her frequent returns to India demonstrate an application of the Essential Question for Unit 1—for although she was a world traveler, Rama Rau embraced her Indian roots.

SETTING A PURPOSE

Direct students to use the Setting a Purpose prompt to focus their reading.

EL ## ENGLISH LEARNER SUPPORT

Use Various Grammatical Structures Have students locate the detail in paragraph 1 that describes the setting for the sisters' first day at the school. *("a hot, windless morning of a north Indian September")* Point out that that phrase, set off by commas, contains quite a bit of information about the setting—the location, the month, the time of day, and the weather. Work with a small group to check their understanding by restating the information in several sentences with varying grammatical structures. *(It was a September morning. We were living in northern India. There was no wind, and the temperature was hot.)* **LIGHT**

 For **listening support** for students at varying proficiency levels, see the **Text X-Ray** on page 18C.

CRITICAL VOCABULARY

precarious: The "trembling" that Rama Rau mentions suggests a physical instability that mirrors the headmistress's "helpless inability" and the fact that she seems "baffled."

ASK STUDENTS how the word relates to the headmistress's hairstyle. *(Her bun may not be firmly secured, or it may appear about to become undone.)*

By Any Other Name **21**

© Houghton Mifflin Harcourt Publishing Company • Image Credits: (t) ©Sedmi/Getty Images • (b) ©The Print Collector/Alamy

ANALYZE HISTORICAL CONTEXT

Today, we would say that Santha and Premila were homeschooled at first. Their ways of learning would undoubtedly be different in the Anglo-Indian day school. Note that Rama Rau cites both her mother's view and the British government's view of Indian schools. (**Answer:** *Their mother's health doesn't allow her to keep teaching her girls at home, and they will be able to get more official recognition for their studies if they go to a British school.*)

For **reading support** for students at varying proficiency levels, see the **Text X-Ray** on page 18D.

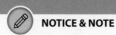

we give you pretty English names. Wouldn't that be more jolly? Let's see, now—Pamela for you, I think." She shrugged in a baffled way at my sister. "That's as close as I can get. And for *you*," she said to me, "how about Cynthia? Isn't that nice?"

4   My sister was always less easily intimidated than I was, and while she kept a stubborn silence, I said "Thank you," in a very tiny voice.

5   We had been sent to that school because my father, among his responsibilities as an officer of the civil service, had a tour of duty to perform in the villages around that steamy little provincial town, where he had his headquarters at that time. He used to make his shorter inspection tours on horseback, and a week before, in the stale heat of a typically postmonsoon[2] day, we had waved goodbye to him and a little procession—an assistant, a secretary, two bearers, and the man to look after the bedding rolls and luggage. They rode away through our large garden, still bright green from the rains, and we turned back into the twilight of the house and the sound of fans whispering in every room.

6   Up to then, my mother had refused to send Premila to school in the British-run establishments of that time, because, she used to say, "You can bury a dog's tail for seven years and it still comes out curly, and you can take a Britisher away from his home for a lifetime and he still remains **insular**." The examinations and degrees from entirely Indian schools were not, in those days, considered valid. In my case, the question had never come up and probably never would have come up if Mother's extraordinary good health had not broken down. For the first time in my life, she was not able to continue the lessons she had been giving us every morning. So our Hindi[3] books were put away, the stories of the Lord Krishna[4] as a little boy were left in midair, and we were sent to the Anglo-Indian school.

7   That first day at school is still, when I think of it, a remarkable one. At that age, if one's name is changed, one develops a curious form of dual personality. I remember having a certain detached and disbelieving concern in the actions of "Cynthia," but certainly no responsibility. Accordingly, I followed the thin, erect back of the headmistress down the veranda to my classroom, feeling, at most, a passing interest in what was going to happen to me in this strange, new atmosphere of School.

8   The building was Indian in design, with wide verandas opening onto a central courtyard, but Indian verandas are usually whitewashed, with stone floors. These, in the tradition of British

insular
(inʹsə-lər) *adj.* narrow-minded or detached from others.

ANALYZE HISTORICAL CONTEXT

Annotate: In paragraph 6, mark the author's reasons for avoiding British schools.

Analyze: Why are the girls sent to the school despite these reasons?

---

[2] **postmonsoon:** after the monsoon, or seasonal heavy rains.
[3] **Hindi:** official language of India.
[4] **Lord Krishna:** in the Hindu religion, human form taken by the god Vishnu. Many Hindu stories recount episodes in the life of Krishna.

© Houghton Mifflin Harcourt Publishing Company

CRITICAL VOCABULARY

insular: The word *insular* comes from the Latin word for "island." For many British citizens, keeping British traditions while living in colonial India helped them feel as if they were still in England.

ASK STUDENTS to cite evidence that supports the idea that the British had an insular attitude. (*The British do not respect schools that they do not run. The headmistress ignores the sisters' birth names and gives them "pretty English names" instead.*)

IMPROVE READING FLUENCY

Targeted Passage   Use paired oral reading to help students review and analyze paragraph 7. Ask students to follow along in their text as you read the paragraph aloud, emphasizing its reflective nature as Rama Rau recalls her younger self. Then allow students to take turns reading the paragraph aloud to each other, correcting themselves as needed. Have them work together to determine how the author's reflection adds meaning to what she felt at the time. (*Santha felt "detached" from "Cynthia" and had little concern for what she might do. Reflecting upon that time, the author refers to her "dual personality."*)

Go to the **Reading Studio** for additional support in developing fluency.

schools, were painted dark brown and had matting on the floors. It gave a feeling of extra intensity to the heat.

9   I suppose there were about a dozen Indian children in the school—which contained perhaps forty children in all—and four of them were in my class. They were all sitting at the back of the room, and I went to join them. I sat next to a small, solemn girl, who didn't smile at me. She had long, glossy black braids and wore a cotton dress, but she still kept on her Indian jewelry—a gold chain around her neck, thin gold bracelets, and tiny ruby studs in her ears. Like most Indian children, she had a rim of black kohl[5] around her eyes. The cotton dress should have looked strange, but all I could think of was that I should ask my mother if I couldn't wear a dress to school, too, instead of my Indian clothes.

10   I can't remember too much about the proceedings in class that day, except for the beginning. The teacher pointed to me and asked me to stand up. "Now, dear, tell the class your name."

11   I said nothing.

12   "Come along," she said, frowning slightly. "What's your name, dear?"

13   "I don't know," I said, finally.

14   The English children in the front of the class—there were about eight or ten of them—giggled and twisted around in their chairs to look at me. I sat down quickly and opened my eyes very wide, hoping in that way to dry them off. The little girl with the braids put out her hand and very lightly touched my arm. She still didn't smile.

15   Most of that morning I was rather bored. I looked briefly at the children's drawings pinned to the wall, and then concentrated on a lizard clinging to the ledge of the high, barred window behind the teacher's head. Occasionally it would shoot out its long yellow tongue for a fly, and then it would rest, with its eyes closed and its belly palpitating, as though it were swallowing several times quickly. The lessons were mostly concerned with reading and writing and simple numbers—things that my mother had already taught me—and I paid very little attention. The teacher wrote on the easel-blackboard words like "bat" and "cat," which seemed babyish to me; only "apple" was new and incomprehensible.

16   When it was time for the lunch recess, I followed the girl with braids out onto the veranda. There the children from the other classes were assembled. I saw Premila at once and ran over to her, as she had charge of our lunchbox. The children were all opening packages and sitting down to eat sandwiches. Premila and I were the only ones who had Indian food—thin wheat chapatis,[6] some vegetable curry, and a bottle of buttermilk. Premila thrust half of it into my hand and

---

[5] **kohl:** dark powder used as eye makeup.
[6] **chapatis:** thin, flat bread.

ANALYZE AUTHOR'S PURPOSE

Annotate: Underline the author's responses in paragraphs 10–14.

Analyze: Why is the author unable to answer this basic question?

 For **speaking support** for students at varying proficiency levels, see the **Text X-Ray** on page 18D.

 ANALYZE AUTHOR'S PURPOSE

Remind students that at the time of this account, Santha is quite young—only five and a half. In addition, when she was asked questions earlier in the memoir, either her sister answered for her (paragraph 2) or Santha mumbled "Thank you" instead of answering directly (paragraph 4). Now, because of what the headmistress has told her, Santha is faced with a challenge from yet another stranger. (**Answer:** *The author can't answer because the name that the teacher expects to hear [Cynthia] is different from the author's true name [Santha].*)

EL ENGLISH LEARNER SUPPORT

Identify Adverbs Have students locate the words that end in *-ly* in paragraphs 12 and 13. (*slightly, finally*) Tell students that these are adverbs and that though some adverbs do not end in *-ly*, many do. Explain that *slightly* tells how the teacher frowned and that *finally* tells when Santha spoke. Work with students to identify the adverbs that end in *-ly* in paragraph 14 and explain how each one functions. (*Quickly tells how Santha sat down;* [very] *lightly tells how the girl with the braids touched Santha's arm.*) **MODERATE**

WHEN STUDENTS STRUGGLE . . .

Relate Context to Conflict As students read this page, have individuals or partners use a chart to list details that show differences between Indian traditions and British traditions. Students should discuss how cultural differences shape the memoir.

Indian Tradition	British Tradition
whitewashed verandas with stone floors	dark brown verandas with mats on floors
customary Indian clothes for girls	cotton dresses
chapatis, vegetable curry, and buttermilk for lunch	sandwiches for lunch

For additional support, go to the **Reading Studio** and assign the following **Level Up Tutorial: Historical and Cultural Context.**

 © Houghton Mifflin Harcourt Publishing Company

TEACH

CONTRASTS AND CONTRADICTIONS

Explain to students that this signpost can be used to emphasize the effects or importance of various **settings**. Remind students that Santha is at school; then have them identify the phrase that reveals the contrasting setting. (*at home*) Finally, have students determine the purpose of the contrast. (**Answer:** *The pleasant details and loving environment of home create a stark contrast to the cold, unfriendly school environment.*)

LANGUAGE CONVENTIONS

Remind students that verbs can show physical action, mental action, or a state of being. Have students identify the verbs in the sentence and tell what they show. (**Answer:** Seemed *shows a state of being;* had seen *shows physical action.*) Review the term *past perfect tense* from page 20. (**Answer:** Seemed *shows what took place during the time of the story;* had seen *shows what took place before that time.*)

■ English Learner Support

Discuss Verb Forms Students may notice other words in paragraph 22 that look like verbs: *wizened, giving,* and *to be.* Tell students that these forms come from verbs but do not do the kind of work that verbs usually do; instead, they act like other parts of speech. To answer the Language Conventions question, students should look for verb forms that work with a subject to express meaning. Guide students to identify *It* as the subject of *seemed* and *I* as the subject of *had seen.*

SUBSTANTIAL

CRITICAL VOCABULARY

sedately: Premila acts with calmness and dignity.

ASK STUDENTS how the difference between the sisters' behavior in paragraph 22 helps show the meaning of *sedately.* (*Santha yells and runs to the car. She is the opposite of Premila, who behaves calmly.*)

---

whispered fiercely that I should go and sit with my class, because that was what the others seemed to be doing.

17   The enormous black eyes of the little Indian girl from my class looked at my food longingly, so I offered her some. But she only shook her head and plowed her way solemnly through her sandwiches.

18   I was very sleepy after lunch, because at home we always took a siesta. It was usually a pleasant time of day, with the bedroom darkened against the harsh afternoon sun, the drifting off into sleep with the sound of Mother's voice reading a story in one's mind, and, finally, the shrill, fussy voice of the ayah[7] waking one for tea.

19   At school, we rested for a short time on low, folding cots on the veranda, and then we were expected to play games. During the hot part of the afternoon we played indoors, and after the shadows had begun to lengthen and the slight breeze of the evening had come up, we moved outside to the wide courtyard.

20   I had never really grasped the system of competitive games. At home, whenever we played tag or guessing games, I was always allowed to "win"—"because," Mother used to tell Premila, "she is the youngest, and we have to allow for that." I had often heard her say it, and it seemed quite reasonable to me, but the result was that I had no clear idea of what "winning" meant.

21   When we played twos-and-threes[8] that afternoon at school, in accordance with my training I let one of the small English boys catch me but was naturally rather puzzled when the other children did not return the courtesy. I ran about for what seemed like hours without ever catching anyone, until it was time for school to close. Much later I learned that my attitude was called "not being a good sport," and I stopped allowing myself to be caught, but it was not for years that I really learned the spirit of the thing.

22   When I saw our car come up to the school gate, I broke away from my classmates and rushed toward it yelling, "Ayah! Ayah!" It seemed like an eternity since I had seen her that morning—a wizened, affectionate figure in her white cotton sari,[9] giving me dozens of urgent and useless instructions on how to be a good girl at school. Premila followed more **sedately**, and she told me on the way home never to do that again in front of the other children.

23   When we got home, we went straight to Mother's high, white room to have tea with her, and I immediately climbed onto the bed and bounced gently up and down on the springs. Mother asked how we had liked our first day in school. I was so pleased to be home and to

---

[7] **ayah:** Anglo-Indian for nanny or maid.

[8] **twos-and-threes:** game similar to tag.

[9] **sari:** long piece of cloth wrapped around the body. a long skirt; the other crosses the chest and shoulder.

CONTRASTS AND CONTRADICTIONS

Notice & Note: What details does Santha remember about home in paragraph 18?

Infer: Why does the author mention this difference between what she usually does and what happens at school?

LANGUAGE CONVENTIONS

Annotate: Mark the verbs in the second sentence of paragraph 22.

Interpret: Which actions take place during the time of the story the author tells? Which actions took place before that time?

sedately
(sĭ-dāt´ lē) *adv.* in a calm and dignified manner.

The pupils of the Jaora School, Indore, India. 3rd August 1928

have left that peculiar Cynthia behind that I had nothing whatever to say about school, except to ask what "apple" meant. But Premila told Mother about the classes, and added that in her class they had weekly tests to see if they had learned their lessons well.

24   I asked, "What's a test?"

25   Premila said, "You're too small to have them. You won't have them in your class for donkey's years." She had learned the expression that day and was using it for the first time. We all laughed enormously at her wit. She also told Mother, in an aside, that we should take sandwiches to school the next day. Not, she said, that she minded. But they would be simpler for me to handle.

26   That whole lovely evening I didn't think about school at all. I sprinted barefoot across the lawns with my favorite playmate, the cook's son, to the stream at the end of the garden. We quarreled in our usual way, waded in the **tepid** water under the lime trees, and waited for the night to bring out the smell of the jasmine. I listened with fascination to his stories of ghosts and demons, until I was too frightened to cross the garden alone in the semidarkness. The ayah found me, shouted at the cook's son, scolded me, hurried me in to supper—it was an entirely usual, wonderful evening.

27   It was a week later, the day of Premila's first test, that our lives changed rather abruptly. I was sitting at the back of my class, in my usual inattentive way, only half listening to the teacher. I had started a rather guarded friendship with the girl with the braids, whose name turned out to be Nalini (Nancy in school). The three other Indian children were already fast friends. Even at that age, it was apparent to all of us that friendship with the English or Anglo-Indian children was out of the question. Occasionally, during the class, my new friend and I would draw pictures and show them to each other secretly.

NOTICE & NOTE

tepid
(tep´id) *adj.* neither hot nor cold; lukewarm.

ANALYZE HISTORICAL CONTEXT

Annotate: Mark what was apparent to the Indian children in paragraph 27.

Infer: Why might such young children consider this a fact?

By Any Other Name   25

 ENGLISH LEARNER SUPPORT

Discuss Idioms Point out the phrase *for donkey's years* (paragraph 25) and share its definition. Explain that it is an idiom—an expression whose meaning is not the same as the literal meaning of the words that form it—and that Premila's having learned it in school relates to the cultural context of the memoir. You might mention that *years* rhymes with *ears* and that a donkey has long ears, so "long years" helps show the meaning of the idiom. Other idioms that refer to a long time include *ages and ages*, *a month of Sundays*, and *forever and a day*. Invite students to name and define other idioms they may know (for example, *raining cats and dogs* = "raining very hard" and *costs an arm and a leg* = "is very expensive"). **ALL LEVELS**

TEACH

ANALYZE HISTORICAL CONTEXT

Suggest that students scan paragraph 27, looking for the word *apparent*, and then paraphrase the rest of the sentence that follows that word. (*There was no way that we were going to be able to be friends with the children who were British or even partly British.*) Invite comments about how the Indian children are treated at school. (**Answer:** *The young Indian children consider this a fact because they have been treated as inferior to the other children.*)

CRITICAL VOCABULARY

tepid: A stream might be expected to have cool water; however, as Rama Rau notes in paragraph 1, the weather is hot, probably raising the water's temperature a bit.

ASK STUDENTS to explain whether they would prefer to swim in cool or tepid water on a hot day. (*Students may say that cool water would be more refreshing.*)

© Houghton Mifflin Harcourt Publishing Company

ENGLISH LEARNER SUPPORT

React to the Language of Imagery Have students reread paragraph 34. Point out that it does little to advance the plot of this narrative; indeed, students could skip directly from paragraph 33 to paragraph 35 without losing track of Rama Rau's story. What purpose, then, does paragraph 34 serve? Use the following activities with students at varying proficiency levels:

- Have students name three things that Santha sees while walking home. (*Answers include dusty hedges, a tonga, and Indian women carrying baskets of vegetables on their heads.*) Point out that these details help readers visualize the setting outside of the school. **SUBSTANTIAL**

- Have students note not only the sights in the paragraph but also a smell that Rama Rau recalls. (*"the faint fragrance from the eucalyptus trees"*) Note that the fragrance is not described as pleasant or unpleasant; then discuss what its purpose might be. (*It helps readers imagine the world in which Santha lives—the world apart from the school.*) **MODERATE**

- In addition to noting sights and smells, challenge students to locate details relating to touch and hearing. (*touch—the sticky pencils and the heat of the day; hearing—Premila's telling her to carry her notebook on her head*) Discuss how these sensory details create images in the reader's mind. **LIGHT**

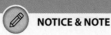

28   The door opened sharply and Premila marched in. At first, the teacher smiled at her in a kindly and encouraging way and said, "Now, you're little Cynthia's sister?"

29   Premila didn't even look at her. She stood with her feet planted firmly apart and her shoulders rigid and addressed herself directly to me. "Get up," she said. "We're going home."

30   I didn't know what had happened, but I was aware that it was a crisis of some sort. I rose obediently and started to walk toward my sister.

31   "Bring your pencils and your notebook," she said.

32   I went back for them, and together we left the room. The teacher started to say something just as Premila closed the door, but we didn't wait to hear what it was.

33   In complete silence we left the school grounds and started to walk home. Then I asked Premila what the matter was. All she would say was, "We're going home for good."

34   It was a very tiring walk for a child of five and a half, and I dragged along behind Premila with my pencils growing sticky in my hand. I can still remember looking at the dusty hedges and the tangles of thorns in the ditches by the side of the road, smelling the faint fragrance from the eucalyptus trees, and wondering whether we would ever reach home. Occasionally a horse-drawn tonga[10] passed us, and the women, in their pink or green silks, stared at Premila and me trudging along on the side of the road. A few coolies[11] and a line of women carrying baskets of vegetables on their heads smiled at us. But it was nearing the hottest time of day, and the road was almost deserted. I walked more and more slowly, and shouted to Premila, from time to time, "Wait for me!" with increasing peevishness. She spoke to me only once, and that was to tell me to carry my notebook on my head, because of the sun.

35   When we got to our house, the ayah was just taking a tray of lunch into Mother's room. She immediately started a long, worried questioning about what are you children doing back here at this hour of the day.

36   Mother looked very startled and very concerned and asked Premila what had happened.

37   Premila said, "We had our test today, and She made me and the other Indians sit at the back of the room, with a desk between each one."

38   Mother said, "Why was that, darling?"

39   She said it was because Indians cheat," Premila added. "So I don't think we should go back to that school."

---

[10]**tonga:** a two-wheeled carriage.
[11]**coolies:** a term referring to unskilled laborers.

TO CHALLENGE STUDENTS...

Consider Another Perspective Paragraphs 36–44 bring Santha's mother to the forefront of the memoir. Challenge students to summarize "By Any Other Name" by relating the events from the mother's perspective. Suggest that students consider these questions as they work:

- How do events reflect the mother's comment about British schools in paragraph 6?

- How do you think she responded to what she learned from Premila about the first day of school (paragraphs 23–25)?

- Why do you think Rama Rau describes her as "very distant," "silent," and "displeased" in paragraph 40?

Have students share their summaries with a partner or a small group. Encourage students to look for similarities to and differences from Santha Rama Rau's own account.

40 Mother looked very distant and was silent a long time. At last she said, "Of course not, darling." She sounded displeased.

41 We all shared the curry she was having for lunch, and afterward I was sent off to the beautifully familiar bedroom for my siesta. I could hear Mother and Premila talking through the open door.

42 Mother said, "Do you suppose she understood all that?"

43 Premila said, "I shouldn't think so. She's a baby."

44 Mother said, "Well, I hope it won't bother her."

45 Of course, they were both wrong. I understood it perfectly, and I remember it all very clearly. But I put it happily away, because it had all happened to a girl called Cynthia, and I never was really particularly interested in her.

ANALYZE AUTHOR'S PURPOSE

Annotate: Mark what the author's mother and sister were wrong about in paragraph 45.

Analyze: Why did the author make a distinction between herself and "Cynthia" as a child?

CHECK YOUR UNDERSTANDING

Answer these questions before moving on to the **Analyze the Text** section on the following page.

1 What conflict do Santha and Premila experience when they meet the headmistress?

A She disapproves of their Indian clothing and food.

B She changes their names to make them easier for her to pronounce.

C They want to take a siesta but are not allowed to.

D She does not want them to interact with the English children.

2 Which of these does Santha learn at school?

F How to spell simple English words like "bat" and "cat."

G How her name is pronounced properly in English.

H That English children play more competitively than she does.

J That a midday siesta is unnecessary for older children.

3 Why does Premila take Santha out of school in the middle of the day?

A Premila's teacher says that Indians cheat.

B Premila is nervous about her afternoon test.

C The girls' father is on his way home from a business trip.

D Santha isn't paying attention in her classes.

✎ ANALYZE AUTHOR'S PURPOSE

Point out that *it* in paragraph 45 and *all that in* paragraph 42 refer to the same topic. Suggest that students reread the dialogue in paragraphs 35–39 to aid their understanding. (**Answer:** *Because she is discouraged from doing any of the things she normally would do, she doesn't feel like herself at school. She's happier to not consider that short-lived but negative experience.*)

✎ CHECK YOUR UNDERSTANDING

Have students answer the questions independently.

Answers:

1. *B*

2. *H*

3. *A*

If they answer any questions incorrectly, have them reread the text to confirm their understanding. Then they may proceed to ANALYZE THE TEXT on page 28.

ENGLISH LEARNER SUPPORT

Oral Assessment Use the following questions to assess students' comprehension and speaking skills. Ask students to respond in short, complete sentences.

1. What does the headmistress make the girls change? (*She gives the girls new names.*)

2. _____ children were more competitive. (*British children were more competitive.*)

3. Premila's teacher says that Indians _____. (*Premila's teacher says that Indians cheat.*) **ALL LEVELS**

ANALYZE THE TEXT

Possible answers:

1. **DOK 2:** *The headmistress smiles helplessly, shakes her head, and shrugs to show that she has given up on ever being able to pronounce the girls' names. It's clear that she doesn't consider learning their names worth the effort she would have to make.*

2. **DOK 3:** *The other Indian girls at the school wear cotton dresses like the British girls; they also bring sandwiches for lunch, not Indian food. They do these things because at that time, prejudice against Indian customs was strong.*

3. **DOK 2:** *Santha chooses to consider the conflict as something that happened to someone else—a girl named Cynthia—and Santha is not "really particularly interested in her." This approach suits the author's purpose because it creates a distance from the event that shows how strange it was.*

4. **DOK 4:** *What the teacher says and does sends a message that Indian children, unlike the British children, can't be trusted. She's an authority figure, so she communicates to the students that it's okay to think and say things like that. Santha's mother passes on a love of learning and the importance of protecting the vulnerable. Her support for Premila's decision to leave school passes on a sense of respect. These messages suggest that one theme of the story is that every individual deserves respect.*

5. **DOK 4:** *The text suggests that children understand more than adults think they do. Santha doesn't always understand why the adults behave the way they do, but she does recognize prejudice.*

RESEARCH

Remind students to verify their findings by checking at least two websites. You may wish to simplify the final question to: What was one effect of the name change?

Connect Students should recall that the headmistress gives the Indian children English names, but Santha does not feel connected to her new name. In their discussion, students may suggest that by relating all of the unpleasantness to school to "Cynthia" and then having no interest in "Cynthia," Santha was able to separate herself from the difficult experience recounted in "By Any Other Name."

 RESPOND

ANALYZE THE TEXT

Support your responses with evidence from the text. 📓 NOTEBOOK

1. **Interpret** What do the headmistress's gestures and expressions tell you about her motivation for changing the girls' names?

2. **Cite Evidence** Name two ways in which the Indian girls who have been at the school for a while imitate the English girls. How do these examples reflect the historical context of the memoir?

3. **Infer** Based on the last paragraph, explain how Santha views the conflict with the headmistress. How does this view fit the author's purpose for writing this memoir?

4. **Analyze** Many ideas are passed from generation to generation. How might Premila's teacher have passed on a prejudice to her students? What values did Santha's mother pass on to her children? Based on your responses, what do you think is the story's theme or insight about life?

5. **Notice & Note** What does the text suggest about how the experience of childhood is remembered? Cite Memory Moments from the text in your answer.

RESEARCH

RESEARCH TIP

The best search terms are very specific, but it's hard to be specific when you're not sure what you're looking for. If you search online, you might start with something like "effects of name change." As you find a story or stories you want to pursue, continue refining your search terms.

How do you think Santha Rama Rau would answer Juliet's question, "What's in a name?" How important do you think a person's name is to his or her sense of identity? Find out more about a situation in which someone's name has been changed, either by their choice or someone else's.

RESEARCH QUESTIONS	WHAT YOU LEARNED
Whose name was changed?	*Boxer Cassius Marcellus Clay, Jr. (1942–2016) became Muhammad Ali in 1964.*
Whose idea was it to change the name?	*Elijah Muhammad, the leader of an organization called the Nation of Islam, chose this name for him.*
Why was the name changed?	*Clay/Ali wanted a name that reflected his conversion to Islam and that put what he called his "slave name" behind him.*
How did the name change affect the person or others around him or her?	*Ali was devoted to his new faith; however, It took several years before the media called him by his adopted name.*

Connect Reread the last paragraph of the story. Recall why the school's headmistress renamed Santha "Cynthia." How did Santha use "Cynthia" to get through a difficult experience? Discuss with a partner or small group.

 LEARNING MINDSET

Belonging Remind students that everyone in the classroom is part of a learning community. Everyone belongs (contrary to what students experienced in the classroom described in "By Any Other Name")—and everyone has something to contribute. As students discuss the Analyze the Text questions, emphasize the importance of respecting each other's contributions. At the same time, allow students to ask classmates, in a tactful way, to expand upon or otherwise clarify their responses.

CREATE AND DISCUSS

Write a Poem Write a free-verse poem about your own name—and your relationship with it.

- ❑ Free verse includes unrhymed lines of varying length. There is no fixed metrical pattern.
- ❑ Include the name your teachers call you, other names people refer to you by, and where they came from.
- ❑ What do all of these names mean to you? How do you feel about having them? Address these questions in your poem.

Discuss with a Small Group Have a discussion about why names matter.

- ❑ Include evidence from your research task.
- ❑ Include insight you gained from the process of writing your free-verse poem.
- ❑ What common patterns and themes do you notice in the information shared by members of your group?

RESPOND

Go to the **Speaking and Listening Studio** for more on participating in collaborative discussions.

RESPOND TO THE ESSENTIAL QUESTION

? How do we engage with others while staying true to ourselves?

Gather Information Review your annotations and notes on "By Any Other Name." Then, add relevant information to your Response Log. As you determine which information to include, think about:

- where names come from and what they say to others about us
- why people have different names at different points in their lives
- what a shift from one name to another can mean to a person and the people around him or her

At the end of the unit, use your notes to help you write a personal essay.

ACADEMIC VOCABULARY

As you write and discuss what you learned from the memoir, be sure to use the Academic Vocabulary words. Check off each of the words that you use.

- ❑ **discriminate**
- ❑ **diverse**
- ❑ **inhibit**
- ❑ **intervene**
- ❑ **rational**

© Houghton Mifflin Harcourt Publishing Company

APPLY

CREATE AND DISCUSS

Write a Poem You may wish to show students a free-verse poem in this book so that they can see the difference between free verse and traditional poetry. Explain that although writers of free-verse poems do not use patterns of rhyme and meter, they still include vivid word choices and create memorable images to express their ideas. Suggest that if students do not have "other" names, they should focus on the meaning of their given name and their feelings about that name.

For **writing support** for students at varying proficiency levels, see the **Text X-Ray** on page 18D.

Discuss with a Small Group Remind students of the importance of courtesy and mutual respect in small-group work. During the discussion, students should not interrupt or make private comments to each other. Looking attentive (through appropriate body language and eye contact) will help them be attentive toward each other—a skill that will help them in other cooperative learning situations.

RESPOND TO THE ESSENTIAL QUESTION

Allow time for students to add details from "By Any Other Name" to their Unit 1 Response Logs.

EL ## ENGLISH LEARNER SUPPORT

Discuss with a Small Group Relate the discussion to Juliet's question: "What's in a name?" (page 19). You may wish to provide these sentence frames to help students organize their thoughts before they share in the cooperative discussion:

- *The person I researched, [name], thought that a name change was important because _____.*

- *As I wrote my poem, I realized that I feel _____ about my name.*
- *My name is important to me because _____.*

Remind students to listen for ideas that come up often in the discussion.

ALL LEVELS

APPLY

CRITICAL VOCABULARY

Answers:

1. a; Expressing interest in other places reflects a more open-minded attitude than focusing on one's home town.

2. b; A painter who forgets supplies is unprepared, but a painter balancing on a wobbly ladder could be in danger of falling.

3. b; A quiet lake would be more calm than a rocky river.

4. a; Coffee is usually served hot, but juice that was left out would be at room temperature.

VOCABULARY STRATEGY:
Foreign Words Used in English

Answers:

1. the current situation or state of things

2. a feeling that you have experienced the same thing before

3. daring and experimental

4. an act of taking power away from a leader by force

RESPOND

WORD BANK
insular
precarious
sedately
tepid

 Go to the **Vocabulary Studio** for more on foreign words used in English.

CRITICAL VOCABULARY

Practice and Apply Mark the letter of the best answer to each question. Then, explain your response.

1. Which statement represents an **insular** attitude?
   a. No place is as great as my home town.
   b. The world is full of interesting places.

2. Which of these could be described as **precarious**?
   a. a house painter who forgot to bring brushes and dropcloths
   b. a house painter standing on one foot on a wobbly ladder

3. Which of the following might happen **sedately**?
   a. a canoe trip on a rocky river
   b. a canoe trip on a quiet lake

4. Which of the following is likely to be **tepid**?
   a. juice that was left out all night
   b. a freshly-poured cup of coffee

VOCABULARY STRATEGY:
Foreign Words Used in English

English speakers use many words from other languages. "By Any Other Name" includes *veranda*, which comes from the Hindi language, and *siesta*, which comes from Spanish.

Practice and Apply Use context clues and a dictionary, if needed, to write the meaning of the boldfaced term in your own words.

1. Tobias is in a rare good mood, so please don't upset the **status quo**.

2. When our 20-point lead began to shrink with minutes to play, I had an odd **déjà vu** about last season and losing the national championship.

3. It may sound old-school today, but there was a time when punk music was aggressively **avant-garde**.

4. The cruel military dictator was overthrown in a violent **coup d'état**.

ENGLISH LEARNER SUPPORT

Articulate Foreign Words Pronouncing foreign words and phrases can be challenging for students whose first language is English; it is even more so for students who are learning English. Spend extra time on the pronunciation of *status quo, déjà vu, avant-garde,* and *coup d'état.* Have students practice saying the terms in isolation and then as part of the sentences in which they appear. As time permits, invite partners or small groups to create and share original sentences using these terms, paying special attention to their articulation. **ALL LEVELS**

LANGUAGE CONVENTIONS:
Appropriate Verb Tense

Use verb tense accurately to indicate when actions or events take place. The author of a memoir uses appropriate verb tense to orient the reader about actions and events in the present day, the past, and the distant past. Different tenses are appropriate, depending on the time and time order in which events happened.

In "By Any Other Name," Santha Rama Rau uses different tenses to indicate when events happened. Here are examples from the memoir:

- The past tense reflects the time when the main event occurred.

    My sister answered for us.

- The past perfect shares events that happened before the main action.

    The headmistress had been in India, I suppose, fifteen years or so . . .

- The present tense allows the author to reflect now on what happened during the event.

    That first day at school is still, when I think of it, a remarkable one.

Practice and Apply Think of an exciting or striking experience you had. Write a few sentences using appropriate verb tenses to describe the experience, events that came before it, and your current perspective on it. When you are finished, share your sentences with a partner. Ask your partner to make a time line of events that matches your use of verb tenses.

> ! Go to the **Grammar Studio** for more on verb tense.

LANGUAGE CONVENTIONS:
Appropriate Verb Tense

Explain that a verb can show physical action (for example, *run, sing, drive, swim*), mental action (for example, *think, remember, guess, study*), or a state of being (for example, *be, become, seem*). Relate the words *tense* and *time* and then ask a volunteer to explain the meaning of *verb tense* in his or her own words. *(Verb tense refers to the time at which a given action or state of being takes place.)*

Explain that the basic tenses are past, present, and future. Rephrase the first example sentence, which is in the past tense, in the present tense *(My sister answers for us)* and the future tense *(My sister will answer for us),* and have students comment on the differences. Use the same sentence to introduce the present perfect tense *(My sister has answered for us),* past perfect tense *(My sister had answered for us),* and future perfect tense *(My sister will have answered for us).*

As you discuss the bulleted explanations, note:

- Writing that deals with past events usually uses past-tense verbs. When students find another tense, they should pause to figure out the purpose for the change.
- If they find a past perfect tense verb (a verb phrase beginning with *had*), they should ask, "What is the earlier action or state of being, and why is it important?" If they find a present-tense verb, they should ask, "How does the writer's thinking now compare to what he or she experienced or thought at the time?"
- Students should apply these questions to their own writing. If they cannot give a reasonable answer, there's a good chance that the change in tense was made in error and needs revision.

Practice and Apply Have partners discuss whether the verb tenses in their sentences are correct, using their time lines as support. *(Students' sentences and time lines will vary.)*

  ENGLISH LEARNER SUPPORT

Use Appropriate Verb Tense Use the following supports with students at varying proficiency levels:

- Write simple sentences and have students identify them as past or past perfect. For example: *We baked a cake. We had baked many cakes before.* **SUBSTANTIAL**
- Work with students to find and record another sentence in "By Any Other Name" that uses the past-perfect tense and one that uses the

present tense. Explain the difference between the tenses and ask them follow-up questions to confirm their understanding. **MODERATE**

- Have students work with partners to write two pairs of sentences. In each pair, one sentence should be in the past tense. In one pair, the other sentence should use the past-perfect tense to express a related idea; in the other, the present tense. Have them trade sentences with another pair and edit the sentences as needed. **LIGHT**

WITHOUT TITLE

Poem by Diane Glancy

GENRE ELEMENTS
LYRIC POETRY

Explain to students that the word *lyric* in *lyric poetry* reflects the idea that early **lyric poems** were meant to be sung to the accompaniment of a lyre, a small harp-like instrument. Because of its free-verse form, "Without Title" is not easily sung; still, the rhythm of the speaker's words creates memorable sound effects. Point out that since lyric poetry expresses a speaker's thoughts and feelings, it usually is written from a first-person point of view. Finally, note that a well-crafted lyric poem will encourage readers to share the poet's feelings about the topic described.

LEARNING OBJECTIVES

- Analyze the impact of historical/cultural settings in literature and make inferences about the theme of a literary text.
- Conduct research about changes in the lives of Native Americans and evaluate the credibility and accuracy of the sources used.
- Write a narrative based on the poem "Without Title."
- Present a narrative as an interpretive reading for the class.
- **Language** Contribute to class discussions about how listening to a poem and identifying its tone can lead to better understanding.

TEXT COMPLEXITY

Quantitative Measures	Without Title	Lexile: N/A
Qualitative Measures	**Ideas Presented** Multiple levels with some implied meanings, requiring greater inferential thinking.	
	Structures Used Largely conventional and explicit, but presented in a free-verse format.	
	Language Used Some subject-area terms and examples of figurative language appear.	
	Knowledge Required Historical/cultural references require some outside knowledge.	

RESOURCES

- Unit 1 Response Log
- Selection Audio
- Reading Studio:
  Notice & Note
- Level Up Tutorial:
  Setting
- Writing Studio:
  Writing Narratives
- Speaking and Listening Studio:
  Delivering Your Presentation
- "Without Title" Selection Test

SUMMARIES

English

The speaker reflects upon her father's connections to his Native American heritage following his migration to a city, where he worked in the meat-packing industry. He provided for his family with the dedication that his ancestors showed when providing for their own during buffalo hunts. Though the speaker's mother discouraged the father from practicing his cultural traditions, the speaker imagines how his heritage remained a part of him.

Spanish

La voz narrativa reflexiona sobre su padre, quien vivió en una ciudad moderna y trabajó en una empacadora pero siempre mantuvo un fuerte sentido de su herencia Cherokee. Él mantuvo a su familia con la dedicación que sus ancestros mostraban cuando mantenían a las suyas durante las cazas de búfalos. El padre siempre pensaba en su herencia pero lo intimidaba la indiferencia de su esposa. Como resultado, aprendió a mantener su herencia para sí mismo, pero siempre estuvo ahí dentro de él.

SMALL-GROUP OPTIONS

Have students work in small groups to read and discuss the selection.

Think-Write-Pair-Share

- Before students read "Without Title," ask: "How does your cultural heritage affect your daily life?"
- Give students a few minutes to reflect and then jot down their responses individually.
- Have students pair up with partners to discuss their responses and create one with which they both agree.
- Call on volunteers to share those responses.
- As students read and discuss the poem, urge them to see how the situation it presents confirms their response, contradicts it, or gives them something new to consider.

Give One, Get One

- Have students record three statements about "Without Title"—an insight, a memorable image, an unanswered question, and so on—using three index cards or strips of notebook paper.
- Gather students in a circle.
- At your signal, each student hands one statement to the student to his or her right and gets one from the student to his or her left. Repeat two times.
- Ask students to look over the statements they now have. Invite comments about how those statements affect their thinking about the poem.

Text X-Ray: English Learner Support
for "Without Title"

Use the Text X-Ray and the supports and scaffolds in the Teacher's Edition to help guide students at different proficiency levels through the selection.

INTRODUCE THE SELECTION
DISCUSS CULTURAL BACKGROUND

Tell students that the speaker of the poem they are about to read is the daughter of a Native American man who struggled to adjust to city life. You may wish to discuss the following:

- Anthropologists usually classify the Native Americans of North America into ten major groups. Subgroups have their own cultural distinctiveness, as well.
- The poem includes references to the historical and cultural background of the speaker's father. Encourage students to think about what ideas the references might suggest about assimilation, or the process of adopting the customs and attitudes of a dominant culture.

CULTURAL REFERENCES

The following words or phrases may be unfamiliar to students:

- *buffalo* (line 1): a large animal hunted for food and other purposes
- *arrow* (line 2): a pointed stick shot from a bow
- *stockyards* (line 5): areas where animals are held before being slaughtered for meat
- *packing house* (line 10): a business that processes and packs meat
- *bow string* (line 17): a string used on a bow for shooting arrows

LISTENING

Interpret Tone

Explain that the ideas and feelings of a poem's speaker can become clearer if parts of the poem are read aloud.

Use the following supports with students at varying proficiency levels:

- Read aloud lines 7–8. Ask: Is the speaker sad? **SUBSTANTIAL**
- Read aloud lines 11–13 in as objective a way as possible. Ask students to identify the tone of the mother's words and then to read aloud the lines in a way that suggests that tone. **MODERATE**
- Have groups of students do a read-around, sentence by sentence. Ask group members to comment upon the tones that they hear. **LIGHT**

SPEAKING

Present a Narrative

Work with students to read the presentation assignment on Student Edition page 39.

Use the following supports with students at varying proficiency levels:

- Have students present their narratives as a series of labeled pictures. Work with them on pronouncing the labels that describe their pictures. **SUBSTANTIAL**
- Guide students as they mark up a copy of their narrative. In particular, have them note places where they want to pause and places where they want to be sure to read with a certain tone (perhaps by using color-coded markers). **MODERATE**
- Invite partners to read aloud their narrative to each other and elicit suggestions about how they think that various parts should be presented. **LIGHT**

READING

Analyze Point of View

Explain to students that knowing the point of view, or perspective, from which ideas are shared can help clarify the message of a text.

Use the following supports with students at varying proficiency levels:

- Ask students to locate the appearances of *I remember* in this poem (lines 14 and 18). Remind speakers of Arabic that English poems are read from left to right. **SUBSTANTIAL**
- Instruct groups of students to list all the first-person references they can find in the poem. Discuss how first-person terms such as *my father* instead of *the man* and *I heard his buffalo grunts like a snore* instead of *he snored like a buffalo* make the tone more personal. **MODERATE**
- Have students discuss how the effect of the poem might be different if it were told from the father's perspective. How might he perceive the city? his wife? his daughter? his traditions? **LIGHT**

WRITING

Write a Narrative

Work with students to read the writing assignment on Student Edition page 39.

Use the following supports with students at varying proficiency levels:

- Have students describe one or two pictures they see when they read the poem. Provide them with sentence frames such as: *Here the father is going _____. The father brings home _____ and _____. The car leaves _____ in the snow and mud.* **SUBSTANTIAL**
- Using think aloud and modeling strategies, help students find and mark up details or phrasing in the poem that they might work into their narrative. **MODERATE**
- Have pairs of students reread the poem, each one choosing two events that they think they would want to include in their narrative. Do their choices agree? What does the answer suggest about how students should proceed with their writing? **LIGHT**

Connect to the
? ESSENTIAL QUESTION

As she writes about her father in "Without Title," Diane Glancy explores the concept of assimilation. Is it possible for people to have a satisfying life if their generations-old heritage differs dramatically from the society in which they now live? What aspects of their heritage would they want to hold close, and why? What kinds of compromises might they need to make? These are just a few of the questions that Glancy raises in "Without Title."

WITHOUT TITLE

Poem by **Diane Glancy**

? ESSENTIAL QUESTION:

How do we engage with others while staying true to ourselves?

32   Unit 1

 LEARNING MINDSET

Growth Mindset   Remind students that a *growth mindset* means believing that you can get smarter by taking on challenges and pushing yourself. "Without Title" presents challenges by focusing on a culture that many students may find unfamiliar (or may have been led to stereotype). Furthermore, its details and ideas are presented in free-verse lyrical poetry rather than prose, and students must use more inferential thinking to analyze it. Encourage students to look at "Without Title" as an opportunity to set higher learning goals and stretch past their comfort zone.

QUICK START

Imagine being suddenly uprooted from your current life and moving to a new place with different customs and a different way of life. What aspects of your current life would you miss? How would this change affect how you think about who you are? Write a brief journal entry exploring your ideas.

ANALYZE SETTING

The setting of a work of literature encompasses much more than simply the time and place where the action occurs. In the poem you will read, the interplay between two historical and cultural settings is crucial to the theme:

- The poem's present is in the late 20th century, in a modern American city.
- The poem's past is in the father's previous Native American culture.

The way the characters think of and react to these settings drives the choices that they make in their lives.

As you read "Without Title," use this chart to record references to the historical and cultural settings. In particular, note how the speaker seems to feel about each of these settings. One example is shown for you.

GENRE ELEMENTS: LYRIC POETRY

- expresses the speaker's thoughts and feelings
- implies, rather than states, the speaker's emotion
- written in free verse without regular meter
- uses the rhythm of natural speech to create its musical quality

DETAIL (LINE NUMBER)	SETTING IT BELONGS TO	SPEAKER'S TONE
buffalo (line 1)	Native American past	sympathetic

QUICK START

Have students discuss a place they would like to move to. Then, encourage them to list several aspects of their current life that they would no longer have. Ask them to reflect on that list before writing a journal entry that connects those losses to their sense of self. What might they gain from such a move? What might they lose? Allow volunteers to share their entries.

ANALYZE SETTING

Students are likely to think of setting in terms of descriptions such as "a moonlit beach in August" or "a wintry morning in Vermont." Discuss the fact that the meaning of *setting* in this poem goes beyond that—it includes cultures and ways of thinking that are connected to certain times and places. "Without Title" focuses on the mental and emotional challenges faced when a person must try to reconcile contrasting settings. As students work on the chart, suggest that they refer to the settings as either "Native American past" or "modern American city" and pay special attention to the speaker's tone.

ENGLISH LEARNER SUPPORT

Share Connections It is quite possible that some students won't have to imagine the "uprootedness" described in the Quick Start activity. As first- or second-generation Americans, they may well understand the challenge of reconciling two cultural settings. Allow such students to express their opinions and feelings about the topic in whatever ways they are most comfortable, and have classmates monitor their understanding of the important details shared.   **ALL LEVELS**

MAKE INFERENCES ABOUT THEME

Explain that the theme of a work usually is a message or insight about some aspect of human life (for example, coming of age) or human nature (for example, the power and value of love). Emphasize that themes often are not stated directly (a notable exception being the morals in Aesop's Fables).

- Point out the title of the poem and discuss how it might help students infer the theme. Ask: What meanings does the word *title* have? *(It can be the name of something, such as a poem. It also can be the way someone is addressed. This kind of title often gives information about a person's occupation or authority.)* What title might the speaker's father have had to describe his occupation or authority? *(The title might have reflected his importance in the tribe he left behind.)*

In addition to the suggestions in the text, offer these tips for inferring the theme of a poem:

- Develop an objective summary of the poem. In a sentence or two, state "what the poem is about"—that is, what are the most important ideas and details that the poet presents.

- Ask what message about life or about people the poem conveys. A poem may have more than one theme, but one probably will be stronger than the others. All themes must be supported by textual evidence.

- Draft a sentence that states the theme (or the strongest theme). Check to make sure there are enough details in the poem to support the theme. Revise the sentence if needed.

✏ ANNOTATION MODEL

Point out that the model includes different annotations to draw attention to different aspects of the poem and to avoid confusion. Ask students how the circled words relate to the first comment. *(They all identify details of a traditional Native American way of life.)* Also point out that the second comment shows that the student sees a purpose in the underlined long *o* sounds. Encourage students to make notes about "why did the poet do this?" as they annotate their text.

MAKE INFERENCES ABOUT THEME

Most often, poets do not state the theme, or message, of a work. Instead, making inferences that lead to the theme is part of the experience of reading the poem. This reader involvement adds impact in a way that merely stating a message could never accomplish.

As you read "Without Title," keep in mind the historical and cultural settings that are central to the poem's theme. The information you record in your setting chart will help you infer what the poet hopes to communicate about the lives of Native Americans. To infer the theme, you will consider the details and the speaker's tone in light of your own experiences and knowledge.

In addition to historical and cultural details, here are some other keys to inferring the theme of a poem:

- **Title:** Some poems have no title or a title that merely tells the subject. But for many poems, the title (and subtitles, such as this poem has) contributes to the overall meaning of the poem.

- **Repetition:** Poets use words sparingly, so if a word, image, or idea is repeated, it's for an important purpose.

- **Changes and shifts:** Changes in people or places, as well as shifts in tone or structure, can signal central ideas in a poem.

ANNOTATION MODEL **NOTICE & NOTE**

As you read "Without Title," make inferences about the poem's theme. Here is how a reader might annotate the beginning of the poem.

It's hard you kn<u>ow</u> without the buffalo,

the shaman, the arrow,

but my father went out each day to hunt

as th<u>ough</u> he had them.

The speaker shows admiration for her father, who has lost his way of life.

A repeated "o" sound is like a chant, as if echoes of the past remain.

BACKGROUND

After World War II, the United States government's Urban Relocation Program promised Native Americans better jobs if they moved to cities and tried to join mainstream American society. **Diane Glancy** *(b. 1941), a writer of Cherokee descent, has explored issues such as the difficulty of assimilation in her many novels, poems, and plays as well as in nonfiction works. Glancy's work has been awarded numerous literary prizes over a career spanning three decades.*

WITHOUT TITLE

for my Father who lived without ceremony

Poem by Diane Glancy

SETTING A PURPOSE

As you read, think about ways in which the life of the speaker's father is different from the traditional life of his people.

It's hard you know without the <u>buffalo</u>,
the <u>shaman</u>,[1] the <u>arrow</u>,
but my father went out each day to <u>hunt</u>
as though he had them.
5   He worked in the stockyards.
All his life he brought us meat.
No one marked his first kill,
no one sang his buffalo song.

---

[1] **shaman:** a person who interacts with the spiritual world.

Notice & Note

You can use the side margins to notice and note signposts in the text.

ANALYZE SETTING

Annotate: Mark details in lines 1–4 that reveal the historical and cultural background of the speaker's father.

Analyze: Why does the speaker begin by sharing details that no longer apply to her father's life?

Without Title   35

BACKGROUND

Have students read the Background note about Diane Glancy. You may wish to note that as a child, Glancy saw that what she knew of her father's Cherokee heritage differed from what she was learning about Native Americans in school. She also recognized that her English-German mother disliked the Cherokee side of the family. (Both of these realizations find voice in "Without Title.") Glancy turned to poetry as a way to explore her self-identity. She has said, "I was born between two heritages and I want to explore that empty space, that place-between-2-places, that walk-in-2-worlds."

SETTING A PURPOSE

Direct students to use the Setting a Purpose prompt to focus their reading.

ANALYZE SETTING

Remind students that they are looking for details relating to the father, so the details may not be things with which they are personally familiar. Discuss the footnoted term *shaman* (line 2) as needed, along with the fact that many Native American groups depended upon buffalo (technically, bison) and used every part of the animal to sustain their way of life. (**Answer:** *These details develop part of the family's cultural background. They also provide context that helps to show why the speaker's father is unhappy.*)

 For **listening support** for students at varying proficiency levels, see the **Text X-Ray** on page 32C.

EL ENGLISH LEARNER SUPPORT

Learn Plural Nouns Point out the noun "buffalo" in the poem. Explain that in English the singular and plural forms of some nouns are the same. Provide other examples such as: *sheep, deer,* and *moose.* In contrast, point out the word "arrows." Remind students that an "s" is added to form the plural of many nouns. Have students practice writing sentences or phrases using regular and irregular plural nouns. **ALL LEVELS**

WHEN STUDENTS STRUGGLE . . .

Describe Settings Have students use a chart to track details relating to the poem's settings. Point out that lines 1–8 focus on the father's heritage, while the rest focuses on his present, with reminders of his heritage.

"Heritage" Details	shaman, first kill (sign of adulthood), buffalo song (prayer of sorrow at taking the buffalo's life but appreciation for what the buffalo provides)
"Present" Details	the city, the packing house, the old car
"Reminders"	red buffalo on his chest, buffalo grunts when snoring

 For additional support, go to the **Reading Studio** and assign the following **LEVEL Up Tutorial: Setting.**

(b) ©jkraft5/Adobe Stock

MAKE INFERENCES ABOUT THEME

Remind students of the speaker's repeated references to buffalo in lines 1–8. Review how those references are a way of talking about her father's heritage. As students read lines 18–22, urge them to look for "heritage" details that intrude upon life in the present. (**Answer:** *These connections point toward the theme that our cultural heritage is always with us and is vital to who we are.*)

English Learner Support

Elaborate Using Comparisons Once students have answered the question, challenge them to review lines 14–17 and locate additional connections between past and present. This time, however, the connections are more complex, for students will need to interpret two examples of **figurative language**. Monitor partners or small groups as they discuss these details:

- "the animal tracks of his car": A car makes tire tracks, not animal tracks. One of the father's ancestors, however, may have ridden a horse when hunting buffalo. The implied comparison of a car to a horse (a metaphor) suggests a connection between past and present.

- "the aerial on his old car waving / like a bow string": The father drives to work so that he can provide for his family, as an ancestor may have gone out with bow and arrow to provide for his family. The stated comparison of a car aerial to a bow string (a simile) again allows the past to intrude into the present.

LIGHT

  For r**eading support** for students at varying proficiency levels, see the **Text X-Ray** on page 32D.

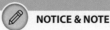 **NOTICE & NOTE**

> Without a vision[2] he had migrated to the city
> 10 and went to work in the packing house.
>   When he brought home his horns and hides
>   my mother said
>   get rid of them.
>   I remember the animal tracks of his car
> 15 backing out the drive in snow and mud,
>   the aerial[3] on his old car waving
>   like a bow string.
>   I remember the silence of his lost power,
>   the red buffalo painted on his chest.
> 20 Oh, I couldn't see it
>   but it was there, and in the night I heard
>   his buffalo grunts like a snore.

---

[2] **vision:** a guiding experience that often comes in a dream or a trance.
[3] **aerial:** a thin, metal antenna.

MAKE INFERENCES ABOUT THEME
Annotate: Mark details in lines 18–22 that make connections between the father's past and present.

Infer: What theme do these connections point toward?

IMPROVE READING FLUENCY

Targeted Passage Have students work with partners to read lines 9–22. Point out that one characteristic of free verse is that the poet's sentences often run through several lines. In this case, lines 9–10 form one sentence, as do lines 11–13, 14–17, 18–19, and 20–22. Therefore, students should not pause at the end of every line. Demonstrate by reading lines 9–10 twice: once with an inappropriate pause at the end of line 9, and then as one continuous sentence. Ask students in each pair to take turns reading the remaining four sentences in this passage. Students also should pause briefly at commas and may want to read each sentence more than once to see whether they can improve their fluency. Tell students to pay attention to intonation.

  Go to the **Reading Studio** for additional support in developing fluency.

✎ CHECK YOUR UNDERSTANDING

Have students answer the questions independently.

Answers:

1. *C*

2. *J*

3. *A*

If they answer any questions incorrectly, have them reread the text to confirm their understanding. Then they may proceed to ANALYZE THE TEXT on page 38.

CHECK YOUR UNDERSTANDING

Answer these questions before moving on to the **Analyze the Text** section on the following page.

1 The father in the poem —

 A has adjusted well to life in the city

 B agrees with his wife's wish to keep the house tidy

 C holds on to thoughts of his past every day

 D makes it clear that his current life is better than his old one

2 The speaker's repeated references to <u>buffalo</u> —

 F make use of multiple meanings in a humorous way

 G reflect a stereotype about Native American culture

 H establish a clear structure for the poem

 J point out the importance of the father's memories

3 Throughout the poem, the speaker makes connections between —

 A the father's past culture and present experiences

 B the competing views of her mother and father

 C positive and negative aspects of life in the city

 D the lives of her generation and those of her father's generation

© Houghton Mifflin Harcourt Publishing Company

Without Title **37**

 ENGLISH LEARNER SUPPORT

Oral Assessment Use the following questions to assess students' comprehension and speaking skills. Ask students to respond in short, complete sentences.

1. What is missing from the father's life? (*He does not practice the cultural traditions of his ancestors.*)

2. Is the buffalo important to the father's past? (*Yes, his memories are very important.*)

3. What does the speaker connect to the father's past culture? (*The speaker connects his present experiences to his past culture.*) **ALL LEVELS**

APPLY

ANALYZE THE TEXT

Possible answers:

1. **DOK 1:** *Contrasts include "hunting" in the stockyards vs. hunting buffalo, a waving aerial on his car vs. a bow string, and buffalo grunts vs. a snore. These contrasts create a wistful, nostalgic tone.*

2. **DOK 2:** *Details such as "It's hard you know," "no one marked his first kill," "without a vision," and the repetition of "buffalo" and "I remember" suggest that the speaker understands how hard it was for her father to take a job in the city. Students may say the speaker didn't intervene in her parents' conflict because she was caught between two cultures.*

3. **DOK 4:** *Theme: Personal identity is strong when it includes a sense of heritage. Summary: The speaker remembers her father, who left his Native American homeland to work at a city stockyard to provide for his family. After his wife orders him to get rid of the horns and hides he brought home from work, the speaker describes him driving away, possibly feeling diminished. The repeated "buffalo" and "I remember"; comparisons between the original culture, in which the father had a strong identity and the city culture, in which he had little sense of identity; and the phrase "the silence of his lost power" all develop the theme.*

4. **DOK 2:** *The title refers to the lack of recognition the father receives. "Without ceremony" could mean he never experienced important cultural rites of passage. These ideas contribute to the theme by emphasizing what is missing in the father's life.*

5. **DOK 4:** *The speaker may feel that her father has remained true to himself, for when he sleeps, his true nature shows through. The father may disagree because he continues to give up his culture, as in the outcome of his argument with his wife.*

RESEARCH

Discuss the fact that a viewpoint can be either stated or implied. Explain that bias can be signaled through word choices that evoke strongly positive or negative feelings; through information that benefits one side of a topic much more so than the other; and through a failure to support statements with evidence.

Extend Students should realize that the poem's information suggests a protest against the loss of traditional ways. Students may not find as strong a sentiment in their sources, but urge them to look for details suggesting a viewpoint on the topic.

 RESPOND

ANALYZE THE TEXT

Support your responses with evidence from the text. 📓 NOTEBOOK

1. **Identify** What details does the speaker use to contrast life in her father's original culture and life in the city? What tone is used to describe these two settings?

2. **Infer** What can you infer about the speaker's feelings toward her father? Why doesn't she try to intervene in the conflict between her parents? Cite evidence from the text to support your answer.

3. **Analyze** What theme about tradition and community does this poem convey? Draft an objective summary and then cite key details that help develop the theme over the course of the poem.

4. **Interpret** What do the poem's title and subtitle mean? How do these ideas relate to the theme of the poem?

5. **Evaluate** Does the speaker think her father has remained true to himself? Would the father agree? Support your response with evidence from the poem.

RESEARCH TIP
Look for sources from a Native American perspective, such as a particular group's history website. Comparing information from sources developed from multiple perspectives can give you a more complete picture of the change your research explores.

RESEARCH

Work with a partner to learn more about changes in the lives of Native Americans. Gather information from at least three sources, evaluating the credibility and accuracy of the information using the criteria below.

TITLE OF SOURCE:	
Who created it?	*Students' research notes should identify at least three sources, analyze viewpoints, evaluate bias, and summarize key information about the culture.*
What viewpoints and/ or biases are expressed?	
What does the source convey about the culture?	

Extend Discuss or write about a connection you can make between your source information and the situation described in "Without Title."

⚙️ LEARNING MINDSET

Belonging In "Without Title," the father retreats in "the silence of his lost power" when he is told that "his horns and hides" don't belong (lines 11–19). Remind students that everyone in your classroom belongs there. Everyone is a valuable member of the class and should support one another as learners. Encourage students to ask for help from you or a classmate if they find themselves struggling to answer questions about this poem.

CREATE AND DISCUSS

Write a Narrative The speaker of "Without Title" gives a clear picture of her family's day-to-day life. Using details from the poem, your research, and your imagination, write a short narrative that depicts one typical day for the family in the poem.

- ❑ Decide who will narrate: the speaker, one of the speaker's parents, or a third-person narrator outside the family.

- ❑ Describe the events of one day through your chosen narrator's voice, incorporating details from the poem.

- ❑ Make sure your narrative builds to a logical conclusion that reflects what the characters experience in the poem.

Present a Narrative Read your completed narrative aloud, clearly and expressively.

- ❑ Consider the personality of your narrator, and use conventions of language the way this person would. For example, how would the register of an outside narrator differ from that of the father?

- ❑ Speak using appropriate volume, pauses for effect, and meaningful gestures to enhance your ideas.

- ❑ Request feedback from listeners on your delivery and ideas.

For help with brainstorming ideas for your narrative, visit the **Writing Studio.**

For help with delivering an oral presentation, visit the **Speaking and Listening Studio.**

RESPOND TO THE ESSENTIAL QUESTION

 ? How do we engage with others while staying true to ourselves?

Gather Information Review your annotations and notes on "Without Title." Then, add relevant information to your Response Log. As you determine which information to include, think about:

- how the father feels about who he is in the poem's two settings
- how the speaker views the father
- the causes and results of compromises people make

At the end of the unit, use your notes to help you write a personal essay.

UNIT 1
RESPONSE LOG

Essential Question:
How do we engage with others while staying true to ourselves?

What, of This Goldfish, Would You Wish?	
By Any Other Name	
Without Title	
from Texas v. Johnson Majority Opinion	
American Flag Stands for Tolerance	

ACADEMIC VOCABULARY

As you write and discuss what you learned from the poem, be sure to use the Academic Vocabulary words. Check off each of the words that you use.

- ❑ **discriminate**
- ❑ **diverse**
- ❑ **inhibit**
- ❑ **intervene**
- ❑ **rational**

CREATE AND DISCUSS

Write a Narrative Suggest that students reread "Without Title" and list details that they want to include (for example, the father's leaving for the packing house in the old car, the mother's distain for Native American culture). Then have them choose a narrator, pointing out that the way that the events of the narrative are described will be colored by the narrator's viewpoint. As students write, remind them that vivid, precise word choices and the inclusion of dialogue can enrich a narrative. Have them review their work and make revisions that help the narrative to better reflect the ideas in the poem.

For **writing support** for students at varying proficiency levels, see the **Text X-Ray** on page 32D.

Present a Narrative As you review the guidelines in the text, urge students to "lose themselves" in the character of their chosen narrator, imagining how that person would tell the story to them. Allow time for students to practice, both by themselves and with a "test audience," and to process feedback before they present their narrative to the class. Remind the class, as well, to be constructive in their feedback. After students have presented their narratives, invite comments about how the narratives influenced students' thinking about the poem.

For **speaking support** for students at varying proficiency levels, see the **Text X-Ray** on page 32D.

RESPOND TO THE ESSENTIAL QUESTION

Allow time for students to add details from "Without Title" to their Unit 1 Response Logs.

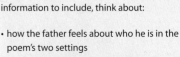 **ENGLISH LEARNER SUPPORT**

Present a Narrative Students may not necessarily use challenging words such as *shaman*, *stockyards*, and *aerial* in their narrative, but they may choose some words whose pronunciation they want to practice before presenting. Provide assistance as needed, perhaps by pairing them with fluent partners. Encourage students to pay attention to sound/symbol relationships as they practice their pronunciation. **SUBSTANTIAL/MODERATE**

from TEXAS *v.* JOHNSON MAJORITY OPINION

Court Opinion by William J. Brennan

GENRE ELEMENTS
COURT OPINION

Explain to students that a **court opinion** is a formal document that expresses the thinking of one or more judges. A court opinion is a **public document,** or a record that anyone is allowed to read. Most of the spoken and written thoughts and decisions of government officials are public documents. Court opinions are important public documents because they influence our laws and how they are enforced. They also guide court opinions in other cases.

LEARNING OBJECTIVES

- Read complex text using a variety of comprehension strategies.
- Identify a writer's claims and evaluate evidence.
- Research First Amendment court cases.
- Write a comparison of formal documents.
- Create a presentation on the First Amendment.
- Use Latin roots to help define words and understand related words.
- Analyze and use commas and other punctuation.
- **Language** With a partner, read aloud using punctuation as a guide to pacing and expression.

TEXT COMPLEXITY

Quantitative Measures	*from* Texas v. Johnson Majority Opinion	Lexile: 1420L
Qualitative Measures	**Ideas Presented** Requires weighing of multiple perspectives and author's purpose.	
	Structures Used Multiple perspectives presented; not chronological.	
	Language Used Unfamiliar and complex domain-specific words; compound/complex sentences.	
	Knowledge Required Understanding of some complex civics concepts; cultural and historical references.	

Online

RESOURCES

- Unit 1 Response Log
- Selection Audio
- Close Read Screencasts: Modeled Discussions
- Reading Studio: Notice & Note
- Writing Studio: Using Textual Evidence
- Speaking and Listening Studio: Using Media in a Presentation
- Vocabulary Studio: Words from Latin
- Grammar Studio: Module 11: Lesson 4: Punctuating Independent Clauses
- *from* Texas *v.* Johnson Majority Opinion / "American Flag Stands for Tolerance" Selection Test

SUMMARIES

English

Supreme Court Justice William Brennan explains the Court's 1989 decision to overturn a Texas law making it illegal to burn the American flag. He confirms the importance of national unity and the flag as a respected symbol of the country, but he rejects the idea that people should be compelled to treat the flag in a special way. He also suggests that allowing people to burn the flag as a form of free speech will actually strengthen overall respect for the flag since protection of free speech is an essential freedom symbolized by the flag.

Spanish

El Juez de la Corte Suprema, William Brennan, explica la decisión de la Corte de 1989 de anular una ley de Texas que ilegalizaba quemar la bandera de Estados Unidos. Él confirma la importancia de la unidad nacional y de la bandera como un símbolo respetado del país, pero rechaza la idea de que haya que forzar a los ciudadanos a tratar la bandera de una manera especial. También sugiere que permitirle a la gente quemar la bandera como una forma de libertad de expresión en realidad refuerza el respeto general por la bandera debido a que la protección de la libertad de expresión es una libertad esencial simbolizada por la misma bandera.

SMALL-GROUP OPTIONS

Have students work in small groups and pairs to read and discuss the selection.

Pinwheel Discussion

- Form groups of 8 (or 6) with 4 students facing out and paired with 4 facing in.
- Provide a question for discussion by all pairs and allow a prescribed amount of time.
- Call on random pairs to summarize their discussion for the class and answer any clarifying questions.
- Have outer students rotate one spot to the right to form a new pair. Repeat the process so that all students work with all others (four rounds for a group of 8).
- Possible questions: How effective is burning the flag in expressing an opinion? Why is the flag so dear to Americans? Why is free speech important?

Think-Pair-Share

- After students have read and analyzed the selection, pose these questions: How does the United States constitutional guarantee of free speech make the country stronger? Why?
- Have students think about the question individually and take notes.
- Then, have pairs discuss their ideas about the question.
- Finally, ask pairs to share their responses with the class.

Text X-Ray: English Learner Support
for *Texas* v. *Johnson Majority Opinion*

Use the Text X-Ray and the supports and scaffolds in the Teacher's Edition to help guide students at different proficiency levels through the selection.

INTRODUCE THE SELECTION
DISCUSS MAJORITY OPINION

In this lesson, students will read and discuss a majority opinion of the United States Supreme Court. Explain the following terms:

- *Majority* is used here as an adjective that describes a number: more than half of the nine Supreme Court justices.
- *Opinion* is used here to explain the decision of the Court.

Note that one of the basic principles of American government is "majority rules" and that judges form opinions that become the basis for interpreting a law. Provide these frames:

- It takes _____ (number) students to form a majority in this class.
- In *Texas* v. *Johnson*, five justices supported the majority _____.

CULTURAL REFERENCES

The following words or phrases from the selection may be unfamiliar to students:

- *We decline* (paragraph 1): the decision is written by one person, Justice Brennan, but he speaks throughout for the other justices who agree, using the pronoun *we*
- *foster by persuasion* (paragraph 2): encourage with convincing support
- *To paraphrase* (paragraph 3): to communicate the same idea with different words

LISTENING

Understand Important Ideas

Throughout the selection, students can practice listening comprehension to ensure their understanding of important information. One example is provided here.

Use the following supports with students at varying proficiency levels:

- Recite a paraphrased version of paragraph 5: We should not punish people for burning the flag. We should convince them they are wrong. To confirm understanding, ask students: *Should we punish people for burning the flag?* **SUBSTANTIAL**
- Read paragraph 5 aloud. Pause after each sentence and confirm students' understanding. **MODERATE**
- Read paragraph 5 aloud. Confirm students' understanding by asking them to provide a summary statement for the paragraph. **LIGHT**

SPEAKING

Identify Claims and Evaluate Evidence

Explain that court opinions usually present claims and evidence to support those claims. Students can practice identifying and stating the claims and evaluating evidence using these activities.

Use the following supports with students at varying proficiency levels:

- Direct students to the first sentence of paragraph 4. Then, have students echo read with you using appropriate pacing. **SUBSTANTIAL**
- Direct students to the first sentence of paragraph 4. Have partners paraphrase the sentence by restating it as a simple declarative sentence that presents the writer's claim. **MODERATE**
- Direct students to the first sentence of paragraph 4. Have partners identify and discuss the author's claim and a sentence in the paragraph that supports it. **LIGHT**

READING

Use Punctuation as a Guide When Reading Aloud

Help students practice reading simple and complex sentences, allowing punctuation to direct their pacing.

Use the following supports with students at varying proficiency levels:

- Point out the commas used in paragraph 1 before reading it aloud. Then, ask students to read it aloud using your reading as a model. **SUBSTANTIAL**
- Point out the commas used in paragraph 1. Then, ask students to read it aloud to a partner using appropriate pacing. **MODERATE**
- Ask students the purpose of the commas used in paragraph 1 before they read it aloud to a partner using appropriate pacing. **LIGHT**

WRITING

Write Comparative Sentences

Work with students to prepare them for the writing assignment on Student Edition page 47.

Use the following supports with students at varying proficiency levels:

- Review the meanings of *both* and *neither* as ways to make comparisons, and then ask students to use them with this frame: *Both dogs were _____. Neither dog was _____.* **SUBSTANTIAL**
- Ask partners to write sentences that use *both* and *neither* in making comparisons. **MODERATE**
- Review the use of the conjunction *but* in making a comparison. Ask students to write a complex, comparative sentence using *but.* **LIGHT**

Connect to the

ESSENTIAL QUESTION

In his *Texas* v. *Johnson* opinion, Supreme Court Justice William J. Brennan explains the reasoning behind the Court's decision to strike down a Texas law that made burning the American flag illegal. His opinion specifies that states may not engage with protesters who have unpopular opinions by arresting them. He also explains that allowing this form of expression is a way for Americans to stay true to the basic ideals of our form of government.

COMPARE ARGUMENTS

To compare arguments, students must understand and remember the claims and evidence used in each argument as well as keep in mind the author's purpose and intended audience. To prepare for this comparison, students need to read the *Texas* v. *Johnson* opinion carefully and keep track of essential information.

COURT OPINION

from TEXAS *v.* JOHNSON MAJORITY OPINION

by **William J. Brennan**
pages 43–45

COMPARE ARGUMENTS

As you read, identify the argument made in each selection. Compare the author's purpose and intended audience for each selection. After you review both selections, you will complete an independent project.

 ## ESSENTIAL QUESTION:

How do we engage with others while staying true to ourselves?

EDITORIAL

AMERICAN FLAG STANDS FOR TOLERANCE

by **Ronald J. Allen**
pages 53–55

LEARNING MINDSET

Growth Mindset Remind students that a growth mindset means believing you can get smarter by taking on challenges and pushing yourself. Encourage students to look for opportunities to set new or higher goals and stretch past their comfort zone. This selection may be the first legal opinion they have attempted to analyze—and it may pose significant challenges to them. Remind them that legal opinions are hard to sort out for readers at all levels and that working to meet these challenges builds important thinking skills that can benefit them in school and beyond.

from **Texas** *v.* **Johnson Majority Opinion**

QUICK START

You have rights that allow you to enjoy your life and to fulfill your potential. But at what point do your wants interfere with someone else's? List two examples of times when your rights could clash with those of another person. Be ready to share one example with the class.

MONITOR COMPREHENSION

Legal documents tend to be complex because the authors use specialized terms that most people do not recognize. Plan to use your background knowledge and reread sections of the text to aid your comprehension. The strategies below will also help you monitor your comprehension.

- **Annotation:** Mark the text with your notes and questions. Underline important ideas. Mark unfamiliar words to look up after your first read. Write notes in the margin as you think about the author's meaning.
- **Notetaking:** Take notes about important ideas. Outlining the text or writing down keywords can help you track your thoughts as you read.
- **Freewriting:** Explore your understanding of the author's meaning by writing down everything that comes to your mind, without stopping, for a certain period of time, such as 2 minutes.

As you read the excerpt from *Texas* v. *Johnson Majority Opinion*, mark the text and keep your own notes.

EVALUATE EVIDENCE

A well-written opinion makes a claim that is supported with evidence. The evidence helps readers to understand how the author came to his or her conclusions. Evidence includes data, anecdotes, and expert opinions. The authors of legal documents usually cite **precedents,** or past legal opinions, as evidence for their opinion. Use an organizer like the one below to record Brennan's claims and to track the evidence he uses to support them.

**GENRE ELEMENTS:
COURT OPINION**

- expresses the opinion of the majority—the group of judges who have decided the case
- clearly states the judges' verdict at the beginning
- cites court cases from the past as evidence
- acknowledges and addresses counterarguments

CLAIM	EVIDENCE
The flag's special role in society is not in danger.	If the flag's status were in danger, nobody would be offended by the idea of flag burning.

TEACH

QUICK START

Help students remember or imagine possible conflicts over their rights by encouraging them to think of times when they or others were tempted to argue. Some examples include friends or family wanting to watch different TV shows, establishing who is first in line, or agreeing on the volume of music being played. After they have identified conflicts and shared them with the class, ask pairs of students to discuss the outcome of these conflicts (such as an argument, a discussion, a decision by a person in power) and which outcome was the most effective. Pairs can share their conclusions with the class.

MONITOR COMPREHENSION

Note that there is not a single preferred method for students to use in understanding complex text. Some may be most comfortable with annotations; others, with notetaking or with freewriting, or a combination of two strategies, or all three. One way to ensure comprehension is to write a summary sentence for each paragraph after reading it. Students may draw upon their annotations, notes, or freewriting to summarize.

EVALUATE EVIDENCE

Provide students with a larger version of the graphic organizer shown. Tell students that in a legal opinion, textual evidence will be stated explicitly, or outright. Explain that citations of previous rulings are the core evidence of legal opinions. Point out that evidence derived from previous rulings is easily identified in a text since it is always followed by a bracketed citation naming the specific case. Students may work in pairs to complete the chart. Alternatively, have students work individually to complete the chart, but have peers review their findings.

WHEN STUDENTS STRUGGLE . . .

Aid Comprehension Some students may feel overwhelmed by the options available for monitoring comprehension. Give students practice by monitoring their comprehension of either or both of the reading skills lessons on this page in three stages.

1. Have students read through the lesson once, using the annotation strategy.
2. Read through the lesson again using notetaking.
3. Freewrite for one or two minutes on the meaning of the lesson.

Direct students to review their annotations, notes, and freewriting before writing a summary sentence for the lesson. Tell them that they may later use the same three-stage method for monitoring their comprehension of the selection.

TEACH

CRITICAL VOCABULARY

As a clue to determining meaning, point out that *reaffirmation* includes the prefix *re-*, which indicates an act that is repeated. You may wish to point out that *re-* also can mean "back" and that it has that meaning in the word *resilience* (where *re-* is attached to a root rather than to a base word, as in *reaffirmation*).

Answers:

1. *d*

2. *c*

3. *a*

4. *b*

■ English Learner Support

Use Cognates Tell students that one of the Critical Vocabulary words has a direct Spanish cognate (*implicit/implícito*) and a second has a Spanish cognate for the base word (*affirmation/affirmación*). **ALL LEVELS**

LANGUAGE CONVENTIONS

Review the information about commas. Note that commas are generally used to separate information and to indicate a short pause when reading, whether aloud or silently.

Read aloud the example sentence using appropriate pauses indicated by the commas. Then read it aloud a second time without pauses and discuss how the commas allow greater understanding of the sentence. (*The phrase* under our Constitution *is an important modifier for the sentence since it establishes a limitation on considering compulsion. The commas help the reader pause to consider the phrase and its importance.*)

ANNOTATION MODEL

Remind students of the annotation ideas in Monitor Comprehension on page 41, which suggest marking unfamiliar words and important ideas and writing their own ideas and questions in the margin. Point out that students may follow this suggestion or use their own system for marking up the selection in their write-in text. They may want to color-code their annotations using highlighters. Their notes in the margin may include questions about ideas that are unclear or topics they want to learn more about.

CRITICAL VOCABULARY

To preview the Critical Vocabulary words, match the words to their definitions.

1. compulsion	a. the act of verifying or endorsing again
2. implicit	b. the ability to return to a normal state after a change or an injury
3. reaffirmation	c. understood but not expressed
4. resilience	d. forced obligation

LANGUAGE CONVENTIONS

Commas Watching for commas can help you understand a lengthy sentence by dividing it into meaningful parts. Writers use commas to set off a dependent clause or a phrase in a sentence, as in this example from the text:

> The problem is whether, <u>under our Constitution,</u> compulsion as here employed is a permissible means for its achievement.

As you read the court decision, watch for phrases and dependent clauses set off with commas. Take in each chunk of meaning on its own, and then put them back together to fully grasp Justice Brennan's points.

ANNOTATION MODEL

NOTICE & NOTE

Here is how you might annotate the beginning of from *Texas* v. *Johnson Majority Opinion* to monitor your comprehension.

> We <u>decline</u>, therefore, to create for the flag an <u>exception</u> to the (joust) of principles protected by the (First Amendment.) . . .

decline = refuse
exception = a change in rules

"joust" = competition, so principles or rights may compete with each other.

First Amendment covers several freedoms, including free speech.

My version: The rights in the First Amendment conflict, but that doesn't mean that symbols like the flag aren't covered by it.

BACKGROUND

At the 1984 Republican National Convention, people protested the policies of then-President Ronald Reagan. One of the protesters, Gregory Lee Johnson, set an American flag on fire. He was punished with a fine and a jail term for breaking a state law banning flag desecration. He appealed, and the case was sent to the Supreme Court to decide whether flag burning is a form of expression protected by the Constitution. The Court delivered its ruling in 1989. **William J. Brennan** *(1906–1997), who served on the Supreme Court from 1956 to 1990, wrote the majority opinion in the case. His staunch defense of First Amendment rights influenced many significant Court decisions.*

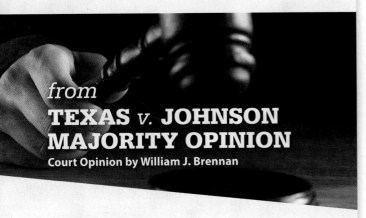

from

TEXAS v. JOHNSON MAJORITY OPINION

Court Opinion by William J. Brennan

PREPARE TO COMPARE

As you read, make notes about the evidence that Brennan uses to support his opinion, and think about his audience and purpose for writing. Use your background knowledge and reread to monitor your comprehension.

1 We decline, therefore, to create for the flag an exception to the joust[1] of principles protected by the First Amendment . . . [2]

2 To say that the government has an interest in encouraging proper treatment of the flag, however, is not to say that it may criminally punish a person for burning a flag as a means of political protest.

> National unity as an end which officials may foster by persuasion and example is not in question. The problem is whether, under our Constitution, **compulsion** as here employed is a permissible means for its achievement.
>
> *[Barnette, 319 U.S. at 640.]*

---
[1] **joust:** competition.
[2] **First Amendment:** the part of the Bill of Rights added to the U.S. Constitution that deals with freedom of speech, among other freedoms.

Notice & Note

You can use the side margins to notice and note signposts in the text.

---

compulsion
(kəm-pŭl´shən) *n.* forced obligation.

MONITOR COMPREHENSION

Annotate: Mark the words that Brennan cites from another legal document.

Interpret Reread the citation. Paraphrase its meaning.

CLOSE READ SCREENCAST

Modeled Discussion In their eBook, have students view the Close Read Screencast, in which readers discuss and annotate the following key passage from the selection:

- the Court's statement of the issues it has considered (paragraphs 1–2)

As a class, view and discuss the video. Then have students pair up to do an independent close read of an additional passage—the Court's explanation of the flag's symbolism (last two sentences of paragraph 4–paragraph 5). Students can record their answers on the Close Read Practice PDF.

 Close Read Practice PDF

BACKGROUND

Have students read the Background note about the Johnson case and Justice Brennan. Explain that the case went to the U.S. Supreme Court after a Texas appeals court reversed Johnson's conviction for burning the flag. That court found that Johnson's actions were a form of symbolic speech that is protected by the First Amendment to the U.S. Constitution. The Supreme Court ruled on two issues: (1) whether burning the flag was a form of expressive conduct, permitting Johnson to invoke the First Amendment; and (2) whether Texas's interest in preserving the flag as a symbol of the United States justified Johnson's conviction.

PREPARE TO COMPARE

Direct students to use the Prepare to Compare prompt to focus their reading.

MONITOR COMPREHENSION

Remind students that legal opinions usually cite (mention) previous court cases that have dealt with similar issues. Authors of legal opinions can use these previous cases as a way to clarify issues and ideas. Brennan quotes from a previous case that involved forcing children to recite the Pledge of Allegiance. (**Answer:** *The question isn't whether officials should encourage national unity. The question is whether the Constitution allows officials to force people to show national unity.*)

For **reading support** for students at varying proficiency levels, see the **Text X-Ray** on page 40D.

CRITICAL VOCABULARY

compulsion: Justice Brennan cites a previous court case that questioned whether the Constitution allows children to be forced to pledge allegiance to the flag.

ASK STUDENTS to explain the compulsion regarding the flag in *Texas v. Johnson*. (*Texas tried to force its citizens to treat the flag in ways that the state deemed to be more respectful by banning the burning of the flag in protest.*)

EVALUATE EVIDENCE

Legal opinions often use the words of previous findings to make a clear statement about the current case. Note that Brennan clearly identifies the source of his thoughts and notes that he is paraphrasing rather than quoting directly. (**Answer:** *Justice Holmes said that one person's action isn't going to change the entire nation's feelings about the flag. As a previous Supreme Court Justice, Holmes's words carry authority.*)

■ English Learner Support

Identify Formal English Note that court opinions are important legal documents and use formal English structures and vocabulary. Identify words used in formal English in the first sentence of paragraph 3 (*fortified, conviction, forbidding, conduct, endanger*). Work with a small group to ensure understanding of each word. Then, ask pairs to rewrite the sentence in less formal English. (*We are sure that preventing punishment for burning the flag won't change most people's attitudes about the flag.*) **LIGHT**

For **listening and speaking support** for students at varying proficiency levels, see the **Text X-Ray** on pages 40C–40D.

CRITICAL VOCABULARY

implicit: The Texas statute implies that society is offended by what the state sees as mistreatment of the flag.

ASK STUDENTS how Brennan uses the state's implicit assumption to support his argument. (*The flag must be special if disrespect of it offends people.*)

reaffirmation: Justice Brennan says that the Court's opinion endorses the principles that the flag symbolizes.

ASK STUDENTS why Justice Brennan makes this reaffirmation. (*The Court agrees with the principles the flag stands for and has made its decision based on them.*)

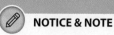
NOTICE & NOTE

Justice William J. Brennan

EVALUATE EVIDENCE

Annotate: Mark the claim Brennan makes about the consequences of the decision.

Interpret: How does Brennan use a court case from the past (*Abrams* v. *United States*) to support this claim?

implicit
(ĭm-plĭs´ĭt) *adj.* understood, but not expressed.

reaffirmation
(rē´ăf-ər-mā´shən) n. the act of verifying or endorsing again.

3   We are fortified in today's conclusion by our conviction that <u>forbidding criminal punishment for conduct such as Johnson's will not endanger the special role played by our flag or the feelings it inspires.</u> To paraphrase Justice Holmes, we submit that nobody can suppose that this one gesture of an unknown man will change our Nation's attitude towards its flag [*Abrams* v. *United States*]. Indeed, Texas' argument that the burning of an American flag "is an act having a high likelihood to cause a breach of the peace," and its statute's **implicit** assumption that physical mistreatment of the flag will lead to "serious offense," tend to confirm that the flag's special role is not in danger; if it were, no one would riot or take offense because a flag had been burned.

4   We are tempted to say, in fact, that the flag's deservedly cherished place in our community will be strengthened, not weakened, by our holding today. Our decision is a **reaffirmation** of the principles of freedom and inclusiveness that the flag best reflects, and of the

---

IMPROVE READING FLUENCY

Targeted Passage Use echo reading to help students use appropriate phrasing and emphasis in reading formal English in paragraph 3. Begin by reading the paragraph aloud, emphasizing pauses and phrasing. Then have students echo your reading as you read it a second and third time, first by pausing after each phrase or clause and then by reading it again with pauses after each sentence. You may choose to conclude with choral reading as all read this complex paragraph aloud together.

Go to the **Reading Studio** for additional support in developing fluency.

conviction that our toleration of criticism such as Johnson's is a sign and source of our strength. Indeed, one of the proudest images of our flag, the one immortalized in our own national anthem, is of the bombardment it survived at Fort McHenry.[3] It is the Nation's **resilience**, not its rigidity, that Texas sees reflected in the flag—and it is that resilience that we reassert today.

5   The way to preserve the flag's special role is not to punish those who feel differently about these matters. It is to persuade them that they are wrong.

---

[3] **Fort McHenry**: War of 1812 battle site in Baltimore. In 1814, poet Francis Scott Key, being held prisoner on a ship nearby, was elated to see the American flag flying there and wrote the poem that became "The Star-Spangled Banner" to celebrate this American victory over the British.

CHECK YOUR UNDERSTANDING

Answer these questions before moving on to the **Analyze the Text** section on the following page.

1 What did the Supreme Court decide should happen to people who burn the flag?

A They should be punished for violating the First Amendment.

B Their punishment should be determined by state laws, not by the Supreme Court.

C Their punishment depends on which of the conflicting rights in the First Amendment is more important.

D They should not be punished because their actions are protected under the First Amendment.

2 What is the purpose of the italicized words such as *Barnette* in the text?

F They identify the authors of Brennan's research sources.

G They identify important court decisions related to this decision.

H They are the names of previously charged flag burners.

J They list officials who disagree about whether flag burning is legal.

3 Which of these describes Brennan's opinion of the American flag?

A It plays a special role in American society.

B Strong laws should protect it from disrespect.

C The government does not have reason to protect it.

D It is of no worth.

LANGUAGE CONVENTIONS

Annotate: Underline the two phrases set off by commas in the first sentence of paragraph 4.

Respond: Reread the sentence without these phrases. What do they add to Brennan's meaning?

resilience
(rĭ-zĭl´yəns) *n.* ability to return to a normal state after a change or an injury.

TEACH

LANGUAGE CONVENTIONS

Note that commas can be important for meaning (such as in separating items in a list) but can also be used to affect style. In this example, the phrases the commas set apart are not essential to the basic meaning of the sentence, but they make the sentence more emphatic. (**Answer:** *Both phrases are unnecessary for meaning but add emphasis to Brennan's ideas.*)

CRITICAL VOCABULARY

resilience: Justice Brennan says that Texas and the Court agree that one of the nation's strengths is its ability to return to normal after a disturbing event.

ASK STUDENTS to explain Justice Brennan's use of the word *resilience* in the phrase "and it is that resilience that we reassert" in paragraph 4. (*The Court's decision confirms that the United States is a resilient nation.*)

CHECK YOUR UNDERSTANDING

Have students answer the questions independently.

Answers:

1. *D*

2. *G*

3. *A*

If they answer any questions incorrectly, have them reread the text to confirm their understanding. Then they may proceed to ANALYZE THE TEXT on page 46.

 ENGLISH LEARNER SUPPORT

Oral Assessment Use the following questions to assess students' comprehension and speaking skills.

1. Did the Supreme Court say that people should be punished for burning the flag? (*no*)

2. Does the First Amendment protect flag burners? (*yes*)

3. Does Justice Brennan think the American flag is important? (*yes*)
    SUBSTANTIAL

ANALYZE THE TEXT

Possible answers:

1. **DOK 4:** *Students may identify* Barnette, 319 U.S. at 640 *or* Abrams v. United States. *The quote from* Barnette *sets up the idea that there is a difference between encouraging national unity and forcing it through law. The information from* Abrams v. United States *supports Brennan's claim that the Court's decision is not going to destroy public opinion of the flag.*

2. **DOK 3:** *Texas argued that flag burning would cause rioting and the loss of the flag's special role in American culture. The Supreme Court argued that the flag's special role was not in danger because if it were, no one would care that it was being burned.*

3. **DOK 3:** *Justice Brennan says that the Supreme Court's decision reaffirms the principles of free speech, specifically freedom and inclusiveness, which are the very principles the flag represents.*

4. **DOK 4:** *The flag flying after the bombardment of Fort McHenry strengthened people's pride in the nation. Similarly, the Supreme Court believes its ruling will increase people's pride in the principles the flag represents.*

5. **DOK 2:** *Justice Brennan's repetition of resilience suggests that he sees the Constitution as strong because it is flexible.*

RESEARCH

Encourage students to carefully read the cases they research. For background information and additional sources to help them better understand the results of court decisions, have them search for reputable newspaper and magazine articles about those cases.

Extend Encourage students to identify and explore opposing viewpoints in each scenario by asking questions. For example: Who suffers when businesses refuse to post political flyers? Who suffers when critiques of politicians cannot be expressed or heard? How is each student affected by disciplinary actions or the lack of discipline? In their discussions, partners may note the conflicts between the rights of private businesses to control their own property and the right to free speech through flyers. Courts have previously ruled that criticizing a political decision is a protected right but that schools do have the right to control speech because insults may lead to conflicts and violence.

 RESPOND

ANALYZE THE TEXT

Support your responses with evidence from the text. NOTEBOOK

1. **Connect** What earlier points of law does Justice Brennan use to support the Supreme Court's opinion in this case? How does the information from previous cases support his claims?

2. **Compare** In its argument to make flag burning a criminal offense, what consequences did Texas predict might happen? How did the Supreme Court interpret the significance of these possible events?

3. **Cite Evidence** How does Justice Brennan support the idea that "the flag's deservedly cherished place in our community will be strengthened, not weakened" by the ruling?

4. **Analyze** How is the image of the flag flying over Fort McHenry related to the central idea of the court opinion?

5. **Infer** Justice Brennan repeatedly uses the word *resilience* to refer to the United States. What does the repetition of this word suggest about his view of the Constitution?

RESEARCH TIP

Many First Amendment cases have been controversial, and some online sources portray a biased, or one-sided, view. To find unbiased summaries of court decisions, look for text on educational (*.edu*) sites or official Supreme Court sites.

RESEARCH

Read the text of the First Amendment on the next page. The U.S. courts have interpreted the language of the amendment many times through the nation's history. Conduct research to find examples of cases in which people challenged court rulings on the basis of the First Amendment. Use an organizer like the one below to summarize your findings by recording which rights in those cases are specifically covered under the First Amendment and which rights are not covered. Share what you learn with a partner.

RIGHTS COVERED BY FIRST AMENDMENT	RIGHTS NOT COVERED BY FIRST AMENDMENT
• the right not to be arrested or prosecuted for stating your opinion	• the right to advocate a particular position in the workplace • the right to disrupt the school environment

Extend With your partner, discuss your opinion whether First Amendment rights have been violated in these scenarios:

❏ A business refuses to allow posting of political flyers.

❏ Someone has been arrested for criticizing a politician's decisions.

❏ A student has been disciplined for insulting another student.

LEARNING MINDSET

Belonging Remind students that court decisions and opinions are very complex and require some special language and reading skills. Encourage students to share the challenges of reading and understanding the material and in answering questions like those in Analyze the Text. Advanced students can often help to explain or address the questions that other students have.

CREATE AND PRESENT

Write a Comparison The Supreme Court determines whether actions are constitutional. In *Texas* v. *Johnson*, the Court's ruling centered around the First Amendment. Compare ideas in Brennan's court opinion and this amendment.

> **First Amendment** *Congress shall make no law respecting an establishment of religion, or prohibiting the free exercise thereof; or abridging the freedom of speech, or of the press; or the right of the people peaceably to assemble, and to petition the Government for a redress of grievances.*

❏ Identify concepts that are discussed in both the Supreme Court's majority opinion and the First Amendment. How does each document address the concepts?

❏ In a paragraph, compare and contrast the two documents. Support your points with examples from both texts.

Create a Multimedia Presentation You will present to the class what you have learned about the First Amendment.

❏ Review your annotations and notes about the selection from *Texas v. Johnson Majority Opinion,* the text of the First Amendment, and your research findings about the amendment. Summarize the rights that it covers and does not cover.

❏ Choose examples to support your summary. Cite cases that dealt with the First Amendment. Save images that illustrate the cases.

❏ Using the information you have gathered, put together a short presentation that will last under five minutes. Summarize your ideas, and then present images and descriptions of exemplary court cases.

 For more on using textual evidence in a comparison, visit the **Writing Studio.**

 For more on using media in a presentation, visit the **Speaking and Listening Studio.**

RESPOND TO THE ESSENTIAL QUESTION

 How do we engage with others while staying true to ourselves?

Gather Information Review your annotations and notes on the selection from *Texas v. Johnson Majority Decision* and highlight those that help answer the Essential Question. Then, add relevant details to your Response Log.

At the end of the unit, use your notes to write a personal essay.

ACADEMIC VOCABULARY
As you write and discuss what you learned from the speech, be sure to use the Academic Vocabulary words. Check off each of the words that you use.

❏ **discriminate**

❏ **diverse**

❏ **inhibit**

❏ **intervene**

❏ **rational**

CREATE AND PRESENT

Write a Comparison Provide students with a Venn diagram or two-column chart to identify concepts in both documents and how they are addressed in each. Then, review what it means to compare (*describe similarities*) and contrast (*describe differences*). Finally, review a format for presenting comparisons and contrasts in a paragraph. Have students summarize their information in a statement and include bullet points for rights that are covered by the First Amendment.

For **writing support** for students at varying proficiency levels, see the **Text X-Ray** on page 40D.

Create a Multimedia Presentation Images could include print photos or illustrations as well as digital images and videos. Encourage students to find images that address the specific rights they list in their summaries. Have students write and practice any voice-overs or other oral statements before their presentation.

RESPOND TO THE ESSENTIAL QUESTION

Allow time for students to add details from *Texas* v. *Johnson Majority Opinion* to their Unit 1 Response Logs.

(EL) ENGLISH LEARNER SUPPORT

Use Basic Language Have Vietnamese-speaking students practice proper past-tense inflections and relate sounds to words used in the selection. Display the words *burned, strengthened, weakened,* and *survived* and read them aloud with students. Next, choral read the sentences from the selection that include these words, emphasizing the *-ed* sound of the past tense.

Have students complete sentence frames using verbs in the past tense— for example: *The court _____ that children did not need to say the Pledge of Allegiance. (ruled)* **SUBSTANTIAL**

CRITICAL VOCABULARY

Answers:

1. *resilience*

2. *implicit*

3. *reaffirmation*

4. *compulsion*

VOCABULARY STRATEGY:

Words from Latin

Possible answers:

- **affirmative:** *strongly supporting; adjective; His affirmative response made us all believe in what he said.*

- **resilient:** *bouncing or leaping back into shape; adjective; The floor was so resilient that dropping the heavy weight didn't make a dent in it.*

- **compulsory:** *something that is forced or required; adjective; He couldn't graduate because he didn't complete all the compulsory courses.*

 RESPOND

WORD BANK
compulsion
reaffirmation
resilience
implicit

CRITICAL VOCABULARY

Practice and Apply Choose which Critical Vocabulary word is most closely associated with the situation in each sentence.

1. Citizens of a town ravaged by hurricanes work together to rebuild each other's homes.

_____

2. Abby asks to borrow the car, but her father raises an eyebrow and looks at her pile of homework.

_____

3. Our grandparents renewed their wedding vows on their 45th anniversary.

_____

4. Anthony wants to go hang out with friends, but has to babysit his little brother instead.

_____

 Go to the **Vocabulary Studio** for more on words from Latin.

VOCABULARY STRATEGY:

Words from Latin

The Critical Vocabulary words *compulsion, reaffirmation,* and *resilience* have Latin roots. Knowing the meaning of a root helps you define the various words derived from it. This chart defines several Latin roots and shows English words that derive from them.

LATIN ROOT AND ITS MEANING	RELATED WORDS
firmus means "strong"	reaffirmation, firmament
resilire means "to leap back"	resilience
pulsus means "to drive, to force"	compulsion, compel

Practice and Apply Use a separate page to explore these roots. For each row of the chart, identify one new word that belongs to the word family. (You may use a dictionary if needed.) For each word you choose, follow these steps:

1. Write a definition that incorporates the meaning of the Latin root.

2. Identify the part of speech.

3. Use the word in a sentence that reflects its meaning.

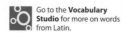 **ENGLISH LEARNER SUPPORT**

Vocabulary Strategy As students identify adjectives that are part of word families and write sentences using them, review the placement of adjectives in English. Note the general placement of adjectives before nouns in English sentences as opposed to the placement after the noun in Spanish, Vietnamese, and other languages. Begin with simple declarative sentences (It is a red door. It was a rainy day.) and identify the noun and adjective. Then supply a list of alternate adjectives (*yellow, white, oak, open, sunny, cloudy, foggy, windy*) and have students identify the correct placement of the adjective. Remind them that this placement is a general rule in English when writing sentences. **SUBSTANTIAL**

LANGUAGE CONVENTIONS:
Commas to Set Off Phrases and Clauses

A **clause** is a group of words that contains a subject and a verb. There are two types of clauses: the **independent clause**, which can stand alone as a sentence, and the **dependent clause**, which cannot stand alone as a sentence. Dependent clauses act as modifiers that add meaning to independent clauses. Dependent clauses often begin with subordinating conjunctions: *as if, as, since, than, that, though, until, whenever, where, while, who,* and *why.*

Phrases include prepositional phrases, such as *across the room* and *on the kitchen counter.*

Separate independent clauses in a compound sentence with a comma and a coordinating conjunction, or use a semicolon if there is no conjunction.

> **Brennan respects the flag, but he defends Johnson's right to burn it.**
> **Brennan respects the flag; he defends Johnson's right to burn it.**

In general, if a clause or phrase appears at the beginning of a sentence, or if it appears in the middle of the sentence, it should be set off with commas. Clauses and phrases at the ends of sentences usually are not set off with commas. Look at the following examples:

> **The judges ruled in favor of Johnson because of the First Amendment.**
> **Because of the First Amendment, the judges ruled in favor of Johnson.**
> **The judges, because of the First Amendment, ruled in favor of Johnson.**

Practice and Apply Write a one-paragraph summary of the court case *Texas v. Johnson* and the Supreme Court's decision. Use prepositional phrases and dependent clauses. (Hint: Use the words *as if, as, since, than, that, though, until, whenever, where, while, who,* and *why* to start dependent clauses.) Vary the placement of phrases and clauses within your sentences. Trade your summary with a partner, and check each other's use of commas.

> ! Go to the **Grammar Studio** for more on using commas.

LANGUAGE CONVENTIONS:
Commas to Set Off Phrases and Clauses

Review the distinction between independent clauses *(can stand alone)* and dependent clauses *(cannot stand alone),* and the distinction between clauses *(have a subject and verb)* and phrases that modify *(are only related to another phrase or clause).*

In general, commas are used to set off (separate) information. Note that there are often choices about using commas with phrases and clauses because a single sentence may be written in a variety of ways.

Illustrate the use of commas to set off dependent clauses in a sentence by rewriting an example sentence. Call attention to the subordinating conjunctions shown in the lesson. Then, display the following sentence:

> "*Since* Brennan respects the flag, he defends Johnson's right to burn it."

Point out that the dependent clause, "Since Brennan respects the flag," modifies "he defends Johnson's right to burn it" because it helps to describe or explain Brennan's motivation for defending Johnson's right.

Practice and Apply Have partners discuss whether commas are used correctly in the paragraph and what effect they have on the reader *(help emphasize a certain point, separate bits or types of information).*

ENGLISH LEARNER SUPPORT

Use Commas in Sentences Provide instruction and practice in comma usage with the following example sentences:

- Combine the sentences using a comma and the conjunction *but*: The sun was bright. It was still cold outside. (*The sun was bright, but it was still cold outside.*) **SUBSTANTIAL**

- Combine the sentences using a comma and the phrase *even though*: It was cold outside. The sun was bright. (*It was cold outside, even though the sun was bright.*) **MODERATE**

- Combine the sentences to use a dependent clause at the beginning followed by a comma: The sun was bright. I had to wear sunglasses. (*Because the sun was bright, I had to wear sunglasses.* **LIGHT**

AMERICAN FLAG STANDS FOR TOLERANCE

Argument by Ronald J. Allen

GENRE ELEMENTS

ARGUMENT

Remind students that the purpose of a written **argument** is to be persuasive about a particular opinion or point of view. To accomplish this purpose, a writer may employ a variety of strategies. For instance, a writer may appeal strongly to readers' emotions, supply factual evidence that backs up the opinion, or both. An argument on a controversial subject intends to spur the reader to action or create a changed opinion. In this lesson, students will analyze the elements of the editorial, the rhetoric used, and the overall success of the argument in achieving its goal.

LEARNING OBJECTIVES

- Evaluate an argument and analyze its rhetoric.
- Research opinions to evaluate credibility and bias.
- Write a letter to the editor that cites evidence.
- Debate using opinions and evidence.
- Understand word connotations.
- Analyze the function of dashes and use them correctly.
- **Language** With teacher support, identify unfamiliar words and define them using context and other supports.

TEXT COMPLEXITY

Quantitative Measures	**American Flag Stands for Tolerance**	Lexile: 1170L
Qualitative Measures	**Ideas Presented** Purpose implied but easily identified from context; requires some inferential reasoning.	
	Structures Used Complex main ideas and details but mostly explicit.	
	Language Used Unfamiliar and high academic words defined; compound/complex sentences.	
	Knowledge Required Understanding of complex civics concepts; cultural and historical references.	

RESOURCES

- Unit 1 Response Log

- Selection Audio

- Close Read Screencasts: Modeled Discussions

- Reading Studio: Notice & Note

- Level Up Tutorial: Analyzing Arguments

- Writing Studio: Using Formal Style

- Speaking and Listening Studio: Listening and Responding Contructively

- Vocabulary Studio: Connotations

- Grammar Studio: Module 12: Lesson 6: Dashes and Parentheses

- *from* Texas *v.* Johnson Majority Opinion / "American Flag Stands for Tolerance" Selection Test

SUMMARIES

English

Ronald J. Allen provides a persuasive argument in an editorial supporting the Supreme Court ruling on flag burning. He notes that U.S. support of free speech sets it apart from most other countries. He identifies the flag as a cherished symbol of American values. According to Allen, the First Amendment prohibits the government from requiring all citizens to follow dogma related to the flag. Allen also notes that the flag's secure place in American culture is proven by how unpopular burning the flag is.

Spanish

Ronald J. Allen da razones persuasivas en un editorial que apoya la decisión de la Corte Suprema acerca de la quema de la bandera. Observa que el apoyo de Estados Unidos a la libertad de expresión lo separa de la mayoría de los países. Identifica a la bandera como un símbolo apreciado de los valores americanos. De acuerdo con Allen, la Primera Enmienda garantiza los derechos más importantes de los ciudadanos. Prohíbe que el gobierno le exija a ninguno de sus ciudadanos el seguimiento de un dogma relacionado con la bandera. Allen también observa que el lugar de la bandera está a salvo en la cultura americana debido a lo impopular que es el acto de quemarla.

SMALL-GROUP OPTIONS

Have students work in small groups to read and discuss the selection.

Three Before Me

- Have students use a collaborative approach for improving the letter to the editor assigned as a response to the editorial.

- Instruct students to write and edit the assigned letter individually.

- Have each student ask three other students to read the letter before it is turned in. Readers may be asked to read for a particular type of error or to edit the entire paper. They can make notes, edits, and suggestions in the margin.

- When editing is complete, ask the original writer to evaluate suggestions and edits and to make appropriate changes before submission.

Numbered Heads Together

- Have students form groups of four. Count off 1-2-3-4 to assign each student a number within a group.

- Pose a question to the class. For example: What does Allen mean by the phrase "freedom of conscience"? Alternatively, ask a question posed in Respond: Analyze the Text.

- Have students discuss responses to the question in their groups.

- Call a number from 1 to 4. Each student with that number responds for the group.

- Change group composition for each question, as needed.

Text X-Ray: English Learner Support
for "American Flag Stands for Tolerance"

Use the Text X-Ray and the supports and scaffolds in the Teacher's Edition to help guide students at different proficiency levels through the selection.

INTRODUCE THE SELECTION
DISCUSS TOLERANCE

In this lesson, students will read about and discuss the symbolism associated with the American flag. Explain the following:

- *Tolerance* means "respecting the beliefs or actions of others."
- *Stands for* means "represents" or "is a symbol of."
- *American Flag Stands for Tolerance* means "The American flag represents respect for the beliefs or actions of others."

Tell students that not everyone agrees on what the American flag stands for. Point out that the root word *tolerate* suggests accepting something that is not desired or favored. Display pictures of two symbols, such as mascots of rival sports teams. Provide these frames:

- *This symbol stands for _____.*
- *We all should show tolerance for _____.*

CULTURAL REFERENCES

The following phrases from the selection may be unfamiliar to students:

- *the Supreme Court . . . held* (paragraph 1): the Supreme Court decided
- *compel the conclusion* (paragraph 2): force people to think
- *by his or her own lights* (paragraph 3): using personal opinions or choices

LISTENING

Verify Comprehension

Confirm listening comprehension by asking students about what they have heard.

Read aloud the first two sentences of paragraph 8. Clarify the meanings of *tolerance, free expression,* and *distasteful.* Use the following supports with students at varying proficiency levels:

- Paraphrase the first two sentences of paragraph 8: The flag stands for tolerance. The flag stands for free expression. Ask thumbs-up and thumbs-down questions to verify comprehension. **SUBSTANTIAL**
- Ask students to quick-write about the meaning of the sentences read aloud. Then, have them share and discuss their notes with a partner. **MODERATE**
- Have students retell the meaning of what they heard to confirm understanding. **LIGHT**

SPEAKING

State Opinions in a Debate

Help students prepare for participation in the debate activity on Student Edition page 57 by saying statements and responses aloud.

Use the following supports with students at varying proficiency levels:

- Help students speak their basic opinion statement using this frame: *I believe that burning the flag should be _____ (allowed/against the law).* **SUBSTANTIAL**
- Help students speak their basic opinion statement and support it using this frame: *I believe that burning the flag as a protest should be _____ (allowed/against the law) because _____.* **MODERATE**
- Help students prepare to respond to opposing opinions during a debate using this frame: *I understand the opposing opinion, but I believe_____ is more important. These are my reasons why: _____.* **LIGHT**

READING

Identify and Understand Unfamiliar Words

Encourage students to take the time to understand unfamiliar words, both in the Word Gaps note on Student Edition page 54 and throughout the lesson.

Use the following supports with students at varying proficiency levels:

- Direct students to read the first two sentences of paragraph 3 and circle any unfamiliar words. Provide supports such as definitions, cognates (*contrario, definitivo*), and simpler synonyms (*hopes* in place of *aspirations*). **SUBSTANTIAL**
- Have students read the first two sentences of paragraph 3, circling unfamiliar words. Provide supports, including definitions, cognates (*aspiración*), and synonyms (*goal, wish*). Model use of the dictionary. **MODERATE**
- Have partners read paragraph 3 and circle unfamiliar words. Have partners work together to define as many words as possible using context clues, before finding remaining definitions in a dictionary. **LIGHT**

WRITING

Outline a Writing Assignment

Work with students to read the writing assignment on Student Edition page 57.

Use the following supports with students at varying proficiency levels:

- Explain that a letter to the editor should contain one clear opinion statement. Use this frame: *I believe that burning the flag should be _____ (allowed/against the law).* **SUBSTANTIAL**
- Guide students in writing a topic sentence that identifies their opinion for a letter to the editor. **MODERATE**
- Have students write topic sentences for each planned paragraph for a letter to the editor. **LIGHT**

Connect to the
ESSENTIAL QUESTION

The *Texas* v. *Johnson* case created controversy around the country. It essentially stated that staying true to ourselves and our American principles meant that laws must permit expression of views that are unpopular. The "American Flag Stands for Tolerance" editorial addresses the case and reactions to it. It also summarizes the Court's view of what it means to stay true to ourselves by staying true to the principles of the First Amendment.

COMPARE ARGUMENTS

To compare arguments, students must understand and remember the claims and evidence used in each argument as well as keep in mind the author's purpose and intended audience. To continue preparing for this comparison, students can use their notes from the previous selection to identify similarities and differences. Remind them that not every idea in a selection will have a clear comparison or contrast in the other. In some cases, writers propose ideas that are not addressed in another piece on the same subject.

COLLABORATE & COMPARE

EDITORIAL

AMERICAN FLAG STANDS FOR TOLERANCE

by **Ronald J. Allen**
pages 53–55

COMPARE ARGUMENTS

Now that you have read the court opinion from *Texas* v. *Johnson Majority Opinion*, you will read a newspaper editorial—a type of argument—that was written in response to the *Texas* v. *Johnson* decision. Compare Allen's argument with the court's opinion. Also consider how the purpose and audience for the texts differ. After you review both selections, you will complete an independent project.

 ESSENTIAL QUESTION:

How do we engage with others while staying true to ourselves?

COURT OPINION

from TEXAS *v.* JOHNSON MAJORITY OPINION

by **William J. Brennan**
pages 43–45

50   Unit 1

American Flag Stands for Tolerance

QUICK START

What is the appropriate way to react if people have opinions that you find hateful or disrespectful? How can you respond in a way that keeps the disagreement from turning into a fight? Discuss this dilemma in a small group.

EVALUATE AN ARGUMENT

Editorials present an author's **argument** about a contested issue. A well-crafted argument contains the following elements:

ELEMENT OF ARGUMENT	DESCRIPTION
Claim	A statement of the overall opinion
Reasons and Evidence	Data, anecdotes, facts, and other examples that support the claim
Counterclaims and Counterarguments	Acknowledgment of reasons an opponent might disagree and arguments against those reasons
Concessions and Rebuttals	Concession: agreement that a counterargument is valid; rebuttal: argument against the counterclaim
Conclusion	Usually a call to action for the reader

As you read "American Flag Stands for Tolerance," evaluate how Allen includes the above elements of an argument.

ANALYZE RHETORIC

Persuasive authors often use **rhetoric**, or specific words and language structures that make a message memorable. They also use **appeals** to a reader's emotions, sense of logic, and sense of justice (beliefs about what is right and wrong). Common rhetorical devices include the following:

- **Parallelism:** a form of repetition in which a grammatical pattern is repeated to create rhythm, link ideas, or evoke emotions
- **Antithesis:** placing two ideas side-by-side to show contrast between them
- **Shifts:** changes in mood, attitude, or point, often signaled by words such as *but, however,* and *although*
- **Logical Fallacy:** an error in reasoning that undermines an argument or renders it invalid

As you read, identify how Allen uses rhetoric to make his points memorable.

GENRE ELEMENTS: ARGUMENT

- states the author's stance on an issue
- supports the opinion with relevant evidence
- addresses potential counterclaims
- ends with a call to action

QUICK START

Students may wish to focus on a specific problem, either real or imagined. A real problem might have involved a student at a sports contest or a large event in which they overheard or were the subject of hateful comments. An imagined problem might be watching a street protest in which someone burned a flag, made offensive gestures, or used hateful words. After students have identified a situation, they can proceed through the questions posed in the text. Also remind them that there is not a single right answer in this type of discussion and that adults and others in the United States and around the world struggle with these issues.

EVALUATE AN ARGUMENT

Note that the process of evaluating evidence as practiced in the excerpt from *Texas* v. *Johnson* is one part of the larger process of evaluating an argument described here. Review the chart that lists the elements of argument and answer any questions. Note that different written arguments may be stronger in one element than another and that space limitations may affect which elements are presented. Explain that every effective argument includes a claim, reasons and evidence, and a conclusion. However, including counterarguments, concessions, and rebuttals makes the argument stronger because they address ideas that readers might use in opposition.

ANALYZE RHETORIC

Explain that the term *rhetoric* includes a wide variety of strategies used in speaking and writing. In persuasive articles such as this argument, using appeals to logic or emotion implies that the reader and the author share some basic ideas or attitudes. An effective appeal convinces the reader that the author shares the reader's attitudes and that they are correct or important.

As they read the selection, suggest that students use the following questions to help them understand and assess the rhetorical devices:

- What rhetorical device is the author using?
- What are the specific details involved? Details may include the ideas placed side-by-side in an antithesis, or the error of a logical fallacy.
- What is the intended effect of the device? For example, the effect may be to emphasize the importance of an idea.
- Does the device achieve the intended effect?

ENGLISH LEARNER SUPPORT

Understand Directionality Make sure that students, especially speakers of Arabic, understand how to read the chart that identifies and explains elements of an argument. Explain that the column headings apply to all the rows beneath it in that same column and that the headings serve as a broad category with specific details listed in the rows beneath. Students should read the chart beginning at the top left, which lists the first element (Claim) and then move from left to right to read its description. They can then move down the chart using the same process and direction.   **SUBSTANTIAL**

CRITICAL VOCABULARY

Encourage students to read all the definitions before deciding which one fits a word. As a clue to the definition of *sanctity*, note that it is derived from the same root word as *sanctuary*.

Answers:

1. *a*

2. *c*

3. *b*

■ English Learner Support

Use Cognates Tell students that two of the Critical Vocabulary words have Spanish cognates: *sanctity/santidad* and *dogma/dogma*. **ALL LEVELS**

LANGUAGE CONVENTIONS

Review the information about dashes. Some students may confuse a dash with a hyphen (-). Tell students that hyphens are used to connect two words or separate syllables in a word, while dashes separate ideas and are used as an option instead of other punctuation.

Reinforce the idea that dashes are an optional type of punctuation a writer may choose to provide more emphasis than other punctuation or to vary the pace of reading. Read each example sentence twice, once with dashes and a second time with the type of punctuation replaced. Note that the differences are very subtle and that the basic information is not changed by the choice of one type of punctuation instead of another.

✎ ANNOTATION MODEL

Remind students of the rhetorical devices listed in Analyze Rhetoric on page 51. Suggest that students read through the selection, specifically looking for rhetorical devices. It may be easier to spot the rhythmic elements of parallelism by reading the text aloud. Have them scan for signal words (*but, however, although*) to identify shifts. Students may use their own systems to note important information, including underlining, circling, using parentheses or brackets, highlighting in different colors, or using special symbols such as a star, check mark, or exclamation point.

GET READY

CRITICAL VOCABULARY

To preview the Critical Vocabulary words, match each word to its definition.

1. icon	a. symbol of deeply held values
2. sanctity	b. traditionally accepted codes and customs
3. dogma	c. sacredness or ultimate importance

LANGUAGE CONVENTIONS

Dashes A **dash** is a punctuation mark that sets a phrase or clause off from other parts of a sentence. Dashes can often take the place of commas, parentheses, or colons and allow a writer freedom to vary the flow of a text. Look at these examples of dashes used in place of other punctuation marks.

Instead of a colon:

Thus, we do have one official dogma—each American may think and express anything he wants.

Instead of parentheses:

The American flag—which is one of our most important symbols—is the subject.

Instead of commas:

We wonder—soon after the court case has been decided—what to do next.

As you read "American Flag Stands for Tolerance," notice how the author uses dashes to set off ideas.

ANNOTATION MODEL

NOTICE & NOTE

Here is how you might annotate to help you identify how Allen uses an appeal to emotion—the reader's patriotism—as a rhetorical device.

> The American flag is a cherished symbol of our national aspirations. It is the closest object to a national icon, rivaled only by the Constitution and the Declaration of Independence. Given the widespread and deeply felt reverence for this symbol of what we perceive to be the best of our civilization, what is the harm in insisting upon a modicum of respect for it?

Allen appeals to readers' patriotism with words like "cherished symbol" and "reverence."

Mentioning the Declaration of Independence and the Constitution connects with other things Americans value.

BACKGROUND

In the court case Texas v. Johnson, the Supreme Court decided, with a vote of 5 justices against 4, that burning the flag was an action protected by the First Amendment to the Constitution. The close vote among the judges reflected the opinion of people around the country. Controversy erupted at the ruling, with people still arguing on all sides. We can read newspaper reports, including editorials, from the time to understand the public sentiment. Law professor **Ronald J. Allen** *published this editorial in the* Chicago Tribune *on June 30, 1989, in response to the* Texas v. Johnson *decision and the uproar that it caused.*

AMERICAN FLAG STANDS FOR TOLERANCE

Editorial by Ronald J. Allen

PREPARE TO COMPARE

As you read, consider your own opinion of the issue. How might your ideas defend or challenge those Allen presents? Mark ideas you agree or disagree with as you read, noting your thoughts on the page.

1   In a controversial decision, the Supreme Court, by the closest possible margin of a 5-to-4 vote, held that a person has a right to express disagreement with governmental policies by burning the American flag. In a decision at least as controversial, the leadership of the People´s Republic of China decided that citizens who peacefully express disagreement with government policies may be slaughtered.[1] On the surface, these two events may seem to bear little relationship to one another, but deep and fundamental lessons can be drawn from their comparison.

2   The American flag is a cherished symbol of our national aspirations. It is the closest object to a national **icon**, rivaled only by the Constitution and the Declaration of Independence. Given the widespread and deeply felt reverence for this symbol of what we perceive to be the best of our civilization, what is the harm

---

[1] **People's Republic of China . . . slaughtered:** In June 1989, government tanks fired on citizens who had gathered in Beijing's Tiananmen Square to demand democratic reforms. Hundreds were killed.

Notice & Note

You can use the side margins to notice and note signposts in the text.

ANALYZE RHETORIC
Annotate: Mark two ideas in paragraph 1 that the author places together in order to contrast them.

Analyze: What is the effect of the author's use of antithesis here?

icon
(ī´kän) *n.* symbol of deeply held values

APPLYING ACADEMIC VOCABULARY

❑ **discriminate**   ❑ **diverse**   ☑ **inhibit**   ☑ **intervene**   ❑ **rational**

Write and Discuss   Have students turn to a partner to discuss the following questions. Guide students to include the academic vocabulary words *inhibit* and *intervene* in their responses. Ask volunteers to share their responses with the class.

- Do you think the Chinese response to protest will **inhibit** people from protesting?
- According to the United States Supreme Court ruling, can authorities **intervene** in people's right to express disagreement with governmental policies?

BACKGROUND

Explain that after the *Texas* v. *Johnson* decision, people around the country expressed opinions explaining their support or opposition to it. Written opinions such as newspaper editorials require people to delineate their views carefully and to explain why they support one side or the other. Reading a variety of newspaper editorials on a particular issue can provide a snapshot of opinions at the time.

PREPARE TO COMPARE

Direct students to use the Prepare to Compare prompt to focus their reading.

✏ ANALYZE RHETORIC

Remind students that analyzing rhetoric means that they analyze how something is presented without necessarily agreeing or disagreeing with the ideas presented. In this example and others, students need to describe the strategies used by the author and analyze their effectiveness. This means that regardless of whether they agree or disagree with what Allen says, they should analyze his approach without being swayed by their emotional reaction to it. (**Answer:** *The author is contrasting the lack of freedom shown by the People's Republic of China's leaders' choice to execute dissenters with the decision of* Texas v. Johnson. *The effect is to emphasize the goodness or rightness of the Supreme Court's position by its contrast to a position that was terribly violent and extreme.*)

CRITICAL VOCABULARY

icon: Allen suggests that the flag is similar to early American documents that are symbols of American values in establishing a new nation.

ASK STUDENTS to explain why the Constitution, the Declaration of Independence, and the flag are the "closest object(s)" to icons. (*All are connected to events and ideas that symbolize American values, but America does not have official icons.*)

EVALUATE AN ARGUMENT

Successful arguments require a clear claim and then reasons and evidence to back up the claim. Help students as necessary to identify the simple claim in the first sentence of paragraph 3, and then the expansion of this claim in the second sentence. (**Answer:** *Allen supports his claim that "The Supreme Court was not wrong" in its decision by stating that "a decision contrary to the one reached would have been a definitive step away from our national aspirations."*)

▶ WORD GAPS

Explain that the formal English used in newspaper editorials may include words that are not common in informal or spoken English. Remind students that in addition to using a dictionary, they may use context clues or other resources on the page to determine a word's meaning. (**Answer:** *Depending on the word circled, students may use a footnote, Critical Vocabulary definition, a dictionary, or context clues to understand the word.*)

📖 For **reading support** for students at varying proficiency levels, see the **Text X-Ray** on page 50D.

CRITICAL VOCABULARY

sanctity: Allen feels that what separates our nation from other nations is Americans' belief that individual freedoms are of the utmost importance.

ASK STUDENTS to give an example of how Americans demonstrate their belief in the sanctity of the human conscience. (*A person can pass out literature or express opinions in public without fear of being arrested.*)

dogma: Allen feels that the beliefs and opinions of private citizens are just as legitimate as the established opinions of the government. No individual or group has the right to impose those beliefs and opinions on another.

ASK STUDENTS to consider the possible dangers in imposing or following dogma. (*Other relevant and helpful ideas may be ignored or put down. The suppression of ideas may lead to dangerous conflict.*)

 NOTICE & NOTE

EVALUATE AN ARGUMENT

Annotate: Mark the claim Allen makes in paragraph 3.

Analyze: How does Allen support this claim?

sanctity
(săngk´tĭ-tē) *n.* sacredness or ultimate importance.

WORD GAPS

Notice & Note: Mark a word in paragraph 4 that might interfere with your understanding.

Interpret: How can you determine what this word means?

dogma
(dôg´mə) *n.* principles or beliefs that an authority insists are true.

---

in insisting upon a modicum[2] of respect for it? After all, no one can seriously equate a prohibition on flag burning with the imposition of governmental orthodoxy[3] in political speech. Any messages that burning the flag might convey easily can be communicated in other ways. Those are powerful points, deserving the greatest respect. If not rebutted,[4] they compel the conclusion that the Supreme Court was wrong in its decision.

3   The Supreme Court was not wrong. Indeed, a decision contrary to the one reached would have been a definitive step away from our national aspirations. A commitment to the intertwined freedoms of conscience and expression is at the core of those aspirations. What most distinguishes our civilization from both its predecessors and its contemporary competitors is a belief in the **sanctity** of the human conscience. Each individual is to have the freedom to develop by his or her own lights, and not by the command of officialdom. That requires not just the right to be let alone, but also the right to communicate with, to learn from and test views in conversations.

4   It is, thus, no surprise that the First Amendment is where it is in the Bill of Rights, for it is first in importance. A concomitant[5] of the commitment to freedom of conscience, in a sense its mirror image, is that no one has better access to truth than anyone else. Official dogma is not better (perhaps no worse) than the beliefs of private citizens.

5   The dissenters[6] in the flag-burning case and their supporters might at this juncture note an irony in my argument. My point is that freedom of conscience and expression is at the core of our self-conception and that commitment to it requires the rejection of official dogma. But how is that admittedly dogmatic belief different from any other dogma, such as the one inferring that freedom of expression stops at the border of the flag?

6   The crucial distinction is that the commitment to freedom of conscience and expression states the simplest and least self-contradictory principle that seems to capture our aspirations. Any other principle is hopelessly at odds with our commitment to freedom of conscience. The controversy surrounding the flag-burning case makes the case well.

7   The controversy will rage precisely because burning the flag is such a powerful form of communication. Were it not, who would care? Thus were we to embrace a prohibition on such communication, we would be saying that the First Amendment protects expression only when no one is offended. That would mean that this aspect of the First Amendment would be of virtually no consequence. It would protect a person only when no protection was needed. Thus, we do have one official dogma—each American may

---

[2] **modicum:** small amount offered as a symbol or gesture.
[3] **orthodoxy:** traditionally accepted codes and customs.
[4] **rebutted:** opposed using reasons and evidence.
[5] **concomitant:** one that occurs or exists concurrently with another.
[6] **dissenters:** those who disagree or refuse to accept.

CLOSE READ SCREENCAST

Modeled Discussion   In their eBook, have students view the Close Read Screencast, in which readers discuss and annotate the following key passage:

- Allen's argument supporting the Supreme Court's decision (paragraph 3)

As a class, view and discuss the video. Then have students pair up to do an independent close read of an additional passage—Allen's beliefs about what the American flag symbolizes (paragraph 8). Students can record their answers on the Close Read Practice PDF.

 Close Read Practice PDF

think and express anything he wants. The exception is expression that involves the risk of injury to others and the destruction of someone else's property. Neither was present in this case.

8   At the core of what the flag symbolizes, then, is tolerance. More than anything else, the flag stands for free expression of ideas, no matter how distasteful. The ultimate irony would have been to punish views expressed by burning the flag that stands for the right to those expressions.

9   . . . Perhaps, though, there is another way to look at it—to acknowledge that not even such a fundamental value as the commitment to freedom of conscience should be free from controversy. With controversy comes debate, enlightenment and renewed commitment. Perhaps, then, we are in the court's debt for not treating the flag-burning case like the simple case it is. Let the controversy rage. After all, it is in robust debate that we are most true to ourselves.

LANGUAGE CONVENTIONS

Annotate: Mark the dash in paragraph 9.

Analyze: How does the dash link two ideas in this sentence?

CHECK YOUR UNDERSTANDING

Answer these questions before moving on to the **Analyze the Text** section on the following page.

1   What is Allen's stance on people who burn the American flag?

  A   No one should be offended when they burn it.

  B   They are making an empty gesture and should be ignored.

  C   They should be punished by the government.

  D   Their offensive act is protected by the First Amendment.

2   Allen believes that, above all, the flag symbolizes tolerance and —

  F   love

  G   patriotism

  H   free expression

  J   law and order

3   What does Allen see as a bright point in the controversy?

  A   The debate it inspires

  B   The attention it gives the flag

  C   The increasing support for the military

  D   The growing tide of people willing to protest

 ENGLISH LEARNER SUPPORT

Oral Assessment   Use the following questions to assess students' comprehension and speaking skills.

1.   Does the author say people have the right to burn the flag? *(yes)*

2.   Does the flag stand for freedom of speech? *(yes)*

3.   Does the author respect the flag? *(yes)*

     SUBSTANTIAL

 ENGLISH LEARNER SUPPORT

Review Multiple Meanings   Point out the word *irony* in the third line of paragraph 8 and note that it was also used in the second line of paragraph 5. Tell students that the Spanish cognate for *irony* is *ironía*. Explain to students that the word *irony* is used to express how something seems out of place or is the opposite of what is expected. Help students to understand the meaning of "the ultimate irony" (paragraph 8). Have pairs read and discuss paragraph 8. Guide students to understand that the author suggests that it would seem *ironic*, or out of place, to punish people for free expressions about the flag when the flag *is* a symbol of free expression.

LIGHT

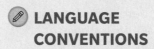 For **listening support** for students at varying proficiency levels, see the **Text X-Ray** on page 50C.

 LANGUAGE CONVENTIONS

Reinforce the idea that dashes are an option that writers can use to replace three other types of punctuation (colon, parentheses, comma). Their intent in choosing to use a dash is to achieve a specific effect. Because dashes are not used as commonly as other punctuation, they draw special attention to a particular clause or phrase. (**Answer:** *The dash links the ideas presented previously and those presented after the dash, or "another way" to consider the topic.*)

CHECK YOUR UNDERSTANDING

Have students answer the questions independently.

Answers:

1.   *D*

2.   *H*

3.   *A*

If they answer any questions incorrectly, have them reread the text to confirm their understanding. Then they may proceed to ANALYZE THE TEXT on page 56.

ANALYZE THE TEXT

Possible answers:

1. **DOK 2:** *The words "cherished," "aspirations," "reverence," "best," and "respect" show Allen's feelings toward the flag. Understanding his attitude toward the flag makes me feel that his argument is stronger because it's clear that he has great respect for the flag, yet he thinks it's important to Americans' belief in freedom that they should be allowed to burn the flag in protest if they wish.*

2. **DOK 4:** *Both "sanctity" and "enlightenment" have strongly positive connotations, which convey a positive attitude, or tone, toward the freedoms Americans share and the commitment to keeping them.*

3. **DOK 4:** *In paragraph 2, Allen states the following counterargument: The flag's status as a cherished symbol commands our respect, and any dissent should be communicated in ways other than the burning of that symbol. By acknowledging an opponent's argument, he builds a foundation for his own argument in paragraph 3 that forcing respect ("the command of officialdom") undermines the freedom Americans value.*

4. **DOK 4:** *The statement is an overgeneralization about people who disagree with Allen. If he had included it, he would have insulted the very audience he is trying to convince, so his argument would have failed.*

5. **DOK 4:** *Allen points out that the First Amendment protects freedom of expression, even when that expression is offensive, as long as it does not cause risk of injury or destruction of someone else's property. He further says that "the flag stands for free expression of ideas, no matter how distasteful" (paragraph 8).*

RESEARCH

Encourage students to list at least four online sources with summaries and assessments of credibility. Remind students that in general, credible sources include established newspapers and research organizations, college affiliations, and government agencies.

Connect Students can discuss criteria for credible sources, including an author's position (*as a professor or historian*) and the publication or site that features it (*established newspapers or reputable organizations*). They might extend their discussion with experiences they have had with sources that are not credible.

◎ **RESPOND**

ANALYZE THE TEXTS

Support your responses with evidence from the text. 📓 NOTEBOOK

1. **Infer** What words or phrases in paragraph 2 convey Allen's feelings about the flag? Does understanding his attitude make you feel that his argument is stronger or weaker? Why?

2. **Analyze** In his editorial, Allen talks about the "sanctity of the human conscience" and the "enlightenment" that comes from debate. Explain how the connotations of these words convey his tone.

3. **Analyze** Allen presents a counterargument involving respect for the flag at the beginning of the editorial. How does this contribute to the structure of his argument? How does he address the counterargument?

4. **Evaluate** A **logical fallacy** is an error in reasoning. Suppose Allen had included this sentence in his editorial: *Anyone who wants to throw flag burners in jail is obviously not a supporter of the Constitution.* In what way is this statement a fallacy? How would this sentence have affected Allen's argument?

5. **Notice & Note** Allen discriminates, or distinguishes, between what people *should* do and what they *should be allowed* to do. How does he reconcile this apparent contradiction in his argument?

RESEARCH TIP
It can be tempting to call a source biased if you disagree with its content. Likewise, it can be easy not to notice bias if you *agree* with a source's bias. To determine whether bias exists, ask yourself how a reader with different views from yours would view the text. Also, check a variety of credible sources.

RESEARCH

Find four online sources that provide opinions or information on the topic of flag burning. Since anyone can post information on the Internet, it's important to analyze sources for **credibility**, or the quality of being trustworthy. For each source you find, ask yourself if it comes from an established organization and if the author's background gives him or her the expertise to address the topic accurately and responsibly. Look for signs of **bias**, or unfairly choosing one side over another, and possible **omissions**, or information purposely left out. Using a chart like the one below, keep track of your sources and describe their credibility.

URL / SOURCE	OPINION OR MAIN IDEA	NOTES ON CREDIBILITY
Sources will vary.	*Burning the flag is bad but not illegal*	*Includes quotes from a Supreme Court justice.*

Connect Share an example of a credible online source with your partner. Explain what factors led you to believe that the author or authors are credible.

WHEN STUDENTS STRUGGLE . . .

Reteaching: Evaluate an Argument Remind students that an important part of evaluating an argument is identifying the author's claims (main points) and the reasons and evidence that support those claims. Have students identify one of Allen's claims in the selection and the evidence used to support it. (*Allen claims that freedom of thought and expression is a basic right and cites the First Amendment to the Constitution, in paragraph 4, to support the claim.*)

 For additional support, go to the **Reading Studio** and assign the following 🔼 **Level Up Tutorial: Analyzing Arguments.**

CREATE AND PRESENT

Write a Letter to the Editor Editors of newspapers and magazines receive letters from the public expressing their reactions to the content of the publications. Some of these letters to the editor are published in future issues. Write a letter to a newspaper editor. In your letter, respond to "American Flag Stands for Tolerance."

❏ Use a business letter format and formal language that addresses an adult.

❏ At the beginning of your letter, state your opinion clearly.

❏ Cite evidence from the editorial to support your opinion.

Debate the Issue People are strongly divided on whether burning the flag should be protected as a form of free speech. You have read multiple opinions about the topic. Use your knowledge to form an opinion, and debate the issue.

❏ Write your opinion as a statement. Draw evidence from the sources you have read to support your opinion. List your pieces of evidence as bullet points for quick reference.

❏ Form debate teams. One side should argue "Burning the flag should be protected as free speech under the First Amendment." The other side should oppose this argument. If all the students in your class agree, choose a group to take the opposite side and find evidence to support it.

❏ Establish the rules of debate. Decide on the order in which people will speak. Assign roles, such as a moderator and panel members. When debating, listen attentively to others, and take notes if you think of something you want to say in response. Use a respectful tone, even when disagreeing with others. After the debate, reevaluate your opinion.

RESPOND

Go to the **Writing Studio** for more on using a formal style in your letter.

Go to the **Speaking and Listening Studio** for more on listening and responding constructively.

RESPOND TO THE ESSENTIAL QUESTION

? How do we engage with others while staying true to ourselves?

Gather Information Review your annotations and notes on "American Flag Stands for Tolerance" and highlight those that help answer the Essential Question. Then, add relevant details to your Response Log.

At the end of the unit, use your notes to write a personal essay.

ACADEMIC VOCABULARY

As you write and discuss what you learned from the argument, be sure to use the Academic Vocabulary words. Check off each of the words that you use.

❏ discriminate
❏ diverse
❏ inhibit
❏ intervene
❏ rational

CREATE AND PRESENT

Write a Letter to the Editor Note that a letter to the editor is meant to be a persuasive argument in the same way as the "American Flag Stands for Tolerance" editorial. Provide students with several examples of a letter to a newspaper editor. Discuss the similarities and differences between an editorial and a letter to the editor. Point out that an effective letter must include a clear statement of their opinion, or claim, evidence and reasons that support their opinion, and a conclusion.

For **writing support** for students at varying proficiency levels, see the **Text X-Ray** on page 50D.

Debate the Issue Some students may have to craft an argument that runs counter to their beliefs. Tell students that examining an issue from all angles is similar to forming a counterargument. Point out that no matter which side students argue, the procedure for making and supporting a claim are the same.

Emphasize the idea that the rules and format of a debate allow for a reasonable discussion and respectful argument about an issue that may be very emotional for some people. By establishing and following the rules as outlined, students can express their opinions and respond to questions in a way that focuses on issues and ideas rather than people or personalities.

Remind students that oral statements in a debate are similar to written arguments and that initially they need to make a clear claim, use reasons and evidence to support the claim, and provide a persuasive conclusion.

For **speaking support** for students at varying proficiency levels, see the **Text X-Ray** on page 50D.

RESPOND TO THE ESSENTIAL QUESTION

Allow time for students to add details from "American Flag Stands for Tolerance" to their Unit 1 Response Logs.

EL ## ENGLISH LEARNER SUPPORT

Write a Letter to the Editor Assist students in writing their letter by establishing their basic claim and supporting reasons and evidence, and then helping them expand on them in full paragraphs. Have them begin with this sentence frame: *I believe _____ because _____.* Once they have established their central claim and support for it, suggest that they expand them into multiple sentences or paragraphs. For example, they might answer the following questions to help them extend their thoughts: *How does flag burning make me feel? Why would someone burn the flag? How does this action affect me, my family, or my community?* **MODERATE**

APPLY

CRITICAL VOCABULARY

Answers:

1. A statue in a church is more of an icon because it is of a religious figure that most people seeing it would revere.

2. Although a swearing-in ceremony involves taking a solemn oath, a religious service would be seen as something more sacred, and more closely tied to the idea of sanctity.

3. A politician who votes against everything is attached to dogma; there is no flexibility on any topic.

VOCABULARY STRATEGY:
Connotations

Answers:

- **reverence:** (synonym, *admiration*) To say, "Given the widespread and deeply felt *admiration* for this symbol" doesn't convey the same sense of the flag as an almost sacred symbol. Therefore, the author may have chosen *reverence* to convey a positive religious connotation.

- **crucial:** (synonym, *critical*) To say, "The *critical* distinction is . . . to capture our aspirations" very nearly conveys the same connotation as *crucial,* because it also conveys a sense of something very important, serious, and under pressure. The author probably chose *crucial* to convey this type of importance.

- **rage:** (synonym, *storm*) To say, "Let the controversy *storm*" might come close to the use of the verb *rage* here. However, *rage* has the advantage of implying violent anger, which is appropriate to the controversy. It has negative connotations in terms of debate and human interactions.

WORD BANK
icon
dogma
sanctity

Go to the **Vocabulary Studio** to learn more about connotations.

CRITICAL VOCABULARY

Practice and Apply Answer each question by incorporating the meaning of the Critical Vocabulary word.

1. Which do you consider more of an **icon,** a statue of a past national leader or a very popular musician?

_____

2. Which do you think better exemplifies **sanctity,** a mayor being sworn into office or a solemn religious service?

_____

3. Who is more attached to **dogma,** a politician who votes against everything or a parent who refuses to change your curfew?

_____

VOCABULARY STRATEGY:
Connotations

A **connotation** is a feeling or value associated with a word. These associations are different from the word's dictionary definition. For example, *cheap* and *inexpensive* have the same meaning, but people tend to have a more negative view of something described as *cheap* than something described as *inexpensive.* Persuasive writers often use connotations to their advantage. **Loaded language** is an effort to appeal to emotions and convince others to share an opinion. Look at the following example:

The American flag is a <u>cherished</u> symbol of our national aspirations. (paragraph 2)

The neutral term *well-liked* has a meaning similar to that of the word *cherished,* but Allen's language would not appeal to readers' emotions in the same way if he called the flag a "well-liked symbol." The positive connotation of the word *cherished* communicates just how loved the American flag is.

Practice and Apply Find these words in the editorial: *reverence* (paragraph 2), *crucial* (paragraph 6), *rage* (paragraph 7). Working with a partner, discuss how the connotations of the words affect the author's meaning.

1. Look up each word and its synonyms.

2. Try using one of the synonyms in place of the word. How does it affect the meaning of the sentence?

3. Discuss and write down the purpose of the author's word choices. Base your answers on the words' connotations.

EL ENGLISH LEARNER SUPPORT

Vocabulary Strategy Work with students to find the three words from the activity (*reverence, crucial, rage*) in a thesaurus and select at least three synonyms for each. Discuss the various connotations for each synonym. For example, they might select *simmer, blow up,* and *smolder* for the verb *rage.* Use pictures (glowing coals for *smolder,* pots on a stove for *simmer*) to help describe the connotations. Ask them to arrange the words in a list from the weakest connotation to the strongest (*smolder, simmer, rage, blow up*). **MODERATE/LIGHT**

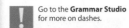

LANGUAGE CONVENTIONS:
Dashes

Like several other forms of punctuation, dashes cause readers to pause. Dashes and pairs of dashes are used to set off or emphasize ideas in place of commas, parentheses, or colons.

Here are two common uses of dashes.

> **!** Go to the **Grammar Studio** for more on dashes.

PURPOSE	EXAMPLE
to set off a definition or explanation	The First Amendment—which addresses the right to free speech, among other things—was cited in the case.
to emphasize a word, a series of words, a phrase, or a clause	This flag—the banner of *all* Americans—matters.

Practice and Apply Find two sentences in your letter to the editor that you can make more effective with the use of dashes. Rewrite your sentences and share them with a partner. Work together to discuss how the dashes affect the way the sentences are read.

LANGUAGE CONVENTIONS:
Dashes

Emphasize the differences between hyphens and dashes: hyphens are often used to connect words while dashes are used to separate them.

Reinforce the idea that writers have many choices of sentence construction and punctuation in communicating complex ideas. For example, the first example sentence combines three distinct ideas: *The First Amendment addresses the right to free speech. The First Amendment addresses other rights. The First Amendment was cited in this case.* Allen chose to combine all of these ideas in a single sentence and used both dashes and commas to help readers understand the content. Discuss the reasons Allen might have chosen this approach. (*Three sentences can be short and choppy, while a single sentence allows the sentence to flow more easily.*)

Point out that sentence length and punctuation contribute to a writer's unique style. Also note that combining several ideas in one sentence is not always a good choice. In some cases, a sentence can become too long and overly complex and may interfere with understanding its content.

Practice and Apply Have partners exchange letters to suggest appropriate sentences for the use of dashes. Once the sentences are rewritten and reviewed for correct usage of dashes, have partners discuss the new sentences. Do the dashes communicate the intended meaning more effectively? If not, students may choose to retain the original construction or punctuation and select a different sentence for the use of dashes.

American Flag Stands for Tolerance   59

 ENGLISH LEARNER SUPPORT

Language and Style Provide instruction and practice in the use of dashes with the following:

- Display the sentence from paragraph 7 that begins, "Thus we do have one official dogma. . . ." Work with students to underscore and rewrite the ideas separated by the dash. (*We share one belief. Americans are free to think and express.*) **SUBSTANTIAL**

- Have partners rewrite the activity's example sentences with commas, parentheses, or colons. **MODERATE**

- Direct students to paragraph 9, sentence 1. Have them rewrite the sentence with a different punctuation choice. (*Perhaps, though, there is another way to look at it: to acknowledge . . .*) **LIGHT**

COMPARE ARGUMENTS

Before small groups begin work to fill in the chart, emphasize that their task is not to compare the ideas presented, but to compare the reasons why each was written. Note that a student's personal feelings or emotional responses to either selection are not relevant to their group task. *(Possible statements: Brennan writes to other legal authorities to explain how the ruling affects the way they will enforce the law. Allen writes to persuade an audience of fellow patriotic Americans to support the Supreme Court's decision.)*

ANALYZE THE TEXTS

Possible answers:

1. **DOK 2:** *Both texts are about how people should be allowed to burn the flag in protest without being criminally punished. Allen's use of emotional language makes his argument more convincing because his ideas become more personal for readers.*

2. **DOK 4:** *As a Supreme Court Justice, Brennan is more credible. His objective tone also makes his opinion sound more authoritative. Allen uses some emotional language that somewhat detracts from his credibility.*

3. **DOK 4:** *Responses will vary. Students should use evidence from the texts to make inferences about how the authors would respond to the current debate they identify.*

4. **DOK 4:** *Brennan's tone is serious and thoughtful, as he is explaining the decision of a group of people—a decision that directly affected the life of one person but has implications about future law enforcement. He uses past court cases as evidence instead of appealing to people's emotions. Allen uses appeals to patriotism to make the tone of his editorial more personal and engaging.*

⊜ **RESPOND**

Collaborate & Compare

from **TEXAS v. JOHNSON MAJORITY OPINION**
Court Opinion
by William J. Brennan

AMERICAN FLAG STANDS FOR TOLERANCE
Argument by Ronald J. Allen

COMPARE ARGUMENTS

While reading you may have noted that, in his editorial, Allen agrees with the Supreme Court's majority decision. In this way, the main opinions that are expressed in the texts overlap. The two authors have different purposes for writing their texts, however, and they consider different audiences when putting together their thoughts.

In a small group, reread both texts to identify clues that indicate who the intended audience is and why each author is writing. Keep track of these clues as shown below. Use your completed chart to draft a statement about the purpose and audience your group identified for each piece based on the clues.

TEXT	CLUES ABOUT PURPOSE	CLUES ABOUT AUDIENCE
from *Texas v. Johnson Majority Opinion*	**We decline, therefore, . . .** *"is not to say that it may criminally punish"*	**[Barnette, 319 U.S. at 640.]** *"We are tempted to say . . . by our holding today."*
"American Flag Stands for Tolerance"	*""The Supreme Court was not wrong"*	*"our national aspirations" "our civilization"*

ANALYZE THE TEXTS

Discuss these questions in your group.

1. **Compare** What ideas are expressed in both the court opinion and the argument? Which selection's argument do you find more convincing? Why?

2. **Evaluate** Does one author seem more credible than the other? Why?

3. **Connect** Arguments about the First Amendment are ongoing. Name a recent event that caused a debate about people's rights. How do you think the authors of these texts would respond to the debate?

4. **Analyze** Compare the tone of the two selections. What makes one selection more serious and thoughtful and the other more emotional?

EL ENGLISH LEARNER SUPPORT

Ask Questions Use the following questions to help students compare the selections.

1. Who were the first people to read Justice Brennan's decision? Who were the first to read Allen's editorial? *(fellow justices, lawyers, people involved in the case; newspaper readers)*

2. What were the effects of Justice Brennan's decision? What were the possible effects of Allen's editorial? *(Johnson wasn't penalized, opinion influences future decisions; editorial influenced public opinion)*

3. Why has Justice Brennan's decision been read many times since it was first written? Why has Allen's editorial been read many times since it was first written? *(Each continues to influence opinions.)* **MODERATE/LIGHT**

RESEARCH AND DISCUSS

Debates, such as those about flag burning, tend to involve heated emotions. People feel passionate about their opinions, and they can take dissenting opinions personally. **De-escalation** refers to strategies that prevent conflicts from getting out of control.

You may have de-escalated a fight between friends by talking to them calmly and pointing out that their positions are both legitimate. In debates about politics, de-escalation keeps everyone respectful and makes it possible to find solutions.

Research de-escalation techniques, and instruct others on what to do when they encounter an offensive opponent.

1. **Research Techniques** Research what experts do to de-escalate heated conflicts. Take notes on recommended strategies that you think might be effective.

RESEARCH TIP
To find strong sources, begin with an Internet search using a keyword such as "de-escalate" and check for sources from reputable sites.

2. **Create a Procedure** Using your notes, write a step-by-step plan for what someone should do when encountering someone who is engaging in a legal, but offensive, activity or expression.

3. **Give Instructions** Role-play a scenario in which you step in to help two people who are involved in a tense, rapidly escalating situation. Give them instructions on how to shift to a calm and respectful conversation. Then, trade roles and follow instructions given by another student. Finally, reflect on your role and the process you used.

RESEARCH AND DISCUSS

Explain that emotional issues and debates about them have occurred throughout U.S. history. Congress originally established rules to allow free expression of opinions, but even those did not always work. Allowing argument without insults, threats, or physical confrontations within a group is a difficult challenge.

1. **Research Techniques** Note that some experts specialize in directing or guiding emotional discussions. They make use of techniques that have worked in a wide range of environments and issues. It makes sense to use what they have learned in dealing with conflicts.

2. **Create a Procedure** Explain that a thoughtful plan can guide someone to calmly and effectively respond to an emotional issue. It can help move a confrontation from a regrettable display of anger to a productive learning experience.

3. **Give Instructions** Tell students that the ability to de-escalate conflict, like any other skill, takes practice to master. Role-playing will allow them to practice behaviors without having to fully engage in the emotions involved. Point out that it will allow them to see an issue from a different point of view when positions are switched. As part of the group's reflections, students may consider whether they were able to understand all sides of the issue by acting as both a supporter and an opponent of a particular position.

TO CHALLENGE STUDENTS . . .

Report on Debate Moderators Explain that televised presidential debates have been standard in presidential elections for more than fifty years. These debates are meant to allow candidates to present their own views on different issues and to question their opponents' views. Political debates typically have moderators, or people who ask questions and guide participants to follow proper debating procedures. Effective moderators keep debaters from interrupting others or speaking longer than allowed.

Have students research presidential debates and present an oral or a multimedia presentation on the role of the moderator. Students may choose to provide an overview of presidential moderators, compare and contrast several, or focus on just one. Guide them in concentrating on the moderators' responses to the behavior of the debaters rather than the content of the debate. They should answer questions such as these: How important and effective was the moderator? Did both sides follow the established procedures and instructions? How effective was the format for communicating positions?

INDEXPENDENT READING

READER'S CHOICE

Setting a Purpose Have students review their Unit 1 Response Logs and think about what they've already learned about how we engage with others while staying true to ourselves. As they choose their Independent Reading selections, encourage them to consider what more they want to know.

NOTICE NOTE

Explain that some selections may contain multiple signposts; others may contain only one. And the same type of signpost can occur many times in the same text.

 LEARNING MINDSET

Setting Goals Tell students that setting goals is an essential skill for developing a learning mindset. Explain that having several small goals (or short-term goals) can make a seemingly huge task easier. Encourage students to set manageable goals for reading the self-selected texts outside of class, such as setting a daily reading schedule or finishing one chapter or a set number of pages each night. Help students create personal progress reports that will help them track their goals and see their successes.

 INDEPENDENT READING

 ESSENTIAL QUESTION:

How do we engage with others while staying true to ourselves?

Reader's Choice

Setting a Purpose Select one or more of these options from your eBook to continue your exploration of the Essential Question.

- Read the descriptions to see which text grabs your interest.
- Think about which genres you enjoy reading.

Notice Note

In this unit, you practiced noticing and noting these signposts: **Tough Questions, Memory Moment,** and **Words of the Wiser.** As you read independently, these signposts and others will aid your understanding. Below are the key questions to ask when you read literature and nonfiction.

Reading Literature: Stories, Poems, and Plays		
Signpost	**Anchor Question**	**Lesson**
Contrasts and Contradictions	Why did the character act that way?	p. 145
Aha Moment	How might this change things?	p. 394
Tough Questions	What does this make me wonder about?	p. 2
Words of the Wiser	What's the lesson for the character?	p. 3
Again and Again	Why might the author keep bringing this up?	p. 145
Memory Moment	Why is this memory important?	p. 3

Reading Nonfiction: Essays, Articles, and Arguments		
Signpost	**Anchor Question(s)**	**Lesson**
Big Questions	What surprised me? What did the author think I already knew? What challenged, changed, or confirmed what I already knew?	p. 220 p. 319 p. 74
Contrasts and Contradictions	What is the difference, and why does it matter?	p. 318
Extreme or Absolute Language	Why did the author use this language?	p. 221
Numbers and Stats	Why did the author use these numbers or amounts?	p. 75
Quoted Words	Why was this person quoted or cited, and what did this add?	p. 221
Word Gaps	Do I know this word from someplace else? Does it seem like technical talk for this topic? Do clues in the sentence help me understand the word?	p. 75

 ENGLISH LEARNER SUPPORT

Develop Fluency Select a passage from a text that matches students' abilities. Read the passage aloud while students follow along silently.

- Choral read the passage with students two or three times. Then, check their comprehension by asking yes/no questions about the passage. **SUBSTANTIAL**
- Have students read and then reread the passage silently. Remind them that the goal is to read at a steady pace and to understand what they

read. Ask them if they noticed any parts of the passage that became easier after they had read it a few times. **MODERATE**

- Allow more fluent readers to select their own texts. Have them read silently, marking sentences or phrases they find challenging. Have students discuss these parts with a partner and restate them in their own words. **LIGHT**

Go to the **Reading Studio** for additional support in developing fluency.

You can preview these texts in Unit 1 of your eBook.

Then, check off the text or texts that you select to read on your own.

MEMOIR

from *The Pleasure of Reading*
Kamila Shamsie

A writer from Pakistan reflects on how books helped her feel connected to the world when she was growing up.

POEM

Magic Island
Cathy Song

This poem explores how recent immigrants embrace a new culture without forgetting their past.

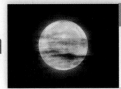

SHORT STORY

The Wife's Story
Ursula K. Le Guin

Is the narrator's husband, who has begun acting strangely, really one of the group, or has he become something else?

ARGUMENT

America: The Multinational Society
Ishmael Reed

What does it really mean to be American? A poet and novelist considers his own experiences.

Collaborate and Share   Discuss with a partner what you learned from at least one of your independent readings.

- Give a brief synopsis or summary of the text.
- Describe any signposts that you noticed in the text and explain what they revealed to you.
- Describe what you most enjoyed or found most challenging about the text. Give specific examples.
- Decide whether you would recommend the text to others. Why or why not?

 Go to the **Reading Studio** for more resources on **Notice & Note.**

INDEPENDENT READING

MATCHING STUDENTS TO TEXTS

Use the following information to guide students in choosing their texts.

from **The Pleasure of Reading**	**Lexile: 1270L**

   Genre: memoir
   Overall Rating: Challenging

Magic Island	**Lexile: N/A**

   Genre: poem
   Overall Rating: Accessible

The Wife's Story	**Lexile: 880L**

   Genre: short story
   Overall Rating: Accessible

America: The Multinational Society	**Lexile: 1440L**

   Genre: argument
   Overall Rating: Challenging

Collaborate and Share   To assess how well students read the selections, walk around the room and listen to their conversations. Encourage students to be focused and specific in their comments.

Online
Ed   **for Assessment**

- Independent Reading Selection Tests

 Encourage students to visit the **Reading Studio** to download a handy bookmark of **NOTICE & NOTE** signposts.

WHEN STUDENTS STRUGGLE . . .

Keep a Reading Log As students read their selected texts, have them keep a reading log for each selection to note signposts and their thoughts about them. Use their logs to assess how well they are noticing and reflecting on elements of their texts.

Reading Log for (title)		
Location	**Signpost I Noticed**	**My Notes about It**

(3) CP Cheah/Flickr/Getty Images (4) ©White Rock/Getty Images

UNIT (1) Task

- **WRITE A PERSONAL ESSAY**

MENTOR TEXT

BY ANY OTHER NAME

Memoir by SANTHA RAMA RAU

LEARNING OBJECTIVES

Writing Task

- Write a personal essay that explores a time when the writer had to decide how to interact with others.
- Use strategies to plan and organize ideas for a personal essay.
- Develop a focused, structured draft.
- Use the Mentor Text as a model for including personal insights and time clues in a personal essay.
- Revise drafts, incorporating feedback from peers.
- Edit drafts to include standard English conventions and the appropriate verb tenses.
- Use a rubric to evaluate writing.
- Publish writing to share it with an audience.
- **Language** Write about a personal experience using time-order words as clues to chronology.

Assign the Writing Task in *Ed.*

Online
Ed

RESOURCES

- Unit 1 Response Log
- Reading Studio: Notice & Note
- Writing Studio: Writing as a Process
- Grammar Studio: Module 7: Lesson 3: Verb Tense

Language X-Ray: English Learner Support

Use the instruction below and the supports and scaffolds in the Teacher's
Edition to help you guide students at different proficiency levels.

INTRODUCE THE WRITING TASK

Explain that in a **personal essay,** the writer expresses an insight based on something he or she experienced. Point out cognates for *personal* in other European languages, such as Spanish (*personal*), Italian (*personale*), French (*personnel*), and German (*persönlich*). As used in *personal essay,* the word means "related to one's own life, relationships, beliefs, and feelings." Emphasize that students' essays should reveal insights they gained through interacting with people.

Remind students that the selections in this unit explore how we engage with others while remaining true to ourselves. Provide sentence frames to help students articulate ideas. For example: *Sometimes you must _____ when dealing with other people.* Help students brainstorm words and phrases to complete the frame, such as *compromise, stand up for your beliefs,* or *hide your feelings.* Have pairs write sentences they can use as they complete the writing task.

WRITING

Use Time Clues

Tell students that their personal essays will explain an insight gained during a past experience. Emphasize the importance of providing time clues.

Use the following supports with students at varying proficiency levels:

- Display three pictures that represent a clear narrative—for example, runners at the starting line, during the race, and at the finish line. Have students label the pictures with time-order words such as *first, second,* and *third* or *first, next,* and *finally.* **SUBSTANTIAL**
- Use sentence frames to help students express time order: *At first, _____. Then _____. Soon after, _____. In the end, _____.* **MODERATE**
- After students complete their drafts, have partners work together to determine whether the verb tenses in their personal essays provide reasonable time clues to the reader. **LIGHT**

SPEAKING

Present, Past, and Past Perfect Tenses

Provide oral practice using the appropriate tense to describe the time and sequence of events.

Use the following supports with students at varying proficiency levels:

- Have students draw pictures that represent actions in present, past, and past perfect tenses. Then ask them to display their pictures and describe them in simple sentences. For example: *We eat dinner. We ate dinner. We had eaten dinner.* **SUBSTANTIAL**
- Ask students to make sentences using each of the three tenses. For example: *We watch that movie. We watched that movie yesterday. We had watched that movie before.* **MODERATE**
- Challenge students to find examples of sentences with present, past, and past perfect tense verbs in a selection from the unit (other than "By Any Other Name"). **LIGHT**

WRITING

WRITE A PERSONAL ESSAY

Read the introductory paragraph on page 64 and discuss the writing task with students. Tell them to refer to the notes they recorded in their Unit 1 Response Logs as they plan and draft their personal essays. Explain that the Response Log will contain ideas from the unit's selections about engaging with others while remaining true to oneself. Reviewing these different perspectives will help make their personal essays more interesting and informed.

USE THE MENTOR TEXT

Point out that students' personal essays will be similar in some ways to "By Any Other Name" by Santha Rama Rau. Emphasize that, like Rama Rau's memoir, their essays will explore a time when they had to decide how to interact with others. Point out that their personal essays will be shorter than "By Any Other Name".

WRITING PROMPT

Review the writing prompt with students. Ask: Are there any parts of the assignment you don't understand? Then discuss and clarify answers to questions, and remind students to consider the Essential Question as they plan and draft their essays.

Discuss the key points that appear on the checklist at the bottom of page 64. Explain that they define the goals of the writing task and will serve as a guide to help students successfully complete it.

 WRITING TASK

Write a Personal Essay

Go to the **Writing Studio** for help writing a narrative such as a personal essay.

This unit focuses on how we relate to people who are different from us. For this writing task, you will write a personal essay about engaging with others despite differences. A personal essay is a work of nonfiction in which an author reflects on the significance of an experience. For an example of a well-written personal essay you can use as a mentor text, review the essay "By Any Other Name."

As you write your essay, you will want to look at the notes you made in your Response Log after reading the texts in this unit.

Writing Prompt

Read the information in the box below.

This is the topic or context for your essay.

> Engaging with those who are different from you can be difficult, but it can also create a new understanding of who you are.

Think carefully about the following question.

This is the Essential Question for the unit. How would you answer this question, based on the texts in this unit?

> How do we engage with others while staying true to ourselves?

Think about events in your own experience that relate to this topic.

Write a personal essay that explores a time when you had to decide how to interact with others.

Be sure to—

Review these points as you write and again when you finish. Make any needed changes or edits.

- ☐ write an introduction that will grab the reader's interest
- ☐ describe a single, meaningful experience in vivid detail
- ☐ use appropriate verb tenses to orient the reader in time
- ☐ conclude with the insight you gained from the experience

64   Unit 1

 LEARNING MINDSET

Belonging   Remind students that everyone makes mistakes, and when we do, a good response is to reflect on what we can learn from them. Ask students to think about a mistake they have made that they're willing to share with others. Ask: Who would like to celebrate what they learned from making a mistake? If students are tentative about speaking, say, "I make mistakes. Let's learn from each other." Then, model how to share a reflection about a mistake you made.

1 Plan

The event you will choose to write about could be anything, such as a time you stood up for what you believed, or a moment when you quietly realized something about yourself. The event doesn't have to be big, but the way you reacted should lead to self-discovery.

Begin brainstorming ideas using the chart below. For each event you list, note its significance and the kinds of readers who would get the most out of your story. Your purpose for writing will be to reflect on your experience and share it with this audience to help them learn an important lesson.

PERSONAL ESSAY BRAINSTORMING CHART		
Experience or Event	**What I Learned from It**	**Who Would Be Interested?**

Background Reading Review the notes you have taken in your Response Log after reading the texts in this unit. The relationships explored in those texts may give you ideas about what experience you want to share in your essay.

© Houghton Mifflin Harcourt Publishing Company

WRITING TASK

Go to **Writing as a Process** for help with planning and drafting.

Notice & Note

From Reading to Writing

As you plan your personal essay, apply what you've learned about signposts in your own writing. Think about how you can incorporate a **Memory Moment** into your essay.

Go to the **Reading Studio** for more resources on **Notice & Note**.

Use the notes from your Response Log as you plan your essay.

UNIT 1 RESPONSE LOG	

---

1 PLAN

Restate the main focus of this writing task: to share an experience in which the student had to decide how to interact with others while staying true to himself or herself. Discuss the topics suggested in the introductory paragraph at the top of page 65 and ask volunteers to suggest others. Explain that their personal essays should describe a moment of self-discovery, in which they show how the event taught them something about themselves. Allow time for students to complete the brainstorming chart.

■ English Learner Support

Complete a Brainstorming Chart Review how the brainstorming chart is organized. Read and discuss the three column headings, and elicit and answer clarifying questions. Model how to complete one row, moving from left to right, paying particular attention to speakers of Arabic. Stress that each horizontal row contains information related to the same event. **SUBSTANTIAL/MODERATE**

▶ NOTICE & NOTE

From Reading to Writing Discuss different ways that students may make memories "come alive" in a personal essay, such as using dialogue or specific, sensory details that allow the reader to experience what it was like to be in that moment.

Background Reading As students plan their personal essays, encourage them to review the notes in their Response Logs for Unit 1.

WHEN STUDENTS STRUGGLE...

Use Partner Brainstorming Have students scan selections to find examples and ideas they might want to use as models for their writing. Then ask pairs to discuss which suggestions they found most interesting and why. Next, have students work independently to complete two rows of their brainstorming charts. When they have finished, let partners compare their charts and give each other feedback.

WRITING

Develop Details Read and discuss the introductory paragraph with students. Emphasize the importance of including specific and vivid details of the event in order to engage the audience.

Explain that the planning chart on page 66 can serve as a working outline as they draft their essays. Display the following headings and discuss each section.

I. Introduction

II. How It Began

III. What Happened

IV. How It Ended

V. Reflection on the Event's Significance

DEVELOP A DRAFT

Remind students to refer to their completed planning charts as they draft their essays. Suggest that they write one paragraph for each section of the outline, resulting in a five-paragraph essay. Emphasize that they can still make changes to their outlines if they decide to include a different example or a more interesting detail.

ENGLISH LEARNER SUPPORT

Create a Narrative Have students create their narrative as a series of labeled pictures. Encourage them to use time-order words in their labels.
SUBSTANTIAL

For **writing support** for students at varying proficiency levels, see the **Language X-Ray** on page 64B.

 WRITING TASK

Go to **Writing as a Process: Task, Purpose, and Audience** for help choosing details that appeal to your audience.

Develop Details To help you choose the most promising idea from your brainstorming chart, consider your readers. While reading some memoirs can be as exciting as watching someone look at themselves in the mirror, *your* personal essay will be much more interesting. How? Because you'll plan vivid details and think about your audience every step of the way. You'll also take care to orient your reader about when, where, and why the event happened. Use the chart below to map out your ideas.

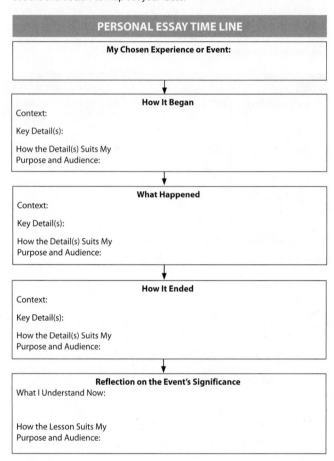

PERSONAL ESSAY TIME LINE

My Chosen Experience or Event:

How It Began
Context:
Key Detail(s):
How the Detail(s) Suits My Purpose and Audience:

What Happened
Context:
Key Detail(s):
How the Detail(s) Suits My Purpose and Audience:

How It Ended
Context:
Key Detail(s):
How the Detail(s) Suits My Purpose and Audience:

Reflection on the Event's Significance
What I Understand Now:

How the Lesson Suits My Purpose and Audience:

Develop a Draft

You might prefer to draft your essay online to make it easier to access from multiple locations.

Now, you're ready to begin drafting your personal essay. Refer to your time line as well as any notes you took as you read the texts in the unit to help guide you as you write. Use word-processing software or an online writing app to make it easier to reword ideas or move sentences around later when you are ready to revise your first draft.

WHEN STUDENTS STRUGGLE . . .

Use Drafting Strategies When students "get stuck," point out that a draft is not a finished piece of writing; it's a first attempt to get ideas on paper. Remind them that:

- They DON'T have to start at the beginning. They can start anywhere they feel comfortable.
- They DON'T have to use perfect grammar.
- They DON'T have to use correct punctuation.
- They DON'T have to spell all words correctly.

Use the Mentor Text

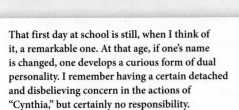

Genre Characteristics

Although a personal essay often describes an event, it does not simply tell a story. The writer describes his or her feelings at the time, as well as thoughts and insights that came later. Note the way the writer reflects on the changing of her name in "By Any Other Name."

That first day at school is still, when I think of it, a remarkable one. At that age, if one's name is changed, one develops a curious form of dual personality. I remember having a certain detached and disbelieving concern in the actions of "Cynthia," but certainly no responsibility.

The author comments on an event she has described, choosing vivid words like "remarkable" and "disbelieving" to tell what she thinks about it now and how it made her feel at the time.

Apply What You've Learned As you describe your life experience, comment on its meaning for you in order to help the reader understand your reactions.

Author's Craft

An author may describe a sequence of events in time order, also known as chronological order. This is an easy way to help readers understand how the ideas are connected. Look at how the author uses time clues like *during* and *after* in the following example to make the order of events clear.

At school, we rested for a short time on low, folding cots on the veranda, and then we were expected to play games. During the hot part of the afternoon we played indoors, and after the shadows had begun to lengthen and the slight breeze of the evening had come up, we moved outside to the wide courtyard.

The author also uses the time clues "for a short time" and "then" to indicate the order of events.

Apply What You've Learned The order of events in your essay should be clear. Use words and phrases that help the reader follow what is happening.

Write a Personal Essay   67

WHY THIS MENTOR TEXT?

"By Any Other Name" is a memoir, but it contains the key elements of a personal essay. Use the instruction below to model how to include insights about a life event and how to use time clues to describe the sequence of events.

USE THE MENTOR TEXT

Genre Characteristics Read aloud the introductory paragraph. Then have students read and discuss the model annotation about genre characteristics in "By Any Other Name." Ask: How does the author connect her actual experience at school with her later insights? *(She uses phrases such as "the first day of school" and "at that age" to let readers know she is reflecting on events that happened in the past. Words and phrases such as "remarkable" and "a certain detached and disbelieving concern" describe how she remembers and thinks about those events now.)*

Author's Craft Ask a volunteer to read aloud the introduction to this section and the example from the mentor text. Point out that, as in the preceding excerpt, the author uses words and phrases to indicate when events happened. Ask: How is the use of time-order words in this model text different from the use of time clues in the previous model? *(In this excerpt, the sequence of events occurred at school during a specific period in the past. In the Genre Characteristics excerpt, time-order clues connect a single event at school to an insight about it from a later time in the author's life.)*

(EL) ENGLISH LEARNER SUPPORT

Use the Mentor Text Use the following supports with students at varying proficiency levels:

- Choral read the first two sentences of the excerpt under Genre Characteristics. Explain the concept of dual personality: two different ways of being. **SUBSTANTIAL**
- Read aloud the Genre Characteristics excerpt. Ask: Which present tense verb connects the author's thoughts with her past experience? (*remember*) **MODERATE**

- Have students read the Author's Craft excerpt. Ask them to list two verbs that are in the simple past tense (*rested, played*) and two verbs that are in the past perfect tense. (*had begun, had come up*) **LIGHT**

WRITING

3 REVISE

Have students evaluate their drafts using the questions posed in the Revision Guide. Then call on students to model their revision techniques.

With a Partner Have students work with peer reviewers to evaluate drafts of their personal essays. Use the following questions as a guide for peer review:

- Which parts of the essay do you think work well?
- Which parts of the essay do you think could be improved?
- What specific suggestions do you have for improving the personal essay?

Encourage students to use the reviewer's comments to add interesting details, examples, dialogue, and vivid language to their personal essays.

---

3 Revise

Go to **Writing as a Process** for help with revising and editing your essay.

On Your Own Once you've captured, sequenced, and elaborated your ideas in a draft, you need to reread what you've written with a fresh eye. Especially since you're writing about your own experience, it may be difficult to read your draft objectively. Try reading it as though you know nothing about the people and events involved. The chart below notes specific elements of a personal essay that might need extra attention.

REVISION GUIDE

Ask Yourself	Tips	Revision Techniques
1. Does the introduction grab the reader's attention?	**Highlight** an attention-getting detail or intriguing dialogue in the first paragraph.	**Add** a vivid detail or dialogue from the event to get readers right into the experience.
2. Is a single event told in a clear sequence?	**Underline** words and phrases that provide time and sequence clues.	**Add** words and phrases that make the sequence of events clear.
3. Are relationships among people and events clear?	**Circle** names of people, places or events. **Highlight** where each is defined or explained.	**Add** explanations about people, places, or events that make their connection to your experience clear.
4. Do vivid details bring the event to life?	**Underline** sensory language and specific details about the experience and its setting.	**Add** descriptive, sensory details about the place and the people.
5. Does the essay reveal why the experience was significant?	**Underline** comments, thoughts, and feelings in your conclusion.	**Add** statements and reflections that explain the event's significance.

ACADEMIC VOCABULARY

As you conduct your peer review, try to use these words.

- ❏ **discriminate**
- ❏ **diverse**
- ❏ **inhibit**
- ❏ **intervene**
- ❏ **rational**

With a Partner After you have worked through the Revision Guide on your own, exchange papers with a partner. Evaluate each other's drafts in a peer review, first noting parts of the essay that you think work well. Then, share a few ideas about how your partner could better engage readers and accomplish his or her purpose in writing. Be sure to provide reasons and specific suggestions.

ENGLISH LEARNER SUPPORT

Use Sensory Details Explain that telling what we see, hear, feel, touch, and taste makes our writing more interesting. Review the five senses by displaying a chart like the one shown. Model examples of sensory language from "By Any Other Name" or other texts. Encourage students to make a similar chart to track and add sensory details to their personal essays.

SUBSTANTIAL/MODERATE

Sense	Vivid Detail
Looks	*"her rimless half-glasses glittered"* (paragraph 3)
Smells	*"the smell of jasmine"* (paragraph 26)
Feels	*"a hot windless morning"* (paragraph 1)
Tastes	
Sounds	*"fans whispering in every room"* (paragraph 5)

④ Edit

Once you have addressed the organization, development, and flow of ideas in your essay, you can look to improve the finer points of your draft. Edit for the proper use of standard English conventions and make sure to correct any misspellings or grammatical errors.

Language Conventions

Appropriate Verb Tenses In "By Any Other Name," the author began in the present and told an event from the past that included flashbacks to prior events. Because a memoir or personal essay may not follow a strict chronological order, it's important to indicate the time using appropriate verb tenses:

- **Present tense verbs** indicate that an action is taking place now. You will probably use this tense when stating the insight of your essay and when commenting on your central event.
- **Past tense verbs** indicate that an action happened in the past. You will use this tense to narrate your central event.
- **Past perfect tense verbs** indicate that an action was completed before an action in the past. You will use this tense to set the context for your central event, telling what happened *before* that event.

The chart contains examples of verb tenses from "By Any Other Name."

Verb Tense	Example from "By Any Other Name"
Present	I <u>remember</u> it all very clearly.
Past	Mother <u>looked</u> very distant and <u>was</u> silent a long time.
Past Perfect	Up to then, my mother <u>had refused</u> to send Premila to school . . .

! For more about verb tenses, visit the **Grammar Studio.**

⑤ Publish

Finalize your essay, and choose the best way to share it with your audience. Consider these options:

- If your audience is your classmates, present your essay as a speech to the class, or post it as a blog on a classroom or school website.
- If your audience is one person, send your essay as a letter.
- If you wrote for members of a certain community—for example, younger children or people who enjoy the same activities or face the same challenges as you—ask permission to post your essay to a website or share it in person where appropriate.

WHEN STUDENTS STRUGGLE . . .

Present, Past, and Past Perfect Tenses Display these sentences: I still recall my first day of school. I wore a blouse that my mother had made for me.

Ask students to identify the present, past, and past perfect verbs. Then have students place the events in a flow chart to clarify the sequence of events.

My mother made a blouse for me.	→	I wore it on the first day of school.	→	Years later, I still recall that day.

④ EDIT

Suggest that students set aside their essays for a period of time before they begin editing for grammar, spelling, and mechanics. They should check to see that each sentence begins with a capital letter and ends with the correct punctuation mark. If they have included any dialogue, it should be in quotation marks. If they are uncertain of the spellings of any words, they should look them up in a dictionary. Their grammar check should include a review of verb tenses.

LANGUAGE CONVENTIONS

Appropriate Verb Tenses Review the definitions of present, past, and past perfect tenses. Discuss the example sentences in the chart. Connect each example to the part of the definition that explains when students should use that particular tense.

Use the sentences below to discuss the correct use of each tense.

I still **remember** my first day at school. (*The writer* **remembers** *now, or in the present moment.*)

Yesterday, my sister **remembered** our lunch. (*The writer's sister* **remembered** *yesterday, or in a past moment.*)

I **had forgotten** the lunch a long time ago. (*The writer* **had forgotten** *long before the sister remembered.*)

Ask: Why might someone writing a personal essay want to use these three tenses? (*Personal essays move back and forth in time. The writer often expresses what he or she thinks now about an event from the past. Sometimes, the writer must describe things that happened even before the past event, usually to provide context for what he or she is writing about.*)

 For **speaking support** for students at varying proficiency levels, see the **Language X-Ray** on page 64B.

⑤ PUBLISH

Note the various publishing options described on page 69. Discuss why adapting a publication method to a specific audience is a good idea. Challenge students to think of other ways to publish their personal essays.

WRITING

USE THE SCORING GUIDE

Have students read the scoring guide. Encourage them to ask any questions they may have about terms or ideas they do not understand. Ask partners to exchange their final personal essays and score them using the scoring guide. Have each peer reviewer write a paragraph explaining the reason for the score he or she awarded for each of the three major categories.

 **WRITING TASK**

Use the scoring guide to evaluate your essay.

	Organization/Progression	Development of Ideas	Use of Language and Conventions
4	• The organization is effective and appropriate to the purpose. • The essay thoroughly addresses the ideas in the writing prompt. • Transitions or sequence words clearly show the relationship among ideas and events.	• The introduction catches the reader's attention with a vivid detail or quotation. • The essay centers on a single, clearly narrated life experience. • The writer makes appropriate and clarifying comments on the narration. • The conclusion expresses the significance and impact of the narrated event with insight.	• Language and word choice are vivid, purposeful, and precise. • Verb tenses consistently orient the reader in time. • Spelling, capitalization, and punctuation are correct. • Grammar and usage are correct.
3	• The organization is for the most part effective and appropriate to the purpose. • The essay adequately responds to the writing prompt. • A few more transitions or sequence words are needed to show relationships among ideas or events.	• The introduction gets right into the event or experience. • The essay mostly focuses on one clearly narrated life experience. • The writer comments on the narration at times. • The conclusion clearly states the significance of the narrated event.	• Language is for the most part specific and clear. • Verb tenses are mostly correct and consistent. • Some spelling, capitalization, or punctuation mistakes are present but do not affect meaning. • Some minor grammar or usage errors occur.
2	• The organization is generally chronological but sometimes unclear. • The writing prompt is evident but only partially addressed in the essay. • Few transitions or sequence words indicate relationships among ideas or events.	• The introduction tells what the essay will discuss but does not grab attention. • The essay shares a vaguely narrated life experience and may go off on tangents. • The writer's comments on the narration are absent or repetitive. • The conclusion hints at or makes a vague statement about the meaning of the narrated event.	• Language is somewhat vague and unclear. • Some errors in verb tense cause reader confusion. • Several errors in spelling, capitalization, or punctuation are present. • Several errors in grammar or usage appear.
1	• The organization is not appropriate to the purpose. • The essay fails to address key points in the writing prompt. • No transitions are used, making the sequence of events difficult to understand.	• The introduction is missing or confusing. • The essay may share multiple, unrelated experiences or fail to share an experience. • No commentary or analysis of events is included. • The conclusion is missing or merely summarizes an event.	• Language is imprecise, incorrect, or inappropriate. • Verb tenses fail to orient the reader in time. • Many errors in spelling, capitalization, or punctuation are present. • Many errors in grammar or usage cause confusion.

WRITING TASK SCORING GUIDE: PERSONAL ESSAY

Reflect on the Unit

In writing your personal essay, you incorporated ideas and techniques you learned from the reading you have done in this unit. Now is a good time to reflect on what you have learned.

Reflect on the Essential Question

- How do we engage with others while staying true to ourselves? How has your answer to this question changed since you started this unit?

- What are some examples from the texts you've read that show how people interact with others without compromising themselves?

Reflect on Your Reading

- Which selections were the most interesting or surprising to you?

- From which selection did you learn the most about engaging with others?

Reflect on the Writing Task

- What difficulties did you encounter while working on your personal essay? How might you avoid them next time?

- What part of the essay was easiest to write? What part was the hardest? Why?

- What improvements or additions did you make to your essay as you were revising?

UNIT 1 SELECTIONS

- "What, of This Goldfish, Would You Wish?"
- "By Any Other Name"
- "Without Title"
- from *Texas* v. *Johnson Majority Opinion*
- "American Flag Stands for Tolerance"

© Houghton Mifflin Harcourt Publishing Company

REFLECT ON THE UNIT

Read the headings of the three major categories for reflection. Review the questions under each heading and discuss how they relate to the unit's essential question, reading selections, and writing task. Ask students to independently write notes on how they would respond to each question. After they have written their notes, have them join small groups to discuss their reflections. Circulate during group discussions and try to identify topics that generate lively interactions. Include these topics as discussion points for a whole-class discussion that wraps up the unit.

🧠 LEARNING MINDSET

Self-Reflection Explain the importance of being able to recognize one's own strengths and weaknesses while developing a learning mindset that embraces growth. As students reflect on the unit, encourage them to consider questions such as the following: Were there times when I realized I needed help? Did I ask questions about things that were unclear? After completing my work, did I take time to go back, looking for errors and ways to improve it? Am I proud of the work I turned in?

UNIT 2

Instructional Overview and Resources

	Instructional Focus	**Online** **Ed** Resources
Unit Introduction **How We See Things**	**Unit 2 Essential Question** **Unit 2 Academic Vocabulary**	**Stream to Start:** How We See Things **Unit 2 Response Log**

ANALYZE & APPLY

 **"Coming to Our Senses"** Science Essay by Neil deGrasse Tyson Lexile 1310L ▶ **NOTICE & NOTE** READING MODEL **Signposts** • Big Questions • Numbers and Stats • Word Gaps	**Reading** • Analyze Development of Ideas • Analyze Tone **Writing:** Write an Explanation **Speaking and Listening:** Give a Presentation **Vocabulary:** Reference Sources **Language Conventions:** Parallel Structure	**Audio** **Close Read Screencasts:** Modeled Discussions **Reading Studio:** Notice & Note **Level Up Tutorial:** Analyzing Arguments **Writing Studio:** Evaluating Research Sources **Speaking and Listening Studio:** Speaking in a Discussion **Vocabulary Studio:** Reference Sources
 **Mentor Text** **"The Night Face Up"** Short Story by Julio Cortázar Lexile 1210L	**Reading** • Make Inferences • Analyze Plot Structure **Writing:** Write an Analysis **Speaking and Listening:** Discuss Opinions **Vocabulary:** Denotation and Connotation **Language Conventions:** Complex Sentences	**Audio** **Reading Studio:** Notice & Note **Level Up Tutorial:** Plot: Sequence of Events; Reading for Details **Writing Studio:** Using Textual Evidence **Speaking and Listening Studio:** Participating in Collaborative Discussions **Vocabulary Studio:** Connotation and Denotation **Grammar Studio:** Module 4: Lesson 5: Sentence Structure
"Mirror" Poem by Sylvia Plath	**Reading** • Analyze Speaker • Analyze Figurative Language **Writing:** Write a Poem **Speaking and Listening:** Discuss	**Audio** **Reading Studio:** Notice & Note **Level Up Tutorial:** Reading for Details **Speaking and Listening Studio:** Participating in Collaborative Discussions

SUGGESTED PACING: 30 DAYS	Unit Introduction	Coming to Our Senses						The Night Face Up						Mirror		
	1	2	3	4	5	6	7	8	9	10	11	12	13	14	15	16

English Learner Support	Differentiated Instruction	Assessment
• Learn New Expressions • Learning Strategies		

English Learner Support	Differentiated Instruction	Assessment
• Text X-Ray • Develop Vocabulary • Use Cognates • Identify Formal and Informal English • Develop Vocabulary • Understand Language Structures • Read and Paraphrase • Oral Assessment • Express Opinions • Use Support from Peers and Teachers • Use a Variety of Sentence Patterns	**When Students Struggle** • Use Strategies • Analyze Evidence • Use Reference Sources **To Challenge Students** • Analyze Development of Ideas	**Selection Test**
• Text X-Ray • Make Inferences • Use Cognates • Expand Reading Skills • Learn Spelling Rules • Respond Orally • Monitor Understanding • Oral Assessment • Understand Spoken Language • Vocabulary Strategy • Use Complex Sentences	**When Students Struggle** • Analyze Plot Structure • Analyze Details **To Challenge Students** • Analyze Point of View	**Selection Test**
• Text X-Ray • Use Academic Language • Compare Similar Words • Understand Figurative Language • Rephrase Poetic Statements • Oral Assessment • Compare Cultural Views	**When Students Struggle** • Analyze Details **To Challenge Students** • Connect "Mirror" to Folklore	**Selection Test**

The World as 100 People/A Contribution to Statistics

Independent Reading

End of Unit

17 〉 18 〉 19 〉 20 〉 21 〉 22 〉 23 〉 24 〉 25 〉 26 〉 27 〉 28 〉 29 〉 30

UNIT 2 Continued

	Instructional Focus	Online Ed Resources

COLLABORATE & COMPARE

"The World as 100 People" Infographic by Jack Hagley	**Reading** • Interpret Graphics • Analyze Motives	🔊 **Audio** **Reading Studio:** Notice & Note **Level Up Tutorial :** Reading Graphic Aids
"A Contribution to Statistics" Poem by Wisława Szymborska	**Reading** • Analyze Literary Devices • Analyze Structure **Writing:** Write a Letter **Speaking and Listening:** Give Instructions	🔊 **Audio** **Reading Studio:** Notice & Note **Writing Studio:** Writing for a Specific Audience and Purpose **Speaking and Listening Studio:** Giving and Following Instructions
Collaborate and Compare	**Reading:** Compare Details **Speaking and Listening:** Research and Present	**Speaking and Listening Studio:** Delivering a Multimedia Presentation

Online Ed INDEPENDENT READING

The Independent Reading selections are only available in the eBook. 📖 **Go to the Reading Studio for more information on Notice & Note.**	"Before I got my eye put out" Poem by Emily Dickinson	"What Our Telescopes Couldn't See" Essay by Pippa Goldschmidt **Lexile 1210L**

END OF UNIT

Writing Task: Write a Short Story **Speaking and Listening Task: Produce a Podcast** **Reflect on the Unit**	**Writing:** Write a Short Story **Language Conventions:** Use Complex Sentences **Speaking and Listening:** Produce a Podcast	**Unit 2 Response Log** **Mentor Text:** "The Night Face Up" **Reading Studio:** Notice & Note **Writing Studio:** Writing Narratives **Speaking and Listening Studio:** Using Media in a Presentation **Grammar Studio:** Module 4: Lesson 5: Sentence Structure

English Learner Support	Differentiated Instruction	Online Ed Assessment
• Text X-Ray • Use Visual Support • Discuss Motives • Use Prereading Supports • Discuss Directionality and Language Structure • Use Cognates • Oral Assessment	**When Students Struggle** • Discuss Motives	Selection Test
• Text X-Ray • Use Idioms • Use Support to Develop Vocabulary • Use Grammatical Structures • Analyze Idioms • Oral Assessment • Write a Letter	**When Students Struggle** • Compare and Contrast	Selection Test
• Ask Questions	**When Students Struggle** • Synthesize Ideas	
from *Big Bang: The Origin of the Universe* Informational Text by Simon Singh **Lexile 1270L**	"By the Waters of Babylon" Short Story by Stephen Vincent Benét **Lexile 820L**	Selection Tests
• Language X-Ray • Understand Academic Language • Complete a Group Story Starter • Identify Vivid Sensory Language • Use Vivid Sensory Details • Use Signal Words in Complex Sentence Frames • Adapt the Short Story	**When Students Struggle** • Mine Memories • Use Sentence Frames to Map Plot • Take Notes	Unit Test

HOW WE SEE THINGS

? Connect to the
ESSENTIAL QUESTION

Ask a volunteer to read aloud the Essential Question. Have students consider their point of view regarding something they can all relate to, such as the importance of school sports as part of the educational experience. Point out that not all their viewpoints will be the same. Then have them think about how their perspective may affect what they think they know about the situation. Ask them, for example, how their point of view might be affected by their own interest or lack of interest in playing sports. What do they *think* they know and what do they *really know* about the situation? How does their point of view compare to the student next to them?

■ English Learner Support

Learn New Expressions Make sure students understand the Essential Question. If necessary, explain the following phrase:

- *Point of view* means "a way of looking at or thinking about something."

Help students restate the question in simpler language: How does our way of looking at things affect our thinking?
ALL LEVELS

DISCUSS THE QUOTATION

Henry David Thoreau (1817–1862) was an American essayist, poet, and a prominent transcendentalist (*transcendentalism* was a philosophical movement that began in the early 1830s). Thoreau's book *Walden*, which reflects on simple living in nature, is his best known work. Ask students to read and reflect upon the quotation. Then have them discuss the meaning of Thoreau's words. What is the difference between looking at something and seeing it? How can our point of view affect whether we just look at something or really see it?

? ESSENTIAL QUESTION:

How does our point of view shape what we think we know?

 The question is not what you look at, but what you see.

Henry David Thoreau

⚙ LEARNING MINDSET

Curiosity Ask students to share a book, band, or hobby they have recently discovered. Explain that curiosity—the desire to discover new things—is often what leads to deeper, more engaged learning. Have students think about how they could apply the skills they learn in class to explore what interests them outside of school. For example, using their reading skills could help them dive deeper into genres they like and allow them to discover new interests.

ACADEMIC VOCABULARY

Academic Vocabulary words are words you use when you discuss and write about texts. In this unit you will practice and learn five words.

☑ differentiate   ☐ incorporate   ☐ mode   ☐ orient   ☐ perspective

Study the Word Network to learn more about the word **differentiate**.

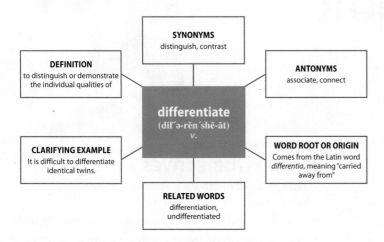

SYNONYMS
distinguish, contrast

DEFINITION
to distinguish or demonstrate the individual qualities of

ANTONYMS
associate, connect

differentiate
(dĭf´ə-rĕn´shē-āt)
v.

CLARIFYING EXAMPLE
It is difficult to differentiate identical twins.

WORD ROOT OR ORIGIN
Comes from the Latin word *differentia*, meaning "carried away from"

RELATED WORDS
differentiation, undifferentiated

Write and Discuss Discuss the completed Word Network with a partner, making sure to talk through all of the boxes until you both understand the word, its synonyms, antonyms, and related forms. Then, fill out Word Networks for the remaining four words. Use a dictionary or online resource to help you complete the activity.

 Go online to access the Word Networks.

RESPOND TO THE ESSENTIAL QUESTION

In this unit, you will explore how individual perspective shapes our beliefs. As you read, you will revisit the **Essential Question** and gather your ideas about it in the **Response Log** that appears on page R2. At the end of the unit, you will have the opportunity to write a **short story** about how things are not as they first appear. Filling out the Response Log will help you prepare for this writing task.

 You can also go online to access the Response Log.

ACADEMIC VOCABULARY

As students complete Word Networks for the remaining four vocabulary words, encourage them to include all the categories shown in the completed network if possible, but point out that some words do not have clear synonyms or antonyms. Some words may also function as different parts of speech—for example, *orient* may also be a noun or adjective.

differentiate (dĭf´ə-rĕn´shē-āt´) *v.* To distinguish or demonstrate the individual qualities of. (Spanish cognate: *diferenciar*)

incorporate (ĭn-kôr´pə-rāt) *v.* To absorb or make part of a whole. (Spanish cognate: *incorporar*)

mode (mōd) *n.* A way or means for expressing or doing something. (Spanish cognate: *modo*)

orient (ôr´ ē-ənt) *v.* To place or align in relation to something else. (Spanish cognate: *oriente*)

perspective (pər-spĕk´tĭv) *n.* A viewpoint from a particular position; an outlook or standpoint. (Spanish cognate: *perspectiva*)

RESPOND TO THE ESSENTIAL QUESTION

Direct students to the Unit 2 Response Log. Explain that students will use it to record ideas and details from the selections that help answer the Essential Question. When they work on the writing task at the end of the unit, their Response Logs will help them think about what they have read and make connections between the texts.

ENGLISH LEARNER SUPPORT

Learning Strategies Use this strategy to help students build concept and language attainment in this unit:

- Explain that several of the selections in this unit use scientific and technical language that students may not be familiar with such as *astronomy* (paragraph 1) in the science essay, "Coming to Our Senses."

- Before students read each selection, display some of the key words and phrases students may not know. Model how to use print or online resources to find out what these words and phrases mean, including

those that use visual images to convey meaning. Then, guide students to find the words or phrases in the selection, circle or highlight them, and copy a basic definition that you provide in the margin of their books.

- During and after the lesson, prompt students to use these words and phrases when they respond orally and in writing to questions about the selection.

ALL LEVELS

READING MODEL

COMING TO OUR SENSES

Science Essay by **Neil deGrasse Tyson**

GENRE ELEMENTS
INFORMATIONAL TEXT

Remind students that the main purpose of informational text is to present facts and information. A **science essay** is one type of informational text. In a science essay, the author introduces a key idea, often one that is new or surprising. Because a science essay often deals with challenging concepts, the author may use analogies, or comparisons, to move from familiar concepts to more complex ideas. A science essay often uses scientific terminology; these terms may or may not be explained, depending upon assumptions that the author makes about the audience. The tone of a science essay is generally serious, but the author can also use humor or irony to make a point.

LEARNING OBJECTIVES

- Analyze how the author develops a central idea and achieves a certain tone.
- Research an instrument used to study a given scientific topic.
- Write an explanation that elaborates upon a concept or idea from the selection.
- Discuss the draft of an explanation with a partner and then present the finished explanation to a group.
- Use print or digital resources to define or explain references from the selection.
- Use parallel structure in writing.
- **Language** Use domain-specific vocabulary and language structures to discuss tools that scientists use.

TEXT COMPLEXITY

Quantitative Measures	Coming to Our Senses	Lexile: 1310L
Qualitative Measures	**Ideas Presented** Mostly explicit, but with some implied meanings; use of irony and sarcasm.	
	Structures Used Organization of main ideas and details is complex, but sequential.	
	Language Used Many Tier II and III words; many technical (scientific) terms used.	
	Knowledge Required More complex science concepts.	

RESOURCES

- Unit 2 Response Log
- Selection Audio
- Close Read Screencasts: Modeled Discussions
- Reading Studio: Notice & Note
- Level Up Tutorial: Analyzing Arguments
- Writing Studio: Evaluating Research Sources
- Speaking and Listening Studio: Speaking in a Discussion
- Vocabulary Studio: Reference Sources
- "Coming to Our Senses" Selection Test

SUMMARIES

English

Thanks to our five senses, humans can perceive much about the world around us. At the same time, our ability to develop scientific instruments that enhance and augment our senses has allowed us to examine and come to understand most of what we now know about the universe and how it works. In modern times, to rely merely on our five senses to understand the world is dangerous; we must seek to expand our awareness by continuing to develop tools that transcend our senses.

Spanish

Gracias a nuestros cinco sentidos, los humanos podemos percibir mucho acerca del mundo que nos rodea. Al mismo tiempo, nuestra capacidad para desarrollar instrumentos científicos que mejoran y aumentan nuestros sentidos nos ha permitido examinar y llegar a entender la mayoría de las cosas que ahora conocemos sobre el universo y sobre cómo funciona. En tiempos modernos, confiar únicamente en nuestros cinco sentidos para entender al mundo es peligroso: debemos buscar expandir nuestra conciencia, continuando el desarrollo de las herramientas que trascienden nuestros sentidos.

SMALL-GROUP OPTIONS

Have students work in small groups to read and discuss the selection.

Jigsaw with Experts

- Divide the selection into the following four parts: paragraphs 1–3, 4–10, 11–15, and 16–18.
- Have students count off, or assign each student one of those sections.
- After they have read the text, have students form groups with other students who read the same section. Each expert group should discuss its section.
- Then, have students form new groups with a representative for each section. These jigsaw groups should discuss all the sections and the selection as a whole.

Think-Write-Pair-Share

- After students have read and analyzed "Coming to Our Senses," pose these questions: What is Tyson's thesis? Do you agree with it? Why or why not?
- Have students think about the questions individually and write down their ideas.
- Then, have pairs discuss their ideas about the questions.
- Ask a few volunteers to share some of the key ideas of their discussions.

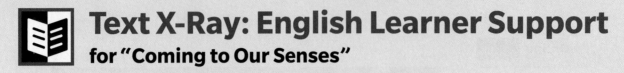

Text X-Ray: English Learner Support
for "Coming to Our Senses"

Use the Text X-Ray and the supports and scaffolds in the Teacher's Edition to help guide students at different proficiency levels through the selection.

INTRODUCE THE SELECTION
DISCUSS THE FIVE SENSES

In this lesson, students will need to be able to discuss the five senses. Read aloud paragraphs 1–2 with students and point out these phrases: *five senses* and *register information*. Provide the following explanations:

- The *five senses* are vision, hearing, smell, taste, and touch.
- When we *register information* with our senses, we become aware of it and pay attention to it.

Explain to students that people depend on their senses to survive and to learn about the world. Have volunteers share how they or others use one or more senses to take in information. Supply the following sentence frame:

- *(I/People) use (my/their) sense of _____ to register information about _____.*

CULTURAL REFERENCES

The following words or phrases may be unfamiliar to students:

- *fortune-telling psychics* (paragraph 6): people who claim to have the power to tell future events
- *TV hotlines* (paragraph 6): a part of some TV shows in which viewers call in—in this case, to have their fortune told
- *lottery* (paragraph 6): a game in which people buy numbered tickets in hopes of winning money
- *sci-fi series* (paragraph 8): a science fiction TV show whose story is told over a set of episodes
- *starship* (paragraph 8): a ship that travels through space
- *common sense* (paragraph 16): people's natural ability to understand the world and make good choices

LISTENING

Understand General Meaning

Have students identify the main topic or central idea of the modified Edwin P. Hubble quotation in paragraph 10.

Use the following supports with students at varying proficiency levels:

- Teach the term *science tools*. Draw students' attention to the phrase beginning with *telescopes* and ending with *spectrum* and explain that it is a list of *science tools*. Ask: Does the passage say we use *both* our senses *and* science tools to explore the universe? (*yes*) **SUBSTANTIAL**
- Read the excerpt aloud, adding the phrase *science tools such as* after the phrase *along with*. Then have partners state a main idea of the passage using this frame: *In addition to _____, we also need _____ to _____.* **MODERATE**
- Read the excerpt aloud, pointing out that students don't need to understand how each listed tool works in order to understand the main idea. Then have pairs of students work together to write a sentence that tells what the passage is mostly about. **LIGHT**

SPEAKING

Use Content-Area Vocabulary

Have students use content-area vocabulary to discuss some of the tools that scientists use.

Use the following supports with students at varying proficiency levels:

- Display photos of a microscope and a telescope. Say each word and have students say it after you. Briefly explain the function of each: *We can use a microscope to see bacteria; we can use a telescope to see planets.* Ask: Which tool can we use to see planets? (*a telescope*) Which tool can we use to see bacteria? (*a microscope*) **SUBSTANTIAL**
- Display a list of science tools such as a microscope, telescope, compass, and seismograph. Provide frames to help partners ask and answer questions: *Which tool do scientists use to _____? Scientists use _____ to _____.* **MODERATE**
- Display a list of science tools. Ask partners to use the words *measure, determine,* and *observe* to discuss the purposes of each tool. **LIGHT**

READING

Read for Main Idea and Details

Work with students to reread and analyze paragraphs 4–5 of the selection.

Use the following supports with students at varying proficiency levels:

- Read aloud paragraphs 4–5. Paraphrase paragraph 4: *What else can we learn about our environment beyond what we can observe with our senses?* Point out that paragraph 5 addresses the questions in paragraph 4. Then ask: Do science tools help us learn about our environment? (*yes*) **SUBSTANTIAL**
- Read aloud paragraphs 4–5. Then ask: Are our five senses the best tools for decoding how nature works? Why or why not? **MODERATE**
- Have pairs read paragraphs 4–5 and identify one sentence that states the central idea. (*If we want to know what's out there, then we require detectors that can do more than the ones we are born with.*) **LIGHT**

WRITING

Write an Explanation

Work with students to help them develop and improve their work on the writing assignment on Student Edition page 87.

Use the following supports with students at varying proficiency levels:

- Work with students to choose a topic to write about. Write the topic in the center of a word web. Then model how to use an online encyclopedia to learn facts about the topic. Record facts in the web. Then use the facts to write a few short sentences. Have students copy the sentences into their notebooks. **SUBSTANTIAL**
- Provide scaffolding to help students organize their explanations: *(Topic) _____ is/are (definition or explanation) _____. Fact #1: _____. Fact #2: _____. Fact #3: _____. I think that _____. I was surprised that _____.* **MODERATE**
- Remind students of the transitions they can use to make facts and examples clear in their writing: *first, second, third, another,* and *finally.* (You also might explain that the words can be incorporated into phrases such as these: *the first interesting fact, another interesting fact, a third fact I found interesting.*) Have pairs find three places in their explanations where they can use a transition. **LIGHT**

EXPLAIN THE SIGNPOSTS

Explain that **NOTICE & NOTE Signposts** are significant moments in the text that help readers understand and analyze works of fiction or nonfiction. Use the instruction on these pages to introduce students to asking **Big Questions** and to using the **Numbers and Stats** and **Word Gaps** signposts. Then use the selection that follows to have students apply the Big Questions and signposts to a text.

For a full list of the fiction and nonfiction signposts, see p. 130.

▶ BIG QUESTIONS

Explain to students that when they read a nonfiction text, asking **Big Questions** can help them connect with and understand the author's **thesis**, or main idea, and the **evidence** used to support it. Tell students that in the upcoming selection, they will focus on the following Big Question: *What changed, challenged, or confirmed what I already knew?* Let students know that the answers to this question will vary, depending on the reader's prior knowledge of the topic.

Read aloud the example passage. Use modeling as you discuss how the reader used the Big Question to understand the author's idea about the acuity of human senses.

Tell students that when they encounter a main point, an unfamiliar concept, or a new idea, they should pause, mark it in their consumable text, and ask themselves the anchor question: *What changed, challenged, or confirmed what I already knew?*

Notice & Note

READING MODEL

COMING TO OUR SENSES

For more information on these and other signposts to Notice & Note, visit the **Reading Studio**.

You are about to read the science essay "Coming to Our Senses." In it, you will notice and note signposts that will give you clues about the ideas and information in the essay. Here are a question to ask and two signposts to look for as you read this science essay and other works of nonfiction.

Break down the parts of this **Big Question** as you read by asking yourself these smaller questions:

Does this fit what I already know about the topic?

How does this add to what I already knew?

Why doesn't this information match what I thought I knew?

▶ **Big Questions** Any time someone gives you information—in a speech or a nature show for example—you'll make some mental connections between what you already know and these new ideas. Without even thinking about it, you categorize these connections as things you already know, things that extend what you already know, and things that are completely new to you.

These categories apply to information you read, too. When you read about the world around you, your view of the world should change—even if it is in a very small way. By making connections to your own life, you will be able to read more carefully and attentively. Ask yourself this Big Question: *What challenged, changed, or confirmed what I already knew?*

Here is how a student might use this Big Question to mark and more deeply understand the author's ideas while reading "Coming to Our Senses":

> 2   When thought of as an ensemble of experimental tools, our senses enjoy an astonishing acuity and range of sensitivity. Our ears can register the thunderous launch of the space shuttle, yet they can also hear a mosquito buzzing a foot away from our head. Our sense of touch allows us to feel the magnitude of a bowling ball dropped on our big toe, just as we can tell when a one-milligram bug crawls along our arm.

Which parts confirmed something you already knew or had experienced?	I've had some of these experiences with sound and touch.
How do these examples challenge what you thought about the acuity of human senses?	The details about bugs are striking because they're so specific. I never realized how fine-tuned our senses are.

74   Unit 2

Numbers and Stats Think about the difference between a football team winning 24–21 and winning 49–0. What do you learn by looking at the score? What does the score indicate about the matchup?

As you read, look for meaning in numbers and statistics, including those spelled out as words. Not every number is important; you have to decide which numbers develop an idea and which merely provide context.

Here is how a student might mark Numbers and Stats in the essay:

> 3   . . . For example, if you increase the energy of a sound's volume by a factor of 10, your ears will judge this change to be rather small. Increase it by a factor of 2 and you will barely notice. . . .

What numbers or statistics are important or surprising?	Numbers related to increasing volume are surprising.
Why did the author include these numbers?	They illustrate ways that our senses are not very sensitive at all.

Word Gaps Imagine that you're in a garden and notice a striped caterpillar. The gardener excitedly tells you that it's a monarch larva in its fifth instar, almost ready to shed its exoskeleton to pupate and metamorphose inside its chrysalis. If you don't know much about butterflies, this might sound like another language.

That's how reading is sometimes, when you come across multiple words you don't know. Don't give up. Instead, look for clues that help you decode them.

In this example, a student marked her own Word Gaps in the essay:

> 3   . . . The stellar magnitude scale of brightness, the well-known acoustic decibel scale, and the seismic scale for earthquake severity are each logarithmic, in part because of our biological propensity to see, hear, and feel the world that way. . . .

What words confuse me? Why?	All of these scientific terms are new to me.
What clues help me understand the words and the passage?	The footnotes give definitions and the text provides clues like "brightness" and "earthquake severity."

When you read and encounter phrases like these, pause to see if it's a **Numbers and Stats** signpost:

"The percentage of voters in their 20s rose by…"

"More than fifty million stars…"

"The runner improved her time by three minutes …"

Anchor Question
When you notice this signpost, ask: Why did the author use these numbers or amounts?

Anchor Questions
When you notice words that don't seem to make sense, ask yourself:

- Do I know this word from someplace else?

- Can I find clues in the sentence to help me understand the word?

- Does this seem like technical talk for experts on this topic?

WHEN STUDENTS STRUGGLE . . .

Use Strategies Model applying strategies to figure out the meaning of the word *acoustic* in paragraph 3: "Do I know this word from someplace else? I've seen this word before; I've heard of *acoustic* music. Can I find clues in the sentence to help me understand the word? Well, I see that the passage refers to the way that we use our senses to 'see, hear, and feel the world.' Brightness refers to sight and earthquakes have to do with touch—so acoustic must relate to hearing. Does this seem like technical talk for experts on this topic? Yes, the phrase *acoustic decibel scale* sounds technical. A scale is used to measure, so maybe an acoustic decibel scale is a way of measuring sound."

NUMBERS AND STATS

Explain that **Numbers and Stats** are often used in informational texts, such as this science essay, to illustrate a point or provide evidence for a **thesis**, or central idea. Discuss with students why numbers might provide convincing **evidence.**

Read aloud the example passage. Point out that increasing an amount by a factor of ten means multiplying it by ten, and an increase by a factor of two means multiplying by two, or doubling the amount. These numbers help support the author's point that significant increases in the energy of a sound's volume are not noticed much by humans.

Tell students when they spot Numbers and Stats, they should pause, mark it in their consumable text, and ask themselves the anchor question: *Why did the author use these numbers or amounts?*

WORD GAPS

Explain that **Word Gaps** may occur when words are unfamiliar or when words have more than one meaning. Explain that **nonfiction texts,** such as science essays or textbook chapters, may contain technical language or subject-area vocabulary that results in Word Gaps.

Read aloud the example passage. Model how to ask questions about unfamiliar words. Then point out how one reader answered the questions shown below the passage.

Tell students that when they experience a Word Gap, they should pause, mark it in their consumable text, and ask themselves the anchor questions: *Do I know this word from someplace else? Can I find clues in the sentence to help me understand the word? Does this seem like technical talk for experts on this topic?*

APPLY THE SIGNPOSTS

Have students use the selection that follows as a model text to apply the signposts. As students encounter signposts, prompt them to stop, reread, and ask themselves the anchor questions that will help them understand the essay's main ideas and important details.

Tell students to continue to look for these and other signposts as they read the other selections in the unit.

ANALYZE & APPLY

COMING TO OUR SENSES

Science Essay by **Neil deGrasse Tyson**

In this science essay, Neil deGrasse Tyson argues that as powerful as our five senses are, they are limited, and their limits shape our view of the universe. He argues that's why humans need to continue developing scientific tools and discovering new ways of knowing that enhance our natural senses, broaden our point of view, and expand our awareness of the wonderfully complex universe that surrounds us.

? **ESSENTIAL QUESTION:**

How does our point of view shape what we think we know?

76   Unit 2

LEARNING MINDSET

Effort Remind students that effort is necessary for growth and that success usually requires hard work. Tell students that this science essay presents technical vocabulary and concepts. Let students know they may they find it challenging at first to understand all of the points, but the effort they make to do so will pay off. Encourage students by explaining that they don't have to understand every single science term and concept to understand the essay's main ideas and important details. Also point out that they will have multiple opportunities to read and discuss the ideas in the essay. Through these interactions, they will become more familiar with key terms and more confident about understanding the key points of the essay.

TEACH

QUICK START

Some people use sensory deprivation to reduce stress. Would temporarily being deprived of information from your eyes, ears, and other senses be torture, or would it help you relax and focus? Share your ideas with a partner.

ANALYZE DEVELOPMENT OF IDEAS

The central idea of a nonfiction text is developed through the use of a thesis, evidence, examples, and a conclusion. Analyzing the evidence and examples and how they work together can help you determine the thesis of an essay.

GENRE ELEMENTS: SCIENCE ESSAY

- the author introduces a key idea, often a surprising one
- uses analogies to move from familiar concepts to complex ideas
- may use scientific terminology or refer to established theories
- generally sticks to facts, not the author's opinions

PARTS OF AN ESSAY	EXAMPLE FROM TEXT
A **thesis** is the main idea the writer wants to make about a topic. It may be stated or inferred.	**Does there exist a way of knowing that transcends our biological interfaces with the environment?**
Strong **evidence** supports the idea. Each piece of evidence builds upon the next to develop the argument.	**In nearly every case, the job of scientific apparatus is to transcend the breadth and depth of our senses.**
Examples make the ideas interesting and relevant to the reader. They tell *who, what, when, where, why,* and *how.*	**If we were born with magnetic detectors, the compass would never have been invented because we wouldn't ever need one.**
A **conclusion** explains and summarizes the main idea developed by all of the evidence and examples.	**Discovering new ways of knowing has always heralded new windows on the universe . . . [We are] always coming to our senses.**

ANALYZE TONE

The author of this essay, Neil deGrasse Tyson, communicates his ideas with irony and sarcasm. Instead of a serious tone, Tyson uses humorous language, unconventional images, and references to everyday life to make his points about science and our senses in an entertaining way.

EXAMPLES FROM TEXT	TYPE OF IRONY
And here's a news headline none of us has seen, "Psychic Wins the Lottery."	sarcastic reference to everyday life
Without hardware to help our analysis, and without a particular urge to lick the stuff, all we can report back to the starship is, "Captain, it's a blob."	unconventional image
"If a tree falls in the forest and nobody is around to hear it, does it make a sound?" My best answer is, "How do you know it fell?" But that just gets people angry.	humorous language

Coming to Our Senses   77

QUICK START

Have students read the Quick Start activity. Explain that as it is used here, *sensory deprivation* means that a person is prevented from using his or her senses to take in information about the immediate environment. Briefly explain, or have students speculate on, how this could be done (*for example, with blindfolds and earplugs*). Invite volunteers to share how they think they would respond to sensory deprivation.

ANALYZE DEVELOPMENT OF IDEAS

Discuss the information in the table. Point out that using a question to introduce a thesis captures readers' attention and sets a purpose for reading. Have students suggest various types of evidence a science writer might use in an essay. (*facts gathered through testing and research, numbers and statistics, and other verifiable pieces of information*) Explain that examples are helpful when explaining a new, difficult, or abstract idea. For example, a writer who wants to explain the term *orbit* might provide the example of how Earth moves around the sun. Compare the examples of the thesis and the conclusion and discuss how they are related.

ANALYZE TONE

Point out that when a writer uses verbal irony or sarcasm in a piece of informational writing, the writer communicates one thing but means another. Read aloud the first example in the table and ask students why it is sarcastic. (*Tyson is saying that if psychics were as powerful as they claim to be, then they would be able to predict winning lottery numbers and make a lot of money.*) Note that the second example is based on the TV show *Star Trek*. Discuss why the image is unconventional. (*Most science writers wouldn't refer to a fictional TV series to make a point or use imprecise words such as* blob. *In addition, people don't usually use their sense of taste to analyze an unknown substance.*)

ENGLISH LEARNER SUPPORT

Develop Vocabulary Explain that when someone is being *ironic*, that person says the opposite of what he or she means; when someone is being *sarcastic,* that person also says the opposite of what he or she means, but usually does so to be funny or to criticize a person or an idea. Then explain that when a person is being literal, that person is saying precisely what he or she means; there are no extra meanings. Say the following sentences, using appropriate intonation and expression, and have students identify whether you are being ironic, sarcastic, or literal each time: I'm hungry. (*literal*) An empty pizza box. Gee, thanks for saving me a slice. (*sarcastic*) I'm so glad I didn't eat breakfast. I'm not hungry at all. (*ironic*)

MODERATE/LIGHT

TEACH

CRITICAL VOCABULARY

Encourage students to read all the sentences before deciding which word best completes each one. Remind them to look for context clues that match the precise meaning of each word.

Answers:

1. *transcend*
2. *acuity*
3. *propensity*
4. *stimuli*

■ English Learner Support

Use Cognates Tell students that each of the Critical Vocabulary words has a Spanish cognate *(transcend/ trascender, acuity/agudeza, propensity/propensión,* and *stimuli/estímulos).* **ALL LEVELS**

LANGUAGE CONVENTIONS

Review the information about parallel structure. As you read aloud the example sentences, ask students to identify the subject and verb in each sentence and explain what makes the two sentences parallel in structure. *(The subjects are similar: our ears/our eyes. They both govern the verb* can register.*)*

ANNOTATION MODEL

Students can review the Reading Model introduction if they have questions about any of the signposts. Suggest that they underline important phrases or circle key words that help them identify signposts. They may want to color-code their annotations by using a different color highlighter for each signpost. Point out that they may follow this suggestion or use their own system for marking up the selections in their write-in texts.

CRITICAL VOCABULARY

acuity   stimuli   propensity   transcend

To see how many Critical Vocabulary words you already know, use them to complete the sentences.

1. Working hard in school will help you to _____ many obstacles.

2. A hawk has remarkable visual _____ to help it see prey from afar.

3. The advanced theater students showed a strong _____ for acting.

4. We can detect even faint _____ , such as a bug landing on our arm.

LANGUAGE CONVENTIONS

Parallel Structure In this lesson, you will learn about **parallel structure,** the repetition of a pattern of words or phrases in a text. This technique helps writers organize and emphasize ideas.

Here is an example from the article:

Our ears can register the thunderous launch of the space shuttle. . . . And our eyes can register the bright sandy terrain on a sunny beach. . . .

The parallel constructions make a clear connection between the abilities of two different senses. As you read "Coming to Our Senses," note the author's use of parallel structure.

ANNOTATION MODEL   NOTICE & NOTE

As you read, ask **Big Questions** and notice and note signposts, including **Numbers and Stats** and **Word Gaps.** Here is an example of how one reader responded to the opening paragraphs of "Coming to Our Senses":

> Among our five senses, sight is the most special to us. Our eyes allow us to register information not only from across the room but also from across the universe. Without vision, the science of astronomy would never have been born and our capacity to measure our place in the universe would have been hopelessly stunted. Think of bats. Whatever bat secrets get passed from one generation to the next, you can bet that none of them is based on the appearance of the night sky.

> *I never thought about it this way, but of course this makes sense.*

> *Why does he say this? Can bats not see at all, or is vision just not important to them?*

EL ENGLISH LEARNER SUPPORT

Develop Vocabulary Explain that *register,* in the second sentence of the Annotation Model, is a multiple-meaning word. Point out that if you *register information,* you notice it. Display this frame: *Our _____ allow(s) us to register _____.* Have students practice using the verb *register* by completing the frame with the name of a sense organ (eyes, ears, nose, skin, and tongue) and a type of information. (Example: *Our eyes allow us to register colors. Our ears allow us to register loud music at a rock concert and soft whispers in the library.*) **SUBSTANTIAL/MODERATE**

BACKGROUND

Neil deGrasse Tyson (b. 1958) is an American astrophysicist and director of the Hayden Planetarium at the American Museum of Natural History. But he is best known for helping to explain science to the public through his many books and television appearances. Tyson is the author of The Pluto Files: The Rise and Fall of America's Favorite Planet and Death by Black Hole and Other Cosmic Quandaries. He also hosted the TV series Cosmos: A Spacetime Odyssey and the PBS miniseries Origins and NOVA ScienceNOW.

COMING TO OUR SENSES
Science Essay by Neil deGrasse Tyson

SETTING A PURPOSE

As you read, pay attention to the details the author provides about humans' five senses. Evaluate these details to help you determine the key ideas in the essay.

> Equipped with his five senses, man explores the universe around him and calls the adventure science.
>
> —Edwin P. Hubble (1889–1953),
> The Nature of Science

1   Among our five senses, sight is the most special to us. Our eyes allow us to register information not only from across the room but also from across the universe. Without vision, the science of astronomy would never have been born and our capacity to measure our place in the universe would have been hopelessly stunted. Think of bats. Whatever bat secrets get passed from one generation to the next, you can bet that none of them is based on the appearance of the night sky.

2   When thought of as an ensemble of experimental tools, our senses enjoy an astonishing **acuity** and range of sensitivity. Our ears can register the thunderous launch of the space shuttle, yet they can also hear a mosquito buzzing a foot away from our head. Our

Notice & Note

You can use the side margins to notice and note signposts in the text.

ANALYZE TONE

Annotate: Mark the humorous image about bats that the author presents.

Infer: Why might the author begin a serious scientific essay with a humorous image?

acuity
(ə-kyoō ˈĭ-tē) n. critical perceptiveness; awareness.

Coming to Our Senses   79

BACKGROUND

Have students read the background about Neil deGrasse Tyson. Ask students to share what they know about the work of astrophysicists. Point out that one of Tyson's goals as a scientist is to engage young people in the study of science. Explain that he was instrumental in "demoting" Pluto from "full planet" to "dwarf planet" status. This caused many elementary school children to write him letters of protest, defending Pluto's planetary status.

SETTING A PURPOSE

Direct students to use the Setting a Purpose prompt to focus their reading. Check that they recall what the five senses are (sight, hearing, touch, smell, and taste).

ANALYZE TONE

Explain that bats find their way around by using their sense of hearing. They use echolocation, a system, like sonar, in which they make sounds that bounce back off surrounding objects to learn the location of those objects. Point out that bats aren't, in fact, blind, but that the author uses humor to make a point. Have students explain the point of the joke. (Astronomy wouldn't have existed without the ability to observe the sky.) (**Answer:** Tyson's humorous example emphasizes the importance of the sense of sight. His humor is a good way to engage readers at the beginning of the essay.)

CLOSE READ SCREENCAST

Modeled Discussion   In their eBook, have students view the Close Read Screencast, in which readers discuss and annotate paragraph 3.

As a class, view and discuss the video. Then have students pair up to do an independent close read of an additional passage—Tyson's restatement of his central idea (paragraph 17). Students can record their answers on the Close Read Practice PDF.

 Close Read Practice PDF

CRITICAL VOCABULARY

acuity: The five human senses allow us to perceive a great deal of information about the world around us.

ASK STUDENTS to explain how using all five of our senses can result in increased acuity. (By seeing, listening, touching, tasting, and smelling, we become more aware of the world around us than we would be if we used only one sense.)

NUMBERS AND STATS

Science writers such as Tyson often cite numbers and statistics (which may appear as words instead of numerals) in order to support a point they want to make. Such information tends to make a writer's ideas more convincing. (**Answer:** *Each measurement refers to an extreme that human senses can register.*)

 ## ANALYZE DEVELOPMENT OF IDEAS

Briefly review that questions can be used to engage the audience, introduce an idea, or advance an argument. (**Answer:** *He will identify things that we can't sense on our own and methods of detecting these things that go beyond what our senses can do.*)

For **reading support** for students at varying proficiency levels, see the **Text X-Ray** on page 74D.

CRITICAL VOCABULARY

stimuli: Tyson uses *stimuli* to refer to changes that we notice and react to with our senses.

ASK STUDENTS to identify the stimuli Tyson discusses in this selection. (*He discusses a change in light, such as a solar eclipse, or a change in volume, such as the increase in decibels of music.*)

propensity: Tyson explains that humans have a tendency to behave in a certain way because of our biology.

ASK STUDENTS to cite one example from the text of humans' propensity for experiencing stimuli. (*As humans, we notice that the sky has darkened during an eclipse only after the sun is covered 90%.*)

transcend: Tyson explains that our knowledge goes beyond what we experience with our senses due to our use of tools and machines that can be used for scientific investigation.

ASK STUDENTS to name one "tool of science" that allows us to transcend our sense of sight. (*a microscope or telescope*)

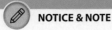 ## NOTICE & NOTE

NUMBERS AND STATS

Notice & Note: Mark the measurements that appear in this paragraph.

Analyze: How do these measurements help the author illustrate the sensitivity of human senses?

stimuli
(stĭm´yə-lī) *n.* things that cause a response or reaction.

propensity
(prə-pĕn´sĭ-tē) *n.* a tendency to behave in a certain way.

transcend
(trăn-sĕnd´) *v.* to go beyond or rise above.

ANALYZE DEVELOPMENT OF IDEAS

Annotate: Mark the important questions that tell the thesis, or main idea.

Predict: How do you think the author will develop this thesis?

---

sense of touch allows us to feel the magnitude of a bowling ball dropped on our big toe, just as we can tell when a one-milligram bug crawls along our arm. Some people enjoy munching on habañero peppers while sensitive tongues can identify the presence of food flavors to the level of parts per million. And our eyes can register the bright sandy terrain on a sunny beach, yet these same eyes have no trouble spotting a lone match, freshly lit, hundreds of feet across a darkened auditorium.

3   But before we get carried away in praise of ourselves, note that what we gain in breadth we lose in precision: we register the world's **stimuli** in logarithmic[1] rather than linear increments. For example, if you increase the energy of a sound's volume by a factor of 10, your ears will judge this change to be rather small. Increase it by a factor of 2 and you will barely notice. The same holds for our capacity to measure light. If you have ever viewed a total solar eclipse you may have noticed that the Sun's disk must be at least 90 percent covered by the Moon before anybody comments that the sky has darkened. The stellar magnitude scale of brightness, the well-known acoustic decibel scale, and the seismic scale for earthquake severity[2] are each logarithmic, in part because of our biological **propensity** to see, hear, and feel the world that way.

4   What, if anything, lies beyond our senses? Does there exist a way of knowing that **transcends** our biological interfaces with the environment?

5   Consider that the human machine, while good at decoding the basics of our immediate environment—like when it's day or night or when a creature is about to eat us—has very little talent for decoding how the rest of nature works without the tools of science. If we want to know what's out there then we require detectors other than the ones we are born with. In nearly every case, the job of scientific apparatus is to transcend the breadth and depth of our senses.

6   Some people boast of having a sixth sense, where they profess to know or see things that others cannot. Fortune-tellers, mind readers, and mystics are at the top of the list of those who lay claim to mysterious powers. In doing so, they instill widespread fascination in others, especially book publishers and television producers. The questionable field of parapsychology[3] is founded on the expectation that at least some people actually harbor such talents. To me, the biggest mystery of them all is why so many fortune-telling psychics

[1] **logarithmic:** capable of being raised by repeated multiplication of itself; exponential.
[2] **stellar magnitude scale . . . acoustic decibel scale . . . seismic scale:** systems of measurement for the brightness of starlight, the loudness of sounds, and the intensity of earthquakes.
[3] **parapsychology:** the study of unexplainable or supernatural mental phenomena.

 ## IMPROVE READING FLUENCY

Targeted Passage Use echo reading to help students use appropriate pacing, intonation, phrasing, and expression in reading in paragraphs 4–5. Begin by reading the passage aloud, modeling how to use punctuation as a guide to phrasing and intonation. Then have students echo your reading as you read it a second and third time, first by pausing after each phrase or clause and then reading it again with pauses after each sentence. You may choose to conclude with paired oral reading to give students more practice reading the passage aloud.

Go to the **Reading Studio** for additional support in developing fluency.

choose to work the phones on TV hotlines instead of becoming insanely wealthy trading futures contracts on Wall Street.[4] And here's a news headline none of us has seen, "Psychic Wins the Lottery."

7   Quite independent of this mystery, the persistent failures of controlled, double-blind experiments to support the claims of parapsychology suggest that what's going on is nonsense rather than sixth sense.

8   On the other hand, modern science wields dozens of senses. And scientists do not claim these to be the expression of special powers, just special hardware. In the end, of course, the hardware converts the information gleaned from these extra senses into simple tables, charts, diagrams, or images that our inborn senses can interpret. In the original *Star Trek* sci-fi series, the crew that beamed down from their starship to the uncharted planet always brought with them a tricorder—a handheld device that could analyze anything they encountered, living or inanimate, for its basic properties. As the tricorder was waved over the object in question, it made an audible spacey sound that was interpreted by the user.

9   Suppose a glowing blob of some unknown substance were parked right in front of us. Without some diagnostic tool like a tricorder to help, we would be clueless to the blob's chemical or nuclear composition. Nor could we know whether it has an electromagnetic

WORD GAPS

Notice & Note: Mark the words or phrases in paragraph 9 that you don't know or that you find confusing.

Analyze: What clues in the passage help you understand these words? What do you already know about these words?

---

[4] **trading futures contracts on Wall Street:** a form of speculative investment in which someone agrees to pay a fixed price for an item at a future date. The success of the investment is measured by the difference between the agreed-upon price and the actual market price on that future date.

▶ WORD GAPS

Remind students that when they encounter unfamiliar or confusing vocabulary, they can ask themselves: Do I know this word from someplace else? Does it seem like technical talk for this topic? Can I find clues in the text to help me understand the word? Have students share the words they identified with a partner and try answering those three questions. Then invite volunteers to identify clues in the text that helped them figure out some of the words. (*Answers will vary depending on words selected.*)

■ English Learner Support

Identify Formal and Informal English Work with a small group. Remind students that Tyson is a science writer who likes to make science interesting and fun for people of all ages. Therefore, he uses some informal words and expressions that you wouldn't see in many other science essays. Identify words and phrases in informal English in paragraph 9. (*blob, parked right in front of us, clueless to*) Ask pairs to rewrite each sentence in more formal English. (*Suppose a glowing object of some unknown substance appeared in front of us. Without a diagnostic tool such as a tricorder, we would not be able to determine the object's chemical or nuclear composition.*)

Then have students practice speaking using informal and formal English. Have students take turns using the informal and formal words they identified in spoken sentences; ask other students whether the sentences are informal or formal.

MODERATE/LIGHT

APPLYING ACADEMIC VOCABULARY

❑ **differentiate** ☑ **incorporate** ☑ **mode** ❑ **orient** ❑ **perspective**

Write and Discuss Have students turn to a partner to discuss the following questions. Guide students to include the academic vocabulary words *incorporate and mode* in their responses. Ask volunteers to share their responses with the class.

- What kinds of scientific technology do we often **incorporate** into our study of the universe?
- How do the **modes** of information discussed in the text differ?

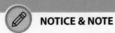
ANALYZE DEVELOPMENT OF IDEAS

Have pairs review the two passages together, with one student turning to page 79 and the other to page 82. (**Answer:** *Both quotations express the idea of understanding the universe, but the second one clarifies that we need much more than our five senses to do this; in other words, we need scientific technology.*)

■ English Learner Support

Develop Vocabulary Point out that both passages begin with the phrase *equipped with*. Explain that if someone is *equipped with* something, that person has something useful. For example, most students are *equipped with* paper and pencils. Ask students to point to something else they are equipped with that is useful in class. Then guide students to complete this frame: *Our senses are useful for learning about the universe because _____. (they help us observe our surroundings)* **ALL LEVELS**

 For **listening and speaking support** for students at varying proficiency levels, see the **Text X-Ray** on pages 74C–D.

LANGUAGE CONVENTIONS

Remind students that parallel structure is a technique in which a writer repeats a pattern of words or phrases within the same sentence or paragraph, often to emphasize important ideas. (**Answer:** *The repetition shows that the sentences beginning with* Tune into . . . *have something in common: all three are kinds of wavelengths that Tyson says would be helpful for people to be able to see.*)

---

field, or whether it emits strongly in gamma rays, x-rays, ultraviolet, microwaves, or radio waves. Nor could we determine the blob's cellular or crystalline structure. If the blob were far out in space, appearing as an unresolved point of light in the sky, our five senses would offer us no insight to its distance, velocity through space, or its rate of rotation. We further would have no capacity to see the spectrum of colors that compose its emitted light, nor could we know whether the light is polarized.

10   Without hardware to help our analysis, and without a particular urge to lick the stuff, all we can report back to the starship is, "Captain, it's a blob." Apologies to Edwin P. Hubble, the quote that opens this chapter, while poignant and poetic, should have instead been:

> (Equipped with our five senses) along with telescopes and microscopes and mass spectrometers and seismographs and magnetometers and particle accelerators and detectors across the electromagnetic spectrum, (we explore the universe around us and call the adventure science)

ANALYZE DEVELOPMENT OF IDEAS

Annotate: Reread this quotation and the one that opens the science essay. Mark two things the two versions have in common. Underline a difference you see in the second quotation.

Compare: How are these quotations alike? How are they different?

LANGUAGE CONVENTIONS

Annotate: Mark the repeated phrase you see at the beginnings of sentences in paragraph 11.

Respond: How does repeating this structure help clarify Tyson's point?

11   Think of how much richer the world would appear to us and how much earlier the nature of the universe would have been discovered if we were born with high-precision, tunable eyeballs. Dial up the radio-wave part of the spectrum and the daytime sky becomes as dark as night. Dotting that sky would be bright and famous sources of radio waves, such as the center of the Milky Way, located behind some of the principal stars of the constellation Sagittarius. Tune into microwaves and the entire cosmos glows with a remnant from the early universe, a wall of light set forth 380,000 years after the big bang. Tune into x-rays and you immediately spot the locations of black holes, with matter spiraling into them. Tune into gamma rays and see titanic explosions scattered throughout the universe at a rate of about one per day. Watch the effect of the explosion on the surrounding material as it heats up and glows in other bands of light.

12   If we were born with magnetic detectors, the compass would never have been invented because we wouldn't ever need one. Just tune into Earth's magnetic field lines and the direction of magnetic north looms like Oz[5] beyond the horizon. If we had spectrum analyzers within our retinas, we would not have to wonder what we were breathing. We could just look at the register and know whether the air contained sufficient oxygen to sustain human life. And we would have learned thousands of years ago that the stars and nebulae in the Milky Way galaxy contain the same chemical elements found here on Earth.

---

[5] **Oz:** the magical city and destination for characters in L. Frank Baum's *The Wonderful Wizard of Oz.*

(EL) ENGLISH LEARNER SUPPORT

Understand Language Structures Read aloud the first sentence of paragraph 11. Explain that *high-precision, tunable eyeballs* basically means "eyes as powerful as telescopes." Point out that the author uses the word *if* and the verbs *were born, would appear,* and *would have been discovered* to suggest possible results of a condition, or something that is imagined or not real—having more powerful vision. Note that helping verbs such as *would, could,* and *might* are often used to express conditions in different tenses because conditions may have possible effects on the past, present, or future. Then read aloud the rest of the paragraph, explaining that the actions described in each sentence are dependent on the condition introduced in the first sentence. Have partners work together to rewrite each sentence to include the conditional clause *If we were born with eyes as powerful as telescopes, we could . . . .* **MODERATE/LIGHT**

13 And if we were born with big eyes and built-in Doppler motion detectors, we would have seen immediately, even as grunting troglodytes,[6] that the entire universe is expanding—with distant galaxies all receding from us.

14 If our eyes had the resolution of high-performance microscopes, nobody would have ever blamed the plague and other sicknesses on divine wrath. The bacteria and viruses that made us sick would be in plain view as they crawled on our food or as they slid through open wounds in our skin. With simple experiments, we could easily tell which of these bugs were bad and which were good. And of course postoperative infection problems would have been identified and solved hundreds of years earlier.

15 If we could detect high-energy particles, we would spot radioactive substances from great distances. No Geiger counters necessary. We could even watch radon gas seep through the basement floor of homes and not have to pay somebody to tell us about it.

16 The honing of our senses from birth through childhood allows us, as adults, to pass judgment on events and phenomena in our lives, declaring whether they "make sense." Problem is, hardly any scientific discoveries of the past century flowed from the direct application of our five senses. They flowed instead from the direct application of sense-transcendent mathematics and hardware. This simple fact is entirely responsible for why, to the average person, relativity, particle physics, and 10-dimensional string theory make no sense. Include

---

[6] **troglodyte:** a primitive creature or a cave dweller.

BIG QUESTIONS

Notice & Note: Mark ideas in paragraphs 14 and 15 that challenge what you know about the dangers around us.

Draw Conclusions: Which improvements to our senses would benefit humanity the most? Why?

Coming to Our Senses   83

BIG QUESTIONS

Remind students of the anchor question: *What challenged, changed, or confirmed what I already knew?* Point out to students that this Notice & Note asks for one part of this question—what *challenged* them. Tell students if they already knew about these dangers, they could instead mark what *confirmed* what they already knew. (**Possible answer:** *Students might point out that if our vision enabled us to see down to a molecular level, then we might be able to detect harmful gases and know when cancer cells and harmful bacteria and viruses are in our bodies.*)

TO CHALLENGE STUDENTS . . .

Analyze Development of Ideas Have students, working individually or with partners, review paragraphs 11–15 and then paragraphs 16–17. Instruct them to discuss these questions: What main points does Tyson make? What evidence does he use to support these points? What commonly held belief is he trying to counter? How well do you think he makes his case? Ask students to write and share a paragraph explaining their thinking and supporting it with evidence from the text.

TEACH

ANALYZE DEVELOPMENT OF IDEAS

Direct students to paragraph 18. Explain that the word *heralded* means "signaled." Ask students to break down the word *supersentient* to figure out what it means and then paraphrase it. (*having extra-strong senses*) Then have students mark the text and paraphrase the author's conclusion. (**Answer:** *In a way, we continue to evolve through the development of technology that enhances our perception.*)

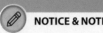
in the list black holes, wormholes, and the big bang. Actually, these ideas don't make much sense to scientists either, or at least not until we have explored the universe for a long time, with all the senses that are technologically available. What emerges, eventually, is a newer and higher level of "common sense" that enables a scientist to think creatively and to pass judgment in the unfamiliar underworld of the atom or in the mind-bending domain of higher-dimensional space. The twentieth-century German physicist Max Planck made a similar observation about the discovery of quantum mechanics:

> *Modern Physics impresses us particularly with the truth of the old doctrine which teaches that there are realities existing apart from our sense-perceptions, and that there are problems and conflicts where these realities are of greater value for us than the richest treasures of the world of experience.*
> (1931, p. 107)

17   Our five senses even interfere with sensible answers to stupid metaphysical questions like, "If a tree falls in the forest and nobody is around to hear it, does it make a sound?" My best answer is, "How do you know it fell?" But that just gets people angry. So I offer a senseless analogy, "Q: If you can't smell the carbon monoxide, then how do you know it's there? A: You drop dead." In modern times, if the sole measure of what's out there flows from your five senses then a precarious life awaits you.

18   Discovering new ways of knowing has always heralded <u>new windows on the universe</u> that tap into our <u>growing list of nonbiological senses</u>. Whenever this happens, a <u>new level of majesty and complexity in the universe reveals itself to us, as though we were technologically evolving</u> into supersentient beings, always coming to our senses.

ANALYZE DEVELOPMENT OF IDEAS

Annotate: Mark the words, phrases, and sentences that help you understand the author's conclusion.

Paraphrase: What is the author's conclusion? Explain it in your own words.

WHEN STUDENTS STRUGGLE...

Analyze Evidence Explain that when writers make an analogy, as Tyson does in paragraph 17, they are explaining one thing by comparing it to something else. Direct students to identify what Tyson is comparing. (*questions about hearing a tree fall and smelling carbon dioxide*) Explain that carbon monoxide is an odorless gas that is deadly. Then work with students to explain how the questions are similar. (*The first question raises the possibility that a tree that falls without anyone to hear it doesn't make a sound. Tyson's question suggests that you could ask a similar question about whether carbon*

monoxide is present if you can't smell it.) Invite volunteers to state the point of this analogy. (*to show that we shouldn't rely only on our senses because they can't give us all of the information we need*)

 For additional support, go to the Reading Studio and assign the following [LEVEL UP] **Level Up Tutorial: Analyzing Arguments.**

CHECK YOUR UNDERSTANDING

Answer these questions before moving on to the **Analyze the Text** section on the following page.

1 The author shares ideas in a tone that is —

A serious and dry

B informative yet humorous

C lighthearted and imprecise

D enthusiastic yet ill-informed

2 The information about scientific instruments is used to —

F describe various ways scientists gather information

G provide a detailed overview of the latest technology

H compare science fiction with actual developments

J illustrate how our five senses are superior to artificial means

3 Which idea is supported by the essay?

A Science is sometimes wrong and has to revise statements.

B Popular culture makes many valid observations about science.

C Scientists are the most important people in our society.

D We can always expand our awareness of the world around us.

 CHECK YOUR UNDERSTANDING

Have students answer the questions independently.

Answers:

1. *B*

2. *F*

3. *D*

If they answer any questions incorrectly, have them reread the text to confirm their understanding. Then they may proceed to ANALYZE THE TEXT on page 86.

EL ENGLISH LEARNER SUPPORT

Oral Assessment Use the following questions to assess students' comprehension and speaking skills.

1. Would you describe the tone of the essay as serious or informative yet humorous? *(informative yet humorous)*

2. Which best describes the purpose of the evidence the author includes about scientific instruments: to provide a thorough overview of current technology, or to describe ways in which scientists gather information? *(to describe ways in which scientists gather information)*

3. Does the essay support the idea that we can always expand our awareness of the world around us? *(yes)* **SUBSTANTIAL/MODERATE**

ANALYZE THE TEXT

Possible answers:

1. **DOK 1:** *Tyson notes that our senses are powerful, but we have to use scientific instruments to truly understand the world around us. Tyson develops this thesis with evidence and examples of the capabilities and limits of our senses and how they are expanded upon by scientific tools.*

2. **DOK 2:** *Our senses don't always notice small changes. We cannot observe things that are very small, like bacteria and germs, or very far away, like celestial bodies, without the help of scientific instruments. Sometimes our senses can fool us or fail to detect something important, like carbon monoxide.*

3. **DOK 3:** *Tyson points out the flawed ideas of parapsychology in contrast to the proven record of science in helping us to understand the world. This comparison helps to show why science is very important.*

4. **DOK 4:** *The tone is effective because it engages readers and points them to the ideas that Tyson considers most accurate and important.*

5. **DOK 4:** *Our five senses really are amazing. We can see a tiny light or hear a very faint sound. Despite this amazing sensitivity, there is much more to the universe that we can't sense.*

RESEARCH

Tell students that they may find it useful to narrow a broad topic such as *hurricanes* or *cancer* by pairing it with a word such as *instruments*, *technology*, or *tools*.

Connect Have students share their research in small groups. After each student has presented information on a topic, urge the group to discuss other applications of that technology before moving on to the next student.

 RESPOND

ANALYZE THE TEXT

Support your responses with evidence from the text. 📓 NOTEBOOK

1. **Identify** What is the thesis that the author develops throughout this essay? What evidence and examples support that thesis?

2. **Summarize** What are some of the limitations of our five senses? Give a few examples from the text.

3. **Compare** The author compares parapsychology and science. Why does Tyson compare these two methods of learning about the world? What differences does he find?

4. **Evaluate** The author uses an ironic, sarcastic tone throughout the essay. Was his tone effective in helping him make his point? Why or why not?

5. **Notice & Note** Give one example of how this essay challenged your understanding of science and of your five senses. Support your ideas with text evidence.

RESEARCH

RESEARCH TIP
You can ask a question in a search engine, such as "How can you measure global temperature changes?" Look for key words on each page that you find, and then search for any specific instruments that are mentioned. Remember to use reliable websites, such as those maintained by a university or research agency.

Scientists use many instruments to find out about the world around them. Choose a scientific topic, such as hurricanes, cancer, nanotechnology, rainforests, or another topic. Then find out more about one of the instruments scientists use to study that topic. Draw a sketch in the chart of the instrument and record 2–3 facts about what the scientific instrument does.

TOPIC	SCIENTIFIC INSTRUMENT	PICTURE	FACTS
nanotechnology	nanorobots or nanobots (tiny robots controlled by a computer) for heart surgery	Illustrations will vary.	Tiny robots, guided by magnetic charges, they can be used in heart surgery. They can deliver drugs and break through blocked arteries.

Connect Share your work with a small group. Explain how the instrument you researched has helped scientists widen their understanding of the world. Discuss other ways this scientific instrument could be used.

© Houghton Mifflin Harcourt Publishing Company

⚙ LEARNING MINDSET

Problem Solving Remind students that everyone runs into problems from time to time but that most problems can be solved with effort and persistence. Emphasize that there are many different problem-solving strategies, including trying various solutions, being patient, and asking for help. Model aloud a problem-solving approach: "If I'm not finding a good scientific instrument, it could be that I need to change my search terms, or maybe I need to refine my research question. I'll try a few different searches and be patient; after all, it may take a few tries before I find anything useful. Then, if I'm still having trouble, I might ask a peer or the teacher to give me some tips."

CREATE AND PRESENT

Write an Explanation Choose one of the concepts or ideas Neil deGrasse Tyson mentions in this science essay. Write 1–2 paragraphs about this topic. Some possible topics may include carbon monoxide, black holes, bacteria and viruses, X-rays, a solar eclipse, or our senses.

❏ Introduce the topic and state your main idea.

❏ Provide some facts that tell more about the topic. You may choose to do some quick independent research about the topic. Also include details from "Coming to Our Senses."

❏ Share your own thoughts about this topic. What surprised or interested you? Were your ideas confirmed or challenged?

Give a Presentation Share your paragraph and research with a partner. Discuss how we use scientific instruments to study each partner's topic.

❏ Listen to what your partner wrote and ask thoughtful questions to clarify facts or ideas.

❏ Share your research. Make at least one change or addition to your writing based on your partner's feedback.

❏ Check that you included a clear main idea.

❏ Join with another group and present your revised paragraphs. Listen respectfully to others. When it is your turn to speak, make eye contact with your audience and speak with a slow, steady pace.

RESPOND TO THE ESSENTIAL QUESTION

? How does our point of view shape what we think we know?

Gather Information Review your annotations and notes on "Coming to Our Senses." Then, add relevant details to your Response Log. As you determine which information to include, think about:

• how we use our senses to understand the world

• how scientific instruments help us learn

• why we should be open to learning more about our world

At the end of the unit, use your notes to help you write a short story.

 For more on evaluating research sources, visit the **Writing Studio**.

For help with speaking in a discussion, visit the **Speaking and Listening Studio**.

ACADEMIC VOCABULARY
As you write and discuss what you learned from the article, be sure to use the Academic Vocabulary words. Check off each of the words that you use.

❏ **differentiate**

❏ **incorporate**

❏ **mode**

❏ **orient**

❏ **perspective**

UNIT 2 RESPONSE LOG

Coming to Our Senses   87

CREATE AND PRESENT

Write an Explanation Remind students that there are various ways in which writers can introduce a topic; for example, they might pose a rhetorical question or include an interesting or surprising fact. Explain that since students are writing only a paragraph or two, they should limit their introduction to one or two sentences. Suggest that it may make sense for them to organize their ideas by explaining their topic in one paragraph and then providing their own comments about it in a second paragraph.

For **writing support** for students at varying proficiency levels, see the **Text X-Ray** on page 74D.

Give a Presentation Inform students that scientists often write papers and present them to their peers at meetings and conferences. Before doing so, they often go through a peer review stage, in which they have other scientists comment on their work. Have pairs of students take turns presenting their paragraphs and receiving feedback on their writing. Afterward, circulate around the room and check to ensure that students are making at least one substantive revision. Then have two or three pairs of students gather and take turns presenting their revised paragraphs within each larger group.

RESPOND TO THE ESSENTIAL QUESTION

Allow time for students to add details from "Coming to Our Senses" to their Unit 2 Response Logs.

EL ENGLISH LEARNER SUPPORT

Express Opinions Display these sentence frames and use them to model how to give polite feedback to a partner before the presentation:

I think that the _____ is _____.

These are some of the things I liked: _____, _____, and _____.

I'm a little confused about _____.

The _____ is missing, so you should add that.

You might work a little more on _____ because _____.

I think once you _____, the paragraph will be _____.

Have pairs of students use the frames to give feedback on their partner's writing.
MODERATE/LIGHT

CRITICAL VOCABULARY

Possible answers:

1. *No; if you had high visual acuity, your vision would be very good, and you would not need glasses.*

2. *I would respond to my cell phone more quickly because it might be a very important call—perhaps even an emergency.*

3. *My room would be tidy because I always try to keep my things organized.*

4. *You would not be able to classify the songs easily; they might mix genres or have a few traits of a genre but then do something associated with a different genre.*

VOCABULARY STRATEGY:
Reference Sources

Possible answers:

1. **Edwin P. Hubble** *was one of the leading astronomers of the 20th century. The Hubble Telescope is named after him. He discovered that there were other galaxies outside the Milky Way.*

2. *In a* **double-blind experiment,** *both the scientist and the subject being studied are kept unaware regarding the experimental conditions being used. This is a way to randomize the experiment and avoid bias.*

3. **The** *Star Trek* **sci-fi series** *was a TV show that ran during the 1960s. In it, Captain Kirk and the crew of the Starship Enterprise explore the galaxy and represent the United Federation of Planets.*

4. **Geiger counters** *are used to detect radioactive emissions*

■ English Learner Support

Use Support from Peers and Teachers Have partners work together to complete the Practice and Apply activity. Help them choose which reference source to use to locate each name, term, or topic. Once they locate each item, have them draw an illustration and label it or write one sentence about it, depending on their proficiency level.
ALL LEVELS

 RESPOND

WORD BANK
acuity
stimuli
propensity
transcend

Go to the **Vocabulary Studio** for more on reference sources.

CRITICAL VOCABULARY

Practice and Apply Demonstrate an understanding of each Critical Vocabulary word by responding to each question and explaining your answer. Use a dictionary or the definitions in the text to help you understand the meanings of the words.

1. If you possess high visual **acuity**, would you need glasses? Explain.

   _____

2. Which of these **stimuli** would be more likely to make you respond quickly: a ringing cell phone or the smell of cookies baking?

   _____

3. If you have a **propensity** for organization, is your room messy or tidy?

   _____

4. If a singer's songs **transcend** musical genres, would you be able to easily classify the songs as country or rock?

   _____

VOCABULARY STRATEGY:
Reference Sources

The author of the essay incorporates pop culture, historical, and scientific references into the text. For example, Tyson mentions a *total solar eclipse*, which is a scientific phenomenon that people rarely get to observe. Some readers may not be familiar with this event.

To determine the meaning of an unknown word, name, or reference, consult general and specialized reference materials, both print and digital. These may include college-level or bilingual dictionaries, encyclopedias, and online search engines that can lead you to specialized online resources that will help you identify more obscure references.

Practice and Apply Use print or digital resource materials to define or explain each reference from the essay.

1. Edwin P. Hubble

   _____

2. double-blind experiment

   _____

3. the *Star Trek* sci-fi series

   _____

4. Geiger counters

   _____

WHEN STUDENTS STRUGGLE . . .

Use Reference Sources Display several physical or digital reference resources, such as a dictionary, an encyclopedia, and a science book. Point out key features of each reference tool and model using each one to look something up. Ask students which reference sources would be most helpful for gathering information about each of the items in the Practice and Apply activity. (*Each item could probably be found in a print or digital encyclopedia; a definition of a Geiger counter probably would appear in a dictionary; by visiting a library or doing a keyword search at a library website, you could find out which books would be likely to have information on these topics.*)

LANGUAGE CONVENTIONS:
Parallel Structure

Parallel structure is a technique in which authors repeat words or phrases within the same sentence or paragraph. Using parallel structure helps authors organize and clarify their thoughts, and it helps emphasize important ideas. Parallel structure can make writing more interesting, lyrical, and rhythmic.

In "Coming to Our Senses," Neil deGrasse Tyson uses parallel structure in different ways.

• To draw connections between seemingly different concepts:

> **Our eyes allow us to register information <u>not only from across the room but also from across the universe.</u>**

Here, the author uses parallel structure within a sentence to compare and draw connections between two very different distances: across a room and across the universe.

• To add rhythm and continuity throughout the essay:

> **<u>If we were born with</u> magnetic detectors, . . .**
>
> **And <u>if we were born with</u> big eyes and built-in Doppler motion detectors, . . .**

Here, the author starts two different paragraphs with similar phrasing. This carries his ideas throughout different paragraphs and emphasizes the conditional nature of his argument.

Practice and Apply Do you believe it is important for humans to continue to explore space? Write one or two paragraphs that express your position on this issue, supporting your thinking with evidence and examples. Use parallel structure both within a sentence and between sentences by starting or ending two sentences in similar ways. When you are finished, share your sentences with a partner. Ask your partner to mark the examples of parallel structure.

Coming to Our Senses 89

LANGUAGE CONVENTIONS:
Parallel Structure

Review the information about parallel structure. Direct students to the first example from "Coming to Our Senses." Display the same sentence with the phrases stacked in this way to highlight the parallel structures:

> Our eyes allow us to register information
>
> not only
>
> from across the room
>
> but also
>
> from across the universe.

Point out that the repetition of the words *from across the* makes it clear that the structures are parallel and that the parallel elements are prepositional phrases. Demonstrate how you could change the statement with other parallel words, phrases, or clauses—for example: Our eyes allow us to register information not only <u>quickly</u> but also <u>accurately</u>.

Display this example: Our sense of hearing permits us to distinguish not only sounds of distant thunder but also we can hear low whispers. Ask students to stack the phrases as you did with the example sentence, identify the error in structure, and write a corrected sentence. (*Error:* sounds *is a noun and* we can *is a subject plus verb, so the structures aren't parallel. Corrected sentence: Our sense of hearing permits us to distinguish not only sounds of distant thunder but also low whispers.*)

Practice and Apply After students have completed their paragraphs and exchanged their writing with a partner, call on volunteers to share the parallel structures they used with the class.

ENGLISH LEARNER SUPPORT

Use a Variety of Sentence Patterns Provide instruction and practice in parallel structure with the following example sentences:

• Provide this frame: *I like _____, _____, and _____.* Model how to complete the frame with three parallel nouns. (*Example: I like soccer, baseball, and football.*) **SUBSTANTIAL**

• Provide this frame: *I like not only _____ but also _____.* Model how to complete it with parallel structures. (*I like not only studying science but also reading about science topics.*) Then have pairs of students take turns completing it. **MODERATE**

• Have students write their own sentences using *not only/but also* and *neither/nor.* Have them write one sentence using noun phrases and one using verb phrases. Have them read their sentences aloud. **LIGHT**

MENTOR TEXT

THE NIGHT FACE UP

Short Story by Julio Cortázar, translated by Paul Blackburn

This story serves as a **mentor text,** a model for students to follow when they come to the Unit 2 Writing Task: Write a Short Story.

GENRE ELEMENTS
SHORT STORY

Remind students that a **short story** includes the four basic elements of fiction: setting, characters, plot, and theme. Remind students that a theme is an underlying message about life or human nature that a writer wants the reader to understand. Explain that a story usually begins with an exposition that introduces the characters and setting. Authors choose how to develop their characters in the story. They might give detailed descriptions or reveal information about them slowly as the plot develops.

LEARNING OBJECTIVES

- Analyze character and plot development and structure.
- Make inferences.
- Research ancient Aztec culture.
- Write a literary analysis.
- Discuss opinions about parallel plots.
- Identify denotative and connotative meanings.
- Use complex sentence structure.
- **Language** Use expressions such as *I think* and *I agree* to express opinions about plot.

TEXT COMPLEXITY

Quantitative Measures	"The Night Face Up"	Lexile: 1210L
Qualitative Measures	**Ideas Presented** Multiple levels of meaning, with greater demand for inference.	
	Structures Used Complex; parallel plot lines.	
	Language Used Mostly explicit, some figurative language.	
	Knowledge Required Cultural references make heavier demands.	

RESOURCES

- Unit 2 Response Log
- Selection Audio
- Reading Studio:
  Notice & Note
- Level Up Tutorial:
  Plot: Sequence of Events; Reading
  for Details
- Writing Studio:
  Using Textual Evidence
- Speaking and Listening Studio:
  Participating in Collaborative
  Discussions
- Vocabulary Studio:
  Connotation and Denotation
- Grammar Studio: Module 4: Lesson
  5: Sentence Structure
- "The Night Face Up" Selection Test

SUMMARIES

English

Driving to work, a man crashes his motorcycle while trying to avoid hitting a woman who steps out into the street. He is injured and taken to the hospital. As the man passes in and out of consciousness, he dreams he is being chased by the Aztecs through a deep, dark forest. The Aztecs want to capture him to use as a human sacrifice in an ancient ritual known as the "war of blossoms." The hospital scenario and the darker manhunt scenario switch back and forth as parallel plots, leaving the reader to decide which scenario is "real" and which is a dream.

Spanish

Al conducir al trabajo a través de calles pintorescas, un hombre choca en su motocicleta al tratar de evitar chocar con una mujer que camina hacia la calle. El hombre resulta herido y lo llevan al hospital. Mientras el hombre sale y vuelve en sí, sueña que es perseguido por los Aztecas a través de un bosque oscuro y profundo. Los Aztecas quieren capturarlo para usarlo como un sacrificio humano en un antiguo ritual conocido como la "guerra de las flores". La perspectiva del hospital y la aun más oscura perspectiva de la persecución cambian de adelante hacia atrás como tramas paralelos, dejando que el lector decida qué trama es "real" y cuál es un sueño.

SMALL-GROUP OPTIONS

Have students work in small groups to read and discuss the selection.

Double-Entry Journal

- Model the structure of a two-column format. Divide each page down the middle by drawing a line from top to bottom. The heading on the left side should be "Quotes from the Text," and the heading on the right side should be "My Notes."
- Have students record significant events, important details, or puzzling passages from the text in the left column.
- Ask students to write their own thoughts opposite the quoted text in the right column.
- Have students share and discuss their notes in small groups.

Think-Pair-Share

- After students have read and analyzed "The Night Face Up," pose this question: Which of the parallel plots is "real," and which is a dream? Why?
- Have students think about the question individually, and then review the text and their notes.
- With partners, have students discuss their ideas about the question.
- Finally, ask pairs to share their responses with the whole class.

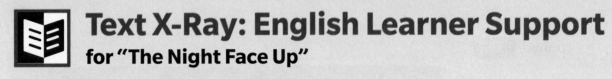

Text X-Ray: English Learner Support
for "The Night Face Up"

Use the Text X-Ray and the supports and scaffolds in the Teacher's Edition to help guide students at different proficiency levels through the selection.

INTRODUCE THE SELECTION
DISCUSS SHIFT IN SETTING

In this lesson, students will need to be able to recognize shifts in the story's narrative from one setting to another. The two parallel plots in the story present very different cultural and historical settings. Read paragraphs 5 and 6 and explain that this is the moment in the story where the first shift occurs. Point out the word *dream* as a clue to a shift in the setting.

- Dreams are thoughts that occur in someone's mind during sleep.
- The first setting in this story is a modern city. The second setting is a jungle in an ancient time.
- The *setting* is when and where the story takes place.

Guide students to recall another story they've read or movie they've seen that had different settings. Initiate discussion with the following sentence frame:

- The story took place in _____ and _____.

CULTURAL REFERENCES

The following cultural references may be unfamiliar to some students :

- *Aztecs* (paragraph 6): early people who lived during the 14th century in what is now central Mexico. The Aztecs built a large, powerful empire. They were known for practicing human sacrifice, or killing a person to appeal to a god. The empire ended in 1521 when the Spanish invaded.
- *big lake* (paragraph 7): The Aztec capital of Tenochitlán was built in a marshy area of islands in Lake Texcoco. Mexico City is located there now.

LISTENING

Identify Sensory Details

Explain that authors use sensory details to give readers a vivid description of people, places, and events, enabling readers to form mental images from the author's words.

Have students listen as you read aloud paragraphs 6–7. Use the following supports with students at varying proficiency levels.

- Reread the first three sentences of paragraph 7. Guide students to "act out" what they hear. For example, cover your nose when mentioning the odor and crouch at the "unexpected sound." **SUBSTANTIAL**
- Ask: What sense first tells the character something is different? *(smell)* What makes him shake? *(an unexpected sound)* What does he see? *(the glare of the fire)* **MODERATE**
- Have students identify words and phrases associated with the sense of smell. *(reek, foul, marshy smell, fresh composite fragrance, cloying incense)* **LIGHT**

SPEAKING

Share and Discuss Opinions

Support student participation in the discussion activity on Student Edition page 103.

Use the following supports with students at varying proficiency levels.

- Before students meet with their discussion groups, have them practice expressing their opinions about the ending: *I think that the Aztec setting is _____. (real* or *a dream).* **SUBSTANTIAL**
- Provide these frames for students to express opinions about the story's ending: *The setting I think is real is _____ because _____. The setting I think is a dream is _____ because _____.* **MODERATE**
- Have students use expressions such as the following to add information to group members' ideas: *I agree with your point about _____, but I also think that _____ .* **LIGHT**

READING

Understand Setting and Plot

Help students trace the parallel plots in the story.

Use the following supports with students at varying proficiency levels.

- Think aloud to help students identify words and phrases in paragraph 1 that describe a modern setting. For example: The words *motorcycle, jewelry store,* and *tall downtown buildings* let me know that this part of the story is set in a modern time. **SUBSTANTIAL**
- Have partners discuss details in the story that help them infer shifts from one setting to another. Provide this sentence frame: *The words _____ tell me that the setting is changing.* **MODERATE**
- Prompt students to silently read the modern scenes in sequence and then read the manhunt scenes in sequence. Ask partners to discuss how reading the scenes in sequence clarifies the order of events. **LIGHT**

WRITING

Write an Analysis

Support student participation in the writing activity on Student Edition page 103.

Use the following supports with students at varying proficiency levels.

- Provide and discuss model theme statements, such as "Things aren't always what they seem" or "Dreams can take us to amazing but frightening places." **SUBSTANTIAL**
- Have students review and mark key words in the writing prompt to ensure they understand the activity. **MODERATE**
- Have students create an outline before they begin to write. Make sure their outline includes an introductory theme statement, points about how the theme is conveyed in the body, and a conclusion that reiterates the theme. **LIGHT**

Connect to the
ESSENTIAL QUESTION

In "The Night Face Up," author Julio Cortázar weaves parallel plots to create an intriguing story about a young man who drifts in and out of two dramatically different worlds. Characters in both worlds throughout the story offer varied points of view of events as they unfold. For the reader, what appears real may actually be an illusion or dream.

MENTOR TEXT

At the end of the unit, students will be asked to write a short story. "The Night Face Up" provides a model for how to write a dramatic story using parallel plots and descriptive details to describe setting, characters, and events.

THE NIGHT FACE UP

Short Story by **Julio Cortázar**

translated by Paul Blackburn

? ESSENTIAL QUESTION:

How does our point of view shape what we think we know?

LEARNING MINDSET

Persistence Remind students that persistence is an important part of a learning mindset because it pushes one to keep on doing something—or trying to do something—even though it may seem difficult. Explain to students that the use of parallel plots in this story may be challenging to understand, but with persistence students can understand the settings, characters, and events that ultimately unfold.

QUICK START

The idea of dreams versus reality plays a central role in the story you are about to read. Think of three words that describe how you feel when you wake from a vivid dream. Share and discuss your words with a partner.

MAKE INFERENCES

Inferences are logical guesses based on clues in the text and on your prior knowledge. "The Night Face Up" includes events in two very different settings. As you read, you can use story details to make inferences about the cultural environments and historical periods in the story. This will help you to develop a clear picture of the two worlds in which the protagonist finds himself. Record your inferences and the clues that helped you make them as shown.

EVIDENCE/CLUES FROM THE TEXT	→	INFERENCE
Setting 1: But they kept him for a good while in a room with that hospital smell, filling out a form, getting his clothes off, and dressing him in a stiff, grayish smock. They moved his arm carefully, it didn't hurt him. The nurses were constantly making wisecracks, and if it hadn't been for the stomach contractions he would have felt fine, almost happy.		The man is hurt and in a hospital, but he feels like he is in good hands. The people taking care of him are happy and competent.
Setting 2: He had to press forward, to stay out of the bogs and get to the heart of the forest. Groping uncertainly through the dark, stooping every other moment to touch the packed earth of the trail, he took a few steps.		The man is in a dark, swampy forest. He is frightened and uncertain and is being chased.

ANALYZE PLOT STRUCTURE

When two plots share equal time and importance in a story, they are called **parallel plots**. A story with this structure moves back and forth between the plots. In "The Night Face Up," the author uses parallel plots that develop alongside each other and share a main character. As you read this story, use the questions below to analyze the parallel plots.

- How does the parallel plot structure create **tension**, or a sense of anxious anticipation?

- What is the **tone** of each plot? Are the tones similar or different?

- What is the **pace**, or speed, of each plot? Does the action of each plot move at the same or different paces?

- How does the author **bridge**, or connect, the two plots so that the story flows smoothly from one plot line to the other?

GENRE ELEMENTS: SHORT STORY

- includes the four basic elements of fiction—setting, characters, plot, and theme

- may use a nonlinear or disrupted plot structure, such as parallel plots

- can be read in one sitting

The Night Face Up 91

QUICK START

Have students read the Quick Start prompt and discuss feelings resulting from vivid dreams with a partner. Invite pairs to share any feelings they had in common with the class. Then discuss connections between dreams and reality as a class.

MAKE INFERENCES

Remind students that understanding a story's events, characters, and settings involves not only analyzing what the text says explicitly, but also making inferences, or logical assumptions based on text evidence and their own knowledge and experience. Work with students to identify words and phrases in the evidence given in the chart that supports the inference. For example, *moved his arm carefully* and *making wisecracks* support the inference that the people who are taking care of the main character are happy and competent.

■ English Learner Support

Make Inferences Have students review a selection they've recently read and practice making inferences about the setting. Ask questions such as: Where and when does the story take place? How do you know? What details give you clues about the setting? **MODERATE**

ANALYZE PLOT STRUCTURE

Explain that parallel plots share equal importance and, generally, equal space in a story. Point out that "The Night Face Up" is structured so that parallel plots mirror each other, with the narration shifting back and forth between the two plots. Consider having students use a two-column chart with a column for each story to take notes about the tension, tone, and pace of each plot and on how the plots are connected.

CRITICAL VOCABULARY

Encourage students to read both answer choices before choosing the correct one.

Answers:

1. *b. a home-cooked meal*

2. *b. follow directions*

3. *a. donating supplies to a shelter*

4. *a. a religious leader*

5. *a. frosted glass*

■ English Learner Support

Use Cognates Tell students that one of the Critical Vocabulary words has a Spanish cognate: *lucid/lúcido.*
ALL LEVELS

LANGUAGE CONVENTIONS

Review the information about complex sentences with students. Read aloud the example sentence, pausing after the dependent clause to reinforce that it cannot stand alone as a complete sentence. Then read aloud the independent clause and ask students whether they think it can stand alone as a complete sentence and why.

Ask students how the dependent clause connects with ideas in the independent clause. *(The information in the dependent clause explains why is was "too late for a simple solution.")*

✎ ANNOTATION MODEL

Draw students' attention to the Annotation Model showing one reader's analysis of the story's shift in setting and tone. Point out that they may follow this model or use their own system for marking up the selection in their write-in text. They may want to color-code their annotations by using highlighters. Their notes in the margin may include questions about ideas that are unclear or topics they want to learn more about.

◎ **GET READY**

CRITICAL VOCABULARY

To preview the vocabulary words, choose the best answer to each question.

1. Which of the following might give you a feeling of **solace**?
   a. a difficult homework assignment
   b. a home-cooked meal

2. Which of the following describes something a **lucid** person might do?
   a. hallucinate
   b. follow directions

3. Which of the following is a **beneficent** act?
   a. donating supplies to a shelter
   b. throwing away a recyclable bottle

4. Which person has the authority to **consecrate** something?
   a. a religious leader
   b. a healthcare professional

5. Which of the following describes something that is **translucent**?
   a. frosted glass
   b. a cement wall

LANGUAGE CONVENTIONS

A **complex sentence** has an independent clause and one or more dependent clauses. An independent clause can stand alone as a sentence; a dependent, or subordinate, clause cannot. Complex sentences like the one below from the story show the relationship between ideas or events:

<u>When he saw that the woman standing on the corner had rushed into the crosswalk while he still had the green light,</u> it was already somewhat too late for a simple solution.

In the example text, the dependent clause is underlined twice and the independent clause is underlined once. This complex sentence reflects the character's thought process.

Cortázar also uses sentence fragments and run-on sentences to reflect the character's thoughts. As you read, look for complex sentences, run-ons, and fragments and consider the effect these have on style and flow.

ANNOTATION MODEL   **NOTICE & NOTE**

As you read, notice how the story moves between the two parallel plots and make notes about the tone, pace, and tension in each. In the model, you can see one reader's response to the first transition between plots in "The Night Face Up."

A woman's hands were arranging his head, he felt that they were moving him from one <u>stretcher</u> to another. The <u>man in white</u> came over to him again, <u>smiling</u>, something gleamed in his right hand. He <u>patted his cheek</u> and made a sign to someone stationed behind.

It was unusual as a dream because it was full of smells, and he never dreamt smells. First a <u>marshy smell</u>, there to the left of the trail the swamps began already, <u>the quaking bogs from which no one ever returned.</u>

> He is in a hospital. People are taking care of him. The tone is reassuring.
>
> He is dreaming of being in a jungle. The tone has an anxious edge.

BACKGROUND

Julio Cortázar *(1914–1984) was an Argentine teacher, novelist, and short-story writer. A vocal opponent of the Argentinian government, Cortázar fled to Paris in 1951, where he remained until his death. He is best known for deftly weaving fantasy, hallucinations, and dreams into his fiction, as he does in this story. The Aztec sacrifice alluded to in this work was an important part of Aztec religious life. Human victims were usually prisoners of war or slaves; their sacrifice was thought to appease the gods and to make the gods stronger.*

NOTICE & NOTE ✏

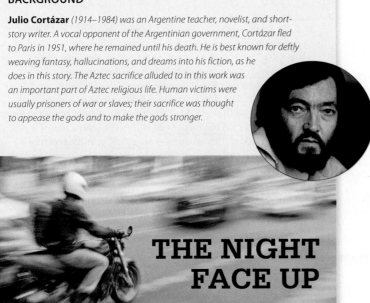

THE NIGHT FACE UP

Short Story by Julio Cortázar
translated by Paul Blackburn

SETTING A PURPOSE

As you read, pay attention to the details that help you develop a mental image of the story's two cultural and historical settings.

And at certain periods they went out to hunt enemies; they called it the war of the blossom.*

1   Halfway down the long hotel vestibule,[1] he thought that probably he was going to be late, and hurried on into the street to get out his motorcycle from the corner where the next-door superintendent let him keep it. On the jewelry store at the corner he read that it was ten to nine; he had time to spare. The sun filtered through the tall downtown buildings, and he—because for himself, for just going along thinking, he did not have a name—he swung onto the machine, savoring the idea of the ride. The motor whirred between his legs, and a cool wind whipped his pantslegs.

---
* The war of the blossom was the name the Aztecs gave to a ritual war in which they took prisoners for sacrifice. It is metaphysics to say that the gods see men as flowers, to be so uprooted, trampled, cut down. –Ed. [Cortázar's note]
[1] **vestibule:** a hall or entryway next to a building's exterior door.

Notice & Note

You can use the side margins to notice and note signposts in the text.

BACKGROUND

Have students read the Background note. Add that Julio Cortázar also wrote under the pseudonym Julio Denis. He was a citizen of both Argentina and France. Explain that Cortázar's interest in fantasy and the supernatural was nurtured when he was a child and first read stories by Edgar Allan Poe.

SETTING A PURPOSE

Direct students to use the Setting a Purpose prompt to focus their reading.

EL **ENGLISH LEARNER SUPPORT**

Expand Reading Skills Pair English learners with proficient English speakers. Have students mark this page and all subsequent pages of the story:

- Mark the first line when events take place in the time of the Aztecs.
- Mark the first line when events take place during modern times.

Ask students what items or places mentioned on the first page of the story show that these events take place during modern times. *(hotel, motorcycle, jewelry store, downtown buildings, machine, motor)* **ALL LEVELS**

ANALYZE PLOT STRUCTURE

Remind students that **setting** is the time and place of the action of a story. Explain that **tone** is a writer's attitude toward a place, character, or event. Examples of words used to describe tone include *serious, sarcastic,* or *humorous.*
(Answer: *The details convey a relaxed, peaceful tone, until the woman rushes into the street. The reader knows this because the character is enjoying the familiar sights and sensations of his ride.)*

For **reading support** for students at varying proficiency levels, see the **Text X-Ray** on page 90D.

■ English Learner Support

Learn Spelling Rules Display the word *lucid*. Explain *-ly* is added to the end of the adjective to make it an adverb: *lucidly*. Provide a sample sentence, such as: He smelled smoke and lucidly decided to call 911. Provide examples of regular adverbs, such as *slowly, quickly,* and *sadly*. Make sure students know that not all words follow this rule. Then have students practice adding *-ly* to make other regular adverbs with words such as *bad, clear,* and *calm*.
SUBSTANTIAL

CRITICAL VOCABULARY

solace: The man feels relieved and takes comfort in knowing that the accident wasn't his fault.

ASK STUDENTS why the man's only solace is knowing that he is not at fault. *(The man is in pain, his motorcycle is wrecked, and his day is ruined, so his only comfort is knowing that he's not responsible for the accident.)*

lucid: The man is able to think clearly after the accident even though he isn't well.

ASK STUDENTS What signs show the man is lucid? *(He can think clearly enough to understand what has happened to him and to provide information to the officer.)*

ANALYZE PLOT STRUCTURE
Annotate: Mark several details in paragraph 2 that help establish the setting of the first parallel plot.

Cite Evidence: Based on these details, how would you describe the tone of this part of the story? Cite evidence in your answer.

solace
(sŏl´ ĭs) *n.* source of relief and comfort.

lucid
(loo´sĭd) *adj.* thinking rationally and clearly.

2   He let the ministries[2] zip past (the pink, the white), and a series of stores on the main street, their windows flashing. Now he was beginning the most pleasant part of the run, the real ride: a long street bordered with trees, very little traffic, with spacious villas whose gardens rambled all the way down to the sidewalks, which were barely indicated by low hedges. A bit inattentive perhaps, but tooling along on the right side of the street, he allowed himself to be carried away by the freshness, by the weightless contraction of this hardly begun day. This involuntary relaxation, possibly, kept him from preventing the accident. When he saw that the woman standing on the corner had rushed into the crosswalk while he still had the green light, it was already somewhat too late for a simple solution. He braked hard with foot and hand, wrenching himself to the left; he heard the woman scream, and at the collision his vision went. It was like falling asleep all at once.

3   He came to abruptly. Four or five young men were getting him out from under the cycle. He felt the taste of salt and blood, one knee hurt, and when they hoisted him up he yelped, he couldn't bear the pressure on his right arm. Voices which did not seem to belong to the faces hanging above him encouraged him cheerfully with jokes and assurances. His single **solace** was to hear someone else confirm that the lights indeed had been in his favor. He asked about the woman, trying to keep down the nausea which was edging up into his throat. While they carried him face up to a nearby pharmacy, he learned that the cause of the accident had gotten only a few scrapes on the legs, "Nah, you barely got her at all, but when ya hit, the impact made the machine jump and flop on its side . . ." Opinions, recollections of other smashups, take it easy, work him in shoulders first, there, that's fine, and someone in a dust coat giving him a swallow of something soothing in the shadowy interior of the small local pharmacy.

4   Within five minutes the police ambulance arrived, and they lifted him onto a cushioned stretcher. It was a relief for him to be able to lie out flat. Completely **lucid**, but realizing that he was suffering the effects of a terrible shock, he gave his information to the officer riding in the ambulance with him. The arm almost didn't hurt; blood dripped down from a cut over the eyebrow all over his face. He licked his lips once or twice to drink it. He felt pretty good, it had been an accident, tough luck; stay quiet a few weeks, nothing worse. The guard said that the motorcycle didn't seem badly racked up, "Why should it," he replied. "It all landed on top of me." They both laughed, and when they got to the hospital, the guard shook his hand and wished him luck. Now the nausea was coming back little by little; meanwhile they were pushing him on a wheeled stretcher toward a pavilion further back, rolling along under trees full of birds, he shut

---
[2] **ministries:** government offices.

IMPROVE READING FLUENCY

Targeted Passage Use echo reading to help students use appropriate phrasing and emphasis. Begin by reading paragraph 3 aloud, emphasizing pauses and phrasing. Then have students echo your reading as you read it a second time, first by pausing after each phrase or clause and then reading it again with pauses after each sentence. Conclude by having students read the paragraph aloud together.

Go to the **Reading Studio** for additional support in developing fluency.

his eyes and wished he were asleep or chloroformed.[3] But they kept him for a good while in a room with that hospital smell, filling out a form, getting his clothes off, and dressing him in a stiff, grayish smock. They moved his arm carefully, it didn't hurt him. The nurses were constantly making wisecracks, and if it hadn't been for the stomach contractions he would have felt fine, almost happy.

5   They got him over to X-ray, and twenty minutes later, with the still-damp negative lying on his chest like a black tombstone, they pushed him into surgery. Someone tall and thin in white came over and began to look at the X-rays. A woman's hands were arranging his head, he felt that they were moving him from one stretcher to another. The man in white came over to him again, smiling, something gleamed in his right hand. He patted his cheek and made a sign to someone stationed behind.

6   It was unusual as a dream because it was full of smells, and he never dreamt smells. First a marshy smell, there to the left of the trail the swamps began already, the quaking bogs from which no one ever returned. But the reek lifted, and instead there came a dark, fresh composite fragrance, like the night under which he moved, in flight from the Aztecs. And it was all so natural, he had to run from the Aztecs who had set out on their manhunt, and his sole chance was to find a place to hide in the deepest part of the forest, taking care not to lose the narrow trail which only they, the Motecas, knew.

7   What tormented him the most was the odor, as though, notwithstanding the absolute acceptance of the dream, there was something which resisted that which was not habitual, which until that point had not participated in the game. "It smells of war," he

---

[3] **chloroformed:** made unconscious by inhaling an anesthetic.

ANALYZE PLOT STRUCTURE

Annotate: Mark three details in paragraph 6 that help establish the setting and tone of the second parallel plot.

Analyze: How is the tone of the second plot different from the tone of the first plot? Cite text evidence in your answer.

 ANALYZE PLOT STRUCTURE

Help students understand descriptions related to **setting** and **tone**. Ask volunteers to describe experiences being near swamps, honing in on smells and other sensations. Then have students describe what a character being pursued might feel like. (**Answer:** *The tone of the second plot is anxious, wild, and ominous. The narrator describes earthy smells, darkness, and details about being pursued and needing to hide. It's very different from the calm and peaceful tone of the first setting.*)

EL ENGLISH LEARNER SUPPORT

Respond Orally   Pair English language learners with students fluent in English to create two-column "tone charts," with one column labeled "Calm" and the other labeled "Tense." Encourage students in each pair to take turns reading aloud the words and phrases that illustrate each type of tone—calm or tense. Have them speak in a voice that reflects the tone. For example, they might speak soothingly and in a drawn out voice when saying "enjoying the pleasure of keeping awake." When saying "horrible blast of that foul smell," they might speak brusquely in a clipped voice. Encourage students to use facial expressions when speaking as well.
MODERATE

For **listening support** for students at varying proficiency levels, see the **Text X-Ray** on page 90C.

TO CHALLENGE STUDENTS...

Analyze Point of View   Explain that each character in a story has a perspective, or point of view, about the events and the other characters. Ask students to consider what the woman or one of the men who helped the crash victim might have thought about the accident. What might their description or retelling of the accident be? Challenge students to create a short monologue in which they describe and retell the events surrounding the accident from a minor character's perspective. Alternatively, have students work in small groups to develop a skit in which each student, acting as a different character, describes the accident from that character's point of view.

TEACH

AGAIN AND AGAIN

Remind students that this signpost refers to recurring words, images, or events. Ask students what sense the author focuses on in this parallel **plot.** (*smell*) Why is this sense noteworthy in this part of the story? (*The man had never dreamt smells.*) Have students discuss what the "smell of war" in ancient times might smell like. (**Answer:** *These details tell the reader something bad is about to occur; the man may face an enemy.*)

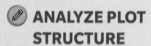 ANALYZE PLOT STRUCTURE

Remind students that the plots switch back and forth. For the story to be effective, the author includes a bridge or connector that orients each plot so that the narration flows smoothly. Parallel plots are often connected by a common character, event, or theme. The two plots usually converge in a final scene. (**Answer:** *The author uses sleep and wakefulness as the bridge between the two plots.*)

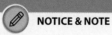 **NOTICE & NOTE**

AGAIN AND AGAIN

Notice & Note: Mark the sensory details in this paragraph that appear again and again.

Predict: How do these details change the mood and tone of this plot? What do you predict will happen next?

ANALYZE PLOT STRUCTURE

Annotate: Mark where the setting changes from the jungle to the hospital.

Analyze: How does the author bridge, or connect, the two plots so that the story flows smoothly from one plot line to the other?

---

thought, his hand going instinctively to the stone knife which was tucked at an angle into his girdle of woven wool. An unexpected sound made him crouch suddenly stock-still and shaking. To be afraid was nothing strange, there was plenty of fear in his dreams. He waited, covered by the branches of a shrub and the starless night. Far off, probably on the other side of the big lake, they'd be lighting the bivouac[4] fires; that part of the sky had a reddish glare. The sound was not repeated. It had been like a broken limb. Maybe an animal that, like himself, was escaping from the smell of war. He stood erect slowly, sniffing the air. Not a sound could be heard, but the fear was still following, as was the smell, that cloying incense of the war of the blossom. He had to press forward, to stay out of the bogs and get to the heart of the forest. Groping uncertainly through the dark, stooping every other moment to touch the packed earth of the trail, he took a few steps. He would have liked to have broken into a run, but the gurgling fens[5] lapped on either side of him. On the path and in darkness, he took his bearings. Then he caught a horrible blast of that foul smell he was most afraid of, and leaped forward desperately.

8   "You're going to fall off the bed," said the patient next to him. "Stop bouncing around, old buddy."

9   He opened his eyes and it was afternoon, the sun already low in the oversized windows of the long ward. While trying to smile at his neighbor, he detached himself almost physically from the final scene of the nightmare. His arm, in a plaster cast, hung suspended from an apparatus with weights and pulleys. He felt thirsty, as though he'd been running for miles, but they didn't want to give him much water, barely enough to moisten his lips and make a mouthful. The fever was winning slowly and he would have been able to sleep again, but he was enjoying the pleasure of keeping awake, eyes half-closed, listening to the other patients' conversation, answering a question from time to time. He saw a little white pushcart come up beside the bed, a blond nurse rubbed the front of his thigh with alcohol and stuck him with a fat needle connected to a tube which ran up to a bottle filled with a milky, opalescent liquid. A young intern arrived with some metal and leather apparatus which he adjusted to fit onto the good arm to check something or other. Night fell, and the fever went along dragging him down softly to a state in which things seemed embossed as through opera glasses,[6] they were real and soft and, at the same time, vaguely distasteful; like sitting in a boring movie and thinking that, well, still, it'd be worse out in the street, and staying.

10   A cup of a marvelous golden broth came, smelling of leeks, celery, and parsley. A small hunk of bread, more precious than a

---

[4] **bivouac:** a temporary camp.
[5] **fens:** wet, swampy land.
[6] **opera glasses:** small binoculars.

96   Unit 2

APPLYING ACADEMIC VOCABULARY

☑ **differentiate**   ☐ **incorporate**   ☐ **mode**   ☑ **orient**   ☑ **perspective**

Have students turn to a partner to discuss the following questions. Guide students to include the academic vocabulary words *differentiate, orient,* and *perspective* in their responses. Ask volunteers to share their responses with the class.

- What text details help readers **differentiate** between each plot?
- Why is it difficult for the narrator to **orient** himself?
- From whose **perspective** is the story told?

whole banquet, found itself crumbling little by little. His arm hardly hurt him at all, and only in the eyebrow where they'd taken stitches a quick, hot pain sizzled occasionally. (When the big windows across the way turned to smudges of dark blue,) he thought it would not be difficult for him to sleep. Still on his back so a little uncomfortable, running his tongue out over his hot, too-dry lips, he tasted the broth still, and with a sigh of bliss, he let himself drift off.

11   First there was a confusion, as of one drawing all his sensations, for that moment blunted or muddled, into himself. He realized that he was running in pitch darkness, although, above, the sky criss-crossed with treetops was less black than the rest. "The trail," he thought, "I've gotten off the trail." His feet sank into a bed of leaves and mud, and then he couldn't take a step that the branches of shrubs did not whiplash against his ribs and legs. Out of breath, knowing despite the darkness and silence that he was surrounded, he crouched down to listen. Maybe the trail was very near, with the first daylight he would be able to see it again. Nothing now could help him to find it. The hand that had unconsciously gripped the haft of the dagger climbed like a fen scorpion up to his neck where the protecting amulet[7] hung. Barely moving his lips, he mumbled the supplication of the corn which brings about the **beneficent** moons, and the prayer to Her Very Highness, to the distributor of all Motecan possessions. At the same time he felt his ankles sinking deeper into the mud, and the waiting in the darkness of the obscure grove of live oak grew intolerable to him. The war of the blossom had started at the beginning of the moon and had been going on for three days and three nights now. If he managed to hide in the depths of the forest, getting off the trail further up past the marsh country, perhaps the warriors wouldn't follow his track. He thought of the many prisoners they'd already taken. But the number didn't count, only the **consecrated** period. The hunt would continue until the priests gave the sign to return. Everything had its number and its limit, and it was within the sacred period, and he on the other side from the hunters.

12   He heard the cries and leaped up, knife in hand. As if the sky were aflame on the horizon, he saw torches moving among the branches, very near him. The smell of war was unbearable, and when the first enemy jumped him, leaped at his throat, he felt an almost-pleasure in sinking the stone blade flat to the haft into his chest. The lights were already around him, the happy cries. He managed to cut the air once or twice, then a rope snared him from behind.

13   "It's the fever," the man in the next bed said. "The same thing happened to me when they operated on my duodenum.[8] Take some water, you'll see, you'll sleep all right."

---

[7] **amulet:** a charm or necklace believed to have protective powers.
[8] **duodenum (dōō-ə-dē´nəm):** part of the small intestine.

LANGUAGE CONVENTIONS
Annotate: Place brackets around the second-to-last sentence in paragraph 10. Underline the independent clause within this sentence. Then circle the dependent, or subordinate clause.

Analyze: How are the ideas in the independent and subordinate clauses related in this sentence?

beneficent
(bə-nĕf´ĭ-sənt) *adj.* beneficial; producing good.

consecrate
(kŏn´sĭ-krāt) *v.* to make or define as sacred.

LANGUAGE CONVENTIONS

Remind students that a **complex sentence** consists of an independent clause and one or more dependent clauses. The independent clause can stand alone as a complete sentence; the dependent clause cannot. In this example, the dependent clause gives context for the independent clause. (**Answer:** *The dependent clause explains when the protagonist thinks he will be able to sleep.*)

CRITICAL VOCABULARY

beneficent: The man mumbles words and prayers that he hopes will bring about the moons that will be beneficial to him.

ASK STUDENTS in what way the man thinks moons might be beneficent. (*He may think that certain phases of the moon bring good luck or help crops grow.*)

consecrate: The manhunt could only take place during the period that was defined as sacred.

ASK STUDENTS who determines the consecrated period and why. (*The priests determine the period, because they decide what is sacred.*)

ANALYZE PLOT STRUCTURE

Point out to students that the **pace** is the rate or speed at which a story progresses. Various techniques can be used to speed up or slow down the pace. For example, an author might use shorter sentences, brief descriptions, and more action to create a fast pace. Conversely, the author could use longer sentences, longer descriptions, and less action to create a slower pace. Explain that as a story advances to its climax, or point of ultimate dramatic tension, the pace often quickens. (**Answer:** *The pace of this plot is slow, steady, and predictable. The protagonist moves very little; he spends time recalling what happened.*)

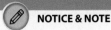

NOTICE & NOTE

ANALYZE PLOT STRUCTURE

Annotate: Mark the physical actions that the main character takes in paragraph 14.

Evaluate: Based on these details, how would you describe the pace, or speed, of the plot that takes place in the hospital? Cite evidence from the text in your answer.

14   Laid next to the night from which he came back, the tepid shadow of the ward seemed delicious to him. A violet lamp kept watch high on the far wall like a guardian eye. You could hear coughing, deep breathing, once in a while a conversation in whispers. Everything was pleasant and secure, without the chase, no . . . But he didn't want to go on thinking about the nightmare. There were lots of things to amuse himself with. He began to look at the cast on his arm, and the pulleys that held it so comfortably in the air. They'd left a bottle of mineral water on the night table beside him. He put the neck of the bottle to his mouth and drank it like a precious liqueur. He could now make out the different shapes in the ward, the thirty beds, the closets with glass doors. He guessed that his fever was down, his face felt cool. The cut over the eyebrow barely hurt at all, like a recollection. He saw himself leaving the hotel again, wheeling out the cycle. Who'd have thought that it would end like this? He tried to fix the moment of the accident exactly, and it got him very angry to notice that there was a void there, an emptiness he could not manage to fill. Between the impact and the moment that they picked him up off the pavement, the passing out or what went on, there was nothing he could see. And at the same time he had the feeling that this void, this nothingness, had lasted an eternity. No, not even time, more as if, in this void, he had passed across something, or had run back immense distances. The shock, the brutal dashing against the pavement. Anyway, he had felt an immense relief in coming out of the black pit while the people were lifting him off the ground. With pain in the broken arm, blood from the split eyebrow, contusion on the knee; with all that, a relief in returning to daylight, to the day, and to feel sustained and attended. That was weird. Someday he'd ask the doctor at the office about that. Now sleep began to take over again, to pull him slowly down. The pillow was so soft, and the coolness of the mineral water in his fevered throat. The violet light of the lamp up there was beginning to get dimmer and dimmer.

15   As he was sleeping on his back, the position in which he came to did not surprise him, but on the other hand the damp smell, the smell of oozing rock, blocked his throat and forced him to understand. Open the eyes and look in all directions, hopeless. He was surrounded by an absolute darkness. Tried to get up and felt ropes pinning his wrists and ankles. He was staked to the ground on a floor of dank, icy stone slabs. The cold bit into his naked back, his legs. Dully, he tried to touch the amulet with his chin and found they had stripped him of it. Now he was lost, no prayer could save him from the final . . . From afar off, as though filtering through the rock of the dungeon, he heard the great kettledrums of the feast. They had carried him to the temple, he was in the underground cells of Teocalli[9] itself, awaiting his turn.

---

[9] **Teocalli** (tē´ə-kăl´ē): an ancient Mexican terraced pyramid and temple.

16   He heard a yell, a hoarse yell that rocked off the walls. Another yell, ending in a moan. It was he who was screaming in the darkness, he was screaming because he was alive, his whole body with that cry fended off what was coming, the inevitable end. He thought of his friends filling up the other dungeons, and of those already walking up the stairs of the sacrifice. He uttered another choked cry, he could barely open his mouth, his jaws were twisted back as if with a rope and a stick, and once in a while they would open slowly with an endless exertion, as if they were made of rubber. The creaking of the wooden latches jolted him like a whip. Rent, writhing, he fought to rid himself of the cords sinking into his flesh. His right arm, the strongest, strained until the pain became unbearable and he had to give up. He watched the double door open, and the smell of the torches reached him before the light did. Barely girdled by the ceremonial loincloths, the priests' acolytes[10] moved in his direction, looking at him with contempt. Lights reflected off the sweaty torsos and off the black hair dressed with feathers. The cords went slack, and in their place the grappling of hot hands, hard as bronze; he felt himself lifted, still face up, and jerked along by the four acolytes who carried him down the passageway. The torchbearers went ahead, indistinctly lighting up the corridor with its dripping walls and a ceiling so low that the acolytes had to duck their heads. Now they

---

[10]**acolytes:** people who assist in religious services.

MAKE INFERENCES

Annotate: In paragraph 16, mark three historical and cultural details that help develop the setting of the Aztec plot.

Infer: Based on the details you marked, how would you describe the historical period and the culture of the Aztecs? Cite evidence in your answer.

The Night Face Up   99

 MAKE INFERENCES

Remind students that **inferences** are logical guesses based on clues in the text and on the students' prior knowledge. Point out that details about the objects in the scene, such as wooden latches, ceremonial loincloths, and torchbearers, allow the reader to infer that an ancient ritual is taking place. (**Answer:** *The forbidding rituals seem to be an important part of the culture and time. The ceremony has clearly happened before.*)

 ENGLISH LEARNER SUPPORT

Monitor Understanding Support students in making inferences about the setting. Read aloud paragraph 16, pausing after each event to have students retell it in their own words. Encourage students to seek clarification as needed to confirm understanding.

- (*man finds himself in a cold, dark place unable to move*)
- (*man screams and thinks of friends being sacrificed*)
- (*doors open and people approach the struggling man*)
- (*man is carried down a passageway*)

Ask students to make an inference about the setting. Provide this sentence frame as needed: *The Aztec setting is _____.* **MODERATE/LIGHT**

WHEN STUDENTS STRUGGLE . . .

Analyze Plot Structure To help students understand how the plots converge, have students use a plot sequence chart like the one below to record and analyze the series of events at the end of the story.

| The man discovers he's in an Aztec dungeon. | → | | → | |

 For additional support, go to the **Reading Studio** and assign the following **Level Up Tutorial: Plot: Sequence of Events.**

AHA MOMENT

Tell students that this signpost occurs when a **character** realizes or finally understands something. In the final scene, the two plots converge. Ask students to identify words and phrases that signal an Aha Moment. *(For a second he thought he had gotten there...But...he knew now...)*
(**Answer:** *The character realizes that he is going to die. The final scene suggests that the Aztec plot was reality, and the modern plot was a dream.)*

CRITICAL VOCABULARY

translucent: The bottle of water on the night table makes a semi-transparent and indistinct figure.

ASK STUDENTS why the translucent shape of the bottle stands out. *(The shadow is dark; the bottle of water allows some light to show through it.)*

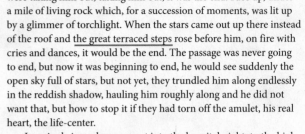

NOTICE & NOTE

translucent
(trăns-lōō´sənt) *adj.* semi-transparent; indistinct.

> **AHA MOMENT**
>
> **Notice & Note:** What does the main character suddenly realize in the second half of paragraph 17? Mark at least two clues in the text.
>
> **Infer:** What does this realization suggest about the man's fate?

were taking him out, taking him out, it was the end. Face up, under a mile of living rock which, for a succession of moments, was lit up by a glimmer of torchlight. When the stars came out up there instead of the roof and the great terraced steps rose before him, on fire with cries and dances, it would be the end. The passage was never going to end, but now it was beginning to end, he would see suddenly the open sky full of stars, but not yet, they trundled him along endlessly in the reddish shadow, hauling him roughly along and he did not want that, but how to stop it if they had torn off the amulet, his real heart, the life-center.

17   In a single jump he came out into the hospital night, to the high, gentle, bare ceiling, to the soft shadow wrapping him round. He thought he must have cried out, but his neighbors were peacefully snoring. The water in the bottle on the night table was somewhat bubbly, a **translucent** shape against the dark azure shadow of the windows. He panted, looking for some relief for his lungs, oblivion for those images still glued to his eyelids. Each time he shut his eyes he saw them take shape instantly, and he sat up, completely wrung out, but savoring at the same time the surety that now he was awake, that the night nurse would answer if he rang, that soon it would be daybreak, with the good, deep sleep he usually had at that hour, no images, no nothing . . . It was difficult to keep his eyes open, the drowsiness was more powerful than he. He made one last effort, he sketched a gesture toward the bottle of water with his good hand and did not manage to reach it, his fingers closed again on a black emptiness, and the passageway went on endlessly, rock after rock, with momentary ruddy flares, and face up he choked out a dull moan because the roof was about to end, it rose, was opening like a mouth of shadow, and the acolytes straightened up, and from on high a waning moon fell on a face whose eyes wanted not to see it, were closing and opening desperately, trying to pass to the other side, to find again the bare, protecting ceiling of the ward. And every time they opened, it was night and the moon, while they climbed the great terraced steps, his head hanging down backward now, and up at the top were the bonfires, red columns of perfumed smoke, and suddenly he saw the red stone, shiny with the blood dripping off it, and the spinning arcs cut by the feet of the victim whom they pulled off to throw him rolling down the north steps. With a last hope he shut his lids tightly, moaning to wake up. For a second he thought he had gotten there, because once more he was immobile in the bed, except that his head was hanging down off it, swinging. But he smelled death, and when he opened his eyes he saw the blood-soaked figure of the executioner-priest coming toward him with the stone knife in his hand. He managed to close his eyelids again, although

---

WHEN STUDENTS STRUGGLE . . .

Analyze Details   Have students work in pairs and use dictionaries to define descriptive phrases the author uses to develop the historical setting. Have each pair write the meanings of the phrases and a sentence using each phrase in a chart.

Phrase	Meaning	Sentence
waning moon		
terraced steps		

 For additional support, go to the **Reading Studio** and assign the following [LEVEL] **Level Up Tutorial: Reading for Details.**

he knew now he was not going to wake up, that he was awake, that the marvelous dream had been the other, absurd as all dreams are—a dream in which he was going through the strange avenues of an astonishing city, with green and red lights that burned without fire or smoke, on an enormous metal insect that whirred away between his legs. In the infinite lie of the dream, they had also picked him off the ground, someone had approached him also with a knife in his hand, approached him who was lying face up, face up with his eyes closed between the bonfires on the steps.

CHECK YOUR UNDERSTANDING

Answer these questions before moving on to the **Analyze the Text** section on the following page.

1 The story's parallel plots concern —

A a modern hospital and an Aztec ritual

B a pedestrian and a motorcyclist

C the two sides of an ancient war

D a busy city and a beautiful jungle

2 Which of the following is a similarity the two plots share?

F A sense of fear and concern hangs over all of the events.

G The protagonist is lying on his back while others control his fate.

H Despite his difficulties, the protagonist is optimistic about his future.

J It is entirely the protagonist's fault that he is in a dire situation.

3 What seems to be true of the protagonist at the end of the story?

A He will make a full recovery from his motorcycle accident.

B He lives in Aztec times and is going to be sacrificed.

C He will continue to suffer from nightmares as a result of the accident.

D He is living simultaneously in two different realities.

The Night Face Up   101

CHECK YOUR UNDERSTANDING

Have students answer the questions independently.

Answers:

1. *A*

2. *G*

3. *B*

If they answer any questions incorrectly, have them reread the text to confirm their understanding. Then they may proceed to ANALYZE THE TEXT on page 102.

 ENGLISH LEARNER SUPPORT

Oral Assessment Use the following questions to assess students' comprehension and speaking skills.

1. Where do the story's two plots take place? *(in a modern city and an Aztec jungle)*

2. What do the two plots have in common? *(The character is lying on his back, while other people control what happens to him.)*

3. What do you learn about the character at the end of the story? *(He lives in Aztec times and is going to be killed.)* **ALL LEVELS**

APPLY

ANALYZE THE TEXT

Possible answers:

1. **DOK 4** *Beginning the narrative with the plot about the motorcycle accident suggests that this plot is the reality not the dream. This heightens the surprise a reader may feel at the end of the story.*

2. **DOK 4** *Cortázar echoes this scene in the second plot when the priest approaches the man with a knife in his hand (paragraph 17). This mode of narration ties the two plots together, and increases the reader's interest in how they are connected.*

3. **DOK 3** *In the manhunt plot, the smells include dampness and oozing rock (paragraph 15), which are unpleasant. In the motorcycle accident plot, the smells are pleasing, such as the smell of leeks, celery, and parsley in the broth (paragraph 10). The difference in smells affects the tone of each plot by making the accident plot seem comforting and safe while the manhunt is foreboding and dangerous.*

4. **DOK 2** *At the beginning of the story, the protagonist is in control as he rides his motorcycle. He becomes injured and no longer has as much control as he did, but the reader still perceives him to be safe (paragraphs 4–5, 9–10). As the story moves forward, the protagonist is revealed to be hunted and less safe. By the end of the story, the reader learns that the protagonist has no control and is about to lose his life (paragraph 17).*

5. **DOK 4** *At one point, the narrator realizes he does not remember the moment of the accident (paragraph 14). At the end of the story, the narrator realizes that the hospital is a dream, while the Aztec sacrifice is reality. These moments suggest his mental struggle; he wants to hold on to the hospital reality but eventually has no choice but to accept that it is only a dream.*

RESEARCH

Remind students to confirm any information they find by checking multiple websites and assessing the credibility of each one.

Extend Invite students to share information they discover about Aztec games and leisure activities. Discuss similarities and differences between games and leisure activities enjoyed today.

ANALYZE THE TEXT

Support your responses with evidence from the text. NOTEBOOK

1. **Analyze** Cortázar begins the narrative with the plot concerning the motorcycle accident rather than the one about the manhunt. Why is this choice an effective way to structure the story?

2. **Evaluate** The author structures the story so that the parallel plots mirror each other. For example, the author describes a scene in which the protagonist is x-rayed, taken to surgery, and approached by a doctor. Where in the second plot does the author echo this scene? What is the effect of this mode of narration?

3. **Compare** In both plots, the author frequently refers to smells. Explain how the descriptions of smells differ in each plot. How do these differences affect the tone of each plot?

4. **Infer** The protagonist is never named, but his reality and his ongoing dream make up the parallel plots of the story. How does the reader's perception of the protagonist change throughout the story? Cite text evidence to support your ideas.

5. **Notice & Note** Identify two moments in "The Night Face Up" when the main character has a realization. What do these Aha Moments suggest about the man's changing state of mind and his lucidity?

RESEARCH

RESEARCH TIP
Be sure to document the sources you use in order to give proper credit to the people who created them and to avoid plagiarism. Depending on the type of source you use, the elements of a source citation may include the title, the author's name, the publisher's name and location, date of publication or creation, URL, and page numbers.

Ancient Aztec culture was highly developed. It included sophisticated cities, complex religious beliefs, and advances in math, science, and the arts. With a partner, conduct research to learn more about ancient Aztec culture. Record what you learn in the chart.

ASPECT OF AZTEC CULTURE	DETAILS
architecture	*Basic tools were used to construct sophisticated cities.*
education	*Education happened in the home and in organized schools.*
arts	*The Aztecs were skilled with metal and ceramics.*
economy	*Trading was part of the Aztec economy.*

Extend Conduct additional research on Aztec culture to learn about games and leisure activities. Are any of the games and activities that you discovered still enjoyed today?

LEARNING MINDSET

Problem Solving If students get stuck when trying to respond to the Analyze the Text questions, encourage them to apply problem-solving strategies as they work through the questions. For example, students might consider the first question from a different angle by asking themselves what inferences they might have made about the story if it began with the Aztec plot. How might this difference in plot structure have impacted their response to the story's ending? Considering the question from this angle can help students draw conclusions about the effectiveness of the plot structure the author used.

CREATE AND DISCUSS

Write an Analysis Write a one-page analysis of the story's **theme**, or central message about human nature or the human experience. Include information about how this theme is conveyed through the different story elements. Review your notes and annotations in the text before you begin.

- ❏ Introduce your analysis by revealing the theme.
- ❏ In the body of your analysis, describe how the theme is conveyed through the characters, plot, imagery, tone, and setting. Include specific details from the text to support your ideas.
- ❏ In your conclusion, remind readers of the theme and leave them with something to think about.

Discuss Opinions With a small group, discuss the ending of "The Night Face Up." Is the Aztec setting "real," or could it just be a dream?

- ❏ As a group, review the story, paying particular attention to the places where the story shifts from one plot to another and to the final paragraph.
- ❏ Then discuss whether the Aztec setting is real or a dream, using story details for support. As you discuss, listen closely to one another and ask questions to help clarify ideas.
- ❏ Finally, end the discussion by listing the opinion of each member in your group.

RESPOND TO THE ESSENTIAL QUESTION

 How does our point of view shape what we think we know?

Gather Information Review your annotations and notes on "The Night Face Up." Then, add relevant information to your Response Log. As you determine which information to include, think about:

- the protagonist's attitude about life when he is in the hospital setting
- how this point of view changes during the manhunt
- how your point of view shapes your ideas about what is real and what is a dream in the story

At the end of the unit, use your notes to help you write a short story.

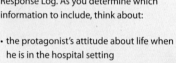

RESPOND

Go to the **Writing Studio** for help in using textual evidence in your analysis.

Go to the **Speaking and Listening Studio** for help with having a group discussion.

ACADEMIC VOCABULARY
As you write and discuss what you learned about "The Night Face Up," be sure to use the Academic Vocabulary words. Check off each of the words that you use.

- ❏ **differentiate**
- ❏ **incorporate**
- ❏ **mode**
- ❏ **orient**
- ❏ **perspective**

CREATE AND DISCUSS

Write an Analysis Have students review their notes and annotations to help them determine a theme, or message about human nature or the human experience that might apply to the story. As they write their analyses, remind students to clearly explain how the text details and examples they include connect to and support their ideas about the story's theme. When students have finished, invite them to share their analyses with the class.

For **writing support** for students at varying proficiency levels, see the **Text X-Ray** on page 90D.

Discuss Opinions Provide students with questions to generate discussion, such as: At what point in the story did you decide that the setting is real or a dream? Do you think the author wants the reader to feel certain about which plot is real? Remind students to cite text evidence to support their opinions. Then have them share their views with the class as a whole. Accept all reasonable responses.

For **speaking support** for students at varying proficiency levels, see the **Text X-Ray** on page 90D.

■ English Learner Support

Understand Spoken Language After students listen to peers speak, provide them with a frame, such as the following, to help them express what they heard: _____ _thinks that the Aztec setting is (real/a dream) because _____._
SUBSTANTIAL

RESPOND TO THE ESSENTIAL QUESTION

Allow time for students to add details from "The Night Face Up" to their Unit 2 Response Logs.

APPLY

CRITICAL VOCABULARY

Possible answers:

1. *I visited a temple. I could tell that it was a sacred,* <u>consecrated</u> *place because it had many religious symbols and an awe-inspiring feel.*

2. *I sought* <u>solace</u> *after the death of my pet. I was very upset and needed some comfort.*

3. *I can tell someone is not completely* <u>lucid</u> *if their eyes are half-closed and what they are saying doesn't make sense.*

4. *I behaved in a* <u>beneficent</u> *manner when I woke up early and made breakfast for my family last Saturday. I even did the dishes afterward. Everyone benefited from having a tasty breakfast.*

5. *A* <u>translucent</u> *material might be used for curtains in my living room. It prevents people outside from seeing inside but still lets light in.*

VOCABULARY STRATEGY:
Denotation and Connotation

Answers:

reek denotation: *an overpowering smell of something rotting or unsafe*

reek connotation: *strongly negative*

fragrance denotation: *a pleasant, sweet smell*

fragrance connotation: *positive; enjoyable*

odor denotation: *a distinctive smell*

odor connotation: *neutral or slightly negative*

 RESPOND

WORD BANK
solace
lucid
beneficent
consecrate
translucent

 Go to the **Vocabulary Studio** for more on connotation and denotation.

CRITICAL VOCABULARY

Practice and Apply Answer each question in a complete sentence that demonstrates your understanding of the meaning of each Critical Vocabulary word.

1. Have you ever visited a place or seen an item that was **consecrated**? Explain.

2. When have you sought **solace**? Why?

3. How can you tell someone is not completely **lucid**? Explain.

4. When did you behave in a **beneficent** manner? Explain.

5. Where might a **translucent** material be used in your home? Why?

VOCABULARY STRATEGY:
Denotation and Connotation

A word's literal meaning or definition is called its **denotation**. A word may also have an implied meaning, an association that evokes a particular emotion. This is the word's **connotation**. The emotions that words evoke range from positive to neutral to negative. Consider the meaning of the word *solace* in this sentence:

After a hard day, Bella went for a healing hike in the desert, where she found <u>solace</u> in the beautiful atmosphere and peaceful sounds.

The denotation of the word *solace* is "a source of relief and comfort." Finding solace in something connotes a positive feeling of relief and happiness.

Practice and Apply Find these three words in "The Night Face Up." Look up the words, and then decide on their connotations based on what you find in a dictionary or in the text. Work in a group to discuss denotation and connotation. Record the words and your group's ideas in the chart.

WORD	DENOTATION	CONNOTATION
reek (paragraph 6)		
fragrance (paragraph 6)		
odor (paragraph 7)		

 ENGLISH LEARNER SUPPORT

Vocabulary Strategy Give students additional practice in determining the denotation and connotation of other words from the text. Display the following words: *yell, moan, cry; gentle, soft, peacefully.* Have pairs of mixed proficiency levels look up the words in a dictionary and discuss the denotation and connotation of the words. Have students practice spelling the words. **ALL LEVELS**

LANGUAGE CONVENTIONS:
Complex Sentences

A **complex sentence** contains one independent, or main, clause and one or more subordinate, or dependent, clauses. The subordinate clause(s) expresses ideas that are less important than, but related to, the main idea. Here is an example from the story:

> subordinate clause
> **While they carried him face up to a nearby pharmacy, he learned that the cause of the accident had gotten only a few scrapes on the legs.**
> (paragraph 3)   independent clause

> Go to the **Grammar Studio** for more on using complex sentences.

Julio Cortázar uses complex sentences in "The Night Face Up" for a variety of purposes and effects:

- To convey the narrator's frantic, worried situation:

    If he managed to hide in the depths of the forest, getting off the trail further up past the marsh country, perhaps the warriors wouldn't follow his track. (paragraph 11)

- To show how events are related in time and to create suspense:

    When the stars came out up there instead of the roof and the great terraced steps rose before him, on fire with cries and dances, it would be the end. (paragraph 16)

Good writers may also deliberately use incorrect sentence structures to achieve certain effects:

- A **sentence fragment** is a part of a sentence that is punctuated as if it were a complete sentence. Sentence fragments are often used in stories to make dialogue sound authentic.
- There are two kinds of **run-on sentences**. In the first, two or more sentences are run together without any punctuation marks to separate them. In the second, the writer uses a comma instead of a period between sentences. This second type of run-on is called a **comma splice**. Run-on sentences, used sparingly, can create a sense of frantic urgency, an effect Cortázar achieves in this story.

Practice and Apply Take a closer look at a piece of your own writing, such as the writing you did in response to "The Night Face Up." Revise it by combining shorter sentences to create three complex sentences. Check for and correct any fragments or run-on sentences in your work.

LANGUAGE CONVENTIONS:
Complex Sentences

Remind students that they can use complex sentences in their own writing to improve clarity, style, and sentence effectiveness. Point out that students should avoid unintentional splices, run-ons, and fragments in formal writing. Explain that a sentence fragment does not express a complete thought and may be confusing to a reader or listener. Some run-ons have missing punctuation; a comma splice is a type of run-on in which a sentence has only a comma where a conjunction or other punctuation mark is needed. Discuss the following examples:

FRAGMENT: Reached for his water glass on the table.

CORRECTED: He reached for his water glass on the table.

RUN-ON: He reached for the water glass on the table it tipped over it spilled all over the floor.

CORRECTED: As he reached for the water glass on the table, it tipped over and spilled all over the floor.

COMMA SPLICE: He reached for his water glass, it was empty.

CORRECTED: He reached for his water glass, but it was empty.

Practice and Apply Have partners review and discuss each other's revised sentences. *(Revisions will vary but should correctly incorporate complex sentences and correct any fragments or run-on sentences.)*

 ENGLISH LEARNER SUPPORT

Use Complex Sentences Use the following supports with students at varying proficiency levels:

- Read fragments, run-ons, and correct sentences aloud. Ask students to raise their hand when they hear the correct sentences. For example: *Sat down; The man sat down he was tired; The man sat down because he was tired.* **SUBSTANTIAL**

- Have students find other complex sentences in "The Night Face Up" and copy them in their notebook. Ask them to underline the dependent clause in each sentence. **MODERATE**

- Have students find a complex sentence in "The Night Face Up," and use it as a model to write their own complex sentence. Ask partners to share their sentences and identify the independent and dependent clauses. **LIGHT**

MIRROR
Poem by **Sylvia Plath**

GENRE ELEMENTS
LYRIC POETRY

Students may be surprised to identify a nonliving object as the **speaker of a poem.** Explain that this unusual choice gets readers' attention and may help readers think more carefully about the ideas that the poet presents. Encourage students to read "Mirror" to identify both its key ideas and the emotions that help make those ideas clear. In addition, remind students that **lyric poems** have a musical quality that sometimes—as in "Mirror"—is based on speech patterns, not traditional meters. You may wish to illustrate by comparing prose sentences to examples of iambic and anapestic meters.

LEARNING OBJECTIVES

- Analyze the thoughts and feelings of a poem's speaker and the figurative language that expresses a poem's ideas.
- Conduct research about figurative language in other Plath poems and create a poster to share the results.
- Write a poem that includes figurative language to explore "Mirror" from the viewpoint of a different speaker.
- Present the completed poem to a small group and then discuss physical appearance as part of a person's identity.
- **Language** Identify figurative language to help express ideas in a poem.

TEXT COMPLEXITY

Quantitative Measures	Mirror		Lexile: N/A
Qualitative Measures	**Ideas Presented** Multiple levels with use of nonliteral language and subtle meanings.		
	Structures Used Largely conventional and explicit, but presented in a free-verse format.		
	Language Used Sentences contain figurative language. Meanings are implied, but support is offered.		
	Knowledge Required Topic is easily envisioned, requiring no special knowledge.		

RESOURCES

- Unit 2 Response Log
- 🔊 Selection Audio
- 📖 Reading Studio: Notice & Note
- Level Up Tutorial: Reading for Details
- 💬 Speaking and Listening Studio: Participating in Collaborative Discussions
- ✓ "Mirror" Selection Test

SUMMARIES

English

The speaker is a mirror, which describes itself as truthful, unbiased, unaffected by emotion, and faithfully exact—in short, godlike. It spends much of its time meditating upon the wall that it faces. The mirror then introduces a woman who comes each morning to look at her reflection. The woman may want to find out "what she really is," but she prefers the softer image she presents when seen in candlelight or moonlight. What the "exact" mirror shows her upsets her deeply—namely, that her youth has faded and old age is approaching.

Spanish

La voz narrativa es un espejo, que se describe a sí mismo como honesto, imparcial, no afectado por emociones y fielmente exacto; en resumen, divino. Pasa la mayoría de su tiempo meditando sobre la pared que ve. Luego, el espejo presenta a una mujer que viene cada mañana a mirar su reflejo. La mujer puede querer descubrir "qué es ella realmente", pero prefiere la imagen suave que presenta al verse bajo la luz de una vela o de la luna. Lo que el espejo "exacto" le muestra la ofende profundamente; concretamente, que su juventud se ha desvanecido y la vejez se aproxima.

SMALL-GROUP OPTIONS

Have students work in small groups to read and discuss the selection.

Write-Around

- When students meet in groups, tell each group member to initial a sheet of paper and then write a comment or question about the poem.
- Have students pass their paper to the right.
- Instruct students to think about the comment or question they receive and then to write a brief response.
- Have students pass the papers around until everyone has written a response to each paper and has his or her paper back.
- Encourage students to incorporate the comments on their paper into their discussions of "Mirror" within small groups or as a class.

Numbered Heads Together

- Divide students into groups of four and tell them to number off (1, 2, 3, and 4) within each group.
- Pose this question about "Mirror" to all the groups: "If the woman is so upset by her reflection, why does she come back to the mirror every day?"
- Instruct groups to discuss their thoughts and then to form a response to share with the class.
- Call out a number—1, 2, 3, or 4. Have the student with that number in each group share the group's response.
- Invite students to compare the responses and create at least one interpretation with which everyone agrees. Repeat with a new question.

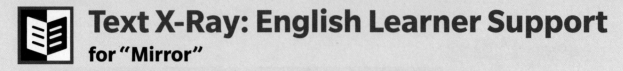

Text X-Ray: English Learner Support
for "Mirror"

Use the Text X-Ray and the supports and scaffolds in the Teacher's Edition to help guide students at different proficiency levels through the selection.

INTRODUCE THE SELECTION
DISCUSS REFLECTIONS

In this lesson, students will need to be able to distinguish between two meanings of the word *reflect*. Read the Setting a Purpose note aloud and explain the following:

- Mirrors *reflect* because they show back an image of whatever is before them. Other things that *reflect* include water and shiny surfaces, but mirrors show back images with greatest accuracy.

- We sometimes *reflect* in our thoughts, which means that we think deeply and quietly about something.

As students read "Mirror," encourage them to consider how both meanings of *reflect* apply to the speaker.

CULTURAL REFERENCES

The following words or phrases may be unfamiliar to students:

- *silver* (line 1): A basic mirror is made from a flat piece of glass that is coated with a silvery metal on the back. At one time, actual silver was used. Today, the metal is more likely to be aluminum.

- *faithfully* (line 13): accurately, truthfully

- *an agitation of hands* (line 14): moving or waving hands about as a way of showing unhappiness or anger

LISTENING

Analyze a Poem's Speaker

Point out that in some poems, the speaker is the poet. At other times, the poet invents a speaker—and in this poem, the speaker is an object. Explain that this choice means that we need to look at the poem's ideas in a special way.

Have students listen as you read the poem aloud. Use the following supports with students at varying proficiency levels:

- Tell students to respond *yes* or *no* to some questions about what they just heard. For example, ask: Is the mirror the speaker in the poem? *(yes)* Is the woman in the poem happy? *(no)* **SUBSTANTIAL**

- Have students respond to questions about the speaker. For example, ask: What does the mirror mean when it says, "I have no preconceptions"? Tell students that *pre-* means "before" and that *conceptions* refers to ideas. *(I don't know about things before I reflect them.)* What does the mirror think the woman wants from it? *(to know what she really is)* **MODERATE**

- After students listen to the poem, have partners discuss how the speaker feels toward the woman. Display and explain the following terms to help students express their ideas: *proud, bored, superior, better than*. **LIGHT**

SPEAKING

Discuss Main Ideas

Have students discuss the main ideas in the poem, citing evidence to support their views.

Use the following supports with students at varying proficiency levels:

- Display and read aloud this sentence: *The mirror in this poem shows a woman a picture of herself.* Have students say it aloud back to you and then practice saying it to each other. **SUBSTANTIAL**
- Have small groups orally complete these sentence frames: *In the mirror, the woman sees that she _____. (is growing old) This thought upsets her, but she still _____. (comes to look at herself)* **MODERATE**
- Ask partners to discuss questions they would like to ask the mirror. What can the answers tell them about the mirror and the woman? **LIGHT**

READING

Analyze Statements of Identification

Point out to students that the speaker of this poem claims to have certain characteristics and to take certain actions. Both kinds of statements help it to identify itself.

Work with students to reread the first stanza (lines 1–9). Then use the following supports with students at varying proficiency levels:

- Reread lines 1–4 with students following along. Point out *exact* and review that a mirror reflects precisely what is in front of it. Then ask: Is a mirror truthful? *(yes)* **SUBSTANTIAL**
- Have small groups create a graphic organizer (such as a T-Chart), listing things that the mirror says it is and does in the first stanza. Invite groups to compare their findings. **MODERATE**
- Have partners identify the two *I am* statements in the first stanza *(lines 1 and 4)*. Ask: How are these statements true of any mirror? How would you feel if a person were saying these things about himself or herself? **LIGHT**

WRITING

Write a Poem

Work with students to help them with the writing assignment on Student Edition page 113.

Use the following supports with students at varying proficiency levels:

- After students have chosen a speaker, help them complete a simile to use in their poem: *My speaker is a _____. This speaker is like a _____.* **SUBSTANTIAL**
- Have partners share their ideas for speakers. Have them write one simile describing each of their speakers to use in their poems. Remind them to use the words *like* or *as*. **MODERATE**
- Have students work with a partner to discuss their ideas for a speaker and then write a simile and a metaphor about each speaker to use in their poems. Remind them that metaphors do not use the words *like* or *as* to express a comparison. **LIGHT**

Connect to the
 ? **ESSENTIAL QUESTION**

In Sylvia Plath's "Mirror," the speaker, named in the poem's title, considers its own existence and that of the woman who uses it to gaze at her reflection. The mirror's ability to show the woman an accurate image of herself goes unappreciated. What the woman sees in her reflection reminds her of an upsetting truth that she is reluctant to admit—but that the mirror clearly recognizes.

MIRROR

Poem by **Sylvia Plath**

? **ESSENTIAL QUESTION:**

How does our point of view shape what we think we know?

106   Unit 2

⚙ LEARNING MINDSET

Effort   Remind students that effort is necessary for growth and, ultimately, for success. As you read and discuss "Mirror," use modeling, such as thinking aloud, to show students that putting effort into understanding a poem pays off. When you see students doing the same—for example, in the questions and comments they note while reading, the questions they ask, and their contributions to class discussions—be sure to reinforce their efforts. If they stumble along the way, encourage them to keep going and remind them that we all grow when we work to overcome challenges.

GET READY

QUICK START

Is a mirror's reflection of you an accurate depiction of who you are? When you stand in front of a mirror, what parts of you does the mirror reflect? What parts does it miss? Record your thoughts below. Then, share them with a partner.

WHAT THE MIRROR REFLECTS	WHAT THE MIRROR CANNOT SEE

ANALYZE SPEAKER

In poetry, the **speaker** is the voice that "talks" to the reader. The speaker is not always the same as the poet, even in a poem that uses *I* and *me*. A poet chooses a particular speaker to convey a message and to elicit the reader's emotions. The speaker may be a child, an adult, an animal, or an object. The speaker could be a baby, a dog, or the wind.

When you read a poem, identify the speaker and the subject. Use the poem's words and images to help you get a sense of who the speaker is. Ask the following questions:

- What is the speaker paying attention to in the poem?
- What thoughts and feelings does the speaker express?
- What is the speaker's tone, or attitude, toward the subject?

As you read "Mirror," use this chart to record your inferences about the speaker and the details that led you to make these inferences.

INFERENCES ABOUT THE SPEAKER	DETAILS FROM THE POEM

GENRE ELEMENTS: LYRIC POETRY
- expresses the speaker's thoughts and feelings
- implies, rather than states, the speaker's emotion
- written in free verse without regular meter
- uses the rhythm of natural speech to create its musical quality

TEACH

QUICK START

Ask students to think about the many times they check out their reflection over the course of a day. Suggest that they think about these questions: What do I expect to see? What do I wish I could see? Then have students read the Quick Start questions. As they work on the chart and then share their responses, point out that a mirror cannot "see" someone from every angle at the same time and also that it cannot see a person's thoughts and feelings. When students read "Mirror," challenge them to consider how well the speaker can "see" the woman who looks into it.

ANALYZE SPEAKER

Point out that a poem's speaker does not always directly address the reader. The speaker in "Mirror" voices its thoughts to the world at large, seemingly without expecting a response. When students read a poem, they should make the effort to understand what the speaker is like, for that speaker's point of view will shape the message of the poem. In "Mirror," therefore, students should go beyond saying, "The speaker is a mirror." Instead, they should look for details that show how it describes itself and its role in the life of the woman who looks into it. Encourage students to use the chart, reminding them of the importance of supporting their ideas with text evidence.

 ENGLISH LEARNER SUPPORT

Use Academic Language Review the chart. Then use the following supports with students at different proficiency levels.

- Make sure students understand words and phrases in the chart, such as *inferences, speaker,* and *poet.* Work with them to fill in the blank sections, providing text that they can copy into their charts as needed. Supply the following sentence frames: *The speaker is _____. Details that tell me who the speaker is are _____ and _____.* **SUBSTANTIAL**

- Have students review the first paragraph, which gives examples of different kinds of speakers. Have them write sentences with details about one of these speakers, and challenge partners to identify the speaker. **MODERATE**

- Invite students to write brief paragraphs with different speakers, without identifying the speakers' identity. Then have them exchange their paragraphs with a partner to see if they can identify the speaker. **LIGHT**

ANALYZE FIGURATIVE LANGUAGE

Explain that figurative language is based on a comparison that is not literally true. The things that are compared are quite different from each other—but by suggesting a comparison between them, a writer engages the reader's imagination and points to a memorable idea.

Help students apply the concept of figurative language to the examples in the text:

- **Simile:** Point out the word *like*. Explain that the snow is compared to a blanket; then ask students why that comparison makes sense. (*Snow covers a landscape in a way that smooths over details, much as a blanket covers a bed and softens the edges of whatever is beneath it.*)

- **Metaphor:** Invite students to explain the comparison. (*Flowers are compared to a carpet. The comparison indicates that there are many colorful flowers, growing closely together.*) Explain that the absence of *like* or *as* can make metaphors more powerful figures of speech than similes.

- **Personification:** In "Mirror," students will immediately see that Sylvia Plath has personified a mirror. You may wish to note that personification also works on a sentence level; for example, "The angry storm poured out its wrath on the tiny village" suggests that weather can feel and act upon a human emotion.

■ English Learner Support

Compare Similar Words At first glance, the word *simile* could be mistaken for *smile*. Point out that even though the words differ by only one letter, they are not related. Sound out the three syllables of *simile* and the single syllable of *smile*; have students repeat. **SUBSTANTIAL/MODERATE**

🖉 ANNOTATION MODEL

Point out that although the model illustrates only one note, that note has a lot to say—not only about a use of figurative language but also about the poem's speaker. Have students read the line in question a few times and then the reader's comment about it. Ask students how the words in the line personify the mirror. (*They suggest that the mirror can see and swallow.*) Then invite students to paraphrase the reader's note about the speaker. (*I wonder whether the writer means that the mirror is destructive—or just that it is objective.*) Remind students to note in the margins questions and ideas that are unclear or topics they want to learn more about.

ANALYZE FIGURATIVE LANGUAGE

Figurative language communicates ideas beyond the literal meaning of the words. Figurative language uses ordinary words in unusual ways and forces a reader to look at familiar things in a new way. Similes, metaphors, and personification are three figures of speech that poets use to create meaning.

A **simile** is a stated comparison between two things that are actually unlike, but that have something in common. A simile contains the words *like* or *as*.

> The snow settled on the roof *like* a comforting blanket.

A **metaphor** is a figure of speech that makes a comparison between two unlike things that have something in common. It does not contain the words *like* or *as*.

> The flowers *are* a carpet of color.

Personification is a figure of speech in which human qualities are attributed to an animal, object, or idea. In some poems, poets use personification by making the speaker the voice of the animal, object, or idea.

> The tree *stretched its arms* to the sky.

ANNOTATION MODEL   NOTICE & NOTE 🖉

As you read, watch for figurative language. Analyze how it adds meaning to the poem's message. This model shows one reader's notes about lines from "Mirror."

> I am silver and exact. I have no preconceptions.
>
> <u>Whatever I see I swallow immediately</u>
>
> Just as it is, unmisted by love or dislike.

The verb "swallow" makes me think the mirror wants to devour what it sees, which is a little disturbing. Or maybe the mirror means that it doesn't judge what it sees.

BACKGROUND

Sylvia Plath *(1932–1963) was born in Boston and won literary awards as a teen for her stories and poems. She attended Cambridge University in London as a Fulbright Scholar. There, she met and married poet Ted Hughes. Plath's intensely personal and complex poems explore the painful dilemmas of her own life as poet, wife, mother, and daughter. A critic called her final poems a "triumph for poetry at the moment that they are a defeat for their author." After her premature death, her reputation continued to grow, and in 1982, her* Collected Poems *received the Pulitzer Prize.*

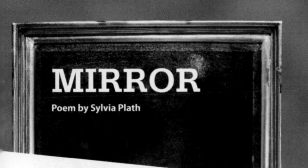

MIRROR

Poem by Sylvia Plath

SETTING A PURPOSE

As you read, consider how you react to what you see when you look in the mirror and compare this to the reaction of the woman in the poem.

> I am silver and exact. I have <u>no preconceptions</u>.[1]
> Whatever I see I swallow immediately
> Just as it is, <u>unmisted by love or dislike.</u>
> I am <u>not cruel, only truthful</u> –
> 5   The eye of a little god, <u>four-cornered.</u>
> Most of the time I meditate on the opposite wall.
> It is pink, with speckles. I have looked at it so long
> I think it is a part of my heart. But it flickers.
> Faces and darkness separate us over and over.

---
[1] **preconception:** an opinion in advance, a bias.

Notice & Note

You can use the side margins to notice and note signposts in the text.

ANALYZE SPEAKER

Annotate: Mark the words that help you identify and understand the speaker.

Infer: Why does the speaker claim "I am not cruel, only truthful?" Do you agree with the speaker? Why or why not?

WHEN STUDENTS STRUGGLE . . .

Analyze Details "Mirror" is a free-verse poem, but it has a structure: two stanzas of nine lines each. Have students annotate the poem to track details that point to the focus of each stanza. Encourage students to look for details related to the speaker and the ideas the speaker wants to convey. Have them write a summary statement about each stanza with the following sentence frame: *Stanza 1/2 is mostly about _____.*

 For additional support, go to the **Reading Studio** and assign the following [LEVEL UP] **Level Up Tutorial: Reading for Details.**

BACKGROUND

After students read the Background note, explain that people often turn to writing as a way to process their feelings about personal challenges. As a result, some lyric poems have a sad or grim tone. The speaker in "Mirror" may not show such emotion (or any emotion at all), but the woman who looks into it certainly does.

You may wish to note that Sylvia Plath kept several journals. Explain that a note that she made in November 1959 seems especially relevant to the poem they are about to read: "What horrifies me most is the idea of being useless: well-educated, brilliantly promising, and fading out into an indifferent middle-age."

SETTING A PURPOSE

Direct students to use the Setting a Purpose prompt to focus their reading.

✎ ANALYZE SPEAKER

Tell students that they should look for ways in which the mirror describes its physical appearance and the way that it thinks. (**Answer:** *A mirror, as an object, has no emotion. It is truthful because it reflects life as it really is. Students may agree or disagree with the mirror's description but should offer a reasonable explanation for their view.*)

■ English Learner Support

Understand Figurative Language Point out the unusual word *unmisted* in line 3. Explain that the speaker compares the emotions of love and dislike to mist, or fog. Invite students to briefly share experiences that they have had with fog. Then work with them to complete these sentences:

- Mist, or fog, can be a problem because ____. (*it keeps you from seeing physical objects clearly*)

- The speaker says that the feelings of love and dislike are like mist because ____.(*they keep you from seeing people or situations the way they actually are*)

- Therefore, being "unmisted" is a good characteristic for a mirror to have because ____. (*a mirror always should present an accurate reflection*)

MODERATE/LIGHT

 For **reading support** for students at varying proficiency levels, see the **Text X-Ray** on page 106D.

✎ ANALYZE FIGURATIVE LANGUAGE

Review the three kinds of figurative language introduced in this lesson. The entire poem personifies the mirror, so remind students of the difference between a simile (with its use of *like* or *as*) and a metaphor. Point out that not every comparison in this stanza describes the mirror. **(Answer:** *The mirror compares itself to the woman and seems to understand her. It has insight but no emotional stake in her responses to her reflection. It objectively observes her need for approval and her unhappiness, as well as the changes that age is making to her appearance.)*

■ English Learner Support

Rephrase Poetic Statements As students read the second stanza, discuss the meanings of these words that may cause confusion:

- *reaches* (line 11): the extent or depth of something (a noun in this context, not a verb)

- *agitation* (line 14): the state of being strongly upset (Rub and wring your hands to demonstrate what "an agitation of hands" might look like.)

- *terrible* (line 18): causing great fear (more than merely "unpleasant," as the word often is used)

When students seem to understand these words, have them meet in small groups that include at least one fluent student to tell, in their own words, what is happening in the second stanza. Instruct them not to summarize; rather, have them go through the stanza, line by line. Ask more fluent students to offer help as needed. Some lines will require more rephrasing than others (especially lines 12, 14, and 17–18); have the groups work together on these. **ALL LEVELS**

 For **listening support** for students at varying proficiency levels, see the **Text X-Ray** on page 106C.

ANALYZE FIGURATIVE LANGUAGE

Annotate: What does the mirror compare itself to in the second stanza? Mark the words and phrases that help you understand this comparison.

Analyze: How would you describe the mirror's attitude toward the woman?

10 Now I am a lake. A woman bends over me,
Searching my reaches for what she really is.
Then she turns to those liars, the candles or the moon.
I see her back, and reflect it faithfully.
She rewards me with tears and an agitation of hands.
15 I am important to her. She comes and goes.
Each morning it is her face that replaces the darkness.
In me she has drowned a young girl, and in me an old woman
Rises toward her day after day, like a terrible fish.

TO CHALLENGE STUDENTS . . .

Connect "Mirror" to Folklore Tell students that some cultures believe that mirrors can be a portal for souls. For that reason, people may cover mirrors when a person dies, lest the person's soul become trapped in the mirror or wait there until it can possess a living person. Present these questions regarding "Mirror":

- In what sense could it be said that a soul has entered the mirror? *(A "young girl"—the woman's younger self—has "drowned" in the mirror.)*

- In what sense could it be said that a soul is lurking within the mirror? *(An "old woman" in the mirror—the woman's future self—is rising toward the woman, wanting to overtake her.)*

CHECK YOUR UNDERSTANDING

Answer these questions before moving on to the **Analyze the Text** section on the following page.

1 The first stanza suggests that the mirror —

   A schemes to make the woman unhappy

   B welcomes the faces that interrupt its meditation

   C lacks any emotion, even a beating heart

   D is critical, passing judgment on all it sees

2 In the second stanza, the candles and the moon are called liars because they —

   F come and go instead of being constantly present

   G alter the woman's perception of reality

   H seem to be harsh and judgmental

   J are at war with the mirror

3 What does the terrible fish in line 18 represent?

   A The mirror's anger toward the woman

   B Society's overemphasis on appearances

   C The reality of growing old

   D The sadness of the young girl

CHECK YOUR UNDERSTANDING

Have students answer the questions independently.

Answers:

1. *C*

2. *G*

3. *C*

If they answer any questions incorrectly, have them reread the text to confirm their understanding. Then they may proceed to ANALYZE THE TEXT on page 112.

EL ENGLISH LEARNER SUPPORT

Oral Assessment Use the following questions to assess students' comprehension and speaking skills. Ask students to respond in short, complete sentences.

1. In the first stanza, what is most likely true about the mirror? *(It lacks any emotion, even a beating heart.)*

2. In the second stanza, why are the candles and the moon called liars? *(They alter the woman's perception of reality.)*

3. In line 18, what does the terrible fish represent? *(It represents the reality of growing old.)* **ALL LEVELS**

ANALYZE THE TEXT

Possible answers:

1. **DOK 2:** *The mirror (the speaker) seems conflicted. It states that it is objective and offers the truth with no emotion—"just as it is." But then it also seems lonely and sad, as it stares at a wall all day. Seeing itself as god-like may reflect the mirror's sense of superiority over the woman.*

2. **DOK 4:** *The mirror is bored with meditating on the pink wall. The flickering means that the mirror's view is interrupted as people and nighttime change its view. The wall is different from the mirror's heart because it changes and is not constant.*

3. **DOK 3:** *Candles and the moon have subtle and even romantic lighting. They "lie" because their lighting fails to create an accurate image of people. The woman turns to them, however, because they cover up evidence of her aging.*

4. **DOK 4:** *The woman is agitated because she does not like to see herself as aging. The fact that she cries and has "an agitation of hands" when she views her image but still returns to the mirror each morning for another look shows that she is conflicted.*

5. **DOK 4:** *The theme may be that people often do not want to admit truths about themselves, especially the truth about aging. "People" are embodied in the woman, who always is "searching for what she really is." When she sees her youthfulness "drowned" and an older self that "rises" toward her, she is upset and turns to the "liars" of representations that are kinder but not accurate. Still, she is haunted by the truth and must check her mirrored reflection each day.*

RESEARCH

Point out that students are not analyzing the poems' themes (which may be quite grim) but are looking for examples of figurative language. Ask partners to try to locate two examples in each poem. Encourage them to experiment with a variety of layouts before creating their final poster.

Extend Students should focus on the immediate meaning of an example, but allow students to relate that meaning to a larger idea in the poem if they wish. In particular, encourage students who chose examples from the same poem or poems to compare their interpretations.

RESPOND

ANALYZE THE TEXT

Support your responses with evidence from the text. ☰ NOTEBOOK

1. **Infer** Reread the first stanza. What is your impression of the speaker? What does the phrase "The eye of a little god" suggest about the mirror's personality?

2. **Analyze** Reread lines 6–9. How does the mirror feel about its daily meditation? What does the line "But it flickers" mean? How does this make the wall different from the mirror's heart?

3. **Draw Conclusions** Reread line 13. If the candles and the moon are "liars," why does the woman turn to them? How does this metaphor reveal the mirror's perspective?

4. **Analyze** In the second stanza, why is the woman agitated that the lake (mirror) reflects her "faithfully"? How does the woman's reaction support the idea that she is conflicted?

5. **Synthesize** What is the theme, or message, of this poem? Explain your answer using evidence from the poem as support.

RESEARCH TIP
When citing a poem, put quotation marks around the poem's title. The book in which the poem is located should be in italics if typed or underlined if handwritten. Remember to include the date of publication and the publisher's name. For a poem found online, include the URL.

RESEARCH

Collaborate with a partner and choose 2–3 other poems by Sylvia Plath. Then, create a poetry poster to present them. Your poster should include the following:

- the full text of each poem, typed or written neatly and pasted on the poster

- lines from the poems that contain examples of metaphor, simile, or personification

- a brief explanation of why you chose each poem

TITLE OF POEM	EXAMPLE LINE(S)	TYPE OF FIGURATIVE LANGUAGE
Responses will vary		

Extend Explain what each example of figurative language helps readers to understand.

LEARNING MINDSET

Problem Solving Remind students that everyone runs into problems when learning something new, including making meaning from an unfamiliar poem. Working hard to solve those problems creates a sense of accomplishment and builds skills that can be used in other problem-solving situations. Model working through a problem related to one of the Analyze the Text questions, or invite students to share how they did so. Make sure students understand that there can be various ways of solving a problem and that they should be patient with themselves as they work.

CREATE AND DISCUSS

Write a Poem The poem "Mirror" is unusual because the speaker is an object—the mirror. Write a similar poem with a different speaker, such as the woman, the wall, the candles, or the moon. Or, you might write from the perspective of an outside narrator who knows the thoughts and feelings of both the mirror and the woman—like an omniscient narrator in fiction.

❏ Choose the speaker of your "Mirror" poem.

❏ Jot down notes about how the speaker feels and what the speaker notices. Your poem could be humorous or serious.

❏ Use similes, metaphors, or personification to convey the speaker's attitude.

Discuss The speaker in "Mirror" says that the woman is searching for "what she really is." In a small group, discuss whether mirrors show people the most accurate versions of themselves. Use details from the poem and personal experience to support your ideas.

❏ Read the poem aloud in your group. Share and discuss ideas that you and other group members wrote down in the Quick Start.

❏ Discuss societal values concerning appearance and the kinds of judgments and distorted thinking this might lead to.

❏ Consider how looking in the mirror can have positive and negative consequences.

❏ Discuss ways in which people can embrace their identities and achieve confidence in a society that is so focused on appearance.

 Go to the **Speaking and Listening Studio** for more on participating in a discussion.

RESPOND TO THE ESSENTIAL QUESTION

 How does our point of view shape what we think we know?

Gather Information Review your annotations and notes on "Mirror." Then, add relevant ideas to your Response Log. As you decide which ideas to include, think about:

• the difference between our physical appearance and our inner self
• the acceptance of our personal identity
• the difference between our own desires and the demands of society

At the end of the unit, use your notes to help you write a short story.

UNIT 2 RESPONSE LOG

? Essential Question:
How does our point of view shape what we think we know?

Coming to Our Senses	
The Night Face Up	
Mirror	
The World as 100 People	
A Contribution to Statistics	

ACADEMIC VOCABULARY
As you write and discuss what you learned from the poem, be sure to use the Academic Vocabulary words. Check off each of the words that you use.

❏ **differentiate**
❏ **incorporate**
❏ **mode**
❏ **orient**
❏ **perspective**

Mirror 113

CREATE AND DISCUSS

Write a Poem If students choose a speaker that appears in "Mirror," urge them to review the poem to see what the mirror says about it. (For example, the mirror makes an assumption about why the woman looks closely at the mirror [line 11] and calls the candles and moon "liars" [line 12].) In their poem, students may want to show whether their speaker confirms or contradicts the mirror's viewpoint. If students choose an outside narrator as the speaker, suggest that they jot down a statement about the relationship between the woman and the mirror and then build upon that rather than going into detail about the other objects in the poem. Students may find it helpful to write three or four sentences from the viewpoint of their speaker and then adapt those into poetic form, deciding where to place line breaks and experimenting with using figurative language to express ideas. In addition, remind students that "Mirror" is a free-verse poem and that they need not be concerned about a pattern of rhyme or meter unless they want the extra challenge and have already made decisions about figurative language.

📖 For **speaking and writing support** for students at varying proficiency levels, see the **Text X-Ray** on page 106D.

Discuss Remind students to be attentive while listening to one another's poems. As students review their Quick Start responses and enter into discussion, encourage them to remember that a mirror can show only people's appearance, not their thoughts and feelings. Remind them to support their ideas about appearance with evidence—examples from popular culture, personal experience, and so on. Invite group representatives to share with the class ideas about how to live with a confidence that is not based on physical appearance.

RESPOND TO THE ESSENTIAL QUESTION

Allow time for students to add details from "Mirror" to their Unit 2 Response Logs.

 ENGLISH LEARNER SUPPORT

Compare Cultural Views The Discuss activity gives English learners a good opportunity to share their home culture while internalizing basic language and learning new language structures. Remind mixed-ability groups that our society includes people from a wide variety of cultural groups. Provide students with sentence frames such as these to encourage them to share what it means to embrace their identity in their home culture. Have students write the sentences and then read them aloud.

• *In my home culture, a person's physical appearance [is/is not] important because _____.*
• *_____ is a meaningful part of who I really am.* **ALL LEVELS**

THE WORLD AS 100 PEOPLE

Infographic by **Jack Hagley**

GENRE ELEMENTS
INFOGRAPHIC

Explain that an **infographic** presents information in a more visual form than plain text does. It combines text with elements such as charts and images to communicate information. An infographic often includes text features such as titles, headings, labels, numbers, and explanatory information. Images, colors, and designs also help communicate information. In this lesson, students will interpret the infographic "The World as 100 People" and consider the designer's motives for creating it.

LEARNING OBJECTIVES

- Analyze and interpret an infographic.
- Discuss data and information presented in an infographic.
- Evaluate the motives behind a media presentation and the use of print and graphic features to achieve specific purposes.
- Conduct research about other statistics and synthesize information gathered.
- Create and deliver a multimedia presentation.
- **Language** Use correct verbs in writing.

TEXT COMPLEXITY

Quantitative Measures	The World as 100 People	Lexile: N/A
Qualitative Measures	**Ideas Presented** Infographic is explicit, but introductory text requires some inferential reasoning.	
	Structures Used Introductory text presents ideas chronologically; infographic uses text (title, headings, and subheadings) and graphics.	
	Language Used Vocabulary not defined at point of use. Many Tier II and III words.	
	Knowledge Required Requires no special knowledge or experience. Context familiar or easily envisioned.	

RESOURCES

- Unit 2 Response Log
- Selection Audio
- Reading Studio: Notice & Note
- Level Up Tutorial:
  Reading Graphic Aids
- "The World as 100 People" /
  "A Contribution to Statistics"
  Selection Test

SUMMARIES

English

Designer Jack Hagley used a simple list of statistics about the lives and living conditions of people around the world to create a colorful infographic. The circle depicts 14 categories, each of which is broken down into statistical percentages (the number of people out of 100). For example, within the *Age* category, there are three groups of people: out of 100 people, 26 are aged 0–14, 66 are aged 15–44, and 8 are aged 65+. The infographic's circular design represents the world; the colors are meant to evoke the flags of many nations.

Spanish

El diseñador Jack Hagley utilizó una sencilla lista de estadísticas acerca de las vidas y las condiciones de vida de gente alrededor del mundo para crear una infografía colorida. El círculo representa 14 categorías, cada una es descompuesta en porcentajes analíticos (del número de gente entre 100). Por ejemplo, en la categoría de la EDAD, hay tres grupos de personas: de 100 personas, 26 están entre los 0 y 14 años; 66 tienen edades entre 15 y 44; y 8 tienen más de 65 años. El diseño de esta infografía circular representa al mundo; los colores evocan las banderas de muchas naciones.

SMALL-GROUP OPTIONS

Have students work in small groups to read and discuss the selection.

Reciprocal Teaching

- Present students with question words (*who, what, when, where, why*, and *how*).
- Instruct students, working independently, to write 3–5 questions about information in the infographic, using those words. (Students don't need to be able to answer the questions they write.)
- Arrange students into pairs or groups of three.
- Each student should offer at least two questions for group discussion, without repeating another student's question.
- Tell groups to reach consensus on the answer to each question and support it with text evidence.

Pinwheel Discussion

- Display a series of questions such as these for students to discuss: Explain the motives behind the design that Jack Hagley chose. What are some categories that you think Hagley should have included? What information is the most surprising to you, and why?
- Have students form groups of four, six, or eight, with half the students sitting facing out and the other half of the group sitting facing in.
- Instruct students in the inner circle to remain in place throughout the discussion and students in the outer circle to rotate to their right after discussing each question.
- Continue the rotation until all questions have been discussed.

Text X-Ray: English Learner Support
for "The World as 100 People"

Use the Text X-Ray and the supports and scaffolds in the Teacher's Edition to help guide students at different proficiency levels through the selection.

INTRODUCE THE SELECTION
DISCUSS POPULATION DATA

In this lesson, students will read an infographic that summarizes data and statistics on the world population. Explain the following terms:

- *Data* are facts or numbers that you can analyze, or look at carefully. *Data* is an unusual word because it looks singular but actually is plural.
- The *population* is the total number of people who live in a place or the total number from which data is collected.

Invite volunteers to share what data they would like to collect about the school population. Provide these frames:

- *The total _____ of the school is about _____.*
- *I would like to collect this _____: How many students _____?*

CULTURAL REFERENCES

The following words or phrases from the Artist's Statement may be unfamiliar to students:

- *chain e-mail*: an email note that is forwarded, or shared with many people
- *studio*: a place where an artist or designer works
- *first draft*: the earliest version of something that is written or designed (drawn)

LISTENING

Understand Important Details

Explain that you are going to do a dictation. You will read aloud some numerical data about different groups of people; as you do so, students should record the numbers they hear.

Use the following supports with students at varying proficiency levels:

- Review the numbers 1–20 and the tens up to 100. Then dictate ten numbers and have students write them in a list. Have students read back to you the numbers you dictated. **SUBSTANTIAL**
- Select a category from "The World as 100 People" (*Age*, for example: people 14 or younger, between 15 and 64, or over 65) and dictate the statistical data to students. Explain that the equivalent of "50 out of 100 people" is 50/100. So if you say "50 out of 100 people are female," students may write "50 percent female" or "50/100 female." Check students' work. **MODERATE**
- Select a category from "The World as 100 People" and dictate the statistical data to students. Have students record both the numerical data and the descriptions of each group. Then have partners compare what they wrote and check their spelling. **LIGHT**

SPEAKING

Use Academic Language in Class Discussions

Introduce the word *category*. Encourage students to use the word as they discuss the infographic on Student Edition page 118.

Use the following supports with students at varying proficiency levels:

- Introduce each category by saying, "This category is about _____," and have students repeat the category name. Then check comprehension by saying, "Point to the _____ category." **SUBSTANTIAL**

- Display these frames: *Which category are _____ grouped under? They are under the _____ category.* Model asking and answering questions about the infographic: *Which category are rural areas and urban areas grouped under? They are in the "Area" category.* **MODERATE**

- Have students work with a partner and take turns asking and answering questions about each category in the infographic. **LIGHT**

READING

Read an Infographic

Explain that one way to read an infographic is to look for information that you find interesting or surprising.

Use the following supports with students at varying proficiency levels:

- Read aloud the data in the *Language* category. Ask students to point to any language(s) they speak Then ask if they speak a language that is one of the 62 languages not listed by name. **SUBSTANTIAL**

- Have students read the *Language* category. Then ask them what information surprised them and why. Provide these frames: *I am surprised that _____. I thought that _____, but I see that _____.* **MODERATE**

- Tell students to read the infographic and find one thing that's interesting and one thing that's surprising. Then have them share their ideas with a partner. **LIGHT**

WRITING

Use Correct Verbs to Cite Sources

Explain that there are certain language structures that are used to write sentences about information that comes from sources. Knowing these patterns will help students edit for correct verb tense, subject-verb agreement, and clause structure on Student Edition page 129.

Use the following supports with students at varying proficiency levels:

- Ask a volunteer to state a sentence—for example, *It is raining*. Model how to write a sentence stating what the volunteer said—for example, *Binh says that it is raining*. Have another volunteer say a sentence. Guide students in writing it. **SUBSTANTIAL**

- Display this example: "Hagley's infographic states that 30 out of 100 people can access the Internet." Explain that when writers use someone else's ideas, they must include that person's name and a verb such as *states*. Point out that the verb is usually present tense and must agree with the subject. Guide students to write sentences based on the infographic with correct verb usage. **MODERATE**

- Have students check the sentences they wrote in the Research and Present activity. Make sure they have included a word such as *states* or *writes* to introduce another writer's ideas. Point out that when they paraphrase, the word following *states* or *writes* is always *that*; if they quote, then they do not use *that*; instead they use quotation marks. **LIGHT**

TEACH

Connect to the
ESSENTIAL QUESTION

"The World as 100 People" is an infographic that presents statistics about people around the world. The designer's point of view helped shape his decisions about which information to include and how to present it. The infographic may, in turn, influence readers' points of view by challenging what they think they know about the world.

COMPARE DETAILS

Ask students to think about weather reports they see on local TV. Point out that meteorologists often compare a statistic (number fact) about that day's conditions—for example, the high temperature or the amount of rainfall—to the related statistic from another year (such as one year ago or a record-setting date). Discuss how such a comparison helps viewers understand how typical or atypical that day's conditions are.

Explain that in this Collaborate & Compare lesson, students will compare a variety of statistical details about people, presented in two different kinds of text. To make effective comparisons, students must interpret the information and ideas presented in each text, and they must consider how the details reflect the designer's or author's message and purpose.

INFOGRAPHIC
THE WORLD AS 100 PEOPLE

by **Jack Hagley**
pages 117–119

COMPARE DETAILS

As you read, notice how the ideas in both texts relate to the world around you, as well as how they help you understand ideas through mathematics. Then, look for ways that the ideas in the two texts relate to each other. After you read both selections, you will collaborate with a small group on a final project.

ESSENTIAL QUESTION:

How does our point of view shape what we think we know?

POEM
A CONTRIBUTION TO STATISTICS

by **Wisława Szymborska**
pages 123–125

114   Unit 2

LEARNING MINDSET

Effort   Remind students that effort is necessary for growth and that hard work is necessary for success. Tell students that this infographic presents a lot of information in a format that may be new to them. Let students know that although they may find interpreting the graphic a little challenging at first, they will see that the effort they make in doing so will pay off. Encourage students by explaining that they will have multiple opportunities to interpret the graphic, discuss the information it contains with peers, and compare it with another selection. Through these various interactions, they will become more familiar with the infographic and more confident about interpreting its content.

The World as 100 People

QUICK START

You can be classified in a wide range of groups: teenagers, Americans, athletes, people who live in suburbs, etc. With a group, brainstorm all the ways that you can statistically classify the world population.

Demographic	by age
Geographic	by country
Personal	by hobbies

INTERPRET GRAPHICS

Graphics can sometimes communicate information more clearly than words. Texts often include one of more of the following types of graphics:

TYPE OF GRAPHIC	WHAT IT DOES
Tables	Large amounts of data organized in a logical order that makes it easier for a reader to see and understand the data
Graphs	Two-dimensional representations of data that help the reader understand the relationships among the data
Photographs and Drawings	Visual illustrations of a topic discussed in a text that can show details that are difficult to explain in words
Diagrams	Illustrations that show the relationship of parts in an object or the steps in a process
Infographics	Combinations of charts, text, and images to create a visual that communicates statistical information

GENRE ELEMENTS: INFOGRAPHIC

- provides numerical information
- uses a visual representation
- combines elements of charts, text, and images

QUICK START

Point out that there are usually many ways that a population can be classified, or grouped. For example, a student population could be classified by ages, by grade levels, by students who take the bus or walk to school, and by many other criteria. After students have completed the Quick Start activity and shared their ideas in groups, ask each group to share its brainstormed list of categories. Did students choose similar categories? What categories were the most surprising? Did any of the categories change students' thinking about the world or how to classify people in it? Invite students to share their findings.

INTERPRET GRAPHICS

Help students understand that in order to interpret graphics, they should begin by considering what type of graphic they are viewing and what information it presents. Next, they should consider the specific ways in which information is presented. How is the information organized? What can readers learn from titles, headings, or labels? Finally, they should consider the purpose of the graphic. Does it present data, "tell a story," or convey a message—a point that the creator wants the reader to think about and remember? Explain to students that answering questions such as these will help them interpret the infographic they are about to read.

🄴🄻 ENGLISH LEARNER SUPPORT

Use Visual Support Display an example of each type of graphic listed in the table. Include examples of environmental print, such as street signs or product labels. Also include materials used frequently in the classroom. Encourage volunteers to read aloud familiar words. As you review each term, point to the example graphic, say its name, and have students repeat it. Check students' comprehension by asking them questions such as these, based on their proficiency level: Which graphic would you use to show how to build something? Why? (*A diagram would be best because it would show*

each step in the building process.) How are an infographic, a drawing, and a table alike? (*All present information graphically, with lines or designs that are drawn.*) How do they differ? (*An infographic blends text, images, and other designs; a drawing may not include text; a table usually includes lines and text but no images.*) **ALL LEVELS**

ANALYZE MOTIVES

Point out that the word *motives* refers to a person's reasons for doing something. Explain that just as a writer has reasons for choosing facts or details and presenting them in a particular way, the creator of the infographic "The World as 100 People" had reasons for choosing the information he did and for designing the graphic in a particular way.

■ English Learner Support

Discuss Motives Introduce the word *motive,* have students repeat the word after you, and define it. Display these frames: *I _____. What was your motive? I _____.* Then model this short dialogue, with a volunteer in the role of speaker B:

> A: I came to school early today.
>
> B: What was your motive?
>
> A: I wanted to review my lesson plan.

Have partners take turns producing their own brief dialogues about motives. **SUBSTANTIAL/MODERATE**

✎ ANNOTATION MODEL

Point out to students that as they examine "The World as 100 People," they should mark and make note of details that might suggest the designer's motives and purpose. These details might include headings, labels, and design features such as style of the illustration or the colors used. Point out that students may want to color-code their annotations using highlighters. Their notes in the margin may include questions about ideas that are unclear or topics they want to learn more about. You may wish to point out that students' notes need not always be as detailed as seen in the example but that they should include enough detail to jog students' memories when referring to them later.

 GET READY

ANALYZE MOTIVES

Even though graphics present objective data, the creators of graphics make choices about how to present this data. Designers may choose to include or exclude certain types of data based on the point they hope to make and the overall purpose of the graphic.

For example, the creator of the infographic "The World as 100 People" chose to include data about age, religion, and literacy but did not include data about car ownership or types of employment.

When examining "The World as 100 People," think about why the designer chose to include each category and how doing so serves the purpose of the graphic.

ANNOTATION MODEL **NOTICE & NOTE**

Here is how a student might annotate to analyze the motives of the infographic's creator.

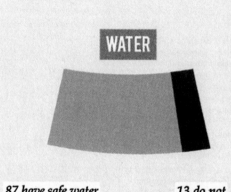

WATER

87 have safe water   *13 do not*

> The infographic tells me that, out of every 100 people, 87 people have safe drinking water and 13 people do not.
>
> That means 13 out of every 100 people have to spend time and energy getting safe water to drink—time and energy they can't use to work or to gather food.
>
> This data matters because access to clean drinking water is necessary for life.

WHEN STUDENTS STRUGGLE . . .

Discuss Motives Read aloud the text and student notes in the Annotation Model. Ask: What type of information does the infographic contain? *(facts about drinking water)* What might be the designer's motive for telling people that 13 out of 100 people do not have safe water to drink? *(perhaps to make readers more aware of other people and their needs)* Tell students that asking and answering similar questions will help them analyze and understand the designer's motives.

 For additional support, go to the **Reading Studio** and assign the following ⬛ **Level Up Tutorial: Reading Graphic Aids.**

BACKGROUND

Representing statistical information in terms of a small group of people is popular in advertising ("Three out of five dentists recommend . . .") because it makes a point easy to understand. This infographic both shares information and makes some persuasive points. The Artist's Statement by designer **Jack Hagley** *provides context for choices he made, including why he chose this particular shape for the infographic.*

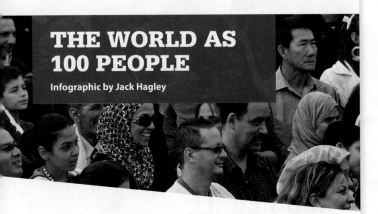

THE WORLD AS 100 PEOPLE

Infographic by Jack Hagley

PREPARE TO COMPARE

As you read the statement and infographic that follow, think about how the data relates to the world around you. What parts of the data confirm your expectations? What data surprises you? Why?

ARTIST'S STATEMENT

When I was a boy in the '90s, my mother had a printout of a chain e-mail pinned to the wall in our kitchen. It was called "The World as 100 People," and it was just a simple list. I never forgot it because it was a simple but clever idea – a child could understand it without knowing the concept of percentages. One day, I didn't have any other work to do and I was sitting in my studio. The idea and the method came to me very quickly. I knew that I wanted to make it round, like the world. I wanted to use colors that might remind people of flags. I made the first draft in the morning and it was on the Internet by the afternoon.

Notice & Note

You can use the side margins to notice and note signposts in the text.

ANALYZE MOTIVES

Annotate: Mark the text that describes the author's inspiration for creating the infographic.

Analyze: Why might this type of infographic appeal to a child? What information does it make easier to understand?

The World as 100 People   117

BACKGROUND

Have students read the Background note. Remind students that statistical information refers to a set of numerical data, such as the number of Americans between the ages of 14 and 18. Then point out that when artists and designers show their work, they often provide what's called an "artist's statement." An artist's statement often focuses on the central concept or message of a single work or a collection of works. It may explain what inspired the creation of the work, or it may give reasons why the work was created in a certain way. It also may reveal the artist's point of view on a subject or the artist's goal or purpose.

PREPARE TO COMPARE

Direct students to use the Prepare to Compare prompt to focus their reading.

ANALYZE MOTIVES

Clarify that Hagley had been thinking about the concept of "The World as 100 People" since childhood ("I never forgot it") but that he didn't create the infographic until he was an adult. Make sure students understand that the original "The World as 100 People" was simply a list of numbers and descriptions, not an infographic like the one that he himself would later create. (**Answer:** *This type of infographic might appeal to a child because it has a plain circular shape, because it is colorful, and because it is simple to use. It makes certain statistics about the world's people—and comparisons of those statistics—easy to understand because it does not require the reader to calculate percentages; rather, it uses "plain" numbers and blocks of color.*)

 ENGLISH LEARNER SUPPORT

Discuss Motives Remind students that motives are the reasons why someone does something. Explain that to discuss motives, or reasons, students need to be able to ask and answer questions with *why*. Provide these frames and have students use them to ask and answer questions about the infographic and the designer's motives in making it the way he did: *Why did the designer _____? He did that because _____.* **MODERATE/LIGHT**

ENGLISH LEARNER SUPPORT

Use Prereading Supports Preteach the following topic-related vocabulary: *literacy, poverty, nutrition, shelter, undernourished, urban, rural, continent,* and *gender.* Introduce the words one at a time by writing or displaying each word, having students repeat the word, defining or explaining the word, giving an example, then quickly checking their comprehension. For example, you might say, "Literacy: repeat after me, 'literacy,' (students say the word). *Literacy* means being able to read and write. We say a country has high literacy if many people can read and write. If a person cannot read or write, does that person have literacy, or need literacy?" *(The person needs literacy.)*
SUBSTANTIAL/MODERATE

For **listening and speaking support** for students at varying proficiency levels, see the **Text X-Ray** on pages 114C–114D.

ENGLISH LEARNER SUPPORT

Discuss Directionality and Language Structure Explain that like other text in English, the information in an infographic is often read from top to bottom and from left to right. Tell students that in this infographic, however, the designer's intentions aren't clear. The content can be read from left to right around the circle, like a clock; readers can also begin with any category that interests them. Ask students to comment on the directionality that appeals to them.

Have students read aloud the paired labels under "Literacy." *(83 able to read & write, 17 unable)* Explain that the "unable" means "unable to read & write"; that is, some words in the paired label are understood. Challenge students to complete these statistics:

- for "College": 93 do not *(93 do not have a college degree)*
- for "Internet": 70 cannot *(70 cannot access the Internet)*
- for "Phones": 25 do not *(25 do not have cell phones)*
- for "Water": 13 do not *(13 do not have safe water)*
ALL LEVELS

For **reading support** for students at varying proficiency levels, see the **Text X-Ray** on page 114D.

The **WORLD** *as* **100 PEOPLE**

118   Unit 2

ENGLISH LEARNER SUPPORT

Use Cognates Have Spanish-speaking students review the infographic in pairs and identify cognates: *gender/género, religion/religión, Internet/Internet, poverty/pobreza, nutrition/nutrición, language/lenguaje, area/área, continent/continent.* Ask students if they see a word that looks like a cognate of the Spanish word *colegio* but has a slightly different meaning. *(college)* Invite a student to explain the different meanings. *(In English, college is a two-year or four-year school that many students attend after high school. In Spanish, colegio can mean a middle school, a high school, or a private school.)*   **ALL LEVELS**

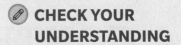 CHECK YOUR UNDERSTANDING

Have students answer the questions independently.

Answers:

1. *D*

2. *G*

3. *A*

If they answer any questions incorrectly, have them reread the text to confirm their understanding. Then they may proceed to ANALYZE THE TEXT on page 126.

CHECK YOUR UNDERSTANDING

Answer these questions before moving on to the next selection.

1 Which of the following is true of this infographic?

A It represents everything we need to know about people.

B Its design shows that it is inaccurate and biased.

C It includes only people who live in the United States.

D It provides a quick view of some key population facts.

2 The categories in the infographic are —

F topics that people often argue about

G characteristics for which factual information is available

H based on emotions more than on hard data

J arranged in order of their importance in people's lives

3 The concept of showing the world's population as 100 people —

A makes it easy to understand challenges most people in the world face

B reveals the difficulty that many children and adults have with math

C distorts and oversimplifies the world's population

D shows how the people in all of the categories overlap with each other

The World as 100 People   119

 ENGLISH LEARNER SUPPORT

Oral Assessment Use the following questions to assess students' comprehension and speaking skills. Ask students to respond in short, complete sentences.

1. Which of the following is true? The infographic includes everything we need to know about people. *(no)* The infographic's design shows that the information is not correct. *(no)* The infographic includes only people who live in the U.S. *(no)* The infographic provides a quick view of some important population facts. *(yes)*

2. What kind of information do the categories on the infographic show? *(They are characteristics for which factual information is available.)*

3. What does the idea of showing the world's population as 100 people help readers understand? *(It makes it easier to understand challenges most people in the world face.)* **ALL LEVELS**

A CONTRIBUTION TO STATISTICS

Poem by **Wisława Szymborska**

GENRE ELEMENTS
POEM

Remind students that **poems** can take many forms, but they share some things in common. Most poems are arranged into lines and stanzas. They also use figurative language and literary devices. Poems may use **parallelism** (a repeated grammatical construction) and **shifts** (changes in tone or focus). Most poems express a **theme**, or a message about life, which sometimes is stated directly but more often requires readers to do some inferential thinking.

LEARNING OBJECTIVES

- Analyze literary devices in a poem.
- Analyze the use of text structure to achieve an author's purpose.
- Conduct additional research on a category from the infographic and appropriately credit the source(s) of information.
- Write a friendly letter to provide or request advice.
- Give step-by-step oral instructions for solving a problem.
- **Language** Use correct verbs in a letter.

TEXT COMPLEXITY

Quantitative Measures	A Contribution to Statistics	Lexile: N/A
Qualitative Measures	**Ideas Presented** Multiple levels with subtle, implied meanings and purpose; use of irony.	
	Structures Used Poem follows a consistent pattern; stanzas follow a parallel structure.	
	Language Used Mostly explicit, but with some figurative language and idioms.	
	Knowledge Required Most of the text deals with subjects and situations that are familiar or easily envisioned.	

RESOURCES

- Unit 2 Response Log
- 🔊 Selection Audio
- 📖 Reading Studio:
  Notice & Note
- 📄 Writing Studio:
  Writing for a Specific Audience
  and Purpose
- 💬 Speaking and Listening Studio:
  Giving and Following Instructions;
  Delivering a Multimedia
  Presentation
- ☑ "The World as 100 People" /
  "A Contribution to Statistics"
  Selection Test

SUMMARIES

English

This poem conveys the speaker's estimation of how many people out of 100 exhibit various behaviors, hold various values, and exhibit various moral strengths and weaknesses. By inventing her own categories and "statistics" for human behavior, the speaker expresses her own point of view on human nature and the human condition.

Spanish

Este poema transmite la estimación del poeta de cuántas personas entre cada 100 demuestran varios comportamientos, tienen varios valores y presentan varias fuerzas y debilidades morales. Al crear sus propias categorías y "estadísticas" del comportamiento humano, el poeta expresa su punto de vista con respecto a la naturaleza y la condición humana.

 ## SMALL-GROUP OPTIONS

Have students work in small groups to read and discuss the selection.

Think-Pair-Share

- After students have read and analyzed "A Contribution to Statistics," pose this question: "What do you think the title of the poem means?"
- Have students think about the question individually and take notes.
- Then, have pairs discuss their ideas about the question.
- Finally, ask pairs to share their responses with the class.

Triple-Entry Journal

- Have students use a notebook or journal for recording Triple-Entry Journal notes.
- Model how to divide a page into three columns. Have students label the columns from left to right, "Quotations from the Text," "My Notes," and "My Partner's Notes."
- In the first column, have students record passages from the text that they found interesting, important, or confusing.
- In the middle column, have students write their own reactions, interpretations, or questions.
- Instruct partners to exchange journals. In the third column, have students write responses either to the quotation from the text or to their partner's notes.

Text X-Ray: English Learner Support
for "A Contribution to Statistics"

Use the Text X-Ray and the supports and scaffolds in the Teacher's Edition to help guide students at different proficiency levels through the selection.

INTRODUCE THE SELECTION
DISCUSS THE TITLE

Read aloud the title of the selection. Provide these explanations:

- If someone makes a *contribution* to something, that person gives something or adds something.
- *Statistics* refers to collecting, organizing, and studying numerical (number) data.

Explain that statistics help us understand the characteristics of a population. *Characteristics* are the things that describe groups within the total population. Model pronouncing *contribution, statistics*, and *characteristics*. Then guide students to use the words to complete these frames:

- *When I work in a group, I make a _____ by _____.*
- *If you study _____, you _____.*
- *Most students share these _____: they _____ and _____.*

CULTURAL REFERENCES

The following phrases may be unfamiliar to students:

- *suffering illusions* (line 14): having ideas that are not true and that may hurt you later
- *fleeting youth* (line 15): the years when a person is young that seem to pass quickly
- *forced by circumstances* (line 28): when a person has to do something, especially something unpleasant, because of special pressures or circumstances
- *ballpark figures* (line 30): approximate numbers

LISTENING

Listen for Details

Explain that listening for details, or certain information, will help students build listening comprehension skills and understand more of what they hear.

Use the following supports with students at varying proficiency levels:

- Say: "Listen as I read the poem. Write the numbers you hear. For example, if I say, 'Out of ten people,' you write '10.'" (Model writing "10.") "If you hear no number, write a dash (—)." (Model writing a dash.) Read aloud the first stanza. Have students write the number they hear. *(100)* Continue in this way through each stanza. **SUBSTANTIAL**
- Read aloud each stanza. Ask literal questions such as, "How many people always know better?" and have students answer in complete sentences. **MODERATE**
- Display literal and inferential questions about stanzas 1–6, such as "How many people always know better?" (*literal*) and "According to the poem, how do most people who admire others feel?" (*inferential*). Read aloud stanzas 1–6 and have students answer each question orally or in writing. Repeat with the rest of the poem. **LIGHT**

SPEAKING

Express Opinions and Give Advice

Read aloud the "Give Instructions" part of the Create and Discuss assignment on Student Edition page 127. Check that students understand the task. Then scaffold the language structures they will need to complete the task.

Use the following supports with students at varying proficiency levels:

- Model expressing a problem and seeking advice. Say: "I doubt every step—that means I worry too much." (Pantomime worry.) "I texted my friend. She hasn't answered. Is she mad at me? What should I do?" Elicit or provide some words of advice such as *relax, believe in yourself, don't worry*. Then role-play the conversation with students. Have them provide advice, using the imperative form of the verbs. **SUBSTANTIAL**

- Provide sentence starters to help partners take turns asking for and offering advice: *I think you should _____. You also can _____.* **MODERATE**

- Ask students to role-play giving advice to a friend about how to solve a problem. Have students use the words *first, next, then*, and *finally* to make each step clear. **LIGHT**

READING

Expand Reading Skills

Explain that poems are meant to be read aloud and that doing so will help students understand the poem better.

Use the following supports with students at varying proficiency levels:

- Have students echo read lines 1–5 with you. Paraphrase *doubting every step* as "worrying a lot or not believing in themselves." Explain that *nearly all the rest* means "almost 48 people out of 100." Repeat with other stanzas. **SUBSTANTIAL**

- Select several stanzas for students to read aloud. Preteach idioms and unfamiliar words and phrases. Have partners take turns reading, stopping at the end of each stanza to paraphrase what they have read. **MODERATE**

- Ask students to read the poem independently and to seek clarification of any words, phrases, or structures by checking a reference source, asking a peer, or asking you or an aide. Have students keep track of learned words, phrases, and structures in a language notebook. **LIGHT**

WRITING

Use Modal Verbs

Read aloud the "Write a Letter" part of the Create and Discuss assignment on Student Edition page 127. Explain that when you give people advice, you tell them what you think they should do or what would be good for them to do.

Introduce or review the modal verbs *should, could, can*, and *might*. Use the following supports with students at varying proficiency levels to help them edit their letters:

- Introduce *should* and *could*. Have students repeat the words. Explain that the *l* is silent and the *ou* is pronounced like the *oo* in *wood* or *stood*. Have students use each word in a sentence offering advice. **SUBSTANTIAL**

- Explain the differences in meaning between the modals *should, could, can*, and *might*. Have students use at least two of the verbs in their letter. **MODERATE**

- Have students check their use of modal verbs, making sure that the words are spelled correctly and are followed by the correct form of the main verb in the sentence. **LIGHT**

TEACH

Connect to the
ESSENTIAL QUESTION

Like the infographic "The World as 100 People," the poem "A Contribution to Statistics" classifies and quantifies people by aspects of their lives. However, the point of view expressed in the poem is considerably more subjective, or personal. The poem presents invented statistics about various human characteristics in order to convey ideas about life and about people's motives and behaviors.

COMPARE DETAILS

Have students reflect upon "The World as 100 People." Call on volunteers to suggest the message that its creator had in mind. (**Possible answers:** *What we consider to be important in human life today is a complex mix of characteristics; many people have to go without certain aspects of life that we consider important.*)

Point out that even though the infographic and the poem are different genres, they both use details to express a message about people around the world. To prepare to compare the two texts, students need to read the poem carefully, note numbers and other information the poet conveys and ask themselves how these details compare to those in the infographic. They also should consider the poet's purpose and how that purpose may have influenced her choice of details and the message that she wished to communicate to readers.

COLLABORATE & COMPARE

POEM

A CONTRIBUTION TO STATISTICS

by **Wisława Szymborska**
pages 123–125

COMPARE DETAILS

Now that you have examined the infographic "The World as 100 People," read "A Contribution to Statistics" and explore how this poem expresses similar ideas. As you read, think about how the author uses literary devices and poetic structure to analyze people and their experiences. After you are finished, you will collaborate with a small group on a final project that involves an analysis of both texts.

 ### ESSENTIAL QUESTION:

How does our point of view shape what we think we know?

INFOGRAPHIC

THE WORLD AS 100 PEOPLE

by **Jack Hagley**
pages 117–119

120   Unit 2

 ## LEARNING MINDSET

Persistence   Remind students that a persistence mindset means not giving up on something that seems tough at first but, instead, continuing to work on it. Tell students that like most poems, "A Contribution to Statistics" communicates feelings and ideas indirectly, through the use of literary devices, poetic structure, and word choice. Explain that for most readers, inferring the meaning of a poem becomes easier with multiple readings, careful examination, and discussion. Therefore, encourage students to persist in reading and rereading even if the message is not immediately evident. You might suggest they say to themselves, "I know that I can understand this poem if I keep examining the details and thinking about them."

A Contribution to Statistics

QUICK START

During any given day, each human being experiences a range of emotions from jubilation to sadness and from doubt to confidence. Think about a day in which you experienced numerous emotions. Discuss your experience with your group.

ANALYZE LITERARY DEVICES

Literary devices are techniques writers use to communicate their ideas to readers. The use of literary devices often enhances a writer's work and leads readers to a deeper understanding of the writer's message. Here are three devices used in the poem:

Idioms are phrases or expressions whose meaning is different from their literal meaning. The figurative meaning of an idiom usually develops over time and is often specific to a particular culture or language.

IDIOM IN POEM	FIGURATIVE MEANING
glad to lend a hand	happy to help another person do something

Parallelism repeats a grammatical construction to show a connection between ideas.

PARALLELISM IN POEM	HOW IT LINKS IDEAS
Those who always know better —fifty-two, doubting every step —nearly all the rest,	The poem repeatedly uses the structure of presenting a human characteristic followed by a long dash and a statistical estimate of it.

Shifts occur when the writer's tone or focus changes. Shifts help keep a reader interested in a text and can enhance the clarity of a writer's presentation.

SHIFT IN POEM	EFFECT ON TONE
glad to lend a hand if it doesn't take too long —as high as forty-nine,	The first line seems very positive, but the second line shifts to show that convenience may be more important than kindness for some people.

GENRE ELEMENTS: POETRY
- uses figurative language and literary devices
- expresses a theme, or a message about life
- is arranged in lines and stanzas

TEACH

QUICK START

After students share their experiences, ask them to make some generalizations about the emotions that people experience and also to think about how these emotions might affect human characteristics and behavior. For example, who is more likely to help another: a person who's often happy, or a person who's often angry? Why? After pairs discuss their ideas, have pairs share them with the larger group.

ANALYZE LITERARY DEVICES

Point out that writers use a range of devices to communicate their ideas to readers and that **idioms**, **parallelism**, and **shifts** are just a few of those. Review each type of device, its definition, example, and related explanation. Then have students work in groups to create or locate two or three more examples of each type of device. Ask groups to discuss the effects each device may have on an author's message and tone. (If necessary, remind students that the **tone** of a literary work expresses the writer's attitude toward his or her subject. A tone may be described as angry, sad, amused, and so on.)

 ## ENGLISH LEARNER SUPPORT

Use Idioms Explain the meaning of the idiom *lend a hand*. Check that students understand that when we lend something to someone, we let someone use it for a time; when we lend a hand, we are lending our help (something that our hands can do) or giving someone our help for a time. Point out that if you are *glad* to do something, you are happy to do it. Model the following exchange and then have pairs repeat it: "Could you help me with this?" "Sure! I'm glad to lend you a hand." Point out the placement of the pronoun *me* and explain that in the answer, you would switch the pronoun to *you*: "I would be happy to lend you a hand." Finally, have pairs or small groups describe a time when they were glad to lend someone a hand.

ALL LEVELS

TEACH

ANALYZE STRUCTURE

Emphasize that a stanza may consist of a varying number of lines, even within the same poem. Review the structure of "A Contribution to Statistics." Point out how the first line of the poem is a stanza of its own and how it introduces all of the other stanzas.

As students read, have them identify the human characteristic or quality expressed at the beginning of each stanza and the number of people the poet claims have that quality. Students should consider the numbers and the way the poet writes them. For example, in the second stanza, she writes "fifty-two," but in the third stanza, she writes "nearly all the rest." Point out the repeated structure of characteristic followed by statistic; explain that it allows her to highlight contrasts and thus convey both a tone and a theme.

ANNOTATION MODEL

Point out that as students read the poem, they may find it helpful to mark the topic (characteristic) and the number (statistic) in each stanza. They may also find it helpful to color-code their annotations using highlighters or use some other system to help them analyze structure or identify literary devices. Also remind students that in addition to answering the questions in the margins, they are free to write their own notes, including paraphrases, comments, or questions about ideas that are unclear or topics they want to learn more about.

ANALYZE STRUCTURE

Poems are often divided into stanzas, with an extra line space separating lines. A **stanza** functions in a way similar to a paragraph in a story or essay, forming a meaningful section of the work. A very long stanza may provide context or detail, while a very short stanza will usually make an important point.

In "A Contribution to Statistics," Szymborska uses the stanzas to communicate her theme. In each stanza, the poem presents a human characteristic followed by a statistic. The predictable structure of the stanzas links the poet's ideas and heightens their impact.

As you read, note the topic or characteristic that each stanza explores as shown below. Considering all of the stanza topics together can help you understand the poem's theme, or message about human nature.

ANNOTATION MODEL

NOTICE & NOTE

Make annotations to help you analyze the structure of a poem. In this model, you can see one reader's notes about the beginning of "A Contribution to Statistics."

> Out of a hundred people ← — The poet is creating each stanza in relation to 100 people.
>
> Those who always know better
> —fifty-two,
>
> doubting every step
> —nearly all the rest,
>
> The first topic is overconfidence. This sets up a contrast with the next topic, which is insecurity.

Use Support to Develop Vocabulary   Introduce or review the words *characteristic* and *statistic*. Explain that a *characteristic* is the way we describe a person or thing. For example, a person's characteristics could be friendly, smart, and funny. A *statistic* is a number that defines a *characteristic*. For example, in the sentence "Half of the students in our class have brown hair," the *statistic* is "half of the students" and the *characteristic* is "have brown hair." Provide students with a T-chart or two-column graphic organizer. Have students label the left column "Characteristic" and the right column "Statistic." Ask pairs of students to complete the organizer for the second and third stanzas of "A Contribution to Statistics." Then have students meet in small groups to compare their organizers. Have students complete the chart for the rest of the stanzas in the poem. **ALL LEVELS**

BACKGROUND

Wisława Szymborska *(1923–2012) was a poet and essayist. Szymborska lived in Poland her entire life and had to continue her education in underground classes during World War II. The poet often employed literary devices to write about philosophy, obsessions, war, and sometimes quirky subjects. Some of her poetry appeared in songs and pop culture and was translated into many languages. She won the 1996 Nobel Prize in Literature and was still working on new poetry at the time of her death at age 88.*

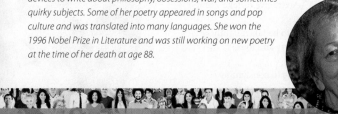

A CONTRIBUTION TO STATISTICS

Poem by Wisława Szymborska
translated by Stanislaw Barańczak and Clare Cavanagh

PREPARE TO COMPARE

This poem uses the same approach to analyzing people as the infographic does. Watch for similarities and differences between the details Szymborska and Hagley choose as you read.

> Out of a hundred people
>
> Those who always know better
> —fifty-two,
>
> doubting every step
> 5 —nearly all the rest,
>
> glad to lend a hand
> if it doesn't take too long
> —as high as forty-nine,
>
> always good,
> 10 because they can't be otherwise
> —four, well maybe five,

(b) ©Rawpixel.com/Shutterstock

Notice & Note

You can use the side margins to notice and note signposts in the text.

ANALYZE STRUCTURE
Annotate: Mark the first three stanzas in the poem. What pattern do they establish?

Paraphrase: Restate lines 1–5 in your own words. Remember to maintain the order and meaning of the original text.

BACKGROUND

Have students read the background about the poet, Wisława Szymborska. Explain that in this case the word *underground* means "secret." Remind students that in Nazi-controlled lands during World War II (1939–1945), many Jewish people and members of other groups were killed and that harsh restrictions were placed on those who were not. Ask students to make predictions about how being a young adult during World War II may have shaped the poet's point of view on human nature. Have students share their ideas with a partner or small group.

PREPARE TO COMPARE

Direct students to use the Prepare to Compare prompt to focus their reading.

✏️ ANALYZE STRUCTURE

Have students focus on the second and third stanzas and consider how the dashes help to clarify the structure. Encourage students to remember that Szymborska sets up a pattern in which each stanza (after the first) identifies a characteristic, followed by a statistic. Explain that the question is asking them to mark details that make that pattern clear. Point out that it may be helpful to mark the characteristics and the statistics in different ways (by underlining and circling or by using different colors). (**Answer:** *If you look at one hundred people, fifty-two of these people will always think they know better than you do about something, while nearly all of the rest of the one hundred will doubt every action they take.*)

■ English Learner Support

Use Grammatical Structures Explain that looking for and recognizing patterns in language can help a person master it. Point out that the poem begins with "Out of a hundred people / Those who . . . " and that every stanza, from the third stanza on, begins with a word that could follow that phrase if the verb *are* were added. To give students practice using this pattern, have them take turns reading the first half of each stanza by adding "Those who [are]" or "People who [are]" before each characteristic. For example, they might read the beginning of line 4 as "Those who [are] doubting every step."

MODERATE/LIGHT

📖 For **listening** and **reading support** for students at varying proficiency levels, see the **Text X-Ray** on pages 120C–120D.

WHEN STUDENTS STRUGGLE . . .

Compare and Contrast Have students begin a Venn diagram to help them start thinking about comparing the poem to the infographic. Start by having students record a genre label and the topic of each text. *(infographic and poem; statistics or categories of people)* Ask students what the purpose of the infographic is. *(to provide basic number facts about the lives of people around the world)* Have students record that. Then ask: What kind of contribution might the poet want to make to statistics? That is, what ideas might she want to add? Tell students to record the purpose after they have read the poem, along with other notes on the similarities and differences in the texts.

TEACH

ANALYZE LITERARY DEVICES

Have a volunteer read aloud the stanza that begins at line 27. Then ask students how the word *ballpark* affects the tone of the stanza. (**Answer:** *The speaker is saying that it is better not to know even a general estimate of the number of people who are cruel when circumstances force them to be that way. The statement suggests that the number is so high that the speaker doesn't want to think about it. The resulting tone can be seen either as serious and sad, or as wry—that is, funny in an ironic way.*)

■ English Learner Support

Analyze Idioms Explain that a *ballpark* is where people play a game such as baseball; if students have ever watched baseball on TV, then they have seen a ballpark. Point out that this is its literal meaning. Explain that in this stanza, however, *ballpark figures* is an idiom that has nothing to do with sports. It is just a guess or estimate that is close to what the real number is. For example, if the real price for a car is $28,998, then a price in ballpark figures might be $28,000 or $29,000 or even $30,000. However, $5,000 is not in the ballpark because it's not even close to the actual price. Go on to explain that an **idiom** is a type of figurative language—a group of words with a special meaning that is different from the literal meaning of each word alone. **Figurative language** is language used in a creative way; **literal language** means words that have plain meanings. Work with students to create a list of idioms and their literal explanations (for example, *in the doghouse*/"in trouble"; *scared to death*/"very scared").

SUBSTANTIAL/MODERATE

ANALYZE LITERARY DEVICES

Remind students that when writers use **parallelism**, they repeat a grammatical structure to show a connection between ideas. Urge students to consider both repetition and parallelism as they analyze lines 41–45. (**Answer:** *The structure of the two stanzas beginning in lines 41 and 43 is parallel. Like the rest of the poem, both stanzas begin with a characteristic and then present a number. Because the word* righteous *is repeated in both stanzas and and understanding is added the second time, the poet emphasizes that far fewer people [three vs. thirty-five] are both righteous and understanding. The contrast suggests that a fair number of people believe in doing the right thing but that very few truly care about understanding other people.*)

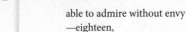

able to admire without envy
—eighteen,

15 suffering illusions
induced by fleeting youth
—sixty, give or take a few,

not to be taken lightly
—forty and four,

20 living in constant fear
of someone or something
—seventy-seven,

capable of happiness
—twenty-something tops,

harmless singly,
25 savage in crowds
—half at least,

cruel
when forced by circumstances
—better not to know
30 even ballpark figures,

ANALYZE LITERARY DEVICES

Annotate: Mark the word *ballpark* in line 30.

Evaluate: A number "in the ballpark" is approximate, not precise. How does this idiom affect the tone of this stanza?

wise after the fact
—just a couple more
than wise before it,

taking only things from life
35 —thirty
(I wish I were wrong),

hunched in pain,
no flashlight in the dark
—eighty-three
40 sooner or later,

ANALYZE LITERARY DEVICES

Annotate: Mark a word that is repeated in lines 41–45.

Analyze: How does the author use repetition and parallelism to show a contrast here?

righteous
—thirty-five, which is a lot,

IMPROVE READING FLUENCY

Targeted Passage Use echo reading to help students apply appropriate phrasing, pacing, and expression in reading lines 37–50. Read those lines aloud, modeling how to read some lines (for example, 37–38 and 43–44) as a sentence and how to use punctuation (dashes and commas) as signals to pause. Then have students echo your reading as you read those lines a second and third time.

 Go to the **Reading Studio** for additional support in developing fluency.

righteous
and understanding
45 —three,

worthy of compassion
—ninety-nine,

mortal
—a hundred out of a hundred.
50 Thus far this figure still remains unchanged.

CHECK YOUR UNDERSTANDING

Answer these questions before moving on to the **Analyze the Text** section on the following page.

1 The statistics in the poem —

A indicate the poet's assessments of human nature

B are based on scientific surveys of how people act

C help the reader predict how people react in particular circumstances

D show that the poet has a negative view of human behavior

2 The poem's structure —

F emphasizes the rhythm and rhyme of the statistics the poet chose

G is predictable to allow the reader to focus on the poet's message about humanity

H arranges the statistics in numerical order to show what characteristics are less and more important

J moves from humorous examples to increasingly serious ones

3 What is the meaning of the final stanza of the poem?

A The negatives of life outweigh the positives of life.

B Each person should try to live the best life he or she can.

C There is no way to avoid the ups and downs of life.

D Every person dies regardless of how they live their life.

NOTICE & NOTE

CONTRASTS AND CONTRADICTIONS

Notice & Note: Mark the contrast that appears at the end of this poem.

Interpret: Why might you find the ending surprising or jarring?

CONTRASTS AND CONTRADICTIONS

Have students mark the text that contrasts with the poem's **structure** in the rest of the poem. (**Answer:** *The line "a hundred out of a hundred" contrasts with the numbers given previously, which were all under 100. By "mortal," the poet means that all people will die one day. This statement is surprising or jarring because all of the previous characteristics were subjective generalizations, whereas mortality is a stark fact.*)

CHECK YOUR UNDERSTANDING

Have students answer the questions independently.

Answers:

1. *A*

2. *G*

3. *D*

If they answer any questions incorrectly, have them reread the text to confirm their understanding. Then they may proceed to ANALYZE THE TEXT on page 126.

ENGLISH LEARNER SUPPORT

Oral Assessment Use the following questions to assess students' comprehension and speaking skills. Ask students to respond in short, complete sentences.

1. Which of the following is true about the statistics in the poem? They show the poet's views of human nature. *(yes)* They are based on scientific surveys of how people act. *(no)* They help the reader guess how people react in certain cases. *(no)* They show that the poet has a negative view of human behavior. *(no)*

2. Which of the following is true about the poem's structure? It stresses the rhythm and rhyme of the statistics. *(no)* Its steady pattern helps readers think about the poet's message about people. *(yes)* It arranges the statistics in numerical order to show what characteristics are less and more important. *(no)* It moves from funny examples to more serious ones. *(no)*

3. What is the meaning of the final stanza of the poem? *(All people die regardless of how they live their life.)* **ALL LEVELS**

APPLY

ANALYZE THE TEXTS

Possible answers:

1. **DOK 3:** *The use of an infographic makes it much easier for the reader to view and understand large amounts of data. If the data were presented in a table or in paragraph form, it would be too overwhelming for most people to view or thoroughly understand.*

2. **DOK 2:** *Continent, gender, and age represent the most basic information about people. It could be that the designer placed them there so that they would stand out or would be read first.*

3. **DOK 4:** *The poem suggests that many people have weaknesses of character: out of every 100 people, few people are always good ("four, well maybe five"), and even fewer are righteous and understanding (three); few can admire without envy (eighteen); seventy-seven are living in constant fear; and it's "better not to know" how many are "cruel / when forced by circumstances." Yet virtually all, ninety-nine out of a hundred, are "worthy of compassion."*

4. **DOK 4:** *The poem's predictable structure makes the connections among the poet's ideas clear, so readers can focus on how these statistics apply to themselves or people they know.*

5. **DOK 4:** *The poet is using specific numbers to measure aspects of human nature that defy statistical measurement. The title of the poem implies that the poet is contributing something to statistics—this "contribution" being an acknowledgement that there is more to people than can be counted in numbers.*

RESEARCH

Have students begin by reviewing the categories that Hagley used in his infographic. Then have them select one to research. You might have students predict which categories will be relatively stable (for example, gender or religion) and which ones might change significantly from year to year (for example, Internet use). If students have trouble locating information, review useful search terms such as "world literacy data" or "percentage of people who can read." Once students have located their data, invite them to present it to the class, making sure to credit their information source(s).

Extend Discuss with students ways they can look at a given category from another point of view. They could reimagine data using geography. For example, if they want to show the number of people out of 100 that live on each continent, they might use a color key with warm colors indicating greater populations and cool colors for smaller populations.

 RESPOND

ANALYZE THE TEXTS

Support your responses with evidence from the text. 📓 NOTEBOOK

1. **Draw Conclusions** How does the use of an infographic help you to better understand the data presented in "The World as 100 People"?

2. **Make Inferences** Why do you think the creator of the infographic "The World as 100 People" placed the data about continent, gender, and age at the top of the graphic?

3. **Analyze** Based on the numbers used in the poem, what is the poet's opinion of humanity? Use text evidence in your answer.

4. **Evaluate** How effective do you find the predictable, parallel structure of this poem in communicating a message about human nature? Support your response with examples from the poem.

5. **Notice & Note** How does the poet's use of specific numbers relate to the title and ultimate message of the poem? Use text evidence in your answer.

RESEARCH TIP
It's best to begin a research project by creating a research question. Before you begin researching, decide exactly what you are looking for. If you cannot find the information you need, be willing to alter your research question.

RESEARCH

Choose one statistical category from the infographic to explore further. Determine if your research matches Hagley's infographic or if the conditions have changed in the years since he created the graphic. Be sure to credit the source of the information you use.

Possible answers:

CATEGORY	RECENT DATA	SOURCE
Water	30 out of 100 people lack access to safe water at home	World Health Organization website

Extend Create a color-coded map that shows how your chosen statistic plays out in various countries or on different continents.

⚙️ LEARNING MINDSET

Problem Solving Remind students that everyone runs into problems at times when learning something new, but most problems can be solved with effort and persistence. Note the importance of understanding the cause of the problem. Other problem-solving strategies include trying various solutions, being patient, and asking for help. Remind students that every problem they solve will build self-confidence. You might say, "If I have trouble finding new data on one of Hagley's categories, then I should consider what the source of my struggle might be. Do I need to change my question or my search terms? Is my focus either too broad or too narrow? Identifying the problem will help me find a solution."

CREATE AND DISCUSS

Write a Letter Choose one statistical category from Szymborska's poem, and write a friendly letter to a real or imagined person who fits into that category.

- ❏ Review the format of a friendly letter.
- ❏ Identify the audience of the letter.
- ❏ Provide advice to or request advice from your reader about a topic related to the category you chose.

Give Instructions In pairs, ask a partner a question related to a problem Szymborska identifies in her poem. For example, "What can I do to be able to admire someone without feeling envious of them?"

- ❏ Provide step-by-step instructions to your partner for solving the problem they ask about.
- ❏ Then, switch roles and ask a question of your partner. Listen to your partner carefully and take notes about what was said.

RESPOND TO THE ESSENTIAL QUESTION

 How does our point of view shape what we think we know?

Gather Information Review your annotations and notes on "The World as 100 People" and "A Contribution to Statistics." Then, add relevant details to your Response Log. As you determine which information to include, think about

- what the statistics in the poem and infographic reveal about the human condition
- which statistics or ideas surprised you
- which statistics you would like to learn more about

At the end of the unit, you will use your notes to write a short story.

RESPOND

 Go to the **Writing Studio** for more on writing for a specific audience and purpose.

 Go to the **Speaking and Listening Studio** for more on giving and following instructions.

ACADEMIC VOCABULARY

As you write and discuss what you learned about "The World as 100 People" and "A Contribution to Statistics," be sure to use the Academic Vocabulary words. Check off each of the words that you use.

- ❏ **differentiate**
- ❏ **incorporate**
- ❏ **mode**
- ❏ **orient**
- ❏ **perspective**

APPLY

CREATE AND DISCUSS

Write a Letter Remind students how each stanza of Szymborska's poem identifies a human characteristic, or category of people. Check that students understand the task. Review the parts of a friendly letter: date, address, salutation, body, closing, signature, and optional postscript. Explain that in a friendly letter, the language is usually informal (casual but not impolite). Once students have completed their letters, invite them to exchange letters with a partner to read.

For **writing support** for students at varying proficiency levels, see the **Text X-Ray** on page 120D.

Give Instructions Give students a moment to skim the poem to locate a potential problem that they could ask for advice about. Encourage students to choose a new topic rather than the characteristic that they chose when writing their letter. Have students take a few minutes to think of the question that they would like to ask. Then have partners take turns asking and answering their questions. You can model the activity by selecting a problem not mentioned in the poem (e.g., *bullying people on the Internet*), posing a question (*How can we stop bullying on the Internet?*), and providing instructions for solving it (*First, form an interested group. Next, identify sites to monitor. Then brainstorm ways to respond to bullying comments.*). Note that clear instructions include words such as *first, next,* and *then.*

For **speaking support** for students at varying proficiency levels, see the **Text X-Ray** on page 120D.

RESPOND TO THE ESSENTIAL QUESTION

Allow time for students to add details from "The World as 100 People" and "A Contribution to Statistics" to their Unit 2 Response Logs.

🔵 ENGLISH LEARNER SUPPORT

Write a Letter Use the following supports with students at different proficiency levels:

- Guide students to write a short letter. "Share the pen" and have students copy the finished letter. Focus on a request for advice and select someone famous to write to—for example, "Dear [famous person], I would like your advice. Many people doubt every step. They worry too much. How can they be strong like you?" **SUBSTANTIAL**

- Provide a frame to help scaffold the writing task. For the body, provide a simple frame such as this one requesting advice: *I would like your _____. This is the problem: Some people _____. How can _____?* **MODERATE**

- Have students write their letters independently. If they are writing to seek advice, ask them to include descriptive details about the problem. If they are writing to offer advice, have them provide several problem-solving steps. **LIGHT**

© Houghton Mifflin Harcourt Publishing Company

COMPARE TEXTS

Before groups complete the two graphic organizers, remind students that the nature of the details included in the infographic and the poem are quite different: The infographic includes details based on fact; they can be verified by sources. The poem includes details that were invented by the poet; they cannot be verified by sources. Point out that this distinction is important to keep in mind as they consider each message the details convey.

ANALYZE THE TEXTS

Possible answers:

1. **DOK 2:** *Both the infographic and the poem convey aspects of the human condition—what life is like for many people.*

2. **DOK 2:** *The infographic uses actual statistics; the poem uses made-up statistics based on the author's point of view on various human traits or behaviors.*

3. **DOK 3:** *Both the infographic and the poem encourage readers to think about what they are reading and potentially inspire them toward positive change. The infographic brings awareness to specific topics regarding the world population. The purpose of the poem may be to raise emotional awareness and encourage readers to care more about the people around them.*

4. **DOK 4:** *There are a great many differences in the lives of people around the world. As the infographic indicates, there are people who are privileged but others who live hard lives. The poem also suggests that people's lives are very diverse—at least, that there are different types of people—but it closes with the idea that one thing all people have in common is that they will die one day.*

Collaborate & Compare

THE WORLD AS 100 PEOPLE
Infographic by Jack Hagley

A CONTRIBUTION TO STATISTICS
Poem by Wislawa Szymborska

COMPARE DETAILS

The infographic and the poem are based on the same idea but emphasize different details. In a small group, complete the charts to track the details and their effect on the message of the infographic and the poem.

"The World as 100 People"

DETAIL FROM TEXT	MESSAGE
Literacy	Almost a fifth of people cannot read or write.
Housing	Almost a fourth of the world's population is homeless.
Internet	The Internet is available to only 30 out of every 100 people.
Poverty	Almost half of the world's population lives in extreme poverty.

"A Contribution to Statistics"

DETAIL FROM TEXT	MESSAGE
able to admire without envy —eighteen,	Most people feel envy.
not to be taken lightly —forty and four,	People—and their circumstances—should be taken seriously by others.
capable of happiness —twenty-something tops,	Relatively few people are able to find happiness. This may suggest either that life can be difficult for many or that most people are difficult to please.
worthy of compassion —ninety-nine,	Almost everyone is worthy of the compassion of others.

ANALYZE THE TEXTS

Discuss these questions in your group.

1. **Compare** What are the similarities between the infographic and poem?

2. **Contrast** What are the differences between the two?

3. **Evaluate** How are the purposes of the texts similar? Different?

4. **Synthesize** What have you learned about the world's population from these two texts?

ENGLISH LEARNER SUPPORT

Ask Questions Use the following questions to help students compare the selections.

1. Which text uses facts, or true information? Which text expresses feelings?

2. How is the infographic like the poem? How are the infographic and the poem different?

3. Which text did you understand better? Which text did you like more? Why?

   ALL LEVELS

RESEARCH AND PRESENT

Now, your group can continue exploring the ideas in these texts by researching more statistics and using them to create a multimedia presentation. Follow these steps:

Go to the **Speaking and Listening Studio** for help with delivering a multimedia presentation.

1. **Develop a Question** In your group, brainstorm what the members of your group would like to learn more about. Decide what statistics you could find about the area of interest your group selects. Select a statistic that is not included on the infographic "The World as 100 People."

2. **Gather Information** Try a variety of methods for locating valid, relevant sources of statistical information. You might search in a library database or conduct an online search. If you do not find sources that answer your original question, modify your research question to a related topic and try again. Document each source using an approved citation format.

3. **Synthesize Ideas** Draw a conclusion about your question using information from two or more sources. You can use a chart to record the information you find.

My Question:	
Source 1:	Source 2:
Source 1 Information:	Source 2 Information:
My Answer:	

4. **Present to the Class** Your group will present what you have learned in a brief multimedia presentation. You will share your original question, the information you gathered, and an answer in the form of a statistic with elaboration. Present images and graphics to support your ideas. Be sure to compare the idea you present with the details in the infographic and the poem. Which of the two works does your topic best fit?

WHEN STUDENTS STRUGGLE . . .

Synthesize Ideas Remind students that when they synthesize ideas, they take individual pieces of information from different sources and combine them in order to gain a better understanding of a subject. For example, if you find that one research report states that 30 people out of 100 can access the Internet and another says that 25 people can access the Internet, then you might synthesize those two pieces of information by combining them into one statement—for example, *Research indicates that anywhere from 25 to 30 people out of 100 have Internet access.* Guide students to synthesize their research in the graphic organizer above.

RESEARCH AND PRESENT

Explain that a multimedia presentation includes two or more of these elements: speech, writing, visuals (images and graphics), audio, and video. Point out that for this activity, students could create their own infographic, show slides, or work with other media formats suited to their topic. Guide students to develop presentations appropriate for the classroom.

1. **Develop a Question** As students develop questions, circulate among the groups and check that the questions are appropriate for the level of research you expect students to conduct. Make sure that the statistic is not already included in "The World as 100 People."

2. **Gather Information** Discuss the meaning of sources that are *valid* and *relevant*. Explain that *valid* sources provide accurate, factual information that can be verified by other sources. Explain that *relevant* sources are sources that are on topic and also current. (For example, a magazine article from 20 years ago would not contain relevant facts about how many people today have access to the Internet.) Let students know the citation format you want them to use and provide them with examples of that format.

3. **Synthesize Ideas** Explain that when researchers synthesize ideas, they combine information from various sources to make a solid whole. You might use the analogy of braiding together three pieces of string to make a rope. While researching, students should look for two or three different sources to provide the same facts and then use them as a basis for a strong conclusion.

4. **Present to the Class** Before students give their multimedia presentations, review with them these elements of effective presentation: eye contact, purposeful gestures, and clear speech (appropriate rate, volume, and enunciation). Also let students know that each person in the group should present some of the information. Allow groups time to rehearse before giving their presentations.

 For **writing support** for students at varying proficiency levels, see the **Text X-Ray** on page 114D.

INDEPENDENT READING

READER'S CHOICE

Setting a Purpose Have students review their Unit 2 Response Logs and think about what they've already learned about how our point of view shapes what we think we know. As they choose their Independent Reading selections, encourage them to consider what more they want to know.

NOTICE NOTE

Explain that some selections may contain multiple signposts; others may contain only one. And the same type of signpost can occur many times in the same text.

 LEARNING MINDSET

Curiosity Tell students that curiosity leads to deeper, more engaged learning. Explain that it is a key skill for developing a learning mindset—and one of the first steps in overcoming the challenges that accompany learning any new skill. Have students focus on the selection that most intrigues them. Encourage them to try satisfying that curiosity, even if the selection is more challenging than what they typically read.

 INDEPENDENT READING

ESSENTIAL QUESTION:

How does our point of view shape what we think we know?

Reader's Choice

Setting a Purpose Select one or more of these options from your eBook to continue your exploration of the Essential Question.

· Read the descriptions to see which text grabs your interest.

· Think about which genres you enjoy reading.

Notice Note

In this unit, you practiced asking a **Big Question** and noticing and noting two signposts: **Numbers and Stats** and **Word Gaps**. As you read independently, these signposts and others will aid your understanding. Below are the anchor questions to ask when you read literature and nonfiction.

Reading Literature: Stories, Poems, and Plays		
Signpost	**Anchor Question**	**Lesson**
Contrasts and Contradictions	Why did the character act that way?	p. 145
Aha Moment	How might this change things?	p. 394
Tough Questions	What does this make me wonder about?	p. 2
Words of the Wiser	What's the lesson for the character?	p. 3
Again and Again	Why might the author keep bringing this up?	p. 145
Memory Moment	Why is this memory important?	p. 3

Reading Nonfiction: Essays, Articles, and Arguments		
Signpost	**Anchor Question(s)**	**Lesson**
Big Questions	What surprised me? What did the author think I already knew? What challenged, changed, or confirmed what I already knew?	p. 220 p. 319 p. 74
Contrasts and Contradictions	What is the difference, and why does it matter?	p. 318
Extreme or Absolute Language	Why did the author use this language?	p. 221
Numbers and Stats	Why did the author use these numbers or amounts?	p. 75
Quoted Words	Why was this person quoted or cited, and what did this add?	p. 221
Word Gaps	Do I know this word from someplace else? Does it seem like technical talk for this topic? Do clues in the sentence help me understand the word?	p. 75

© Houghton Mifflin Harcourt Publishing Company

 ENGLISH LEARNER SUPPORT

Develop Fluency Select a passage from a text that matches students' abilities. Read the passage aloud while students follow along silently.

· Echo read the passage by reading aloud one sentence and then having students repeat the sentence back to you. Check their comprehension by asking yes/no questions about the passage. **SUBSTANTIAL**

· Have students read the passage silently and write down one question they have. As a class, review the questions and discuss possible answers. Model how to use text details and context clues to increase comprehension. **MODERATE**

· Allow more fluent readers to select their own texts. Set a specific time for students to read silently. Have them write a brief summary. Then, provide them with a longer period of time to reread. Ask students to review what they wrote before and make any necessary revisions. **LIGHT**

Go to the **Reading Studio** for additional support in developing fluency.

You can preview these texts in Unit 2 of your eBook.

Then, check off the text or texts that you select to read on your own.

POEM

Before I got my eye put out
Emily Dickinson

Read what one of our most famous poets has to say about how we see things.

ESSAY

What Our Telescopes Couldn't See
Pippa Goldschmidt

When we look to the skies, what do we miss seeing here on Earth?

INFORMATIONAL TEXT

from *Big Bang: The Origin of the Universe*
Simon Singh

Find out how an ancient genius measured how far it is around the Earth, using only a stick and a well.

SHORT STORY

By the Waters of Babylon
Stephen Vincent Benét

A young narrator sets off on his own to try to understand a post-apocalyptic world he has only heard rumors of.

Collaborate and Share   Discuss with a partner what you learned from at least one of your independent readings.

- Give a brief synopsis or summary of the text.
- Describe any signposts that you noticed in the text, and explain what they revealed to you.
- Describe what you most enjoyed or found most challenging about the text. Give specific examples.
- Decide whether you would recommend the text to others. Why or why not?

Go to the **Reading Studio** for more resources on **Notice & Note.**

INDEPENDENT READING

MATCHING STUDENTS TO TEXTS

Use the following information to guide students in choosing their texts.

Before I got my eye put out
   Genre: poem
   Overall Rating: Accessible

What Our Telescopes Couldn't See   Lexile: 1210L
   Genre: essay
Overall Rating: Challenging

from **Big Bang : The Origin of the Universe**   Lexile: 1270L
   Genre: informational text
   Overall Rating: Accessible

By the Waters of Babylon   Lexile: 820L
   Genre: short story
   Overall Rating: Accessible

Collaborate and Share   To assess how well students read the selections, walk around the room and listen to their conversations. Encourage students to be focused and specific in their comments.

 for Assessment

- Independent Reading Selection Tests

 Encourage students to visit the **Reading Studio** to download a handy bookmark of **NOTICE & NOTE** signposts.

WHEN STUDENT STRUGGLE . . .

Keep a Reading Log As students read their selected texts, have them keep a reading log for each selection to note signposts and their thoughts about them. Use their logs to assess how well they are noticing and reflecting on elements of the texts.

Reading Log for (title)		
Location	**Signpost I Noticed**	**My Notes about It**

UNIT ② Tasks

- **WRITE A SHORT STORY**
- **PRODUCE A PODCAST**

MENTOR TEXT

THE NIGHT FACE UP

Short Story by Julio Cortázar

LEARNING OBJECTIVES

Writing Task

- Write a short story in which things are revealed to be different from how they first appeared.
- Use strategies to plan and organize ideas for a short story.
- Develop a focused, structured draft of a short story.
- Use the Mentor Text as a model for a short story.
- Revise drafts incorporating feedback from peers.
- Edit drafts to incorporate standard English conventions.
- Use a rubric to evaluate writing.
- Publish writing to share it with an audience.
- **Language** Practice using vivid sensory details in a short story.

Speaking and Listening Task

- Adapt a short story into a podcast.
- Present a short story podcast to an audience.
- Use appropriate verbal and nonverbal techniques.
- Listen actively to a podcast presentation.
- **Language** Identify, form, and use complex sentences in speaking.

Assign the Writing Task in *Ed.*

Online

RESOURCES

- Unit 2 Response Log

- Reading Studio: Notice & Note

- Writing Studio: Writing Narratives

- Speaking and Listening Studio: Using Media in a Presentation

- Grammar Studio: Module 4: Lesson: 5 Sentence Structure

Language X-Ray: English Learner Support

Use the instruction below and the supports and scaffolds in the Teacher's Edition to help you guide students at different proficiency levels.

INTRODUCE THE WRITING TASK

Explain that a **short story** is a brief work of narrative fiction, typically with five essential elements: character(s), setting, plot, conflict, and theme. Most stories have one main character and a few secondary characters. Characters may be people, animals, strange creatures, and even objects. Setting provides the time and place of the short story. The plot consists of a series of events that lead to a climax and resolution. The conflict in a short story may involve two people, a person and nature, or an internal struggle within the main character. Short stories express a theme, or a general truth about life.

Note that the selections in this unit deal with the theme of how our point of view shapes what we think we know. Use sentence frames to help students explore the ideas related to this theme to help them prepare to write their stories. For example: *I discovered something about myself when I _____. Sometimes you can see someone every day and then suddenly _____.* Assist students as they brainstorm words and phrases such as *had to help an elderly relative* and *you realize you had never seen the real person.* Have pairs of students work together to write original sentences about appearance versus reality.

WRITING

Use Sensory and Descriptive Details

Tell students that as they work on their short stories they should plan how to include vivid details that describe or relate to sight, sound, and other sensory experiences.

Use the following supports with students at varying proficiency levels:

- Have students close their eyes while you give them clues about a mystery person, place, or thing, and then have students suggest something that fits the description. *I am round. I feel warm. I taste sweet. I am a _____.* **SUBSTANTIAL**
- Have students add sensory details to complete sentence frames. For example: *The _____ bird landed nearby and began singing _____.* **MODERATE**
- Have students expand kernel sentences with sensory details. For example: *The boy danced. The small boy with bright red hair danced to the band's rolling rhythms.* **LIGHT**

SPEAKING AND LISTENING

Use Complex Sentences

Using model paragraphs from the mentor text and other texts, provide oral practice in which students identify, form, and use complex sentences.

Use the following supports with students at varying proficiency levels:

- Read aloud the first two sentences of paragraph 13 of the mentor text as students follow along. Have students orally identify the complex sentence. **SUBSTANTIAL**
- Read aloud the first two sentences of paragraph 13 of the mentor text. Have students orally identify the complex sentence and its independent clause. **MODERATE**
- Tell partners to find and read aloud two examples of complex sentences in another unit selection. **LIGHT**

WRITING

WRITE A SHORT STORY

Read the introductory paragraph with students and discuss the writing task with them. Encourage students to refer to the notes they recorded in their Unit 2 Response Logs before they begin planning and writing a draft. Emphasize that their Response Logs will contain a variety of ideas about how our experiences shape our expectations and affect what we think we see or know. Note that these different perspectives will be useful in making their short stories more suspenseful and entertaining.

USE THE MENTOR TEXT

Explain to students that their short stories will be similar to "The Night Face Up" by Julio Cortázar. Emphasize that, like Cortázar's short story, their stories will have a setting, narrator, and main character. They will also contain a central conflict and use a variety of narrative techniques to develop character, plot, theme, and suspense or surprise. The ending of their story should resolve the central conflict in a way that makes sense and satisfies readers. Remind students of the importance of including vivid sensory language and descriptive details as a way to keep readers engaged.

WRITING PROMPT

Discuss the prompt with students. Encourage them to ask questions about any part of the assignment they find unclear. Emphasize that the purpose of their short story is to entertain readers with a narrative that reveals the way something is different from how it first appeared.

Review the checklist of key points that students should consider as they write their short stories.

Write a Short Story

Go to the **Writing Studio** for help writing a narrative, such as a short story.

This unit focuses on the sometimes surprising differences between how we see things and how they really are. Look back at the texts from this unit, and think about the ways in which things are not as they may first appear in these texts. Use those surprising insights as the basis of a suspenseful or surprising narrative of your own. For an example of a short story you can use as a mentor text, review the story "The Night Face Up."

As you write your story, you will want to look at the notes you made in your Response Log after reading the texts in this unit.

HOW WE SEE THINGS

Writing Prompt

Read the information in the box below.

This is the starting point or premise for your story.

> We often see what we expect to see, based on what we already have experienced.

Think carefully about the following question.

This is the Essential Question for the unit. How would you answer this question, based on the texts in this unit?

> How does our point of view shape what we think we know?

Pay attention to the words that describe exactly what you are supposed to write.

Write a short story in which things are revealed to be different from how they first appeared.

Be sure to—

Review these points as you write and again when you finish. Make any needed changes or edits.

- ❏ begin by introducing a setting, a narrator, a main character, and a distinct point of view
- ❏ have an engaging plot with a central conflict
- ❏ use a variety of narrative techniques to develop characters, plot, theme, and suspense or surprise
- ❏ include sensory language and descriptive details
- ❏ end with a logical and satisfying resolution to the conflict

---

 LEARNING MINDSET

Asking for Help   Emphasize that there are many strategies for solving problems, but a common one is to ask someone for help. Remind students to consider who they think can offer useful suggestions for the task at hand. Discuss a range of possible sources of help such a teacher, a classmate, an older sibling, or a parent or guardian. Stress that students should not think that asking for help is an admission of failure in any way. Tell them that they should think of "asking for help" as a "working smarter" strategy.

① Plan

Before you begin to write a short story, you need to have an idea. Begin by brainstorming, discussing, and journaling about experiences, events, or conflicts you know about that involved an element of suspense or surprise. Then, freewrite about any of these ideas. Use your imagination to create fictional characters, setting, plot, conflict, and theme related to this experience or event. Remember that even though this is a fictional account, you may use ideas from real life to help you get started. Use the chart below to plan your story.

SHORT STORY PLANNING CHART	
Topic, Experience, or Event:	
Characters:	Setting:
Conflict:	Resolution:
Theme or Message:	

Background Reading Review the notes you have taken in your Response Log after reading the texts in this unit. These texts provide background reading that will help you think about what you want to say in your story.

Notice & Note
From Reading to Writing

As you plan your short story, apply what you've learned about signposts to your own writing. Think about how you can incorporate an **Aha Moment** into your short story.

Go to the **Reading Studio** for more resources on **Notice & Note**.

Use the notes from your Response Log as you plan your story.

UNIT 2 RESPONSE LOG

Write a Short Story   133

WHEN STUDENTS STRUGGLE . . .

Mine Memories Have students briefly list five memories and then do the following:

- Choose the memory they think others might find interesting.
- Try to figure out why the memory is still important to them.
- Think about other memories that provide insights into the main one.
- Imagine how someone else in the memory might describe the event(s).

When students have finished the brainstorming activity, give them a few minutes to freewrite (or prewrite) a scene or some dialogue for their stories or to share ideas with a partner.

① PLAN

Read the introductory text. Then, review some of the techniques students will benefit from as they plan their short stories. Suggest that students think about favorite stories, TV shows, or movies that begin with an element of suspense. Ask: What did you want to know after the beginning of the story? Did you eventually find out what you wanted to know? Provide students with sufficient time to complete the Short Story Planning Chart. Remind them that changing ideas and thinking of new ones is a natural part of the planning process.

■ English Learner Support

Understand Academic Language Review the meaning of key academic vocabulary used in the chart such as *experience, event, conflict, character, setting, plot,* and *theme.* Ask volunteers to explain the meaning of each term in their own words. When students do not know exact English words, encourage them to convey their ideas through description. For example, a student may describe a conflict as "the thing that is wrong," instead of "problem." Record the term and key words related to it on the board. Organize small groups of students with a range of language proficiencies and encourage them to discuss these terms and their importance as a way to provide further clarification.
ALL LEVELS

▶ NOTICE & NOTE

From Reading to Writing Discuss different ways that students may introduce Aha Moments into their stories. Point out that Aha Moments can be used at several points in a story to help move the plot along and give the reader insight into how a character is growing or changing.

Background Reading As students plan their short stories, encourage them to review the notes in their Response Logs for Unit 2. Suggest that they briefly scan the unit selections to identify examples of text elements and language use they might use as models in their own writing.

WRITING

Organize Your Ideas Emphasize the importance of organizing ideas in an outline before students begin a draft of their short story. Display the diagram of the five stages of a plot. Work with students to prepare a list of bulleted items that highlight key points for each stage.

Remind students that the beginning of a short story sets the stage by introducing the main character, the setting, and the conflict in a way that immediately captures the reader's attention.

As the story develops, the reader learns more about the characters and events that build toward the story's most exciting moment, or climax.

After the climax, the reader learns about how the conflict will be resolved. In the ending, the reader finds out the final outcome of the story and how it affected the main character(s).

② DEVELOP A DRAFT

Encourage students to follow their graphic organizers and/ or outlines as they draft their short stories. Emphasize that these planning materials are only a first step in writing and, if new ideas come to them during the drafting stage, they should feel free to change their plans.

■ English Learner Support

Complete a Group Story Starter Model the task of writing an engaging beginning to a short story by using a starter sentence such as: *Have you ever heard the expression, "Seeing is believing"? Well, _____,* or *In my dreams, I kept seeing the same thing over and over again. Then I realized _____.* Encourage volunteers to suggest ways they might finish the starter sentences. **SUBSTANTIAL/MODERATE**

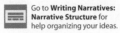

Go to **Writing Narratives: Narrative Structure** for help organizing your ideas.

Organize Your Ideas Combine the techniques you identified in the texts with your own ideas. Consider these points:

- How does the story begin? What can you do to grab the attention of your readers right from the start?
- How does the plot develop? How does the sequence of events lead to a climax—a turning point or moment of greatest intensity and excitement? Pay attention to how you develop the element of surprise or suspense.
- How is the conflict resolved? Is there a moment of sudden insight? How does the story end?
- Who will tell what happens—a character in the story or a narrator observing and reporting events? Whose thoughts will readers understand?
- What details will bring your setting and characters to life for readers?

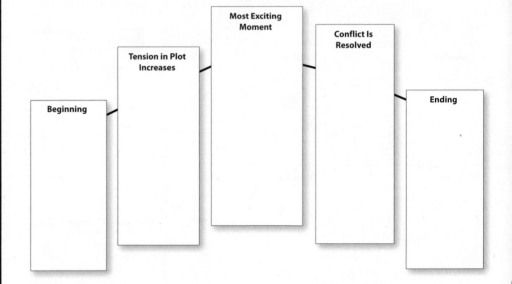

You might prefer to draft your story online.

② Develop a Draft

Once you have completed your planning activities, you will be ready to begin drafting your short story. Refer to your graphic organizers and/or the outline you have created, as well as any notes you took as you studied the texts in the unit. These will provide a kind of map for you to follow as you write. Finish a first draft and then read it over before you decide to make changes or move sentences around.

WHEN STUDENTS STRUGGLE . . .

Use Sentence Frames to Map Plot Have students use a sequence of numbered sentence frames like the ones below to help plan a plot they might use in their short stories.

1. The story begins with (or when) _____.

2. A problem that _____, the main character, has is _____.

3. The _____ tries to solve the problem by _____.

4. The main problem is solved when _____.

5. At the end, _____ realizes _____.

WRITING TASK

Use the Mentor Text

Author's Craft

Sensory and descriptive details can be very effective in evoking a setting. Note the way the author uses an appeal to the sense of smell when introducing the Aztec setting in "The Night Face Up."

> It was unusual as a dream because it was full of smells, and he never dreamt smells. First a marshy smell, there to the left of the trail the swamps began already, the quaking bogs from which no one ever returned. But the reek lifted, and instead there came a dark, fresh composite fragrance, like the night under which he moved, in flight from the Aztecs.

The author brings the scene to life for readers by describing the smells using precise, vivid language.

Apply What You've Learned Be creative in your use of sensory and descriptive details when you describe your setting.

Genre Characteristics

In a story that creates suspense by playing with the reader's sense of reality, the author may drop clues, possibly false, that lead the reader to lean toward one conclusion or another. Notice how Cortázar does this as his protagonist lies in the hospital.

> He tried to fix the moment of the accident exactly, and it got him very angry to notice that there was a void there, an emptiness he could not manage to fill. Between the impact and the moment that they picked him up off the pavement, the passing out or what went on, there was nothing he could see. And at the same time he had the feeling that this void, this nothingness, had lasted an eternity.

Does this mean that the other reality is true, or is this just a description of a temporary loss of memory?

Apply What You've Learned Making the reader wonder what's going on can create suspense and mystery.

WHY THIS MENTOR TEXT?

"The Night Face Up" expresses the following relevant theme: what we think we know shapes the way we experience the world. Use the instruction below to model how sensory and descriptive details can establish setting and the way carefully chosen memories and insights can develop suspense.

USE THE MENTOR TEXT

Author's Craft Have a volunteer read aloud the introduction to this section and the example from the Mentor Text. Ask: How does the author use the sense of smell to build suspense about the setting? *(Words such as "marshy" and "reek" make the setting of the bog seem unpleasant and scary.)*

Genre Characteristics Discuss the use of suspense and clues. Ask a volunteer to read aloud the example from Cortázar's story. Ask: What words does Cortázar use to create suspense about what is real and what is imagined? *(emptiness, nothing he could see, void, nothingness, eternity)*

For **writing support** for students of varying proficiency levels, use the **Language X-Ray** on page 132B.

 ENGLISH LEARNER SUPPORT

Identify Vivid Sensory Language Use the following supports with students at varying proficiency levels:

- Read aloud paragraph 1 of "The Night Face Up" and discuss the last two sentences. Ask: Which sense does "the sun filtered through the downtown buildings" refer to? *(sight)* Which senses are referred to in the last sentence? *("whirred"/sound, "cool wind"/touch)* **SUBSTANTIAL**

- Have groups of three or four students find examples of vivid sensory language in paragraph 8 of "The Night Face Up." Have students organize their examples according to taste, touch, sight, hearing, and

smell. Tell group members to discuss their examples and assess the effectiveness of each. **MODERATE**

- Have pairs of students create a five-column chart, with the following column labels: SIGHT, HEARING, TASTE, TOUCH, and SMELL. Have students work together to identify examples of vivid sensory language in "The Night Face Up" or another selection from the unit. Instruct students to insert these examples into the table. Have partners select several of their favorite examples to present to the class for further discussion. **LIGHT**

WRITING

③ REVISE

Have students evaluate their drafts by answering each question posed in the Revision Guide. Call on volunteers to model their revision techniques.

With a Partner Invite students to work with peer reviewers to evaluate their short story drafts. Encourage students to team up with classmates whom they don't usually work with to gain new perspectives and strengthen collaboration skills.

Use the following questions as a guide for peer review:

- Are the events of the story told in an easy-to-follow sequence?
- Has the writer used vivid language and sensory details that make the story interesting?
- Is the conflict clearly described and eventually resolved?

Encourage students to use the reviewer's comments to revise or add vivid sensory details that build suspense as they further develop their short stories.

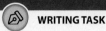 **WRITING TASK**

 Go to **Writing Narratives: The Language of Narrative** for help making your story more engaging.

③ Revise

On Your Own The best fiction writers know that a draft is only a beginning. In fact, some of the most important and creative work is done in the revision process, including bringing realism and color to a story by introducing vivid descriptions, sensory details, suspenseful elements, and effective narrative techniques. Use the Revision Guide below to help you make your writing stronger.

REVISION GUIDE		
Ask Yourself	**Tips**	**Revision Techniques**
1. Does the narrative begin in an engaging way and introduce characters, setting, conflict, and point of view?	**Underline** the engaging opening and **mark** clues about the characters, setting, conflict, or point of view.	**Revise** your introduction to begin with action or dialogue, and **add** details about characters, setting, conflict, or narrator.
2. Do narrative techniques and precise language bring the story and characters to life?	**Underline** dialogue, sensory details, and vivid verbs.	**Add** dialogue, sensory details, and vivid verbs where they are lacking.
3. Does the central conflict develop in a logical and engaging way?	**Mark** points at which the conflict advances the plot. **Underline** phrases or sentences that build suspense.	**Revise** passages that do not advance the plot. **Add** phrases or sentences that build suspense.
4. Is surprise used effectively to bring the conflict to its peak?	**Mark** surprising passages.	**Add** a surprising event or narration that links the surprise to the central conflict.
5. Does the conclusion resolve the conflict in a logical way?	**Underline** the explanation of how the conflict is resolved.	**Add** dialogue or narration that logically resolves the conflict.

ACADEMIC VOCABULARY
As you conduct your peer review, try to use these words.

- ❏ differentiate
- ❏ incorporate
- ❏ mode
- ❏ orient
- ❏ perspective

With a Partner After you revise based on the points above, exchange stories with a partner. Evaluate each other's drafts in a peer review. Point out parts of the story that work well, and ask questions about any confusing or unrealistic events or characters. Provide concrete suggestions for improving the draft as appropriate.

 ENGLISH LEARNER SUPPORT

Use Vivid Sensory Details Have small groups of students brainstorm lists of vivid sensory words, as in these examples, and practice using them in oral and written sentences.

- **Sight:** sparkling, gloomy, gigantic, cloudy, bright
- **Sound:** roaring, sizzle, whisper, howling, thunderous
- **Taste:** sour, sweet, spicy, creamy, bitter, salty
- **Touch:** bumpy, freezing, damp, soft, smooth, slimy
- **Smell:** aroma, perfume, fragrant, putrid, whiff   **SUBSTANTIAL/MODERATE**

4 Edit

No matter how good your story is, readers will not fully appreciate it if they are confused by misspellings or other problems with language conventions. Edit for proper use of standard English conventions and make sure to correct any misspellings and usage or grammatical errors.

Language Conventions

Use Complex Sentences A complex sentence includes an independent clause and one or more dependent clauses.

- An **independent clause** has a subject and a verb and can stand alone. If two independent clauses are joined only by a comma, they form a **comma splice.** When no punctuation joins them but they are in the same sentence, they form a **run-on sentence.**
- A **dependent clause** has a subject and a verb and cannot stand alone. It can act as an adverb or an adjective, modifying another part of the sentence. If it is not attached to an independent clause, it is a **sentence fragment.**

! Go to the **Grammar Studio** for help with complex sentences.

Here are examples of complex sentences from "The Night Face Up":

Type of Dependent Clause	Examples from Text
Adverb Clause	**When the big windows across the way turned to smudges of dark blue,** he thought it would not be difficult for him to sleep.
Adjective Clause	A young intern arrived with some metal and leather apparatus **which he adjusted to fit onto the good arm to check something or other.**

5 Publish

Finalize your story and choose a way to share it with your audience. Consider these options:

- Read your story aloud to the class.
- Produce your story as a podcast to be posted on a classroom or school website.

4 EDIT

Suggest that students read their drafts aloud multiple times. During their first reading, have students listen for sentence fragments—groups of words that are only phrases or dependent clauses. Remind students that every complete sentence contains at least one independent clause. During their second reading, suggest that students listen for run-on sentences, which contain two or more independent clauses that are not properly joined with a conjunction or a punctuation mark. A third reading might focus on comma splices, in which two independent clauses are connected only by a comma.

LANGUAGE CONVENTIONS

Use Complex Sentences Review the key elements of a complex sentence: one independent, or main, clause and at least one dependent, or subordinate, clause. Remind students that an independent clause can stand alone as a sentence. In contrast, a dependent clause needs another clause to make a complete sentence. Explain that complex sentences allow writers to make connections between closely related ideas and to provide sentence variety in their writing.

Display the complex sentences below. Then have volunteers identify the independent and dependent clause in each. Underline the independent clause twice and the dependent, or subordinate, clause once.

- *After the man character was in an accident, an ambulance took him to the hospital.*
- *If he hadn't swerved to avoid hitting the woman, he might not have been injured.*

As students read each sentence aloud, have them note a slight pause after the introductory dependent clause. Explain that if the dependent clause comes first in a sentence, it is set off by a comma, as in the examples above. Note that if the dependent clause comes after the independent clause, often no comma separates them, as shown here:

- *The main character had a strange dream after he had fallen asleep.*

5 PUBLISH

Discuss the suggested publishing options. Note that both types of publication involve a dramatic reading of descriptive details and dialogue spoken by characters. Ask: *Can you think of ways in which a dramatic reading of a short story might differ from a podcast?* Remind students that their narratives should include all the required elements of a short story.

(EL) ENGLISH LEARNER SUPPORT

Use Signal Words in Complex Sentence Frames Point out the signal words in these sentence frames: *If _____, then _____. Although _____, she _____. While _____, they _____.* Instruct pairs or small groups of students to use these frames to write original sentences based on the selection or topic of their choice. Ask: Can you think of other signal words that might be used to form complex sentence frames? **MODERATE/LIGHT**

WRITING

USE THE SCORING GUIDE

Give students time to read and study the scoring guide. Encourage them to ask questions about any ideas, sentences, phrases, or words they find unclear. Tell partners to exchange their final short stories and score them using the guidelines. Have each student reviewer write a paragraph explaining the reason for the score he or she awarded for each major category.

Use the scoring guide to evaluate your short story.

WRITING TASK SCORING GUIDE: SHORT STORY

	Organization/Progression	Development of Ideas	Use of Language and Conventions
4	• The sequence of events is effective, clear, and logical. • Virtually all events serve the plot and/or the character development. • The pace and organization keep the reader curious about what will happen next.	• The beginning of the story catches the reader's attention and establishes the conflict. • The conflict of the story is developed and resolved in a logical and interesting way. • The theme emerges from the plot events and character development. • The story is told from a distinct point of view that advances the theme or tone.	• Language and word choice is precise and descriptive. • Complex sentences are used effectively to build tension. • Text is free from unintended sentence fragments, run-on sentences, and comma splices. • Spelling, capitalization, and punctuation are correct. • Grammar and usage are correct.
3	• The sequence of events is, for the most part, effective, clear, and logical. • Most events serve the plot and/or the character development. • The pace and organization sometimes make the reader curious about what will happen next.	• The beginning of the story catches the reader's attention fairly well and establishes the conflict. • The conflict of the story is developed and resolved fairly well. • For the most part, the theme emerges from the plot events and character development. • The story's point of view is clear and consistent.	• Language is for the most part specific and descriptive. • Complex sentences are used. • There are some unintended sentence fragments, run-on sentences, and comma splices. • There are some spelling, capitalization, and punctuation mistakes. • Some grammar and usage errors occur.
2	• The sequence of events is sometimes confusing. • Only some events serve the plot and/or the character development. • The pace and organization rarely make the reader curious about what will happen next.	• The beginning of the story does not catch the reader's attention well and the establishment of the conflict is vague. • The conflict of the story needs to be better developed and resolved. • The theme does not emerge from the plot events and character development well, but it does exist. • The point of view is vague but generally sticks with either the first or third person.	• Language is somewhat vague and lacking in detail. • There are unintended sentence fragments, run-on sentences, and comma splices. • Conventions including spelling, capitalization, punctuation, grammar, and usage, are often incorrect but do not make reading difficult.
1	• The sequence of events is mostly unclear. • Events do not serve the plot and/or the character development. • The pace and organization do not make the reader curious about what will happen next.	• The beginning of the story does not catch the reader's attention and the conflict is missing. • The conflict of the story is not developed or resolved. • The theme does not emerge from the plot events and character development. • The point of view is inconsistent and confusing.	• Language is inappropriate for the text. • There are many unintended sentence fragments, run-on sentences, and comma splices. • Many spelling, capitalization, and punctuation errors are present. • Grammatical and usage errors interfere with the writer's meaning.

Produce a Podcast

You will now adapt your short story into a podcast that your classmates can listen to. You also will listen to their podcasts, ask questions to better understand what they are trying to accomplish, and help them improve their work.

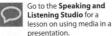 Go to the **Speaking and Listening Studio** for a lesson on using media in a presentation.

1 Adapt Your Story as a Podcast

Review your short story and use the chart below to guide you as you adapt your story for a podcast, including the creation of a script, music, or other sound effects.

PODCAST PLANNING CHART		
Beginning	How will you revise the story's beginning to capture listener's attention? Is there a way to effectively use sound effects or music?	
Voices	Will you read the story by yourself? Could you use classmates to read certain characters' dialogue?	
Transitions	Are there parts of your story that should be simplified? Can you use audio signals to help identify changes in time or place?	
Sound	Should you use music in your podcast? Are there sound effects that will help you create a mood of suspense or surprise?	

Produce a Podcast **139**

SPEAKING AND LISTENING

PRODUCE A PODCAST

Introduce students to the Speaking and Listening Task by discussing the differences between reading aloud a short story and presenting it as a podcast. Discuss the idea that even though a reading might be dramatic, it still involves just one person making the presentation. Note that students might wish to engage other classmates in their podcasts to read dialogue spoken by different characters or to create sound effects. Discuss how music and other sound effects might be used to express the story's location(s). Ask: How might you alert the listener to changes in time and place? *(There might be different sounds or music for different locations and scene changes.)*

1 ADAPT YOUR STORY AS A PODCAST

Have students read the questions for each major topic listed in the left-hand column of the chart. Discuss some general principles for converting a written short story into a podcast. Ask: How will the listeners know which characters are speaking? How will the setting be indicated? Will all the scenes and dialogue from the written story be needed in the podcast? Encourage students to prepare by listening to short story podcasts online.

For **speaking and listening support** for students at varying proficiency levels, see the **Language X-Ray** on page 132B.

■ English Learner Support

Listen to Media Listen to high-interest podcasts with students. Define unfamiliar words and phrases or concepts. Ask students to pay attention to a particular element, such as voices. Ask: How many people are speaking? How do you know who is speaking? **ALL LEVELS**

SPEAKING AND LISTENING

② PRACTICE WITH A PARTNER OR GROUP

Practice Effective Verbal Techniques Have volunteers read each checklist item. Model the effective use of each verbal technique. After each modeling activity, have volunteers demonstrate how they would use the technique. Be sure to establish a recording location for students to practice microphone skills or demonstrate how they can practice using smartphones, tablets, or computers.

Create Your Podcast Have volunteers read each of the checklist items. If students are using their classroom, a music practice room, or a media center in the school, establish a schedule that provides students with adequate time. Review any rules for proper equipment use before students begin their recording. If available, model the use of school editing software or pre-select open source software for student use. When considering music and other sound effects, have students think about the mood they want to create.

Provide and Consider Advice for Improvement Discuss elements of the podcast students should focus on as they listen. Ask: Is it clear which character is speaking? Have the scene and mood been communicated effectively? Are the plot events clearly presented?

Encourage students to consider the suggestions from other students about their podcasts. Ask: Which suggestions do you think would be most helpful in improving your podcast? How would using these suggestions change your podcast?

③ POST YOUR PODCAST

Set aside time for all students to post their podcasts and to listen to the podcasts made by other students in the class. Have students share how their classmates' feedback helped them improve their podcasts.

SPEAKING AND LISTENING TASK

As you work to improve your own podcast and those of your classmates, follow these rules of constructive criticism:

- ❑ be objective about the podcaster's purpose
- ❑ begin feedback with the strong points of the work
- ❑ provide honest but respectful criticism that includes concrete suggestions for improvement

② Practice with a Partner or Group

When your script is ready and you've decided whether to include music and/or sound effects, practice before you record your podcast.

Practice Effective Verbal Techniques

- ❑ **Enunciation** Be sure not to swallow the ends of letters or words. Pronounce each letter, such as a final *g* in *going* or *beginning*.
- ❑ **Voice Modulation and Pitch** Adjust your voice and pitch to display appropriate emotion and emphasis for the content.
- ❑ **Speaking Rate** Adjust your rate of speaking to the emotion or mood of the content to ensure the listeners' interest.
- ❑ **Microphone Skills** Practice speaking into a microphone to ensure appropriate volume and to avoid distracting feedback from the microphone, such as pops or hisses.

Create Your Podcast

- ❑ **Recording Location** If your school doesn't have a music practice room or a studio, record in a space with as little background noise as possible.
- ❑ **Recording** If you make a mistake while recording, just continue. If you can edit, pause and go back to the beginning of a paragraph so that you can incorporate your correction more smoothly.
- ❑ **Editing** If your school has audio editing software, or if you can download an open source app, tighten up the transitions between segments of your recorded podcast.
- ❑ **Music** Find appropriate free music from a site such as archive.org or the Library of Congress music collection. Always check copyright restrictions before using someone else's music.

Provide and Consider Advice for Improvement

As an audience, listen closely. Take notes about ways that podcasters can improve their presentations and more effectively present their stories.

As a podcaster, pay attention to feedback and consider ways to improve your podcast to make it more effective. Remember to ask for suggestions about your music and sound effects, if you chose to use them.

③ Post Your Podcast

Use the advice you received during practice to make final changes to your podcast. Then, make it available to your classmates on your school's website. Reflect on listeners' comments to improve future podcasts.

© Houghton Mifflin Harcourt Publishing Company

WHEN STUDENTS STRUGGLE...

Take Notes Form groups of three students to listen to the podcasts and divide note-taking tasks among them. Designate one student to listen to the podcast for key elements of a good short story, such as character, setting, plot, dialogue, and theme. Have a second student focus on the use of effective verbal techniques, making brief notes about items that need improvement. A third student should focus on the technical aspects of the podcast, commenting on the recording quality, editing, and the sound/music choices.

Reflect on the Unit

When you were writing your short story, you were inspired by your thoughts about the reading you have done in this unit. Now is a good time to reflect on what you have learned.

Reflect on the Essential Question

- How does our point of view shape what we think we know? How has your answer to this question changed since you first considered it when you started this unit?

- What are some examples from the texts you've read that show how our point of view shapes what we think of as reality?

Reflect on Your Reading

- Which selections were the most interesting or surprising to you?

- From which selection did you learn the most about the differences between what is real and what we think is real?

Reflect on the Writing Task

- What difficulties did you encounter while working on your short story? How might you avoid these challenges the next time?

- What part of the short story was the easiest to write? What was the most difficult to write? Why?

- What improvements did you make to your story as you were revising?

UNIT 2 SELECTIONS
"Coming to Our Senses"
"The Night Face Up"
"Mirror"
"The World as 100 People"
"A Contribution to Statistics"

Reflect on the Unit   141

REFLECT ON THE UNIT

Have students think about the three major points of reflection they are being asked to consider. Tell students to work independently and note how they would respond to each question. After students have completed their individual reflections, bring them together in small groups to discuss their responses. Circulate among students during these discussions and note questions that seem to generate the liveliest conversations. Wrap up the unit with a whole-class discussion focused on these questions.

LEARNING MINDSET

Problem Solving Prompt students to reflect on how our point of view shapes what we see and know—but also how we approach problems. For example, talk about how people may find themselves in unhealthy relationships and not realize how these are negatively impacting their lives. One of the first steps in problem solving is often just figuring out what the problem truly is—to recognize it, identify it, name it. Then, once the problem has been seen for what it truly is, figuring out solutions that are likely to work becomes much more possible.

Instructional Overview and Resources

	Instructional Focus	Online Resources
 **Unit Introduction** **The Natural World**	**Unit 3 Essential Question** **Unit 3 Academic Vocabulary**	**Stream to Start:** The Natural World **Unit 3 Response Log**

ANALYZE & APPLY

	Instructional Focus	Resources
"My Life as a Bat" Short Story by Margaret Atwood **Lexile 1020L** **NOTICE & NOTE** READING MODEL **Signposts** • Memory Moment • Contrasts and Contradictions • Again and Again	**Reading** • Analyze Structure • Analyze Language **Writing:** Write an Analysis **Speaking and Listening:** Present Research **Vocabulary:** Reference Sources **Language Conventions:** Colons	**Audio** **Close Read Screencasts:** Modeled Discussions **Reading Studio:** Notice & Note **Level Up Tutorial:** Summarizing **Writing Studio:** Writing Informative Texts **Speaking and Listening Studio:** Giving a Presentation **Vocabulary Studio:** Using Reference Sources **Grammar Studio:** Module 12: Lesson 2: Colons
Mentor Text **"Joyas Voladoras"** Essay by Brian Doyle **Lexile 1170L**	**Reading** • Analyze Style • Analyze Structure **Writing:** Write an Explanation **Speaking and Listening:** Participate in a Panel Discussion **Vocabulary:** Denotation and Connotation **Language Conventions:** Parallelism	**Audio** **Reading Studio:** Notice & Note **Level Up Tutorials:** Main Idea and Supporting Details; Connotations and Denotations **Writing Studio:** Synthesizing Research Information **Speaking and Listening Studio:** Participating in Collaborative Discussions **Vocabulary Studio:** Denotation and Connotation
"Find Your Park" Public Service Advertisement by National Park Service	**Reading** • Analyze Media Techniques and Purposes **Writing:** Write a Letter to the Editor **Speaking and Listening:** Give Instructions	**Level Up Tutorial:** Taking Notes and Outlining **Writing Studio:** Writing Arguments **Speaking and Listening Studio:** Speaking Constructively

SUGGESTED PACING:
30 DAYS

Unit Introduction	My Life as a Bat	Joyas Voladoras	Find Your Park
1	2 3 4 5 6	7 8 9	10 11 12 13 14

English Learner Support	Differentiated Instruction	Online Ed Assessment
• Learn Vocabulary		

English Learner Support	Differentiated Instruction	Assessment
• Text X-Ray • Make Comparisons with Similes • Use Cognates • Use Context Clues for Vocabulary • Understand Language Conventions • Oral Assessment • Write an Analysis • Critical Vocabulary • Language Conventions	**When Students Struggle** • Use a Sketch to Stretch • Use a Graphic Organizer	**Selection Test**
• Text X-Ray • Develop Vocabulary • Use Prior Knowledge • Use Support to Read • Develop Vocabulary to Build Understanding • Oral Assessment • Participate in a Panel Discussion • Use Vocabulary Strategies • Use Parallel Structure	**When Students Struggle** • Determine Meaning • Understand Denotation and Connotation **To Challenge Students** • Create a Multimodal Presentation	**Selection Test**
• Text X-Ray • Monitor Understanding • Understand Maps • Oral Assessment • Write a Letter to the Editor	**When Students Struggle** • Analyze Media	**Selection Test**

The Seventh Man / Carry

15 > 16 > 17 > 18 > 19 > 20 > 21 > 22 > 23 > 24 > 25

Independent Reading

26 > 27

End of Unit

28 > 29 > 30

UNIT 3 Continued

	Instructional Focus	Online Resources

COLLABORATE & COMPARE

"The Seventh Man"
Short Story by Haruki Murakami
Lexile 910L

Reading
- Analyze Symbol and Theme
- Analyze Plot

Writing: Write a Vignette

Speaking and Listening: Discuss with a Small Group

Vocabulary: Figurative Language

Language Conventions: Complex Sentences

Audio

Reading Studio: Notice & Note

Level Up Tutorials: Plot: Sequence of Events; Figurative Language

Speaking and Listening Studio: Participating in Collaborative Discussions

Grammar Studio: Module 4: Lesson 5: Sentence Structure

"Carry"
Poem by Linda Hogan

Reading
- Analyze Symbol and Theme
- Analyze Free Verse

Writing: Write a Free-Verse Poem

Speaking and Listening: Discuss with a Small Group

Audio

Reading Studio: Notice & Note

Level Up Tutorial: Imagery

Speaking and Listening Studio: Participating in Collaborative Discussions

Collaborate and Compare

Reading: Compare Themes

Speaking and Listening: Create and Share

Online Ed INDEPENDENT READING

The Independent Reading selections are only available in the eBook.

Go to the Reading Studio for more information on Notice & Note.

from *Hope for Animals and Their World*
Argument by Jane Goodall
Lexile 1300L

"Sea Stars"
Essay by Barbara Hurd
Lexile 1210L

END OF UNIT

Writing Task: Write an Explanatory Essay

Writing: Write an Explanatory Essay

Language Conventions: Parallel Structure

Speaking and Listening: Deliver a Multimedia Presentation

Speaking and Listening Task: Deliver a Multimedia Presentation

Unit 3 Response Log

Mentor Text: "Joyas Voladoras"

Reading Studio: Notice & Note

Writing Studio: Writing Informative Texts

Speaking and Listening Studio: Using Media in a Presentation

Reflect on the Unit

English Learner Support	Differentiated Instruction	Online Ed Assessment
• Text X-Ray • Discuss with a Small Group • Use Cognates • Analyze Figurative Language • Reinforce Meaning • Use Varying Sentence Types • Confirm Understanding • Understand Vocabulary • Develop Vocabulary • Learn Expressions • Decode Words • Explain with Detail • Oral Assessment	**When Students Struggle** • Identify Figurative Language • Analyze Plot Structure **To Challenge Students** • Analyze Personification • Present a Movie Proposal	**Selection Test**
• Text X-Ray • Understand Directionality • Confirm Understanding • Comprehend Language Structures • Oral Assessment • Discuss with a Small Group	**When Students Struggle** • Analyze Imagery	**Selection Test**
• Answer Questions	**To Challenge Students** • Explore Themes in Visual Art	
"Starfish" Poem by Lorna Dee Cervantes	"Wolves" Short Story by José Luis Zárate **Lexile 740L**	**Selection Tests**
• Language X-Ray • Understand Academic Language • Write a Group Essay • Use the Mentor Text • Use Parallel Structures • Adapt the Essay	**When Students Struggle** • Brainstorm Topics • Draft the Essay • Take Notes **To Challenge Students** • Design an Exhibit	**Unit Test**

THE NATURAL WORLD

Ask a volunteer to read aloud the Essential Question. Have students pause to reflect on their relationship with nature. Then ask for examples of how they interact with nature and how it interacts with them. What are the effects of these interactions? Prompt them to consider whether these interactions create a mutually beneficial relationship. Do they take more from nature than they give?

■ English Learner Support

Learn Vocabulary Make sure students understand the Essential Question. If necessary, explain the following terms:

- *Effect* means "a change that is the result of an action."
- *Affect* means "to have an influence on or create a change in something."
- *Nature* means "the world of living things and the outdoors."

Help students restate the question in simpler language: How do we change nature and how does nature change us?
SUBSTANTIAL/MODERATE

DISCUSS THE QUOTATION

Tell students that Terry Tempest Williams (1955) is an American author, conservationist, and activist whose work often focuses on the American West, especially Utah. Explain that her work explores a range of topics, from nature preservation to our relationship to nature. Ask students to read the quotation. Then have them consider how Williams might answer the Essential Question. Do you think she would agree that nature affects us by reminding us "what it means to be human"?

? ESSENTIAL QUESTION:

What effect do we have on nature, and how does nature affect us?

> " Wildness reminds us what it means to be human, what we are connected to rather than what we are separate from. "
>
> Terry Tempest Williams

⚙ **LEARNING MINDSET**

Setting Goals Ask students if they have ever made a New Year's resolution. Did they follow through or did they struggle to stick to their resolution? Share a past experience with a failed resolution and talk about how it might have been easier to achieve with the help of setting goals. Explain that setting goals can help track progress and divide work into more manageable tasks. Remind students about the importance of setting goals that they are comfortable with, because everyone learns at different speeds and has unique needs.

ACADEMIC VOCABULARY

Academic Vocabulary words are words you use when you discuss and write about texts. In this unit you will practice and learn five words.

☑ advocate   ❏ discrete   ❏ domain   ❏ evoke   ❏ enhance

Study the Word Network to learn more about the word **advocate**.

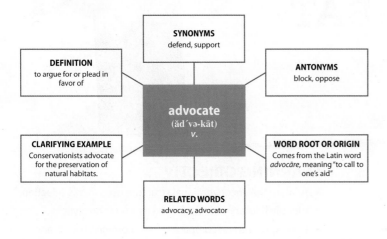

Write and Discuss Discuss the completed Word Network with a partner, making sure to talk through all of the boxes until you both understand the word, its synonyms, antonyms, and related forms. Then, fill out Word Networks for the remaining four words. Use a dictionary or online resource to help you complete the activity.

 Go online to access the Word Networks.

RESPOND TO THE ESSENTIAL QUESTION

In this unit, you will read various genres that explore how we affect nature and how it affects us. As you read, you will revisit the **Essential Question** and gather your ideas about it in the **Response Log** that appears on page R3. At the end of the unit, you will have the opportunity to write an **explanatory essay** about an interaction between humans and nature. Filling out the Response Log will help you prepare for this writing task.

 You can also go online to access the Response Log.

ACADEMIC VOCABULARY

As students complete Word Networks for the remaining four vocabulary words, encourage them to include all the categories shown in the completed network if possible, but point out that some words do not have clear synonyms or antonyms. Some words may also function as different parts of speech—for example, *advocate* can function as a verb or a noun.

>**advocate** (ăd´və-kāt´) *v.* To argue for or plead in favor of. (Spanish cognate: *abogado*)

>**discrete** (dĭ-skrēt´) *adj.* Made up of separate or distinct things or parts. (Spanish cognate: *discreto*)

>**domain** (dō-mān´) *n.* A sphere of activity.

>**evoke** (ĭ-vōk´) *v.* To give rise to; draw forth; produce. (Spanish cognate: *evocar*)

>**enhance** (ĕn-hăns´) *v.* To make better, or add to the value or effectiveness.

RESPOND TO THE ESSENTIAL QUESTION

Direct students to the Unit 3 Response Log. Explain that students will use it to record ideas and details from the selections that help answer the Essential Question. When they work on the writing task at the end of the unit, their Response Log will help them think about what they have read and make connections between the texts.

READING MODEL

MY LIFE AS A BAT

Short Story by **Margaret Atwood**

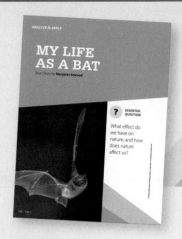

GENRE ELEMENTS
FICTION

Remind students that **fiction** allows an author to communicate thoughts, feelings, and information through imagined events. A **short story** is a work of fiction that often centers on a single idea and can usually be read in one sitting. Note that some fiction is extremely realistic and involves events and feelings that are easy for readers to believe, while other fiction involves situations and descriptions that require the reader to accept or imagine a world of fantastic possibilities, such as time travel, animals that think or talk like humans, or beings with superhuman powers.

LEARNING OBJECTIVES

- Analyze the unconventional structure used in this selection.
- Identify figurative language and its effects on style.
- Research bats and compare facts to common beliefs about bats.
- Write an analysis comparing facts with common misperceptions about bats.
- Present research findings and respond to questions.
- Use reference sources to deepen vocabulary knowledge.
- Understand and use colons in written work.
- **Language** Recognize sensory descriptions in the text.

TEXT COMPLEXITY

Quantitative Measures	My Life as a Bat	Lexile: 1020L
Qualitative Measures	**Ideas Presented** Includes multiple levels of meaning and multiple themes.	
	Structures Used Unconventional story structure with numbered heads and multiple flashbacks/memories.	
	Language Used Some figurative language requiring interpretation.	
	Knowledge Required Single perspective with unfamiliar aspects; some cultural and literary knowledge useful.	

Online **Ed**

RESOURCES

- Unit 3 Response Log
- Close Read Screencasts: Modeled Discussions
- Selection Audio
- Reading Studio: Notice & Note
- Level Up Tutorial: Summarizing
- Writing Studio: Writing Informative Texts
- Speaking and Listening Studio: Giving a Presentation
- Vocabulary Studio: Using Reference Sources
- Grammar Studio: Module 12: Lesson 2: Colons
- "My Life as a Bat" Selection Test

SUMMARIES

English

This short story is divided into numbered sections which explain the narrator's belief that he or she was a bat in a previous incarnation. Many sections include complex descriptions and emotions from the perspective of a bat; these challenge conventional wisdom about bats and suggest that humans' fear of and aggression toward bats is based entirely on misinformation and superstition.

Spanish

Margaret Atwood utiliza su formato único para formular preguntas acerca de las actitudes humanas hacia los murciélagos. Su cuento corto provee secciones numeradas que explican la creencia del narrador de que él o ella fue un murciélago en una encarnación pasada. Muchas secciones incluyen descripciones y emociones complejas desde la perspectiva de un murciélago; que cuestionan la sabiduría popular acerca de los murciélagos y sugieren que los humanos son enemigos agresivos y violentos de los murciélagos que se basan enteramente en supersticiones y falta de información.

SMALL-GROUP OPTIONS

Have students work in small groups to read and discuss the selection.

Three Before Me

- Tell students they will use a collaborative approach to improve their assigned research analysis of information about bats.
- Have each student write and edit the research analysis individually.
- Then have each student ask three other students to read the analysis and do one of the following: peer edit the entire draft or check it for a particular type of error. Tell students they can make notes, edits, and suggestions in the margin. You might suggest that reviewers initial each comment in case the writer has follow-up questions.
- When editing is complete, ask writers to review their peers' suggestions and edits and make appropriate changes.

Reciprocal Teaching

- Form groups of 2–3 students.
- Have students write three or more discussion prompts related to the selection, using these stems: *The most surprising thing I learned about bats was _____. I don't know why the narrator _____. I liked/didn't like the story because _____. After reading the story, I realized that bats _____.*
- In their small groups, have each student offer one or more of their prompts for discussion.
- Tell students to ask clarifying questions and discuss each prompt.
- When discussion is complete, have groups prepare a summary of their discussions and share it with the class.

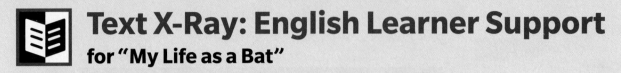

Text X-Ray: English Learner Support
for "My Life as a Bat"

Use the Text X-Ray and the supports and scaffolds in the Teacher's Edition to help guide students at different proficiency levels through the selection.

INTRODUCE THE SELECTION
DISCUSS REINCARNATION/PREVIOUS LIVES

In this lesson, students will read observations by a narrator who believes in reincarnation and previous lives. Explain the following terms:

- *Reincarnation* is a term used in Eastern religions such as Buddhism and Hinduism to describe a continuing cycle of death and rebirth into a different human or animal form.
- *Previous lives* is a more modern and less religious idea related to the same process. There are nonreligious people who offer to help others discover their previous lives.

Explain that *reincarnation* and *previous lives* are controversial ideas among people following non-Eastern religions. Provide these frames:

- Reincarnation *involves a person's ____ and return in a different ____.*
- *Some people claim they can help people ____ previous lives.*

CULTURAL REFERENCES

The following words or phrases from the selection may be unfamiliar to students:

- *the previous-life market* (paragraph 4): a business in which people pay to discover their previous lives
- *1952 housewives living in California split-levels* (paragraph 4): a reference to a person's life that is implied to be ordinary and boring
- *Dracula* (paragraph 18): a real-life count who, in fictional stories, was a vampire who could turn into a bat
- *a radiator grille* (paragraph 25): the front of a car, often from the 1950s, decorated with narrow ridges or posts

LISTENING

Understand Important Ideas

Explain that you are going to read text aloud and then ask questions about it so that students can practice their listening comprehension skills. Point out that sharpening their listening comprehension skills will also help students develop stronger reading and speaking skills.

Explain that an "incendiary device" is something that causes a fire to start. Read aloud paragraph 19. Then use the following supports with students at varying proficiency levels:

- Say, Close your eyes. Show me thumbs up for *yes* and thumbs down for *no*. This text is about bats. *(yes)* This text is about bats in World War II. *(yes)* This text is about bats in movies. *(no)* This text is about bats in the United States. *(no)* **SUBSTANTIAL**
- Ask these questions and have students answer them orally: What country were bats going to be released in? What time were bats going to be released? Why was each bat going to have an incendiary device tied to it? **MODERATE**
- Ask the following question orally and have students write an answer: What was the goal of the experiments done on bats during World War II? **LIGHT**

SPEAKING

Speak with Emphasis

Explain that in English, speakers sometimes emphasize, or stress, a certain word in a sentence in order to make an idea clear or express an opinion.

Write these two sentences on the board, with the words *like* and *don't* underlined: I *like* bats. I *don't* like bats. Then use the following supports with students at varying proficiency levels:

- Read the first sentence aloud, giving a thumbs-up sign. Have students repeat the sentence with the same emphasis. Read the second sentence aloud, giving a thumbs-down sign. Have students repeat the sentence with the same emphasis. **SUBSTANTIAL**
- Read each sentence aloud, modeling the appropriate emphasis. Then have students complete this frame to give their opinion about the selection: I (liked/didn't like) "My Life as a Bat" because _____. **MODERATE**
- Use the example sentences to model how to emphasize a word to express an opinion. Then write these sentences on the board: 1. *Bats* are amazing! 2. Bats *are* amazing! 3. Bats are *amazing!* Guide students to read each sentence aloud with the appropriate emphasis. Discuss the subtle difference in meaning in each sentence. **LIGHT**

READING

Recognize Sensory Descriptions

Discuss how this author uses many sensory descriptions to provide vivid images.

Use the following supports with students at varying proficiency levels:

- Read aloud paragraphs 6 and 7 as students follow along. Ask students to circle each color word they read (*red, white, white, blue*) and underline one phrase that has to do with sound. (*furious noise*) Explain that *furious* means "angry," so a "mouth emitting furious noise" is someone shouting in anger. **SUBSTANTIAL**
- Have students reread paragraph 8 and identify words that appeal to their senses of smell, hearing, and touch/temperature. **MODERATE**
- Have pairs of students reread paragraphs 6–9 and make a list of sensory words and phrases that appeal to at least four of the five senses. **LIGHT**

WRITING

Write Comparative Sentences

Read aloud the Write an Analysis directions on Student Edition page 155. Explain that in their analysis, students will write sentences that compare two or more things.

Use the following supports with students at varying proficiency levels:

- Guide students to compare bats in the story with bats in real life. Display these sentence frames and have students copy them as you model how to make comparisons: *Bats in the story _____. Bats in real life _____.* **SUBSTANTIAL**
- Have students use these frames to write sentences compare facts and beliefs about bats: *Unlike in the movies, real bats don't _____. People think that bats _____, but they actually _____.* **MODERATE**
- Have pairs of students refer to the chart on page 154. Ask students to write two sentences that compare and two that contrast using *and* and *but* to connect ideas. **LIGHT**

EXPLAIN THE SIGNPOSTS

Explain that **NOTICE & NOTE Signposts** are significant moments in the text that help readers understand and analyze works of fiction or nonfiction. Use the instruction on these pages to introduce students to the signposts **Memory Moment, Contrasts and Contradictions,** and **Again and Again.** Then use the selection that follows to have students apply the signposts to a text.

For a full list of the fiction and nonfiction signposts, see page 206.

 ## MEMORY MOMENT

Tell students that a **Memory Moment** involves a character or narrator describing events or feelings from the past. In some cases, an author will provide an obvious clue, such as a character saying "I remember when. . . ." In other cases, the moment is not so clearly introduced.

One clue to identifying a Memory Moment is that the action of the story stops and the reader's attention is directed to a memory or previous event. In many cases, a story being told in the present tense will shift to past tense as the memory is described.

A Memory Moment can provide readers with important information. For example, it can help develop the **plot** by explaining events in the past. It can introduce or reinforce a **theme** that is woven into the narrative. The information from the past can help readers understand **character development** and how a character has been affected by previous events.

When an author interrupts the flow of a story to include a Memory Moment, it usually means that the author considers the memory to be important information for the reader to know.

Read the first two sentences of the example passage and model how they indicate a Memory Moment: I notice that the character is describing nightmares from the past rather than current events.

Read the example passage aloud. Discuss the way it is annotated and the information in the chart. In this case, the Memory Moment provides important information about how the narrator views human beings.

Tell students that when they notice a Memory Moment, they should pause and mark it in their consumable texts and ask the anchor question: *Why might this memory be important to the character?*

MY LIFE AS A BAT

You are about to read the short story "My Life as a Bat." As you read, you will notice and note signposts that will help you identify and analyze the story's structure and the author's use of language. Here are three key signposts to look for as you read this short story and other works of fiction.

> For more information on these and other signposts to Notice & Note, visit the **Reading Studio.**

When you read and encounter a phrase like these, pause to see if it's a **Memory Moment** signpost:

"I remembered when . . ."

"that reminded me of . . ."

"I always thought of the time when . . ."

"Something like this had happened before . . ."

"We used to . . ."

▶ **Memory Moment** Has a friend ever stopped to tell you a story from his or her past? Was it a funny story? The story of an important event? Friends share stories to get to know each other better. Think about what you learned about your friend from the story he or she told you.

When an author includes a memory or a flashback, it can reveal important information about a character. Some of the things you can learn about a character from a **Memory Moment** are:

- strengths and weaknesses
- fears and desires
- opinions and perspectives
- motivations and obstacles

Read this part of "My Life as a Bat" to see how a student might annotate a Memory Moment:

Anchor Question
When you notice this signpost, ask: Why might this memory be important to the character?

6 I have recurring nightmares.
7   In one of them, I am clinging to the ceiling of a summer cottage while a red-faced man in white shorts and a white V-necked T-shirt jumps up and down, hitting at me with a tennis racket. There are cedar rafters up here, and sticky flypapers attached with tacks, dangling like toxic seaweeds. I look down at the man's face, foreshortened and sweating, the eyes bulging and blue, the mouth emitting furious noise. . . .

What memory is introduced?	a nightmare of being attacked by an angry man inside a house
What does the memory reveal about the narrator's opinions?	The narrator sees humans as ugly and irrational and a threat to her safety.

Contrasts and Contradictions Have you ever heard the saying "cruel to be kind?" The idea of this contradiction is that it is kinder to be brutally honest with a person in order to help him or her in the long term.

Contrasts and Contradictions can also highlight important elements in a story. They can establish a character's world view, create tension in the story's mood, or signal plot developments. They may help to better define an idea or experience by setting it up against what it is not. Taking note of contradictions and contrasts can help you more fully understand a story.

Here is how a student might annotate a contrast in "My Life As a Bat":

> 5 . . . When they kill, they kill <u>without mercy, but without hate</u>. . . .

Anchor Question
When you notice this signpost, ask: What point is the author making with this contrast?

What ideas are contrasted?	mercy and hate
Why is this an important distinction to the narrator?	The contrast shows bats as neither good nor evil.

Again and Again Imagine that a friend keeps mentioning a big basketball game coming up next week. You already know about the game, so why keep talking about it? Clearly, it's important to your friend. Maybe she's worried about it.

Authors repeat words, phrases, and imagery to make a point. Repetition can reveal important information about the characters or setting. **Again and Again** signposts may foreshadow future events or develop a story's theme.

In this example, a student underlined repeated elements:

> 3   Consider also: previous lives have entered the world of commerce. Money can be made from them. *You were* Cleopatra, *you were* a Flemish duke, *you were* a Druid priestess, and money changes hands. If the stock market exists, so must previous lives.

Pause to see if it's an **Again and Again** signpost when you see repetition of:

words

phrases

colors

images

descriptions

Anchor Question
When you notice this signpost, ask: Why might the author bring up this idea again and again?

What phrase or idea is repeated?	You were
What does this repetition accomplish in the text?	It sounds like someone might be told they were all of these things or that someone goes around telling many people stories about previous lives.

WHEN STUDENTS STRUGGLE . . .

Use a Sketch to Stretch If students are having trouble identifying or understanding Memory Moments, they can use a sketch to help visualize them. Ask them to think of a comic book or graphic novel that uses thought balloons to show what a character is thinking. Memory Moments are points in the story where a character or narrator stops to remember something from the past. Students can visualize the character in the story with a thought balloon and sketch the thoughts or memory. Then they can ask the anchor question: *Why might this memory be important to the character?*

CONTRASTS AND CONTRADICTIONS

Explain that authors may place words or phrases that describe different ideas or attitudes near each other to highlight the differences most vividly. **Contrasts and Contradictions** often surprise the reader. Read aloud the example sentence and note the underlined phrases *without mercy* and *without hate*. Ask students what the phrases describe. *(ways of killing)* Ask: How do these descriptions encourage comparisons to human actions? *(They encourage readers to think about the ways that humans kill compared to the ways bats kill.)*

Contrast and Contradictions can make readers consider **character development** when a character takes unexpected or surprising actions. They can also highlight **internal conflicts** in a character or reinforce a **theme** or a question that recurs throughout the selection.

Tell students that when they spot a Contrast or Contradiction, they should pause, mark it in their consumable text, and ask themselves the anchor question: *What point is the author making with this contrast?*

AGAIN AND AGAIN

Note that when words or phrases appear **Again and Again** in a sentence, paragraph, or story, they may be intended to draw the reader's attention to features of the **plot** or **setting,** to the use of **symbolism,** or to **character development.** In some cases, the repetition is clear, while in others the reader may need to be alert to notice images or ideas that recur in different parts of the story. Read aloud the example passage, emphasizing the words that are italicized. Ask: Who is saying these repeated words? What do I think when I hear them?

Tell students that when they spot this signpost, they should pause, mark it in their consumable text, and ask themselves the anchor question: *Why might the author bring up this idea again and again?*

APPLY THE SIGNPOSTS

Have students use the selection that follows as a model text to apply the signposts. As students encounter signposts, prompt them to stop, reread, and ask themselves the anchor questions that will help them understand the author's intentions. Tell students to continue to look for these and other signposts as they read the other selections in the unit.

TEACH

 Connect to the
ESSENTIAL QUESTION

Our natural world is an intricate system of connections in which a small change in one area may cause significant ripple effects in other areas. This short story provides a unique view of these relationships by describing the world through the eyes and mind of a creature that is understood and loved by few humans. This story shows some of the effects we have on nature—and also exposes the effects nature has on us by highlighting some of our irrational fears and reactions.

MY LIFE AS A BAT

Short Story by **Margaret Atwood**

? **ESSENTIAL QUESTION:**

What effect do we have on nature, and how does nature affect us?

 LEARNING MINDSET

Curiosity Display the terms *Who? What? Why? Where?* and *How?* Ask students what the terms have in common. *(They are all questions.)* Explain that curiosity—or the inclination to learn something—is a valuable trait. Tell students that asking questions is one way to connect with what they are reading. Exploring ideas, books, and skills can also add to their understanding of the world. Point out that this selection will challenge students to consider the world around them through different eyes. It will also ask them to use new analysis skills, learn new words, and research new subjects. Encourage students to be curious and think about how this unusual text relates to their lives and how what they are learning can help outside of class.

QUICK START

Imagine what life would be like if you were an animal. Quickwrite about what animal you would be. What would you be afraid of? What would humans seem like to you? Would you avoid them or live near them?

ANALYZE STRUCTURE

Most stories follow a **structure** that includes these elements:

- **Exposition:** introduces characters, setting, and conflict.
- **Rising Action:** introduces complications and builds suspense.
- **Climax:** the most exciting part; makes the conflict's outcome clear.
- **Falling Action:** eases tension and shows main character's response.
- **Resolution:** reveals how events turn out; also called the denouement.

In this story, the author dispenses with traditional narrative structure. Instead, she arranges events, conflicts, and reflections using an informative essay format with numbered heads. Readers must piece together the narrative to determine the order and significance of events. When reading any story that uses an unusual narrative structure, consider the effect of the author's choices: How does the structure maintain reader interest and develop theme? How does it help you make, correct, and confirm predictions?

ANALYZE LANGUAGE

An author's language can create vivid images, convey specific meanings, and set the mood or tone of the story. Figurative language and sensory descriptions are two ways that authors use language.

Figurative language makes imaginative comparisons between dissimilar things. **Similes** are comparisons that use the words *like* or *as*; **metaphors** are comparisons that are implied rather than stated.

Sensory descriptions rely on the senses to convey vivid images. An author will show how something looks, tastes, sounds, smells, or feels.

To analyze the language that Margaret Atwood uses in "My Life as a Bat," form a mental image of what the language describes. Then, ask yourself questions such as the ones in the following examples.

- **Simile:** "flypapers . . . dangling like toxic seaweeds." In what way are the items being compared similar? What feeling does the word *toxic* convey?
- **Metaphor:** "his breath, . . . the breath of the monster." Is the man really a monster? What does this comparison suggest about him or his likely actions? What is the narrator's **tone**, or attitude, toward him?
- **Sensory description:** "sound of water trickling through limestone . . . a glistening hush." What senses does this description rely on? How does the description enhance, or strengthen, the imagery of the story?

GENRE ELEMENTS: SHORT STORY

- centers on the thoughts and actions of one or more characters
- includes a narrator who may or may not be a character
- contains one or more settings
- includes a series of events or actions that may be told in or out of order

My Life as a Bat   147

QUICK START

Have students read the Quick Start instructions. If they struggle to answer the questions, prompt them with the following suggestions: First, think of an animal that you like or respect. Then, imagine the world that animal lives in. Does it live in a desert, a forest, the mountains, or even cities? Do other animals or humans threaten that animal? Next, think of an animal that scares you or that you find unpleasant and ask yourself the same questions.

ANALYZE STRUCTURE

Note that authors have a variety of structures to choose from in fiction. The most common is a chronological structure that begins at a particular point and describes events as they occur after that. In that structure, an author may use **flashbacks** to describe events before the beginning of the narrative.

In this short story, the author uses an unusual structure that challenges readers in much the same way that the story itself challenges readers to see the world from a different perspective. Using numbered headings presents the story as if it were a nonfiction, informational article and reinforces the idea that the point of view of a bat is a rational, factual perspective.

ANALYZE LANGUAGE

Explain that an author's choice of language helps establish and define the author's style. In this selection, the author uses **figurative language** to help readers see or imagine scenes that are unfamiliar to them.

Point out that people often use figurative language in conversations to help them describe things. Offer some common examples:

- **Similes:** *It was so loud it sounded like thunder. It was as bright as day when they turned the porch lights on.*
- **Metaphors:** *I was a slug this morning. He was a bear on the first day of class.*
- **Sensory descriptions:** *I love the smell of warm cookies fresh from the oven. I love the taste of lemonade on a hot day. I love the feeling of a cozy blanket.*

Invite volunteers to suggest other examples of figurative language or sensory descriptions.

EL ENGLISH LEARNER SUPPORT

Make Comparisons with Similes   Students may need additional support to understand similes. Help them see how a simile compares things that are mostly different but that share something in common. For example, a person and a tree are very different, but if an author writes, "The basketball player was as tall as a tree," then readers can imagine that the basketball player was very tall. Explain that similes exaggerate certain qualities that are not literally true (a person is not *really* as tall as most trees) to create images and feelings. Provide practice making comparisons using these frames: *The day was as hot as _____. She ran as fast as _____. The smooth water was like _____.*   **ALL LEVELS**

© Houghton Mifflin Harcourt Publishing Company

TEACH

CRITICAL VOCABULARY

Encourage students to read all the sentences before deciding which words fit in the blanks. As a clue to the definition of *consensus,* tell students that it is derived from the root word *consent.*

Answers:

1. *denizen*
2. *consensus*
3. *incendiary*
4. *interlude*
5. *subtleties*

■ **English Learner Support**

Use Cognates Tell students that the root word for one of the Critical Vocabulary words has a Spanish cognate: *subtle/ sutil.* **ALL LEVELS**

LANGUAGE CONVENTIONS

Review the information about **colons** and note that like commas and dashes, colons signal for a reader to pause. However, the uses of colons tend to be more limited: to introduce a list, to introduce a direct quotation, or to set up an explanation of a preceding idea. The example sentence describes something the narrator does not like (heads of human hair) and then provides the reason why after the colon.

Like a period, a colon indicates that the reader should come to a full stop before continuing. However, what follows the colon refers to information from the sentence that immediately precedes the colon.

ANNOTATION MODEL

Remind students of the signposts listed on pages 144–145 and the information on story structure and figurative language on page 147. Point out that the model shown illustrates how one student reacted to the story structure and the narrator's surprising statements early in the story. Briefly discuss the example annotations. Emphasize that students may use suggestions from the text for their annotations or develop their own system. Their notes in the margin may include questions and ideas about the text (as in the model) as well as information that is unclear or topics they want to learn more about.

 GET READY

CRITICAL VOCABULARY

consensus	interlude	subtleties	incendiary	denizen

To see how many Critical Vocabulary words you already know, use them to complete the sentences.

1. I am a(n) _____ of the town where I live.

2. When the whole class agrees, we have a(n) _____.

3. The graduation party invitation specified no _____ materials, such as fireworks.

4. Our coach gave us a brief _____ between running laps so we could get a drink of water.

5. The _____ of foreign languages take time to distinguish.

LANGUAGE CONVENTIONS

Colons Writers can use colons to introduce a list or a direct quotation. A colon may also set up an explanation of a preceding idea. A reader pauses at a colon to prepare for what comes after it. Here is an example from the story:

There was also my dislike for headfuls of human hair, so like nets or the tendrils of poisonous jellyfish: I feared entanglements.

A colon is set at the end of a word and is followed by a space. As you read, watch for ways that Atwood uses colons for effect.

ANNOTATION MODEL   **NOTICE & NOTE**

As you read, notice and note signposts, including **Memory Moment, Contrasts and Contradictions,** and **Again and Again**. Here is an example of how one reader responded to the structure and the author's use of language in the opening of "My Life as a Bat":

> **1. Reincarnation** ←
> In my previous life I was a bat.
>
>   If you find previous lives amusing or unlikely, you are not a serious person. Consider: a great many people believe in them, and if sanity is a general consensus about the content of reality,[who are you to disagree?]

Sets up story structure

Surprising statement

Narrator is speaking directly to the reader.

BACKGROUND

Margaret Atwood *(b. 1939) has published more than fifty works of fiction, poetry, and nonfiction. This Canadian author uses her keen intellect and sharp wit to explore ideas about nature, science, the search for identity, social criticism, and human rights. Her award-winning novels include* The Handmaid's Tale, *which was made into a movie and award-winning television series,* Cat's Eye, Alias Grace, *and* Oryx and Crake.

MY LIFE AS A BAT

Short Story by Margaret Atwood

SETTING A PURPOSE

As you read, make predictions about what each section of the story will be about and how it will contribute to the story's structure.

1. Reincarnation

1   In my previous life I was a bat.

2   If you find previous lives amusing or unlikely, you are not a serious person. Consider: a great many people believe in them, and if sanity is a general **consensus** about the content of reality, who are you to disagree?

3   Consider also: previous lives have entered the world of commerce. Money can be made from them. *You were Cleopatra,[1] you were a Flemish duke, you were a Druid priestess,* and money changes hands. If the stock market exists, so must previous lives.

4   In the previous-life market, there is not such a great demand for Peruvian ditch-diggers as there is for Cleopatra; or for Indian latrine-cleaners, or for 1952 housewives living in California split-levels. Similarly, not many of us choose to remember our lives as vultures, spiders, or rodents, but some of us do. The fortunate

---
[1] **Cleopatra:** Queen of Egypt in the first century B.C.E.

Notice & Note

You can use the side margins to notice and note signposts in the text.

consensus
(kən-sĕn´səs) *n.*
agreement.

ANALYZE STRUCTURE

Annotate: Mark two details in paragraphs 1–4 that help explain the section heading.

Analyze: What role does this section play in the structure of the story? Cite evidence in your answer.

My Life as a Bat   149

BACKGROUND

After students read the Background paragraph, note the various genres that the author has used and the wide variety of subjects she has written about. Ask students to speculate on how her experience writing in different genres might affect her work in fiction. How might a background as a poet affect her work in writing fiction? *(She might be skilled in the use of figurative or vivid language.)* How might a background in nonfiction and science writing affect her work in writing fiction? *(Her references to scientific subjects may be based on factual knowledge.)*

SETTING A PURPOSE

Direct students to use the Setting a Purpose prompt to focus their reading.

✏ ANALYZE STRUCTURE

Note that the author uses an unusual **structure** for a fictional short story. Numbered section headings are more commonly used in nonfiction texts, such as informational articles. Explain that in this story, this structure serves different purposes. It suggests that the narrator of the story is a reliable reporter of factual information. It also allows the author to shift subjects quickly without transitions. (**Answer:** *This section serves as exposition. It introduces the narrator and a core conflict: conventional wisdom about past lives as an animal and the narrator's own opinion on the matter.*)

CRITICAL VOCABULARY

consensus: The narrator points out that many people agree that there are past lives.

ASK STUDENTS why consensus is part of determining whether someone is sane. *(One indicator of whether someone is sane is whether he or she views reality in the same way as most other people.)*

APPLYING ACADEMIC VOCABULARY

☑ **advocate**   ☑ **discrete**   ☐ **domain**   ☐ **evoke**   ☐ **enhance**

Write and Discuss Have students turn to a partner to discuss the following questions. Guide students to include the academic vocabulary words *advocate* and *discrete* in their responses. Ask volunteers to share their responses with the class.

- What position do you think the narrator is trying to **advocate**?
- Discuss which species the narrator considers superior, citing text evidence of **discrete** characteristics of the two species.

(b) ©CreativeNature.nl/Adobe Stock

ANALYZE LANGUAGE

Explain that authors can use **figurative language** to create a variety of effects. In this paragraph, it is used to convey the fear and tension felt by the narrator in the nightmare. However, in paragraph 25, the author uses similes to compare a bat's nose to a dead leaf and a radiator grille. These comparisons create vivid images, but not tension. Authors choose language that creates the **mood** or feeling they want to communicate. (**Answer:** *The comparison of the sticky flypaper to toxic seaweed creates tension by presenting the flypaper as dangerous and deadly. The comparison of the noises the man makes to something great and ominous rising in and out of cresting waves creates tension by imparting a sense of foreboding.*)

▶ **MEMORY MOMENT**

Point out that the entire section "Nightmares" is in a sense a Memory Moment in that it recounts the narrator's thoughts and memories rather than current actions. Guide students to think about why this memory may be important to the **character** of the narrator. The memories of nightmares that are described vividly by the narrator emphasize the importance of the narrator's belief in a previous life and her experiences as a bat rather than a human. (**Answer:** *The memory of being a bat is largely positive; the narrator recalls specific details with a tone of pleasant nostalgia. This becomes a nightmare when humans become involved, separating the bat from its home.*)

For **reading support** for students at varying proficiency levels, see the **Text X-Ray** on page 144D.

CRITICAL VOCABULARY

interlude: The narrator suggests that living as an animal may be a peaceful break after living as a human.

ASK STUDENTS to explain why the narrator may see an animal's life as an "interlude of grace." (*The narrator sees the memory of life as an animal as "fortunate" and a "resting place" compared to the conflicts experienced by humans.*)

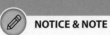 **NOTICE & NOTE**

interlude
(ĭn´tər-lōōd) *n.* a time of rest between two tasks.

ANALYZE LANGUAGE

Annotate: Mark two similes in paragraph 7.

Analyze: How do the comparisons that the author makes create tension?

MEMORY MOMENT

Notice & Note: Mark positive images and impressions in paragraph 9.

Draw Conclusions: How does the narrator feel about the memory of being a bat? Why is this passage a "nightmare"?

few. Conventional wisdom has it that reincarnation as an animal is a punishment for past sins, but perhaps it is a reward instead. At least a resting place. An **interlude** of grace.

5   Bats have a few things to put up with, but they do not inflict. When they kill, they kill without mercy, but without hate. They are immune from the curse of pity. They never gloat.

2. Nightmares

6   I have recurring nightmares.

7   In one of them, I am clinging to the ceiling of a summer cottage while a red-faced man in white shorts and a white V-necked T-shirt jumps up and down, hitting at me with a tennis racket. There are cedar rafters up here, and sticky flypapers attached with tacks, dangling like toxic seaweeds. I look down at the man's face, foreshortened and sweating, the eyes bulging and blue, the mouth emitting furious noise, rising up like a marine float, sinking again, rising as if on a swell of air.

8   The air itself is muggy, the sun is sinking; there will be a thunderstorm. A woman is shrieking, "My hair! My hair!" and someone else is calling, "Anthea! Bring the stepladder!" All I want is to get out through the hole in the screen, but that will take some concentration and it's hard in this din of voices, they interfere with my sonar.[2] There is a smell of dirty bathmats—it's his breath, the breath that comes out from every pore, the breath of the monster. I will be lucky to get out of this alive.

9   In another nightmare I am winging my way—flittering, I suppose you'd call it—through the clean-washed demilight before dawn. This is a desert. The yuccas are in bloom, and I have been gorging myself on their juices and pollen. I'm heading to my home, to my home cave,

---

[2] **sonar:** a system for identifying objects with reflected sound.

CLOSE READ SCREENCAST

Modeled Discussions In their eBook, have students view the Close Read Screencast, in which readers discuss and annotate the following key passage:

  • a description of the narrator's nightmare about a man launching an attack with a tennis racket (paragraph 7)

As a class, view and discuss the video. Then have students pair up to do an independent close read of an additional passage describing the narrator's longing to return to life as a bat (paragraph 25). Students can record their answers on the Close Read Practice PDF.

 Close Read Practice PDF

where it will be cool during the burnout of day and there will be the sound of water trickling through limestone, coating the rock with a glistening hush, with the moistness of new mushrooms, and the other bats will chirp and rustle and doze until night unfurls again and makes the hot sky tender for us.

10   But when I reach the entrance to the cave, it is sealed over. It's blocked in. Who can have done this?

11   I vibrate my wings, sniffing blind as a dazzled moth over the hard surface. In a short time the sun will rise like a balloon on fire and I will be blasted with its glare, shriveled to a few small bones.

12   Whoever said that light was life and darkness nothing?

13   For some of us, the mythologies are different.

3. Vampire Films

14   I became aware of the nature of my previous life gradually, not only through dreams but through scraps of memory, through hints, through odd moments of recognition.

15   There was my preference for the **subtleties** of dawn and dusk, as opposed to the vulgar blaring hour of high noon. There was my déjà vu experience in the Carlsbad Caverns—surely I had been there before, long before, before they put in the pastel spotlights and the cute names for stalactites and the underground restaurant where you can combine claustrophobia and indigestion and then take the elevator to get back out.

16   There was also my dislike for headfuls of human hair, so like nets or the tendrils of poisonous jellyfish: I feared entanglements. No real bat would ever suck the blood of necks. The neck is too near the hair. Even the vampire bat will target a hairless extremity—by choice a toe, resembling as it does the teat of a cow.

17   Vampire films have always seemed ludicrous to me, for this reason but also for the idiocy of their bats—huge rubbery bats, with red Christmas-light eyes and fangs like a sabertoothed tiger's, flown

CONTRASTS AND CONTRADICTIONS

Notice & Note: Mark a statement in this section that expresses the opposite of conventional thinking.

Compare: How does this statement serve to contrast humans and bats?

subtleties
(sŭt´l-tēz) *n.* fine details or nuances.

ANALYZE LANGUAGE

Annotate: In paragraph 15, mark a context clue for the meaning of the commonly used foreign phrase *déjà vu*.

Analyze: How does the use of the phrase *déjà vu* support the narrator's claim of a past life?

My Life as a Bat   151

CONTRASTS AND CONTRADICTIONS

Explain that the author continues a pattern of surprising statements that illustrate the differences between the lives of bats and the lives of humans. This fundamental difference is at the heart of the story and serves as a **theme** that appears in all sections of the story. Ask students what the conventional thinking is about light and darkness. (*Light is necessary for life and darkness is emptiness and not important.*) Discuss how paragraph 13 serves to contrast humans and bats. (**Answer:** *The sentence highlights the idea that bats have the opposite point of view on the importance of light and darkness that people do.*)

ANALYZE LANGUAGE

Tell students that *déjà vu* is a French phrase meaning "already seen." Explain that the narrator's belief in reincarnation as described in the first section paints many of the descriptions in the story as something akin to déjà vu: if a person has lived a previous life and remembers it, then there is a good chance that a person will feel that they have already been to a new place or that they have seen or felt a unique experience before. Ask students why the narrator may have referenced déjà vu. (*Culturally people often accept the mystery of déjà vu without much thought, so referencing the concept can help readers relate to the narrator.*) (**Answer:** *The narrator expresses familiarity with caves and the habitats of bats. This feeling of having been there before creates a connection between the narrator and a previous life.*)

CRITICAL VOCABULARY

subtleties: The narrator likes the soft light of morning and evening.

ASK STUDENTS why this supports the narrator's connection to bats. (*Like bats, the narrator does not like bright light.*)

ENGLISH LEARNER SUPPORT

Use Context Clues for Vocabulary Point out the Spanish cognate for the word *context* (*contexto*) and review how context can be used in determining meanings of unfamiliar words. Model the following approach to provide a meaning for the word *tendrils* in paragraph 16. Say:

- Context clues appear in words and sentences near the unfamiliar word.
- In the same sentence, *tendrils* are compared to *headfuls of human hair* and *nets.*
- In the same sentence, this fear of *tendrils* is described as fear of *entanglements.*

- Using these clues, I can guess that *tendrils* work like nets and hair that a bat might get tangled in.
- I know that jellyfish have things like vines that hang down from their body.
- *Tendrils* must be something that can tangle a person or animal like a net.
- Now I can use a dictionary to see if I figured out the meaning of the word.
  MODERATE/LIGHT

TEACH

AGAIN AND AGAIN

Tell students that sometimes readers must infer the reason why an author uses repetition. Ask students how they feel about bats at this point in the story. How does the repetition of the idea of death affect readers' understanding of the relationship between bats and humans? (**Answer:** *By this point in the story, the reader may identify or sympathize with bats. The repetition of the idea of death emphasizes how badly humans treat bats.*)

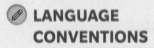 For **listening support** for students at varying proficiency levels, see the **Text X-Ray** on page 144C.

LANGUAGE CONVENTIONS

Review that a **colon** is a way to separate words and ideas from each other and often indicates that the words following it help explain the words before it. (**Answer:** *The information following the colon clarifies that humans experience loathing for the skin and flesh of bats in particular, not all those with skin and flesh.*)

■ English Learner Support

Understand Language Conventions Read aloud paragraph 23. Invite students to ask for clarification of any unfamiliar words. Then help students understand how the colon is used in the last sentence of the paragraph. Ask students how the meaning would change if the sentence ended where the colon is. (*It would mean that we loathe all those who have skin and flesh.*) Ask how the information after the colon adds meaning. (*It makes it clear that we loathe the skin and flesh of bats because they are different from our own.*) Have pairs of students write a sentence about bats that uses a colon to introduce an explanation.

MODERATE/LIGHT

CRITICAL VOCABULARY

incendiary: The bats would be equipped with small bombs intended to start fires.

ASK STUDENTS what the result of a small incendiary device deep inside a structure would be. (*It would start a fire that would be difficult to extinguish.*)

denizen: The narrator explains that the bat's unusual face makes it look like an alien from the planet Pluto.

ASK STUDENTS to explain the characteristics that denizens of a bat colony would have. (*Denizens of a bat colony would be individuals of a particular species of bat.*)

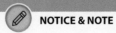

in on strings, their puppet wings flapped sluggishly like those of an overweight and degenerate bird. I screamed at these filmic moments, but not with fear; rather with outraged laughter, at the insult to bats.

18   O Dracula, unlikely hero! . . . Why was it given to you by whoever stole your soul to transform yourself into bat and wolf, and only those? Why not a vampire chipmunk, a duck, a gerbil? Why not a vampire turtle? Now that would be a plot.

4. The Bat as Deadly Weapon

19   During the Second World War they did experiments with bats. Thousands of bats were to be released over German cities, at the hour of noon. Each was to have a small **incendiary** device strapped onto it, with a timer. The bats would have headed for darkness, as is their habit. They would have crawled into holes in walls, or secreted themselves under the eaves of houses, relieved to have found safety. At a preordained moment they would have exploded, and the cities would have gone up in flames.

20   That was the plan. Death by flaming bat. The bats too would have died, of course. Acceptable megadeaths.

21   The cities went up in flames anyway, but not with the aid of bats. The atom bomb had been invented, and the fiery bat was no longer thought necessary.

22   If the bats had been used after all, would there have been a war memorial to them? It isn't likely.

23   If you ask a human being what makes his flesh creep more, a bat or a bomb, he will say the bat. It is difficult to experience loathing for something merely metal, however ominous. We save these sensations for those with skin and flesh: a skin, a flesh, unlike our own.

5. Beauty

24   Perhaps it isn't my life as a bat that was the interlude. Perhaps it is this life. Perhaps I have been sent into human form as if on a dangerous mission, to save and redeem my own folk. When I have gained a small success, or died in the attempt—for failure, in such a task and against such odds, is more likely—I will be born again, back into that other form, that other world where I truly belong.

25   More and more, I think of this event with longing. The quickness of heartbeat, the vivid plunge into the nectars of crepuscular flowers, hovering in the infrared of night; the dank lazy half-sleep of daytime, with bodies rounded and soft as furred plums clustering around me, the mothers licking the tiny amazed faces of the newborn; the swift love of what will come next, the anticipations of the tongue and of the infurled, corrugated and scrolled nose, nose like a dead leaf, nose like a radiator grille, nose of a **denizen** of Pluto.

Sidebar notes

incendiary
(ĭn-sĕn′dē-ĕr-ē) *adj.*
intended to cause fire; flammable.

AGAIN AND AGAIN

Notice & Note: Mark instances of the idea of death in paragraph 20.

Infer: Why might the narrator be emphasizing this idea?

LANGUAGE CONVENTIONS

Annotate: Mark the colon in paragraph 23.

Interpret: How does the information that follows the colon add to the meaning of the sentence?

denizen
(dĕn′ĭ-zən) *n.*
a resident.

WHEN STUDENTS STRUGGLE . . .

Use a Graphic Organizer A graphic organizer can help students track content for each numbered section. Guide them as necessary to fill in information for all five sections.

Section Title	Summary of Content	Details
1. Reincarnation	Establishes idea of narrator living previously as a bat	
2. Nightmares	Introduces view of humans through a bat's eyes	

 For additional support, go to the **Reading Studio** and assign the following Level Up Tutorial: Summarizing.

26 <u>And in the evening, the supersonic hymn of praise to our Creator, the Creator of bats,</u> who appears to us in the form of a bat and who gave us all things: water and the liquid stone of caves, the woody refuge of attics, petals and fruit and juicy insects, and the beauty of slippery wings and sharp white canines and shining eyes.

27 What do we pray for? We pray for food as all do, and for health and for the increase of our kind; and for deliverance from evil, which cannot be explained by us, which is hair-headed and walks in the night with a single white unseeing eye, and stinks of half-digested meat, and has two legs.

28 Goddess of caves and grottoes: bless your children.

ANALYZE STRUCTURE

Annotate: Mark two details in the section "Beauty" that describe the future the narrator envisions.

Analyze: How does this section serve as a resolution for the story?

CHECK YOUR UNDERSTANDING

Answer these questions before moving on to the **Analyze the Text** section on the following page.

1 How does the author structure this story?

  A As a stream-of-consciousness reflection on the narrator's thoughts

  B As a collection of very short stories that are increasingly serious

  C In chronological order showing a sequence of events in the narrator's life

  D In sections that include brief scenes or facts to illustrate ideas

2 References to popular culture and historical events serve to —

  F use funny stories to keep the interest of readers who don't like bats

  G show how the lives of bats and humans have always been intertwined

  H illustrate why the narrator considers humans to be evil

  J reveal that the narrator is wrong about how much humans value bats

3 Which statement best reflects the narrator's attitude toward the relationship between bats and people?

  A People fear bats, yet humans are the real monsters.

  B People and bats should appreciate each other more.

  C Bats have good reason to attack people like they do.

  D Bats miss out on the day, yet people miss out on the night.

My Life as a Bat   153

ANALYZE STRUCTURE

Note the title of section 5 and explain that it prepares the reader for a subject unlike those in other sections. It can be seen as the **resolution** of the story, presenting a unique perspective on life, in comparison to the previous sections that refer to "deadly weapons," "vampires," and "nightmares." Explain that the internal tension described by the narrator has built with each successive section, and that the structure of both fiction and nonfiction generally leads to some sort of resolution or conclusion. (**Answer:** *This section resolves the narrator's internal conflict between being a bat and being a human by suggesting that the narrator has chosen to identify more with bats than with humans. The section also serves to reiterate a primary theme of the story: people's fear of bats is unreasonable, as people cause more harm to bats than they do to us.*)

CHECK YOUR UNDERSTANDING

Have students answer the questions independently.

Answers:

 1. *D*

 2. *G*

 3. *A*

If they answer any questions incorrectly, have them reread the text to confirm their understanding. Then they may proceed to ANALYZE THE TEXT on page 154.

ENGLISH LEARNER SUPPORT

Oral Assessment Use the following questions to assess students' comprehension and speaking skills. Ask students to respond in complete sentences.

  1. What device does the author use to structure the story? (*The author uses numbered sections that include brief scenes or facts to illustrate ideas.*)

  2. Why does the author refer to vampire stories and events from history? (*The author uses references to vampire stories and history to show that the lives of bats and humans have always been connected.*)

  3. What is the narrator's view of the relationship between bats and humans? (*The narrator shows that people fear bats, but that people are a greater danger to bats than the other way around.*) **MODERATE/LIGHT**

APPLY

ANALYZE THE TEXT

Possible answers:

1. **DOK 4:** *Humor helps develop the narrator because it's mostly directed at humans. For example, the narrator uses a humorous example to comment that there isn't a great demand in the previous-life market for "Peruvian ditch-diggers" or "Indian latrine-cleaners." In contrast, at the end of the story, the narrator speaks seriously and reverently about bats.*

2. **DOK 2:** *To the nocturnal bat, the sun burns fiercely in daytime ("the burnout of day"). So, in the nightmare, the narrator is "blasted" with the sun's glare and "shriveled to a few small bones."*

3. **DOK 3:** *The narrator contrasts the beauty of bats ("bodies rounded and soft as furred plums") with the hideousness of humans. The morality of bats and humans is contrasted. Bats "kill without mercy, but without hate"; they do not pity or gloat. It is implied that humans do all these things. The experiments on using bats as incendiary devices, the man swatting at the narrator with a tennis racket, and the nightmare about the sealed cave all show humans as evil aggressors. These contrasts develop a theme suggesting that humans are not as advanced a species as they think they are.*

4. **DOK 4:** *The narrative structure progresses from exposition through rising action until it reaches the climax about how cruelly humans were prepared to treat bats in World War II. The structure and the headings help readers make predictions to some extent, but each section holds surprises. For example, in section 4, it becomes clear that humans are the "deadly" ones, not bats.*

5. **DOK 4:** *The essential contradiction lies in the fact that bats are considered "creepy" and people flee from them and fear them, when in fact bats not only pose no danger to people but are instead directly threatened by them.*

RESEARCH

Suggest that partners divide up the task of paraphrasing their research findings among their sources and then review each other's work to ensure that they're using their own words and not plagiarizing from their sources.

Extend Help students understand the power of misconceptions. Suggest that they consider the views they held about bats before beginning this selection and try to identify the source of the information. Have them discuss whether the information was founded on scientific fact or was influenced by popular media such as sensational movies or scary Halloween stories.

RESPOND

ANALYZE THE TEXT

Support your responses with evidence from the text. NOTEBOOK

1. **Analyze** Throughout the story, the author uses wry, humorous language in the form of exaggeration and irony. Give an example of humor from the text. How does the humor develop the character of the narrator?

2. **Interpret** The narrator, as a bat, describes the sun rising "like a balloon on fire" (paragraph 11). What meaning is conveyed by this simile in the context of the nightmare?

3. **Compare** What are some of the main contrasts the narrator makes between humans and bats? Cite specific statements as well as stories that imply the differences. What theme about people is developed through these contrasts?

4. **Evaluate** How did the narrative structure and section headings help you make, correct, and confirm predictions about where the story would go? How do the structure and headings help develop a theme?

5. **Notice & Note** Consider the way the narrator contrasts ideas about and images of bats in the sections "Vampire Films," "The Bat as Deadly Weapon," and "Beauty." Explain how comparison and contrast help to highlight an essential contradiction between people's perceptions of bats and bats in reality.

RESEARCH TIP
Paraphrase the information from a source to better track important information. Mark the text where you find descriptions about bats. Write the details in your own words to guide your research.

RESEARCH

"My Life as a Bat" includes many details about bats that counteract misconceptions people hold about them. With a partner, choose one aspect of bats listed below, and conduct research to determine how accurately the story reflects the facts.

ASPECTS OF BATS	STORY DETAILS	RESEARCH FINDINGS	POPULAR MISCONCEPTIONS
where they live	*rafters/attics, caves in the dark*	*live in colonies*	*only live in caves or attics and are solitary*
how they behave			
what they eat			
what they look like			

Extend With a partner, review your research and determine how accurate the descriptions in the story were and whether popular misconceptions have any basis in fact. Discuss reasons for any differences, including faulty reasoning, bias, or conflicting information.

LEARNING MINDSET

Try Again Review the learning process as one that includes mistakes. Note that a successful inventor such as Thomas Edison reportedly failed in a thousand experiments before understanding the technology required for making a light bulb. To gain new understanding, all learners make mistakes. If there are no mistakes, learners never stretch their minds and grow. Encourage students to share with a partner, a small group, or the class, a mistake they made in analyzing this selection. Support students in acknowledging mistakes as a positive step and in seeing the classroom as a safe place to take chances as a way to develop new skills and gain knowledge.

CREATE AND PRESENT

Write an Analysis Write a three-to four-paragraph essay in which you compare and contrast the facts that you found in your research and those that were included in the selection.

❏ Introduce the topic and discuss the selection's focus on bats and life as a bat.

❏ Then, discuss the accuracy of facts and descriptions that the story provides. Use evidence from your research to support or refute both details from the story and popular misconceptions about bats.

❏ In your final paragraph, state your conclusion about the overall accuracy of the facts included in "My Life as a Bat."

Present Research Share your findings in a brief presentation about the accuracy of facts about bats in "My Life as a Bat."

❏ Review your analysis and choose a few facts or descriptions to illustrate your analysis. Create a three-factor Venn diagram to compare the story details and facts that you have chosen.

❏ Display the diagram and discuss the information you chose to include.

❏ Present your conclusion about the accuracy of the facts and descriptions about bats in "My Life as a Bat." Invite your audience to ask questions at the end of your presentation.

RESPOND TO THE ESSENTIAL QUESTION

 What effect do we have on nature, and how does nature affect us?

Gather Information Review your annotations and notes on "My Life as a Bat." Then, add relevant information to your Response Log. As you determine which information to include, think about:

• the opinions and attitude of the narrator
• the language the author uses to build meaning
• the non-traditional structure of the story

At the end of the unit, use your notes to help you write an explanatory essay.

RESPOND

 Visit the **Writing Studio** for more on writing informative texts.

 Go to the **Speaking and Listening Studio** for help with giving a presentation.

TIP: Here is an example of a three-factor Venn diagram. Commonalities should appear in overlapping areas.

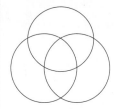

ACADEMIC VOCABULARY

As you write and discuss what you learned from the short story, be sure to use the Academic Vocabulary words. Check off each of the words that you use.

❏ advocate
❏ discrete
❏ domain
❏ evoke
❏ enhance

CREATE AND PRESENT

Write an Analysis Review with students the prompt for writing the analysis and clarify any misunderstandings. Suggest an approach to take for planning their writing, such as creating an informal outline. Remind students to refer to their research notes to cite sources of information that support the accuracy or inaccuracy of story details and popular misconceptions. Note that their conclusion should follow naturally from the previous paragraphs and that it should be supported by cited evidence.

 For **writing support** for students at varying proficiency levels, see the **Text X-Ray** on page 144D.

Present Research Guide students in completing the three-factor Venn diagram as necessary. Help them identify the three different areas that were the focus of their research (*story details, research, and misconceptions*). Suggest that they review the notes from their research (page 154) to identify similarities and differences for the diagram.

Once the diagram is complete, encourage students to practice for the presentation. Note that their presentation could follow the outline suggested for the written analysis above. Reinforce the idea that any conclusions they present should be supported by their research sources. Also have students consider how they will introduce information in their diagram.

 For **speaking support** for students at varying proficiency levels, see the **Text X-Ray** on page 144D.

RESPOND TO THE ESSENTIAL QUESTION

Allow time for students to add details from the selection "My Life as a Bat" to their Unit 3 Response Logs.

EL ENGLISH LEARNER SUPPORT

Write an Analysis Review the common organization of an analysis essay that involves an introductory paragraph, body paragraphs that develop the subject, and a conclusion that sums up the information that has been presented. Work with students to develop topic sentences using these frames:

• *The short story "My Life as a Bat" focuses on _____.*
• *Many people think they know that bats _____.*
• *In fact, bats _____.*
• *Overall, the story presents _____ information about bats.*

Once students have created topic sentences, work with them on developing the sentences into paragraphs by including details and factual information.
MODERATE/LIGHT

CRITICAL VOCABULARY

Answers:

1. *According to the narrator in the story, humans hold a **consensus** that bats make their flesh creep more than a bomb does.*

2. *The **interlude** gives the bats a chance to sleep.*

3. *Some of the **subtleties** inside a bat colony include the chirping and rustling in the clusters of bats and the tender care of newborns by mothers.*

4. *Military strategists might use **incendiary** devices because fires can cause mass destruction.*

5. *Bats are **denizens** of caves and other dark places.*

VOCABULARY STRATEGY:
Reference Sources

Answers:

1. *agreement, accord, unanimity; a thesaurus was used because it provides synonyms*

2. *a period of rest; a piece of music that comes between parts of a longer composition; a dictionary lists different word uses*

3. *sŭt'l-tēz; this pronunciation was found in the glossary and also in a dictionary*

4. *Middle English, from Latin* incendiārius, *from incendium, fire, from incendere, to set on fire; a dictionary provides this information about etymology*

5. *noun: den-i-zen; a dictionary provides this information about part of speech and syllable division*

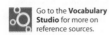 **RESPOND**

WORD BANK
consensus
interlude
subtleties
incendiary
denizen

 Go to the **Vocabulary Studio** for more on reference sources.

CRITICAL VOCABULARY

Practice and Apply Answer the questions to demonstrate your understanding of each Critical Vocabulary word.

1. What **consensus** do humans hold about bats?

2. What do bats usually do in the **interlude** between dawn and dusk?

3. What are some of the **subtleties** of life inside a bat colony?

4. Why might military strategists use **incendiary** weapons?

5. What environments can a bat be considered a **denizen** of?

VOCABULARY STRATEGY:
Reference Sources

If you come across an unfamiliar word while reading, look first for a footnote on the page. If one is not provided, you can use the context—the words and sentences around the unfamiliar word—to help you determine the meaning. If context is not helpful, turn to a reference source, such as a **glossary**, **dictionary**, or **thesaurus**. For advanced or foreign terms, you may need to consult a college-level or bilingual dictionary.

GLOSSARY	DICTIONARY	THESAURUS
Where it is found: at the back of the book in which the word is used	**Where it is found:** library; Internet; print and digital versions	**Where it is found:** library; Internet; print and digital versions
What it includes: pronunciation; definition as it is used in the text	**What it includes:** part of speech; syllable division; pronunciation; definitions; synonyms; etymology	**What it includes:** synonyms; shades of meaning

Practice and Apply Use reference sources to find the specified information about each of the Critical Vocabulary words. Write your answers and explain which reference source you used and why.

1. Write three synonyms for **consensus**.

2. Write two different uses of the word **interlude**.

3. Write the pronunciation for **subtleties**.

4. Write the etymology, or origin, of the word **incendiary**.

5. Write the part of speech and syllable division for **denizen**.

 ENGLISH LEARNER SUPPORT

Critical Vocabulary Provide practice in recognizing and pronouncing English words with silent letters. Note that in Spanish there are just a few instances in which written letters are silent in pronunciation (*the letter* h *in most cases and the letter* u *in certain cases*) but that there are many silent letters in English. Point out the letter *b* in *subtleties* and the *e* at the end of *interlude*. In most cases, the *e* at the end of a word in English will be silent in pronunciation; however, there are not simple rules for the pronunciation of a *b* within a word. Provide examples of each (*device, game, horse; debt, doubt*) and have students practice pronunciations in a small group or with a partner. **SUBSTANTIAL**

© Houghton Mifflin Harcourt Publishing Company

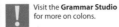

LANGUAGE CONVENTIONS: Colons

A writer's use of punctuation helps clarify meaning for the reader by showing places of emphasis or change of tone. In "My Life as a Bat," Margaret Atwood uses colons not only for meaning but also to create an engaging style.

> Visit the **Grammar Studio** for more on colons.

Colons are used to introduce lists, as in the following passage from the story:

And in the evening, the supersonic hymn of praise to our Creator, the Creator of bats, who appears to us in the form of a bat and who gave us all things: water and the liquid stone of caves, the woody refuge of attics, petals and fruit and juicy insects, and the beauty of slippery wings and sharp white canines and shining eyes.

Colons can also be used to introduce direct quotations, as in this example:

Atwood suggests that humans could learn from animals' lives: "When they kill, they kill without mercy, but without hate. They are immune from the curse of pity. They never gloat."

Colons can be used to provide examples or clarify and expand on the clause or clauses that precede it, such as:

Consider: a great many people believe in them, and if sanity is a general consensus about the content of reality, who are you to disagree?

Additionally, colons can be used to precede a direct address, such as:

Goddess of caves and grottoes: bless your children.

Practice and Apply Look back at the presentation you created about bats. Revise your written presentation to include at least one colon. Then, discuss with a partner how the colon clarifies or enhances the meaning of your ideas.

LANGUAGE CONVENTIONS: Colons

Note that authors can choose from several different types of punctuation to achieve the effect they want. For example, commas, parentheses, and dashes can each be used in a variety of ways to create a particular style or for certain emphasis.

Review each of the four uses for colons and focus on the examples provided. Note that a colon is a more formal type of punctuation and that it can help establish an authoritative or poetic tone. Illustrate this aspect of colon usage with the list in the first example: Substitute the words "who gave us things like" for "who gave us all things:" and discuss how this change would affect the tone. Point out that the colon has the effect of equating "all things" with the particular things listed after the colon; it therefore elevates those things in importance.

Practice and Apply Partners can consider the effectiveness of the colon by switching to a different type of punctuation, such as a dash. Note that differences may be subtle and that punctuation is one of the tools writers use to establish a writing style, to focus attention on one particular idea, or to emphasize a key point or idea. *(Students' answers will vary depending on their use of colons in their written presentations.)*

 ENGLISH LEARNER SUPPORT

Language Conventions Use the following supports with students at varying proficiency levels:

- Display this incorrect sentence and help students add a colon and commas in the right places: A bat is scary looking it has fur wings and a strange nose. *(A bat is scary looking: it has fur, wings, and a strange nose.)* **SUBSTANTIAL**

- Have partners write a sentence in which they use a colon to introduce a quotation from the story. *(Sentences will vary.)* **MODERATE**

- Direct students to write one sentence using a colon to introduce a list and another sentence using a colon to introduce a quotation, using the examples above as models. *(Sentences will vary.)* **LIGHT**

MENTOR TEXT

JOYAS VOLADORAS

Essay by **Brian Doyle**

This essay serves as a **mentor text,** a model for students to use when they come to the Unit 3 Writing Task: Writing an Explanatory Essay.

GENRE ELEMENTS
EXPLANATORY ESSAY

Remind students that the main purpose of informational text is to present facts and information. An explanatory essay is one type of informational text. In an explanatory essay, the author explores and explains a single topic. The essay presents factual information supported with evidence. It may also include the author's own thoughts or experiences to invite the reader to consider an everyday topic in more depth or from a different point of view.

LEARNING OBJECTIVES

- Analyze the author's style, diction, and syntax.
- Analyze how main ideas and details support the central idea of an essay.
- Conduct research using multiple sources, and evaluate the effectiveness of search methods.
- Write a one- or two-paragraph explanatory text.
- Participate in a panel discussion and work toward consensus.
- Analyze context to distinguish the denotative and connotative meanings of words.
- Revise drafts to use parallel constructions.
- **Language** Use *I think* to express opinions in a panel discussion.

TEXT COMPLEXITY

Quantitative Measures	Joyas Voladoras	Lexile: 1170L
Qualitative Measures	**Ideas Presented** Many explicit; also implied meanings and extended metaphors.	
	Structures Used Primarily explicit; some implicit coherence between paragraphs.	
	Language Used Many Tier II and III words; figurative language including metaphors and similes.	
	Knowledge Required Some complex concepts; biology subject matter may not be familiar to all.	

RESOURCES

- Unit 3 Response Log
- 🔊 Selection Audio
- 📖 Reading Studio: Notice & Note
- Level Up Tutorials: Main Idea and Supporting Details; Connotations and Denotations
- ▤ Writing Studio: Synthesizing Research Information
- 💬 Speaking and Listening Studio: Participating in Collaborative Discussions
- Vocabulary Studio: Denotation and Connotation
- ✅ "Joyas Voladoras" Selection Test

SUMMARIES

English

Through a series of facts and lyrical descriptions, the essay conveys the remarkable design and workings of a tiny hummingbird heart and then the heart of the largest creature on Earth, the blue whale. After generalizing that mammals, birds, reptiles, fish, insects, and mollusks all have hearts, the essay concludes by musing over all that may be held in a heart over the course of a lifetime.

Spanish

A través de una serie de hechos y descripciones líricas, el ensayo transmite el sorprendente diseño y funcionamiento del corazoncito del colibrí, y luego explica el corazón de la criatura más grande de la Tierra, la ballena azul. Después de generalizar que los mamíferos, aves, reptiles, peces, insectos y moluscos tienen corazones, el ensayo concluye reflexionando sobre todo lo que puede ser retenido en un corazón a lo largo de una vida.

👥 SMALL-GROUP OPTIONS

Have students work in small groups to read and discuss the selection.

Double-Entry Journal

- Have students draw a line down the center of a sheet of notebook or loose-leaf paper.
- Ask students to title the left column "Quotes from 'Joyas Voladores'" and the right column "My Notes."
- Have students record interesting, confusing, or surprising text passages in the left column.
- Then, beside each passage, have them write their own interpretation, paraphrase, or question in the right column.

Numbered Heads Together

- After students have read and analyzed "Joyas Voladoras," pose this question: What do you think the author's message is in this essay?
- Have students form groups of four and number themselves 1–4 within each group.
- Ask students to discuss their responses to the question within each group.
- Then, call a number from 1 to 4. Have each student with that number respond for the group.

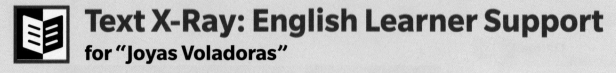

Text X-Ray: English Learner Support
for "Joyas Voladoras"

Use the Text X-Ray and the supports and scaffolds in the Teacher's Edition to help guide students at different proficiency levels through the selection.

INTRODUCE THE SELECTION
DISCUSS THE HEART AND ITS FUNCTION

In this lesson, students will need to be able to discuss the heart and how it works. Display a diagram of the human heart and the upper respiratory system. Point out the heart and its chambers, the arteries, and the lungs. Provide the following explanations:

- The *heart* is a *muscle* that pumps blood.
- A *chamber* is a hollow (empty) space in the heart used to help move blood to and from the lungs.
- When we breathe, our *lungs* fill with *oxygen*. Our lungs send blood with oxygen to our hearts.
- Tubes called *arteries* carry the blood to the rest of our bodies.

Have students use the diagram to identify and/or form simple sentences using each of the terms you introduced.

CULTURAL REFERENCES

The following words or phrases may be unfamiliar to students:

- *first white explorers* (paragraph 1): the first people who came to America from Europe in the late 1400s and 1500s.
- *burn out* (paragraph 3): to use up all of one's energy.
- *waaaaay* (paragraph 4): the author's made-up spelling of *way*; in slang, *way* means very much or a whole lot.
- *second glance* (paragraph 6): a closer look; used here to indicate possible romantic interest.
- *I have something to tell you* (paragraph 6): a sentence that people often use before they tell someone bad news or something sad or difficult to say.

LISTENING

Understand Main Points and Important Details

Have students identify the main topic or idea of a passage.

Preteach the terms *mammals, reptiles, insects, mollusks, worms,* and *bacteria.* Then have students listen as you read aloud paragraph 5. Use the following supports with students at varying proficiency levels:

- Tell students you will ask some questions about what they just heard. Model that they should give a thumbs-up if the answer is *yes* and a thumbs-down for *no.* Then ask: Do bacteria have hearts? *(no)* Do most animals have hearts? *(yes)* **SUBSTANTIAL**
- Ask questions such as the following and have students answer in complete sentences: What is the passage mostly about? *(It is about living things.)* **MODERATE**
- Have pairs of students work together to write a sentence about the main idea of the passage. **LIGHT**

SPEAKING

Use *I Think* to Express Opinions

Review the panel discussion instructions on Student Edition page 167. Explain that when students express an opinion, they often begin a sentence with *I think*.

Use the following supports with students at varying proficiency levels:

- Introduce these sentence frames: *I think _____. I don't think _____.* Then provide some simple statements about the heart. Pantomime or provide illustrations to support meaning. Have students complete the frame to express an opinion about the heart. **SUBSTANTIAL**
- Provide longer frames to help students share their ideas: *I think the ideal heart would have _____. I think the ideal heart would be _____.* **MODERATE**
- Explain that an opinion can begin with *I think* or *I think that*; both are correct. Have partners take turns using each form to introduce their opinions about the features of the ideal heart. **LIGHT**

READING

Read for Main Idea and Details

Draw students' attention to paragraph 4. Remind them that a main idea is supported by details and other examples from the text.

Work with students to reread paragraph 4. Use the following supports with students at varying proficiency levels:

- Read aloud each sentence and pause after reading it to restate it in simplified language. Then, have students find, circle, and read aloud familiar words. **SUBSTANTIAL**
- Echo read the paragraph with students, pausing to paraphrase and explain as necessary. Then have pairs of students take turns rereading the paragraph and paraphrasing the main idea and important details. **MODERATE**
- Have pairs of students read the paragraph together and discuss its main idea and key details. Monitor their progress and help explain challenging language as needed. Then have partners work together to write a short summary. **LIGHT**

WRITING

Use Adjectives and Adverbs to Evaluate Research

Read the writing assignment on Student Edition page 167. Explain that when you *evaluate* something, you explain what worked well and what did not.

Use the following supports with students at varying proficiency levels:

- Provide this question: What does a heart do? Model looking up the heart in a learner's dictionary or an encyclopedia. Read aloud the information and paraphrase it. Have students complete this sentence frame: *The heart pumps _____.* Next, introduce the word *useful*. Model writing a simple evaluation using the word *useful* (e.g., *The dictionary was useful*). **SUBSTANTIAL**
- Display sample adjectives and adverbs students may use to evaluate their research: *helpful/ unhelpful, useful, clear, confusing, [worked] well.* Provide these sentence frames to help students use adjectives and adverbs to write evaluations of their research process: *_____ was/was not useful. _____ worked/didn't work well.* **MODERATE**
- Have students write their explanations independently. Explain how they can use adjectives and adverbs to evaluate their research process as they write. Circulate to provide support. **LIGHT**

JOYAS VOLADORAS

Essay by **Brian Doyle**

? Connect to the
ESSENTIAL QUESTION

In his essay, author Brian Doyle presents amazing facts about the tiny hummingbird and the enormous blue whale. He points out that, no matter the size, virtually all of the world's creatures have hearts. In this way, Doyle invites readers to consider how all living things are connected—and indirectly invites us to ponder what effect we may have on nature, and what effect nature may have on us.

MENTOR TEXT

At the end of the unit, students will be asked to write an explanatory essay. "Joyas Voladoras" models the elements of this genre, providing students with an example of how a writer presents a central idea about a single topic, includes facts and details, and incorporates his or her own point of view.

? ESSENTIAL QUESTION:

What effect do we have on nature, and how does nature affect us?

LEARNING MINDSET

Effort   Remind students that effort is necessary for growth and that hard work leads to success. Tell students that this essay presents a lot of descriptive words and figurative language. Let students know they may find it challenging at first to understand all of the vocabulary and poetic language Doyle uses, but the effort they make will pay off. Point out to students that they will have multiple opportunities to read and discuss the essay. Working at becoming more familiar with the language and vocabulary in the essay will help them to better understand the main message.

QUICK START

Think about the human heart. Make a list of words that come to mind when you think about the heart. Share your list with a partner and discuss the kinds of words you chose, such as anatomical words or emotional words, and what the idea of the heart means to you.

ANALYZE STYLE

Writers craft their work with a particular **style.** Two key elements of style are diction and syntax. **Diction** includes the author's word choices and register (language that sounds academic or casual, for example). **Syntax** involves the types of sentences and grammatical structures that a writer employs. Prose may be written in a straightforward and direct style, or a more lyrical style that evokes an emotional reaction in readers.

In this essay, Doyle intertwines scientific facts with figurative language and vivid descriptions to take readers on a philosophical journey that explores what the heart means to different animals. He varies his syntax from simple, factual sentences to long, winding sentences that build meaning and emotional impact. As you read, look closely at Doyle's style choices and note their effect.

GENRE ELEMENTS: EXPLANATORY ESSAY

- explores and explains a single topic
- may include the writer's own thoughts or experiences
- provides factual information supported with evidence
- invites the reader to consider an everyday topic in more depth

ANALYZE STRUCTURE

Writers of informational essays choose logical structures to clearly convey key ideas. One or more **main ideas** are supported with **details** that explain or provide examples. Different sections of a text may have main ideas that relate to the central idea of the whole text. The **central idea,** or what the writer wants you to learn about the topic, may be directly stated or implied.

You can track main ideas and details as you read using a graphic organizer.

TOPIC:		
MAIN IDEA:	MAIN IDEA:	MAIN IDEA:
KEY DETAILS:	KEY DETAILS:	KEY DETAILS:
CENTRAL MESSAGE:		

Consider the way that the information is organized in the essay and how that organization helps the reader identify the central message.

Joyas Voladoras 159

QUICK START

Explain that *anatomical* means "having to do with the structure and function of the body." Then have students complete the activity.

ANALYZE STYLE

Review the information about style on page 159. To illustrate how style affects meaning, display a simple sentence, such as *I walked down the street.* Ask students whether it's a straightforward or lyrical (poetic) style. *(straightforward)* Discuss elements of diction—word choice and register. Have students suggest a more formal and a less formal way to say the same thing. *(I strolled along the main avenue. / I jetted down the street.)* Then have students suggest words that would make the walking seem happier and sadder. *(skipped, plodded)* Have pairs of students work together to revise the syntax by adding a phrase or clauses that tell when, how, or where the action took place.

ANALYZE STRUCTURE

Discuss with students the difference between a central idea that is stated and one that is implied. You might illustrate the difference with a simple example, such as this one: "Imagine a friend tells you she just saw a movie. She talks about how suspenseful it was and how great the actors were and how the ending completely surprised her. How did your friend probably feel about the movie?" *(She probably loved it.)* Is this central idea stated or implied? *(Implied.)* How did you know how your friend felt? *(Possible response: It was clear from the details she provided.)* If your friend wrote a movie review, what would her stated central idea be? *(Possible response: This is a really suspenseful movie worth seeing.)* Guide students through the table at the bottom of page 159, pointing out how students can use it to outline the organization of the essay as they read it.

© Houghton Mifflin Harcourt Publishing Company

(EL) ENGLISH LEARNER SUPPORT

Develop Vocabulary Read aloud the instruction on how to "analyze" style. Explain these words and phrases in the second paragraph: *intertwines* means mixes; *figurative language* includes words used in special ways to create pictures in readers' minds; *take readers on a philosophical journey* (itself an example of figurative language) means that the author writes about things that make readers think deeply about life; if something has an *emotional impact,* it has a strong effect on how people feel. Have students record these words and phrases in their books or notebook, along with explanations and their own example sentences or illustrations.

ALL LEVELS

TEACH

CRITICAL VOCABULARY

Encourage students to read both answer choices before selecting one.

Answers:

1. *b*

2. *b*

3. *a*

LANGUAGE CONVENTIONS

Review the information about parallel structure. Read aloud the example sentences. Ask students to identify the subject and verb in each sentence and explain what makes the three sentences parallel in structure. *(The subjects are the same. Each begins with the noun phrase "A hummingbird's heart.")*

✎ ANNOTATION MODEL

Read the excerpt aloud and point out to students that the first four sentences combined are shorter than the fifth sentence of the paragraph. Discuss the style (particularly word choice and syntax) of the paragraph. Ask questions such as these: What are some facts the author included? What are some colorful words and phrases the author used? What images do those words create? Why might the author have chosen to include all those details in a single sentence? Remind students that as they read the rest of the essay, they should make notes on style, as well as on the main ideas and details they encounter in the essay.

■ English Learner Support

Develop Vocabulary Display the words *elephantine* and *infinitesimal* in the annotated paragraph. Point out the word parts *elephant* and *infinite* and their meanings. Say each word aloud, modeling the syllable stress in your pronunciation. Explain each word. Have students say the words and then use them in this frame: *The _____ blue whale eats tons of _____ shellfish called "krill."* **ALL LEVELS**

 GET READY

CRITICAL VOCABULARY

taut	harrowed	felled

Choose the synonym for each word to see how many of the Critical Vocabulary words you already know.

1. **taut**   **a.** uncomfortable   **b.** stretched

2. **harrowed**   **a.** remembered   **b.** pained

3. **felled**   **a.** struck down   **b.** traveled with

LANGUAGE CONVENTIONS

Parallelism An author's sentence structure can affect a text's force and clarity. **Parallelism** is the use of similar grammatical constructions to express related ideas or ideas of equal importance. Writers create parallel sentences, clauses, or phrases using the same parts of speech in the same order, as in this example from the essay you will read:

A hummingbird's heart beats ten times a second. A hummingbird's heart is the size of a pencil eraser. A hummingbird's heart is a lot of the hummingbird.

This use of parallelism repeats the subject "A hummingbird's heart" followed by a verb phrase to link three facts about the subject. As you read, notice how Doyle uses parallelism to create meaning.

ANNOTATION MODEL   **NOTICE & NOTE**

As you read, note the author's style along with the essay's structure. Mark word choices that stand out to you, especially those that carry strong emotional connotations. Mark also where the structure shifts from one main idea to another. In the model, you can see one reader's notes about "Joyas Voladoras":

Consider the hummingbird for a long moment. A hummingbird's heart beats ten times a second. A hummingbird's heart is the size of a pencil eraser. A hummingbird's heart is a lot of the hummingbird. [*Joyas voladoras*, flying jewels, the first white explorers in the Americas called them, and the white men had never seen such creatures, for hummingbirds came into the world only in the Americas, nowhere else in the universe, more than three hundred species of them whirring and zooming and nectaring in hummer time zones nine times removed from ours, their hearts hammering faster than we could clearly hear if we pressed our elephantine ears to their infinitesimal chests.]

> *Short sentences with facts*
>
> *Long, winding sentence with musical language and expressive words that show movement or imitate natural sounds*

© Houghton Mifflin Harcourt Publishing Company

 ENGLISH LEARNER SUPPORT

Use Prior Knowledge Tell students that when they see an unfamiliar word, they should look for parts of the word they recognize. Point to the image of the hummingbird on page 158. Say the word *hummingbird* and have students repeat it. Point out the two word parts: *humming* and *bird* (a word they may already know). Model humming and explain that a hummingbird gets its name because of the humming sound its wings make. Have students repeat the word *hummingbird* and use it in a sentence. **SUBSTANTIAL/MODERATE**

BACKGROUND

*We are often fascinated by extremes in nature: minute, complex organisms that function at a high level of efficiency, as well as enormous animals that make us feel insignificant by comparison. In this essay, **Brian Doyle** (1956–2017) explores the heart from both of these angles, as well as from an emotional one. Doyle wrote several books of essays, including* The Wet Engine, *a meditation on the heart.*

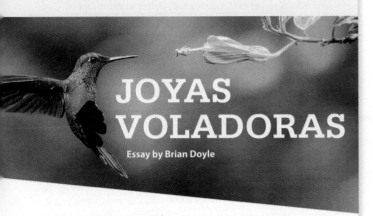

JOYAS VOLADORAS

Essay by Brian Doyle

SETTING A PURPOSE

As you read, pay attention to the author's style and what the arrangement of the ideas in the text makes you think and feel.

1   Consider the hummingbird for a long moment. A hummingbird's heart beats ten times a second. A hummingbird's heart is the size of a pencil eraser. A hummingbird's heart is a lot of the hummingbird. *Joyas voladoras,* flying jewels, the first white explorers in the Americas called them, and the white men had never seen such creatures, for hummingbirds came into the world only in the Americas, nowhere else in the universe, more than three hundred species of them whirring and zooming and nectaring in hummer time zones nine times removed from ours, their hearts hammering faster than we could clearly hear if we pressed our elephantine ears to their infinitesimal chests.

2   Each one visits a thousand flowers a day. They can dive at sixty miles an hour. They can fly backward. They can fly more

---

[1] **infinitesimal:** so small it cannot be measured.

Notice & Note

You can use the side margins to notice and note signposts in the text.

CONTRASTS AND CONTRADICTIONS

Notice & Note: What words are synonyms for *big* and *small*? Mark the synonyms in the last sentence of paragraph 1.

Analyze: What contrast is presented here? What idea does the contrast help to define?

Joyas Voladoras   161

BACKGROUND

Have students read the background about Brian Doyle. Ask students which minute and which enormous hearts they expect Doyle to write about. *(the hummingbird and the blue whale)* Ask a Spanish speaker to translate the title "Joyas Voladoras." *(flying jewels)* Ask students why hummingbirds might be called that. *(because they are brightly colored, like jewels)*

SETTING A PURPOSE

Direct students to use the Setting a Purpose prompt to focus their reading.

▶ CONTRASTS AND CONTRADICTIONS

Remind students that when an author contrasts two things in writing, readers should ask themselves why that difference is important. Have students identify the two things the author contrasts in paragraph 1 and use them to **draw conclusions** about why the author makes this contrast. (***Answer:*** *The words* elephantine *and* infinitesimal *help to emphasize the contrast between a human ear and a hummingbird's heart, which underscores the smallness and fragility of the hummingbird's heart and the size and danger of the world around it.*)

TO CHALLENGE STUDENTS . . .

Create a Multimodal Presentation   Have students work with a partner to reread the selection and choose several instances of surprising facts and startling imagery. Challenge students to research photographs, music, or video—or to create their own artwork—that enhances and supports the facts and imagery they have chosen. Have students discuss how to use media to complement the author's style. Then have student pairs work together to create a multimodal presentation that incorporates text from the selection and visual or aural media. Invite student pairs to share their presentations with the class.

ANALYZE STYLE

Remind students that **syntax,** or sentence structure, is one of the elements that characterizes an author's style of writing. After students identify the beginning and end of the last sentence of paragraph 2, ask them to evaluate the effect of the sentence and how it might reflect the author's message. (**Answer:** *This very long sentence expresses the great variety of hummingbird species and how amazing each one is. This style emphasizes the author's sense of awe at these tiny birds.*)

ANALYZE STRUCTURE

Briefly review with students how most informational texts are organized by **main ideas** and **supporting details,** that those main ideas relate to the central idea of the whole text, and that the central idea may be stated directly or implied.

Then, have students mark the main idea of paragraph 4. Point out that in this paragraph, the first sentence states a factual main idea that serves to introduce and unify all the details in the paragraph, but that in this paragraph, there are important details that tie to the central message of the entire essay. Have students consider this central message as they answer the two questions. (**Answer:** *The first sentence of the paragraph establishes a contrast with the tiny heart of a hummingbird. It also adds to the central message—both the whale and the hummingbird have hearts. It makes clear that the essay explores different kinds of hearts and that the heart is amazing regardless of size. Details in the paragraph also suggest that the central message has to do with not only the physical heart, but also the emotional heart of each animal.*)

CRITICAL VOCABULARY

taut: Doyle uses the word *taut* to describe the arteries of a hummingbird.

ASK STUDENTS to explain why Doyle describes hummingbird arteries as taut. (*He is describing the differences between hummingbird hearts and arteries and those of humans; he wants to show how hard hummingbird hearts are working, so he describes the arteries—which carry blood to the rest of the body—as being pulled really tight.*)

 NOTICE & NOTE

ANALYZE STYLE
Annotate: Mark the beginning and end of the last sentence of paragraph 2.

Evaluate: What is the effect of naming so many species and restating ideas in this lengthy sentence? How does this style add impact to the author's ideas?

taut
(tôt) *adj.* pulled tight; tense.

ANALYZE STRUCTURE
Annotate: Mark a key idea in paragraph 4.

Analyze: How does this idea relate to the ideas in paragraphs 1–3? What does this relationship reveal about the central message of the essay?

than five hundred miles without pausing to rest. But when they rest they come close to death: on frigid nights, or when they are starving, they retreat into torpor, their metabolic rate slowing to a fifteenth of their normal sleep rate, their hearts sludging nearly to a halt, barely beating, and if they are not soon warmed, if they do not soon find that which is sweet, their hearts grow cold, and they cease to be. Consider for a moment those hummingbirds who did not open their eyes again today, this very day, in the Americas: bearded helmetcrests and booted racket-tails, violet-tailed sylphs and violet-capped woodnymphs, crimson topazes and purple-crowned fairies, red-tailed comets and amethyst woodstars, rainbow-bearded thornbills and glittering-bellied emeralds, velvet-purple coronets and golden-bellied star-frontlets, fiery-tailed awlbills and Andean hillstars, spatuletails and pufflegs, each the most amazing thing you have never seen, each thunderous wild heart the size of an infant's fingernail, each mad heart silent, a brilliant music stilled.

3   Hummingbirds, like all flying birds but more so, have incredible enormous immense ferocious metabolisms.[2] To drive those metabolisms they have race car hearts that eat oxygen at an eye-popping rate. Their hearts are built of thinner, leaner fibers than ours. Their arteries are stiffer and more **taut.** They have more mitochondria in their heart muscles—anything to gulp more oxygen. Their hearts are stripped to the skin for the war against gravity and inertia, the mad search for food, the insane idea of flight. The price of their ambition is a life closer to death; they suffer more heart attacks and aneurysms[3] and ruptures than any other living creature. It's expensive to fly. You burn out. You fry the machine. You melt the engine. Every creature on earth has approximately two billion heartbeats to spend in a lifetime. You can spend them slowly, like a tortoise, and live to be two hundred years old, or you can spend them fast, like a hummingbird, and live to be two years old.

4   The biggest heart in the world is inside the blue whale. It weighs more than seven tons. It's as big as a room. It is a room, with four chambers. A child could walk around in it, head high, bending only to step through the valves. The valves are as big as the swinging doors in a saloon. This house of a heart drives a creature a hundred feet long. When this creature is born it is twenty feet long and weighs four tons. It is waaaaay bigger than your car. It drinks a hundred gallons of milk from its mama every day and gains two hundred pounds a day, and when it is seven or eight years old it endures an unimaginable puberty and then it essentially disappears from human ken,[4] for next to nothing is known of the mating habits, travel patterns, diet, social

---

[2] **metabolism:** the process of turning food into energy.
[3] **aneurysm:** a blood-filled sac in a blood vessel caused by disease or trauma.
[4] **ken:** understanding.

IMPROVE READING FLUENCY

Targeted Passage Use echo reading to help students use appropriate pacing, phrasing, and expression in reading in paragraph 3. Begin by reading the passage aloud, modeling how to use punctuation and sentence length as guides to phrasing. Also model how to read multi-syllabic words, as in the phrase "incredible enormous immense ferocious metabolisms," with appropriate pacing and word stress. Then have students echo your reading as you read it a second and third time. You may choose to conclude with paired oral reading to give students more practice reading the passage aloud.

 Go to the **Reading Studio** for additional support in developing fluency.

© Houghton Mifflin Harcourt Publishing Company • Image Credits: ©Franco Banfi/Getty Images

NOTICE & NOTE

Joyas Voladoras   163

ENGLISH LEARNER SUPPORT

Use Support to Read Work with a small group. Have students create a chart titled "Blue Whale Facts." Then have them create four columns labeled "Heart," "Size & Growth," "Life," and "Talk." Check that students understand each of these terms. Assign pairs to one of the four topics. Have each pair read paragraph 4 and find words and phrases that relate to their assigned topic and list them under the appropriate columns.

Blue Whale Facts			
Heart	Size & Growth	Life	Talk
weighs more than seven tons	a hundred feet long	mating habits unknown	penetrating moaning cries

Once partners have completed the task, have each pair share their list of words and phrases with the whole group. Explain important terms that students can't figure out on their own and that will be helpful for them to learn. You might also point out the multiple-meaning words *chamber* and *tongue*.

MODERATE/LIGHT

WHEN STUDENTS STRUGGLE . . .

Determine Meaning Some students may struggle interpreting the implied meanings in the essay. Have them reread each paragraph and record facts they learn in a chart like the one below.

Paragraph	Facts	Feelings

Then, ask them to reread the paragraph a second time and record how details in the paragraph make them feel about the subject. Have students continue with the other paragraphs in the essay. Finally, guide students to state a central message about the essay.

 For additional support, go to the **Reading Studio** and assign the following **Level Up Tutorial: Main Idea and Supporting Details.**

LANGUAGE CONVENTIONS

Remind students that **parallel structure** is a technique in which authors repeat a pattern of words or phrases within the same sentence or across sentences in a paragraph, often to emphasize important ideas. (**Answer:** *This repetition makes clear the wide variety of hearts in the natural world.*)

 For **listening and reading support** for students at varying proficiency levels, see the **Text X-Ray** on pages 158C–158D.

EL ENGLISH LEARNER SUPPORT

Develop Vocabulary to Build Understanding

Provide visual support and explanations to help students understand key words and phrases.

- For paragraph 5, provide visual support for the terms *mammals, reptiles, turtles, insects, mollusks,* and *unicellular bacteria*.
  SUBSTANTIAL/MODERATE
- Read aloud paragraph 6. Pause to explain key words and phrases. Make a list of words that relate to injury or damage. (*bruised and scarred, scored and torn, repaired, patched, fragile and rickety*) Then create a list on the board titled "Things that make our hearts open to pain." Guide students to paraphrase and list things from the paragraph that make our hearts open to pain. (*falling in love, having a child, a car accident, bad news, seeing an injured animal, aging parents*).
  MODERATE/LIGHT

CRITICAL VOCABULARY

harrowed: Doyle speculates that fear of getting hurt prevents people from revealing what's in their hearts.

ASK STUDENTS to name some things that might make a heart feel harrowed. (*fear of losing a loved one; fear of rejection*)

felled: Doyle suggests that, no matter how hard people try to protect themselves, the heart remains vulnerable.

ASK STUDENTS what Doyle means when he says a heart can be "felled by a woman's second glance." (*the emotions created by romantic interest*)

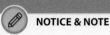

NOTICE & NOTE

life, language, social structure, diseases, spirituality, wars, stories, despairs, and arts of the blue whale. There are perhaps ten thousand blue whales in the world, living in every ocean on earth, and of the largest mammal who ever lived we know nearly nothing. But we know this: the animals with the largest hearts in the world generally travel in pairs, and their penetrating moaning cries, their piercing yearning tongue, can be heard underwater for miles and miles.

5   Mammals and birds have hearts with four chambers. Reptiles and turtles have hearts with three chambers. Fish have hearts with two chambers. Insects and mollusks have hearts with one chamber. Worms have hearts with one chamber, although they may have as many as eleven single-chambered hearts. Unicellular bacteria have no hearts at all; but even they have fluid eternally in motion, washing from one side of the cell to the other, swirling and whirling. No living being is without interior liquid motion. We all churn inside.

6   So much held in a heart in a lifetime. So much held in a heart in a day, an hour, a moment. We are utterly open with no one, in the end—not mother and father, not wife or husband, not lover, not child, not friend. We open windows to each but we live alone in the house of the heart. Perhaps we must. Perhaps we could not bear to be so naked for fear of a constantly **harrowed** heart. When young we think there will come one person who will savor and sustain us always; when we are older we know this is the dream of a child, that all hearts finally are bruised and scarred, scored and torn, repaired by time and will, patched by force of character, yet fragile and rickety forevermore, no matter how ferocious the defense and how many bricks you bring to the wall. You can brick up your heart as stout and tight and hard and cold and impregnable[5] as you possibly can and down it comes in an instant, **felled** by a woman's second glance, a child's apple breath, the shatter of glass in the road, the words "I have something to tell you", a cat with a broken spine dragging itself into the forest to die, the brush of your mother's papery ancient hand in the thicket of your hair, the memory of your father's voice early in the morning echoing from the kitchen where he is making pancakes for his children.

LANGUAGE CONVENTIONS

Annotate: Mark examples of parallelism in paragraph 5.

Analyze: How does the use of parallel structure link the ideas in this paragraph?

harrowed
(hăr´ōd) *adj.* greatly distressed.

felled
(fĕld) *v.* knocked down.

---

[5] **impregnable:** impossible to get through or past.

APPLYING ACADEMIC VOCABULARY

☐ **advocate**   ☐ **discrete**   ☐ **domain**   ☑ **enhance**   ☑ **evoke**

Write and Discuss Have students turn to a partner to discuss the following questions. Guide students to include the academic vocabulary words *enhance* and *evoke* in their responses. Ask volunteers to share their responses with the class.

- How does parallel structure **enhance** readers' understanding of the essay?
- What emotions does the author **evoke** in paragraph 6 through vivid descriptions?

CHECK YOUR UNDERSTANDING

Have students answer the questions independently.

Answers:

1. *A*

2. *H*

3. *B*

If they answer any questions incorrectly, have them reread the text to confirm their understanding. Then they may proceed to ANALYZE THE TEXT on page 166.

CHECK YOUR UNDERSTANDING

Answer these questions before moving on to the **Analyze the Text** section on the following page.

1 Which sentence best describes the way ideas are presented in the essay?

  A Factual information is followed by intensely personal reflections.

  B The way that the brain controls the heart's function is explained.

  C Claims about mammal and bird hearts are presented and refuted.

  D Vivid pictures of life in the wild support the author's opinion.

2 What ideas about the heart provide the overall structure of this essay?

  F How hummingbird hearts function and why they burn out so fast

  G How little is known about either blue whales or hummingbirds

  H Relative sizes of hearts and emotions attributed to the heart

  J Why the heart matters to animals and humans

3 Why did the author most likely begin the essay by discussing hummingbirds?

  A Hummingbirds are more interesting than other animals.

  B Hummingbirds represent how fragile life can be.

  C Hummingbirds represent the adaptability of nature.

  D Hummingbirds are unique to the Americas.

ENGLISH LEARNER SUPPORT

Oral Assessment Use the following questions to assess students' comprehension and speaking skills. Ask students to respond in short, complete sentences.

1. How are ideas presented in the essay? (*Facts are followed by the author's own ideas.*)

2. Which of the following ideas about the heart provide the main structure of the essay? How hummingbird hearts work and why they burn out

fast. (*no*) How we know very little about blue whales and hummingbirds. (*no*) The sizes of different hearts and the feelings that we relate to the heart. (*yes*) Why the heart is important to animals and humans. (*no*)

3. Why did the essay begin with hummingbirds? (*They show how fragile life is.*) **MODERATE/LIGHT**

ANALYZE THE TEXT

Possible answers:

1. **DOK 4:** *The author's central message is that the heart is amazing, both in its physical function and in its metaphorical ability to love. He develops this message through examples across the range of nature and evocative images that readers can relate to; for example, in paragraph 4, the author describes the heart of the blue whale.*

2. **DOK 2:** *The author means that no matter how close we are to others, no one else can ever truly understand the inner workings of our heart—our capacity for love, our weaknesses, or who or what holds our deepest affections.*

3. **DOK 3:** *The heart is discussed figuratively in the final paragraph of the essay. This figurative discussion recasts the meaning of earlier facts about hummingbird and blue whale hearts as a more figurative reflection on life, love, and losses.*

4. **DOK 4:** *The compounded adjectives allow the author to capture all of the denotations and connotations of the different synonyms, piling them onto the noun to show the myriad of emotions the author felt when considering the wonder of the heart and its capabilities. This style helps create a sense of awe, implying that a single word is insufficient to describe something so impressive.*

5. **DOK 4:** *The repeated reference to time serves to remind the reader that life is fleeting.*

RESEARCH

Tell students that they can choose a question about how the heart functions or a question about feelings associated with the heart. If students choose a question concerning feelings, check that they understand how to pose a clear question that can be researched online or in a printed reference work. If students need some ideas about authoritative sources for "matters of the heart," suggest that they visit psychology sites or popular science sites. *(Students' journal entries will vary but should include thorough notes and thoughtful reflections.)*

 RESPOND

ANALYZE THE TEXT

Support your responses with evidence from the text. 📓 NOTEBOOK

1. **Analyze** What is the central message of the essay? What main ideas and details lead to the central message? Cite text evidence.

2. **Interpret** What does the writer mean by the phrase "we live alone in the house of the heart" in the last paragraph?

3. **Compare** How does the writer's use of the word *heart* shift in the last paragraph of the essay? How does this affect the meaning of the earlier parts of the essay?

4. **Evaluate** In paragraph 3, the author uses the phrase "incredible enormous immense ferocious metabolisms." What effect do the compounded adjectives have on his tone?

5. **Notice & Note** The writer mentions time throughout the essay. What is significant about this repetition?

RESEARCH TIP
Take notes on the information you find in your sources. Record the author and book or article title of the source along with the notes that you take so you will be able to find the information again.

RESEARCH

Think about the topic of the heart. What do you wonder about it? Pose a question and decide how you will go about answering it. Try multiple search methods and examine multiple sources as you research answers to your question. Notice how effective each source was in answering the question. Complete the following journal entries. Record the information you found and evaluate the effectiveness of each search method.

My Question: _____

Source 1: _____

Notes: _____

_____

How effective was this method? Do I need to change my approach? _____

Source 2: _____

Notes: _____

_____

How effective was this method? Do I need to change my approach? _____

_____

My Answer: _____

🛠 LEARNING MINDSET

Try Again Explain to students that it's okay to make mistakes—in fact, mistakes can teach us a lot. Tell students about a mistake you made while researching something and what you learned from it. Ask students, in small groups, to share some mistakes they made while researching and what they learned from those mistakes. Before students share, point out that you'd like everybody to feel free to speak and that when one person in a group is speaking, everyone else should listen quietly and respectfully.

CREATE AND PRESENT

Write an Explanation Write a one- to two-paragraph explanation in which you present the question that you posed about the heart, describe your research findings, and discuss the answer that you developed.

- ❏ Introduce the topic and the question that guided your research.

- ❏ Evaluate your research process and the sources that you used. Highlight the important information you learned from each of the sources.

- ❏ State the answer to the question you asked. Discuss how this knowledge adds to your understanding of the heart.

Participate in a Panel Discussion Use your research, along with the information in "Joyas Voladoras," to consider how the ideal heart would function.

- ❏ Gather your notes and write an opening statement that includes one way that the ideal heart would function.

- ❏ Follow rules for discussion by listening attentively while others talk, building on others' ideas, and considering everyone's ideas. Support your own ideas in the discussion with information from your research.

- ❏ Work toward a consensus on a list of features or functions of the ideal heart. Display a list of those features or functions as they are agreed upon.

 Go to the **Writing Studio** for more on synthesizing research information.

 Go to the **Speaking and Listening Studio** for help with participating in a discussion.

RESPOND TO THE ESSENTIAL QUESTION

 What effect do we have on nature, and how does nature affect us?

Gather Information Review your annotations and notes on "Joyas Voladoras." Then, add relevant information to your Response Log. As you determine which information to include, think about:

- the central message of the essay
- the author's style, including his diction and syntax
- the purpose each paragraph plays in the structure of the essay

At the end of the unit, use your notes to help you write an explanatory essay.

ACADEMIC VOCABULARY
As you write and discuss what you learned from the explanatory essay, be sure to use the Academic Vocabulary words. Check off each of the words that you use.

- ❏ **advocate**
- ❏ **discrete**
- ❏ **domain**
- ❏ **evoke**
- ❏ **enhance**

UNIT 3
RESPONSE LOG

CREATE AND PRESENT

Write an Explanation Discuss the task with students. Point out that the bullet points on page 167 can serve as a rough outline for students' writing.

For **writing support** for students at varying proficiency levels, see the **Text X-Ray** on page 158D.

Participate in a Panel Discussion Inform students that a panel discussion is a focused discussion in which experts share research and their own points of view on a topic. Have students form groups and choose a moderator and a notetaker. Tell students that you would like each of them to take turns presenting their own ideas about how the ideal heart would function, and to support those ideas with their research. The notetaker will record their ideas. The moderator will help all students equally share the time. Once all students have presented, the moderator will help the entire group come to a consensus.

For **speaking support** for students at varying proficiency levels, see the **Text X-Ray** on page 158D.

RESPOND TO THE ESSENTIAL QUESTION

Allow time for students to add details from "Joyas Voladoras" to their Unit 3 Response Logs.

 ## ENGLISH LEARNER SUPPORT

Participate in a Panel Discussion Display these frames and use them to model how to agree and politely disagree with group members in a collaborative discussion.

I liked _____'s idea that _____.

I agree with _____ that _____.

You have a good point, but I think _____.

We could also _____.

Then guide students to use the frames to agree with, disagree with, or build on comments made by group members. **ALL LEVELS**

CRITICAL VOCABULARY

Answers:

1. *A line that is either too taut or not taut enough may be difficult to walk on.*

2. *Narrowly avoiding a car accident would leave me feeling harrowed.*

3. *A person can feel knocked down by strong emotions, just as a tree can be felled by a lumberjack.*

VOCABULARY STRATEGY:
Denotation and Connotation

Possible answers:

1. *Connotation: painful. Synonyms: cold, bitter. The first synonym isn't extreme enough, while the second is too extreme for the sentence's meaning.*

2. *Connotation: wild. Synonyms: insane, absurd. The synonyms don't work because searching for food is neither a sign of mental illness nor silly.*

3. *Connotation: incessant and powerful. Synonyms: stir, move. The connotations of the synonyms are too weak for this idea.*

■ ENGLISH LEARNER SUPPORT

Use Vocabulary Strategies Work with a small group of students. Read aloud each of the three Critical Vocabulary words. Then, provide example sentences that explain the denotation and connotation of each word. For example: *A rope is taut when it is pulled very tight. If the arteries of a hummingbird are stretched taut, they are so tight they may break. So the word taut suggests a feeling of fear or danger.* Explain that the denotation, or dictionary definition, of *taut* is "pulled very tight," while one connotation of taut is "something that is so tight it is in danger of breaking." Have pairs look up definitions for each of the Practice and Apply words. Model how to pronounce each word. Ask students to read their definitions and share what feelings the words suggest based on those definitions. **ALL LEVELS**

 RESPOND

WORD BANK
taut
harrowed
felled

 Go to the **Vocabulary Studio** for more on denotation and connotation.

CRITICAL VOCABULARY

Practice and Apply Use the Critical Vocabulary words to answer each question. Discuss your responses with a partner.

1. In what ways might a tightrope walker be affected by how **taut** the line is?

2. What is an experience that might leave you feeling **harrowed**?

3. How can **felled** refer both to cutting down trees and to feeling strong emotions?

VOCABULARY STRATEGY:
Denotation and Connotation

The **denotation** of a word is the meaning found in a dictionary. The **connotation** of a word refers to the feelings or ideas associated with it. In writing "Joyas Voladoras," Brian Doyle chose words for both their denotations and their connotations. In this sentence, he describes the heart as *harrowed*: "Perhaps we could not bear to be so naked for fear of a constantly harrowed heart." The denotation of *harrowed* is "greatly distressed." But by choosing *harrowed*, Doyle suggests that the heart is not just distressed, but tormented to a great degree. This chart shows the connotations and denotations of the remaining Critical Vocabulary words:

WORD	DENOTATION	CONNOTATION
taut	tense	stretched to breaking point
felled	knocked down	overpowered

Practice and Apply Work with a partner to brainstorm at least two synonyms for these words from the essay. Note the connotation of each original word, and discuss how the connotation of each synonym changes the meaning of the original sentence.

1. frigid (paragraph 2)

_____

2. mad (paragraph 3)

_____

3. churn (paragraph 5)

_____

WHEN STUDENTS STRUGGLE . . .

Understand Denotation and Connotation Review the information on Student Edition page 168. Explain that context, or the way in which a word is used, may add a certain connotation, or feeling, to a word. Provide these examples: *It was a chilly day. She gave me a chilly smile.* Discuss how the connotation of the word *chilly* is negative in the second sentence. Then guide students to complete the Practice and Apply. Have students begin by copying the original sentence and circling each practice word (*frigid, mad,* and *churn*). Then have students write two synonyms for each word and read each new sentence aloud. Ask students to explain how the connotation of each synonym changes the meaning of the original sentence.

For additional support, go to the **Reading Studio** and assign the following Level Up Tutorial: Connotations and Denotations.

LANGUAGE CONVENTIONS:
Parallelism

A writer's use of parallelism helps reinforce meaning for readers by emphasizing connections among ideas. It is also used to enhance style by creating a rhythm. In "Joyas Voladoras," Brian Doyle uses parallelism in both ways.

Parallelism can be created using words:

> . . . whirring and zooming and nectaring . . .

Parallelism can be created using phrases:

> . . . their penetrating moaning cries, their piercing yearning tongue . . .

Parallelism can be used across sentences:

> Mammals and birds have hearts with four chambers. Reptiles and turtles have hearts with three chambers. Fish have hearts with two chambers. Insects and mollusks have hearts with one chamber. . . .

Often, a main idea or other piece of important information interrupts a series of parallel phrases or sentences. The stark shift between the regular pattern and the new construction helps to highlight that information or imagery as important.

> . . . each the most amazing thing you have never seen, each thunderous wild heart the size of an infant's fingernail, each mad heart silent, a brilliant music stilled.

Practice and Apply Look back at the explanation you wrote about your research. Revise your written presentation to include at least one instance of parallelism. Then, read the section containing the parallelism aloud to a partner and discuss which ideas your parallelism has linked.

LANGUAGE CONVENTIONS:
Parallelism

Review the information about parallel structure. Direct students to the first example, from paragraph 1. Ask students if they recognize the grammar structure that was repeated. Point out that in this example, the repeated structure is a present participle (a verb form ending in -*ing*) that may be used as an adjective to describe something, in this case "three hundred species" of hummingbirds. Explain that repeating an action, either as a participle or as a verb, can evoke a sense of movement and propel a sentence forward.

Direct students to the second example, from paragraph 4. Discuss the structure that's repeated (a noun phrase that begins with a pronoun and includes two present participles used as adjectives). (You might also check that students understand that in this context, *tongue* means language.)

Direct students to the fourth example, from paragraph 2. Point out how each phrase begins with *each* until the last phrase breaks that pattern. Ask what the effect of that is. (*It draws more attention to the words "a brilliant music stilled."*) Ask what conclusion students can draw from this evidence. (*The author feels that the birds are amazing creatures and is sad that any should die.*)

Practice and Apply Encourage students to add one instance of parallelism across sentences and one within sentences. Once students have completed their writing and exchanged it with a partner, ask volunteers to share the parallel structures they used with the class.

ENGLISH LEARNER SUPPORT

Use Parallel Structure Provide instruction and practice in parallel structure with the following example sentences:

- Display pictures of the heart and draw content from them to model how to write three parallel structures. For example: *The heart works hard. The heart pumps blood. The heart keeps us alive.* **SUBSTANTIAL**

- Provide these frames: *The heart _____. The heart _____. The heart _____.* Have pairs of students take turns completing the frames to write sentences that they could add to their explanations. **MODERATE**

- Have pairs of students review their explanations. Ask them to find a place to add three parallel structures followed by a contrasting structure, as in the last example on page 169. Then have students check their partner's work. **LIGHT**

FIND YOUR PARK

Public Service Advertisement by
The National Park Service

GENRE ELEMENTS
PUBLIC SERVICE ADVERTISEMENT

Briefly review with students that the purpose of an advertisement is to persuade a target audience. Point out that a public service advertisement (PSA) is one type of advertisement. Explain that like commercial ads, a PSA combines images and words to make an emotional impact. It may also be multimodal, combining print, audio, and video. Point out that, unlike commercial ads, the goal of a PSA is to raise awareness or change attitudes. It therefore tends to have a broader audience than most commercial ads.

LEARNING OBJECTIVES

- Analyze media techniques and purpose.
- Research a national park and create an advertisement for it.
- Write a letter to support the creation of a national park.
- Give oral instructions about how to create a public service advertisement.
- **Language** Write a persuasive letter that uses verbs correctly.

TEXT COMPLEXITY

Quantitative Measures	Find Your Park	Lexile: N/A
Qualitative Measures	**Ideas Presented** Explicit and direct; purpose or stance clear.	
	Structures Used Primarily explicit; images and text features clarify points.	
	Language Used Explicit, familiar language.	
	Knowledge Required Cultural and historical references.	

Online Ed

RESOURCES

- Unit 3 Response Log
- Level Up Tutorial: Taking Notes and Outlining
- Writing Studio: Writing Arguments
- Speaking and Listening Studio: Speaking Constructively
- "Find Your Park" Selection Test

SUMMARIES

English

With fast-cut images and a punchy voice-over, this National Park Service public service advertisement (PSA) makes a compelling case for why national parks are important and why we should get out and discover them.

Spanish

Con imágenes rápidas y una narración incisiva, este Anuncio al Servicio Público (ASP) del Servicio Nacional de Parques crea un caso convincente sobre por qué los parques nacionales son importantes y por qué debemos salir a explorarlos.

SMALL-GROUP OPTIONS

Have students work in small groups to view and discuss the media selection.

Trivia Game

- After students have viewed and analyzed "Find Your Park," have pairs draw on all they have learned to write national park trivia questions.
- Have students write each question on one side of an index card and the answer on the other.
- Then have two or three pairs join together.
- Have groups shuffle the cards and take turns drawing cards and answering questions. Or, have students in one group exchange all of their questions with those of another group before they play the game.

Think-Pair-Share

- After students have read and analyzed "Find Your Park," pose this question: Do you think tax money should be spent on maintaining our national parks? Why or why not?
- Have students think about the question individually and take notes.
- Then, have pairs discuss their ideas about the question, drawing on information gleaned from the video, class discussion, and research to support their views.
- Finally, ask pairs to share their responses with the class.

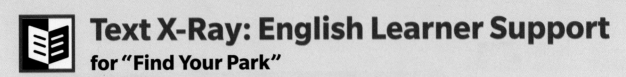

Text X-Ray: English Learner Support
for "Find Your Park"

Use the Text X-Ray and the supports and scaffolds in the Teacher's Edition to help guide students at different proficiency levels through the selection.

INTRODUCE THE SELECTION
DISCUSS NATIONAL PARKS

In this lesson, students will need to be able to discuss the benefits of national parks. Introduce the following key ideas:

- U.S. national parks are areas of land set aside for visitors to respectfully enjoy.
- National parks protect land, water, plants, and animals.
- Parks preserve history and culture. They help us learn about and remember important people, traditions, and events.

Ask students to name things they might see or do at a national park. List them under the headings *Nature, History, People,* and *Culture.* Then discuss whether students think national parks are important and why.

CULTURAL REFERENCES

The following historical figures featured in the PSA video may be unfamiliar to students:

- Booker T. Washington (1856–1915): American educator; author of *Up from Slavery*
- Clara Barton (1821–1912): Civil War nurse, founder of the American Red Cross
- Theodore Roosevelt (1858–1919): U.S. president (1901–1909); national park champion
- Henry David Thoreau (1817–1862): author of *Walden* (1854)
- Harriet Tubman (c. 1820–1913): famous abolitionist
- Thomas Edison (1847–1931): inventor of the first practical incandescent lamp (light bulb)
- César Chávez (1927–1993): farm worker organizer

LISTENING

Understand Main Points and Key Details

Tell students they are going to listen to the video and write down main points and key details.

Use the following supports with students at varying proficiency levels:

- Have students write these words and phrases on index cards: *nature, history, important people,* and *activities.* Ask students to close their eyes and listen as you play the PSA. Have students hold up the appropriate card when they hear that topic referenced. *(nature: 00:00–00:16; history: 00:17–22; important people: 00:23–31; activities: 00:32–39)* **SUBSTANTIAL**
- Play one section of the PSA. Have students write at least one sentence or idea they heard in that section. **MODERATE**
- Play the first section of the PSA, stopping at the first break in the narration. Have students record as much as they can. Then have them compare their dictation with that of a partner. Continue with the rest of the PSA. **LIGHT**

SPEAKING

Use High-Frequency Words to Describe

Have students watch the video without audio to describe what they see.

Use the following supports with students at varying proficiency levels:

- Introduce these sentence frames: *There is/are _____. _____ are _____-ing.* Then play the PSA with the audio off. Point to and name things you see. List them on the board and have everyone repeat them. Model using the words and frames to form short sentences. (*There is a river. Fish are swimming.*) Replay the video and have students say words, phrases, or sentences about what they see. **SUBSTANTIAL**

- Play the PSA once with the audio off. Ask students to identify things they see. List them on the board. Then replay the video twice and have students take turns narrating the video to a partner. **MODERATE**

- Have students play the video with the audio turned off. Have them take turns narrating the video to a partner. Have students include the words *history, art, culture, heroes,* and *leaders* in their narration. **LIGHT**

READING

Read and Summarize

Provide students with a transcript of the PSA video to read.

Use the following supports with students at varying proficiency levels:

- Select a segment of the transcript to read with students. Read aloud each sentence, modeling correct intonation and phrasing and explaining key terms. Have students echo read it after you. After reading the entire segment, ask simple comprehension questions, such as "Where do fish live?" (*oceans, rivers*) **SUBSTANTIAL**

- Echo read the transcript with students, pausing to paraphrase and explain as necessary. Then have pairs of students take turns rereading the transcript and summarizing the main idea and important details. **MODERATE**

- Have pairs of students read the transcript together and discuss its main idea and key details. Monitor their progress and help explain challenging language as needed. Then have partners work together to write a short summary. **LIGHT**

WRITING

Write a Letter to the Editor

Read aloud the writing assignment on Student Edition page 173. Explain that certain verbs and verb forms are often used to persuade, or to try to get someone else to agree with a position.

Use the following supports with students at varying proficiency levels:

- Introduce *need to* and *should*. Then model using each verb or verb phrase to write a sentence about why a new national park is needed. Have students copy the sentences and include drawings or translations in their home language to support meaning. **SUBSTANTIAL**

- Introduce *need to, have to,* and *should*. Then guide students to use the verbs to write sentences about why a new national park is needed. **MODERATE**

- Have pairs of students work together to use *need to, have to, should,* and *must* to write sentences about why a new national park is needed. **LIGHT**

Connect to the
ESSENTIAL QUESTION

Just as human activity can have a huge impact on nature, experiencing nature can have a profound effect on people. Those two facts are why our first national parks were created: they were established to preserve and protect natural spaces so that they could be enjoyed by all for many generations to come.

QUICK START

Check that students understand that a *nature preserve* refers to an area where wildlife and natural resources are protected. If necessary, list national parks, state parks, nature preserves, or living history museums in your area that students may be familiar with. Mention any parks that your school visits on field trips.

ANALYZE MEDIA TECHNIQUES AND PURPOSES

Point out that sounds from a particular environment, such as birds chirping in a forest or people cheering in a crowd, are often called *ambient sounds*. For each sound and visual element, ask students to think of examples from videos or full-length movies they have seen.

Suggest that students use these questions to help them analyze sound and visual elements in the video:

- What music, sound effects, or ambient sounds does the video use? What mood, or feeling, do they convey?
- How might you describe the voice-over narration? What does the narration add to the video?
- What visual elements are used? What message do they convey?

■ English Learner Support

Monitor Understanding Play a brief video clip and use it to introduce the terms *sound effects*, *voice-over narration*, *images*, and *juxtaposition* (of images). Pause the video to discuss each example. Think aloud to help students identify the elements. For example: "I'm listening to a woman speaking. She is telling about the images, or pictures, in the video. This element is called voiceover narration." Then tell students to watch or listen for each element in "Find Your Park." **ALL LEVELS**

ANALYZE & APPLY

MEDIA

FIND YOUR PARK

Public Service Advertisement by
The National Park Service

ESSENTIAL QUESTION:

What effect do we have on nature, and how does nature affect us?

QUICK START

Have you ever visited a national park, state park, nature preserve, or living history museum? What surprised you? Discuss your experiences.

ANALYZE MEDIA TECHNIQUES AND PURPOSES

A media message may be created for many **purposes**, or reasons: to entertain, to share information, to persuade. Underlying any of these purposes may be a specific motive. For example, the maker of a media message may have a social, commercial, or political goal in mind. Many messages are created with a combination of purposes and motives.

GENRE ELEMENTS: PUBLIC SERVICE ADVERTISEMENT

- addresses a wide, public audience
- provides information free of charge to raise awareness or change attitudes
- includes images and words with an emotional impact
- is multimodal: print, audio, or video

Public Service Advertisements, or **PSAs**, are messages created to give the public useful, helpful information rather than to sell something. They may appear in magazines, and on billboards, radio, and television. The main purpose of a PSA is to provide needed information, but a PSA may also make a persuasive appeal. Media techniques such as those listed can give you clues about the motives behind an audiovisual message.

Sound Elements

MUSIC AND SOUND EFFECTS	Sounds from nature and music can work to build a particular mood that affects the emotional response of the viewer.
VOICE-OVER NARRATION	Word choices can appeal to viewer emotions, but so can the speaker's vocal expression, emphasis, and pace.

Visual Elements

IMAGES	Art, photos, animation, graphs, and video can work together to share information and create emotional appeal.
WORDS	Onscreen text in the form of titles, subtitles, captions, or visual guides to the narration can emphasize key ideas.
JUXTAPOSITION	Sequencing shots implies a connection between ideas or events, adding meaning in ways that enhance the message.

170 Unit 3

BACKGROUND

The National Park Service was established to preserve meaningful places, moments in history, and monuments. The National Park Service is a bureau of the U.S. Department of the Interior, led by a director appointed by the president and voted in by the Senate. Over 20,000 people work for the National Park Service and over 300,000 people volunteer at the parks to preserve these national treasures and educate the public about them. More than 400 areas in the United States and its territories—including American Samoa, Guam, Puerto Rico, and the Virgin Islands—provide the public with history, archeology, and a celebration of wildlife and the natural world, to be protected for all time.

SETTING A PURPOSE

Consider what you think of or feel when you hear the phrase National Parks. *As you view and listen to the video, adjust your view of parks as needed based on the evidence presented in the PSA.* NOTEBOOK

To view the video, log in online and select **"FIND YOUR PARK"** from the unit menu.

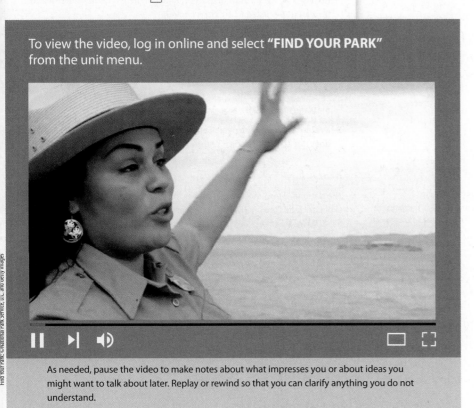

As needed, pause the video to make notes about what impresses you or about ideas you might want to talk about later. Replay or rewind so that you can clarify anything you do not understand.

WHEN STUDENTS STRUGGLE . . .

Analyze Media   Have partners view the video. Suggest that they play the video once without stopping or taking notes, and then discuss what they learned and what was unclear. Next, have them replay the video, pausing it each time the word *PARK* appears to review the segment they have just watched. Ask students to jot down important ideas or questions they have about what they have viewed, using a graphic organizer like the one below.

Video Segment	Notes and Questions

 For additional support, go to the **Reading Studio** and assign the following Level Up Tutorial: Taking Notes and Outlining.

BACKGROUND

Show a map of National Parks to students. Check that students understand that American Samoa, Guam, Puerto Rico, and the U.S. Virgin Islands are territories held by the United States. Then ask volunteers to share knowledge they may have about the founding of the National Park Service. *(In 1872, Congress established Yellowstone as the first National Park. The United States authorized more parks in the years that followed. In 1916, President Woodrow Wilson signed the act that created the National Park Service.)*

SETTING A PURPOSE

Direct students to use the Setting a Purpose prompt to focus their viewing.

 For **listening, speaking, and reading support** for students at varying proficiency levels, see the **Text X-Ray** on pages 170C–170D.

🔵 ENGLISH LEARNER SUPPORT

Understand Maps   With students, look at maps, signs, or other environmental print in the classroom. Have volunteers identify basic vocabulary and familiar features and images.   **ALL LEVELS**

ANALYZE MEDIA

Possible answers:

1. DOK 3:

NATURE	HISTORY/ CULTURE	PEOPLE	ACTIVITIES	OVERALL IMPRESSION
oceans, rocks, fish, birds, mountains, trees, grass	monuments/ memorials, battle re-enactments, inventions (railroad, plane, light bulb), works of art from diverse cultures (murals, carvings, beads)	Harriet Tubman, Thomas Edison, César Chávez, Booker T. Washington, Clara Barton, Henry David Thoreau, Presidents Lincoln & Roosevelt	hiking, kayaking, camping, bicycling, celebrations of culture, many fun things to do	wide range of activities and topics to suit various interests; everyone can find something to enjoy

2. DOK 4: *A strong percussive rhythm plays in the background; four times it stops (along with the narration), the word PARK appears, and viewers hear ambient sounds. These breaks divide the PSA into four segments.*

3. DOK 4: *The cuts are fast-paced, which helps to present national parks as active and exciting.*

4. DOK 4: *Just as the shots are short, the narration also consists of short, punchy clauses. This keeps the pace quick and fun, which may appeal to viewers.*

5. DOK 4: *The PSA achieves its purpose of encouraging people to value and use the park system. The rapid succession of images set to a lively rhythm and the punchy narration communicate the many interesting things the parks offer. The content conveys the historical, cultural, and environmental importance of our parks. The call to action, "Go find your park," encourages viewers to enjoy our country's parks.*

RESEARCH

Encourage students to use images and text in creative ways. Ask them to target a specific audience, such as outdoor athletes.

Connect Students may wish to think about preservation of parks in terms of visiting "dos" and "don'ts," as well as supporting policies and actions.

RESPOND

ANALYZE MEDIA

Support your responses with evidence from the PSA. NOTEBOOK

1. **Cite Evidence** The PSA sequences images and words in categories to build toward an overall impression of its subject. List examples of details from each category to map the structure of the message.

NATURE→	HISTORY / CULTURE→	PEOPLE→	ACTIVITIES→	OVERALL IMPRESSION

2. **Analyze** Describe the interaction between the music and the onscreen text reading "PARK." How does this interaction help organize the PSA into the categories listed in the chart above?

3. **Evaluate** How would you characterize the pace, or speed, of cuts between images? How does this pace serve the purpose of motivating viewers to go visit a National Park?

4. **Analyze** What kinds of sentence lengths and structures are used in the voiceover? How do these types of sentences enhance the pacing and message of the PSA?

5. **Evaluate** What is the overall effect of this PSA? Explain how it does or does not achieve its purpose through media techniques.

RESEARCH

The National Park Service has 417 areas that provide a wide variety of experiences for the public. Research one National Park: What features does it have? Why should people visit? What audience might enjoy it most? Record what you learn about your chosen park in the chart, and then create a poster advertising it.

NATIONAL PARK		
Features	Reasons to Visit	Target Audience
Students' responses will vary; check that charts include clear reasons and a specific target audience.		

Connect In the video, the narrator describes the experiences offered by the National Park Service as fun. With a small group, discuss how visitors can enjoy the park system and at the same time help to preserve it.

RESEARCH TIP
Be sure to check the websites you use to ensure that they are reliable and credible sources of information. The best place to begin your research on a National Park is the National Park Service's official website, www.nps.gov.

ENGLISH LEARNER SUPPORT

Oral Assessment To gauge comprehension and speaking skills, conduct an informal assessment. Walk around the class, talking with students, and asking these questions:

- What is the video about? *(our national parks)* **SUBSTANTIAL**
- What sound elements does the video use? *(music/drums, narration, ambient sounds)* **MODERATE**
- What are different ways in which people can enjoy our national parks? *(People can enjoy activities in nature, such as hiking, camping, or kayaking; they can also learn about important people, historical events, art, and cultural celebrations.)* **LIGHT**

CREATE AND PRESENT

Write a Letter to the Editor Write a letter to the editor advocating for a new National Park. Your proposed park may be a real place you have visited or a place you imagine. Your letter should be brief, about 100–200 words long.

- ❏ Use a business letter format and formal language for your letter.
- ❏ State your thesis clearly, and support it with facts and details.
- ❏ End your letter with a call to action.

Give Instructions Consider the PSA video and the poster you created for the Research task. Then, develop instructions that a younger student could follow for creating a compelling advertisement.

- ❏ Remember what you found compelling about the PSA video and what you used to make your own poster PSA compelling.
- ❏ Deliver the instructions to create a compelling PSA using clear and detailed steps in a logical sequence.
- ❏ Review the instructions with a partner and make suggestions about how your partner might improve his or her instructions. Listen closely and respectfully to all ideas.

 RESPOND

 For more on writing arguments, visit the **Writing Studio.**

 For more on speaking constructively, visit the **Speaking and Listening Studio.**

RESPOND TO THE ESSENTIAL QUESTION

 ? What effect do we have on nature, and how does nature affect us?

Gather Information Review your notes on "Find Your Park." Then, add relevant information to your Response Log. As you determine which information to include, think about:

- the reasons for creating a national park system
- what experiences the parks offer to the public
- how people can interact with nature by using the national parks

At the end of the unit, use your notes to write an explanatory essay.

UNIT 3 RESPONSE LOG

ACADEMIC VOCABULARY

As you write and discuss what you learned from the public service advertisement, be sure to use the Academic Vocabulary words. Check off each of the words that you use.

- ❏ advocate
- ❏ discrete
- ❏ domain
- ❏ evoke
- ❏ enhance

Find Your Park   173

© Houghton Mifflin Harcourt Publishing Company

CREATE AND PRESENT

Write a Letter to the Editor Briefly review how formal business language differs from language students might use in a personal letter or email. If necessary, share samples of letters to the editor from local media. You might also point out that while a letter to the editor may be addressed to a single *reader* (e.g., the editor of a local media outlet), writers usually have a broader *audience* in mind. Have students identify an audience and keep it in mind as they draft their letters.

For **writing support** for students at varying proficiency levels, see the **Text X-Ray** on page 170D.

Give Instructions Have students jot down notes about what made the PSA video and their own poster compelling. Remind them to consider visual elements and sound elements. Then have them choose whether they want to give instructions for making a print or a video PSA. As they draft their instructions, remind them to use sequence words such as *first, next,* and *then* to signal each step clearly. Once they have completed their drafts, have partners take turns delivering their instructions and giving feedback on both their content and delivery.

RESPOND TO THE ESSENTIAL QUESTION

Allow time for students to add details from "Find Your Park" to their Unit 3 Response Logs.

 ## ENGLISH LEARNER SUPPORT

Write a Letter to the Editor Use these suggestions to support students' writing.

- Choose a place in your community, such as a nearby river. Display pictures of it and/or display it on a map. Ask questions such as these to elicit oral input from students: What is this? (*a river*) What can you do there? (*fish, swim*) Then use the information to model writing a simple letter about the place. Have students copy the finished letter. **SUBSTANTIAL**

- Provide pairs of students with a cloze letter. For example, the body might read: *We need a new park in (place name). The reason that (place) is important is _____.* Have pairs work together to write their letter. **MODERATE**

- Have students draft their letters, then exchange them with a partner to check that the letters meet task guidelines. **LIGHT**

THE SEVENTH MAN

Short Story by **Haruki Murakami**
translated by **Jay Rubin**

GENRE ELEMENTS
SHORT STORY

Remind students that a **short story** is a work of fiction that centers on a single idea and can usually be read in one sitting. Short stories include the basic elements of fiction: plot, character, setting, and theme. Generally, a short story has one main conflict that involves the characters and keeps the story moving. In this lesson, students will analyze plot structure and identify symbols that develop the story's **theme,** or the underlying message about life or human nature that the writer wants to communicate.

LEARNING OBJECTIVES

- Analyze symbol and theme.
- Conduct research about typhoons.
- Write a vignette that uses a symbol to communicate theme.
- Discuss symbols and the development of theme.
- Identify and analyze figurative language.
- Use complex sentences correctly.
- **Language Objective** Identify and analyze figurative language using the terms *metaphor, simile,* and *personification.*

TEXT COMPLEXITY

Quantitative Measures	The Seventh Man	Lexile: 910L
Qualitative Measures	**Ideas Presented** Multiple levels of meaning; use of symbolism.	
	Structures Used Primarily explicit; multiple points of view; varies from chronological order.	
	Language Used Mostly explicit; some figurative language.	
	Knowledge Required More complexity in theme.	

RESOURCES

- Unit 3 Response Log
- Selection Audio
- Reading Studio: Notice & Note
- Level up Tutorials: Plot: Sequence of Events; Figurative Language
- Speaking and Listening Studio: Participating in Collaborative Discussions
- Grammar Studio: Module 4 Lesson 5: Sentence Structure
- "The Seventh Man"/"Carry" Selection Test

SUMMARIES

English

As this frame story begins, the seventh man in a group tells about the most devastating event of his life. The narration then shifts to his recounting his childhood experience of losing his best friend to a tsunami. He describes the far-reaching effects of that loss, including a great sense of guilt, recurrent nightmares, and a paralyzing fear of water and drowning. Years later, he overcomes his fear by revisiting his friend's artwork and returning to his hometown, the scene of the disaster.

Spanish

En esta historia, un narrador en tiempo presente en tercera persona presenta al séptimo hombre de un grupo que está contando los sucesos más devastadores de sus vidas. La narración cambia al punto de vista del séptimo hombre, mientras recuenta la experiencia de perder a su mejor amigo en un tsunami, durante su niñez. El séptimo hombre describe los efectos trascendentales de su pérdida, entre ellos las pesadillas recurrentes y su miedo paralizante al agua y a ahogarse. Mucho después en su vida, el séptimo hombre supera su miedo al volver a visitar el arte de su amigo y al regresar a su pueblo natal, la escena del desastre.

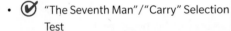 SMALL-GROUP OPTIONS

Have students work in small groups to read and discuss the selection.

Three-Minute Review

- After students have read "The Seventh Man" for the first time, organize them into pairs or triads.
- Pose a question to guide a group review, such as "Is the seventh man's fear of water rational? Why or why not?"
- Set the timer for three minutes. During that time, have students discuss possible answers to the question and then write at least one clarifying question to be handed in per group.
- Discuss each group's questions as a class.

Numbered Heads Together

- Have students form groups of four. Count off 1-2-3-4 to assign each student a number within a group.
- Ask a question posed in Respond: Analyze the Text.
- Have students discuss responses to the question in their groups.
- Call a number from 1 to 4. The student with that number responds for the group.

Text X-Ray: English Learner Support
for "The Seventh Man"

Use the Text X-Ray and the supports and scaffolds in the Teacher's Edition to help guide students at different proficiency levels through the selection.

INTRODUCE THE SELECTION
DISCUSS CHARACTER

In this lesson, students will need to be able to discuss the effects of a natural disaster on a fictional character. Read paragraphs 1–2 aloud and explain the following:

- An adult man is the main character of the story. He is talking about an event that occurred during his childhood.
- He talks quietly, as if it is difficult for him to discuss the event.
- The man says that he was almost swept away, or pulled out to sea, by a giant wave.
- In Japan, where this story takes place, huge waves called tsunamis sometimes come ashore during storms.

Discuss students' predictions about the story. Ask volunteers to share what they think happened during the event and how it affected the man's life.

CULTURAL REFERENCES

The following words or phrases may be unfamiliar to students:

- *seascapes* (paragraph 11): paintings or drawings of the sea or ocean
- *eye of the storm* (paragraph 16): the center of a storm, in which wind or precipitation slows down or almost stops before severe weather begins again
- *breakwater* (paragraph 25): a concrete barrier that keeps water back; also called a *dike,* or *dyke*

LISTENING

Create Mental Images

Tell students that creating mental images as they read can help them understand the action of the story. Encourage students to sketch the scene as you read. Tell students that the narrator was afraid of the image of his friend inside the wave for many years.

Have students listen as you read aloud paragraph 38. Use the following supports with students at varying proficiency levels:

- Tell students to respond *yes* or *no* to questions about what they just heard. For example: Does the narrator think he really saw K. in the wave? *(yes)* Was K. smiling? *(yes)* **SUBSTANTIAL**
- Work with students to generate words to complete the sentence: *The description helps readers understand the narrator's feelings of _____. (helplessness, shock, terror)* **MODERATE**
- Have partners work together to write sentences describing how they think the narrator felt when he saw K. in the wave. **LIGHT**

SPEAKING

Discuss Plot Structure

Tell students that in a frame story, the main story is introduced by another, less-detailed story, or "frame," that sets the scene for the telling of the main story. The "frame" may return at the end of the main story, as well.

Have students discuss the structure of the plot so that they understand the concept of a frame story. Use the following supports with students at varying proficiency levels:

- Read aloud paragraphs 1–3. Help students identify the spoken dialogue within quotation marks. Ask: Who is speaking in the story? *(the seventh man)* **SUBSTANTIAL**

- Have students note the sudden change in the text starting in paragraph 10. Ask students to identify who is talking. *(The seventh man is talking about his childhood.)* When did the events he describes happen? *(They happened in the past.)* **MODERATE**

- Have partners identify and discuss the flash-forward in paragraph 47, where the narrator takes a break from talking about events in the past to return to the present. **LIGHT**

READING

Analyze Figurative Language

Explain to students that figurative language emphasizes ideas by communicating meanings beyond the literal meanings of words.

Review the terms *simile, metaphor,* and *personification.* Then use the following supports with students at varying proficiency levels:

- Read aloud paragraph 6. Explain that "it" refers to the huge wave. Ask students to underline the verb the author uses to describe the action of the wave. *(swallowed)* **SUBSTANTIAL**

- Have small groups work together to identify the personification in paragraph 6. Then have them complete this sentence: *The personification of the wave shows _____. (how powerful it was)* **MODERATE**

- Have small groups of students identify and discuss other examples of figurative language in the text. Have them share which examples of figurative language create the most vivid images for them. **LIGHT**

WRITING

Write a Vignette

Work with students to clarify and support their preparation for the creative writing assignment on Student Edition page 193.

Explain that a **vignette** is a short description of a character or idea. A vignette should create a mood or a feeling and express a theme. Use the following supports with students at varying proficiency levels:

- Explain that an author's choice of words helps create a mood or feeling. Help students list words to describe a mood or feeling they might create in a vignette. *(happiness, mystery, fear, curiosity, bravery, sadness)* **SUBSTANTIAL**

- Write this theme on the board: It is important to face one's fears. Have partners work together to complete the sentence frame: *The man says that it is important to face your fears because _____.* **MODERATE**

- Have students freewrite about something that might symbolize fear in their own lives. **LIGHT**

? Connect to the ESSENTIAL QUESTION

Both the short story "The Seventh Man" and the poem "Carry" address themes of how humans relate to and are affected by nature. In "The Seventh Man," nature's tremendous power has a devastating effect on a man's life.

COMPARE THEMES

Comparing texts of different genres can give students a deeper understanding of common themes in literature. Tell students that in this Collaborate & Compare lesson, they will read the short story "The Seventh Man" and the poem "Carry." Ask students to look for the theme, or the author's message about life, as they read the short story. Tell them to pay attention to symbols in the short story that relate to nature and think about how these symbols may hint at the story's themes. Identifying themes in the short story will help students get ready to analyze themes of the poem.

SHORT STORY

THE SEVENTH MAN

by **Haruki Murakami**
pages 177–191

COMPARE THEMES

As you read, notice how authors working in two different genres address similar themes. What are the texts' messages about the world in general? How do the authors express those messages? After you read both selections, you will work on a final project about the texts' themes.

ESSENTIAL QUESTION:

What effect do we have on nature, and how does nature affect us?

POEM

CARRY

by **Linda Hogan**
pages 199–201

LEARNING MINDSET

Effort   Remind students that effort is necessary for growth and that it takes hard work to succeed at something. It may be difficult for students to infer theme from a literary work and then find thematic similarities between two literary works of different genres. Praise students for their attempts to identify and compare themes within these two selections. Offer feedback as students work to analyze and compare the selections: "I noticed you put a lot of effort into your reading today. When you had difficulty with a section, you stopped, took a breath, and kept going."

The Seventh Man

QUICK START

In the 1930s, President Franklin Roosevelt told the American people, "The only thing we have to fear is fear itself." What do you think Roosevelt meant by that? Do you agree? Why or why not? Share your thoughts with a partner.

ANALYZE SYMBOL AND THEME

A **symbol** is a person, place, object, or activity that stands for something beyond itself. Our culture has established common symbols, such as doves (peace), red roses (love), and flags (countries). Writers can use these symbols to make connections among ideas without stating them explicitly.

In a text, recurring symbols make up a pattern called a **motif**. Symbols and motifs help develop a text's theme. The **theme** of a work is the underlying message about life or human nature that the writer wants to communicate.

As you read "The Seventh Man," look for symbols and motifs like the ones shown in the chart. Write what each might represent.

GENRE ELEMENTS: SHORT STORY

- centers around characters, conflict, and plot development
- usually focuses on one or very few settings, moments in time, and characters
- can usually be read in one sitting

SYMBOL OR MOTIF	WHAT IT MIGHT REPRESENT
wave/sea	fear, loss, change
typhoon	destructive power of nature, supernatural force powerlessness, loss of control
K.'s paintings	innocence, peaceful nature, childhood, happiness

ANALYZE PLOT

Stories are often told in chronological, or linear, order, meaning that the narrator tells plot events in the order in which the characters experience them. Within a linear plot, an author can depart from the main time line for effect. For example, a **flashback** interrupts the chronological flow of a story with an account of a prior event relevant to the present action of the story. "The Seventh Man" is structured as a **frame story,** in which a present-day narrator relates the main story, which happens in the past, and then returns to the present day. Mapping plot events sequentially in a graphic organizer will help you keep track of the actual order of events in a story.

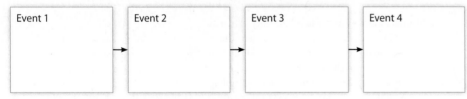

As you read, think about how each plot event affects the plot as a whole.

© Houghton Mifflin Harcourt Publishing Company

QUICK START

Tell students that this quotation comes from President Roosevelt's first inaugural address, delivered on March 4, 1933, in the midst of the economic crisis known as the Great Depression. Many people were unemployed, had lost their life savings, and struggled to feed themselves and their families. President Roosevelt encouraged Americans to fight the feeling of paralyzing fear during this difficult and unstable time in the country's history. In the speech, President Roosevelt went on to say that "this great nation will endure as it has endured, will revive and will prosper." Invite students to share a time in their own lives when they felt a paralyzing fear. Did they overcome this fear? How?

ANALYZE SYMBOL AND THEME

Discuss the terms *symbol, motif,* and *theme* with students. Explain that a **symbol** stands for something beyond itself. Ask students to identify symbols they may have encountered in literature, films, or daily life, and to explain what each of these symbols represents. In literature, a **motif** is a recurrent image or symbol that helps develop and reinforce the theme of the work. Remind students that as they read and identify symbols and motifs, they should consider how these elements develop the story's **theme.** Help students preview the chart so that they can look for symbols as they read and think about their meanings and importance in the story.

ANALYZE PLOT

Review with students that the events of a story's **plot** are not always presented in chronological, or sequential, order. Authors may choose to deviate from a chronological, or linear, plot to provide information about a character or to create an effect, such as mystery, suspense, or tension. Explain that the main character of this frame story is an older man who describes an event that happened long ago in his past. The short story begins and ends in the present, with the man talking about this event to an audience. Help students create a chart to identify the sequential order of the plot's events. Guide students to consider why the author structured the story this way and to think about how the unconventional structure helps underscore the story's theme.

APPLY

CRITICAL VOCABULARY

Remind students to read all the sentences before deciding which word best completes each one.

Answers:

1. *permeate*

2. *frail*

3. *sociable*

4. *reconciliation*

5. *delirium*

6. *premonition*

7. *entranced*

8. *sentiment*

■ English Learner Support

Use Cognates Tell students that several of the Critical Vocabulary words have Spanish cognates: *frail/frágil, delirium/delirio, sociable/sociable, premonition/premonición, sentiment/sentimiento,* and *reconciliation/reconciliación.*
ALL LEVELS

LANGUAGE CONVENTIONS

Review the information on complex sentences with students. Make sure students understand the difference between an independent clause, which can stand alone as a sentence, and a dependent clause, which cannot. Read the example sentence aloud and ask a volunteer to identify the independent clause and the dependent clause. Explain that authors use complex sentences to show how ideas are connected and to create variety in their writing.

ANNOTATION MODEL

Remind students that they may mark details from the text that indicate symbols and theme and that help identify the order of plot events. Point out that they may follow the Annotation Model or use their own system for marking up the selection in their write-in text. They may want to color-code their annotations by using highlighters. Their notes in the margin may include questions and comments about the story.

◎ GET READY

CRITICAL VOCABULARY

frail	entranced	delirium	sociable
premonition	permeate	sentiment	reconciliation

To see how many Critical Vocabulary words you already know, use them to complete the sentences.

1. The musty odor of my wet dog began to _____ my room.
2. The _____ old man had trouble walking up the stairs.
3. At the party, I pledged to be _____ and talk to others.
4. After the argument, we shook hands and had a _____.
5. She was in a _____, confused about where she was.
6. My dream was a _____ that my grandmother would visit.
7. The child was_____, transfixed by the cartoon.
8. The _____ in the heartfelt poem was touching.

LANGUAGE CONVENTIONS

Complex Sentences To add interest, writers vary sentence structure. A **complex sentence** includes an independent clause and at least one dependent clause. An independent clause can stand alone as a sentence. A dependent clause has a subject and verb, but does not express a complete thought.

In this complex sentence from the story, the underlined dependent clause adds information to the independent clause.

"It happened one September afternoon <u>when I was ten years old</u>."

As you read the selection, notice how the author uses complex sentences to create variety and elaborate on ideas.

ANNOTATION MODEL

NOTICE & NOTE

Here is how you might annotate to help you analyze symbols.

"A huge wave nearly swept me away," said the seventh man, almost whispering.

"It happened one September afternoon when I was ten years old."

The man was the last one to tell his story that night. The hands of the clock had moved past ten. The small group that huddled in a circle could hear the <u>wind tearing through the darkness outside</u>, heading west. <u>It shook the trees, set the windows to rattling, and moved past the house with one final whistle.</u>

The wind might symbolize either real or emotional turmoil that people need to protect themselves from. It sets an ominous tone for the story the seventh man will tell.

BACKGROUND

*As a boy, **Haruki Murakami** (b. 1949) preferred reading American paperbacks to studying traditional Japanese literature. He went on to become a novelist and short-story writer known for his unique and whimsical works that break away from typical Japanese forms. Murakami combines mystery, comedy, and fantasy in his work while keeping his messages practical, profound, and believable.*

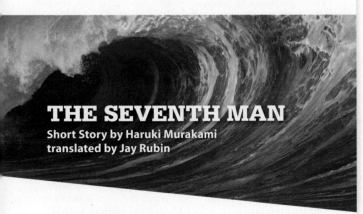

THE SEVENTH MAN

Short Story by Haruki Murakami
translated by Jay Rubin

PREPARE TO COMPARE

As you read the author's vivid descriptions and figurative language, create mental images of the story's setting and events. You might find it useful to sketch the images that come up for you. As the story is set in the author's home country of Japan, call upon your prior knowledge of the country to help you picture the setting.

Notice & Note

You can use the side margins to notice and note signposts in the text.

1   "A huge wave nearly swept me away," said the seventh man, almost whispering.

2   "It happened one September afternoon when I was ten years old."

3   The man was the last one to tell his story that night. The hands of the clock had moved past ten. The small group that huddled in a circle could hear the wind tearing through the darkness outside, heading west. It shook the trees, set the windows to rattling, and moved past the house with one final whistle.

4   "It was the biggest wave I had ever seen in my life," he said. "A strange wave. An absolute giant."

5   He paused.

The Seventh Man   177

BACKGROUND

Have students read the Background and information about the author. Explain to students that the main character in this story is tragically affected by a tsunami—a giant wave—that strikes his hometown. Point out that Murakami is known for his eclectic style and unique vision. Explain that "The Seventh Man" draws upon American realism as well as Japanese surrealism, which introduces dreamlike and fantastic elements.

PREPARE TO COMPARE

Direct students to use the Prepare to Compare prompt to focus their reading.

 For **reading support** for students at varying proficiency levels, see the **Text X-Ray** on page 174D.

WHEN STUDENTS STRUGGLE . . .

Identify Figurative Language   Encourage students to identify examples of figurative language as a way to help them understand the story's symbolism.

Simile	*"the house would creak and shudder as if a huge hand were shaking it"* (paragraph 13)
Metaphor	*"it was just a great big circus"* (paragraph 12)
Personification	*"it swallowed everything that mattered most to me"* (paragraph 6)

For additional support, go to the **Reading Studio** and assign the following **Level Up Tutorial: Figurative Language.**

TEACH

For **reading support** for students at varying proficiency levels, see the **Text X-Ray** on page 174D.

 ANALYZE PLOT

Review with students that a **frame story** is a story told within a narrative setting, or "frame." Help students identify the frame of "The Seventh Man" as a group of people in the present sharing stories late one stormy night (paragraph 3). The seventh and final person to tell his story to the group begins talking about a storm he experienced long ago, when he was a boy. In the frame, the man sets up the story he is about to tell as the most tragic event of his life. Paragraph 10 begins the **flashback,** or the interruption of the action of the present (the frame) to describe events of the past. Explain to students that the words "I grew up" signal that the seventh man is now the first-person narrator. (**Answer:** *The perspective of the narrator's story allows him to reflect on the experience. The author structures the tale this way because it will have more impact through the character's reflection on the past than it would as an isolated event.*)

■ English Learner Support

Reinforce Meaning Draw a picture frame on the board so that students can visualize how a frame surrounds something. Explain that the frame of the story is the part of the text that identifies the seventh man as a part of a group of people in the present. The frame "surrounds" the part of the story that takes place in the past. Point out that the narrator uses the third-person pronoun *he* to describe the man in paragraphs 1–9. In paragraph 10, the pronoun *I* shows that the narration shifts to the man's point of view. Ask: Does the action of the story in paragraphs 1–9 happen in the past, or present? (*present*) Does the action of the story in paragraph 10 happen in the past, or present? (*past*)
SUBSTANTIAL/MODERATE

CRITICAL VOCABULARY

frail: The narrator describes his friend K. as skinny and small with a delicate face and pale complexion.

ASK STUDENTS whether someone who was frail would be likely to be active or athletic. (*Someone who is frail, or physically weak, would not likely be an active or athletic person.*)

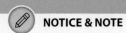

6   "It just barely missed me, but in my place it swallowed everything that mattered most to me and swept it off to another world. I took years to find it again to recover from the experience—precious years that can never be replaced."

7   The seventh man appeared to be in his mid-fifties. He was a thin man, tall, with a moustache, and next to his right eye he had a short but deep-looking scar that could have been made by the stab of a small blade. Stiff, bristly patches of white marked his short hair. His face had the look you see on people when they can't quite find the words they need. In his case, though, the expression seemed to have been there from long before, as though it were part of him. The man wore a simple blue shirt under a grey tweed coat, and every now and then he would bring his hand to his collar. None of those assembled there knew his name or what he did for a living.

8   He cleared his throat, and for a moment or two his words were lost in silence. The others waited for him to go on.

9   "In my case, it was a wave," he said. "There's no way for me to tell, of course, what it will be for each of you. But in my case it just happened to take the form of a gigantic wave. It presented itself to me all of a sudden one day, without warning. And it was devastating."

10   I grew up in a seaside town in the Province of S. It was such a small town, I doubt that any of you would recognize the name if I were to mention it. My father was the local doctor, and so I led a rather comfortable childhood. Ever since I could remember, my best friend was a boy I'll call K. His house was close to ours, and he was a grade behind me in school. We were like brothers, walking to and from school together, and always playing together when we got home. We never once fought during our long friendship. I did have a brother, six years older, but what with the age difference and differences in our personalities, we were never very close. My real brotherly affection went to my friend K.

11   K. was a **frail**, skinny little thing, with a pale complexion and a face almost pretty enough to be a girl's. He had some kind of speech impediment,[1] though, which might have made him seem retarded to anyone who didn't know him. And because he was so frail, I always played his protector, whether at school or at home. I was kind of big and athletic, and the other kids all looked up to me. But the main reason I enjoyed spending time with K. was that he was such a sweet, pure-hearted boy. He was not the least bit retarded, but because of his impediment, he didn't do too well at school. In most subjects, he could barely keep up. In art class, though, he was great. Just give him a pencil or paints and he would make pictures that were so full of life that even the teacher was amazed. He won prizes in one contest after another, and I'm sure he would have become a famous painter if he had continued with his art into adulthood. He liked to do seascapes. He'd go out to the shore for hours, painting. I would often sit beside

---
[1] **impediment** (ĭm-pĕd´ə-mənt): an obstacle.

ANALYZE PLOT
Annotate: Mark details that indicate "The Seventh Man" is a frame story (a story within a story).

Analyze: Why do you think the author structures his tale this way?

frail
(frāl) *adj.* physically weak.

 ENGLISH LEARNER SUPPORT

Confirm Understanding Review with students that the seventh man is telling a story about a huge wave that nearly pulled him out to sea when he was young. Read paragraph 6 aloud to students, emphasizing "it swallowed everything that mattered most to me and swept it off to another world." Discuss how the word *"swallowed"* helps them visualize the wave. Ask: What effect did the wave have on the man's life? (*The wave was like an animal swallowing everything that was important to the man. It destroyed his life.*) **LIGHT**

him, watching the swift, precise movements of his brush, wondering how, in a few seconds, he could possibly create such lively shapes and colors where, until then, there had been only blank white paper. I realize now that it was a matter of pure talent.

12   One year, in September, a huge typhoon[2] hit our area. The radio said it was going to be the worst in ten years. The schools were closed, and all the shops in town lowered their shutters in preparation for the storm. Starting early in the morning, my father and brother went around the house nailing shut all the storm doors, while my mother spent the day in the kitchen cooking emergency provisions. We filled bottles and canteens with water, and packed our most important possessions in rucksacks for possible evacuation. To the adults, typhoons were an annoyance and a threat they had to face almost annually, but to the kids, removed as we were from such practical concerns, it was just a great big circus, a wonderful source of excitement.

13   Just after noon the color of the sky began to change all of a sudden. There was something strange and unreal about it. I stayed outside on the porch, watching the sky, until the wind began to howl and the rain began to beat against the house with a weird dry sound, like handfuls of sand. Then we closed the last storm door and gathered together in one room of the darkened house, listening to the radio. This particular storm did not have a great deal of rain, it said, but the winds were doing a lot of damage, blowing roofs off houses and capsizing[3] ships. Many people had been killed or injured by flying debris. Over and over again, they warned people against leaving their homes. Every once in a while, the house would creak and shudder as if a huge hand were shaking it, and sometimes there would be a great crash of some heavy-sounding object against a storm door. My father guessed that these were tiles blowing off the neighbors' houses. For lunch we ate the rice and omelettes my mother had cooked, waiting for the typhoon to blow past.

14   But the typhoon gave no sign of blowing past. The radio said it had lost momentum almost as soon as it came ashore at S. Province, and now it was moving north-east at the pace of a slow runner. The wind kept up its savage howling as it tried to uproot everything that stood on land.

15   Perhaps an hour had gone by with the wind at its worst like this when a hush fell over everything. All of a sudden it was so quiet, we could hear a bird crying in the distance. My father opened the storm door a crack and looked outside. The wind had stopped, and the rain had ceased to fall. Thick, grey clouds edged across the sky, and patches of blue showed here and there. The trees in the yard were still dripping their heavy burden of rainwater.

---

[2] **typhoon** (tī-foon´): a tropical storm forming in the Pacific or Indian Ocean, consisting of violent winds and rain.

[3] **capsize** (kăp´sīz): flip upside-down in water.

CONTRASTS AND CONTRADICTIONS

Notice & Note: In paragraphs 13–15, mark where the weather changes drastically.

Analyze: How does the contrast in the descriptions of the weather change the tone of the story?

ENGLISH LEARNER SUPPORT

Understand Vocabulary   Read aloud paragraph 12 to students. Draw students' attention to the footnote for the word "typhoon" and ask a volunteer to read the word's definition aloud. Explain that "typhoon" and "hurricane" are both names for severe tropical storms, or cyclones. Typhoons occur in the western Pacific and Indian oceans while hurricanes occurs in the Atlantic and northern Pacific oceans.

Have students note how the narrator compares the typhoon to a "great big circus." Ask students to describe a circus (*fun, exciting, maybe a little scary*). Discuss how a storm might be like a circus to the children in the narrator's town. (*Both the storm and the circus are fun and exciting but a little dangerous; the storm, like a circus, is not something that happens all the time.*) Then discuss why adults might view the storm differently. (*Adults have to get ready for the storm to keep their families and houses safe.*) **MODERATE**

▶ **CONTRASTS AND CONTRADICTIONS**

Explain to students that noticing **contrasts** in setting, such as the sudden environmental changes that are part of a big storm, can help draw their attention to the theme of the story. Ask: How might these changes in the setting affect the characters in the story? (*It seems that the storm has stopped, so maybe the characters think they are safe.*) Discuss how the contrast impacts the tone and mood of the story. (***Answer:** The sudden onslaught of the storm increases tension, but its sudden ceasing seems even more ominous.*)

IMPROVE READING FLUENCY

Targeted Passage   Use paragraph 12 to model fluent reading. Have students follow along in their books as you read aloud the text with appropriate expression, phrasing, and emphasis. Then, have partners take turns reading aloud paragraph 13 to each other. Encourage students to provide feedback and support for correct pronunciation and appropriate expression. Remind students that when they are reading fiction aloud for an audience, they should pace their reading so the audience has time to visualize the action.

Go to the **Reading Studio** for additional support in developing fluency.

TEACH

ENGLISH LEARNER SUPPORT

Develop Vocabulary Read aloud paragraph 16 to students. Explain that an *intermission* is a short pause. Draw a simple illustration of the swirl-like shape of a typhoon or hurricane. Explain that the "eye of the storm" is the area of calm weather at the center of the storm. Explain that as the storm moves along the land, the eye passes over the land. As the storm continues to move along the land, the eye passes and the winds and rain of the outer part of the storm resume. Ask students to raise their hands if they think it is safe to go out in the eye of a storm. (*Students may think it is not safe because the storm will start again in a short time.*) **SUBSTANTIAL**

 ANALYZE PLOT

Tell students that **foreshadowing** is when an author provides hints that suggest future events in a story. Foreshadowing creates suspense and makes readers eager to find out what will happen. (***Answer:*** *The foreshadowing fills the reader with a sense of dread, partly because the reader already knows that something terrible involving the ocean happens in the narrator's life.*)

ANALYZE PLOT

Annotate: Mark details in paragraphs 25 and 26 that seem to foreshadow future plot events.

Evaluate: How does foreshadowing affect the tone of this part of the story?

16   "We're in the eye of the storm," my father told me. "It'll stay quiet like this for a while, maybe fifteen, twenty minutes, kind of like an intermission. Then the wind'll come back the way it was before."

17   I asked him if I could go outside. He said I could walk around a little if I didn't go far. "But I want you to come right back here at the first sign of wind."

18   I went out and started to explore. It was hard to believe that a wild storm had been blowing there until a few minutes before. I looked up at the sky. The storm's great "eye" seemed to be up there, fixing its cold stare on all of us below. No such "eye" existed, of course: we were just in that momentary quiet spot at the center of the pool of whirling air.

19   While the grown-ups checked for damage to the house, I went down to the beach. The road was littered with broken tree branches, some of them thick pine boughs that would have been too heavy for an adult to lift alone. There were shattered roof tiles everywhere, cars with cracked windshields, and even a doghouse that had tumbled into the middle of the street. A big hand might have swung down from the sky and flattened everything in its path.

20   K. saw me walking down the road and came outside.

21   "Where are you going?" he asked.

22   "Just down to look at the beach," I said.

23   Without a word, he came along with me. He had a little white dog that followed after us.

24   "The minute we get any wind, though, we're going straight back home," I said, and K. gave me a silent nod.

25   The shore was a 200-yard walk from my house. It was lined with a concrete breakwater—a big dyke that stood as high as I was tall in those days. We had to climb a short flight of steps to reach the water's edge. This was where we came to play almost every day, so there was no part of it we didn't know well. In the eye of the typhoon, though, it all looked different: the color of the sky and of the sea, the sound of the waves, the smell of the tide, the whole expanse of the shore. We sat atop the breakwater for a time, taking in the view without a word to each other. We were supposedly in the middle of a great typhoon, and yet the waves were strangely hushed. And the point where they washed against the beach was much farther away than usual, even at low tide. The white sand stretched out before us as far as we could see. The whole, huge space felt like a room without furniture, except for the band of flotsam[4] that lined the beach.

26   We stepped down to the other side of the breakwater and walked along the broad beach, examining the things that had come to rest there. Plastic toys, sandals, chunks of wood that had probably once been parts of furniture, pieces of clothing, unusual bottles, broken crates with foreign writing on them, and other, less recognizable

---
[4] **flotsam** (flŏt´səm): pieces of floating debris.

TO CHALLENGE STUDENTS . . .

Analyze Personification Encourage students to explore how nature is personified throughout this short story. Have students research the literary term **pathetic fallacy,** the attribution of human emotions to things that are not human—in this case, nature. Have students work in small groups to discuss the following:

- Why does the author use pathetic fallacy in "The Seventh Man"?
- How does the portrayal of nature change throughout the story?
- How does Murakami's use of pathetic fallacy compare to examples of pathetic fallacy within other texts you have read?

ANALYZE SYMBOL AND THEME

Remind students that the figurative language in the author's vivid descriptions of the waves and water help develop the symbolism of the story. Ask: What figurative language does the author use to describe the waves and the water? *(He compares them to a dangerous and stealthy animal, like a snake or a lion).* Discuss how this language helps readers understand what the waves and ocean symbolize. (**Answer:** *The author is making the statement that nonliving parts of nature have a destructive power similar to that of wild animals and are capable of harming people.)*

items: it was like a big candy store. The storm must have carried these things from very far away. Whenever something unusual caught our attention, we would pick it up and look at it every which way, and when we were done, K.'s dog would come over and give it a good sniff.

27   We couldn't have been doing this more than five minutes when I realized that the waves had come up right next to me. Without any sound or other warning, the sea had suddenly stretched its long, smooth tongue out to where I stood on the beach. I had never seen anything like it before. Child though I was, I had grown up on the shore and knew how frightening the ocean could be—the savagery with which it could strike unannounced.

28   And so I had taken care to keep well back from the waterline. In spite of that, the waves had slid up to within inches of where I stood. And then, just as soundlessly, the water drew back—and stayed back. The waves that had approached me were as unthreatening as waves can be—a gentle washing of the sandy beach. But something ominous about them—something like the touch of a reptile's skin—had sent a chill down my spine. My fear was totally groundless—and totally real. I knew instinctively that they were alive. They knew I was here and they were planning to grab me. I felt as if some huge, man-eating beast were lying somewhere on a grassy plain, dreaming of the moment it would pounce and tear me to pieces with its sharp teeth. I had to run away.

ANALYZE SYMBOL AND THEME

Annotate: Mark details that suggest what the waves and ocean symbolize in paragraphs 27 and 28.

Analyze: What message about nature is the author communicating through this use of symbolism?

The Seventh Man   181

© Houghton Mifflin Harcourt Publishing Company • Image Credits: ©Media Worldimages/Alamy Stock Photo/Alamy

ENGLISH LEARNER SUPPORT

Learn Expressions   Read aloud paragraph 26. Draw students' attention to the phrase "it was like a big candy store." Discuss how children might view a candy store as a fun place where they can look at a variety of sweets. Have students use this frame to explain why the author compares the beach to a candy store: *A candy store and the beach both have _____ . (a variety of interesting things to look at)* **MODERATE**

TEACH

LANGUAGE CONVENTIONS

Read aloud the first three sentences of paragraph 30, emphasizing the dramatic effect of the sentence variety. Review with students that a **complex sentence** includes an independent clause and at least one dependent clause. An **independent clause** can stand alone as a sentence. A **dependent clause** has a subject and verb but does not express a complete thought. In the third sentence of paragraph 30—a complex sentence—the first dependent clause, "Actually, before I heard the rumble," helps to show the sequence of the two sounds. The second dependent clause, "as though a lot of water was surging up through a hole in the ground," helps to describe the weirdness of the sound that the narrator heard first. (**Answer:** *The two short sentences create anticipation of what will happen. The long sentence creates tension and a sense of the first-hand experience as the narrator tries to understand what is happening.*)

🔵 ENGLISH LEARNER SUPPORT

Decode Words Read aloud paragraph 33 and point out the consonant digraphs in the words *do*dge and *ducking*. Pronounce the words several times, with students repeating them after you. Explain that *to dodge* means "to avoid" and that *ducking* means "lowering your head and/or body to avoid being hit." Have students mimic you as you model the action. Explain that the narrator is able to get out of the wave's way by hiding behind the breakwater, or dyke—a wall constructed to protect the shore. **SUBSTANTIAL**

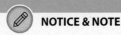 **NOTICE & NOTE**

LANGUAGE CONVENTIONS

Annotate: Circle the independent clause and underline the dependent clauses in the third sentence of paragraph 30.

Evaluate: What is the effect of this complex sentence following two simple sentences?

29   "I'm getting out of here!" I yelled to K. He was maybe ten yards down the beach, squatting with his back to me, and looking at something. I was sure I had yelled loud enough, but my voice did not seem to have reached him. He might have been so absorbed in whatever it was he had found that my call made no impression on him. K. was like that. He would get involved with things to the point of forgetting everything else. Or possibly I had not yelled as loudly as I had thought. I do recall that my voice sounded strange to me, as though it belonged to someone else.

30   Then I heard a deep rumbling sound. It seemed to shake the earth. Actually, before I heard the rumble, I heard another sound, a weird gurgling, as though a lot of water was surging up through a hole in the ground. It continued for a while, then stopped, after which I heard the strange rumbling. Even that was not enough to make K. look up. He was still squatting, looking down at something at his feet, in deep concentration. He probably did not hear the rumbling. How he could have missed such an earth-shaking sound, I don't know. This may seem odd, but it might have been a sound that only I could hear—some special kind of sound. Not even K.'s dog seemed to notice it, and you know how sensitive dogs are to sound.

31   I told myself to run over to K., grab hold of him, and get out of there. It was the only thing to do. I *knew* that the wave was coming, and K. didn't know. As clearly as I knew what I ought to be doing, I found myself running the other way—running full speed toward the dyke, alone. What made me do this, I'm sure, was fear, a fear so overpowering it took my voice away and set my legs to running on their own. I ran stumbling along the soft sand beach to the breakwater, where I turned and shouted to K.

32   "Hurry, K.! Get out of there! The wave is coming!" This time my voice worked fine. The rumbling had stopped, I realized, and now, finally, K. heard my shouting and looked up. But it was too late. A wave like a huge snake with its head held high, poised to strike, was racing towards the shore. I had never seen anything like it in my life. It had to be as tall as a three-story building. Soundlessly (in my memory, at least, the image is soundless), it rose up behind K. to block out the sky. K. looked at me for a few seconds, uncomprehending. Then, as if sensing something, he turned towards the wave. He tried to run, but now there was no time to run. In the next instant, the wave had swallowed him.

33   The wave crashed on to the beach, shattering into a million leaping waves that flew through the air and plunged over the dyke where I stood. I was able to dodge its impact by ducking behind the breakwater. The spray wet my clothes, nothing more. I scrambled back up on to the wall and scanned the shore. By then the wave had turned and, with a wild cry, it was rushing back out to sea. It looked like part of a gigantic rug that had been yanked by someone at the other end of the earth. Nowhere on the shore could I find any trace of K., or of his dog. There was only the empty beach. The receding wave

---

APPLYING ACADEMIC VOCABULARY

☐ **advocate**   ☐ **discrete**   ☐ **domain**   ☑ **evoke**   ☑ **enhance**

Write and Discuss   Have students turn to a partner to discuss the following questions. Guide students to use the academic vocabulary words *evoke* and *enhance* in their responses. Ask volunteers to share their responses with the class.

- What feelings does the author's description of K. **evoke?**
- How does the author's use of personification in paragraph 32 **enhance** your understanding of the wave?

had now pulled so much water out from the shore that it seemed to expose the entire ocean bottom. I stood along on the breakwater, frozen in place.

34   The silence came over everything again—a desperate silence, as though sound itself had been ripped from the earth. The wave had swallowed K. and disappeared into the far distance. I stood there, wondering what to do. Should I go down to the beach? K. might be down there somewhere, buried in the sand . . . But I decided not to leave the dyke. I knew from experience that big waves often came in twos and threes.

35   I'm not sure how much time went by—maybe ten or twenty seconds of eerie emptiness—when, just as I had guessed, the next wave came. Another gigantic roar shook the beach, and again, after the sound had faded, another huge wave raised its head to strike. It towered before me, blocking out the sky, like a deadly cliff. This time, though, I didn't run. I stood rooted to the sea wall, **entranced**, waiting for it to attack. What good would it do to run, I thought, now that K. had been taken? Or perhaps I simply froze, overcome with fear. I can't be sure what it was that kept me standing there.

36   The second wave was just as big as the first—maybe even bigger. From far above my head it began to fall, losing its shape, like a brick wall slowly crumbling. It was so huge that it no longer looked like a real wave. It was like something from another, far-off world, that just happened to assume the shape of a wave. I readied myself for the moment the darkness would take me. I didn't even close my eyes. I remember hearing my heart pound with incredible clarity.

37   The moment the wave came before me, however, it stopped. All at once it seemed to run out of energy, to lose its forward motion and simply hover there, in space, crumbling in stillness. And in its crest, inside its cruel, transparent tongue, what I saw was K.

38   Some of you may find this impossible to believe, and if so, I don't blame you. I myself have trouble accepting it even now. I can't explain what I saw any better than you can, but I know it was no illusion, no hallucination. I am telling you as honestly as I can what happened at that moment—what really happened. In the tip of the wave, as if enclosed in some kind of transparent capsule, floated K.'s body, reclining on its side. But that is not all. K. was looking straight at me, smiling. There, right in front of me, so close that I could have reached out and touched him, was my friend, my friend K. who, only moments before, had been swallowed by the wave. And he was smiling at me. Not with an ordinary smile—it was a big, wide-open grin that literally stretched from ear to ear. His cold, frozen eyes were locked on mine. He was no longer the K. I knew. And his right arm was stretched out in my direction, as if he were trying to grab my hand and pull me into that other world where he was now. A little closer, and his hand would have caught mine. But, having missed, K. then smiled at me one more time, his grin wider than ever.

39   I seem to have lost consciousness at that point. The next thing I knew, I was in bed in my father's clinic. As soon as I awoke the

entranced
(ĕn-trănsd´) *adj.* filled with wonder and delight.

AGAIN AND AGAIN

Notice & Note: In paragraphs 36–38, mark ways in which the description of the second huge wave differs from previous descriptions of waves in the story.

Synthesize: How does this description of the second huge wave elaborate on the story's motif of waves?

The Seventh Man   183

AGAIN AND AGAIN

Ask students to describe how the narrator explains his vision of the second wave. Does he think it was illusion or hallucination? *(He thinks it really happened.)* Explain to students that noticing images that occur Again and Again in a text can help them pinpoint important **motifs** (repeated symbols) within a text. Tell students that the wave is a motif of this short story. The narrator describes two waves coming ashore. The first wave overcomes K. on the beach. As the second wave strikes, the narrator sees an image of K. inside the wave. Discuss how this new information adds to or changes the wave motif of the story. (**Answer:** *The motif of the wave as a threatening force is reinforced by the terrifying image of K. in the wave.*)

■ English Learner Support

Use Cognates Tell students that *illusion* and *hallucination* (paragraph 38) have Spanish cognates: *ilusión* and *alucinación*. **ALL LEVELS**

For **listening support** for students at varying proficiency levels, see the **Text X-Ray** on page 174C.

CRITICAL VOCABULARY

entranced: The narrator says he "stood rooted to the sea wall, entranced, waiting for [the wave] to attack."

ASK STUDENTS to explain why the narrator felt entranced. What would a synonym be for the word *entranced*? *(The narrator felt entranced because he felt filled with wonder or fear at the power of the wave and could not move. A synonym might be "paralyzed" or "mesmerized.")*

nurse went to call my father, who came running. He took my pulse, studied my pupils, and put his hand on my forehead. I tried to move my arm, but couldn't lift it. I was burning with fever, and my mind was clouded. I had been wrestling with a high fever for some time, apparently. "You've been asleep for three days," my father said to me. A neighbor who had seen the whole thing had picked me up and carried me home. They had not been able to find K. I wanted to say something to my father. I had to say something to him. But my numb and swollen tongue could not form words. I felt as if some kind of creature had taken up residence in my mouth. My father asked me to tell him my name, but before I could remember what it was, I lost consciousness again, sinking into darkness.

40   Altogether, I stayed in bed for a week on a liquid diet. I vomited several times, and had bouts of **delirium**. My father told me afterwards that I was so bad that he had been afraid that I might suffer permanent neurological[5] damage from the shock and high fever. One way or another, though, I managed to recover—physically, at least. But my life would never be the same again.

41   They never found K.'s body. They never found his dog, either. Usually when someone drowned in that area, the body would wash up a few days later on the shore of a small inlet to the east. K.'s body never did. The big waves probably carried it far out to sea—too far for it to reach the shore. It must have sunk to the ocean bottom to be

delirium
(dĭ-lîr´ē-əm) *n.* a state of mental confusion.

---

[5] **neurological** (noor-ə-lŏj´ĭ-kəl): having to do with the body's nervous system.

© Houghton Mifflin Harcourt Publishing Company • Image Credits: ©Caran Handy/Alamy

---

CRITICAL VOCABULARY

delirium: High fever or shock may cause delirium. Someone experiencing "bouts of delirium" suffers from periods of mental confusion, hallucinations, or incoherent speech.

ASK STUDENTS why the narrator fell ill and was delirious. *(The narrator experienced a traumatic shock, witnessing his friend get pulled out to sea by a giant wave. The shock causes him to lose consciousness and become sick.)*

 ENGLISH LEARNER SUPPORT

Reinforce Meaning Ask a volunteer to read the footnote for the word *neurological*. Point out that the word's Spanish cognate is *neurológico*. Ask: What could have caused neurological damage in the narrator? *(shock and fever)* **MODERATE**

eaten by the fish. The search went on for a very long time, thanks to the cooperation of the local fishermen, but eventually it petered out[6]. Without a body, there was never any funeral. Half crazed, K.'s parents would wander up and down the beach every day, or they would shut themselves up at home, chanting sutras[7].

42   As great a blow as this had been for them, though, K.'s parents never chided me for having taken their son down to the shore in the midst of a typhoon. They knew how I had always loved and protected K. as if he had been my own little brother. My parents, too, made a point of never mentioning the incident in my presence. But I knew the truth. I knew that I could have saved K. if I had tried. I probably could have run over and dragged him out of the reach of the wave. It would have been close, but as I went over the timing of the events in my memory, it always seemed to me that I could have made it. As I said before, though, overcome with fear, I abandoned him there and saved only myself. It pained me all the more that K.'s parents failed to blame me and that everyone else was so careful never to say anything to me about what had happened. It took me a long time to recover from the emotional shock. I stayed away from school for weeks. I hardly ate a thing, and spent each day in bed, staring at the ceiling.

43   K. was always there, lying in the wave tip, grinning at me, his hand outstretched, beckoning. I couldn't get that picture out of my mind. And when I managed to sleep, it was there in my dreams—

---

[6] **peter out:** gradually come to an end.
[7] **sutras** (soo´trəs)**:** short Buddhist texts.

TEACH

ANALYZE SYMBOL AND THEME

Ask a volunteer to read aloud the first dream the narrator describes that features K. (paragraph 43). Have another volunteer read aloud the second dream (paragraph 44). Point out that many people believe that in our dreams, our unconscious minds communicate through images and symbols. (**Answer:** *The symbolism of the dream reflects how the narrator's peaceful, carefree childhood is destroyed when he witnesses K.'s death. The narrator feels the burden of the memory and his guilt that he could not save K.*)

CRITICAL VOCABULARY

sociable: The narrator says he is not overly sociable, or friendly, but he does have a few friends.

ASK STUDENTS to describe the qualities of a sociable person. *(Someone who is sociable is friendly, outgoing, not shy; likes to make new friends.)*

premonition: A premonition, like a hunch, is a feeling about something that may happen in the future.

ASK STUDENTS what the narrator's premonition is about. *(The narrator has a premonition that he will drown.)*

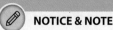

ANALYZE SYMBOL AND THEME

Annotate: In paragraph 44, mark phrases from the narrator's dream that seem to contain symbols.

Interpret: How would you interpret the symbolism in the narrator's dream?

except that, in my dreams, K. would hop out of his capsule in the wave and grab my wrist to drag me back inside with him.

44 And then there was another dream I had. I'm swimming in the ocean. It's a beautiful summer afternoon, and I'm doing an easy breaststroke far from shore. The sun is beating down on my back, and the water feels good. Then, all of a sudden, someone grabs my right leg. I feel an ice-cold grip on my ankle. It's strong, too strong to shake off. I'm being dragged down under the surface. I see K.'s face there. He has the same huge grin, split from ear to ear, his eyes locked on mine. I try to scream, but my voice will not come. I swallow water, and my lungs start to fill.

45 I wake up in the darkness, screaming, breathless, drenched in sweat.

46 At the end of the year I pleaded with my parents to let me move to another town. I couldn't go on living in sight of the beach where K. had been swept away, and my nightmares wouldn't stop. If I didn't get out of there, I'd go crazy. My parents understood and made arrangements for me to live elsewhere. I moved to Nagano Province in January to live with my father's family in a mountain village near Komoro. I finished elementary school in Nagano and stayed on through junior and senior high school there. I never went home, even for holidays. My parents came to visit me now and then.

47 I live in Nagano to this day. I graduated from a college of engineering in the City of Nagano and went to work for a precision toolmaker in the area. I still work for them. I live like anybody else. As you can see, there's nothing unusual about me. I'm not very **sociable**, but I have a few friends I go mountain climbing with. Once I got away from my hometown, I stopped having nightmares all the time. They remained a part of my life, though. They would come to me now and then, like debt collectors at the door. It happened when I was on the verge of forgetting. And it was always the same dream, down to the smallest detail. I would wake up screaming, my sheets soaked with sweat.

sociable
(sō´shə-bəl) *adj.* able to enjoy the company of others.

48 That is probably why I never married. I didn't want to wake someone sleeping next to me with my screams in the middle of the night. I've been in love with several women over the years, but I never spent a night with any of them. The terror was in my bones. It was something I could never share with another person.

49 I stayed away from my hometown for over forty years. I never went near that seashore—or any other. I was afraid that if I did, my dream might happen in reality. I had always enjoyed swimming, but after that day I never even went to swim in a pool. I wouldn't go near deep rivers or lakes. I avoided boats and wouldn't take a plane to go abroad. Despite all these precautions, I couldn't get rid of the image of myself drowning. Like K.'s cold hand, this dark **premonition** caught hold of my mind and refused to let go.

premonition
(prĕm-ə-nĭsh´ən) *n.* an unproven feeling that something specific will happen.

50 Then, last spring, I finally revisited the beach where K. had been taken by the wave.

WHEN STUDENTS STRUGGLE . . .

Analyze Plot Structure Have students work with a partner to sequence plot events in a graphic organizer. Draw students' attention to paragraph 47, in which the narrator begins to talk about his life in the present day and what has happened over the decades since he saw his friend swept away by the wave. Discuss why the narrator moved away from his hometown after the accident and why this event is important to the plot as a whole. *(He was having horrible nightmares about K.'s death. The fact that the narrator had to move away from his hometown and his parents shows how traumatic the event was.)*

  For additional support, go to the **Reading Studio** and assign the following **Level Up Tutorial: Plot: Sequence of Events.**

51   My father had died of cancer the year before, and my brother had sold the old house. In going through the storage shed, he had found a cardboard carton crammed with childhood things of mine, which he sent to me in Nagano. Most of it was useless junk, but there was one bundle of pictures that K. had painted and given to me. My parents had probably put them away for me as a keepsake of K., but the pictures did nothing but reawaken the old terror. They made me feel as if K.'s spirit would spring back to life from them, and so I quickly returned them to their paper wrapping, intending to throw them away. I couldn't make myself do it, though. After several days of indecision, I opened the bundle again and forced myself to take a long, hard look at K.'s watercolors.

52   Most of them were landscapes, pictures of the familiar stretch of ocean and sand beach and pine woods and the town, and all done with that special clarity and coloration I knew so well from K.'s hand. They were still amazingly vivid despite the years, and had been executed with even greater skill than I recalled. As I leafed through the bundle, I found myself steeped in warm memories. The deep feelings of the boy K. were there in his pictures—the way his eyes were opened on the world. The things we did together, the places we went together began to come back to me with great intensity. And I realized that his eyes were my eyes, that I myself had looked upon the world back then with the same lively, unclouded vision as the boy who had walked by my side.

53   I made a habit after that of studying one of K.'s pictures at my desk each day when I got home from work. I could sit there for hours with one painting. In each I found another of those soft landscapes of childhood that I had shut out of my memory for so long. I had a sense, whenever I looked at one of K.'s works, that something was permeating my very flesh.

54   Perhaps a week had gone by like this when the thought suddenly struck me one evening: I might have been making a terrible mistake all those years. As he lay there in the tip of the wave, surely K. had not been looking at me with hatred or resentment; he had not been trying to take me away with him. And that terrible grin he had fixed me with: that, too, could have been an accident of angle or light and shadow, not a conscious act on K.'s part. He had probably already lost consciousness, or perhaps he had been giving me a gentle smile of eternal parting. The intense look of hatred I thought I saw on his face had been nothing but a reflection of the profound terror that had taken control of me for the moment.

55   The more I studied K.'s watercolor that evening, the greater the conviction with which I began to believe these new thoughts of mine. For no matter how long I continued to look at the picture, I could find nothing in it but a boy's gentle, innocent spirit.

ANALYZE SYMBOL AND THEME

Annotate: Mark details in paragraphs 52 and 53 that show the narrator's emotional response to K.'s paintings.

Analyze: What might the paintings symbolize to the narrator?

permeate
(pûr´mē-āt) *v.* to spread through an area.

✏️ **ANALYZE SYMBOL AND THEME**

Point out to students that decades have passed since the disaster occurred and the narrator moved away from his hometown, but the narrator is still paralyzed by his fear and guilt over K.'s death. Ask: Why do you think the man hesitates to open the bundle of pictures? *(He is afraid of being reminded of the terror of K.'s death.)* Ask students to describe the narrator's feelings as he finally looks at K.'s artwork. *(warm, happy, full of life)* Discuss what the paintings might symbolize to the man at this point in his life. (**Answer:** *The paintings may symbolize his carefree, innocent childhood and his friendship with K.*) Ask: How might this symbol be important to the theme of the short story? *(Once the narrator is able to think about the past in a positive way, he can get over his fear.)*

WHEN STUDENTS STRUGGLE . . .

Analyze Plot Structure   Remind students of the difficulty the narrator had in revisiting K.'s artwork. Discuss how the artwork helps the narrator change. *(He remembers his childhood friendship with K. in a positive light and then has a sudden realization about his vision of K. in the wave.)* Then have partners work together to identify the narrator's "terrible mistake" and tell what he now understands that he didn't before. *(The narrator misinterpreted the boy's grin, and he now understands that his friend was saying goodbye.)* Ask students to explain why this realization is important to the plot as a whole. *(The narrator decides to return to his hometown to visit the beach where K. died.)*

CRITICAL VOCABULARY

permeate: The narrator describes a feeling that something is permeating, or spreading through, his body as he looks at K.'s artwork.

ASK STUDENTS to describe a feeling that permeates through them as they look at something that was important to them as children. *(A feeling of happiness permeates through me as I look at an old toy that I used to love.)*

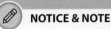
56   I went on sitting at my desk for a very long time. There was nothing else I could do. The sun went down, and the pale darkness of evening began to envelop the room. Then came the deep silence of night, which seemed to go on forever. At last, the scales tipped, and dark gave way to dawn. The new day's sun tinged the sky with pink.

57   It was then I knew I must go back.

58   I threw a few things in a bag, called the company to say I would not be in, and boarded a train for my old hometown.

59   I did not find the same quiet, little seaside town that I remembered. An industrial city had sprung up nearby during the rapid development of the Sixties, bringing great changes to the landscape. The one little gift shop by the station had grown into a mall, and the town's only movie theater had been turned into a supermarket. My house was no longer there. It had been demolished some months before, leaving only a scrape on the earth. The trees in the yard had all been cut down, and patches of weeds dotted the black stretch of ground. K.'s old house had disappeared as well, having been replaced by a concrete parking lot full of commuters' cars and vans. Not that I was overcome by **sentiment.** The town had ceased to be mine long before.

sentiment
(sĕn′tə-mənt) *n.* the emotion behind something.

CRITICAL VOCABULARY

sentiment: The change in his hometown does not cause the narrator to feel any strong emotion, or sentiment.

ASK STUDENTS to discuss whether or not they are surprised that the narrator shows little emotion in response to the changes in his hometown. *(It's not surprising that the narrator doesn't feel that much emotional connection to the town because he moved away so long ago.)*

WHEN STUDENTS STRUGGLE...

Identify Figurative Language   Have students work in small groups to review and share their charts tracking figurative language—including simile, metaphor, and personification—throughout the story. Ask students to discuss with their groups how the figurative language helps them understand the symbols of the storm and the wave/water throughout the text.

   For additional support, go to the **Reading Studio** and assign the following 🔲 **Level Up Tutorial: Figurative Language.**

60   I walked down to the shore and climbed the steps of the breakwater. On the other side, as always, the ocean stretched off into the distance, unobstructed, huge, the horizon a single straight line. The shoreline, too, looked the same as it had before: the long beach, the lapping waves, people strolling at the water's edge. The time was after four o'clock, and the soft sun of late afternoon embraced everything below as it began its long, almost meditative descent to the west. I lowered my bag to the sand and sat down next to it in silent appreciation of the gentle seascape. Looking at this scene, it was impossible to imagine that a great typhoon had once raged here, that a massive wave had swallowed my best friend in all the world. There was almost no one left now, surely, who remembered those terrible events. It began to seem as if the whole thing were an illusion that I had dreamed up in vivid detail.

61   And then I realized that the deep darkness inside me had vanished. Suddenly. As suddenly as it had come. I raised myself from the sand, and, without bothering to take off my shoes or roll up my cuffs, walked into the surf and let the waves lap at my ankles.

The Seventh Man   189

WHEN STUDENTS STRUGGLE . . .

Analyze Plot Structure Have students continue their work with a partner to finish mapping out the plot events of the story in sequential order. Invite student pairs to share their completed graphic organizers with the class.

For additional support, go to the **Reading Studio** and assign the following **Level Up Tutorial: Plot: Sequence of Events.**

TEACH

 ANALYZE PLOT

Discuss with students the narrator's experience of revisiting the beach where K. died. Have students describe the mood and tone of this scene. *(peaceful, meditative, gentle)* Then ask students to paraphrase what the narrator tells the group of people listening to his story in the present (the frame). *(He says he is trying to restart his life and he is grateful that he is no longer living in fear.)* Discuss how the frame structure is an effective way of communicating the story's theme. (**Answer:** *Returning to the present amplifies the statements the man made before telling his story. By framing his story with present-day reflections, the author uses the story as an illustration of his theme of salvation, recovery, and reconciliation.)*

 ANALYZE SYMBOL AND THEME

Discuss how the symbol of the wave changes throughout the story. Ask: What does the wave symbolize at the beginning of the story, when it swallows K.? *(terrible power, fear, loss)* How does the narrator feel about the wave near the end of the story? *(He does not feel frightened of it any more.)* How is the narrator able to overcome his paralyzing fear and start to change his life? *(He looks at K.'s artwork and remembers their friendship; he revisits the scene of the accident.)* Discuss how the change in the symbolism helps students identify the theme of the story. (**Answer:** *A theme of the story is that it is more damaging to try to avoid our fears than to face them directly.)*

CRITICAL VOCABULARY

reconciliation: The narrator describes the gentle waves on the beach "fondly washing [his] feet," as if the waves are seeking a reconciliation, or the end of a conflict.

ASK STUDENTS to explain how the description of the waves seeking reconciliation is an example of figurative language. *(The waves are personified with human qualities.)*

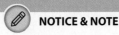 **NOTICE & NOTE**

reconciliation
(rĕk-ən-sĭl-ē-ā´shən) *n.* the act of coming to an agreement.

ANALYZE PLOT

Annotate: Mark the shift back to the present day that occurs in paragraph 64.

Interpret: How does returning to the present add meaning to the man's story? Complete a plot diagram or time line of the story's events.

ANALYZE SYMBOL AND THEME

Annotate: Mark the details in paragraphs 64–66 that reveal what the narrator has learned from his experience.

Synthesize: Based on these and other details, what do you think is the theme of "The Seventh Man"?

---

62   Almost in **reconciliation,** it seemed, the same waves that had washed up on the beach when I was a boy were now fondly washing my feet, soaking black my shoes and pant cuffs. There would be one slow-moving wave, then a long pause, and then another wave would come and go. The people passing by gave me odd looks, but I didn't care.

63   I looked up at the sky. A few grey cotton chunks of cloud hung there, motionless. They seemed to be there for me, though I'm not sure why I felt that way. I remembered having looked up at the sky like this in search of the "eye" of the typhoon. And then, inside me, the axis[8] of time gave one great heave. Forty long years collapsed like a dilapidated house, mixing old time and new time together in a single swirling mass. All sounds faded, and the light around me shuddered. I lost my balance and fell into the waves. My heart throbbed at the back of my throat, and my arms and legs lost all sensation. I lay that way for a long time, face in the water, unable to stand. But I was not afraid. No, not at all. There was no longer anything for me to fear. Those days were gone.

64   I stopped having my terrible nightmares. I no longer wake up screaming in the middle of the night. And I am trying now to start life over again. No, I know it's probably too late to start again. I may not have much time left to live. But even if it comes too late, I am grateful that, in the end, I was able to attain a kind of salvation, to effect some sort of recovery. Yes, grateful: I could have come to the end of my life unsaved, still screaming in the dark, afraid.

65   The seventh man fell silent and turned his gaze upon each of the others. No one spoke or moved or even seemed to breathe. All were waiting for the rest of his story. Outside, the wind had fallen, and nothing stirred. The seventh man brought his hand to his collar once again, as if in search for words.

66   "They tell us that the only thing we have to fear is fear itself; but I don't believe that," he said. Then, a moment later, he added: "Oh, the fear is there, all right. It comes to us in many different forms, at different times, and overwhelms us. But the most frightening thing we can do at such times is to turn our backs on it, to close our eyes. For then we take the most precious thing inside us and surrender it to something else. In my case, that something was the wave."

---

[8] **axis** (ăk´sĭs): a line around which other things rotate.

TO CHALLENGE STUDENTS . . .

Present a Movie Proposal Ask students to think about how this story might translate onto a big screen. Have students work in small groups to write and present a proposal, or "pitch," for a blockbuster movie based on the story. Each proposal should include a plot summary, suggestions for a musical score and special effects, ideas about a director, descriptions of actors who might be cast in various roles, ideas about locations, and a proposed budget. Explain that the goal of the pitch is to persuade others to fund the project.

CHECK YOUR UNDERSTANDING

Answer these questions before moving on to the **Analyze the Text** section on the following page.

1 The story's narrator is haunted by —

  A his overwhelming fear of violent storms

  B his sorrow over the loss of his childhood home

  C his guilt over failing to save K. from the wave

  D his jealousy of his friend's artistic talent

2 What does the narrator do after the storm has passed?

  F He finds and promotes K.'s accomplished artwork.

  G He moves to another town and does not return for many years.

  H He walks the seawall attempting to find K. and his dog.

  J He runs back to the house to tell his family what has happened.

3 The narrator decides to go back to his hometown after he —

  A learns that his father is dying from cancer

  B finishes his engineering studies in another city

  C recognizes that his nightmares have kept him from getting married

  D receives a collection of K.'s paintings and looks at them

The Seventh Man   191

CHECK YOUR UNDERSTANDING

Have students answer the questions independently.

Answers:

  1. *C*

  2. *G*

  3. *D*

If they answer any questions incorrectly, have them reread the text to confirm their understanding. Then they may proceed to ANALYZE THE TEXT on page 192.

 ENGLISH LEARNER SUPPORT

Oral Assessment Use the following questions to assess students' comprehension and speaking skills.

  1. What can't the story's narrator forget? *(his guilt over not having saved K. from the wave)*

  2. What does the narrator do after the storm? *(He moves to another town.)*

  3. What event makes the narrator return? *(He looks at a collection of K.'s paintings.)*

  SUBSTANTIAL/MODERATE

APPLY

ANALYZE THE TEXT

Possible answers:

1. **DOK 4:** *The frame story provides a setting that holds readers' attention, making them wonder about the narrator's past. If the story were strictly chronological, readers would have to wait longer to put the story in perspective.*

2. **DOK 2:** *At the end of the story, the narrator describes the wave as something that represents fear for him. In paragraph 9, he is telling the rest of the group that each of them has something that represents fear in the same way the wave did for him.*

3. **DOK 2:** *The huge wave that swallowed K. may symbolize change, loss, the end of childhood, or uncontrollable fear. Students should cite evidence from the text that describes the wave as a frightening, threatening animal that "swallowed" up K. and destroyed the narrator's innocence, changing his life forever.*

4. **DOK 4:** *As an adult, the seventh man believes that it's more frightening to run away from your fears. He first "turned his back" on K. to save himself and ran from the huge wave, with devastating consequences. Throughout most of his life, the man ran from his fear—leaving his hometown, avoiding water, deciding not to marry. Only when he returns to the village of his youth and faces the sea again is he able to let go of his fear and try to restart his life.*

5. **DOK 4:** *The seventh man say that if you do not face whatever frightens you, you "take the most precious thing inside [you] and surrender it" to that fear. This advice reflects the story's theme about the power of unresolved fear.*

RESEARCH

Remind students to conduct research on credible websites. Guide them to search scholarly articles by following links to web addresses ending in *.edu*. They also may try organizations devoted to historical topics—for example, by looking for links ending in *.org*. Newspapers and government websites (*.gov*) may have primary sources.

Extend Students' social media posts should share an appropriate storm-related fact and include an image.

 RESPOND

ANALYZE THE TEXT

Support your responses with evidence from the text. **NOTEBOOK**

1. **Evaluate** Why is the frame story structure an effective way to tell this story? What effect would using a strictly chronological order of events have on the story?

2. **Interpret** In paragraph 9, the narrator says, "In my case, it was a wave," . . . "There's no way for me to tell, of course, what it will be for each of you. . . ." What does he mean by this?

3. **Infer** What might the huge wave symbolize? Support your response with evidence from the story and your own experience.

4. **Analyze** In the last paragraph, the narrator says he disagrees with the saying that "the only thing we have to fear is fear itself." How does the author develop this message about fear?

5. **Notice & Note** What advice does the narrator pass down to his listeners? How do these Words of the Wiser reflect the story's theme?

RESEARCH TIP

When looking online for the answer to a question, you can always type the question directly into the search engine. To save time, you can leave out the unimportant words from your question. For example, "major typhoons history" will give you almost the same results as searching for "What were the major typhoons throughout history?"

RESEARCH

The narrator of the story experienced a typhoon as a child. Typhoons, cyclones, and hurricanes are all the same kind of storm; they are given different names depending on where on Earth they occur. Think of some questions about these storms that you would like to answer through online research. You might have questions about historically significant typhoons, the damage they can cause, how people prepare for them, or how people rebuild in the storm's aftermath.

Use multiple versions of the chart below to list your questions before you go online. Then, record the answers as you find them. Remember to keep track of your sources.

Question: *Do typhoons cause tsunamis?*	
Answer: *A tsunami is a series of giant waves usually caused by earthquakes or underwater volcanic eruptions. Sometimes tropical cyclones (typhoons) can cause tsunamis.*	**Source:** *Sources will vary.*

Extend Choose a social media platform. Write a post telling the most interesting fact you learned about typhoons, and choose a picture that you could attach to your post. Share your post and a picture with a small group.

192   Unit 3

⚙ LEARNING MINDSET

Try Again Tell students that sometimes they think they know the answer to a question but then find out they were incorrect. Remind students that it's OK (and expected) to make mistakes. It's how we learn. If students are having trouble with the Analyze the Text questions, encourage them to go back to the text and reread to clarify their understanding. Invite students to share their mistakes and how they learned from them. Remind students that the classroom is a "risk-free" zone where students can feel free to take risks and make mistakes.

RESPOND

CREATE AND DISCUSS

Write a Vignette A **vignette** is a short description, usually under one thousand words, that explores an idea or theme. Vignettes do not depend on short story elements such as plot events. Rather, they use words to create a snapshot of the unifying idea. Think about the theme you identified for "The Seventh Man." Write a vignette communicating your ideas about the theme. Use one or more symbols to talk about the theme.

❏ Think about how the theme relates to your experiences.

❏ What person, place, object, or activity from your own experience could stand as symbols of this theme?

❏ Use your ideas about theme and symbolism to write a vignette. Explore your thoughts or describe a scene in which you observe the symbol and ponder its importance. Share your vignette with a partner.

Discuss with a Small Group With some of your classmates, discuss the story's use of symbols and motifs, and work together to write a statement of theme that combines your perspectives.

❏ Come to the group discussion with notes about symbols and the development of theme in "The Seventh Man." Briefly explain your ideas when it's your turn. Listen actively and respond appropriately to other group members, and ask clarifying questions if you'd like more information about what they're thinking.

❏ There are several possibilities for the story's theme, and different group members might have picked up on different ones. See if you can find common ground to write a statement about the overall theme. The statement should include the theme and a few supporting examples.

❏ If your group can't come to a consensus, write separate statements and show how they are related.

 Go to the **Speaking and Listening Studio** for help with participating in a collaborative discussion.

RESPOND TO THE ESSENTIAL QUESTION

? What effect do we have on nature, and how does nature affect us?

Gather Information Review your annotations and notes on "The Seventh Man" and highlight those that help answer the Essential Question. Then, add relevant details to your Response Log.

At the end of the unit, use your notes to write an explanatory essay.

ACADEMIC VOCABULARY
As you write and discuss what you learned from the story, be sure to use the Academic Vocabulary words. Check off each of the words that you use.

❏ **advocate**

❏ **discrete**

❏ **domain**

❏ **evoke**

❏ **enhance**

The Seventh Man   193

APPLY

CREATE AND DISCUSS

Write a Vignette Guide students to follow the directions for writing shown in the list on page 193. Remind students that one theme, or message about life, of the selection is the importance of facing our fears so that they do not take over our lives. Have students brainstorm ideas for symbols in their own lives that represent fear in a similar way that the wave represents the seventh man's fear. Remind students that a vignette is a short, descriptive sketch. Tell students that their vignette should focus on describing their symbol, their own thoughts about it, and how they interact with it.

For **writing support** for students at varying proficiency levels, see the **Text X-Ray** on page 174D.

Discuss with a Small Group Remind students that different readers may find different themes in the same work of fiction. Encourage students to revisit their charts analyzing the story's symbols and motifs (such as wave/ sea, typhoon, soundlessness, K.'s paintings) to frame their discussion of possible themes of the story. Explain that some groups may agree on a single theme of the story, while other groups may decide to identify multiple themes.

RESPOND TO THE ESSENTIAL QUESTION

Allow time for students to add details from "The Seventh Man" to their Unit 3 Response Logs.

ENGLISH LEARNER SUPPORT

Discuss with a Small Group Restate the discussion prompt as a question: What do you think is the theme of this short story? Then have small groups, representing varied proficiencies, discuss the story's symbols and motifs, compare their charts, decide on a theme they can agree on, and write their statement about the theme with a few supporting details from the text. Provide these sentence frames to help students formulate ideas for the discussion: *An important symbol of the short story is ____. This symbol represents ____. One important theme of the short story is ____.* **MODERATE/LIGHT**

CRITICAL VOCABULARY

Possible answers:

1. *I could help a frail person having trouble at the grocery store by putting her groceries on the checkout counter. .*

2. *The starry night sky is one scene that has always entranced me.*

3. *I feel most sociable in situations where I'm with a small group of people I know well.*

4. *In my friend's yearbook, I would include the sentiment that she's important to me.*

5. *I could help two friends reach a reconciliation by asking them to explain their points of view about the argument they're having.*

6. *Signs of delirium could be that a person is confused about where he is and what day it is.*

7. *If a person had a premonition that something bad was going to happen, he might change his plans or be extra cautious.*

8. *I could open curtains and blinds during the day and add lamps for nighttime so the light would permeate the whole room.*

VOCABULARY STRATEGY:
Figurative Language

1. *The first example is a metaphor comparing the preparations for the typhoon to a circus. The second example is a simile comparing the beach to a large, empty room. The third example is personification, giving the wave the human characteristic of a "cruel . . . tongue."*

2. *The first example shows how, even though the storm is a serious matter for the adults, the change of routine is fun for the kids, who don't understand how destructive the storm could be. The image helps the reader visualize the scene and also helps explain how unprepared the narrator and K. are when the wave approaches. The second example helps the reader visualize what the narrator and K. are looking at—a huge, empty space stretching before them. They have no idea that the waves will come rushing back in. The third example suggests that the wave is a living thing capable of making the decision to kill K.*

3. *Students should locate and discuss three other examples of figurative language in the story.*

RESPOND

WORD BANK

frail	entranced
delirium	sociable
premonition	permeate
sentiment	reconciliation

CRITICAL VOCABULARY

Practice and Apply Answer each question using the Critical Vocabulary word in a complete sentence.

1. How could you help a **frail** person at the grocery store?

2. What is one scene that has **entranced** you?

3. During what situations do you feel the most **sociable**?

4. What kind of **sentiment** is appropriate when signing a friend's yearbook?

5. How could you help two friends reach a **reconciliation**?

6. What signs would tell you that a person was experiencing **delirium**?

7. How might a **premonition** affect someone's plans?

8. How could you change a room to make light **permeate** it?

VOCABULARY STRATEGY:
Figurative Language

By now, you are familiar with many types of **figurative language,** including similes, metaphors, and personification. If you read too quickly or the comparison the writer is making with figurative language is subtle, you may miss its impact. To get the most from figurative language in a text:

• Pause when you notice a clue word such as *like* or *as* or when you see a reference to something that doesn't seem to fit.
• Note what two things or ideas are being compared.
• Identify what they have in common to understand the writer's point.

Practice and Apply Working with a partner, locate the following examples of figurative language in the story. Then, follow the steps below:

> **. . . but to the kids, removed as we were from such practical concerns, <u>it was just a great big circus</u> . . .** (paragraph 12)

> **The whole, huge <u>space felt like a room without furniture</u> . . .** (paragraph 25)

> **And in its crest, <u>inside its cruel, transparent tongue,</u> what I saw was K.** (paragraph 37)

1. Is the figurative language an example of simile, metaphor, or personification? Form a mental image of the two things being compared. Determine what qualities of the two things are similar and different.

2. With your partner, discuss the effect of the figurative language. For example, does it help you visualize a scene or better understand the story's theme?

3. Find and discuss three other examples of figurative language in the story.

ENGLISH LEARNER SUPPORT

Analyze Figurative Language Provide students with additional practice in understanding figurative language. Stress that figurative language goes beyond the literal meanings of words. Draw students' attention to the metaphor that compares the storm to a circus (first example). Ask: Is there really a circus in town? (*No, the town just seems like a circus to the children because there is so much activity.*) Emphasize that the author makes the comparison between two unlike things (*a circus/a storm*) to show how excited the children in the story feel. Have pairs of students work together to read aloud the example sentences and identify figurative language.

MODERATE

LANGUAGE CONVENTIONS:
Complex Sentences

A **clause** is a group of words with a subject and a verb. A **complex sentence** combines an **independent clause**, which can stand by itself as a sentence, with one or more **dependent clauses**, which cannot. Dependent clauses add meaning to independent clauses by acting as modifiers. Dependent clauses often begin with words or phrases called subordinating conjunctions such as: *as if, as, since, than, that, though, until, whenever, where, while, because, who,* and *why*. Subordinating conjunctions clarify the connection between clauses. A comma follows a dependent clause when it begins the sentence.

Look at the following examples of complex sentences from "The Seventh Man." The bold parts represent dependent clauses that add information to the independent clause:

> **Whenever something unusual caught our attention,** we would pick it up and look at it every which way . . .

> I did not find the same quiet, little seaside town **that I remembered.**

Reread paragraph 13 of "The Seventh Man." Notice how the author uses a variety of sentences. There are short, simple sentences such as "There was something strange and unreal about it." The sentence right after it—"I stayed outside on the porch . . ."—is a complex sentence with multiple clauses. Sentence variety enhances the rhythm of a story's language and adds interest for the reader.

Practice and Apply Choose a paragraph from "The Seventh Man." How do the sentences vary? Are there simple, complex, and compound sentences within it? Try rewriting several of the sentences, keeping the meaning of the text but changing the sentences' complexity.

! Go to the **Grammar Studio** for more on complex sentences.

LANGUAGE CONVENTIONS:
Complex Sentences

Review the information about complex sentences with students. Make sure students understand the terms *independent clause* and *dependent clause*. Ask: Which of these expresses a complete thought? *(independent clause)* Emphasize that a dependent clause adds meaning to an independent clause by acting as a modifier.

Tell students that one way to identify a dependent clause is to look for subordinating conjunctions such as *after, as, as if, as though, because, since, so, than, that, though, until, when, whenever, where, wherever, while, who,* and *why*. The subordinating conjunction helps show how the independent clause and the dependent clause are related. Remind students that authors use complex sentences to connect ideas in the writing, as well as to vary the rhythm of their writing.

Practice and Apply Review the sentence types: simple, compound, and complex. Remind students that a **compound sentence** consists of two or more independent clauses joined with commas and coordinating conjunctions. Have student pairs compare their work to identify different sentence types and rewrite several sentences, changing the structure but not the overall meaning. *(Students' responses will vary depending on the paragraph chosen but should accurately identify and change sentence types.)*

 ENGLISH LEARNER SUPPORT

Use Varying Sentence Types Use the following supports with students at varying proficiency levels:

- Direct students to the first two sentences of paragraph 41. Note that these are simple sentences, but can be combined into a compound sentence using the coordinating conjunction *and*. Help them rewrite the sentences as a compound sentence using correct punctuation. Discuss reasons writers choose different types of sentences. **SUBSTANTIAL**

- Direct students to the first two sentences of paragraph 41. Ask them to rewrite the sentences as a compound sentence using the coordinating conjunction *and*. Discuss reasons writers choose different types of sentences. **MODERATE**

- Ask students to work in pairs to choose a paragraph from the text and read it aloud. Have students identify the sentence types within their paragraph. **LIGHT**

CARRY

Poem by **Linda Hogan**

GENRE ELEMENTS
FREE VERSE

Remind students that **free verse** is a type of poetry that does not contain regular patterns of rhythm or rhyme. Rather, the rhythm of free verse poetry is more like that of everyday speech. Likewise, poets writing free verse do not have to fit their words into a set structure. The poet's arrangement of words and phrases, use or omission of punctuation, and varying line length all work together to add to the poem's meaning. Like other kinds of poetry, free verse uses figurative language and sensory details to create meaning and express themes. Tell students that after they have read the poem, they will compare the short story "The Seventh Man" and the poem "Carry" to explore related themes.

LEARNING OBJECTIVES

- Analyze symbol and theme in free verse poetry.
- Conduct research on photographic evidence of unusual occurrences in nature.
- Write a free verse poem.
- Discuss images of water in the poem "Carry."
- **Language Objective** Use sensory words to discuss imagery.

TEXT COMPLEXITY

Quantitative Measures	Carry		Lexile: N/A
Qualitative Measures	**Ideas Presented** Multiple levels of meaning; use of symbolism.		
	Structures Used Complex; free verse.		
	Language Used Implied meanings; figurative language.		
	Knowledge Required More complexity in theme; experiences may be less familiar.		

Online Ed

RESOURCES

- Unit 3 Response Log
- Selection Audio
- Reading Studio: Notice & Note
- Level Up Tutorial: Imagery
- Speaking and Listening Studio: Participating in Collaborative Discussions
- "The Seventh Man" / "Carry" Selection Test

SUMMARIES

English

The speaker in this poem by Native American writer Linda Hogan describes pulling a live fish from a body of water; trailing the fish is the decayed body of a dead hawk. This unusual image begins the poet's reflection on the dual nature of water, as both life-giving and life-destroying. The poem creates a mood of reverence and awe for the beauty, power, and mystique of nature.

Spanish

El narrador de este poema de la escritora indígena americana Linda Hogan describe cómo es sacar a peces vivos del agua; encuentra en la corriente, detrás del pez, el cuerpo descompuesto de un halcón muerto. Con esta imagen inusual comienza la reflexión del poeta acerca de la naturaleza dual del agua, porque otorga vida, pero también la destruye. Este poema crea una atmósfera de reverencia y sobrecogimiento debido a la belleza, el poder y el misticismo de la naturaleza.

SMALL-GROUP OPTIONS

Have students work in small groups to read and discuss the selection.

Think-Pair-Share

- After reading "Carry," pose a question to the class—for example, "How does the poem communicate a message about nature and people's place within it?"
- Ask students to consider the question individually and to jot down a response.
- Have students meet with partners and collaborate on a shared response.
- Optional: Student pairs may consult other pairs to reach a new consensus.
- Call upon pairs or larger groups to share and compare their responses in a whole-class discussion.

Focus on Details

- After students have read "Carry" at least once, have them break into small groups.
- Assign each group a detail to focus on as they examine the poem: rhythm, sensory language, line breaks, figurative language, and repetition.
- Read the poem aloud to students and have them take notes on their assigned detail and the way in which it affects the poem as a whole.
- Afterward, allow students time to discuss their observations within the group and form a summary statement. Then have each group share its findings with the class.

Text X-Ray: English Learner Support
for "Carry"

Use the Text X-Ray and the supports and scaffolds in the Teacher's Edition to help guide students at different proficiency levels through the selection.

INTRODUCE THE SELECTION
DISCUSS POETRY

In this lesson, students will need to be able to discuss elements of **poetry.** Explain the following terms:

- **Free verse** is poetry that does not contain regular patterns of rhythm or rhyme.
- A **line** is the core unit of a poem. Point out that line breaks, or where a line ends, may have a period or comma. Other times, poets break the line in the middle of a phrase or sentence.
- **Repetition** is a technique in which a sound, word, phrase, or line is repeated. Repetition can help emphasize meaning and create rhythm.

Discuss other poems that students have read. Was the poem written in free verse, or did it have a regular pattern of rhythm or rhyme? What techniques did the poet use to emphasize ideas?

CULTURAL REFERENCES

Explain that the person who wrote this poem is Native American. Native Americans, or American Indians, are people who lived in the land now known as the United States before Europeans arrived. Many different groups of Native Americans live in the United States today, each with its own distinct culture and traditional beliefs.

The following words or phrases may be unfamiliar to students:

- *gasping* (line 4): struggling to breathe
- *element* (line 4): one of the four substances—earth, air, fire, and water—once thought to make up all things
- *hawk* (line 7): a bird that hunts other animals
- *talons* (line 8): the claws of a bird
- *scale* (line 10): one of many hard parts of a fish's skin

LISTENING

Identify Elements of Poetry

Have students listen to the poem. Draw students' attention to the natural, conversational rhythm of this free-verse poem. Review the terms *rhyme, speaker, images,* and *mood.*

Use the following supports with students at varying proficiency levels:

- Have students hold up a green card (for *yes*) or a red card (for *no*) in response to questions after they listen to the poem. Ask: Did you notice any rhyming words? *(no)* Did you notice any repeated words or phrases? *(yes)* **SUBSTANTIAL**
- Ask students to listen for the word *carry* in the poem. Have students point to where the word *carry* appears. *(the title and line 28)* Ask: What does *carry* mean? *(to take from one place to another)* **MODERATE**
- Ask students to identify the two speakers in the poem. Ask follow-up questions: Who pulled the fish from the water? *(the human speaker)* Who says, "I will carry you down to a world you never knew or dreamed"? *(the water)* **LIGHT**

SPEAKING

Discuss with a Small Group

Work with students to read the discussion activity on Student Edition page 203.

Use the following supports with students at varying proficiency levels:

- Tell students that poetry uses imagery, or descriptions that help the reader imagine how something looks, sounds, smells, tastes, or feels. Invite students to create drawings that illustrate sensory images and then describe the senses shown. **SUBSTANTIAL**

- Provide examples of imagery in the poem and then have students answer questions about the senses the images appeal to—for example: What do the words "broken mirror" describe? *(the water)* What does a broken mirror look like? *(has cracks but is shiny and smooth in parts)* What would happen if you touched a broken mirror? *(It could hurt you.)* **MODERATE**

- Invite partners to share their favorite image in the poem. Then have partners discuss these questions: How does this image make me feel? Which of the five senses does this image appeal to? **LIGHT**

READING

Understand Theme

Explain to students that theme in a work of literature is an idea about life that the author wants to share.

Write this possible theme on the board: *Water, like nature, is both life-giving and life-destroying*. Use the following supports with students at varying proficiency levels:

- Review the terms *life-giving* and *life-destroying*. Ask yes or no questions such as the following: Do people and animals need water to live? *(yes)* Can water also cause death? *(yes)* **SUBSTANTIAL**

- Have pairs of students use a chart to find evidence in the text that supports water as "life-giving" and evidence that supports water as "life-destroying." **MODERATE**

- Have partners work together to paraphrase lines 24–32 from the poem. Have students describe the tone of the "speaker," water. Ask: Does the voice of the water sound inviting? Threatening? Frightening? Peaceful? Loving? **LIGHT**

WRITING

Write a Free-Verse Poem

Work with students to read the writing assignment on Student Edition page 203.

Use the following supports with students at varying proficiency levels:

- Provide a web graphic organizer to help students begin to write sensory descriptions of their photograph. In the center have them place a copy of their photograph. In the surrounding five circles, have them write the five senses: sight, hearing, smell, taste, and touch. **SUBSTANTIAL**

- Have students complete one or several of the following sentence stems to help them create sensory descriptions: *My image looks like _____. My image sounds like _____. My image smells like _____. My image tastes like _____. My image feels like _____.* **MODERATE**

- Reteach the terms *metaphor, simile,* and *personification*. Invite students to use at least three examples of any of these types of figurative language in their poems. **LIGHT**

TEACH

Connect to the
ESSENTIAL QUESTION

The free-verse poem "Carry" by Native American poet Linda Hogan employs figurative language to create vivid, rich descriptions of nature and water. The poem explores the dual characteristics of water as both nurturing and destructive, as well as the relationship between humans and nature and our part within the cycle of life.

COMPARE THEMES

Have students take a few moments to reflect upon their reading of "The Seventh Man." Ask: What message about people's relationship with nature did the short story convey? *(Nature [a storm] can be a powerful, destructive force; nature can also help us heal and renew ourselves.)* Direct students to use the Compare Themes prompt to focus their reading of the poem and to prepare them to compare the themes of the two works.

POEM

CARRY

by **Linda Hogan**

pages 199–201

COMPARE THEMES

Now that you've read "The Seventh Man," read "Carry" and explore how this poem addresses a theme similar to that of the short story. As you read, ask yourself what ideas the author expresses about life or human nature and whether those ideas overlap with the ideas Haruki Murakami explores in "The Seventh Man." After you are finished, you will work on a final project that involves an analysis of both texts.

? ESSENTIAL QUESTION:

What effect do we have on nature, and how does nature affect us?

SHORT STORY

THE SEVENTH MAN

by **Haruki Murakami**

pages 177–191

Carry

QUICK START

Whether you live in a city, a rural area, or the suburbs, you have many opportunities to observe the natural world. Moments when you consider the night sky, a body of water, or windblown leaves might trigger thoughts about your place in the world. Talk with a partner about a time when you observed an aspect of the natural world. Describe what you noticed and what you thought about.

ANALYZE SYMBOL AND THEME

The **theme** of a work is the message about life that the writer wants to communicate. Because readers make inferences in order to determine a text's theme, a text may reveal different meanings to different readers. Your interpretation of theme will be valid if you base it closely on evidence from the text.

To determine a theme in "Carry," look for clues in the poem's images and descriptive details, and think about the writer's use of symbols. A **symbol** is a person, place, object, or activity that stands for something beyond itself.

As you read "Carry," pay attention to how the writer uses details to shape and refine particular themes. This chart can help guide your analysis:

GENRE ELEMENTS: POETRY

- uses figurative language, including personification
- includes poetic elements, such as rhythm and rhyme
- may or may not be structured in stanzas
- includes imagery that appeals to the senses
- expresses a theme, or message about life

TEXT EVIDENCE TO CONSIDER	EXAMPLES	ANALYSIS AND QUESTIONS
metaphors and similes that create strong images	"water's broken mirror"	This image is beautiful but also dark. Is water used as a symbol throughout the poem? If so, what might it represent?
descriptive details that create a mood or feeling	"like a silver coin stretched thin/ enough to feed us all"	This simile creates an image of water as a life-giving force. What broad idea does the water represent?
personification that conveys feelings or emotions	"and water is never lonely"	Here, human characteristics are associated with water. What does this add to water's symbolic meaning?
title	"Carry"	Carry can mean "to hold" or "to support." What or who is carrying something? What are they carrying?

QUICK START

As students discuss the Quick Start prompt, have them consider how their observations of nature made them feel as individuals in the world. What emotions did their observations evoke? For example, students may describe their emotional responses to nature as feelings of wonder, fear, or peace. Invite student pairs to share their observations of the natural world and their thoughts and feelings.

ANALYZE SYMBOL AND THEME

Explain to students that analyzing the poem's figurative language, images, symbols, and descriptive details will help them infer the poem's theme. Remind students that an **inference** is a logical conclusion that is based on clues in the text and on a reader's own experience. Their inferences about the theme of the poem should be based on evidence in the poem as well as their knowledge and experience.

Help students preview the chart so that they can look for elements of the poem as they read and think about their meanings and importance in the poem. Review the terms *metaphor, simile,* and *personification.* Remind students to look for symbols in the poem that may stand for something beyond themselves.

ENGLISH LEARNER SUPPORT

Understand Directionality Reinforce the directionality of English for native speakers of Arabic and other languages by reviewing how to read the Analyze Symbol and Theme chart. Explain that each column heading applies to the text in all the rows beneath it. To read the chart, students should begin at top left. The top row, left column introduces the first text evidence—metaphors and similes. After reading this description, students should track to the right to see where they should write examples of metaphors and similes in the text. Point out the final column: Analysis and Questions. Tell students that they should write their thoughts and questions about the poem's metaphors and similes here. Guide students through the remaining rows of the chart, explaining the text evidence in each row. Tell them the final row of the chart, "title," refers to the poem's title, "Carry." **SUBSTANTIAL/MODERATE**

APPLY

ANALYZE FREE VERSE

Reinforce that free verse does not follow regular patterns of rhythm or rhyme. The poet is "free" to structure the poem in a way that achieves a rhythm more like that of everyday speech. Have students quickly scan the poem and ask them if the lines are about the same length. *(No; the line lengths vary.)* Does each line end with a period or comma? *(No; sentences may stretch over multiple lines, with no punctuation at the end of some lines.)* Read aloud the first four lines of the poem, pausing briefly at the end of the first line to let the image of the broken mirror sink in. Model how to pause appropriately when you reach a comma or a period.

ANNOTATION MODEL

Remind students that they may underline, circle, or otherwise mark details from the text that indicate figurative language, symbols, and theme as well as characteristics of free verse, including rhythm, syntax (the arrangement of words and phrases), and line length. Point out that they may want to color-code their annotations by using highlighters. Have them use the margins for questions and comments about the poem.

 GET READY

ANALYZE FREE VERSE

"Carry" is written in a poetic style known as **free verse**. Free verse poetry is characterized by:

- rhythm that is similar to spoken language
- a flow that creates a particular tone
- unconventional structure which gives freedom to enhance meaning through word placement and varying line lengths

When reading a free verse poem, pause only when you would normally pause while speaking, such as when you reach a punctuation mark. Since poets writing free verse do not have to fit their words into a set structure, they are free to add to the poem's meaning through syntax—the arrangement of words and phrases—and different line lengths.

You may have read poems about nature written long ago and noticed that they fit into specific poem structures, such as sonnets. Though structured poetry was very prevalent in the 19th century and earlier, modern nature poetry is often in free verse form.

ANNOTATION MODEL

NOTICE & NOTE

Here is how a student might annotate to analyze the elements of free verse in the poem's first lines:

> From water's broken mirror
> we pulled it,
> alive and shining,
> gasping the painful other element of air.
> It was not just fish.
> There was more.

The first four lines make up one sentence. I can read it as if I am speaking. Different parts of the sentence are on different lines to emphasize the different ideas—the setting, the speaker's action, a description, and what the fish is doing.

BACKGROUND

Linda Hogan (b. 1947) grew up in Oklahoma and Colorado. A member of the Chickasaw Nation, Hogan has received many awards and honors for her writing. She is a strong advocate for preserving endangered species, and her work reflects her deep interest in environmental issues, native cultures, and spirituality. Hogan says of her writing, "It takes perseverance. I will do it over and over again until I get it right." Her poetry collections include The Book of Medicines and Rounding the Human Corners. Her first novel, Mean Spirit, was a finalist for the Pulitzer Prize.

CARRY
Poem by Linda Hogan

PREPARE TO COMPARE

Both "The Seventh Man" and "Carry" feature water as an irresistible natural force. As you read "Carry," think about how the poet's exploration of water and its strength echoes details from the short story. How do the speaker of the poem and the narrator of the story feel about water? How are their feelings similar?

(B) ©Miguel Lasa/Steve Bloom Images/Alamy

From water's broken mirror
we pulled it,
alive and shining,
gasping the painful other element of air.
5 It was not just fish.
There was more.
It was hawk, once wild with
hunger, sharp talons
locked into the dying twist
10 and scale of fish,
its long bones
trailing like a ghost
behind fins
through the dark, cold water.

Notice & Note

You can use the side margins to notice and note signposts in the text.

Carry 199

ENGLISH LEARNER SUPPORT

Comprehend Language Structure Explain that a pronoun stands in for a nearby noun. Usually, the noun comes before the pronoun. Sometimes, however, the noun follows the pronoun—for example, "From water's broken mirror / we pulled it, / alive and shining, / gasping the painful other element of air. / It was not just fish." Have students discuss how they discovered that the pronoun *it* referred to a fish. *(At first, the reader is unsure what it refers to. The poem goes on to describe pulling something "alive" and "shining" and "gasping" from the water. At this point, students may infer that it is a fish.)* Have partners review the rest of the poem for pronouns, circle each pronoun, and underline the noun it replaces. **MODERATE/LIGHT**

BACKGROUND

Have students read the Background note. Tell students that Linda Hogan is an important Native American writer. Explain that Hogan did not intend to become a writer, but she began writing on her lunch break from her job. She eventually earned a degree in creative writing from the University of Colorado. In 2007, Hogan was recognized for her writing accomplishments by becoming part of the Chickasaw Nation Hall of Fame.

Hogan's poems, plays, and novels grow from her belief that Earth and all who live on it are sacred and closely connected. Her works address the need to protect Earth from damage caused by humans. Encourage students to look for expressions of Hogan's philosophy as they read the poem "Carry."

PREPARE TO COMPARE

Direct students to use the Prepare to Compare prompt to focus their reading.

ENGLISH LEARNER SUPPORT

Confirm Understanding Use the following supports with students at varying proficiency levels:

- Read aloud lines 1–14. Ask students if there are any words that are unfamiliar. Clarify the meanings of any unfamiliar words. Write the words on the board and draw lines to separate the syllables. Pronounce the words several times, with students repeating them after you. **SUBSTANTIAL**

- Have students look for language that helps them picture the water. *("water's broken mirror" [line 1], "dark, cold water" [line 14])* **MODERATE**

- Ask students to identify figurative language that describes the hawk. Then have students discuss what the hawk might symbolize. **LIGHT**

TEACH

ANALYZE FREE VERSE

Remind students that the unconventional structure of free verse allows the poet freedom to convey meaning through word placement and varying line lengths. Ask students to pay attention to the rhythm and flow of the words as you read aloud lines 15–23. (**Answer:** *These lines are one long sentence with many pauses, which makes it sound conversational.*)

ANALYZE SYMBOL AND THEME

Ask students to identify descriptions of water earlier in the poem and contrast them. (*"broken mirror," "dark, cold water," "beautiful . . . like a silver coin stretched thin," "smooth as skin," "rough hands," "never lonely."*) What is the effect of these contrasting descriptions? (*Water is contradictory—it gives life, but also takes it away.*)

Point out to students that beginning in line 24, water becomes the speaker of the poem. What does the water say to the reader? (*"come close," "Come near," "I will carry you," "I will gather you"*) What mood, or feeling or atmosphere, is conveyed through the personification? (**Answer:** *A mysterious mood is created. Personifying the water makes it seem as if it has a consciousness and a will. This emphasizes the water's power; it is a symbol for the immense power of nature, which can destroy, create, and transform at will, despite the wishes or needs of living things. Water can have a direct, personal effect on us.*)

For **listening and reading support** for students at varying proficiency levels, see the **Text X-Ray** on pages 196C–196D.

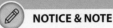 **NOTICE & NOTE**

ANALYZE FREE VERSE

Annotate: Mark the places where you would pause while reading aloud lines 15–23.

Analyze: How does the poet structure the lines in a way that keeps it close to "sounding" like natural speech?

ANALYZE SYMBOL AND THEME

Annotate: Mark an example of personification in lines 26–32.

Analyze: How does this personification develop the water as a symbol?

---

15 It was beautiful, that water,
  like a silver coin stretched thin
  enough to feed us all,
  smooth as skin before anyone knew
  the undertow's[1] rough hands
20 lived inside it, working everything down
  to its absence,
  and water is never lonely,
  it holds so many.
  It says, come close, you who want to swallow me;
25 already I am part of you.
  Come near. I will shape myself around you
  so soft, so calm
  I will carry you
  down to a world you never knew or dreamed,
30 I will gather you
  into the hands of something stronger,
  older, deeper.

---

[1] **undertow:** a strong current below the surface of water.

APPLYING ACADEMIC VOCABULARY

☑ **advocate** ☐ **discrete** ☑ **domain** ☐ **evoke** ☐ **enhance**

Write and Discuss Have students turn to a partner to discuss the following questions. Guide students to use the academic vocabulary words *advocate* and *domain* in their responses. Ask volunteers to share their responses with the class.

- In what ways does the poet **advocate** for nature in this poem?
- What message about life does this poem communicate concerning the **domain** of nature?

CHECK YOUR UNDERSTANDING

Answer these questions before moving on to the **Analyze the Text** section on the following page.

1 What does the speaker find?

  A A large fish swimming in the river

  B An undertow beneath the surface of the water

  C A friend who will provide solace

  D A hawk that has died catching its prey

2 The voice that speaks from line 24 to the poem's end is that of —

  F the fish

  G the hawk

  H the water

  J the poet

3 The speaker considers the water —

  A beautiful and peaceful

  B deceptive and powerful

  C rich and teeming with life

  D inspiring and mysterious

© Houghton Mifflin Harcourt Publishing Company

Carry **201**

CHECK YOUR UNDERSTANDING

Have students answer the questions independently.

Answers:

  1. *D*

  2. *H*

  3. *B*

If they answer any questions incorrectly, have them reread the text to confirm their understanding. Then they may proceed to ANALYZE THE TEXT on page 202.

(EL) ENGLISH LEARNER SUPPORT

Oral Assessment Use the following questions to assess students' comprehension and speaking skills.

  1. At the beginning of the poem, what does the speaker say they pulled from the water? *(a live fish and the bones of a hawk that tried to catch it)*

  2. Who is the speaker of the poem in lines 24–32? *(the water)*

  3. Which word pair better describes the water in the poem: "deceptive and powerful," or "beautiful and peaceful"? *("deceptive and powerful")* **MODERATE/LIGHT**

ANALYZE THE TEXT

Possible answers:

1. **DOK 2:** *A live fish is pulled from the water. A dead hawk is attached to the fish, and its body trails behind the fish as the fish is pulled from the water. The image in these lines creates a somber, contemplative mood in the poem.*

2. **DOK 4:** *Two of the sentences are long, with many clauses, and both give vivid descriptions of the setting and the narrator's discovery. The two shorter sentences ("It was not just a fish. There was more.") emphasize that something unexpected has happened—the narrator has found something strange besides the fish.*

3. **DOK 2:** *The water is not empty, and many things can be found beneath its surface—like the fish and the hawk. Line 20 also mentions "working everything down," which suggests that many things are under the water's surface.*

4. **DOK 2:** *Water acts as a symbol of nature—both nature's life-giving abundance and its ability to deal out death—throughout the poem.*

5. **DOK 3:** *All living things are part of nature. We are sustained by nature and ultimately ended by it. Nature provided the fish as life-sustaining food for the hawk, yet the fish ultimately led the hawk to its death.*

RESEARCH

Remind students that they are looking for *unaltered* images that show unusual or bizarre natural phenomena, animal encounters, or other surprising occurrences in nature. Guide students to use search terms such as "strange weather phenomenon" or "bizarre animals." Invite students to share their search terms. Remind students to use only reputable websites and select images with complete photo credits.

Extend Remind students that seeing is not always believing. Discuss the credibility of the pictures' sources. Reinforce that because of the prevalence of photo-editing tools, most of the photographic images we see today are enhanced in some way. Help student pairs examine their photos for signs of photo-editing. Look for differences in color, brightness, and focus throughout the image. Does one area of the photograph appear lower in quality than the rest?

RESPOND

ANALYZE THE TEXT

Support your responses with evidence from the text. NOTEBOOK

1. **Summarize** Review what is stated explicitly in lines 1–14 and write a brief summary of what the speaker describes. How does the image created in these lines affect the **mood**, or emotion, of the poem?

2. **Analyze** In lines 1–14, the author uses sentences of different lengths. How do these varied sentence lengths affect your reading of the poem?

3. **Interpret** Explain what is meant by lines 22–23: "and water is never lonely, / it holds so many." Support your interpretation with evidence from other lines.

4. **Interpret** Review the descriptions of water in the poem. What does the water symbolize?

5. **Cite Evidence** What theme about our connection with nature does this poem convey? Support your theme statement with evidence from the poem.

RESEARCH

In this poem, Hogan describes a bizarre natural image. Sometimes strange things happen in nature, and photographs of unusual occurrences get spread around social media. Of course, it is important to study the picture for signs that it is may not actually represent reality. Photo-editing programs enable people to alter images drastically.

Look online for photographs of surprising occurrences in nature. For instance, you might think about unusual animal encounters or the strange effects of severe weather. Record your findings in a chart like the one below.

RESEARCH TIP
To examine the credibility of a photo you find online, ask:

• Is it on a reputable website or on a site that anyone can post to?

• Is it credited to a photographer or photo agency?

• Does the photo appear to be altered digitally? Look for differences in focus and color, as well as awkward angles.

SOURCE OF IMAGE (URL)	BRIEF DESCRIPTION OF IMAGE	WHAT MAKES THE PICTURE UNUSUAL?
Sources will vary.	*Bhupathy's purple frog*	*This animal doesn't even look like a frog. The caption says it spends almost all its life underground in India.*
Sources will vary.	*lightning that strikes up*	*Most lightning strikes from the sky toward the ground; ground-to-sky lightning is very rare.*
Sources will vary.	*a preserved human body found in Denmark bog*	*The body looks remarkably well preserved—like a mummy—but the article says he lived more than 2,300 years ago.*

Extend Choose one of the pictures you found and share it with a partner. Talk about why you find the picture striking. Examine each other's photos for signs that it might be altered, and help each other find new images if necessary.

WHEN STUDENTS STRUGGLE . . .

Analyze Imagery Remind students that a poem's **imagery** often points to the poem's **theme.** Encourage them to ask these questions as they think about the imagery in "Carry":

• What do I picture when I read this?

• How are the images related to each other and the poem as a whole?

• What ideas do they express? What do I already know about these ideas?

 For additional support, go to the **Reading Studio** and assign the following Level Up Tutorial: Imagery.

CREATE AND DISCUSS

Write a Free-Verse Poem Write a free-verse poem about the photograph that you researched and shared with your partner.

❏ Write a description of the image. Assuming that your reader will not have access to the photograph, use sensory details in your description. Read through your description and decide how you would like to structure lines of poetry to communicate your ideas.

❏ In your poem, use figurative language such as metaphor, simile, and personification to help the reader connect to the photo.

❏ With a partner, practice reading your poem aloud. Explain the messages about nature that your poems contain.

Discuss with a Small Group In "Carry," descriptions of water are central to the poem's meaning. Discuss the choices the poet made in her use of water imagery.

 Go to the **Speaking and Listening Studio** for help with participating in a collaborative discussion.

❏ Form a small group of three or four students to analyze the descriptions of water throughout the poem.

❏ For each image of water in the poem, ask questions about what feelings or ideas the author wanted to convey. For example, why did the poet choose to use a "broken mirror" as an image?

❏ Consider how the images of water develop—from an inanimate object to a powerful living force—throughout the poem.

❏ The members of your group may have different ideas about the poem, but see if you can find common ground about your understanding of the poem. Set rules to ensure that everyone is able to contribute equally, if needed. Write a summary that includes the most important insights from the discussion.

RESPOND TO THE ESSENTIAL QUESTION

 What effect do we have on nature, and how does nature affect us?

Gather Information Review your annotations and notes on "Carry" and highlight those that help answer the Essential Question. Then, add relevant details to your Response Log.

At the end of the unit, use your notes to write an explanatory essay.

ACADEMIC VOCABULARY

As you write and discuss what you learned from the poem, be sure to use the Academic Vocabulary words. Check off each of the words that you use.

❏ advocate
❏ discrete
❏ domain
❏ evoke
❏ enhance

Carry   **203**

CREATE AND DISCUSS

Write a Free-Verse Poem Review the terms *sensory details, metaphor, simile,* and *personification* with students. Have students brainstorm figurative language describing their images until they have quite a few examples of each type to choose from as they write their poem.

Remind students that free verse does not follow a regular pattern of rhyme or rhythm. Students' free-verse poems should flow naturally, as does everyday speech. Have students imagine that they are describing the image they have chosen to a close friend, selecting the most effective descriptions and figurative language. As students write, have them consider the message about nature they want to convey.

 For **writing support** for students at varying proficiency levels, see the **Text X-Ray** on page 196D.

Discuss with a Small Group Encourage group members to share all insights about the poem in a respectful manner. Ask students to include insights that compare and contrast poems within the group so that every member's interpretations and thoughts are represented in each group's written summary.

For **speaking support** for students at varying proficiency levels, see the **Text X-Ray** on page 196D.

RESPOND TO THE ESSENTIAL QUESTION

Allow time for students to add details from "Carry" to their Unit 3 Response Logs.

 ENGLISH LEARNER SUPPORT

Discuss with a Small Group Allow students to work with a partner to reread the poem aloud and review the text for descriptions of water. Suggest that students sort descriptive words and phrases into two groups: one group of light, positive images related to water (for example, *"beautiful . . . like a silver coin"*) and one group of dark, negative images (*"down to a world you never knew or dreamed"*). Provide sentence frames to help students formulate questions for discussion: *The poet describes water as a "broken _____." The poet describes _____ as "dark" and "cold."* **SUBSTANTIAL/MODERATE**

RESPOND

COMPARE THEMES

Preview the chart with students. Stress that while both selections feature water, the authors' conclusions, themes, or messages about water may differ. As groups of students collaborate to complete the chart, encourage students to refer to their notes and, if they wish, to reread the short story or the poem.

ANALYZE THE TEXTS

Possible answers:

1. **DOK 3:** *The themes of the power, mystery, and vastness of nature appear in both texts. Murakami's narrator, however, spends most of the story haunted by the power of nature, as it caused the death of his friend, and makes peace with his fear only at the end of the story. On the other hand, the speaker in "Carry" shows respectful awe of this power, speaking in almost magical terms of an underwater world "you never knew or dreamed."*

2. **DOK 4:** *Hogan uses the hawk as a symbol of the unpredictability of nature. The hawk, a predator, should have killed the fish easily; instead, it ends up dead, "its long bones trailing like a ghost." As the speaker in the poem catches a fish (presumably to eat), she is reminded by the hawk of the death that awaits her, too. In "The Seventh Man," the narrator revisits his friend's watercolors, a symbol of the narrator's and K.'s carefree and innocent childhood. Reminded of the beauty of the natural world and his place in it, the narrator is able to push through his fear of water and reclaim his life.*

3. **DOK 4:** *Students will mention different mental images inspired by the texts—for example, the image of people fishing in a large, peaceful body of water and pulling a live fish and dead hawk from the water. Students may also recall visualizing the terrifying moment when K. appears, grimacing and beckoning from within the crest of the wave. These memorable images help readers relate to the texts personally, connect with the experiences of the characters, and encourage deeper appreciation and understanding of the themes of the works.*

4. **DOK 3:** *Murakami is a native of Japan, an island nation in the Pacific Ocean that depends on the ocean for much of its food but also experiences severe tropical storms and other natural disasters. These factors could have influenced Murakami to use a typhoon and a tsunami to explore the theme of the power of nature. Hogan is a member of the Chickasaw Nation and grew up in Oklahoma and Colorado. Native American culture emphasizes a respect and reverence for nature and its power, as well as a deep understanding of people's place within the natural order.*

Collaborate & Compare

THE SEVENTH MAN
Short Story
by Haruki Murakami

CARRY
Poem by Linda Hogan

COMPARE THEMES

Now that you have read "The Seventh Man" and "Carry," you can compare how the authors developed themes in their work. The short story and the poem explore a similar idea—the unstoppable power of water—even though the conclusions they draw about that idea are different. Analyzing how the authors built their themes will give you insight into each writer's craft.

Both authors rely on setting, events, the narrator's or speaker's thoughts, and word choice to develop the idea of water as a force that cannot be overcome. With a partner, review the texts. Use a chart like the one below to record your thoughts about the authors' use of narrative elements to develop a theme. Cite specific text evidence where you can. You will use the information from your chart to create a project about the themes in both texts.

	"THE SEVENTH MAN"	"CARRY"
Setting	*Responses will vary, but should include evidence from both selections as needed.*	
Key Events		
Narrator's or Speaker's Thoughts		
Use of Language		

ANALYZE THE TEXTS

Discuss these questions in your group.

1. **Compare** What themes did you discover in both "The Seventh Man" and "Carry"? How do the authors' attitudes toward those themes differ?

2. **Evaluate** Both authors use symbolism. Choose a symbol from each text and evaluate how the author uses it to enrich the text.

3. **Connect** How did creating mental images help you understand both texts? Cite examples from each text when explaining.

4. **Compare** Reread the biographies of Murakami and Hogan. How might their cultural backgrounds—Japanese and Native American, respectively—or geography have shaped their attitudes toward the topic of nature?

 ENGLISH LEARNER SUPPORT

Answer Questions Use the following questions to help students compare the selections.

1. What is a theme of "The Seventh Man"? What is a theme of "Carry"? Do the two selections share the same theme? If not, how are they different?

2. Identify a symbol in either "The Seventh Man" or "Carry." How does this symbol help you understand the selection?

3. Think about the images you imagined as you read the selections. What image stands out? Why is this image important to the selection? **MODERATE/LIGHT**

CREATE AND SHARE

Now, you will create a project showing your understanding of how Murakami and Hogan both use the topic of water to express themes about our world. Imagine the "seventh man"—the narrator of the short story—and the speaker in the poem as characters. They are both looking at powerful bodies of water. What messages about the world would they like to pass along to an audience as they gaze at the water? Create a two-sided piece of artwork expressing their messages.

1. **Plan Your Artwork** Create a two-sided piece of artwork using a medium you are comfortable with, such as drawing or creating a collage from images printed from a computer. Think about what each character would want to communicate about nature.

   My Ideas: _____

   _____

   _____

   _____

2. **Write Statements** What "universal truths" about nature and humanity would each character want to share with an audience? Write a statement for each character, in his or her own voice, and add it to your artwork.

   Statement 1: _____

   _____

   _____

   _____

   Statement 2: _____

   _____

   _____

   _____

3. **Present** Present your artwork to your group. Different group members may have different interpretations of the authors' themes. Consider how the topic of water—a major part of the natural world—allowed two writers working in different genres to express universal ideas about our world. Support your ideas with quotations from both texts as you present your artwork.

© Houghton Mifflin Harcourt Publishing Company

CREATE AND SHARE

Tell students that they will work independently to create artwork that visually expresses the themes of the two works "The Seventh Man" and "Carry." Have students imagine the narrator of "The Seventh Man" and the speaker of "Carry" standing on the shore of a body of water. Encourage students to freewrite about what both characters see, feel, and think as they stand at the water. What message about life, the world, or nature does each character want to communicate to us?

1. **Plan Your Artwork** Encourage students to choose a medium they feel comfortable with—for example, painting, drawing, cartooning, or collage-making. Emphasize that the images they present should represent the narrator's and speaker's feelings and perception of water. For example, the narrator of "The Seventh Man" fears the power of water. Ask: How can you visually represent the seventh man's feelings about the water? How can you show how he is able to overcome his fear?

2. **Write Statements** Guide students to think about what each character wants to express to the audience. How would each character express this message? Guide students to think about each character's unique voice as they write their statements. Encourage students to add their statements to their artwork in a creative way.

3. **Present** Have students present and share their artwork with their group. Remind students that different interpretations of theme are valid if they are well supported with evidence from the text. Encourage group members to ask questions about the presenter's artwork. For example, why did you choose a certain image? What specific quotations from the text support your interpretation?

TO CHALLENGE STUDENTS . . .

Explore Themes in Visual Art Challenge students to explore how nature is represented in Japanese and Native American visual art, including paintings, sculpture, woodblock prints, and so on. Have students research Japanese and Native American visual artists, either historical or contemporary. Some examples include Katsushika Hokusai, Hiroshi Yoshida, R. C. Gorman, and Shonto Begay. Have students collect a few examples of artwork that they feel make a strong statement about nature and/or people's relationship to nature. Then have students work in small groups to share the artwork they selected and discuss the following:

- What elements of nature appear in the artwork?
- What is the artist trying to say through the artwork?
- How does the artist's message compare to the message of either "The Seventh Man" or "Carry"?

INDEQPENDENT READING

READER'S CHOICE

Setting a Purpose Have students review their Unit 3 Response Log and think about what they've already learned about the effect we have on nature and it has on us. As they choose their Independent Reading selections, encourage them to consider what more they want to know.

NOTICE NOTE

Explain that some selections may contain multiple signposts; others may contain only one. The same type of signpost may occur many times in the same text.

 LEARNING MINDSET

Plan/Predict Tell students that planning is essential to completing work efficiently and exceptionally. Encourage students to create a plan for reading the self-selected texts outside of class, for example, mapping out the steps toward completing their reading. Consider having students create a chart to plan their work and track their progress.

 INDEPENDENT READING

 ESSENTIAL QUESTION:

What effect do we have on nature, and how does nature affect us?

Reader's Choice

Setting a Purpose Select one or more of these options from your eBook to continue your exploration of the Essential Question.

· Read the descriptions to see which text grabs your interest.

· Think about which genres you enjoy reading.

Notice Note

In this unit, you practiced noticing and noting three signposts: **Memory Moment, Contrasts and Contradictions,** and **Again and Again**. As you read independently, these signposts and others will aid your understanding. Below are the anchor questions to ask when you read literature and nonfiction.

Reading Literature: Stories, Poems, and Plays		
Signpost	**Anchor Question**	**Lesson**
Contrasts and Contradictions	Why did the character act that way?	p. 145
Aha Moment	How might this change things?	p. 394
Tough Questions	What does this make me wonder about?	p. 2
Words of the Wiser	What's the lesson for the character?	p. 3
Again and Again	Why might the author keep bringing this up?	p. 145
Memory Moment	Why is this memory important?	p. 3

Reading Nonfiction: Essays, Articles, and Arguments		
Signpost	**Anchor Question(s)**	**Lesson**
Big Questions	What surprised me? What did the author think I already knew? What challenged, changed, or confirmed what I already knew?	p. 220 p. 319 p. 74
Contrasts and Contradictions	What is the difference, and why does it matter?	p. 318
Extreme or Absolute Language	Why did the author use this language?	p. 221
Numbers and Stats	Why did the author use these numbers or amounts?	p. 75
Quoted Words	Why was this person quoted or cited, and what did this add?	p. 221
Word Gaps	Do I know this word from someplace else? Does it seem like technical talk for this topic? Do clues in the sentence help me understand the word?	p. 75

 ENGLISH LEARNER SUPPORT

Develop Fluency Select a passage from a text that matches students' reading abilities. Read the passage aloud while students follow along silently.

· Echo read the passage by reading aloud one sentence and having students repeat the sentence back to you. Then check their comprehension by asking yes/no questions. **SUBSTANTIAL**

· Have partners take turns quietly reading the passage aloud to each other. Set time limits that will allow each student the opportunity to be the reader and listener twice. Ask them to discuss what they noticed

while listening to each other read. Explain that making observations and giving feedback regarding their partner's reading habits will help them recognize their own. **MODERATE**

· Allow more fluent readers to select their own texts. Set a specific time for students to read silently. Check their comprehension by asking for a written or oral summary of the text. **LIGHT**

 Go to the **Reading Studio** for additional support in developing fluency.

You can preview these texts in Unit 3 of your eBook.

Then, check off the text or texts that you select to read on your own.

ARGUMENT

from **Hope for Animals and Their World**
Jane Goodall

The world's leading expert on chimpanzees explains why we should care about a little insect that has a big impact.

ESSAY

Sea Stars
Barbara Hurd

Consider the ability of the sea star to regenerate and the drama of its life from low to high tide, with truths that echo in human lives as well.

POEM

Starfish
Lorna Dee Cervantes

This poem explores the human fascination with starfish: their life cycle, beauty, and ocean habitat.

SHORT STORY

Wolves
José Luis Zárate

Nature both frightens us and draws us in, in this fantastic tale from Mexico.

Collaborate and Share   Discuss with a partner what you learned from at least one of your independent readings.

- Give a brief synopsis or summary of the text.
- Describe any signposts that you noticed in the text and explain what they revealed to you.
- Describe what you most enjoyed or found most challenging about the text. Give specific examples.
- Decide whether you would recommend the text to others. Why or why not?

Go to the **Reading Studio** for more resources on **Notice & Note.**

INDEPENDENT READING

MATCHING STUDENTS TO TEXTS

Use the following information to guide students in choosing their texts.

from **Hope for Animals and Their World**   Lexile: 1300L
   Genre: argument
   Overall Rating: Challenging

Sea Stars   Lexile: 1210L
   Genre: essay
   Overall Rating: Challenging

Starfish
   Genre: poem
   Overall Rating: Accessible

Wolves   Lexile: 740L
   Genre: short story
   Overall Rating: Accessible

Collaborate and Share   To assess how well students read the selections, walk around the room and listen to their conversations. Encourage students to be focused and specific in their comments.

Online
Ed   **for Assessment**

- Independent Reading Selection Tests

Encourage students to visit the **Reading Studio** to download a handy bookmark of **NOTICE & NOTE** signposts.

WHEN STUDENTS STRUGGLE . . .

Keep a Reading Log   As students read their selected texts, have them keep a reading log for each selection to note signposts and their thoughts about them. Use their logs to assess how well they are noticing and reflecting on elements of their texts.

Reading Log for (Title)		
Location	**Signpost I Noticed**	**My Notes About It**

UNIT ③ Tasks

- **WRITE AN EXPLANATORY ESSAY**
- **DELIVER A MULTIMEDIA PRESENTATION**

MENTOR TEXT

JOYAS VOLADORAS

Informative Essay by
BRIAN DOYLE

LEARNING OBJECTIVES

Writing Task

- Write an explanatory essay about an aspect of nature and people's relationship to it.
- Use strategies to plan, research, and organize ideas for an explanatory essay.
- Develop a focused, structured draft.
- Use the Mentor Text as a model for writing an engaging introduction and using a narrative structure to present information.
- Revise drafts, incorporating feedback from peers.
- Edit drafts to incorporate parallel structure.
- Use a rubric to evaluate writing.
- Publish writing to share it with an audience.
- **Language** Write about nature using newly acquired vocabulary.

Speaking and Listening Task

- Adapt an explanatory essay into a multimedia presentation.
- Deliver a multimedia presentation to an audience.
- Listen actively to a multimedia presentation.
- **Language** Use increasingly complex and specific language to present ideas orally.

Assign the Writing Task in **Ed**.

Online

RESOURCES

- Unit 3 Response Log
- Reading Studio: Notice & Note
- Writing Studio: Writing Informative Texts
- Speaking and Listening Studio: Using Media in a Presentation

Language X-Ray: English Learner Support

Use the instruction below and the supports and scaffolds in the Teacher's Edition to help you guide students at different proficiency levels.

INTRODUCE THE WRITING TASK

Define an **explanatory essay** as a type of writing that explains something. It uses facts and information and can include personal opinions. For example, an explanatory essay might explain how a computer works or why animals need to sleep. If appropriate, point out that the word *explanatory* translates as *explicativo* in Spanish.

Point out that the selections in this unit focus on how we affect nature and how nature affects us. Use sentence frames to help students explore ideas related to this topic—for example: *Nature is all around us, even ____*. Assist students as they brainstorm phrases such as *in a big city* and *if we don't notice it*. Have pairs of students work together to write an original sentence about the topic of people's relationships with nature. Explain that they might use sentences like these as main ideas for their essays.

WRITING

Use New Vocabulary

Tell students to write about nature using the vocabulary they have learned in this unit.

Use the following supports with students at varying proficiency levels:

- Display photographs depicting scenes from the selections in this unit, such as a park ranger, a hummingbird, a blue whale, a bat, and a beach. Prompt students to recall terms related to the photographs and create a word bank. Instruct students to write three short sentences using these words. **SUBSTANTIAL**
- Use sentence frames to help students write about nature. For example: *People need nature because ____. Nature creates challenges for people when ____.* **MODERATE**
- Ask students to use vocabulary learned in this unit to write about people's relationships with nature and to cite examples from selections in the unit. **LIGHT**

SPEAKING

Present Information

Tell students that in a **multimedia presentation**, the presenter speaks to the audience while also sharing media, such as photos and video clips.

Use the following supports with students at varying proficiency levels:

- In small groups, have students choose an image relevant to one of the unit selections. Then ask groups to choose a word to say about the image they selected. **SUBSTANTIAL**
- Allow students extra time to practice with partners. If they stumble over certain sentences, encourage them to revise their scripts. They should practice speaking while sharing media until the presentation runs smoothly. **MODERATE**
- With a partner, have students practice their presentations, focusing on enunciation, gestures, and eye contact. **LIGHT**

WRITING

WRITE AN EXPLANATORY ESSAY

Have a volunteer read the introductory paragraph, and then discuss the writing task with students. Encourage them to refer to the notes they recorded in the Unit 3 Response Log before they begin planning and writing a draft. Explain that the Response Log will contain ideas about various aspects of nature and our relationship to it that may be useful as they plan their explanatory essays.

USE THE MENTOR TEXT

Explain to students that their explanatory essays will be similar to "Joyas Voladoras" by Brian Doyle. Like Doyle's essay, theirs will have a central message with main ideas supported by evidence found in research or personal experiences. Their introduction will include an interesting observation, a quotation, or a detail that engages readers, and their conclusion will tell readers why the topic is important. Remind students of the importance of including precise and vivid words throughout their essays.

WRITING PROMPT

Discuss the prompt with students. Encourage them to ask questions about any part of the assignment they find unclear. Emphasize that the purpose of their explanatory essay is to explain to readers a specific aspect of nature and our relationship to it. Review the checklist of key points that students should consider as they write their essays.

 **WRITING TASK**

Write an Explanatory Essay

 Go to the **Writing Studio** for help writing informative texts.

This unit focuses on our relationship with nature and wildness. For this writing task, you will write an explanatory essay focusing on one aspect of nature. In it, you will give a clear explanation of this aspect of nature and our relationship to it. For an example of a well-written explanatory essay you can use as a mentor text, review the essay "Joyas Voladoras."

As you write your essay, you will want to look at the notes you made in your Response Log after reading the texts in this unit.

Writing Prompt

Read the information in the box below.

This is the topic or context for your essay.

> Human beings are a part of nature and have a complex relationship with it.

Think carefully about the following question.

Mark the two most important words, phrases, or ideas in the prompts.

> What effect do we have on nature, and how does nature affect us?

Now mark the word or words that identify the question you must answer in your essay.

Write an explanatory essay about a specific aspect of nature and our relationship to it.

Be sure to—

Review these points as you write and again when you finish. Make any needed changes or edits.

- ❏ maintain a narrow focus on your specific topic
- ❏ engage readers with an interesting observation, quotation, or detail
- ❏ organize central ideas in a logically structured body that clearly develops the thesis
- ❏ support ideas with evidence from research and experience
- ❏ emphasize ideas using precise and vivid word choices
- ❏ conclude by addressing the significance of the specific topic

---

 ## LEARNING MINDSET

Seeking Challenges Remind students that being willing to take risks and tackle new challenges is essential to the learning mindset. In fact, overcoming challenges is a key to developing skills and intelligence. Point out that when Brian Doyle set out to write "Joyas Voladoras," he may have known very little about hummingbirds and blue whales. Instead of feeling intimidated, he challenged himself to gather facts and details about these animals that would interest his readers and support his ideas about the heart. Encourage students to take a similar approach as they begin planning their explanatory essays.

1 Plan

To decide what your explanatory essay will be about, begin with a general topic that interests you, and then do research to focus on one specific aspect of that topic. Also explore your own experiences with the specific topic to develop an idea about your relationship with it. You can then draft a thesis statement and identify a specific purpose for your writing and the audience that might get the most from your ideas. Use the chart below to help you plan.

EXPLANATORY ESSAY PLANNING CHART

Focused Topic:	
Source 1: Information:	
Source 2: Information:	
Source 3: Information:	
My Experience	
Thesis Statement: **Purpose for Writing:** **Specific Audience:**	

Go to **Writing Informative Texts: Developing a Topic** for help planning your essay.

Notice & Note

From Reading to Writing

As you plan your explanatory essay, apply what you've learned about signposts to your own writing. Think about how you can incorporate **Numbers and Stats** into your essay.

Go to the **Reading Studio** for more resources on Notice & Note.

Use the notes from your Response Log as you plan your essay.

UNIT 3 RESPONSE LOG

Background Reading Review the notes you have taken in your Response Log after reading the texts in this unit. These texts provide background reading that will help you formulate the key ideas in your essay.

Write an Explanatory Essay **209**

---

1 PLAN

Read the introductory text. Emphasize that students' topics will be about nature. If necessary, provide questions such as the following to inspire their thinking: Would you like to know more about deserts, mountains, or coral reefs? Which animals that you have seen or heard about do you find most interesting? Why? Do earthquakes or volcanic eruptions interest you? What about extreme weather? Then review the key elements of the planning chart. Explain to students that although not every source they examine during their initial research will turn out to be useful in writing about their final topic, this research is still an important part of the process.

■ English Learner Support

Understand Academic Language Remind students that the introduction to each of their explanatory essays should provide an observation, quotation, or detail that will grab the reader's interest.

Be sure to reinforce the idea that the introduction to each essay must also include a clear **thesis,** or controlling idea, that expresses the central idea of the essay.

Organize small groups of students with a range of language proficiencies and have them discuss ideas for their introductions, especially each student's thesis statement. **MODERATE/LIGHT**

For **writing support** for students at varying proficiency levels, see the **Language X-Ray** on page 208B.

NOTICE & NOTE

From Reading to Writing Discuss the focus of the **Numbers and Stats** signpost, in which the writer provides specific numbers or statistical information. Emphasize that not every number students encounter in their research will enhance their essays. Before including a number or statistic, they should ask themselves whether it will be interesting to readers and will clearly support an idea they want to express.

Background Reading As students plan their explanatory essays, encourage them to review their notes in the Unit 3 Response Logs. Suggest that they look back at the unit's selections to identify information that may help them select topics.

WHEN STUDENTS STRUGGLE . . .

Brainstorm Topics Have students fold a blank sheet of paper into four equal parts and then label each part with a general category—for example: Places, Animals, Processes, and Seasons.

- Give students three minutes to list some specific topics within each general category that might interest them.
- Encourage students to write questions about any of the topics.
- Have students note key words related to specific topics they may use for research.

Have students identify the topic they find most interesting. Suggest that they get feedback from a partner about ways in which they can make their topic interesting to their readers.

Write an Explanatory Essay **209**

WRITING

Organize Your Ideas Emphasize to students the importance of organizing their ideas in an outline before beginning to draft their explanatory essays. Tell students that their outlines may include one main section for each paragraph of the essay. Provide the following sample based on the chart.

I. Introduction: Describe the eruption of Mount Vesuvius.

II. Main Idea/Example 1 with Evidence: How does a volcano form?

III. Main Idea/Example 2 with Evidence: How do we know whether a volcano will erupt?

IV. Main Idea/Example 3 with Evidence: What can we do to prevent damage from a volcanic eruption?

V. Conclusion: Describe current research and end with a statement about the power of natural forces.

Remind students that they can further outline body paragraphs using the specific evidence from their research activities.

② DEVELOP A DRAFT

Remind students to follow their outlines as they draft their explanatory essays. However, emphasize that an outline is only a first step in writing. If new ideas come to them during the drafting stage, they can make changes to their plans.

■ English Learner Support

Write a Group Essay Work in small groups with students who require direct support. Together, write an explanatory paragraph that responds to the writing prompt. Begin by drafting a thesis statement that reflects the Essential Question and will serve as a guidepost for the explanation.
MODERATE

 **WRITING TASK**

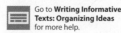 Go to **Writing Informative Texts: Organizing Ideas** for more help.

Organize Your Ideas After you have researched your topic, organize your information in a way that's appropriate to your topic, purpose, and audience.

- To explain a process over time, choose chronological order.
- To tell what happens and the result, use cause-and-effect organization.
- You can present several key ideas in order of importance.
- You might even mix structures or incorporate a brief narrative passage that shows the effect your topic has had on you.

For any text structure, you will need to provide specific details, examples, and commentary to make your essay engaging and informative. Create an outline or use the chart below to organize your essay.

EXPLANATORY ESSAY OUTLINE
INTRODUCTION WITH THESIS:
BODY
Idea or Example 1:
Evidence:
Idea or Example 2:
Evidence:
Idea or Example 3:
Evidence:
CONCLUSION

② Develop a Draft

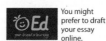 You might prefer to draft your essay online.

As you write your draft, refer to your outline as well as any notes you took on the texts in the unit. Draft electronically to make it easier to make changes or move sentences around later when you are revising.

WHEN STUDENTS STRUGGLE . . .

Draft the Essay Students often struggle as they try to get started on their drafts, even if they have a good outline. An effective way to have them begin is by writing their thesis statements. If they are still struggling, encourage them to start with a body paragraph they feel confident about. Explain that once they have begun writing, they will likely find that their ideas flow more freely. Emphasize that a first draft is not meant to be perfect. At this stage, students are just getting their ideas down; they will have time to revise and edit their writing later.

Use the Mentor Text

Author's Craft

An intriguing detail or an interesting quotation can be a good way to start an explanatory essay. It will catch your audience's attention and lead the way into the rest of the essay.

> Consider the hummingbird for a long moment.
> A hummingbird's heart beats ten times a second.
> A hummingbird's heart is the size of a pencil eraser.
> A hummingbird's heart is a lot of the hummingbird. . . .

The writer begins with fascinating facts that make the reader want to know more.

Apply What You've Learned Begin your essay in a way that makes people want to keep reading. An interesting fact about your topic is one good possibility.

Genre Characteristics

An explanatory essay often has sections that use a narrative structure. This can be a highly effective way to provide information.

> . . . When this creature is born it is twenty feet long and weighs four tons. It is waaaaay bigger than your car. It drinks a hundred gallons of milk from its mama every day and gains two hundred pounds a day, and when it is seven or eight years old it endures an unimaginable puberty and then it essentially disappears from human ken . . .

The author tells about the blue whale as though it were a character in a story.

Apply What You've Learned Use a narrative structure, when it's appropriate, to make your explanation clear and draw in your reader.

WHY THIS MENTOR TEXT?

"Joyas Voladoras" provides a good example of explanatory writing. To develop his ideas about hearts in general, the author explains how the hearts of hummingbirds and blue whales function. Use the instruction below to model how an intriguing detail can grab a reader's attention and how different text structures can be effective for explaining aspects of the natural world.

USE THE MENTOR TEXT

Author's Craft Have a volunteer read aloud the introduction to this section and the example from the mentor text. Ask: In what ways does this text capture readers' interest? *(The repetition of "A hummingbird's heart" creates a rhythm that engages readers, and each sentence introduces an interesting new fact about a hummingbird's heart.)*

Genre Characteristics Discuss the introductory text. Ask a volunteer to read aloud the example from Brian Doyle's essay. Ask: How can you tell that this excerpt from a paragraph has a narrative structure? *(The excerpt describes a process with a beginning, middle, and end. It tells the story of the creature's birth, development, and eventual disappearance from human observation.)*

Discuss other types of paragraph structures that might be used to develop ideas in an explanatory essay. For example, chronological order may be a good structure for explaining how to do something or how a process works. Ask: What structure might be appropriate for describing the results of some action or event? *(cause and effect)*

🔵 ENGLISH LEARNER SUPPORT

Use the Mentor Text Use the following supports with students at varying proficiency levels:

- Read aloud paragraph 4 from the mentor text. Help students identify the events in the narrative and the transitions used to connect them (*then, when*). Draw pictures as needed to clarify the meaning of each sentence. **SUBSTANTIAL**

- Have pairs draw a three-picture sequence that shows the beginning, middle, and end of the narrative about the blue whale in the passage from the mentor text. **MODERATE**

- Have small groups of students read paragraph 2 of "Joyas Voladoras" on page 164. Ask each group to draft a brief narrative paragraph that summarizes the life of a hummingbird, using the passage about the blue whale as a model. **LIGHT**

WRITING

③ REVISE

Have students evaluate their drafts by answering each question posed in the Revision Guide. Call on volunteers to model their revision techniques.

With a Partner Have students work with a peer reviewer to evaluate the drafts of their explanatory essays. Use the following questions as a guide for peer review:

- Does the beginning of the essay grab the reader's attention with an engaging detail?
- Does the introduction include a thesis statement that clearly responds to the writing prompt?
- Are the ideas presented in a logical order?
- Are key ideas supported with evidence?
- Has the writer used precise and vivid language that makes the explanation interesting for the reader?
- Does the conclusion clearly state why the topic is important?

Encourage students to use their reviewer's comments as they further develop their explanatory essays.

③ Revise

 Go to **Writing Informative Texts: Precise Language and Vocabulary** for help revising your essay.

On Your Own A memorable explanatory essay is carefully crafted, in part through thoughtful revision, to achieve its purpose. Your revisions should make your explanation both clearer and more engaging. Use the chart below to focus on specific elements to make your writing stronger.

REVISION GUIDE

Ask Yourself	Tips	Revision Techniques
1. Does the introduction engage readers and state a clear thesis about a focused topic?	**Mark** an engaging idea in the introduction. **Underline** the thesis statement.	**Add** an attention-getting detail to the introduction and add a thesis statement
2. Are ideas organized logically?	**Note** the central idea explored in each paragraph.	**Reorder** evidence to focus each paragraph on one idea.
3. Is each key idea supported with evidence from research or experience?	**Number** each supporting fact, example, or quotation for a key idea.	**Add** facts, details, examples, or quotations to support ideas with only one or two pieces of support.
4. Do precise and vivid word choices effectively communicate ideas about the specific topic?	**Mark** precise word choices in each section of the essay.	**Revise** vague word choices to make them more precise and descriptive.
5. Does the conclusion effectively summarize ideas and address the importance of the topic?	**Underline** the restated thesis or summary of ideas in the conclusion.	**Add** a restatement of the thesis or summary of the essay's ideas.

ACADEMIC VOCABULARY
As you conduct your peer review, try to use these words.

- ❑ advocate
- ❑ discrete
- ❑ domain
- ❑ evoke
- ❑ enhance

With a Partner After revising your draft, exchange papers with a partner for a peer review focused on evaluating how clear and engaging the writing is. Begin with the aspects you think work best in your partner's draft, and then note confusing passages and provide concrete suggestions for revision.

When receiving feedback from your partner, listen attentively and ask questions to make sure you fully understand the revision suggestions.

4 Edit

Once you have addressed the organization, development, and flow of ideas in your essay, you can look to improve the finer points of your draft. Edit for the proper use of standard English conventions and make sure to correct any misspellings and grammatical errors.

Language Conventions

Parallel Structure Strategic use of **parallel structure**—using the same grammatical structure for two or more elements—can guide your readers to make meaningful links between your ideas and also make your writing flow more smoothly.

- **Within a sentence**, parallel construction involves repeated parts of speech or structures in two or more phrases or clauses.
- **Within a paragraph**, parallel construction may involve two or more sentences and is often used for emphasis.

Here are examples of parallel construction from "Joyas Voladoras":

CONSTRUCTION	EXAMPLE FROM TEXT
Within a sentence	. . . more than three hundred species of them **whirring and zooming and nectaring in hummer time zones** . . .
Within a paragraph	. . . It's expensive to fly. **You burn out. You fry the machine. You melt the engine.** . . .

5 Publish

Finalize your essay and choose a way to share it with your audience. Consider these options:

- Post your essay as a blog on a classroom or school website.
- Produce your essay as a multimedia presentation.

4 EDIT

Encourage students to read their drafts aloud multiple times. During their first reading, have students focus on the clarity of their ideas. During their second reading, suggest that students listen for precise and vivid word use. During a third reading, students should listen for the use of parallel structure in their essays.

LANGUAGE CONVENTIONS

Parallel Structure Review the key elements of parallel structure within sentences and paragraphs. Remind students that parallel structure helps make writing flow smoothly.

Have volunteers read the examples of parallel construction from "Joyas Voladoras." Ask: In the first example, what creates parallel structure within the sentence? (*There are three verbs in a row ending in -ing:* whirring, zooming, nectaring.) In what way does the second example show parallel structure? (*Three short sentences begin with* you *and have simple predicates with related verbs:* burn out, fry, melt.)

5 PUBLISH

Discuss the suggested publishing options. If possible, have students post their explanatory essays as blog posts on a school website. Encourage other students to read the essays and write courteous comments and suggestions. Encourage students to respond to the comments.

ENGLISH LEARNER SUPPORT

Use Parallel Structures Display the following sentences. Encourage students to combine them in one sentence that has parallel structure.

- How much and what kind of food whales eat depends on their size.
- How much and what kind of food whales eat depends on their age.
- How much and what kind of food whales eat depends on local marine life.

After students have combined the sentences, have pairs write similar examples and trade them with partners to form sentences with parallel structures. **MODERATE/LIGHT**

WRITING

USE THE SCORING GUIDE

Allow students time to read the scoring guide. Encourage them to ask questions about any ideas, sentences, phrases, or words they find unclear. Tell partners to exchange their final explanatory essays and score them using the guidelines. Have each student reviewer write a paragraph explaining the reason for the score he or she awarded for each major category.

 **WRITING TASK**

Use the scoring guide to evaluate your essay.

	Organization/Progression	Development of Ideas	Use of Language and Conventions
WRITING TASK SCORING GUIDE: EXPLANATORY ESSAY			
4	• The organization is effective and appropriate to the purpose, and includes a purposeful narrative passage. • All ideas are focused on a specific aspect of nature. • Transitions clearly show the relationships among ideas.	• The introduction catches the reader's attention and clearly states a thought-provoking thesis. • Key ideas are well developed with clear main ideas supported by specific and well-chosen facts, details, examples, and quotations. • The conclusion effectively synthesizes ideas and expresses the importance of the topic.	• Word choice is purposeful and precise. • Parallel structure is used correctly where appropriate. • Spelling, capitalization, and punctuation are correct. • Grammar and usage are correct.
3	• The organization is, for the most part, effective and appropriate to the purpose. • Most ideas are focused on one aspect of nature. • Transitions generally clarify the relationships among ideas.	• The introduction states the thesis but could be more engaging. • Key ideas are adequately developed and supported with evidence. • The conclusion synthesizes ideas and summarizes information.	• Word choices are generally clear. • Parallel structure is used correctly in one or two instances. • There are some spelling, capitalization, and punctuation mistakes. • Some grammatical and usage errors occur but do not interfere with understanding.
2	• The organization is evident but is not always appropriate to the purpose. • Extraneous ideas draw the focus away from the main topic at times. • Relationships among ideas are sometimes unclear.	• The introduction is not engaging and the thesis statement does not express a clear point. • Some ideas are supported with evidence. • The conclusion may merely summarize key ideas or restate the thesis.	• Word choices are occasionally vague. • An attempt is made to use parallel structure. • Spelling, capitalization, and punctuation are often incorrect. • Flawed grammar and usage sometimes make reading difficult.
1	• Organization is not evident or not appropriate to the purpose. • Nature is addressed generally; a specific topic is not evident. • Connections among ideas are missing, making the writer's ideas difficult to understand.	• The introduction and the thesis statement are missing or confusing. • Development of ideas is minimal, with inappropriate, vague, or missing support. • The conclusion is absent or fails to summarize ideas.	• Word choices are vague or inaccurate. • Parallel construction is lacking. • Many spelling, capitalization, and punctuation errors are present. • Grammatical and usage errors make the writer's ideas unclear.

TO CHALLENGE STUDENTS

Design an Exhibit Challenge students to adapt their essays for an exhibit about interactions between humans and nature. Encourage them to incorporate various types of visuals and interactive displays.

Deliver a Multimedia Presentation

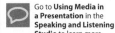

SPEAKING AND
LISTENING TASK

You will now adapt your explanatory essay into a multimedia presentation that you can deliver to your classmates. You also will watch and listen to their presentations, ask questions to better understand their ideas, and provide feedback.

Go to **Using Media in a Presentation** in the **Speaking and Listening Studio** to learn more.

1 Adapt Your Essay as a Multimedia Presentation

Use the chart below to guide you as you adapt your essay into a script and gather media for your presentation. You may also choose to create a storyboard rather than a script.

MULTIMEDIA PRESENTATION PLANNING CHART		
Title and Introduction	How will you revise your title and introduction to capture the listener's attention? Is there a more concise way to state your controlling idea or thesis?	
Purpose and Audience	What text structure, vocabulary, language, and tone are appropriate for your intended purpose and audience?	
Effective Language and Organization	Which parts of your essay should be simplified? Where can you link ideas with transitions such as *first*, *second*, and *finally*?	
Media	What types of media best illustrate your written ideas? Are there sections of writing that can be removed and replaced with audio or video of the phenomenon you are explaining?	

SPEAKING AND LISTENING

DELIVER A MULTIMEDIA PRESENTATION

Introduce students to the Speaking and Listening Task by discussing how delivering a multimedia presentation based on an explanatory text is different from simply reading it aloud. Tell students they will have the opportunity to gather and create audio and visual materials to make their topic more engaging for an audience. Explain that they will need to adapt the way they present information so that a live audience, rather than a reader, can easily understand it. A reader can read difficult or complex information more slowly or even go back and reread it, but an audience cannot. Therefore, a speaker or presenter must plan carefully to help his or her audience follow along.

1 ADAPT YOUR ESSAY AS A MULTIMEDIA PRESENTATION

Have students read the questions in each row of the chart and note their responses in the third column. Discuss some general principles for explaining ideas in a multimedia presentation. *(speak at a reasonable pace; use illustrations, video, and recordings for clarification)* Note that visuals can also be used to show the audience the structure of a presentation, serving the same function as headings in a text.

ENGLISH LEARNER SUPPORT

Adapt the Essay Use the following supports with students at varying proficiency levels:

- Instruct students to find or draw images of nature that are important to them. Tell them to display the images and describe each in a word or two. **SUBSTANTIAL**

- Review the questions in the Multimedia Presentation Planning Chart to confirm students' comprehension of key ideas. Then have students work independently to apply the questions to their explanatory essays. **MODERATE**

- Have students discuss the questions in the Multimedia Presentation Planning Chart with a partner before they begin writing their answers independently. **LIGHT**

SPEAKING AND LISTENING

② CREATE YOUR MULTIMEDIA PRESENTATION

If your school does not provide multimedia presentation software, have students explore free online sources.

Put the Media Together Discuss each of the three elements that students should include in a slideshow: text, images, and credits. Lead them to understand that placing a lot of text on a slide forces the audience to read it while also listening to the speaker, which causes confusion and reduces the impact of both parts of the presentation. Similarly, they should limit the number of images they use, including enough to help explain their main ideas but not so many that the audience becomes overwhelmed. If students plan to use a computer or other presentation devices for their presentations, be sure to provide adequate accessibility and, if necessary, training.

Practice with a Partner or Group Remind students of the importance of practicing their presentations in advance of delivering them. Suggest that they work in small groups of three or four students. Emphasize that the first practice sessions will enable them to get a sense of how long their presentations are and what explanations and visuals work best for an audience.

Encourage listeners to make notes about two things they liked and two suggestions for improvement. Encourage presenters to consider the suggestions as they revise their presentations. Ask: Which suggestions do you think would be most helpful in improving your presentation? What would you need to do to incorporate these changes into the presentation?

 For **speaking support** for students at varying proficiency levels, see the **Language X-Ray** on page 208B.

③ DELIVER YOUR PRESENTATION

Schedule time for all students to make their final presentations. After everyone has finished, encourage students to discuss how their classmates' suggestions helped them improve their presentations.

 **SPEAKING AND LISTENING TASK**

As you work to improve your presentations, follow these discussion rules:

❑ listen closely to each other
❑ don't interrupt
❑ stay on topic
❑ ask only helpful, relevant questions
❑ provide only clear, thoughtful, and direct answers

② Create Your Multimedia Presentation

When you've adapted your essay and decided on what kinds of visuals and sounds you want, use online search engines to help you find what you need. Use only elements for which you have permission or for which permission is not required. (Most sources allow use in educational settings.)

Put the Media Together

If you use slideshow software, pay attention to these things:

❑ **Text** Keep any text you use to a minimum. Let your images speak for themselves; you can provide any needed commentary in your speech.

❑ **Images** Use images that are high enough resolution to be clear and easily seen.

❑ **Credits** You will need to give credit to your information sources. Create a slide for the end of your presentation that gives the sources for all the media you have used.

Practice with a Partner or Group

Show your presentation to a partner or small group and ask for help in revising and improving it.

As a listener, take notes about ways that presenters can improve their content and media and more effectively enunciate, use purposeful gestures, and make eye contact. Paraphrase and summarize each presenter's key ideas and main points to confirm your understanding, and ask questions to clarify any confusing ideas.

As a presenter, listen closely to questions and feedback, and consider ways to revise your presentation to make it more effective. Remember to ask for suggestions about your visuals and audio to make your presentation clearer and more engaging.

③ Deliver Your Presentation

Use the advice you received during practice to make final changes to your presentation. If possible, practice incorporating your media before presenting to troubleshoot any technical problems. Then, deliver your presentation to your classmates.

WHEN STUDENTS STRUGGLE . . .

Take Notes Have students work in groups of three, focusing on different aspects of listening to the multimedia presentations. Designate one student to listen to the presentation for examples of an engaging introduction and logical organization. Have a second student listen for the use of precise and vivid words. A third student should focus on the technical aspects of the presentation, commenting on the quality of visuals, sound, and editing.

Reflect on the Unit

When you were writing your explanatory essay, you synthesized your ideas about the reading you have done in this unit. Now is a good time to reflect on what you have learned.

Reflect on the Essential Question

- What effect do we have on nature, and how does nature affect us? How has your answer to this question changed since you first considered it when you started this unit?

- What are some examples from the texts you've read that show our relationship with nature?

Reflect on Your Reading

- Which selections were the most interesting or surprising to you?

- From which selection did you learn the most about how nature affects us or how we affect nature?

Reflect on the Writing Task

- What difficulties did you encounter while working on your explanatory essay? How might you avoid them next time?

- What part of the essay was the easiest and what part was the hardest to write? Why?

- What improvements did you make to your essay as you were revising?

UNIT 3 SELECTIONS
- "My Life as a Bat"
- "Joyas Voladoras"
- "Find Your Park"
- "The Seventh Man"
- "Carry"

REFLECT ON THE UNIT

Have students reflect on the questions independently and write some notes in response to each one. Then have students meet with partners or in small groups to discuss their reflections. Circulate during these discussions to identify the questions that are generating the liveliest conversations. Wrap up with a whole-class discussion focused on these questions.

 LEARNING MINDSET

Self-Reflection Remind students that an important part of developing a learning mindset is reflecting on the behaviors and strategies that led them to succeed or fail at various tasks. Identifying what works for them will allow them to build on past successes and learn from past mistakes. As students reflect on this unit, encourage them to consider these questions: Did I set a high standard for myself at the start of the unit? When I was struggling, did I ask for help or try a different approach to get back on track? Did I review my work for possible errors? Am I proud of the work I turned in?

Instructional Overview and Resources

	Instructional Focus	**Online Ed Resources**
 **Unit Introduction** **Hard-Won Liberty**	**Unit 4 Essential Question** **Unit 4 Academic Vocabulary**	**Stream to Start:** Hard-Won Liberty **Unit 4 Response Log**

ANALYZE & APPLY

"Letter from Birmingham Jail" Argument by Martin Luther King Jr. Lexile 1190L **NOTICE & NOTE** READING MODEL **Signposts** • Big Questions • Quoted Words • Extreme or Absolute Language	**Reading** • Analyze Argument • Analyze Rhetorical Devices **Writing:** Write a Friendly Letter **Speaking and Listening:** Present Research **Vocabulary:** Context Clues **Language Conventions:** Repetition and Parallelism	🔊 **Audio** **Close Read Screencasts:** Modeled Discussions **Reading Studio:** Notice & Note **Level Up Tutorial:** Analyzing Arguments **Writing Studio:** Task, Purpose, Audience **Speaking and Listening Studio:** Giving a Presentation **Vocabulary Studio:** Using Context Clues
"Elsewhere" Poem by Derek Walcott	**Reading** • Analyze Poetic Structure • Analyze Motif **Writing:** Write an Analysis **Speaking and Listening:** Discuss with a Group	🔊 **Audio** **Reading Studio:** Notice & Note **Level Up Tutorial:** Rhyme **Writing Studio:** Citing Text Evidence **Speaking and Listening Studio:** Participating in Collaborative Discussions
"The Hawk Can Soar" Memoir by Randi Davenport Lexile 790L	**Reading** • Analyze Diction and Syntax • Analyze Text Structure **Writing:** Design a Web Page **Speaking and Listening:** Discuss with a Small Group **Vocabulary:** Allusions **Language Conventions:** Purposeful Fragments	🔊 **Audio** **Reading Studio:** Notice & Note **Level Up Tutorials:** Paraphrasing; Summarizing; Taking Notes and Outlining **Writing Studio:** Publishing with Technology **Speaking and Listening Studio:** Participating in Collaborative Discussions **Grammar Studio:** Module 1: Lesson 1: Sentences and Sentence Fragments

SUGGESTED PACING: **30 DAYS**	**Unit Introduction**	**Letter from Birmingham Jail**	**Elsewhere**	**The Hawk Can Soar**	**The Briefcase**
	1	2 3 4 5 6	7 8	9 10 11 12	13 14 15 16

English Learner Support	Differentiated Instruction	Assessment
• Learn Vocabulary		

English Learner Support	Differentiated Instruction	Assessment
• Text X-Ray • Create Definitions • Discuss Words of Contrast • Vocabulary Strategy • Make Personal Connections • Analyze Verb Tenses • Use Cognates • Interpret New Vocabulary • Use Informal Language • Understand Word Parts • Discuss Rhetorical Questions • Discuss Prefixes • Discuss Allusions • Analyze Conclusions • Use Synonyms • Understand Negative • Understand Connotation • Discuss the Subjunctive Statements • Elaborate on Ideas • Discuss Informal Language • Build Vocabulary • Recognize Repetition • Oral Assessment • Discuss Visuals • Build Grammar Knowledge • Work with Others • Expand Reading Skills • Listen for Intonation • Vocabulary Strategy • Understand Pronoun Use • Use Double Negatives • Language Conventions • Preteach Content	**When Students Struggle** • Sketch to Stretch • Understand Purpose • Analyze Arguments • Understand Comparisons **To Challenge Students** • Conduct Research	**Selection Test**
• Text X-Ray • Understand Directionality • Ask for Information • Oral Assessment • Using New Vocabulary	**When Students Struggle** • Identify Rhyme • Draw Conclusions **To Challenge Students** • Plan an Interview	**Selection Test**
• Text X-Ray • Use Cognates • Discuss Verb Tenses • Make a Timeline • Understand Vocabulary • Oral Assessment • Discuss with a Small Group • Confirm and Clarify Understanding • Analyze Allusions • Analyze Purposeful Fragments	**When Students Struggle** • Monitor Understanding • Take Discussion Notes	**Selection Test**

Letter to Viceroy, Lord Irwin / Gandhi: The Rise to Fame

Independent Reading

End of Unit

17 18 19 20 21 22 23 24 25 26 27 28 29 30

UNIT 4 Continued

	Instructional Focus	**Online Ed** Resources

ANALYZE & APPLY

"The Briefcase"
Short Story by Rebecca Makkai
Lexile 860L

Reading
• Analyze Character
• Analyze Theme

Writing: Write a Letter

Speaking and Listening: Deliver a Summary

Vocabulary: Discipline-Specific Terms

Language Conventions: Semicolons

🔊 **Audio**

Reading Studio: Notice & Note

Level Up Tutorial: Author's Style

Writing Studio: Persuasive Techniques

Speaking and Listening Studio: Giving a Presentation

Vocabulary Studio: Discipline-Specific Terms

Grammar Studio: Module 12: Lesson 1: Semicolons

COLLABORATE & COMPARE

Mentor Text

from "Letter to Viceroy, Lord Irwin"
Letter by Mohandas K. Gandhi
Lexile 1210L

Reading
• Analyze Argument
• Analyze Rhetoric

Writing: Write an Analysis

Speaking and Listening: Share Information

Vocabulary: Denotations and Connotations

Language Conventions: Active and Passive Voice

🔊 **Audio**

Reading Studio: Notice & Note

Level Up Tutorial: Elements of an Argument

Writing Studio: Writing Arguments

Speaking and Listening Studio: Participating in Collaborative Discussions

Vocabulary Studio: Denotations and Connotations

from Gandhi: The Rise to Fame
Documentary Film by BBC

Reading
• Analyze Motives
• Analyze Media Techniques

Writing: Create a Multimodal Presentation

Speaking and Listening: Present and Lead a Discussion

Speaking and Listening Studio: Using Media in a Presentation

 Online Ed

Collaborate and Compare

Reading: Compare Accounts

Speaking and Listening: Compare and Debate

Speaking and Listening Studio: Tracing a Speaker's Argument

INDEPENDENT READING

The Independent Reading selections are only available in the eBook.

 Go to the Reading Studio for more information on Notice & Note.

 from "Speech at the March on Washington"
Speech by Josephine Baker
Lexile 860L

 "The Book of the Dead"
Short Story by Edwidge Danticat
Lexile 920L

END OF UNIT

Writing Task: Write an Argument

Speaking and Listening Task: Deliver an Argument

Reflect on the Unit

Writing: Write an Argument

Language Conventions: Correct Writing Conventions

Speaking and Listening: Deliver an Argument

Unit 4 Response Log

Mentor Text: from "Letter to Viceroy, Lord Irwin"

Reading Studio: Notice & Note

Writing Studio: Writing Arguments

Speaking and Listening Studio: Giving a Presentation

Grammar Studio: Capitalization; Modules 11–12: Punctuation; Module 13: Spelling

English Learner Support		Differentiated Instruction	Online Ed Assessment
• Text X-Ray • Use Cognates • Use Graphic Organizers • Understand Theme • Understand Semicolons • Provide Teacher and Peer Support • Recognize Sounds • Understand Dialogue	• Understand Conflict • Understand Imagery • Oral Assessment • Write a Letter • Deliver a Summary • Build Vocabulary • Use a Variety of Sentence Patterns	**When Students Struggle** • Read and Explain • Read and Discuss **To Challenge Students** • Explore Themes	**Selection Test**
• Text X-Ray • Apply Directionality • Use Cognates • Internalize New Vocabulary • Discuss Connotation • Clarify Grammar Issues	• Understand Passive Voice • Oral Assessment • Share Information • Vocabulary Strategies • Language Conventions	**When Students Struggle** • Analyze Rhetoric **To Challenge Students** • Analyze Perspective	**Selection Test**
• Text X-Ray • Understand Viewpoint and Motive • Use Cognates • Analyze Juxtaposition • Present and Lead a Discussion		**When Students Struggle** • Analyze Media • Conduct Research	**Selection Test**
• Analyze Accounts in Different Media		**To Challenge Students** • Practice and Apply	

"Cloudy Day" Poem by Jimmy Santiago Baca		*from* "Crispus Attucks" History by Kareem Abdul-Jabbar **Lexile 970L**	**Selection Tests**

English Learner Support	Differentiated Instruction	Assessment
• Language X-Ray • Understand Academic Language • Develop a Thesis Statement with a Claim • Use the Mentor Text • Use Transitions in Arguments • Use a Checklist to Edit Writing • Adapt the Argument	**When Students Struggle** • Make Claims • Improving Writing Flow • Use Visuals	**Unit Test**

HARD-WON LIBERTY

? Connect to the ESSENTIAL QUESTION

Ask a volunteer to read aloud the Essential Question. Have students pause to reflect on the term "free." Ask for examples of what it means to feel free. Have students work together to create a list of things they think most people need in order to feel free. Encourage them to draw on both their personal experience and knowledge of history.

■ English Learner Support

Learn Vocabulary Make sure students understand the Essential Question. If necessary, explain the following term:

- *Free* means "not confined; not controlled by another" or "able to act as one wishes."

Help students restate the question in simpler language: What helps us feel free? **SUBSTANTIAL/MODERATE**

DISCUSS THE QUOTATION

Tell students that Jawaharlal Nehru (1889–1964) was part of Mahatma Gandhi's independence movement to free India from British rule. After India gained independence, Nehru became the country's first prime minister. Ask students to read the quotation carefully and take a moment to reflect. Have them discuss what Nehru means by "walk to freedom." Ask students to recall what they decided was necessary in order to feel free. Have them consider how easy or difficult it is to obtain those things.

? ESSENTIAL QUESTION:

What do we need in order to feel free?

 There is no easy walk to freedom anywhere. "

Jawaharlal Nehru

218   Unit 4

⚙ LEARNING MINDSET

Effort Explain the importance of effort. Discuss how in order to improve their skills, students must apply the necessary amount of effort. Emphasize that hard work leads to success. Prompt students to think of something they became better at with hard work, such as playing an instrument or sport, learning how to use a new app or tool, or improving time management or an academic skill. Be sure to offer positive feedback to students for their continued effort.

ACADEMIC VOCABULARY

Academic Vocabulary words are words you use when you discuss and write about texts. In this unit you will practice and learn five words.

 ☑ comprehensive ☐ equivalent ☐ incentive ☐ innovate ☐ subordinate

Study the Word Network to learn more about the word **comprehensive**.

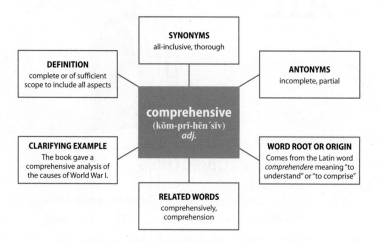

SYNONYMS
all-inclusive, thorough

DEFINITION
complete or of sufficient scope to include all aspects

comprehensive
(kŏm-prĭ-hĕn´sĭv)
adj.

ANTONYMS
incomplete, partial

CLARIFYING EXAMPLE
The book gave a comprehensive analysis of the causes of World War I.

WORD ROOT OR ORIGIN
Comes from the Latin word *comprehendere* meaning "to understand" or "to comprise"

RELATED WORDS
comprehensively, comprehension

Write and Discuss Discuss the completed Word Network with a partner, making sure to talk through all of the boxes until you both understand the word, its synonyms, antonyms, and related forms. Then, fill out Word Networks for the remaining four words. Use a dictionary or online resource to help you complete the activity.

 Go online to access the Word Networks.

RESPOND TO THE ESSENTIAL QUESTION

In this unit, you will read various genres that explore what we need in order to feel free. As you read, you will revisit the **Essential Question** and gather your ideas about it in the **Response Log** that appears on page R4. At the end of the unit, you will have the opportunity to write an **argument** about what it means to be free. Filling out the Response Log will help you prepare for this writing task.

You can also go online to access the Response Log.

ACADEMIC VOCABULARY

As students complete Word Networks for the remaining four vocabulary words, encourage them to include all the categories shown in the completed network if possible, but point out that some words do not have clear synonyms or antonyms. Some words may also function as different parts of speech—for example, *equivalent* can function as an adjective or a noun.

comprehensive (kŏm´prĭ-hĕn´sĭv) *adj.* Complete or of sufficient scope to include all aspects.

equivalent (ĭ-kwĭv´ə-lənt) *adj.* Equal to or similar. (Spanish cognate: *equivalente*)

incentive (ĭn-sĕn´tĭv) *n.* Something that induces effort or motivates action. (Spanish cognate: *incentivo*)

innovate (ĭn´ə-vāt´) *v.* To change or develop through new or original methods, processes, or ideas. (Spanish cognate: *innovar*)

subordinate (sə-bôr´dn-ĭt) *adj.* Belonging to a lower or inferior class or rank; secondary. (Spanish cognate: *subordinado*)

RESPOND TO THE ESSENTIAL QUESTION

Direct students to the Unit 4 Response Log. Explain that students will use it to record ideas and details from the selections that help answer the Essential Question. When they work on the writing task at the end of the unit, their Response Log will help them think about what they have read and make connections between the texts.

LETTER FROM BIRMINGHAM JAIL

Argument by **Martin Luther King Jr.**

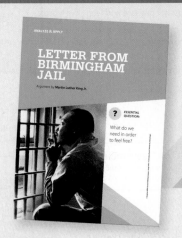

GENRE ELEMENTS
ARGUMENT

Remind students that one of the purposes for writing is to persuade. The intent of an **argument** is to persuade readers—persuade them to agree with the writer's claim (or, at least, to agree that the claim is valid), to take a certain action, or both. In this lesson, students will explore how Martin Luther King Jr. powerfully presents and supports his claims about the Civil Rights movement in "Letter from Birmingham Jail," a letter that has become a seminal document in the history of the United States.

LEARNING OBJECTIVES

- Analyze how the author develops an argument and uses rhetorical devices to make it powerful and memorable.
- Research another leader of the Civil Rights movement.
- Write a friendly letter about the person researched.
- Give a brief, formal speech about the person researched.
- Use context clues to define words and discuss their nuances.
- Identify and use examples of repetition and parallelism.
- **Language** Analyze the effect of punctuation on phrasing.

TEXT COMPLEXITY

Quantitative Measures	Letter from Birmingham Jail	Lexile: 1190L
Qualitative Measures	**Ideas Presented** Much is literal and straightforward; purpose and stance are clear.	
	Structures Used Organization of main ideas and details is complex but mostly explicit.	
	Language Used Many unfamiliar, academic, or domain-specific words; complex sentence structures.	
	Knowledge Required Specialized knowledge required; somewhat complex civics concepts; many religious references, but with footnotes.	

RESOURCES

- Unit 4 Response Log

- Selection Audio

- Close Read Screencasts: Modeled Discussions

- Reading Studio: Notice & Note

- Level Up Tutorial: Analyzing Arguments

- Writing Studio: Task, Purpose, Audience

- Speaking and Listening Studio: Giving a Presentation

- Vocabulary Studio: Using Context Clues

- "Letter from Birmingham Jail" Selection Test

SUMMARIES

English

Martin Luther King Jr. was criticized by a group of clergymen for his "unwise and untimely" protests against racial injustice in Birmingham, Alabama. In "Letter from Birmingham Jail," his response to his critics, King describes the conditions that prompted the protests; defends his role in the protests; explains the steps involved in planning nonviolent direct action; criticizes moderates who decry injustice but don't take action against it; and expresses his hope that a day of racial equality will come.

Spanish

Martin Luther King Jr. fue criticado por un grupo de clérigos por sus protestas "poco sabias y prematuras" en contra de la injusticia racial en Birmingham, Alabama. En "Carta desde la cárcel de Birmingham", su respuesta a sus críticos, King describe las condiciones que fomentaron las protestas; defiende su papel en las protestas; explica los pasos involucrados en la planificación de acciones directas de no violencia; critica a los moderados quienes condenan la injusticia pero no luchan en contra de ella; y expresa su esperanza de que un día la igualdad racial llegará.

SMALL-GROUP OPTIONS

Have students work in small groups to read and discuss the selection.

Gallery Walk

- Tape large sheets of paper on the walls and write a question or topic addressed in the letter at the top of each (for example, conditions being protested, action steps, main claims, and key supporting evidence).

- Form students into small groups or pairs in front of each sheet. Have them discuss the topic or question and write their ideas on the sheet.

- After all groups have had a chance to note something, signal groups to move to the next sheet and repeat the activity. Continue until all students have responded to all topics or questions.

- As a class, discuss students' ideas.

Think-Pair-Share

- After students have read and analyzed "Letter from Birmingham Jail," tell them that the letter is considered by many to be the most important piece of writing from the Civil Rights movement. Ask: Why do you think this is so? What makes the content of the letter so important?

- Instruct students to think about the questions individually and take notes about their responses.

- Then have pairs discuss their ideas about the questions and choose the two or three ideas that they consider most important.

- Invite pairs to share their responses with the class.

Text X-Ray: English Learner Support
for "Letter from Birmingham Jail"

Use the Text X-Ray and the supports and scaffolds in the Teacher's Edition to help guide students at different proficiency levels through the selection.

INTRODUCE THE SELECTION
DISCUSS SEGREGATION

In this lesson, students will need to discuss the racial segregation that the Civil Rights movement worked to end. Read aloud the Background note and explain the term *lunch counter segregation*. Some stores had a small, casual restaurant, where a cook worked on one side of a counter and served customers who sat on stools on the other side. In the early 1960s, most lunch counters in the South refused to serve African Americans. Explain that segregation extended to public facilities, standards for voting—indeed, almost every aspect of life.

Discuss what students may know about the Civil Rights movement or what methods they would use to change a segregationist culture. Use these sentence frames:

- *I know that the Civil Rights movement* ____.
- *I think the best way to end* segregation *would be* ____.

CULTURAL REFERENCES

The following words or phrases may be unfamiliar to students:

- *Southern Christian Leadership Conference* (paragraph 2): the Civil Rights organization that grew out of the Montgomery Bus Boycott, with Martin Luther King Jr. as its first president
- *white power structure* (paragraph 5): the white people in control of government and business; many of them wanted to keep segregation.
- *The nations of Asia and Africa . . . political independence* (paragraph 14): Between the end of World War II and the early 1960s, about four dozen countries in Asia and Africa gained partial or full independence from their colonial rulers.

See also the footnotes in the selection.

LISTENING

Discuss Rhetorical Questions

Help students identify and use rhetorical questions.

Use the following supports with students at varying proficiency levels:

- Tell students that you will read a few questions. Model that they should give a thumbs up if the question has a specific answer and a thumbs down if it is so obvious that no answer is needed (i.e., a rhetorical question). Ask: What time is it? *(up)* What is the capital of our state? *(up)* Don't we all deserve a little fun in our lives? *(down)* We all believe in fun, right? *(down)* **SUBSTANTIAL**
- Read the following to pairs and ask them to explain why it is a rhetorical question: Are you here in class today? *(The answer is obvious; the students are in class.)* **MODERATE**
- Read the following to students and ask them to explain why it is a rhetorical question: What is wrong with the world today? *(There is no single, specific answer.)* **LIGHT**

SPEAKING

Analyze Rhythm in Language

Remind students that Martin Luther King Jr. was a preacher. Have students examine the rhythm of the language in his letter and consider how it may have assisted his effectiveness as a public speaker.

Use the following supports with students at varying proficiency levels:

- Echo read the first two sentences of paragraph 24 aloud, using appropriate pauses and emphasis, pausing after each phrase, clause, or sentence. Then echo read the sentences without pauses and emphasis. Ask students to comment on the difference in the two readings. **SUBSTANTIAL**
- Echo read the first two sentences of paragraph 24 aloud, using appropriate pauses and emphasis. Then ask volunteers to read each of the sentences aloud. Discuss the importance of rhythm in the sentences. **MODERATE**
- Read the first two sentences of paragraph 24 aloud, using appropriate pauses and emphasis. Then ask partners to read the sentences to each other with similar pauses and emphasis. Ask them to discuss the importance of the rhythm in the reading. **LIGHT**

READING

Analyze Punctuation and Phrasing

Have students use punctuation as a guide to analyze some statements from King's letter.

Use the following supports with students at varying proficiency levels:

- Direct students to the very long sentence that begins in the 6th line of paragraph 14 ("But when you have seen . . .") and ends on the 17th line of the paragraph (". . . then you will understand why we find it difficult to wait."). Explain that the semicolons and dash are used to separate ideas. Discuss how the punctuation helps readers understand the sentence. **SUBSTANTIAL**
- Direct students to the very long sentence that begins in the 6th line of paragraph 14. Point out the semicolons and dash, and ask students to identify their purposes. **MODERATE**
- Direct students to the very long sentence that begins in the 6th line of paragraph 14. Ask them to identify the punctuation used and its purposes. **LIGHT**

WRITING

Write a Friendly Letter

Work with students to help them develop and improve their work on the writing assignment on Student Edition page 245.

Use the following supports with students at varying proficiency levels:

- Guide students to complete the following pair of sentences about the person they researched: *[Name] was important to the Civil Rights movement because _____. What he/she did matters today because _____.* **SUBSTANTIAL**
- Provide scaffolding to help students organize the body of their letters: *[Name] was important to the Civil Rights movement because _____ . A few facts you should know about [name] are: 1. _____; 2. _____; and 3. _____ . What [name] did matters today because _____ .* **MODERATE**
- Remind students that their tone should be friendly, casual, and respectful. Use the following as a model: *Some of the people whom King praises in his letter were white journalists. Ralph McGill, for example, . . .* Have students work in groups to share and check the tone of some of their sentences. **LIGHT**

EXPLAIN THE SIGNPOSTS

Explain that **NOTICE & NOTE Signposts** are significant moments in the text that help readers understand and analyze works of fiction or nonfiction. Use the instruction on these pages to introduce students to asking **Big Questions** and to using the **Quoted Words** and **Extreme or Absolute Language** signposts. Then use the selection that follows to have students apply the Big Questions and signposts to a text.

For a full list of the fiction and nonfiction signposts, see page 304.

BIG QUESTIONS

Remind students that **Big Questions** are questions that readers can ask as a way of connecting with and understanding what they read. Tell students that in the upcoming selection, they will focus on the following Big Question: *What surprised me?* Let students know that the answers to this question will vary, depending on the reader's prior knowledge of the topic. In this case, students probably know something about Martin Luther King Jr. and his views—but how he defended his views, both in words and in actions, may give students something new to consider.

Read aloud the example passage. Use a Think Aloud to model the reader's surprise at reading King's reference to his critics as "my fellow clergymen." Use the reader's comments about the second note to point out that mere surprise is not the point of this Big Question; rather, the surprise should be a springboard to thinking through the new information and raising questions related to it. Doing so is part of the way in which students can **analyze arguments** and even **analyze rhetorical devices** that add power to an argument.

Urge students to look for "the new" as they read. Tell them that when they encounter new information, a new interpretation of familiar information, a new viewpoint, or even possibly unreliable information they should pause, mark it in their consumable text, and ask themselves the anchor question: *What surprised me?*

LETTER FROM BIRMINGHAM JAIL

For more information on these and other signposts to Notice & Note, visit the **Reading Studio**.

You are about to read the argument "Letter from Birmingham Jail." In it, you will notice and note signposts that provide clues about the argument's claims and evidence. Here are a key question and two signposts to look for as you read this argument and other nonfiction writing.

Big Question Have you ever watched a TV commercial or listened to a classmate's student council campaign speech and thought, *"REALLY?"* When you're presented with an idea that's hard to believe, determine whether the information makes you wonder about something new or is simply untrue.

A nonfiction writer may share fascinating, true information with you—or the writer may have a bias or purpose that affects how believable the information is. As you read, be prepared to ask yourself: *What surprised me?* Look for:

- New information ("I didn't know that!")
- Suspicious information ("Seriously? Is that really true?")
- Clarifying information ("Oh! Now I get it!")
- A different perspective ("I hadn't thought of it that way.")

Here is how a student might mark surprising elements in King's letter.

> April 16, 1963
> My Dear Fellow Clergymen:
>
> 1 While confined here in the Birmingham city jail, <u>I came across your recent statement calling my present activities "unwise and untimely."</u> Seldom do I pause to answer criticism of <u>my work and ideas.</u> If I sought to answer all the criticisms that cross my desk, my secretaries would have little time for anything other than such correspondence in the course of the day, and I would have no time for constructive work. But since I feel that you are men of genuine good will and that your criticisms are sincerely set forth, <u>I want to try to answer your statement</u> in what I hope will be patient and reasonable terms.

What surprised you?	That Dr. King wrote to "fellow clergymen" who had criticized him.
Why did it surprise you? What other questions does it bring to mind?	I thought the letter was to the public or maybe political officials. What religious leaders criticized Dr. King, and what did they say?

Quoted Words Backing up your ideas with documented evidence and expert opinions shows that you really know your topic. The same is true of professional writers and speakers. A strong argument is supported by:

- Personal Perspectives: the experience or views of an ordinary person
- Voices of Authority: an expert view, from someone with relevant credibility
- Documented Facts: verifiable information that supports an idea or claim

Here a student annotated part of King's letter that uses **Quoted Words**:

> 15   . . . One has not only a legal but a moral responsibility to obey just laws. Conversely, one has a moral responsibility to disobey unjust laws. I would agree with St. Augustine that "an unjust law is no law at all."

Any time you see quotation marks in an argument or informational text, pause to see whether they share important information or an expert opinion about the topic.

Anchor Question
When you notice this signpost, ask: Why is this person quoted, and what do the quoted words add?

Who is quoted?	Saint Augustine
Why did the author include the quote? What did it add?	The words of a saint will resonate with an audience of clergy. It also shows that this is not a new or revolutionary idea.

Extreme or Absolute Language If a friend tells you that you *have* to play this new game because it has *the most intense plot line* and you'll be a *complete loser* if you don't, you should ask: Why all the extreme language?

In nonfiction, absolute words like *every, always, never,* or words that end in *-est* should also catch your attention. When you see extreme or absolute language, don't just accept it; determine why the author is using it.

In this example, a student marked **Extreme or Absolute Language:**

> 26   I have just received a letter from a white brother in Texas. He writes: "All Christians know that the colored people will receive equal rights eventually, but it is possible that you are in too great a religious hurry. . . . "

Anchor Question
When you notice this signpost, ask: Why would the author use this language? What does this reveal about the author's biases or purpose?

What is extreme about this statement?	It doesn't acknowledge that some Christians don't "know" this and assumes that eventual equality will just happen. It also dismisses people's need for equality.
What does this language reveal about purpose, bias, or perspective?	It reflects the letter writer's perspective that things are going fine, which he may see because he isn't really affected by inequality.

WHEN STUDENTS STRUGGLE . . .

Sketch to Stretch Some students may grasp material better if they visualize text details and then use drawing to interpret them. Ask students to reread the excerpts from "Letter from Birmingham Jail" and find a detail to visualize (for example, refusing to obey an unjust law). Then have them sketch the image they have envisioned and include the text of the detail in the sketch (in this case, the quoted words from St. Augustine, which include the extreme language, "no law at all"). Have students meet in small groups to share their sketches and their thoughts about how sketching helped them make sense of details and ideas in the text.

QUOTED WORDS

Explain that **Quoted Words** are information that comes from an authority—either an expert on a topic or someone who took part in or witnessed an event. Quoted Words can help students **analyze arguments** by offering support for important ideas. The information often will appear in quotation marks; but if not, there should be a reference to the source.

Read aloud the example passage and direct students to the quoted statement at the end. Explain that St. Augustine lived about 1,600 years before King wrote this letter. Point students to the reader's second comment to see why King might have wanted to use such an "old" quotation. Then ask students what idea the quoted words support. (*They support the idea that if a law is unfair, a person who disobeys that law is in the right.*)

Tell students when they spot Quoted Words, they should pause, mark the words in their consumable text, and ask themselves the anchor question: *Why is this person quoted, and what do the quoted words add?*

EXTREME OR ABSOLUTE LANGUAGE

Explain that **Extreme or Absolute Language** is all about word choice. Point out that we call words such as *every, nothing,* and *always* "absolute" because they do not allow for exceptions or compromise. Also explain that extreme language often exaggerates, as in *Everyone knows that. . . .* Noticing Extreme or Absolute Language can help students **analyze rhetorical devices.**

Read aloud the example passage and discuss the reader's comments, making sure students understand that the extreme language comes from a critic, not from King.

Tell students when they spot Extreme or Absolute Language, they should pause, mark it in their consumable text, and ask themselves the anchor questions: *Why would the author use this language? What does this reveal about the author's biases or purpose?*

APPLY THE SIGNPOSTS

Have students use the selection that follows to apply the signposts. As students encounter signposts, prompt them to stop, reread, and ask themselves the anchor questions that will help them understand King's argument.

Tell students to continue to look for these and other signposts as they read the other selections in the unit.

ANALYZE & APPLY

LETTER FROM BIRMINGHAM JAIL

Argument by **Martin Luther King Jr.**

In "Letter from Birmingham Jail," Martin Luther King Jr. defends what some critics called his "unwise and untimely" use of nonviolent protest to draw attention to injustice in Birmingham, Alabama. With logical reasoning and skillful rhetoric, King makes his case as one who is "compelled to carry the gospel of freedom" because he believes that freedom is "the goal of America."

 ESSENTIAL QUESTION:

What do we need in order to feel free?

222 Unit 4

 LEARNING MINDSET

Seeking Challenges As students preview "Letter from Birmingham Jail," they may be daunted by the length and depth of King's classic defense. Indeed, the text requires careful reading. Explain the importance of trying new things—in this case, working through a sometimes difficult yet very important text—and remind students that trying things that are hard is essential for learning. When students show understanding of aspects of the text, acknowledge their effort to work through a challenge; and if a response shows a lack of understanding, correct them, but also encourage them for taking the risk in responding at all.

QUICK START

Have you ever asked permission to do something new? Did you plan your case in advance? Did you anticipate and address possible reasons you might be told no? How did it go? Freewrite about your experience.

ANALYZE ARGUMENT

A well-crafted argument includes these elements:

- A clear **claim** stating the writer's position on the issue or problem

- Relevant and appealing **reasons** and **evidence** that support the claim

- **Counterarguments** that anticipate and rebut, or refute, opposing views

- **Concession** acknowledging a valid point made by the opposition

- A convincing **conclusion,** often with a call to action

An effective argument will appeal to the interests of a specific audience and work toward a clear goal or purpose. Look for these features as you read.

GENRE ELEMENTS: ARGUMENT

- makes claims to persuade an audience

- includes evidence to support claims

- contains personalized appeals to connect with the audience

- includes rhetorical devices that strengthen the message

- acknowledges and disproves counterclaims through concession and rebuttal

ANALYZE RHETORICAL DEVICES

Rhetoric is the art or study of using language effectively and persuasively. A **rhetorical device** is a technique writers use to enhance their arguments and communicate more effectively. King's letter uses these devices:

RHETORICAL DEVICE	HOW IT WORKS	EXAMPLE FROM TEXT
appeals	These include *ethos*: establishes authority or credibility *pathos*: speaks to emotions *logos*: uses logic or reason	I have the honor of serving as president of the Southern Christian Leadership Conference. . . .
antithesis	Contrasting ideas are presented via parallel language.	Injustice anywhere is a threat to justice everywhere. . . .
parallelism	The use of similar grammatical constructions to express ideas that are related or equal in importance.	I . . . am here because I was invited here. I am here because I have organizational ties here.
shift	A change in mood or tone, often signaled by words like *but* or *however*. Here, King shifts the meaning of *extremist* from negative to positive.	Was not Jesus an extremist for love: . . . the question is not whether we will be extremists, but what kind of extremists we will be. . . .

Point by point, King uses these and other techniques to show that each of the clergymen's criticisms is a **logical fallacy**, a statement based on an error in reasoning. As you read, keep in mind King's point and the techniques he uses to prove it.

(EL) ENGLISH LEARNER SUPPORT

Vocabulary Strategy Help students define and remember terms from the reading skills that may be unfamiliar. Create a 3-column chart on the board with the following terms in the first column: *antithesis, appeal, claim, concession, conclusion, counterclaim, counterargument, ethos, evidence, fallacy, logos, pathos, reason*. Have pairs or small groups use a reference source or create a definition in the second column. Lead the class in a discussion of the terms and encourage students to write down notes (such as mnemonics) in the third column to help them remember the definitions. **ALL LEVELS**

QUICK START

Have students read the set of Quick Start questions and identify occasions that might require a planned argument (for example, requesting financial help in making a purchase or asking for a later curfew). Discuss why it would be important to plan an approach and to anticipate a negative response. As students freewrite, instruct them to include some comments about why they think that their argument was either effective or weak. Invite a few volunteers to share their experiences.

ANALYZE ARGUMENT

Point out that the purpose of an argument is to persuade. Then display the six boldfaced terms and discuss each one. You may wish to categorize the terms as follows:

- *Presenting the writer's viewpoint:* **claim** (the writer's position); **reasons** (supportive statements of logic); **evidence** (proof that the reasons are valid); **conclusion** (a review of the main point, stated in a memorable way).

- *Facing opposing viewpoints:* **concession** (acknowledging merit in the other viewpoint); **counterargument** (arguing against that viewpoint). You might also add **counterclaim** from the Genre Elements list, but distinguish counterclaim from counterargument.

Emphasize the importance of understanding the audience. Discuss why it would be important to address an argument to an audience that had the power to do something about the issue at hand—and why a strong argument might still resonate with people who are reading it decades after it was written.

ANALYZE RHETORICAL DEVICES

Discuss the terms *ethos, pathos,* and *logos* and work with students to identify the parallel language in the examples of antithesis *(anywhere/everywhere)* and parallelism *("I am here [in Birmingham] because . . . here")*. Note that a shift can turn a negative into a positive (as King does in the example) but that the opposite also is true. As you relate the concept of logical fallacy to King's letter, point out that a counterclaim is not necessarily a logical fallacy (for a counterclaim can be well reasoned and may need to be conceded) and that writers need to be alert to spot and correct logical fallacies in their own arguments.

TEACH

CRITICAL VOCABULARY

Encourage students to read each question carefully and to consider context clues before making an answer choice.

Answers (sentences will vary):

1. **b;** *When people have a desire for revenge, it may <u>manifest</u> itself in a desire to <u>retaliate</u> against the person who wronged them.*

2. **a;** *I think that society would become a mess if we ever declared a <u>moratorium</u> on <u>mores</u>.*

3. **a;** *Sometimes it takes a powerful <u>provocation</u> to stir people out of their <u>complacency</u>.*

4. **a;** *The speaker was not <u>cognizant</u> of the effect of his words, which <u>precipitated</u> a walkout by some members of the audience.*

■ English Learner Support

Use Cognates Tell students that several of the Critical Vocabulary words have Spanish cognates: *moratorium/moratoria, precipitate/precipitar, complacency/complacencia, manifest/manifestar, provocation/provocación.*

ALL LEVELS

LANGUAGE CONVENTIONS

Emphasize the difference between **repetition** and **parallelism**: When students see exactly the same word or phrase repeated, they are seeing repetition; when they see a repeated structure, with some word variations (for example, a string of clauses beginning with *if*, or a set of statements with the same subject but different future-tense verbs), they are seeing parallelism. "The white moderate" quotation is an example of parallelism because it is the structure that is repeated (and only the subject *who* is repeated).

ANNOTATION MODEL

Students can review the **NOTICE & NOTE** Reading Model or the Reading Skills descriptions if they have questions about signposts or other possible annotations. Suggest that they underline important phrases or circle key words that help them identify important points. They may want to color-code their annotations by using a different color highlighter for each type of annotation. Point out that they may follow this suggestion or use their own system for marking up the selections in their write-in texts.

  GET READY

CRITICAL VOCABULARY

cognizant	moratorium	retaliate	precipitate
complacency	manifest	mores	provocation

Mark the letter of the best answer to each question. Then, explain your response to a partner using both words.

1. Which of the following would be used when talking about revenge?
   a. manifest   **b. retaliate**
2. Which of the following would be used when talking about values?
   a. mores   **b. moratorium**
3. Which of the following happens when someone incites or inflames a situation?
   a. provocation   **b. complacency**
4. Which of the following would be used when talking about being aware?
   a. cognizant   **b. precipitate**

LANGUAGE CONVENTIONS

Repetition is a technique in which a word or phrase is repeated for emphasis or unity. **Parallelism** is the repetition of grammatical structures to express ideas that are related or equal in importance. This example is from the letter:

. . . the white moderate, <u>who</u> is more devoted to "order" than to justice; <u>who</u> prefers a negative peace . . . <u>who</u> constantly says . . .

Notice how King uses repetition and parallelism to strengthen his argument.

ANNOTATION MODEL   **NOTICE & NOTE**

Here is how a student marked the opening of "Letter from Birmingham Jail."

April 16, 1963

<u>My Dear Fellow Clergymen:</u>

     While confined here in the Birmingham city jail, I came across <u>your recent statement calling my present activities "unwise and untimely."</u> Seldom do I pause to answer criticism of my work and ideas. If I sought to answer all the criticisms that cross my desk, my secretaries would have little time for anything other than such correspondence in the course of the day, and I would have no time for constructive work. <u>But since I feel that you are men of genuine good will and that your criticisms are sincerely set forth,</u> I want to try to answer your statement in what I hope will be patient and reasonable terms.

> King establishes audience and his own credibility—he's one of them.
>
> He explains why he's writing.
>
> He's not overly sensitive to criticism.
>
> He's polite and respectful.

BACKGROUND

Martin Luther King Jr. (1929–1968) *led a nonviolent protest in 1963 against lunch counter segregation in Birmingham, Alabama. He was jailed along with many of his supporters. While in jail, King wrote this letter in response to the local clergy. As a Baptist minister and civil rights leader, King helped to organize the 1963 March on Washington, where he delivered his "I Have a Dream" speech. His leadership was crucial in passing the Civil Rights Act of 1964. That year, he received the Nobel Peace Prize. King was assassinated in 1968.*

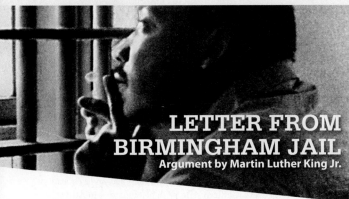

LETTER FROM BIRMINGHAM JAIL
Argument by Martin Luther King Jr.

SETTING A PURPOSE

As you read, monitor your understanding of King's lengthy and detailed argument by using a graphic organizer, note-taking, or annotations. Watch for and note key ideas he uses to make his case.

April 16, 1963
My Dear Fellow Clergymen: Close Read

1   While confined here in the Birmingham city jail, I came across your recent statement calling my present activities "unwise and untimely." Seldom do I pause to answer criticism of my work and ideas. If I sought to answer all the criticisms that cross my desk, my secretaries would have little time for anything other than such correspondence in the course of the day, and I would have no time for constructive work. But since I feel that you are men of genuine good will and that your criticisms are sincerely set forth, I want to try to answer your statement in what I hope will be patient and reasonable terms.

2   I think I should indicate why I am here in Birmingham, since you have been influenced by the view which argues against "outsiders coming in." I have the honor of serving as president

Notice & Note

You can use the side margins to notice and note signposts in the text.

QUOTED WORDS

Notice & Note: Mark the direct quotation in paragraph 2. Who is being quoted?

Interpret: Why are these words central to King's argument?

CLOSE READ SCREENCAST

Modeled Discussion   In their eBook, have students view the Close Read Screencasts, in which readers discuss and annotate two key passages:

- King's introduction to his letter (paragraph 1)
- King's discussion of just and unjust laws (paragraph 15)

As a class, view and discuss the video. Then have students pair up to do an independent close read of paragraph 37—King's request for southern white ministers to support integration because it is morally right to do so. Students can record their answers on the Close Read Practice PDF.

 Close Read   **Close Read Practice PDF**

BACKGROUND

After students read the Background note, explain that Martin Luther King Jr.'s position on nonviolent direct action was influenced by the views and methods of India's Mohandas Gandhi. The lunch counter protest mentioned in the note was part of The Birmingham Campaign—various nonviolent actions that protested segregation in the city. The protests were ruled illegal, but King continued to protest, and he was arrested. News and photos of reprisals against the protesters shocked the nation and got the White House involved. Negotiations led to early steps of desegregation (including desegregation of the lunch counters), but civil rights struggles would continue to involve King after his release. A federal U.S. holiday, celebrated on the third Monday of each January, was established in 1983 to honor King's far-reaching accomplishments and legacy.

SETTING A PURPOSE

Direct students to use the Setting a Purpose prompt to focus their reading.

▶ QUOTED WORDS

Remind students that the Quoted Words signpost encourages them to think about the authority of relevant people or groups. (**Answer:** *The people who don't want to see protest organizers enter the city are the source of the quotation. The words are important because they begin to make the case that African Americans in Birmingham needed organizational help to effectively draw attention to the prejudice that they faced in that city.*)

■ English Learner Support

Understand Word Parts   Point out that *outsider* is related to *outside* and that both words include the prefix *out-*. Explain that *out-* can refer to something that is outside or something that exists at or comes from a distance. Ask students to define the word *outsider*. ("a person who comes from the outside" or "a person left out of a group") Display these selection words and have pairs work to define each word by drawing on context as well as what they know about the prefix *out-*: *outgoing* (paragraph 12), *outlawing* (paragraph 15), *outlet* (paragraph 30), *outlines* (paragraph 38), and *outcome* (paragraph 44). **LIGHT**

ANALYZE RHETORICAL DEVICES

Tell students that all of the **allusions** in paragraph 3 come from the Bible. *The Macedonian call for aid* is explained in a footnote, but you may wish to explain the others:

- *the prophets of the eighth century B.C.:* Amos, Hosea, Isaiah, and Micah, all of whom have books named for them in the Bible

- *"thus saith the Lord":* a way of declaring that a prophet's message came directly from God

- *the Apostle Paul:* an early convert to Christianity who traveled extensively, founded many churches, and wrote most of the epistles (letters) that are part of the New Testament

(**Answer:** *King's audience is Christian clergymen, so they would be likely to appreciate and be persuaded by religious allusions, especially references to the Bible.*)

■ English Learner Support

Discuss Allusions Students may not realize that they already have incorporated some allusions into their knowledge of English. Discuss these examples:

- "The actor's success is a *Cinderella* story." = "The actor grew up in poverty but, surprisingly, became very successful." (literature)

- "The team had a good season but *went down like the Titanic* in the playoffs." = "The team suffered a major defeat in its playoff game." (historical event)

- "She was a *Good Samaritan* that day." = "She helped someone who was in trouble." (Bible)

Have students brainstorm and discuss other common allusions. **MODERATE/LIGHT**

CRITICAL VOCABULARY

cognizant: King is aware that communities and states are connected.

ASK STUDENTS how King was cognizant of injustices in Birmingham if he did not live there. (*King was informed by an affiliate organization that was present in Birmingham.*)

NOTICE & NOTE

ANALYZE RHETORICAL DEVICES

Annotate: Paragraph 3 is an extended **allusion,** an indirect reference to a famous person, place, event, or literary work. Mark the people, places, events, and/or literary works to which King alludes in this paragraph.

Connect: Why does King include religious allusions in his letter?

cognizant
(kŏg´nĭ-zənt) *adj.* aware or conscious of.

of the Southern Christian Leadership Conference, an organization operating in every southern state, with headquarters in Atlanta, Georgia. We have some eighty-five affiliated organizations across the South, and one of them is the Alabama Christian Movement for Human Rights. Frequently we share staff, educational and financial resources with our affiliates. Several months ago the affiliate here in Birmingham asked us to be on call to engage in a nonviolent direct-action program if such were deemed necessary. We readily consented, and when the hour came we lived up to our promise. So I, along with several members of my staff, am here because I was invited here. I am here because I have organizational ties here.

3   But more basically, I am in Birmingham because injustice is here. Just as the prophets of the eighth century B.C. left their villages and carried their "thus saith the Lord" far beyond the boundaries of their home towns, and just as the Apostle Paul left his village of Tarsus and carried the gospel of Jesus Christ to the far corners of the Greco-Roman world, so am I compelled to carry the gospel of freedom beyond my own home town. Like Paul, I must constantly respond to the Macedonian call for aid.[1]

4   Moreover, I am **cognizant** of the interrelatedness of all communities and states. I cannot sit idly by in Atlanta and not be concerned about what happens in Birmingham. Injustice anywhere is a threat to justice everywhere. We are caught in an inescapable

---

[1] **Macedonian call for aid:** according to the Bible (Acts 16), the apostle Paul received a vision calling him to preach in Macedonia, an area north of Greece.

WHEN STUDENTS STRUGGLE . . .

Understand Purpose To help students understand King's purpose in writing the letter and to practice citing text evidence, read aloud paragraph 1. Ask students to identify King's audience. (*"My Dear Fellow Clergymen"*) Then ask how these people described King's protest activities. (*"unwise and untimely"*) Direct students to the final sentence in this paragraph and ask them to explain why King is writing this letter to the clergymen. (*"to answer your statement"*) Have partners read paragraphs 2–3. Ask them to cite evidence that answers these questions:

- Who invited King to Birmingham? (*"the affiliate here in Birmingham"*)
- Why did he accept that invitation? (*"because injustice is here"*)

network of mutuality, tied in a single garment of destiny. Whatever affects one directly, affects all indirectly. Never again can we afford to live with the narrow, provincial "outside agitator" idea. Anyone who lives inside the United States can never be considered an outsider anywhere within its bounds.

5   You deplore the demonstrations taking place in Birmingham. But your statement, I am sorry to say, fails to express a similar concern for the conditions that brought about the demonstrations. I am sure that none of you would want to rest content with the superficial kind of social analysis that deals merely with effects and does not grapple with underlying causes. It is unfortunate that demonstrations are taking place in Birmingham, but it is even more unfortunate that the city's white power structure left the Negro community with no alternative.

6   In any nonviolent campaign there are four basic steps: collection of the facts to determine whether injustices exist; negotiation; self-purification; and direct action. We have gone through all these steps in Birmingham. There can be no gainsaying the fact that racial injustice engulfs this community. Birmingham is probably the most thoroughly segregated city in the United States. Its ugly record of brutality is widely known. Negroes have experienced grossly unjust treatment in the courts. There have been more unsolved bombings of Negro homes and churches in Birmingham than in any other city in the nation. These are the hard, brutal facts of the case. On the basis of these conditions, Negro leaders sought to negotiate with the city

EXTREME OR ABSOLUTE LANGUAGE

Notice & Note: Mark uses of the word *never* and other absolute language in paragraph 4.

Connect: How might King's choice of words make it difficult for his audience to disagree with him?

EXTREME OR ABSOLUTE LANGUAGE

Remind students that absolute language does not allow for any exceptions or any compromises. Discuss the fact that *never* is an example of absolute language because it means "not ever," "not at all," and "at no time." (**Answer:** *King's word choice makes disagreement difficult because it emphasizes the idea that there cannot be any exceptions when it comes to justice.*)

■ English Learner Support

Understand Negative Statements In several languages (including Cantonese, Korean, Russian, Spanish, and Tagalog), negative statements do not include helping verbs. Direct students to "Never again can we afford" in paragraph 4 and point out the helping verb *can*. Then say a few simpler negative statements, stressing the helping verb (for example, I <u>do</u> not like cold weather, I <u>will</u> not go to the party, and [after explaining that *cannot* is a single word] I <u>cannot</u> find my keys) and have students repeat each one.

SUBSTANTIAL/MODERATE

ENGLISH LEARNER SUPPORT

Build Vocabulary Using a whiteboard, display paragraph 5. Mark the following words and phrases: *deplore, fails to, superficial,* and *grapple with.* Explain that each one is a stronger way of expressing something that could have been said more simply and objectively (*dislike, does not, basic,* and *deal with,* respectively). Have students repeat these sentences in random order, substituting the word or phrase from paragraph 5: I <u>dislike</u> broccoli. The movie <u>does not</u> make much money. I gave the article a <u>basic</u> reading. The committee will have to <u>deal with</u> that problem tomorrow. As students continue to read King's letter, have them look for other words and phrases that he chose for their powerful impact. **MODERATE**

ANALYZE ARGUMENT

Point out the sentence in paragraph 6 that introduces the list of actions already taken: "We have gone through all of these steps in Birmingham". Ask students to identify the structure King uses in this section of his **argument** (*main idea and supporting details*) and discuss why it is effective. (**Answer:** *King is responding to the claim that his work is "untimely" by detailing evidence to show that the work is, in fact, long overdue. The depth of the detail shows that plans for the protests were carefully thought out and not a rush to action that might harm the movement.*)

EL ENGLISH LEARNER SUPPORT

Discuss Visuals Give students a few moments to examine the photograph on this page and to think about what King has said in his letter thus far. Then have them meet in mixed-proficiency groups to discuss the following questions:

- What does the photo show? (*Someone is spraying people with water.*)

- A fire hose has high water pressure. How does that feel? (*It probably hurts.*)

- Why do you think the people are being sprayed? (*to get them to stop doing something—perhaps to stop protesting*)

- Who do you think is spraying them? (*people who do not want them to protest; members of "the city's white power structure" [paragraph 5]*)

If enough students speak the same primary language, allow them to work together to translate the questions into that language. **ALL LEVELS**

CRITICAL VOCABULARY

moratorium: Because of promises made by local merchants, leaders of the Alabama Christian Movement for Human Rights agreed to suspend their demonstrations in Birmingham.

ASK STUDENTS why the leaders of the Alabama Christian Movement for Human Rights agreed to a moratorium on all direct actions. (*They wanted to show that they would honor the negotiated terms.*)

 NOTICE & NOTE

ANALYZE ARGUMENT
Annotate: Mark details in paragraphs 6–9 that list steps King and his associates have taken in Birmingham.

Analyze: How does going into such detail about these actions support King's argument?

moratorium
(môr-ə-tôr´ē-əm) *n.* a temporary suspension or agreed-upon delay.

fathers. But the latter consistently refused to engage in good-faith negotiation.

7   Then, last September, came the opportunity to talk with leaders of Birmingham's economic community. In the course of the negotiations, certain promises were made by the merchants—for example, to remove the stores' humiliating racial signs.[2] On the basis of these promises, the Reverend Fred Shuttlesworth and the leaders of the Alabama Christian Movement for Human Rights agreed to a **moratorium** on all demonstrations. As the weeks and months went by, we realized that we were the victims of a broken promise. A few signs, briefly removed, returned; the others remained.

8   As in so many past experiences, our hopes had been blasted, and the shadow of deep disappointment settled upon us. We had no

[2] **racial signs:** signs that marked segregated areas of buildings and other facilities.

alternative except to prepare for direct action, whereby we would present our very bodies as a means of laying our case before the conscience of the local and the national community. Mindful of the difficulties involved, we decided to undertake a process of self-purification. We began a series of workshops on nonviolence, and we repeatedly asked ourselves: "Are you able to accept blows without **retaliating?**" "Are you able to endure the ordeal of jail?" We decided to schedule our direct-action program for the Easter season, realizing that except for Christmas, this is the main shopping period of the year. Knowing that a strong economic withdrawal program³ would be the by-product of direct action, we felt that this would be the best time to bring pressure to bear on the merchants for the needed change.

9   Then it occurred to us that Birmingham's mayoralty election was coming up in March, and we speedily decided to postpone action until after election day. When we discovered that the Commissioner of Public Safety, Eugene "Bull" Connor, had piled up enough votes to be in the run-off, we decided again to postpone action until the day after the run-off so that the demonstrations could not be used to cloud the issues. Like many others, we waited to see Mr. Connor defeated, and to this end we endured postponement after postponement. Having aided in this community need, we felt that our direct-action program could be delayed no longer.

10   You may well ask: "Why direct action? Why sit-ins, marches and so forth? Isn't negotiation a better path?" You are quite right in calling for negotiation. Indeed, this is the very purpose of direct action. Nonviolent direct action seeks to create such a crisis and foster such a tension that a community which has constantly refused to negotiate is forced to confront the issue. It seeks so to dramatize the issue that it can no longer be ignored. My citing the creation of tension as part of the work of the nonviolent-resister may sound rather shocking. But I must confess that I am not afraid of the word "tension." I have earnestly opposed violent tension, but there is a type of constructive, nonviolent tension which is necessary for growth. Just as Socrates⁴ felt that it was necessary to create a tension in the mind so that individuals could rise from the bondage of myths and half-truths to the unfettered realm of creative analysis and objective appraisal, so must we see the need for nonviolent gadflies to create the kind of tension in society that will help men rise from the dark depths of prejudice and racism to the majestic heights of understanding and brotherhood.

retaliate
(rĭ-tăl´ē-āt) v. to respond in kind to having been acted upon, often with harmful intent.

LANGUAGE CONVENTIONS

Annotate: Mark the instances of the word *tension* in paragraph 10. How many times does King use the word?

Evaluate: How do the meaning and tone of *tension* change over the course of the paragraph? How does this repetition help King make a point?

---

³ **economic withdrawal program:** boycott.
⁴ **Socrates:** (c. 470–399 BCE) Greek philosopher and major influence in the development of Western thought.

Letter from Birmingham Jail   229

LANGUAGE CONVENTIONS

Suggest that students look at the language around each instance of the word *tension* to help them consider its tone and meaning. If necessary, explain that *tension* is a stressful feeling, a feeling of anxiety that most people want to do something to settle. (**Answer:** *At first,* tension *seems to be a negative word. However, King makes it positive when he explains the idea of "constructive, nonviolent* tension *which is necessary for growth"—that is,* tension *as a way to encourage positive change. The repetition of* tension *indicates that because it is a result of nonviolent direct action, King finds it valuable and wants to see it become part of the resolution of an unjust situation.*)

APPLYING ACADEMIC VOCABULARY

❏ comprehensive ☑ equivalent ☑ incentive ❏ innovate ❏ subordinate

Write and Discuss Have students turn to a partner to discuss the following questions based on paragraph 10. Guide students to include the academic vocabulary words *equivalent* and *incentive* in their responses. Ask volunteers to share their responses with the class.

• What is the **equivalent** of Socrates' ideas in the Civil Rights movement?
• What was King's **incentive** for choosing nonviolent direct action in Birmingham?

CRITICAL VOCABULARY

retaliate: The workshops on nonviolence were designed to ensure that participants in direct actions would not react in a harmful way even if harm came to them.

ASK STUDENTS what might happen if participants retaliated against police who struck blows. (*Participants and police officers would both get injured, and participants would fail to win the support of the larger population.*)

TEACH

ANALYZE RHETORICAL DEVICES

Remind students that **antithesis** involves two things: contrasting words and parallel language. When students have identified the example of antithesis in paragraph 14, briefly discuss its parallel language. Point out that "jetlike speed" and "horse-and-buggy pace" are grammatically parallel because they are both noun phrases. Then call on one or more volunteers to read the entire sentence aloud in a way that highlights its contrasts. (**Answer:** *These contrasting ideas remind King's audience that the United States is moving more slowly than other countries are when it comes to securing greater freedom for its people. The statement may be part of the way that King shames his audience into taking action.*)

ENGLISH LEARNER SUPPORT

Expand Reading Skills Read paragraph 13 with students. Ask: Which sentence expresses the main idea? *(the first sentence)* Prompt students to restate the main idea in their own words. *(Oppressors never give freedom to the oppressed; the oppressed must fight for it.)* Point out that King provides details to support this main idea in paragraph 14. Have pairs or small groups of students work together to review paragraph 14 and explain how King supports this main idea. Provide this frame: *He gives many examples to show how African Americans have been _____ by_____ . (He gives many examples to show how African Americans have been mistreated and oppressed by mobs, police, and those that support segregation.)*

MODERATE

NOTICE & NOTE

11 The purpose of our direct-action program is to create a situation so crisis-packed that it will inevitably open the door to negotiation. I therefore concur with you in your call for negotiation. Too long has our beloved Southland been bogged down in a tragic effort to live in monologue rather than dialogue.

12 One of the basic points in your statement is that the action that I and my associates have taken in Birmingham is untimely. Some have asked: "Why didn't you give the new city administration time to act?" The only answer that I can give to this query is that the new Birmingham administration must be prodded about as much as the outgoing one, before it will act. . . . My friends, I must say to you that we have not made a single gain in civil rights without determined legal and nonviolent pressure. Lamentably, it is an historical fact that privileged groups seldom give up their privileges voluntarily. Individuals may see the moral light and voluntarily give up their unjust posture; but, as Reinhold Niebuhr[5] has reminded us, groups tend to be more immoral than individuals.

13 We know through painful experience that freedom is never voluntarily given by the oppressor; it must be demanded by the oppressed. Frankly, I have yet to engage in a direct-action campaign that was "well timed" in the view of those who have not suffered unduly from the disease of segregation. For years now I have heard the word "Wait!" It rings in the ear of every Negro with piercing familiarity. This "Wait" has almost always meant "Never." We must come to see, with one of our distinguished jurists, that "justice too long delayed is justice denied."

14 We have waited for more than 340 years for our constitutional and God-given rights. The nations of Asia and Africa are moving with jetlike speed toward gaining political independence, but we still creep at horse-and-buggy pace toward gaining a cup of coffee at a lunch counter. Perhaps it is easy for those who have never felt the stinging darts of segregation to say, "Wait." But when you have seen vicious mobs lynch your mothers and fathers at will and drown your sisters and brothers at whim; when you have seen hate-filled policemen curse, kick and even kill your black brothers and sisters; when you see the vast majority of your twenty million Negro brothers smothering in an airtight cage of poverty in the midst of an affluent society; when you suddenly find your tongue twisted and your speech stammering as you seek to explain to your six-year-old daughter why she can't go to the public amusement park that has just been advertised on television, and see tears welling up in her eyes when she is told that Funtown is closed to colored children, and see

ANALYZE RHETORICAL DEVICES

Annotate: To create **antithesis**, a writer contrasts ideas using parallel language. Mark the example of antithesis near the beginning of paragraph 14.

Compare: How do these contrasting ideas support King's argument?

---

[5] **Reinhold Niebuhr:** (1892–1971) American theologian whose writings address moral and social problems.

230   Unit 4

IMPROVE READING FLUENCY

Targeted Passage Hearing examples of fluent reading can help students, so model a fluent, expressive reading of paragraph 13. Have students follow along in their texts as you read aloud, focusing on King's phrasing and tone. For example, read the first sentence as "We know / through painful experience / that freedom / is never voluntarily given / by the oppressor; / it must be demanded / by the oppressed." In addition, distinguish the sarcastic tone in the quoted *"well timed"* from the confrontational tone of *"Wait!"* As time permits, invite students to read the paragraph aloud, with greater fluency.

 Go to the **Reading Studio** for additional support in developing fluency.

ominous clouds of inferiority beginning to form in her little mental sky, and see her beginning to distort her personality by developing an unconscious bitterness toward white people; when you have to concoct an answer for a five-year old son who is asking: "Daddy, why do white people treat colored people so mean?"; when you take a cross-country drive and find it necessary to sleep night after night in the uncomfortable corners of your automobile because no motel will accept you; when you are humiliated day in and day out by nagging signs reading "white" and "colored"; when your first name becomes "nigger," your middle name becomes "boy" (however old you are) and your last name becomes "John," and your wife and mother are never given the respected title "Mrs."; when you are harried by day and haunted by night by the fact that you are a Negro, living constantly at tiptoe stance, never quite knowing what to expect next, and are plagued with inner fears and outer resentments; when you are forever fighting a degenerating sense of "nobodiness"—then you will understand why we find it difficult to wait. There comes a time when the cup of endurance runs over, and men are no longer willing to be plunged into the abyss of despair. I hope, sirs, you can understand our legitimate and unavoidable impatience.

15   You express a great deal of anxiety over our willingness to break laws. This is certainly a legitimate concern. Since we so diligently urge people to obey the Supreme Court's decision of 1954 outlawing segregation in the public schools,[6] at first glance it may seem rather paradoxical for us consciously to break laws. One may well ask: "How can you advocate breaking some laws and obeying others?" The answer lies in the fact that there are two types of laws: just and unjust. I would be the first to advocate obeying just laws. One has not only a legal but a moral responsibility to obey just laws. Conversely, one has a moral responsibility to disobey unjust laws. I would agree with St. Augustine[7] that "an unjust law is no law at all."

16   Now, what is the difference between the two? How does one determine whether a law is just or unjust? A just law is a man-made code that squares with the moral law or the law of God. An unjust law is a code that is out of harmony with the moral law. To put it in the terms of St. Thomas Aquinas:[8] An unjust law is a human law that is not rooted in eternal law and natural law. Any law that uplifts human personality is just. Any law that degrades human personality is unjust. All segregation statutes are unjust because segregation distorts the soul and damages the personality. It gives the segregator a false sense of superiority and the segregated a false sense of inferiority.

---

[6] **Supreme Court . . . public schools:** The U.S. Supreme Court's decision in the case *Brown v. Board of Education of Topeka, Kansas.*

[7] **St. Augustine:** North African bishop (AD 354–430) regarded as a founder of Christianity.

[8] **St. Thomas Aquinas:** noted philosopher and theologian (1225–1274).

ANALYZE ARGUMENT

Annotate: Mark the concession that King makes in paragraph 15.

Connect: How does this concession work to support King's argument?

Close Read

ANALYZE ARGUMENT

Remind students that when a writer offers a **concession**, he or she admits that the opposing point of view makes a valid point. The writer may well disagree with that point, but he or she understands why the opponent says it and why many people may agree with it. Elicit that King uses the phrase *a legitimate concern* to concede the point that breaking the law is a serious matter. (**Answer:** *The concession shows that King has heard and understands the fears of his audience—in short, that he is a reasonable person.*)

■ English Learner Support

Understand Pronoun Use   Students may be confused by King's repeated use of the pronoun *one* in paragraph 15. Explain that here, *one* is not a reference to the number (1); it is a rather formal way of saying *every person* or *all people*. Have students say the sentences in which *one* is the subject, using *every person* instead of *one*. (You may wish to point out that King really means "people who are criticizing me" but that *one* softens the tone and helps make the statement more acceptable to his audience.) Have students write a sentence using *all people*. Then ask them to edit the sentence, revising *all people* to the pronoun *one*.

MODERATE

For **reading support** for students at varying proficiency levels, see the **Text X-Ray** on page 220D.

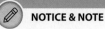
 ENGLISH LEARNER SUPPORT

Preteach Content Explain that paragraph 17 presents a complex argument that uses some difficult language and concepts and that King presents further explanations in paragraphs 18 and 19. Paraphrase the content of paragraph 17 as follows: *Fair, or just, laws treat all groups of people the same. Unfair, or unjust, laws discriminate against certain groups and treat them unfairly.* Note that King must provide these distinctions because many laws at the time discriminated against African Americans and treated them unfairly. Ask students to reread the paragraph and ask questions about unfamiliar vocabulary and meanings.

ALL LEVELS

 ENGLISH LEARNER SUPPORT

Create Definitions Explain that in paragraph 17, King presents definitions of *unjust law* and *just law* in an effective way. Effective definitions begin by naming the larger group (category) to which the term belongs (here, *code*) and then saying something that shows how that term is different from other members of the group (often in a clause beginning with *that*). Have students state simple definitions of the following words, using this frame: *A [term] is a [category] that. . . .* :

- shoe (Example: A shoe is a piece of clothing that is worn on the feet.)

- heart (Example: A heart is an organ that moves blood throughout the body.)

- square (Example: A square is a shape that has four equal sides.)

To extend the activity, have students go back into paragraph 16 and find the definitions that King gives there. Which definitions of just laws and unjust laws are easiest to understand—those in paragraph 16 or those in paragraph 17?

LIGHT

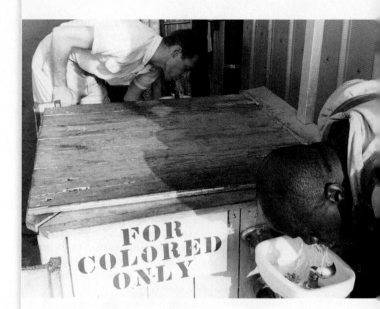

Segregation, to use the terminology of the Jewish philosopher Martin Buber,[9] substitutes an "I-it" relationship for an "I-thou" relationship and ends up relegating persons to the status of things. Hence segregation is not only politically, economically and sociologically unsound, it is morally wrong and sinful. Paul Tillich[10] has said that sin is separation. Is not segregation an existential expression of man's tragic separation, his awful estrangement, his terrible sinfulness? Thus it is that I can urge men to obey the 1954 decision of the Supreme Court, for it is morally right; and I can urge them to disobey segregation ordinances, for they are morally wrong.

17   Let us consider a more concrete example of just and unjust laws. An unjust law is a code that a numerical or power majority group compels a minority group to obey but does not make binding on itself. This is *difference* made legal. By the same token, a just law is a code that a majority compels a minority to follow and that it is willing to follow itself. This is *sameness* made legal.

18   Let me give another explanation. A law is unjust if it is inflicted on a minority that, as a result of being denied the right to vote, had no part in enacting or devising the law. Who can say that the legislature of Alabama which set up that state's segregation laws was democratically elected? Throughout Alabama all sorts

---

[9] **Martin Buber:** influential philosopher (1878–1965) with a great impact on Jewish and Christian theology.

[10] **Paul Tillich:** (1886–1965) influential German-American philosopher and Christian theologian.

 ENGLISH LEARNER SUPPORT

Make Personal Connections Throughout this selection, English Learners are encouraged to speak and write about King's ideas and his ways of expressing them; but the fact that some students are English Learners means that they come from another culture—and perhaps a culture in which similar injustices have occurred or are still occurring. They may also see injustices occurring in American society. Be alert to students who feel stress because they are making a strong personal connection (such as when they study the photograph on this page). Encourage them to freewrite about their ideas and feelings in their primary language and, if they wish, to share those ideas and feelings during class or small-group discussion. **ALL LEVELS**

of devious methods are used to prevent Negroes from becoming registered voters, and there are some counties in which, even though Negroes constitute a majority of the population, not a single Negro is registered. Can any law enacted under such circumstances be considered democratically structured?

19   Sometimes a law is just on its face and unjust in its application. For instance, I have been arrested on a charge of parading without a permit. Now, there is nothing wrong in having an ordinance which requires a permit for a parade. But such an ordinance becomes unjust when it is used to maintain segregation and to deny citizens the First-Amendment privilege of peaceful assembly and protest.

20   I hope you are able to see the distinction I am trying to point out. In no sense do I advocate evading or defying the law, as would the rabid segregationist. That would lead to anarchy. One who breaks an unjust law must do so openly, lovingly, and with a willingness to accept the penalty. I submit that an individual who breaks a law that conscience tells him is unjust, and who willingly accepts the penalty of imprisonment in order to arouse the conscience of the community over its injustice, is in reality expressing the highest respect for law.

21   Of course, there is nothing new about this kind of civil disobedience. It was evidenced sublimely in the refusal of Shadrach, Meshach and Abednego to obey the laws of Nebuchadnezzar,[11] on the ground that a higher moral law was at stake. It was practiced superbly by the early Christians, who were willing to face hungry lions and the excruciating pain of chopping blocks rather than submit to certain unjust laws of the Roman Empire. To a degree, academic freedom is a reality today because Socrates practiced civil disobedience. In our own nation, the Boston Tea Party[12] represented a massive act of civil disobedience.

22   We should never forget that everything Adolf Hitler did in Germany was "legal" and everything the Hungarian freedom fighters[13] did in Hungary was "illegal." It was "illegal" to aid and comfort a Jew in Hitler's Germany. Even so, I am sure that, had I lived in Germany at the time, I would have aided and comforted my Jewish brothers. If today I lived in a Communist country where certain principles dear to the Christian faith are suppressed, I would openly advocate disobeying that country's antireligious laws.

23   I must make two honest confessions to you, my Christian and Jewish brothers. First, I must confess that over the past few years I have been gravely disappointed with the white moderate. I have

---

[11] **refusal ... Nebuchadnezzar:** Biblical account of three Hebrews condemned for refusing to worship an idol as required by the King of Babylon. The three were miraculously protected from the flames into which they were thrown.

[12] **Boston Tea Party:** a 1773 protest against the British Tea Act in which American colonists dumped 342 chests of tea into Boston Harbor.

[13] **Hungarian freedom fighters:** participants in the 1956 revolt against Hungary's Soviet-backed government.

ANALYZE RHETORICAL DEVICES

Annotate: Mark the allusions in paragraphs 21 and 22.

Evaluate: Are these allusions an effective way to support the idea of civil disobedience? Why or why not?

BIG QUESTIONS

Notice & Note: What surprising idea does King express in paragraph 23?

Interpret: Why might King's audience find this idea surprising? How might readers react to this statement?

Letter from Birmingham Jail   233

ANALYZE RHETORICAL DEVICES

Have students read the footnotes and also offer additional explanations for the allusions that are not footnoted. Explain that the **allusions** illustrate the idea of disobeying a legal law because a contrasting moral law is felt to be more important. (***Answer:*** *The allusions are effective. King's audience almost certainly would agree that all of the "law-breaking" people mentioned had done the right thing. In addition, the allusions encourage King's audience to see Civil Rights protesters as part of this long tradition.*)

■ English Learner Support

Interpret New Vocabulary In paragraph 21, King introduces the term *civil disobedience*. Explain that the term refers to people refusing to obey certain laws because they feel the laws are morally wrong. Ask: According to King, how did Shadrach, Meshach, and Abednego practice civil disobedience? (*They refused to worship what they believed was a false god, even when the law said they had to do so.*) If the photograph on page 232 were meant to show civil disobedience, what activity would it show? (*The African American man drinking at the "white" fountain.*)

ALL LEVELS

▶ BIG QUESTIONS

Have students paraphrase the second sentence in paragraph 23. Or model a possible answer: *I am very disappointed that many white people who are not segregationists do nothing to help the Civil Rights movement.* Then have a volunteer read aloud sentence 3 and discuss what might make that idea surprising and why King prefaces the idea by writing, "I have almost reached the regrettable conclusion. . . ." Discuss the importance of King's message in this paragraph to his argument. (***Answer:*** *Members of King's audience probably think of themselves as white moderates and therefore would be surprised that King, their "fellow clergyman," would say this about them. If present-day readers think of themselves in the same way, they would be similarly surprised.*)

WHEN STUDENTS STRUGGLE . . .

Analyze Arguments Remind students that an argument presents the writer's point of view but also must consider opposing viewpoints. Review the fact that King favored breaking some laws, even though other clergymen opposed that course of action. Then have partners work to paraphrase paragraphs 20 and 21. Follow up by having one partner argue for one minute in favor of breaking some laws and then the other partner argue against it.

For additional support, go to the Reading Studio and assign the following **Level Up Tutorial: Analyzing Arguments.**

ANALYZE RHETORICAL DEVICES

Review the term **logical fallacy.** Suggest that students look for language in paragraph 25 that indicates that King has doubts about or is surprised by what he has been told. (**Answer:** *King offers the examples of blaming the victim of a robbery for causing the crime and of blaming Socrates and Jesus for their own executions.*)

■ English Learner Support

Discuss Rhetorical Questions In part, King makes his point about the logical fallacy by asking rhetorical questions in paragraph 25. Students who are learning English may think that every question requires an answer, but tell them that a **rhetorical question** does not, either because there is no answer or because the answer is so obvious that it need not be said. Writers use rhetorical questions to grab the attention of their audience and to emphasize ideas. Read students the three "Isn't this like . . . ?" questions that King asks in paragraph 25 and have them explain why they are rhetorical questions. (*The answer to all three is obvious: "Of course it is!"*) **LIGHT**

For **listening and speaking support** for students at varying proficiency levels, see the **Text X-Ray** on page 220C–220D.

CRITICAL VOCABULARY

precipitate: King does not agree with the clergymen's assertion that the peaceful direct action caused the police to act violently toward participants.

ASK STUDENTS to identify what King argues did *not* precipitate, or cause, a man to be robbed. (*"his possession of money"*)

---

almost reached the regrettable conclusion that the Negro's great stumbling block in his stride toward freedom is not the White Citizen's Counciler or the Ku Klux Klanner,[14] but the white moderate, who is more devoted to "order" than to justice; who prefers a negative peace which is the absence of tension to a positive peace which is the presence of justice; who constantly says: "I agree with you in the goal you seek, but I cannot agree with your methods of direct action"; who paternalistically believes he can set the timetable for another man's freedom; who lives by a mythical concept of time and who constantly advises the Negro to wait for a "more convenient season." Shallow understanding from people of good will is more frustrating than absolute misunderstanding from people of ill will. Lukewarm acceptance is much more bewildering than outright rejection.

24   I had hoped that the white moderate would understand that law and order exist for the purpose of establishing justice and that when they fail in this purpose they become the dangerously structured dams that block the flow of social progress. I had hoped that the white moderate would understand that the present tension in the South is a necessary phase of the transition from an obnoxious negative peace, in which the Negro passively accepted his unjust plight, to a substantive and positive peace, in which all men will respect the dignity and worth of human personality. Actually, we who engage in nonviolent direct action are not the creators of tension. We merely bring to the surface the hidden tension that is already alive. We bring it out in the open, where it can be seen and dealt with. Like a boil that can never be cured so long as it is covered up but must be opened with all its ugliness to the natural medicines of air and light, injustice must be exposed, with all the tension its exposure creates, to the light of human conscience and the air of national opinion before it can be cured.

25   In your statement you assert that our actions, even though peaceful, must be condemned because they **precipitate** violence. But is this a logical assertion? Isn't this like condemning a robbed man because his possession of money precipitated the evil act of robbery? Isn't this like condemning Socrates because his unswerving commitment to truth and his philosophical inquiries precipitated the act by the misguided populace in which they made him drink hemlock? Isn't this like condemning Jesus because his unique God-consciousness and never-ceasing devotion to God's will precipitated the evil act of crucifixion? We must come to see that, as the federal courts have consistently affirmed, it is wrong to urge an individual to cease his efforts to gain his basic constitutional rights because the quest may precipitate violence. Society must protect the robbed and punish the robber.

[14]**White . . . Klanner:** members of white-supremacist groups.

precipitate
(prĭ-sĭp´ĭ-tāt) *v.* to cause something to happen rapidly or unexpectedly.

ANALYZE RHETORICAL DEVICES

Annotate: Mark the logical fallacy about peaceful protests that King introduces in paragraph 25.

Evaluate: What examples does King use to refute this fallacy?

ENGLISH LEARNER SUPPORT

Analyze Conclusions Explain that a **conclusion** is a judgment based on related details or events. Help students trace the development of a conclusion. Direct students to King's conclusions about white moderates that appear in the final two sentences of paragraph 23. Read the sentences aloud and define words and phrases students may not understand (*shallow, good will, frustrating, absolute, ill will, lukewarm acceptance, bewildering, outright rejection*). Then explain that King based his conclusions on specific reasons. Work with students to reread paragraph 23 aloud, pausing after each relative clause that provides a reason for King's disappointment in order to help students monitor their understanding. Encourage students to paraphrase each reason. **LIGHT**

26　　I had also hoped that the white moderate would reject the myth concerning time in relation to the struggle for freedom. I have just received a letter from a white brother in Texas. He writes: "All Christians know that the colored people will receive equal rights eventually, but it is possible that you are in too great a religious hurry. It has taken Christianity almost two thousand years to accomplish what it has. The teachings of Christ take time to come to earth." Such an attitude stems from a tragic misconception of time, from the strangely irrational notion that there is something in the very flow of time that will inevitably cure all ills. Actually, time itself is neutral; it can be used either destructively or constructively. More and more I feel that the people of ill will have used time much more effectively than have the people of good will. We will have to repent in this generation not merely for the hateful words and actions of the bad people but for the appalling silence of the good people. Human progress never rolls in on wheels of inevitability; it comes through the tireless efforts of men willing to be coworkers with God, and without this hard work, time itself becomes an ally of the forces of social stagnation. We must use time creatively, in the knowledge that the time is always ripe to do right. Now is the time to make real the promise of democracy and transform our pending national elegy into a creative psalm[15] of brotherhood. Now is the time to lift our national policy from the quicksand of racial injustice to the solid rock of human dignity.

27　　You speak of our activity in Birmingham as extreme. At first I was rather disappointed that fellow clergymen would see my nonviolent efforts as those of an extremist. I began thinking about the fact that I stand in the middle of two opposing forces in the Negro community. One is a force of **complacency**, made up in part of Negroes who, as a result of long years of oppression, are so drained of self-respect and a sense of "somebodiness" that they have adjusted to segregation; and in part of a few middleclass Negroes who, because of a degree of academic and economic security and because in some ways they profit by segregation, have become insensitive to the problems of the masses. The other force is one of bitterness and hatred, and it comes perilously close to advocating violence. It is expressed in the various black nationalist groups that are springing up across the nation, the largest and best known being Elijah Muhammad's Muslim movement.[16] Nourished by the Negro's frustration over the continued existence of racial discrimination, this movement is made up of people who have lost faith in America, who have absolutely

---

[15]**elegy . . . psalm:**　an elegy is a lament for the dead; a psalm is a song of praise.

[16]**black nationalist . . . Elijah Muhammad's Muslim movement:**　groups that proposed economic and social independence for African American communities, including the Nation of Islam, founded in 1930 and led by Elijah Muhammad (1897–1975) from 1934 until his death.

QUOTED WORDS

Notice & Note: Mark the quotation King provides in paragraph 26.

Analyze: How does King use his rebuttal of this quotation as a key part of his argument?

complacency
(kəm-plā′sən-sē) *n.* contented self-satisfaction.

Letter from Birmingham Jail　235

QUOTED WORDS

Have students identify the quotation by looking for quotation marks in paragraph 26. Elicit that this quotation comes from a critic but not from one of the critics to whom King is writing. (**Answer:** *King's rebuttal of the idea that equal rights will come "eventually" underscores the idea that the time for taking direct action is now.*)

■ **English Learner Support**

Understand Connotation　Display this sentence from line 8, paragraph 26: "Such an attitude stems from a tragic misconception of time, from the strangely irrational notion that there is something in the very flow of time that will inevitably cure all ills." To help students understand King's rebuttal, point out the words *tragic* and *irrational* and explain that both words have a negative connotation; that is, people associate negative emotions (such as sadness or anxiety) to both of them. Guide partners as they use reference sources to identify and share other words in this paragraph that have negative connotations. (*Examples include* hateful, appalling, *and* stagnation.) **MODERATE/LIGHT**

 ENGLISH LEARNER SUPPORT

Elaborate on Ideas　Direct students to this statement from paragraph 26: "We must use time creatively, in the knowledge that the time is always ripe to do right." Explain that *the time is ripe* means "it is a good or appropriate time." Have students use their primary language to write a hypothetical example of a "ripe" time for doing something good (for example, helping someone who is being bullied, or visiting a lonely relative in a nursing home instead of waiting for a "more convenient time"). Work with students to translate their responses into English. As students read on, urge them to think of examples that help to clarify King's other ideas. **MODERATE**

CRITICAL VOCABULARY

complacency: King expresses the idea that some African Americans are content with the way society is structured.

ASK STUDENTS to explain the two reasons why some African Americans are complacent. (*They are "so drained of self-respect" from "long years of oppression," or they "profit" in some way from segregation.*)

ENGLISH LEARNER SUPPORT

Recognize Repetition Read paragraph 31 aloud and have students raise their hands or clap each time they hear *extremist*, *extremists*, or *extremism*. (Students will not become aware of the repetition until the second sentence. Acknowledge when students recognize the first instances of repetition and then encourage everyone to listen for and identify the remaining appearances.) **SUBSTANTIAL**

CRITICAL VOCABULARY

manifest: King explains why the long-suppressed desire for civil rights is finally becoming apparent.

ASK STUDENTS to identify the two reminders that have manifested within and without the African American man. *("his birthright of freedom" and "that it can be gained")*

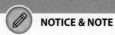

NOTICE & NOTE

repudiated Christianity, and who have concluded that the white man is an incorrigible "devil."

28   I have tried to stand between these two forces, saying that we need emulate neither the "do-nothingism" of the complacent nor the hatred and despair of the black nationalist. For there is the more excellent way of love and nonviolent protest. I am grateful to God that, through the influence of the Negro church, the way of nonviolence became an integral part of our struggle.

29   If this philosophy had not emerged, by now many streets of the South would, I am convinced, be flowing with blood. . . .

30   Oppressed people cannot remain oppressed forever. The yearning for freedom eventually **manifests** itself, and that is what has happened to the American Negro. Something within has reminded him of his birthright of freedom, and something without has reminded him that it can be gained. Consciously or unconsciously, he has been caught up by the *Zeitgeist*,[17] and with his black brothers of Africa and his brown and yellow brothers of Asia, South America and the Caribbean, the United States Negro is moving with a sense of great urgency toward the promised land of racial justice. If one recognizes this vital urge that has engulfed the Negro community, one should readily understand why public demonstrations are taking place. The Negro has many pent-up resentments and latent frustrations, and he must release them. So let him march; let him make prayer pilgrimages to the city hall; let him go on freedom rides—and try to understand why he must do so. If his repressed emotions are not released in nonviolent ways, they will seek expression through violence; this is not a threat but a fact of history. So I have not said to my people: "Get rid of your discontent." Rather, I have tried to say that this normal and healthy discontent can be channeled into the creative outlet of nonviolent direct action. And now this approach is being termed extremist.

31   But though I was initially disappointed at being categorized as an extremist, as I continued to think about the matter I gradually gained a measure of satisfaction from the label. Was not Jesus an extremist for love: "Love your enemies, bless them that curse you, do good to them that hate you, and pray for them which despitefully use you, and persecute you." Was not Amos[18] an extremist for justice: "Let justice roll down like waters and righteousness like an ever-flowing stream." Was not Paul an extremist for the Christian gospel: "I bear in my body the marks of the Lord Jesus." Was not Martin Luther[19] an extremist: "Here I stand; I cannot do otherwise, so help me God."

manifest
(măn´ə-fĕst) *v.* to show or reveal.

---

[17] ***Zeitgeist*** (tsīt´gīst): German for "the spirit of the time," referring to the attitudes and beliefs of most people living during a period.

[18] **Amos:** Hebrew prophet whose words are recorded in the Old Testament book bearing his name.

[19] **Martin Luther:** (1483-1546) German monk who launched the Protestant Reformation.

WHEN STUDENTS STRUGGLE . . .

Analyze Arguments Guide student pairs to trace the development of a claim by completing a graphic organizer. Direct students to read paragraph 30. Tell students that as they read they should consider King's opinion regarding "oppressed people," the reasons for his opinion, and the specific actions he thinks "oppressed people" should take. Have students create a two-column chart with the first row of the left column labeled "Opinion," the second row of the left column labeled "Reasons," and the third row of the left column labeled "Action." Ask students to write their notes next to the appropriate label in the right column.

And John Bunyan:[20] "I will stay in jail to the end of my days before I make a butchery of my conscience." And Abraham Lincoln: "This nation cannot survive half slave and half free." And Thomas Jefferson: "We hold these truths to be self-evident, that all men are created equal . . ." So the question is not whether we will be extremists, but what kind of extremists we will be. Will we be extremists for hate or for love? Will we be extremists for the preservation of injustice or for the extension of justice? In that dramatic scene on Calvary's hill[21] three men were crucified. We must never forget that all three were crucified for the same crime—the crime of extremism. Two were extremists for immorality, and thus fell below their environment. The other, Jesus Christ, was an extremist for love, truth and goodness, and thereby rose above his environment. Perhaps the South, the nation and the world are in dire need of creative extremists.

32   I had hoped that the white moderate would see this need. Perhaps I was too optimistic; perhaps I expected too much. I suppose I should have realized that few members of the oppressor race can understand the deep groans and passionate yearnings of the

---

[20] **John Bunyan:** (1628-1688) English preacher and writer, author of *The Pilgrim's Progress*.
[21] **Calvary's hill:** the site of Jesus' crucifixion.

 ## ENGLISH LEARNER SUPPORT

Build Grammar Knowledge Review King's use of the word *extremist* in paragraph 31. Tell students that the *-ist* suffix usually means that the word refers to a person; for example, a *cartoonist* is a person who draws cartoons, and a *geologist* is a person who studies geology. Point out that King says *an extremist* and that *an* is called an article. (You may wish to review the differences among the articles *a, an,* and *the*.) In many languages, an article is not used before a noun unless there is a need for emphasis. Encourage students to monitor their speech and writing and to self-correct if they catch themselves dropping the article.
SUBSTANTIAL/MODERATE

 ## ENGLISH LEARNER SUPPORT

Listen for Intonation Direct students to these sentences from paragraph 31 (near the top of page 237): "Will we be extremists for hate or for love? Will we be extremists for the preservation of injustice or for the extension of justice?" Point out that these are rhetorical questions. Explain the meanings of the terms *preservation* and *extension*. Ask students to paraphrase the phrases "preservation of injustice" and "extension of justice." (*protecting laws that are wrong; providing fair laws for everyone*)

Then read each rhetorical question aloud, modeling appropriate pacing, emphasis, and intonation. Ask students to use a "thumbs up" sign to indicate rising intonation and a "thumbs down" sign to indicate falling intonation. (*"thumbs up" for rising intonation at "for hate" and "thumbs down" for falling intonation at "for love"; "thumbs up" for rising intonation at "for the preservation of injustice" and "thumbs down" for falling intonation at "for the extension of justice"*) Also point out how you emphasized the words *hate* and *love* in the first question and *injustice* and *justice* to show contrast.

Read the questions a second time and have students echo read them. Then ask pairs of students to take turns reading the questions aloud with the proper intonation.
MODERATE/LIGHT

ANALYZE ARGUMENT

Point out the word *disappointment* in the instructions and have students look for a form of that word at the beginning of paragraph 33. (**Answer:** *Because King praises the "notable exceptions," the contrast he goes on to make between them and "the white religious leadership of this community" in general becomes more pronounced.*)

■ English Learner Support

Use Double Negatives Direct students to this statement in paragraph 33: "I am not unmindful of the fact that each of you has taken some significant stands on this issue." Point out the phrase *not unmindful* and tell students that it is an example of a double negative. In many languages (Spanish and Russian, for example), a double negative is correct for expressing strong negativity, but most uses are considered incorrect in formal, standard English (for example, *we didn't have no money* or *I never saw nothing*). However, in uses such as *not unmindful,* the double negative works—it is an attention-getting way of expressing a thought in a more subtle way. Help students explain the effective use of double negatives in these sentences:

- You may not have heard of this band, but it is *not unknown* around the city.

- He has a hard time being on time; in fact, his lateness is *never unexpected.* **LIGHT**

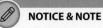
ANALYZE ARGUMENT

Annotate: Mark the disappointment that King uses to begin a new section of his argument in paragraph 33.

Analyze: How do the concessions King makes in paragraph 33 strengthen the point he makes in subsequent paragraphs?

oppressed race, and still fewer have the vision to see that injustice must be rooted out by strong, persistent and determined action. I am thankful, however, that some of our white brothers in the South have grasped the meaning of this social revolution and committed themselves to it. They are still all too few in quantity, but they are big in quality. Some—such as Ralph McGill, Lillian Smith, Harry Golden, James McBride Dabbs, Ann Braden and Sarah Patton Boyle—have written about our struggle in eloquent and prophetic terms. Others have marched with us down nameless streets of the South. They have languished in filthy, roach-infested jails, suffering the abuse and brutality of policemen who view them as "dirty nigger-lovers." Unlike so many of their moderate brothers and sisters, they have recognized the urgency of the moment and sensed the need for powerful "action" antidotes to combat the disease of segregation.

33   Let me take note of my other major disappointment. I have been so greatly disappointed with the white church and its leadership. Of course, there are some notable exceptions. I am not unmindful of the fact that each of you has taken some significant stands on this issue. I commend you, Reverend Stallings, for your Christian stand on this past Sunday, in welcoming Negroes to your worship service on a nonsegregated basis. I commend the Catholic leaders of this state for integrating Spring Hill College several years ago.

34   But despite these notable exceptions, I must honestly reiterate that I have been disappointed with the church. I do not say this as one of those negative critics who can always find something wrong with the church. I say this as a minister of the gospel, who loves the church; who was nurtured in its bosom; who has been sustained by its spiritual blessings and who will remain true to it as long as the cord of life shall lengthen.

35   When I was suddenly catapulted into the leadership of the bus protest in Montgomery, Alabama,[22] a few years ago, I felt we would be supported by the white church. I felt that the white ministers, priests and rabbis of the South would be among our strongest allies. Instead, some have been outright opponents, refusing to understand the freedom movement and misrepresenting its leaders; all too many others have been more cautious than courageous and have remained silent behind the anesthetizing security of stained glass windows.

36   In spite of my shattered dreams, I came to Birmingham with the hope that the white religious leadership of this community would see the justice of our cause and, with deep moral concern, would serve as the channel through which our just grievances could reach the power structure. I had hoped that each of you would understand. But again I have been disappointed.

[22] **bus protest in Montgomery, Alabama:** the 1955–1956 boycott that ended segregated seating in Montgomery's transportation system.

TO CHALLENGE STUDENTS . . .

Conduct Research In paragraph 35, King refers to his role in the Montgomery Bus Boycott. The event is briefly summarized in a footnote, but invite small groups of students to do some research to learn more about it. Ask students to find and share answers to these questions:

- What prompted the boycott, and how was Rosa Parks involved? How did Martin Luther King Jr. become involved?

- What demands did the African American bus riders make?

- Why did the boycott end? Why is it considered important for the Civil Rights movement and King's career?

37   I have heard numerous southern religious leaders admonish their worshipers to comply with a desegregation decision because it is the law, but I have longed to hear white ministers declare: "Follow this decree because integration is morally right and because the Negro is your brother." In the midst of blatant injustices inflicted upon the Negro, I have watched white churchmen stand on the sideline and mouth pious irrelevancies and sanctimonious trivialities. In the midst of a mighty struggle to rid our nation of racial and economic injustice, I have heard many ministers say: "Those are social issues, with which the gospel has no real concern." And I have watched many churches commit themselves to a completely otherworldly religion which makes a strange, un-Biblical distinction between body and soul, between the sacred and the secular.

38   I have traveled the length and breadth of Alabama, Mississippi and all the other southern states. On sweltering summer days and crisp autumn mornings I have looked at the South's beautiful churches with their lofty spires pointing heavenward. I have beheld the impressive outlines of her massive religious-education buildings. Over and over I have found myself asking: "What kind of people worship here? Who is their God? Where were their voices when the lips of Governor Barnett dripped with words of interposition and nullification? Where were they when Governor Wallace[23] gave a clarion call for defiance and hatred? Where were their voices of support when bruised and weary Negro men and women decided to rise from the dark dungeons of complacency to the bright hills of creative protest?"

39   Yes, these questions are still in my mind. In deep disappointment I have wept over the laxity of the church. But be assured that my tears have been tears of love. There can be no deep disappointment where there is not deep love. Yes, I love the church. How could I do otherwise? I am in the rather unique position of being the son, the grandson and the great-grandson of preachers. Yes, I see the church as the body of Christ. But, oh! How we have blemished and scarred that body through social neglect and through fear of being nonconformists.

40   There was a time when the church was very powerful—in the time when the early Christians rejoiced at being deemed worthy to suffer for what they believed. In those days the church was not merely a thermometer that recorded the ideas and principles of popular opinion; it was a thermostat that transformed the **mores** of society. Whenever the early Christians entered a town, the people in power became disturbed and immediately sought to convict the Christians

mores
(môr´āz) *n.* established customs and conventions.

---

[23] **Gov. Barnett . . . Gov. Wallace:** Ross Barnett (1898–1987) and George Wallace (1919–1998), segregationist governors of Mississippi and Alabama, respectively, during the 1960s.

ENGLISH LEARNER SUPPORT

Discuss Words of Contrast Review the contrast that King makes in paragraph 33. Then tell students that some English words and phrases signal contrasts and that King uses two of them in paragraphs 34–36, where he elaborates on his disappointment. Help students construct a three-column chart that lists the contrast word, the paragraph where it is found, and the things that are being contrasted. Begin with the signal word *but* in paragraphs 34 and 36 and the signal word *instead* in paragraph 35. Have students find the three additional appearances of *but* in paragraphs 37–39 and discuss as necessary what is contrasted in each case.

You may wish to share a few other words and phrases that signal contrasts, such as *however, in contrast*, and *on the other hand*. Invite students to share how they express contrasts in their primary language.
SUBSTANTIAL/MODERATE

WHEN STUDENTS STRUGGLE . . .

Understand Comparisons Help students understand King's claim in paragraphs 40–42 with a comparison chart. Explain and discuss difficult terms: *thermostat, God-intoxicated, astronomically, infanticide, ineffectual, archdefender, status quo, sanction.*

Churches of the Past	Churches in King's Time
very powerful	weak, ineffectual
disturbed those in power	consoled those in power
transformed society	defended the status quo

CRITICAL VOCABULARY

mores: King states that the church determined the established customs and conventions of society.

ASK STUDENTS to compare the mores of a society that would allow infanticide and gladiatorial contests with our own. (*Accept all reasonable responses.*)

© Houghton Mifflin Harcourt Publishing Company

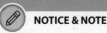

ENGLISH LEARNER SUPPORT

Analyze Verb Tenses Remind students that a verb's tense expresses the time at which an action takes place. Work through paragraph 44, sentence by sentence, identifying examples of past-tense, present-tense, and future-tense verbs. Point out verbs that are basic sight vocabulary. Clarify any confusion about the use of these tenses. Then discuss how the verb tenses in the paragraph express the following:

- *past tense:* injustices that African Americans faced for many years

- *present tense:* King's thoughts about the current state of civil rights in the United States

- *future tense:* King's assurance that the time will come when his goals will become reality

ALL LEVELS

ENGLISH LEARNER SUPPORT

Use Informal Language Read the first two sentences in paragraph 44 with students. Work with students to informally paraphrase the ideas conveyed in these sentences. (*He hopes the church will do the right thing. But if it doesn't, he's not worried about the future.*)

MODERATE

for being "disturbers of the peace" and "outside agitators." But the Christians pressed on, in the conviction that they were "a colony of heaven," called to obey God rather than man. Small in number, they were big in commitment. They were too God-intoxicated to be "astronomically intimidated." By their effort and example they brought an end to such ancient evils as infanticide and gladiatorial contests.[24]

41   Things are different now. So often the contemporary church is a weak, ineffectual voice with an uncertain sound. So often it is an archdefender of the status quo. Far from being disturbed by the presence of the church, the power structure of the average community is consoled by the church's silent—and often even vocal—sanction of things as they are.

42   But the judgment of God is upon the church as never before. If today's church does not recapture the sacrificial spirit of the early church, it will lose its authenticity, forfeit the loyalty of millions, and be dismissed as an irrelevant social club with no meaning for the twentieth century. Every day I meet young people whose disappointment with the church has turned into outright disgust.

43   Perhaps I have once again been too optimistic. Is organized religion too inextricably bound to the status quo to save our nation and the world? Perhaps I must turn my faith to the inner spiritual church, the church within the church, as the true *ekklesia*[25] and the hope of the world. But again I am thankful to God that some noble souls from the ranks of organized religion have broken loose from the paralyzing chains of conformity and joined us as active partners in the struggle for freedom. They have left their secure congregations and walked the streets of Albany, Georgia, with us. They have gone down the highways of the South on tortuous rides for freedom. Yes, they have gone to jail with us. Some have been dismissed from their churches, have lost the support of their bishops and fellow ministers. But they have acted in the faith that right defeated is stronger than evil triumphant. Their witness has been the spiritual salt that has preserved the true meaning of the gospel in these troubled times. They have carved a tunnel of hope through the dark mountain of disappointment.

44   I hope the church as a whole will meet the challenge of this decisive hour. But even if the church does not come to the aid of justice, I have no despair about the future. I have no fear about the outcome of our struggle in Birmingham, even if our motives are at present misunderstood. We will reach the goal of freedom in Birmingham and all over the nation, because the goal of America is freedom. Abused and scorned though we may be, our destiny is tied

[24]**ancient evils . . . contests:** despicable past practices of killing unwanted babies and of forcing men to fight to the death for sport.

[25]*ekklesia* (ĭ-klē´zē-ə): a Greek term meaning "an assembly of people for worship," often translated into English as "church."

ENGLISH LEARNER SUPPORT

Discuss Prefixes Remind students that English words can have multiple parts. A **prefix** is a word part added to the beginning of a word. Prefixes have their own unique meanings, and understanding those meanings will help students define unfamiliar words. Point out these words in paragraph 45, explaining that the prefix (underlined here) in each case means "not": <u>un</u>armed, <u>non</u>violent, <u>in</u>humane. Point out other words with prefixes: *ineffectual* and *uncertain* (paragraph 41), *inextricably* (paragraph 43), and *immoral* (paragraph 46). Discuss the meanings of the root words and how the prefixes change those meanings.

MODERATE/LIGHT

up with America's destiny. Before the pilgrims landed at Plymouth, we were here. Before the pen of Jefferson etched the majestic words of the Declaration of Independence across the pages of history, we were here. For more than two centuries our forebears labored in this country without wages; they made cotton king; they built the homes of their masters while suffering gross injustice and shameful humiliation—and yet out of a bottomless vitality they continued to thrive and develop. If the inexpressible cruelties of slavery could not stop us, the opposition we now face will surely fail. We will win our freedom because the sacred heritage of our nation and the eternal will of God are embodied in our echoing demands.

45   Before closing I feel impelled to mention one other point in your statement that has troubled me profoundly. You warmly commended the Birmingham police force for keeping "order" and "preventing violence." I doubt that you would have so warmly commended the police force if you had seen its dogs sinking their teeth into unarmed, nonviolent Negroes. I doubt that you would so quickly commend the policemen if you were to observe their ugly and inhumane treatment of Negroes here in the city jail; if you were to watch them push and curse old Negro women and young Negro girls; if you were to see them slap and kick old Negro men and young boys; if you were to observe them, as they did on two occasions, refuse to give us food because we wanted to sing our grace together. I cannot join you in your praise of the Birmingham police department.

46   It is true that the police have exercised a degree of discipline in handling the demonstrators. In this sense they have conducted themselves rather "nonviolently" in public. But for what purpose? To preserve the evil system of segregation. Over the past few years I have consistently preached that nonviolence demands that the means we use must be as pure as the ends we seek. I have tried to make clear that it is wrong to use immoral means to attain moral ends. But now I must affirm that it is just as wrong, or perhaps even more so, to use moral means to preserve immoral ends. Perhaps Mr. Connor and his policemen have been rather nonviolent in public, as was Chief Pritchett in Albany, Georgia, but they have used the moral means of nonviolence to maintain the immoral end of racial injustice. As T. S. Eliot has said: "The last temptation is the greatest treason: To do the right deed for the wrong reason."

47   I wish you had commended the Negro sit-inners and demonstrators of Birmingham for their sublime courage, their willingness to suffer and their amazing discipline in the midst of great **provocation**. One day the South will recognize its real heroes. They will be the James Merediths,[26] with the noble sense of purpose that

---

[26] **James Merediths:** people like James Meredith, who endured violent opposition from whites to become the first African American to attend the University of Mississippi.

ANALYZE ARGUMENT

Annotate: Mark King's counterargument to the clergymen's praise for the police keeping "order" and "preventing violence."

Analyze: How does this counterargument strengthen King's argument?

provocation
(prŏv-ə-kā'shən) *n.* an action intended to elicit an angered response.

IMPROVE READING FLUENCY

Targeted Passage   Use paired oral reading to help students track key details while reading complex text. Have partners take turns reading paragraph 45 aloud. After the second sentence, have them pause and ask: If the police kept order and prevented violence, then why does King say that he is troubled? The next sentence gives the answer, but it is a long, complicated sentence. Tell partners to continue taking turns as readers but to pause at each semicolon (;) to rephrase, ask questions, and share insights. When they reach the end, have students explain the final sentence by sharing details from the paragraph.

 Go to the **Reading Studio** for additional support in developing fluency.

ANALYZE ARGUMENT

Before students mark paragraph 45, suggest that they consider how King's use of "warmly commended" in the second sentence differs from his use of it in the third sentence. (**Answer:** *The counterargument—that there are many instances of Birmingham police mistreating African Americans that King calls his audience to see—emphasizes King's argument that racial injustice exists in the city but that his audience has failed to recognize it and to seek to change it.*)

■ English Learner Support

Use Synonyms   Point out the forms of the verbs *see, observe,* and *watch* in paragraph 45. Explain that these are synonyms—words with the same, or nearly the same, meaning. Elicit that all three words refer to taking in information visually. Call on volunteers to name additional synonyms with that meaning. (*Examples include* view, look at, *and* witness.) Invite students to share some words in their primary language with similar meanings.   **SUBSTANTIAL**

■ English Learner Support

Discuss the Subjunctive   Point out the four examples of "if you were [infinitive]" in paragraph 45. Explain that King's phrasing shows the use of the subjunctive mood; its approximate meaning is "if you saw these police actions." Explain that King is making the point that if his readers saw all of the bad treatment of African Americans by police, they would not praise the police for avoiding violence.

Explain that the subjunctive mood is more common in languages such as Spanish, and it is used less and less often in English. Someone writing in English today probably would replace that phrasing with the past perfect tense (*if you had observed . . . had watched . . . had seen . . . had observed*), which King himself used in the first "I doubt" sentence in the paragraph. Have students practice using the subjunctive in English with this frame: *If I were you, I would _____.*   **LIGHT**

CRITICAL VOCABULARY

provocation: King points out that the demonstrators received no praise for their refusal to respond with violence even when they were faced with actions intended to elicit anger.

ASK STUDENTS to identify the type of provocation James Meredith endured. (*He faced "jeering and hostile mobs."*)

TEACH

▶ QUOTED WORDS

Remind students that this signpost encourages them to think about words that have the ring of authority. You may wish to point out that the woman mentioned is "Mother Pollard," a well-respected member of King's church, who was very active during the Montgomery Bus Boycott and who often encouraged King in his efforts. Explain that although her quoted statement is not expressed in standard English, it is still important and eloquent. (**Answer:** *The choice of this quotation, with its "ungrammatical profundity," shows that anyone—regardless of gender, age, or level of education—can act heroically and feel empowered for having made a difference. Furthermore, the choice is not merely a matter of the words, but also of the fact that the words come from a woman who had been the target of injustice longer than most and who decided to take action against it.*)

■ English Learner Support

Discuss Informal Language The fact that attention is drawn to an ungrammatical statement may concern some students. Remind students of the difference between formal and informal English and between standard and nonstandard English. Use the quotation in paragraph 47, however, to point out that language doesn't necessarily have to be "perfect" to be powerful. Ask students to restate the sentence in formal, grammatical English, then discuss reasons the original is more powerful in this context.

ALL LEVELS

ANALYZE ARGUMENT

After students mark the concluding sentence in paragraph 50, invite students to summarize it in their own words. (Example: Let us hope that racial injustice will end someday soon and that we all can live as equals.) (**Answer:** *The conclusion is effective because it reminds readers of the issue but expresses hope that a resolution will come.*)

 NOTICE & NOTE

QUOTED WORDS

Notice & Note: Mark the quotation in paragraph 47 that uses humor and ungrammatical sentences.

Respond: What is the effect of King's choice to quote this woman?

ANALYZE ARGUMENT
Annotate: Mark the long sentence in paragraph 50 that summarizes King's argument and message.

Evaluate: Do you think this conclusion enhances King's argument? Why or why not?

enables them to face jeering and hostile mobs, and with the agonizing loneliness that characterizes the life of the pioneer. They will be old, oppressed, battered Negro women, symbolized in a seventy-two-year-old woman in Montgomery, Alabama, who rose up with a sense of dignity and with her people decided not to ride segregated buses, and who responded with ungrammatical profundity to one who inquired about her weariness: "My feets is tired, but my soul is at rest." They will be the young high school and college students, the young ministers of the gospel and a host of their elders, courageously and nonviolently sitting in at lunch counters and willingly going to jail for conscience' sake. One day the South will know that when these disinherited children of God sat down at lunch counters, they were in reality standing up for what is best in the American dream and for the most sacred values in our Judaeo-Christian heritage, thereby bringing our nation back to those great wells of democracy which were dug deep by the founding fathers in their formulation of the Constitution and the Declaration of Independence.

48   Never before have I written so long a letter. I'm afraid it is much too long to take your precious time. I can assure you that it would have been much shorter if I had been writing from a comfortable desk, but what else can one do when he is alone in a narrow jail cell other than write long letters, think long thoughts and pray long prayers?

49   If I have said anything in this letter that overstates the truth and indicates an unreasonable impatience, I beg you to forgive me. If I have said anything that understates the truth and indicates my having a patience that allows me to settle for anything less than brotherhood, I beg God to forgive me.

50   I hope this letter finds you strong in the faith. I also hope that circumstances will soon make it possible for me to meet each of you, not as an integrationist or a civil-rights leader but as a fellow clergyman and a Christian brother. Let us all hope that the dark clouds of racial prejudice will soon pass away and the deep fog of misunderstanding will be lifted from our fear-drenched communities, and in some not too distant tomorrow the radiant stars of love and brotherhood will shine over our great nation with all their scintillating beauty.

   Yours for the cause of Peace and Brotherhood,

   Martin Luther King, Jr.

 **CHECK YOUR UNDERSTANDING**

Have students answer the questions independently.

Answers:

1. *B*

2. *H*

3. *D*

If they answer any questions incorrectly, have them reread the text to confirm their understanding. Then they may proceed to ANALYZE THE TEXT on page 244.

CHECK YOUR UNDERSTANDING

Answer these questions before moving on to the **Analyze the Text** section on the following page.

1 King wrote this letter because —

A doing so kept him occupied and helped to pass the time while in jail

B he wanted to respond to criticism from a group of fellow clergymen

C he needed to consider what he had done to wind up in jail

D it helped him to organize his thoughts about his own motivations

2 King mainly supports his ideas using —

F acknowledgment of the many helpful good deeds of the police and public officials

G emotional arguments centered on his own personal experience with discrimination

H examples from the Bible and history that illustrate the fight against injustice

J overstatement and exaggeration of the obstacles faced by African Americans

3 King's argument makes clear that racial segregation is —

A something that only happens in the South

B solely the responsibility of its victims to change

C a necessary evil that will eventually pass

D an inhumane and immoral practice

Letter from Birmingham Jail   243

 ENGLISH LEARNER SUPPORT

Oral Assessment Use the following questions to assess students' comprehension and speaking skills.

1. What was King's reason for writing this letter? *(He is answering some clergymen who criticized him.)*

2. What kinds of examples does King use to support his ideas? *(He names people from the Bible and from history who fought injustice.)*

3. What does King want his audience to understand about racial segregation? *(He wants to show that racial segregation is wrong and that it should end.)* **SUBSTANTIAL/MODERATE**

APPLY

ANALYZE THE TEXT

Possible answers:

1. **DOK 4:** *King defines a just law as "a man-made code that squares with the moral law or the law of God." An unjust law, on the other hand, is "a code that is out of harmony with moral law." He is responding to the view that there is no justification for selectively breaking laws. He reasons that belief in a moral law provides the incentive for disobeying an unjust law.*

2. **DOK 2:** *The four basic steps are: (1) "collection of the facts to determine whether injustices exist," (2) "negotiation," (3) "self-purification," and (4) "direct action." In Birmingham, King's organization began by gathering evidence that racial injustice was widespread in the community; next, they tried to negotiate with city and business leaders; then they held workshops to ensure that participants would be nonviolent and could endure the hardship of jail; and finally they took direct action in the form of sit-ins and marches.*

3. **DOK 3:** *King is referring to the fact that African Americans had often been told to "Wait" for equal rights but never saw any progress. He provides descriptive examples and personal experiences to illustrate denied rights and ongoing injustices.*

4. **DOK 4:** *King writes that the communities and states of the United States are interrelated. He uses valid reasoning, saying that citizens are part of a mutual network that can be affected directly or indirectly, but that those effects will impact everyone.*

5. **DOK 4:** *King quotes the clergymen who wrote to him and other critics, the Bible and religious leaders throughout history, political leaders including Lincoln and Jefferson, and ordinary people including his son and an elderly protester. This broad range of sources provides a solid base for King's argument.*

RESEARCH

Leaders are named in paragraphs 7, 27, 32, and 47. Suggest that students do an initial search on two or three names to assess sources of information before settling on one person to research in depth.

Extend Encourage students to check information in at least two reliable sources. If students find discrepancies, remind them to review the reliability of the sources (for example, a government or university site as opposed to a personal blog) and then, if needed, to check one or two more reliable sources.

 RESPOND

ANALYZE THE TEXT

Support your responses with evidence from the text. 📓 NOTEBOOK

1. **Analyze** How does King define just and unjust laws? To what opposing view is he providing a counterargument? Consider how defining certain laws as unjust provides an incentive for his readers to support his actions.

2. **Summarize** According to King, what are the four basic steps in a nonviolent campaign, and how did King's organization follow these steps in Birmingham?

3. **Draw Conclusions** King says that "This 'Wait' has almost always meant 'Never.'" To what does he refer, and how does he defend his position?

4. **Analyze** Discuss whether King uses valid reasoning when he states that "Injustice anywhere is a threat to justice everywhere." What evidence does he provide to support this idea? What appeal does he use?

5. **Notice & Note** Review the letter to identify all of the people King quotes. How would you categorize these people? What is the effect of King's quoting so many kinds of people on his overall argument?

RESEARCH

RESEARCH TIP
Finding at least two different sources for each fact will help you verify that individual facts are accurate.

King refers to other leaders who were part of the Civil Rights movement. Choose one of them to research. Seek credible sources; avoid those with these flaws:

- **Bias:** overly favoring one side on a controversial topic
- **Omission:** leaving out information that doesn't support a particular bias
- **Misconceptions:** basing ideas on incorrect information
- **Faulty Reasoning:** drawing illogical conclusions from information

Record what you learn in a chart similar to this one.

CIVIL RIGHTS FIGURE	ACCOMPLISHMENTS	INFORMATION SOURCES
Responses will vary.		

Extend If you find conflicting information in your sources, visit multiple sources. Verification of an idea in multiple reliable resources should be considered valid.

⚙ LEARNING MINDSET

Asking for Help Because "Letter from Birmingham Jail" is a complex text, students may stumble when trying to answer the Analyze the Text questions. Remind students to ask for help if they cannot answer a question or if they feel unsure of their answer—help from classmates, from you (the teacher), even from parents. Tell students to think of asking for help as a way to "try smarter." As students seek help in getting "unstuck," have them ask the people helping them to explain their reasoning; then encourage students to use similar techniques as they continue to work on their own.

CREATE AND PRESENT

Write a Friendly Letter Write a one-page letter that shares with a friend what you have learned in your research and why it matters.

- ❏ Keep the tone friendly and casual.
- ❏ Treat this serious information with respect.
- ❏ Explain what you have learned in terms you and your friend can understand and relate to.

Present Research Give a brief, formal speech that shares what you learned about the Civil Rights leader you researched.

- ❏ Explain what you have learned, citing evidence from reliable sources.
- ❏ Connect your research to the information in Dr. King's letter.
- ❏ Include images or video of the person you researched if available.

RESPOND

Go to the **Writing Studio** for help with writing for a certain task, purpose, and audience.

Go to the **Speaking and Listening Studio** for help with giving a speech.

RESPOND TO THE ESSENTIAL QUESTION

What do we need in order to feel free?

Gather Information Review your annotations and notes on "Letter from Birmingham Jail." Then, add relevant information to your Response Log. As you determine which information to include, think about:

- what some people sacrifice to preserve freedom for all
- why those in power must recognize that freedom cannot be delayed
- why power should not be preserved by oppressing others

At the end of the unit, use your notes to help you write an argument.

UNIT 4 RESPONSE LOG

Essential Question: What do we need in order to feel free?

Letter from Birmingham Jail	
Glassheart	
The Hawk Can Soar	
The Briefcase	
Open Letter to Viceroy Lord Irwin	
from Gandhi: The Rise to Fame	

ACADEMIC VOCABULARY

As you write and discuss what you learned from the argument, be sure to use the Academic Vocabulary words. Check off each of the words that you use.

- ❏ **comprehensive**
- ❏ **equivalent**
- ❏ **incentive**
- ❏ **innovate**
- ❏ **subordinate**

CREATE AND PRESENT

Write a Friendly Letter Have students use their findings from the Research activity to write a compelling main idea that will help them focus their thinking. If necessary, review the parts of a friendly letter:

- heading (the writer's address, the date)
- greeting
- body (where the writer shares ideas and information)
- closing
- signature
- postscript (optional)

Remind students that they are presenting information, but with a friendly, casual tone. As students edit their letters, suggest that they get input from peers about how they can take a personal approach to convey factual content.

For **writing support** for students at varying proficiency levels, see the **Text X-Ray** on page 220D.

Present Research As in the letter-writing activity, have students review their research and create one or two sentences that will help them focus their thinking and provide the main point that they want to get across in their speech. Point out that the support for their main point should come from their research but also should refer to The Birmingham Campaign and specifically to King's "Letter from Birmingham Jail." Remind students that their speech, unlike the letter in the previous activity, should have a formal tone. Provide assistance to students who want to display images or video as part of their presentation.

RESPOND TO THE ESSENTIAL QUESTION

Allow time for students to add details from "Letter from Birmingham Jail" to their Unit 4 Response Logs.

ENGLISH LEARNER SUPPORT

Work with Others Provide students with a main-idea-and-details organizer. Ask them to work in pairs or small groups to complete it, listing points they want to make about the Civil Rights leader they researched and any connections they find between that leader and information in King's letter. Then have small groups of varied proficiencies discuss and compare their organizers, even if they chose different people to research. Ask them to exchange ideas about how best to present their information. Encourage students to practice with a partner or small group and to use feedback to refine their presentation. **ALL LEVELS**

CRITICAL VOCABULARY

Possible answers:

1. Losing a point in a game because of a foul might make someone angry enough to <u>retaliate</u>, or seek revenge, against someone.

2. A flood might cause a <u>moratorium</u> on building roads because the water would make it impossible to work. Potholes also might cause a <u>moratorium</u> because construction workers probably would be needed to make repairs rather than work on construction.

3. If I am <u>cognizant</u> of your plans, I know about them.

4. A movie that reflects <u>mores</u> would show traditional practices.

5. If a motive <u>manifests</u> itself, that means the reason for the crime becomes clear; this can make it easier or harder to prove a suspect's guilt, depending on whether the motive fits for the suspect.

6. Breaking a treaty would be the more likely <u>provocation</u> for a war.

7. A person who shows <u>complacency</u> might give in to demands or not react to them at all.

8. If my actions <u>precipitate</u> an accident, that means that I cause rather than prevent it.

VOCABULARY STRATEGY:
Context Clues

Possible answers:

1. A <u>moderate</u> holds mainstream political beliefs and prefers order to confrontation. King presents a negative view of "the white moderate," who lacks the commitment to make radical change.

2. <u>Condemned</u> means judged and punished harshly for an action considered a crime or otherwise harmful to others. King repeats the word to show how those in power, out of fear of unwelcome results, frequently mistreat those who are working for good.

3. An <u>extremist</u> is a person who takes or advocates action that is bold, unconventional, and even risky in order to support or defend a point of view. Because King labels Jesus, the prophet Amos, the apostle Paul, Martin Luther, John Bunyan, Abraham Lincoln, and Thomas Jefferson as "extremists", the word takes on the meaning of someone who takes bold action for a good cause.

RESPOND

CRITICAL VOCABULARY

WORD BANK
cognizant
moratorium
retaliate
precipitate
complacency
manifest
mores
provocation

Practice and Apply Answer each question in a complete sentence by thinking about the meaning of the Critical Vocabulary word.

1. Which might cause someone to **retaliate**: Losing a point in a game because of a foul or getting a well-deserved award?

2. Would a flood or potholes cause a **moratorium** on road construction?

3. If I am **cognizant** of your plans, do I know about them or not?

4. If a movie reflects a society's **mores**, does it show traditional or unconventional practices?

5. If a motive for a crime begins to **manifest** itself, will it be easier or harder to prove the suspect's guilt?

6. What might be a **provocation** for war, breaking a treaty or signing one?

7. If you show **complacency**, how do you respond to demands?

8. If my actions **precipitate** an accident, do I cause or prevent it?

VOCABULARY STRATEGY:
Context Clues

 Go to the **Vocabulary Studio** for more on using context clues.

A word's **context**, the words and sentences that surround it, often gives clues to its meaning. Context can also add shades of meaning to a word. Consider how context shapes the meaning of the word *tension* in King's letter:

DEFINITION	CONTEXT CLUES
tension: a strained relationship	. . . Nonviolent direct action seeks to . . . foster such a **tension** that a community . . . is forced to confront the issue. . . . I have earnestly opposed violent **tension**, but there is a type of constructive, nonviolent **tension** which is necessary for growth.

King's use of *tension* describes a force that can be positive. Think about how replacing it with *conflict* might change King's intended meaning.

Practice and Apply Use context clues to define these words. Verify your definitions in a print or online dictionary. Discuss how King adds nuances to each word's meaning in the context of his letter.

1. moderate (paragraph 23)

_____

2. condemned/condemning (paragraph 25)

_____

3. extremist (paragraph 31)

_____

EL ENGLISH LEARNER SUPPORT

Vocabulary Strategy Provide students with additional practice in using context clues. Display the following words and their placement in King's letter: *mutuality* (paragraph 4), *negotiate* (paragraph 6), *endurance* (paragraph 14), *inevitability* (paragraph 26), *latent* (paragraph 30). Have students work in pairs to determine each word's meaning as it is used in the letter by analyzing context clues and then checking their definition in a print or digital dictionary. Have partners meet with other pairs to compare their work.

MODERATE/LIGHT

LANGUAGE CONVENTIONS:
Repetition and Parallelism

Repetition is a technique in which a sound, word, or phrase is repeated for emphasis or unity. **Parallelism** is the use of similar grammatical forms to express ideas that are related or equal in importance. King skillfully uses repetition and parallelism to make his message resonate with his audience. Consider the following examples and their effects:

EXAMPLES FROM TEXT	EFFECTS
when you have seen vicious mobs . . . **when you** have seen hate-filled policemen . . . **when you** see the vast majority of your twenty million Negro brothers smothering . . . **when you** suddenly find your tongue twisted . . . **when you** have to concoct an answer . . . **when you** take a cross-country drive . . . **when you** are humiliated . . . **when you** are harried by day and haunted by night . . . **when you** are forever fighting . . . —**then you** will understand why we find it difficult to wait.	Starting each subordinate clause with the words *when you* and then varying the parallellism at the end with the word *then* emphasizes and dramatizes King's point that African Americans have waited long enough for their constitutional and God-given rights.
To a degree, academic freedom is a reality today because Socrates practiced **civil disobedience**. In our own nation, the Boston Tea Party represented a massive act of **civil disobedience**. We should never forget that everything Adolf Hitler did in Germany was "**legal**" and everything the Hungarian freedom fighters did in Hungary was "**illegal**." It was "**illegal**" to aid and comfort a Jew in Hitler's Germany.	Not only are the words *legal* and *illegal* repeated, they are contrasted as opposites to stress the unfairness of their application. King repeats *civil disobedience* to stress the distinction between what is legal or illegal.
Was not Jesus an extremist for love . . . **Was not** Amos an extremist for justice . . . **Was not** Paul an extremist for the Christian gospel . . . **Was not** Martin Luther an extremist . . . **And** John Bunyan . . . **And** Abraham Lincoln . . . **And** Thomas Jefferson . . . So the question is not whether **we will be extremists**, but what kind of **extremists we will be**. **Will we be extremists** for hate or for love? **Will we be extremists** for the preservation of injustice or for the extension of justice?	The repetition of the words *extremist* and *and* along with the parallelism created by the repeating phrase *was not* and the clause *we will be/will we be* link King's approach to that of other religious and historical figures.

Practice and Apply Locate other examples of repetition and parallel structure in King's letter and consider their effects. Then, look back at the speech you wrote for this selection's Create and Present activity. Revise your speech to include an example of repetition and parallelism. Discuss with a partner the effects of your revisions.

LANGUAGE CONVENTIONS:
Repetition and Parallelism

Remind students that repetition is the repeating of the same word or phrase and that parallelism is the repeating of the same structure. Explain that when we say that these techniques can make a message *resonate*, we mean that the techniques can call forth or suggest images, feelings, and memories that echo in the audience's mind. To emphasize how King's use of repetition and parallelism sounds, read aloud, or ask volunteers to read aloud, the examples in the table or the original passages in the text. Ask students to discuss how listening to these examples makes them feel and what, if any, images or memories the examples call forth.

Practice and Apply Students can find several examples of repetition and parallelism in the letter—for example, the repetition of "*Wait*" in paragraphs 13 and 14 and the parallelism in defining a just law as opposed to an unjust law in paragraph 16. Then have students work individually or in pairs, depending upon their proficiency, to incorporate repetition and parallelism into their speech. You might suggest that students build upon a phrase or structure already in their speech instead of trying to create something completely new. Invite students to share and comment upon their revisions.

 ENGLISH LEARNER SUPPORT

Language Conventions Use the following supports with students at varying proficiency levels:

- Read each example aloud as students follow along. When you come to a boldfaced word or phrase, pause and have students read it aloud with you. **SUBSTANTIAL**

- Have partners explain, in their own words, why the first and third examples illustrate not only repetition but also parallelism. (*The examples show repeated structures as well as repeated words.*) Then

have them explain why the second example is powerful, even without parallelism. (*The events that King uses the repetition to describe are events that probably would move his audience.*) **MODERATE**

- Focus on the way that King creates an effect by changing "when you" to "then you" in the first example and by changing the statement "we will be extremists" to a question in the third example. Discuss why these changes are effective. **LIGHT**

ELSEWHERE

Poem by Derek Walcott

GENRE ELEMENTS
POETRY

Remind students that **poetry** has many elements that differentiate it from other genres. Structural elements of poetry include lines and stanzas, which may have regular meter and rhyme, and devices such as repetition and figurative language to develop a theme.

In this lesson, students will examine structural elements of poetry, such as rhyme and meter, as well as the use of motif. This will help them unpack the meaning and analyze the effect of the poem.

LEARNING OBJECTIVES

- Analyze poetic structure, including the use of rhyme and motif.
- Create a correctly formatted reference citation for a source.
- Write an analysis of the poem's effectiveness and cite supporting evidence.
- Discuss the analysis and the poem's impact with a small group.
- **Language** Identify and discuss rhyme scheme in poetry.

TEXT COMPLEXITY

Quantitative Measures	"Elsewhere"	Lexile: N/A
Qualitative Measures	**Ideas Presented** Multiple levels of meaning; use of symbolism; greater demand for inference.	
	Structures Used Four-line stanzas; free verse.	
	Language Used Meanings implied; more figurative language; more inference demanded.	
	Knowledge Required More complexity in theme; references may make heavier demands.	

RESOURCES

- Unit 4 Response Log
- Selection Audio
- Reading Studio: Notice & Note
- Level Up Tutorial: Rhyme
- Writing Studio: Citing Text Evidence
- Speaking and Listening Studio: Participating in Collaborative Discussions
- "Elsewhere" Selection Test

SUMMARIES

English

In this poem, the speaker describes a number of incidents of oppression happening "somewhere" around the world—unnamed places where people are victims of torture, war, slavery, and extreme punishment. We who are "here" are only "free for a while," while "elsewhere" there is suffering and "nothing is free." The speaker makes the point that the "darker crime" is our doing nothing to alleviate the suffering, no matter what "career of conscience" we have adopted in claiming to feel sympathy for oppressed people.

Spanish

En este poema, Derek Walcott describe un número de incidentes relacionados a la opresión que ocurren en "algún lugar" en el mundo; sitios sin nombre, donde la gente sufre las crueldades de la tortura, la guerra, la esclavitud y el castigo. Nosotros que estamos "aquí", en un lugar más "seguro", solo somos "libres por un tiempo", mientras que en "otros sitios" hay sufrimiento y "nada es gratis". Explica que el "crimen más oscuro" es no hacer nada para aliviar el sufrimiento, sin importar que "carrera de consciencia" hayamos adoptado.

SMALL-GROUP OPTIONS

Have students work in small groups to read and discuss the selection.

Jigsaw with Experts

- Have students form groups of five and then number off one to five.
- Have each student read and take notes about two stanzas in "Elsewhere." Student one will work with the first and second stanzas, and so on.
- After reading the poem, have students form expert groups with others who read the same stanzas (ones with ones, twos with twos, and so on) and share their notes.
- Then have students form new jigsaw groups with a representative for each pair of stanzas. (Each group should have at least one student from each of the expert groups.) These groups should discuss all the stanzas in turn and then the poem as a whole.

Think-Pair-Share

- After students have read and analyzed "Elsewhere," pose this question: Why did Walcott repeat the word *somewhere* instead of specifically identifying locations and events?
- Have students think about the question individually and take notes.
- Then have pairs discuss their ideas about the question and formulate a shared response.
- Finally, ask pairs to share their responses with the class.

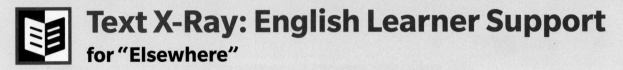

Text X-Ray: English Learner Support
for "Elsewhere"

Use the Text X-Ray and the supports and scaffolds in the Teacher's Edition to help guide students at different proficiency levels through the selection.

INTRODUCE THE SELECTION
DISCUSS OPPRESSION

In this lesson, the topic of oppression may result in strong emotions and opinions from students. Explain and discuss the following as a group:

- What is oppression? *(prolonged cruel or unjust treatment)* Have students read lines 1–4 and 9–12; ask them what words help them visualize the oppressive scenes the speaker describes. Before reading the entire poem, prompt them to consider the messages these scenes send to a reader. Ask students to consider how oppression links to the Essential Question: What is preventing the people in these scenes from feeling free?

- Brainstorm examples of oppression. Ask students to think about instances of oppression from history or current events. Elicit a variety of responses that show how oppression can take many forms. Use this sentence frame to support discussion: *In ___ , people experience oppression by ___.*

CULTURAL REFERENCES

The following words or phrases may be unfamiliar to students:

- *Caribbean* (Background): a region southeast of North America that consists of the Caribbean Sea, its islands, and the surrounding coasts
- *barbed wire* (line 3): twisted strands of wire with sharp points at regular intervals, used in fencing
- *shawled* (line 5): covered, usually with a piece of cloth
- *conference* (line 13): a meeting to share ideas about a topic
- *comrade* (line 17): a friend or companion
- *rifle butt* (line 23): the end piece of the gun that is held against the shoulder when firing
- *stanzas* (line 31): one type of division for a poem
- *massacres* (line 36): the act of killing large numbers of people
- *conscience* (line 38): a sense of right and wrong

LISTENING

Understand the Central Idea

As they listen, draw students' attention to the poem's theme: oppression and cruelty can happen anywhere.

Use the following supports with students at varying proficiency levels.

- Read the poem aloud for students, one stanza at a time, and have them follow along. After each stanza, pause and clarify new vocabulary, using images as necessary. Confirm comprehension by asking questions after each stanza and clarify misconceptions. **SUBSTANTIAL**

- As you read and discuss each stanza, have students identify the different types of oppression or cruelty that they notice in the poem. After reviewing their notes, prompt students to answer this question: What kinds of acts has Walcott described in his poem? *(slavery, torture, murder)* **MODERATE**

- Have partners take turns speaking and listening to each other as they discuss this question: Why doesn't Walcott name a location where these acts occur? *(because they occur in many locations)* Ask them to find evidence in the poem to support their conclusions. **LIGHT**

SPEAKING

Discuss Types of Rhyme

Students will discuss and practice identifying the types of rhyme introduced at the beginning of the selection.

Use the following supports with students at varying proficiency levels.

- Review the different types of rhyme discussed at the beginning of the selection: exact rhyme, slant rhyme, and eye rhyme. Display examples from the poem to help them visualize the words. Read the example aloud and model identifying the rhyme scheme. For example: *food* and *blood* are eye rhymes; *food* and *mood* are exact rhymes. **SUBSTANTIAL**
- After reviewing types of rhyme, have students reread aloud lines 13–16 in pairs. Ask them to discuss with their partner what they notice about these words: *rage, outrage, page, foliage, camouflage.* Guide them to recognize the words that are exact rhymes and those that are eye rhymes. **MODERATE**
- Have students reread aloud lines 13–16 with partners and determine which words form which types of rhymes, and explain why. **LIGHT**

READING

Understand Motif

Explain to students that motifs—repeated images, ideas, or themes—can help reinforce the overall theme of a work. As students read, they should explore the motif of location in "Elsewhere."

Use the following supports with students at varying proficiency levels.

- Display the first two stanzas and read them aloud, modeling the left-to-right directionality of reading English by pointing to the words as you read. Use images to help students understand new vocabulary. Guide students to understand that *somewhere* refers to a different place in each stanza. **SUBSTANTIAL**
- As they read the poem, guide students in marking words that relate to location. Then discuss the significance of these words: Why do you think the author used *here, somewhere,* or *elsewhere* instead of location names? *(to indicate that it could be anywhere in the world)* **MODERATE**
- Have students summarize the location motif in the poem. Provide questions for them to consider: What does Walcott mean by somewhere? *(injustice isn't isolated; it occurs in many locations)* What does this unnamed location remind me of? *(Answers will vary.)* **LIGHT**

WRITING

Write an Analysis

Work with students to carefully read and understand each step of the assignment on Student Edition page 255.

Use the following supports with students at varying proficiency levels.

- Support students to write their analysis by providing sentence stems: *I think this poem would make readers _____. I believe this because _____. The phrase _____ makes me feel _____.* **SUBSTANTIAL**
- Support students' use of grade-level vocabulary by providing key terms to use in their analysis: *theme, motif, stanza, rhyme.* **MODERATE**
- After students write their analysis, have them trade their work with a partner and review it for clarity of ideas and standard grammar usage, circling mistakes. Then ask students to trade back and edit errors identified in their own work. **LIGHT**

Connect to the
? ESSENTIAL QUESTION

Throughout human history, people have struggled to free themselves from oppression. The aftermath of European colonization and the institution of slavery continue to shape the lives of many people in the Caribbean region.

ELSEWHERE

Poem by **Derek Walcott**

248   Unit 4

? ESSENTIAL QUESTION:

What do we need in order to feel free?

WHEN STUDENTS STRUGGLE . . .

Identify Rhyme   Have individuals or partners create a chart to record examples of the different kinds of rhyme in the poem. Encourage students to refer to the chart on page 249 for examples.

Exact Rhyme	Slant Rhyme	Eye Rhyme

 For additional support, go to the **Reading Studio** and assign the following LEVEL **Level Up Tutorial: Rhyme.**

QUICK START

What's going on right now, somewhere else in the world, that concerns you? Is there a war or a refugee crisis or a tyrannical leader committing atrocities against his own people? What is it like to live in a relatively peaceful, stable place knowing that these things are going on in another part of the world? Turn to a partner and share your thoughts.

ANALYZE POETIC STRUCTURE

"Elsewhere" is written in four-line **stanzas,** or groups of lines, in **free verse,** which does not contain regular patterns of rhythm or rhyme. In free verse, the natural flow of lines often mimics the rhythm and flow of everyday speech.

Instead of exact rhymes, the poet may create interest with other structures, including slant rhyme and eye rhyme. End rhyme that is not exact but approximate is called **slant rhyme**, such as *seventh* and *heaven* or *crime* and *scream*. An **eye rhyme** appeals to the eye rather than to the ear. It pairs words with similar spellings but different sounds, such as *enough* and *although* or *mane* and *men*. Add your own examples to the chart below.

GENRE ELEMENTS: POETRY

- explores an idea using figurative language and imagery
- might be arranged in lines and stanzas, which may have regular meter and rhyme
- may use devices such as repetition and symbolism to develop a theme
- the speaker may or may not be the poet's own voice

RHYME TYPE	HOW IT WORKS	EXAMPLES	ALSO CALLED
exact rhyme	a pair of words end in similar or identical sounds	heat > complete stab > taxicab stranglehold > marigold dish > squish	full rhyme perfect rhyme
slant rhyme	a pair of words include the same vowel or consonant sound	care > dear shape > keep grudge > bridge detach > unpack	half rhyme imperfect rhyme near rhyme oblique rhyme off rhyme
eye rhyme	a pair of words have similar spellings but are pronounced differently	love > move through > tough laughter > slaughter enemies > flies	sight rhyme visual rhyme

Elsewhere 249

ENGLISH LEARNER SUPPORT

Understand Directionality Reinforce the directionality of English by reviewing how to read the chart of rhyme types on this page. Explain that each column heading applies to the text in all the cells directly beneath it. To read this chart, students should begin at the top left. Ask a volunteer to trace with a finger the order in which a reader would read the information in the top row. Have students follow along to see how exact rhyme works, read some examples, and learn other names for this kind of rhyme. Suggest that students use colored pencils to lightly shade charts, if doing so will help their understanding.
SUBSTANTIAL

QUICK START

In their discussions, encourage students to give specific examples to support their ideas. To help focus their discussion, ask: How do you learn about what is happening in another part of the world? What makes a society stable?

ANALYZE POETIC STRUCTURE

Tell students that a poem's **rhyme scheme** is its pattern of end rhymes. Most traditional forms, such as sonnets, have a strict rhyme scheme. Most free verse poems, such as "Elsewhere," have a varying pattern of rhyme (or no rhyme at all).

Explain that rhyme scheme can appear in a single stanza or that it can be a "chain," with the same pattern repeated in every stanza. "Elsewhere" does not have a "chain," but students can identify the rhyme scheme in individual stanzas and can mark the rhymes with letters of the alphabet. To illustrate, read aloud the first stanza of the poem. Ask students which lines rhyme. (*first/third, second/fourth*) Have students place an *a* after the first and third lines and a *b* after the second and fourth lines. Then read aloud the second stanza and have students identify its rhyme scheme. (*The rhyming words are different; but like the first stanza, the first and third lines rhyme, as do the second and fourth.*) Elicit that in the third stanza, the same rhyme ends all four lines. You may wish to have students work together to identify the rhyme scheme in each of the other stanzas. You also may wish to point out, later, that the rhyme scheme falls apart toward the end of the poem and discuss with students why that might be so.

To help students understand how free verse varies from traditional metrical poetry, explain that in metrical poetry, stressed and unstressed syllables are arranged in a regular pattern, with each line having the same number of syllables. In free verse, however, line length is not determined by a count of syllables or stresses. The length of a line is often determined by the idea in the line, and lines are often written the way they are spoken, with varying meter.

Write lines 29–30 of "Elsewhere" on the board and guide students in scanning them, emphasizing the stressed syllables aloud. Discuss the effect of this irregular rhythm. (*The four stressed syllables in line 29 evoke an ominous feeling.*)

As they read this poem and others, have students look for examples of different meter and think about the effect of regular and irregular meter.

TEACH

ANALYZE MOTIF

Make sure that students understand the reference to Martin Luther King Jr.'s "I Have a Dream" speech. If necessary, review some of the ideals expressed through King's "dream" motif. (Examples: *the dream that children will be judged by their character rather than their skin color; that black children and white children will consider themselves sisters and brothers*)

Review the plots of the folk tales for students who may be unfamiliar with them. Discuss how the motifs are central to the themes.

Encourage students to pay attention to the repeating motif of location in "Elsewhere." The places referred to by the poet are not named. What idea does this motif emphasize? What is the effect on the reader?

ANNOTATION MODEL

Refer students to the chart in Analyze Poetic Structure on page 249. Point out that the last word in each line in the model is an exact rhyme. (The *e* in the final *-est,* however, sounds slightly different: "ih" or "eh.") Remind students to look for examples of different kinds of rhyme in the poem and to mark these in the text. They may want to color-code their annotations using highlighters. Their notes in the margin, like the reader's notes in the model, can include questions about ideas that are unclear or topics they want to learn more about.

ANALYZE MOTIF

Within a work of literature, a **motif**, or repeated image, idea, or theme, can tie ideas together. For example, in his famous speech, Martin Luther King Jr. expresses hope for many different things, using the motif "I have a dream" to tie them all together. A motif is more concrete than a theme, though it can contribute to the development of both mood and theme within a work.

Complete the chart with the primary motif that occurs in each folk tale:

"The Three Little Pigs"	*weak animals outwitting their enemy*
"The Boy Who Cried Wolf"	*consequences for lying*
"Cinderella"	*the wicked stepmother*

The poem "Elsewhere" employs the motif of location. Although a location is never specified, the poem makes reference to a place using the words *somewhere, here, where,* or *elsewhere.* As you read, notice how this motif adds to the poem's meaning and tone.

ANNOTATION MODEL

NOTICE & NOTE

As you read, look for the various types of rhyme and the use and effect of location-related words. This model shows one reader's notes about a stanza from "Elsewhere":

That <u>somewhere</u> there was an ar<u>rest</u>.

<u>Somewhere</u> there was a small harv<u>est</u>

of bodies in the truck. Soldiers <u>rest</u>

<u>somewhere</u> by a road, or smoke in a for<u>est</u>.

All lines end with -est words. Use of "somewhere" 3x creates distant, disconnected mood.
Does the "where" matter? Are they the same or different?

BACKGROUND

Derek Walcott *(1930–2017), a Caribbean poet and playwright, was raised on the tiny island of Saint Lucia. Of African, English, and Dutch descent, Walcott lost his father at a young age. Guided by his schoolteacher mother, Walcott published his first poem at age 14. About fifty years later, he won the Nobel Prize for Literature. Walcott's work explores the complex racial, cultural, and colonial history of the Caribbean. This poem is dedicated to English poet Stephen Spender, whose poetry examined themes of social injustice.*

ELSEWHERE
Poem by Derek Walcott

SETTING A PURPOSE
As you read, connect the impressions in this poem with real incidents of oppression that you have heard about around the world.

(For Stephen Spender)

Somewhere a white horse gallops with its mane
plunging round a field whose sticks
are ringed with barbed wire, and men
break stones or bind straw into ricks.[1]

5   Somewhere women tire of the shawled sea's
weeping, for the fishermen's dories[2]
still go out. It is blue as peace.
Somewhere they're tired of torture stories.

---

[1] **ricks:** stacks of hay.
[2] **dories:** rowboats.

Elsewhere   251

Notice & Note

You can use the side margins to notice and note signposts in the text.

ANALYZE MOTIF
Annotate: Mark the recurring use of *somewhere* in lines 1–20.

Interpret: What is the effect of the repetition? Where are these places and what do they have in common?

TEACH

BACKGROUND

Provide students with some context about Caribbean history. Explain that much of the Caribbean was colonized by European powers, such as the British, the French, and the Dutch. Enslaved people were forcibly brought from parts of Africa to work the land. Walcott's family reflects this colonial influence; both of his grandmothers were probably descendants of slaves. Some Caribbean islands are still colonies of European nations, though most, including the island of Saint Lucia where Walcott grew up, have gained independence. The United States has been involved in the affairs and conflicts of many Caribbean nations, including Cuba, Haiti, and the Dominican Republic.

SETTING A PURPOSE

Direct students to use the Setting a Purpose prompt to focus their reading.

ANALYZE MOTIF

Point out that *Somewhere* is the first word of several stanzas. The insistent repetition of this motif underscores the fact that people are experiencing oppression and cruelty—and suffering greatly—in "one third, or one seventh of this planet" (lines 22–23). The fact that these locations are not named emphasizes the point that the oppression occurs in more places than can be identified. Those who are oppressed and treated with cruelty include enslaved men who do backbreaking labor (lines 3–4), people who are tortured and imprisoned, people who are arrested and killed by military forces (lines 9–12), and writers who are silenced (lines 17–20). **(Answer:** *This repetition may make readers wonder whether these references are to one place or many. The places are not identified, but what they have in common is that people in all of them are suffering.)*

For **listening and reading support** for students at varying proficiency levels, see the **Text X-Ray** on pages 248C– 248D.

TO CHALLENGE STUDENTS . . .

Plan an Interview Have partners take on the roles of journalists and develop at least five questions to ask Walcott during an interview. Questions might include the following:

- Why do you write about oppression?
- Why did you not specifically identify the locations in "Elsewhere"?
- Do you think that writing can make a difference in people's lives? How?

Students should take turns representing Walcott and the journalist during the interview. After the interview, encourage them to draw conclusions about Walcott and his subject matter.

ANALYZE POETIC STRUCTURE

Explain to students that because *rage*, *outrage*, and *page* are exact rhymes, the reader expects other words ending in *-age* to rhyme with them. The fact that *foliage* and *camouflage* are eye rhymes that don't rhyme with the first three *-age* words or with each other draws more attention to the ideas they express. The sudden shift to eye rhymes draws the reader's attention to the imagery in lines 15 and 16. (**Answer:** *They make the reader wonder what makes foliage look like camouflage. Perhaps, what was once beautiful has been changed by violence and become something to hide in.*)

 For **speaking support** for students at varying proficiency levels, see the **Text X-Ray** on page 248D.

 ## ANALYZE POETIC STRUCTURE

Point out how the first five stanzas use an unspecified "somewhere" repeatedly. It could be anywhere in the world—or all over the world. Beginning with the sixth stanza, the focus shifts. We're "here," and "free for a while." This shift puts an emotional distance between "here" and "elsewhere" that implies tentative safety from the dangers mentioned earlier. (**Answer:** *As the title of the poem, "Elsewhere," suggests, this cruelty is happening around the world—everywhere but "here," where we are [temporarily, at least] free.*)

 ## ENGLISH LEARNER SUPPORT

Ask for Information Read the poem aloud. Encourage students to ask for information by raising their hand when they hear unfamiliar words or expressions. Have a volunteer model asking for information about *comrade* or *hollowed faces.*
SUBSTANTIAL

 NOTICE & NOTE

ANALYZE POETIC STRUCTURE
Annotate: Mark examples of eye rhyme in the third and fourth stanzas.

Analyze: How do these words that look like they should rhyme, but don't, affect your reading of the poem?

ANALYZE POETIC STRUCTURE
Annotate: Mark the new location words used in the sixth stanza.

Analyze: What is the effect of this shift? Why do you think the writer included it?

That somewhere there was an arrest.
10 Somewhere there was a small harvest
of bodies in the truck. Soldiers rest
somewhere by a road, or smoke in a forest.

Somewhere there is the conference <u>rage</u>
at an <u>outrage</u>. Somewhere a <u>page</u>
15 is torn out, and somehow the <u>foliage</u>
no longer looks like leaves but <u>camouflage</u>.

Somewhere there is a comrade,
a writer lying with his eyes wide open
on a mattress ticking,[3] who will not read
20 this, or write. How to make a pen?

And <u>here</u> we are free for a while, but
<u>elsewhere</u>, in one-third, or one-seventh
of this planet, a summary[4] rifle butt
breaks a skull into the idea of a heaven

25 where nothing is free, where blue air
is paper-frail, and whatever we write
will be stamped twice, a blue letter,
its throat slit by the paper knife of the state.

Through these black bars
30 hollowed faces stare. Fingers
grip the cross bars of these stanzas
and it is here, because somewhere else

---

[3] **ticking:** strong fabric, usually striped, used for mattress covers.
[4] **summary:** quickly done.

252   Unit 4

IMPROVE READING FLUENCY

Targeted Passage Students may need additional support in pronouncing words with suffixes that look the same but do not rhyme with each other or other rhyming words. To help students respond to the first guided reading question on this page, read aloud lines 13–14, emphasizing the words *rage*, *page*, and *outrage*. Have students repeat the words. Then read aloud lines 15–16, emphasizing the final syllables of *foliage* and *camouflage*. Define the words for students. Then have students echo your reading as you read the stanza a second and third time, pausing after each line. You may choose to conclude with choral reading as all read this stanza aloud together.

 Go to the **Reading Studio** for additional support in developing fluency.

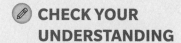

their stares fog into oblivion
thinly, like the faceless numbers
35 that bewilder you in your telephone
diary. Like last year's massacres.

The world is blameless. The darker crime
is to make a career of conscience,
to feel through our own nerves the silent scream
40 of winter branches, wonders read as signs.

CHECK YOUR UNDERSTANDING

Have students answer the questions independently.

Answers:

1. *D*

2. *G*

3. *C*

If they answer any questions incorrectly, have them reread the text to confirm their understanding. Then they may proceed to ANALYZE THE TEXT on page 254.

CHECK YOUR UNDERSTANDING

Answer these questions before moving on to the **Analyze the Text** section on the following page.

1 The poem repeats the idea of "Somewhere" because —

   A the speaker has heard about these crimes but is unsure where they occurred

   B it would be unsafe for the writer to name the place where these events happened

   C the repetition is needed to show where each new sentence begins

   D these events are so pervasive that the location could be anywhere

2 How does the poet describe the reactions of people not directly affected by the events described?

   F They understand that events in other places are not their problem.

   G They feel overwhelmed by how many people are affected.

   H They defeat oppression by writing letters and poems.

   J They know how lucky they are to be free.

3 Which is an important idea emphasized throughout the poem?

   A Living overseas is dangerous.

   B People experience grief for lost loved ones.

   C Oppression and cruelty can happen anywhere.

   D Writers are an important voice for freedom.

 ENGLISH LEARNER SUPPORT

Oral Assessment Use the following questions to assess students' comprehension and speaking skills. Ask students to respond in short, complete sentences.

1. Why does the poet repeat the idea of "Somewhere"? (*He repeats the idea because the events could be occurring in many places.*)

2. How does the poet describe the reactions of people "here," who are not directly affected by these events? (*They feel overwhelmed to hear about the oppression.*)

3. What is an important idea in the poem? (*People can be oppressed and treated badly anywhere.*)
   SUBSTANTIAL/MODERATE

APPLY

ANALYZE THE TEXT

Possible answers:

1. **DOK 2:** *The horse, which represents freedom, is able to run only within a field ringed by barbed wire; the horse's proximity to the prisoners doing forced labor suggests that the prisoners were once free, but now, like the horse, they are fenced in.*

2. **DOK 4:** *The remaining lines take place "here," where great suffering and abuse are not supposed to happen. "Here" people have the luxury of forgetting about these things.*

3. **DOK 3:** *The stanzas compare the stares of "hollowed faces" from behind black prison bars with the telephone numbers that the owner doesn't recognize. The black bars also represent the lines of the poem, which remind us of things that are easy to forget, "like last year's massacres."*

4. **DOK 4:** *Sometimes awful things happen to innocent people. The "darker crime" is often committed by those of us who think we're somehow protected from those things. We might talk about being aware or concerned, to make a "career of conscience," but not do anything about the evil.*

5. **DOK 3:** *The poem makes the point that the world isn't divided into "here" versus "elsewhere." We must actively oppose injustice wherever it happens. We are all responsible. The poet wants us to recognize that our own freedom may be limited or temporary.*

RESEARCH

Tell students that proper citation requires careful attention to detail and lends authority to their writing. Encourage students to exchange their citations and use an online source to review and peer-edit each other's citations.

Extend Remind students to discuss their ideas respectfully and work collaboratively to reach a consensus. Prompt them to consider various perspectives and to think about examples and other evidence from the poem that supports their ideas.

RESPOND

ANALYZE THE TEXT

Support your responses with evidence from the text. 📓 NOTEBOOK

1. **Interpret** Reread lines 1–4. What might the horse represent in the poem? Where is the horse, and what is the significance of that location?

2. **Analyze** If the first 20 lines of the poem take place "somewhere," where do the remaining 20 take place? Explain.

3. **Draw Conclusions** Reread lines 29–36. What are "like the faceless numbers / that bewilder you in your telephone / diary"? What is being compared in these two stanzas?

4. **Analyze** What does the poet express about the world in the final stanza by using phrases such as "darker crime" and "a career of conscience"? Cite text evidence in your answer.

5. **Evaluate** What might be the social function of this poem with its "somewhere" motif? What does the writer want us to take away from the experience of reading the poem?

RESEARCH

RESEARCH TIP
If you need help formatting your source citations, you can consult online sources such as the MLA Style Center (style.mla.org) or EasyBib (www.easybib.com).

Find an online news story that relates to an idea in the poem. Complete the chart below, and create a correctly formatted reference citation for your result. Your citation should include key information: the author (if known), the specific source title, the title of any larger source it comes from, the publisher and publication date. Here is how to format a citation of an online article.

author ⟶ United States Holocaust Memorial Museum. "Political Prisoners." ⟵ title / URL
source publication ⟶ Holocaust Encyclopedia. https://www.ushmm.org/wlc/en/article.php?ModuleId=10007656. Accessed on January 24, 2019. ⟵ date accessed

KEY IDEA FROM THE POEM:	SEARCH TERMS I MIGHT USE:
Responses may vary; citations should include all required information.	
WEB LINK TO ARTICLE	
MLA CITATION	

Extend Discuss what you learned with a partner, and come to a consensus about how effectively the poem addresses the problem of oppression in the world.

WHEN STUDENTS STRUGGLE...

Draw Conclusions Some students may need additional support in understanding the third question in Analyze the Text. Explain that the slash marks indicate line breaks, and draw their attention to lines 34–36 of the poem from which the quote is excerpted. Then read the two stanzas aloud and coach students to identify what is being compared by asking guiding questions. Ask: What is the first stanza describing? (*people being held as prisoners*) What point is Walcott making about telephone numbers with no names attached? (*They are easily forgotten.*)

CREATE AND DISCUSS

Write an Analysis Write an analysis that argues the effectiveness of Walcott's poem. Might it stir readers to find out more about the problems that exist "elsewhere"? Why or why not? Cite evidence from the poem and your own experience.

- ❏ Review your notes and annotations from before, during, and after reading the poem.
- ❏ Reread the poem and take notes on your reaction to it. Note whether and how your reaction changed as a result of rereading the poem.
- ❏ Support your analysis with evidence from the poem and what you know from other sources.

Discuss with a Group Meet with a small group to share your analysis and discuss the poem's impact.

- ❏ Provide specific lines as text evidence and paraphrase or summarize the evidence in support of your interpretation.
- ❏ Keep your comments brief and listen closely as others share theirs. Write down at least one relevant question or meaningful observation you might share in response to something someone else says.
- ❏ After everyone has participated, review similarities and differences in your analyses. What can you conclude as a group?

 Go to the **Writing Studio** for more on citing text evidence.

 Go to the **Speaking and Listening Studio** for more on participating in a discussion.

RESPOND TO THE ESSENTIAL QUESTION

 What do we need in order to feel free?

Gather Information Review your notes and annotations on "Elsewhere," then add relevant information to your Response Log. As you determine which information to include, think about:

- What does "freedom" look like?
- Who among us is really, truly free?
- What does it mean to *feel* free? Is it enough just to feel it, and what would that require?

At the end of the unit, use your notes to help you write an argument.

ACADEMIC VOCABULARY
As you write and discuss what you learned from the poem, be sure to use the Academic Vocabulary words. Check off each of the words that you use.

- ❏ comprehensive
- ❏ equivalent
- ❏ incentive
- ❏ innovate
- ❏ subordinate

CREATE AND DISCUSS

Write an Analysis To begin, have students reread the poem and take notes on their reactions. Have them think about whether they are moved more by one example than another. If so, why? Have them choose one example, such as the writer who has been killed, and explore how the language might stir readers to learn more and take action.

For **writing support** for students at varying proficiency levels, see the **Text X-Ray** on page 248D.

Discuss with a Group Have students discuss their ideas about the effectiveness of the poem. Encourage them to listen attentively and respectfully. If students do not understand a comment made by another group member, they should ask questions to clarify meaning. Comments will vary but should be supported by evidence from the poem.

RESPOND TO THE ESSENTIAL QUESTION

Allow time for students to add details from "Elsewhere" to their Unit 4 Response Logs.

ENGLISH LEARNER SUPPORT

Use New Vocabulary Restate the discussion prompt in Write an Analysis as a question: Is the poem effective? Discuss what the word *effective* means and display words and phrases such as *explains ideas well* and *makes valid points* to help students grasp its meaning. Then, have students work with partners to answer the question. Provide these sentence frames to help them formulate their ideas for their discussions and writing: *The poet describes people who _____. The description of _____ makes me feel _____. I want to ask the poet _____. In conclusion, I think the poem is effective because _____.* **SUBSTANTIAL/MODERATE**

THE HAWK CAN SOAR
Memoir by Randi Davenport

GENRE ELEMENTS
MEMOIR

Remind students that a **memoir** is a written account of an important experience in the author's life. The author's feelings or attitudes about the experience are evident in the voice, mood, and tone of the memoir, which the author conveys through the use of stylistic elements such as diction and syntax. Like any narrative, the sequence of events does not always follow chronological order. In this lesson, students will read to understand how the author uses the genre of a memoir to share thoughts about her disability.

LEARNING OBJECTIVES

- Analyze diction, syntax, and overall text structure.
- Conduct research about a degenerative disease.
- Design a web page to share information gained through research.
- Discuss with a small group how the memoir relates to the theme of Hard-Won Liberty.
- Explain specific allusions.
- Identify the functions of purposeful fragments and distinguish purposeful fragments from incomplete but purposeless thoughts.
- **Language** Explain how the memoir's syntax and tone help readers understand an unfamiliar experience.

TEXT COMPLEXITY

Quantitative Measures	**The Hawk Can Soar**	Lexile: 790L
Qualitative Measures	**Ideas Presented** Mostly explicit, but requires some inferential reasoning.	
	Structures Used Primarily one perspective; may vary from simple chronological order.	
	Language Used Vocabulary not defined at point of use; uses purposeful fragments.	
	Knowledge Required Experiences may be less familiar to many; cultural and literary allusions.	

RESOURCES

- Unit 4 Response Log
- Selection Audio
- Reading Studio: Notice & Note
- Level Up Tutorials: Paraphrasing; Summarizing; Taking Notes and Outlining
- Writing Studio: Publishing with Technology
- Speaking and Listening Studio: Participating in Collaborative Discussions
- Grammar Studio: Module 1: Lesson1: Sentences and Sentence Fragments
- "The Hawk Can Soar" Selection Test

SUMMARIES

English

In her 30s, author Randi Davenport begins to experience physical symptoms of weakness and lack of control. Diagnosed with an incurable degenerative neuromuscular disease, Davenport adjusts her activities and her expectations as her mobility deteriorates. She describes her struggle and her determination to sustain a spirit that can soar even as her body lets her down.

Spanish

En sus 30, la autora Randi Davenport comienza a experimentar síntomas de debilidad y falta de control. Al ser diagnosticada con una enfermedad neuromuscular degenerativa incurable, Davenport ajusta sus actividad y expectaciones a medida que su movilidad se deteriora. Describe su lucha y su determinación para mantener un espíritu que pueda surgir, incluso a pesar de que su cuerpo le falle.

SMALL-GROUP OPTIONS

Have students work in small groups to read and discuss the selection.

Reciprocal Teaching

- After students have read the memoir, present them with a list of generic question stems *(What? Who? Where? When? Why? How?)*.
- Instruct students to work independently to write three to five questions about the memoir, using the question stems. They do not need to know the answers.
- Group students into teams of three and have each student offer two questions for group discussion.
- Guide groups to reach consensus on the answer to each question and cite text evidence that supports the answer.

Three-Minute Review

- Pause during reading or discussion of the memoir and direct students to spend three minutes reviewing what they have read.
- Set a timer and have pairs or triads work together to reread, review class notes, and write clarifying questions about the memoir. You may want to suggest they focus on one aspect of the author's style or structure or on a specific topic such as living with a chronic disease.
- When the time is up, ask volunteers from each group to share and discuss their clarifying questions.

Text X-Ray: English Learner Support
for "The Hawk Can Soar"

Use the Text X-Ray and the supports and scaffolds in the Teacher's Edition to help guide students at different proficiency levels through the selection.

INTRODUCE THE SELECTION
DISCUSS DISABILITY

In this lesson, students will need to discuss the author's challenge of coping with a disability that developed when she was an adult. Explain words that describe her initial physical symptoms:

- When you're **weak,** you have little strength.
- When you **quake,** you shake.
- When you **stiffen,** you feel hard and tense.
- When you feel **fatigue,** you are very tired.

Have volunteers share how it might feel for a healthy person to begin to experience serious physical symptoms. Encourage students to listen closely and respond to each other.

CULTURAL REFERENCES

The following words or phrases may be unfamiliar to students:

- *full expression* (paragraph 3): all symptoms are clearly apparent
- *a fighter* (paragraph 7): someone who is strong and doesn't give up easily
- *saving grace* (paragraph 7): something that makes a difficult situation easier to take
- *escape fate:* (paragraph 7): avoid what must happen
- *epiphany:* (paragraph 12): a moment in which something important is realized
- *this narrative in America* (paragraph 12): a popular type of story in America, such as one in which someone overcomes a great hardship

LISTENING

Interpret Tone

Explain that reading aloud can help students notice the author's syntax—the pattern and arrangement of words and sentences. Explain that syntax often contributes to the tone of a text.

Have students listen as you read aloud paragraph 5. Emphasize syntax as you read. Use the following supports with students at varying proficiency levels:

- Tell students that you will ask some questions about the tone of the paragraph. Model giving a thumbs up or down for the answer. Does the author seem nervous? Do the short sentences make the author seem scared? **SUBSTANTIAL**
- Reread the first six sentences of paragraph 5. Ask students to describe the sentences. *(short, incomplete)* Ask them to identify the tone. *(scared, nervous, desperate)* **MODERATE**
- Have students work in pairs to describe the syntax and identify the tone of the paragraph. **LIGHT**

SPEAKING

Discuss the Introduction

Have students discuss how the author uses specific details to introduce herself as someone with a disability.

Use the following supports with students at varying proficiency levels:

- Read aloud the first three sentences of paragraph 1. Have students read aloud the sentences back to you. **SUBSTANTIAL**
- Have one student read aloud the first three sentences of paragraph 1. Then have a partner paraphrase aloud. **MODERATE**
- Invite partners to read aloud paragraph 1 together. Encourage them to break down words they find difficult to pronounce into individual parts. Have them discuss how they feel reading specific descriptions of the author's disability. **LIGHT**

READING

Analyze Text Structure

Remind students that authors do not always tell stories in chronological order. Remind them that understanding the order of events is important to comprehending the text.

Use the following supports with students at varying proficiency levels:

- Reread paragraphs 3–4 aloud to students as they follow along. Then ask students to locate the phrase "It begins for me in my 30s." Think aloud: This phrase lets me know that the author's illness began when she was in her 30s. **SUBSTANTIAL**
- Have students reread paragraphs 3–4. Then instruct them to find evidence to support the fact that the author has not lived with the disease for her entire life. Supply a sentence frame: *I know that the author became sick as an adult because* _____. **MODERATE**
- Have partners reread paragraphs 3–4 and identify when the author began experiencing symptoms. Have them discuss why the author might not reveal that information until paragraph 4. **LIGHT**

WRITING

Design a Web Page

Work with students to complete the writing assignment on Student Edition page 265.

Use the following supports with students at varying proficiency levels:

- Provide sentence frames that students can use as they begin planning their web page: _____ *will be the topic of my web page. I chose this topic because* _____. **SUBSTANTIAL**
- Using Think Aloud and modeling strategies, help students brainstorm features to help them structure information. For example, say: *I think I will include a bulleted list to display the evidence I gathered. This list will make it easier for users to understand my ideas.* **MODERATE**
- Have partners review each other's work. Ask: Which features did the writer use to structure the information? Which features might be added to improve the work? **LIGHT**

THE HAWK CAN SOAR

Memoir by **Randi Davenport**

? Connect to the
ESSENTIAL QUESTION

In her memoir "The Hawk Can Soar," Randi Davenport describes how a degenerative neuromuscular disease affects her daily life and shares thoughts about how her physical limitations affect her ideas about personal freedom.

? ESSENTIAL QUESTION:

What do we need in order to feel free?

 LEARNING MINDSET

Questioning   In "The Hawk Can Soar," students meet an author who questions her life. Use this idea as a springboard to encourage students to feel comfortable about asking questions as they read and discuss this memoir. Welcome students' questions and their curiosity; remind students that asking questions is a great way to check their understanding and learn new things. Suggest that students keep a record of questions that lead them to new ideas.

QUICK START

Have you ever lost the ability to do something you normally could do because of an illness or injury? How did it make you feel? Discuss your experience with the class.

ANALYZE DICTION AND SYNTAX

To understand how the author uses language to inform and shape the perception of readers, you need to analyze the author's diction and syntax. **Diction** refers to the author's choice of words. **Syntax** is the pattern and arrangement of words or other elements of sentence structure. The author's diction and syntax contribute to the mood, voice, and tone of the text. **Mood** is the atmosphere or feeling the writer creates for readers. **Voice** is the unique way of writing that allows a reader to sense the writer's personality. **Tone** is the author's attitude toward the subject or topic.

EXAMPLE FROM TEXT	TECHNIQUE AND EFFECT
I'm also weak. Spastic.	**Syntax:** short sentence followed by a fragment: contributes to a matter-of-fact, casual voice; emphasizes the word *spastic*
. . . transmitted in an autosomal dominant pattern, the geneticist said.	**Diction:** formal, medical terminology creates a sterile, impersonal tone

ANALYZE TEXT STRUCTURE

Text structure is the way an author organizes a text to show connections between events and to develop ideas. The text structure of this memoir provides information about the author's disease in the context of narrative passages, which are not in chronological order.

Use the graphic organizer below to track events in the memoir that happen before and after the author's diagnosis.

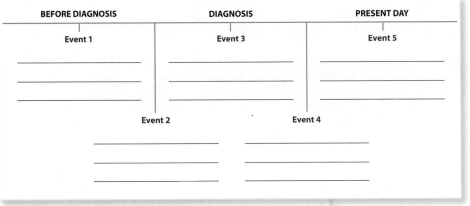

GENRE ELEMENTS: MEMOIR

- self-written account that describes a significant experience in the author's life
- includes the author's feelings and attitude toward the experience
- includes purposeful stylistic choices to create voice, mood, and tone
- events may not be told in chronological order

The Hawk Can Soar 257

QUICK START

Share an anecdote about a time when your own activities were affected by illness or injury. Suggest that students jot down adjectives that describe their feelings as they recall similar experiences—perhaps a seasonal illness, a sports injury, or even a long-term and chronic condition. Invite volunteers to share their responses with the class. After you discuss various ways in which people respond to physical limitations, tell students to compare and contrast some of the points made during the discussion with what Randi Davenport says in "The Hawk Can Soar."

ANALYZE DICTION AND SYNTAX

Help students understand the terms and concepts related to **diction** and **syntax.** Read aloud the examples in the chart. Model thinking about how the formal diction, or word choice, in the second example creates a formal, impersonal **tone.** Then guide students to understand that in the first example, the use of the contraction *I'm* and the purposeful use of a fragment convey an informal, conversational tone. Point out that both examples contribute to the author's **voice.** You may wish to have students speculate about the **mood** that the author creates, but explain that students will need to read more of the selection to form an accurate view.

ANALYZE TEXT STRUCTURE

Explain that readers can often use verb tense to help determine the sequence of events in a narrative. In this memoir, however, Davenport mostly uses present-tense verbs. This writing style creates for the reader a sense of experiencing events along with the writer. Tell students to look for signals such as "when," "by this time," and "soon" to help them determine chronological sequence and decide where to place events on their timelines.

CRITICAL VOCABULARY

Answers:

1. *b*

2. *a*

3. *a*

4. *a*

5. *b*

■ English Learner Support

Use Cognates   Tell students that four of the Critical Vocabulary words have Spanish cognates: *irrefutable/ irrefutable, insidious/insidioso, atrophy/atrofiarse, occult/ oculto*. **ALL LEVELS**

LANGUAGE CONVENTIONS

If necessary, explain that a **fragment** is missing a subject, a verb, or both. Point out that people often use fragments in casual conversation and have volunteers offer examples.

Read aloud the example. Then read aloud the following: "I tell myself that I'm working too hard. I'm trying to do too much." Ask students to compare the two versions and discuss how the fragment affects the tone. (*The difference is subtle, but the example with the fragment sounds more like someone engaged in casual conversation. It also puts a little more emphasis on* Trying to do too much, *as if the author is exasperated or disappointed.*)

ANNOTATION MODEL

Remind students about the annotation ideas they have learned about and used in past units. Encourage students to use the system that works best for them. Urge them also to mark details that catch their interest and to make marginal comments—interpretations, questions, and so on—as they read. As students examine the model, point out that the reader used brackets to identify details relating to the author's disability and made comments about both the content and the style in the passage.

CRITICAL VOCABULARY

To see how many Critical Vocabulary words you already know, mark the correct answer to each question.

1. Which of the following is **irrefutable**?
   a. A dollar bill is better than a dollar coin.
   b. A dollar bill is worth 100 cents.

2. Which of the following is an example of an **insidious** rumor?
   a. It spreads and ruins a person's reputation.
   b. It is ignored and believed to be false.

3. Which of the following might result in muscle **atrophy**?
   a. a person's broken leg in a cast for months
   b. a person lifting weights in the gym

4. Which of the following is an example of a **contemptuous** action?
   a. pointing and laughing at someone who fell
   b. comforting someone who is hurt

5. Which of the following is an example of an **occult** location?
   a. a covered bus stop on a busy sidewalk
   b. a mysterious grove hidden deep in a forest

LANGUAGE CONVENTIONS

Purposeful Fragments   In this lesson, you will learn about the intentional use of fragments in writing. While a fragment is usually an error, an author may choose to use fragments for effect, as in this example from the text:

I tell myself that I'm working too hard. <u>Trying to do too much.</u>

This fragment reflects the author's thought process. As you read, note other fragments that develop a conversational tone and emphasize key ideas.

ANNOTATION MODEL   **NOTICE & NOTE**

As you read, note the author's use of diction and syntax to shape the reader's perception of her experience and mark descriptions that explain the author's unique experiences. Here are one reader's notes about "The Hawk Can Soar":

> [I push the walker] in front of me, its front wheels larger than the wheels in back. [My right leg drags a little. My right foot drops.] <u>When I don't have the rollator in front of me—when I try to walk unaided</u>—I have to bring my right hand up to my waist to create my own version of balance. [Elbow clamped to my side. . . .]

descriptions of the author's challenges

Syntax reflects that the author is not in control, her elbow is.

BACKGROUND

Novelist and essayist **Randi Davenport** *earned a MA in creative writing and a PhD in literature from Syracuse University. One of her award-winning books,* The Boy Who Loved Tornadoes, *is about her son's struggle with mental illness. In addition to writing, Davenport has also worked with state officials in North Carolina to change policies to provide more help for people with mental illnesses.*

THE HAWK CAN SOAR

Memoir by Randi Davenport

SETTING A PURPOSE

In this memoir, the author describes an experience that may be unfamiliar to you. As you read, monitor your understanding, pausing to ask questions or rereading to clear up your understanding of what the author experiences.

1   I push the walker in front of me, its front wheels larger than the wheels in back. My right leg drags a little. My right foot drops. When I don't have the rollator[1] in front of me—when I try to walk unaided—I have to bring my right hand up to my waist to create my own version of balance. Elbow clamped to my side. Stiffness where most other people have swing.

2   I'm also weak. Spastic. I wear braces for balance and support. How many times has some bio-technician cradled my feet in his or her hands, stroking the wrapping in place from which a new brace will be cast? I cannot count, but I recall each time as if it were the same as the time before, the same as the time yet to come.

---

[1] **rollator:** a frame on wheels used to provide support and balance for walking.

Notice & Note

You can use the side margins to notice and note signposts in the text.

ANALYZE DICTION AND SYNTAX

Annotate: Mark a repeated structure in paragraph 2.

Analyze: How does this repetition reflect what the author understands about her disease?

The Hawk Can Soar   **259**

BACKGROUND

Note that Davenport has a special interest in helping readers understand various illnesses. In *The Boy Who Loved Tornadoes,* she writes about the disabling effects of mental illness. Discuss with students that mental illness is a condition affecting someone's thinking or emotional state, which may affect how that person relates to others. Examples include depression and anxiety. In "The Hawk Can Soar," Davenport discusses how she copes with restrictions on her mobility.

SETTING A PURPOSE

Direct students to use the Setting a Purpose prompt to focus their reading.

For **speaking support** for students at varying proficiency levels, see the **Text X-Ray** on page 256D.

ANALYZE DICTION AND SYNTAX

Point out that earlier in paragraph 2, the author notes "how many times" technicians have cast new braces for her. Have students consider how she may feel about the continuing need for such support. (***Answer:*** *The repeated structure at the end of the paragraph—an example of parallelism—emphasizes that the author has been coping with this disease for some time and has come to understand that it will continue to dominate her life. Her attitude seems to be one of resignation, or acceptance that her situation will not improve.*)

WHEN STUDENTS STRUGGLE . . .

Monitor Understanding   Read aloud the first couple of paragraphs of the memoir. Model how to monitor understanding by pausing to paraphrase or summarize, ask clarifying questions, and reread as needed. Suggest that students pause to monitor their understanding after the following paragraphs: paragraph 3, paragraph 6, paragraph 8, paragraph 10, paragraph 15, and then at the end of the selection.

 For additional support, go to the **Reading Studio** and assign the following **Level Up Tutorials: Paraphrasing** and **Summarizing.**

ANALYZE TEXT STRUCTURE

Make sure students understand that in paragraph 4 the author transitions from describing her current symptoms to backtracking to recount how her disability first manifested and then began to affect her mobility. Remind students that she uses the present tense to discuss these past events. (**Answer:** *The first event occurs in her 30s, when her foot goes out from under her while running. She experiences other symptoms over time. She does not give specific times for the next events, but she stiffens, has difficulty with rising from a chair, can't climb stairs, and suffers from extreme fatigue.*)

For **reading support** for students at varying proficiency levels, see the **Text X-Ray** on page 256D.

■ English Learner Support

Discuss Verb Tenses In several languages (including Cantonese, Haitian Creole, Korean, Tagalog, and Vietnamese), verbs do not change form to express tense. Students have been learning that in English, verbs do change form to express tense. As a result, there may be some confusion over the fact that the author uses the present tense to talk about past events in paragraphs 4 and beyond. Model for students how the first part of paragraph 4 would be expressed in past tense: *It began for me in my 30s. When I was out running, my right foot went out from under me.* Work with students to restate the rest of the paragraph with past-tense verbs. **SUBSTANTIAL/MODERATE**

For **listening support** for students at varying proficiency levels, see the **Text X-Ray** on page 256C.

 NOTICE & NOTE

ANALYZE TEXT STRUCTURE

Annotate: Mark words that indicate the passage of time in paragraph 4.

Analyze: How does the author's disease progress? Start your timeline with the first event.

3   My hands quake with tremors, as do my father's hands and as did his father's hands before him. But I'm the lucky one. I'm the one who gets the disease, a rare form of motor neuron disease, in its full expression. My father and grandfather didn't even know they had a disease — *transmitted in an autosomal dominant pattern,*[2] the geneticist said. They stopped being able to walk in their 70s and 80s and decided that this was caused by other things, perhaps by the nature of being old men, or a failure of the will to move, or the inconstant beating of their own blood.

4   It begins for me in my 30s. When I'm out running, my right foot goes out from under me, then comes back into position. It's nothing, I think. But over time, it happens more and more frequently. And other things come too, in silent waves: I stiffen like a tree trunk. I cannot easily rise from a chair. I cannot climb a flight of stairs. I cannot live my life without being overcome with profound fatigue, an exhaustion so deep and unmeasurable that I weep when I don't have the strength to make dinner.

5   I tell myself that I'm working too hard. Trying to do too much. That all single parents are beset by weariness without end. I stop running and walk instead. When I can no longer walk any distance,

---

[2] *autosomal dominant pattern:* a disease that requires only one copy of the gene to be inherited to transmit the disease.

EL ENGLISH LEARNER SUPPORT

Make a Timeline To support students in determining the sequence of events in the memoir, provide them with a timeline graphic organizer. As you read, emphasize the time-order words and phrases, and work with students to identify time-order clues in the memoir.

- Provide a timeline that is partially filled in with the development and diagnosis of Davenport's condition. Have them work with partners to place events on the timeline as they occur in the memoir. **SUBSTANTIAL/MODERATE**
- Provide students with a blank timeline and sentence stems: *The first sign of disability happened when _____. Next, she _____. After that _____.* **LIGHT**

After reading, have students display, compare, and discuss their timelines.

I go to the gym. When I can no longer tolerate the gym, I go to the pool. But each new environment is a landscape of loss. What I could do and no longer can. What I can't do an **irrefutable** presence, as if lack has a shape and a weight.

6   A colleague at work points out my constant limp. I shrug. By this time, I have seen neurologists at Duke and Johns Hopkins. They're baffled. Something is wrong — on exam, my big toes point up, my reflexes jump, my muscles catch, my index finger shivers in a sign of a spinal lesion — but they can't say what. Only when I finally see a neuromuscular disease specialist at the big teaching hospital in Chapel Hill, N.C., do I find the doctor who knows what's gone wrong. In time, he delivers the news that I cannot be cured. I can only grow worse, my disability increasing in **insidious** increments that he will track by seeing me every three months.

7   Time passes. We watch, this doctor and I, as my disease moves through me. It's languid, quiet, but it moves. I grow weaker. I **atrophy** in discrete regions — my right foot and then my left and then my right hand — but I don't waste. I grow fat from immobility and then I grow thin again. I want to live as who I was, not as what this disease makes of me. This idea is a chimera[3] but it helps me to think that I am fighting. I am a fighter. I always have been, even when I cannot win. At other times in my life, I might have viewed this as a pathological neurosis akin to tilting at windmills. Now I think of it as a saving grace. These tales I tell myself. The way I plan to escape fate. All to keep myself going.

8   Eventually, however, I am disabled. Disabled. Like this word is the sum total of my existence. That dragging leg. That dropping foot. That unbearable fatigue. A woman with a rollator moving slowly through the world. These things signal my difference whenever I move. They are obvious. Unrestrained.

9   Soon, I leave my university career. I slowly begin to disappear from view. The things I have earned seem ever further away. This is the nature of this difference, I realize. The way disability stands in for everything you were or ever would have been. Even when you say it will not. Even when you refuse its existence. Disability is **contemptuous** of your refusal. It scoffs at your desperate concern. It pushes forward and it drags you after it.

10   I develop a serious side effect. A co-morbidity[4], my doctors call it. I nearly die. It doesn't matter that I said I would fight to stay upright. It doesn't matter that I have resisted the wheelchair. My body has other plans and it doesn't consult me. It is my own and yet it is blind to my dreams. My desires. Weirdly, I begin to understand that I am but a part of my body. My body is not a part of me.

---

[3] **chimera** (kī-mîr´ə): a mental illusion or fabrication.
[4] **co-morbidity** (kō-môr-bĭd´ ĭ-tē): an incidence of two diseases or disorders in the same person

irrefutable
(ĭ-rĕf´yə-tə-bəl) *adj.* impossible to disprove; unquestionable.

insidious
(ĭn-sĭd´ē-əs) *adj.* spreading harmfully in a subtle way.

atrophy
(ăt´rə-fē) *v.* to deteriorate due to disease, injury, or lack of use.

ANALYZE DICTION AND SYNTAX
Annotate: Mark the phrase "tilting at windmills" in paragraph 7.

Interpret: This phrase is an allusion to *Don Quixote*, in which a character who imagines he is a knight attempts to battle windmills. How does this reference fit the author's approach to her illness?

contemptuous
(kən-tĕmp´chŏŏ-əs) *adj.* scornful.

ANALYZE DICTION AND SYNTAX

Explain that an **allusion** is a reference to a famous person, place, event, or work of literature. An allusion can be used as a kind of shorthand to convey ideas. The phrase "tilting at windmills" brings to mind complex ideas and attitudes connected with the story of Don Quixote, and the visual image alone suggests the futility of taking on some fights. (**Answer:** *The author is affirming her instinct to fight the disease. She might once have thought it was crazy to do so, the way Don Quixote was crazy to think that windmills were knights, but now she prefers to keep fighting.*)

CRITICAL VOCABULARY

irrefutable: To Davenport, the decline of her physical abilities is so obvious that it cannot be denied.

ASK STUDENTS why irrefutable facts might be important in the field of medicine. (*Facts that cannot be denied or disproven form a solid basis for diagnosing an illness.*)

insidious: Davenport's disability will continue to get worse little by little, stealthily and relentlessly.

ASK STUDENTS to discuss why an insidious disease might be difficult to treat. (*It begins without much warning, often with confusing symptoms that make diagnosis difficult.*)

atrophy: Davenport loses function in different parts of her body, such as her right foot and right hand.

ASK STUDENTS to discuss how atrophy of just one hand would affect a person's daily life. (*The inability to use a hand due to atrophy or weakness would make nearly every mundane activity, such as getting dressed, very difficult.*)

contemptuous: Davenport compares disability to a person who disrespects her.

ASK STUDENTS to discuss the relationship between power and contemptuous behavior. (*People with great power often scoff at, or look down on, those who are weaker or are unable to fight against them.*)

APPLYING ACADEMIC VOCABULARY

❏ comprehensive ☑ equivalent ❏ incentive ❏ innovate ☑ subordinate

Discuss Have students turn to a partner to discuss the following questions based on paragraph 10. Guide students to include the academic vocabulary words *equivalent* and *subordinate* in their responses. Ask volunteers to share their responses with the class.

- How is Davenport's battle against her disability **equivalent** to Don Quixote's battle against windmills?
- Why does Davenport feel **subordinate** to her own body?

© Houghton Mifflin Harcourt Publishing Company

LANGUAGE CONVENTIONS

Remind students that one reason for using a **fragment** is to emphasize a point. Suggest that students consider how the author feels about being the object of attention. (**Answer:** *The fragment emphasizes that the author is aware that people often look at her because of her disability. The fragment suggests a tone of slight annoyance.*)

ANALYZE DICTION AND SYNTAX

Remind students that **connotations** are not the same as dictionary definitions (**denotations**); rather, they have to do with the feelings that words evoke. Words with positive connotations suggest hope, happiness, acceptance, and so on; words with negative connotations suggest displeasure, sadness, hatred, and the like.

Review Davenport's encounter with the hawk and then discuss ways in which she and it are alike. (*Both would like to be free; both have their freedom limited by forces they cannot control.*) (**Answer:** *These words and phrases contrast the hawk's opportunity for freedom with the limits imposed on the author by her disease. Together, they develop the idea that the author must find a different sort of freedom.*)

ALL LEVELS

■ English Learner Support

Understand Vocabulary Read aloud paragraphs 16–18 and invite students to ask for clarification of any words that are unfamiliar. Then ask students to draw images that represent the words "dreary morning," "strains against its bindings," "my heart lifts," and "hawk rises and spreads its wings." Have students compare the feelings evoked by the drawings to the feelings, or **tone,** that the author evokes in paragraph 16. Have students note which drawings evoke positive feelings and which evoke negative feelings.

ALL LEVELS

CRITICAL VOCABULARY

occult: As Davenport drives along the road home, which she can see, she considers the "road" of what the rest of her life will be like, which she cannot "see," or know.

ASK STUDENTS why, according to paragraph 6, the cause of Davenport's physical problems was occult at first. (*Despite testing her, specialists were unable to tell why she was experiencing the problems.*)

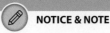

NOTICE & NOTE

LANGUAGE CONVENTIONS
Annotate: Mark a purposeful fragment in paragraph 14.

Analyze: How does the fragment you marked contribute to the tone of the memoir?

ANALYZE DICTION AND SYNTAX
Annotate: In paragraphs 16–18, circle words with positive connotations, and underline words with negative connotations.

Interpret: How do these contrasting words shape your perception of the encounter with the hawk?

occult
(ə-kŭlt´) *adj.* mysterious or hidden.

---

11   Thus subordinated, I live. And I keep on living.

12   This story should end with an epiphany, a moment when I discover that I can still soar. How we love this narrative in America! The ultimate act of bootstrapping[5]: refusing to give in to a body you cannot control and that medicine is helpless to cure.

13   And I nearly have such a moment. Leaning against my car in a gas station by the side of a highway, pumping gas, I see a man standing next to a pickup truck, an unremarkable sight save that he has a huge hawk on his arm. The hawk is unblinded, its hood draped over its neck like a collar, but it is lashed to the glove on the man's arm like a dog to a post. Unaccountably, it sees me and tilts its head and then tilts its head again.

14   What are you looking at? I think. As I so often think. But I wave to the man and call, "Beautiful bird."

15   He nods and says they've been out hunting.

16   It's a dreary morning, mist hanging in veils over the fields, a purplish tinge to the distant trees. I cannot imagine hunting in the rain with a bird aloft but then I do. The rivulets of water standing in the farm ditches. The fresh scent of the pines. The breeze lifting the sky and then lifting the sky again, each cloud turning. For just a moment, my heart lifts and, as if to answer me, the hawk rises and spreads its wings and then flaps back into place. Gives itself a shake as it strains against its bindings and then looks at me again, the expressionless light of its eyes seeming to say, What're you going to do?

17   Nothing, I say. I can do nothing.

18   I finish pumping my gas, and holding onto the side of my car for balance, I return the nozzle to its cradle, turn and climb back into the driver's seat and point my car south, toward home. A few minutes later, the man and the hawk are gone and nothing is left but the road ahead, **occult,** unknown, and yet so familiar by now that I feel every turn in my failing neurons. In my ever hopeful bones.

---

[5] **bootstrapping:** to develop using one's own work, without help from others.

CHECK YOUR UNDERSTANDING

Have students answer the questions independently.

Answers:

1. C

2. H

3. A

If students answer any questions incorrectly, have them reread the text to confirm their understanding. Then they may proceed to **ANALYZE THE TEXT** on page 264.

CHECK YOUR UNDERSTANDING

Answer these questions before moving on to the **Analyze the Text** section on the following page.

1 What has happened to the author?

  A She has always had a disability, as did her father and grandfather.

  B She learned she could have had a genetic disease but was lucky.

  C She gradually loses motor skills due to an incurable disease.

  D She is surprised to learn that she has a neurological disorder.

2 As the memoir concludes —

  F the author has an epiphany

  G a hawk soars above the long road

  H the author drives toward home

  J a hawk hunts for prey in a field

3 Which of these best describes the tone of the selection?

  A Helpless but hopeful

  B Joyful but nostalgic

  C Angry but forgiving

  D Fearful but brave

The Hawk Can Soar   263

ENGLISH LEARNER SUPPORT

Oral Assessment Use the following questions to assess students' comprehension and speaking skills.

1. What causes the author to become disabled? *(She has an incurable disease that affects her motor skills.)*

2. What does the author do at the end of the memoir? *(She drives toward home.)*

3. Name two words that describe the tone, or the author's feelings, in this memoir. *(The words* helpless *and* hopeful *best describe the tone.)* **SUBSTANTIAL/MODERATE**

ANALYZE THE TEXT

Possible answers:

1. **DOK 4:** *Completed timelines should reflect this sequence: In her 30s the author begins to have motor problems; increasing exhaustion causes her to change her activities; she begins to limp; she visits multiple doctors before arriving at a diagnosis; she loses mobility and leaves her job; she nearly dies and must rely on a rolling walker; she sees the hawk. Because Davenport begins near the end of this sequence, the reader already knows what the small signs of trouble will lead to, but the reader does not know whether Davenport will redefine how to feel free.*

2. **DOK 4:** *The author personifies her disability by describing it as "contemptuous," scoffing at her and dragging her along. She portrays it as a relentless bully that she must confront constantly as it begins to take over her life.*

3. **DOK 2:** *The author nearly had an epiphany thinking about a hawk soaring over a field and feeling her heart soar, but instead she is struck with the reality that the hawk is now tethered and unable to fly. She and the hawk can "do nothing" but wait and hope for small moments in which they can feel free.*

4. **DOK 3:** *Although she has seen what the disease did to her father and grandfather, she knows that her case is more severe. And although she knows her diagnosis and how the disease has progressed so far, she can't really know what it will be like to experience it until she arrives at that point.*

5. **DOK 4:** *The author repeats the idea of living. No matter how this disease progresses, she will continue to adapt and live as fully as she can, which is a theme of the memoir.*

RESEARCH

Review the Research Tip with students. Share with students that some researchers think Lou Gehrig may not have had ALS but instead may have suffered from CTE (Chronic Traumatic Encephalopathy), which has similar symptoms. Suggest possible research questions students might consider: What are the symptoms? How is it diagnosed? What is the treatment for the disorder?

Connect Instruct students to use information they gathered in their research to consider the variety of everyday challenges people with disabilities face. Encourage students to consider simple tasks and activities that others take for granted. Ask each group to come up with a list of recommendations about how society can be more inclusive.

 RESPOND

ANALYZE THE TEXT

Support your responses with evidence from the text. 📓 NOTEBOOK

1. **Analyze** The events of the memoir are not in chronological order. Use your timeline to help you describe the order of events. What is the effect of the way the author structures this text?

2. **Critique** Reread paragraph 9. How does the author personify the idea of disability? How does this personification communicate her ongoing experience through a series of parallel sentences?

3. **Infer** In paragraph 13, the author says, "And I nearly have such a moment." What moment did she nearly have, and why did it not come to pass?

4. **Cite Evidence** In paragraph 18, the author describes the road using antonyms: "unknown, yet so familiar." Using evidence from the text, explain what is unknown and what is familiar to the author about her metaphorical road ahead.

5. **Evaluate** What idea does the author repeat in paragraph 11? How might this very short paragraph serve as a statement of the memoir's theme, or message?

RESEARCH

RESEARCH TIP
If you're not sure where to start your search, try searching for a list of degenerative diseases and then consider what interests you. For example, a baseball fan might choose to learn more about amyotrophic lateral sclerosis (ALS) and how it affected Lou Gehrig.

The author of "The Hawk Can Soar" suffers from a degenerative disease. Learn about another degenerative disease. Develop a plan for your research, such as determining general keywords and formulating a question to answer. Use a chart such as the one below to track how your plan and question change as you gather more information.

Initial question: *Responses will vary.*	Best information source:
Revised question:	Best information source:
What I learned:	How my plan changed:

Connect In paragraph 9, the author states, "I slowly begin to disappear from view." With a small group, discuss what people with the disability you researched do to keep from "disappearing," as well as what others can do to see the person.

🛠 LEARNING MINDSET

Asking for Help As students answer the Analyze the Text questions and work on the postreading activities, there may be times when they feel "stuck" and are unsure of how to proceed. Remind students that at such times, they should ask for help in order to move forward again. Establish guidelines for seeking help from peers, from you (as the teacher), and from people outside the classroom. Encourage students to use those guidelines, and reinforce the efforts of students who do so and make progress as a result.

CREATE AND DISCUSS

Design a Web Page Use your research findings to create a web page about your research topic.

❏ Objectively introduce and develop your topic using concise sentences and a formal style.

❏ Use features such as boldfaced headings, sidebars, bulleted lists, and images to incorporate evidence and structure your information.

❏ Create your web page online or represent your page using a word processing program or a handwritten mock-up.

Discuss with a Small Group Have a discussion about how the memoir "The Hawk Can Soar" relates to the theme of Hard-Won Liberty. In what way is the author striving for freedom?

❏ Have group members prepare ideas and gather evidence from the memoir.

❏ Listen actively and respectfully to the members of your group. Ask questions for clarification if needed.

❏ Respond to questions appropriately.

Go to the **Writing Studio** for more on publishing with technology.

Go to the **Speaking and Listening Studio** for help with having a group discussion.

RESPOND TO THE ESSENTIAL QUESTION

 What do we need in order to feel free?

Gather Information Review your annotations and notes on "The Hawk Can Soar." Then, add relevant information to your Response Log. As you determine which information to include, think about:

• what keeps people from feeling free
• why people fight against odds
• how changes and loss affect our sense of freedom

At the end of the unit, use your notes to help you write an argument.

ACADEMIC VOCABULARY
As you write and discuss what you learned from the memoir, be sure to use the Academic Vocabulary words. Check off each of the words that you use.

❏ comprehensive
❏ equivalent
❏ incentive
❏ innovate
❏ subordinate

APPLY

CREATE AND DISCUSS

Design a Web Page Remind students to cite each source they use in their research. After they finish the first draft of their web pages, have students form peer groups to critique each other's work. Remind them to check for these features:

• links to more information
• content that is easy to scan
• use of illustrations and other graphics
• text that is easy to scan

For **writing support** for students at varying proficiency levels, see the **Text X-Ray** on page 256D.

Discuss with a Small Group Encourage all students to participate in the discussion. Suggest that they begin by identifying a quotation in the memoir that relates to the theme of Hard-Won Liberty. As students discuss how Davenport strives for freedom, encourage them to ask each other questions to confirm or clarify their understanding and to support their ideas by citing evidence.

■ English Learner Support

Confirm and Clarify Understanding Review the theme of Hard-Won Liberty and make sure students understand its meaning and significance. Help students participate in the group discussion by asking questions to connect the main ideas of the selection they have just read with the theme.
 MODERATE

RESPOND TO THE ESSENTIAL QUESTION

Allow time for students to add details from "The Hawk Can Soar" to their Unit 4 Response Logs.

WHEN STUDENTS STRUGGLE . . .

Take Discussion Notes Tell students that listening carefully during the discussion will help them evaluate others' points of view and make thoughtful comments. Suggest that students use a three-column chart to take notes during the discussion. In the left-hand column they can write the points they want to make; in the middle column they can write evidence from the memoir that supports their points; and in the right-hand column they can take notes on other speakers' points during the discussion. Remind students to look for connections between other speakers' points and their own ideas and evidence from the memoir.

 For additional support, go to the Reading Studio and assign the following **Level Up Tutorial: Taking Notes and Outlining.**

CRITICAL VOCABULARY

Possible answers:

1. An **irrefutable** fact about life is that everything that is living will eventually die.

2. Spreading and believing gossip is an **insidious** problem because it attacks people and makes even the truth seem hard to believe.

3. A muscle might **atrophy** if it isn't used for a long time—a problem that astronauts at the International Space Station counter through exercise.

4. A person might be **contemptuous** of someone or something that he or she feels is inferior or worthless.

5. The dense code that the average user can't understand makes computer programming seem **occult** to some people.

VOCABULARY STRATEGY:
Allusions

Possible answers:

1. **Achilles' heel** refers to a small weakness that can lead to a downfall. In Greek mythology, the young Achilles was dipped in the river Styx to make him invulnerable, but his mother held him by the heel, so it was still vulnerable. In battle as an adult, Achilles was struck in that heel by a poison arrow and died.

2. **The handwriting is on the wall** refers to an indication of future disaster or failure. In the Bible, King Belshazzar sees a floating hand writing on the wall; the prophet Daniel interprets the writing to mean that the king's rule is coming to an end and his kingdom will be divided up.

3. **It's Greek to me** refers to hearing or reading an explanation that seems to make no sense. In Shakespeare's The Tragedy of Julius Caesar, a character asked to relay what was said explains that he doesn't know because he doesn't understand Greek.

4. **[Met] his/her Waterloo** refers to a complete or utter defeat. In history, Waterloo was the location in Belgium of Napoleon's final defeat (1815).

 RESPOND

CRITICAL VOCABULARY

WORD BANK
irrefutable
insidious
atrophy
contemptuous
occult

Practice and Apply Answer each item using the Critical Vocabulary word in your response.

1. What is an **irrefutable** fact about life?

   _____

2. What is a problem that you would consider **insidious**?

   _____

3. What is a reason why a muscle might **atrophy**?

   _____

4. Why might someone act **contemptuous**?

   _____

5. What is **occult** about computer programming?

   _____

VOCABULARY STRATEGY:
Allusions

An **allusion** is an indirect reference to a literary work or to a historical person, place, or event. In "The Hawk Can Soar," the author uses the allusion "tilting at windmills." When you encounter an expression such as this one that does not at first make sense, you can quickly research the allusion in a print or online dictionary to validate your understanding of its meaning.

Practice and Apply Research these common allusions. Then, explain the meaning in your own words and describe the source.

1. Achilles' heel

   _____

2. The handwriting is on the wall.

   _____

3. It's Greek to me.

   _____

4. met his/her Waterloo

   _____

 ## ENGLISH LEARNER SUPPORT

Analyze Allusions Tell students that the general meaning of an allusion can often be inferred from context clues, but finding out about the source of the allusion will increase their understanding. Invite students to think of familiar allusions in their primary language. Have them research the source of their allusions.

- Have students explain the meaning and source of their allusions to a partner.
  SUBSTANTIAL
- Have students explain the allusions to a partner and use them in original sentences.
  MODERATE/LIGHT

LANGUAGE CONVENTIONS:
Purposeful Fragments

Although it is grammatically incorrect, a writer may intentionally use a sentence fragment, or incomplete sentence, as a stylistic choice for effect. Fragments create a particular tone, breaking up the flow of writing. If not used appropriately, fragments can cause confusion, so they are not used in formal pieces of writing, such as a letter to a business.

In "The Hawk Can Soar," fragments are used in the following ways.

- To emphasize an idea

   Disabled. Like this word is the sum total of my existence.

- To develop tone

   That dragging leg. That dropping foot. That unbearable fatigue.

- To create a voice

   In my ever hopeful bones.

Practice and Apply Read the following examples. Determine whether the fragment is a purposeful fragment or an incomplete thought. Explain your choices.

1. I want to live as I did before my injury. Before everything changed.

_____

_____

2. Sometimes life is unfair. Sometimes not.

_____

_____

3. She wears a brace on her leg. And on her back.

_____

_____

4. The hawk lifts its wings. Tries to fly, but can't.

_____

_____

5. The road ahead is a mystery. Winding and unfamiliar.

_____

_____

> Go to the **Grammar Studio** for more on sentence fragments.

LANGUAGE CONVENTIONS:
Purposeful Fragments

Discuss with students the various reasons for choosing to use fragments. Remind students that using purposeful fragments in writing creates a conversational tone and may hint at the writer's emotion. Suggest that pausing before and after fragments can give students the chance to think about their purpose and meaning.

Practice and Apply

Possible answers:

1. *purposeful fragment, to emphasize the word* before *and the fact that the injury changed everything*

2. *purposeful fragment, to create a casual, conversational tone*

3. *incomplete thought because the fragment doesn't add or amplify anything*

4. *incomplete thought because it is conveying information rather than providing emphasis*

5. *either; it could be purposeful if the writer is emphasizing the road's mystery, or it could be an incomplete thought that should be joined to the previous sentence*

ENGLISH LEARNER SUPPORT

Analyze Purposeful Fragments Use the following supports with students at varying proficiency levels:

- Have students identify fragments in paragraph 8 of "The Hawk Can Soar" and copy them into their notebooks. Make sure students understand how each fragment relates to the text that precedes it and follows it. **SUBSTANTIAL**

- Have partners identify fragments in paragraph 5 of "The Hawk Can Soar" and discuss the effect, or tone, created by each. **MODERATE**

- Direct students to paragraph 7 of "The Hawk Can Soar" and ask them to read aloud the last complete sentence and the two fragments that follow it. Have students rewrite the fragments as complete sentences; then have them read aloud and compare the author's version with their revised version. Discuss with students how the purposeful fragments affect the tone of the passage. **LIGHT**

THE BRIEFCASE

Short Story by Rebecca Makkai

GENRE ELEMENTS
SHORT STORY

Remind students that a **short story** includes the basic elements of fiction — setting, characters, plot, conflict, and theme. Told from one perspective and focusing on one character, "The Briefcase" is a short story that shows how the setting can profoundly drive both character development and plot. Encourage students to notice details—which are often ambiguous—about the time and place of this story. The mood and sense of foreboding also come from these elements.

LEARNING OBJECTIVES

- Analyze development of character and theme in a short story.
- Choose a research question to refine and expand upon as research progresses.
- Write a persuasive letter that uses specific details from the short story.
- Summarize a short story and predict what might logically happen to the main character.
- Use a range of methods to define discipline-specific vocabulary.
- Self- and peer-edit drafts for correct use of semicolons.
- **Language** Explain the key term *semicolon* and use semicolons correctly.

TEXT COMPLEXITY

Quantitative Measures	The Briefcase	Lexile: 860L
Qualitative Measures	**Levels of Meaning/Purpose** Multiple levels of meaning (multiple themes).	
	Structures Somewhat complex story concepts.	
	Language Conventionality and Clarity Some unfamiliar language.	
	Knowledge Demands Somewhat unfamiliar situation.	

RESOURCES

- Unit 4 Response Log
- Selection Audio
- Reading Studio: Notice & Note
- Level Up Tutorial: Author's Style
- Writing Studio: Persuasive Techniques
- Speaking and Listening Studio: Giving a Presentation
- Vocabulary Studio: Discipline-Specific Terms
- Grammar Studio: Module 12: Lesson 1: Semicolons
- "The Briefcase" Selection Test

SUMMARIES

English

The protagonist, an unnamed chef in an unnamed country, is a political prisoner who is unexpectedly freed. A professor is arrested in his stead; the chef assumes his identity by taking his discarded shirt and briefcase. The chef moves to another city and goes into hiding. As time goes on, he begins to believe he is the professor. When the professor's wife finds and confronts him, the chef tries to persuade her to let him really become the professor.

Spanish

El protagonista, un chef sin nombre de un país sin nombre, es un prisionero político. Luego de ser liberado inesperadamente, asume la identidad de un profesor de física que también estaba arrestado. El chef toma la camisa y el maletín del profesor, se muda a otra ciudad y se esconde. A medida que pasa el tiempo, empieza a creer que él es el profesor. Cuando la esposa del profesor lo encuentra y le confronta, el chef trata de persuadirla para que le permita que realmente se convierta en el profesor.

SMALL-GROUP OPTIONS

Have students work in small groups and pairs to read and discuss the selection.

Buzz Group

- Form groups of 3–4 and pose a question to discuss. Set a time limit and prompt all students to take notes on the discussion.
- Next, have students agree on one response, citing evidence from the story.
- Assign or let students choose a speaker for their group. Group members should share their notes with the speaker. Randomly pick a speaker from one of the groups to go first.
- The following speakers should frame their response as a reply to the previous speaker.

Pyramids

- Ask each student to review the story and pick the two questions they found most challenging.
- Pair up students to discuss answers to their questions.
- Then have pairs form groups of four and collaborate on a combined set of answers or on any other challenging questions.
- Finally, have one representative from each group report the group's conclusion on which question they found most challenging, and why.

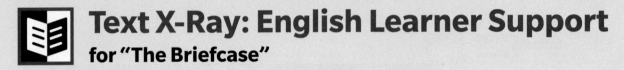

Text X-Ray: English Learner Support
for "The Briefcase"

Use the Text X-Ray and the supports and scaffolds in the Teacher's Edition to help guide students at different proficiency levels through the selection.

INTRODUCE THE SELECTION
DISCUSS POLITICAL IMPRISONMENT

The topic of political imprisonment and authoritarian government may be challenging for students to discuss. Consider these whole-group activities:

- Discuss political prisoners students may be familiar with, such as Nelson Mandela. Guide students to understand that political prisoners are those deemed a threat by the current government because of their political beliefs.
- Brainstorm ideas about what kind of government would jail people based on their political beliefs. Discuss how this government might come into power *(often violently)*, be structured *(often as an autocracy)*, and keep its power *(often with fear and harsh punishments for "crimes" against the state)*.

Emphasize how these governments control their citizens so that students can better understand the story's main character. Guide students in taking notes during the discussion to use as a reference when they read the selection.

CULTURAL REFERENCES

The following words or phrases may be unfamiliar to students:

- *Using modern astronomical data, construct . . . a proof that the sun actually revolves around the Earth* (paragraph 6): this is a clear impossibility, as the Earth revolves around the sun and all astronomical data will show this
- *mandoline* (paragraph 14): a tool used for thinly slicing food
- *plate-sized canvas, delicate oils* (paragraph 20): an oil painting
- *trenches* (paragraph 20): holes dug into battlefields where soldiers would hide from enemy fire; miserable and dangerous places
- *Minister P——— of the Interior* (paragraph 23): a person of high government rank in charge of the internal matters of the country

LISTENING

Understand Character Development

Have students listen as you read aloud paragraphs 7–12, when the chef first takes on the identity of the professor. Give students a graphic organizer to take notes on details that show character and plot development.

Use the following supports with students at varying proficiency levels:

- Confirm understanding by asking questions. Model giving a thumbs up if the answer is yes, and a thumbs down for no. Ask: Does the chef feel he is doing the right thing by taking on the professor's identity? *(yes)*; Does the chef contact the professor's wife? *(no)* **SUBSTANTIAL**
- Confirm understanding by discussing the following questions: How does the chef become more confident in taking on the professor's identity? *(by making comparisons between himself and the professor)*; Why does the chef feel no guilt for taking on the professor's identity? *(He believes he is doing the right thing.)* **MODERATE**
- As they listen, have students identify details that they think show how the character develops. Pause at key points to support students' understanding. **LIGHT**

SPEAKING

Discuss Punctuation

Draw students' attention to paragraph 5. Explain that a writer may use punctuation—in this selection, dashes and a semicolon—to help reveal a character's traits.

Use the following supports with students at varying proficiency levels:

- Model identifying the dashes and semicolon in the paragraph. Discuss how dashes can stop the flow of ideas or set text apart for emphasis, and how semicolons can closely link ideas or signal a pause. **SUBSTANTIAL**

- Have pairs reread the paragraph and mark dashes and the semicolon. Then guide students in discussing the writer's use of punctuation. *(Dashes suggest a pause in the story, where the narrator adds a comment; semicolons link clauses together to show how one action leads to another.)* **MODERATE**

- Have pairs reread the paragraph and discuss what the punctuation suggests about the character's thoughts. *(He feels guilty; he wants to feel better about his actions.)* **LIGHT**

READING

Analyze Character

Read aloud paragraph 1. Explain that the beginning of this story tells readers some key information about the main character—the prisoner. Explain that readers can learn more about the character by studying his words or phrases as they read the selection.

Use the following supports with students at varying proficiency levels:

- Choral read the first paragraph. Prompt students to think about how the main character is feeling. Allow students to answer in their primary language by pointing to images that represent feelings or by drawing. **SUBSTANTIAL**

- Have partners reread the first paragraph. Then guide them in identifying words and phrases, such as "a line of miserable monkeys," that they can use to understand how the character is feeling. **MODERATE**

- Prompt small groups to discuss the character's thoughts in the first paragraph and what they tell them about the character. Then, have them use a graphic organizer to track the character's thoughts and actions as they read. **LIGHT**

WRITING

Write a Letter

Provide students with a model of a personal letter to use as a guide for the writing assignment on Student Edition page 281.

Use the following supports with students at varying proficiency levels:

- Review the model letter and point out its main features, such as the greeting, closing, and paragraphing. Then discuss the contents and how it is organized. **SUBSTANTIAL**

- In small groups, have students review the model letter. Talk about what they will say in their letters. Then, have them choose words and phrases from the story to use in their letters. **MODERATE**

- On their own, have students use the model letter as an outline and replace the contents with the points they want to make. Then, choose words and phrases to use or adapt for their letters. **LIGHT**

Connect to the
ESSENTIAL QUESTION

"The Briefcase" explores the ways totalitarian governments affect the lives and freedoms of their citizens. These governments use any and all means they can to control citizens' speech, thoughts, and actions and to put down any and all opposition. The protagonist in this selection requires a new identity to feel free—and even then he is trapped by his own lies.

THE BRIEFCASE

Short Story by **Rebecca Makkai**

ESSENTIAL QUESTION:

What do we need in order to feel free?

🧠 LEARNING MINDSET

Questioning Discuss the value of asking questions with students. Explain that any reasonable question is welcome, as it shows curiosity and a desire to learn more. In addition, if they have a question, other students probably do, as well. This selection will likely generate many questions from students, so encourage them to ask. Then suggest various strategies for them to find the answers, including rereading a passage, asking a classmate, or bringing it to your attention before, during, or after class.

QUICK START

Life events may cause us to question or even change who we are. Think of an experience in your life that changed you or your sense of yourself. Write one or two paragraphs about that time, describing how you changed.

ANALYZE CHARACTER

Characters are the people who participate in the events in a story. Like real people, they display certain qualities and develop and change over time. You can understand characters through their thoughts, action, dialogue, and interactions with other characters. The setting also affects characterization in a story. Characters' **motivations**, or reasons for doing what they do, advance the plot of a story and reveal its theme.

In this story, only one character is fully developed. As you read, ask yourself about these key elements of character to analyze this unnamed main character.

SETTING	Do the time, place, or cultural setting affect the character?
PHYSICAL DESCRIPTION	Do the physical descriptions of the character relate to his identity?
ACTIONS	What do his actions and reactions reveal about him?
MOTIVATIONS	What drives the character to make the choices he does?
THOUGHTS	What does he think about? What do his thoughts reveal about him?
INTERACTIONS	With whom does he interact? What does each interaction reveal about him?
CHANGES	How does he change throughout the story?

ANALYZE THEME

The **theme** is the central idea of a story. It is the moral, life lesson, or insight about life or human nature that the author wants to convey. Themes may be universal, such as "Money can't buy happiness" or "Love conquers all," or they may be more specific to the story. An author might state a theme directly, but most often readers must infer theme, relying on character development and unfolding events to make an educated guess about what message the author wants to convey.

To infer theme as you read, consider:
- the character's actions, thoughts, and motivations
- the character's interactions with others
- how the character changes over the course of the story
- unfolding events in the plot
- setting and its effect on the plot

**GENRE ELEMENTS:
SHORT STORY**
- uses the basic elements of setting, characters, plot, conflict, and theme
- focuses on one or two main characters and a single plot with minimal subplots
- can be read in its entirety in one sitting

QUICK START

Have students read the Quick Start prompt and ask them what kinds of events can change people's lives. Seek a variety of responses, both positive and negative, so that students do not feel pressure to reflect on and write about only negative or traumatic life experiences. Ask volunteers to share a summary of their writing with the class or a small group.

ANALYZE CHARACTER

Help students understand the relationship between *action* and *motivation*. **Action** is what a character does; **motivation** is his or her reasons for those actions. Explain that a character's motivations are the driving force behind the plot and provide insight into theme. Discuss with students why someone might be motivated to assume a new identity. *(The person might be a fugitive or simply might want to start a new life).*

ANALYZE THEME

Acknowledge that readers may differ in their interpretation of a story's **theme**, in part because every reader brings personal experiences to his or her understanding of the story. Readers can determine the theme by following the actions and motivations of the main character. Suggest that students highlight the actions, thoughts, and motivations of the protagonist, or main character, as they read "The Briefcase." Their annotations should include their thoughts and questions about the protagonist and how he changes.

TEACH

CRITICAL VOCABULARY

Have students read all of the sentences before deciding which word belongs in each sentence. Remind students to consider how context clues can help guide them to the correct word for each sentence.

Answers:

1. *havoc*

2. *equidistant*

3. *flagrantly*

4. *flail*

5. *inversion*

6. *transpire*

■ English Learner Support

Use Cognates Tell students a few of the Critical Vocabulary words have Spanish cognates (*equidistant/equidistante, flagrant/flagrante* in the adjective form, *inversion/inversion, transpire/transpirar*). Explain that the cognate *transpirar* has two possible meanings; make sure students understand that this vocabulary word is synonymous with *tener lugar,* which means "to occur," rather than *sudar,* which means "to sweat."
ALL LEVELS

LANGUAGE CONVENTIONS

Review the information about semicolons. Explain that writers use semicolons for three main purposes: to link two independent clauses, to link an independent clause with another clause that begins with a conjunctive adverb (such as *therefore, meanwhile, also,* or *however*), and to separate items in a list when the items already contain commas.

Read the example sentence aloud and ask students about the writer's purpose in using a semicolon. *(The semicolon is used to link two independent clauses. The writer has done this to show that these two ideas are connected.)*

✎ ANNOTATION MODEL

Remind students of the suggestions for making inferences about character and theme on page 269. Point out that they may want to use these to guide how and what they annotate as they read. They may also want to color-code their annotations and use their notes in the margins to include questions and notes about ideas or topics that they are unsure about or want to learn more about.

CRITICAL VOCABULARY

flail	inversion	equidistant
transpire	flagrantly	havoc

To see how many Critical Vocabulary words you already know, use them to complete the sentences.

1. The tornado caused _____ in the neighborhoods where it touched down.

2. The two buildings are _____ from the street.

3. I have rarely seen rudeness displayed so _____.

4. He began to _____ his arms wildly to shoo the bee away.

5. The _____ of roles at my company means I am my former boss's new manager.

6. It was easy to predict what would _____ by the end of the movie.

LANGUAGE CONVENTIONS

Semicolons In this lesson, you will learn about how writers use semicolons (;) to link closely related ideas in independent clauses. Here is an example from the story:

Surely he could not teach at the university; surely he could not slip into the man's bed unnoticed.

As you read "The Briefcase," note the author's use of semicolons and how they link ideas to create coherence.

ANNOTATION MODEL   **NOTICE & NOTE**

As you read, note the main character's thoughts, actions, and interactions with others. Generate questions that will lead you to deepen your understanding. Here is one reader's response to the main character's initial appearance:

> He thought how strange that a <u>political prisoner</u>, marched through town in a line, chained to the man behind and chained to the man ahead, should take comfort in the fact that this had happened before. [He thought of other chains of men on other islands of the Earth, and he thought how since there have been men there have been prisoners.] [He thought of mankind as a line of miserable monkeys chained at the wrist, dragging each other back into the ground.]

Who is the prisoner? What did he do?

takes comfort in universal suffering

seems resigned to his fate; hopeless

BACKGROUND

The protagonist of "The Briefcase" is a political prisoner in an unnamed country, a man arrested for associating with the wrong people. Political prisoners are detained, imprisoned, and sometimes executed, without benefit of trial or jury, due to political associations or beliefs that conflict with those of the people in power. Such detentions happen all over the world under regimes that hold absolute power over the people and the press. In this story, author **Rebecca Makkai** *(b. 1978) examines this issue through the lens of basic astronomy.*

THE BRIEFCASE

Short Story by Rebecca Makkai

SETTING A PURPOSE

As you read, pay attention to details that reveal the protagonist's character. Write down questions you generate before you read, during your reading, and after you read. Your questions will lead you to a deeper understanding of the main character's motivations and will help you infer the theme.

1   He thought how strange that a political prisoner, marched through town in a line, chained to the man behind and chained to the man ahead, should take comfort in the fact that all this had happened before. He thought of other chains of men on other islands of the Earth, and he thought how since there have been men there have been prisoners. He thought of mankind as a line of miserable monkeys chained at the wrist, dragging each other back into the ground.

2   In the early morning of December first, the sun was finally warming them all, enough that they could walk faster. With his left hand, he adjusted the loop of steel that cuffed his right hand to the line of doomed men. His hand was starved, his wrist was thin, his body was cold: the cuff slipped off. In one beat of the heart he looked back to the man behind him and forward to the man limping ahead, and

ANALYZE CHARACTER
Annotate: Mark words or phrases in paragraph 2 that describe the main character.

Infer: What can you tell about the main character based on these descriptions?

The Briefcase   **271**

BACKGROUND

Have students read the Background note about political prisoners. Tell students that people's sense of identity often changes as different life events affect them and reshape their sense of who they are. This has happened with some political prisoners in history who eventually rose to positions of power. The most famous may be Nelson Mandela, who was the first black president of South Africa. Prior to that, Mandela spent 27 years in prison for trying to end apartheid, that nation's oppressive policy of racial segregation.

SETTING A PURPOSE

Direct students to use the Setting a Purpose prompt to focus their reading.

ANALYZE CHARACTER

Explain to students that writers often use a character's thoughts and actions to describe the character. Encourage them to mark these as well as descriptive words about the character to get an idea of what the main character is like. (**Answer:** *He is treated poorly and malnourished. He is lonely and dejected as he assumes the other prisoners are thinking about loved ones, as he does. He is not attempting to free himself.*)

For **reading support** for students at varying proficiency levels, see the **Text X-Ray** on page 268D.

ENGLISH LEARNER SUPPORT

Use Graphic Organizers   Students may find the plot of this story difficult to follow as it includes flashbacks, and the passing of time is not always made explicit. Provide students with a graphic organizer, such as a timeline, to track events as they occur in the story as well as to record events that took place prior to the narrative. When there is a shift in time or a major plot development, stop during a shared reading and ask students to record it on their graphic organizer. For more advanced students, ask them to identify which words and phrases they used to determine whether the event is taking place in the present or in a flashback.
ALL LEVELS

ANALYZE THEME

Have students identify the major plot development that occurs in paragraph 5. Remind students of the list of considerations to infer **theme** at the beginning of the selection. Have students work in small groups to analyze who is to blame for the professor being taken prisoner. Have volunteers share their ideas. If groups disagree, hold a class discussion on how this shapes our perception of the chef, and encourage them to explore how being taken prisoner has affected his sense of identity and how this relates to the story's theme. (**Answer:** *The chef has freed himself and the soldiers have taken a professor prisoner in his place. The soldiers are to blame, as they do not seem to care who they take prisoner but rather seem intent on having the right number of prisoners. Had the chef not been taken prisoner and starved, he probably would not have stolen the professor's identity. He has become desperate.*)

■ English Learner Support

Understand Theme Explain that a theme is the central idea of a story. It may be an idea or insight that is universal or specific to the story. First, review the list of considerations to infer theme at the beginning of the selection. After students have read the story, discuss these examples. Then go through the story together to infer theme.

The character's actions/thoughts/motivations: the chef feels guilt for the professor taking his place in the prison line, so he decides to take the professor's place in life

The character's interactions with others: the chef writes letters to the professor's friends but is mostly alone

How the character changes throughout the story: the chef becomes convinced that he is the professor

Unfolding events in the plot: the professor's widow arrives at the post office

Setting and its effects on the plot: a country where everyone is found to be a political prisoner forms the basis of the plot.

After reviewing examples, demonstrate how to combine these details to make inferences about the theme. For example: *The chef's decision to take the professor's life and correspond with his colleagues shows how confused his sense of identity has become after being a prisoner.* **ALL LEVELS**

CRITICAL VOCABULARY

flail: Makkai compares the papers flying out of the briefcase to doves thrashing about in the alley.

ASK STUDENTS why they think the chef chased down the *flailing* papers. (*to keep someone from catching him or because they might have value*)

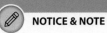

knew that neither saw his naked, red wrist; each saw only his own mother weeping in a kitchen, his own love on a bed in white sheets and sunlight.

3   He walked in step with them to the end of the block.

4   Before the war this man had been a chef, and his one crime was feeding the people who sat at his tables in small clouds of smoke and talked politics. He served them the wine that fueled their underground newspaper, their aborted revolution. And after the night his restaurant disappeared in fire, he had run and hidden and gone without food — he who had roasted ducks until the meat jumped from the bone, he who had evaporated three bottles of wine into one pot of cream soup, he who had peeled the skin from small pumpkins with a twist of his hand.

5   And here was his hand, twisted free of the chain, and here he was running and crawling, until he was through a doorway. It was a building of empty classrooms — part of the university he had never attended. He watched from the bottom corner of a second-story window as the young soldiers stopped the line, counted 199 men, shouted to each other, shouted at the men in the panicked voices of children who barely filled the shoulders of their uniforms. One soldier, a bigger one, a louder one, stopped a man walking by. A man in a suit, with a briefcase, a beard — some sort of professor. The soldiers stripped him of his coat, his shirt, his leather case, cuffed him to the chain. They marched again. And as soon as they were past — no, not that soon; many minutes later, when he had the stomach — the chef ran down to the street and collected the man's briefcase, coat and shirt.

6   In the alley, the chef sat against a wall and buttoned the professor's shirt over his own ribs. When he opened the briefcase, papers flew out, a thousand doves **flailing** against the walls of the alley. The chef ran after them all, stopped them with his feet and arms, herded them back into the case. Pages of numbers, of arrows and notes and hand-drawn star maps. Here were business cards: a professor of physics. Envelopes showed his name and address — information that might have been useful in some other lifetime, one where the chef could ring the bell of this man's house and explain to his wife about empty chains, empty wrists, empty classrooms. Here were graded papers, a fall syllabus, the typed draft of an exam. The question at the end, a good one: "Using modern astronomical data, construct, to the best of your ability, a proof that the sun actually revolves around the Earth."

7   The chef knew nothing of physics. He understood chemistry only insofar as it related to the baking time of bread at various elevations or the evaporation rate of alcohol. His knowledge of biology was limited to the deboning of chickens and the behavior

NOTICE & NOTE

ANALYZE THEME
Annotate: Mark the major plot development that occurs in paragraph 5.

Analyze: Who is to blame for what happens to the professor? How does the chef respond to this injustice?

flail
(flāl) *v.* to thrash or wave about wildly.

APPLYING ACADEMIC VOCABULARY

☑ comprehensive   ☐ equivalent   ☐ incentive   ☑ innovate   ☐ subordinate

Write and Discuss Have students turn to a partner and discuss the following questions. Guide students to include the academic vocabulary words *comprehensive* and *innovate* in their responses.

• Does the chef have a **comprehensive** set of reasons for his actions?

• How does the professor's question **innovate** astronomy instruction?

of *Saccharomyces cerevisiae*, common bread yeast. And what did he know at all of moving bodies and gravity? He knew this: he had moved from his line of men, creating a vacuum — one that had sucked the good professor in to fill the void.

8   The chef sat on his bed in the widow K—'s basement and felt, in the cool leather of the briefcase, a second vacuum: here was a vacated life. Here were salary receipts, travel records, train tickets, a small address book. And these belonged to a man whose name was not blackened like his own, a man whose life was not hunted. If he wanted to live through the next year, the chef would have to learn this life and fill it — and oddly, this felt not like a robbery but an apology, a way to put the world back in balance. The professor would not die, because he himself would become the professor, and he would live.

9   Surely he could not teach at the university; surely he could not slip into the man's bed unnoticed. But what was in this leather case, it seemed, had been left for him to use. These addresses of friends; this card of identification; this riddle about the **inversion** of the universe.

10   Five cities east, he now gave his name as the professor's, and grew out his beard so it would match the photograph on the card he now carried in his pocket. The two men did not, anymore, look entirely dissimilar. To the first name in the address book, the chef had written a typed letter: "Am in trouble and have fled the city. Tell my dear wife I am safe, but for her safety do not tell her where I am. If you are able to help a poor old man, send money to the following post box . . . I hope to remain your friend, Professor T—."

11   He had to write this about the wife; how could he ask these men for money if she held a funeral? And what of it, if she kept her happiness another few months, another year?

12   The next twenty-six letters were similar in nature, and money arrived now in brown envelopes and white ones. The bills came wrapped in notes — (Was his life in danger? Did he have his health?) — and with the money he paid another widow for another basement, and he bought weak cigarettes. He sat on café chairs and drew pictures of the universe, showed stars and planets looping each other in light. He felt, perhaps, that if he used the other papers in the

inversion
(ĭn-vûr´zhən) *n.*
reversal or upside-down placement.

LANGUAGE CONVENTIONS

Annotate: Mark the semicolon that links two independent clauses in paragraph 11.

Analyze: What is the effect of using a semicolon here instead of a period?

The Briefcase   273

LANGUAGE CONVENTIONS

Review the information about **semicolons** being used to link two closely related ideas in independent clauses. Explain that a semicolon also creates less of a pause between clauses and quickens the pace of the reading. Have them focus on why Makkai may have wanted a subtler pause between these clauses. (**Answer:** *The clauses are linked with a semicolon to show how the second clause explains the first. This emphasizes how the chef has begun a complex chain of lies to maintain his false identity.*)

■ English Learner Support

Understand Semicolons Tell students that semicolons are used to link two independent clauses. The clauses linked by the semicolon can function as two distinct sentences; however, connecting them with a semicolon, instead of separating them with a period, demonstrates that they are closely related. Semicolons also take the place of a conjunction like *and*. Review the semicolon in the first sentence of paragraph 11. Explain how it demonstrates that the second clause explains the first. Have students find another semicolon in the story and practice explaining how the clauses relate to each other (*paragraphs 15, 16, 20*).
MODERATE/LIGHT

For **listening and speaking support** for students at varying proficiency levels, see the **Text X-Ray** on pages 268C–268D.

WHEN STUDENTS STRUGGLE . . .

Read and Explain Makkai's complex sentence structures may challenge some students. Have students create a graphic organizer to keep track of the colons, semicolons, and dashes in paragraphs 8–11, with one column for location and another for function. Ask: Does the punctuation closely link ideas? Does it indicate an abrupt pause?

 For additional support, go to the **Reading Studio** and assign the following Level Up Tutorial: **Author's Style.**

CRITICAL VOCABULARY

inversion: The riddle reverses an idea about the universe.

ASK STUDENTS to identify the idea about astronomy in this riddle and what the *inversion* of this idea is. (*The original idea is that Earth revolves around the sun; the inversion of this is the idea that the sun revolves around Earth.*)

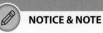
ANALYZE THEME

Remind students of the list of considerations to infer **theme** at the beginning of the selection. Have students work in pairs to infer how the chef is changing. Explain that they can use what they already learned about the chef's character, and combine it with information from paragraph 13 to make inferences about what is happening to him. Point out that in this section of the story, the chef and the professor have more similarities than differences and how this could relate to the theme. (**Answer:** *The chef is starting to think of himself as the professor. He uses logical language such as "ergo" and says he has "the hands of the professor" and as such he is "now the professor." The chef is assuming a new identity.*)

■ English Learner Support

Provide Teacher and Peer Support Provide additional scaffolding and processing time for the question on this page by asking students to first identify how the chef and the professor are similar. Form pairs or small groups of mixed proficiency levels and have students take turns reading aloud paragraphs 13–15 while listeners follow along and note similarities. Then, have them compare and discuss their notes. Ask students to think about how the chef has changed since the beginning of the story. **ALL LEVELS**

ANALYZE THEME

Annotate: Mark the sentence in paragraph 13 that summarizes the chef's answer to the professor's question.

Infer: What does this answer reveal about how the chef's character is changing?

equidistant
(ē-kwĭ-dĭs´tənt) *adj.*
at equal distance from.

---

briefcase, he must also make use of the question. Or perhaps he felt that if he could answer it, he could put the universe back together. Or perhaps it was something to fill his empty days.

13 He wrote in his small notebook: "The light of my cigarette is a fire like the sun. From where I sit, all the universe is **equidistant** from my cigarette. Ergo,[1] my cigarette is the center of the universe. My cigarette is on Earth. Ergo, the Earth is the center of the universe. <u>If all heavenly bodies move, they must therefore move in relation to the Earth, and in relation to my cigarette.</u>"

14 His hand ached. These words were the most he had written since school, which had ended for him at age sixteen. He had been a smart boy, even talented in languages and mathematics, but his mother knew these were no way to make a living. He was not blessed, like the professor, with years of scholarship and quiet offices and leather books. He was blessed instead with chicken stocks and herbs and sherry. Thirty years had passed since his last day of school, and his hand was accustomed now to wooden spoon, mandoline, peeling knife, rolling pin.

15 Today, his hands smelled of ink, when for thirty years they had smelled of leeks. They were the hands of the professor; ergo, he was now the professor.

16 He had written to friends A through L, and now he saved the rest and wrote instead to students. Here in the briefcase's outermost pocket were class rosters from the past two years; letters addressed to those young men care of the university were sure to reach them. The

---

[1] **Ergo** (ûr´gō): the Latin equivalent of "therefore."

274 Unit 4

IMPROVE READING FLUENCY

Targeted Passage Have students work with partners to read paragraphs 13–17. First, use paragraph 13 to model how to read a fictional narrative. Have students follow along in their books as you read the text with appropriate phrasing and emphasis. Then, have partners take turns reading aloud each paragraph. Encourage students to provide feedback and support for pronouncing multisyllabic words. Remind students that when they are reading aloud for an audience, they should pace their reading so that the audience has time to understand what is being read.

 Go to the **Reading Studio** for additional support in developing fluency.

CRITICAL VOCABULARY

equidistant: The chef says that everything in the universe is an equal distance from his cigarette.

ASK STUDENTS to discuss what the chef may mean when he says that all of the universe could be *equidistant* from a spot on Earth. (*The chef may be thinking broadly or metaphorically that everything is far away from him.*)

amounts they sent were smaller, the notes that accompanied them more inquisitive. What exactly had **transpired**? Could they come to the city and meet him?

17   The post box, of course, was in a different city than the one where he stayed. He arrived at the post office just before closing, and came only once every two or three weeks. He always looked through the window first to check that the lobby was empty. If it was not, he would leave and come again another day. Surely one of these days, a friend of the professor would be waiting there for him. He prepared a story, that he was the honored professor's assistant, that he could not reveal the man's location but would certainly pass on your kindest regards, sir.

18 If the Earth moved, all it would take for a man to travel its distance would be a strong balloon. Rise twenty feet above, and wait for the Earth to turn under you; you would be home again in a day. But this was not true, and a man could not escape his spot on the Earth but to run along the surface. Ergo, the Earth was still. Ergo, the sun was the moving body of the two.

19   No, he did not believe it. He wanted only to know who this professor was, this man who would teach his students the laws of the universe, then ask them to prove as true what was false.

20 On the wall of the café: plate-sized canvas, delicate oils of an apple, half-peeled. Signed, below, by a girl he had known in school. The price was more than a month of groceries, and so he did not buy it, but for weeks he read his news under the apple and drank his coffee. Staining his fingers in cheap black ink were the signal fires of the world, the distress sirens, the dispatches from the trenches and hospitals and abattoirs[2] of the war; but here, on the wall, a sign from another world. He had known this girl as well as any other: had spoken with her every day, but had not made love to her; had gone to her home one winter holiday, but knew nothing of her life since then. And here, a clue, perfect and round and unfathomable. After all this time: apple.

21   After he finished the news, he worked at the proof and saw in the coil of green-edged skin some model of spiraling, of expansion. The stars were at one time part of the Earth, until the hand of God peeled them away, leaving us in the dark. They do not revolve around us: they escape in widening circles. The Milky Way is the edge of this peel.

22   Outside the café window, a beggar screeched his bow against a defeated violin. A different kind of case, open on the ground, this one

---

[2] **abattoirs** (ăb´ə-twärs): slaughterhouses.

The Briefcase   275

---

transpire
(trăn-spīr´) v. to happen or occur.

ANALYZE CHARACTER
Annotate: Mark text in paragraph 17 that describes the chef's habits of approaching and entering the post office.

Infer: What do these habits reveal about the chef?

 ANALYZE CHARACTER

Review the key elements of **character** at the beginning of the selection. Have students work in pairs to consider what the chef's **actions** reveal about his **motivations.** Have students continue to discuss the questions about his thoughts, interactions, how he has changed, and how he is affected by the setting of the story. Their answers can be recorded as annotations or on a graphic organizer for understanding character development. (**Answer:** *The chef is paranoid about being discovered or caught, so he is very careful.*)

EL ENGLISH LEARNER SUPPORT

Recognize Sounds Display the vocabulary word *transpire* and say it aloud. Point out that the *e* is silent. Explain that "silent *e*" at the end of the word makes the long *i* vowel sound. Discuss other example words that follow this rule, such as *note, fire,* and *state.*
SUBSTANTIAL/MODERATE

TO CHALLENGE STUDENTS . . .

Explore Themes After they have read the **story**, ask students what role women play in the chef's life. Point out the brief but telling scenes about the chef's relationships with his landlady and his lover. The story climaxes in the confrontation between the chef and the professor's wife. Have students work in small groups to discuss the importance of women in the story. Prompt them to consider what we learn about the chef through his relationships. Ask: Are there ways in which the women highlight different parts of his personality? Tell students to think about how the female characters relate to the theme of identity. Ask: Why does the chef feel so strongly attracted to the professor's wife? Invite students to present their ideas to the rest of the class.

CRITICAL VOCABULARY

transpire: The professor's students all want to know what happened to him.

ASK STUDENTS to summarize what *transpired* as the professor walked down the street. (*He was captured by guards to take the chef's place as a prisoner.*)

ANALYZE CHARACTER

Remind students that the chef's emotional state and thoughts will help them infer the theme. Have students compare the chef's current feelings with his feelings at the beginning of the story. Ask them how he has changed, and whether or not they think his situation has improved. Encourage them to connect their understanding of the chef to possible themes in the story. (**Answer:** *The chef exists in uncertainty; he is in constant fear of being discovered and grows more afraid. A possible theme is that oppression and fear change people profoundly and make them yearn for some certainty.*)

 **NOTICE & NOTE**

ANALYZE CHARACTER

Annotate: Mark text that explains why the chef is no longer reading current newspapers.

Infer: What does this change reveal about the chef's state of mind?

collecting the pennies of the more compassionate passers-by. The café owner shooed him away, and the chef sighed in guilty relief that he would not have to pass, on the way out, his double.

23 After eight months in the new city, the chef stopped buying his newspapers on the street by the café and began instead to read the year-old news the widow gave him for his fires. Here, fourteen months ago: Minister P—— of the Interior predicts war. One day he found that in a box near the widow's furnace were papers three, four, five years old. Pages were missing, edges eaten. He took his fragments of yellowed paper to the café and read the beginnings and ends of opinions and letters. He read reports from what used to be his country's borders.

24 When he had finished the last paper of the box, he began to read the widow's history books. The Americas, before Columbus; the oceans, before the British; the Romans, before their fall.

25 History was safer than the news, because there was no question of how it would end.

26 He took a lover in the city and told her he was a professor of physics. He showed her the stars in the sky and explained that they circled the Earth, along with the sun.

27 That's not true at all, she said. You tease because you think I'm just a silly girl.

28 No, he said and touched her neck, You are the only one who might understand. The universe has been folded inside out.

29 A full year had passed, and he paid the widow in coins. He wrote to friends M through Z. I have been in hiding for a year, he wrote. Tell my dear wife I have my health. May time and history forgive us all.

30 A year had passed, but so had many years passed for many men. And after all what was a year, if the Earth did not circle the sun?

31 The Earth does not circle the sun, he wrote. Ergo: The years do not pass. The Earth, being stationary, does not erase the past nor escape towards the future. Rather, the years pile on like blankets, existing at once. The year is 1848; the year is 1789; the year is 1956.

32 If the Earth hangs still in space, does it spin? If the Earth were to spin, the space I occupy I will therefore vacate in an instant. This city will leave its spot, and the city to the west will usurp its place. Ergo, this city is all cities at all times. This is Kabul; this is Dresden; this is Johannesburg.[3]

33 I run by standing still.

---

[3] **Kabul . . . Dresden . . . Johannesburg:** cities in Afghanistan, Germany, and South Africa, respectively.

 ## ENGLISH LEARNER SUPPORT

Understand Dialogue Students may have difficulty identifying spoken language without the use of quotation marks. To guide students' identification of dialogue, display paragraphs 26–28 and help volunteers mark up the lines of dialogue:

- Underline clue words that indicate who is speaking. (*"she said," "he said"*)
- Circle the words that the lover speaks. (*"That's not true at all," "You tease because you think I'm just a silly girl."*)
- Box the words that the chef speaks. (*"No," "You are the only one.... The universe has been folded inside out."*) **SUBSTANTIAL/MODERATE**

34 At the post office, he collects his envelopes of money. He has learned from the notes of concerned colleagues and students and friends that the professor suffered from infections of the inner ear that often threw off his balance. He has learned of the professor's wife, A—, whose father died the year they married. He has learned that he has a young son. Rather, the professor has a son.

35   At each visit to the post office, he fears he will forget the combination. It is an old lock, and complicated: F1, clockwise to B3, back to A6, forward again to J3. He must shake the little latch before it opens. More than forgetting, perhaps what he fears is that he will be denied access — that the little box will one day recognize him behind his thick and convincing beard, will decide he has no right of entry.

36   One night, asleep with his head on his lover's leg, he dreams that a letter has arrived from the professor himself. They freed me at the end of the march, it says, and I crawled my way home. My hands are bloody and my knees are worn through, and I want my briefcase back.

37   In his dream, the chef takes the case and runs west. If the professor takes it back, there will be <u>no name left for the chef, no place on the Earth</u>. The moment his fingers leave the leather loop of the handle, <u>he will fall off the planet.</u>

38 He sits in a wooden chair on the lawn behind the widow's house. Inside, he hears her washing dishes. In exchange for the room, he cooks all her meals. It is March, and the cold makes the hairs rise from his arms, but the sun warms the arm beneath them. He thinks, the tragedy of a moving sun is that it leaves us each day. Hence the Aztec sacrifices, the ancient rites of the eclipse. If the sun so willingly leaves us, each morning it returns is a stay of execution, an undeserved gift.

39   Whereas: If it is we who turn, how can we so **flagrantly** leave behind that which has warmed us and given us light? If we are moving, then each turn is a turn away. Each revolution a revolt.

40 The money comes less often, and even old friends who used to write monthly now send only rare, apologetic notes, a few small bills. Things are more difficult now, their letters say. No one understood when he first ran away, but now it is clear: After they finished with the artists, the journalists, the fighters, they came for the professors. How wise he was, to leave when he did. Some letters come back unopened, with a black stamp.

41   Life is harder here, too. Half the shops are closed. His lover has left him. The little café is filled with soldiers. The beggar with the violin has disappeared, and the chef fears him dead.

ANALYZE CHARACTER

Annotate: Mark text in the description of the chef's dream that reveals what he fears most.

Analyze: What does this dream suggest about the chef's conflicted feelings about the professor?

flagrantly
(flā′grənt-lē) *adv.* in a blatantly or conspicuously offensive manner.

ANALYZE CHARACTER

Ask students to explain what emotions are in conflict for the chef. Have students continue to reflect on how the chef's thoughts and emotions have developed over the story. Encourage students to predict how the story will end for the chef based on his growing fear. (**Answer:** *The chef feels afraid that the professor will return to take his identity back, but he also feels guilt. He knows he has had someone killed for his own survival. He is becoming more afraid as time goes on, not less.*)

■ English Learner Support

Understand Conflict Tell students that conflicting emotions are feelings that oppose, or are different from, each other. For example: *good/bad, happy/sad, brave/scared.* Explain that they can use language and context to decipher the emotions they are reading about. For example, paragraph 37 says, "the chef takes the case and runs west." The words "takes" and "runs" show the reader that the chef is afraid and becoming paranoid. He might run, or try to escape, at the slightest provocation. Now, refer students back to paragraph 8 and have them practice finding language that demonstrates the chef's earlier emotions. Ask them to discuss how they conflict with the emotions later revealed during his dream. **LIGHT**

WHEN STUDENTS STRUGGLE . . .

Read and Discuss Help students examine the chef's inner dialogue by reviewing the professor's question at the end of paragraph 6. Emphasize that the professor is asking his students to prove something that isn't true. Then have students reread paragraph 38 and chart the chef's theory about the sun:

The moving sun leaves each day >> Aztecs made sacrifices for it >>
Therefore it returns >> We are still undeserving of its return

Discuss how the ideas of "Aztec sacrifices" and "an undeserved gift" relate to the chef's circumstances. (*He is grateful for escaping execution but feels guilty and undeserving because someone was sacrificed in his place.*)

CRITICAL VOCABULARY

flagrantly: The chef questions how Earth can turn away from the sun in such a blatantly offensive way.

ASK STUDENTS to identify what "we" or Earth flagrantly leaves behind. (*warmth and light from the sun*)

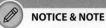

ANALYZE CHARACTER

Remind students of the guiding questions at the beginning of the selection to focus their analysis of the chef's **character**. Explain that in this scene, the chef is finally caught by the professor's wife, which means his fears have come true. Tell students that it will be useful to pay attention to his thoughts, motivations, and physical description to determine how he reacts. Prompt students to discuss what people's reactions to frightening situations reveal about their character. (**Answer:** *He struggles to respond to her and points to his "beard" and "shirt" in an attempt to prove his false identity, showing his desperation and fear as he feels the world closing in on him.*)

■ English Learner Support

Understand Dialogue Repeat the activity on page 276 to help students identify spoken language without the use of quotation marks. To guide students' identification of dialogue, display paragraphs 46–57 and invite volunteers to mark up the lines.

- Underline clue words that indicate who is speaking. (*e.g., "she says," "He begins to say"*)
- Circle the words that the professor's wife speaks. (*e.g., "Forgive me for coming"*)
- Box the words that the chef speaks. (*e.g., "You are the widow."*) **SUBSTANTIAL/MODERATE**

ANALYZE THEME

Remind students that the chef's emotional state and thoughts will help them infer the **theme**. Explain that the first sentence of paragraph 57 demonstrates his desperation because he wishes for more time to prove that he is the professor. This and other actions show that the chef knows that if he is caught in his lies, he will lose the professor's identity and be taken away again. His desperation drives him to continue to try to convince the wife—and to some extent, himself—that he is the professor. The chef's continued attempts demonstrate the theme of unknown or uncertain identity. (**Answer:** *He will be taken prisoner again, and we presume that he will be killed.*)

ANALYZE CHARACTER

Annotate: Mark the woman's actions and words in paragraphs 45–54.

Analyze: What do the chef's responses to these words and actions reveal about him?

42   One afternoon, he enters the post office two minutes before closing. The lobby is empty but for the postman and his broom.

43   The mailbox is empty as well, and he turns to leave but hears the voice of the postman behind him. You are the good Professor T——, no? I have something for you in the back.

44   Yes, he says, I am the professor. And it feels as if this is true, and he will have no guilt over the professor's signature when the box is brought out. He is even wearing the professor's shirt, as loose again over his hungry ribs as it was the day he slipped it on in the alley.

45   From behind the counter, the postman brings no box, but a woman in a long gray dress, a white handkerchief in her fingers.

46   She moves towards him, looks at his hands and his shoes and his face. Forgive me for coming, she says, and the postman pulls the cover down over his window and vanishes. She says, No one would tell me anything, only that my husband had his health. And then a student gave me the number of the box and the name of the city.

47   He begins to say, You are the widow. But why would he say this? What proof is there that the professor is dead? Only that it must be; that it follows logically.

48   She says, I don't understand what has happened.

49   He begins to say, I am the good professor's assistant, madam — but then what next? She would ask questions he has no way to answer.

50   I don't understand, she says again.

51   All he can say is, This is his shirt. He holds out an arm so she can see the gaping sleeve.

52   She says, What have you done with him? She has a calm voice and wet, brown eyes. He feels he has seen her before, in the streets of the old city. Perhaps he served her a meal, a bottle of wine. Perhaps, in another lifetime, she was the center of his universe.

53   This is his beard, he says.

54   She begins to cry into the handkerchief. She says, Then he is dead. He sees now from the quiet of her voice that she must have known this long ago. She has come here only to confirm.

55   He feels the floor of the post office move beneath him, and he tries to turn his eyes from her, to ground his gaze in something solid: postbox, ceiling tile, window. He finds he cannot turn away. She is a force of gravity in her long gray dress.

56   No, he says. No, no, no, no, no, I am right here.

57   No, he does not believe it, but he knows that if he had time, he could prove it. And he must, because he is the only piece of the professor left alive. The woman does not see how she is murdering her husband, right here in the post office lobby. He whispers to her: Let me go home with you. I'll be a father to your son, and I'll warm your bed, and I'll keep you safe.

ANALYZE THEME

Annotate: In paragraph 57, mark the text that reveals the chef's desperation.

Infer: What will happen to the chef if he loses the professor's identity?

ENGLISH LEARNER SUPPORT

Understand Imagery Explain to students that the author uses imagery to convey the chef's emotion in the scene. Imagery is the use of vivid language to represent objects, actions, or ideas. Often, the imagery being described is not what is actually occurring. For example, in paragraph 55, the chef feels the floor start to move under him. Tell students that this doesn't mean the floor is actually moving, but instead describes the chef feeling that he is losing control, or balance, and might fall to the floor if he doesn't focus. By describing the scene this way, the author gives the reader a sense of how lost the chef suddenly feels as his lie is being discovered. Point out the first sentence in paragraph 60 and coach students in describing how the imagery reveals the chef's emotions. **SUBSTANTIAL/MODERATE**

58   He wraps his hands around her small, cold wrists, but she pulls loose. She might be the most beautiful woman he has ever seen.

59   As if from far away, he hears her call to the postmaster to send for the police.

60   His head is light, and he feels he might float away from the post office forever. It is an act of will not to fly off, but to hold tight to the Earth and wait. If the police aren't too busy to come, he feels confident he can prove to them that he is the professor. He has the papers, after all — and in the **havoc** of war, what else will they have the time to look for?

61   She is backing away from him on steady feet, and he feels it like a peeling off of skin.

62   If not the police, perhaps he'll convince a city judge. The witnesses who would denounce him are mostly gone or killed, and the others would fear to come before the law. If the city judge will not listen, he can prove it to the high court. One day he might convince the professor's own child. He feels certain that somewhere down the line, someone will believe him.

havoc
(hăv´ək) *n.* destructive disorder or chaos.

CHECK YOUR UNDERSTANDING

Answer these questions before moving on to the **Analyze the Text** section on the following page.

1 Why does the chef have the professor's briefcase?

   A The professor dropped it when taken prisoner in the chef's place.

   B He found it on the street and picked it up, hoping it might be helpful.

   C He feels a responsibility to tell the professor's family what happened.

   D It was left in the restaurant where the chef worked before his arrest.

2 What is the chef's strategy for survival?

   F He conceals his location and asks the professor's friends for money.

   G He plans to marry the professor's wife and help raise their son.

   H He takes a job in a new restaurant where no one knows him.

   J He has no strategy because he knows how hopeless his situation is.

3 At the end of the story —

   A the chef finally understands the professor's question

   B he has been evicted from his room because he has no more money

   C his disguise has convinced the professor's son that he is his father

   D the chef's secret has been discovered

The Briefcase   279

ENGLISH LEARNER SUPPORT

Oral Assessment   Use the following questions to assess students' comprehension and speaking skills. Ask students to respond in short, complete sentences.

1. Why does the chef have the professor's briefcase? (*The professor dropped it when he was taken prisoner.*)

2. What does the chef do to survive? (*He keeps his location a secret and writes to the professor's friends to send him money.*)

3. What happens at the end of the story? (*His secret is discovered.*)
    SUBSTANTIAL/MODERATE

CHECK YOUR UNDERSTANDING

Have students answer the questions independently.

Answers:

1. *A*

2. *F*

3. *D*

If they answer any questions incorrectly, have them reread the text to confirm their understanding. Then they may proceed to ANALYZE THE TEXT on page 280.

CRITICAL VOCABULARY

havoc: The war has resulted in chaos and destruction.

ASK STUDENTS why no one would be able to check on the chef's identity in the midst of *havoc*. (*Records may have been destroyed, or those that do exist may be in dangerous places.*)

ANALYZE THE TEXT

Possible answers:

1. **DOK 3:** *He fears he won't remember the combination to his box at the post office; he's afraid that even the box will turn him away (paragraph 35); he dreams about the professor finding him (paragraph 36).*

2. **DOK 2:** *The chef's justification is that the act was a kind of apology for trading places with the professor; keeping the professor's identity alive will put the world back in balance (paragraph 8).*

3. **DOK 2:** *The beggar has lost his "real" life and is doing what he must to survive. The chef does not want to walk past him because he sees himself in the beggar and doesn't want to be reminded that he is more like the beggar than the professor.*

4. **DOK 4:** *The astronomy question invites students to prove a theory that isn't true. This relates to the chef because he is living a life that is not true. If he can solve the riddle, then he also has the ability to make his own lie believable (paragraphs 12–13, 18–19).*

5. **DOK 3:** *Answers will vary. The chef does not believe his own lie. In paragraphs 51 and 53, he says, "This is his shirt" and "This is his beard." When he realizes that his life as the professor is ending, he tries to convince himself of his own lie. In paragraph 57, he says, "No, he does not believe it, but he knows that if he had time, he could prove it."*

RESEARCH

Make sure that students understand how to identify whether or not a source is credible. Focus especially on how to tell the difference between objective and subjective articles. Model how to refine and refocus research questions. For example, an initial question—*Why are people still imprisoned as political prisoners today?*—could be modified as follows: *What countries imprison people for political crimes? Where and why are people imprisoned for acts of political protest?*

Extend To encourage students to notice similarities between famous political prisoners and the governments that imprisoned them, have students do a gallery walk. Give partners chart paper and have them put their questions and findings on it. Then tape the chart paper to the wall. Have students walk around the room and take notes of their comparisons.

RESPOND

ANALYZE THE TEXT

Support your responses with evidence from the text. NOTEBOOK

1. **Cite Evidence** What evidence does the author provide that the chef, even after a year in hiding, fears discovery?

2. **Summarize** How does the chef justify the theft of the professor's briefcase and identity?

3. **Interpret** In what way is the beggar outside the café the chef's "double"? Why does the chef not want to walk past him?

4. **Analyze** Throughout the story, the author revisits the astronomy question. What is the connection between this question and the story's theme?

5. **Draw Conclusions** Does the chef ever begin to believe his own lie? Cite evidence from the story to support your answer.

RESEARCH

RESEARCH TIP
As you find information and begin to write it in the chart, be sure to document every source you use so that you can give proper credit. The main elements of a source citation are the author name, publisher name, publisher location (for books), date created or published, title, URL (for websites), and page number(s).

A political prisoner is imprisoned for his or her political beliefs or actions. With a partner, research political imprisonment around the world. Begin your research with an initial question. As you learn more, use your findings to generate, modify, and refine more questions to refocus your research plan. Use credible sources, such as objective news outlets or nonprofit websites (.org). Add your questions and research findings to the chart.

QUESTIONS	FINDINGS
Initial question:	*Findings will vary, but students should locate credible sources and modify their questions as appropriate.*
Modified question:	
Final question:	

Extend Compare findings with others. How do the political prisoners' beliefs and actions compare? What comparisons can you make among the governments that imprisoned them? What conclusions can you draw about political prisoners?

LEARNING MINDSET

Asking for Help Before pairs research and discuss political imprisonment, encourage them to take advantage of the different perspectives and ideas everyone in the classroom can offer that might help them generate, modify, and refine their research questions. For example, pairs might exchange drafts of their questions or early findings with another pair and ask for feedback to help them refine and refocus their efforts. Or assign students or ask for volunteers to serve as an advisor-of-the-day and be the initial person others ask for help that day.

CREATE AND PRESENT

Write a Letter Assume the identity of the chef. Write a letter to the professor's son in which you attempt to convince him that you could serve as his father.

- ❏ Gather details from the story that support the chef's idea that he has become the professor.

- ❏ Write a brief letter to the son based on the details you have gathered from the text. Address the son, using a voice and logic suited to the chef's character.

- ❏ Make sure you use specificity and detail when you mention events and relationships of which the chef would be aware.

Deliver a Summary Summarize the story to classmates while maintaining meaning and logical order. Conclude with a prediction of what happens next to the chef.

- ❏ Review your notes about the chef's character and motivations. Outline the key events of the story, including the chef's actions and reactions.

- ❏ Based on what you know about the chef and the flow of the story, make a logical prediction about what happens to him after the story ends.

- ❏ If you have trouble expressing ideas about physics or political imprisonment, use strategies including synonyms, descriptions, or analogies as needed.

RESPOND TO THE ESSENTIAL QUESTION

 What do we need in order to feel free?

Gather Information Review your annotations and notes on "The Briefcase." Then add relevant information to your Response Log. As you determine which information to include, think about:

- the chef's actions and motivations
- what happened to the professor
- the setting's effects on character and plot
- themes in the story

At the end of the unit, use your notes to help you write an argument.

 Go to the **Writing Studio** for more on persuasive techniques.

 Go to the **Speaking and Listening Studio** for help with presentations.

ACADEMIC VOCABULARY
As you write about and discuss the short story, be sure to use the Academic Vocabulary words. Check off each of the words that you use.

- ❏ **comprehension**
- ❏ **equivalent**
- ❏ **incentive**
- ❏ **innovate**
- ❏ **subordinate**

CREATE AND PRESENT

Write a Letter Use each check box as a step in the writing process. First, have students work in groups to gather details from the story that support the chef's idea that he has become the professor. Give each student in the group a section of the story to reread for these details. Have them share their findings with the rest of the group and note what details they should mention in their letters.

Tell students to pay attention to the voice of the chef and how it changes in their assigned section. Explain that voice consists of the way a character speaks and what he thinks about himself and the world. After students have written their letters, have pairs read each other's letters and give feedback on adding more specificity and detail.

For **writing support** for students at varying proficiency levels, see the **Text X-Ray** on page 268D.

Deliver a Summary Explain that effective summaries have the major developments in plot and character presented in chronological order. Project a summary of a popular movie and ask students what makes it successful. Students are likely to point out that it is concise, contains only relevant information, and uses connecting words and phrases.

To prepare students for writing their summary, instruct them to make a timeline that shows events, the chef's actions, and the ways that he changes. The timeline will help them put events such as flashbacks in chronological order. It will also help them predict what happens to the chef, based on logical next steps.

When students deliver their summary and prediction, have them respond to questions from the rest of the class about how they came to their predictions.

RESPOND TO THE ESSENTIAL QUESTION

Allow time for students to add details from "The Briefcase" to their Unit 4 Response Logs.

EL ENGLISH LEARNER SUPPORT

Deliver a Summary To assist students as they review their notes, have students of varying proficiency levels work together to identify phrases that can be used to summarize key points in the story. If students have created timelines, encourage them to share their timelines and use them as an additional resource for their summaries.

Before students deliver their summaries, have them create or provide a word bank of specific, relevant academic terms they can use to clearly express their ideas about physics or political imprisonment. **ALL LEVELS**

APPLY

CRITICAL VOCABULARY

Answers:

1. *He resisted arrest because flailing means that he was throwing his arms around.*

2. *The professor's test question asks students to prove that the sun revolves around Earth. This is an inversion because it is the opposite of what is true.*

3. *The sun and the moon are both the same distance from the chef because equidistant means "an equal distance"; therefore, everything in the universe is the same distance from the chef.*

4. *The professor's wife hoped to find out what had happened to her husband.*

5. *The guards were unconcerned about the law. They were obvious, or flagrant, about their disrespect and were not worried about being caught breaking the law.*

6. *Everyday life was confusing, chaotic, and full of destruction.*

VOCABULARY STRATEGY:
Discipline-Specific Terms

Practice and Apply Review the options for determining the meanings of unfamiliar words: context clues, encyclopedias, or technical dictionaries.

- Using context clues is reading or rereading the text around the unfamiliar term to infer its meaning.
- Digital and print encyclopedias contain information on many subjects. Inform students that online encyclopedias often can be edited by anyone, so students always should verify their findings at a credible website.
- Technical dictionaries contain definitions of terms that are highly specialized to a particular field or subject.

Discuss situations in which it would be most appropriate to rely on context clues and when it may be necessary to use print or digital resources.

1. *a common type of yeast used to make bread*

2. *ancient practice of killing people to please the gods*

3. *information related to the study of all extraterrestrial objects and phenomena; astronomical data includes star charts, planetary charts, measurements, orbit charts*

 RESPOND

WORD BANK
flail
inversion
equidistant
transpire
flagrantly
havoc

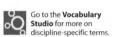 Go to the **Vocabulary Studio** for more on discipline-specific terms.

CRITICAL VOCABULARY

Practice and Apply Answer each question to demonstrate your understanding of the Critical Vocabulary words. Then, explain your responses.

1. If the professor's arms were **flailing** when he was seized, did he resist arrest or comply meekly?

   _____

2. When the chef reads the professor's test question, he interprets it as an **inversion**. Why?

   _____

3. If the chef believes that all things in the universe are **equidistant** from him, is the sun farther from the chef than the moon?

   _____

4. The professor's wife tracked down the chef to determine what had **transpired**. What did she hope to find out?

   _____

5. The guards **flagrantly** disregarded the law in seizing the professor. How concerned were they about being caught making an unlawful arrest?

   _____

6. The war created **havoc** in the chef's country. What might you assume everyday life was like for people?

   _____

VOCABULARY STRATEGY:
Discipline-Specific Terms

The author of this story uses terms from cooking, physics, and history. Context clues, encyclopedias, or technical dictionaries can help you determine the meaning of an unfamiliar term specific to a particular field or discipline.

Practice and Apply Read these sentences from the story. Use context clues or other resources to write the meaning of each boldfaced term.

1. His knowledge of biology was limited to the deboning of chickens and the behavior of ***Saccharomyces cerevisiae***, common bread yeast.

   _____

2. Hence the **Aztec sacrifices**, the ancient rites of the eclipse. If the sun so willingly leaves us, each morning it returns is a stay of execution, an undeserved gift.

   _____

3. Using modern **astronomical data**, construct, to the best of your ability, a proof that the sun actually revolves around Earth.

   _____

ENGLISH LEARNER SUPPORT

Build Vocabulary Use the following supports for students at varying proficiency levels:

- Review the Critical Vocabulary words and their meanings. Guide groups of three to outline and then role-play a news report using all of the words accurately. Provide students with visual images as resources. Coach them in choosing images or in making their own drawings to help communicate their news report. **SUBSTANTIAL/MODERATE**

- Have groups of three write a script for a news report, using all of the Critical Vocabulary words accurately, and then present it to the class. **LIGHT**

LANGUAGE CONVENTIONS:
Semicolons

Writers use semicolons for three main purposes:

- to link two independent clauses, setting them off from each other without using a conjunction such as *and* or *but*
- to link an independent clause with another clause that begins with a conjunctive adverb (such as *therefore, meanwhile, also,* or *however*)
- to separate items in a list when the items already contain commas

Makkai uses semicolons to provide structure and organization in her writing, but she also uses them to influence meaning. Read this sentence from the story:

> Surely he could not teach at the university; surely he could not slip into the man's bed unnoticed.

The author could have separated the two independent clauses with a period, but placing them in the same sentence shows that the two thoughts are closely connected. By setting them off from each other in the same sentence without using a conjunction, Makkai lets the reader deduce how they are related. Now, read this sentence from the story:

> They were the hands of the professor; ergo, he was now the professor.

In this example, the semicolon links two thoughts, and a conjunctive adverb (*ergo*) shows that the second thought results from the first.

Practice and Apply Look back at the letter you wrote to the professor's son. Revise your letter to link two independent clauses with semicolons. Then, discuss with a partner how using semicolons helps clarify the meaning of your letter.

Go to the **Grammar Studio** for more on semicolons.

LANGUAGE CONVENTIONS:
Semicolons

Explain that linking ideas with semicolons contributes to the tone of "The Briefcase." Write the following sentences from the selection on the board and ask students to describe how linking the clauses affects the tone.

Illustrate the idea of stylistic choices by rewriting several of the example sentences with different punctuation and discussing the effect.

- He had to write this about the wife; how could he ask these men for money if she held a funeral? [paragraph 11] *(Linking the clauses shows the chef's thought process.)*
- The year is 1848; the year is 1789; the year is 1956. [paragraph 31] *(It connects the ideas as a list; the tone is factual, like something the professor would write.)*

Practice and Apply When students have completed their revisions, they should be able to explain how they and their partners have used semicolons for clarity.

 ## ENGLISH LEARNER SUPPORT

Use a Variety of Sentence Patterns Review the three main purposes of semicolons and provide practice in their use with the last sentence from paragraph 2.

- Ask students to identify the semicolon. Point out that the semicolon is used in this example to link two closely related ideas. Discuss why the writer might have used a semicolon instead of a period. *(The details given after the semicolon support the idea presented before the semicolon.)* **MODERATE**

- Ask pairs to discuss the use of the semicolon in the sentence and explain the meaning and significance of the sentence. *(The prisoners have not noticed that the chef is suddenly free. They are preoccupied with their own thoughts and despair.)* Then have students practice writing sentences using semicolons and review each other's work. **LIGHT**

MENTOR TEXT

from LETTER TO VICEROY, LORD IRWIN

Letter by **Mohandas K. Gandhi**

This letter serves as a **mentor text**, a model for students to follow when they come to the Unit 4 Writing Task: Write an Argument.

GENRE ELEMENTS
ARGUMENT

Remind students that in an **argument** a writer presents a claim, or position, and then supports it with relevant, credible facts and examples. The writer also will anticipate and respond to counterclaims and use language persuasively—for example, by utilizing rhetorical devices and language structures designed to sway the audience. In this lesson, students will explore how Gandhi appeals to a British official and reinforces his argument to try to accomplish social change.

LEARNING OBJECTIVES

- Analyze the elements of an argument and the use of rhetorical devices.
- Conduct research on an event of civil disobedience through a primary source.
- Write an analysis evaluating the strength of Gandhi's argument.
- Discuss the topic of civil disobedience with a partner.
- Identify and interpret denotative and connotative meanings of words.
- **Language** Discuss active and passive voice.

TEXT COMPLEXITY

Quantitative Measures	Letter to Viceroy, Lord Irwin	Lexile: 1210L
Qualitative Measures	**Ideas Presented** Mostly literal, explicit meaning; more than one purpose, but easily identifiable.	
	Structures Used Text organization is somewhat complex, but clearly stated and generally sequential.	
	Language Used Complex and varied sentence structure, with some allusive language.	
	Knowledge Required Historical references require some background knowledge.	

RESOURCES

- Unit 4 Response Log
- Selection Audio
- Reading Studio: Notice & Note
- Level Up Tutorial: Elements of an Argument
- Writing Studio: Writing Arguments
- Speaking and Listening Studio: Participating in Collaborative Discussions
- Vocabulary Studio: Denotations and Connotations
- *from* "Letter to Viceroy, Lord Irwin" / *from* Gandhi: The Rise to Fame Selection Test

SUMMARIES

English

In this letter, Mohandas K. Gandhi writes to Lord Irwin, the Viceroy, or governor, of British-controlled India, to inform him of his plans to protest the oppressive British rule of the Indian people through nonviolent civil disobedience. Gandhi describes how the Indian people have suffered under British rule and appeals to the Viceroy to change the way the British treat the Indian people.

Spanish

En esta carta, Mohandas K. Gandhi, le escribe a Lord Irwin, un oficial británico, para informarle de sus planes de protestar en contra del opresivo régimen británico sobre el pueblo de la India a través de la desobediencia civil no violenta. Gandhi describe cómo el pueblo indio ha sufrido bajo el régimen británico y apela al Virrey para cambiar la manera en que los británicos tratan al pueblo indio.

SMALL-GROUP OPTIONS

Have students work in small groups to read and discuss the selection.

Three-Minute Review

- After students have read "Letter to Viceroy, Lord Irwin" for the first time, direct students to form groups of two or three students each.
- Pose a question to guide a group review, such as "What is Gandhi's main argument?"
- Set the timer for three minutes. During that time, have students discuss possible answers to the question and then write at least one clarifying question to be handed in per group.
- Ask volunteers to share their answers and discuss each group's clarifying question.
- Repeat with another question or topic.

Numbered Heads Together

- Have students form groups of four. Count off 1-2-3-4 to assign each student a number within a group.
- Pose a question to the class, such as "Why does Gandhi consider British rule over India to be a curse?" Alternatively, ask a question posed in Respond: Analyze the Text.
- Have students discuss responses to the question in their groups.
- Call out a number from one to four. Each student with that number responds for the group.
- Repeat with another question as time allows.

Text X-Ray: English Learner Support
for the excerpt from "Letter to Viceroy, Lord Irwin"

Use the Text X-Ray and the supports and scaffolds in the Teacher's Edition to help guide students at different proficiency levels through the selection.

INTRODUCE THE SELECTION
DISCUSS THE BACKGROUND FOR GANDHI'S ARGUMENT

To help students understand the context for the "Letter to Viceroy, Lord Irwin," read the Background note aloud and discuss the following terms:

- British colonial government (a system in which the British controlled other countries and territories)
- nonviolent (or non-violent) *protest* (a method used to attempt to bring about social or political change)
- prohibition (an order or law that prevents something from being done)

Have students use the terms to complete these sentence frames orally:

- *After 1858, the _____ ruled India as one of its colonies.*
- *Gandhi objected to the _____ against Indians producing salt.*
- *When this letter was written, Gandhi had already carried out _____ in South Africa.*

Briefly discuss the strength of conviction Gandhi must have had to stand up to the forces ruling his country.

CULTURAL REFERENCES

The following words or phrases may be unfamiliar to students:

- civil disobedience (paragraph 1): refusal to obey certain laws; a means of political protest
- proposed conference (paragraph 6): meetings planned by the British government to consider India's future
- Independence Movement (paragraph 10): organized efforts to free India from British rule, which began in the 1850s and continued until India gained independence in 1947
- telegram (paragraph 11): a message sent by telegraph (a method for sending messages using electrical signals transmitted along wires)

LISTENING

Analyze an Argument

Have students listen as you read aloud paragraphs 3–5 to help prepare them for analyzing Gandhi's argument. Explain footnotes as needed.

Use the following supports with students at varying proficiency levels:

- Point out that Gandhi begins his argument by stating a cause and its effects. Review the terms *cause* and *effect*, and then ask students: "According to Gandhi, what is the cause of India's problems?" *(British rule)* **SUBSTANTIAL**
- Ask students to cite some of the words Gandhi uses to describe the effects of British rule in India. *(impoverished, exploitation, serfdom, degraded, helplessness)* Display the words and brief definitions for students to copy. **MODERATE**
- Have student pairs discuss words Gandhi uses to describe the effects of British rule and the connotation of these words. Have them think of synonyms. **LIGHT**

SPEAKING

Discuss Active and Passive Voice

Explain that the voice of a verb determines whether its subject performs or receives the action. While active voice is generally preferred, sometimes writers use the passive voice for a purpose.

Use the following supports with students at varying proficiency levels:

- Read aloud the first sentence in paragraph 2: "I must not be misunderstood." Have students choral read the sentence again with you and then explain why it is in the passive voice. **SUBSTANTIAL**
- Guide students to rephrase the first sentence in paragraph 2 using the active voice. As a group, discuss which voice made a stronger impression on them as readers and why. **MODERATE**
- Have students rephrase the first sentence in paragraph 2 using the active voice and then read aloud both it and the original sentence. Then have them discuss which structure is more effective in the context of Gandhi's speech and why. **LIGHT**

READING

Interpret Statements in an Argument

Explain that authors use a variety of techniques to craft an effective argument. These techniques include thought-provoking word choices and comparisons.

Use the following supports with students at varying proficiency levels:

- Read aloud paragraph 8. Help students complete this sentence frame: *In this paragraph, Gandhi is making a comparison between _____ and _____. (the British; his family)* **SUBSTANTIAL**
- Have small groups discuss the use of the word *weapon* in paragraph 8. Ask groups to complete this sentence stem: *The weapon that Gandhi is referring to is _____. (the practice of nonviolent protest)* **MODERATE**
- Have groups reread paragraph 8. Ask: "How might the comparison of the British to family members affect Gandhi's audience?" *(The Viceroy might understand that Gandhi does not intend to harm the British because he would not harm members of his own family).* **LIGHT**

WRITING

Write an Analysis

Work with students as they prepare their two-paragraph analysis of Gandhi's argument as described on Student Edition page 293.

Use the following supports with students at varying proficiency levels:

- Ask students: "Do you think Gandhi made a strong argument in his letter to the Viceroy? Have them give a thumbs-up sign for yes, or a thumbs-down for no. Prompt them to give a reason for their response. **SUBSTANTIAL**
- Have students review their notes. Then guide them in creating an outline showing the order in which they will make their points in both paragraphs. **MODERATE**
- Provide a list of sentence frames to help students refine their analysis. For example: *In paragraph _____, Gandhi emphasizes _____. Gandhi's reference to _____ serves to _____. Gandhi uses the rhetorical device _____ to _____.* Then help students construct and write a reason for their response. **LIGHT**

TEACH

? Connect to the ESSENTIAL QUESTION

Explain that Mohandas Gandhi was a leader in India's movement to gain independence from Great Britain and freedom for the people of India. In 1930, when Gandhi wrote the letter, Great Britain had ruled in India for decades. Prior to that, European commercial interests, including the British East India Company, operated in and eventually controlled parts of India. Under foreign rule, the Indian people lacked political freedom and were subjected to unfair taxes, racial and cultural discrimination, and poverty.

MENTOR TEXT

At the end of the unit, students will be asked to write an argument. "Letter to Viceroy, Lord Irwin" provides a model for how a writer can craft an effective argument that includes a claim, reasons, evidence, and rhetoric.

COMPARE ACCOUNTS

Start students thinking about primary and secondary sources. Tell students that Gandhi's letter to Lord Irwin is a primary source, written in his own words. Explain that a primary source—for example, a letter, a diary, or a photograph—is produced by someone who participated in an event. In contrast, the documentary film *Gandhi: The Rise to Fame* was produced after Gandhi's death and is a secondary source of information. Explain that a secondary source is produced by someone who studied or learned about an event but did not participate in it. Secondary sources include documentaries, biographies, and analyses.

LETTER

from LETTER TO VICEROY, LORD IRWIN

by **Mohandas K. Gandhi**
pages 287–291

COMPARE ACCOUNTS

As you read the letter and view the documentary, notice how Gandhi presents his argument to Lord Irwin and how the film portrays the resulting nonviolent protest. How do these different formats affect your understanding of Gandhi's leadership in a movement to bring justice to the Indian people? After you review both selections, you will collaborate with a small group on a final project.

 ESSENTIAL QUESTION:

What do we need in order to feel free?

DOCUMENTARY FILM

from GANDHI: THE RISE TO FAME

by **BBC**
page 299

LEARNING MINDSET

Questioning Some students may find the language or style of Gandhi's letter to be challenging. In addition, Gandhi references historical events that may be unfamiliar to students. Remind students that asking questions demonstrates curiosity and leads to learning new things. Encourage students to ask questions about unfamiliar ideas, phrases, or references in the letter. Prompt them to search for answers to historical or fact-based questions on their own, using reliable print and online resources, and to share what they learn with their classmates.

from Letter to Viceroy, Lord Irwin

QUICK START

Many countries throughout history have gained independence from rule by a foreign government. How does a fight for freedom get its start? With a group, discuss how one person might begin a movement for independence.

ANALYZE ARGUMENT

A formal argument sets forth a specific and well supported claim. Gandhi's letter attempts to sway the British Viceroy to improve the living conditions of the Indian people. As you analyze his argument, consider these elements:

ELEMENTS TO CONSIDER	CRITERIA FOR EVALUATION
Claim: the central point of an argument	Should be specific and reasonable
Reasons: the logical support for a claim	Must be **valid**—both accurate and relevant. Faulty reasoning, or logical fallacy, can weaken the argument.
Evidence: facts, details, examples, and anecdotes that elaborate on reasons	Must provide solid support. Irrelevant or insufficient evidence weakens a writer's argument.
Counterarguments: points that refute a counterclaim, or an argument against the central claim	Like a claim, must be supported by reasons and evidence

GENRE ELEMENTS: ARGUMENT

- makes a claim that states the central point
- provides logical and accurate reasons for a claim
- includes evidence to support reasons
- includes counterarguments that address potential counterclaims

ANALYZE RHETORIC

A writer uses **rhetoric** to effectively communicate ideas to an audience. A writer can construct a strong argument by establishing credibility and using an appropriate tone. The use of rhetoric can determine whether readers accept or reject an argument. Rhetoric includes these devices:

- **Appeals:** An appeal to logic, emotions, or the character of the speaker can strengthen the power of an argument.
- **Antithesis:** Opposing ideas linked in a sentence can provide a strong contrast, examine pros and cons, and make the argument more memorable.
- **Parallelism:** The repetition of words, phrases, and grammatical patterns can be used to emphasize points and provide a rhythm.
- **Shifts:** A shift in rhetoric is a change from one idea to another to prove a point. Shifts can be signaled by conjunctions such as *but* or *however*.

As you read, notice how Gandhi uses these devices to convince Lord Irwin.

from Letter to Viceroy, Lord Irwin   285

QUICK START

Have students read the Quick Start question and invite them to share their responses with the group. First encourage students to think of freedom movements that they know about. Then ask them to think of leaders associated with those movements. Brainstorm a list of those leaders' characteristics or experiences.

ANALYZE ARGUMENT

As a group, review the elements of an **argument** included in the chart. Share this graphic organizer to help students understand the connections between claims, reasons, and evidence and the role that counterarguments often play.

Consider having students use this organizer to analyze and evaluate Gandhi's argument.

ANALYZE RHETORIC

Guide students through the bulleted list of **rhetorical devices**. Tell students that identifying these devices will help them to understand an author's message and purpose. Suggest that students use these questions to help them identify rhetorical devices in the text and understand their meaning and purpose:

- What does this statement mean?
- How does it create emphasis?
- What is its effect on the audience?

ENGLISH LEARNER SUPPORT

Apply Directionality Demonstrate the directionality of English using the Analyze Argument chart. Explain that each column heading applies to the text in all the rows directly beneath it (a vertical direction). Model how to read the chart by tracing with your finger the first example of Elements to Consider from the first row, top left, and then tracking to the right (a horizontal direction) to Criteria for Evaluation.

- Have a volunteer trace directionality while you read the chart aloud. **SUBSTANTIAL**
- Have a volunteer trace directionality while a partner reads the chart aloud. **MODERATE**

TEACH

CRITICAL VOCABULARY

Remind students to read all of the sentences before deciding which word best completes each one.

Answers:

1. *unpalatable*
2. *humility*
3. *iniquitous*
4. *peremptory*
5. *unadulterated*

■ English Learner Support

Use Cognates   Tell students that three of the Critical Vocabulary words have Spanish cognates: *humility/humilidad, iniquitous/inicuo,* and *peremptory/perentorio.*
ALL LEVELS

LANGUAGE CONVENTIONS

Review the information about active and passive voice. Display the example sentences. Ask a volunteer to circle the subject in the first sentence. (*protesters*) Repeat for the second sentence. (*demands*) Next, ask a volunteer to underline the verb used is the first sentence. (*shouted*) Repeat for the second sentence. (*were shouted*) Point out that in the passive sentence, the subject "demands" performs no action, but the subject in the first sentence "protesters" does.

⊘ ANNOTATION MODEL

Remind students that they may underline, circle, highlight, or otherwise mark elements of argument and examples of rhetoric they identify in the text. Have them use the margins for questions and comments about the text.

CRITICAL VOCABULARY

unpalatable   unadulterated   humility   iniquitous   peremptory

To preview the Critical Vocabulary words, fill in the blank with the word that best completes each sentence.

1. The milk had spoiled, so it was _____ to drink.

2. When she was honored, the activist showed _____ by saying that her contributions were merely simple acts.

3. The laws that keep many people from finding affordable housing are _____.

4. Learning to drive is _____ to actually getting your license.

5. I can drink safely from the stream because the water is _____.

LANGUAGE CONVENTIONS

Active and Passive Voice A sentence may express an idea in either the active or the passive voice. In **active voice,** the subject of the sentence performs the action. In **passive voice,** the subject is acted on rather than doing the action. Here is an example:

Active Voice: The protesters shouted demands as they marched down the street.
Passive Voice: Demands were shouted by the protesters as they marched down the street.

Most writing uses active voice. As you read Gandhi's letter, pay attention to where he strategically uses passive voice to achieve his persuasive goals.

ANNOTATION MODEL

NOTICE & NOTE ⊘

Here is how a reader might annotate to identify a specific appeal that Gandhi uses:

> Before embarking on Civil Disobedience and taking the risk I have dreaded to take all these years, I would fain approach you and find a way out. My personal faith is absolutely clear. I cannot intentionally hurt any thing that lives, much less fellow-human beings even though they may do the greatest wrong to me and mine.

The author tries to persuade the reader that he is credible by making an appeal to his own ethical character.

BACKGROUND

Mohandas K. Gandhi *(1869–1948), often called "Mahatma" ("Great Soul"), helped lead the Indian drive for independence from British rule. The Salt March protested living conditions endured by the Indian people, including a high tax on salt and a prohibition against producing it independently. Gandhi wrote this letter on March 2, 1930. The British colonial government refused Gandhi's demands. On April 6, Gandhi broke the law at the end of the Salt March by picking up handfuls of salt from the seashore. This action sparked a national campaign of nonviolent protest that led to independence from Britain in 1947.*

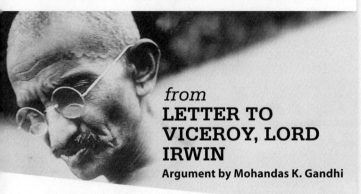

from
LETTER TO VICEROY, LORD IRWIN
Argument by Mohandas K. Gandhi

PREPARE TO COMPARE

As you read, make notes about Gandhi's claim and the reasons and evidence he uses to support his argument. This will help you compare his letter with the information and statement made about the march in the video that follows.

Dear Friend,

1 Before embarking on Civil Disobedience and taking the risk I have dreaded to take all these years, I would fain[1] approach you and find a way out. My personal faith is absolutely clear. I cannot intentionally hurt any thing that lives, much less fellow-human beings even though they may do the greatest wrong to me and mine. *Whilst therefore I hold the British rule to be a curse, I do not intend to harm a single Englishman or any legitimate interest he may have in India.*

2 I must not be misunderstood. Though I hold the British rule in India to be a curse, I do not therefore consider Englishmen in general to be worse than any other people on earth. I have the privilege of claiming many Englishmen as dearest friends. Indeed

---
[1] **fain:** with pleasure.

> **Notice & Note**
>
> You can use the side margins to notice and note signposts in the text.

ANALYZE ARGUMENT
Annotate: Mark the counterclaim Gandhi anticipates in paragraph 2.

Interpret: What counterargument does Gandhi make to refute this counterclaim?

from Letter to Viceroy, Lord Irwin **287**

BACKGROUND

After students read the Background note, expand their knowledge by telling them that Gandhi began his career as a lawyer, training in England and practicing In South Africa. His first civil rights efforts took place there, leading nonviolent protests against the discrimination Indians faced in South Africa. Less than a year after helping India achieve independence, Gandhi was shot and killed by an extreme Hindu nationalist. People around the world mourned his death.

PREPARE TO COMPARE

Direct students to use the Prepare to Compare prompt to focus their reading.

 For **listening, speaking, and reading support** for students at varying proficiency levels, see the **Text X-Ray** on pages 284C–284D.

ANALYZE ARGUMENT

Explain to students that an effective argument anticipates and responds to **counterclaims**, showing why they are not valid or not as reasonable as the writer's own claim. After students have marked the counterclaim, call on a volunteer to identify Gandhi's **counterargument**. (**Answer:** *Gandhi refutes this idea by saying that English people are some of his "dearest friends" and praising the courage of some English writers.*) Finally, remind students that Gandhi's audience is a very important British official—specifically, the Viceroy of India, who governed India on behalf of Great Britain. Briefly discuss how Gandhi's counterargument may have affected the viceroy. (**Answer:** *Gandhi's identification with the English makes it more likely that an English official would be willing to hear his argument.*)

IMPROVE READING FLUENCY

Targeted Passage Read aloud the first paragraph of the letter while students follow along silently. Model appropriate pacing, intonation, and expression. Stress the last sentence, in which Gandhi emphasizes his nonviolent approach. Then have students choral read the same passage.

 Go to the **Reading Studio** for additional support in developing fluency.

TEACH

 ANALYZE RHETORIC

Review the fact that **antithesis** is a **rhetorical device** in which opposing ideas are linked in a sentence in order to show contrast or make an argument more memorable. Ask students to quietly reread the sentence in which they marked the two forces before answering the Compare question. (***Answer:*** *Although these forces are on opposing political sides, Gandhi makes clear that they have more similarities than differences. Nonviolence is the opposite of both of these forces.*)

EL **ENGLISH LEARNER SUPPORT**

Internalize New Vocabulary Display the word *dumb* and have students pronounce it after you. Then explain that the meaning in the text is not the most widely used meaning—that is, "stupid." Rather, Gandhi uses the primary meaning of *dumb*: "silent" or "unable to speak." His diction reminds the Viceroy that Gandhi represents his fellow Indians, who are unable to make their views effectively known.

ALL LEVELS

 AGAIN AND AGAIN

Briefly review the meaning and importance of **repetition** as a rhetorical device. After students have marked their text, read aloud the paragraph, emphasizing Gandhi's use of the verb *serve*. (***Answer:*** *Gandhi is emphasizing his history of serving the British. He uses repetition to show the Viceroy that Gandhi is not his enemy.*)

CRITICAL VOCABULARY

unpalatable: Gandhi acknowledges that some truths may be unpleasant to hear.

ASK STUDENTS to discuss why British officials may find the truth about British rule unpalatable. (*The truth states a negative view of their involvement in India.*)

unadulterated: Gandhi describes his vision of nonviolence as pure and having no exceptions.

ASK STUDENTS to discuss why nonviolence must be unadulterated to be effective. (*If nonviolence is tainted by violence or corruption, it loses its impact and credibility.*)

 NOTICE & NOTE

unpalatable
(ŭn-păl´ə-tə-bəl) *adj.*
unpleasant or unacceptable.

ANALYZE RHETORIC
Annotate: Gandhi uses antithesis in paragraph 6 to explain his approach. Mark the two forces Gandhi states that his nonviolent force is opposing.

Compare: Are these two forces more alike or more different? How might nonviolence counter both of them?

unadulterated
(ŭn-ə-dŭl´tə-rā-tĭd) *adj.*
pure and untainted.

AGAIN AND AGAIN
Notice & Note: Mark the verb Gandhi repeats several times in paragraph 8.

Infer: What point does this repetition emphasize?

---

much that I have learnt of the evil of British rule is due to the writings of frank and courageous Englishmen who have not hesitated to tell the **unpalatable** truth about that rule.

3 And why do I regard the British rule as a curse?

4 It has impoverished the dumb millions by a system of progressive exploitation and by a ruinously expensive military and civil administration which the country can never afford.

5 It has reduced us politically to serfdom.[2] It has sapped the foundations of our culture, and, by the policy of disarmament,[3] it has degraded us spiritually. Lacking inward strength, we have been reduced by all but universal disarmament to a state bordering on cowardly helplessness.

6 . . . If India is to live as a nation, if the slow death by starvation of her people is to stop, some remedy must be found for immediate relief. The proposed conference is certainly not the remedy. It is not a matter of carrying conviction by argument. The matter resolves itself into one of matching forces. Conviction or no conviction Great Britain would defend her Indian commerce and interest by all the forces at her command. India must consequently evolve force enough to free herself from that embrace of death. It is common cause that, however disorganized and for the time being insignificant it may be, the party of violence is gaining ground and making itself felt. Its end is the same as mine. But I am convinced that it cannot bring the desired relief to the dumb millions. And the conviction is growing deeper and deeper in me that nothing but **unadulterated** non-violence can check the organized violence of the British Government. Many think that non-violence is not an active force. It is my purpose to set in motion that force as well against the organized violent force of the British rule as the unorganized violent force of the growing party of violence. To sit still would be to give rein to both the forces above mentioned. Having an unquestioning and immovable faith in the efficacy of non-violence as I know it, it would be sinful on my part to wait any longer. . . .

7 I know that in embarking on non-violence, I shall be running what might fairly be termed a mad risk, but the victories of truth have never been won without risks, often of the gravest character. Conversion of a nation that has consciously or unconsciously preyed upon another far more numerous, far more ancient and no less cultured than itself is worth any amount of risk.

8 I have deliberately used the word conversion. For my ambition is no less than to convert the British people through non-violence and thus make them see the wrong they have done to India. I do not seek to harm your people. I want to serve them even as I want to serve my own. I believe that I have always served them. I served them up

---

[2] **serfdom:** the lowest class of a feudal system, which held people in bondage.
[3] **disarmament:** the reduction or elimination of weapons.

APPLYING ACADEMIC VOCABULARY

☐ **comprehensive** ☑ **equivalent** ☑ **incentive** ☐ **innovate** ☐ **subordinate**

Write and Discuss Have students turn to a partner to discuss the following questions. Guide students to include the academic vocabulary words *equivalent* and *incentive* in their responses. Ask volunteers to share their responses with the class.

- Does Gandhi believe that nonviolence is **equivalent** to violence? Why or why not?
- What are the **incentives** for the "mad risk" Gandhi is willing to take in service of his cause?

to 1919 blindly. But when my eyes were opened, and I conceived non-cooperation the object still was to serve them. I employed the same weapon that I have in all **humility** successfully used against the dearest members of my family. If I have equal love for your people with mine, it will not long remain hidden. It will be acknowledged by them even as the members of my family acknowledged it after they had tried me for several years. If the people join me as I expect they will, the sufferings they will undergo, unless the British nation sooner retraces its steps, will be enough to melt the stoniest hearts.

9   The plan through civil disobedience will be to combat such evils as I have sampled out.

10   If we want to sever the British connection it is because of such evils. When they are removed the path becomes easy. Then the way to friendly negotiation will be open. If the British commerce with India is purified of greed, you will have no difficulty in recognizing our independence. I respectfully invite you then to pave the way for an immediate removal of those evils and thus open a way for a real conference between equals, interested only in promoting the common good of mankind through voluntary fellowship and in arranging terms of mutual help and commerce suited to both. You have unnecessarily laid stress upon the communal problems that unhappily affect this land. Important though they undoubtedly are for the consideration of any scheme of government, they have little bearing on the greater problems which are above communities and which affect them all equally. *But if you cannot see your way to deal with these evils and my letter makes no appeal to your heart, on the 11th day of this month, I shall proceed with such co-workers of the*

humility
(hyo͞o-mĭl´ĭ-tē) *n.*
modesty; lack of superiority
over others.

from Letter to Viceroy, Lord Irwin   289

WHEN STUDENTS STRUGGLE . . .

Analyze Rhetoric Have partners use a chart to list examples of rhetorical devices.

Rhetorical Device	Example from the text
Appeal to emotion	*(paragraph 4) "It has impoverished the dumb millions by a system of progressive exploitation and by a ruinously expensive military..."*
Parallelism	*(paragraphs 4 and 5) repetition of the phrase "it has"*

 For additional support, go to the **Reading Studio** and assign the following **Level Up Tutorial: Elements of an Argument.**

 ENGLISH LEARNER SUPPORT

Discuss Connotation Explain to students that words have both denotations, or dictionary definitions, and connotations, or associated meanings and emotions. Connotations can be used in an argument to help persuade the audience.

- Reread paragraph 10. Point out that Gandhi describes a future relationship between Great Britain and India after greed has been eliminated from the relationship. Guide students to identify the words Gandhi uses to describe this future relationship. (*friendly, conference, equals, common good, voluntary fellowship, mutual help*)

- Ask how these words might affect the Viceroy. (*The positive connotations might help persuade the Viceroy to think positively about Gandhi's argument.*) **LIGHT**

ENGLISH LEARNER SUPPORT

Clarify Grammar Issues Distinguishing tenses can be a challenge for speakers of several Asian languages (including Cantonese, Mandarin, Vietnamese, Korean, Burmese, and Tagalog). These languages do not use tense-markers; in some, the present tense can be used for future action. Spend some time, therefore, discussing the use of tenses in paragraphs 8–10. In particular, focus on Gandhi's "if" statements in this passage, most of which couple a present-tense situation with its future-tense likely outcome. **ALL LEVELS**

CRITICAL VOCABULARY

humility: Gandhi expresses no superiority over others; he views himself as equal to others, including both the poor and the Viceroy.

ASK STUDENTS to discuss how humility may have contributed to Gandhi's success as a leader. (*People are willing to listen to and follow someone with whom they can identify and who does not exhibit arrogance or abuse of social power.*)

✏️ LANGUAGE CONVENTIONS

Point out that students are sometimes advised to avoid using the passive voice in written assignments, so they may wonder why a writer would choose to use the passive voice when trying to persuade an audience. Reread the sentence aloud. Then ask for volunteers to paraphrase the sentence using the active voice. As a group, decide whether such a change would have a positive or negative effect on the audience. Would using an active voice create an aggressive tone? (**Answer:** *The passive voice emphasizes the message of the sentence. Gandhi isn't attacking the Viceroy; he is appealing to him to understand the "Indian cause." Using "I" would place more emphasis on Gandhi.*)

■ English Learner Support

Understand Passive Voice Read aloud paragraph 12. Prompt students to ask clarifying questions to ensure their understanding. Then, explain that the passive voice is often used to remove the connection between the person doing the action and the action itself. For Gandhi, this meant putting the focus not on himself, but on his" sacred duty."
MODERATE/LIGHT

CRITICAL VOCABULARY

iniquitous: Gandhi thinks that the salt tax is the most immoral and cruel of the British demands on the Indian people.

ASK STUDENTS to identify why Gandhi finds the salt tax so iniquitous. (*The law is evil because it disproportionately affects India's poorest people.*)

peremptory: Gandhi says that he requires himself, by virtue of his commitment to civil disobedience, to send the letter to the Viceroy.

ASK STUDENTS to discuss how Gandhi's reminder that this letter is peremptory may affect the Viceroy. (*The Viceroy may not interpret the letter as a threat. He may see that he is dealing with a person of good faith and character.*)

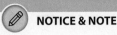

✏️ NOTICE & NOTE

iniquitous
(ĭ-nĭk′wĭ-təs) *adj.*
wicked, evil.

LANGUAGE CONVENTIONS
Annotate: Mark the subject of the first sentence of paragraph 12.

Respond: How might the tone of this sentence change if the subject were "I"? What is the effect of Gandhi's wording in this key sentence?

peremptory
(pə-rĕmp′tə-rē) *adj.*
imperative; required; not able to be denied.

Ashram[4] *as I can take to disregard the provisions of the Salt laws. I regard this tax to be the most* **iniquitous** *of all from the poor man's standpoint. As the Independence Movement is essentially for the poorest in the land, the beginning will be made with this evil. The wonder is, that we have submitted to the cruel monopoly[5] for so long. It is, I know, open to you to frustrate my design by arresting me. I hope that there will be tens of thousands ready in a disciplined manner to take up the work after me, and in the act of disobeying the Salt Act to lay themselves open to the penalties of a law that should never have disfigured the Statute-book.*

11   I have no desire to cause you unnecessary embarrassment or any at all so far as I can help. If you think that there is any substance in my letter, and if you will care to discuss matters with me, and if to that end you would like me to postpone publication of this letter, I shall gladly refrain on receipt of a telegram to that effect soon after this reaches you. You will however do me the favor not to deflect me from my course unless you can see your way to conform to the substance of this letter.

12   This letter is not in any way intended as a threat, but is a simple and sacred duty **peremptory** on a civil resister. Therefore I am having it specially delivered by a young English friend, who believes in the Indian cause and is a full believer in non-violence and whom Providence[6] seems to have sent to me as it were for the very purpose.

I remain,
Your Sincere friend,

M K Gandhi

M.K. Gandhi

---

[4] **Ashram:** a secluded residence of a Hindu religious leader and followers.
[5] **monopoly:** the complete and exclusive control of a product or service.
[6] **Providence:** God or a supernatural power.

TO CHALLENGE STUDENTS . . .

Analyze Perspective Challenge students to examine multiple perspectives on a topic. Have them respond to the following prompt:

> Write a letter to Gandhi that argues in support of British rule in India. Reference outside historical sources for background information.

Tell students that the reasons they provide should accurately reflect the British position, or the position of those in India who support some form of British rule. Direct them to anticipate and respond to counterclaims and to use a formal style and appropriate word choice.

NOTICE & NOTE

CHECK YOUR UNDERSTANDING

Answer these questions before moving on to the **Analyze the Text** section on the following page.

1 Why did Gandhi want to meet with the Viceroy?

   A To discuss a proposed conference

   B To find a way out of his planned civil disobedience

   C To inform the Viceroy about the party of violence

   D To request help for his family

2 What evil did Gandhi describe as the main point of the letter?

   F The risks of civil disobedience

   G An expensive military

   H The Independence Movement

   J British rule of India

3 What did Gandhi say would happen if the letter had no effect?

   A He and his followers would disobey the Salt Act.

   B He would be arrested and put in prison.

   C He would ask his followers to protest violently.

   D He would no longer serve English people.

CHECK YOUR UNDERSTANDING

Have students answer the questions independently.

Answers:

1. *B*

2. *J*

3. *A*

If they answer any questions incorrectly, have them reread the text to confirm their understanding. Then they may proceed to ANALYZE THE TEXT on page 292.

 ENGLISH LEARNER SUPPORT

Oral Assessment   Use the following questions to assess students' comprehension and speaking skills.

1. What is the main point of Gandhi's letter? (*Gandhi wants to meet with the Viceroy. He does not want to strike unless he absolutely has to.*)

2. What does Gandhi think is evil and wrong? (*the British controlling India*)

3. What does Gandhi say will happen if the Viceroy does not agree to meet? (*Gandhi and his followers will take part in nonviolent protest against the Salt Act.*)

SUBSTANTIAL/MODERATE

ANALYZE THE TEXT

Possible answers:

1. **DOK 4:** *Gandhi's central claim is that British rule in India should end. He cites the Indian people's poverty, exploitation, political serfdom, and spiritual degradation as reasons in support of his claim.*

2. **DOK 4:** *Gandhi acknowledges his audience, makes his claim, provides reasons for his claim, and then proposes at least two solutions for the problem. His order of ideas is effective because it is logical while not being adversarial.*

3. **DOK 3:** *Gandhi uses the word* curse *early in the letter and the word* conversion *midway through the letter. These word choices are significant because one has a negative connotation and one has a positive connotation. Their placement shows a progression from the negative to the positive.*

4. **DOK 3:** *Gandhi says that he will proceed with co-workers of the Ashram to disregard the provisions of the salt laws. He supports this action because the tax targets the poorest in the land.*

5. **DOK 4:** *Gandhi offers not to publish the letter if the Viceroy will meet and discuss it. If the Viceroy will not meet or conform to the letter, Gandhi asks him not to try to stop him. He then shifts to say that this is not a threat. This affects the tone by showing that Gandhi is willing to talk but is also firm in his decision to carry out his protest.*

RESEARCH

Remind students to conduct research on credible websites. Newspapers, educational institutions (*.edu*), and government websites (*.gov*) may have primary sources. Students also may try organizations devoted to historical topics—for example, by looking for links ending in *.org*. Guide students to use secondary sources for background information and contextual support.

Extend Encourage students to be respectful and to display a positive attitude when others are sharing what they have learned. To show understanding, ask student listeners to complete the following sentence frames:

One thing I learned about _____ is _____.

One thing I wondered about is _____.

RESPOND

ANALYZE THE TEXT

Support your responses with evidence from the text. NOTEBOOK

1. **Analyze** Identify Gandhi's central claim in this letter. What key reasons does he provide to support this claim?

2. **Evaluate** Notice how Gandhi structures his argument. Why is this order of ideas effective?

3. **Draw Conclusions** Identify the places where Gandhi uses the words *curse* and *conversion*. Why are these word choices significant, and how do they affect his tone?

4. **Cite Evidence** How does Gandhi support his choice of the first action to take against the evils of British rule?

5. **Notice & Note** What contrasting ideas or rhetorical shift do you notice in the last two paragraphs of Gandhi's letter? What effect does this shift have on the tone of the letter?

RESEARCH

RESEARCH TIP
Choose carefully as you look for primary sources. Use valid, reliable sources that relate to authentic historical events.

Explore another act or event of civil disobedience through a primary source such as a letter. A **primary source** contains original, firsthand information. It may be an eyewitness account, letter, diary, interview, speech, or autobiography. A **secondary source,** on the other hand, provides someone else's version of a primary source. It may be a news article, a documentary, a biography, or encyclopedia entry. Keep track of your sources in a chart like the one shown.

EVENT	URL/ SOURCE	PARAPHRASED OR QUOTED INFORMATION
Responses will vary.	*Sources used should be reliable.*	*Paraphrases and quotations should accurately reflect the sources used.*

Extend Share what you learn with a small group. Be sure to identify your sources.

LEARNING MINDSET

Asking for Help Encourage students to think of various people who can be sources of support and encouragement. From teachers, coaches, and other adults at school, to staff at nonprofit or community organizations, and to friends and relatives, students may be surprised at how many people in the school and community can be a source of support—but only if asked. Remind students to ask for help when they need it (as a sign of strength and of taking responsibility for themselves) and to keep asking until they find someone who can help.

CREATE AND DISCUSS

Write an Analysis Overall, how would you evaluate the strength of Gandhi's argument?

❏ Write a one-paragraph analysis of his claims, reasons, evidence, and rhetoric, providing examples from the text of the letter.

❏ Then, discuss in a second paragraph why you think this argument failed to persuade the Viceroy to change the conditions imposed on the Indian people or even to respond to Gandhi.

Share Information Now that you have read and analyzed "Letter to Viceroy, Lord Irwin" and researched another event of civil disobedience, meet with a partner to share what you have learned about civil disobedience. Delve deeper into the information by doing the following:

❏ Support the information you share using pictures or timelines.

❏ Take notes during your discussion.

❏ Ask and respond to questions as needed.

RESPOND

 Go to **Writing Arguments: Building Effective Support** in the **Writing Studio** help with your analysis.

 Go to the **Speaking and Listening Studio** for help with collaborative discussions.

RESPOND TO THE ESSENTIAL QUESTION

 What do we need in order to feel free?

Gather Information Review your annotations and notes on Gandhi's letter and highlight those that help you answer the Essential Question. Then, add relevant details to your Response Log.

At the end of the unit, use your notes to write an argument.

ACADEMIC VOCABULARY
As you write and discuss what you learned from the argument in the letter, be sure to use the Academic Vocabulary words. Check off each of the words that you use.

❏ **comprehensive**

❏ **equivalent**

❏ **incentive**

❏ **innovate**

❏ **subordinate**

CREATE AND DISCUSS

Write an Analysis Have students use the following questions to prepare outlines before they begin drafting their paragraphs.

• Is Gandhi's claim clear and reasonable? Are his reasons clear and logical?

• Does Gandhi's evidence support his claim and reasons? Is his rhetoric persuasive?

• Why might the letter have failed to persuade the Viceroy?

For **writing support** for students at varying proficiency levels, see the **Text X-Ray** on page 284D.

Share Information Encourage students to ask each other questions to clarify meaning and draw out details. Explain that the process of asking and answering questions can lead to greater understanding for both partners.

RESPOND TO THE ESSENTIAL QUESTION

Allow time for students to add details from "Letter to Viceroy, Lord Irwin" to their Unit 4 Response Logs.

 ENGLISH LEARNER SUPPORT

Share Information After pairs share what they have learned with each other, encourage them to compare information with another pair of students. Then have both pairs work together as a small group to summarize their common understanding of **civil disobedience.** Provide them with a graphic organizer, such as a web diagram, to organize their ideas. Invite each group to share its graphic organizer with the class. **MODERATE/LIGHT**

CRITICAL VOCABULARY

Answers:

1. *a. A sandwich covered with mold is unpalatable because it is unpleasant or unacceptable to eat.*

2. *a. A sterile beaker of distilled water is unadulterated because it is pure and untainted.*

3. *b. A race winner thanking his coach shows humility because the winner does not emphasize superiority over the other contestants.*

4. *b. A career criminal robbing people's homes is iniquitous because he or she shows no remorse and is motivated by greed.*

5. *a. A passport carried by a traveler to China is peremptory because it is required in order to enter the country.*

VOCABULARY STRATEGY:
Denotations and Connotations

Possible answers:

1. *I **feared** the growing, barking dog in my neighbor's yard./I **dreaded** the days I had to walk to school. While both words mean "to be frightened or scared," dreaded has the connotation of deep fear or anxiety about a future situation.*

2. *The speaker's criticisms were **unpleasant** to hear./Many listeners protested the speaker's **unpalatable** words. While both words mean "something that is not enjoyable," the connotation of unpalatable is much stronger.*

3. *The mother remained **silent** as she cleaned the mess in the kitchen./The first responders were struck **dumb** by the amount of damage caused by the tornado. While both words mean "to not say a word," dumb has the connotation of being unable to speak because of shock.*

4. *The tree fell, **weakened** by the recent hurricane./Over the years, the pipes steadily **degraded** with rust. While both words mean "to break down or lose strength," degraded has the connotation of losing strength over a long period of time.*

5. *By dinnertime, he felt great **hunger** because he had not had lunch./The refugees faced **starvation** because of dwindling food supplies. While both words mean "the need to eat," the connotation of starvation is a life-threatening condition.*

6. *It is **wrong** not to respect other people's property./Most religions consider stealing to be **sinful**. While both words mean "not right," the connotation of sinful is a greater moral crime.*

 RESPOND

CRITICAL VOCABULARY

WORD BANK
unpalatable
unadulterated
humility
iniquitous
peremptory

Practice and Apply Mark which of the two situations best fits the word's meaning. Discuss with a partner why your choice is the best response.

1. **unpalatable**
   a. a sandwich covered with mold
   b. a sandwich too large to eat

2. **unadulterated**
   a. a sterile beaker of distilled water
   b. a precise mixture of water and iodine

3. **humility**
   a. a race winner pumping his fist in the air
   b. a race winner thanking his coach

4. **iniquitous**
   a. a hungry person stealing an apple
   b. a career criminal robbing people's homes

5. **peremptory**
   a. a passport carried by a traveler to China
   b. a map of Beijing bought by a tourist

 Go to the **Vocabulary Studio** for more on denotations and connotations.

VOCABULARY STRATEGY:
Denotations and Connotations

To persuade his audience, Gandhi uses words with strong **connotations**, or associated meanings and emotions. For example, he uses the Critical Vocabulary word *iniquitous*, which has a negative connotation of something that is not only wrong but also immoral. How would the meaning of the sentence change if the word *unjust* was used instead? *Unjust* has a **denotation**, or dictionary meaning, similar to that of *iniquitous*, but it carries a less immoral connotation.

Practice and Apply Analyze the nuances presented by each pair of words with similar denotations. Note that the boldfaced words are from the letter. Use each word in a sentence, and then explain the connotation of each word.

1. feared/**dreaded** (paragraph 1)

   _____

2. unpleasant/**unpalatable** (paragraph 2)

   _____

3. silent/**dumb** (paragraph 4)

   _____

4. weakened/**degraded** (paragraph 5)

   _____

5. hunger/**starvation** (paragraph 6)

   _____

6. wrong/**sinful** (paragraph 6)

   _____

EL # ENGLISH LEARNER SUPPORT

Vocabulary Strategies Provide students with additional practice in understanding denotations and connotations. Read aloud several words from the letter. For each word, ask: "Positive, or negative?" Then have students work in pairs to reread passages from the text. Ask them to make two lists: one for words with a positive connotation and one for words with a negative connotation. Encourage students to discuss how Gandhi's word choices help him more effectively persuade readers. Finally, ask: When can you use connotations to your advantage? *(in essays of argument and persuasion, in stories to establish a mood)* When might it be less appropriate to use charged words? *(in writing that is supposed to be unbiased or objective, such as a news article or research report)* **ALL LEVELS**

LANGUAGE CONVENTIONS
Active and Passive Voice

The subject of a sentence may either perform or receive the action expressed in a verb. In **active voice,** which is the more commonly used of the two voices, the subject of the sentence performs the action. In "Letter to Viceroy, Lord Irwin," Gandhi uses the active voice to express the action taken by the subject, British rule ("It"):

It has reduced us politically to serfdom.

The active voice makes clear Gandhi's belief that British rule has actively taken away the rights of the Indian people.

Sometimes, a writer may choose passive voice, in which the subject receives the action. A form of *be* (*am, is, are, was, were*) and a past participle of the verb form passive voice. Here, the subject ("we") does not perform the action stated in the verb:

Lacking inward strength, we have been reduced . . . to a state bordering on cowardly helplessness.

Gandhi's use of the passive voice emphasizes that the Indian people are being acted upon, rather than being able to take action themselves.

Notice that even though the main verb in these two sentences is the same, the voice is different because of the helping verbs used.

Practice and Apply Identify each sentence as active or passive voice. Then, rewrite each sentence using the other voice, and evaluate the effect of each version.

1. Great Britain would defend her Indian commerce and interest by all the forces at her command.

   _____

   _____

2. The same weapon was employed by me.

   _____

   _____

3. You are respectfully invited to pave the way for an immediate removal of those evils.

   _____

   _____

from Letter to Viceroy, Lord Irwin   295

LANGUAGE CONVENTIONS:
Active and Passive Voice

Review the information about active and passive voice with students. To ensure that students understand how passive sentences are constructed, have them use a dictionary or other classroom resource to look up the following: **helping (or auxiliary) verb** and **past participle**. Tell students to write the definition or description of these terms with a few examples in their notebook. (*A helping, or auxiliary, verb helps to form tenses of other verbs. Examples:* be, do, have. *A past participle expresses a completed action and is used to form passive voice. Examples:* dropped, dumped, tossed.)

Practice and Apply
Possible answers:

1. *Active;* Her Indian commerce and interest would be defended by Great Britain by all the forces at her command. (The change places the emphasis on Indian commerce and interest.)

2. *Passive;* I employed the same weapon. (The change places the emphasis on Gandhi rather than the weapon.)

3. *Passive;* I respectfully invite you to pave the way for an immediate removal of those evils. (The change places the emphasis on Gandhi rather than Lord Irwin.)

ENGLISH LEARNER SUPPORT

Language Conventions Use the following supports with students at varying proficiency levels:

- Read aloud sentences from Gandhi's letter. Tell students to say "active" if the sentence is written in active voice or "passive" if it is written in the passive voice. **SUBSTANTIAL**

- Have students work with partners to find examples of active voice and passive voice within Gandhi's letter. Tell students to label the sentences as either "active" or "passive." Encourage students to consider why Gandhi chose to word the sentence in the way he did. **MODERATE**

- Ask students to rewrite the sentences they labeled in the letter from active voice to passive voice and vice versa. Encourage them to discuss the effect such a change would have on Gandhi's message. **LIGHT**

from GANDHI: THE RISE TO FAME

Documentary Film by BBC

GENRE ELEMENTS
DOCUMENTARY FILM

Tell students that a **documentary film** is meant to "document," or provide evidence about, its subject using the medium of film. While all documentary films are works of nonfiction, they may be made for different purposes—for example, to inform, entertain, or persuade an audience. In this lesson, students will watch part of a documentary film about Mohandas K. Gandhi and the 1930 Salt March. They will analyze the filmmakers' purposes in making the film, as well as the techniques used to convey their message. Students will then compare Gandhi's "Letter to Viceroy, Lord Irwin" with the film.

LEARNING OBJECTIVES

- Analyze a filmmaker's motive in making a documentary and the media techniques used to convey that motive.
- Locate an online biography of Gandhi and use information contained in it to provide context for the film clip.
- Create a multimodal presentation that illustrates how media coverage affects our perceptions of an event.
- Lead a group discussion of reactions to a multimodal presentation.
- **Language** Discuss techniques used in documentary filmmaking, including interviews, voiceover, juxtaposition, and their effects on viewers.

TEXT COMPLEXITY

Quantitative Measures	Gandhi: The Rise to Fame	Lexile: N/A
Qualitative Measures	**Ideas Presented** Mostly explicit, but requires some inferential reasoning.	
	Structures Used Organization of main ideas and details is complex with multiple perspectives, but clearly stated and sequential.	
	Language Used Includes some unfamiliar, academic, or domain-specific words.	
	Knowledge Required Cultural and historical references require some specialized knowledge.	

Online Ed

RESOURCES

- Unit 4 Response Log

- Speaking and Listening Studio: Using Media in a Presentation; Tracing a Speaker's Argument

- ✓ *from* "Letter to the Viceroy, Lord Irwin" / *from* Gandhi: The Rise to Fame Selection Test

SUMMARIES

English

This documentary film, the second film in a three-part series, discusses Gandhi's rise to fame from his beginnings as a lawyer through his emergence as a powerful figure in Indian politics. The film retraces Gandhi's movements in India and interviews people who knew him personally. Narrator Mishal Husain explores Gandhi's philosophy of nonviolence and details the events and aftermath of the 1930 Salt March.

Spanish

Este documental, el segundo de una serie de tres partes, discute cómo Gandhi llega a la fama desde sus inicios como abogado hasta su surgimiento como una figura poderosa en la política de la India. La película vuelve sobre los pasos de Gandhi en la India y entrevista a gente que lo conoció personalmente. El narrador, Mishal Husain, explora la filosofía de no violencia de Gandhi y detalla los eventos y el resultado de la Marcha de la Sal de 1930.

SMALL-GROUP OPTIONS

Have students work in small groups to view and discuss the selection.

Think-Pair-Share

- After viewing the film clip, pose a question to the class—for example, "How did the film's depiction of Gandhi compare with what you learned when you read his letter?"
- Ask students to consider the question individually and to jot down a response.
- Have students meet with partners and collaborate on a shared response.
- Optional: Student pairs may consult other pairs to reach a new consensus.
- Call upon pairs or larger groups to share and compare their responses in a whole-class discussion. Repeat with a new question or topic about the film.

Reciprocal Teaching

- After students have viewed the film clip, provide them with a list of question stems. For example: *Why do you think ___? What does the narrator mean when she says ___? What was the result of ___? Why is ___ important?*
- Ask students to work independently to create at least two questions about the film using the stems. Encourage students to rewatch the film as needed.
- Group students into teams of three or four. Ask each student to present their questions for group discussion.
- Guide groups to answer each question, citing evidence from the film to support their answers.

Text X-Ray: English Learner Support
for the documentary film *Gandhi: The Rise to Fame*

Use the Text X-Ray and the supports and scaffolds in the Teacher's Edition to help guide students at different proficiency levels through the selection.

INTRODUCE THE SELECTION
DISCUSS FILM TECHNIQUES

In this lesson, students will analyze how some filmmakers convey information and a message about a historical topic. Ask students to name documentary films they have seen—perhaps a presentation of some aspect of the natural world, or a historical event, or a famous concert. Invite comments regarding what students remember about their choices and why they think that choice had an impact on them. Then introduce the Gandhi film.

Explain that since there is no actual footage of the Salt March and Gandhi is no longer alive to speak about the events, the filmmakers rely on a variety of techniques, including an interview with an associate of Gandhi, voiceover narration, and the juxtaposition of historical images with footage showing modern-day India. Have students briefly review Gandhi's letter to Lord Irwin. Explain that students will compare that letter with the clip from the documentary film in terms of both content and format.

CULTURAL REFERENCES

The following words or phrases may be unfamiliar to students:

- *Mahatma*: a Hindu title of honor; when used with *the*, a reference to Gandhi
- *crass*: lacking an understanding of what is acceptable or proper
- *satyagraha*: a Hindi word that means "to insist on truth"
- the *Ashram*: Gandhi's religious retreat; in general, a place where people gather away from others to practice the Hindu religion
- *Nehru*: a contemporary of Gandhi who became the first prime minister of the independent India in 1947
- *parliamentarians*: members of the British legislature
- *sari*: a garment worn by some Asian women that consists of cloth draped around one's body

LISTENING

Identify Purpose and Tone

Remind students that a film, like a written work, has a purpose, or goal. Tell students that documentary films, like written works, may use tone to help reach that goal, which may be to convey a specific message or perspective about the subject.

Have the class listen as you play the beginning of *Gandhi: The Rise to Fame*. Pause the film after about two and one-half minutes. Guide students to identify the purpose and tone of the film based on this introduction. Review the terms *purpose* and *tone*. Use the following supports with students at varying proficiency levels:

- Ask students: How do you think the narrator views Gandhi? Tell them to give a thumbs-up sign for a positive view and a thumbs-down sign for a negative view. **SUBSTANTIAL**
- Guide students to understand the narrator's tone toward Gandhi. Coach students to identify the narrator's words and tone of voice that provide evidence for whether she has a positive or a negative view of Gandhi. **MODERATE**
- Discuss the conflict outlined in the opening of the film. Ask: Does the narrator portray the British in a positive manner or in a negative manner? Prompt students to cite language used to support their opinion. **LIGHT**

SPEAKING

Discuss Media Techniques

Review with students the examples of media techniques used by documentary filmmakers on Student Edition page 298.

Use the following supports with students at varying proficiency levels:

- Ask questions such as the following to gauge students' understanding of the techniques: What did you learn about Gandhi from the interviews? What surprised you about the historical photos and film clips? How did the music and sound make you feel? Invite students to use drawings and their home language to demonstrate understanding of these film techniques. **SUBSTANTIAL**
- Briefly explain each technique used in the film clip and then have students answer questions to demonstrate understanding. For example: Why do you think the narrator chose to interview someone who knew Gandhi personally? **MODERATE**
- Invite partners to use the list of techniques and discuss these questions: What was the film's message? How did the media techniques help make that message clear? **LIGHT**

READING

Understand Directionality

Remind students that there are many different types of documentaries with different motives, or purposes. Review the basic use of charts for presenting information.

Read aloud the information about analyzing purposes and motives on Student Edition page 297 while students follow along. Use the following supports with students at varying proficiency levels:

- Model how to read the chart by tracing with your finger as you read the first row, *Type of Documentary*, and then track to the right to read the *Possible Subject* and *Main Purpose*. **SUBSTANTIAL**
- Have students trace directionality while they choral read the chart aloud. **MODERATE**
- Ask students guiding questions to make sure that they understand the chart. For example: What types of documentaries are listed? What are the main purposes for a documentary film? **LIGHT**

WRITING

Write a Narrative

Support students as they complete the narrative portion of the multimodal presentation assignment on Student Edition page 301.

Use the following supports with students at varying proficiency levels:

- To help students focus their narrative, provide a Main Idea and Details organizer. Guide students to understand that the main idea is the event they selected and that the details are their perceptions of what happened. **SUBSTANTIAL**
- Provide sentence frames to help students organize their writing and introduce key details. For example: *In my opinion, _____ . _____ is important because _____. An interesting point is _____.* **MODERATE**
- Provide, or have students create, a list of transitional words and phrases. Encourage students to use at least three of them in their narrative. **LIGHT**

TEACH

Connect to the
ESSENTIAL QUESTION

The excerpt from the documentary film *Gandhi: The Rise to Fame* enables students to learn more about the opinions that both British and Indian people had regarding the topic of Indian independence. It also highlights the fact that Gandhi viewed the salt tax as an important symbol of British oppression of the Indian people. While some people thought Gandhi was out of touch, the Salt March garnered worldwide attention and ultimately became a turning point in India's campaign for independence.

COMPARE ACCOUNTS

Have students take a few moments to reread or reflect upon their experience of reading "Letter to Viceroy, Lord Irwin." Ask students to keep Gandhi's letter in mind as they prepare to learn more about Gandhi and the results of the Salt March. Let students know that they will have an opportunity to take notes on an excerpt from the documentary film *Gandhi: The Rise to Fame*—notes that will help them to compare the two genres.

DOCUMENTARY FILM

from

GANDHI: THE RISE TO FAME

by **BBC**

page 299

COMPARE ACCOUNTS

Now that you've read "Letter to Viceroy, Lord Irwin," view an excerpt from the documentary film "Gandhi: The Rise to Fame." As you watch, think about how the clip relates to the concerns Gandhi stated in his letter as well as new information that you learn about him. After viewing, you will collaborate with a small group on a final project that involves an analysis of the text and the film.

ESSENTIAL QUESTION:

What do we need in order to feel free?

LETTER

from

LETTER TO VICEROY, LORD IRWIN

by **Mohandas K. Gandhi**

pages 287–291

296   Unit 4

from **Gandhi: The Rise to Fame**

QUICK START

A small action by one person can change history. We can learn about the action if at least one witness tells or shows others what happened. Why is it important for a witness to be reliable and accurate? How can technology be both a reliable and unreliable witness? Discuss with a partner.

ANALYZE MOTIVES

Filmmakers create documentaries on a wide variety of subjects for different **motives**, or purposes. Here are a few examples:

TYPE OF DOCUMENTARY	POSSIBLE SUBJECT	MAIN PURPOSE
music	a concert performance	to entertain
history	an event or person's life	to inform
social issue	a current problem	to persuade
nature or science	animal behavior	to inform

Documentaries may have more than one purpose, depending on how the filmmakers' viewpoints and motives influence their choice of content and narration. This documentary centers on information about a historical figure. Viewers can examine the details provided for clues that reveal the filmmakers' motives, particularly those that show a positive or negative perspective on the subject.

Use the chart below to note a brief description of clues you see or hear in the film that help you determine the purpose and motive of the documentary.

GENRE ELEMENTS: DOCUMENTARY FILM

- has an on-screen or voiceover narrator who provides context
- includes interviews with key people, experts, or eyewitnesses
- includes location shots of places discussed
- may use music and sound to enhance the message
- features archival film footage and/or photos of historical events

CLUE	POSITIVE OR NEGATIVE?	MOTIVE OR PURPOSE

from Gandhi: The Rise to Fame   297

QUICK START

To focus students' discussion, ask them to consider how various types of technology available today—for example, the Internet, social media, mobile phones with video capability, 24-hour news media—influence our knowledge and interpretation of important events. How do students judge the accuracy of these sources? Call on volunteers to share their ideas with the class.

ANALYZE MOTIVES

Remind students that they may watch the film clip multiple times as they work to complete the chart. You may also choose to have students work with a partner or small group to complete this activity. Tell students that although this documentary's main purpose is to inform, students also should look for clues that provide either positive or negative information about Gandhi and the Salt March. Once students have completed their charts, invite volunteers to share their entries with the class.

For **reading support** for students at varying proficiency levels, see the **Text X-Ray** on page 296D.

 ENGLISH LEARNER SUPPORT

Understand Viewpoint and Motive To help students identify the filmmaker's viewpoint and motives, ask the following questions:

- What main ideas and events does the film emphasize? *(the Salt March and its aftermath)*
- What is the motive or purpose for the film? *(to inform and to entertain)*
- What is the narrator's point of view about Gandhi? *(She admires him and seems impressed by his determination.)* **SUBSTANTIAL/MODERATE**

TEACH

ANALYZE MEDIA TECHNIQUES

Remind students that the film *Gandhi: The Rise to Fame* is a documentary, which is a film that explores the facts related to an event or person. Unlike Gandhi's "Letter to Viceroy, Lord Irwin," which is a primary source, the documentary film is a secondary source, produced many years after the events it depicts. However, in a documentary, filmmakers may make use of primary sources, including interviews, photographs and film footage, documents, and direct quotations from people who lived during the time period covered in the film, in order to improve the accuracy and thoroughness of their presentation. Discuss how some of the techniques identified in the text make use of both primary and secondary sources. (For example, the narration, voiceover, and interviews may incorporate eyewitness accounts, and the juxtaposed images may include photographs taken at the time and/or event discussed.)

As students watch the film clip, remind them to make notes about the various techniques in the chart on page 298. Students can add details from follow-up discussions as well.

■ English Learner Support

Use Cognates Read aloud the text's discussion of media techniques. Encourage students to ask for clarification of any unfamiliar words. Point out that some of the terms included here have Spanish cognates: *narration/narración, juxtaposition/yuxtaposición, music/música,* and *sound/sonido.*
SUBSTANTIAL/MODERATE

 For **speaking support** for students at varying proficiency levels, see the **Text X-Ray** on page 296D.

ANALYZE MEDIA TECHNIQUES

Documentary filmmakers use techniques such as these to present their topics:

Narration is the commentary spoken by a narrator to explain, inform, and offer opinions to the audience from the filmmaker about the subject.

Voiceover is the narrator speaking while the film shows people, locations, or events.

Interviews may show the narrator speaking with and asking questions of people who are experts on the subject, or who were a part of, knew, or were influenced by a historical event or person.

Juxtaposition is the close placement of two images or scenes in order to compare and contrast or show a relationship. In a historical documentary, archival photos and film clips of people and places from the past may be juxtaposed with current photos and film of where events occurred.

Music and sound can be used to create drama, to appeal to emotions, and to enhance the realism of a place or the description of an event.

As you view the clip from *Gandhi: The Rise to Fame*, watch for uses of media techniques. Use the following chart to list these techniques and note your ideas about how they helped to inform or persuade you as the audience.

MEDIA TECHNIQUE	EFFECT OF TECHNIQUE

ENGLISH LEARNER SUPPORT

Analyze Juxtaposition To help students analyze the effect of juxtaposition, work with them to discuss an example from the film. Model the pronunciation and review the meaning of the term. Ask all students to say the word and have them contribute to a paraphrase of the definition. Then show the film from minute 1:53 to 2:04. Ask the following:

- What images does the filmmaker use in this section of the film? (*the ocean, salt mounds and people working, the narrator in the train, and a landscape*)
- Are the images current, or historical? (*both; the ocean, the narrator in*

the train, and the landscape are current, while the image of the salt and the people working is historical)

- Ask students to juxtapose the image of the workers in the salt works with the image of the narrator on the train using the following sentence frames: *When I _____ the image of the people working in the _____ with the image of the _____ on the train, I notice that _____. Because of what I observe, I think that the struggle of Gandhi and the people was _____.*

MODERATE/LIGHT

BACKGROUND

In 2009, the British Broadcasting Corporation (BBC) aired a three-part documentary series on the life and legacy of Mohandas Gandhi. In it, British-born journalist Mishal Husain retraces Gandhi's steps, interviews those who knew him personally, and provides context for historical footage and photos. Husain's heritage is Pakistani, but her grandfather served in the Indian army before partition, the division of the former British colony into the independent nations of India and Pakistan.

PREPARE TO COMPARE

As you view the film, keep Gandhi's argument in mind. Write down any questions you generate during viewing.

To view the video, log in online and select **"from GANDHI: THE RISE TO FAME"** from the unit menu.

As needed, pause the video to make notes about how the filmmaker and narrator tell about Gandhi and the Salt March. Replay or rewind so that you can clarify anything you do not understand.

from Gandhi: The Rise to Fame   299

TEACH

BACKGROUND

Have students read the Background information. Tell them that *The Rise to Fame* is the second episode in the three-part *Gandhi* documentary series. The titles of the other parts of the film series are *The Making of the Mahatma* and *The Road to Freedom*. The series is largely chronological, following Gandhi from his early years to his life as a public figure to his final years.

PREPARE TO COMPARE

Direct students to use the Prepare to Compare prompt to focus their viewing and listening.

> 📖 For **listening support** for students at varying proficiency levels, see the **Text X-Ray** on page 296C.

WHEN STUDENTS STRUGGLE . . .

Analyze Media Have students view the film excerpt with partners. After they have watched it one time to get an overall "feel" for the depiction of the event, ask them to watch it again while taking notes in a chart like the one on page 298. Students should feel free to take additional notes that are not directly related to media techniques. Have students pause as needed to take notes and clarify understanding. Invite partners to compare notes afterward.

ANALYZE MEDIA

Possible answers:

1. **DOK 2:** *The film clip begins with Gandhi nearing 60 at the end of the 1920s and believing that independence for India seemed nearly impossible. A thoughtless decision on governance by the British, however, caused Gandhi to organize a political campaign that brought India's struggle for independence to the whole world. The narrator provides this context in a voiceover.*

2. **DOK 2:** *The narrator explains the history of the Salt March while the film shows contemporary India in the places where it happened. Historic black-and-white film clips are juxtaposed with some of these same locations. The effect is to show that history had and still has a great impact on the people and the country.*

3. **DOK 4:** *The filmmakers use current location shots of the narrator at the beach where Gandhi gathered salt and at the current salt works where a large protest was staged. Viewers see a note Gandhi wrote to journalists, a historic film clip of Gandhi walking with followers, and gathering crowds at the protest juxtaposed with the narrator at these sites. This creates a contrast of peaceful places today that were once the scene of dramatic events. Music is used for additional drama. The narrator's reading of a journalist's eyewitness account of the soldiers striking down the protesters is dramatized with drum beats, followed by silence to emphasize the seriousness of what happened.*

4. **DOK 2:** *Gandhi wrote, "The hopes I have for you, you must fulfill them." The companion passed the words on to the schoolchildren to encourage them to think about what Gandhi would hope for them to do as independent people in India.*

5. **DOK 4:** *This media piece may have been created to emphasize critical events in India's history. It was also a personal exploration by the narrator, who wanted answers to questions she had about her own history.*

RESEARCH

Encourage students to seek out multiple reliable sources of online information to confirm dates and other facts.

Extend Prompt students to use the online biography to fill in any missing information or answer questions they may have after watching the film.

RESPOND

ANALYZE MEDIA

Support your responses with evidence from the video. NOTEBOOK

1. **Summarize** At what point in history does the film clip begin? How does the narrator provide context?

2. **Interpret** What is the effect of the filmmakers' use of past and present juxtapositions?

3. **Analyze** There are no videos of the protest at the commercial salt works. To portray what happened, the video uses a combination of documentary techniques. What are these techniques? What effect do they have?

4. **Infer** Why does the former companion of Gandhi tell the schoolchildren what Gandhi wrote to him in a book? How does this use of Gandhi's words enhance the documentary?

5. **Evaluate** Why might this media piece have been created? What strategies were used in the video to advance its purpose? Complete the chart below. *Possible answers are shown.*

APPROACH	EXAMPLE	INTENT OR EFFECT
facts	*Gandhi's 240-mile walk to purify salt from the sea*	*to make a bold statement against the Salt Tax*
opinions	*the greatest political campaign of the 20th century*	*to emphasize the importance of what Gandhi did*
scenes	*close-ups of current salt workers dumping salt*	*to represent the marchers falling when struck down*
interviews	*narrator's talk with a man who spent 10 years with Gandhi*	*to present a primary account of Gandhi*

RESEARCH TIP
It's always easier to begin a research project by creating a research plan. First, identify exactly what you want to learn. Then, create a step-by-step plan to guide your search.

RESEARCH

Find a brief online biography of Gandhi to provide context for the video clip. Note any information that conflicts with the video's view of Gandhi.

VIDEO	ONLINE BIOGRAPHY
Responses will vary.	

Extend How does the online biography complement the viewpoint expressed in the documentary?

WHEN STUDENTS STRUGGLE . . .

Conduct Research Once students have located a reliable online biography of Gandhi, provide them with a main idea and details organizer or web diagram. Encourage students to use the organizer to synthesize information that they learn about Gandhi from the online biography. Students can then compare information in the graphic organizer with notes they took when they analyzed *Gandhi: The Rise to Fame.*

CREATE AND PRESENT

Create a Multimodal Presentation The news reports of Gandhi's Salt March and the protests at the salt works had a worldwide effect on perceptions of British rule in India. Write and create a brief multimodal presentation that illustrates how media coverage affects our perceptions of a particular event.

❏ Choose a specific event to feature in your presentation. Gather research on how the media covered this event. What was focused on in a limited time or space? How might this choice have affected audience perceptions of the event? How were these perceptions reflected in follow-up reports?

❏ Plan to use the most effective communication modes and technology, including written, oral, visual, and audio. You might do a podcast or photo essay. You could also include music, sound, recordings, and film clips.

❏ Outline your presentation and then write a narrative that describes the event and explains your perceptions of what happened.

Present and Lead a Discussion With a small group, lead a discussion of impressions and reactions to your presentation.

❏ Before you begin, list questions, such as the following: What was your perception of the event? How did the choice of media affect your perception? What might have been inadequately addressed by the choice of media? How would different coverage change your perceptions? Where do you see evidence of the viewpoint of a reporter or filmmaker?

❏ Restate or replay parts of your presentation to aid in the discussion. Make sure that everyone in the group has an opportunity to express ideas, opinions, and questions.

 Go to the **Speaking and Listening Studio** for help using media in a presentation.

RESPOND TO THE ESSENTIAL QUESTION

? What do we need in order to feel free?

Gather Information Review your annotations and notes on the excerpt from *Gandhi: The Rise to Fame*. Think about Gandhi's methods and accomplishments. Then, add relevant details to your Response Log.

At the end of the unit, use your notes to write an argument.

ACADEMIC VOCABULARY
As you write and discuss what you learned about Gandhi, be sure to use the Academic Vocabulary words. Check off each of the words that you use.

❏ **comprehensive**
❏ **equivalent**
❏ **incentive**
❏ **innovate**
❏ **subordinate**

from Gandhi: The Rise to Fame 301

CREATE AND PRESENT

Create a Multimodal Presentation As students plan their multimodal presentation, help them pinpoint an event by providing the following list of questions:

• What events have been covered in the media recently?

• Does the event I'm considering for my presentation interest me? How much do I know about it already?

• What format and technology will I use in my presentation? Do I have the skills needed to use these effectively?

Once students have selected an event, remind them to develop a clear outline. From there, they can write a detailed narrative.

 For **writing support** for students at varying proficiency levels, see the **Text X-Ray** on page 296D.

Present and Lead a Discussion Invite students to agree upon rules for conducting the discussion. They may wish all group members to respond after being called upon, to keep their remarks within a time limit, and to invite questions from the audience.

Remind students to come to the discussion well prepared. Students may wish to review their presentation beforehand so they can anticipate questions and rehearse talking points. Remind students to participate fully, to listen actively, and to respond thoughtfully and with respect to others.

RESPOND TO THE ESSENTIAL QUESTION

Allow time for students to add details from the excerpt from *Gandhi: The Rise to Fame* to their Unit 4 Response Logs.

EL ## ENGLISH LEARNER SUPPORT

Present and Lead a Discussion Restate the discussion prompt as a question: How did the media that I chose for my multimodal presentation affect how my audience perceived the topic? Have students write a statement (in their home language, if they wish) of what they wanted their presentation to achieve. Then give students a few minutes to list the media that they used. Turn some of the questions from the text into sentence frames to help students formulate their ideas for the discussion: *Because I used [type of media], my audience understood _____. If I had included [type of media], maybe my audience would have understood _____ better.*

SUBSTANTIAL/MODERATE

APPLY

COMPARE ACCOUNTS

Emphasize that students should use the Venn diagram to compare how the letter and film formats affected their overall understanding of Gandhi's beliefs and actions. As groups of students collaborate to complete the diagram, encourage students to refer to their notes and, if they wish, to reread the text of "Letter to Viceroy, Lord Irwin" or to rewatch the film clip.

ANALYZE THE ACCOUNTS

Possible answers:

1. **DOK 2:** *The formal word choice in the letter shows that its audience was the Viceroy, while the language of the documentary reflects that its audience is more modern and interested in learning about Gandhi.*

2. **DOK 4:** *The letter is more closely focused on presenting an effective argument, while the film seeks to provide a wider historical panorama of an important figure in India's history. An argument would be more likely to use order of importance to organize ideas; a biography would use chronological order to provide context.*

3. **DOK 3:** *The letter's strength lies in the fact that it is a primary source. The firsthand account presents an argument from a renowned figure. A weakness might be that some audiences may find the vocabulary and formality of the letter difficult, or they may lack sufficient understanding of this time in India's history. The documentary film has the strength of a contemporary viewpoint, and the visual medium would engage visual learners to better understand the topic. A weakness might be a secondhand point of view that dilutes the historical facts.*

4. **DOK 4:** *The letter provides Gandhi's argument in his own words, while the images, narration, and music in the documentary combine to give audiences a rich understanding of Gandhi.*

💬 **RESPOND**

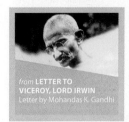

from **LETTER TO VICEROY, LORD IRWIN**
Letter by Mohandas K. Gandhi

from **GANDHI: THE RISE TO FAME**
Documentary Film by BBC

302   Unit 4

Collaborate & Compare

COMPARE ACCOUNTS

When you compare two or more perspectives of the same material in different formats or genres, you **synthesize** the information, making connections and building on key ideas. Sometimes you can get a more thorough understanding of the topic by experiencing the material in different formats. This especially is true for historical topics when you can read, view, or hear both a primary source and a secondary source, such as a letter and a film about the topic.

In a small group, complete the Venn diagram to show some similarities and differences in the information, arguments, ideas, and points of view presented in the letter and the film. One example is completed for you.

Letter   **Both**   **Film**

"Letter to Viceroy, Lord Irwin": Gandhi's own words before the Salt March   *both justify the salt issues as a valid protest*   *Gandhi: Rise to Fame: emphasizes the Salt March and its aftermath*

ANALYZE THE ACCOUNTS

Discuss these questions in your group.

1. **Interpret** Describe the tone and word choice of the author and narrator, providing examples from the letter and film. What can you infer from those word choices about the purposes of each account?

2. **Evaluate** In the documentary, the history of Gandhi's rise to fame is documented in chronological order with the use of present-day narration and commentary interspersed with some supporting archival images. Why is this an effective way to organize a biography but not an argument, as was presented in the letter?

3. **Compare** What are some of the strengths and weaknesses of both the letter and the film?

4. **Synthesize** How do the film and letter work together to create a fuller picture of Gandhi than either could alone?

TO CHALLENGE STUDENTS . . .

Practice and Apply Prompt students to find out more about Gandhi or a specific event they're interested in by asking a research question, such as "Why was the Salt March important?" In addition to Gandhi's letter and the BBC documentary film, suggest that students use a source from their previous research or find a new one that is also reliable. Have students identify information that is common among all three sources and information that differs. Ask them to identify and evaluate the reasons behind the differences. Then have students write or present a brief response to their research question based on information from all three sources.

COMPARE AND DEBATE

Now, your group can continue exploring the ideas in these different formats by participating in a debate to answer this question: Which format communicates Gandhi's ideas more effectively, the letter or the film?

Follow these steps:

1. **Form teams** of two to three students each with half defending the letter as more effective and half defending the film clip.

2. **Gather evidence** from both the letter and the film to support your team's position. Prepare a chart such as the following to help you gather evidence.

Key Idea	How Best To Communicate Idea	Why This Medium is Effective	Why Other Medium is Less Effective

3. **Follow the rules** of debating:
   - ❏ Appoint a **moderator** to present the topic and goals of the debate, keep track of the time, keep the debate moving, and introduce and thank the participants.
   - ❏ As a participant, anticipate possible **opposing claims**. Include evidence in your preparation to counter those claims.
   - ❏ Follow the **moderator's instructions** on whose turn it is to speak and how much time each speaker has.
   - ❏ Maintain a **respectful presentation** for the exchange of ideas.

4. **Write a brief evaluation** of which side presented a more compelling argument.

RESPOND

Go to the **Speaking and Listening Studio** to find more information on tracing a speaker's argument.

APPLY

COMPARE AND DEBATE

The following tips can help the classroom debate go smoothly.

1. **Form teams** Depending on your class, you may allow students to choose their own groups, or you may assign students to groups based on their preference to defend the letter or the film clip.

2. **Gather evidence** As students prepare the evidence charts, remind them to go back and review all of the notes they've taken—for both the letter and the film clip.

3. **Follow the rules** You may choose to act as the moderator, or choose a student (or volunteer) to take on this role. As students prepare for the debate, encourage them to practice and refine their opening statements and monitor how much time each speaker is taking. Remind them to anticipate and practice responding to opposing claims.

4. **Write a brief evaluation** Provide guiding questions to help students evaluate the results of the debate. For example:
   - How effectively did the team present reasons and evidence?
   - Was the team effective in countering opposing claims? Why or why not?
   - How well did team members follow the rules of the debate and treat everyone with respect?

 ENGLISH LEARNER SUPPORT

Analyze Accounts in Different Media Review the terms *documentary, medium, point of view,* and *purpose.* Then have students compare the letter and the film as follows.

- Instruct students to reread the letter to note which parts they find most striking, memorable, or persuasive. In pairs, have them discuss whether these parts could be communicated as effectively through video. Next, ask students to watch the film clip again, noting the parts that make the strongest impression on them. Have them discuss in pairs whether the same effects of the film clip could have been achieved in print. **MODERATE/LIGHT**

- Instruct students to make a chart reflecting their analyses. Have students list what is emphasized in each source, what features of the medium are used to emphasize the details listed, and what they conclude about whether the same details could be treated as effectively in the other medium. **LIGHT**

INDEPENDENT READING

READER'S CHOICE

Setting a Purpose Have students review their Unit 4 Response Log and think about what they've already learned about what we need in order to feel free. As they choose their Independent Reading selections, encourage them to consider what more they want to know.

NOTICE NOTE

Explain that some selections may contain multiple signposts; others may contain only one. The same type of signpost may occur many times in the same text.

LEARNING MINDSET

Persistence Tell students that persistence is about not giving up when tasks get challenging. Explain that persistence is an important part of having a learning mindset because effort is the key to growth. Ask students for examples of positive thinking that show persistence, for example, "I know I can do this if I keep trying."

 INDEPENDENT READING

? ESSENTIAL QUESTION:

What do we need in order to feel free?

Reader's Choice

Setting a Purpose Select one or more of these options from your eBook to continue your exploration of the Essential Question.

- Read the descriptions to see which text grabs your interest.
- Think about which genres you enjoy reading.

Notice & Note

In this unit, you practiced asking a **Big Question** and noticing and noting two signposts: **Extreme or Absolute Language** and **Quoted Words.** As you read independently, these signposts and others will aid your understanding. Below are the anchor questions to ask when you read literature and nonfiction.

Reading Literature: Stories, Poems, and Plays		
Signpost	**Anchor Question**	**Lesson**
Contrasts and Contradictions	Why did the character act that way?	p. 145
Aha Moment	How might this change things?	p. 394
Tough Questions	What does this make me wonder about?	p. 2
Words of the Wiser	What's the lesson for the character?	p. 3
Again and Again	Why might the author keep bringing this up?	p. 145
Memory Moment	Why is this memory important?	p. 3

Reading Nonfiction: Essays, Articles, and Arguments		
Signpost	**Anchor Question**	**Lesson**
Big Questions	What surprised me? What did the author think I already knew? What challenged, changed, or confirmed what I already knew?	p. 220 p. 319 p. 74
Contrasts and Contradictions	What is the difference, and why does it matter?	p. 318
Extreme or Absolute Language	Why did the author use this language?	p. 221
Numbers and Stats	Why did the author use these numbers or amounts?	p. 75
Quoted Words	Why was this person quoted or cited, and what did this add?	p. 221
Word Gaps	Do I know this word from someplace else? Does it seem like technical talk for this topic? Do clues in the sentence help me understand the word?	p. 75

 ENGLISH LEARNER SUPPORT

Develop Fluency Select a passage from a text that matches students' reading abilities. Read the passage aloud while students follow along silently.

- Echo read the passage by reading aloud one sentence and then having students repeat the sentence back to you. Then check their comprehension by asking yes/no questions. **SUBSTANTIAL**
- Have students read and then reread the passage silently. Have them time their reading to track improvements. Check their comprehension by asking yes/no questions. **MODERATE**

- Ask students to select a text and slowly read the passage, marking unfamiliar words or features. Check their comprehension by discussing their notes and having students identify key points in the reading. **LIGHT**

 Go to the **Reading Studio** for additional support in developing fluency.

You can preview these texts in Unit 4 of your eBook.

Then, check off the text or texts that you select to read on your own.

SPEECH

from **Speech at the March on Washington**
Josephine Baker

An international musical and political icon speaks about civil rights at the 1963 March on Washington.

SHORT STORY

The Book of the Dead
Edwidge Danticat

A young Haitian-American sculptor must come to terms with her father's troubled past.

POEM

Cloudy Day
Jimmy Santiago Baca

A poet explores his ability to survive and endure his time in prison.

HISTORY

from **Crispus Attucks**
Kareem Abdul-Jabbar

Learn the story of Crispus Attucks, an African American remembered as the first American to die in the Revolutionary War.

Collaborate and Share   Discuss with a partner what you learned from at least one of your independent readings.

- Give a brief synopsis or summary of the text.
- Describe any signposts that you noticed in the text and explain what they revealed to you.
- Describe what you most enjoyed or found most challenging about the text. Give specific examples.
- Decide whether you would recommend the text to others. Why or why not?

 Go to the **Reading Studio** for more resources on **Notice & Note.**

MATCHING STUDENTS TO TEXTS

Use the following information to guide students in choosing their texts.

from **Speech at the March on Washington** Lexile: 860L
   Genre: speech
   Overall Rating: Accessible

The Book of the Dead   Lexile: 920L
   Genre: short story
   Overall Rating: Accessible

Cloudy Day
   Genre: poem
   Overall Rating: Accessible

from **Crispus Attucks**   Lexile: 970L
   Genre: history
   Overall Rating: Accessible

Collaborate and Share   To assess how well students read the selections, walk around the room and listen to their conversations. Encourage students to be focused and specific in their comments.

 Online **for Assessment**

- Independent Reading Selection Tests

Encourage students to visit the **Reading Studio** to download a handy bookmark of **NOTICE & NOTE** signposts.

WHEN STUDENTS STRUGGLE . . .

Keep a Reading Log   As students read their selected texts, have them keep a reading log for each selection to note signposts and their thoughts about them. Use their logs to assess how well they are noticing and reflecting on elements of their texts.

Reading Log for (Title)		
Location	**Signpost I Noticed**	**My Notes About It**

UNIT 4 Tasks

- **WRITE AN ARGUMENT**
- **DELIVER AN ARGUMENT**

MENTOR TEXT

LETTER TO VICEROY, LORD IRWIN

Letter by
Mohandas K. Gandhi

LEARNING OBJECTIVES

Writing Task

- Write an argument about what freedom means.
- Use strategies to plan and organize ideas for an argument.
- Develop a focused, structured draft of an argument.
- Use the Mentor Text as a model for an argument.
- Revise drafts for use of claims and counterclaims.
- Revise drafts incorporating reasons and evidence.
- Edit drafts to incorporate standard English conventions.
- Use a rubric to evaluate writing.
- Publish writing to share it with an audience.
- **Language** Identify and discuss correct end punctuation in sentences.

Speaking and Listening Task

- Adapt an argument into an oral presentation.
- Deliver a presentation to an audience.
- Listen actively to a presentation.
- **Language** Practice using a variety of sentence types.

Assign the Writing Task in **Ed.**

Online

RESOURCES

- Unit 4 Response Log
- Reading Studio: Notice & Note
- Writing Studio: Writing Arguments
- Speaking and Listening Studio: Giving a Presentation
- Grammar Studio: Capitalization; Modules 11–12: Punctuation; Module 13: Spelling

Language X-Ray: English Learner Support

Use the instruction below and the supports and scaffolds in the Teacher's Edition to help you guide students at different proficiency levels.

INTRODUCE THE WRITING TASK

Explain that an **argument** is a type of writing in which the author takes a position on a topic and then offers reasons backed by evidence to support that position. In the introduction, the writer discusses the topic in a general way, explains why it is important, and then states a position by making a claim expressed in a clear, concise thesis statement. The body of an argument develops the claim with reasons and supporting evidence. Counterclaims, or opposing arguments, are also discussed to provide additional support. Paragraphs are presented in a logical order with smooth transitions from one to the next. The conclusion restates the thesis with a claim, synthesizes the key points of the argument, and offers a new insight.

Point out that the selections in this unit deal with the theme of what we need in order to feel free. Provide sentence frames to help students explore ideas related to this theme. For example: *In order to feel free, a person needs to* _____ . Assist students as they brainstorm words and phrases such as *have equal rights in society*. Have pairs of students work together to write an original thesis statement related to freedom.

WRITING

Use Correct End Punctuation

Emphasize the importance of using correct end punctuation to make sentence meaning clear.

Use the following supports with students at varying proficiency levels:

- Review examples of the four sentences types: declarative, interrogative, imperative, and exclamatory. Note the end punctuation for each type of sentence. **SUBSTANTIAL**
- Instruct students to delete the semicolons and add end punctuation to these sentences: *Gandhi was born in India; Do you know when Gandhi wrote to the Viceroy; Read Gandhi's letter; How brave Gandhi was.* **MODERATE**
- Once students have completed drafts of their arguments, have them work with a partner to determine if they used correct end punctuation. **LIGHT**

SPEAKING AND LISTENING

Listen to Pitch and Pauses

Provide oral practice in hearing pitch and identifying pauses in different types of sentences.

Use the following supports with students at varying proficiency levels:

- Read paragraphs 2–3 of Gandhi's letter. Tell students to raise their hands when they hear a question. **SUBSTANTIAL**
- Read paragraph 4 of Gandhi's letter. Have students raise their hands every time they hear a pause that indicates the end of a sentence. **MODERATE**
- Discuss how pauses and changing pitch help a listener. Ask: Why do we pause after a sentence? How does changing pitch help us understand sentence meaning? **LIGHT**

WRITING

WRITE AN ARGUMENT

Have a volunteer read aloud the introductory paragraph and then discuss the writing task with students. Encourage them to review the notes they made in the Unit 4 Response Log before they begin planning and writing their drafts.

USE THE MENTOR TEXT

Explain to students that their arguments will have the same key features found in "Letter to Viceroy, Lord Irwin" by Mohandas K. Gandhi and "Letter from Birmingham Jail" by Martin Luther King Jr. Like these arguments, theirs will present and develop a clear and specific claim, their reasons for making it, and evidence to support it. Their arguments will also discuss counterarguments, or arguments with an opposing position. Remind students that they should use effective transitions to connect ideas and maintain a formal tone. Emphasize that in the conclusion, they should briefly summarize their claim and the key evidence presented in their argument and include a thought-provoking idea for their readers to consider.

WRITING PROMPT

Discuss the prompt with students and review the checklist of key points they should consider as they write their arguments. Encourage them to ask questions about any part of the assignment they do not understand. Emphasize that the goal of their arguments is to make and support a claim about what freedom means to them.

 WRITING TASK

Write an Argument

 Go to the **Writing Studio** for help writing an argument.

This unit explores the idea of freedom, what it means, and what people have done to become free. For this writing task, you will write an argument that reveals what freedom means to you. For an example of a well-written argumentative text you can use as a mentor text, review Gandhi's "Letter to Viceroy, Lord Irwin" or King's "Letter from Birmingham Jail."

As you write your argument, you will want to look at the notes you made in your Response Log after reading the texts in this unit.

Writing Prompt

Read the information in the box below.

This is the topic or context for your argument.

> Freedom means different things to different people.

Think carefully about the following question.

This is the Essential Question of the unit. Circle the most important words in the question.

> What do we need in order to feel free?

Now mark the words that identify exactly what you are supposed to write.

Write an argument about what freedom means to you.

Be sure to—

Review these points as you write and again when you finish. Make any needed changes.

- ❏ make a clear, specific claim
- ❏ develop the claim with valid reasons and relevant evidence
- ❏ anticipate and address counterclaims, or opposing arguments, by providing counterarguments
- ❏ use transitions to link reasons and evidence to the claim
- ❏ maintain a formal tone through the use of standard English
- ❏ conclude by effectively summarizing the argument and leaving readers with a thought-provoking idea

---

LEARNING MINDSET

Belonging Remind students that the classroom is a learning community and that they are all valuable members of it. Emphasize the importance of everyone making contributions during class activities, such as by taking on the roles of timekeeper, notetaker, facilitator, or presenter during small-group discussions. Point out that by encouraging each other throughout the writing process, they'll help both themselves and their classmates feel like part of the team. During peer reviews, remind them to be supportive and make constructive suggestions to help improve each other's arguments.

① Plan

Writing an argument depends on good planning. Think about the selections you've read in this unit and the questions they raise about political, physical, and emotional freedom. Does the meaning of freedom vary from person to person and culture to culture, or is it more universal? Use the word web below to help you explore your thoughts and feelings about freedom. Include ideas from the unit texts.

You also need to think about what you hope to achieve in your argument and for whom you are writing—your purpose and your audience.

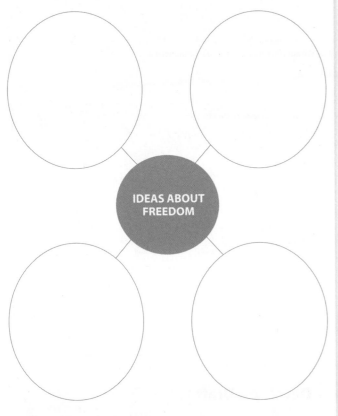

IDEAS ABOUT FREEDOM

Background Reading Review the notes you have taken in your Response Log after reading the texts in this unit. These texts provide background reading that will help you think about what you want to say in your argument.

WRITING TASK

Go to **Writing Arguments: What Is a Claim?** for help planning your argument.

Notice & Note

From Reading to Writing

As you plan your argument, apply what you've learned about signposts to your own writing. Think about how you can incorporate **Quoted Words** into your argument.

Go to the **Reading Studio** for more resources on Notice & Note.

Use the notes from your Response Log as you plan your argument.

UNIT 4
RESPONSE LOG

① PLAN

Read the introductory text. Discuss the three dimensions of freedom mentioned: political, physical, and emotional. If necessary, model questions for thought: Do you think the three types of freedom are equal to one another, or do you think one is more important than the others? Does freedom depend on who you are or where you live? Are the principles of freedom the same for everyone, everywhere? Before students complete the word web, remind them to think about the purpose and audience of their arguments.

■ English Learner Support

Understand Academic Language Emphasize that students will be asking themselves questions about freedom and filling in the web with their ideas. First, make sure they understand the terms *purpose* and *audience*. Tell them that their purpose is to make a claim about the meaning of freedom. To do this, they will compare different ideas about freedom. Organize small groups of students with a range of language proficiencies and encourage group discussion of examples of claims that might be made about the meaning of freedom. **ALL LEVELS**

▶ NOTICE & NOTE

From Reading to Writing Discuss the focus of the Quoted Words signpost in which the writer provides the exact words of an expert or someone who was a participant or a witness to an event. Emphasize that a Quoted Words signpost is a good moment to ask, "How are this person's words important to the idea of freedom?"

Background Reading Encourage students to review the notes in their Response Log for Unit 4. Explain that these notes will contain ideas that they may find useful as they plan their arguments.

WHEN STUDENTS STRUGGLE . . .

Make Claims Have students work in small groups to brainstorm possible topics about the meaning of freedom based on different types of claims.

- Have students complete a graphic organizer such as a word web or two-column chart that provides five spaces labeled *fact, definition, cause and effect, values,* and *policies.*
- Explain that the goal is to record one example for each type of claim. Tell students to rotate among group members with each offering a suggestion for a possible claim.
- After five minutes or so, call on volunteers to read aloud the suggestions and discuss each example and the type of claim it represents.

Organize Your Ideas Discuss the importance of organizing ideas in an outline before students begin drafting their arguments. Review the chart's headings and explain that students can combine the information on their chart into an outline as the basis for a well-thought-out five-paragraph argument. Connect the ideas in the planning chart with a traditional outline, like the one below:

I. Introduction: Claim and Counterclaim

II. Reason 1 with Evidence

III. Reason 2 with Evidence

IV. Reason 3 with Evidence

V. Conclusion: Summary of Argument and Thought-Provoking Idea

② DEVELOP A DRAFT

Remind students to follow their outlines as they draft their arguments. Emphasize that an outline is a preliminary step in the writing process. Remind students that if new ideas come to them during the drafting stage, they can and should make changes to their plans.

■ English Learner Support

Develop a Thesis Statement with a Claim Emphasize the importance of drafting a clear thesis statement that contains a claim that can be debated. Remind students that the goal of an argument is to take a side and defend it. To support students, provide the following sentence frames:

- *I believe that true freedom can only be achieved by _____.*
- *One reason I believe this is _____.*
  SUBSTANTIAL/MODERATE

WRITING TASK

Go to **Writing Arguments: Building Effective Support** for help developing and organizing your ideas.

Organize Your Ideas Use the chart below to write an outline with a clear thesis statement. Your thesis should express the claim you want to support. Acknowledge a counterclaim, or opposing view, that you will address by providing a counterargument. Then, clearly organize your reasons and relevant evidence, progressing logically from one idea to the next. Conduct more research to find additional details and examples you need. Write a conclusion that follows logically from the information you've presented.

ARGUMENT: THE NATURE OF FREEDOM		
Thesis with Claim:		
Why the audience might not agree (counterclaim):		
Why the audience should agree:		
Reason 1	Reason 2	Reason 3
Evidence	Evidence	Evidence
Conclusion:		

You might prefer to draft your essay online.

② Develop a Draft

Once you have completed your planning activities, you can begin drafting your argument. Use your outline or graphic organizer to keep your argument on track. Refer to any notes you took as you studied the texts in the collection so that you can use evidence from multiple texts. Use word processing software or an online writing app to make it easier to make changes or move sentences around later when you are ready to revise your first draft.

© Houghton Mifflin Harcourt Publishing Company

WHEN STUDENTS STRUGGLE . . .

Improving Writing Flow Students often have difficulty getting started when tackling a new task, such as writing an argument. Discuss the following suggestions:

- Students should set aside a specific time and place to work on their drafts, and shut off any distractions (for example, a TV, smartphone, and background music).
- Students should "dive in" where they are most comfortable, even if that is not the first paragraph based on their outlines.
- Students should focus on the content and ideas of their arguments.
- At this point, they should not be concerned with mechanical details such as grammar, usage, punctuation, and spelling.

WRITING TASK

Use the Mentor Text

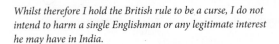

Genre Characteristics

In any argument, it's crucial to write a clear thesis statement with your claim. If your reader doesn't understand the core of your argument, the rest of what you write will not fully make sense, no matter how well you write it. Notice how Gandhi states his claim in the first paragraph of "Letter to Viceroy, Lord Irwin."

> *Whilst therefore I hold the British rule to be a curse, I do not intend to harm a single Englishman or any legitimate interest he may have in India.*

> Gandhi makes a clear, strong statement by stating that British rule is a curse.

Apply What You've Learned State your claim clearly in the first paragraph of your argument.

Author's Craft

When pressing home an argument, authors frequently use repetition to make their points more effectively. Gandhi uses the repetition of grammatical structure, or parallel structure, when he gives evidence for why he considers British rule over India a curse.

> It has impoverished the dumb millions by a system of progressive exploitation and by a ruinously expensive military and civil administration which the country can never afford.
> It has reduced us politically to serfdom. It has sapped the foundations of our culture, and, by the policy of disarmament, it has degraded us spiritually.

> The repetition of the words "It has . . ." indicates three points he is making.

Apply What You've Learned When you present evidence for your claim, use words effectively as well as clearly.

Write an Argument 309

WHY THIS MENTOR TEXT?

Gandhi's "Letter to Viceroy, Lord Irwin" provides a good example of an argument. Use the instruction below to model how a thesis statement with a claim forms the central idea of an argument and how the use of grammatical repetition can enhance the effectiveness of supporting examples.

USE THE MENTOR TEXT

Genre Characteristics Discuss the introductory text. Ask a volunteer to read aloud the example of an effective claim from Gandhi's argument. Ask: How does Gandhi's claim grab the readers' attention? *(the use of the word* curse, *which is then balanced by the rational behavior he says he will engage in by not harming any English person or interest in India)*

Discuss other ways to develop a thesis statement with a claim in an argument. Ask: What type of claim might be appropriate if you want to argue the idea that we often misunderstand what is meant by the word *freedom*? *(definition)*

Author's Craft Have a volunteer read aloud the introduction to this section and the example from the mentor text. Tell students to underline the three clauses that begin with "It has." Discuss the meaning of each clause and how the repetition ties together the three reasons.

(EL) ENGLISH LEARNER SUPPORT

Use the Mentor Text Use the following supports with students at varying proficiency levels:

- Read aloud the Genre Characteristics introduction, and use gestures to help students understand the phrase "core of the argument." **SUBSTANTIAL**

- Read aloud the Author's Craft introduction, and invite students to ask about any words or phrases that are unclear. Demonstrate parallel structure by listing the four repeated phrases from the excerpt on the board. **MODERATE**

- Read aloud the repetition of the words *it has* _____ in the second excerpt. Have students write two or three statements about the meaning of freedom using repetition. For example: *Freedom is not* _____. *Freedom is* _____. Then have partners read their statements to each other, giving feedback about the effectiveness of the repetition. **LIGHT**

WRITING

3 REVISE

Have students determine how they can improve their drafts by answering each question posed in the Revision Guide. Call on volunteers to model their revision techniques.

With a Partner Have students work with peer reviewers to evaluate drafts of their arguments. Use the following questions as a guide for peer review:

- Is my claim specific, and does it express where I stand?
- Which reasons are not clearly stated?
- Does my evidence support my claim and the reasons I have presented?
- Will my concluding insight engage my readers and encourage them to think about the topic further?

Encourage students to carefully evaluate reviewers' comments as they further develop their arguments.

WRITING TASK

3 Revise

Go to **Writing Arguments: Formal Style** for help revising your argument.

On Your Own When you revise your draft, check for clear organization and the inclusion of all elements of your argument. As you revise, think about whether you have achieved your purpose for your intended audience. The Revision Guide will help you focus on specific elements to make your writing stronger.

REVISION GUIDE

Ask Yourself	Tips	Revision Techniques
1. Does the introduction state a clear claim?	**Underline** the claim.	**Add** a claim or **revise** the claim to make it clearer.
2. Does the argument address one or more counterclaims?	**Mark** both the counterclaim and the response to it.	**Add** a counterclaim and counterargument that addresses the counterclaim.
3. Are reasons and evidence presented in a logical, organized way?	**Mark** each important idea and the supporting reasons or evidence.	**Reorganize** ideas to make the structure more logical.
4. Are appropriate and varied transitions used to link ideas?	**Note** transitions that move ideas smoothly from paragraph to paragraph.	**Add** transition words and phrases to provide continuity.
5. Does the conclusion give the reader something to think about?	**Underline** the concluding insight offered to readers.	**Add** a final, thought-provoking statement about freedom.
6. Is an appropriately formal tone used throughout the argument?	**Highlight** each academic word or phrase that contributes to a formal tone.	**Replace** informal word choices and sentence structures as needed.

ACADEMIC VOCABULARY
As you conduct your peer review, try to use these words.

- ❏ comprehensive
- ❏ equivalent
- ❏ incentive
- ❏ innovate
- ❏ subordinate

With a Partner After you have worked through the Revision Guide on your own, exchange papers with a partner. Evaluate each other's drafts in a peer review, using the chart to guide you. Give your partner specific suggestions for improving clarity, organization, and the development of ideas.

When receiving feedback from your partner, listen attentively and ask questions to make sure you fully understand the revision suggestions.

ENGLISH LEARNER SUPPORT

Use Transitions in Arguments Explain that good writers use transitions to link ideas. Introduce students to transitional words and phrases common in arguments. For example:

- *Illustrate by examples:* for example, for instance, in other words, such as
- *Addition:* and, in addition to, also, furthermore
- *Consequence:* because, since, so, as a result of
- *Contrast:* however, nevertheless, on the one (other) hand, in spite of
- *Summary:* in conclusion, therefore, finally, accordingly

Encourage students to use a few of these transitional phrases in their arguments.
SUBSTANTIAL/MODERATE

4 Edit

After you have drafted and revised your argument, there is one final step before you're ready to publish. In the editing process, you will make sure that your writing meets the conventions of grammar, spelling, and word usage.

Language Conventions

Correct Writing Conventions One definition of a **convention** is a way of doing things that most people accept. In a sense, writing is all about conventions. We agree to spell words in a certain way, using certain patterns of letters to stand for the sounds we use. We also agree to use a period to show that we've finished a sentence and quotation marks to indicate that we are using someone else's words.

All of these conventions make text easier to read. Ignoring the conventions of grammar, spelling, punctuation, and capitalization can indicate either that you don't care about what you're communicating or that you did not spend enough time on your writing. Either way, you are signaling to the reader that they don't need to take your argument seriously.

Finally, while it may be tempting to set some words in all capital letters for emphasis when you are writing an argument, departing from this convention tells readers that they can't trust what you're saying. Reserve capital letters for proper nouns, initials, and the beginnings of sentences, and let your logical and well-crafted argument speak for itself.

 Go to the **Grammar Studio** to learn more about conventions of capitalization, punctuation, and spelling.

5 Publish

When you choose a way to share your argument, consider who your audience is and what method of publication they would find understandable, clear, and convincing. Consider these options:

- Deliver your argument as an oral presentation.
- Use online software to prepare a slide show presentation.
- Present your argument as a letter to the editor. Submit it to your school or community newspaper or an online magazine.

© Houghton Mifflin Harcourt Publishing Company

Write an Argument   311

WRITING

4 EDIT

Encourage students to read their drafts aloud multiple times. During their first reading, have students focus on the clarity of their ideas and the use of transitions. During their second reading, suggest that students focus on grammar and usage. During a third reading, students should focus on the punctuation and spelling in their arguments.

For **writing support** for students at varying proficiency levels, use the **Language X-Ray** on page 306B.

LANGUAGE CONVENTIONS

Correct Writing Conventions Remind students that they have studied writing conventions this year and in previous grades. Make sure that students understand what is involved in each of the four major areas—grammar, usage, punctuation, and spelling—and are comfortable with any associated academic vocabulary.

Review checklists for grammar, usage, punctuation, and spelling that you may have previously handed out. Alternatively, have groups of three or four students prepare checklists of their own in one of these four areas. Discuss student-composed checklists and have students make any necessary corrections. Then, use the checklists to create a class handbook.

5 PUBLISH

Discuss the three publishing options suggested. Have students identify the challenges that each option presents and the types of changes that would be required to transform their written arguments into oral or visual presentations. Encourage students who listen to, watch, or read the arguments of their classmates to make notes and offer comments about things they liked and any suggestions they have for improvement.

EL ENGLISH LEARNER SUPPORT

Use a Checklist to Edit Writing Teach and model how to use a checklist (supplied by you or created by students) to edit for grammar, usage, punctuation, and spelling. For example, for standard grammar and usage, review rules for subject-verb agreement, pronoun agreement, and appropriate verb tenses. For spelling, use sentence frames to remind students of the relationships between sounds and letters: *The word _____ is pronounced _____. Therefore it is spelled _____. This word is spelled correctly/incorrectly because _____.*
ALL LEVELS

WRITING

USE THE SCORING GUIDE

Allow students time to read the scoring guide. Encourage them to ask questions about any ideas, sentences, phrases, or words they find unclear. Tell partners to exchange their final arguments and score them using the guidelines. Have each student reviewer write a paragraph explaining the reason for the score he or she awarded in each major category.

Use the scoring guide to evaluate your argument.

	WRITING TASK SCORING GUIDE: ARGUMENT		
	Organization/Progression	**Development of Ideas**	**Use of Language and Conventions**
4	• The organization is effective and appropriate to the purpose. • All ideas center on a specific claim. • Transitions clearly show the relationships among ideas.	• The introduction catches the reader's attention and clearly states the claim. • Reasons are compelling and supported by evidence including quotations and facts. • A counterclaim is effectively presented and addressed. • The conclusion synthesizes the ideas, effectively summarizes the argument, and provides a thought-provoking insight.	• Language and word choice is purposeful and precise. • The style is appropriately formal. • Spelling, capitalization, and punctuation are correct. • Grammar and usage are correct.
3	• The organization is, for the most part, effective and appropriate to the purpose. • Most ideas are focused on the claim. • A few more transitions are needed to show the relationship among ideas.	• The introduction could be more engaging. The claim is stated. • Appropriate reasons for the claim are supported by relevant evidence. • A counterclaim is presented and addressed. • The conclusion summarizes the argument effectively.	• Language is for the most part specific and clear. • The style is generally formal. • Minor spelling, capitalization, and punctuation mistakes do not interfere with the message. • Some grammar and usage errors occur but do not cause confusion.
2	• The organization is evident but is not always appropriate to the purpose. • Only some ideas are focused on the claim presented in the thesis. • Relationships among ideas are sometimes unclear.	• The introduction is not engaging. A vague claim is stated. • One or more reasons may be provided but lack sufficient evidence. • A counterclaim may be hinted at or not adequately addressed. • The conclusion merely restates the claim.	• Language is somewhat vague and unclear. • The style is often informal. • Spelling, capitalization, and punctuation are often incorrect. • Several errors in grammar and usage appear.
1	• The organization is not apparent. • Ideas are often tangential to a claim. • No transitions are used, making the argument difficult to understand.	• The introduction is missing or fails to make a claim. • Reasons are irrelevant or unsupported by evidence. • A counterclaim is either absent or not addressed. • The conclusion is missing.	• The style of language is inappropriate for the text. • Many spelling, capitalization, and punctuation errors make reading difficult. • Grammatical and usage errors cause significant confusion.

Deliver an Argument

 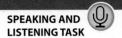

You will now prepare to deliver your argument as an oral presentation to your classmates. You also will listen to your classmates' arguments, ask questions to better understand their ideas, and help them improve their presentations.

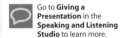 Go to **Giving a Presentation** in the **Speaking and Listening Studio** to learn more.

① Adapt Your Argument for Presentation

Review your argument, and use the chart below to guide your presentation.

DELIVERING AN ARGUMENT PLANNING CHART		
Title and Introductory Paragraph	How can you revise your introduction to capture listeners' attention and make a powerful statement of your claim?	
Audience	What information will your audience already know about your claim? What counterclaims might they make? How will you address those counterclaims?	
Effective Language and Organization	Which parts of your argument should be simplified? Where can you add transitions to clarify relationships among ideas? How can you make your conclusion stronger?	
Delivery	What words or ideas might you emphasize with your voice or gestures to make your argument more convincing?	

Deliver an Argument **313**

DELIVER AN ARGUMENT

Introduce students to the Speaking and Listening Task. Ask: How is delivering and listening to an oral argument different from reading the argument silently? How can a presenter help listeners better understand the connections between ideas being presented? Emphasize the importance of highlighting ideas by adjusting reading rate, volume, and gestures; of employing counterarguments strategically; and of repeating key ideas as the argument proceeds.

① ADAPT YOUR ARGUMENT FOR PRESENTATION

Review the organization of the Delivering an Argument Planning Chart. Have students scan the four major sections in the left-hand column, moving from top to bottom. Have volunteers read aloud the questions for each major section that appear in the second column.

Model how to go about answering questions when students are uncertain of what is being requested or how to achieve the desired results. For example, when considering the title and introduction, suggest that students might open with a surprising statement, personal example, or memorable quotation to grab listeners' attention.

ENGLISH LEARNER SUPPORT

Adapt the Argument Use the following supports with students at varying proficiency levels:

- Help students identify effective gestures they can use when reading their introductions aloud. **SUBSTANTIAL**
- Review the questions in the chart to confirm student comprehension of key ideas. Then have students work independently to apply the questions to their arguments. **MODERATE**
- Have students discuss the questions in the chart with a partner before they begin writing their answers independently. **LIGHT**

② PRACTICE WITH A PARTNER OR GROUP

Review the discussion rules presented in the margin and provide students with an opportunity to ask questions about them. Review the information and tips about effectively using verbal and nonverbal techniques, ensuring that all the terms and ideas are clear. If necessary, model the techniques while reading aloud the mentor text.

Provide and Consider Advice for Improvement Read the introductory text about the role of listeners to practice presentations of oral arguments. Discuss the importance of taking notes about key ideas as well as brief comments that evaluate the presenter's use of verbal and nonverbal techniques. Ask: How can you use the notes you take while listening to students' oral arguments? *(to provide specific comments and suggestions for improvement)*

Emphasize the importance of mutual respect between listeners and presenters during practice presentations. Encourage presenters to ask questions about comments and suggestions they find confusing. Explain that, in the end, presenters must decide which comments they will incorporate into their final presentations.

 For **speaking and listening support** for students at varying proficiency levels, see the **Language X-Ray** on page 306B.

③ DELIVER YOUR ARGUMENT

Schedule time for students to make their final presentations. To make the best use of time, you may want to break the class into smaller groups and have students present to each other. Another strategy would be to schedule presentations over the course of several days. Encourage students to discuss how their classmates' suggestions helped them improve their presentations.

 SPEAKING AND LISTENING TASK

As you work to improve your own delivery and that of your classmates, follow these discussion rules:

- ❏ listen attentively
- ❏ be respectful and considerate of other students' feelings
- ❏ stay focused on one student's work at a time
- ❏ raise questions and counterarguments that might not have occurred to the author
- ❏ be clear and specific in your suggestions for improvement

② Practice with a Partner or Group

When you have adapted your argument, practice with a partner or group to improve your delivery.

Practice Effective Verbal Techniques

- ❏ **Enunciation.** Consider replacing words that you stumble over if you can find effective alternatives. Rearrange sentences that are not as understandable in speech as in writing.
- ❏ **Voice Modulation and Pitch** Use your voice to express enthusiasm, emphasis, or emotion.
- ❏ **Speaking Rate** Adjust your speaking rate to the points in your argument. Pause briefly at points you want your audience to ponder or consider carefully.
- ❏ **Volume** Adjust your volume to the size of the room and the distance of the audience.

Practice Effective Nonverbal Techniques

- ❏ **Eye Contact** Try to make eye contact with everyone in your audience at least once.
- ❏ **Facial Expression** Use facial expressions as well as your words and your voice to show your audience your feelings about various points of your argument.
- ❏ **Gestures** Don't force gestures, but add them if they improve meaning and interest.

Provide and Consider Advice for Improvement

As a listener, pay close attention to how effectively each speaker expresses and supports a point of view. Take notes about ways that presenters can improve their deliveries and more effectively use verbal and nonverbal techniques. Paraphrase and summarize each presenter's key ideas and main points to confirm your understanding, and ask questions to clarify any confusing ideas.

As a presenter, listen closely to questions and consider ways to revise your delivery to make sure your points are clear and logically sequenced. Remember to ask for suggestions about how you might make your delivery more interesting.

③ Deliver Your Argument

Use the advice you received during practice to make final changes to your argument delivery. Then, using effective verbal and nonverbal techniques, present your argument to your classmates.

WHEN STUDENTS STRUGGLE . . .

Use Visuals Explain that visuals can help a presenter remember key ideas and the structure of their presentation, and establish proper pacing. Discuss using slides, drawings, photos, or other images for the following elements for students giving an oral or slide show presentation:

- title
- thesis statement
- a summary
- opening quotation
- an important example
- counterarguments or contrasting ideas
- a final thought for further consideration

Point out that all text displayed should be concise and readable, and may include decorative elements for added emphasis.

Reflect on the Unit

In this writing task, you wrote about your idea of the meaning of freedom in the light of ideas and insights from the readings in this unit. Now is a good time to reflect on what you have learned.

Reflect on the Essential Question

- What do we need in order to feel free? How has your answer to this question changed since you first considered it when you started this unit?

- What are some examples from the texts you've read that show what freedom means to people?

Reflect on Your Reading

- Which selections were the most interesting or surprising to you?

- From which selection did you learn the most about the nature of freedom?

Reflect on the Writing Task

- What difficulties did you encounter while working on your argument? How might you avoid them next time?

- What part of the argument was the easiest and what part was the hardest to write? Why?

- What improvements did you make to your argument as you were revising?

UNIT 4 SELECTIONS
- "Letter from Birmingham Jail"
- "Elsewhere"
- "The Hawk Can Soar"
- "The Briefcase"
- *from* "Letter to Viceroy, Lord Irwin"
- *from Gandhi: The Rise to Fame*

Reflect on the Unit   315

REFLECT ON THE UNIT

Have students reflect independently on the questions presented under each of the three major headings. Tell students to think about each question and write notes on how they would respond. After students have completed these tasks, have them form small groups to discuss their responses. During these discussions, circulate about the classroom and note questions that seem to produce the liveliest conversations. Use these questions as the basis for a whole-class discussion that wraps up the unit.

 LEARNING MINDSET

Try Again Explain to students that it's natural for everyone learning a new skill or new information to make mistakes. Stress that the important thing is to use the mistake as an opportunity to grow. Encourage students to understand the value of making mistakes by presenting an account of how you or someone you know about learned by making a mistake and trying again by using a different strategy. For example, point out how sports teams respond after a loss: they'll go over which plays worked (and which didn't) and practice on improving certain plays or learning new ones. Emphasize that often it takes several attempts to succeed at learning anything worthwhile, whether a new skill, new concepts, or a new play for a sports team.

Instructional Overview and Resources

		Online **Resources**
	Instructional Focus	

Unit Introduction
Responses to Change

Instructional Focus
Unit 5 Essential Question
Unit 5 Academic Vocabulary

Resources
Stream to Start: Responses to Change
Unit 5 Response Log

ANALYZE & APPLY

from "Total Eclipse"
Essay by Annie Dillard
Lexile 760L

NOTICE & NOTE READING MODEL

Signposts
• Contrasts and Contradictions
• Extreme or Absolute Language
• Big Questions

Reading
• Analyze Literary Nonfiction
• Analyze Style

Writing: Write a Comparison

Speaking and Listening: Share Your Opinion

Vocabulary: Figurative Meanings

Language Conventions: Sentence Variety

🔊 **Audio**

Reading Studio: Notice & Note

Level Up Tutorials: Author's Style; Literal and Figurative Meanings

Writing Studio: Quoting and Paraphrasing Sources

Speaking and Listening Studio: Sharing Opinions in Collaborative Discussions

Grammar Studio: Module 4: Lesson 5: Sentence Structure

Mentor Text

from *The Fever*
Science Writing by Sonia Shah
Lexile 1150L

Reading
• Analyze Text Structure
• Analyze Purpose and Audience

Writing: Write a Procedural Brochure

Speaking and Listening: Follow and Give Instructions

Vocabulary: Affixes

Language Conventions: Subject-Verb Agreement

🔊 **Audio**

Reading Studio: Notice & Note

Level Up Tutorial: Cause-and-Effect Organization

Writing Studio: Writing Informative Texts

Speaking and Listening Studio: Participating in Collaborative Discussions

Vocabulary Studio: Affixes

Grammar Studio: Module 5: Lesson 2: Subject-Verb Agreement

"A Sound of Thunder"
Short Story by Ray Bradbury
Lexile 710L

Reading
• Analyze Plot and Setting
• Make Inferences

Writing: Write a Story

Speaking and Listening: Deliver a Sales Pitch

Vocabulary: Synonyms and Antonyms

Language Conventions: Transitions

🔊 **Audio**

Close Read Screencasts: Modeled Discussions

Reading Studio: Notice & Note

Level Up Tutorial: Author's Style; Setting

Writing Studio: Writing Narrative Texts

Speaking and Listening Studio: Delivering Your Speech

Vocabulary Studio: Synonyms and Antonyms

SUGGESTED PACING: 30 DAYS

Unit Introduction	*from* Total Eclipse	*from* The Fever	A Sound of Thunder
1	2 3 4 5 6	7 8 9 10 11	12 13 14 15 16 17

English Learner Support		Differentiated Instruction	Online Ed Assessment
• Build New Vocabulary			

English Learner Support		Differentiated Instruction	Assessment
• Text X-Ray • Use Cognates • Grasp Language Structures • Distinguish Verb Tenses • Practice Working with Synonyms	• Oral Assessment • Discuss Word Meanings • Language Conventions	**When Students Struggle** • Monitor, Annotate, and Ask • Clarify the Author's Meaning • Understand Complicated Text	**Selection Test**
• Text X-Ray • Use Cognates • Use Apostrophes • Understand Expressions • Summarize • Understand Idioms • Oral Assessment	• Discuss with a Small Group • Vocabulary Strategy • Identify Subject-Verb Agreement	**When Students Struggle** • Use Prereading Support • Identify Supporting Details **To Challenge Students** • Explore Electron Microscopy	**Selection Test**
• Text X-Ray • Use Cognates • Check Understanding • Understand Contractions • Confirm Understanding • Understand Plural Nouns • Understand Dashes • Practice Phonology • Analyze Onomatopoeia	• Analyze Description • Analyze Characterization • Analyze Idioms • Discuss Syntax • Oral Assessment • Discuss Connotations • Vocabulary Strategy • Language Conventions	**When Students Struggle** • Understand Style • Contrast Settings **To Challenge Students** • Conduct Research • Explore Figurative Language	**Selection Test**

5 P.M., Tuesday, August 23, 2005 18 > 19 > 20

from **Rivers and Tides/ Sonnets to Orpheus, Part Two, XII** 21 > 22 > 23 > 24 > 25

Independent Reading 26 > 27

End of Unit 28 > 29 > 30

UNIT 5 Continued

| | Instructional Focus | Online Ed Resources |

ANALYZE & APPLY

"5 P.M., Tuesday, August 23, 2005"
Poem by Patricia Smith

Reading
• Analyze Word Choice
• Create Mental Images

Writing: Write a Literary Analysis

Speaking and Listening: Give a Poetry Reading

 Audio

Reading Studio: Notice & Note

Level Up Tutorials: Historical and Cultural Context; Figurative Language

Writing Studio: Writing Analytical Texts

Speaking and Listening Studio: Delivering Your Recitation

COLLABORATE & COMPARE

from *Rivers and Tides*
Documentary Film by Thomas Riedelsheimer

· ·

"Sonnets to Orpheus, Part Two, XII"
Poem by Rainer Maria Rilke

Reading
• Analyze Media Techniques
• Analyze Purpose and Theme

Writing: Create a Reflection

Speaking and Listening: Share and Discuss Opinions

Audio

Reading Studio: Notice & Note

Level Up Tutorial: Analyzing Visuals

Speaking and Listening Studio: Participating in Collaborative Discussions

Collaborate and Compare

Reading: Compare Themes Across Genres

Speaking and Listening: Compare and Presents

Speaking and Listening Studio: Giving a Presentation

Online Ed INDEPENDENT READING

The Independent Reading selections are only available in the eBook.

 Go to the Reading Studio for more information on Notice & Note.

"The Norwegian Rat"
Short Story by Naguib Mahfouz
Lexile 990L

"After the Storm"
Memoir by Orhan Pamuk
Lexile 1330L

END OF UNIT

Writing Task: Write a Research Report

Reflect on the Unit

Writing: Write a Research Report

Language Conventions: Crediting a Source

Unit 5 Response Log

Mentor Text: from *The Fever*

Reading Studio: Notice & Note

Level Up Tutorial: Paraphrasing; Summarizing

Writing Studio: Conducting Research; Using Textual Evidence

Grammar Studio: Module 12: Lesson 4: Quotation Marks

English Learner Support	Differentiated Instruction	Online **Ed** Assessment
• Text X-Ray • Use Prereading Supports • Identify Personification • Analyze Metaphors • Oral Assessment	**When Students Struggle** • Identify Extended Metaphor • Provide Contextual Support • Analyze Figurative Language	**Selection Test**
• Text X-Ray • Analyze the Media • Use Content Area Vocabulary • Use Strategies to Decode Words • Develop Vocabulary • Use Present Perfect Verb Structure • Understand Ideas • Oral Assessment • Expand Vocabulary • Create a Reflection	**When Students Struggle** • Analyze Media	**Selection Tests**
• Ask Questions		
from *Simplexity* Science Writing by Jeffrey Kluger **Lexile 1490L**	from *The Metamorphosis* Novella by Franz Kafka **Lexile 1110L**	**Selection Tests**
• Language X-Ray • Understand Academic Language • Use Source Information • Use the Mentor Text • Spell Singular and Plural Forms • Use Correct Subject-Verb Agreement with Compound Subjects	**When Students Struggle** • Paraphrase Quotations • Use Note Cards **To Challenge Students** • Use Direct Quotations	**Unit Test**

Connect to the
? ESSENTIAL QUESTION

Ask a volunteer to read aloud the Essential Question. Have students pause to reflect. Prompt them to discuss changes that have occurred around them recently. Examples might include new cafeteria rules or an extreme weather event. Tell students to reflect on how they have handled these and other changes. What can we learn about ourselves based on our reactions to change?

■ English Learner Support

Build New Vocabulary Make sure students understand the Essential Question. If necessary, explain the following terms:

- *Changes* means "acts of altering, modifying, or making different."
- *Reveal* means "to make known something that is hidden."

Help students restate the question in simpler language: When things around us change, what do we learn about ourselves? **SUBSTANTIAL/MODERATE**

DISCUSS THE QUOTATION

Tell students that a proverb is "a short, pithy saying in frequent and widespread use that expresses a basic truth or practical precept." Have them read the proverb and take a moment to reflect. Discuss what the difference between building a wall and building a windmill might be. Suggest that students consider the difference between trying to keep out the winds of change and adapting to these winds. Have students discuss how the way we deal with change reveals who we are.

UNIT ⑤

RESPONSES TO CHANGE

? ESSENTIAL QUESTION:

How do changes around us reveal who we are?

> " When the wind of change blows, some build walls while others build windmills. "
>
> Chinese Proverb

 LEARNING MINDSET

Plan Discuss how planning helps make completing assignments and reaching other goals more manageable and efficient. Talk about how strengthening planning skills now will help students in the future, whether in school, at work, or with family and friends. For example, ask students to think about times they have planned to meet up with friends somewhere (for example, at a park, the movies, or a school event). Did they agree in advance about a time and place to meet? Do they plan how to get to and from the event from their homes? Give them examples of how they can apply planning skills in their lives right now, such as using a calendar to keep track of assignments, important events, and progress toward their academic and personal goals.

ACADEMIC VOCABULARY

Academic Vocabulary words are words you use when you discuss and write about texts. In this unit you will practice and learn five words.

☑ abstract ☐ evolve ☐ explicit ☐ facilitate ☐ infer

Study the Word Network to learn more about the word **abstract.**

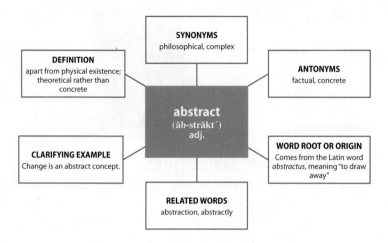

Write and Discuss Discuss the completed Word Network with a partner, making sure to talk through all of the boxes until you both understand the word, its synonyms, antonyms, and related forms. Then, fill out Word Networks for the remaining four words. Use a dictionary or online resource to help you complete the activity.

 Go online to access the Word Networks.

RESPOND TO THE ESSENTIAL QUESTION

In this unit, you will explore how changes reveal who people really are. As you read, you will revisit the **Essential Question** and gather your ideas about it in the **Response Log** that appears on page R5. At the end of the unit, you will have the opportunity to write a **research report** about how people reveal who they are through their responses to changes around them. Filling out the Response Log will help you prepare for this writing task.

 You can also go online to access the Response Log.

ACADEMIC VOCABULARY

As students complete Word Networks for the remaining four vocabulary words, encourage them to include all the categories shown in the completed network if possible, but point out that some words do not have clear synonyms or antonyms. Some words may also function as different parts of speech—for example, *abstract* can be an adjective, noun, or verb.

abstract (ăb-străkt´) *adj.* Apart from physical existence; theoretical rather than concrete. (Spanish cognate: *abstracto*)

evolve (ĭ-vŏlv´) *v.* To change or develop gradually over time.

explicit (ĭk-splĭs´ĭt) *adj.* Clearly stated or expressed. (Spanish cognate: *explícito*)

facilitate (fə-sĭl´ĭ-tāt´) *v.* To make something easier. (Spanish cognate: *facilitar*)

infer (ĭn-fûr´) *v.* To deduce from evidence or reason. (Spanish cognate: *inferir*)

RESPOND TO THE ESSENTIAL QUESTION

Direct students to the Unit 5 Response Log. Explain that students will use it to record ideas and details from the selections that help answer the Essential Question. When they work on the writing task at the end of the unit, their Response Logs will help them think about what they have read and make connections between the texts.

READING MODEL
from TOTAL ECLIPSE
Essay by **Annie Dillard**

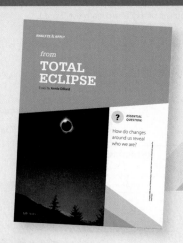

GENRE ELEMENTS
LITERARY NONFICTON

Remind students that **literary nonfiction** is like other nonfiction in that it shares factual information and real experiences and may include real people and places. It is distinguished as "literary," however, because it uses literary techniques such as figurative language and narration to convey a personal involvement in the event or topic. Autobiographies, biographies, speeches, and essays may be written as literary nonfiction.

LEARNING OBJECTIVES

- Analyze literary nonfiction as a genre and the author's style in an example of the genre.
- Conduct research to find and document another person's account of a total eclipse.
- Write a comparison between Dillard's account of a total eclipse and the account found through research.
- Discuss the power of eclipses in human imagination.
- Interpret examples of figurative language.
- Write in a variety of sentence structures.
- **Language** Discuss elements of an author's style.

TEXT COMPLEXITY

Quantitative Measures	Total Eclipse	Lexile: 760L
Qualitative Measures	**Ideas Presented** Some simple facts in the first half; second half contains more complex ideas because they are subjective and very impressionistic.	
	Structures Used Generally in chronological order but with some shifts in time and perspective.	
	Language Used Historical allusions and a heavy reliance on metaphors impose demands.	
	Knowledge Required A basic knowledge of astronomy may be beneficial but is not necessary to understand the essay; however, some knowledge of early human history is expected.	

from Total Eclipse 318B

Online Ed

RESOURCES

- Unit 5 Response Log
- 🔊 Selection Audio
- 📖 Reading Studio: Notice & Note
- LEVEL UP Level Up Tutorial: Author's Style; Literal and Figurative Meanings
- Writing Studio: Quoting and Paraphrasing Sources
- 💬 Speaking and Listening Studio: Sharing Opinions in Collaborative Discussion
- ❗ Grammar Studio: Module 4: Lesson 5: Sentence Structure
- ✅ "Total Eclipse" Selection Test

SUMMARIES

English

The experience of a total eclipse is unlike anything you would imagine, even if you knew every detail of what would happen and why. It is a dramatic experience that can alter perceptions, affect emotions, and make people feel dislocated in time and space. The only way to fully understand what it is like is to be present during one—and Dillard's poetic descriptions of this experience make doing that a very tantalizing prospect.

Spanish

La experiencia de un eclipse total no se parece a nada que puedas imaginar incluso si conoces cada detalle de lo que sucede y por qué. Es una experiencia dramática, que altera la percepción y afecta emocionalmente, que puede hacerte sentir temporalmente dislocado en el tiempo y el espacio. La única manera de entenderlo completamente es estando presente durante uno; y la descripción poética de Dillard sobre esta experiencia la convierte en un proyecto muy tentador.

SMALL-GROUP OPTIONS

Have students work in small groups to read and discuss the selection.

Jigsaw with Experts

- After students have read the selection, have the class break into four groups.
- Assign each group its own paragraph from among the "impressionistic" paragraphs 5–8.
- Have members of each group individually read and take notes on their paragraph.
- Reconvene the original groups and have these new "experts" on this paragraph discuss their observations and questions.
- Form four new "jigsaw" groups that consist of an "expert" from each original group. Have the new groups discuss paragraphs 5–8 as a whole.

Double-Entry Journals

- Have students divide a blank page in their notebooks vertically down the middle.
- Tell students to record in the left column text passages that strike them as important, surprising, or confusing and to note the paragraph number for each passage.
- To the right of each passage, have students write an interpretation or restatement of the text and one observation.
- Convene the class and, starting with the first paragraph, proceed through the selection, having students share the passages and their observations.

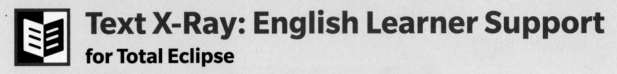

Text X-Ray: English Learner Support
for Total Eclipse

Use the Text X-Ray and the supports and scaffolds in the Teacher's Edition to help guide students at different proficiency levels through the selections.

INTRODUCE THE SELECTION
DISCUSS SUBJECTIVITY AND OBJECTIVITY

Introduce the concept of subjectivity by explaining that a **subjective** account is one in which the author includes his or her own ideas, feelings, sensations, and experiences as opposed to attempting to filter out anything personal when reporting on a topic. You may want to explain that some psychologists and philosophers argue that, since we can never know reality independent of our minds, we can never experience anything as truly objective. Explain that in writing, being **objective** refers to reporting without bias or personal commentary or editorializing.

Ask students whether they prefer subjective or objective writing and why. Supply sentence frames such as the following:

- *I like _____ more than _____ because _____ .*
- *I trust the information in _____ accounts more than that in _____ accounts because _____ .*

CULTURAL REFERENCES

The following phrases or references may be unfamiliar to students:

- *Usually it is a bit of a trick to keep your knowledge from blinding you* (paragraph 1): Knowledge can influence you to see or find only what you expect to see or find, figuratively blinding you to aspects of an experience.
- *It [the sky] does not appear to eat the sun* (paragraph 2): This is a reference to the common depiction in myths of the sun being eaten by a demon or an animal.
- *19th-century tinted photograph* (paragraph 5): Most 19th-century photographs were monochromatic but could be produced on dyed printing papers or colored by hand, usually with paints. Either way, the color tended to fade over time.
- *Zagros mountains . . . Euphrates valley* (paragraph 7): This area of western Asia, also called Mesopotamia, is believed to be where humans invented farming, astronomy, and other key elements of civilization.

LISTENING

Create Mental Images

Read aloud one of the highly descriptive paragraphs from the second half of the selection such as paragraph 6, 7, or 8. Ask students to envision what is being described as they listen to you.

Use the following supports with students at varying proficiency levels:

- Have students sketch the scene or some particular aspect of it. **SUBSTANTIAL**
- Ask students to draw and label what they just heard about. Encourage them to use vocabulary that they heard you use in your reading of the passage. **MODERATE**
- Ask students to quick-write about what they just heard. **LIGHT**

SPEAKING

Analyze Author's Style

In small groups, have students discuss word choices, images, sentence structures, and other aspects of Dillard's style they noticed while reading her essay.

Listen in to discussions to make sure students are incorporating word choices, sentence structures, and tone into their conversations. Use the following supports with students at varying proficiency levels:

- Give groups the following sentence frames to use in their discussions:
  I like the way Dillard describes _____ because _____.
  This is a long sentence. In it, Dillard shows us that _____. **SUBSTANTIAL**
- Before the discussion, have groups review the elements of an author's style on Student Edition page 321. Ask groups to find another example of each one in Dillard's essay. **MODERATE**
- Have groups discuss elements of the author's style and read aloud to one another examples of those elements from the essay. **LIGHT**

READING

Read Silently

Encourage students to do sustained silent reading of Dillard's account from 1979 and/or other people's accounts of their experiences of the 2017 total eclipse.

Use the following supports with students at varying proficiency levels:

- Have partners who speak the same primary language read a short account and summarize it in their primary language. **SUBSTANTIAL**
- Ask students to read a short account and then write 2–3 sentences about it. **MODERATE**
- Tell students to take notes on the accounts they read, recording the stages of the eclipse the author recounts or dwells upon and, if appropriate, characteristics of the author's style. **LIGHT**

WRITING

Write a Comparison

Work with students to help them draft the comparison they have been assigned to write on Student Edition page 329.

Use the following supports with students at varying proficiency levels:

- Help students develop an accurate understanding of scientific and academic terms by guiding them in reading about this phenomenon in a text that is written in their primary language (or guide them in listening to an audio version) before they begin writing. **SUBSTANTIAL**
- Instruct groups of students to compile a list of what they think are the most significant elements of Dillard's account. Urge individuals to refer to this list when looking for points of comparison between Dillard's description and the 2017 account they found. **MODERATE**
- Remind students to include in their introductions a reference to the difference between literary nonfiction and informational nonfiction. Allow them to work with a partner to find examples of these in Dillard's essay that they may want to cite. **LIGHT**

Notice & Note

EXPLAIN THE SIGNPOSTS

Explain that **NOTICE & NOTE Signposts** are significant moments in the text that help readers understand and analyze works of fiction or nonfiction. Use the instruction on these pages to introduce students to the signposts **Contrasts and Contradictions** and **Extreme or Absolute Language,** and to asking **Big Questions** as they read. Then use the selection that follows to have students apply the signposts and Big Questions to a text.

For a full list of the fiction and nonfiction signposts, see page 382.

▶ CONTRASTS AND CONTRADICTIONS

Explain that some **Contrasts and Contradictions** occur when an author's **style** places words or phrases that describe extremely different ideas, opinions, or experiences near each other, to startle readers into noticing important differences. They may also directly tell readers that what they are about to read will not match their expectations. In the example passage, the author points out that what you experience during an eclipse is so convincing that you simply can't cling to any wild theories about eclipses you may have had prior to that experience. In other words, the experience of viewing a total eclipse is not what you would expect and, consequently, the following account will not conform to any preconceived notions you may have had.

Read the example passage aloud. Discuss the way it is annotated and the fact that the student's first annotation is a generalization derived from the contrast as well as from the first idea presented in the paragraph.

Tell students that when they spot an example of Contrasts and Contradictions, they should pause, mark it in their consumable text, and ask the anchor question: *What is the difference, and why does it matter?*

from TOTAL ECLIPSE

For more information on these and other signposts to Notice & Note, visit the **Reading Studio**.

You are about to read an excerpt from the literary nonfiction essay "Total Eclipse." In it you will encounter signposts that will give you insight into the author's experience of a total eclipse. Here are two key signposts to look for and a big question to keep in mind as you read nonfiction.

When you see phrases like these, pause to see if it's a **Contrasts and Contradictions** signpost:

"On the other hand, . . ."

"However, . . ."

"Instead, . . ."

"You might be surprised to learn . . ."

Contrasts and Contradictions Imagine trying to catch up with a friend after a big game, when everyone in the crowd is wearing your team's color. Luckily, your friend is wearing her lucky psychedelic bandanna, so she stands out in the crowd.

When you read, sometimes the most important thing will stand out as well. Authors set up **Contrasts and Contradictions** to make sure you'll pay attention when it matters most. When you read nonfiction, watch for:

- a contrast between what you would expect and what the author says
- a contrast between two ideas or approaches to the topic
- a contradiction about something stated earlier in a text

Here is how a student marked this signpost in "Total Eclipse":

Anchor Question
When you notice this signpost, ask: What is the difference, and why does it matter?

1 . . . Usually it is a bit of a trick to keep your knowledge from blinding you. But during an eclipse it is easy. What you see is much more convincing than any wild-eyed theory you may know.

What two ideas does the author contrast?	How we usually think about things and how that way of thinking changes during an eclipse.
What is the effect of this contrast?	It emphasizes how the experience of viewing a total eclipse is completely different from what you would expect.

Extreme or Absolute Language Remember in elementary school, when an exclamation like "I love that shirt!" was met with a sarcastic "Then why don't you marry it?" Extreme language should be met with that kind of skepticism.

Nonfiction authors share information or real experiences. So when an author seems to exaggerate, it gets your attention. **Extreme or Absolute Language** may emphasize what matters to the author or reveal a bias about the topic.

Here is how a student marked Extreme or Absolute Language in the essay:

> 2   You may read that the moon has something to do with eclipses. I have <u>never</u> seen the moon yet. <u>You do not see the moon.</u> So near the sun, it is as <u>completely invisible</u> as the stars are by day....

When you encounter words and phrases like these, pause to see if it's an **Extreme or Absolute Language** signpost:

"Everyone knows that . . ."

never or *always*

words ending in *-est*

"We must all agree . . ."

Anchor Question
When you notice this signpost, ask: Why did the author use this language?

What does the author describe with extreme or absolute language?	She describes the moon as completely invisible, even though it is the reason for the eclipse.
What effect does extreme or absolute language have on your understanding?	It makes it clear that even though I would expect to see the moon during an eclipse, there is no way that I would.

Big Questions Maybe you've had the experience of a friend telling you a story that involves people you don't know. If your friend assumes you know these people, the story might make no sense at all to you.

You might have the same experience reading nonfiction. An author may not be able to provide *all* of the background knowledge you might need to understand the topic in one essay. Instead, he or she must decide what information it's safe to assume that you already know. When you read nonfiction, ask yourself: *What did the author think I already knew?*

Here is how a student might annotate with this **Big Question** in mind:

> 1   What you see in an eclipse is <u>entirely different from what you know</u>. It is especially <u>different for those of us whose grasp of astronomy is so frail</u> that, given a flashlight, a grapefruit, two oranges, and 15 years, we still could not figure out which way to set the clocks for daylight saving time. . . .

What does the author think I already know?	She thinks I might know some basic astronomy but not much.
How does this fit with what I actually know, and how does this affect my reading?	Her example is funny because it shows no understanding at all; I know more than that, but this introduction makes the scientific information friendly.

Notice & Note   319

WHEN STUDENTS STRUGGLE . . .

Monitor, Annotate, and Ask If students are confused by Dillard's figurative language or stymied by a desire to understand what's causing certain phenomena, have them circle whatever they want to comprehend better. Next, direct them to draw a line from this text to a blank area and, in the blank area, write a question about it. In small groups, have students share their questions and what they know about the answers. If any answers remain unknown at the end of the discussion, invite volunteers to research the answers online.

 For additional support, go to the **Reading Studio** and assign the following **Level Up Tutorial: Author's Style.**

EXTREME OR ABSOLUTE LANGUAGE

Explain that in speeches and some other nonfiction texts, **Extreme or Absolute Language**—language that does not allow for exceptions, compromise, or question—is often used to persuade. In literary essays, however, authors often use such language for emphasis. For example, "It was the hottest day ever" is most likely an exaggeration the author made simply to emphasize the heat of the day. Therefore, the presence of extreme or absolute language may signal that exaggerations and overgeneralizations are just characteristics of the author's **style.**

Read aloud the example passage and discuss the reader's comments. Help students understand that Dillard uses extreme and absolute language to dramatically emphasize and make absolutely clear what she is conveying.

Tell students when they spot Extreme or Absolute Language, they should pause, mark it in their consumable text, and ask themselves the anchor question: *Why did the author use this language?*

BIG QUESTIONS

Remind students that **Big Questions** are questions that readers can ask as a way of connecting with and understanding what they read. Tell students that in the upcoming selection, they will focus on the following Big Question: *What did the author think I already knew?*

Read aloud the example passage, emphasizing the words that are underlined. Ask: *What does the author think you already know?*

Tell students that when they encounter a surprising detail or example, or an unfamiliar concept or new idea, they should pause, mark it in their consumable text, and ask themselves the anchor question: *What does the author think I already know?*

APPLY THE SIGNPOSTS

Have students use the selection that follows as a model text to apply the signposts and ask the Big Questions. As students encounter signposts, prompt them to stop, reread, and ask themselves the anchor questions that will help them understand the author's intentions. Tell students to continue to look for these and other signposts as they read the other selections in the unit.

ESSENTIAL QUESTION:

How do changes around us reveal who we are?

Connect to the
ESSENTIAL QUESTION

Pulitzer Prize-winning writer Annie Dillard describes her experience of watching a total solar eclipse. In so doing, she reveals much about her frame of reference as well as how surprised she was by the way in which the change in her environment affected her.

from

TOTAL ECLIPSE

Essay by **Annie Dillard**

320   Unit 5

LEARNING MINDSET

Grit   Remind students that the part of our brain we use to plan, set goals, maintain our commitment to those goals, and diligently work to achieve them is like a muscle, which can be strengthened with use. Encourage students with this fact because, in essence, it means that everyone can develop grit (perseverance or stick-to-it-iveness). Promote the notion of establishing daily "grit goals"—that is, goals small enough to be manageable and achievable, specific enough to be measurable, and few enough not to be overwhelming. For instance, to create one goal have students complete this sentence: *"Just for today, I will _____."* Emphasize that *any* effort to stick to a goal strengthens the part of their brain that helps them to achieve their goals. Foster an attitude of recognizing and appreciating effort—big steps and small ones—when working toward a goal.

QUICK START

Events of nature can often leave us questioning reality. How might a powerful storm or some rare phenomenon such as hail leave you disoriented? Discuss your reaction with the class.

ANALYZE LITERARY NONFICTION

Literary nonfiction shares factual information, ideas, or experiences using literary techniques, such as figurative language and narration. The author of literary fiction has a specific purpose, audience, and message in mind. Literary nonfiction can include essays like Annie Dillard's as well as autobiographies, biographies, and speeches. How can you tell the difference between literary nonfiction and other informational texts?

- Look for artistic descriptions that go beyond simple explanation.
- Take notice of how the author interprets what he or she is explaining or describing. Watch for evidence presented in a lyrical or poetic manner.
- Be aware of how the author becomes involved with the topic or the subject of their reporting. Often the author will describe his or her reactions to events.

ANALYZE STYLE

Style is the particular way literature is written to produce a desired effect. Style is not just *what* is said but *how* it is said. Here are some of the key elements that contribute to an author's style:

ELEMENT	EXAMPLE FROM TEXT	EFFECT
word choice	**Only the thin river held a trickle of sun.**	expresses how unsubstantial this usually strong force of nature is
tone	**What you see is much more convincing than any wild-eyed theory you may know.**	friendly and informal; seems to be chatting directly with the reader
sentence structure	**It gets narrower and narrower, as the waning moon does, and, like the ordinary moon, it travels alone in the simple sky.**	long and meandering sentence mirrors the slow process of the moon across the sun's face and creates a pensive mood

As you read, pay attention to how Annie Dillard uses style to recreate the effect of experiencing the eclipse.

GENRE ELEMENTS: LITERARY NONFICTION

- shares factual information, ideas, or experiences
- develops a key insight about the topic that goes beyond the facts
- uses literary techniques such as figurative language and narration
- reflects a personal involvement in the topic

from Total Eclipse   321

TEACH

QUICK START

Invite volunteers to describe extreme or amazing displays of nature that they have experienced. After each student completes an account, ask a reflection question such as one of these: How did this experience affect you? What were you thinking as you experienced this? What are your thoughts about this event now?

ANALYZE LITERARY NONFICTION

Review with students the hallmarks of informational texts:

- provide factual information
- often explain an idea or teach a process
- typically use text features such as subheadings
- appear in many forms from news reports to science texts

Then for each characteristic you've mentioned, discuss how works of literary nonfiction depart from the general characteristics of informational texts—for example:

- present factual information: still factual but may also incorporate narration and personal observations, interpretations, and experiences
- written to inform or explain: author's primary purpose is not necessarily to inform or explain
- use of text features: rare in literary nonfiction
- can be news reports or science texts: literary nonfiction is typically more lyrical, poetic, and personal or subjective; usually takes the form of an essay, speech, autobiography, or biography

ANALYZE STYLE

Explain that elements of style might include figurative language, allusions, and other literary devices that help to create a particular effect. Encourage students to use a chart like the one on page 321 to record elements of Dillard's style as they read, adding rows for figurative language, allusions, and other literary devices.

Element	Example from Text	Effect
figurative language		
allusions		
other literary devices		

CRITICAL VOCABULARY

Suggest that students try out the words in each sentence before committing to their answers. Remind them that context clues may hint at the meaning of the missing word.

Answers:

1. *recede*
2. *saturate*
3. *wane*
4. *hue*

■ English Learner Support

Use Cognates Tell students that the Spanish cognate for the Critical Vocabulary word *saturate* is *saturar*.
ALL LEVELS

LANGUAGE CONVENTIONS

Review what the text says about sentence lengths and patterns. Encourage students to recall and provide the names of other writers who have used sentence lengths and patterns to achieve a particular effect. (For an example in this book, refer students to the first paragraph of "The Briefcase" by Rebecca Makkai in Unit 4 and help them to notice how she has reproduced long chains with her sentence structures and their lengths and how doing so serves to reinforce the content.) Then tell them to be on the lookout for Dillard's artful use of sentence structures to achieve specific effects.

ANNOTATION MODEL

Remind students that in Analyze Style on page 321 they were asked to record in a chart examples of Dillard's word choices, tone, and sentence structures. Point out that this reader takes note of Dillard's word choices by underlining significant words and phrases and writing notes about them in the side margin. Tell students that they can use this method, too.

◎ GET READY

CRITICAL VOCABULARY

wane	saturate	hue	recede

To see how many Critical Vocabulary words you already know, use them to complete the sentences.

1. As the falling tide began to _____ , we gathered shells left behind.

2. Water began to _____ the furniture as the flood waters rose.

3. The moon will _____ each month until it temporarily disappears from view.

4. The artist mixed paints until she had the perfect _____ for the sky.

LANGUAGE CONVENTIONS

Sentence Variety Mixing sentence lengths and patterns can engage readers and develop a particular mood or tone. Read this example from the essay:

What you see in an eclipse is entirely different from what you know. It is especially different for those of us whose grasp of astronomy is so frail that, given a flashlight, a grapefruit, two oranges, and 15 years, we still could not figure out which way to set the clocks for daylight saving time.

The long, winding second sentence sounds almost like Dillard is thinking aloud about a confusing science demonstration from the past. As you read, notice how she varies sentence lengths to grab your attention and express her ideas.

ANNOTATION MODEL   NOTICE & NOTE

As you read, notice and note the author's use of style and elements of literary nonfiction. In this model, you can see how one reader marked the text.

> Stuck up into that unworldly sky was the cone of Mount Adams, and the alpenglow was upon it. The alpenglow is that red light of sunset which holds out on snowy mountaintops long after the valleys and tablelands are dimmed. "Look at Mount Adams," I said, and that was the last sane moment I remember.
>
>   I turned back to the sun. It was going. The sun was going, and the world was wrong. The grasses were wrong; they were platinum. Their every detail of stem, head, and blade shone lightless and artificially distinct as an art photographer's platinum print.

Details about the setting create a strange mood

Preview of what is to come

Repetition of the word "wrong" emphasizes the strangeness of the experience.

🔵 ENGLISH LEARNER SUPPORT

Grasp Language Structures The annotation model offers an opportunity to review prepositional phrases. Tell students that a **prepositional phrase** is a phrase that begins with a preposition—a word such as *at, by, for, from in, of, on, into, to, with,* and *upon.* If necessary, review that a **phrase** is a group of words that does not contain both a subject and its verb but instead functions as a part of speech. Then work with students to identify some of the prepositional phrases in the model. (*into that unworldly sky; of Mount Adams; upon it; of sunset; on snowy mountaintops; at Mount Adams; of stem, head, and blade; as an art photographer's platinum print*) Ask: What do these prepositional phrases add to this text? (*They make it more descriptive by adding information that tells* what kind *and* where; *they clarify what the author means when she says such things as "Look" and "Their every detail."*)
MODERATE/LIGHT

BACKGROUND

In a solar eclipse, the moon passes between Earth and the sun. While solar eclipses are not rare, totality (seeing the sun completely covered) can be viewed only from a narrow band on Earth. **Annie Dillard** *(b. 1945) won the Pulitzer Prize for the book* Pilgrim at Tinker Creek, *which details her extended stay at a cabin while pondering life's big questions. "Total Eclipse," Dillard's first-hand account of a total solar eclipse she witnessed in Washington State in 1979, comes from her essay collection* Teaching a Stone to Talk.

from

TOTAL ECLIPSE

Essay by Annie Dillard

SETTING A PURPOSE

As you read, use Annie Dillard's vivid descriptions and figurative language to develop a mental image of what the experience of viewing a total eclipse would be like.

1   What you see in an eclipse is entirely different from what you know. It is especially different for those of us whose grasp of astronomy is so frail that, given a flashlight, a grapefruit, two oranges, and 15 years, we still could not figure out which way to set the clocks for daylight saving time. Usually it is a bit of a trick to keep your knowledge from blinding you. But during an eclipse it is easy. What you see is much more convincing than any wild-eyed theory you may know.

2   You may read that the moon has something to do with eclipses. I have never seen the moon yet. You do not see the moon. So near the sun, it is as completely invisible as the stars are by day. What you see before your eyes is the sun going through phases. It gets narrower and narrower, as the **waning** moon does, and, like the ordinary moon, it travels alone in the simple sky. The sky is of course background. It does not appear to eat the

---

Notice & Note

You can use the side margins to notice and note signposts as you read.

EXTREME OR ABSOLUTE LANGUAGE

Notice & Note: Mark examples of extreme or absolute language in paragraph 1.

Analyze: How do these word choices prepare the reader to learn about the experience of viewing an eclipse?

---

wane
(wān) *v.*
to gradually decrease in size or intensity.

---

from Total Eclipse   323

BACKGROUND

Read aloud the Background note. Some students may have heard about—or even witnessed—the total eclipse of the sun that occurred on August 21, 2017. Encourage students to share their experiences and invite others to ask them questions about it. If no one has heard about or experienced that total eclipse, invite students to imagine what witnessing such an event might be like. Discuss whether they think that knowing the scientific explanation for this event would influence what they thought and felt during such an event.

SETTING A PURPOSE

Direct students to use the Setting a Purpose prompt to focus their reading.

▶ EXTREME OR ABSOLUTE LANGUAGE

The word choices in paragraph 1 are one way the author alerts readers to the big surprise that awaits them if they ever are lucky enough to actually experience an eclipse. Discuss with students the strong language Dillard uses, such as *entirely* and *frail*, and how it can shape readers' expectations—and understanding—of what an eclipse is really like. **(Answer:** *These word choices dislodge readers from their potentially bored sense of certainty by putting them on notice that they are about to be surprised and disoriented. Dillard helps to prepare readers to be dazzled by what they will read by telling them to discard their expectations as inadequate or even wrong.)*

CRITICAL VOCABULARY

wane: What happens to the sun's light during an eclipse is much like what happens to the moon's light over the course of a month: the amount of light gradually decreases.

ASK STUDENTS how this comparison to the waning moon helps them to visualize an eclipse. *(Since readers are familiar with how the moon looks as it progresses through its various phases, the comparison can help them to envision what they will see during an eclipse.)*

WHEN STUDENTS STRUGGLE . . .

Clarify the Author's Meaning Explain that Dillard's statement about general scientific knowledge in paragraph 1 ("given a flashlight, a grapefruit . . . for daylight saving time.") is not supposed to make sense. Note that daylight saving time is not based on scientific principles; it is simply a system used to save energy by taking advantage of longer daylight hours. Dillard humorously makes the point that many people do not have a solid grasp of science.

  For additional support, go to the **Reading Studio** and assign the following **Level Up Tutorial: Literal and Figurative Meanings.**

ENGLISH LEARNER SUPPORT

Distinguish Verb Tenses Use paragraphs 3 and 4 to remind students about some uses of the past tense and present tense. In paragraph 3, point out the first few past-tense verbs (*was, freshened, blew*) and invite students to identify other past-tense verbs in the two paragraphs. (*grew, were dissolving, held; deepened, was, said,* and [again] *was*) Explain that all of the verbs in paragraph 3 are in the past tense, for they describe an experience that happened in the past. Most of the verbs in paragraph 4 are also in the past tense, and for the same reason. Then point out these exceptions:

- "A dark sky usually loses color" = present-tense verb because the statement describes something that is always true
- "The alpenglow . . . are dimmed" = present-tense verbs because the statement is a definition that is always true
- ". . . the last sane moment I remember" = present-tense verb to show the lasting impact of that memory **SUBSTANTIAL/MODERATE**

CRITICAL VOCABULARY

saturate: The sky was so soaked with indigo that it was a deeper shade of blue than people ever see.

ASK STUDENTS what else Dillard conveys beside the vividness of the indigo by saying "This was a saturated, deep indigo, up in the air." (*Since we normally associate saturation with liquid, by describing the air as* saturated *she is emphasizing how abnormal everything has become.*)

hue: As the eclipse began, normal colors disappeared, replaced by colors that "never [were] seen on Earth."

ASK STUDENTS to describe the hues of the landscape as Dillard now sees them. (*Dillard now sees only a range of metallic hues. For example, all the grasses—every detail of them—look platinum.*)

---

sun; it is far behind the sun. The sun simply shaves away; gradually, you see less sun and more sky.

3 The sky's blue was deepening, but there was no darkness. The sun was a wide crescent, like a segment of tangerine. The wind freshened and blew steadily over the hill. The eastern hill across the highway grew dusky and sharp. The towns and orchards in the valley to the south were dissolving into the blue light. Only the thin river held a trickle of sun.

4 Now the sky to the west deepened to indigo, a color never seen. A dark sky usually loses color. This was a **saturated**, deep indigo, up in the air. Stuck up into that unworldly sky was the cone of Mount Adams,[1] and the alpenglow was upon it. The alpenglow is that red light of sunset which holds out on snowy mountaintops long after the valleys and tablelands are dimmed. "Look at Mount Adams," I said, and that was the last sane moment I remember.

5 I turned back to the sun. It was going. The sun was going, and the world was wrong. The grasses were wrong; they were platinum. Their every detail of stem, head, and blade shone lightless and artificially distinct as an art photographer's platinum print. This color has never been seen on Earth. The **hues** were metallic; their finish was matte. The hillside was a 19th-century tinted photograph from which the tints had

saturate
(săch´ə-rāt) *v.*
to soak with liquid to the point where nothing more can be absorbed.

hue
(hyōō) *n.*
a color, shade, or tint.

---

[1] **Mount Adams:** a volcano in the Cascades mountain range in southern Washington State.

IMPROVE READING FLUENCY

Targeted Passage Use echo reading to help students use appropriate pacing, phrasing, and expression in reading paragraphs 3–4. Begin by reading the passage aloud, modeling how to use punctuation and sentence length as guides to phrasing. Also model how to read multi-syllabic words, such as *steadily, dissolving, deepened,* and *indigo,* with appropriate pacing and word stress. Then have students echo your reading as you read it a second and third time. You may choose to conclude with paired oral reading to give students more practice reading the passage aloud.

 Go to the **Reading Studio** for additional support in developing fluency.

faded. All the people you see in the photograph, distinct and detailed as their faces look, are now dead. The sky was navy blue. My hands were silver. All the distant hills' grasses were finespun metal which the wind laid down. I was watching a faded color print of a movie filmed in the Middle Ages; I was standing in it, by some mistake. I was standing in a movie of hillside grasses filmed in the Middle Ages. I missed my own century, the people I knew, and the real light of day.

6   I looked at Gary. He was in the film. Everything was lost. He was a platinum print, a dead artist's version of life. I saw on his skull the darkness of night mixed with the colors of day. My mind was going out; my eyes were **receding** the way galaxies recede to the rim of space. Gary was light-years away gesturing inside a circle of darkness, down the wrong end of a telescope. He smiled as if he saw me; the stringy crinkles around his eyes moved. The sight of him, familiar and wrong, was something I was remembering from centuries hence from the other side of death. Yes, that is the way he used to look, when we were living. When it was our generation's turn to be alive. I could not hear him; the wind was too loud. Behind him the sun was going. We had all started down a chute of time. At first it was pleasant; now there was no stopping it. Gary was chuting away across space moving and talking and catching my eye, chuting down the long corridor of separation. The skin on his face moved like thin bronze plating that would peel.

Mount Adams,
Cascade Range,
Washington

from Total Eclipse   325

ANALYZE LITERARY NONFICTION

Annotate: Mark imaginative comparisons that appear in paragraph 5.

Analyze: Why does the author choose this style to describe what she sees?

recede
(rĭ-sēd´) *v.*
to move back or away from something.

CONTRASTS AND CONTRADICTIONS

Notice & Note: Underline what Gary is doing in paragraph 6, and circle how the author perceives him.

Infer: Why is there such a strong contrast between how Gary is acting and how Dillard sees him?

ANALYZE LITERARY NONFICTION

Remind students that not all comparisons use the words *like* or *as*. Metaphors, for example, make comparisons by stating that one thing *is* another. Then point out that while Dillard's imaginative comparisons may begin as literal descriptions of her perceptions, they veer into the more fantastical realm when she begins saying such things as the scene is a "movie filmed in the Middle Ages." (**Answer:** *She wants readers to sense that there was a primitive aspect to this event—a quality that made her feel a kinship to people who lived during an age when such a phenomenon would have been feared. She wants to convey that this event tapped into a primeval, or ancient and original, part of her brain and sense of identity.*)

CONTRASTS AND CONTRADICTIONS

Help students to imagine Gary as the author sees him. Tell them to imagine what she describes as if it might be portrayed in a film. (**Answer:** *Dillard wants to emphasize that even ordinary things such as smiling and talking seem bizarre and otherworldly during an eclipse.*)

For **listening support** for students at varying proficiency levels, see the **Text X-Ray** on page 318C.

WHEN STUDENTS STRUGGLE . . .

Understand Complicated Text One of the hallmarks of Dillard's style is her occasional use of complicated sentences, dense with meaning. Guide students through one example—the sentence in paragraph 6 beginning with "The sight of him . . ."

- Explain that "was remembering" is the past progressive tense of "I remember" and that *hence* is a shortened form of *henceforth*, meaning "in the future." Help students paraphrase "I was remembering from centuries hence." (*I was recalling from hundreds of years in the future.*) Ask students why she is stating an impossibility. (*to show how strange and surreal her perceptions have become*)

- Point out the statement that follows the colon. Explain that Dillard imagines that this would be her thought if she and Gary met in the future, after both of them had died.

CRITICAL VOCABULARY

recede: Her eyes were moving away from Gary.

ASK STUDENTS what Dillard seems to mean by saying that her "eyes were receding." (*She seems to mean that her visual perception was changing drastically, causing her to perceive what she was looking at as if she had zoomed far away from it.*)

BIG QUESTIONS

Before students attempt to answer the questions, help them to analyze why she says "the river we called River" by asking volunteers to speculate on why a group of people might refer to a river simply as River. (*Dillard is trying to convey the idea that this time period was so early and these people's range so limited that they knew only one river and so had no need to distinguish rivers with individual names.*) (**Answer:** *Students might say that she thinks they already know where ancient civilization began, what people in this civilization ate, the tools they used, and how they gathered food. Students should note that to better understand her historical allusions, they could search online.*)

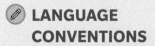

LANGUAGE CONVENTIONS

Remind students that using a variety of sentences makes the reading experience more enjoyable. What students choose to mark up will be subjective. Accept all reasonable interpretations of "very short" and "very long." (**Possible answer:** *The short sentences convey the author's shock at what she has witnessed. The longer sentences lend a poetic, reflective tone to that emotion. Together they express her full experience.*)

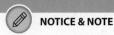

NOTICE & NOTE

BIG QUESTIONS

Notice & Note: Mark historical allusions the author makes in paragraph 7.

Evaluate: What does the author think you know about ancient civilizations? How could you fill in any knowledge gaps?

LANGUAGE CONVENTIONS

Annotate: Underline very short sentences and mark brackets around very long sentences in paragraph 8.

Analyze: How does mixing these two very different sentence types affect the mood of this passage?

7   The grass at our feet was wild barley. It was the wild einkorn wheat which grew on the hilly flanks of the Zagros Mountains, above the Euphrates valley, above the valley of the river we called River. We harvested the grass with stone sickles, I remember. We found the grasses on the hillsides; we built our shelter beside them and cut them down. That is how he used to look then, that one, moving and living and catching my eye, with the sky so dark behind him, and the wind blowing. God save our life.

8   From all the hills came screams. A piece of sky beside the crescent sun was detaching. It was a loosened circle of evening sky, suddenly lighted from the back. It was an abrupt black body out of nowhere; it was a flat disk; it was almost over the sun. That is when there were screams. At once this disk of sky slid over the sun like a lid. The sky snapped over the sun like a lens cover. The hatch in the brain slammed. Abruptly it was dark night, on the land and in the sky. In the night sky was a tiny ring of light. The hole where the sun belongs is very small. A thin ring of light marked its place. There was no sound. The eyes dried, the arteries drained, the lungs hushed. There was no world. We were the world's dead people rotating and orbiting

ENGLISH LEARNER SUPPORT

Practice Working with Synonyms Students probably are familiar with single-word synonyms, or words with the same (or nearly the same) meaning. For example, the word *screams* in the first sentence of paragraph 8 has synonyms such as *cries*, *shrieks*, and *yells*. Explain that synonyms can occur in phrases, too. In paragraph 8, point out these phrases: *a piece of sky, a loosened circle of evening sky, an abrupt black body out of nowhere, a flat disk.* Explain that all of these are synonyms that refer to the shadow of the moon. Invite students to describe this detail in their primary language and then in English. Encourage them to use synonyms to clarify their understanding as they continue to read, as well. **LIGHT**

around and around, embedded in the planet's crust, while the Earth rolled down.]Our minds were light-years distant, forgetful of almost everything. Only an extraordinary act of will could recall to us our former, living selves and our contexts in matter and time. We had, it seems, loved the planet and loved our lives, but could no longer remember the way of them. We got the light wrong. In the sky was something that should not be there. In the black sky was a ring of light. It was a thin ring, an old, thin silver wedding band, an old, worn ring. It was an old wedding band in the sky, or a morsel of bone. There were stars. It was all over.

NOTICE & NOTE

ANALYZE STYLE

Annotate: Mark repeated words and ideas in the last four sentences of paragraph 8.

Analyze: How does this repetition emphasize what Dillard sees and how she thinks about it?

CHECK YOUR UNDERSTANDING

Answer these questions before moving on to the **Analyze the Text** section on the following page.

1 In this excerpt, Dillard's central focus is —

   A the moment when a solar eclipse reaches totality

   B a time when she experienced a bizarre hallucination

   C learning that she and her husband perceived the world differently

   D how the wisdom of other times in history applies today

2 Dillard's writing style in the essay serves to —

   F objectively teach readers key facts about eclipses

   G reflect her disoriented state of mind during the experience

   H amuse readers with her humor about her limited understanding

   J persuade readers that nothing is more amazing than an eclipse

3 What was the main effect of experiencing the eclipse?

   A Dillard lost her memory of events before the eclipse.

   B People became physically separated from each other.

   C No one was able to speak or hear during totality.

   D The appearances of everyday things changed dramatically.

TEACH

ANALYZE STYLE

Have a student read the first of these four sentences aloud, pausing only where there are commas. Ask: What do Dillard's unusual punctuation and repetition convey? *(Dillard's punctuation and repetition suggest that she is mesmerized by what she is seeing and just trying to put the sight into apt words.)* (**Possible answer:** *The repetition reveals that this was the strongest visual impression the author was left with and suggests that this is something timeless, never-ending, and ritual-based.*)

For **speaking support** for students at varying proficiency levels, see the **Text X-Ray** on page 318D.

CHECK YOUR UNDERSTANDING

Have students answer the questions independently.

Answers:

  1. *A*

  2. *G*

  3. *D*

If they answer any questions incorrectly, have them reread the text to confirm their understanding. Then they may proceed to ANALYZE THE TEXT on page 328.

ENGLISH LEARNER SUPPORT

Oral Assessment Use the following questions to assess students' comprehension and speaking skills. Ask students to respond in short, complete sentences.

  1. What is the central focus of this essay? *(The central focus is the moment when a solar eclipse reaches totality.)*

  2. What does Dillard's writing style reveal about her state of mind during the eclipse? *(Dillard's writing style reveals her disoriented state of mind during the experience.)*

  3. What was the main effect of experiencing the eclipse? *(The main effect of experiencing the eclipse was that the appearance of everyday things changed dramatically.)* **MODERATE/LIGHT**

ANALYZE THE TEXT

Possible answers:

1. **DOK 2:** *She alludes to 19th-century tinted photographs, the Middle Ages, the ancient farming times in the Zagros Mountains of present day Iran, and stone sickles cutting wild barley and ancient wild einkorn wheat. These suggest that Dillard has a reverence for the experience; it causes her to feel connected to the earliest people to experience this; and they lend her description a primeval quality.*

2. **DOK 3:** *Students may note some or all of the following things: a lens cover, detaching pieces of sky, a black body, flat disk, a ring of light, an old thin silver wedding band, a morsel of bone. These images describe what the eclipse looks like, remain consistent with her allusions, and evoke a sense of timelessness and awe.*

3. **DOK 2:** *The moon moves between Earth and the sun, blocking most or part of the sun's light, depending on the viewer's location. In the places where the alignment of the moon and sun are exact, everything appears in a rare dimmed light.*

4. **DOK 4:** *Accept all answers supported by examples from the text, including those that state a preference for a more objective, scientific tone. Sample answer: Her subjective, imaginative account communicates the strangeness of the experience quite well, as evidenced in the passage where she describes the grasses turning platinum or metallic.*

5. **DOK 4:** *Sample answer: Merely relating what was observable would not convey the fullness of the experience and how it affected those present as effectively as does including strange images and perceptions that contrast and contradict readers' expectations of a scientific account.*

RESEARCH

Remind students that their summaries should accurately represent the main ideas, events, and impressions of each account according to its author without any additional explanations, commentary, or observations of their own. Also remind students to document their sources accurately and completely.

Extend Prompt students to focus on the eyewitness accounts they researched when evaluating Dillard's experience.

 RESPOND

ANALYZE THE TEXT

Support your responses with evidence from the text. ▤ NOTEBOOK

1. **Interpret** What historical allusions does the author make? How do these allusions contribute to the tone of the essay?

2. **Compare** To what other things does the author compare what she sees during the eclipse? What message or main idea do these images reflect?

3. **Summarize** What actually happens during the total eclipse?

4. **Critique** Did you think that the author's word choices and tone helped the reader appreciate a total eclipse? Cite examples from the essay.

5. **Notice & Note** How does contrast and contradiction serve as a better way of describing a true event than merely relating what was observed?

RESEARCH

Many witnesses have written their own accounts of solar eclipses. Research eyewitness accounts of the 2017 total solar eclipse that was visible in much of the United States. Summarize what you learn during your research, and document the sources using a standard method of citation.

RESEARCH TIP
Documenting your sources gives credit for the information cited. Research the person or organization that is providing the information. Are there complaints about their accuracy or doubts cast by other professional news sources? If so, search for more reliable sources of information.

Source 1 Citation:	*Sources will vary but citations should be complete, accurate, and appropriate for the type of source used.*
Summary:	*Summaries will vary depending on the source used. Summaries should be succinct and clear and retain the meaning and logic of the original account.*
Source 2 Citation:	
Summary:	

Extend With a small group, evaluate how typical Dillard's experience is for people who experience an eclipse.

⚙ **LEARNING MINDSET**

Questioning Remind students that questioning can help them identify and fill in gaps in their understanding. It is also a great way to initiate research and learning.

Encourage students to ask questions in classroom discussions. Also, note that questioners may not want to be "rewarded" for their questions by being assigned the job of finding answers. Rewarding a question with an assignment of homework can discourage students from asking questions in the future. Instead, consider writing all questions in a central place (for example, "a parking lot") as they are asked, and then allow any interested volunteers to select a question to research.

WRITE AND SHARE

Write a Comparison Write a two-paragraph comparison between Annie Dillard's description and the 2017 eyewitness eclipse account you researched.

❏ Introduce the topic and explain the sources of these two accounts, emphasizing that Dillard's account is literary nonfiction while the researched account is likely informational nonfiction.

❏ Include similarities and differences between these accounts, using appropriate register and vocabulary—in particular, accurate scientific and academic terms.

❏ Support your ideas with quotations and paraphrases.

Share Your Opinion Have a discussion and share your opinion.

❏ Explain why eclipses still capture human imagination, even though we can now predict them and understand them better.

❏ Use appropriate tone and voice, expressing your ideas in a reasonable and academic way that still sounds like you.

❏ Be respectful of other peoples' and eras' knowledge and belief systems, recognizing that you might have different knowledge and beliefs.

❏ Support ideas with details from both texts.

 Go to the **Writing Studio** for help with quoting and paraphrasing sources.

 Go to the **Speaking and Listening Studio** for help with sharing your opinion during a group discussion.

RESPOND TO THE ESSENTIAL QUESTION

? How do changes around us reveal who we are?

Gather Information Review your annotations and notes on *from* Total Eclipse. Then, add relevant information to your Response Log. As you determine which information to include, think about:

- why people long ago became upset when the sun disappeared during a total eclipse
- why people thought a total eclipse was a sign
- what effect an eclipse has after it passes

At the end of the unit, use your notes to help you write a research report.

UNIT 5
RESPONSE LOG

ACADEMIC VOCABULARY
As you write and discuss what you learned from the literary nonfiction essay, be sure to use the Academic Vocabulary words. Check off each of the words that you use.

❏ abstract
❏ evolve
❏ explicit
❏ facilitate
❏ infer

from Total Eclipse **329**

WRITE AND SHARE

Write a Comparison Remind students that they can use a comparison-contrast chart or Venn diagram to aid them in their initial analysis of the similarities and differences between the accounts. If students have more than three main points to make, you might allow them to use only a single quotation or paraphrase to support each of their main points.

 For **reading and writing support** for students at varying proficiency levels, see the **Text X-Ray** on page 318D.

Share Your Opinion Remind students to listen actively and speak using appropriate discussion rules, maintaining an awareness of verbal and nonverbal cues. Also remind them to respond thoughtfully and tactfully.

RESPOND TO THE ESSENTIAL QUESTION

Allow time for students to add details from the excerpt from "Total Eclipse" to their Unit 5 Response Logs.

APPLYING ACADEMIC VOCABULARY

❏ abstract   ❏ evolve   ☑ explicit   ❏ facilitate   ☑ infer

Write and Discuss Have students turn to a partner to discuss the following questions. Guide students to include the academic vocabulary words *explicit* and *infer* in their responses. Ask volunteers to share their responses with the class.

- What **explicit** details from the account made a strong impression on you?
- What might you **infer** about Dillard's desire to see another total solar eclipse?

CRITICAL VOCABULARY

Possible answers:

1. *Because waning daylight would mean it was getting darker, it would be evening.*

2. *If rain saturated, or soaked into, my backpack, I would hurry to get someplace where I could dry out everything that was inside it.*

3. *The bright green hue of a rainbow is like new leaves in spring with light shining through them.*

4. *A farmer might plant fresh crops in the wet and enriched soil once the water recedes and the land is no longer covered in water.*

VOCABULARY STRATEGY:
Figurative Meanings

Possible answers:

1. *The part of the sun that you can see shining gets smaller and smaller.*

2. *Features of the landscape were slowly disappearing.*

3. *People had all begun to seem different, as if they were from an earlier era, and there was no end in sight to this rapidly shifting perspective.*

4. *His skin appeared to be brittle and fragile.*

 RESPOND

WORD BANK
wane
saturate
hue
recede

CRITICAL VOCABULARY

Practice and Apply Answer each question, incorporating the meaning of the Critical Vocabulary word in your response.

1. If daylight began to **wane**, would it be morning or evening?

2. How would you react if rain started to **saturate** your backpack?

3. How would you describe any **hue** of a rainbow?

4. What might a farmer do when flood waters **recede**?

VOCABULARY STRATEGY:
Figurative Meanings

Figurative language develops an idea through an imaginative comparison. In some cases, a word with a concrete meaning is used to describe an abstract idea or process. For example, the Critical Vocabulary word *recede* in paragraph 6 is not used literally. When Dillard says her "eyes were receding the way galaxies recede to the rim of space," her eyes aren't actually going anywhere; she is sharing her reaction to describe vividly how distant and strange Gary looks.

Practice and Apply Explain the meaning of the figurative language in each example from the selection.

1. **The sun simply shaves away; gradually, you see less sun and more sky.**

2. **The towns and orchards in the valley to the south were dissolving into the blue light.**

3. **We had all started down a chute of time.**

4. **The skin on his face moved like thin bronze plating that would peel.**

 ENGLISH LEARNER SUPPORT

Discuss Word Meanings If students need help incorporating the meaning of each word into their answers to the Critical Vocabulary questions, use the following supports with students at varying proficiency levels:

- Encourage students to discuss the meaning of each word with a partner until they feel that they can explain the meaning verbally before writing. **MODERATE**

- Tell students to determine whether they have explained the words' meanings accurately by sharing their responses with a partner, soliciting feedback, and revising as necessary. **LIGHT**

LANGUAGE CONVENTIONS:
Sentence Variety

Writers vary sentences as an element of style. If every sentence were the same length or pattern, readers might lose interest. A change in **syntax,** or sentence structure, can signal an important idea or a change in mood. Dillard mixes short and simple sentences with long, stream-of-consciousness sentences in the excerpt from "Total Eclipse." Here are some examples from the essay:

- Simple: Subject and Predicate
  Everything was lost.

- Compound: Two Independent Clauses Combined with a Conjunction
  The sky's blue was deepening, but there was no darkness.

- Compound: Two Independent Clauses Combined with Semicolon
  He smiled as if he saw me; the stringy crinkles around his eyes moved.

- Complex: One Independent Clause with One Dependent Clause
  In the sky was something that should not be there.

Practice and Apply Write your own sentences of varying lengths and patterns using examples found in the essay as models. Your sentences can be about your own experiences with strange situations like an eclipse. When you have finished, compare your sentences with a partner.

 Go to the **Grammar Studio** for more on sentence variety.

APPLY

LANGUAGE CONVENTIONS:
Sentence Variety

Review the fact that an **independent clause** is a group of words with a subject and verb that can stand alone as a sentence.

Next, review the fact that a **dependent clause** is a group of words that cannot stand alone as a sentence because it is subordinate to, or dependent on, an independent clause. Writers link dependent clauses to independent ones with words such as *who, which, that, where, when, while, because,* and *since.*

Call on volunteers to read aloud the various examples and to comment about how mixing the kinds of sentences makes the writing more interesting.

Practice and Apply Demonstrate how to vary a sentence as an example for students' own writing by using sentence frames such as these:

_____ *[was/were]* _____.

The _____ *[was/were]* _____, *but there [was] no* _____ .

In the _____ *[was/were]* _____ *that* _____.

 ENGLISH LEARNER SUPPORT

Language Conventions Help students use a variety of sentences in their writing by providing the following supports with students at varying proficiency levels:

- Instruct students to find a few sentences in the essay that they like and copy them into their notebooks. Have them work in small groups to write new sentences. **SUBSTANTIAL**

- When students meet with a partner to compare sentences, encourage each student to experiment with using one or two of the partner's models for their own sentences. Encourage them to consider expanding the sentence variety in their responses. **MODERATE**

- Have students use their sentences as the basis for a paragraph, adding details where desired. Remind students to include a topic sentence and appropriate transitions to connect ideas. **LIGHT**

MENTOR TEXT
from THE FEVER
Science Writing by **Sonia Shah**

This article serves as a **mentor text,** a model for students to follow when they come to the Unit 5 Writing Task: Write a Research Report.

GENRE ELEMENTS
INFORMATIONAL TEXT

There are many forms of **informational text,** such as news articles, essays, and science writing. Informational text provides factual information and cites sources as needed. It is organized with a clear structure and includes a clearly stated or implied thesis, evidence to support ideas, and a conclusion. In this lesson, students will analyze text structure as they explore the topic of the excerpt from *The Fever*.

LEARNING OBJECTIVES

- Analyze the structure of a text.
- Analyze author's purpose and audience.
- Research methods of preventing the spread of a specific disease.
- Write a procedural brochure or public service announcement.
- Work in small groups to analyze a complex process.
- Analyze and use subject-verb agreement.
- Learn how to use knowledge of affixes to expand vocabulary.
- **Language** Identify examples and supporting evidence in the text.

TEXT COMPLEXITY

Quantitative Measures	*from* **The Fever**	Lexile: 1150L
Qualitative Measures	**Ideas Presented** Mostly offers basic information; explicit and direct.	
	Structures Used Text structure easily identified as cause-and-effect and narration.	
	Language Used Complex sentence structure; mostly Tier II and Tier III words.	
	Knowledge Required Explores complex scientific ideas.	

Online Ed

RESOURCES

- Unit 5 Response Log

- Selection Audio

- Reading Studio: Notice & Note

- Level Up Tutorial: Cause-and-Effect Organization

- Writing Studio: Writing Informative Texts

- Speaking and Listening Studio: Participating in Collaborative Discussions

- Vocabulary Studio: Affixes

- Grammar Studio: Module: 5 Lesson 2: Subject-Verb Agreement

- *The Fever* Selection Test

SUMMARIES

English

Diseases have plagued humans for hundreds of thousands of years. Some of the most virulent, such as smallpox and measles, have killed millions of people. Over time, however, vaccines have been developed for these diseases, and diseases have been greatly diminished. Not so with malaria, a disease spread by the bite of a mosquito. The mosquito is an ancient parasite that continues to thrive. Millions of people around the world die from its bite every year.

Spanish

Las enfermedades han plagado a los humanos por cientos de miles de años. Algunas de las más virulentas, como la viruela y el sarampión, han matada a millones de personas. Sin embargo, con el tiempo, se han desarrollado vacunas para estas enfermedades y así se han reducido muchísimo. Pero este no es el caso de la malaria, una enfermedad propagada por la picada de un mosquito. El mosquito es un parásito antiguo que sigue prosperando. Millones de personas alrededor del mundo mueren por su picada cada año.

SMALL-GROUP OPTIONS

Have students work in small groups to read and discuss the selection.

Pinwheel Discussion

- Form groups of eight, with four students seated (or standing) facing in and four students seated (or standing) facing out.

- Have students in the inner circle remain stationary during the discussion.

- Have students in the outer circle move to their right after discussing each question.

- Control the discussion by providing a different question for each rotation. Sample questions:
  - What are some contagious diseases?
  - Why is malaria known as one of the deadliest diseases?
  - How did *Plasmodium* probably evolve?

Think-Write-Pair-Share

- After students have read and analyzed the excerpt from *The Fever*, pose these questions: Most malaria victims live in tropical and sub-tropical regions. Why do you think this is? Why is it difficult to eradicate malaria in these areas?

- Have students think about the questions individually and write down their ideas.

- Then have pairs discuss their ideas about the questions.

- Finally, ask pairs to share their responses with the class.

Text X-Ray: English Learner Support
for the excerpt from *The Fever*

Use the Text X-Ray and the supports and scaffolds in the Teacher's Edition to help guide students at different proficiency levels through the selection.

INTRODUCE THE SELECTION
DISCUSS EVOLUTION

In this lesson, Sonia Shah explores the development and effects of the *Plasmodium* pathogen, which causes malaria. Explain and discuss the following:

- What is evolution? (*The term refers to genetic changes in a population over time that can result in the development of a new species.*) Prompt students to share examples, such as birds evolving from dinosaurs.
- What are pathogens? (*They are disease-causing agents. A virus, bacterium, or fungus can be a pathogen, as can a parasite.*) Start a list of diseases caused by these pathogens, such as measles and tuberculosis.

Review paragraph 1 with students and explain its key terms. Writing down these terms and their meanings to use as a reference when they read will help students understand the selection better.

CULTURAL REFERENCES

The following words or phrases may be unfamiliar to students:

- *measles and smallpox* (paragraph 1): highly contagious diseases. Measles has been almost eradicated, while smallpox has been completely eradicated.
- *scores* (paragraph 1): large numbers of something
- *tenacity* (paragraph 2): extreme persistence
- *antiquity* (paragraph 2): the quality of being old
- *protozoan* (paragraph 4): like a single-celled organism that moves about freely
- *barnacle* (paragraph 5): type of marine crustacean
- *hardwired* (paragraph 6): capable of doing something through inheriting the skill genetically
- *entomological* (paragraph 8): to do with insects

LISTENING

Identify Subject-Verb Agreement

Before reading paragraph 2 aloud, make sure that students understand subject-verb agreement. Model examples on the board, clearly marking each subject and verb.

Read paragraph 2 aloud for students. Then: use the following supports with students at varying proficiency levels:

- When discussing subject-verb agreement, note that it can seem contradictory. For example: The boy [no s] smile**s**. The boy**s** smile [no s]. Write several similar sentences and ask students to determine when the subject is singular and when it is plural. **SUBSTANTIAL**
- Have students follow along as you read and mark the subject-verb agreement that they notice. **MODERATE**
- With partners, have students discuss the sentences they marked. Encourage them to explain the parts of the sentences. For example: _____ *is the subject and* _____ *is the verb. They are [singular or plural].* **LIGHT**

SPEAKING

Follow and Give Instructions

Use the following supports to coach students through the Follow and Give Instructions assignment on page 341. Encourage students to keep instructions simple, making them easy to follow.

Use the following supports with students at varying proficiency levels:

- Model how to create a flowchart and tell students to make one in order to distinguish the steps of one of the complex processes in the selection. Then, help students explain it in their own words. For example: *The barnacle is born as an independent creature. Then, it attaches itself to the shells of crabs. It sucks its food from the crab's body.* **SUBSTANTIAL**
- With students, brainstorm ideas for processes at school. For example: *taking a test, getting lunch in the cafeteria, playing sports in gym class.* Model how to create a flowchart and have students make one to distinguish the steps for the school process they chose. **MODERATE**
- As groups discuss the steps to their processes, encourage them to keep track of terms that help make instructions clear, such as *first, then,* and *finally.* **LIGHT**

READING

Identify Examples and Supporting Evidence

Explain that authors include text details, examples, and other evidence to support their thesis, or main idea. As they read, prompt students to note the evidence Shah uses to support her argument.

Use the following supports with students at varying proficiency levels:

- Before students read paragraph 5, simplify the vocabulary and sentence structures. Display pictures of a barnacle and a crab; point out their basic features. Then ask students to read the simplified version of paragraph 5. **SUBSTANTIAL**
- In pairs, ask students to reread paragraph 4. Their goal is to locate the two examples of how creatures that are not parasites are beneficial. (*Bees pollinate flowers; predators cull weak animals from herds.*) **MODERATE**
- Ask students to reread paragraph 6 and underline the evidence for the idea that *Plasmodium* was originally a plantlike creature. (*last sentence of paragraph*) How would they state this information in their own words? **LIGHT**

WRITING

Write a Procedural Brochure

Explain that a brochure is a folded booklet of one or more pages, used to convey information in a concise, easy-to-read way. Then, work with students to develop and create their brochures.

Use the following supports with students at varying proficiency levels:

- Give students pre-designed brochures that include sentence stems for students to complete, such as *This brochure is about preventing _____. Characteristics of this disease include [three bullets for students to write].* **SUBSTANTIAL**
- Guide students in choosing information from their research chart to include in their brochure. Guide them to write simple sentences based on their research. **MODERATE**
- Have partners review each other's brochure. Encourage them to ask questions and give useful feedback. Provide sentence stems: *I like how you explained _____. What did you mean by _____? I think it would be helpful if you said more about _____.* **LIGHT**

Connect to the
ESSENTIAL QUESTION

Sometimes the smallest changes have the greatest impact on who we are, individually and as a species. In this selection, students will learn about the origins of malaria, a disease caused by a pathogen that is not at all like the creature from which it developed. The ways in which it changed are surprising, but its deadly impact on humans through the millennia are frustratingly predictable.

MENTOR TEXT

At the end of the unit, students will be asked to write a research report. The excerpt from *The Fever* provides a model for how a writer can use endnotes to cite sources.

from
THE FEVER
HOW MALARIA HAS RULED HUMANKIND FOR 500,000 YEARS

Science Writing by **Sonia Shah**

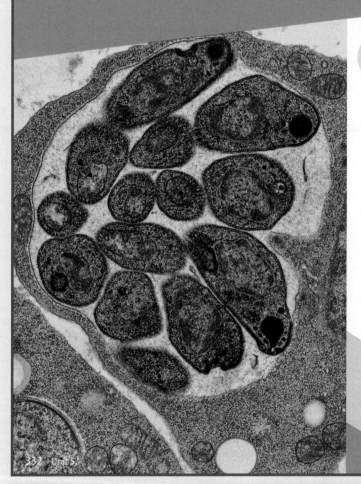

? ESSENTIAL QUESTION:

How do changes around us reveal who we are?

Color enhanced Transmission Electron Micrograph (TEM) showing malaria (*Plasmodium cathemerium*) infecting blood.

332   Unit 5

LEARNING MINDSET

Grit Discuss the value of grit with your students. Explain that our brains are muscles; the more we work them, the stronger they become. An essential part of grit is adapting flexible thinking patterns. Explain that approaching a challenge with flexible thinking means adapting to the problem and viewing the attempts to solve it as learning opportunities. Prompt students to think about the title of the selection and the photograph that accompanies the title. Ask questions such as the following and have students share what comes to mind: Does "science writing" intimidate you? Have you seen similar images before? Encourage students to approach this article with flexible thinking to help in understanding the text.

QUICK START

You're about to learn about a microscopic change that altered the course of human history. What is a small change that you can think of that has had far-reaching effects? Discuss your ideas with a partner.

ANALYZE TEXT STRUCTURE

The structure of a text refers to the purposeful arrangement of ideas and information to achieve a particular goal. With a clear structure, the author can clearly communicate facts in an informational text. Here are some structural elements an author may use:

- **Thesis:** The thesis is the central idea for an entire text that is expressed in one or two sentences.

- **Evidence:** The information that supports a thesis may include facts, quotations, examples, statistics, or narration of personal experiences.

- **Conclusion:** A conclusion is a statement of belief based on evidence, experience, and reasoning. A valid conclusion logically follows from facts or statements. A **deductive** conclusion follows from a generalization or premise. An **inductive** conclusion may be a broad generalization that comes from specific facts and examples.

- **Organizational Structures or Patterns:** The most common organizational text patterns are cause-and-effect, chronological, comparison-and-contrast, classification, deductive (general to specific) or inductive (specific to general) reasoning, order of importance, problem-solution, sequential, and spatial (physical relationships).

As you read the excerpt, note the text structures the author uses, including cause-and-effect and narration. Identifying text structures will help you understand the author's purpose and audience, as well as the topic.

ANALYZE PURPOSE AND AUDIENCE

An author's main **purpose** for writing informational text may be to inform, but authors may also write nonfiction text to:

- express thoughts or feelings
- explain
- persuade
- entertain

The **audience** likely determines the author's purpose. An author has in mind particular readers and will construct the text to appeal to those readers. For example, an author may explain technical research to an audience of fellow experts. Another author may narrate the story of a significant event for readers who are interested in history and especially in a specific time period.

Readers can determine the purpose and audience by paying attention to the topic and the language the author uses.

GENRE ELEMENTS: INFORMATIONAL TEXT

- provides factual information and cites sources as needed
- includes evidence to support ideas
- is organized in a clear structure
- includes many forms, such as news articles and essays

from The Fever 333

WHEN STUDENTS STRUGGLE . . .

Use Prereading Support Review the cause-and-effect text structure. Then have individuals or partners use a chart to trace the cause and effect of the development of the malaria parasite.

CAUSE   ⟶   EFFECT

CAUSE   ⟶   EFFECT

CAUSE   ⟶   EFFECT

 For additional support, go to the **Reading Studio** and assign the following **Level Up Tutorial: Cause-and-Effect Organization.**

QUICK START

Give students an example of a small change that might have far-reaching effects, such as choosing to walk instead of taking the bus, or eating fresh fruit instead of a sugary snack. Suggest what the far-reaching effects of these changes might be. *(getting healthier; feeling better about oneself)*

ANALYZE TEXT STRUCTURE

Tell students that analyzing text elements will make it easier for them to understand important information in a text. Review the text elements in the bulleted list. To help students analyze these elements in the selection, suggest that they ask themselves these questions as they read:

- What is the author's thesis? *(Malaria, unlike most killer diseases that are eradicated over time, continues to thrive, "wild and untamed.")*

- What evidence does the author provide to support her thesis? *(After discussing malaria's persistent ability to kill compared to other diseases, the author explains that the reason malaria continues to thrive is its characteristics as a parasite.)* Should she include more details to support her thesis? *(Some students may feel that some of the explanation is unclear or that not enough information is provided to support the author's thesis.)*

- What conclusion does the author draw from the evidence? *(Given that the* Plasmodium *pathogen was originally a plantlike creature and thus a benefit to life, it's ironic that it is now a ruthless parasite.)*

- What structures or patterns does the author use to organize her thesis? *(Comparison and contrast is the main pattern the author uses. She compares malaria to other diseases and the* Plasmodium *parasite to a parasitic barnacle. She also uses a cause-and-effect structure.)*

ANALYZE PURPOSE AND AUDIENCE

As they read, have students consider the author's main purpose for writing this informational text. As her audience, students are non-experts about the subject. Encourage students to look for the ways the author tries to make the scientific and historical facts clear and understandable to non-experts.

TEACH

CRITICAL VOCABULARY

If students are not confident they have chosen the correct word to complete each sentence, encourage them to look for context clues that match the meaning of each word.

Answers:

1. *vestige*
2. *malevolence*
3. *intrinsic*
4. *virulence*
5. *anomalous*

■ English Learner Support

Use Cognates Tell students that one of the Critical Vocabulary words has a direct Spanish cognate (*intrinsic/ intrínseco*). **ALL LEVELS**

LANGUAGE CONVENTIONS

Review the information about subject-verb agreement. Read aloud the example sentence and have students underline the subject and circle the verbs. Write the sentence on the board and bracket the words between the verbs *examine* and *identifies*. Point out that parts of a compound verb always are separated by at least one word (usually a conjunction) and often by additional words and phrases. Remind students that most singular verbs end with -s. Elicit several examples. (*singular verbs: is, takes, sits, makes, has; plural verbs: are, take, sit, make, have*)

✎ ANNOTATION MODEL

Remind students that an author's purpose might be to inform, express thoughts or feelings, persuade, or entertain. Point out that in this example, the reader has noted that the author's purpose is to share information with non-experts. Words such as *reckless killers* and *unremarkable* are not aimed at an expert audience. To determine the author's purpose and audience as they read, students can use their own system for marking up the selection in their write-in text. They may want to color-code their annotations using highlighters. Their notes in the margin may include questions about ideas and information that are unclear or topics they want to learn more about.

 GET READY

CRITICAL VOCABULARY

| virulence | malevolence | anomalous | intrinsic | vestige |

To see how many Critical Vocabulary words you already know, use them to complete the sentences.

1. The tornado left only a(n) _____ of the house that had once been there.

2. _____ was clear in the movie villain's angry expression.

3. Desert plants have a(n) _____ ability to survive in hot, dry conditions.

4. The flu spread with such _____ that many people were soon sick.

5. The snowstorm was a(n) _____ event for late spring.

LANGUAGE CONVENTIONS

Subject-Verb Agreement One or more phrases may come between a subject and verb. An intervening phrase does not change the number (singular or plural) that the verb should take. A singular verb must agree with a singular subject, and a plural verb must agree with a plural subject. Here is an example:

An anthropologist examines in painstaking detail the condition of ancient human bones and identifies diseases the people had.

The subject of this sentence is "an anthropologist." The main verb "examines" agrees with the singular subject. The singular verb "identifies" also agrees with the subject and not with the plural "bones" in the intervening phrase.

ANNOTATION MODEL   NOTICE & NOTE

As you read, note language and details that help you determine the author's purpose and intended audience. Here is how one reader marked the text:

> In Europe, when those pathogens first emerged, they were probably reckless killers, taking millions of lives. The survivors learned how to withstand the diseases' ravages, though, and in time both measles and smallpox settled into being unremarkable childhood illnesses, felling scores only when encountering virgin populations, such as those in the New World of the fifteenth century.

Author shares basic information that an expert in science or history would already know; purpose is to help curious non-experts understand the topic.

BACKGROUND

The only disease that has been eradicated worldwide by vaccine is smallpox. With routine immunizations and monitoring of breakouts, it is possible that one day the disease of measles may be eliminated worldwide, too. Malaria, a disease traced to the Plasmodium parasite in Africa thousands of years ago, still kills millions of people, especially young children. Malaria is a leading cause of death and disease in developing countries. In this book excerpt, investigative journalist **Sonia Shah** *(b. 1969) explores the causes, treatments, and effects of malaria. Shah's writing on wide-ranging topics, including science, politics, and human rights, has won numerous awards.*

from
THE FEVER:
HOW MALARIA HAS RULED HUMANKIND FOR 500,000 YEARS
Science Writing by Sonia Shah

SETTING A PURPOSE

As you read, pay attention to details that help you draw a conclusion about how Plasmodium *developed into the form it takes today. Also, note the sources the author cites for those details.*

1   Most pathogens mellow as they age. It's enlightened self-interest, as the theory goes. Diminishing **virulence** is a superior strategy for survival. It doesn't make much sense for a pathogen to rapidly destroy its victim—a dead body just means it's time to move on. Take measles and smallpox, for example. In Europe, when those pathogens first emerged, they were probably reckless killers, taking millions of lives. The survivors learned how to withstand the diseases' ravages, though, and in time both measles and smallpox settled into being unremarkable childhood illnesses, felling scores only when encountering virgin populations, such as those in the New World of the fifteenth century.[1]

2   Which begs the question as to malaria's tenacity and continuing **malevolence**. Malaria has been plaguing humans in Africa for some five hundred thousand years, with the first

---

[1] Roy Porter, *The Greatest Benefit to Mankind* (New York: W. W. Norton, 1997), 25.

Notice & Note

You can use the side margin to notice and note signposts as you read.

virulence
(vĭr´yə-ləns) *n.* the quality of aggressively causing disease.

ANALYZE TEXT STRUCTURE
Annotate: Mark details about how measles and smallpox changed over time.

Interpret: Why does the author begin by explaining the progression of diseases other than malaria?

malevolence
(mə-lĕv´ə-ləns) *n.* the quality of having a harmful influence.

from The Fever   335

BACKGROUND

Provide some additional information about malaria—its cause (the bite of an *Anopheles* mosquito infected with the *Plasmodium* pathogen) and its symptoms (fever, chills, and a flu-like illness). Point out that many programs designed to control and prevent malaria, such as spraying insecticides and using mosquito nets, have been successful. However, mosquitoes are tenacious, especially in tropical and subtropical areas, and all it takes to contract the disease is one bite.

SETTING A PURPOSE

Direct students to use the Setting a Purpose prompt to focus their reading.

 ## ANALYZE TEXT STRUCTURE

Remind students that a **thesis** may be directly stated or implied. **(Answer:** *In this passage, the author explains the usual progression of familiar diseases in order to contrast them with the virulence of malaria.)*

> **EL** ### ENGLISH LEARNER SUPPORT
>
> **Use Apostrophes** Many students mistakenly use apostrophes with possessive pronouns. Point out the word *It's* in the second sentence of paragraph 1 and *its* in the fourth sentence. Show how *it's* is a contraction of *it* and *is*. Emphasize that *its* is always possessive. Provide examples (*It's raining, its color*) and elicit more examples from students. **SUBSTANTIAL/MODERATE**

CRITICAL VOCABULARY

virulence: Pathogens can aggressively cause disease.

ASK STUDENTS to compare the virulence of the three diseases. (*Measles and smallpox are rarely fatal, but malaria regularly kills people.*)

malevolence: The author asks why malaria is so harmful.

ASK STUDENTS to explain why malaria is considered malevolent. (*It continues to cause great suffering.*)

WHEN STUDENTS STRUGGLE...

Identify Supporting Details Remind students that supporting details include examples, statistics, and other information in a text that serve as evidence in support of the thesis and key ideas. Model how to identify supporting details using the Background information. For example: *When I read that smallpox has been "eradicated worldwide" and measles "may be eradicated worldwide," I asked myself why malaria "still kills millions of people." I can assume that the "causes, treatments, and effects" of malaria that will be discussed in the scientific writing are different than those of smallpox and measles. Now I can put these details together to support the Background's main idea that the deadly diseases of smallpox and measles have been largely conquered by vaccine—but not malaria.*

Feeding female *Anopheles merus* mosquito; a member of the *A. gambiae* species complex, *A. merus* is a known vector for the parasitic disease malaria.

BIG QUESTIONS

Remind students that authors choose language that reflects their assumptions about their **targeted audience**, especially what the members of that audience already know. For example, language explaining a complex scientific topic might have a specific vocabulary and a complex syntax that may be understood only by experts in the author's field. In contrast, language that includes familiar vocabulary and accessible syntax might make the topic more understandable to an audience of non-experts. In some cases, the author's tone can be detached; here, it is friendly as she explains a complex scientific topic. (**Answer:** *The author includes some scientific details but provides examples and explanations that would be familiar to non-experts. Expressions like "the drama of life" and "strengthening its fabric" are familiar phrases that show her appealing to curious and somewhat educated people but not serious scientists.*)

■ English Learner Support

Understand Expressions Remind students that every language has an abundance of unique terms and expressions. An author who wants to achieve a friendly tone probably will use some terms and expressions that are rather conversational in nature. Point out the phrase "a cheater at the game of life" in paragraph 4. Give students a few examples of games and ask them how some players might try to cheat the other players. Then discuss the phrase "the game of life." Ask: What kinds of rules might apply to a person's life? Have students discuss expressions that are similar in their native languages. **MODERATE**

For **reading support** for students at varying proficiency levels, see the **Text X-Ray** on page 332D.

---

encounters between human, mosquito, and malaria parasite probably occurring around the time our ancestors discovered fire. Malaria existed in Africa before then, too, feeding on the birds, chimps, and monkeys that lived in the canopy.[2] We've had plenty of time—our entire evolutionary history, in fact—to adapt to malaria, and it to us. Or, at least, to devise tools and strategies to blunt its appetite. And yet, despite the millennia-long battles between us, malaria still manages to infect at least three hundred million of us—that is one out of twenty-one human beings on the planet—and kills nearly one million, year after year. As an extinguisher of human lives, write the malariologists Richard Carter and Kamini Mendis, malaria historically and to this day "has few rivals."[3] It remains essentially wild and untamed, despite its great antiquity.

3 And experts such as Terrie Taylor have spent lifetimes trying to figure out why.

BIG QUESTIONS

Notice & Note: Mark details in paragraph 4 that reveal what the author thinks you already know.

Infer: How does the author's language reveal the audience she is speaking to?

4 One simple reason for malaria's ferocity is that the protozoan creature that causes the disease is, by definition, a cheater at the game of life. It is a parasite, a creature that can eke out its livelihood only by depleting others of theirs. The rest of us all do our obscure little part in the drama of life, weaving ourselves deeper into local ecology and strengthening its fabric, the bees pollinating the flowers, predators culling the herds of their weakest members. Parasites don't help anyone. They're degenerates.

5 Take the parasitic barnacle, *Sacculina carcini*. It is born with a head, mouth, segmented body, and legs, just like any respectable barnacle. But then, because it is a parasite, it stops developing into

---

[2] Andrew Spielman and Michael D'Antonio, *Mosquito: A Natural History of Our Most Persistent and Deadly Foe* (New York: Hyperion, 2001), 44-45.
[3] Richard Carter and Kamini Mendis, "Evolutionary and Historical Aspects of the Burden of Malaria," *Clinical Microbiology Reviews* 15, no. 4 (October 2002): 570.

IMPROVE READING FLUENCY

Targeted Passage Use echo reading to help students use appropriate phrasing and emphasis in reading paragraph 4. Begin by reading the paragraph aloud, demonstrating how punctuation clues can be used to emphasize pauses and phrasing. Then have students echo your reading as you read it a second and third time, first by pausing after each phrase or clause and then reading it again with pauses after each sentence. You may choose to conclude with choral reading as all read the paragraph aloud together.

Go to the **Reading Studio** for additional support in developing fluency.

an independent creature. It burrows into the shells of the crabs off of which it will spend its life feeding. There it loses its segments, its legs, its tail, and even its mouth, devolving into a pulsing plantlike form, little more than a blob with tendrils sucking food from the forlorn crab's body.[4] It's the very definition of repellent. In 1883, Scottish lecturer Henry Drummond called parasitism "one of the gravest crimes of nature" and a "breach of the law of Evolution." Who can blame him?[5]

6   And yet parasites such as *Plasmodium* are not **anomalous** on this earth. According to science writer Carl Zimmer, one third of all described species practice the parasitic lifestyle.[6] To be fair, for *Plasmodium*, parasitism arose as an accommodation to newfound opportunities, not because of any **intrinsic** quality or irreversible mechanism within it. *Plasmodium* did not start out life hardwired to steal. This killer first emerged on the planet as a plantlike creature, most likely some kind of aquatic algae. We know this because 10 percent of the proteins in modern-day *Plasmodium* parasites contain **vestiges** of the machinery of photosynthesis.[7]

anomalous
(ə-nŏm´ə-ləs) *adj.* unusual; different from the norm.

intrinsic
(ĭn-trĭn´zĭk, -sĭk) *adj.* of or relating to the essential nature of a thing.

vestige
(vĕs´tĭj) *n.* a visible trace of something that once existed.

---

[4] Carl Zimmer, *Parasite Rex: Inside the Bizarre World of Nature's Most Dangerous Creatures* (New York: Touchstone, 2000), 17.
[5] Ibid., 17-18.
[6] David J. Marcogliese and Judith Price, "The Paradox of Parasites," *Global Bio-diversity* 3 (1997): 7-15.
[7] "Herbicide Hope for Malaria," BBC News, January 31, 2003.

Color enhanced scanning electron micrograph of *Plasmodium gallinaceum* invading mosquito midgut.

APPLYING ACADEMIC VOCABULARY

❏ **abstract**   ☑ **evolve**   ❏ **explicit**   ❏ **facilitate**   ☑ **infer**

Write and Discuss Have students discuss the following questions with a partner. Guide students to use the academic vocabulary words *evolve* and *infer* in their responses. Ask volunteers to share their responses with the class.

- How did malaria's ancestors **evolve** into parasites of the *Anopheles* mosquito?
- What can you **infer** about why more parasites are not fatal to human beings?

EL ENGLISH LEARNER SUPPORT

Summarize Read aloud paragraph 5. Discuss any vocabulary that might be unfamiliar to students. Then have them work with a partner to summarize the development of the barnacle parasite by marking their consumable text or sketching. Explain that they should include only the most important details. Have students write a summary of one or two sentences. Then have them review their work and mark ways in which the summary might be improved, such as replacing an unimportant detail with a more important one. (*Sample summary: The barnacle becomes a parasite by burrowing into a crab's shell. It loses body parts and becomes a blob that sucks nutrients from the crab.*)
LIGHT

CRITICAL VOCABULARY

anomalous: The malaria pathogen has much in common with other parasites; it is not unusual or anomalous.

ASK STUDENTS to identify the trait the malaria pathogen shares with other parasites. (*They attach themselves to other living creatures that provide the sustenance they need.*)

intrinsic: The malaria pathogen's essential, or intrinsic, nature was not originally that of a killer.

ASK STUDENTS what this fact suggests about malaria's intrinsic qualities and why it may be so difficult to eradicate this disease. (*It is malleable, or changeable; it adapts to new opportunities.*)

vestige: Traces of evidence suggest that malaria evolved from a plantlike creature.

ASK STUDENTS to explain why a vestige of evidence is sufficient to draw this conclusion. (*Scientists can get a lot of information from a small amount of material.*)

ANALYZE PURPOSE AND AUDIENCE

Remind students that **evidence**, one of the text elements they have been studying, is included in informational texts in order to support the author's thesis. In many cases, the evidence comes from outside sources; those sources are cited as footnotes on the same page or as endnotes. (**Answer:** *The author includes the information to show the causes and effects of the pathogen's development. She cites her sources for this information to give proper credit and to show that this information is accurate.*)

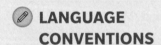

ENGLISH LEARNER SUPPORT

Understand Idioms Chorally read the first sentence of paragraph 7. Point out the idiom *rubbed shoulders with* and explain that it means "met and communicated with." Work with students to practice using the phrase in their own sentences. Have students use the expression informally in a sentence they might say about friends at a party and also in a sentence that might appear in a formal report about politicians or business leaders at an official event. Have students say their sentences aloud.

MODERATE/LIGHT

LANGUAGE CONVENTIONS

Tell students to find the subject and then mark phrases as they recognize them. First, have students find prepositions, which signal prepositional phrases. Then have students find phrases set off by commas. Without those phrases in the way, students will be better able to see the verb. (**Answer:** *The subject of the sentence is creature, so the verb must be singular. By reading the sentence without intervening phrases, students can find the singular phrasal verb turns into.*)

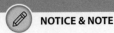 **NOTICE & NOTE**

ANALYZE PURPOSE AND AUDIENCE
Annotate: Mark the superscript numbers in paragraph 7 and key details related to these numbers.
Interpret: What is the author's purpose for including this information?

LANGUAGE CONVENTIONS
Annotate: Mark phrases in paragraph 8 that come between the subject and verb.
Evaluate: How do you know there is agreement between the subject and verb?

7   *Plasmodium's* ancestors probably rubbed shoulders with the eggs and larvae of mosquitoes, similarly floating on sun-dappled waters.[8] When the mosquitoes took wing, malaria's ancestors likely went quietly along with them.[9] It must have happened, then and again, that when a mosquito pierced a bird or chimp or some other blood-filled creature, malaria's algae ancestors fell into the wound. Most probably died. But through the blind ticking clock of evolution, one day some subset of the interlopers found themselves thriving in those crimson seas, and a vampiric parasite was born.

8   Such are the ironies of surviving on this protean planet. A creature at the very bottom of the zoological scale, a humble being beneficently converting sunlight into living tissue (and thereby providing the basis for the planet's entire food chain), turns into one of the most ruthlessly successful parasites ever known, commanding two separate spheres of the living world, human and entomological.[10]

9   Henry Drummond would have been appalled.

---

[8] Graeme O'Neill, "Pathways to Destruction," *The Bulletin*, February 12, 2003.
[9] Carter and Mendis, "Evolutionary and Historical Aspects of the Burden of Malaria," 564-94.
[10] Lewis W. Hackett, *Malaria in Europe: An Ecological Study* (London: Oxford University Press, 1937), 201.

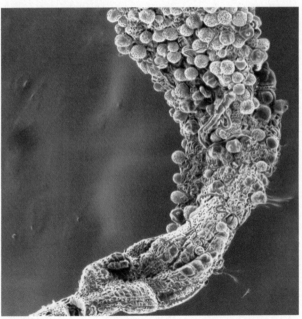

Colored scanning electron micrograph of the stomach wall of a mosquito *Anopheles stephansii* infected with malarial parasites *Plasmodium sp.*

TO CHALLENGE STUDENTS . . .

Explore Electron Microscopy Discuss the photograph of a malaria parasite on the stomach wall of the infected *Anopheles* mosquito and have students read the caption. Invite individuals or partners to research electron microscopy and gather information about how scientists are using this technology to diagnose diseases and test possible cures. Prompt students to find electron micrographs of various pathogens and write captions for them. Then have them share their research with the class. Have students discuss how the improvement of this technology might yield even more information in the fight against disease.

CHECK YOUR UNDERSTANDING

Answer these questions before moving on to the **Analyze the Text** section on the following page.

1 What is different about the pathogen that causes malaria, compared with other pathogens?

   A It is not as well understood by researchers.

   B It is the only disease carried by mosquitoes.

   C It has not become less deadly over the centuries.

   D It never traveled from its home continent to other places.

2 The author discusses barnacles in this passage because —

   F they are parasites, just like *Plasmodium*

   G they develop to adulthood in the same way as *Plasmodium*

   H their existence shows how common repellent creatures are in nature

   J their way of life is the exact opposite of *Plasmodium's*

3 How did the malaria pathogen develop?

   A Like measles and smallpox, it began in Europe and spread to the New World.

   B It first existed in chimps and monkeys living in trees in Africa.

   C It originated in barnacles as part of their parasitic burrowing.

   D An ancient, algae-like aquatic creature was taken up by mosquitoes.

from The Fever   339

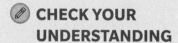 CHECK YOUR UNDERSTANDING

Have students answer the questions independently.

Answers:

  1. C

  2. F

  3. D

If they answer any questions incorrectly, have them reread the text to confirm their understanding. Then they may proceed to ANALYZE THE TEXT on page 340.

 ## ENGLISH LEARNER SUPPORT

Oral Assessment Use the following questions to assess students' comprehension and speaking skills. Ask students to respond in short, complete sentences.

  1. What is the difference between the pathogen that causes malaria and other pathogens? *(The pathogen that causes malaria has not become less deadly over time.)*

  2. Why does the author discuss barnacles in the selection? *(Barnacles are parasites, like* Plasmodium.*)*

  3. How did the malaria pathogen develop? *(It began as an ancient plantlike creature that was taken up by mosquitoes.)*
    ALL LEVELS

ANALYZE THE TEXT

Possible answers:

1. **DOK 2:** *The author's purpose was to inform curious readers about a disease that has had a devastating impact on humanity. She cites sources, makes comparisons to familiar things, and uses a clear cause-and-effect structure to describe her subject.*

2. **DOK 3:** *The author states that malaria today still infects three hundred million people and kills one million people every year in spite of efforts to control it.*

3. **DOK 4:** *The author describes how a barnacle develops into a parasite and feeds off crabs. Her simple and detailed description gives readers a clear and easily understood example of what a parasite does in language they can easily understand. They can apply this example to the way the malaria parasite behaves: its ancestors learned to thrive by living off the blood collected by mosquitoes.*

4. **DOK 2:** *The author uses a cause-and-effect organizational pattern. She first explains what caused Plasmodium as a plantlike creature to come into contact with the eggs and larvae of mosquitoes and the effect this had of connecting the algae with mosquitoes. This is the cause of how the algae came into contact with animals and humans through mosquito bites and the effect this had of further changing the algae into a parasite.*

5. **DOK 4:** *Earlier, the author quoted Drummond's extremely negative view of parasites. By saying that Drummond would be appalled, the author points out that even by parasitic standards, malaria is a horrible—"ruthlessly successful"—disease.*

RESEARCH

As students conduct their research, remind them not only to check the date of information but also to evaluate the source. Reliable sources on the Internet include reputable news publishers and organizations with websites ending in *.gov* or *.edu*.

Extend Students will probably learn that scientists discover these methods by performing a series of experiments and/or coming up with common sense solutions.

RESPOND

ANALYZE THE TEXT

Support your responses with evidence from the text. ☷ NOTEBOOK

1. **Infer** What was the author's purpose for writing this informational text? How do you know?

2. **Cite Evidence** The author writes that malaria is "essentially wild and untamed." Cite evidence from the text that supports her claim.

3. **Evaluate** Review paragraph 5. How does the author's description of a parasitic barnacle help readers to understand how malaria operates?

4. **Identify Patterns** Describe the organizational pattern the author uses to explain the process of how *Plasmodium* developed.

5. **Notice & Note** How does the extreme language in the final sentence of the excerpt sum up the author's point?

RESEARCH TIP
Make sure that sources are reliable and up-to-date. Check the date when information was posted on the Internet or the copyright year of print resources. Also check the origin of the information and make sure that authors or agencies are relevant and considered experts.

RESEARCH

Investigate recommended methods of preventing the spread of a specific disease. The method might be steps in a process or specific procedures to follow at home or in a public space. To develop ideas, you can read recent news articles or discuss options in a small group. Keep track of your sources and key information in the chart.

DISEASE	TIPS FOR PREVENTION	SOURCES
Responses will vary. Students should focus on a specific disease and cite credible sources of key information.		

Extend To extend your research, look for information that tells how experts discovered these methods for preventing specific diseases. Discuss what you find with a small group.

🛠 LEARNING MINDSET

Questioning If students get stuck when trying to respond to the Analyze the Text questions, encourage them to ask clarifying questions. Remind them that asking questions can open up new ways of thinking that they hadn't tried before. Prompt students to apply questioning strategies to work through their stumbling blocks. For example, provide sample questions to get them started: *How can I try this a different way? What do I already know about _____? How did I reach this conclusion? What steps did I miss?* Encourage students to look at the problem from a different perspective and to ask multiple questions. Emphasize that there are no bad questions and that everyone works through a problem differently.

CREATE AND EVALUATE

Write a Procedural Brochure Share the information you have gathered from your research by writing a procedural brochure or a public service announcement. A brochure is a folded booklet of one or more pages. A public service announcement can be written or spoken to alert people to an issue, such as a health or safety topic.

 Go to the **Writing Studio** for more on writing informative texts.

- ❏ Consider your audience. You will be informing professionals in a particular field or place, or adults who need clear and specific information on a topic.

- ❏ Use headings and lists to make your information easily accessible.

- ❏ Organize your information succinctly. Introduce your purpose and main idea, list and describe a procedure or recommendations in a logical order, and conclude with a summary statement.

Follow and Give Instructions In the excerpt, Sonia Shah describes a complex process that occurs in nature. Work with a small group to focus on a complex process that occurs at school.

 Go to the **Speaking and Listening Studio** for help with having a group discussion.

- ❏ As a group, identify a process.

- ❏ Choose specific tasks within your group, such as documenting steps, gathering supplies, and testing the process.

- ❏ Take turns giving and following the instructions you develop.

- ❏ Write a paragraph reflecting on and evaluating the role you had in the process.

RESPOND TO THE ESSENTIAL QUESTION

 How do changes around us reveal who we are?

Gather Information Review your annotations and notes on the excerpt from *The Fever*. Then, add relevant information to your Response Log. As you determine which information to include, think about:

- how malaria has affected the human species
- how scientists have dedicated themselves to figuring out how to conquer malaria
- how a plant can turn into a killer

At the end of the unit, use your notes to help you write a research report.

ACADEMIC VOCABULARY
As you write and discuss what you learned from the science writing, be sure to use the Academic Vocabulary words. Check off each of the words that you use.

- ❏ **abstract**
- ❏ **evolve**
- ❏ **explicit**
- ❏ **facilitate**
- ❏ **infer**

CREATE AND EVALUATE

Write a Procedural Brochure The directions in this section can serve as a guide for students' work. Brochures and public service announcements should be concise and well organized, and the language should be appropriate for whichever audience the student chooses to inform.

For **writing support** for students at varying proficiency levels, see the **Text X-Ray** on page 332D.

Follow and Give Instructions The instructions will vary depending on the process chosen but should be clear and easy to follow.

For **speaking support** for students at varying proficiency levels, see the **Text X-Ray** on page 332D.

RESPOND TO THE ESSENTIAL QUESTION

Allow time for students to add details from *The Fever* to their Unit 5 Response Logs.

EL ENGLISH LEARNER SUPPORT

Discuss with a Small Group As needed, help students identify a complex process that occurs at their school. Explain that the term *complex process* refers to a way of doing something that has many parts or steps in it. Then have students work in their groups to identify such a process at school. (*An example might be taking a test, which would involve several steps including studying for the test, alone or with another student. Students studying together might have different study habits, and those could be discussed.*) Before they begin, have each group determine the responsibilities of its members. Provide these sentence frames to help them formulate their ideas for the discussion: *The process is important because _____. The most important instructions are to _____ and _____.* **SUBSTANTIAL/MODERATE**

CRITICAL VOCABULARY

Possible answers:

1. ... it caused many people to be hospitalized.

2. ... keep practicing free throws until they each had made 20 in a row.

3. ... it had to be conducted again to get more consistent results.

4. ... that I need to interact with my friends every day.

5. ... we accidentally spilled a whole bag of trail mix.

VOCABULARY STRATEGY:
Affixes

Have students use a dictionary to find and define words with the listed affixes. Make sure that students clearly define each word and use it correctly in a sentence.

Answers will vary but should resemble the following:

parasite: *something that is abnormal and feeds on others; an organism that feeds off others*

The parasite invaded the host's blood.

aquatic: *characteristic of water; pertaining to water*

Aquatic algae can be found in ponds.

entomological: *having to do with entomology (the study of insects)*

The entomological conference focused on invasive insects.

 RESPOND

WORD BANK
virulence
malevolence
anomalous
intrinsic
vestige

CRITICAL VOCABULARY

Practice and Apply Complete each sentence, incorporating the meaning of the Critical Vocabulary word in your response.

1. This year's flu strain demonstrated its **virulence** when . . .

_____

2. Some players joked that **malevolence** was behind the coach's instruction to . . .

_____

3. Because the results of the experiment were **anomalous**, . . .

_____

4. Something **intrinsic** to my personality is . . .

_____

5. We tried to leave no **vestige** of our presence on the hiking trail, but . . .

_____

Go to the **Vocabulary Studio** for more on affixes.

VOCABULARY STRATEGY:
Affixes

Affixes include prefixes and suffixes. Affixes are common in terms used in scientific writing. Knowing the meaning of affixes helps to understand technical or discipline-based vocabulary. The word *malevolence* contains the Latin prefix *mal-*, which means "bad." Here are other examples:

AFFIX	MEANING	EXAMPLE
para-	Greek prefix meaning "feeding beside, disordered, abnormal"	*parasite*
-ic	Latin suffix meaning "characteristic of"	*aquatic*
-al	Latin suffix meaning "pertaining to"	*entomological*

Practice and Apply Follow these steps for each example word in the chart.

1. Define the word using the meaning of the affix.

2. Use a print or online resource, such as a technical dictionary or a glossary, to clarify or validate the definition.

3. Use the word in a sentence that accurately reflects its meaning.

EL ## ENGLISH LEARNER SUPPORT

Vocabulary Strategy Provide students with examples of prefixes and suffixes as visual support. Then have them find more words with affixes in the selection. **ALL LEVELS**

Prefix	Meaning	Examples
un-	not	unsure, unready
re-	again	replace, retry
Suffix	**Meaning**	**Examples**
-ful	full of	stressful, plentiful
-less	without	helpless, thoughtless

APPLY

LANGUAGE CONVENTIONS:
Subject-Verb Agreement

The excerpt from *The Fever* contains several complex and compound sentences, some of which include phrases or clauses that intervene between the subject and the verb. Here is an example from the text:

> And yet, despite the millennia-long battles between us, malaria still manages to infect at least three hundred million of us—that is one out of twenty-one human beings on the planet—and kills nearly one million, year after year.

The subject of the sentence is *malaria*. The compound verbs *manages* and *kills* agree with the singular subject. Notice that the verb *kills* appears after the intervening clause *that is one out of twenty-one human beings on the planet*. This clause does not change the number the verb should take. The verb *kills* agrees with the singular subject *malaria* and not with the plural *human beings* in the intervening clause.

Practice and Apply Underline the subject and circle the verbs in each of the following sentences. Look for intervening phrases or clauses. Then, write and revise the sentences in which the subject and the verb do not agree.

1. Over time, survivors (learn) how to withstand the ravages of disease and (passes) along some immunity to the next generation.

_____

_____

2. A parasite (ekes) out a livelihood and at the same time (depletes) others of their lives.

_____

_____

3. We (weave) ourselves deeper into local ecology and (strengthen) its fabric.

_____

_____

4. A killer (emerges) on the planet as a plantlike creature, most likely some kind of aquatic algae, and then (evolve) into a parasite.

_____

_____

> Go to the **Grammar Studio** for more on subject-verb agreement.

LANGUAGE CONVENTIONS:
Subject-Verb Agreement

Practice and Apply

1. *Students should underline* survivors *and circle* learn *and* passes. *The subject of the sentence is* survivors, *which is plural; the verb* passes *is singular and thus is incorrect. Students should revise the sentence to change* passes *to* pass.

2. *Students should underline* parasite *and circle* ekes *and* deplete. *In this sentence, the prepositional phrase* at the same time *intervenes. If students read the sentence without it, the need for a singular verb to agree with* parasite *is clear. They should revise the sentence to change* deplete *to* depletes.

3. *Students should underline* We *and circle* weave *and* strengthen. *The plural subject,* we, *agrees with both verbs, which are also plural. No corrections are needed.*

4. *Students should underline* killer *and circle* emerges *and* evolve. *Reading a sentence while leaving out phrases that are set off by commas, such as "most likely some kind of aquatic algae," can help students find the verb that needs to agree with the singular subject* killer. *Students should revise the sentence to change* evolve *to* evolves.

EL ENGLISH LEARNER SUPPORT

Identify Subject-Verb Agreement Provide instruction and practice in identifying the verb or verbs that agree with the subject in each sentence.

- The flowers (is, are) very dry and (need, needs) water. *are, need*
- Ellen and Juan (are, is) going on a hike and (plan, plans) to have a picnic. *are, plan*
- My sister (play, plays) the piano well, and she (like, likes) it. *plays, likes*
- My friend (doesn't, don't) live near school and (has, have) to take the bus. *doesn't, has*

SUBSTANTIAL/MODERATE

A SOUND OF THUNDER

Short Story by **Ray Bradbury**

GENRE ELEMENTS
SCIENCE FICTION

Write the term **science fiction** on the board. Point to each word individually and explain to students that these words are paradoxical, or contradictory. Explain that science is grounded in facts, data, and theories that can be proven or disproven through observation or experimentation. Fiction, on the other hand, is by definition something that is made up or imagined. In "A Sound of Thunder," author Ray Bradbury fuses the scientific concept of time travel with his richly imagined settings, characters, and plot to create a tale that not only entertains but also conveys a message about the potential results of seemingly inconsequential actions.

LEARNING OBJECTIVES

- Analyze plot and setting in a short story and make inferences about plot events and characters.
- Research the origins of the "butterfly effect" and its relation to chaos theory.
- Write a story about time travel.
- Create and present a sales pitch for a company offering excursions into the past or future.
- Identify and analyze synonyms and antonyms.
- Discuss and use transitions that signal cause-and-effect relationships.
- **Language** Discuss the use of description and dialogue in telling a story.

TEXT COMPLEXITY

Quantitative Measures	**A Sound of Thunder**	Lexile: 710L
Qualitative Measures	**Ideas Presented** Single, literal meaning; purpose and stance are clear.	
	Structures Used Settings vary in time, but chronological order of events is clear.	
	Language Used Heavy use of descriptive language, including figurative language; many complex sentence structures.	
	Knowledge Required Some descriptive language may require special knowledge; a few historical references may make heavier demands.	

RESOURCES

- Unit 5 Response Log

- Selection Audio

- Close Read Screencasts: Modeled Discussions

- Reading Studio: Notice & Note

- Level Up Tutorial: Author's Style; Setting

- Writing Studio: Writing Narrative Texts

- Speaking and Listening Studio: Delivering Your Speech

- Vocabulary Studio: Synonyms and Antonyms

- "A Sound of Thunder" Selection Test

SUMMARIES

English

In the year 2055, Eckels signs on with Time Safari, Inc., and travels 60 million years into the past, along with two other customers and two guides, to hunt a *Tyrannosaurus rex*. Travis, one of the guides, warns them to stay on the specially built Path to avoid harming anything in the past (besides the dinosaur) and thus potentially change the world they left. When the dinosaur appears, Eckels loses his nerve; overwhelmed, he wanders off the Path. The hunting party returns to 2055—and discovers that the death of a prehistoric butterfly, unknowingly killed by Eckels, has changed their world in dramatic and ominous ways.

Spanish

En el año 2055, Eckels firma con Time Safari, Inc. y viaja 60 millones de años al pasado, junto con otros dos clientes y dos guías, para cazar un Tiranosaurio Rex. Travis, uno de los guías, les advierte que se queden en el camino que ha sido creado específicamente para no dañar nada del pasado (aparte del dinosaurio) y así potencialmente cambiar el mundo que dejaron. Cuando aparece el dinosaurio, Eckels pierde su valentía; abrumado, se sale del camino. El grupo de cazadores regresa al año 2055 y descubre que la muerte de una mariposa prehistórica, que Eckles mató sin saberlo, ha cambiado su mundo de una manera dramática y ominosa.

SMALL-GROUP OPTIONS

Have students work in small groups to read and discuss the selection.

Write-Around

- When students meet in groups, tell each group member to initial a sheet of paper and then write a comment or question about the story.

- At your signal, students pass their paper to the right.

- Instruct students to write a brief response to the comment or question they receive.

- Have students pass the papers around until everyone has responded to all other papers and has received his or her paper again.

- Encourage students to incorporate the comments on their paper into their discussions of "A Sound of Thunder."

Numbered Heads Together

- Have students form groups of four. Count off 1-2-3-4 to assign each student a number within a group.

- Pose a question to the class, such as "How did the trip to the past both fulfill and crush the hunters' dreams?" Alternatively, ask a question posed in Respond: Analyze the Text on page 360.

- Instruct students to discuss responses to the question in their groups.

- Call out a number from one to four. Have the student with that number respond for the group.

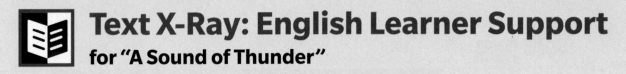

Text X-Ray: English Learner Support
for "A Sound of Thunder"

Use the Text X-Ray and the supports and scaffolds in the Teacher's Edition to help guide students at different proficiency levels through the selection.

INTRODUCE THE SELECTION
DISCUSS TIME TRAVEL

In this lesson, students will need to discuss the idea of traveling through time and the possible results of doing so. Have students read the sign in paragraph 1 of "A Sound of Thunder" and ask:

- Where do the people who come to this business want to go?
- What do they want to do there?
- Do you think this is a safe thing to do?

Encourage students to name a date or era in the past that they would like to visit. What would they want to do while there? Then ask students to hypothesize about the potential consequences of their time travel. Guide them to think about both positive and negative events that could happen. Finally, have students conclude by stating whether they would or would not travel back in time if such travel were possible.

CULTURAL REFERENCES

The following words or phrases may be unfamiliar to students:

- *dictatorship* (paragraph 8): a form of government led by someone whose word is law, with no limits on their power
- *militarist* (paragraph 8): a person who favors a strong military and taking military action as a way of solving problems
- *Tyrannosaurus rex* (paragraph 10): a large, carnivorous dinosaur usually placed in the late Mesozoic Era of prehistory
- *social temperament* (paragraph 40): the ways in which groups of people think about interacting with each other

See also the footnotes in the selection.

LISTENING

Create Mental Images

Tell students that creating images in their mind while they listen will help them to understand a story's setting and appreciate an author's skill with description.

Have students listen as you read aloud paragraph 5 of "A Sound of Thunder." Use the following supports with students at varying proficiency levels:

- Before reading, use pictures to support understanding of *a mass, a snaking . . . of wires; an aurora; a gigantic bonfire*; and other descriptive terms that contain words that may be new to students. After reading the paragraph for themselves, have students draw and label the mental image they created. **SUBSTANTIAL**
- Invite students to use sentence frames to describe mental images in the paragraph: *There was an image of _____ in my mind. I could see _____ and hear _____.* **MODERATE**
- Have students quickwrite about the mental images they created. **LIGHT**

SPEAKING

Discuss Sequence

Remind students that although events in "A Sound of Thunder" happen in different time periods, the events follow a logical sequence. Have students examine "sequence" details in the story.

Use the following supports with students at varying proficiency levels:

- Tell students to note words and phrases that tell the order of events as you read paragraph 44 aloud. Discuss what *When* and *Then* convey. **SUBSTANTIAL**
- Explain that sequence isn't always signaled by certain words or phrases. Read aloud paragraphs 57–66. Ask volunteers to summarize in their own words the sequence of events. **MODERATE**
- Draw students' attention to paragraphs 72–87. Have partners discuss, in sequence, the events leading directly to the death of the prehistoric butterfly. Instruct them to find the text that describes each event. **LIGHT**

READING

Contrast Description and Dialogue

Point out that much of this story is a mix of passages of dialogue and passages of description. Discuss how the two kinds of passages work together.

Use the following supports with students at varying proficiency levels:

- Draw students' attention to paragraphs 69 and 79. Ask: Do these paragraphs focus on description or dialogue? *(description)* Then have students review paragraphs 70–78 and repeat the question. *(dialogue)* **SUBSTANTIAL**
- Ask students to comment about the differences between paragraphs 69 and 79 and paragraphs 70–78. Elicit that the descriptive paragraphs are longer and give details about the setting; the paragraphs of dialogue are shorter and focus more on action and characterization. **MODERATE**
- Have partners read paragraphs 69–79 and complete these sentence frames: *During the dialogue, Eckels and Travis____. As readers, we come to see the T. rex as ____, ____, and ____because of Bradbury's description.* **LIGHT**

WRITING

Write a Story

Work with students to complete the writing assignment on Student Edition page 361.

Use the following supports with students at varying proficiency levels:

- Monitor students as they review the notes they took while reading "A Sound of Thunder." Ask: What other time would you want your characters to explore? Why would you want them to go there? **SUBSTANTIAL**
- Provide sentence frames that students can use as they draft their story: *My characters will visit the year ____. They will have a problem with ____ because ____. They will discuss ____ a lot in their dialogue.* **MODERATE**
- Remind students that Bradbury used vivid, powerful descriptions and figurative language to bring the prehistoric past to life. Have students brainstorm with a partner and write down ideas for figurative language they can use in their story. **LIGHT**

A SOUND OF THUNDER

Short Story by **Ray Bradbury**

? Connect to the
ESSENTIAL QUESTION

School portraits reveal how students have changed from one year to the next. Studying history shows students how their community, the nation, and the world have changed over generations. When millions of years are involved, the changes are more dramatic. As students read Ray Bradbury's classic, "A Sound of Thunder," they will travel to the primeval past with a group of hunters. There, they will see how the setting reveals the heart of one hunter —and how his actions cause unanticipated changes.

? ***ESSENTIAL QUESTION:***

How do changes around us reveal who we are?

 LEARNING MINDSET

Grit As students analyze and make inferences about "A Sound of Thunder," remind them that they will grow in their learning if they work hard and remain flexible in their thinking. Encourage a determination to succeed, but remind students that they shouldn't consider their first try their only try. Even if they stumble as they work, they can learn from the experience if they refuse to quit—and they can apply what they learn to future attempts.

QUICK START

If you could travel to any place in time—past or future—where would you go? What would you want to do or see there? Turn and talk about your ideas with a partner.

ANALYZE PLOT AND SETTING

Every story has a **setting**—a time and place for its action. For science fiction writers, the setting may be in any place in the past, present, or future. "A Sound of Thunder" takes place in two distinct settings—the far distant future and the prehistoric past.

In some stories, the setting is just a backdrop to the **plot**, or sequence of events. In "A Sound of Thunder," the action centers on characters who travel through time, and the setting directly affects the way the plot unfolds.

As you read, note how the setting causes events to happen, or causes them to happen in a certain way, at different stages of the plot. Use a chart like this:

EXPOSITION / RISING ACTION	CLIMAX	FALLING ACTION / RESOLUTION

MAKE INFERENCES

When you make an **inference** while reading, you make a logical guess based on information in a text and your own knowledge, including what you know about genre conventions, or characteristics of a particular type of story. Use your understanding of science fiction characteristics to help you make predictions and draw conclusions about characters, settings, and events in "A Sound of Thunder." Use a chart like this one to record them:

TEXT DETAILS / SCIENCE FICTION CONVENTIONS	MY PREDICTIONS AND CONCLUSIONS

GENRE ELEMENTS: SCIENCE FICTION

• usually set in the future or in a different reality
• presents an imagined view of the past or future
• based on scientific facts and theories
• comments in some way on present-day society

QUICK START

Have students read the Quick Start and make a few notes about their time-traveling destination. After partners discuss their ideas, invite students to share with the class. Students may be especially interested in the reasons for such a journey—for example, to witness a historical event that interests them, to satisfy their curiosity about future technology, or even to try to change history. As students read how Eckels reacts when faced with the reality of another time, ask them how they think the reality of their chosen time might differ from the way they first imagined it.

ANALYZE PLOT AND SETTING

Discuss the definition of **setting** and invite students to describe the settings of some favorite stories or movies. Explain that the setting can change during the course of a story. Point out that in "A Sound of Thunder," the settings are so critical that they almost are characters in themselves.

Check students' understanding of the **plot** stages in the chart headings. Remind students that the plot of a story is built upon conflict; then encourage them to watch for a variety of conflicts in this story. Emphasize, however, that students are to use the chart to note not merely the plot details but the effect of the setting upon the various stages of the plot.

MAKE INFERENCES

Help students understand that an **inference** is something that they assume to be true based on the evidence at hand (in this case, text details) and their own prior knowledge or past experience (in this case, their understanding of the past and science fiction characteristics). Discuss the list of science fiction elements, inviting volunteers to name stories, movies, or TV shows that illustrate each one. As students read the story and complete the chart, suggest that they use highlighting or another form of marking to distinguish specific text details from general science fiction conventions and to distinguish predictions from conclusions.

TEACH

CRITICAL VOCABULARY

Encourage students to read carefully, focusing on the part of each question that sounds like a definition, and to try more than one Critical Vocabulary word before settling on an answer.

Answers:

1. *undulate*

2. *subliminal*

3. *expendable*

4. *paradox*

5. *subtle*

■ English Learner Support

Use Cognates Tell students that several of the Critical Vocabulary words have Spanish cognates: *subtle/sutil, paradox/paradoja, undulate/ondular, subliminal/subliminal.*
ALL LEVELS

LANGUAGE CONVENTIONS

You may wish to explain that the word *transition* comes from the Latin word *transire*, which means "to go across." In that sense, a word or phrase that serves as a transition "goes across" from one idea to another, like a bridge. The ideas that the transitions in the text connect are causes and their effects. Display the example; then circle the transition *thus* and use arrows to show how it connects a cause (killing even a small plant or animal) to a potential effect (destroying "an important link in a growing species"). Point out the other examples of cause-and-effect transition words. As students encounter these transitions in "A Sound of Thunder," suggest that they stop and ask, "What is the important detail here? What kind of change has it produced?"

✎ ANNOTATION MODEL

Call on a volunteer to read aloud the model passage. Point out the first comment and the fact that the reader has marked a sentence that gives the basic idea of the story. Ask students why they think the reader asked a question in the second comment. (*The reader probably is wondering about the connection between time travel and safaris.*) Remind students that they may use highlighting or a variety of markings to note text details as they read. Urge them to use the margins for questions, interpretations, and other comments about the text.

 GET READY

CRITICAL VOCABULARY

| expendable | subtle | paradox | undulate | subliminal |

To see how many Critical Vocabulary words you already know, answer the following questions.

1. What word means to move in a smooth, wave-like motion?

2. What word means something that exists below the level of consciousness?

3. What word means that something is unnecessary?

4. What word means a statement that combines ideas that are opposites?

5. What word means something that is hard to detect?

LANGUAGE CONVENTIONS

Transitions Authors use transitions, or connecting words, to show readers how the details in a paragraph are related. Some common transitions show relationships of comparison and contrast. Other transitions, like the one in this line of dialogue from the story, point out a cause-and-effect relationship.

cause
↓

"Not knowing it, we might kill an important animal, a small bird, a roach, a flower even, thus destroying an important link in a growing species."

↑   ↑
transition   effect

The transition word *thus* introduces an effect of killing even a small plant or animal. Other transition words that signal cause-and-effect relationships include *because, consequently, as a result,* and *therefore.* As you read "A Sound of Thunder," watch Bradbury's use of transitions to show cause and effect.

ANNOTATION MODEL   **NOTICE & NOTE**

As you read, use story details and your knowledge of science fiction conventions to make inferences about the setting and plot. Here is how one reader made inferences about setting and plot in "A Sound of Thunder":

TIME SAFARI, INC.
Safaris to any year in the past.
You name the animal.
We take you there.
You shoot it.

Time travel is technology of the future—story is probably set in the future.

What kind of animals would you travel to the past to hunt?

BACKGROUND

Although **Ray Bradbury** *(1920–2012) is best known as a science fiction writer for Fahrenheit 451, he was never comfortable with that label. Bradbury also wrote imaginative short stories, novels, poems, plays, and nonfiction. At age 12, he wrote his own sequel to a popular novel because he couldn't wait for the next book to be published. In high school, he bought a ten-dollar typewriter and wrote for the school newspaper. At 19, he sold newspapers until he could support himself—about three years later—on his writing alone. Bradbury once remarked that having total recall of every book he's ever read helped his writing.*

A SOUND OF THUNDER

Short Story by Ray Bradbury

SETTING A PURPOSE

As you read, imagine yourself in the main character's role. Consider how you might react in the situations this character faces and what actions you might take.

> **Notice & Note**
>
> You can use the side margins to notice and note signposts in the text.

1   The sign on the wall seemed to quaver under a film of sliding warm water. Eckels felt his eyelids blink over his stare, and the sign burned in this momentary darkness:

> # TIME SAFARI, INC.
> Safaris to any year in the past.
> You name the animal.
> We take you there.
> You shoot it.

BACKGROUND

After students read the Background note, point out that Ray Bradbury developed a passion for writing science fiction at a young age and that he worked hard to achieve his goals. In that sense, he can serve as an inspiration for young people today. "A Sound of Thunder," one of his best-known short stories, shows not only Bradbury's skill as a writer but also his love for holding his readers' attention with a thrilling tale. You may wish to share this comment from his preface to *Zen in the Art of Writing* (1990): "And what, you ask, does writing teach us? First and foremost, it reminds us that we *are* alive and that it is gift and a privilege, not a right . . . So while our art cannot, as we wish it could, save us from wars, privation, envy, greed, old age, or death, it can revitalize us amidst it all."

SETTING A PURPOSE

Direct students to use the Setting a Purpose prompt to focus their reading.

🗨 ENGLISH LEARNER SUPPORT

Check Understanding   The sign for Time Safari, Inc., may not seem important at first, but students will discover that it plays a key role in the outcome of the story. As needed, point out the following:

• *Safari* comes from *safar,* an Arabic word meaning "journey." Early safaris had the same purpose as the one in this story: to travel in order to find and kill exotic animals in their natural surroundings. Most safaris today are much more environmentally conscious, emphasizing viewing and photographing animals in the wild.

• The *Inc.* in the first line is an abbreviation for *Incorporated.* It means that the government recognizes Time Safari as having the legal right to do business. (Students will learn later that Time Safari stays in business by paying bribes to government officials.)

• The company's name is followed by four sentences, but students may recognize that the first one is a fragment. Suggest that students preface it with the words *We offer* to make the meaning clear.

Have students state the meaning of the sign, first in their primary language and then in English.   **ALL LEVELS**

ANALYZE PLOT AND SETTING

Explain to students that consequences are results or effects. Remind students that before they started reading, they learned that *consequently* is a transition that signals a cause-and-effect relationship. Point out that this is just one of many cause-and-effect details in the story. (**Answer:** *The safari sounds highly dangerous and possibly illegal. The severe consequences may indicate that the government does not approve of the safari company and the risks it takes. The official's warning suggests that Eckels may disobey the rules and get himself and the company into trouble.*)

For **listening support** for students at varying proficiency levels, see the **Text X-Ray** on page 344C.

NOTICE & NOTE

ANALYZE PLOT AND SETTING

Annotate: In paragraph 4, mark the consequences for disobeying instructions.

Infer: Why do you think the consequences are so severe? Make a prediction about what Eckels will do later in the story based on the official's warning.

2   A warm phlegm gathered in Eckels's throat; he swallowed and pushed it down. The muscles around his mouth formed a smile as he put his hand slowly out upon the air, and in that hand waved a check for ten thousand dollars to the man behind the desk.

3   "Does this safari guarantee I come back alive?"

4   "We guarantee nothing," said the official, "except the dinosaurs." He turned. "This is Mr. Travis, your Safari Guide in the Past. He'll tell you what and where to shoot. If he says no shooting, no shooting. If you disobey instructions, there's stiff penalty of another ten thousand dollars, plus possible government action, on your return."

5   Eckels glanced across the vast office at a mass and tangle, a snaking and humming of wires and steel boxes, at an aurora[1] that flickered now orange, now silver, now blue. There was a sound like a gigantic bonfire burning all of Time, all the years and all the parchment calendars, all the hours piled high and set aflame.

6   A touch of the hand and this burning would, on the instant, beautifully reverse itself. Eckels remembered the wording in the advertisements to the letter. Out of chars and ashes, out of dust and coals, like golden salamanders, the old years, the green years, might leap; roses sweeten the air, white hair turn Irish-black, wrinkles vanish; all, everything fly back to seed, flee death, rush down to their beginnings, suns rise in western skies and set in glorious easts, moons eat themselves opposite to the custom, all and everything cupping one in another like Chinese boxes,[2] rabbits into hats, all and everything returning to the fresh death, the seed death, the green death, to the time before the beginning. A touch of a hand might do it, the merest touch of a hand.

7   "Unbelievable." Eckels breathed, the light of the Machine on his thin face. "A real Time Machine." He shook his head. "Makes you think. If the election had gone badly yesterday, I might be here now running away from the results. Thank God Keith won. He'll make a fine President of the United States."

8   "Yes," said the man behind the desk. "We're lucky. If Deutscher had gotten in, we'd have the worst kind of dictatorship. There's an anti-everything man for you, a militarist, anti-Christ, anti-human, anti-intellectual. People called us up, you know, joking but not joking. Said if Deutscher became President they wanted to go live in 1492. Of course it's not our business to conduct Escapes, but to form Safaris. Anyway, Keith's President now. All you got to worry about is—"

9   "Shooting my dinosaur," Eckels finished it for him.

10   "A *Tyrannosaurus rex*. The Tyrant Lizard, the most incredible monster in history. Sign this release. Anything happens to you, we're not responsible. Those dinosaurs are hungry."

11   Eckels flushed angrily. "Trying to scare me!"

---

[1] **aurora:** a colorful display of light that appears at night in the skies near the North and South Poles.

[2] **Chinese boxes:** a set of decorated boxes in which each fits into the next-larger one.

WHEN STUDENTS STRUGGLE . . .

Understand Style   One of the hallmarks of Bradbury's style is his practice of listing a series of descriptive phrases that make the same point but with different words and references to build an image in readers' minds. Paragraph 6 is an excellent example of that style. It causes readers to slow down and savor the language, but that very fact can cause confusion for some readers. Work with a group of students to analyze this paragraph, starting with the third sentence. Explain that the details are various ways of describing time as running backward. Students need not interpret every detail in the description, but encourage them to comment about details that catch their attention. Have them use the same process with other passages in the story.

For additional support, go to the **Reading Studio** and assign the following **Level Up Tutorial: Author's Style.**

12   "Frankly, yes. We don't want anyone going who'll panic at the first shot. Six Safari leaders were killed last year, and a dozen hunters. We're here to give you the severest thrill a *real* hunter ever asked for. Traveling you back sixty million years to bag the biggest game in all of Time. Your personal check's still there. Tear it up."

13   Mr. Eckels looked at the check. His fingers twitched.

14   "Good luck," said the man behind the desk. "Mr. Travis, he's all yours."

15   They moved silently across the room, taking their guns with them, toward the Machine, toward the silver metal and the roaring light.

16   First a day and then a night and then a day and then a night, then it was day-night-day-night-day. A week, a month, a year, a decade! A.D. 2055. A.D. 2019, 1999! 1957! Gone! The Machine roared.

17   They put on their oxygen helmets and tested the intercoms.

18   Eckels swayed on the padded seat, his face pale, his jaw stiff. He felt the trembling in his arms, and he looked down and found his hands tight on the new rifle. There were four other men in the Machine. Travis, the Safari Leader; his assistant, Lesperance; and two other hunters, Billings and Kramer. They sat looking at each other, and the years blazed around them.

19   "Can these guns get a dinosaur cold?" Eckels felt his mouth saying.

20   "If you hit them right," said Travis on the helmet radio. "Some dinosaurs have two brains, one in the head, another far down the spinal column. We stay away from those. That's stretching luck. Put your first two shots into the eyes, if you can, blind them, and go back into the brain."

21   The Machine howled. Time was a film run backward. Suns fled and ten million moons fled after them. "Think," said Eckels. "Every hunter that ever lived would envy us today. This makes Africa seem like Illinois."

A Sound of Thunder   349

ENGLISH LEARNER SUPPORT

Understand Contractions Languages other than English have a variety of ways of forming contractions, and some languages have very few contractions. (Spanish, for example, has only two contractions: *al [a + el] and del [de + el].*) Explain that in English, contractions have an apostrophe that takes the place of one or more letters when combining a noun or pronoun with a verb or when combining a verb with the word *not*.

Make sure that students understand the meaning of these contractions in paragraphs 12 and 14: *don't, who'll, We're, check's, he's.* Read aloud paragraphs 12–14, replacing the contractions with their longer versions *(do not, who will, We are, check is, he is)*. Then read the paragraphs again, using the contractions. Discuss how the contractions make the official's comments sound like ordinary English conversation.

SUBSTANTIAL/MODERATE

CLOSE READ SCREENCAST

Modeled Discussion In their eBook, have students view the Close Read Screencast, in which readers discuss and annotate the third sentence of paragraph 6, a description of the reversal of time.

As a class, view and discuss the video. Then have students pair up to do an independent close read of paragraphs 139–142. Students can record their answers on the Close Read Practice PDF.

 Close Read Practice PDF

MAKE INFERENCES

Clarify any references with which students seem unfamiliar (for example, *Alexander* as Alexander the Great). (**Answer:** *These are religious and military/political leaders. Together, they represent not only a spectrum of accomplishments but also the best and worst human instincts. Travis mentions them here to emphasize that there is no human reason in this prehistoric time.*)

EL ENGLISH LEARNER SUPPORT

Confirm Understanding Students who are learning English may be confused by some of the idioms and other expressions that appear in paragraphs 19–21. Have students read the sentences in which these expressions appear; then explain each expression:

* *get . . . cold:* completely (In this case, it means to kill a dinosaur so that there is no question but that it is dead.)

* *stretching luck:* asking for too much, especially when risk is involved

* *This makes Africa seem like Illinois:* This place is exotic but extremely dangerous. (In Eckels's time, Africa was the most exotic and dangerous place for hunters, who would target lions, elephants, and so on. Hunting a dinosaur would be far more exotic and dangerous—so much so that it would make hunting in Africa seem as boring as living somewhere that was known for agriculture instead of hunting—a place like Illinois.)

Later on page 350, you may wish to explain *finicky business* (paragraph 32) as "something that is difficult to get right." **ALL LEVELS**

LANGUAGE CONVENTIONS

Explain that paragraph 38 is packed with potential effects of killing just one mouse in the prehistoric past (paragraph 34). Bradbury's highly descriptive style puts some distance between the various effects—some of which are built on causes that were effects of a previous situation, but all of which stem from the death of the one mouse. (**Answer:** *Travis is trying to make sure the hunters understand that they must be extremely careful and that the sequence of effects that could result from harming something in the prehistoric jungle is grave beyond all understanding.*)

 NOTICE & NOTE

MAKE INFERENCES

Annotate: Mark the names of the historic and classical figures that Travis alludes to in paragraph 25.

Infer: What ideas do you associate with these well-known figures? Why do you think Travis mentions them at this particular moment?

LANGUAGE CONVENTIONS

Annotate: In paragraph 38, number the steps in the cause-and-effect sequence chain, and mark the transition words that connect the steps.

Analyze: What point is Travis trying to impress on the travelers? How do transitions emphasize this point?

22   The Machine slowed; its scream fell to a murmur. The Machine stopped.

23   The sun stopped in the sky.

24   The fog that had enveloped the Machine blew away and they were in an old time, a very old time indeed, three hunters and two Safari Heads with their blue metal guns across their knees.

25   "Christ isn't born yet," said Travis. "Moses has not gone to the mountain to talk with God. The Pyramids are still in the earth, waiting to be cut out and put up. *Remember* that. Alexander, Caesar, Napoleon, Hitler—none of them exists."

26   The men nodded.

27   "That"—Mr. Travis pointed—"is the jungle of sixty million two thousand and fifty-five years before President Keith."

28   He indicated a metal path that struck off into green wilderness, over steaming swamp, among giant ferns and palms.

29   "And that," he said, "is the Path, laid by Time Safari for your use. It floats six inches above the earth. Doesn't touch so much as one grass blade, flower, or tree. It's an anti-gravity metal. Its purpose is to keep you from touching this world of the Past in any way. Stay on the Path. Don't go off it. I repeat. *Don't go off.* For *any* reason! If you fall off, there's a penalty. And don't shoot any animal we don't okay."

30   "Why?" asked Eckels.

31   They sat in the ancient wilderness. Far birds' cries blew on a wind, and the smell of tar and an old salt sea, moist grasses, and flowers the color of blood.

32   "We don't want to change the Future. We don't belong here in the Past. The government doesn't *like* us here. We have to pay big graft³ to keep our franchise. A Time Machine is finicky business. Not knowing it, we might kill an important animal, a small bird, a roach, a flower even, thus destroying an important link in a growing species."

33   "That's not clear," said Eckels.

34   "All right," Travis continued, "say we accidentally kill one mouse here. That means all the future families of this one particular mouse are destroyed, right?"

35   "Right."

36   "And all the families of the families of the families of that one mouse! With a stamp of your foot, you annihilate first one, then a dozen, then a thousand, a million, a *billion* possible mice!"

37   "So they're dead," said Eckels. "So what?"

38   "So what?" Travis snorted quietly. "Well, what about the foxes that'll need those mice to survive? For want of ten mice, a fox dies. For want of ten foxes, a lion starves. For want of a lion, all manner of insects, vultures, infinite billions of life forms are thrown into chaos and destruction. Eventually it all boils down to this: Fifty-nine million years later, a cave man, one of a dozen in the *entire world*,

³ **graft:** bribes.

APPLYING ACADEMIC VOCABULARY

☐ **abstract**   ☐ **evolve**   ☑ **explicit**   ☑ **facilitate**   ☐ **infer**

Write and Discuss Have students turn to a partner to discuss the following questions based on paragraph 29. Guide students to include the academic vocabulary words *explicit* and *facilitate* in their responses. Ask volunteers to share their responses with the class.

* What **explicit** warning about the Path does Travis give to the hunters, and why?

* What is the Path like? How do those qualities **facilitate** the hunt?

goes hunting wild boar or saber-toothed tiger for food. But you, friend, have *stepped* on all the tigers in that region. By stepping on *one* single mouse. So the cave man starves. And the cave man, please note, is not just *any* **expendable** man, no! He is an *entire future nation.*[5] From his loins would have sprung ten sons.[6] From *their* loins one hundred sons, and thus onward to a civilization. Destroy this one man, and you destroy a race, a people, an entire history of life. It is comparable to slaying some of Adam's grandchildren. The stomp of your foot, on one mouse, could start an earthquake, the effects of which could shake our earth and destinies down through Time, to their very foundations. With the death of that one cave man, a billion others yet unborn are throttled in the womb.[7] Perhaps Rome never rises on its seven hills. Perhaps Europe is forever a dark forest, and only Asia waxes healthy and teeming. Step on a mouse and you crush the Pyramids. Step on a mouse and you leave your print, like a Grand Canyon, across Eternity. Queen Elizabeth might never be born, Washington might not cross the Delaware, there might never be a United States at all. So be careful. Stay on the Path. *Never step off!*"

39 "I see," said Eckels. "Then it wouldn't pay for us even to touch the *grass*?"

40 "Correct. Crushing certain plants could add up infinitesimally. A little error here would multiply in sixty million years, all out of proportion. Of course maybe our theory is wrong. Maybe Time *can't* be changed by us. Or maybe it can be changed only in little **subtle** ways. A dead mouse here makes an insect imbalance there, a population disproportion later, a bad harvest further on, a depression, mass starvation, and, finally, a change in *social* temperament in far-flung countries. Something much more subtle, like that. Perhaps only a soft breath, a whisper, a hair, pollen on the air, such a slight, slight change that unless you looked close you wouldn't see it. Who knows? Who really can say he knows? We don't know. We're guessing. But until we do know for certain whether our messing around in Time *can* make a big roar or a little rustle in history, we're being careful. This Machine, this Path, your clothing and bodies, were sterilized, as you know, before the journey. We wear these oxygen helmets so we can't introduce our bacteria into an ancient atmosphere."

41 "How to we know which animals to shoot?"

42 "They're marked with red paint," said Travis. "Today, before our journey, we sent Lesperance here back with the Machine. He came to this particular era and followed certain animals."

43 "Studying them?"

44 "Right," said Lesperance. "I track them through their entire existence, noting which of them lives longest. Very few. How many times they mate. Not often. Life's short. When I find one that's going to die when a tree falls on him, or one that drowns in a tar pit, I note the exact hour, minute, and second. I shoot a paint bomb. It leaves

expendable
(ĭk-spĕn′də-bəl) *adj.* worth sacrificing to gain an objective.

subtle
(sŭt′l) *adj.* so slight as to be difficult to detect or describe.

A Sound of Thunder 351

ENGLISH LEARNER SUPPORT

Understand Plural Nouns In several languages (including Cantonese, Hmong, Korean, Tagalog, and Vietnamese), nouns do not change form to indicate a plural. Direct students to paragraph 38 and the use of *-s* or *-es* to indicate plurals in words such as *foxes, years, tigers, hills,* and *Pyramids,* as well as changing *-y* to *-i* before adding *-es* in *destinies.* In addition, point out *mice* and *grandchildren* and explain that *mice and grandchildren,* not *mouses* and *grandchilds,* are the correct plurals in English. You also may wish to explain that plural nouns are referred to with plural pronouns (for example, *the effects of which could shake our earth and **destinies** down through Time, to **their** very foundations*); languages such as Cantonese and Korean do not require the kind of pronoun-antecedent agreement that English does.
SUBSTANTIAL/MODERATE

CRITICAL VOCABULARY

expendable: In the scenario that Travis describes, every early human is essential. Not one of them should be allowed to die.

ASK STUDENTS how the official's words to Eckels in paragraph 4 show that he considers Eckels expendable. *(The official won't promise that Eckels won't die on the safari. Whether Eckels lives or dies, the company will get its fee.)*

subtle: Travis points out that even a tiny change—something that might be unnoticed at first—might have a devastating ripple effect.

ASK STUDENTS to name three subtle details that Travis says might change the world as the hunters know it. *(any three: a crushed blade of grass, a dead mouse, a soft breath, a whisper, a hair, pollen on the air)*

IMPROVE READING FLUENCY

Targeted Passage Have students work with partners to read with expression. First, model how to read expressively. Have students follow along in their books as you read paragraph 29 aloud, using commas as a guide for pauses and italicized words as a guide for special emphasis. Then, have partners take turns reading aloud paragraph 38, a few sentences at a time. Encourage students to provide feedback and support for pronouncing multisyllabic words. Remind students that when they are reading aloud for an audience they should pace their reading so the audience has time to understand difficult concepts, such as Travis is trying to explain to Eckels in this paragraph.

 Go to the **Reading Studio** for additional support in developing fluency.

MAKE INFERENCES

Before students respond, have them sum up, in a sentence or two, the main idea of the lecture that Travis gives Eckels in paragraphs 32–40. (*Example: If we harm anything other than our target, no matter how unimportant it seems, we could change history—and the world we know—in dramatic ways.*) (**Answer:** *Responses will vary but should express the idea that the results could be disastrous.*)

EL ENGLISH LEARNER SUPPORT

Understand Dashes Explain that one of the functions of dashes in English is to indicate an unfinished statement. Take students back to paragraph 8, where the official's comment ends with a dash: *"All you got to worry about is—"*. In this case, the eager Eckels supplies the rest of the statement, in paragraph 9: *"Shooting my dinosaur," Eckels finished it for him.* In paragraph 52, no character finishes Travis's statement because the implication is clear. A gun that goes off could harm something besides the targeted dinosaur, and Travis has just spent several paragraphs explaining the potentially disastrous effects of such an event.

SUBSTANTIAL/MODERATE

 For **speaking support** for students at varying proficiency levels, see the **Text X-Ray** on page 344D.

CRITICAL VOCABULARY

paradox: Lesperance explains that it would be an impossible contradiction if he, while returning to the present during his earlier visit, met himself traveling to the past with Travis and the hunters.

ASK STUDENTS to explain what is paradoxical about the statement *I am a liar.* (*If the person who says this really is a liar, then he or she is telling the truth—but he or she can't be telling the truth if he or she is a liar.*)

 NOTICE & NOTE

paradox
(păr´ə-dŏks) *n.* something that has or seems to have contradictory qualities.

MAKE INFERENCES
Annotate: Mark Travis's words in paragraph 52.

Infer: Finish Travis's sentence at the end of the paragraph.

a red patch on his side. We can't miss it. Then I correlate our arrival in the Past so that we meet the Monster not more than two minutes before he would have died anyway. This way, we kill only animals with no future, that are never going to mate again. You see how *careful* we are?"

45 "But if you came back this morning in Time," said Eckels eagerly, "you must've bumped into *us*, our Safari! How did it turn out? Was it successful? Did all of us get through—alive?"

46 Travis and Lesperance gave each other a look.

47 "That'd be a **paradox**," said the latter. "Time doesn't permit that sort of mess—a man meeting himself. When such occasions threaten, Time steps aside. Like an airplane hitting an air pocket. You felt the Machine jump just before we stopped? That was us passing ourselves on the way back to the Future. We saw nothing. There's no way of telling *if* this expedition was a success, *if* we got our monster, or whether all of us—meaning *you*, Mr. Eckels—got out alive."

48 Eckels smiled palely.

49 "Cut that," said Travis sharply. "Everyone on his feet!"

50 They were ready to leave the Machine.

51 The jungle was high and the jungle was broad and the jungle was the entire world forever and forever. Sounds like music and sounds like flying tents filled the sky, and those were pterodactyls soaring with cavernous gray wings, gigantic bats of delirium and night fever. Eckels, balanced on the narrow Path, aimed his rifle playfully.

52 "Stop that!" said Travis. "Don't even aim for fun, blast you! If your guns should go off—"

53 Eckels flushed. "Where's our *Tyrannosaurus*?"

54 Lesperance checked his wristwatch. "Up ahead. We'll bisect his trail in sixty seconds. Look for the red paint! Don't shoot till we give the word. Stay on the Path. *Stay on the Path!*"

55 They moved forward in the wind of morning.

56 "Strange," murmured Eckels. "Up ahead, sixty million years, Election Day over. Keith made President. Everyone celebrating. And here we are, a million years lost, and they don't exist. The things we worried about for months, a lifetime, not even born or thought of yet."

57 "Safety catches off, everyone!" ordered Travis. "You, first shot, Eckels. Second, Billings. Third, Kramer."

58 "I've hunted tiger, wild boar, buffalo, elephant, but now, this is *it*," said Eckels. "I'm shaking like a kid."

59 "Ah," said Travis.

60 Everyone stopped.

61 Travis raised his hand. "Ahead," he whispered. "In the mist. There he is. There's His Royal Majesty now."

62 The jungle was wide and full of twitterings, rustlings, murmurs, and sighs.

EL ENGLISH LEARNER SUPPORT

Practice Phonology Students who speak a variety of primary languages may struggle with the pronunciation of *r*-controlled vowels. This story can give them plenty of practice. For example, direct students to paragraphs 42–44. Read aloud, and then have students repeat after you, these examples of words with *r*-controlled vowels: *marked, here, particular, certain, their, entire, more,* and *future.* Then move to these groups of words: *before our journey, a tar pit, I correlate our arrival,* and *You see how* careful *we are.* If students stumble, repeat the word or group of words and have them try again, encouraging them with each success. **SUBSTANTIAL**

63   Suddenly it all ceased, as if someone had shut a door.

64   Silence.

65   A sound of thunder.

66   Out of the mist, one hundred yards away, came *Tyrannosaurus rex.*

67   "It," whispered Eckels. "It . . ."

68   "Sh!"

69   It came on great oiled, resilient, striding legs. It towered thirty feet above half of the trees, a great evil god, folding its delicate watchmaker's claws close to its oily reptilian chest. Each lower leg was a piston, a thousand pounds of white bone, sunk in thick ropes of muscle, sheathed over in a gleam of pebbled skin like the mail[4] of a terrible warrior. Each thigh was a ton of meat, ivory, and steel mesh. And from the great breathing cage of the upper body those two delicate arms dangled out front, arms with hands which might pick up and examine men like toys, while the snake neck coiled. And the head itself, a ton of sculptured stone, lifted easily upon the sky. Its mouth gaped, exposing a fence of teeth like daggers. Its eyes rolled, ostrich eggs, empty of all expression save hunger. It closed its mouth in a death grin. It ran, its pelvic bones crushing aside trees and bushes, its taloned feet clawing damp earth, leaving prints six inches

---

[4] **mail:** flexible metal armor.

ENGLISH LEARNER SUPPORT

Analyze Onomatopoeia Display and pronounce the word *onomatopoeia.* Explain that onomatopoeia is a word that imitates the sound it describes. Give *pop, splash, fizz, mumble,* and *click* as examples and have students sound out each one for themselves. Next, direct students to paragraphs 62–65. Discuss the onomatopoeic words that describe jungle sounds in paragraph 62: *twitterings, rustlings, murmurs, sighs.* Then have students contrast those sounds with the *silence* of paragraphs 63 and 64—and with the onomatopoeic *thunder* that breaks that silence.

LIGHT

TO CHALLENGE STUDENTS . . .

Explore Figurative Language Paragraph 69 is another excellent example of Bradbury's descriptive style. Invite groups of students to discuss the figurative language in this paragraph, explaining how each example helps them visualize the *Tyrannosaurus rex.* Here are a few examples; students can find others:

a great evil god	*the snake neck coiled*
its delicate watchmaker's claws	*a fence of teeth like daggers*
Each lower leg was a piston	*Its eyes rolled, ostrich eggs*
pebbled skin like the mail of a terrible warrior	*It ran with a gliding ballet step*

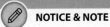
TEACH

For **reading support** for students at varying proficiency levels, see the **Text X-Ray** on page 344D.

▶ AHA MOMENT

Have students recall previous details that suggest that Eckels may be losing his initial confidence—for example, his pale face and trembling arms during the transition to the past (paragraph 18), his questioning about whether Lesperance might already know how this safari will turn out (paragraph 45), and his pale smile (paragraph 48). (**Answer:** *Eckels may be in shock now or overwhelmed by what he sees. The safari leaders have killed dinosaurs before, so Eckels is probably wrong.*)

CRITICAL VOCABULARY

undulate: The moving insects on the dinosaur's skin make its skin seem to rise and fall.

ASK STUDENTS to describe what it would look like to see a group of dancers undulating across a stage. (*The dancers would move up and down, or back and forth, giving the appearance of waves in motion.*)

354   Unit 5

AHA MOMENT

Notice & Note: Mark what Eckels suddenly realizes in paragraph 72.

Predict: Do you think Eckels is right? What science fiction characteristics can help you correct or confirm this prediction?

undulate
(ŭn′jə-lāt) *v.* to move in waves.

---

deep wherever it settled its weight. It ran with a gliding ballet step, far too poised and balanced for its ten tons. It moved into a sunlit arena warily, its beautifully reptilian hands feeling the air.

70   "Why, why," Eckels twitched his mouth. "It could reach up and grab the moon."

71   "Sh!" Travis jerked angrily. "He hasn't seen us yet."

72   "It can't be killed." Eckels pronounced this verdict quietly, as if there could be no argument. He had weighed the evidence and this was his considered opinion. The rifle in his hands seemed a cap gun. "We were fools to come. This is impossible."

73   "Shut up!" hissed Travis.

74   "Nightmare."

75   "Turn around," commanded Travis. "Walk quietly to the Machine. We'll remit one half your fee."

76   "I didn't realize it would be this *big*," said Eckels. "I miscalculated, that's all. And now I want out."

77   "It *sees* us!"

78   "There's the red paint on its chest!"

79   The Tyrant Lizard raised itself. Its armored flesh glittered like a thousand green coins. The coins, crusted with slime, steamed. In the slime, tiny insects wriggled, so that the entire body seemed to twitch and **undulate** even while the monster itself did not move. It exhaled. The stink of raw flesh blew down the wilderness.

80   "Get me out of here," said Eckels. "It was never like this before. I was always sure I'd come through alive. I had good guides, good safaris, and safety. This time, I figured wrong. I've met my match and admit it. This is too much for me to get hold of."

81   "Don't run," said Lesperance. "Turn around. Hide in the Machine."

82   "Yes." Eckels seemed to be numb. He looked at his feet as if trying to make them move. He gave a grunt of helplessness.

83   "Eckels!"

84   He took a few steps, blinking, shuffling.

85   "Not *that* way!"

86   The Monster, at the first motion, lunged forward with a terrible scream. It covered one hundred yards in six seconds. The rifles jerked up and blazed fire. A windstorm from the beast's mouth engulfed them in the stench of slime and old blood. The Monster roared, teeth glittering with sun.

87   Eckels, not looking back, walked blindly to the edge of the Path, his gun limp in his arms, stepped off the Path, and walked, not knowing it, in the jungle. His feet sank into green moss. His legs moved him, and he felt alone and remote from the events behind.

88   The rifles cracked again. Their sound was lost in shriek and lizard thunder. The great level of the reptile's tail swung up, lashed sideways. Trees exploded in clouds of leaf and branch. The Monster

twitched its jeweler's hands down to fondle at the men, to twist them in half, to crush them like berries, to cram them into its teeth and its screaming throat. Its boulder-stone eyes leveled with the men. They saw themselves mirrored. They fired at the metallic eyelids and the blazing black iris.

89   Like a stone idol, like a mountain avalanche, *Tyrannosaurus* fell. Thundering, it clutched trees, pulled them with it. It wrenched and tore the metal Path. The men flung themselves back and away. The body hit, ten tons of cold flesh and stone. The guns fired. The Monster lashed its armored tail, twitched its snake jaws, and lay still. A fount of blood spurted from its throat. Somewhere inside, a sac of fluids burst. Sickening gushes drenched the hunters. They stood, red and glistening.

90   The thunder faded.

91   The jungle was silent. After the avalanche, a green peace. After the nightmare, morning.

92   Billings and Kramer sat on the pathway and threw up. Travis and Lesperance stood with smoking rifles, cursing steadily.

93   In the Time Machine, on his face, Eckels lay shivering. He had found his way back to the Path, climbed into the Machine.

94   Travis came walking, glanced at Eckels, took cotton gauze from a metal box, and returned to the others, who were sitting on the Path.

95   "Clean up."

96   They wiped the blood from their helmets. They began to curse too. The Monster lay, a hill of solid flesh. Within, you could hear the sighs and murmurs as the furthest chambers of it died, the organs malfunctioning, liquids running a final instant from pocket to sac to spleen, everything shutting off, closing up forever. It was like standing by a wrecked locomotive or a steam shovel at quitting time, all valves being released or levered tight. Bones cracked; the tonnage of its own

A Sound of Thunder 355

ENGLISH LEARNER SUPPORT

Analyze Description Display paragraph 96, another strong example of Bradbury's descriptive style. Elicit that here Bradbury is describing the death of the *T. rex*. Work through the paragraph, one sentence at a time. Ask students to read aloud and comment about the various details—what images they bring to mind (for example, the comparison of the dying beast to a wrecked locomotive) and how they are meant to make readers feel (for example, the poignancy in the snapping of the forearms that Bradbury previously compared to delicate watchmaker's claws in paragraph 69 and to jeweler's hands in paragraph 88). Invite students to suggest some details that they would add to the paragraph.
MODERATE/LIGHT

ENGLISH LEARNER SUPPORT

Practice Phonology Students whose primary language is Spanish, Arabic, Hindu-Urdu, or Haitian Creole may struggle with the pronunciation of the *th* sound. To provide some practice, direct students to paragraphs 84–89. Read aloud, and then have students repeat after you, these examples of words that begin with the *th* sound: *that, them, their, themselves, thundering,* and *throat*. Then move to these words that end with the *th* sound: *with, mouth, teeth,* and *Path*. As before, repeat words that seem to cause students special trouble and encourage students as you see progress. **SUBSTANTIAL**

TEACH

ANALYZE PLOT AND SETTING

Read aloud, or invite a volunteer to read aloud, paragraph 109. Suggest that students focus on Travis's statement, "But it isn't *that* so much, no," as the introduction to his greatest source of anger toward Eckels. (**Answer:** *The setting in the distant past is crucial to events because any change that Eckels has caused then may drastically alter the men's present [in the year 2055].*)

---

flesh, off balance, dead weight, snapped the delicate forearms, caught underneath. The meat settled, quivering.

97   Another cracking sound. Overhead, a gigantic tree branch broke from its heavy mooring, fell. It crashed upon the dead beast with finality.

98   "There." Lesperance checked his watch. "Right on time. That's the giant tree that was scheduled to fall and kill this animal originally." He glanced at the two hunters. "You want the trophy picture?"

99   "What?"

100   "We can't take a trophy back to the Future. The body has to stay right here where it would have died originally, so the insects, birds, and bacteria can get at it, as they were intended to. Everything in balance. The body stays. But we *can* take a picture of you standing near it."

101   The two men tried to think, but gave up, shaking their heads.

102   They let themselves be led along the metal Path. They sank wearily into the Machine cushions. They gazed back at the ruined Monster, the stagnating mound, where already strange reptilian birds and golden insects were busy at the steaming armor.

103   A sound on the floor of the Time Machine stiffened them. Eckels sat there, shivering.

104   "I'm sorry," he said at last.

105   "Get up!" cried Travis.

106   Eckels got up.

107   "Go out on that Path alone," said Travis. He had his rifle pointed. "You're not coming back in the Machine. We're leaving you here!"

108   Lesperance seized Travis's arm. "Wait—"

ANALYZE PLOT AND SETTING

Annotate: In paragraph 109, mark Travis's explanation of why he is angry.

Analyze: How does the setting influence events in this part of the story?

109   "Stay out of this!" Travis shook his hand away. "This fool nearly killed us. But it isn't *that* so much, no. It's his *shoes*! Look at them! <u>He ran off the Path. That *ruins* us! We'll forfeit! Thousands of dollars of insurance! We guarantee no one leaves the Path. He left it. Oh, the fool! I'll have to report to the government. They might revoke our license to travel. Who knows *what* he's done to Time, to History!"</u>

110   "Take it easy, all he did was kick up some dirt."

111   "How do we *know*?" cried Travis. "We don't know anything! It's all a mystery! Get out of here, Eckels!"

112   Eckels fumbled his shirt. "I'll pay anything. A hundred thousand dollars!"

113   Travis glared at Eckels's checkbook and spat. "Go out there. The Monster's next to the Path. Stick your arms up to your elbows in his mouth. Then you can come back with us."

114   "That's unreasonable!"

115   "The Monster's dead, you idiot. The bullets! The bullets can't be left behind. They don't belong in the Past; they might change anything. Here's my knife. Dig them out!"

---

116   The jungle was alive again, full of the old tremorings and bird cries. Eckels turned slowly to regard the primeval[5] garbage dump, that hill of nightmares and terror. After a long time, like a sleepwalker he shuffled out along the Path.

117   He returned, shuddering, five minutes later, his arms soaked and red to the elbows. He held out his hands. Each held a number of steel bullets. Then he fell. He lay where he fell, not moving.

118   "You didn't have to make him do that," said Lesperance.

119   "Didn't I? It's too early to tell." Travis nudged the still body. "He'll live. Next time he won't go hunting game like this. Okay." He jerked his thumb wearily at Lesperance. "Switch on. Let's go home."

120   1492. 1776. 1812.

121   They cleaned their hands and faces. They changed their caking shirts and pants. Eckels was up and around again, not speaking. Travis glared at him for a full ten minutes.

122   "Don't look at me," cried Eckels. "I haven't done anything."

123   "Who can tell?"

124   "Just ran off the Path, that's all, a little mud on my shoes—what do you want me to do—get down and pray?"

125   "We might need it. I'm warning you, Eckels, I might kill you yet. I've got my gun ready."

126   "I'm innocent. I've done nothing!"

127   1999. 2000. 2055.

128   The Machine stopped.

129   "Get out," said Travis.

130   The room was there as they had left it. But not the same as they had left it. The same man sat behind the same desk. But the same man did not quite sit behind the same desk.

131   Travis looked around swiftly. "Everything okay here?" he snapped.

132   "Fine. Welcome home!"

133   Travis did not relax. He seemed to be looking at the very atoms of the air itself, at the way the sun poured through the one high window.

134   "Okay, Eckels, get out. Don't ever come back."

135   Eckels could not move.

136   "You heard me," said Travis. "What're you *staring* at?"

137   Eckels stood smelling of the air, and there was a thing to the air, a chemical taint so subtle, so slight, that only a faint cry of his **subliminal** senses warned him it was there. The colors, white, gray, blue, orange, in the wall, in the furniture, in the sky beyond the window, were . . . were . . . And there was a *feel*. His flesh twitched. His hands twitched. He stood drinking the oddness with the pores of his body. Somewhere, someone must have been screaming one of those whistles that only a dog can hear. His body screamed silence

---

[5] **primeval:** primitive; of the earliest times.

subliminal
(sŭb-lĭm´ə-nəl) *adj.* below the level of awareness.

ENGLISH LEARNER SUPPORT

Discuss Syntax Begin by defining the word *syntax* for students. *(the way words are combined to form phrases and sentences)* Read aloud paragraph 130, one sentence at a time, and have students repeat after you. Students may be a little confused by the sentence fragments and by the odd placement of the phrase *did not quite*. Discuss how the strangeness of this paragraph's structure reflects the possibility that Eckels's leaving the Path in the past may indeed have altered the present. **ALL LEVELS**

CRITICAL VOCABULARY

subliminal: At some level—a level that Eckels cannot analyze with his mind—Eckels's body senses a change in the world.

ASK STUDENTS how feeling inexplicably nervous when entering a room might be an example of a subliminal message. *(The nervousness might come because the body senses danger but cannot communicate that information in words to the brain.)*

WHEN STUDENTS STRUGGLE . . .

Contrast Settings Help student pairs examine the difference between the "present" that opens the story and the "present" that concludes it. Suggest that they use a T-chart such as this to record details that they then can bring into class discussion of the story. A few details have been provided.

The "Original" 2055	The "New" 2055
nothing mentioned about the air	chemical taint to the air
sign spelled correctly	spelling on sign very different

 For additional support, go to the **Reading Studio** and assign the following **Level Up Tutorial: Setting.**

ANALYZE PLOT AND SETTING

After students respond, make sure they understand the importance of paragraphs 140–143, the cause of the changes. (**Answer:** *The words on the sign are spelled differently, and Deutscher rather than Keith will be the next president. Voters have elected a leader who is described in paragraph 8 as "an anti-everything man . . . a militarist, anti-Christ, anti-human, anti-intellectual" and whose election some people feared so much that they were willing to move to the past to escape his rule. In this "new" country, it seems that strength and toughness are valued over reason and possibly education, based on the writing on the sign.*)

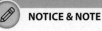

ANALYZE PLOT AND SETTING

Annotate: In paragraphs 138–145, mark the things that are different from the way they were before the trip.

Interpret: What do the differences reveal about how the country has changed?

in return. Beyond this room, beyond this wall, beyond this man who was not quite the same man seated at this desk that was not quite the same desk . . . lay an entire world of streets and people. What sort of world it was now, there was no telling. He could feel them moving there, beyond the walls, almost, like so many chess pieces blown in a dry wind. . . .

138   But the immediate thing was the sign painted on the office wall, the same sign he had read earlier today on first entering.

139   Somehow, the sign had changed:

> ## TYME SEFARI INC.
> Sefaris tu any yeer en the past.
> Yu naim the animall.
> Wee taek yu thair.
> Yu shoot itt.

140   Eckels felt himself fall into a chair. He fumbled crazily at the thick slime on his boots. He held up a clod of dirt, trembling, "No, it *can't* be. Not a *little* thing like that. No!"

141   Embedded in the mud, glistening green and gold and black, was a butterfly, very beautiful and very dead.

142   "Not a little thing like *that*! Not a butterfly!" cried Eckels.

143   It fell to the floor, an exquisite thing, a small thing that could upset balances and knock down a line of small dominoes and then big dominoes and then gigantic dominoes, all down the years across Time. Eckels's mind whirled. It *couldn't* change things. Killing one butterfly couldn't be *that* important! Could it?

144   His face was cold. His mouth trembled, asking: "Who—who won the presidential election yesterday?"

145   The man behind the desk laughed. "You joking? You know very well. Deutscher, of course! Who else? Not that fool weakling Keith. We got an iron man now, a man with guts!" The official stopped. "What's wrong?"

146   Eckels moaned. He dropped to his knees. He scrabbled at the golden butterfly with shaking fingers. "Can't we," he pleaded to the world, to himself, to the officials, to the Machine, "can't we take it *back*, can't we *make* it alive again? Can't we start over? Can't we—"

147   He did not move. Eyes shut, he waited, shivering. He heard Travis breathe loud in the room; he heard Travis shift his rifle, click the safety catch, and raise the weapon.

148   There was a sound of thunder.

CHECK YOUR UNDERSTANDING

Have students answer the questions independently.

Answers:

1. *B*

2. *H*

3. *D*

If they answer any questions incorrectly, have them reread the text to confirm their understanding. Then they may proceed to ANALYZE THE TEXT on page 360.

CHECK YOUR UNDERSTANDING

Answer these questions before moving on to the **Analyze the Text** section on the following page.

1 What kind of business does Time Safari, Inc. operate?

   A They sell watches with bands made from exotic animal skins.

   B They offer trips back in time to hunt extinct animals.

   C They make virtual-reality, time-travel games.

   D They research and report on environmental issues.

2 Why are the travelers warned to be careful not to step off the Path?

   F The safari company wants to be sure travelers are safe.

   G Once a person steps off the Path, they can never get back on.

   H Changing anything in the past could drastically alter the future.

   J The Path offers the best vantage point for shooting dinosaurs.

3 What does Eckels do that has such far-reaching consequences?

   A He attempts to kill a large dinosaur.

   B He chooses to go on a dangerous safari.

   C He leaves his boot in the past.

   D He accidentally kills a butterfly.

A Sound of Thunder   359

ENGLISH LEARNER SUPPORT

Oral Assessment Use the following questions to assess students' comprehension and speaking skills.

1. What kind of service does Time Safari, Inc., provide? *(It takes customers into the past so that they can hunt animals that are extinct in the present.)*

2. Why are people supposed to stay on the Path that the company has built? *(If they were to step off the Path, they might do something that would change the future.)*

3. What does Eckels do that has a huge effect? *(He steps off the Path and accidentally steps on a butterfly, killing it.)* **SUBSTANTIAL/MODERATE**

APPLY

ANALYZE THE TEXT

Possible answers:

1. **DOK 3:** *The two scenes convey the immense effects that were caused by stepping on a prehistoric butterfly. The author is emphasizing the ideas that even an insignificant action can have major repercussions and that individuals have the power to change the course of history. Students may cite the changed sign or election result.*

2. **DOK 4:** *In the beginning of the story, readers learn that technological advances have made time travel possible. The whole story is based on the idea of being able to travel to different times and places. In the prehistoric setting, the dinosaur so terrifies Eckels that he stumbles off the Path and kills a butterfly. By the end of the story, it's clear that his action has affected the future—at the cost of his own life.*

3. **DOK 2:** *Travis is furious that the future has changed, for the worse, as a result of Eckels's stepping off the Path. His short temper with Eckels in the past and his forcing Eckels to retrieve the bullets suggest that Travis is liable to react quickly and cruelly.*

4. **DOK 4:** *The message is that actions can have unintended and even disastrous consequences. The setting—a present that becomes a different present because of a past action—dramatically illustrates the theme.*

5. **DOK 4:** *When Eckels asks, "Can't we start over?" the clear answer to his question is "No." This points to the theme that small actions can have monumental effects and that we are not exempt from the consequences of our actions, even actions that are unintentional.*

RESEARCH

Depending upon time constraints and students' proficiency, allow students to conduct their research in pairs or small groups. Remind students to check their findings in at least two reliable sources.

Connect Invite group representatives to share their ideas. You also may wish to ask them whether their research supports the commonly held idea that the term *butterfly effect* is based on Bradbury's story. (*It is not; the term comes from Lorenz's work.*)

 RESPOND

ANALYZE THE TEXT

Support your responses with evidence from the text. 📓 NOTEBOOK

1. **Draw Conclusions** The story begins and ends in the future. What is significant about these two scenes? What do you think the author wanted you to notice or think about in them? Cite textual evidence to support your conclusions.

2. **Analyze** How did the two settings influence the way story events unfolded? Cite evidence from the text to support your analysis.

3. **Infer** What motivates Travis to shoot Eckels at the end of the story? Support your response with evidence from the text.

4. **Synthesize** What theme or message does this story convey? In what ways is setting important to the theme? Cite evidence from the text to support your response.

5. **Notice & Note** Think about the Tough Questions Eckels asks at the end of the story. What theme might these questions support?

RESEARCH TIP
A source that seems factual at first may turn out to be based on opinion or personal interpretation. Make sure the sources you use are authored by a recognized authority on your subject from a respected university or institution. Also, ask yourself whether the author seems to have a bias.

RESEARCH

The scientific concept called the "butterfly effect" states that a single small change can alter the future in momentous ways. Explore this concept by conducting research to answer the questions in the chart below.

QUESTION	ANSWER
Who was Edward Lorenz?	*Edward Lorenz was a meteorologist who found through mathematical modeling that small events may have major effects on weather far away.*
How did the butterfly effect get this name?	*It was named for the idea that an event as small as a butterfly flapping its wings could result in a tornado thousands of miles away.*
What is chaos theory?	*Chaos theory is a mathematical field concerning complex systems with interrelated variables that initially appear to be random.*
How is the butterfly effect connected to chaos theory?	*Small changes at the beginning of a dynamic system (like the flapping of a butterfly's wings) are what make these systems appear to be chaotic.*

Connect How does "A Sound of Thunder" reflect the butterfly effect and chaos theory? Based on your research, which scientific elements in "A Sound of Thunder" now seem realistic? Discuss your ideas in a small group.

360 Unit 5

LEARNING MINDSET

Questioning On these Respond pages, students are asked several questions. Remind students that they, too, should ask questions and feel comfortable about doing so. When they ask questions, students show that they are open to considering new ideas and trying new things. Suggest the following as possible ways of asking questions:

- asking themselves about various ways to approach a challenging question
- asking classmates for clarification during discussions and presentations
- asking you or peers for feedback as they work on the Research activity or the Create and Present activities

CREATE AND PRESENT

Write a Story Write your own story about characters who travel through time. What technological advances will allow your characters to time travel?

❑ Decide on your main and supporting characters and develop two settings for your story: the characters' present setting and the past or future setting to which they travel.

❑ Determine the problems characters will encounter and whether these problems will be solved. Use a timeline to help you figure out what will happen in the beginning, middle, and end of your story.

❑ Consider telling the story in the first-person, using the main character as your narrator. Develop a strong and engaging voice, using dialogue to reveal reactions.

Deliver a Sales Pitch Imagine that you have a time travel company. Deliver a sales pitch to convince listeners that the adventures they will have if they take a trip with your company are worth the high price you charge.

❑ Create a company name and slogan. Then choose the adventures you will offer, for example witnessing important historical events or shopping for fashions of the future.

❑ Use persuasive language and details that will stimulate interest in the adventures you offer.

❑ Incorporate visuals or other media to enhance your presentation.

❑ Deliver your pitch with an engaging and persuasive tone, adequate volume, and effective pauses. Rehearse before delivering it to the class.

Go to the **Writing Studio** for more on writing a short story.

Go to the **Speaking and Listening Studio** for help with delivering a speech.

RESPOND TO THE ESSENTIAL QUESTION

 ? How do changes around us reveal who we are?

Gather Information Review your annotations and notes on "A Sound of Thunder." Then add relevant information to your Response Log. As you determine which information to include, think about:

- the kinds of changes people experience
- how behavior in times of crisis reveals character
- what kinds of situations require courage or strength

At the end of the unit, use your notes to help you write a research report.

UNIT 5 RESPONSE LOG

ACADEMIC VOCABULARY

As you write and discuss what you learned about "A Sound of Thunder," be sure to use the Academic Vocabulary words. Check off each of the words that you use.

❑ **abstract**

❑ **evolve**

❑ **explicit**

❑ **facilitate**

❑ **infer**

CREATE AND PRESENT

Write a Story Explain that although students' stories have the same topic as "A Sound of Thunder," they need not copy the idea of changing one time due to an action in the past. (Note that students here have the option of writing about a trip to the future, not just the past.) Students may come up with very different themes, as well. Remind students of the following points:

- Most engaging stories are built upon a conflict. Given the instructions, students should build their stories upon an external conflict of some kind.

- If students choose to include a first-person narrator, they should have the narrator refer to himself or herself with first-person pronouns.

- In revealing reactions, students should use dialogue to "show" rather than "tell." (Example: Instead of writing, "I was astounded," students might have the narrator say, "You've got to be kidding!")

- As students edit their stories, suggest that they ask peers for feedback regarding how smoothly the story moves from one time period to another.

 For **writing support** for students at varying proficiency levels, see the **Text X-Ray** on page 344D.

Deliver a Sales Pitch Briefly discuss how Time Safari, Inc., attracted customers: The company understood who their target customers were (hunters) and then crafted advertising to appeal to their interests (being able to hunt a creature that no one in their own time could hunt—"the biggest game in all of Time"). Urge students to do the same by considering these questions: Who would be most interested in traveling to the past? To the future? How can I persuade those people to give my company their money (probably a lot of money)? Suggest that students search for still images or videos that depict what their potential customers might see.

RESPOND TO THE ESSENTIAL QUESTION

Allow time for students to add details from "A Sound of Thunder" to their Unit 5 Response Logs.

EL ENGLISH LEARNER SUPPORT

Discuss Connotations Remind students that many words, in addition to having a dictionary definition, or denotation, also have a connotation; that is, many words have positive or negative feelings associated with them. Discuss how connotations may guide choices of words and phrases such as these in the sales pitch:

- Will customers take a *trip*, or a *voyage?*

- In the past, will they see *interesting events*, or *world-changing events?*

- In the future, will they *observe an amazing new time*, or *a world they now can only dream about?* **ALL LEVELS**

CRITICAL VOCABULARY

Possible answers:

1. *Social media interactions are more expendable because they tend to be shallower and less meaningful than face-to-face interactions.*

2. *A shrug is more subtle because it could have a lot of different meanings.*

3. *"Less is more" is more of a paradox because, while having less of something can increase its impact—and therefore be "more"—it's still less, too.*

4. *Undulating pain from the injury would feel as if it were coming in waves instead of being constant.*

5. *The design of the logo of my favorite fast-food place sends a subliminal message that always makes me want to eat there.*

VOCABULARY STRATEGY:
Synonyms and Antonyms

In paragraph 38, for example, students could mark *destroy, slaying, stomp, throttled,* and *crush*. Findings in a thesaurus may include the following:

- Synonyms: *obliterate, eradicate, stamp (out), decimate*
- Antonyms: *conserve, protect, preserve*

 RESPOND

WORD BANK
expendable
subtle
paradox
undulate
subliminal

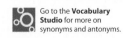 Go to the **Vocabulary Studio** for more on synonyms and antonyms.

CRITICAL VOCABULARY

Practice and Apply Answer each question, incorporating the meaning of the Critical Vocabulary word in your explanation.

1. Which would you consider more **expendable**, interacting through social media or interacting in person?

2. Which is more **subtle**, a sigh or a shrug?

3. Which is a greater **paradox**: "Less is more" or "Love hurts"?

4. What would you feel if the pain from an injury were to **undulate**?

5. How might a **subliminal** idea affect your behavior?

VOCABULARY STRATEGY:
Synonyms and Antonyms

A **synonym** is a word with a meaning similar to that of another word. An **antonym** is a word with a meaning opposite of another word. A synonym for the Critical Vocabulary word *undulate* appears in the first paragraph of the story: *quaver*. Both words mean "to fluctuate." Other synonyms for *undulate* include *ripple* and *billow*.

Sometimes an unfamiliar word will have a synonym or an antonym in the context of a sentence or paragraph. Knowing the meaning of the word's synonym or antonym can help you figure out its meaning. You can find synonyms and antonyms in a thesaurus. In a dictionary, synonyms are often given as part of the definition of a word.

Practice and Apply Search through the story to find all the synonyms and antonyms for the word *annihilate* in paragraph 36. Use a thesaurus to find other synonyms and antonyms. Record the words in the chart.

SYNONYMS OF *ANNIHILATE*	ANTONYMS OF *ANNIHILATE*

 ENGLISH LEARNER SUPPORT

Vocabulary Strategy Give students additional practice in finding and using synonyms and antonyms. Display the following words from early in "A Sound of Thunder": *disobey* (paragraph 4), *sound* and *gigantic* (paragraph 5), *vanish* (paragraph 6), *thin* and *badly* (paragraph 7). Have students work in pairs to select a few synonyms and antonyms for each word. Compile a master list and invite students to use some of the words in original sentences. You also may wish to invite students to share synonyms and antonyms for some of these words from their primary language. **MODERATE/LIGHT**

LANGUAGE CONVENTIONS:
Transitions

Transitions are words and phrases that connect ideas in writing, making the ideas easier to understand. Many ideas in "A Sound of Thunder" have a cause-and-effect relationship. Ray Bradbury uses well-placed transitions to guide readers through chains of causes and effects.

Note the underlined transitions in this passage of dialogue from the story. The repeated use of the transition "for want of" helps readers understand the momentous effects that could result from the death of a single mouse.

"Well, what about the foxes that'll need those mice to survive? <u>For want of</u> ten mice, a fox dies. <u>For want of</u> ten foxes, a lion starves. <u>For want of</u> a lion, all manner of insects, vultures, infinite billions of life forms are thrown into chaos and destruction."

In addition, the transitions allow Bradbury to briefly but clearly describe the long sequence of effects. Without transitions such as those listed in the chart below, the ideas in this section would be difficult to follow.

TRANSITIONS THAT SHOW CAUSE-AND-EFFECT RELATIONSHIPS		
accordingly	as a result	because
consequently	due to	eventually
for this reason	hence	if . . . then
in that case	owing to	since
so	therefore	thus

Practice and Apply Revise your time travel story to add at least two transitional phrases that show cause-and-effect relationships. Discuss with a partner how each transition improves the meaning, flow, and cohesion of your writing.

LANGUAGE CONVENTIONS:
Transitions

Discuss the use of *for want of* in the example, explaining that it is a more unusual way of saying *because*. Rephrase it as follows: *Because ten mice are now gone, a fox dies. Because ten foxes are now gone, a lion starves. . . .* Illustrate some uses of the transitions in the chart by naming a cause-and-effect event in "A Sound of Thunder" and creating sentences using various transitions:

- Because (Since) Eckels stepped off the Path, he changed history.
- Due to (Owing to) Eckels's fear and carelessness, his world changed dramatically.
- Eckels stepped on a butterfly; therefore (for this reason, thus, so, consequently, as a result, accordingly), he altered the future.
- If you don't want to change history, then you shouldn't travel through time.

Practice and Apply Point out that most of these transitions can appear in various sentence structures; what matters most is that they clearly indicate which event is the cause and which is the effect. Monitor students as they work, answering questions and making suggestions (for example, checking where cause-and-effect relationships exist in their stories). As students meet with partners, remind them that revisions will vary but should incorporate cause-and-effect transitions from the chart.

 ENGLISH LEARNER SUPPORT

Language Conventions Use the following supports with students at varying proficiency levels:

- Review the transitions in the chart with students. Make sure that students recognize the difference between cause-and-effect transitions and transitions that show time (such as *later*) or contrast (such as *however*). **SUBSTANTIAL**
- Before students revise their stories, have them work with partners to create original sentences that use a few of the transitions in the chart.

Doing this can help them see how to identify and distinguish between causes and effects. **MODERATE**

- Ask students to choose four transitions from the chart and write two sentences for each one, with each sentence placing the transition in a different spot. Have them share their sentences and explain their choices about sentence structure. **LIGHT**

5 P.M., TUESDAY, AUGUST 23, 2005

Poem by **Patricia Smith**

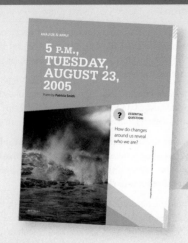

GENRE ELEMENTS
POETRY

Remind students that **lyric poetry** attempts to recreate emotions and experiences by using figurative language and words with specific connotations, and by incorporating sensory details that can be used to create mental images. In lyric poetry, meaning is often expanded by the arrangement of words and lines.

In this lesson, students will examine a poet's word choice, which includes figures of speech and words with connotative meanings. They will construct mental images through word choice, imagery, and figurative language. This will help them appreciate the **extended metaphor** of the poem (a comparison of unlike things that share some similarities developed at length in a text) and analyze its effect.

LEARNING OBJECTIVES

- Analyze word choice, including figurative language and words with strong connotations, and the mental images such language creates.
- Research hurricane development and compare facts to the poem's depiction.
- Write a literary analysis to interpret the effect of personification in the poem.
- Give a poetry reading.
- **Language**   Experiment with ways of reading a poem aloud.

TEXT COMPLEXITY

Quantitative Measures	5 P.M., Tuesday, August 23, 2005	Lexile: N/A
Qualitative Measures	**Ideas Presented** Multiple levels of meaning; use of extended metaphor and personification.	
	Structure Used Complex; use of free verse.	
	Language Used Somewhat complex; more figurative language used.	
	Knowledge Required Helpful to know about Hurricane Katrina or hurricanes in general.	

RESOURCES

- Unit 5 Response Log
- Selection Audio
- Reading Studio: Notice & Note
- Level Up Tutorials: Historical and Cultural Context; Figurative Language
- Writing Studio: Writing Analytical Texts
- Speaking and Listening Studio: Delivering Your Recitation
- ⊘ "5 P.M., Tuesday, August 23, 2005" Selection Test

SUMMARIES

English

This poem centers on the development of Hurricane Katrina several days before anyone realized how forceful it would become. The poem serves as an extended metaphor in which the speaker of the poem is the storm itself. The power of nature and respecting natural forces are themes of the poem.

Spanish

Este poema se centra en el desarrollo del Huracán Katrina, varios días antes de que alguien supiera lo fuerte que sería. El poema sirve como una metáfora extendida en que la voz narrativa es la misma tormenta. El poder de la naturaleza y el respeto a las fuerzas de la naturaleza son temas del poema.

SMALL-GROUP OPTIONS

Have students work in small groups to read and discuss the selection.

Numbered Heads Together

- After students have read and analyzed "5 P.M., Tuesday, August 23, 2005," have them form groups of four and then number off 1-2-3-4 within the group.
- Ask students to discuss the following question: How effective was the poet's comparison of a developing hurricane to a woman?
- After students discuss their responses in their groups, call out a number from 1 to 4. That "numbered" student from each group then shares the key ideas from the group's discussion with the whole class.
- Repeat with another topic or question, such as: What is the significance of the word *harbors* in line 17?

Jigsaw with Experts

- Divide the poem into four parts (for example, A = the epigraph; B = lines 1–10; C = 11–18; and D = 19–22). Then have students form expert groups and assign each group a lettered part.
- Have each expert group read, discuss, and take notes about its assigned part of the poem.
- After discussing their assigned part, have students form new jigsaw groups with a representative for each part of the poem. (Each group should have at least one "A," one "B," and so on.)
- Jigsaw groups should discuss the parts of the poem in order and then discuss it as a whole.

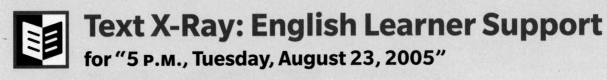

Text X-Ray: English Learner Support
for "5 P.M., Tuesday, August 23, 2005"

Use the Text X-Ray and the supports and scaffolds in the Teacher's Edition to help guide students at different proficiency levels through the selection.

INTRODUCE THE SELECTION
DISCUSS HURRICANES

In this lesson, students will read a poem that personifies Hurricane Katrina. Explain and discuss the following:

- Paraphrase the background information on page 367, noting that Hurricane Katrina began forming as a tropical depression (a smaller storm) on August 23, 2005. Over the next few days, Katrina evolved into one of the most powerful hurricanes ever to hit U.S. soil.

- Point out that the date in the poem's title is the same as the date in the background information. Ask students to consider why the author chose to use a date in the title.

- Before reading, ask students to share what they know about hurricanes and other natural disasters such as floods and earthquakes. Use these sentence frames: *I know that hurricanes _____. Natural disasters can be very harmful to communities because _____.*

CULTURAL REFERENCES

The following words or phrases may be unfamiliar to students:

- *reconnaissance aircraft* (epigraph): planes that explore an area to gather information
- *tropical depression* (epigraph): a storm with winds of less than 39 miles per hour
- *muted* (line 1): muffled, subdued
- *thrashing* (line 4): to move wildly
- *belittle* (line 5): to treat as unimportant or contemptible
- *unbridled* (line 12): unrestrained, uncontrolled
- *chaos* (line 17): a condition of great disorder or confusion
- *dawning* (line 21): a first appearance; a beginning

LISTENING

Understand Personification

Have students listen as you read lines from the poem aloud. Read at an easy-to-follow pace so they can understand content and the personification used.

Use the following supports with students at varying proficiency levels:

- Tell students that the poem uses personification by giving a nonhuman thing (a storm) human qualities. Read line 11 aloud several times; then explain that the storm is speaking this line. Ask which word in the line signals a human quality for the nonhuman storm. *(I)* **SUBSTANTIAL**

- Tell students that the poem uses personification by giving a nonhuman thing (a storm) human qualities. Read line 11 aloud several times. Ask what human qualities the storm has in this line. *(It can speak, and it has emotions.)* **MODERATE**

- Read line 11 aloud several times. Ask how the storm is personified in this line. *(It can speak and feel emotions.)* **LIGHT**

SPEAKING

Give a Poetry Reading

Tell students that many poems are meant to be spoken. Help students prepare for the poetry reading assignment on Student Edition page 371 by practicing reading the original poem aloud.

Use the following supports with students at varying proficiency levels:

- As you read the poem aloud, model appropriate breathing, body language, and tone to demonstrate the poem's full impact. Then have students echo read as you read the poem aloud again. **SUBSTANTIAL**

- Guide students in reading the poem aloud with you. Help them identify descriptive words and phrases that imply tone. For example: *thrashing, how dare, belittle, thunder*. Have students discuss what tone these words suggest for speakers. **MODERATE**

- Have pairs discuss words and phrases that can help guide them in reading the poem aloud with appropriate emphasis and pacing. Then, have them take turns reading the poem aloud to each other. **LIGHT**

READING

Create Mental Images

Explain that writers use word choice, imagery, and figurative language to help readers visualize or create a mental image of their writing. Prompt students to note the images that come to mind as they read the poem.

Use the following supports with students at varying proficiency levels:

- Help students as necessary to read lines 1–8. Ask them to make a sketch of one mental image the lines create for them. **SUBSTANTIAL**

- Have students read lines 11–18. Ask them to make a sketch of one mental image the lines create for them. **MODERATE**

- Have students read lines 1–18. Ask them to sketch at least two mental images the lines create for them. **LIGHT**

WRITING

Write a Literary Analysis

Explain personification—the giving of human qualities to a nonhuman subject—in the poem. Then work with students to help them develop and improve their literary analysis for the assignment on Student Edition page 371.

Use the following supports with students at varying proficiency levels:

- Use think aloud and modeling strategies to help students identify the human qualities of the storm and include them in their written analysis. **SUBSTANTIAL**

- Before they write, prompt students to describe each example of personification. Encourage them to answer clarifying questions in writing such as the following: What does it tell me about the speaker? How does it shape the image I have of the hurricane? **MODERATE**

- Have students work with partners to plan their writing using an outline. Provide sentence stems: _____ *reminded me of* _____. *Line(s)* _____ *created a strong image because* _____. **LIGHT**

Connect to the
? ESSENTIAL QUESTION

Ask a volunteer to read aloud the Essential Question. Discuss the kinds of changes that can reveal who we are. Those might be internal—such as making a decision about one's values or direction in life. Changes also result from external factors—including natural disasters and extreme weather events such as hurricanes. Ask students to think of the changes that can result in people's lives as a result of these kinds of external events.

5 P.M., TUESDAY, AUGUST 23, 2005

Poem by **Patricia Smith**

? ESSENTIAL QUESTION:

How do changes around us reveal who we are?

QUICK START

The poem you are about to read relies on what the reader already knows about the potential violence of a hurricane, in particular Hurricane Katrina, which devastated New Orleans in August 2005. Think about the power of a hurricane. With a partner, discuss what you know or can imagine about the strength of hurricanes, and make a list of the potential damage these storms can cause. Consider the impact a hurricane would have in different geographic areas, such as cities, rural areas, and coastal towns.

HURRICANE DAMAGE
1.
2.
3.
4.

ANALYZE WORD CHOICE

Poetry packs a lot of meaning into a small space, so poets must choose and arrange their words carefully. Using **figurative language**, or words that communicate meaning beyond a literal interpretation, is one way that poets can add extra dimensions to their poems. Many types of figurative language create meaning through comparison:

TYPES OF FIGURATIVE LANGUAGE
A **metaphor** implies a comparison between two unlike things. The comparison draws attention to a key characteristic that both things share.
Personification gives human qualities to a nonhuman subject. Like a metaphor, personification makes a comparison between two things that are dissimilar in order to shed new light on one or both of them.
An **extended metaphor** is a comparison developed at length, often continuing across several stanzas or throughout an entire poem.

Poets also choose words for their **connotative** meanings, or the feelings associated with them. By interpreting the figurative and connotative language in a poem, readers can infer the speaker's **tone**, or attitude, toward the subject, which often reveals the poet's meaning.

As you read this poem, look for comparisons. Note the two things being compared and the meaning or emotions that the comparisons evoke. Also notice the connotations of the words Smith uses.

**GENRE ELEMENTS:
LYRIC POETRY**

- attempts to recreate emotions and experiences
- uses figurative language and sensory details
- words and lines are arranged to add meaning

TEACH

QUICK START

Have students read the Quick Start suggestions and invite them to brainstorm everything they know about hurricanes. They may have seen movies or TV shows about hurricanes, seen photographs of the devastation they cause, or read about them in newspapers or online. Have they or someone they know experienced a hurricane? Invite them to discuss hurricanes and their effects on families, the community, and the region.

ANALYZE WORD CHOICE

Help students understand that these types of **figurative language** are used to make a comparison. To make sure students understand each boldfaced term in the chart, have them work together in pairs to paraphrase the meaning of each term. Students can take turns explaining a term while their partner finds examples in the poem.

The concept of **connotative** meaning might be difficult. Explain that the connotations of words evoke feelings and establish **tone.** Point out the word *belittle* in line 5 of the poem. Explain that other words or phrases, such as *make light of* or *dismiss,* mean roughly the same thing, but they don't carry the harsher tone that *belittle* implies. Then ask students to consider the word *harbors* in line 17. Tell them that it has a similar meaning to *contains* and *shelters.* Ask what connotation *harbors* has that would explain why the poet chose this word. (*The words* shelters *and* contains *do not have the emotional impact of* harbors, *which implies a larger and grander gesture, as well as protection.*)

As students read the poem, prompt them to identify examples of figurative language and words with connotative meanings that suggest a specific tone.

ENGLISH LEARNER SUPPORT

Use Prereading Supports Draw students' attention to the chart showing three types of figurative language. Read each entry aloud. Explain that poets use figurative language to compare things and convey ideas. Display the word *personification* and ask students what root word it contains (*person*). Next, explain that personification compares nonhuman things to people and the way they look and act. Tell them that in the poem they are about to read, a hurricane is compared to a woman. Have them discuss with a partner the ways a hurricane might be compared to a person. What does a hurricane look like? How does it act? (*It might be muscular, angry, loud, unpredictable, dangerous.*) **ALL LEVELS**

TEACH

CREATE MENTAL IMAGES

Tell students that poets use imagery to stir our feelings and create a mood. An image is a representation of anything we can see, hear, taste, touch, or smell. Sensory details can make a thing, person, or place vivid and easy to imagine.

Explain that effective readers construct mental images as they read a text. Tell students that in the poem they are about to read, a hurricane is personified as a woman. After they read the poem, ask students to sketch the woman they see in their minds. Have them compare and discuss their drawings.

 For **reading support** for students at varying proficiency levels, see the **Text X-Ray** on page 364D.

 ANNOTATION MODEL

Remind students that word choice and imagery help readers visualize details, as demonstrated in the model. Tell students that they may use their own system for marking up the selection in their write-in text. They may want to color-code their annotations using highlighters. Their notes in the margin may include questions about ideas that are unclear or topics they want to learn more about.

 GET READY

CREATE MENTAL IMAGES

Creating mental images means using your imagination to form pictures in your mind. Through word choice, imagery, and figurative language, poets help readers visualize the ideas in the poems they write.

In the poem you are about to read, poet Patricia Smith uses personification to characterize a storm as a living person. In addition, she uses sensory description and vivid verbs to create a powerful impression of the storm's appearance and movement. For example, the following excerpt from the poem presents an image that readers can easily picture.

> A muted thread of gray light

As you read "5 P.M., Tuesday, August 23, 2005," creating mental images of the storm will help you understand Smith's characterization of it. You might use the side margin to note or sketch the pictures the poem creates in your mind. Ask yourself whether the images remind you of feelings or experiences that you have had.

ANNOTATION MODEL   NOTICE & NOTE

As you read, note examples of figurative language, imagery, and word choices that stand out to you. Here are one reader's notes about the beginning of the poem:

> A muted <u>thread of gray light</u>, <u>hovering ocean</u>, <u>becomes throat</u>, pulls in <u>wriggle</u>, anemone, kelp, <u>widens</u> with the want of it.

I can picture a wispy cloud, dangling down to touch the ocean and then growing powerful, like a sea creature.

WHEN STUDENTS STRUGGLE . . .

Identify Extended Metaphor To help students understand the extended metaphor and personification in the poem, have them work together to complete the following chart.

Words that suggest the human body	throat, mouth, hair, eye, body, teeth, hips
Words that suggest the speaker is a living being	my thirst, me, I, feed me, myself, breath

 For additional support, go to the **Reading Studio** and assign the following **Level Up Tutorial: Figurative Language.**

BACKGROUND

A hurricane develops in stages. At any point, the storm may either fall apart or become more organized and intense, progressing to the next stage. In the first stage, a tropical disturbance occurs, in which loosely-organized, heavy rain clouds develop. The storm system draws moisture from the warm, humid air on the ocean's surface. This warm air rises and cooler air moves down to replace it, creating a swirling pattern of winds, a tropical depression. If the winds reach 39 to 73 miles per hour, the depression becomes a tropical storm. At 74 miles per hour, the storm becomes a hurricane.

5 P.M., TUESDAY, AUGUST 23, 2005

Poem by Patricia Smith

On August 23, 2005, a tropical depression formed off the southern coast of the United States. It developed over the next few days into Hurricane Katrina, one of the most powerful and devastating hurricanes to ever hit U.S. soil. Katrina's massive winds and torrential rainfall created a storm surge of more than 25 feet, breaching a crucial levee and plunging most of the city of New Orleans under water. The hurricane resulted in at least 1,800 deaths and left a lasting impact on the Gulf Coast and its inhabitants.

Patricia Smith *(b. 1955) is an award-winning poet, performance artist, and four-time National Poetry Slam champion. She is known for using personas—first-person voices that range from gang members to monsters of Greek mythology—to expose uncomfortable truths about situations that most people don't want to face. Her work evokes such themes as self-destruction, betrayal, and vindictiveness, highlighting the spiritual and political impact of the subjects she explores. This poem appears in her book* Blood Dazzler, *a collection that traces the environmental and human costs of Hurricane Katrina. The book earned Smith a National Book Award nomination in 2008.*

BACKGROUND

Have students read the Background information about hurricanes and Hurricane Katrina. To help students appreciate the ferocity of the storm, explain that by the time Katrina hit the Gulf Coast, the winds measured 100–140 miles per hour, and rain fell at the rate of about one inch per hour. While the hurricane caused massive destruction across 400 miles of the coast (as well as inland), the damage caused in New Orleans has become one of the most lasting images of the storm's devastating power. When the storm was finished, 80 percent of New Orleans was under water. Most of this flooding was the result of breaks in the levee that holds back the water from Lake Pontchartrain. In some flooded areas, the water was so deep that people had to climb onto the roof of their home and wait there to be rescued. While the city and other coastal areas have made significant progress toward recovery in the years since, the process of rebuilding continues.

Explain that just as Shakespeare's plays were meant to be performed, so too are Smith's poems. Her *persona* poetry lends itself to performance. In a *persona* poem, the writer becomes another person, an animal, or an object—even a hurricane!

SETTING A PURPOSE

Direct students to use the Setting a Purpose prompt to focus their reading.

WHEN STUDENTS STRUGGLE . . .

Provide Contextual Support Tell students that this poem describes the beginning of a hurricane. Have students read the first paragraph of the Background note on page 367 and then the epigraph, or opening quote, from the National Hurricane Center on page 368. For those students unfamiliar with the vocabulary, define *disturbance, moisture, swirling,* and *depression.* Have them record the words and their definitions. Explain that acquiring this background knowledge will help them better understand the poem, including the opening quote. Ask partners to summarize what happens during the first phases of a tropical depression and discuss what they learn. Then ask them to keep this information in mind as they read the poem.

 For additional support, go to the **Reading Studio** and assign the following **Level Up Tutorial: Historical and Cultural Context.**

CREATE MENTAL IMAGES

Readers often form mental images when the text makes connections to their own feelings through personification. In lines 1–10, have students look for words or phrases that portray feelings they can connect with—for example: "my thirst, treat me". (**Answer:** *The storm has a throat, mouth, hair, and eye; it feels thirst and human emotions. The images created in students' minds will vary.*)

■ English Learner Support

Identify Personification Model ways to determine personification. Offer this example: *The bread jumped out of the toaster.* Have students consider if the bread is doing something that people do to determine that the bread is being personified. Model again with this example: *The stairs groaned as I walked up them.* Practice with more examples; then discuss personification in the poem. **LIGHT**

ANALYZE WORD CHOICE

Remind students that a metaphor compares two unlike things with some shared characteristics. An extended metaphor develops a comparison at length. Point out the phrases that extend the metaphor in lines 20–22: "every woman begins as weather," "knows her hips," and "Every woman / harbors a chaos." Challenge students to think of other extended metaphors to describe a fierce storm. (**Answer:** *The developing hurricane is compared to a powerful, dangerous person with human hair, body, and teeth. The metaphor creates a feeling of dread and vulnerability.*)

■ English Learner Support

Analyze Metaphors Explain that a metaphor draws attention to a characteristic shared by two unlike things. Model an example: *The classroom was a zoo.* Calling the classroom a zoo likens it to a noisy, unruly environment. Do the same modeling with other examples. Then, guide students to decipher the metaphor in line 15 of the poem.

ALL LEVELS

For **listening and reading support** for students at varying proficiency levels, see the **Text X-Ray** on pages 364C–364D.

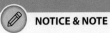

NOTICE & NOTE

Notice & Note

You can use the side margin to notice and note signposts in the text.

CREATE MENTAL IMAGES

Annotate: Mark examples of personification in lines 1–10.

Analyze: In what ways is the storm described as human? What images does this create in your mind?

ANALYZE WORD CHOICE

Annotate: In lines 15–18, mark phrases that develop an extended metaphor.

Interpret: What is being compared in these lines? What effect does this comparison have in the poem?

SETTING A PURPOSE

As you read, note words and phrases that reveal the speaker's character. Write down any questions you generate during reading.

"Data from an Air Force reserve unit reconnaissance aircraft . . . along with observations from the Bahamas and nearby ships . . . indicate the broad low pressure area over the southeastern Bahamas has become organized enough to be classified as tropical depression twelve."

—NATIONAL HURRICANE CENTER

1 A muted thread of gray light, hovering ocean,
   becomes throat, pulls in wriggle, anemone, kelp,[1]
   widens with the want of it. I become
   a mouth, thrashing hair, an overdone eye. How dare
5 the water belittle my thirst, treat me as just
   another
   small
   disturbance,

   try to feed me
10 from the bottom of its hand?

   I will require praise,
   unbridled winds to define my body,
   a crime behind my teeth
   because

15 every woman begins as weather,
   sips slow thunder, knows her hips. Every woman
   harbors a chaos, can
   wait for it, straddling a fever.

   For now,
20 I console myself with small furies,
   those dips in my dawning system. I pull in
   a bored breath. The brine[2] shivers.

---

[1] **anemone, kelp:** sea anemones are brightly colored, tentacled sea creatures; kelp is a kind of seaweed.
[2] **brine:** salt water or sea water.

368   Unit 5

IMPROVE READING FLUENCY

Targeted Passage Have partners do paired oral readings of the poem. Students should take turns reading the stanzas. Remind them to follow print cues such as punctuation and to pause briefly at the end of each line. Then, encourage students to read the poem with expression. Prompt them to read it forcefully, visualizing a hurricane's powerful winds and rain.

 Go to the **Reading Studio** for additional support in developing fluency.

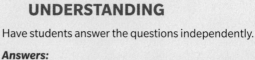 **CHECK YOUR UNDERSTANDING**

Have students answer the questions independently.

Answers:

1. *C*

2. *J*

3. *A*

If they answer any questions incorrectly, have them reread the text to confirm their understanding. Then they may proceed to ANALYZE THE TEXT on page 370.

CHECK YOUR UNDERSTANDING

Answer these questions before moving on to the **Analyze the Text** section on the following page.

1 This poem mainly describes —

A the anger of a woman as compared to a hurricane

B the effect of a hurricane on the people and places it hits

C the development of a hurricane compared to a woman

D how fragile a developing storm can be

2 The introductory text from the National Hurricane Center serves to —

F list the facts that the poem will address

G set up the structure and focus of the poem

H contrast with the poem's ideas about the storm

J provide context for what the poem will describe

3 The last stanza in the poem suggests that —

A the storm has not yet become a hurricane

B the storm has blown over

C the storm is just a dream

D the storm has ended, leaving the ocean calm again

ENGLISH LEARNER SUPPORT

Oral Assessment Use the following questions to assess students' comprehension and speaking skills. Ask students to respond in short, complete sentences.

1. What does the poem mainly describe? *(It describes the development of a hurricane. It compares the hurricane to a woman.)*

2. Why is the quotation from the National Hurricane Center helpful? *(It gives information about the development of the hurricane, which the poem will describe.)*

3. What does the last stanza in the poem suggest about the storm? *(The storm hasn't become a hurricane yet. It is still developing.)*
   SUBSTANTIAL/MODERATE

APPLY

ANALYZE THE TEXT

Possible answers:

1. **DOK 3:** *The quotation establishes that the poem is about a hurricane. It provides a stark contrast to the poem: the language in the quotation is very clinical; there is no drama to it; and it speaks of the storm as an inanimate object. The quotation says the storm is a broad low pressure area over part of the Bahamas and is classified as a tropical depression. The poem, on the other hand, uses vibrant language; establishes a dramatic and ominous tone; and speaks of the hurricane as a powerful, determined living being.*

2. **DOK 3:** *The hurricane is personified. The use of the first-person pronouns ("I," "me," "my"); the references to a body ("mouth," "thrashing hair," "my body," "my teeth," "hips," "breath"); and the comparison to a woman all give it human qualities.*

3. **DOK 4:** *The speaker's tone is patient, confident, and threatening. The patience and confidence are evident in the way the speaker recognizes that she is just a growing storm now, but she will soon be a full-blown hurricane ("I will"; "For now"). The threatening tone is evident in the way the speaker reacts to being challenged ("How dare the water belittle my thirst") and what she will soon unleash ("Every woman harbors a chaos"; "The brine shivers").*

4. **DOK 2:** *Words cited will vary. Students may note words with strong connotations, such as "thrashing," "unbridled," "chaos," and "furies." Sensory description and vivid verbs create a feeling of dread in the anticipation of a powerful, uncontrollable force.*

5. **DOK 2:** *Personification and imagery develop the poem's theme that natural forces are powerful and need to be respected—they cannot be treated lightly.*

RESEARCH

Tell students to use organizations dedicated to weather topics—such as the National Oceanic and Atmospheric Administration (NOAA) and others listed in their books—to research facts about hurricanes. As they research and take notes, encourage them to pause occasionally to compare specific details to the poem. Then, have them compile their findings in a Venn diagram.

Extend Remind students that tone is often established by words with connotative meanings (the feelings associated with the word). Have them look for connotative words in their articles.

 RESPOND

ANALYZE THE TEXT

Support your responses with evidence from the poem. 📓 NOTEBOOK

1. **Draw Conclusions** What information does the quotation from the National Hurricane Center at the poem's beginning convey? Paraphrase it, maintaining a logical order. Why did Smith include this quotation?

2. **Cite Evidence** What nonhuman subject is personified in the poem? Identify specific words and phrases that give the subject human qualities.

3. **Analyze** Describe the speaker's tone in this poem. What words and phrases does the poet use to establish this tone?

4. **Interpret** What words and phrases from the poem helped you develop a mental image of a hurricane gaining strength? What mood did this mental image create?

5. **Infer** What ultimate **theme**, or deeper message about life, does the poet convey through the personification and imagery in the poem?

RESEARCH

RESEARCH TIP
When you conduct research on natural disasters and weather-related phenomena, look for information from organizations dedicated to these topics, such as the National Oceanic and Atmospheric Administration (NOAA), National Weather Service, or Federal Emergency Management Agency (FEMA).

Patricia Smith uses figurative language and imagery to describe the development of a hurricane. How does her description compare to the stages in the development of a real hurricane? With a partner, conduct research to learn about these stages. Take notes about what you learn. Then, compare this information with the details in the poem. Which details about hurricanes are similar in both sources? Which details are different? Record your ideas in the Venn diagram.

Details in the Poem   **Both**   **Facts from Research**

Findings will vary but should accurately compare details about hurricane development in the poem with facts about how hurricanes develop.

Extend Read a newspaper article that was written about Hurricane Katrina as it happened. Compare the tone of the article to the tone of the poem. Note the words and phrases in the article that create the tone. Then discuss how reading the article helped you better understand the poem.

WHEN STUDENTS STRUGGLE . . .

Analyze Figurative Language Work with students to fill in a three-column chart.

Term	Definition	Example
metaphor	implied comparison between two unlike things	lines 1–2: light compared to a throat
personification	gives human qualities to something nonhuman	line 12: a storm has a body
extended metaphor	comparison through several lines, paragraphs, stanzas	lines 1–22: the storm is a woman

 For additional support, go to the **Reading Studio** and assign the following 📖 **Level Up Tutorial: Figurative Language.**

CREATE AND PRESENT

Write a Literary Analysis In the poem "5 P.M., Tuesday, August 23, 2005," Patricia Smith uses personification to describe the storm that will eventually become Hurricane Katrina. Write a paragraph to interpret the effect of the personification in the poem.

❏ Identify the storm's human qualities. Remember that personification can refer to emotions as well as physical characteristics.

❏ Describe what each example of personification means and what it tells you about the speaker's attitude or frame of mind.

❏ Write a topic sentence for your paragraph that states a theme or key idea conveyed through the personification. Support your interpretation with details from the poem.

Give a Poetry Reading Patricia Smith is a National Poetry Slam Champion, and this poem, like most others, is meant to be spoken. Work with a small group to adapt the poem for a male voice and practice reading it aloud.

❏ Discuss which words and phrases in the poem stand out. How should those words be spoken? Ominously? Angrily?

❏ Think about how the poem could have instead personified the hurricane as male. Discuss what words and phrases could be substituted to adapt this poem for a male voice.

❏ Memorize, practice, and recite your adaptation, using your voice and body language, to contribute to a class poetry reading.

RESPOND TO THE ESSENTIAL QUESTION

? How do changes around us reveal who we are?

Gather Information Review your annotations and notes on "5 P.M., Tuesday, August 23, 2005." Then, add relevant information to your Response Log. As you determine which information to include, think about:

- how our need for respect can dictate our responses to others
- the way we hold on to grudges and feed our anger over time
- that storms are out of anyone's control but can bring out the best and worst in people

At the end of the unit, use your notes to help you write a research report.

RESPOND

Go to the **Writing Studio** for more on writing analytical text.

Go to the **Speaking and Listening Studio** to learn more about presenting a recitation.

ACADEMIC VOCABULARY

As you write and discuss what you learned about "5 P.M., Tuesday, August 23, 2005," be sure to use the Academic Vocabulary words. Check off each of the words that you use.

❏ **abstract**
❏ **evolve**
❏ **explicit**
❏ **facilitate**
❏ **infer**

CREATE AND PRESENT

Write a Literary Analysis Before they begin writing, suggest that students review the instruction about figurative language, imagery, and personification on pages 365–366. Remind students to support their ideas with relevant evidence from the poem.

 For **writing support** for students at varying proficiency levels, see the **Text X-Ray** on page 364D.

Give a Poetry Reading Readers should expressively interpret the poem. Have small groups use unique markings to separately identify words as well as phrases with figurative and connotative meanings, as well as words and phrases that indicate a female speaker. (Note that there may be overlap.) Encourage students to be prepared to explain and support any substitutions they make. The readings should demonstrate an understanding of pace and tone, and the summaries should reflect an understanding of the speaker's role in the poem.

For **speaking support** for students at varying proficiency levels, see the **Text X-Ray** on page 364D.

RESPOND TO THE ESSENTIAL QUESTION

Allow time for students to add details from "5 P.M., Tuesday, August 23, 2005" to their Unit 5 Response Logs.

from RIVERS AND TIDES
Documentary Film by **Thomas Riedelsheimer**

SONNETS TO ORPHEUS, PART TWO, XII
Poem by **Rainer Maria Rilke**

GENRE ELEMENTS
DOCUMENTARY FILM

Briefly review with students that a **documentary film** presents factual information on a topic. Many documentaries focus on one person and use images, interviews, and narration to convey information and impressions that help the audience form a picture of that person's life and work.

POEM

Remind students that a **sonnet** is one type of lyric poem. Point out that a sonnet (which means "little song") consists of 14 lines, and like other poetry, uses imagery and figurative language to express emotions and ideas.

LEARNING OBJECTIVES

- Analyze characteristics of multimodal and digital texts.
- Analyze purpose and theme in a poem.
- Compare themes across genres.
- Make connections to personal experiences, ideas in other texts, and society.
- Create and present a reflection.
- Share and discuss opinions about the selection themes and human nature.
- **Language** Use adjectives of quantity to express opinions about human nature.

TEXT COMPLEXITY

Quantitative Measures	Rivers and Tides	Lexile: N/A
	Sonnets to Orpheus	Lexile: N/A
Qualitative Measures	**Ideas Presented** Multiple levels of meaning.	
	Structures Used Implicit themes and relationships between images and narration.	
	Language Used Many Tier I and some Tier II words; mostly simple sentence structures.	
	Knowledge Required Basic knowledge of sculpture and artistic process; some knowledge of Greek legends.	

Online

RESOURCES

- Unit 5 Response Log
- Selection Audio
- Reading Studio: Notice & Note
- Level Up Tutorial: Analyzing Visuals
- Speaking and Listening Studio: Participating in Collaborative Discussions; Giving a Presentation
- *Rivers and Tides* / "Sonnets to Orpheus, Part Two, XII" Selection Test

SUMMARIES

English

The clip from *Rivers and Tides* juxtaposes two similar sculptures. Time-lapse reveals the effects of time: ocean tides cover up one sculpture and meadow grasses grow around the other. Andy Goldsworthy shares his thoughts after seeing his sculpture disappear beneath the waves.

In "Sonnets to Orpheus, Part Two, XII" Rilke uses imagery of fire, water, and wind to urge readers to embrace change and celebrate its elemental and transformative power.

Spanish

Este fragmento de *Ríos y mareas* yuxtapone dos esculturas semejantes. Los intervalos prefijados revelan el efecto del tiempo: las mareas cubren una escultura y el césped de la pradera crece alrededor de la otra. Andy Goldsworthy comparte sus pensamientos luego de ver su escultura desaparecer bajo las olas.

En "Sonetos para Orfeo, parte dos, XII" Rilke utiliza las imágenes del fuego, agua y viento para urgir a los lectores a aceptar el cambio y celebrar su poder transformativo.

SMALL-GROUP OPTIONS

Have students work in small groups to read and discuss the selection.

Think-Pair-Share

- After students have viewed the clip from *Rivers and Tides*, pose this question: "Could you make something and let it be destroyed as Andy Goldsworthy does? Why or why not?"
- Have students think about the question individually and take notes.
- Then, have pairs discuss their ideas about the question.
- Finally, ask pairs to share their responses with the class.

Triple-Entry Journal

- Have students divide a page into three columns and label the columns "Quotations from the Poem," "My Notes," and "My Partner's Notes."
- In the first column, instruct students to record passages from "Sonnets to Orpheus" that they found interesting, important, or confusing.
- In the middle column, have students write their own reactions, interpretations, or questions.
- Then, have partners exchange journals. Instruct them to use the third column to write responses either to the quotations from the text or to their partner's notes.

Text X-Ray: English Learner Support
for *Rivers and Tides* and "Sonnets to Orpheus, Part Two, XII"

Use the Text X-Ray and the supports and scaffolds in the Teacher's Edition to help guide students at different proficiency levels through the two selections.

INTRODUCE THE SELECTION
DISCUSS CHANGE

In this lesson, students will need to be able to discuss change and its effects. Provide the following explanations:

- Change is a *natural process.* When something changes, it becomes different.
- In nature, forces such as water, fire, and wind can *destroy* things people build—these forces break them or ruin them.
- Big changes can create shock and upheaval in people's lives. *A shock* is something sudden that surprises you. *Upheaval* is change that causes a lot of trouble or confusion.

Prompt students to give specific examples of the following: natural processes, something that causes shock, something that causes upheaval, and a change that destroys something.

CULTURAL REFERENCES

The following words or phrases may be unfamiliar to students:

- *filmmaker* (p. 375): a person who makes a movie
- *sculpture* (p. 375): a piece of art made by shaping, cutting, or stacking materials such as wood or stone
- *work* (film interview): a piece of art
- *a figure from mythology* (p. 377): a character from a story about gods and goddesses
- *Apollo* (p. 377): the Greek god of music, poetry, and future-telling
- *Orpheus* (poem title): a hero in Greek stories who was known for music and poetry

LISTENING

Understand Key Details

Tell students they are going to listen to the video and record main points and key details. Introduce the words *cone* and *sculpture.*

Use the following supports with students at varying proficiency levels:

- Play Goldsworthy's interview for students. Ask yes/no questions, such as these: Did Goldsworthy make a cone out of stone? *(yes)* Did the sea carry his cone far away? *(no)* Was he happy to give his cone to the sea as a gift? *(yes)* Have students respond by nodding or shaking their heads. **SUBSTANTIAL**
- Play Goldsworthy's interview for students. Ask questions and have students answer in complete sentences: Where was the sculpture that Goldsworthy is talking about in the interview? *(It was by the sea.)* **MODERATE**
- Display this question and tell students to listen for the answer in the video clip: How does Goldsworthy describe what the sea does to the cone he built? Play Goldsworthy's interview for students. Have students write their answer to the question. *(He says that the sea took the cone as a gift and made more of it than he could have ever hoped for.)* **LIGHT**

SPEAKING

Use *Few, Some, Many,* and *Most* to Share Opinions

Read the Share and Discuss Opinions activity on Student Edition page 379. Explain that the words *few, some, many,* and *most* will help students share their opinions about human nature.

Use the following supports with students at varying proficiency levels:

- Take a quick poll, such as how many people like various ice cream flavors. Record the results on the board. Display this frame: _____ *people like* _____. Then use the data to model how to form sentences with *few, some,* and *many*. **SUBSTANTIAL**
- Display the words *few, some, many,* and *most* and review their meanings. Then ask students questions and have them use one of the words in their answer. For example: Do most people want their lives to stay the same? (*Many like their lives as they are, but some are always wanting change.*) **MODERATE**
- Have pairs of students take turns making generalizations with *few, some, many,* and *most*. **LIGHT**

READING

Read and Summarize

Have students reread the poem and summarize its key images and central message.

Use the following supports with students at varying proficiency levels:

- Display images of a fire, an ice cube, a water fountain, and the wind blowing. Display and introduce the terms *flame, rigid, fountain,* and *wind*. Have students read the words with you. Read the poem aloud. Point to the image mentioned in each stanza. Paraphrase each stanza. Then ask questions such as these: What is another word for *hard*? (*rigid*) What makes things bright? (*fire*). **SUBSTANTIAL**
- Echo-read the poem with students, pausing to paraphrase and explain as necessary. At the end of each stanza, ask questions to check comprehension. **MODERATE**
- Have pairs of students read the poem together and stop to paraphrase each stanza. **LIGHT**

WRITING

Use Gerunds in a Presentation Script

Read the Create a Reflection assignment on Student Edition page 379. Tell students that gerunds will be helpful for writing their scripts. Explain that a gerund is a type of noun derived from a verb form ending in *-ing*.

Use the following supports with students at varying proficiency levels:

- Display images of familiar life changes such as moving, growing up, changing schools, and graduating and then display several images from nature. Model writing a sentence that links the two images. For example, "Growing up is like the end of summer because you can't play anymore." Repeat with other images. **SUBSTANTIAL**
- Provide sentence frames. Have students write sentences about their images by completing the frames with gerunds. **MODERATE**
- Have pairs of students take turns describing their images orally. Then have them write several sentences about the images using gerunds. **LIGHT**

TEACH

 Connect to the
ESSENTIAL QUESTION

Change is an inevitable part of life. The clip from the documentary film *Rivers and Tides* and the poem "Sonnets to Orpheus, Part Two, XII" remind us of the changes occurring all around us constantly, and they invite us to examine our own response to those changes.

COMPARE THEMES ACROSS GENRES

Point out that *Rivers and Tides* is a clip from a documentary film and "Sonnets to Orpheus, Part Two, XII" is a poem. Ask students to speculate on some tools that a filmmaker or a poet might use to convey a message to an audience. Remind students that a theme is a message about life or human nature and usually isn't directly stated but must instead be inferred. Tell students that as they view and read each selection, they should think about what message the details convey. This consideration will prepare them to compare themes across the two genres.

DOCUMENTARY FILM

from
RIVERS AND TIDES

by **Thomas Riedelsheimer**
page 375

COMPARE THEMES ACROSS GENRES

As you view and read, notice how the ideas in both the film and the text relate to your own experiences, as well as how they relate to the experiences of other people you know. Then, look for ways that the ideas in the two texts relate to each other. After you view and read both selections, you will collaborate with a small group on a final project.

 ESSENTIAL QUESTION:

How do changes around us reveal who we are?

POEM

SONNETS TO ORPHEUS, PART TWO, XII

by **Rainer Maria Rilke**
page 376–377

372   Unit 5

 LEARNING MINDSET

Grit   Review with students the benefits of working hard and adopting flexible thinking patterns. (*Someone who works hard will eventually reach a goal; someone with flexible thinking is less discouraged by setbacks—if one solution to a problem fails, the person can try another solution.*) As students watch the clip from *Rivers and Tides*, ask them to think about what they can learn about grit from watching the artist Andy Goldsworthy practice his art.

QUICK START

How do you relate to the natural world and changes that occur within it? What effect do the changes you notice have on you? With a group, discuss how human beings see themselves in the changes that occur in nature.

ANALYZE MEDIA TECHNIQUES

Like a writer, a filmmaker works to develop ideas in a logical fashion. The **central idea** is the most important idea about a topic that a film conveys. Filmmakers use a combination of media elements, including storytelling and production elements, to express a central idea. Storytelling elements are nontechnical elements that filmmakers use to help convey the central idea.

GENRE ELEMENTS: DOCUMENTARY FILM

- presents a factual account of a specific topic
- focuses on a central idea about the topic
- incorporates visuals, sound, and special effects
- uses setting, mood, and sequence to convey the central idea

STORYTELLING ELEMENTS	WHAT THEY DO
Setting: the locations in which a film is shot	Settings can be an integral part of how a filmmaker conveys the central idea.
Mood: the atmosphere created by visual and sound elements	Mood helps support the central idea by reinforcing what the viewer is seeing.
Sequence: the order in which images are presented	A filmmaker presents images in a logical order. Sometimes this is a chronological order, but other times, the images or scenes are shown in an order that helps the viewer relate the ideas being shown.

In addition to storytelling elements, filmmakers use production elements such as those listed below to help them convey the central idea.

PRODUCTION ELEMENTS	EXAMPLES
Visual elements help the filmmaker convey connections among ideas.	• **camera shot:** a single, continuous view taken by a camera • **camera angle:** the angle at which the camera is positioned during the recording of a shot or image
Sound elements may give additional information and set the mood for a scene.	• **music:** instrumental and vocal compositions • **voice-over:** the voice of an unseen narrator • **sound effects:** sounds other than speech and music that are used to make a scene seem more realistic
Special effects are manipulated video images that can heighten drama and create mood.	• **speed:** fast-or slow-motion sequences • **lighting:** unusually bright or dim lighting and changes in lighting • **time-lapse:** starting and stopping filming to connect images from one time period to the same images in another time period

© Houghton Mifflin Harcourt Publishing Company

from Rivers and Tides / Sonnets to Orpheus, Part Two, XII   373

QUICK START

Point out that the natural world refers to the physical environment around us. Ask students to quickly name some changes that take place in the natural world. Changes might include melting snow, blossoming flowers, decreasing daylight, and so on. Then have groups complete the activity.

ANALYZE MEDIA TECHNIQUES

Review each of the **storytelling and production elements** and ask students to name some examples from popular movies that illustrate each concept.

Suggest that students use these questions to help them analyze media techniques as they view *Rivers and Tides:*

- What are the settings?
- What kinds of shots and angles does the filmmaker use? How are they sequenced?
- What do you learn from the interview?
- How do music and sound affect the mood?
- What special effects are used? What effect do they have?

 ## ENGLISH LEARNER SUPPORT

Analyze the Media Read aloud each of the boldface storytelling and production elements, along with the related description or example. Use visual aids such as still photographs or video screenshots to help reinforce meaning. Then confirm students' understanding of the terms by asking either-or questions such as these: Is setting a person or a place? *(a place)* Is mood a feeling or a place? *(a feeling)* Is time-lapse a visual element or a sound element? *(a visual element)*

SUBSTANTIAL/MODERATE

 ## ENGLISH LEARNER SUPPORT

Use Content Area Vocabulary Have students create a glossary of elements that filmmakers use to express ideas. Ask them to list each element, describe it in their own words, and include a familiar example from a video clip, movie, television program, or commercial. Students can add drawings or screenshots to illustrate concepts.

MODERATE/LIGHT

ANALYZE PURPOSE AND THEME

Explain that directors often use **juxtaposition** to show that they want to compare or contrast two ideas.

Suggest that students use these questions to help them analyze theme as they view *Rivers and Tides*:

- What elements are juxtaposed in the film clip?

- What is similar about the two things that are juxtaposed? What is different?

- What might be the filmmaker's reason for juxtaposing those things? What ideas do the images convey?

Then remind students that after they view the film, they will read the poem "Sonnets to Orpheus, Part Two, XII." Point out that, like the film, the poem has a theme. Explain that students should pay attention to details as they read the poem so that they can be prepared to discuss how the themes of the two works of art are similar or different.

ENGLISH LEARNER SUPPORT

Use Strategies to Decode Words Display the word *juxtaposition*. Break it down into two parts: *juxta position*. Point out that the word has a Spanish cognate (*yuxtaposición*) that is also made up of two parts (*yuxta posición*). Explain that like its Spanish relative, the English word *juxtaposition* comes from two Latin words meaning *next to* and *put* or *place*. Model pronouncing the word. Point out the short vowel sounds and the syllable stress on the fourth syllable. Have students repeat the word with you. **ALL LEVELS**

GET READY

ANALYZE PURPOSE AND THEME

As you view the clip from *Rivers and Tides*, think about the purpose of the images, sounds, and **juxtaposition**, or side-by-side placement of key elements in the film. If you were to summarize the clip for someone who had not seen it, what details would you emphasize? What theme is the director trying to communicate using these details? Use the chart below to track details in the clip and infer how they point toward a particular purpose.

DETAIL IN THE CLIP	PURPOSE IT IMPLIES

After viewing the clip from *Rivers and Tides,* you will read a poem that expresses a similar purpose and theme. You can add details from the poem to this chart to help you understand both works.

 ENGLISH LEARNER SUPPORT

Develop Vocabulary Explain or review the meanings of *purpose, theme, emphasize,* and *communicate*. Then ask students to imagine they are asked to plan a school dance. Their *purpose* is to make all students at their school feel welcome at the dance. Ask pairs of students to pick a *theme*—a message they want to share with their peers (for example, "Our differences make our school fun."). Ask students what details they would *emphasize* in the dance—such as the types of music and decorations—in order to *communicate* their theme. Provide frames to help students construct a response: *I would emphasize _____ and _____. My purpose would be to communicate this theme: _____.* **ALL LEVELS**

BACKGROUND

Andy Goldsworthy (b. 1956) is a British artist who creates sculptures from items found in nature. Unlike most sculptors, Goldsworthy creates work that he knows will be destroyed by nature relatively quickly. Goldsworthy has photographed many of his works and has held exhibits primarily featuring photographs of his sculptures. Director **Thomas Riedelsheimer** (b. 1963) is also a photographer and recently worked with Goldsworthy on the documentary Leaning into the Wind.

PREPARE TO COMPARE

Pay attention to settings in the film clip and how they affect your perception of the artist's work. Note any questions you generate during viewing. This information will help you compare the film with the poem that follows it.

To view the video, log in online and select **"from RIVERS AND TIDES"** from the unit menu.

As needed, pause the video to make notes about what impresses you or about ideas you might want to talk about later. Replay or rewind so that you can clarify anything you do not understand.

from Rivers and Tides   375

WHEN STUDENTS STRUGGLE . . .

Analyze Media Students may have difficulty describing the video clip because it does not show events from beginning to end. Have partners describe the film clip using a chart like this to record their ideas.

	Details (Description)	**Effect (on Mood or Message)**
Settings		
Juxtaposed images		
Music/Sound effects		

 For additional support, go to the **Reading Studio** and assign the following **Level Up Tutorial: Analyzing Visuals.**

TEACH

BACKGROUND

Have students read the Background note about artist Andy Goldsworthy and director Thomas Riedelsheimer. You may want to clarify for students that Andy Goldsworthy is the subject of the film—the film is about his art and how he works. When students talk about the film or how it is made, they are talking about the work of Riedelsheimer.

For **listening support** for students at varying proficiency levels, see the **Text X-Ray** on page 372C.

PREPARE TO COMPARE

Direct students to use the Prepare to Compare prompt to focus their viewing.

🗨 ENGLISH LEARNER SUPPORT

Use Present Perfect Verb Structure After playing the video, use the following activity to introduce the present perfect verb structure and have students practice using it. Provide students with the following sentence frames:

I _____ simply _____ the piece to be destroyed by the sea. (haven't, made)

The work _____ been _____ to the sea as a gift. (has, given)

Play the part of the video in which Andy Goldsworthy is interviewed (from 1:55 to 2:52). Have students complete the sentences using the missing parts of each verb phrase. If students have trouble completing the frames the first time, play the clip again.

Choral read the sentences with students. Point out the helping verbs and the past participles in each verb phrase. Have students explain the meaning of each sentence in their own words. *(I made the piece for other reasons, not just to be destroyed by the sea; the work is a gift to the sea.)* Point out that the present perfect structure is often used when the speaker is describing events that have recently happened. Consider having students write their own sentences using the present perfect verb structure. **ALL LEVELS**

BACKGROUND

Have students read the Background note about the poet, Rainer Maria Rilke. Explain that if an artist or writer's works are *lauded*, they are greatly respected and praised. Point out that "Sonnets to Orpheus" is a series of 55 lyrical poems written in two parts. Remind students that in lyrical poetry a single speaker expresses personal thoughts and feelings. Invite volunteers to share anything they recall about Orpheus. Point out that Orpheus was a mythical musician and poet and that throughout the entire collection of "Sonnets to Orpheus," Rilke writes about the relationship of poetry and art to life.

PREPARE TO COMPARE

Direct students to use the Prepare to Compare prompt to focus their reading.

 For **reading support** for students at varying proficiency levels, see the **Text X-Ray** on page 372D.

ANALYZE PURPOSE AND THEME

Before students answer the question, ask them to think about the various changes that they have experienced in their own lives. Then have partners take turns sharing their interpretations of what it means to "want the change" and explaining how that idea relates to their own lives. You might also clarify for students that the first sentence of the poem does not sum up the entire theme of the poem but suggests a larger message. (**Answer:** *Responses will vary.*)

ENGLISH LEARNER SUPPORT

Understand Ideas Read aloud lines 1–2 of the poem. Explain that when a person is *inspired*, something has caused the person to feel full of new ideas and hope. Explain that a *flame* is a part of a fire. Ask: Does the speaker think that the reader should be inspired by "the flame"? (*yes*) Does the speaker think that change should bring the reader hope? (*yes*) **SUBSTANTIAL**

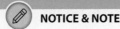 **NOTICE & NOTE**

BACKGROUND

Rainer Maria Rilke *(1875–1926) was born in Prague. At age 11, he was sent to military school, but his uncle made sure he was schooled in literature, his true passion. In 1901, Rilke married Clara Westhoff, who had studied with the sculptor Auguste Rodin. Rilke became Rodin's secretary. In Paris, Rilke's poetry evolved into verses that used simple vocabulary to describe everyday subjects. Sonnets to Orpheus reveals what poetry means to him and is considered one of his best works. His works were lauded by European artists of his time, and his unique style of lyrical poetry continues to place him among the masters of his craft.*

SONNETS TO ORPHEUS, PART TWO, XII

**Poem by Rainer Maria Rilke
translated by Anita Barrows and Joanna Macy**

Notice & Note

You can use the side margins to notice and note signposts in the text.

ANALYZE PURPOSE AND THEME

Annotate: Mark the first sentence of the poem.

Interpret: How would you restate this theme in a way that applies to your own life?

PREPARE TO COMPARE

As you read the poem, keep the ideas about change that you gathered from the Rivers and Tides *film clip in mind.*

Want the change. Be inspired by the flame
Where everything shines as it disappears.
The artist, when sketching, loves nothing so much
as the curve of the body as it turns away.

5 What locks itself in sameness has congealed[1].
Is it safer to be gray and numb?
What turns hard becomes rigid
and is easily shattered.

---

[1] **congealed:** solidified.

IMPROVE READING FLUENCY

Targeted Passage Use echo reading to help students read lines 1–8 of the poem with appropriate phrasing, intonation, and expression. Read those lines aloud. As you do so, model how to use punctuation as a guide to phrasing and intonation. After reading, point out the sentences that span two lines (lines 1–2, 3–4, and 7–8) and point out that they should be read without pausing at the end of lines 1, 3, and 7. Then have students echo your reading as you read lines 1–8 a second and third time.

Go to the **Reading Studio** for additional support in developing fluency.

Pour yourself like a fountain.
10 Flow into the knowledge that what you are seeking
finishes often at the start, and, with ending, begins.

Every happiness is the child of a separation
it did not think it could survive. And Daphne, becoming a laurel,
dares you to become the wind.

ANALYZE PURPOSE AND THEME

Annotate: Mark the reference to Daphne, a figure from mythology who chose being turned into a laurel tree over being pursued by the god Apollo.

Infer: How does the allusion to mythology elaborate on the poem's theme?

CHECK YOUR UNDERSTANDING

Answer these questions before moving on to the **Analyze the Text** section on the following page.

1 A major theme of the poem is that —

   A art and literature are important

   B change makes us feel alive

   C nature is full of surprises

   D we crave feeling safe and secure

2 How is "sameness" described in the poem?

   F As the only way to avoid a separation

   G As the way most people live

   H As both dull and fragile

   J As how all things must end

3 What images in the poem show positive change?

   A Fire burning, water flowing, and wind blowing

   B An artist, knowledge, and a tree

   C Things congealed, numb, and shattered

   D Disappearing, finishing, and separating

TEACH

 ANALYZE PURPOSE AND THEME

Invite students to share anything they recall about the story of Daphne or the god Apollo. If necessary, remind students that in Greek and Roman mythology, Apollo was a son of Zeus and considered very powerful. Explain that Daphne was the beautiful daughter of a less important river god. (**Answer:** *Answers will vary. Students may say that the allusion adds to the poem's theme of celebrating change because change is what saves and protects Daphne from Apollo. Just as Daphne welcomes her transformation into a laurel, readers should also welcome change.*)

CHECK YOUR UNDERSTANDING

Have students answer the questions independently.

Answers:

   1. *B*

   2. *H*

   3. *A*

If they answer any questions incorrectly, have them reread the text to confirm their understanding. Then they may proceed to ANALYZE THE TEXTS on page 378.

 ENGLISH LEARNER SUPPORT

Oral Assessment Use the following questions to assess students' comprehension and speaking skills. Ask students to respond in short, complete sentences.

1. What message about change does the poem give readers? (*Change can inspire us and bring happiness.*)

2. How is "sameness" described in the poem? (*It is described as both dull and fragile.*)

3. What images in the poem show positive change? (*The images of fire burning, water flowing, and wind blowing all show positive change.*)
   ALL LEVELS

APPLY

ANALYZE THE TEXTS

Possible answers:

1. **DOK 4:** *The filmmaker uses time-lapse photography to show one rock sculpture being covered by a rising tide and another by growing plants. In real life, these changes would take hours or days/weeks. By using time-lapse to capture these changes, the filmmaker conveys the idea that change is constantly taking place all around us.*

2. **DOK 3:** *Responses will vary. Students may say that the close-up images show how the sculptures were built and how they have meaning in a very personal way. The shots taken from farther away might show how the art has less impact as the memory of it fades. This might also show how the art is only temporary.*

3. **DOK 2:** *Responses will vary. Students may point out that Goldsworthy describes his work as a gift and says that the sea made more of it than he could have hoped. They may interpret this to mean that the sea heightened Goldsworthy's experience of creating art. Goldsworthy may have ended his statement by saying that despite all the changes, upheavals, and shocks in our lives, the experience of living enriches us in unimaginable ways.*

4. **DOK 2:** *The poem's central idea is that it is better to be flexible and to flow with changes than to be rigid. Rilke uses the image of a substance that turns hard and then shatters as a negative example of what happens when people are rigid and try to avoid change. The poem encourages the reader to "want change" and to be like water or the wind, always moving.*

5. **DOK 2:** *Fire, light, water, and wind are always moving and changing. Because these are essential elements of nature, they support the theme that change itself is essential.*

ANALYZE MEDIA

Have students record their notes in the chart independently and then share their ideas in a small group. Once students have had a chance to discuss the topic, have them work collaboratively or independently to create a product that captures the central message in Goldsworthy's work.

Extend Invite students to present their work and share the unifying theme with the whole class. *(Change is an unavoidable part of life, and the more we accept that, the more we can be in harmony with nature.)*

 RESPOND

ANALYZE THE TEXTS

Support your responses with evidence from the texts.   ▤ NOTEBOOK

1. **Analyze** What special effect does the film use to help the viewer link the sculptures to the idea of time and changes over time?

2. **Compare** What effect does the filmmaker's use of close-up shots of the artist's work and shots taken from farther away have on your understanding of the connections between the sculptures?

3. **Infer** Think about the end of Goldsworthy's statement about what his work might represent. How do you think that statement might be finished, based on the film clip and your own experience?

4. **Summarize** What central idea about change does Rilke's poem convey? Support your answer with evidence from the poem.

5. **Identify Patterns** What do Rilke's images of elements like fire, light, water, and wind have in common? How do these images support the poem's theme?

ANALYZE MEDIA

Analyze the way music, juxtapositions, time lapses, and interviews are used in the clip from *Rivers and Tides*. First, use the chart below to record your ideas about the effects each technique creates in the clip. Then consider how these techniques work together to develop an overall impression of Goldsworthy's work. Present your ideas about this in a paragraph, a poster, a podcast, or an oral presentation.

Possible answers:

MEDIA TECHNIQUE	EFFECT IN THE CLIP
music	*The music is quiet but also rather suspenseful. The rhythm reminds viewers of the passage of time and it helps draw attention to the changes that are happening to the art as time passes.*
juxtaposition	*The juxtaposition of similar sculptures in different settings helps viewers see how both sculptures connect to nature and undergo change.*
time lapse	*Time-lapse photography shows what happens to the art as time passes and as nature takes its course, changing the art in a completely natural way, rather than a destructive way.*
interview	*The interview with the artist shows how the artist feels about seeing the sea come in and cover his artwork and the lessons he learns from that.*

Extend What is the unifying theme that these impressions point to?

⚙ LEARNING MINDSET

Questioning Review the value of asking questions. Remind students that asking questions can sometimes help a person get "unstuck." You might model this by saying, "I want to record notes about the film in this chart. But I'm not sure what to write about the music. I don't see how music is related to Goldsworthy's work. So I ask myself, 'How would I describe the style of the music? What does it sound like? How does the music make me feel? How does it relate to the images I'm seeing?'" Then, point out that by asking these questions, you've realized that you want to focus your notes about music on three things—how the music sounds, how the sounds create feelings, and how the sounds contribute to ideas about change.

CREATE AND DISCUSS

Create a Reflection What connections can you make between changes you see in nature or your community and the kinds of major life changes people experience? Share your ideas in a media presentation.

❏ Develop an idea to write about and present by journaling or discussing with a partner.

❏ Take photographs, make video recordings, or organize a collection of existing images of a meaningful change. (Be sure any images made by others are copyright-free or are allowed for classroom use.)

❏ Record an audio track to accompany your visuals that tells what change the visuals show and how that change is a good metaphor for a specific life change—moving, changing schools, growing up, etc.

Share and Discuss Opinions With a small group, discuss your opinions about the connections between changes in nature and changes in human beings. Does Andy Goldsworthy's art represent any changes in your life?

❏ Review the film clip with your group to identify the ideas about change and connections with nature that Goldsworthy makes.

❏ Then, discuss what the changes in nature reveal about human nature. As you discuss, listen closely and ask each other questions to help clarify ideas.

❏ Finally, end your discussion by listing the conclusions of each member of your group.

 Go to the **Speaking and Listening Studio** to learn more about having a group discussion.

RESPOND TO THE ESSENTIAL QUESTION

 How do changes around us reveal who we are?

Gather Information Review your annotations on the clip from *Rivers and Tides* and "Sonnets to Orpheus, Part Two, XII." Pick an image or idea and connect it with an aspect of human nature. Think about the changes in the natural world as you respond. Then, add relevant details to your Response Log.

At the end of the unit, use your notes to write a research report.

ACADEMIC VOCABULARY
As you write and discuss what you learned about change through these works, be sure to use the Academic Vocabulary words. Check off each of the words that you use.

❏ **abstract**
❏ **evolve**
❏ **explicit**
❏ **facilitate**
❏ **infer**

from Rivers and Tides / Sonnets to Orpheus, Part Two, XII   379

CREATE AND DISCUSS

Create a Reflection Point out that the visual part of students' presentations can take the form of a poster, slide show, or video. Explain that in order to create an audio soundtrack, students will need to write the script for voice-over narration. Tell students that it might be helpful if they storyboard their presentation—that is, draw thumbnail sketches to plan how the visuals and narration will work together to communicate their message.

 For **writing support** for students at varying proficiency levels, see the **Text X-Ray** on page 372D.

Share and Discuss Opinions If students need help starting their discussion, provide the following guiding questions:

• Which changes that you noticed in the film were cyclical? Which were permanent?

• What kinds of changes take place in a person's life? What changes are the most difficult? Why?

• What can people learn about life by observing changes in nature and how nature responds to change? What does a person's response to change say about him or her?

Remind students to give everyone in the group a chance to share his or her opinion and for the rest of the group to listen respectfully and be prepared to ask one question for clarification or additional information.

For **speaking support** for students at varying proficiency levels, see the **Text X-Ray** on page 372D.

EL ENGLISH LEARNER SUPPORT

Expand Vocabulary Explain the terms *cyclical, permanent,* and *unexpected.* Provide frames and have students complete them: *It is hard to accept many _____ changes. (permanent) People try to plan for _____ changes. (unexpected) People get used to _____ changes. (cyclical)* **ALL LEVELS**

RESPOND TO THE ESSENTIAL QUESTION

Allow time for students to add details from *Rivers and Tides* and "Sonnets to Orpheus" to their Unit 5 Response Logs.

EL ENGLISH LEARNER SUPPORT

Create a Reflection Use the following supports with students at different proficiency levels:

• Have students supply some images of change, or provide images of your own. Drawing on the images, model writing a brief reflection. Then have students read it aloud with you and copy it. **SUBSTANTIAL**

• Provide sentence frames such as these to scaffold the writing task: *This is_____. It shows_____. This is a good metaphor for _____ because_____. In both cases, _____.* Have partners discuss their images and write the narration together. **MODERATE**

• Have students write their reflections independently and then take turns reading them aloud to a partner and exchanging feedback. **LIGHT**

COMPARE THEMES ACROSS GENRES

Compare Themes Across Genres Remind students that works of art, like works of literature, often communicate a theme, which is usually implied. Readers and viewers can infer the theme by paying attention to details and then summing up how the details are related. Review the chart on page 380. Tell students that they should craft theme statements supported by evidence for each selection.

ANALYZE THE TEXTS

Possible answers:

1. **DOK 4:** *In both the film and the poem, elements of nature are used to illustrate ideas about change, including the idea that change is a positive and unavoidable force.*

2. **DOK 2:** *Goldsworthy uses natural materials to make his art in sculptural form, photographing his artwork to document it, while Rilke uses words to express images in nature that represent change.*

3. **DOK 2:** *Responses will vary. Students may note that Goldsworthy uses only materials in nature because they connect him to the world around him. He seems to want the artwork to be connected to or be a part of the surrounding area; one sculpture is part of the sea and the other is part of the meadow. The way these materials interact with their surroundings helps him express ideas about impermanence, energy, and change; each piece of art is transformed in an interesting way by nature.*

4. **DOK 4:** *Responses will vary. The film and the poem both present daring messages of how individuals can choose to respond to changes in the natural world and in their own lives. Most humans are not naturally inclined to embrace change. Most artists who create sculptures want them to remain visible for as long as possible. Most of us fear and resist change—even changes brought on by natural processes such as aging and dying. The film and the poem suggest that by transcending our natural tendencies, we can become more a part of nature and life as a whole.*

 RESPOND

from **RIVERS AND TIDES**
Documentary Film by
Thomas Riedelsheimer

SONNETS TO ORPHEUS, PART TWO, XII
Poem by Rainer Maria Rilke

Collaborate & Compare

COMPARE THEMES ACROSS GENRES

When you compare two or more texts with the same theme across genres, you synthesize the information, making connections and expanding on key ideas. You can get a more thorough understanding of the theme by comparing texts from different genres—like a documentary film and a poem. Remember that the **theme** of a text is the message about life expressed in the work. A work does not have to be literature, or even use words at all, to communicate a theme.

In a small group, complete the chart shown below. In the center column, write themes expressed in the film clip and the poem. In the right column, note the details in each work that imply its theme.

TITLE OF WORK	STATEMENTS OF THEME	DETAILS THAT IMPLY THEME
from *Rivers and Tides*		
"Sonnets to Orpheus, Part Two, XII"		

ANALYZE THE TEXTS

Discuss these questions in your group.

1. **Connect** What similarities do you see between Andy Goldsworthy's ideas about using nature to make art and the ideas presented in the poem?

2. **Contrast** What differences are there between the art Goldsworthy makes and the ideas in the poem by Rilke?

3. **Infer** Why does Goldsworthy use only materials he finds in nature to make his art? What is his intention, based on what he says in the film?

4. **Synthesize** What have you learned from these sources together about how changes in nature affect humans?

 ENGLISH LEARNER SUPPORT

Ask Questions Use the following questions to help students compare the selections:

1. What idea about change does each selection focus on?

2. How is the film like the poem? How are the film and the poem different?

3. Which selection was more interesting or important to you? Why?
   ALL LEVELS

COMPARE AND PRESENT

Now, your group can continue exploring the key ideas and themes in these texts by collaborating on research to present an overview of the themes. Follow these steps:

1. **Identify Themes** In your group, compile direct statements of theme from both works that you wrote in your charts, and analyze their similarities and differences.

2. **Gather Information** Choose two key images from each work, and draft a statement expressing the theme or main idea of each image. You can use the framework below to synthesize what you learn.

KEY IMAGES	KEY IDEAS / THEMES
Image 1 from film clip:	
Image 2 from film clip:	
Image 1 from poem:	
Image 2 from poem:	

3. **Present an Overview** Create a presentation comparing the view of change in each work. Be sure to cite examples from both works to support the analysis.

 Go to the **Speaking and Listening Studio** for help with giving a presentation.

COMPARE AND PRESENT

Review the task with students. If necessary, clarify that they will collaborate to compare themes in the film and the poem, tie those themes to particular images in each work, and then create a presentation to communicate their findings to the rest of the class.

1. **Identify Themes** As students compare themes, circulate among the groups and provide support.

2. **Gather Information** You might instruct half the group to review the video while the other half reviews the poem. Have students in each half-group record information about their selection and then share their notes with the rest of the group.

3. **Present an Overview** Allow groups time to plan what they are going to say and practice presenting the information before giving their presentations. Let students know that each group member should take part in the presentation.

APPLYING ACADEMIC VOCABULARY

☑ abstract   ☐ evolve   ☑ explicit   ☐ facilitate   ☐ infer

Write and Discuss Have students turn to a partner to discuss the following questions. Guide students to include the academic vocabulary words *abstract* and *explicit* in their responses. Ask volunteers to share their responses with the class.

- What ideas about change in the film and the poem are more **abstract**?
- What ideas about change are made **explicit** in the film and the poem?

INDEPENDENT READING

READER'S CHOICE

Setting a Purpose Have students review their Unit 5 Response Log and think about what they've already learned about how changes around us reveal who we are. As they choose their Independent Reading selections, encourage them to consider what more they want to know.

NOTICE & NOTE

Explain that some selections may contain multiple signposts; others may contain only one. And the same type of signpost can occur many times in the same text.

LEARNING MINDSET

Seeking Challenges Tell students that having a learning mindset means being willing to take risks and try new things despite the fear of failure. Trying hard is important, but so is trying things that *are* hard. Encourage students to challenge themselves by selecting Independent Reading selections that may be slightly higher than their skill level.

 INDEPENDENT READING

? ESSENTIAL QUESTION:

How do changes around us reveal who we are?

Reader's Choice

Setting a Purpose Select one or more of these options from your eBook to continue your exploration of the Essential Question.

• Read the descriptions to see which text grabs your interest.

• Think about which genres you enjoy reading.

Notice & Note

In this unit, you practiced asking **Big Questions** and noticing and noting two signposts: **Contrasts and Contradictions** and **Extreme or Absolute Language.** As you read independently, these signposts and others will aid your understanding. Below are the anchor questions to ask when you read literature and nonfiction.

Reading Literature: Stories, Poems, and Plays		
Signpost	**Anchor Question(s)**	**Lesson**
Contrasts and Contradictions	Why did the character act that way?	p. 145
Aha Moment	How might this change things?	p. 394
Tough Questions	What does this make me wonder about?	p. 2
Words of the Wiser	What's the lesson for the character?	p. 3
Again and Again	Why might the author keep bringing this up?	p. 145
Memory Moment	Why is this memory important?	p. 3

Reading Nonfiction: Essays, Articles, and Arguments		
Signpost	**Anchor Question(s)**	**Lesson**
Big Questions	What surprised me? What did the author think I already knew? What challenged, changed, or confirmed what I already knew?	p. 220 p. 319 p. 74
Contrasts and Contradictions	What is the difference, and why does it matter?	p. 318
Extreme or Absolute Language	Why did the author use this language?	p. 221
Numbers and Stats	Why did the author use these numbers or amounts?	p. 75
Quoted Words	Why was this person quoted or cited, and what did this add?	p. 221
Word Gaps	Do I know this word from someplace else? Does it seem like technical talk for this topic? Do clues in the sentence help me understand the word?	p. 75

 ENGLISH LEARNER SUPPORT

Develop Fluency Select a passage from a text that matches students' abilities. Read the passage aloud while students follow along silently.

• Choral read the passage by having the students read the passage with you. Set a reasonable pace that will demonstrate the benefits of not rushing through the passage. After reading, check comprehension by asking yes/no questions. **SUBSTANTIAL**

• Have students silently read and reread the passage. Ask students to time their reading to track improvements over time. **MODERATE**

• Have students read the same text from the beginning in short timed bursts (3–5 minutes) and mark how far they get each time. The goal is not to rush through the passage but to build familiarity with difficult words. **LIGHT**

 Go to the **Reading Studio** for additional support in developing fluency.

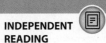

INDEPENDENT READING

You can preview these texts in Unit 5 of your eBook.

Then, check off the text or texts that you select to read on your own.

SHORT STORY

The Norwegian Rat
Naguib Mahfouz

Residents of an apartment building take action to protect themselves from an invasion of rats. But who are the real rats?

MEMOIR

After the Storm
Orhan Pamuk

A Nobel-winning Turkish writer finds meaning in the changes that occur during and after a violent storm.

SCIENCE WRITING

from **Simplexity**
Jeffrey Kluger

How do people react when they have to evacuate in an emergency? The answer is both simple and complicated.

NOVELLA

from **The Metamorphosis**
Franz Kafka

What would you do if you woke up and you weren't human anymore? Would you still be you?

Collaborate and Share   With a partner, discuss what you learned from at least one of your independent readings.

- Give a brief synopsis or summary of the text.
- Describe any signposts that you noticed in the text, and explain what they revealed to you.
- Describe what you most enjoyed or found most challenging about the text. Give specific examples.
- Decide whether you would recommend the text to others. Why or why not?

 Go to the **Reading Studio** for more resources on **Notice & Note.**

MATCHING STUDENTS TO TEXTS

Use the following information to guide students in choosing their texts.

The Norwegian Rat   Lexile: 990L
  Genre: short story
  Overall Rating: Accessible

After the Storm   Lexile: 1330L
  Genre: memoir
  Overall Rating: Challenging

from **Simplexity**   Lexile: 1490L
  Genre: science writing
  Overall Rating: Challenging

from **The Metamorphosis**   Lexile: 1110L
  Genre: novella
  Overall Rating: Accessible

Collaborate and Share   To assess how well students read the selections, walk around the room and listen to their conversations. Encourage students to be focused and specific in their comments.

Online **for Assessment**

- Independent Reading Selection Tests

Encourage students to visit the **Reading Studio** to download a handy bookmark of **NOTICE & NOTE** signposts.

WHEN STUDENTS STRUGGLE . . .

Keep a Reading Log   As students read their selected texts, have them keep a reading log for each selection to note signposts and their thoughts about them. Use their logs to assess how well they are noticing and reflecting on elements of their texts.

Reading Log for (title)		
Location	**Signpost I Noticed**	**My Notes About It**

UNIT 5 Task

• WRITE A RESEARCH REPORT

from **THE FEVER**

Science Writing by Sonia Shah

LEARNING OBJECTIVES

Writing Task

- Write a research report about a specific way humans respond to changes in the world or in their own lives.
- Use strategies to plan and organize ideas.
- Record accurate references to sources used.
- Develop a focused, structured draft.
- Use the Mentor Text as a model for a thesis statement and precise, vivid details.
- Revise drafts, incorporating feedback from peers.
- Edit drafts to incorporate standard English conventions.
- Use a rubric to evaluate writing.
- Publish writing to share it with an audience.
- **Language** Identify correct subject-verb agreement.

Assign the Writing Task in **Ed.**

 Online

RESOURCES

- Unit 5 Response Log

- Reading Studio: Notice & Note

- Level Up Tutorial: Paraphrasing; Summarizing

- Writing Studio: Conducting Research; Using Textual Evidence

- Grammar Studio: Module 12: Lesson 4: Quotation Marks

Language X-Ray: English Learner Support

Use the instruction below and the supports and scaffolds in the Teacher's
Edition to help you guide students at different proficiency levels.

INTRODUCE THE WRITING TASK

In a **research report**, the writer presents information about a specific topic. The introduction briefly identifies the topic and expresses a position in a thesis statement, or controlling idea. The body consists of paragraphs with main ideas and supporting details. The conclusion restates the writer's thesis, synthesizes key points, and may express new insights. The writer accurately cites his or her sources in footnotes or endnotes.

Note that the selections in this unit deal with how people's responses to changes around them reveal who they really are. Use sentence frames to help students explore this theme. For example: *The way someone reacts to a situation tells us _____. We don't really know _____.* Have partners work together to write an original sentence about personal responses to changes around us.

WRITING

Narrow a Topic

Remind students that one of their first tasks is to narrow the topic of their research report so it can be expressed in a concise thesis statement.

Use the following supports with students at varying proficiency levels:

- Give students a broad topic related to the writing task—for example, *adjusting to moving to a new community*. Model how to narrow the topic. List ideas on the board. **SUBSTANTIAL**
- Use sentence frames to help students focus on specific topics, such as: *One response to the death of a family member is _____.* **MODERATE**
- After narrowing their topics, have partners work together to draft thesis statements in one or two concise sentences. **LIGHT**

WRITING

Use Correct Subject-Verb Agreement

Provide practice in which students identify correct subject-verb agreement.

- Read aloud sentence 1 of *The Fever.* Prompt students to raise their hands when they hear the subject. Ask: What is the subject? Is the subject singular or plural? *(pathogens; plural)* What is the verb? Is the verb singular or plural? *(mellow; plural)* Guide students to write the sentence down and mark the subject and verb. **SUBSTANTIAL**
- Read aloud paragraph 3 of *The Fever* and prompt students to identify the subject and verb *(experts, have spent)* and say whether they are singular or plural. Have them rewrite this sentence to include a singular subject and verb. **MODERATE**
- Have partners identify two examples of the subject and verb of a compound or complex sentence in *The Fever.* Have them use these as models for writing sentences. **LIGHT**

WRITING

WRITE A RESEARCH REPORT

Have volunteers read the introductory paragraph, and then engage students in a discussion of the writing task. Encourage students to refer to the notes they recorded in the Unit 5 Response Log before they begin planning and writing a draft. Emphasize that the Response Log will contain a variety of ideas about how people respond to changes in the world or in their own lives as explored in the unit's selections. Note that these different viewpoints will be useful in making students' research reports more informative and interesting.

USE THE MENTOR TEXT

Explain to students that their research reports will be similar to the excerpt from *The Fever* by Sonia Shah. Each report will present accurate information drawn from a variety of reliable sources about a specific way humans respond to changes in their world. Point out that the research report should focus on a narrow topic that addresses a specific research question. It should present information in logically organized paragraphs that connect ideas and evidence with clear transitions. Finally, it should conclude with a paragraph that summarizes the key ideas and supporting points and draws a conclusion about the question posed in the introduction. Encourage students to use precise words and maintain a formal tone and style throughout their research reports.

WRITING PROMPT

Discuss the prompt with students. Encourage them to ask questions about any part of the assignment they do not completely understand. Emphasize that the purpose of their research report is to explain a *specific* way humans respond to changes in their world.

Review the checklist of key points that students should consider as they write their research reports.

 WRITING TASK

Write a Research Report

 Go to the **Writing Studio** for help writing a research report.

The texts in this unit present various perspectives on how we respond to changes around us and how those changes occur. Choose three texts from the unit. Identify a way in which humans respond to major changes, and conduct research about it. Synthesize your findings in a report that develops a clear thesis. For an example of a well-researched report you can use as a mentor text, review the excerpt from *The Fever*.

RESPONSES TO CHANGE

As you write your report, you will want to look at the notes you made in your Response Log after reading the texts in this unit.

Writing Prompt

Read the information in the box below.

> *This is the topic or context for your report.*

> Undergoing change may alter the way someone approaches the world, or it may magnify characteristics he or she already had.

> *This is the Essential Question for the unit. How would you answer this question, based on the texts in this unit?*

Think carefully about the following question.

> How do changes around us reveal who we are?

> *Think about how you will find a specific topic for your report.*

Write a research report about a specific way humans respond to changes in the world or in their own lives.

Be sure to—

> *Review these points as you write and again when you finish. Make any needed changes.*

- ❑ research your topic and keep careful notes about your sources
- ❑ narrow your topic so that it addresses a specific research question
- ❑ clearly structure your ideas and subtopics, linking ideas with transitions
- ❑ smoothly integrate researched information and cite sources correctly
- ❑ use precise word choice and an appropriately formal tone and style
- ❑ end by summarizing your information or drawing a conclusion

---

 LEARNING MINDSET

Try Again Explain to students that it is commonplace for learners to make mistakes, especially when they are trying something for the first time. Emphasize that the key to successful learning is to go back to the original question or task, reread it carefully, and determine what they misunderstood the first time around. For this writing task, have students who are unclear about the assignment review the writing prompt. If possible, provide a personal example of a time you made a mistake while trying to complete a complex task, but then succeeded after trying a new approach. Stress that often it takes several attempts to succeed at new learning tasks.

1 Plan

Begin to formulate a question you have about how humans respond to changes, either personal changes that affect their own lives or larger changes that affect their community or world. This question will guide your research.

Next, gather evidence about your question from credible print or online resources. Skim many sources to get an overview of the general topics they address and determine how credible they seem. Consider the author or organization that created the source, and look for signs of a bias. Reject sources that use faulty reasoning, including making hasty generalizations about human nature based on just a few examples. Once you find credible sources, note important details or quotations in the chart below or on index cards.

RESEARCH REPORT PLANNING CHART

Research Question:

Source:	
Quotation or fact:	Page number or Date accessed:

Source:	
Quotation or fact:	Page number or Date accessed:

Source:	
Quotation or fact:	Page number or Date accessed:

Source:	
Quotation or fact:	Page number or Date accessed:

Source:	
Quotation or fact:	Page number or Date accessed:

 Go to **Conducting Research: Starting Your Research** for help with identifying sources.

Notice & Note

From Reading to Writing

As you plan your research report, apply what you've learned about signposts to your own writing. Think about how you can incorporate **Quoted Words** into your report.

Go to the **Reading Studio** for more resources on **Notice & Note**.

Use the notes from your Response Log as you plan your report.

WRITING

1 PLAN

Make sure students understand that not all sources are equally reliable or credible. When evaluating sources, it is important to know where and how they were published. Most credible scholarly works are reviewed by other scholars, or peers, who check for accuracy. Another matter to check for is the timeliness of the source—for example, is it no longer relevant because this field of knowledge evolves rapidly? Another guiding factor in evaluating the credibility of sources is the audience for whom they were originally written.

EL ENGLISH LEARNER SUPPORT

Understand Academic Language Make sure students understand words and phrases used in the planning chart, such as *source* and *quotation*. Work with them to fill in the blank sections of the chart with possible sources.

NOTICE & NOTE

From Reading to Writing Discuss the different types of **Quoted Words** that students may use in a research report. For example, a writer may quote the opinion or conclusion of someone who is an expert on the topic. Another powerful type of quotation involves citing the words of someone who was a direct witness to or a participant in a related event.

Background Reading As students plan their research reports, encourage them to review the notes in their Response Log for Unit 5. Suggest that they briefly scan the unit's selections to identify examples of text elements they might use as models in their own writing.

WHEN STUDENTS STRUGGLE...

Paraphrase Quotations Have partners work together to scan selections and possible resources while looking for interesting facts they may want to include in their research reports. Have students copy direct quotations from texts and share them with their partner. Then have them paraphrase the quotations and read them back to their partner to see how well they captured the meaning of the original text. Have partners discuss how successful their paraphrases were and then reverse roles.

 For additional support, go to the **Reading Studio** and assign the following [LEVEL] **Level Up Tutorials: Paraphrasing** and **Summarizing.**

WRITING

Organize Your Ideas Emphasize the importance of using an outline to organize their ideas before students begin drafting their research reports. Review the organization of the Research Report Outline. Remind students that their research report must have a clear thesis statement, or controlling idea, expressed in the form of a question the writer has formulated or a statement the writer will prove.

Explain that in the body of the research report each key idea must be developed in a paragraph with a topic sentence and supporting points. Review the format of the planning chart and, if necessary, model where each key idea and its related supporting points are to be recorded.

Remind students that their research report should end with a conclusion that restates the thesis and synthesizes the key ideas and supporting points.

 For **writing support** for students at varying proficiency levels, see the **Language X-Ray** on page 384B.

2 DEVELOP A DRAFT

Encourage students to use their outlines as they begin to draft their research reports. Emphasize that an outline is a preliminary step and that, if new ideas come to them during the drafting stage, students can and should make changes to their outlines. They should feel free to rearrange sections and take their drafts in a different direction if they discover a more effective way to make their key points or a more logical way to order and transition between them.

Encourage students to include direct quotations, paraphrases, and summaries from their research sources. Point out that, although each key point should be supported by sources, the main emphasis of each section should always be on the point itself, not on how many sources or quotes students can fit into that section. **SUBSTANTIAL**

■ English Learner Support

Use Source Information Remind students to have their outlines and their resource notes available as they draft their research reports. **SUBSTANTIAL/MODERATE**

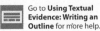 **WRITING TASK**

 Go to **Using Textual Evidence: Writing an Outline** for more help.

Organize Your Ideas After you have researched your topic, you need to organize your information. First, write a thesis statement that identifies your research question. Then, choose the textual and research evidence that most effectively supports your thesis. Decide what organizational pattern you will use for your report, and use this pattern to sort your textual evidence and research information into a logical order. You can use the chart below to make an outline of the points you will cover. You may find that you need to do additional research or omit some information you have gathered.

RESEARCH REPORT OUTLINE
Thesis Statement Identifying the Research Question:
Key Idea 1: Supporting Points:
Key Idea 2: Supporting Points:
Key Idea 3: Supporting Points:
Conclusion That Answers the Research Question:

You might prefer to draft your essay online.

2 Develop a Draft

Use your notes and outline to guide your writing. Your introduction should grab readers' attention and clearly state your thesis. Cite sources for facts, quotations, and examples that elaborate on your ideas, and use introductory phrases to provide context for quotations. Any time you discuss a new text or a new key point, include transitions to help guide your readers.

WHEN STUDENTS STRUGGLE . . .

Use Note Cards Explain that students can create a note card for each key idea or topic in their report. Show students how to label sections of their note cards as in the left column below.

Topic	Source
Paraphrase of information or quotation.	
Date	**Page**

- *Topic: a key idea of your research paper*
- *Source: where the information comes from*
- *Date: when you first noted the source*
- *Page: the page or other location of the source*

Explain that students should place their cards in order as they plan their reports. They can eliminate cards as they narrow their focus.

WRITING TASK

Use the Mentor Text

Genre Characteristics

Using another person's words without credit is called plagiarism and is not acceptable. To avoid plagiarism, paraphrase information and give credit to the source by using footnotes or endnotes, or enclose exact words from the source in quotation marks. Here is an example of paraphrasing and citing a source from *The Fever*:

> **Text:**
> According to the science writer Carl Zimmer, one third of all described species practice the parasitic lifestyle.[4]
>
> **Note:**
> [4] Carl Zimmer, *Parasite Rex: Inside the Bizarre World of Nature's Most Dangerous Creatures* (New York: Touchstone, 2000), 17.

The footnote gives credit to the source where the information was found.

Apply What You've Learned Look carefully through your draft, adding either footnotes or endnotes (whichever your teacher prefers) to document the source of every quotation and every paraphrased fact that isn't common knowledge. The two most accepted methods of source documentation are those of the Modern Language Association (MLA) and the American Psychological Association (APA). For help formatting your citations, see page 389.

Author's Craft

Even when you enclose the exact words from a source in quotation marks, the quoted text still needs to be placed in context for readers by using introductory words. Notice how the author of *The Fever* gives context to a quotation:

> In 1883, Scottish lecturer Henry Drummond called parasitism "one of the gravest crimes of nature . . . "

The introductory words explain who said these words and when.

Apply What You've Learned When you include a quotation, provide some context in the same sentence. You may also give more information in a note inside parentheses.

WHY THIS MENTOR TEXT?

The excerpt from *The Fever* provides a good example of the major elements of a research report. Use the instruction below to help students use the mentor text as a model for paraphrasing text from a source, giving credit to the source with footnotes and endnotes, and providing context for direct quotations introduced as part of a sentence.

USE THE MENTOR TEXT

Genre Characteristics Have a volunteer read the introductory text. Ask: Why is plagiarism unacceptable? (*It is stealing someone else's words.*) How does keeping detailed notes help avoid plagiarism? (*It gives you a record of who said what.*)

Ask a volunteer to read aloud the sample text and the note that accompanies it. Ask: Is the text a paraphrase or a direct quotation? (*paraphrase*) Why might the writer have made a note about this detail? (*because it is an interesting fact and can be used as supporting evidence*)

Author's Craft Have a volunteer read aloud the introduction to this section and the example from the mentor text. Ask: What contextual details are provided to set up the actual quotation? (*the name of the person who is quoted, and the date*) Do you think this context is sufficient? What other details might be included? (*The context is sufficient, but might have included more specific information about Drummond's occupation.*)

 ENGLISH LEARNER SUPPORT

Use the Mentor Text Use the following supports with students at varying proficiency levels:

- Read aloud paragraph 4 of the excerpt from *The Fever*. Ask: What quotation from the paragraph could support its main idea? (*Possible responses: "a cheater at the game of life"; "Parasites don't help anyone. They're degenerates."*) **SUBSTANTIAL**

- Have students work with a partner to write two sentences—one using a direct quotation from the text and the other paraphrasing the quotation. Have partners share their example(s) and discuss when it is most effective to quote or to paraphrase. **MODERATE**

- Have students work independently to write a very brief paraphrase of a passage from the text. Then lead a class discussion about the importance of avoiding plagiarism. **LIGHT**

③ REVISE

Have students answer each question in the Revision Guide and determine how they can improve the drafts of their research reports. Call on volunteers to model their revision techniques.

With a Partner Have students work with peer reviewers to evaluate their research report drafts. Use the following questions as a guide for peer review:

- Is the organization of my report logical?
- Is any evidence unclear? Are more supporting details needed?
- Have I correctly quoted and paraphrased sources?
- What questions do you have about my research?

Encourage students to use the reviewer's feedback to add relevant details and revise for precise word choice and the appropriate tone as they further develop the topic of their research reports.

 For **writing support** for students at varying proficiency levels, see the **Language X-Ray** on page 384B.

■ English Learner Support

Spell Singular and Plural Forms Review that the plural forms of most nouns in English are spelled with -s or -es, as in *vacations* and *beaches.* However, the verbs that agree with these nouns follow the opposite pattern: third-person singular verbs usually end in -s or -es, while the plural verbs do not. Have students copy these sentences for reference as they revise and edit their drafts: *The teacher helps her students. The students learn from the teacher.* **MODERATE**

 **WRITING TASK**

 Go to **Using Textual Evidence: Attribution** for help incorporating research material.

③ Revise

On Your Own Revise your draft to make sure it is clear, coherent, and engaging. Use the chart below as a guide. The Revision Guide will help focus on specific elements to make your writing stronger.

REVISION GUIDE

Ask Yourself	Tips	Revision Techniques
1. Does the introduction grab reader attention and state a clear thesis?	**Mark** the attention-getting opener. Underline the thesis statement or research question.	**Add** an interesting fact, example, or quotation that illustrates the topic. **Add** a thesis or **revise** to clarify it.
2. Is the body of the report logically organized and linked with transitions?	**Note** the topic addressed in each part of the report. **Underline** transitions that link sections or show sequence.	**Rearrange** information as needed to provide a clearer organizational pattern. **Add** transitions that link ideas.
3. Is each key idea in the report supported by text evidence?	**Mark** each piece of evidence for each section of the report.	**Add** supporting evidence from a variety of sources for any sections lacking evidence.
4. Are quotations smoothly integrated into sentences that provide context?	**Underline** sentence parts that provide context for quotations from sources.	**Revise** sentences containing quotations to add context.
5. Are sources correctly cited for quotations and facts that are not common knowledge?	**Mark** quotations and facts. **Mark** their citations in footnotes or endnotes.	**Add** correctly formatted footnotes or endnotes to cite the sources of facts or quotations as needed.
6. Does the conclusion sum up ideas in an insightful way?	**Underline** the summary of ideas in the conclusion.	**Add** a summary or answer to the research question if needed.

ACADEMIC VOCABULARY
As you conduct your peer review, try to use these words.

- ❏ abstract
- ❏ evolve
- ❏ explicit
- ❏ facilitate
- ❏ infer

With a Partner After you have revised your report using the Revision Guide on your own, exchange papers with a partner. Evaluate each other's drafts in a peer review. Look to see whether quotations are smoothly integrated into sentences and that quotations and facts are correctly cited. Be sure you and your partner are using source materials correctly to avoid plagiarism.

In this type of academic writing, it's especially important to respond to what you have read using appropriate register and voice. **Register** refers to the level and context of the writing—a research report should sound like writing suitable for college. But it should also express the writer's **voice,** or unique style of self-expression. Consider reading your report aloud to get your partner's feedback on your register and voice.

 ## ENGLISH LEARNER SUPPORT

Use Correct Subject-Verb Agreement with Compound Subjects Remind students that some simple sentences have compound subjects. In these cases, subject-verb agreement requires careful review.

- Give students an example of a simple sentence with one subject, such as *Elena **likes** doing research.* Then show the same sentence with two subjects joined by the word *and: Elena and Lee **like** doing research.* Point out how the verb *like* changes from singular to plural.

- Next, explain that a sentence with a singular compound subject joined by the word *or* takes a singular verb since it refers to only one element of the compound subject.

    Example: *Either Elena or Lee **likes** doing research.*

Have students write examples of sentences with compound subjects that take either a singular or a plural verb form. Call on volunteers to share their examples and discuss with the class. **LIGHT**

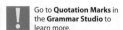

④ Edit

Always give credit to both quoted and paraphrased sources in your research report. It's ethical, and it provides credibility so readers will take your writing seriously. Use footnotes or endnotes to tell the reader where your information came from. Footnotes appear at the bottom of the same page as the information they document; endnotes are grouped together at the end of the report. The notes are numbered in sequence.

> ! Go to **Quotation Marks** in the **Grammar Studio** to learn more.

Crediting a Source

When you present information from a source, you may or may not name that source in the body of your text. However, you must credit the source in your notes. This chart shows a standard footnoting format for three types of sources.

Print Article	Author First Name Last Name, "Article Title," *Magazine or Journal Title,* volume number, issue number (year): page number or numbers.
	David J. Marcogliese and Judith Price, "The Paradox of Parasites," *Global Biodiversity* 3 (1997): 7-15.
Book	Author First Name Last Name, *Book Title* (City of Publication: Publisher, year), page number or numbers.
	Roy Porter, *The Greatest Benefit to Mankind* (New York: W. W. Norton, 1997), 25.
Internet Site	Author First Name Last Name if available, "Title of Web Page," *Publishing Organization or Name of Website,* Publication Month Day, Year, URL (accessed Month Day, Year).
	Tom Phillips, "Brazilian explorers search 'medicine factory' to save lives and rainforest," *The Guardian,* April 27, 2009, http://www.theguardian.com/environment/2009/apr/27/amazon-rainforest-medicine (accessed January 27, 2019).

⑤ Publish

Finalize your research report and choose a way to share it with your audience. Be sure that the report is up to college-level academic standards before you publish it. Consider these options:

- Print your research report and make it available to others.
- Post your research report on a class web page. Embed links to footnotes or endnotes in the citation numbers to help readers locate your sources faster.

Write a Research Report 389

④ EDIT

Tell students that in order to improve their research reports they will need to read their drafts several times. Encourage them to focus on the clarity of their ideas and the evidence they use to support these ideas during their first reading. During their second reading, suggest that students look for places they can add additional evidence. During the third reading, suggest that students focus on their use of effective transitions to connect related ideas and examples.

CREDITING A SOURCE

Emphasize that students are expected to cite sources they have used in a research report. Stress that quoting or paraphrasing the thoughts of others is expected; however, it is essential that they acknowledge the source of the quotations or ideas.

Review the formats and examples of the three types of source citations listed in the chart. Discuss any questions the students may have. Ask: In what ways are all three source notes alike? *(They all begin with the author's first and last name, followed by the title of the work.)* How are the titles of works listed in the sources different from each other? *(The titles of magazine and web articles are placed in quotation marks, whereas the titles of books are italicized.)* With what information do the sources for an article or book end? *(with a page reference)* What does this page indicate? *(where the specific quotation or idea appears in the original source)*

⑤ PUBLISH

Discuss the suggested publishing options. If students print their research reports, provide a place in the classroom where they can store them safely for other students to read. If necessary, provide students with instructions on how to post their research reports on a class web page. Encourage other students to read the research reports and write meaningful comments and helpful suggestions.

TO CHALLENGE STUDENTS . . .

Use Direct Quotations Remind students that a direct quotation must match the original source word for word and must be attributed to the original author.

- Quotations of 40 words or less are set off by quotation marks.

    Example: African American novelist Ralph Ellison said, "When I discover who I am, I'll be free."

- Longer quotations are set off in indented paragraphs with no quotation marks.

Have students select short and long quotations from the selection and explain how to use them correctly in a research report.

WRITING

USE THE SCORING GUIDE

Allow students time to read the scoring guide. Encourage them to ask questions about any ideas, sentences, phrases, or words they find unclear. Tell partners to exchange their final research reports and score them. Have each student reviewer write a paragraph explaining the reason for the score he or she awarded in each category.

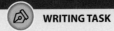

WRITING TASK

Use the scoring guide to evaluate your report.

WRITING TASK SCORING GUIDE: RESEARCH REPORT		
Organization/Progression	**Development of Ideas**	**Use of Language and Conventions**
4 • The organization is effective and appropriate to the purpose. • All ideas are focused on the topic specified in the prompt. • Transitions clearly show the relationship among ideas.	• The introduction is compelling and informative; the thesis statement clearly identifies a research question. • The topic is well developed with clear main ideas supported by specific and well-chosen facts, details, examples, and quotations. • The conclusion effectively summarizes the answer to the research question and makes a thoughtful observation.	• The essay uses formal language, and word choice is purposeful and precise. • Spelling, capitalization, and punctuation are correct. • Grammar and usage are correct. • Several credible research sources are cited using correctly formatted footnotes or endnotes.
3 • The organization is, for the most part, effective and appropriate to the purpose. • Most ideas are focused on the topic specified in the prompt. • Transitions usually connect ideas.	• The introduction is adequate; the thesis statement identifies a research question. • The ideas are sufficiently developed and are supported by specific and appropriate facts, details, examples, and quotations. • The concluding section summarizes the answer to the research question.	• Language is for the most part formal, specific, and clear. • Some minor spelling, capitalization, and punctuation mistakes occur. • Some grammatical and usage errors occur but do not interfere with understanding. • Several credible research sources are cited using footnotes or endnotes with some formatting errors.
2 • The organization is evident but is not always appropriate to the purpose. • Only some ideas are focused on the topic specified in the prompt. • More transitions are needed to show the relationship among ideas.	• The introduction states a vague thesis but does not engage readers. • The development of ideas is minimal. The writer uses facts, details, examples, or quotations that are inappropriate or ineffectively presented. • The conclusion merely restates the thesis.	• Language is somewhat informal, vague, and unclear. • Spelling, capitalization, and punctuation, as well as grammar and usage, are often incorrect and sometimes make the writer's ideas unclear. • Only one or two research sources are cited, using incorrect format.
1 • The organization is absent or not appropriate to the purpose. • Ideas are not focused on the topic specified in the prompt. • No transitions are used, making the report difficult to understand.	• The introduction and the thesis statement are missing or confusing. • The development of ideas is weak. Supporting facts, details, examples, or quotations are unreliable, vague, or missing. • The conclusion is missing.	• Language is inappropriate for the text. • Many spelling, capitalization, and punctuation errors are present. • Frequent grammatical and usage errors cause confusion. • Citations of research sources are missing.

Reflect on the Unit

When you were writing your research report, you gathered and expressed many of your thoughts about the reading you have done in this unit. Now is a good time to reflect on what you have learned.

Reflect on the Essential Question

- How do changes around us reveal who we are? How has your answer to this question changed since you first considered it when you started this unit?

- What are some examples from the texts you've read that show how humans respond to changes around them?

Reflect on Your Reading

- Which selections were the most interesting or surprising to you?

- From which selection did you learn the most about how humans respond to change?

Reflect on the Writing Task

- What difficulties did you encounter while working on your research report? How might you avoid them next time?

- What part of the report was the easiest and what part was the hardest to write? Why?

- What improvements did you make to your report as you were revising?

UNIT 5 SELECTIONS
- from "Total Eclipse"
- from *The Fever*
- "A Sound of Thunder"
- "5 P.M., Tuesday, August 23, 2005"
- from *Rivers and Tides*
- "Sonnets to Orpheus, Part Two, XII"

REFLECT ON THE UNIT

Have students reflect independently on the questions and write their responses. After students have completed these tasks, have them discuss their responses with a partner or in a small group. During these discussions, move about the classroom and note questions that are generating the liveliest conversations. Use these questions as the basis for a whole-class discussion that wraps up the unit.

LEARNING MINDSET

Questioning Explain to students that asking questions is essential all throughout the learning process. At the beginning of a task, asking questions helps clarify the task and goals. For example: What is the task? What am I trying to achieve? During the task, asking questions helps people stay on track, checking their progress and making adjustments as needed. For example: What is going well? What am I struggling with? After the task is completed, asking questions supports self-reflection and solidifies learning. For example: What did I learn from this task that I can build on next time? How can I avoid making similar missteps next time?

Instructional Overview and Resources

	Instructional Focus	**Online Ed Resources**
 **Unit Introduction** **Absolute Power**	**Unit 6 Essential Question** **Unit 6 Academic Vocabulary**	**Stream to Start:** Absolute Power **Unit 6 Response Log**

ANALYZE & APPLY

	Instructional Focus	**Online Ed Resources**
The Tragedy of Macbeth Drama by William Shakespeare **NOTICE & NOTE** READING MODEL **Signposts** • Aha Moment • Again and Again • Tough Questions	**Reading** • Analyze Drama • Analyze Character and Theme **Act I: Writing:** Analysis **Act II: Speaking and Listening:** Discuss **Act III: Speaking and Listening:** Share an Analysis **Act IV: Speaking and Listening:** Participate in a Debate **End of Play: Writing:** Document Information **Speaking and Listening:** Discuss with a Small Group **Vocabulary:** Archaic Language **Language Conventions:** Inverted Sentence Structure	🔊 **Audio** **Close Read Screencasts:** Modeled Discussions **Reading Studio:** Notice & Note **Level Up Tutorials:** Listed at point of use **Writing Studio:** Writing an Analysis **Speaking and Listening Studio:** Participating in Collaborative Discussions
from Macbeth Film by Rupert Goold	**Reading** • Analyze Media Representations **Writing:** Write an Analysis **Speaking and Listening:** Deliver an Argument	**Writing Studio:** Writing an Analysis **Speaking and Listening Studio:** Delivering an Argument

SUGGESTED PACING: 30 DAYS

Unit Introduction	The Tragedy of Macbeth												from Macbeth		
1	2	3	4	5	6	7	8	9	10	11	12	13	14	15	16

English Learner Support

- Build New Vocabulary

Differentiated Instruction

Assessment

- Text X-Ray
- Create a Glossary
- Analyze Drama
- Analyze Inverted Sentences
- Develop Vocabulary
- Guide Pronunciation
- Summarize the Drama
- Confirm Understanding
- Paraphrase Dialogue
- Decode Archaic Language
- Practice Sound Transfer Issues
- Develop Vocabulary to Build Understanding
- Ask and Answer Questions
- Role-Play Dialogue
- Read with Support
- Read and Paraphrase
- Oral Assessment
- Paraphrase
- Analyze a Soliloquy
- Analyze Shakespearean Language
- Analyze Character and Theme

- Answer Questions and Make Inferences
- Rewrite Inverted Language
- Make Predictions to Aid Comprehension
- Understand Figurative Language
- Act Out Dialogue
- Using Side Notes
- Make Inferences
- Paraphrase and Read Aloud
- Compare and Contrast
- Develop Vocabulary to Describe Characters
- Simplify Sentences
- Read and Paraphrase
- Role-Play to Enrich Understanding
- Discuss Visuals
- Discuss Figurative Language
- Analyze Archaic Verbs
- Clarify Pronoun Use
- Develop Vocabulary Through Discussion
- Vocabulary Strategy

When Students Struggle
- Symbols and Metaphors
- Master Literary Terms
- Check Understanding
- Understand Archaic Language
- Analyze an Aside
- Relate Conflict to Plot
- Analyze a Soliloquy
- Interpret Dialogue
- Analyze Dramatic Irony
- Confirm Understanding
- Analyze Figurative Language
- Read Aloud
- Summarize to Check Understanding
- Analyze Dialogue
- Analyze Characters
- Develop Vocabulary to Build Understanding
- Work as Group

- Analyze Characterization
- Trace Character Development
- Connect Events
- Trace Changes in Character

To Challenge Students
- Portray Complex Characters
- Discuss Comic Relief
- Analyze Social Impacts
- Reinterpret a Scene
- Analyze Style
- Analyze Tragic Flaw
- Analyze Character and Theme
- Analyze Verbal Irony
- Analyze Character
- Map the Climax
- Analyze Characterization

Selection Test

- Text X-Ray
- Internalize Vocabulary
- Demonstrate Comprehension

When Students Struggle
- Analyze Media

To Challenge Students
- Use Media

Selection Test

The Macbeth Murder Mystery
17 18 19 20

from **Manga Shakespeare: Macbeth/ Shakespeare and Samurai (and Robot Ninjas?)**
21 22 23 24 25

Independent Reading
26 27

End of Unit
28 29 30

Absolute Power **392B**

PLAN

Instructional Focus

 **Online** Ed **Resources**

ANALYZE & APPLY

"The Macbeth Murder Mystery"
Short Story by James Thurber
Lexile 580L

Reading
• Analyze Satire
• Make Connections
Writing: Write a Narrative
Speaking and Listening: Discuss Perspectives
Vocabulary: Idioms
Language Conventions: Pronoun-Antecedent Agreement

 Audio
Reading Studio: Notice & Note
Level Up Tutorial: Reading for Details
Writing Studio: Writing Narratives
Speaking and Listening Studio: Participating in Collaborative Discussions
Grammar Studio: Module 5: Lesson 8: Pronoun Agreement

COLLABORATE & COMPARE

from Manga Shakespeare: Macbeth
Graphic Novel by Robert Deas and Richard Appignanesi

. . . .

Mentor Text
"Shakespeare and Samurai (and Robot Ninjas?)"
Book Review by Caitlin Perry
Lexile 1480L

Reading
• Analyze Visual Elements
• Analyze Evidence
Writing: Write a Comparison
Speaking and Listening: Deliver a Pitch
Vocabulary: Word Roots
Language Conventions: Parentheses

 Audio
Reading Studio: Notice & Note
Level Up Tutorials: Listed at point of use
Writing Studio: Using Textual Evidence
Speaking and Listening Studio: Delivering Your Speech
Vocabulary Studio: Word Roots
Grammar Studio: Module 12: Lesson 6: Dashes and Parentheses

Collaborate and Compare

Reading: Compare Across Genres
Speaking and Listening: Compare and Present

Speaking and Listening Studio: Delivering Your Argument

Online Ed INDEPENDENT READING

The Independent Reading selections are only available in the eBook.

📖 **Go to the Reading Studio for more information on Notice & Note.**

 from *Holinshed's Chronicles*
History by Raphael Holinshed
Lexile 1630L

 "Why Read Shakespeare?"
Argument by Michael Mack
Lexile 980L

END OF UNIT

Writing Task: Write a Literary Analysis

Reflect on the Unit

Writing: Write a Literary Analysis
Language Conventions: Correct Spelling

Unit 6 Response Log
Mentor Text: "Shakespeare and Samurai (and Robot Ninjas?)"
Reading Studio: Notice & Note
Writing Studio: Writing Informative Texts; Writing as a Process
Grammar Studio: Module 13: Spelling

English Learner Support

Differentiated Instruction

• Text X-Ray
• Use Cognates
• Comprehend Genre
• Identify Antecedents

• Oral Assessment
• Discuss Perspectives
• Pronounce Vocabulary
• Use Pronouns Correctly

When Students Struggle
• Make Connections

To Challenge Students
• Discuss Characters in Satire

Selection Test

• Text X-Ray
• Analyze Visual Elements
• Use Cognates
• Develop Vocabulary
• Develop Vocabulary and Retell Stories
• Reinforce Directionality in Reading
• Develop Vocabulary to Build Understanding

• Create a Glossary
• Read and Paraphrase
• Summarize Reading
• Use Language Conventions
• Oral Assessment
• Write a Comparison
• Vocabulary Strategy
• Use Parentheses

When Students Struggle
• Review the Plot
• Use a Graphic Organizer
• Paraphrase and Predict
• Understand Language Structures

To Challenge Students
• Critique Visual Elements
• Analyze Dialogue

Selection Tests

• Ask Questions

To Challenge Students
• Create an Alternate Format

"Ozymandias"
Poem by Percy Bysshe
Shelley

Julius Caesar, Act III,
Scene 2
Drama by William
Shakespeare

Selection Tests

• Language X-Ray
• Understand Academic Language
• Analyze the Literature
• Use the Mentor Text
• Write Effective Body Paragraphs
• Use Correct Spelling

When Students Struggle
• Small Group Brainstorming

To Challenge Students
• Create Graphic Organizers

Unit Test

Connect to the
? ESSENTIAL QUESTION

Ask a volunteer to read aloud the Essential Question. Have students pause to reflect. Prompt them to give examples of "true power." Point out that students will likely have different opinions about what power is. Then ask students to discuss what sources of power may be.

■ ENGLISH LEARNER SUPPORT

Build New Vocabulary Make sure students understand the Essential Question. If necessary, explain the following terms:

- *Source* means "what something comes from."
- *True* means "real."
- *Power* means "the ability or right to control; the ability to act effectively; strength."

Help students restate the question in simpler language: Where does power come from? **SUBSTANTIAL/MODERATE**

DISCUSS THE QUOTATION

Tell students that *Macbeth* was written by William Shakespeare in 1606. Its gloomy themes reflect the period of political turmoil in which it was written. Queen Elizabeth I had died in 1603 without an heir, and the throne was offered to her distant cousin, who became King James I. Many were unsatisfied with the new king, and there was even an attempt to blow up James and his parliament in the Gunpowder Plot of 1605. *Macbeth* can be viewed as a cautionary tale to warn against regicide (the act of killing a king). Have students read the quotation carefully and take a moment to reflect on it. What kind of person would say this? What message do the words convey? How does that message fit with the historical context of the play?

ABSOLUTE POWER

? ESSENTIAL QUESTION:

What are the sources of true power?

Be bloody, bold, and resolute. Laugh to scorn The power of man, . . .

Macbeth, **Act IV, Scene 1**

392 Unit 6

⚙ LEARNING MINDSET

Growth Mindset Remind students that having a "fixed" mindset can lead a person to believe he or she is simply not good at something or can't learn new skills. Emphasize that learning takes effort and time. Discuss how thinking of mistakes as opportunities to learn and try again can take some pressure off—in other words, mistakes are really just practice. Share the example of Walt Disney, who was fired from a newspaper job for "not being creative enough," and whose early business, Laugh-O-Gram Studios, went bankrupt. Neither incident stopped Disney from putting forth more effort and trying to improve his skills and ventures. Encourage students to find similar examples of people they admire and use their stories as inspiration for reaching for their dreams.

ACADEMIC VOCABULARY

Academic Vocabulary words are words you use when you discuss and write about texts. In this unit you will practice and learn five words.

- ☑ comprise
- ☐ incidence
- ☐ predominant
- ☐ priority
- ☐ ultimate

Study the Word Network to learn more about the word **comprise.**

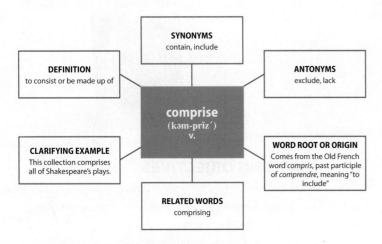

SYNONYMS
contain, include

ANTONYMS
exclude, lack

DEFINITION
to consist or be made up of

comprise
(kəm-prīz´)
v.

CLARIFYING EXAMPLE
This collection comprises all of Shakespeare's plays.

WORD ROOT OR ORIGIN
Comes from the Old French word *compris*, past participle of *comprendre*, meaning "to include"

RELATED WORDS
comprising

Write and Discuss Discuss the completed Word Network with a partner, making sure to talk through all of the boxes until you both understand the word, its synonyms, antonyms, and related forms. Then, fill out Word Networks for the remaining four words. Use a dictionary or online resource to help you complete the activity.

 Go online to access the Word Networks.

RESPOND TO THE ESSENTIAL QUESTION

In this unit, you will explore what true power means to different people. As you read, you will revisit the **Essential Question** and gather your ideas about it in the **Response Log** that appears on page R6. At the end of the unit, you will have the opportunity to write a **literary analysis** about different perspectives of true power. Filling out the Response Log will help you prepare for this writing task.

 You can also go online to access the Response Log.

ACADEMIC VOCABULARY

As students complete Word Networks for the remaining four vocabulary words, encourage them to include all the categories shown in the completed network if possible, but point out that some words do not have clear synonyms or antonyms. Some words may also function as different parts of speech—for example, *ultimate* can also be a noun.

comprise (kəm-prīz´) *v.* To consist or be made up of.

incidence (ĭn´sĭ-dəns) *n.* The occurrence or frequency of something. (Spanish cognate: *incidencia*)

predominant (prĭ-dŏm´ə-nənt) *adj.* Having the most importance, influence, or force. (Spanish cognate: *predominante*)

priority (prī-ôr´ĭ-tē) *n.* Something that is more important or considered more important than another thing. (Spanish cognate: *prioridad*)

ultimate (ŭl´tə-mĭt) *adj.* Concluding a process or progression; final.

RESPOND TO THE ESSENTIAL QUESTION

Direct students to the Unit 6 Response Log. Explain that students will use it to record ideas and details from the selections that help answer the Essential Question. When they work on the writing task at the end of the unit, their Response Logs will help them think about what they have read and make connections between the texts.

READING MODEL

THE TRAGEDY OF MACBETH
Drama by **William Shakespeare**

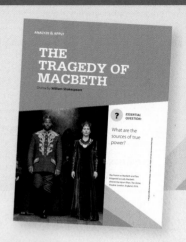

GENRE ELEMENTS
DRAMA

Explain that a **drama** is meant to be performed before an audience; therefore, it provides information that directors and actors can use to bring it to life. That information includes stage directions, speaker tags, and dialogue. Flip to the opening of the play on pages 402–403 to have students identify the cast of characters, stage directions, a speaker tag, and dialogue. Discuss any elements that may need clarification. Explain that in other respects, a drama is much like other works of fiction—it tells a story whose plot is built upon one or more conflicts. Tell students that characterization and theme are both important elements of this play.

LEARNING OBJECTIVES

- Analyze elements of a drama, including character and theme.
- Research a question that remains after reading the play.
- Create a character diagram.
- Collaborate to discuss and create a timeline of key events.
- Paraphrase archaic language.
- Reorder inverted sentence structure.
- **Language** Use *because* and *so* to explain cause-and-effect relationships.

TEXT COMPLEXITY

Quantitative Measures	The Tragedy of Macbeth	Lexile: N/A
Qualitative Measures	**Ideas Presented** Multiple levels of meaning; implicit themes.	
	Structures Used Somewhat complex story concepts.	
	Language Used Archaic, unfamiliar language; inverted sentence structures.	
	Knowledge Required Unfamiliar experience and situation; fairly complex theme.	

RESOURCES

- Unit 6 Response Log
- Selection Audio
- Close Read Screencasts: Modeled Discussions
- Reading Studio: Notice & Note
- Level Up Tutorials: Listed at point of use
- Writing Studio: Writing an Analysis
- Speaking and Listening Studio: Participating in Collaborative Discussions
- *The Tragedy of Macbeth* Selection Test

SUMMARIES

English

Macbeth, a Scottish nobleman, is returning home from a battle in which he defended King Duncan's sovereignty over Scotland. Along the way he meets three witches who prophesy his future. Soon after, he learns that one of their prophecies has come true. This revelation, along with the prompting of Lady Macbeth, causes him to take action to realize another of their prophecies: that he will become king of Scotland. He murders Duncan and persecutes those who do not support him as the new king. The decisions Macbeth makes to pursue this ambition set him on a downward spiral, leading to his eventual downfall.

Spanish

Macbeth, un aristócrata escocés, regresa a casa luego de defender en batalla la soberanía del Rey Duncan sobre Escocia. En su camino, se encuentra a tres brujas, que profetizan su futuro. Luego, se entera de que una de sus predicciones se ha hecho realidad. Esta revelación junto con las presiones de Lady Macbeth hace que tome medidas para que se haga realidad otra de las profecías: que él se convertirá en rey de Escocia. Asesina a Duncan y persigue a aquellos que apoyan a Malcolm, el hijo de Duncan, como el nuevo rey, en lugar de él. Las decisiones que Macbeth toma para conseguir su ambición lo llevan en una espiral descendiente que termina en su ruina.

SMALL-GROUP OPTIONS

Have students work in small groups to read and discuss the selection.

Triple-Entry Journal

- Have students divide a page into three columns and label the columns "Quotations from the Play," "My Notes," and "My Partner's Notes."
- In the first column, have students record lines from *The Tragedy of Macbeth* that they found interesting, important, or confusing.
- In the middle column, have students write their own reactions, interpretations, or questions.
- Then, ask partners to exchange journals. In the third column, have them write responses either to the quotations from the text or to their partner's notes.

Think-Pair-Share

- After students have read *The Tragedy of Macbeth*, pose this question: If you were Macbeth's best friend, what advice would you give him in Act I after he has met the witches? Why?
- Have students think about the question individually and take notes.
- Then, have pairs discuss their ideas about the question.
- Finally, ask pairs to share their responses with the class.

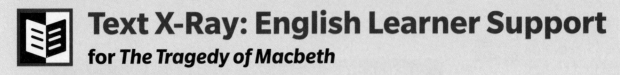

Text X-Ray: English Learner Support
for *The Tragedy of Macbeth*

Use the Text X-Ray and the supports and scaffolds in the Teacher's Edition to help guide students at different proficiency levels through the selection.

INTRODUCE THE SELECTION
DISCUSS AMBITION AND FATE

In this lesson, students will need to be able to discuss how Macbeth's ambition drives his actions and ultimately determines his fate. Provide the following explanations:

- *Ambition* is a strong desire to gain something, such as power.
- *Fate* is what happens to a person or what will happen. If a person's fate is *predetermined*, the outcome is decided or known in advance; no actions can stop it from happening.

Have volunteers share their opinions about whether ambition is good or bad and about whether they think their own actions determine the outcomes of their lives. Supply these sentence frames:

- *I think that ambition is _____.*
- *I think that _____ determine(s) _____.*

CULTURAL REFERENCES

The following words may be unfamiliar to students:

- *assassination:* the murder of someone in power, such as a king (Act I, Scene 7, line 2)
- *deed:* something someone does; an action someone takes (Act I, Scene 7, line 24)
- *revenge:* to punish someone in return for something that person did (Act III, Scene 3, line 18)
- *apparition:* a ghost or figure that appears in the air and then disappears (Act IV, Scene 1, stage directions preceding line 69)
- *prophecy:* a prediction of the future (Act IV, Scene 3, line 157)

See also side glosses throughout the play.

LISTENING

Understand Central Ideas

Read aloud an excerpt from the play to show students how listening to the play's dialogue can help them determine meaning. Tell students when they hear unfamiliar words to try to get a feeling from the words that will help them understand the characters' emotions.

Have students listen as you read aloud lines 17–28 in Act V, Scene 5. Use the following supports with students at varying proficiency levels:

- Explain that in this part of the play, Macbeth finds out that his wife, Lady Macbeth, has died, and soldiers are ready to attack his castle. Then ask students questions about Macbeth. Model how to give a thumbs up if the answer is yes, and a thumbs down for no. Ask: Is Macbeth sad that his wife has died? (*yes*) Is Macbeth happy to be alive? (*no*) **SUBSTANTIAL**
- Tell students to listen for the rhythm of repeated words as you read. Have students mark the repeated words they notice. Then use this sentence frame to help them understand the passage: *The repeated word (s) _____ show that Macbeth feels _____ after his wife has died.* (*The repeated word(s)* tomorrow/day/out *show that Macbeth feels* sad/alone/hopeless *after his wife has died.*) **MODERATE**
- Guide students to listen for words that help them understand what Macbeth is feeling. As you read, have students mark words that show Macbeth's feelings. Ask: How does Macbeth describe life? (*He describes life as slow and meaningless* ["Creeps in this petty pace"].) **LIGHT**

SPEAKING

Use *Because* and *So* to Explain Actions

Read the Discuss with a Small Group activity on Student Edition page 481. Explain that students will use connecting words such as *because* and *so* to explain cause-and-effect relationships.

Use the following supports with students at varying proficiency levels:

- Work with a small group to describe Macbeth. List some adjectives that describe him such as *strong* and *foolish*. Explain the meaning of each word. Then model producing a sentence that explains a simple cause-and-effect relationship, such as *He was strong, so he was a good fighter.* **SUBSTANTIAL**
- Have students refer to their character diagrams. Ask a student to form a sentence about something a character did, such as *Lady Macbeth urged Macbeth to kill King Duncan.* Then ask the student a related Why question. For example: Why did Lady Macbeth want Macbeth to kill King Duncan? Have students respond using a complete sentence with *because* or *so.* **MODERATE**
- Have partners work together to practice presenting their character diagrams. As students describe their characters, have them use the connecting words *so* and *because* to explain actions that their characters took and why. **LIGHT**

READING

Make Inferences

Have students reread Banquo's speech in Act III, Scene 1, lines 1–10, and then make inferences about it.

Use the following supports with students at varying proficiency levels:

- Model reading aloud the stage direction and the first three lines of Banquo's speech. Have students follow along with an index finger or pointer. Then ask these questions: Is Banquo talking about Duncan or Macbeth? *(Macbeth)* Are the Weird Sisters with Banquo now? *(no)* Is Banquo alone? *(yes)* **SUBSTANTIAL**
- Have students read the stage directions and lines 1–10. Then ask: Who is Banquo talking about when he says, "Thou hast it now"? *(Macbeth)* What does Banquo suspect about Macbeth? *(that Macbeth killed Duncan)* What does Banquo hope? *(He hopes that his heirs will be king.)* **MODERATE**
- Have students read the stage directions and lines 1–10. Then ask students to write several sentences explaining the good thoughts and bad thoughts that Banquo is having at this point in the play. **LIGHT**

WRITING

Write Sentences About a Character

Read the writing assignment on Student Edition page 481. Explain that students will use past-tense verbs to describe their characters' actions.

Use the following supports with students at varying proficiency levels, paying particular attention to speakers of Vietnamese:

- List some regular verbs on the board and work with students to write short sentences describing Macbeth's actions. Guide students to add *-ed* to form past tense verbs. Examples: *Macbeth killed Duncan. Macbeth wanted to be king.* **SUBSTANTIAL**
- Drawing on information in their character diagrams, have students write five sentences telling about actions their characters took. Check students' work for the proper *-ed* endings or irregular verb forms. **MODERATE**
- Ask students to write sentences they will use to present their character diagrams to their group. Have students include at least three regular verbs and three irregular verbs in the past tense. **LIGHT**

TEACH

EXPLAIN THE SIGNPOSTS

Explain that **NOTICE & NOTE Signposts** are significant moments in the text that help readers understand and analyze works of fiction or nonfiction. Use the instruction on these pages to introduce students to the signposts **Aha Moment, Again and Again,** and **Tough Questions**. Then use the selection that follows to have students apply the signposts to a text.

For a full list of the fiction and nonfiction signposts, see page 526.

▶ AHA MOMENT

Explain that **Aha Moments** almost always reveal a change in a **character** or signal an important **plot** development. Point out that Aha Moments often are sudden but that plot details may have been building to that moment for some time.

Read aloud the example passage. Point out the underlined text and explain that "Without my stir" means "without my doing anything to make it happen." Ask: What event might make Macbeth king without his doing anything to make it happen? (*The king might die and the people then might want Macbeth to take the crown; the king might die and Macbeth [if unmarried] then might marry the widowed queen.*) Explain that "Without my stir" tells readers that Macbeth now understands that he has an important choice to make: should he leave becoming king strictly up to chance or should he take an active part in becoming king?

Tell students that when they spot an Aha Moment, they should pause, mark it in their consumable texts, and ask the anchor question: *How might this change things?*

 For more information on these and other signposts to Notice & Note, visit the **Reading Studio**.

THE TRAGEDY OF MACBETH

You are about to read the drama *The Tragedy of Macbeth*. In it, you will notice and note signposts that will give you clues about the drama's characters, plot, and themes. Here are three key signposts to look for as you read this drama and other works of fiction.

When you see a phrase like this, pause to see if it's an **Aha Moment:**

"All of a sudden . . ."

"for the first time . . ."

"and just like that . . ."

"I realized . . ."

▶ **Aha Moment** Imagine that you have an important problem to solve. You've been thinking about it from every possible angle, and no solution you consider seems right. One night you give your brain a break and go to bed early . . . and when you wake up the next morning, the perfect solution pops into your head!

This kind of breakthrough is an **Aha Moment**. These moments happen in literature when a character has a sudden realization or comes to understand something fully. Aha Moments tend to:

- signal a new direction in the plot
- indicate character development
- reveal some kind of change
- resolve a character's internal conflict

Here is how a student might mark an Aha Moment in the play:

Anchor Question
When you notice this signpost, ask: How might this change things?

> **Macbeth.** If chance will have me king, why, chance may crown me Without my stir.

What does the character realize?	He may not have to take any action to become king.
How might this moment change things?	He might decide to just enjoy his new title with the anticipation that it will lead to bigger things.

Again and Again When you think of picture books, you probably think of repetition. Repetition of words, ideas, or images helps young readers understand the message. The same is true, but more subtle, in literary works. When a word, phrase, or image comes up **Again and Again,** it may suggest a theme, a symbol, or character motives.

Here is how a student noted repetition of an image:

> **Lady Macbeth.**   The raven himself is hoarse
> That croaks the fatal entrance of Duncan
> Under my battlements. (Act I, Scene 5, lines 35–37)
>
> **Banquo.**   This guest of summer,
> The temple-haunting martlet, does approve . . . (Act I, Scene 6, lines 3–4)

Anchor Question
When you notice this signpost, ask: Why might the author bring this up again and again?

What image is repeated?	references to birds
Why does the author repeat this image?	These birds seem to represent human emotions.

Tough Questions Classic literature is created when main characters face difficult choices. A character's decisions provide insight into internal conflicts, complex personalities, and often suggest themes. Look for moments of confusion, doubt, conflict, and anxiety as you read.

In this example, a student marked a **Tough Question** in the play:

> **Macbeth.** This supernatural soliciting
> Cannot be ill, cannot be good. If ill,
> Why hath it given me earnest of success
> Commencing in a truth? I am Thane of Cawdor.
> If good, why do I yield to that suggestion
> Whose horrid image doth unfix my hair
> And make my seated heart knock at my ribs
> Against the use of nature?

Anchor Question
When you notice this signpost, ask: What does this question make me wonder about?

What tough question is the character facing?	Is the Witches' influence good or bad?
What does this make me wonder about?	whether Macbeth will make the right choice

Notice & Note   395

AGAIN AND AGAIN

Explain that when a word, phrase, or image is used **Again and Again** in a work of literature, it may be a **motif,** or recurrent thematic element in the work. Read aloud the example passage. Explain that in Shakespeare, the raven is often a bad omen or sign.

Tell students when they spot words, phrases, or images Again and Again, they should pause, mark them in their consumable text, and ask themselves the anchor question: *Why might the author bring this up again and again?*

TOUGH QUESTIONS

Explain that in classic literature, the plot is often driven by the **conflict** created by **Tough Questions.**

Read aloud the example passage and point out the Tough Question one reader identified. Explain that the "supernatural soliciting" in the first line refers to a prophecy told to Macbeth. Macbeth is trying to figure out whether he should believe in the prophecy and what he should do about it. Point out how the reader answered the questions below the example passage.

Tell students that when they encounter a Tough Question that a character must answer, they should pause, mark it in their consumable texts, and ask themselves the anchor question: *What does this question make me wonder about?*

APPLY THE SIGNPOSTS

Have students use the selection that follows as a model text to apply the signposts. As students encounter signposts, prompt them to stop, reread, and ask themselves the anchor questions that will help them understand the play's characters and themes.

Tell students to continue to look for these and other signposts as they read the other selections in the unit.

WHEN STUDENTS STRUGGLE . . .

Symbols and Metaphors Guide students to create a chart in which they can track patterns and record meanings of symbols and metaphors. You might provide further support by asking students to look for repeated mention of sleep, clothing, and blood as they read the play.

Category	Example	Meaning
Animals	*sparrows & eagles* (Act I, Scene 2, line 35)	*metaphor: Norwegian soldiers are being compared to weak sparrows; Macbeth and Banquo are being compared to strong eagles.*

 For additional support, go to the **Reading Studio** and assign the following **Level Up Tutorial: Symbols and Allegories.**

CHARACTERISTICS OF SHAKESPEAREAN TRAGEDY

Discuss the terms **tragic hero** and **tragic flaw.** Point out that although the tragic hero is an important person in society, his or her tragic flaw is something with which every reader or audience member can identify. Encourage students to pay particular attention to the ways in which Macbeth's choices, and the motivations for those choices, set up his ultimate fate.

Emphasize the following points about dramatic conventions:

- **Irony** is a contrast between appearance (or expectations) and reality. In **dramatic irony,** what appears to be true to one or more characters is known to be false by the audience because the audience has a more comprehensive picture of the plot and characters.

- A **soliloquy** is delivered by a main character who is alone on stage; an **aside** is delivered when other characters are present, but it is heard only by the audience or another character. Both may point to a character's conflicts and to future plot events.

THE LANGUAGE OF SHAKESPEARE

To help students hear the stressed and unstressed syllables and to realize that **blank verse** is close to the natural rhythms of English, read aloud the example line of iambic pentameter. Explain that thoughts expressed in blank verse do not always appear as in this example—a sentence presented in one end-stopped line. Some sentences can stretch across several lines and can begin or end in the middle of a line (that is, enjambment). Tell students that as they read *Macbeth,* they soon will become accustomed to the "poetic" dialogue.

SHAKESPEAREAN DRAMA

One reason Shakespeare's works have endured for over 400 years is that his characters, whether from history or his imagination, transcend any particular time or place. Many of these characters are archetypes—familiar character types that appear over and over again in literature. The scheming characters and conspiracies at the heart of The Tragedy of Macbeth are as relevant today as they were in Shakespeare's time.

CHARACTERISTICS OF SHAKESPEAREAN TRAGEDY

A **tragedy** is a drama in which a series of actions leads to the downfall of the main character, called the tragic hero. The plot builds to a catastrophe, or a disastrous final outcome. A tragic hero —

- is of high social rank
- has a tragic flaw that leads to a downfall
- suffers ruin or death, but faces this downfall with courage and dignity

Dramatic Conventions As you read, notice how Shakespeare builds suspense with these techniques:

- **Dramatic irony** results when the audience knows something that a character does not know.
- **Soliloquy** is a speech given by a character alone on stage, revealing private thoughts, feelings, and motivations.
- **Aside** is a character's remark, either to the audience or to another character, that no one else on stage is supposed to hear. Like a soliloquy, an aside reveals a character's secret thoughts.

THE LANGUAGE OF SHAKESPEARE

Shakespearean language can be challenging because of its unfamiliar vocabulary and sentence structure, but it shouldn't stop you from getting caught up in the intriguing plot that drives *Macbeth.* Here are some keys to reading Shakespeare's language:

Blank Verse Shakespeare's plays are **verse dramas,** in which most of the dialogue is written in the metrical patterns of poetry. Shakespeare wrote primarily in **blank verse,** or unrhymed lines of iambic pentameter. **Iambic pentameter** is a pattern of rhythm that has five unstressed syllables (�‿), each followed by a stressed syllable (′). Read this line aloud, noticing how the rhythm mimics that of everyday speech:

> ˘ ′ ˘ ′ ˘ ′ ˘ ′ ˘ ′
> *So foul and fair a day I have not seen.*

WHEN STUDENTS STRUGGLE . . .

Master Literary Terms Review these additional terms with students.

- *plot:* the series of related events that happen in a play or other narrative
- *conflict:* a clash or struggle that drives the plot and must be resolved
- *antagonist:* a character who opposes the hero (protagonist)
- *resolution:* the part of the play in which the conflict or problems are settled

Encourage students to create a three-column chart with terms and definitions in the first two columns. As they read, have them complete the third column with text examples.

 For additional support, go to the **Reading Studio** and assign the following Level Up Tutorial: Plot Stages.

Most of *Macbeth* is written in blank verse. In some places, however, Shakespeare broke the pattern to vary the rhythm, create dramatic tension, or distinguish low-ranking characters from those of higher rank.

Rhetorical Devices   In *Macbeth*, characters often attempt to persuade each other as they struggle to reach their goals. One key to persuasion is the use of rhetorical devices such as these:

RHETORICAL DEVICE	EXAMPLE
Repetition: the use of words and phrases more than once to emphasize ideas	Thrice to thine, and thrice to mine And thrice again, to make up nine. —Act I, Scene 3, lines 35–36
Parallelism: the repetition of grammatical structures to express ideas that are related or of equal importance	When the hurly-burly's done, When the battle's lost and won. —Act I, Scene 1, lines 3–4
Rhetorical Questions: the use of questions that require no answer to make the speaker's rightness seem self-evident	Do you not hope your children shall be kings When those that gave the Thane of Cawdor to me Promised no less to them? —Act I, Scene 3, lines 118–120
Antithesis: the use of contrasting ideas within a sentence for effect	Fair is foul, and foul is fair, . . . —Act I, Scene 1, line 10

READING SHAKESPEAREAN DRAMA

Understanding Shakespearean drama can be challenging for modern readers. Use these strategies to help you appreciate and analyze *Macbeth*.

- Study the opening **cast of characters**, which in *Macbeth* will tell you the characters' ranks and how they are related to one another.
- Try to visualize the setting and action by using information in the **stage directions** and **dialogue**.
- Use the **side notes** to understand unfamiliar words and expressions.
- Remember that the end of a line does not necessarily mean the end of a thought. Look closely at each line's punctuation, and try to figure out the meaning of the complete sentence or phrase.
- Paraphrase passages to help you understand the characters' public personas as well as their private schemes. When you **paraphrase** a passage, you restate its key points in your own words.

The Tragedy of Macbeth   397

Explain that writers use **rhetorical devices** for emphasis and persuasion. Review the definitions and examples in the chart. Ask students to explain the effect of each example. Then ask students to provide their own examples of each device. Write their examples on the board and discuss the effect of each. You might begin by illustrating repetition using the following sentence: *We are born to sorrow, pass our time in sorrow, end our days in sorrow.* Have students identify the repeated word and explain what the repetition accomplishes. *(sorrow; No one can avoid sorrow; it is very much part of life.)*

READING SHAKESPEAREAN DRAMA

Direct students to the cast of characters on page 402. Encourage students to refer to this information whenever they feel the need to recall the relationship among various characters.

Tell students that stage directions provide important information about the setting, the action, and the characters. Stage directions will also point out asides and help them determine when dialogue is a soliloquy. Direct students to page 406 and have them identify examples of stage directions and dialogue. Ask students what sounds and movements are described. *(Drums are beating; the witches are dancing in a circle.)* Ask students how they know which events and dialogue occur before and after Macbeth and Banquo arrive. *(The stage directions note when the two characters enter the scene.)*

Point out the side notes, or marginal notes, on page 406. Explain that these notes restate language in modern English and sometimes provide brief explanations. Urge students to get into the habit of skimming these notes as they read the play.

 ENGLISH LEARNER SUPPORT

Create a Glossary   Help students build glossaries or lists of archaic language that they can refer to as they read *Macbeth*.

anon: *soon*	**naught:** *nothing*	**thither:** *there*
durst: *dared*	**nigh:** *near*	**'twixt:** *between*
ere: *before*	**perchance:** *maybe*	**whence:** *where*
fly: *flee, run away*	**prithee:** *please*	**wherefore:** *why*
hark: *listen*	**thence:** *there*	**whither:** *where*
hie: *hurry*	**thine:** *your, yours*	**withal:** *also*
issue: *child, offspring*		

ALL LEVELS

THE TRAGEDY OF MACBETH

Drama by **William Shakespeare**

? Connect to the
ESSENTIAL QUESTION

The Tragedy of Macbeth is a tale of power, ambition, and betrayal. Characters try to convince themselves, other characters, and the audience that their actions in pursuit of power are justified. What are the sources of true power? Do chance or circumstances play a part in someone's rise to power, or is someone's power the sole result of his or her own actions? These are just a few of the power-related questions explored in this play.

? *ESSENTIAL QUESTION:*

What are the sources of true power?

Ray Fearon as Macbeth and Tara Fitzgerald as Lady Macbeth, directed by Iqban Khan, The Globe Theatre, London, England, 2016.

398   Unit 6

 LEARNING MINDSET

Plan Tell students that planning is essential for completing work efficiently and well. Planning will help students learn discipline, a trait that will help them achieve success in their schoolwork and in everyday life. Urge students to make a plan for reading *Macbeth*. Point out that making a plan involves setting goals (for example, understanding characters' motivations), anticipating challenges (for example, understanding Shakespearean English), gathering resources, and keeping track when goals have been met. Help students set goals for reading *Macbeth* based on the class schedule. Discuss aspects of the text they may find challenging and what resources they can use to overcome those hurdles.

QUICK START

Inspirational speakers, politicians, Internet bloggers, television commercials, print ads, and even ordinary people can all be persuasive. People may be tempted or even convinced to do something based on what they read or listen to, even when they doubt and question the information. With a partner, discuss unlikely examples of effective persuasion you have seen or heard.

ANALYZE DRAMA

Use what you learned about the characteristics of Shakespearean tragedy to help you analyze drama, including understanding the characters and plot of *Macbeth*. Watch for ways in which the play's tragic hero, asides, soliloquies, and dramatic irony build suspense and develop a theme.

Use these aspects of drama to help you as you read:

FEATURE	HOW IT HELPS
Cast of Characters	Provides a preview of "who's who" and their relationships with one another
Stage Directions	Tell where and when events occur, describe how actions are performed, and note emotions or how a character says a line of dialogue
Side Glosses	Provide definitions and explanations of unfamiliar terms and expressions

If you still find a passage confusing, read it aloud with a partner and then paraphrase and discuss it.

ANALYZE CHARACTER AND THEME

The **theme** is the insight about life or human nature that the writer wants to communicate. Theme is often developed through characterization, or the way a writer reveals the characters' personalities, and plot. In *The Tragedy of Macbeth*, Shakespeare explores themes related to ambition and power. These themes are supported by the actions, thoughts, and speech of the characters.

Shakespeare shaped the character of Macbeth into a complex and believable character who is driven by ambition. He develops his characters through a range of literary devices, such as:

- **character foils,** or characters who provide a striking contrast to another character. A foil can call attention to certain traits of the main character.
- **soliloquies** and **asides** that reveal a character's motivations and secrets
- **dialogue** that shows what others think about a character
- **responses** of characters to others
- **change** and growth of a character

GENRE ELEMENTS: DRAMA

- is meant to be performed before an audience
- tells a story with a plot, characters, setting, conflict, and theme
- includes stage directions, speaker tags, and dialogue

QUICK START

Have students read the Quick Start. Discuss how each form or practitioner of persuasion mentioned tries to influence its audience. Have partners discuss the prompt. Then call on students to share the examples they named.

ANALYZE DRAMA

Emphasize that as students **analyze drama,** they should look both at individual elements and at ways in which the elements interact as the plot unfolds. Review the information in the chart about some features of a dramatic script and have students find examples in the first few pages of Act I. Urge students to get into the habit of citing act, scene, and line number when they refer to the drama.

ANALYZE CHARACTER AND THEME

Review the information about **theme**—the "lesson" conveyed through a narrative—and how theme may be illustrated through the ways in which characters are portrayed and interact with other characters. Ask students to think of some movies they have seen that showed a character overcoming an obstacle. Discuss how the character's actions and words helped convey the theme of the movie. Then ask students to think of a movie in which a character's actions led to his or her own downfall, as in *The Tragedy of Macbeth*. Discuss the list of literary devices that Shakespeare used to develop his characters; tell students that they will encounter examples of each as they read.

The Tragedy of Macbeth **399**

ENGLISH LEARNER SUPPORT

Analyze Drama Use the text of the play to introduce each of the features of drama listed in the chart. Point to the cast of characters, an example of stage directions, and a side gloss (also called a side note or marginal note). As you say each term, have students repeat it, and then ask a few questions. For example, direct students to the cast of characters and ask: When does the play take place? (*the 11th century*) Where does the play take place? (*in Scotland and in England*) Find the name *Macbeth*. Who is Macbeth? (*a nobleman of Scotland*) Explain that a nobleman is a rich and powerful man. Repeat with the terms *stage directions* and *side gloss*.

SUBSTANTIAL/MODERATE

TEACH

LANGUAGE CONVENTIONS

Work through the information about **inverted sentence structure.** Point out that in modern English, most sentences follow a subject/verb/object sentence order—for example, *Today we begin our study of this famous play.* Then direct students to the example from *Macbeth.* Guide students to locate the subject, verb, and object in the example sentence. Explain that in this context, the verb *dismay* means "surprise and frighten"—in other words, Duncan wonders whether Macbeth and Banquo were surprised and frightened by the Norwegians' attack.

ANNOTATION MODEL

As you discuss the Annotation Model, point out that the reader studied not just the dialogue but also the scene's setting, the stage directions, and the speaker tags. Remind students to annotate dramatic elements they notice as they read the drama—noting interpretations they reach and questions they have—as well as clues about characterization and theme.

 GET READY

LANGUAGE CONVENTIONS

Inverted Sentence Structure In an **inverted sentence,** the usual word order is reversed, usually in one of these ways:

- all or part of the predicate comes before the subject
- a subject comes between a helping verb and a main verb
- a direct object precedes a verb
- a prepositional phrase comes before the noun or verb it modifies

Here is an example from Act 1, Scene 2, of *Macbeth*:

> **Duncan.** Dismayed not this our captains, Macbeth and Banquo?

In the example, the verb precedes the subject.

The sentence could be written in this way:

> Were our captains, Macbeth and Banquo, not dismayed by this?

To understand an inverted sentence, find the subject and verb so you can reorder the ideas.

ANNOTATION MODEL   **NOTICE & NOTE**

As you read, notice the setting in italics and the stage directions that appear in brackets. Also pay attention to who is speaking by referring to the boldface speaker tags. Here is how one reader marked the play's beginning:

> **ACT I**
> **Scene 1** *An open place in Scotland.*
>
> [*Thunder and lightning. Enter three* Witches.]
>
> **First Witch.** When shall we three meet again?
> In thunder, lightning, or in rain?
> **Second Witch.** When the hurly-burly's done,
> When the battle's lost and won.
> **Third Witch.** That will be ere the set of sun.
> **First Witch.** Where the place?
> **Second Witch.**   Upon the heath.
> **Third Witch.** There to meet with Macbeth.

The setting of this first scene is outside during a storm. The first characters we meet are three Witches, who are not named.

Prediction?

They plan to meet Macbeth.

 ENGLISH LEARNER SUPPORT

Analyze Inverted Sentences Display the sentence below and guide students to annotate the subject, verb, and object as shown:

The castle of Macduff | I | will surprise.
o   s   v

Explain how to write this as a modern English sentence: "I will surprise the castle of Macduff." Then have partners rewrite this inverted sentence: "Come, go we to the King." (*Come, we go to the King.*) **LIGHT**

William Shakespeare *(1564–1616) was born in Stratford-upon-Avon to a fairly prosperous family. He attended the local grammar school, studying Latin and classical literature. At age 18, he married Anne Hathaway. They had a daughter and then twins, a boy and a girl.*

Around 1590, Shakespeare moved to London. He worked as an actor and began a successful career as a playwright. As part of a company called the Lord Chamberlain's Men, he performed for Queen Elizabeth I and helped renovate the Globe Theater for its performances. Shakespeare's success enabled him to buy a family home in Stratford, where he returned in 1612. He continued to write until his death four years later at age 52.

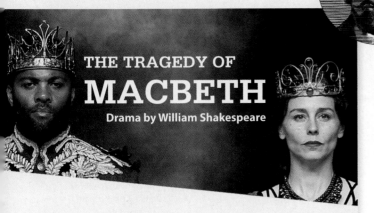

THE TRAGEDY OF
MACBETH
Drama by William Shakespeare

Shakespeare is recognized as the most influential writer in the English language. He mastered the sonnet form, making it his own with his highly original approach; he composed long narrative poems; and he left a dramatic legacy unsurpassed by any playwright before or since. Four centuries later, his plays continue to be performed on stage and made into films.

Shakespeare's plays are often grouped based on when they were written. In the early 1590s, he wrote history plays and comedies with plots derived from earlier stories. In the late 1590s, he wrote comedies, including A Midsummer Night's Dream, *in which he skillfully interwove complex plots to convey his themes. As the century ended, Shakespeare began exploring darker views of human nature in his work. Between 1600 and 1607, he wrote his greatest tragedies, including* Macbeth, Hamlet, *and* King Lear. *His later comedies, such as* The Tempest, *are often called tragicomedies, as they are tinged with sadness.*

After Shakespeare died, his plays were published in an edition known as the First Folio. In the introduction, playwright Ben Jonson wrote that Shakespeare "was not of an age, but for all time."

WILLIAM SHAKESPEARE

Have students read the biography of William Shakespeare. Explain that although Shakespeare wrote his tragedies, comedies, and histories centuries ago, they explore characters and universal themes that speak to people across the ages and around the world—not just Elizabethan England. Shakespeare's works continue to be widely read in classrooms and by casual readers and scholars alike, and his plays are frequently staged and regularly adapted to film. His popularity is not limited to the English-speaking world—his works have been adapted across a wide range of languages and cultures. Because of his timeless characters and themes, as well as the beauty of his language and style, Shakespeare is considered one of the most influential and famous English authors.

BACKGROUND

Have students read the Background note. Discuss how Shakespeare may have based this play on actual people and events and what students think might be the advantages or disadvantages of doing so.

SETTING A PURPOSE

Direct students to use the Setting a Purpose prompt to focus their reading. Offer help as needed as students create their diagrams of character relationships. For example, they can represent the relationships among Duncan and his noblemen using a tree, with blood relations connected by red lines. Point out that not everyone will be connected to this large tree. Characters such as the Witches, Apparitions, and Murderers can be listed separately.

■ English Learner Support

Develop Vocabulary Help students understand words that show rank and power in feudal Scotland. Introduce these terms:

Words for royalty and nobility	
king	leads a country
prince	son of a king
nobleman	a man who has power and a title
earl	a type of nobleman
thane	a noble or man who leads a clan (a group whose members have an ancestor in common)
lord	a man of high rank, such as an earl
lady	a woman of high rank, such as Lady Macbeth

Words for the military	
general	leads an army
officer	high-ranking soldier
captain	follows a general's orders; gives others orders
sergeant	an officer of low rank
soldier	a person in an army who is not an officer

Invite students to take turns asking and answering questions—for example, Who leads an army? (*a general*) Who would be higher in rank: an earl, or a prince? (*a prince*)

MODERATE

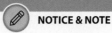

NOTICE & NOTE

Notice & Note

You can use the side margins to notice and note signposts as you read.

BACKGROUND

It is believed that Shakespeare wrote Macbeth *largely to please King James I. The Scottish-born king claimed to be descended from an 11th-century historical figure named Banquo. In* Macbeth, *the Witches predict that Banquo will sire a long line of kings. James's interest in witchcraft—he wrote a book on the subject in 1597—may explain the prominence of the Witches in the play. The play also addressed James's fears of assassination; he had survived several attempts on his life.*

SETTING A PURPOSE

Before you begin reading, use the cast list to make a diagram on a separate piece of paper that shows characters and their relationships. Revisit your diagram at the beginning of each act of the play. Add brief notes about what you learn about the characters.

THE TIME: The 11th century   **THE PLACE:** Scotland and England

CHARACTERS

Duncan, King of Scotland
His Sons
  Malcolm
  Donalbain
Noblemen of Scotland
  Macbeth
  Banquo
  Macduff
  Lennox
  Ross
  Menteith (měn-tēth´)
  Angus
  Caithness (kāth´nĭs)
Fleance (flā´əns), son to Banquo
Siward (syōō´ərd), earl of Northumberland, general of the English forces
Young Siward, his son

Seyton (sā´tən), an officer attending on Macbeth
Son, to Macduff
An English Doctor
A Scottish Doctor
A Porter
An Old Man
Three Murderers
Lady Macbeth
Lady Macduff
A Gentlewoman attending on Lady Macbeth
Hecate (hĕk´ĭt), goddess of witchcraft
Three Witches
Apparitions
Lords, Officers, Soldiers, Messengers, and Attendants

 ## ENGLISH LEARNER SUPPORT

Guide Pronunciation Read through the cast list with students. Pronounce each name; then have students pronounce it with you; and then have students pronounce it on their own. To improve fluency, invite students to create and read aloud sentences about characters' names and relationships, as in these examples:

• Banquo is the father of Fleance.

• I wonder what is the relationship between the Three Witches and Hecate?

• Malcolm and Donalbain are brothers, and King Duncan is their father.

Correct pronunciation as needed. **ALL LEVELS**

ACT I

Scene 1 *An open place in Scotland.*

[*Thunder and lightning. Enter three* Witches.]

First Witch. When shall we three meet again?
In thunder, lightning, or in rain?

Second Witch. When the hurly-burly's done,
When the battle's lost and won.

5 **Third Witch.** That will be ere the set of sun.

First Witch. Where the place?

Second Witch.   Upon the heath.

Third Witch. There to meet with Macbeth.

First Witch. I come, Graymalkin.

Second Witch. Paddock calls.

Third Witch.   Anon.

10 **All.** Fair is foul, and foul is fair,
Hover through the fog and filthy air.

[*They exit.*]

Scene 2 *King Duncan's camp near the battlefield.*

[*Alarum within. Enter* King Duncan, Malcolm, Donalbain,
Lennox, *with* Attendants, *meeting a bleeding* Captain.]

Duncan. What bloody man is that? He can report,
As seemeth by his plight, of the revolt
The newest state.

Malcolm.   This is the sergeant
Who, like a good and hardy soldier, fought
5 'Gainst my captivity.—Hail, brave friend!
Say to the King the knowledge of the broil
As thou didst leave it.

Captain.   Doubtful it stood,
As two spent swimmers that do cling together
And choke their art. The merciless Macdonwald
10 (Worthy to be a rebel, for to that
The multiplying villainies of nature
Do swarm upon him) from the Western Isles
Of kerns and gallowglasses is supplied;

3 hurly-burly: turmoil; uproar.

**8–9 Graymalkin . . .
Paddock:** two demon helpers
in the form of a cat and a toad;
Anon: at once.

[Stage Direction] **Alarum
within:** the sound of a trumpet
offstage, a signal that soldiers
should arm themselves.

5 'Gainst my captivity: to save
me from capture.

6 broil: battle.

9–13 Macdonwald's evils
(**multiplying villainies**) swarm
like insects around him. His
army consists of soldiers (**kerns
and gallowglasses**) from the
Hebrides (**Western Isles**).

The Tragedy of Macbeth, Act I, Scene 2   403

WHEN STUDENTS STRUGGLE . . .

Check Understanding Point out that in lines 1–70 of Scene 2, Malcolm and Duncan learn about a bloody battle. Have students complete a chart like the one below to grasp the key details of that battle.

Who led the battle?	*Macbeth and Banquo on one side; Macdonwald, the King of Norway on the other*
What does Duncan learn about Macbeth?	*Macbeth fought bravely (and brutally) to defeat the opposing armies.*
Where does Duncan learn this information?	*at a camp near the battlefield*
Why does Duncan order Cawdor's execution?	*He is a traitor; he helped the King of Norway.*
How does Duncan plan to reward Macbeth?	*He will make Macbeth the new Thane of Cawdor.*

 For additional support, go to the **Reading Studio** and assign
the following [LEVEL] **Level Up Tutorial: Reading for Details.**

 **ENGLISH LEARNER
SUPPORT**

Summarize the Drama Guide students to begin a chart that they can use to summarize the main events of the drama. To help students summarize Act 1, Scene 1 and Scene 2, use the following supports with students at varying proficiency levels:

- Ask students who is in Act I, Scene 1 and Scene 2. Have students point to the speaker tags in these scenes and copy the names into a simplified version of the chart below. **SUBSTANTIAL**

- Have partners work together to ask and answer Where? Who? What? questions about Scenes 1–2 and add their responses to a chart like the one below. **MODERATE/LIGHT**

Act I, Scene 1	
Where?	*An open place in Scotland*
Who?	*Three Witches*
What?	*They plan to meet with Macbeth after the battle.*

Act I, Scene 2	
Where?	*A camp near a battlefield*
Who?	*King Duncan, his sons Malcolm and Donalbain, the Captain, noblemen Lennox and Ross, Attendants*
What?	*The Captain brings news of a battle. He says that Macbeth and Banquo won against Macdonwald and the King of Norway. He says Macbeth was very brave.*

**ENGLISH LEARNER
SUPPORT**

Confirm Understanding Use the following supports with students at varying proficiency levels:

- Have students point to the names of the characters in the two scenes, sound them out, and pronounce them. **SUBSTANTIAL**

- Model using the question words *where, who,* and *what* to form questions about Scenes 1 and 2. For example, Where is the scene set? Who is in the scene? What happens in the scene? Then have students draw upon information in the chart they created to ask and answer questions about the play so far. **MODERATE/LIGHT**

TEACH

ANALYZE CHARACTER AND THEME

Have students skim the Captain's report to Duncan, looking for Macbeth's name (line 16) and the pronouns referring to him. (**Answer:** *Macbeth is brave, but he is also very fierce and violent. He is described as "Disdaining Fortune," which means that he chooses to take action rather than rely on or even care about luck.*)

■ English Learner Support

Paraphrase Dialogue Instruct pairs or small groups of students to rewrite the Captain's report in modern English. Invite students to share and compare their paraphrases.
MODERATE/LIGHT

NOTICE & NOTE

ANALYZE CHARACTER AND THEME
Annotate: Mark words in the Captain's speech that reveal Macbeth's character traits.

Predict: What kind of person is Macbeth?

19 valor's minion: the favorite of valor, meaning the bravest of all.

22 unseamed him . . . chops: split him open from the navel to the jaw.

25–28 As the rising sun is sometimes followed by storms, a new assault on Macbeth began.

36 sooth: the truth.
37 double cracks: a double load of ammunition.
39–40 The officer claims he cannot decide whether (**except**) Macbeth and Banquo wanted to bathe in blood or make the battlefield as famous as Golgotha, the site of Christ's crucifixion.

45 Thane: a Scottish noble.

And Fortune, on his damnèd quarrel smiling,
15 Showed like a rebel's whore. But all's too weak;
For brave Macbeth (well he deserves that name),
Disdaining Fortune, with his brandished steel,
Which smoked with bloody execution,
Like valor's minion, carved out his passage
20 Till he faced the slave;
Which ne'er shook hands, nor bade farewell to him,
Till he unseamed him from the nave to th' chops,
And fixed his head upon our battlements.

Duncan. O valiant cousin, worthy gentleman!

25 **Captain.** As whence the sun 'gins his reflection
Shipwracking storms and direful thunders break,
So from that spring whence comfort seemed to come
Discomfort swells. Mark, King of Scotland, mark:
No sooner justice had, with valor armed,
30 Compelled these skipping kerns to trust their heels,
But the Norweyan lord, surveying vantage,
With furbished arms and new supplies of men,
Began a fresh assault.

Duncan. Dismayed not this our captains, Macbeth and Banquo?

35 **Captain.** Yes, as sparrows eagles, or the hare the lion.
If I say sooth, I must report they were
As cannons overcharged with double cracks,
So they doubly redoubled strokes upon the foe.
Except they meant to bathe in reeking wounds
40 Or memorize another Golgotha,
I cannot tell—
But I am faint. My gashes cry for help.

Duncan. So well thy words become thee as thy wounds:
They smack of honor both.—Go, get him surgeons.

[*The* Captain *is led off by* Attendants.]
[*Enter* Ross *and* Angus.]
45 Who comes here?

Malcolm.   The worthy Thane of Ross.

Lennox. What a haste looks through his eyes!
So should he look that seems to speak things strange.

Ross. God save the King.

Duncan. Whence cam'st thou, worthy thane?

50 **Ross.** From Fife, great king,
Where the Norweyan banners flout the sky
And fan our people cold.

404   Unit 6

404   Unit 6

Norway himself, with terrible numbers,
Assisted by that most disloyal traitor,
55 The Thane of Cawdor, began a dismal conflict,
Till that Bellona's bridegroom, lapped in proof,
Confronted him with self-comparisons,
Point against point, rebellious arm 'gainst arm,
Curbing his lavish spirit. And to conclude,
60 The victory fell on us.

Duncan.   Great happiness!

Ross. That now Sweno,
The Norways' king, craves composition.
Nor would we deign him burial of his men
Till he disbursèd at Saint Colme's Inch
65 Ten thousand dollars to our general use.

Duncan. No more that Thane of Cawdor shall deceive
Our bosom interest. Go, pronounce his present death,
And with his former title greet Macbeth.

Ross. I'll see it done.

70 **Duncan.** What he hath lost, noble Macbeth hath won.

[*They exit.*]

Scene 3 *A bleak place near the battlefield.*

[*Thunder. Enter the three* Witches.]

First Witch. Where hast thou been, sister?

Second Witch. Killing swine.

Third Witch. Sister, where thou?

First Witch. A sailor's wife had chestnuts in her lap
5 And munched and munched and munched. "Give me," quoth I.
"Aroint thee, witch," the rump-fed runnion cries.
Her husband's to Aleppo gone, master o' th' Tiger;
But in a sieve I'll thither sail
And, like a rat without a tail,
10 I'll do, I'll do, and I'll do.

Second Witch. I'll give thee a wind.

First Witch. Th' art kind.

Third Witch. And I another.

First Witch. I myself have all the other,
15 And the very ports they blow,
All the quarters that they know
I' th' shipman's card.

49–59 Ross has arrived from Fife, where Norway's troops had invaded. There the king of Norway, with the Thane of Cawdor, met Macbeth (described as the husband of **Bellona**, the goddess of war). Macbeth, in heavy armor (**proof**), challenged the enemy.

62 craves composition: wants a treaty.
63 deign: allow.
64 disbursèd at Saint Colme's Inch: paid at Saint Colme's Inch, an island in the North Sea.

66–67 deceive our bosom interest: betray our friendship; **present death:** immediate execution.

6 "Aroint thee, witch," . . . runnion cries: "Go away, witch!" the fatbottomed (**rump-fed**), ugly creature (**runnion**) cries.

7–8 The woman's husband, the master of a merchant ship (**th' Tiger**), has sailed to Aleppo. The witch will pursue him. Witches were thought to sail on strainers (**sieve**).

ENGLISH LEARNER SUPPORT

Decode Archaic Language   Display this sentence from Scene 2, line 70:

What he hath lost, noble Macbeth hath won.

Tell students that this sentence is about the Thane of Cawdor, who fought alongside the King of Norway in rebellion against King Duncan. Circle the two appearances of the word *hath* and explain that *hath* means *has*. Replace *hath* with *has* in the sentence. Read the new sentence with students. Ask this question and have students answer in a complete sentence: What two things has the Thane of Cawdor lost? (*He has lost the battle, and he has lost his title [Thane of Cawdor].*)
MODERATE

ENGLISH LEARNER SUPPORT

Practice Sound Transfer Issues   Use lines 53–60 to guide students whose primary language presents these pronunciation issues:

- Speakers of Vietnamese, Hmong, or Haitian Creole may struggle with the hard /c/ sound, especially distinguishing it from the soft /c/ sound. Have them focus on the hard /c/ sound in *Cawdor, conflict, confronted, self-comparisons, curbing,* and *conclude*.

- Speakers of Burmese, Cantonese, and Mandarin may struggle with the /r/ sound. Have them focus on the /r/ sound in *Norway, traitor, bridegroom, rebellious arm, curbing,* and *victory.* **MODERATE**

AGAIN AND AGAIN

Suggest that students skim the passage twice before identifying the repeated word. Remind students that when they encounter this signpost, they should stop and ask why is this word repeated? Tell students to consider how the repetition may affect the **characters** of Macbeth and Banquo. (**Answer:** *Repeating* hail *shows that the witches are very emphatic. Since it is a word showing honor, the emphatic repetition probably is flattering to Macbeth and Banquo, making them more open to persuasion.*)

■ English Learner Support

Develop Vocabulary to Build Understanding Explain that people once cried, *"Hail!"* to show honor and respect to kings, queens, and other important people. Paraphrase line 48 for students as: *Everyone should show respect to Macbeth! Respect to you, Thane of Glamis!* Model reading lines 49–51 with appropriate phrasing, intonation, and expression. Have students repeat the line aloud, using appropriate phrasing, intonation, and expression.

SUBSTANTIAL/MODERATE

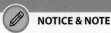

NOTICE & NOTE

14–23 The witch controls the winds, covering all points of a compass (**shipman's card**). She will make the sailor sleepless, keeping his eyelids (**penthouse lid**) from closing. Thus, he will lead an accursed (**forbid**) life for weeks (**sev'nnights**), wasting away with fatigue.

33 posters: quick riders.

36 Nine was considered a magical number by superstitious people.

42–46 aught: anything; **choppy:** chapped; **your beards:** Beards on women identified them as witches.

AGAIN AND AGAIN

Notice & Note: Mark the word the Witches repeat again and again in lines 48–69.

Analyze: What is persuasive about their repetition of this word?

_____

53 are you fantastical: Are you (the Witches) imaginary?

I'll drain him dry as hay.
Sleep shall neither night nor day
20 Hang upon his penthouse lid.
He shall live a man forbid.
Weary sev'nnights, nine times nine,
Shall he dwindle, peak, and pine.
Though his bark cannot be lost,
25 Yet it shall be tempest-tossed.
Look what I have.

Second Witch. Show me, show me.

First Witch. Here I have a pilot's thumb,
Wracked as homeward he did come.

[*Drum within*]

30 **Third Witch.** A drum, a drum!
Macbeth doth come.

All. [*Dancing in a circle*] The Weïrd Sisters, hand in hand,
Posters of the sea and land,
Thus do go about, about,
35 Thrice to thine, and thrice to mine
And thrice again, to make up nine.
Peace, the charm's wound up.

[*Enter Macbeth and Banquo.*]

Macbeth. So foul and fair a day I have not seen.

Banquo. How far is 't called to Forres?—What are these,
40 So withered, and so wild in their attire,
That look not like th' inhabitants o' th' earth
And yet are on 't?—Live you? Or are you aught
That man may question? You seem to understand me
By each at once her choppy finger laying
45 Upon her skinny lips. You should be women,
And yet your beards forbid me to interpret
That you are so.

Macbeth.   Speak, if you can. What are you?

First Witch. All hail, Macbeth! Hail to thee, Thane of Glamis!

Second Witch. All hail, Macbeth! Hail to thee, Thane of Cawdor!

50 **Third Witch.** All hail, Macbeth, that shalt be king hereafter!

Banquo. Good sir, why do you start and seem to fear
Things that do sound so fair? I' th' name of truth,
Are you fantastical, or that indeed
Which outwardly you show? My noble partner
55 You greet with present grace and great prediction
Of noble having and of royal hope,

WHEN STUDENTS STRUGGLE . . .

Understand Archaic Language Remind students that many words and phrases in the play are no longer used. Encourage students to keep a list of unfamiliar expressions. As you read, point out some of the archaic terms and define them. In Scene 2, for example, point out the words *quoth* ("said"), *thither* ("there"), *shalt* ("shall"), and *thine* ("yours"). Ask students to point out other archaic words and help them use context to determine the meaning. For example, on this page the witches say the word *thrice* three times and then say "to make up nine" (lines 35–36). Explain that three times three is nine, so *thrice* must mean "three times."

 For additional support, go to the **Reading Studio** and assign the following [LEVEL UP] **Level Up Tutorial: Use Context Clues.**

Janet Whiteside, Ann Firbank, and Jane Thorne as the Witches and Simon Russell Beale as Macbeth, Almeida Theatre, London.

That he seems rapt withal. To me you speak not.
If you can look into the seeds of time
And say which grain will grow and which will not,
60 Speak, then, to me, who neither beg nor fear
Your favors nor your hate.

First Witch. Hail!

Second Witch. Hail!

Third Witch. Hail!

65 **First Witch.** Lesser than Macbeth and greater.

Second Witch. Not so happy, yet much happier.

Third Witch. Thou shalt get kings, though thou be none.
So all hail, Macbeth and Banquo!

First Witch. Banquo and Macbeth, all hail!

70 **Macbeth.** Stay, you imperfect speakers. Tell me more.
By Sinel's death I know I am Thane of Glamis.
But how of Cawdor? The Thane of Cawdor lives
A prosperous gentleman, and to be king
Stands not within the prospect of belief,
75 No more than to be Cawdor. Say from whence
You owe this strange intelligence or why
Upon this blasted heath you stop our way
With such prophetic greeting. Speak, I charge you.

[Witches *vanish*.]

Banquo. The earth hath bubbles, as the water has,
80 And these are of them. Whither are they vanished?

Macbeth. Into the air, and what seemed corporal melted,
As breath into the wind. Would they had stayed!

54–57 The witches' prophecies of noble possessions (**having**)— the lands and wealth of Cawdor—and kingship (**royal hope**) have left Macbeth dazed (**rapt withal**).

80 whither: where.

81 corporal: physical; real.

The Tragedy of Macbeth, Act I, Scene 3 407

 ENGLISH LEARNER SUPPORT

Summarize the Drama Guide students to summarize what has happened so far in Scene 3 and add it to their charts. For speakers of Arabic, display the completed chart below to reinforce the directionality of English. Review how to begin reading the chart at the top left. The top row, left column asks *Where (does the scene take place)?* Guide students to track right to see where the scene takes place. Then they should move to the middle row, left column. Ask a volunteer to trace with a finger the order in which a reader would read the remaining information in the chart.

Act I, Scene 3	
Where?	*Near a battlefield*
Who?	*Three Witches, Macbeth, Banquo*
What?	*The witches greet Macbeth and Banquo and prophesy to them. They give Macbeth three titles—Thane of Glamis, Thane of Cawdor, and future king. They say that Banquo's descendants will be kings.*

Then have students draw upon information in the chart they created to ask and answer questions about what has happened so far in Scene 3.

MODERATE/LIGHT

EL ENGLISH LEARNER SUPPORT

Ask and Answer Questions Use the following supports with students at varying proficiency levels:

- Ask students who are the characters in this scene. Have them point to the names of the characters in Scene 3, sound them out, and pronounce them. **SUBSTANTIAL**

- Ask students the following questions: Where is Act I, Scene 3 set? Who is in the scene? What happens in the scene? Then have partners take turns asking and answering questions about what has happened so far in Scene 3. **MODERATE/LIGHT**

TEACH

▶ AHA MOMENT

Remind students that an Aha Moment reveals a change in a **character** or an important development in the **plot**. Review the predictions that the witches made: Macbeth will become Thane of Cawdor and king; Banquo's descendants will be kings. Ask: Which prediction comes true here? *(Macbeth becomes Thane of Cawdor.)* Discuss with students how Macbeth responds to this news and how the remaining predictions may affect his actions and the plot. (**Answer:** *Students may say that Macbeth may choose to do nothing and let the witches' predictions come true on their own. Or, he may decide to take action to help these predictions come true.*)

84 insane root: A number of plants were believed to cause insanity when eaten.

92–93 King Duncan hesitates between awe (**wonders**) and gratitude (**praises**) and is, as a result, speechless.

96–97 Although Macbeth left many dead (**strange images of death**), he obviously did not fear death himself.

104 earnest: partial payment.

AHA MOMENT

Notice & Note: Mark the predictions that Banquo and Macbeth realize must be true in lines 107–120.

Predict: How might knowing these future events affect the choices these characters make?

111–116 Whether the former thane of Cawdor allied (**combined**) with the king of Norway or supported the traitor Macdonwald (**did line the rebel**), he is guilty of treasons that deserve the death penalty (**treasons capital**), having aimed at the country's ruin (**wrack**).

Banquo. Were such things here as we do speak about?
Or have we eaten on the insane root
85   That takes the reason prisoner?

Macbeth. Your children shall be kings.

Banquo.   You shall be king.

Macbeth. And Thane of Cawdor too. Went it not so?

Banquo. To th' selfsame tune and words.—Who's here?

[*Enter* Ross *and* Angus.]

Ross. The King hath happily received, Macbeth,
90   The news of thy success, and, when he reads
Thy personal venture in the rebels' fight,
His wonders and his praises do contend
Which should be thine or his. Silenced with that,
In viewing o'er the rest o' th' selfsame day
95   He finds thee in the stout Norweyan ranks,
Nothing afeard of what thyself didst make,
Strange images of death. As thick as hail
Came post with post, and every one did bear
Thy praises in his kingdom's great defense,
100 And poured them down before him.

Angus.   We are sent
To give thee from our royal master thanks,
Only to herald thee into his sight,
Not pay thee.

Ross. And for an earnest of a greater honor,
105 He bade me, from him, call thee Thane of Cawdor,
In which addition, hail, most worthy thane,
For it is thine.

Banquo.   What, can the devil speak true?

Macbeth. The Thane of Cawdor lives. Why do you dress me
In borrowed robes?

Angus.   Who was the Thane lives yet,
110 But under heavy judgment bears that life
Which he deserves to lose. Whether he was combined
With those of Norway, or did line the rebel
With hidden help and vantage, or that with both
He labored in his country's wrack, I know not;
115 But treasons capital, confessed and proved,
Have overthrown him.

Macbeth [*aside*].   Glamis and Thane of Cawdor!
The greatest is behind. [*To Ross and* Angus] Thanks for your pains.
[*Aside to* Banquo] Do you not hope your children shall be kings

---

WHEN STUDENTS STRUGGLE...

Analyze an Aside Remind students that an **aside** is a brief speech that other characters cannot hear but that reveals a character's private thoughts and feelings. Help students distinguish between what Macbeth says to other characters and what he says to himself. Display lines 117–147 and instruct volunteers to do the following:

• Highlight text in which Macbeth addresses other characters.

• Draw a box around text in which Macbeth is speaking to himself.

Then draw a two-column chart with the headings "What He Says" and "What He Thinks." As a class, complete the chart. Encourage students to use a similar method of marking asides from dialogue as they read to help them better understand the motivations of characters. Finally, ask students to explain how differentiating between asides and dialogue helps them understand Macbeth as a character. (*Macbeth is concerned with keeping up appearances, but in his asides he reveals his desires and his true nature to readers.*)

 For additional support, go to the **Reading Studio** and assign the following [LEVEL] **Level Up Tutorial: Character Motivation.**

When those that gave the Thane of Cawdor to me
120 Promised no less to them?

Banquo.   That, trusted home,
Might yet enkindle you unto the crown,
Besides the Thane of Cawdor. But 'tis strange.
And oftentimes, to win us to our harm,
The instruments of darkness tell us truths,
125 Win us with honest trifles, to betray 's
In deepest consequence.—
Cousins, a word, I pray you.   [*They step aside.*]

Macbeth [*aside*].   Two truths are told
As happy prologues to the swelling act
Of the imperial theme.—I thank you, gentlemen.
130 [*Aside*] This supernatural soliciting
Cannot be ill, cannot be good. If ill,
Why hath it given me earnest of success
Commencing in a truth? I am Thane of Cawdor.
If good, why do I yield to that suggestion
135 Whose horrid image doth unfix my hair
And make my seated heart knock at my ribs
Against the use of nature? Present fears
Are less than horrible imaginings.
My thought, whose murder yet is but fantastical,
140 Shakes so my single state of man
That function is smothered in surmise,
And nothing is but what is not.

Banquo.   Look how our partner's rapt.

Macbeth [*aside*]. If chance will have me king, why, chance may
          crown me
Without my stir.

Banquo.   New honors come upon him,
145 Like our strange garments, cleave not to their mold
But with the aid of use.

Macbeth [*aside*].   Come what come may,
Time and the hour runs through the roughest day.

Banquo. Worthy Macbeth, we stay upon your leisure.

Macbeth. Give me your favor. My dull brain was wrought
150 With things forgotten. Kind gentlemen, your pains
Are registered where every day I turn
The leaf to read them. Let us toward the King.
[*Aside to* Banquo] Think upon what hath chanced, and
          at more time,

120 home: fully; completely.
121 enkindle you unto: inflame your ambitions.
123–126 Banquo warns that evil powers often offer little truths to tempt people. The witches may be lying about what matters most (**in deepest consequence**).

144 my stir: my doing anything.

146–147 Come what . . . roughest day: The future will arrive no matter what.
148 stay: wait.
150–152 your pains . . . read them: I will always remember your efforts. The metaphor refers to keeping a diary and reading it regularly.
153–155 Macbeth wants to discuss the prophecies later, after he and Banquo have had time to think about them.

© Houghton Mifflin Harcourt Publishing Company

The Tragedy of Macbeth, Act I, Scene 3   409

ENGLISH LEARNER SUPPORT

Role-Play Dialogue Read and paraphrase the dialogue between Macbeth and Banquo in lines 118–129. Then call on more proficient students to recap the dialogue. *(Macbeth seems to think the prophecy is a good thing. Banquo is not so sure; he thinks the source of the prophecy—the witches—are evil.)* Next, ask partners to role-play the conversation between the two characters. Tell them to use modern language in their role-play, not to read the language verbatim.

MODERATE/LIGHT

TEACH

✏ ANALYZE CHARACTER AND THEME

Ask students what event has taken place just before Scene 4 begins. (*The Thane of Cawdor has been executed.*) Call on a student to summarize what Duncan says to Macbeth in lines 14–21. (*Duncan tells Macbeth that he can't thank him enough for all his help.*) Call on another to summarize Macbeth's response. (*Macbeth says that he doesn't need any thanks from the king as payment because it's his duty to serve the king and to love and honor him.*) (**Answer:** *Students should express their own opinions about the degree of loyalty a king deserves. They may point out that if Macbeth himself aspires to be king, then he would consider loyalty and service from a king's subjects to be appropriate; however, he merely may be saying what is expected of him or what he needs to say in order to flatter the king.*)

■ English Learner Support

Develop Vocabulary to Build Understanding Read aloud Scene 4, lines 22–27 and paraphrase them. Point out and explain the words *service, loyalty,* and *duties.* Then have students use the correct word to complete each sentence frame:

Macbeth and Banquo showed _____ to the king by fighting his enemies. (loyalty)

The king's servants have many _____, such as cooking and cleaning. (duties)

Many soldiers fought in _____ to King Duncan. (service)

MODERATE/LIGHT

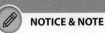

2 those in commission: those who have the responsibility for Cawdor's execution.

6 set forth: showed.

8–11 He died as ... trifle: He died as if he had rehearsed (**studied**) the moment. Though losing his life (**the dearest thing he owed**), he behaved with calm dignity.

14–21 The king feels that he cannot repay (**recompense**) Macbeth enough. Macbeth's qualities and accomplishments are of greater value than any thanks or payment Duncan can give.

ANALYZE CHARACTER AND THEME

Annotate: Mark ideas in lines 22–27 that reflect the duties of a king's subjects.

Evaluate: Do you agree that these duties are appropriate? Do you think Macbeth does? Explain.

28–29 The king plans to give more honors to Macbeth.

The interim having weighed it, let us speak
155 Our free hearts each to other.

Banquo.   Very gladly.

Macbeth. Till then, enough.—Come, friends.

[*They exit.*]

Scene 4 *A room in the king's palace at Forres.*

[*Flourish. Enter* King Duncan, Lennox, Malcolm, Donalbain, *and* Attendants.]

Duncan. Is execution done on Cawdor? Are not
Those in commission yet returned?

Malcolm.   My liege,
They are not yet come back. But I have spoke
With one that saw him die, who did report
5 That very frankly he confessed his treasons,
Implored your Highness' pardon, and set forth
A deep repentance. Nothing in his life
Became him like the leaving it. He died
As one that had been studied in his death
10 To throw away the dearest thing he owed
As 'twere a careless trifle.

Duncan.   There's no art
To find the mind's construction in the face.
He was a gentleman on whom I built
An absolute trust.

[*Enter* Macbeth, Banquo, Ross, *and* Angus.]
                              O worthiest cousin,
15 The sin of my ingratitude even now
Was heavy on me. Thou art so far before
That swiftest wing of recompense is slow
To overtake thee. Would thou hadst less deserved,
That the proportion both of thanks and payment
20 Might have been mine! Only I have left to say,
More is thy due than more than all can pay.

Macbeth. The service and the loyalty I owe
In doing it pays itself. Your Highness' part
Is to receive our duties, and our duties
25 Are to your throne and state children and servants,
Which do but what they should by doing everything
Safe toward your love and honor.

Duncan.   Welcome hither.
I have begun to plant thee and will labor
To make thee full of growing.—Noble Banquo,

30 That hast no less deserved nor must be known
No less to have done so, let me enfold thee
And hold thee to my heart.

Banquo.   There, if I grow,
The harvest is your own.

Duncan.   My plenteous joys,
Wanton in fullness, seek to hide themselves
35 In drops of sorrow.—Sons, kinsmen, thanes,
And you whose places are the nearest, know
We will establish our estate upon
Our eldest, Malcolm, whom we name hereafter
The Prince of Cumberland; which honor must
40 Not unaccompanied invest him only,
But signs of nobleness, like stars, shall shine
On all deservers.—From hence to Inverness,
And bind us further to you.

Macbeth. The rest is labor which is not used for you.
45 I'll be myself the harbinger and make joyful
The hearing of my wife with your approach.
So humbly take my leave.

Duncan.   My worthy Cawdor.

Macbeth [*aside*]. The Prince of Cumberland! That is a step
On which I must fall down or else o'erleap,
50 For in my way it lies. Stars, hide your fires;
Let not light see my black and deep desires.
The eye wink at the hand, yet let that be
Which the eye fears, when it is done, to see.

[*He exits.*]

Duncan. True, worthy Banquo. He is full so valiant,
55 And in his commendations I am fed:
It is a banquet to me.—Let's after him,
Whose care is gone before to bid us welcome.
It is a peerless kinsman.

[*Flourish. They exit.*]

Scene 5 *Macbeth's castle at Inverness.*

[*Enter* Lady Macbeth, *alone, with a letter.*]

Lady Macbeth. [*Reading the letter*] "They met me in the day of
success, and I have learned by the perfect'st report they have more
in them than mortal knowledge. When I burned in desire to
question them further, they made themselves air, into which they
5 vanished. Whiles I stood rapt in the wonder of it came missives
from the King, who all-hailed me 'Thane of Cawdor,' by which

33–35 My plenteous . . . sorrow: The king is crying tears of joy.

39 Prince of Cumberland: the title given to the heir to the Scottish throne.

42 Inverness: site of Macbeth's castle, where the king has just invited himself, giving another honor to Macbeth.

45 harbinger: a representative sent before a royal party to make proper arrangements for its arrival.

ANALYZE DRAMA

Annotate: Mark stage directions at the beginning of Scene 5 that provide important information.

Interpret: How has the scene changed? Whose words are being spoken by Lady Macbeth in lines 1–11?

ANALYZE DRAMA

Discuss the opening of Scene 5 with students. Ask them why Shakespeare may have had Lady Macbeth read the letter aloud. (*He probably wanted the audience to hear her speak the words so that they would know how she learned of the prophecies and what her first thoughts were.*) Ask partners to compare their annotations and their responses to the question. (**Answer:** *This scene is at Macbeth's castle at Inverness. Lady Macbeth is alone, far from the scene of battle. She is reading Macbeth's letter aloud, so she is speaking his words and learning about the witches' prophecy.*)

WHEN STUDENTS STRUGGLE . . .

Relate Conflict to Plot   Help students understand why Macbeth now considers Malcolm a threat. Have them reread lines 33–43. Ask them what Duncan is saying and why this information propels the plot. (*Duncan says that Malcolm is next in line for the throne, so Macbeth likely sees Malcolm as a threat to his goals and may plan to remove him.*) Have pairs create a plot diagram of events in Scenes 1–4. As they read on, urge them to continue plotting key events to understand how the characters' actions build to a climax and then a resolution.

 For additional support, go to the **Reading Studio** and assign the following **Level Up Tutorial: Characters and Conflict.**

ENGLISH LEARNER SUPPORT

Read with Support Tell students that Shakespeare uses the old-fashioned words *thee, thou,* and *thy.* Display the chart below and guide students to identify the modern English equivalents of these words. Have students copy the chart and refer to it as they read.

Shakespeare's English	Modern English
thou	*you (subject)*
thee	*you (object)*
thy	*your*
thine	*yours*

SUBSTANTIAL

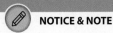 **NOTICE & NOTE**

title, before, these Weïrd Sisters saluted me and referred me to
the coming on of time with 'Hail, king that shalt be.' This have I
thought good to deliver thee, my dearest partner of greatness, that
10 thou might'st not lose the dues of rejoicing by being ignorant of
what greatness is promised thee. Lay it to thy heart, and farewell."

Glamis thou art, and Cawdor, and shalt be
What thou art promised. Yet do I fear thy nature;
It is too full o' th' milk of human kindness
15 To catch the nearest way. Thou wouldst be great,
Art not without ambition, but without
The illness should attend it. What thou wouldst highly,
That wouldst thou holily; wouldst not play false
And yet wouldst wrongly win. Thou'd'st have, great Glamis;
20 That which cries "Thus thou must do," if thou have it,
And that which rather thou dost fear to do,
Than wishest should be undone. Hie thee hither,
That I may pour my spirits in thine ear
And chastise with the valor of my tongue
25 All that impedes thee from the golden round
Which fate and metaphysical aid doth seem
To have thee crowned withal.

[*Enter* Messenger.]

What is your tidings?

Messenger. The King comes here tonight.

Lady Macbeth. Thou'rt mad to say it!
Is not thy master with him? who, were't so,
30 Would have informed for preparation.

Messenger. So please you, it is true. Our Thane is coming.
One of my fellows had the speed of him,
Who, almost dead for breath, had scarcely more
Than would make up his message.

Lady Macbeth. Give him tending.
35 He brings great news.

[Messenger *exits.*]

The raven himself is hoarse
That croaks the fatal entrance of Duncan
Under my battlements. Come, you spirits
That tend on mortal thoughts, unsex me here,
And fill me from the crown to the toe top-full
40 Of direst cruelty. Make thick my blood.
Stop up th' access and passage to remorse,
That no compunctious visitings of nature
Shake my fell purpose, nor keep peace between

13–18 Lady Macbeth fears her husband is too good (**too full o' th' milk of human kindness**) to seize the throne by murder (**the nearest way**). Lacking the necessary wickedness (**illness**), he wants to gain power virtuously (**holily**).

32 had the speed of him: rode faster than he.

35 raven: The harsh cry of the raven, a bird symbolizing evil and misfortune, was supposed to indicate an approaching death.

CLOSE READ SCREENCAST

Modeled Discussion In their eBook, have students view the Close Read Screencast, in which readers discuss and annotate Lady Macbeth's soliloquy in Scene 5, lines 35–44.

Th' effect and it. Come to my woman's breasts
45 And take my milk for gall, you murd'ring ministers,
Wherever in your sightless substances
You wait on nature's mischief. Come, thick night,
And pall thee in the dunnest smoke of hell,
That my keen knife see not the wound it makes,
50 Nor heaven peep through the blanket of the dark
To cry "Hold, hold!"

[*Enter* Macbeth.]

                    Great Glamis, worthy Cawdor,
Greater than both by the all-hail hereafter!
Thy letters have transported me beyond
This ignorant present, and I feel now
55 The future in the instant.

Macbeth.   My dearest love,
Duncan comes here tonight.

Lady Macbeth.   And when goes hence?

Macbeth. Tomorrow, as he purposes.

Lady Macbeth.   O, never
Shall sun that morrow see!
Your face, my thane, is as a book where men
60 May read strange matters. To beguile the time,
Look like the time. Bear welcome in your eye,
Your hand, your tongue. Look like th' innocent flower,
But be the serpent under 't. He that's coming
Must be provided for; and you shall put
65 This night's great business into my dispatch,
Which shall to all our nights and days to come
Give solely sovereign sway and masterdom.

Macbeth. We will speak further.

Lady Macbeth.   Only look up clear.
To alter favor ever is to fear.
70 Leave all the rest to me.

[*They exit.*]

Scene 6 *In front of Macbeth's castle.*

[*Hautboys and Torches. Enter* King Duncan, Malcolm,
Donalbain, Banquo, Lennox, Macduff, Ross, Angus, *and*
Attendants.]

Duncan. This castle hath a pleasant seat. The air
Nimbly and sweetly recommends itself
Unto our gentle senses.

37–51 Lady Macbeth calls on the spirits of evil to rid her of feminine weakness (**unsex me**) and to block out guilt. She wants no normal pangs of conscience (**compunctious visitings of nature**) to get in the way of her murderous plan. She asks that her mother's milk be turned to bile (**gall**) by the unseen evil forces (**murd'ring ministers, sightless substances**) that exist in nature. Furthermore, she asks that the night wrap (**pall**) itself in darkness as black as hell so that no one may see or stop the crime.

60–63 To beguile . . . under 't: To fool (**beguile**) everyone, act as expected at such a time.

65 my dispatch: my management.

67 give solely sovereign sway: bring absolute royal power.

69 To alter . . . fear: To change your expression (**favor**) is a sign of fear.

[Stage Direction] **hautboys:** oboes.

ANALYZE DRAMA

Annotate: Mark King Duncan's impression of Macbeth's castle.

Analyze: What makes this view ironic? What do you know that Duncan does not know?

 ANALYZE DRAMA

Remind students that **dramatic irony** in a play is a situation in which the audience knows something that the characters in a play do not. Call on a student to read aloud Duncan's words when he sees the castle. Point out that Inverness is located on the Ness River, near the northeast coast of Scotland. Invite a volunteer to paraphrase Duncan's description of the castle. *(This castle is in a pleasant location. The air is fresh and sweet.)* (**Answer:** *This view of Macbeth's castle is ironic because it is so positive. The audience knows that what Duncan calls "pleasant" and "sweet" is the place where he will be murdered, if Lady Macbeth has her way.*)

TO CHALLENGE STUDENTS . . .

Portray Complex Characters Remind students that when watching a play, viewers can see how a character acts or feels. When reading, they may rely on stage directions to understand actions and characters. Point out that Shakespeare does not provide detailed stage directions. Instead, readers must pay close attention to details and clues about the characters to determine their feelings, movements, and reactions.

Ask students to reread Act 1, Scene 5, focusing on details that help them visualize how the characters look, feel, and act. Then have students add their own detailed stage directions throughout the scene to help readers visualize the characters and actions. Explain that when staging a play, directors refer to stage directions but also interpret scenes and characters in their own unique way.

ENGLISH LEARNER SUPPORT

Summarize the Drama Guide students to summarize Act I, Scenes 4–6, using the following supports with students at varying proficiency levels:

- Ask students who is in Act I, Scenes 4–6. Have students point to the speaker tags in these scenes and copy the names into a simplified version of the chart below. **SUBSTANTIAL**

- Have partners work together to ask and answer Where? Who? What? questions about Scenes 4–6 and add their responses to a chart like the one below. **MODERATE/LIGHT**

Act I, Scene 4

Where?	The king's palace at Forres
Who?	King Duncan, his sons Malcolm and Donalbain, Lennox, Attendants, Macbeth, Banquo, Ross, Angus
What?	Malcolm tells about the Thane of Cawdor's execution. Duncan thanks Macbeth and Banquo for their help. Duncan says that he will visit Macbeth's castle at Inverness.

Act I, Scene 5

Where?	Macbeth's castle at Inverness
Who?	Lady Macbeth
What?	She reads Macbeth's letter and learns about the prophecies. Then she learns that the king is coming to Inverness.

Act I, Scene 6

Where?	In front of Macbeth's castle
Who?	King Duncan, sons Malcolm and Donalbain, Banquo, Lennox, Macduff, Ross, Angus, Attendants, Lady Macbeth
What?	King Duncan arrives at the castle. Lady Macbeth greets him.

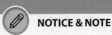

NOTICE & NOTE

3–10 The martin (**martlet**) usually built its nest on a church (**temple**), where every projection (**jutty**), sculptured decoration (**frieze**), support (**buttress**), and convenient corner (**coign of vantage**) offered a good nesting site. Banquo sees the presence of the martin's hanging (**pendant**) nest, a breeding (**procreant**) place, as a sign of healthy air.

16 single business: weak service.

20 we rest your hermits: we can only repay you with prayers. The rich hired hermits to pray for the dead.

21 coursed him at the heels: followed closely.

22 purveyor: one who makes advance arrangements for a royal visit.

25–28 Legally, Duncan owned everything in his kingdom. Lady Macbeth politely says that they hold his property in trust (**compt**), ready to return it (**make their audit**) whenever he wants.

[Stage Direction] **Sewer:** the steward, the servant in charge of arranging the banquet and tasting the king's food; **divers:** various.

Banquo. This guest of summer,
The temple-haunting martlet, does approve,
5 By his loved mansionry, that the heaven's breath
Smells wooingly here. No jutty, frieze,
Buttress, nor coign of vantage, but this bird
Hath made his pendant bed and procreant cradle.
Where they most breed and haunt, I have observed,
10 The air is delicate.

[Enter Lady Macbeth.]

Duncan. See, see, our honored hostess!—
The love that follows us sometime is our trouble,
Which still we thank as love. Herein I teach you
How you shall bid God 'ild us for your pains
And thank us for your trouble.

Lady Macbeth. All our service,
15 In every point twice done and then done double,
Were poor and single business to contend
Against those honors deep and broad wherewith
Your Majesty loads our house. For those of old,
And the late dignities heaped up to them,
20 We rest your hermits.

Duncan. Where's the Thane of Cawdor?
We coursed him at the heels and had a purpose
To be his purveyor; but he rides well,
And his great love (sharp as his spur) hath helped him
To his home before us. Fair and noble hostess,
25 We are your guest tonight.

Lady Macbeth. Your servants ever
Have theirs, themselves, and what is theirs in compt
To make their audit at your Highness' pleasure,
Still to return your own.

Duncan. Give me your hand.

[Taking her hand]

Conduct me to mine host. We love him highly
30 And shall continue our graces towards him.
By your leave, hostess.

[They exit.]

Scene 7 A room in Macbeth's castle.

[Hautboys. Torches. Enter a Sewer, and divers Servants with dishes and service over the stage. Then enter Macbeth.]

WHEN STUDENTS STRUGGLE...

Analyze a Soliloquy To help students understand Macbeth's internal conflict, have them reread his soliloquy from Scene 7, lines 1–28. Work with them to paraphrase and understand the following.

- lines 7–12: Explain that Macbeth is saying that there is punishment ("judgment") for evil in this life. If he does something evil ("teach / Bloody instructions"), then something evil will happen to him ("return / To plague th' inventor").

- lines 12–24. Ask: What are two reasons that the king is at Macbeth's castle in "double trust"? (Macbeth is an unlikely killer because he is related to the king and is both his subject and his host; the king has been such a good king that he doesn't seem to deserve death.)

Ray Fearon as Macbeth and Tara Fitzgerald as Lady Macbeth, directed by Iqban Khan, The Globe Theatre, London, England, 2016.

1–10 If Duncan's murder would have no negative consequences and be successfully completed with his death (**surcease**), then Macbeth would risk eternal damnation. He knows, however, that terrible deeds (**bloody instructions**) often backfire.

Macbeth. If it were done when 'tis done, then 'twere well
It were done quickly. If th' assassination
Could trammel up the consequence and catch
With his surcease success, that but this blow
5 Might be the be-all and the end-all here,
But here, upon this bank and shoal of time,
We'd jump the life to come. But in these cases
We still have judgment here, that we but teach
Bloody instructions, which, being taught, return
10 To plague th' inventor. This even-handed justice
Commends th' ingredience of our poisoned chalice
To our own lips. He's here in double trust:
First, as I am his kinsman and his subject,
Strong both against the deed; then, as his host,
15 Who should against his murderer shut the door,
Not bear the knife myself. Besides, this Duncan
Hath borne his faculties so meek, hath been
So clear in his great office, that his virtues
Will plead like angels, trumpet-tongued, against
20 The deep damnation of his taking-off;
And pity, like a naked newborn babe
Striding the blast, or heaven's cherubin horsed
Upon the sightless couriers of the air,
Shall blow the horrid deed in every eye,
25 That tears shall drown the wind. I have no spur
To prick the sides of my intent, but only
Vaulting ambition, which o'erleaps itself
And falls on th' other—

[*Enter* Lady Macbeth.]

How now? What news?

Lady Macbeth. He has almost supped. Why have you left the chamber?

30 **Macbeth.** Hath he asked for me?

Lady Macbeth.   Know you not he has?

The Tragedy of Macbeth, Act I, Scene 7   415

• lines 25–27: Paraphrase Macbeth's conclusion. Ask: What does Macbeth conclude is his only drive, or motive ("spur / To prick the sides of my intent") in killing the king? (*His strong ambition or "vaulting ambition"*)

 For additional support, go to the **Reading Studio** and assign the following **Level Up Tutorial: Paraphrasing.**

TEACH

► TOUGH QUESTIONS

Remind students that when a character faces Tough Questions, the decisions that he or she makes can give readers insight into his or her internal **conflicts** and can suggest **themes**. Call on students to read aloud the dialogue between Macbeth and Lady Macbeth from lines 31–61. Then ask students what question Lady Macbeth asks and why. (**Answer:** *Lady Macbeth means, "What evil caused you to suggest this idea to me in the first place?" She wants to know what is the point of their scheming if Macbeth will not do anything about it. It is a rhetorical question, so Macbeth is unable to answer it.*)

■ English Learner Support

Read and Paraphrase Read aloud the dialogue between Macbeth and Lady Macbeth from lines 31–61. Paraphrase each speech using simple language. Then have partners work together to orally recap the conversation. Monitor their discussions and provide support as necessary. Then have students draw a simple cartoon of the conversation. Have students write simple speech balloons or captions for their dialogue. **MODERATE/LIGHT**

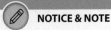
32–35 I have . . . so soon: The praises that Macbeth has received are, like new clothes, to be worn, not quickly thrown away.

35–38 Lady Macbeth sarcastically suggests that Macbeth's ambition must have been drunk, because it now seems to have a hangover (**to look so green and pale**).

39–45 Lady Macbeth criticizes Macbeth's weakened resolve and compares him to a cat in a proverb (**adage**) who wouldn't catch fish because it feared wet feet.

◄ TOUGH QUESTIONS

Notice & Note: Mark the question Lady Macbeth asks in lines 47–48.

Interpret: Paraphrase Lady Macbeth's question. What does she really want to know, and how should Macbeth answer?

54 I have given suck: I have nursed a baby.

60 When each string of a guitar or lute is tightened to the peg (**sticking place**), the instrument is ready to be played.

65–67 Lady Macbeth will get the guards so drunk that their reason will become like a still (**limbeck**), producing confused thoughts.

Macbeth. We will proceed no further in this business.
He hath honored me of late, and I have bought
Golden opinions from all sorts of people,
Which would be worn now in their newest gloss,
35 Not cast aside so soon.

Lady Macbeth.　　　　　Was the hope drunk
Wherein you dressed yourself? Hath it slept since?
And wakes it now, to look so green and pale
At what it did so freely? From this time
Such I account thy love. Art thou afeard
40 To be the same in thine own act and valor
As thou art in desire? Wouldst thou have that
Which thou esteem'st the ornament of life
And live a coward in thine own esteem,
Letting "I dare not" wait upon "I would,"
45 Like the poor cat i' th' adage?

Macbeth.　　　　　Prithee, peace.
I dare do all that may become a man.
Who dares do more is none.

Lady Macbeth.　　　　What beast was't, then,
That made you break this enterprise to me?
When you durst do it, then you were a man;
50 And to be more than what you were, you would
Be so much more the man. Nor time nor place
Did then adhere, and yet you would make both.
They have made themselves, and that their fitness now
Does unmake you. I have given suck, and know
55 How tender 'tis to love the babe that milks me.
I would, while it was smiling in my face,
Have plucked my nipple from his boneless gums
And dashed the brains out, had I so sworn as you
Have done to this.

Macbeth.　　　　　If we should fail—

Lady Macbeth.　　　　　　　We fail?
60 But screw your courage to the sticking place
And we'll not fail. When Duncan is asleep
(Whereto the rather shall his day's hard journey
Soundly invite him), his two chamberlains
Will I with wine and wassail so convince
65 That memory, the warder of the brain,
Shall be a fume, and the receipt of reason
A limbeck only. When in swinish sleep
Their drenchèd natures lie as in a death,
What cannot you and I perform upon
70 Th' unguarded Duncan? What not put upon

WHEN STUDENTS STRUGGLE . . .

Interpret Dialogue Ask volunteers how Lady Macbeth uses shame to pressure her husband into carrying out their plan in lines 47–59. (*First she says that Macbeth isn't a man if he doesn't kill Duncan. Then she says that if she had made a promise to Macbeth, even if it were a promise to kill her own baby, she would do it.*) Then ask students to discuss whether they think that Macbeth admires or fears his wife when he says, in lines 72–74, "bring forth men-children only. . . ."

 For additional support, go to the **Reading Studio** and assign the following **Level Up Tutorial: Making Inferences About Characters.**

His spongy officers, who shall bear the guilt
Of our great quell?

Macbeth.   Bring forth men-children only,
For thy undaunted mettle should compose
Nothing but males. Will it not be received,
75 When we have marked with blood those sleepy two
Of his own chamber and used their very daggers,
That they have done 't?

Lady Macbeth.   Who dares receive it other,
As we shall make our griefs and clamor roar
Upon his death?

Macbeth.   I am settled and bend up
80 Each corporal agent to this terrible feat.
Away, and mock the time with fairest show.
False face must hide what the false heart doth know.

[*They exit.*]

72 quell: murder.

72–74 Bring forth . . . males: Your bold spirit (**undaunted mettle**) is better suited to raising males than females.

79–82 Now that Macbeth has made up his mind, every part of his body (**each corporal agent**) is tightened like a bow. He and Lady Macbeth will deceive everyone (**mock the time**), hiding their evil plan with gracious faces.

CHECK YOUR UNDERSTANDING

Answer these questions before moving on to the **Analyze the Text** section on the following page.

1 What good news occurs near the beginning of the play?

A The King of Norway has been killed in battle.

B Macbeth has been victorious against the King of Norway.

C Macbeth has been named king.

D The Thane of Cawdor has proven his loyalty.

2 What future do the Three Witches predict for Macbeth?

F He will never be killed in battle.

G He will be happier than Banquo in the future.

H His children will become kings, though he will not.

J He will become Thane of Cawdor and King of Scotland.

3 What does Lady Macbeth want Macbeth to do?

A Kill King Duncan to become king

B Return all their property to King Duncan

C Ask King Duncan to make Macbeth heir to the throne

D Order Banquo to kill King Duncan

The Tragedy of Macbeth, Act I   417

ENGLISH LEARNER SUPPORT

Summarize the Drama Guide students to summarize Act I, Scene 7, using the following supports with students at varying proficiency levels:

- Ask students who is in Act I, Scene 7. Have students point to the speaker tags in these scenes and copy the names into a simplified version of the chart below. **SUBSTANTIAL**

- Have partners work together to ask and answer Where? Who? What? questions about Scene 7 and add their responses to a chart like the one below. **MODERATE/LIGHT**

Act I, Scene 7	
Where?	*A room in Macbeth's castle*
Who?	*Macbeth and Lady Macbeth*
What?	*Macbeth says that it is only ambition that would make him kill King Duncan. He decides he should not kill Duncan. Lady Macbeth changes his mind by saying that a real man would be brave enough to do it.*

CHECK YOUR UNDERSTANDING

Have students answer the questions independently.

Answer:

1. *B*

2. *J*

3. *A*

If they answer any questions incorrectly, have them reread the text to confirm their understanding. Then they may proceed to ANALYZE THE TEXT on page 418.

ENGLISH LEARNER SUPPORT

Oral Assessment Use the following questions to assess students' comprehension and speaking skills. Ask students to respond in short, complete sentences.

1. Did Macbeth win in battle? (*Yes, Macbeth won in battle.*)

2. *The witches say Macbeth will become Thane of _____ and King of _____.*
(*The witches say Macbeth will become Thane of Cawdor and King of Scotland.*)

3. *Lady Macbeth wants Macbeth to kill _____. (Lady Macbeth wants Macbeth to kill King Duncan.)* **SUBSTANTIAL/MODERATE**

APPLY

ANALYZE THE TEXT

Possible answers:

1. **DOK 4:** *The first scene foreshadows the violence of the play with thunder and lightning. It also sets up the play's theme of "fair is foul, and foul is fair."*

2. **DOK 3:** *The witches' prediction for Macbeth seems fair, or good, but it actually is foul because it leads him and Lady Macbeth to decide to commit murder. Macbeth appears fair to King Duncan because of his victory in battle, but the audience knows that Macbeth's plans for Duncan are foul.*

3. **DOK 4:** *Before Scene 4, Macbeth thought that to gain the crown, he only needed to rely on the prophecy and would not need to act himself ("without my stir"). In Scene 4, Duncan says that Malcolm is next in line for the throne, so the conflict is intensified once there is a new obstacle between Macbeth and the throne.*

4. **DOK 2:** *Lady Macbeth reveals impatience, ambition, and a lack of compassion by immediately deciding that the king must be killed.*

5. **DOK 4:** *When Malcolm is named heir, Macbeth hopes to hide his "black and deep desires" from the light of the stars. When Lady Macbeth learns of King Duncan's plan to visit, she asks that "thick night" and "the blanket of the dark" hide her planned crime from view. Duncan arrives at the castle at night; Macbeth and Lady Macbeth plan to murder him while everyone else sleeps. The darkness reflects the characters' moral state.*

CREATE AND DISCUSS

Discussions, paragraphs, and Venn diagrams should cite relevant lines from Scene 7 to support ideas.

 RESPOND

ANALYZE THE TEXT

Support your responses with evidence from the text. 📓 NOTEBOOK

1. **Analyze** What is the purpose of the first short scene? Explain.

2. **Draw Conclusions** A paradox is an apparent contradiction that reveals a truth. The witches end the first scene with a paradox: "Fair is foul, and foul is fair." Explain the ways in which this contradiction is shown to be true in Act 1.

3. **Analyze** How is Macbeth's conflict intensified by the events in Scene 4? What lines from his aside in Scene 4 (lines 48–53) develop the audience's understanding of this conflict?

4. **Infer** What does Lady Macbeth's response to the Witches' prophecy reveal about her character?

5. **Notice & Note** Review Act I to find images of darkness or night. How do these repeated references relate to plot events?

CREATE AND DISCUSS

Writing Activity: Analysis The characters of Macbeth and Lady Macbeth may have similar ambitions but they have different feelings and thoughts about their plans.

❏ With a small group, review their major speeches in Scene 7.

❏ Identify what lines 1–28 reveal about Macbeth as he lists the reasons they should not go ahead with the plan. What does he decide?

❏ Consider what is revealed about Lady Macbeth's character through her reaction to Macbeth's decision and her response in lines 47–59.

❏ Summarize their key differences in a paragraph. Share your analysis.

❏ Using your analysis of their differences, create a Venn diagram to compare and contrast Macbeth and Lady Macbeth. List what you know about their differences in the outside sections. Use the middle section to list how they compare. Cite scene and line references to support your conclusions. Discuss your ideas with your group.

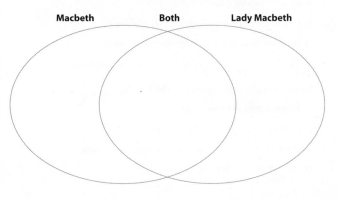

Go to the **Writing Studio** for more on writing an analysis.

SETTING A PURPOSE

As you read, look for details about how Macbeth conceals his plot. Think about the characters involved in and affected by the plot. Continue to fill in your character diagram to show the relationships between characters. Write down any questions you generate during reading.

ACT II

Scene 1 *The court of Macbeth's castle.*

[*Enter* Banquo, *and* Fleance *with a torch before him.*]

Banquo. How goes the night, boy?

Fleance. The moon is down. I have not heard the clock.

Banquo. And she goes down at twelve.

Fleance.   I take 't, 'tis later, sir.

Banquo. Hold, take my sword. [*Giving his sword to* Fleance]
                    There's husbandry in heaven;
5 Their candles are all out. Take thee that too.
A heavy summons lies like lead upon me,
And yet I would not sleep. Merciful powers,
Restrain in me the cursèd thoughts that nature
Gives way to in repose.

[*Enter* Macbeth, *and a* Servant *with a torch.*]

                    Give me my sword.—Who's there?

10 **Macbeth.** A friend.

Banquo. What, sir, not yet at rest? The King's abed.
He hath been in unusual pleasure, and
Sent forth great largess to your offices.
This diamond he greets your wife withal,
15 By the name of most kind hostess, and shut up
In measureless content. [*He gives* Macbeth *a diamond.*]

Macbeth.   Being unprepared,
Our will became the servant to defect,
Which else should free have wrought.

Banquo.   All's well.
I dreamt last night of the three Weïrd Sisters.
20 To you they have showed some truth.

Macbeth.   I think not of them.
Yet, when we can entreat an hour to serve,
We would spend it in some words upon that business,
If you would grant the time.

4–5 The heavens show economy (**husbandry**) by keeping the lights (**candles**) out—it is a starless night.

6 heavy summons: desire for sleep.

13 largess to your offices: gifts to the servants' quarters.

15 shut up: went to bed.

21 can entreat an hour: both have the time.

SETTING A PURPOSE

Direct students to use the Setting a Purpose prompt to focus their reading. Remind them to keep adding to their character diagrams.

🌐 ENGLISH LEARNER SUPPORT

Paraphrase Read aloud Banquo's lines beginning, "There's husbandry in heaven. . ." and ending "Gives way to repose." Then read aloud the side glosses for lines 4–6. Explain that Banquo is tired but does not want to sleep. He fears the "cursèd thoughts" (or bad thoughts) that will come into his mind if he lies down to sleep.

Ask: What bad thoughts is Banquo afraid of? (*He may be worried about the witches' prophecy. He may fear that Macbeth will do something to make his prophecy come true.*) **MODERATE**

WHEN STUDENTS STRUGGLE . . .

Analyze Dramatic Irony Review that **dramatic irony** results when the audience knows something that a character does not know. Read aloud lines 11–16 and the side glosses. Ask: What does Banquo give to Macbeth? Why? (*Banquo gives Macbeth a diamond; It is a gift from King Duncan to Lady Macbeth.*) How is this an example of dramatic irony? (*The king is being kind to Lady Macbeth, not knowing that she wants Macbeth to murder him.*)

 For additional support, go to the **Reading Studio** and assign the following ◼️**Level Up Tutorial: Irony.**

TEACH

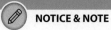
ANALYZE DRAMA

Remind students that a **soliloquy** is a speech that a character delivers when he or she is alone on stage. It often reveals a character's conflict and sometimes it is a way of letting the audience know of a character's secret plans. Call on one or more volunteers to read aloud Macbeth's soliloquy in lines 32–63. Then call on a student to identify what Macbeth sees. (*a dagger in front of him*) Ask what Macbeth means by "a dagger of the mind" in line 37. (*He isn't sure whether the dagger he sees is real or imagined.*) Then ask students to interpret lines 61–63. (*A bell rings. Macbeth interprets it to be a signal of Duncan's approaching death.*) (**Answer:** *This hallucination reveals that Macbeth feels compelled to murder Duncan; he is not in control of his own actions or his fate.*)

■ English Learner Support

Analyze a Soliloquy Work with students to translate lines 32–48 from Macbeth's soliloquy into modern language. Read a few lines at a time, pausing as volunteers summarize them.

- Macbeth sees a dagger in front of him, but it isn't real.
- He draws out his real dagger.
- He sees blood on the dagger, but he knows he is imagining it.

Ask students to use these sentence starters to tell why they think Macbeth is imagining these things:

Macbeth feels guilty that. . . .

His conscience is bothering him because. . . .
SUBSTANTIAL/MODERATE

24–28 Macbeth asks Banquo for his support (**cleave to my consent**), promising honors in return. Banquo is willing to increase (**augment**) his honor provided he can keep a clear conscience and remain loyal to the king (**keep my bosom . . . clear**).

32–42 Macbeth sees a dagger hanging in midair before him and questions whether it is real (**palpable**) or the illusion of a disturbed (**heat-oppressèd**) mind. The floating, imaginary dagger, which leads (**marshal'st**) him to Duncan's room, prompts him to draw his own dagger.

43–44 Either his eyes are mistaken (**fools**) or his other senses are.

45 He sees drops of blood on the blade and handle.

ANALYZE DRAMA

Annotate: Mark what Macbeth imagines seeing during this soliloquy.

Analyze: How does understanding Macbeth's thoughts at this point in the play help you understand the internal conflict he faces?

Banquo.   At your kind'st leisure.

Macbeth. If you shall cleave to my consent, when 'tis,
25 It shall make honor for you.

Banquo.   So I lose none
In seeking to augment it, but still keep
My bosom franchised and allegiance clear,
I shall be counseled.

Macbeth.   Good repose the while.

Banquo. Thanks, sir. The like to you.

[Banquo *and* Fleance *exit.*]

30 **Macbeth.** Go bid thy mistress, when my drink is ready,
She strike upon the bell. Get thee to bed.

[Servant *exits.*]

Is this a dagger which I see before me,
The handle toward my hand? Come, let me clutch thee.
I have thee not, and yet I see thee still.
35 Art thou not, fatal vision, sensible
To feeling as to sight? or art thou but
A dagger of the mind, a false creation
Proceeding from the heat-oppressèd brain?
I see thee yet, in form as palpable
40 As this which now I draw. [*He draws his dagger.*]
Thou marshal'st me the way that I was going,
And such an instrument I was to use.
Mine eyes are made the fools o' th' other senses
Or else worth all the rest. I see thee still,
45 And, on thy blade and dudgeon, gouts of blood,
Which was not so before. There's no such thing.
It is the bloody business which informs
Thus to mine eyes. Now o'er the one-half world
Nature seems dead, and wicked dreams abuse
50 The curtained sleep. Witchcraft celebrates
Pale Hecate's off 'rings, and withered murder,
Alarumed by his sentinel, the wolf,
Whose howl's his watch, thus with his stealthy pace,
With Tarquin's ravishing strides, towards his design
55 Moves like a ghost. Thou sure and firm-set earth,
Hear not my steps, which way they walk, for fear
Thy very stones prate of my whereabouts
And take the present horror from the time,
Which now suits with it. Whiles I threat, he lives.
60 Words to the heat of deeds too cold breath gives.

IMPROVE READING FLUENCY

Targeted Passage Have students work in pairs to present a readers' theater of Macbeth's famous soliloquy in Act II, Scene 1, lines 32–63. First, have one student in each pair act as "director," coaching the "actor" through the lines. Guide student pairs to collaborate to decide the appropriate pacing, intonation, and expression throughout the soliloquy. Circulate throughout the classroom to assist students with speaking rate, accuracy, and expression. Encourage students to practice reading the soliloquy several times to increase fluency, then have the "director" and "actor" trade roles and repeat the exercise. Invite volunteer pairs to perform the soliloquy and explain the choices they made in their dramatic readings.

 Go to the **Reading Studio** for additional support in developing fluency.

[*A bell rings.*]

I go, and it is done. The bell invites me.
Hear it not, Duncan, for it is a knell
That summons thee to heaven or to hell.

[*He exits.*]

Scene 2 *Macbeth's castle.*

[*Enter* Lady Macbeth.]

Lady Macbeth. That which hath made them drunk hath made
    me bold.
What hath quenched them hath given me fire. Hark!—Peace.
It was the owl that shrieked, the fatal bellman,
Which gives the stern'st good-night. He is about it.
5 The doors are open, and the surfeited grooms
Do mock their charge with snores. I have drugged their possets,
That death and nature do contend about them
Whether they live or die.

Macbeth [*within*].   Who's there? what, ho!

Lady Macbeth. Alack, I am afraid they have awaked,
10 And 'tis not done. Th' attempt and not the deed
Confounds us. Hark!—I laid their daggers ready;
He could not miss 'em. Had he not resembled
My father as he slept, I had done 't.

[*Enter* Macbeth *with bloody daggers.*]

                My husband?

Macbeth. I have done the deed. Didst thou not hear a noise?

15 **Lady Macbeth.** I heard the owl scream and the crickets cry.
Did not you speak?

Macbeth.   When?

Lady Macbeth.   Now.

Macbeth.   As I descended?

Lady Macbeth. Ay.

Macbeth.   Hark!—Who lies i' th' second chamber?

Lady Macbeth. Donalbain.

Macbeth.   This is a sorry sight.

Lady Macbeth. A foolish thought, to say a sorry sight.

20 **Macbeth.** There's one did laugh in 's sleep, and one cried "Murder!"
That they did wake each other. I stood and heard them.
But they did say their prayers and addressed them
Again to sleep.

---

62 **knell:** funeral bell.

3 **fatal bellman:** town crier.

5 **surfeited grooms:** drunken servants.

6 **possets:** drinks.

11 **confounds:** destroys. If Duncan survives, they will be killed (as his attempted murderers).

ANALYZE DRAMA
Annotate: Mark brackets around the beginnings and endings of lines 16, 17, and 18.

Interpret: Reread these lines to identify the iambic pentameter. What dramatic effect does Shakespeare achieve by breaking these lines between Lady Macbeth and Macbeth?

✎ ANALYZE DRAMA

Remind students that Shakespeare wrote primarily in **blank verse**, or unrhymed lines of iambic pentameter. Remind them that **iambic pentameter** is a pattern of rhythm that has five unstressed syllables, each followed by a stressed syllable. Explain that in some cases, Shakespeare broke up a single line of iambic pentameter into several lines of dialogue. Direct students to lines 16–18. Have students count the beats of line 16 to identify the last word in the line. (*descended*) Have them repeat this to mark the beginnings and endings of lines 17 and 18. (**Answer:** *Shakespeare broke blank verse lines 16–18 into separate lines of dialogue. Because the dialogue falls within the same line of blank verse, there can't be a pause between speakers as there might otherwise be. This quick delivery of the dialogue increases the tension of the scene.*)

■ English Learner Support

Analyze Shakespearean Language Point to line 14 and read it aloud: "I have done the deed. Didst though not hear a noise?" Guide students to rewrite it in modern English. (*I have done the work—I have killed the king. Didn't you hear a noise?*) Then ask: What noises did Lady Macbeth hear? (*She heard an owl and some crickets. She thought she heard Macbeth say something.*) Explain that Lady Macbeth may have heard Donalbain, Duncan's son, talk in his sleep, or she may have heard one of the servants that Macbeth killed.
ALL LEVELS

AGAIN AND AGAIN

Read lines 24–31 with students. Once students have identified the repeated word, discuss why Macbeth could not bring himself to say "Amen." (**Answer:** *Macbeth couldn't say the holy word because he was committing the unholy act of murder. It suggests that he is being corrupted by his ambition. At this point, however, he is still conscience stricken over what he has done.*)

 NOTICE & NOTE

25 As: as if. He imagines that the sleepers could see him.

AGAIN AND AGAIN

Notice & Note: Mark the repeated word in lines 24–30 that Macbeth cannot say.

Analyze: How does his inability to say this word show a change in his character?

34–38 Sleep eases worries (**knits up the raveled sleave of care**), relieves the aches of physical work (**sore labor's bath**), soothes the anxious (**hurt minds**), and nourishes like food.

Lady Macbeth. There are two lodged together.

Macbeth. One cried "God bless us" and "Amen" the other,
25 As they had seen me with these hangman's hands,
List'ning their fear. I could not say "Amen"
When they did say "God bless us."

Lady Macbeth. Consider it not so deeply.

Macbeth. But wherefore could not I pronounce "Amen"?
30 I had most need of blessing, and "Amen"
Stuck in my throat.

Lady Macbeth.   These deeds must not be thought
After these ways; so, it will make us mad.

Macbeth. Methought I heard a voice cry "Sleep no more!
Macbeth does murder sleep"—the innocent sleep,

King and Queen Macbeth, the Ice Globe Theatre in Jukkasjarvi, Sweden, 2004.

WHEN STUDENTS STRUGGLE...

Confirm Understanding This important scene describes the murder of Duncan. Help students use a sequence chart or make a brief outline listing the key events leading up to and following the murder.

- Lady Macbeth drugs the servants and leaves their daggers ready for Macbeth.
- Macbeth kills Duncan while his wife waits in another room.
- Macbeth hears voices and fears that he has been discovered.
- Macbeth returns to his wife. She scolds him for bringing the daggers and returns to Duncan's room to plant the bloody evidence on his servants.

For additional support, go to the **Reading Studio** and assign the following **Level Up Tutorial: Plot: Sequence of Events.**

35 Sleep that knits up the raveled sleave of care,
   The death of each day's life, sore labor's bath,
   Balm of hurt minds, great nature's second course,
   Chief nourisher in life's feast.

   Lady Macbeth.   What do you mean?

   Macbeth. Still it cried "Sleep no more!" to all the house.
40 "Glamis hath murdered sleep, and therefore Cawdor
   Shall sleep no more. Macbeth shall sleep no more."

   Lady Macbeth. Who was it that thus cried? Why, worthy thane,
   You do unbend your noble strength to think
   So brainsickly of things. Go get some water
45 And wash this filthy witness from your hand.—
   Why did you bring these daggers from the place?
   They must lie there. Go carry them and smear
   The sleepy grooms with blood.

   Macbeth.   I'll go no more.
   I am afraid to think what I have done.
50 Look on 't again I dare not.

   Lady Macbeth.   Infirm of purpose!
   Give me the daggers. The sleeping and the dead
   Are but as pictures. 'Tis the eye of childhood
   That fears a painted devil. If he do bleed,
   I'll gild the faces of the grooms withal,
55 For it must seem their guilt.

   [*She exits with the daggers. Knock within.*]

   Macbeth.   Whence is that knocking?
   How is 't with me when every noise appalls me?
   What hands are here? Ha, they pluck out mine eyes.
   Will all great Neptune's ocean wash this blood
   Clean from my hand? No, this my hand will rather
60 The multitudinous seas incarnadine,
   Making the green one red.

   [*Enter Lady Macbeth.*]

   Lady Macbeth. My hands are of your color, but I shame
   To wear a heart so white.   [*Knock*]

                    I hear a knocking
   At the south entry. Retire we to our chamber.
65 A little water clears us of this deed.
   How easy is it, then! Your constancy
   Hath left you unattended.   [*Knock*]

                    Hark, more knocking.
   Get on your nightgown, lest occasion call us
   And show us to be watchers. Be not lost

LANGUAGE CONVENTIONS

Annotate: Mark the subject and verb in the first part of line 50.

Analyze: What is the effect of placing the verb first in this sentence?

54–55 She'll cover (**gild**) the servants with blood, blaming them for the murder.

59–61 this my hand . . . one red: The blood on my hand will redden (**incarnadine**) the seas.

66–67 Your constancy . . . unattended: Your courage has left you.

68–69 lest . . . watchers: in case we are called for and found awake (**watchers**), which would look suspicious.

The Tragedy of Macbeth, Act II, Scene 2   423

© Houghton Mifflin Harcourt Publishing Company

LANGUAGE CONVENTIONS

Have students reread lines 39–50. Ask what Lady Macbeth wants her husband to do. (*She wants him to return to the king's chamber and place the bloody daggers next to the servants so that it will appear that they killed the king.*) Discuss the effect that the inverted structure has in line 50. (**Answer**: *The placement of "look" emphasizes the guilt Macbeth feels—he can't bring himself to look at what he has done.*)

■ English Learner Support

Paraphrase Write line 50 on the board: "Look on 't again I dare not." Explain that 't is short for the word *it*. Guide students to rewrite the line in subject-verb order, using the word *it* in place of the abbreviation: *I dare not look on it again.* Ask students what Macbeth is afraid to look at. (*He is afraid to look at the king, whom he has just murdered.*)
SUBSTANTIAL/MODERATE

 ## ENGLISH LEARNER SUPPORT

Analyze Character and Theme Work with students to translate lines 56–67 into modern language. Then instruct students to use the following sentence frames to summarize the passage: *Macbeth sees blood on his hands because he just _____. (returned from killing the king) The blood symbolizes _____. (guilt over what he's done) Lady Macbeth also has blood on _____ (her hands). She says she can wash away the blood because _____. (she thinks water will wash away their guilt)* **MODERATE/LIGHT**

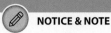

NOTICE & NOTE

ENGLISH LEARNER SUPPORT

Summarize the Drama Guide students to summarize Act II, Scenes 1–2, using the following supports with students at varying proficiency levels:

- Ask students who is in Act II, Scene 1, and Scene 2. Have students point to the speaker tags in these scenes and copy the names into a simplified version of the chart below. **SUBSTANTIAL**

- Have partners work together to ask and answer Where? Who? What? questions about Act II, Scenes 1–2, and add their responses to a chart like the one below. **MODERATE/LIGHT**

Act II, Scene 1	
Where?	*The court of Macbeth's castle*
Who?	*Banquo, Fleance, Macbeth*
What?	*Banquo gives Macbeth a diamond, a gift from King Duncan to Lady Macbeth. Banquo tells Macbeth that he had a dream about the Weird Sisters. Macbeth imagines that he sees a dagger with blood on it.*

Act II, Scene 2	
Where?	*Macbeth's castle*
Who?	*Lady Macbeth, Macbeth*
What?	*Lady Macbeth drugs the king's servants. She leaves their daggers out for Macbeth. Macbeth kills the king and the servants. He tells his wife that he heard men cry, "God bless us" but that he could not say, "Amen." Macbeth hears voices that say that he will sleep no more. Lady Macbeth tells him to put the daggers next to the servants, but Macbeth is afraid to do so. Lady Macbeth goes to put the daggers near the servants. Macbeth sees blood on his hands. Lady Macbeth returns and says that they should go to their room and wash their hands.*

71 To know . . . myself: To come to terms with what I have done, I must lose my conscience.

2 old turning the key: plenty of key turning. Hell's porter would be busy in such evil times.

3 Beelzebub: a devil.

3–11 The porter pretends he is welcoming a farmer who killed himself after his schemes to get rich (**expectation of plenty**) failed, a double talker (**equivocator**) who perjured himself yet couldn't talk his way into heaven, and a tailor who cheated his customers by skimping on material (**stealing out of a French hose**).

31–34 Alcohol is described as a wrestler thrown off (**cast**) by the porter, who thus paid him back (**requited him**) for disappointment in love. *Cast* also means "to vomit" and "to urinate."

424   Unit 6

70   So poorly in your thoughts.

Macbeth. To know my deed 'twere best not know myself.

[*Knock*]

Wake Duncan with thy knocking. I would thou couldst.

[*They exit.*]

Scene 3 *Within Macbeth's castle, near the gate.*

[*Knocking within. Enter a* Porter.]

Porter. Here's a knocking indeed! If a man were porter of hell gate, he should have old turning the key. [*Knock*] Knock, knock, knock! Who's there, i' th' name of Beelzebub? Here's a farmer that hanged himself on th' expectation of plenty. Come in time!
5   Have napkins enough about you; here you'll sweat for 't. [*Knock*] Knock, knock! Who's there, in th' other devil's name? Faith, here's an equivocator that could swear in both the scales against either scale, who committed treason enough for God's sake yet could not equivocate to heaven. O, come in, equivocator.
10 [*Knock*] Knock, knock, knock! Who's there? Faith, here's an English tailor come hither for stealing out of a French hose. Come in, tailor. Here you may roast your goose. [*Knock*] Knock, knock! Never at quiet. —What are you? —But this place is too cold for hell. I'll devilporter it no further. I had thought to have
15 let in some of all professions that go the primrose way to th' everlasting bonfire. [*Knock*] Anon, anon! [*The Porter opens the door to* Macduff *and* Lennox.] I pray you, remember the porter.

Macduff. Was it so late, friend, ere you went to bed
That you do lie so late?

20 **Porter.** Faith, sir, we were carousing till the second cock, and drink, sir, is a great provoker of three things.

Macduff. What three things does drink especially provoke?

Porter. Marry, sir, nose-painting, sleep, and urine. Lechery, sir, it provokes and unprovokes. It provokes the desire, but it takes
25 away the performance. Therefore much drink may be said to be an equivocator with lechery. It makes him, and it mars him; it sets him on, and it takes him off; it persuades him and disheartens him; makes him stand to and not stand to; in conclusion, equivocates him in a sleep and, giving him the lie,
30 leaves him.

Macduff. I believe drink gave thee the lie last night.

Porter. That it did, sir, i' th' very throat on me; but I requited him for his lie, and, I think, being too strong for him, though he took up my legs sometime, yet I made a shift to cast him.

TO CHALLENGE STUDENTS . . .

Discuss Comic Relief Explain that **comic relief** is a technique that playwrights use to provide a break from emotional tension. Have students reread Scene 3, lines 1–17. In groups, ask them to discuss these questions:

- How does Shakespeare use the Porter as comic relief? (*By having the Porter joke about how busy hell is—with the farmer, equivocator, and tailor entering it—the tension from the previous scene is lessened somewhat.*)

- How do the lines spoken by the Porter differ from the lines in the rest of the drama? (*The Porter's lines are in prose rather than blank verse.*) What effect does this choice have? (*It emphasizes the Porter's less formal speech and the fact that he is of a lower social status and that his comic lines are not as important as the other characters'.*)

TEACH

35 **Macduff.** Is thy master stirring?

[*Enter* Macbeth.]

Our knocking has awaked him. Here he comes.

[Porter *exits.*]

Lennox. Good morrow, noble sir.

Macbeth.   Good morrow, both.

Macduff. Is the King stirring, worthy thane?

Macbeth.   Not yet.

Macduff. He did command me to call timely on him.
40 I have almost slipped the hour.

Macbeth.   I'll bring you to him.

Macduff. I know this is a joyful trouble to you,
But yet 'tis one.

Macbeth. The labor we delight in physics pain.
This is the door.

Macduff.   I'll make so bold to call,
45 For 'tis my limited service. [Macduff *exits.*]

Lennox. Goes the King hence today?

Macbeth. He does. He did appoint so.

Lennox. The night has been unruly. Where we lay,
Our chimneys were blown down and, as they say,
50 Lamentings heard i' th' air, strange screams of death,
And prophesying, with accents terrible,
Of dire combustion and confused events
New hatched to th' woeful time. The obscure bird
Clamored the livelong night. Some say the earth
55 Was feverous and did shake.

Macbeth.   'Twas a rough night.

Lennox. My young remembrance cannot parallel
A fellow to it.

[*Enter* Macduff.]

Macduff.   O horror, horror, horror!
Tongue nor heart cannot conceive nor name thee!

Macbeth and Lennox. What's the matter?

60 **Macduff.** Confusion now hath made his masterpiece.
Most sacrilegious murder hath broke ope
The Lord's anointed temple and stole thence
The life o' th' building.

Macbeth.   What is 't you say? The life?

39 timely: early.

40 slipped the hour: missed
the time.

43 physics: cures.

45 limited service:
appointed duty.

**ANALYZE CHARACTER AND
THEME**
Annotate: Mark descriptions in
lines 48–55 of the turmoil that
occurred overnight.

Analyze: How do these natural
events reflect not only what
has occurred inside the castle
but what has occurred within
Macbeth himself?

60–63 Macduff mourns
Duncan's death as the
destruction (**confusion**) of
order and as sacrilegious,
violating all that is holy. In
Shakespeare's time the king
was believed to be God's sacred
representative on earth.

ANALYZE CHARACTER
AND THEME

Have a volunteer read aloud lines 48–55. Ask students
what natural events Lennox is describing. (*There was a
violent storm the night before. The wind blew hard, shaking the
chimneys. There were mournful and frightening sounds. It felt
as if there was an earthquake.*) Then discuss how these events
mirror what has occurred within Macbeth. (**Answer:** *Like the
rough weather and rumbling of the earth, Macbeth's conscience
is filled with confusion and turmoil. Although he wants to be
king, he did not want to murder Duncan.*)

TEACH

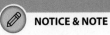

Lennox. Mean you his majesty?

65 **Macduff.** Approach the chamber and destroy your sight
With a new Gorgon. Do not bid me speak.
See and then speak yourselves.

[*Macbeth and* Lennox *exit.*]

                           Awake, awake!
Ring the alarum bell.—Murder and treason!
Banquo and Donalbain, Malcolm, awake!

70 Shake off this downy sleep, death's counterfeit,
And look on death itself. Up, up, and see
The great doom's image. Malcolm. Banquo.
As from your graves rise up and walk like sprites
To countenance this horror.—Ring the bell.

[*Bell rings.*]
[*Enter* Lady Macbeth.]

75 **Lady Macbeth.** What's the business,
That such a hideous trumpet calls to parley
The sleepers of the house? Speak, speak!

Macduff.   O gentle lady,
'Tis not for you to hear what I can speak.
The repetition in a woman's ear

80 Would murder as it fell.

[*Enter* Banquo.]

                      O Banquo, Banquo,
Our royal master's murdered.

Lady Macbeth.   Woe, alas!
What, in our house?

Banquo.   Too cruel anywhere. —
Dear Duff, I prithee, contradict thyself
And say it is not so.

[*Enter* Macbeth, Lennox, *and* Ross.]

85 **Macbeth.** Had I but died an hour before this chance,
I had lived a blessèd time; for from this instant
There's nothing serious in mortality.
All is but toys. Renown and grace is dead.
The wine of life is drawn, and the mere lees

90 Is left this vault to brag of.

[*Enter* Malcolm *and* Donalbain.]

Donalbain. What is amiss?

Macbeth.   You are, and do not know 't.
The spring, the head, the fountain of your blood
Is stopped; the very source of it is stopped.

Side notes

66 new Gorgon: Macduff compares the shocking sight of the corpse to a Gorgon. In Greek mythology, anyone who saw a Gorgon turned to stone.

70 counterfeit: imitation.

72 great doom's image: a picture like the Last Judgment, the end of the world.

73 sprites: spirits. The spirits of the dead were supposed to rise on Judgment Day.

76 trumpet calls to parley: She compares the clanging bell to a trumpet used to call two sides of a battle to negotiation.

86–90 for from . . . brag of: From now on, nothing matters (**there's nothing serious**) in human life (**mortality**); even fame and grace have been made meaningless. The good wine of life has been removed (**drawn**), leaving only the dregs (**lees**).

WHEN STUDENTS STRUGGLE...

Analyze Figurative Language Ask students to define the term *figurative meaning*. *(language such as metaphors, similes, and hyperbole that does not use words or terms literally)* Explain that playwrights use figurative meanings of words to create vivid imagery, to deepen meaning, and to convey a mood. Ask students to identify the metaphor in lines 65–67. *(Macduff compares his shock of seeing the murdered king to being turned to stone by a Gorgon.)* Why is this metaphor effective? *(It conveys Macduff's shock and despair.)*

 For additional support, go to the **Reading Studio** and assign the following **Level Up Tutorial: Figurative Language.**

Macduff. Your royal father's murdered.

Malcolm.   O, by whom?

95 **Lennox.** Those of his chamber, as it seemed, had done 't.
Their hands and faces were all badged with blood.
So were their daggers, which unwiped we found
Upon their pillows. They stared and were distracted.
No man's life was to be trusted with them.

100 **Macbeth.** O, yet I do repent me of my fury,
That I did kill them.

Macduff.   Wherefore did you so?

Macbeth. Who can be wise, amazed, temp'rate, and furious,
Loyal, and neutral, in a moment? No man.
Th' expedition of my violent love

105 Outrun the pauser, reason. Here lay Duncan,
His silver skin laced with his golden blood,
And his gashed stabs looked like a breach in nature
For ruin's wasteful entrance; there the murderers,
Steeped in the colors of their trade, their daggers

110 Unmannerly breeched with gore. Who could refrain
That had a heart to love, and in that heart
Courage to make 's love known?

Lady Macbeth.   Help me hence, ho! **Close Read**

Macduff. Look to the lady.

Malcolm [*aside to* Donalbain]. Why do we hold our tongues,
That most may claim this argument for ours?

Donalbain [*aside to* Malcolm].

115 What should be spoken here, where our fate,
Hid in an auger hole, may rush and seize us?
Let's away. Our tears are not yet brewed.

Malcolm [*aside to* Donalbain].
Nor our strong sorrow upon the foot of motion.

Banquo. Look to the lady.

[Lady Macbeth *is assisted to leave.*]

120 And when we have our naked frailties hid,
That suffer in exposure, let us meet
And question this most bloody piece of work
To know it further. Fears and scruples shake us.
In the great hand of God I stand, and thence

125 Against the undivulged pretense I fight
Of treasonous malice.

Macduff.   And so do I.

96 **badged:** marked.

104–105 He claims his emotions overpowered his reason, which would have made him pause to think before he killed Duncan's servants.

107 breach: a military term to describe a break in defenses, such as a hole in a castle wall.

112 Lady Macbeth faints.

TOUGH QUESTIONS

Notice & Note: Mark the questions Malcolm and Donalbain ask each other in lines 113–116.

Interpret: How do these questions reveal the complicated situation they are in?

120–121 Banquo suggests that they all meet to discuss the murder after they have dressed (**our naked frailties hid**), since people are shivering in their nightclothes (**suffer in exposure**).

123–126 Though shaken by fears and doubts (**scruples**), he will fight against the secret plans (**undivulged pretense**) of the traitor.

The Tragedy of Macbeth, Act II, Scene 3   427

TOUGH QUESTIONS

Call on a student to read aloud lines 113–118. Ask students to **paraphrase** Malcolm's and Donalbain's dialogue. (*Malcolm: "Why don't we say anything? We're the ones who should be saying that we avenged our father's death." Donalbain: "What can we say when we don't know what fate holds in store for us? Let's leave before our fears become a reality."*) Discuss why Malcolm and Donalbain feel that they're in danger. (**Answer:** *The questions show that they feel that they will be accused of Duncan's murder unless they speak up. On the other hand, they fear that if they do speak up, they, too, will be murdered.*)

CLOSE READ SCREENCAST

Modeled Discussion   In their eBook, have students view the Close Read Screencast, in which readers discuss and annotate Scene 3, lines 112–126.

ENGLISH LEARNER SUPPORT

Paraphrase Display lines 127–128:

"Let's briefly put on manly readiness

And meet i' th' hall together."

Explain that Shakespeare used apostrophes where he dropped a letter in a word, or where he left out a word entirely. Explain that "Let's briefly put on manly readiness" means "Let's quickly get dressed." Ask students what words belong after *meet*. *(in the)*

Have mixed-language ability groups study various passages that include apostrophes or inverted word order from Scene 3, filling in missing words and letters and experimenting with word order when necessary. Then have groups work together to paraphrase each passage. **ALL LEVELS**

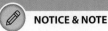

NOTICE & NOTE

129–131 Malcolm does not want to join (**consort with**) the others because one of them may have plotted the murder.

All.   So all.

Macbeth. Let's briefly put on manly readiness
And meet i' th' hall together.

All.   Well contented.

[*All but* Malcolm *and* Donalbain *exit.*]

Malcolm. What will you do? Let's not consort with them.
130 To show an unfelt sorrow is an office
Which the false man does easy. I'll to England.

Donalbain. To Ireland I. Our separated fortune
Shall keep us both the safer. Where we are,
There's daggers in men's smiles. The near in blood,
135 The nearer bloody.

Teatro Regio Torino perform 'Verdi's Macbeth' at Festival Theatre, Edinburgh, Scotland, 2017.

428   Unit 6

TO CHALLENGE STUDENTS . . .

Analyze Social Impacts Act II, Scene 3, would have shocked audiences in Shakespeare's day. Have students discuss why. Provide the following prompts for guidance:

- Briefly research the concept of the divine right of kings and of regicide in Elizabethan times.
- Consider how Macduff's statement about "Confusion" (line 60) fits into the drama's themes.
- Think about the effect of Duncan's murder taking place offstage.

Have students write a summary of their discussion.

Malcolm.   This murderous shaft that's shot
Hath not yet lighted, and our safest way
Is to avoid the aim. Therefore to horse,
And let us not be dainty of leave-taking
But shift away. There's warrant in that theft
140 Which steals itself when there's no mercy left.

[*They exit.*]

Scene 4 *Outside Macbeth's castle.*

[*Enter* Ross *with an* Old Man.]

Old Man. Threescore and ten I can remember well,
Within the volume of which time I have seen
Hours dreadful and things strange, but this sore night
Hath trifled former knowings.

139–140 There's . . . left:
There's good reason (**warrant**) to steal away from a situation that promises no mercy.

1–4 Nothing the old man has seen in 70 years (**threescore and ten**) has been as strange and terrible (**sore**) as this night. It has made other times seem trivial (**hath trifled**) by comparison.

 ENGLISH LEARNER SUPPORT

Summarize the Drama Guide students to summarize Act II, Scene 3, using the following supports with students at varying proficiency levels:

• Ask students who is in Act II, Scene 3. Have students point to the speaker tags in these scenes and copy the names into a simplified version of the chart below. **SUBSTANTIAL**

• Have partners work together to ask and answer Where? Who? What? questions about Act II, Scene 3, and add their responses to a chart like the one below. **MODERATE/LIGHT**

Act II, Scene 3	
Where?	*Within Macbeth's castle*
Who?	*Porter, Macduff, Lennox, Macbeth, Lady Macbeth, Banquo, Malcolm, Donalbain*
What?	*Macduff comes to wake the king only to find the king dead. Macbeth and Lennox go to see the king. Macduff calls the others to awaken. Malcolm and Donalbain learn of their father's death. Macbeth says that he killed the servants because he was so angry at them for their murder of the king. Malcolm decides to go to England; Donalbain decides to go to Ireland.*

TO CHALLENGE STUDENTS . . .

Reinterpret a Scene Tell students that many directors have reinterpreted Shakespeare's plays, setting them in different times and cultures. Instruct small groups of students to rewrite a scene from *Macbeth*, applying the following principles:

• Choose a modern-day setting (to be described in the script).

• Use contemporary language to paraphrase the scene line by line.

• Create roles based on an organizational hierarchy that makes sense in the new setting.

Invite groups to present their scenes to the class.

ENGLISH LEARNER SUPPORT

Summarize the Drama Guide students to summarize Scene 4.

Act II, Scene 4	
Where?	Outside Macbeth's castle
Who?	Ross, Old Man, Macduff
What?	Macduff thinks that it is suspicious that Malcolm and Donalbain left so quickly. He tells Ross that Macbeth will be made king.

Then have partners take turns asking and answering questions about what happened in Scene 4.
MODERATE/LIGHT

 NOTICE & NOTE

6–10 By th' clock . . . kiss it: Though daytime, an unnatural darkness blots out the sun (**strangles the traveling lamp**).

12–13 The owl would never be expected to attack a high-flying (**tow'ring**) falcon, much less defeat one.

15 minions: best or favorites.

17 Contending 'gainst obedience: The well-trained horses rebelliously fought against all constraints.

24 What . . . pretend: Ross wonders what the servants could have hoped to achieve (**pretend**) by killing; **suborned:** hired or bribed.

27–29 He is horrified by the thought that the sons could act contrary to nature (**'gainst nature still**) because of wasteful (**thriftless**) ambition and greedily destroy (**ravin up**) their father, the source of their own life (**thine own lives' means**).

31–32 Macbeth went to the traditional site (**Scone**) where Scotland's kings were crowned.

Ross.   Ha, good father,
5 Thou seest the heavens, as troubled with man's act,
Threaten his bloody stage. By th' clock 'tis day,
And yet dark night strangles the traveling lamp.
Is 't night's predominance or the day's shame
That darkness does the face of earth entomb
10 When living light should kiss it?

Old Man.   'Tis unnatural,
Even like the deed that's done. On Tuesday last
A falcon, tow'ring in her pride of place,
Was by a mousing owl hawked at and killed.

Ross. And Duncan's horses (a thing most strange and certain),
15 Beauteous and swift, the minions of their race,
Turned wild in nature, broke their stalls, flung out,
Contending 'gainst obedience, as they would
Make war with mankind.

Old Man.   'Tis said they eat each other.

Ross. They did so, to th' amazement of mine eyes
20 That looked upon 't.

[*Enter* Macduff.]
                     Here comes the good Macduff.—
How goes the world, sir, now?

Macduff.   Why, see you not?

Ross. Is 't known who did this more than bloody deed?

Macduff. Those that Macbeth hath slain.

Ross.   Alas, the day,
What good could they pretend?

Macduff.   They were suborned.
25 Malcolm and Donalbain, the King's two sons,
Are stol'n away and fled, which puts upon them
Suspicion of the deed.

Ross.   'Gainst nature still!
Thriftless ambition, that will ravin up
Thine own lives' means. Then 'tis most like
30 The sovereignty will fall upon Macbeth.

Macduff. He is already named and gone to Scone
To be invested.

Ross.   Where is Duncan's body?

Macduff. Carried to Colmekill,
The sacred storehouse of his predecessors
35 And guardian of their bones.

APPLYING ACADEMIC VOCABULARY

☑ **comprise** ☑ **incidence** ☐ **predominant** ☐ **priority** ☐ **ultimate**

Write and Discuss Have students turn to a partner to discuss the following questions based on Act II. Guide students to include the academic vocabulary words *comprise* and *incidence* in their responses. Ask volunteers to share their responses with the class.

- What do the unnatural events of this night **comprise** (Scene 3, lines 48–55)?
- There is a great outpouring of grief over Duncan's death. How do you explain this **incidence** of emotion?

Ross.   Will you to Scone?

Macduff. No, cousin, I'll to Fife.

Ross.   Well, I will thither.

Macduff. Well, may you see things well done there. Adieu,
Lest our old robes sit easier than our new.

Ross. Farewell, father.

40 **Old Man.** God's benison go with you and with those
That would make good of bad and friends of foes.

[*All exit.*]

40–41 The old man gives his blessing (**benison**) to Macduff and all those who would bring peace to the troubled land.

CHECK YOUR UNDERSTANDING

Answer these questions before moving on to the **Analyze the Text** section on the following page.

1 Why does Macbeth refuse to go back into the king's bedroom with the bloody knives?

A He is afraid that he has not killed the king and he might still live.

B He is so filled with guilt and remorse that he lacks the courage to return.

C He wants Lady Macbeth to do her share by taking the knives back.

D He thinks it will be harder for someone to catch him if he does not go back.

2 Which of the following is a central theme in Act II?

F The witches' prophecies will ultimately prove false.

G The knocking sounds are the ghost of the king coming back.

H Macbeth deserves the crown more than the king's sons do.

J The king's murder has upset the natural rule of order.

3 What happens to Malcolm and Donalbain at the end of Act II?

A They are found guilty of their father's murder.

B They prepare to assume the throne in Duncan's place.

C They flee because they fear that they, too, will be murdered.

D They accuse Macbeth of having committed Duncan's murder.

The Tragedy of Macbeth, Act II   431

CHECK YOUR UNDERSTANDING

Have students answer the questions independently.

Answers:

1. *B*

2. *J*

3. *C*

If they answer any questions incorrectly, have them reread the text to confirm their understanding. Then they may proceed to ANALYZE THE TEXT on page 432.

 ENGLISH LEARNER SUPPORT

Oral Assessment Use the following questions to assess students' comprehension and speaking skills. Ask students to respond in short, complete sentences.

1. Who kills King Duncan? (*Macbeth kills King Duncan.*)

2. *Macbeth won't go back into the king's bedroom because he feels____.*
(*Macbeth won't go back into the king's bedroom because he feels guilty.*)

3. *At the end of Act II, Malcolm and Donalbain____ because ____. (At the end of Act II, Malcolm and Donalbain leave the castle because they are afraid they will be killed.)* **SUBSTANTIAL/MODERATE**

ANALYZE THE TEXT

Possible answers:

1. **DOK 2:** *Examples include the appearance of the dagger (Scene 1, lines 32–48); the voice after the murder (Scene 2, lines 33–41); Macbeth's refusal to return to the room (Scene 2, lines 48–50); and his words after the discovery of Duncan's death (Scene 3, lines 85–90).*

2. **DOK 4:** *The Porter jokes about being the "porter of hell" and about horrible people coming to his door, implying that Macbeth and Lady Macbeth belong in hell. This humor breaks the tension momentarily so that it can build up again.*

3. **DOK 2:** *Macbeth says he killed Duncan's servants because he was overcome with emotion after learning they murdered the king, but the audience knows Macbeth himself is the guilty party.*

4. **DOK 3:** *Lady Macbeth makes the plans but expects Macbeth to execute them. She both reassures him and mocks him when he has doubts. She knows when she may have pushed him to his limit and is willing to take action to protect them both. Despite their evil deeds, they show a mutual commitment.*

5. **DOK 4:** *The idea of sleep can be interpreted as symbolizing death, as when Lady Macbeth says "The sleeping and the dead are but as pictures." But it also symbolizes innocence. Macbeth and Lady Macbeth pretend to have been sleeping when the murder is discovered, and Macbeth's speech in Scene 2, lines 33–41, emphasizes the idea of sleep as innocence. One theme might be that the evil awakened by selfish ambition will never let one find peace or rest.*

CREATE AND PRESENT

Students' opinions will vary but should be supported by relevant text evidence.

 RESPOND

ANALYZE THE TEXT

Support your responses with evidence from the text. 📓 NOTEBOOK

1. **Summarize** What are some examples of Macbeth's active imagination that add to his internal conflict?

2. **Analyze** What are some things the Porter says that provide comic relief? Why does Shakespeare include them in such a dramatic play?

3. **Infer** How is Macbeth's explanation of why he killed the king's servants an example of dramatic irony? Use text from Scene 3 lines 100–112 to support your answer.

4. **Cite Evidence** What does Shakespeare tell you about Lady Macbeth's and Macbeth's relationship in his description of the murder scene? Cite examples from Scene 2 to support your answer.

5. **Notice & Note** What is the effect of the repeated idea of sleep in Act II? How does this idea point toward a theme?

CREATE AND PRESENT

Discuss Why does Lady Macbeth faint? Is it a distraction, or is it real? Support your conclusion with evidence from the text.

❏ Jot down ideas about what Lady Macbeth does and says in Act II that might explain why she faints.

❏ Use cause-and-effect connecting words to link your ideas.

❏ In a small group, discuss these ideas and your interpretation of her action. Together, draw one or more conclusions about her motives.

❏ Summarize the group discussion and present your ideas to the class.

Go to the **Speaking and Listening Studio** for more on collaborative discussions.

SETTING A PURPOSE

As you read Act III, refer to your character diagram and add any new information you learn about the characters and their relationships.

ACT III

Scene 1 *Macbeth's palace at Forres.*

[*Enter* Banquo.]

Banquo. Thou hast it now—King, Cawdor, Glamis, all
As the Weïrd Women promised, and I fear
Thou played'st most foully for 't. Yet it was said
It should not stand in thy posterity,
5 But that myself should be the root and father
Of many kings. If there come truth from them
(As upon thee, Macbeth, their speeches shine),
Why, by the verities on thee made good,
May they not be my oracles as well,
10 And set me up in hope? But hush, no more.

[*Sennet sounded. Enter* Macbeth *as* King, Lady Macbeth, Lennox,
Ross, Lords, *and* Attendants.]

Macbeth. Here's our chief guest.

Lady Macbeth.   If he had been forgotten,
It had been as a gap in our great feast
And all-thing unbecoming.

Macbeth. Tonight we hold a solemn supper, sir,
15 And I'll request your presence.

Banquo.   Let your Highness
Command upon me, to the which my duties
Are with a most indissoluble tie
Forever knit.

Macbeth.   Ride you this afternoon?

Banquo. Ay, my good lord.

20 **Macbeth.** We should have else desired your good advice
(Which still hath been both grave and prosperous)
In this day's council, but we'll take tomorrow.
Is 't far you ride?

ANALYZE DRAMA
Annotate: Mark what Banquo suspects in lines 1–10.

Infer: What does this soliloquy reveal about Banquo's internal conflict?

[Stage Direction] **Sennet sounded:** A trumpet is sounded.

14–15 A king usually uses the royal pronoun *we*. Macbeth switches to the pronoun *I* with Banquo.

15–18 Banquo says he is duty bound to serve the king.

21 grave and prosperous: thoughtful and profitable.

TEACH

SETTING A PURPOSE

Direct students to use the Setting a Purpose prompt to focus their reading. Remind them to keep adding to their character diagrams.

ANALYZE DRAMA

Ask a volunteer to identify the evidence in lines 1–10 that indicates that Banquo suspects something. (*"Thou hast it now—King, Cawdor, Glamis, all / As the Weïrd Women promised, and I fear / Thou played'st most foully for 't."*) Call on another student to explain what this means. (*Banquo suspects that Macbeth murdered Duncan in order to become king.*) Ask partners to discuss and share what Banquo's internal conflict seems to be. (**Answer:** *Since Banquo's descendants are prophesied to rule Scotland, he doesn't want to interfere with that part of the prophecy; however, he is unhappy about the way that he thinks Macbeth has made his own part of the prophecy come true.*)

For **reading support** for students at varying proficiency levels, see the **Text X-Ray** on page 394D.

EL ENGLISH LEARNER SUPPORT

Paraphrase Read aloud lines 1–10 as students follow along in their texts. Then guide students to paraphrase each line. Review the meanings of *to suspect, prophecy*, and *heirs*. Then have students use the following frames to retell what Banquo is thinking.

Banquo suspects that Macbeth _____ .

According to the prophecy, Macbeth's children _____ .

Banquo believes that his heirs may _____ because _____ . **ALL LEVELS**

TEACH

EL ## ENGLISH LEARNER SUPPORT

Ask and Answer Questions Read aloud the dialogue between Banquo and Macbeth in Scene 1, lines 18–39, as students follow along in their texts. Stop every few lines to paraphrase the text. Then model using the question words *Where, Who,* and *What,* to form questions about it:

Where are Banquo and Fleance going?

Who does Macbeth say is in England and Ireland?

What does Macbeth want everyone to believe about the king's murder?

Have partners take turns asking and answering questions beginning with *Where, Who,* and *What*? **MODERATE/LIGHT**

NOTICE & NOTE

25–27 If his horse goes no faster than usual, he'll be back an hour or two (**twain**) after dark.

29 bloody cousins: murderous relatives (Malcolm and Donalbain); **bestowed:** settled.

32 strange invention: lies; stories they have invented.

33–34 when . . . jointly: when matters of state will require the attention of us both.

40 be master of his time: do what he wants.

43 while: until.

44–45 sirrah: a term of address to an inferior; **Attend . . . pleasure:** Are they waiting for me?

47–48 To be thus . . . safely thus: To be king is worthless unless my position as king is safe.

51 dauntless temper: fearless temperament.

55–56 Banquo's mere presence forces back (**rebukes**) Macbeth's ruling spirit (**genius**). In ancient Rome, Caesar, who became emperor, had the same effect on his rival, Mark Antony.

Banquo. As far, my lord, as will fill up the time
25 'Twixt this and supper. Go not my horse the better,
I must become a borrower of the night
For a dark hour or twain.

Lady Macbeth.   Fail not our feast.

Banquo. My lord, I will not.

Macbeth. We hear our bloody cousins are bestowed
30 In England and in Ireland, not confessing
Their cruel parricide, filling their hearers
With strange invention. But of that tomorrow,
When therewithal we shall have cause of state
Craving us jointly. Hie you to horse. Adieu,
35 Till you return at night. Goes Fleance with you?

Banquo. Ay, my good lord. Our time does call upon 's.

Macbeth. I wish your horses swift and sure of foot,
And so I do commend you to their backs.
Farewell.

[*Banquo exits.*]

40 Let every man be master of his time
Till seven at night. To make society
The sweeter welcome, we will keep ourself
Till suppertime alone. While then, God be with you.

[*Lords and all but* Macbeth *and a* Servant *exit.*]

Sirrah, a word with you. Attend those men
45 Our pleasure?

Servant. They are, my lord, without the palace gate.

Macbeth. Bring them before us.

[*Servant exits.*]

                                   To be thus is nothing,
But to be safely thus. Our fears in Banquo
Stick deep, and in his royalty of nature
50 Reigns that which would be feared. 'Tis much he dares,
And to that dauntless temper of his mind
He hath a wisdom that doth guide his valor
To act in safety. There is none but he
Whose being I do fear; and under him
55 My genius is rebuked, as it is said
Mark Antony's was by Caesar. He chid the sisters
When first they put the name of king upon me
And bade them speak to him. Then, prophet-like,
They hailed him father to a line of kings.

434   Unit 6

WHEN STUDENTS STRUGGLE . . .

Analyze a Soliloquy Remind students that a **soliloquy** is a dramatic device in which a character's private reflections are spoken aloud by that character—as if he or she is speaking only to him- or herself. Its purpose is to reveal the character's innermost thoughts and feelings to the audience. Display lines 47–71 and have volunteers read and interpret each line. As needed, help students understand the following:

- "his royalty of nature" refers to Banquo's integrity and noble behavior
- *valor* means "courage"

- *chid* means "scolded"
- "fruitless crown" and "barren scepter" refer to the fact that, according to the witches' prophecy, no children of Macbeth's will inherit the crown
- "Banquo's issue" and "seeds of Banquo" refer to Banquo's heirs

Then discuss the fact that the soliloquy reveals Macbeth's jealousy and desire for power—and Banquo's apparent nobility and fitness to be king.

 For additional support, go to the **Reading Studio** and assign the following **Level Up Tutorial: Character Motivation.**

60 Upon my head they placed a fruitless crown
   And put a barren scepter in my grip,
   Thence to be wrenched with an unlineal hand,
   No son of mine succeeding. If 't be so,
   For Banquo's issue have I filed my mind;
65 For them the gracious Duncan have I murdered,
   Put rancors in the vessel of my peace
   Only for them, and mine eternal jewel
   Given to the common enemy of man
   To make them kings, the seeds of Banquo kings.
70 Rather than so, come fate into the list,
   And champion me to th' utterance.—Who's there?

[Enter Servant and two Murderers.]

[To the Servant] Now go to the door, and stay there till we call.

[Servant exits.]

Was it not yesterday we spoke together?

Murderers. It was, so please your Highness.

Macbeth.   Well then, now
75 Have you considered of my speeches? Know
   That it was he, in the times past, which held you
   So under fortune, which you thought had been
   Our innocent self. This I made good to you
   In our last conference, passed in probation with you
80 How you were borne in hand, how crossed, the instruments,
   Who wrought with them, and all things else that might
   To half a soul and to a notion crazed
   Say "Thus did Banquo."

First Murderer.   You made it known to us.

Macbeth. I did so, and went further, which is now
85 Our point of second meeting. Do you find
   Your patience so predominant in your nature
   That you can let this go? Are you so gospeled
   To pray for this good man and for his issue,
   Whose heavy hand hath bowed you to the grave
90 And beggared yours forever?

First Murderer.   We are men, my liege.

Macbeth. Ay, in the catalogue you go for men,
   As hounds and greyhounds, mongrels, spaniels, curs,
   Shoughs, water-rugs, and demi-wolves are clept
   All by the name of dogs. The valued file
95 Distinguishes the swift, the slow, the subtle,
   The housekeeper, the hunter, every one
   According to the gift which bounteous nature

60–69 They gave me a childless (**fruitless, barren**) rule, which will be taken away by someone outside my family (**unlineal**). I have committed murder, poisoned (**filed**) my mind, and destroyed my soul (**eternal jewel**) only to benefit Banquo's heirs.

ANALYZE CHARACTER AND THEME
Annotate: Mark passages in lines 47–71 that reveal Macbeth's thoughts about what he has done and how he feels about Banquo.

Infer: What has Macbeth realized? How will he solve this problem?

75–83 Macbeth supposedly proved (**passed in probation**) Banquo's deception (**how you were borne in hand**), methods, and allies. Even a half-wit (**half a soul**) or a crazed person would agree that Banquo caused their trouble.

87–90 He asks whether they are so influenced by the gospel's message of forgiveness (**so gospeled**) that they will pray for Banquo and his children despite his harshness, which will leave their own families beggars.

91–100 The true worth of a dog can be measured only by examining the record (**valued file**) of its special qualities (**particular addition**).

The Tragedy of Macbeth, Act III, Scene 1   435

ANALYZE CHARACTER AND THEME

Read aloud lines 47–71, or ask a volunteer to read them. Discuss what Macbeth's thoughts reveal. (**Answer:** *Macbeth realizes that he has killed Duncan for the ultimate benefit of Banquo's heirs, who—if the witches are correct—will inherit the throne. He sees Banquo as being nobler and more rewarded by the witches. He decides to end Banquo's line, by killing Banquo, rather than allow that to happen.*)

EL ENGLISH LEARNER SUPPORT

Answer Questions and Make Inferences Guide students to understand why Macbeth is meeting with the murderers:

- Direct students to the cast list at the beginning of the play. Ask: How many murderers are there? (*There are three murderers.*) How many murderers appear in Act III, Scene 1? (*two*)

- Ask: Has the audience seen these characters in the play before, or is this the first time? (*This is the first time.*)

- Then read aloud lines 73–74 in Scene 1. Ask: Has Macbeth seen these characters before? (*Yes, yesterday.*)

SUBSTANTIAL/MODERATE

EL ENGLISH LEARNER SUPPORT

Rewrite Inverted Language Students may have difficulty understanding the inverted or other nonstandard sentence structures in the play. Have students make a chart like the one shown and work in pairs to rewrite the lines to help determine their meanings:

Shakespeare's English	Modern English
Line 35: . . . Goes Fleance with you?	Is Fleance going with you?
Line 36: . . . Our time does call upon's.	It's time [to go].
Lines 42–43: . . . we will keep ourself / Till suppertime alone. . . .	We'll stay by ourselves until dinner.

ALL LEVELS

© Houghton Mifflin Harcourt Publishing Company

✏️ **NOTICE & NOTE**

Hath in him closed; whereby he does receive
Particular addition, from the bill
100 That writes them all alike. And so of men.
Now, if you have a station in the file,
Not i' th' worst rank of manhood, say 't,
And I will put that business in your bosoms
Whose execution takes your enemy off,
105 Grapples you to the heart and love of us,
Who wear our health but sickly in his life,
Which in his death were perfect.

Second Murderer.   I am one, my liege,
Whom the vile blows and buffets of the world
Hath so incensed that I am reckless what
110 I do to spite the world.

First Murderer.   And I another
So weary with disasters, tugged with fortune,
That I would set my life on any chance,
To mend it or be rid on 't.

Macbeth.   Both of you
Know Banquo was your enemy.

Murderers.   True, my lord.

115 **Macbeth.** So is he mine, and in such bloody distance
That every minute of his being thrusts
Against my near'st of life. And though I could
With barefaced power sweep him from my sight
And bid my will avouch it, yet I must not,
120 For certain friends that are both his and mine,
Whose loves I may not drop, but wail his fall
Who I myself struck down. And thence it is
That I to your assistance do make love,
Masking the business from the common eye
125 For sundry weighty reasons.

Second Murderer.   We shall, my lord,
Perform what you command us.

First Murderer.   Though our lives—

Macbeth. Your spirits shine through you. Within this hour at most
I will advise you where to plant yourselves,
Acquaint you with the perfect spy o' th' time,
130 The moment on 't, for 't must be done tonight
And something from the palace; always thought
That I require a clearness. And with him
(To leave no rubs nor botches in the work)
Fleance, his son, that keeps him company,
135 Whose absence is no less material to me

103–107 Macbeth will give them a secret job (**business in your bosoms**) that will earn them his loyalty (**grapples you to the heart**) and love. Banquo's death will make this sick king healthy.

111 tugged with: knocked about by.

115–117 Banquo is near enough to draw blood, and like a menacing swordsman, his mere presence threatens (**thrusts against**) Macbeth's existence.

119 bid my will avouch it: justify it as my will.

127 Your spirits shine through you: Your courage is evident.

131–132 something from . . . clearness: The murder must be done away from the palace so that I remain blameless (**I require a clearness**).

135 absence: death.

436   Unit 6

WHEN STUDENTS STRUGGLE . . .

Confirm Understanding   Have small groups discuss how Macbeth manipulates the murderers. Provide these questions: What did Macbeth tell the murderers about Banquo when they met before (lines 73–83)? *(Banquo caused their troubles.)* What do we learn about the murderers in lines 107–113? *(They are desperate to improve their lot in life.)* What does Macbeth tell the murderers in lines 114–125? *(He wants them to kill Banquo.)* Does Macbeth feel guilty now? How has his character changed? *(He doesn't seem to feel guilty; his ambition seems to be winning the battle with his conscience.)*

 For additional support, go to the **Reading Studio** and assign the following 📖 **Level Up Tutorial: Reading for Details.**

Banquo and Fleance, The Conservatory of Theatre and Dance, Southeast Missouri State University, 2014.

Than is his father's, must embrace the fate
Of that dark hour. Resolve yourselves apart.
I'll come to you anon.

Murderers. We are resolved, my lord.

Macbeth. I'll call upon you straight. Abide within.

[Murderers *exit*.]

140 It is concluded. Banquo, thy soul's flight,
If it find heaven, must find it out tonight.

[*He exits*.]

Scene 2 *Macbeth's palace at Forres.*

[*Enter* Lady Macbeth *and a* Servant.]

Lady Macbeth. Is Banquo gone from court?

Servant. Ay, madam, but returns again tonight.

Lady Macbeth. Say to the King I would attend his leisure
For a few words.

Servant. Madam, I will.

[*He exits*.]

Lady Macbeth. Naught's had, all's spent,
5 Where our desire is got without content.

137 Resolve yourselves apart: Decide in private.

139 straight: soon.

4–7 Nothing (**naught**) has been gained; everything has been wasted (**spent**). It would be better to be dead like Duncan than to live in uncertain joy.

The Tragedy of Macbeth, Act III, Scene 2   437

ENGLISH LEARNER SUPPORT

Summarize the Drama Guide students to summarize Act III, Scene 1, using the following supports with students at varying proficiency levels:

• Ask students who is in Act III, Scene 1. Have students point to the speaker tags in this scene and copy the names into a simplified version of the chart below. **SUBSTANTIAL**

• Have partners work together to ask and answer Where? Who? What? questions about Act III, Scene 1, and add their responses to a chart like the one below. **MODERATE/LIGHT**

Act III, Scene 1	
Where?	*Macbeth's palace at Forres*
Who?	*Banquo, Macbeth, Lady Macbeth, Servant, Two Murderers*
What?	*Banquo tells Macbeth that he and his son Fleance are going riding until after dark. Macbeth meets with two murderers. He tells them that Banquo is to blame for their problems. They agree to kill Banquo and Fleance.*

TO CHALLENGE STUDENTS . . .

Analyze Style Remind students that Shakespeare uses iambic pentameter and sometimes an inverted sentence structure. Then instruct pairs of students to do the following: Scan the meter in lines 115–122. Rewrite the following line so that the structure sounds more like usual speech: "And though I could / With barefaced power sweep him from my sight." (*And though I could sweep him from my sight with barefaced power.*) Explain, in writing, how Shakespeare's use of inverted sentence structure affects iambic pentameter. (*Iambic pentameter consists of five metrical feet, each foot consisting of an unaccented syllable followed by an accented syllable. Prepositional phrases begin with an unaccented preposition, so placing them where an unaccented syllable is needed preserves the meter. A traditional structure would interrupt the meter.*)

Dance, Southeast Missouri State University

'Tis safer to be that which we destroy
Than by destruction dwell in doubtful joy.

[*Enter* Macbeth.]

How now, my lord? Why do you keep alone,
Of sorriest fancies your companions making,
10 Using those thoughts which should indeed have died
With them they think on? Things without all remedy
Should be without regard. What's done is done.

Macbeth. We have scorched the snake, not killed it.
She'll close and be herself whilst our poor malice
15 Remains in danger of her former tooth.
But let the frame of things disjoint, both the worlds suffer,
Ere we will eat our meal in fear, and sleep
In the affliction of these terrible dreams
That shake us nightly. Better be with the dead,
20 Whom we, to gain our peace, have sent to peace,
Than on the torture of the mind to lie
In restless ecstasy. Duncan is in his grave.
After life's fitful fever he sleeps well.
Treason has done his worst; nor steel nor poison,
25 Malice domestic, foreign levy, nothing
Can touch him further.

Lady Macbeth.   Come on, gentle my lord,
Sleek o'er your rugged looks. Be bright and jovial
Among your guests tonight.

Macbeth.   So shall I, love,
And so I pray be you. Let your remembrance
30 Apply to Banquo; present him eminence
Both with eye and tongue: unsafe the while that we
Must lave our honors in these flattering streams
And make our faces vizards to our hearts,
Disguising what they are.

Lady Macbeth.   You must leave this.

35 **Macbeth.** O, full of scorpions is my mind, dear wife!
Thou know'st that Banquo and his Fleance lives.

Lady Macbeth. But in them Nature's copy's not eterne.

Macbeth. There's comfort yet; they are assailable.
Then be thou jocund. Ere the bat hath flown
40 His cloistered flight, ere to black Hecate's summons
The shard-borne beetle with his drowsy hums
Hath rung night's yawning peal, there shall be done
A deed of dreadful note.

Lady Macbeth.   What's to be done?

16–22 He would rather have the world fall apart (**the frame of things disjoint**) than be afflicted with such fears and nightmares. Death is preferable to life on the torture rack of mental anguish (**restless ecstasy**).

27 sleek: smooth.

30 present him eminence: pay special attention to him.

32 lave . . . streams: wash (**lave**) our honor in streams of flattery—that is, falsify our feelings.

33 vizards: masks.

37 in them . . . not eterne: Nature did not give them immortality.

39–43 jocund: cheerful; merry; **Ere the bat . . . note:** Before nightfall, when the bats and beetles fly, something dreadful will happen.

TO CHALLENGE STUDENTS . . .

Analyze Tragic Flaw Have students review the conversation between Macbeth and the murderers in Scene 1 and the dialogue between Macbeth and Lady Macbeth in Scene 2. Then have students write a paragraph explaining how Macbeth manipulates the murderers into agreeing to do his bidding. Ask students to include in their analysis details that show how the planning of this murder differs from the planning of Duncan's murder—and how this change signals a change in Macbeth's character and a deepening of his tragic flaw. Work with students to create a format for sharing their analyses.

Macbeth. Be innocent of the knowledge, dearest chuck,
45 Till thou applaud the deed.—Come, seeling night,
Scarf up the tender eye of pitiful day,
And with thy bloody and invisible hand
Cancel and tear to pieces that great bond
Which keeps me pale. Light thickens, and the crow
50 Makes wing to th' rooky wood.
Good things of day begin to droop and drowse,
Whiles night's black agents to their preys do rouse.—
Thou marvel'st at my words, but hold thee still.
Things bad begun make strong themselves by ill.
55 So prithee go with me.

[*They exit.*]

Scene 3 *A park near the palace.*

[*Enter three* Murderers.]

First Murderer. But who did bid thee join with us?

Third Murderer.   Macbeth.

Second Murderer [*to the* First Murderer].
He needs not our mistrust, since he delivers
Our offices and what we have to do
To the direction just.

First Murderer.   Then stand with us.—
5 The west yet glimmers with some streaks of day.
Now spurs the lated traveler apace
To gain the timely inn, and near approaches
The subject of our watch.

Third Murderer.   Hark, I hear horses.

Banquo [*within*]. Give us a light there, ho!

Second Murderer.   Then 'tis he. The rest
10 That are within the note of expectation
Already are i' th' court.

First Murderer.   His horses go about.

Third Murderer. Almost a mile; but he does usually
(So all men do) from hence to th' palace gate
Make it their walk.

[*Enter* Banquo *and* Fleance, *with a torch.*]

Second Murderer. A light, a light!

Third Murderer.   'Tis he.

15 **First Murderer.** Stand to 't.

Banquo. It will be rain tonight.

---

44 chuck: a term of affection.
45 seeling: blinding.

48 great bond: Banquo's life.

50 rooky: gloomy; also, filled with rooks, or crows.

54 Things brought about through evil need additional evil to make them strong.

2–5 He needs . . . just: Macbeth should not be distrustful, since he gave us the orders (**offices**) and we plan to follow his directions exactly.

6 lated: tardy; late.

9 Give us a light: Banquo, nearing the palace, calls for servants to bring a light.

9–11 Then 'tis . . . court: It must be Banquo, since all the other expected guests are already in the palace.

15 Stand to 't: Be prepared.

The Tragedy of Macbeth, Act III, Scene 3   439

© Houghton Mifflin Harcourt Publishing Company

ENGLISH LEARNER SUPPORT

Summarize the Drama Guide students to summarize Act III, Scene 2, using the following supports with students at varying proficiency levels:

- Ask students who is in Act III, Scene 2. Have students point to the speaker tags in this scene and copy the names into a simplified version of the chart below. **SUBSTANTIAL**

- Have partners work together to ask and answer Where? Who? What? questions about Act III, Scene 2, and add their responses to a chart like the one below. **MODERATE/LIGHT**

Act III, Scene 2	
Where?	*Macbeth's palace at Forres*
Who?	*Macbeth and Lady Macbeth*
What?	*Macbeth tells Lady Macbeth that something awful will happen to Banquo and Fleance before nightfall. He doesn't tell her details.*

ENGLISH LEARNER SUPPORT

Make Predictions to Aid Comprehension Before students begin reading Scene 3, invite them to make predictions about what they think will happen to Banquo and Fleance. Provide frames to scaffold their predictions:

I think that _____ and _____ will _____.

I think that the murderers will _____.

I think Macbeth will _____.

Ask more proficient students to use *because* to supply a reason for each of their predictions. **ALL LEVELS**

IMPROVE READING FLUENCY

Targeted Passage Have students echo read as you read Macbeth's speech to Lady Macbeth in Act III, Scene 2, lines 45–55. Before you read, mark short segments of the speech (such as a line or a sentence). Read aloud each section with the appropriate pacing, intonation, and expression and have students echo read as they follow along in their text. After students have echo read the entire speech, have them work in pairs to improve their fluency using this passage.

As one partner reads, have the other partner use a clock or a stopwatch to time the reader to see how long it takes to read the entire passage. Then see if the reader can reduce his or her time on another try. Circulate throughout the room to make sure students are reading fluently and with expression. Have pairs trade roles so that both students have gotten a chance to read and to keep time.

 Go to the **Reading Studio** for additional support in developing fluency.

TEACH

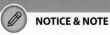

First Murderer.   Let it come down!

[*The three* Murderers *attack.*]

18 Thou mayst revenge: You might live to avenge my death.

Banquo. O, treachery! Fly, good Fleance, fly, fly, fly!
Thou mayst revenge—O slave!

[*He dies.* Fleance *exits.*]

Third Murderer. Who did strike out the light?

19 Was 't not the way: Isn't that what we were supposed to do?

First Murderer.   Was 't not the way?

20 **Third Murderer.** There's but one down. The son is fled.

Second Murderer. We have lost best half of our affair.

First Murderer. Well, let's away and say how much is done.

[*They exit.*]

Scene 4   *The hall in the palace.*

[*Banquet prepared. Enter* Macbeth, Lady Macbeth, Ross, Lennox, Lords, *and* Attendants.]

1 your own degrees: where your rank entitles you to sit.

Macbeth. You know your own degrees; sit down. At first
And last, the hearty welcome.

[*They sit.*]

Lords.   Thanks to your Majesty.

Macbeth. Ourself will mingle with society
And play the humble host.

5 keeps her state: sits on her throne rather than at the banquet table.

5 Our hostess keeps her state, but in best time
We will require her welcome.

Lady Macbeth. Pronounce it for me, sir, to all our friends,
For my heart speaks they are welcome.

[*Enter* First Murderer *to the door.*]

Macbeth. See, they encounter thee with their hearts' thanks.

10 Both sides are even. Here I'll sit i' th' midst.

11 measure: toast. Macbeth keeps talking to his wife and guests as he casually edges toward the door to speak privately with the murderer.

Be large in mirth. Anon we'll drink a measure
The table round. [*Approaching the* Murderer] There's blood upon
    thy face.

Murderer. 'Tis Banquo's then.

Macbeth. 'Tis better thee without than he within.

15 dispatched: killed.

15 Is he dispatched?

Murderer. My lord, his throat is cut. That I did for him.

Macbeth. Thou art the best o' th' cutthroats,
Yet he's good that did the like for Fleance.

19 nonpareil: best.

If thou didst it, thou art the nonpareil.

20 **Murderer.** Most royal sir, Fleance is 'scaped.

WHEN STUDENTS STRUGGLE . . .

Read Aloud   Tell students that one way to better understand Shakespeare's language is to read it aloud. Read aloud Scene 4, lines 12–32, as students follow along in their text. Then discuss the meaning of the passage and ask students to rephrase the language using modern phrases and words. Next have pairs of students practice reading the lines to one another. Ask students to describe how reading aloud helped them better understand the language.

 For additional support, go to the **Reading Studio** and assign the following ⬛ **Level Up Tutorial: Paraphrasing.**

Macbeth [*aside*]. Then comes my fit again. I had else been
   perfect,
Whole as the marble, founded as the rock,
As broad and general as the casing air.
But now I am cabined, cribbed, confined, bound in
25 To saucy doubts and fears.—But Banquo's safe?

Murderer. Ay, my good lord. Safe in a ditch he bides,
With twenty trenchèd gashes on his head,
The least a death to nature.

Macbeth.   Thanks for that.
There the grown serpent lies. The worm that's fled
30 Hath nature that in time will venom breed,
No teeth for th' present. Get thee gone. Tomorrow
We'll hear ourselves again.

[*Murderer exits.*]

Lady Macbeth.   My royal lord,
You do not give the cheer. The feast is sold
That is not often vouched, while 'tis a-making,
35 'Tis given with welcome. To feed were best at home;
From thence, the sauce to meat is ceremony;
Meeting were bare without it.

[*Enter the Ghost of* Banquo, *and sits in* Macbeth's *place.*]

Macbeth [*to* Lady Macbeth]. Sweet remembrancer!—
Now, good digestion wait on appetite
And health on both!

Lennox.   May't please your Highness sit.

40 Macbeth. Here had we now our country's honor roofed,
Were the graced person of our Banquo present,
Who may I rather challenge for unkindness
Than pity for mischance.

Ross.   His absence, sir,
Lays blame upon his promise. Please 't your Highness
45 To grace us with your royal company?

Macbeth. The table's full.

Lennox.   Here is a place reserved, sir.

Macbeth. Where?

Lennox. Here, my good lord. What is 't that moves your Highness?

Macbeth. Which of you have done this?

Lords.   What, my good lord?

50 Macbeth [*to the* Ghost]. Thou canst not say I did it. Never shake
Thy gory locks at me.

23 casing: surrounding.

29 worm: little serpent, that is, Fleance.

31 no teeth for th' present: too young to cause harm right now.

32 hear ourselves: talk together.

32–37 Macbeth must not forget his duties as host. A feast will be no different from a meal that one pays for unless the host gives his guests courteous attention (**ceremony**), the best part of any meal.

37 sweet remembrancer: a term of affection for his wife, who has reminded him of his duty.

40–43 The best people of Scotland would all be under Macbeth's roof if Banquo were present too. He hopes Banquo's absence is due to rudeness rather than to some accident (**mischance**).

46 Macbeth notices Banquo's ghost sitting in the king's chair.

ENGLISH LEARNER SUPPORT

Understand Figurative Language Read aloud Scene 4, lines 25–32. Guide students to interpret the murderer's statement that Banquo is "safe in a ditch." *(Banquo is dead, and his corpse is lying in a ditch. Banquo is not "safe" in the sense that he is protected; rather, he is securely out of the picture and no longer a danger to Macbeth.)*

Then ask students to paraphrase the sentence in lines 29–31. Point out that Macbeth is using a **metaphor**—a creative comparison between two things. Ask students to identify "the grown serpent" *(Banquo)* and "the worm" *(Fleance, Banquo's son).* Explain that the *venom* of a snake is poison that can kill a person. Ask students to explore figurative meanings for venom in this context. *(a desire for revenge)* Then have them interpret the entire metaphor. *(Fleance might kill Macbeth to avenge his father's murder; he might have children, helping to ensure that the prophecy given to Banquo—that Banquo's descendants will rule as kings in the future—will come true.)*

MODERATE/LIGHT

APPLYING ACADEMIC VOCABULARY

❑ comprise   ❑ incidence   ❑ predominant   ☑ priority   ☑ ultimate

Write and Discuss Have students turn to a partner to discuss the following questions regarding Lady Macbeth's response to her husband's actions at the feast (lines 32–37). Guide students to include the academic vocabulary words *priority* and *ultimate* in their responses. Ask volunteers to share their responses with the class.

• What does Lady Macbeth feel should be her husband's **priority** at this feast? Why?

• What seems to be the **ultimate** goal for having this feast? How does Macbeth's behavior threaten that goal?

ENGLISH LEARNER SUPPORT

Act Out Dialogue Direct students to the dialogue in Scene 4, lines 46–60. Assign the roles of Macbeth, Lennox, Lords, and Ross. Take on the role of Lady Macbeth, or assign it to a fluent reader. Have a volunteer play the role of Banquo's Ghost. Tell other students to familiarize themselves with the lines so that they can follow along in their texts.

Have students review their lines. Help them read the dialogue and clarify any unfamiliar words or phrases, such as the following: "Never shake / Thy gory locks at me" (*Don't shake your bloody hair at me*), "fit" (*strange behavior*), "extend his passion" (*make him keep doing what he's doing*), "Feed and regard him not" (*Keep eating and don't pay any attention to him*).

Then do a staged reading of lines 46–60. Ask students to explain why Macbeth sees the Ghost. (*He is feeling guilty because he had Banquo murdered.*)

MODERATE/LIGHT

NOTICE & NOTE

Ross. Gentlemen, rise. His Highness is not well.

Lady Macbeth. Sit, worthy friends. My lord is often thus
And hath been from his youth. Pray you, keep seat.
55 The fit is momentary; upon a thought
He will again be well. If much you note him
You shall offend him and extend his passion.
Feed and regard him not. [*Drawing* Macbeth *aside*] Are you a man?

Macbeth. Ay, and a bold one, that dare look on that
60 Which might appall the devil.

60–68 She dismisses his hallucination as utter nonsense (**proper stuff**). His outbursts (**flaws and starts**) are the product of imaginary fears (**impostors to true fear**) and are unmanly, the kind of behavior described in a woman's story.

Lady Macbeth.   O, proper stuff!
This is the very painting of your fear.
This is the air-drawn dagger which you said
Led you to Duncan. O, these flaws and starts,
Impostors to true fear, would well become
65 A woman's story at a winter's fire,
Authorized by her grandam. Shame itself!
Why do you make such faces? When all's done,
You look but on a stool.

Macbeth. Prithee see there. Behold, look! [*To the* Ghost] Lo, how
    say you?
70 Why, what care I? If thou canst nod, speak too.—
If charnel houses and our graves must send
Those that we bury back, our monuments
Shall be the maws of kites.

71–73 If burial vaults (**charnel houses**) give back the dead, then we may as well throw our bodies to the birds (**kites**), whose stomachs (**maws**) will become our tombs (**monuments**).

[Ghost *exits*.]

Lady Macbeth.   What, quite unmanned in folly?

Macbeth. If I stand here, I saw him.

Lady Macbeth.   Fie, for shame!

75 **Macbeth.** Blood hath been shed ere now, i' th' olden time,
Ere humane statute purged the gentle weal;
Ay, and since too, murders have been performed
Too terrible for the ear. The time has been
That, when the brains were out, the man would die,
80 And there an end. But now they rise again
With twenty mortal murders on their crowns
And push us from our stools. This is more strange
Than such a murder is.

75–78 Macbeth desperately tries to justify his murder of Banquo. Murder has been common from ancient times to the present, though laws (**humane statute**) have tried to rid civilized society (**gentle weal**) of violence.

Lady Macbeth.   My worthy lord,
Your noble friends do lack you.

Macbeth.   I do forget.—
85 Do not muse at me, my most worthy friends.
I have a strange infirmity, which is nothing

85 muse: wonder.

Dmitry Belosselskiy and Zeljko Lucic perform Guiseppe Verdi's opera 'Macbeth', directed by Peter Stein and conducted by Ricardo Muti, Salzburg, 2011.

To those that know me. Come, love and health to all.
Then I'll sit down.—Give me some wine. Fill full.

[*Enter* Ghost.]

I drink to the general joy o' th' whole table
90 And to our dear friend Banquo, whom we miss.
Would he were here! To all and him we thirst,
And all to all.

Lords.   Our duties, and the pledge.

[*They raise their drinking cups.*]

Macbeth [*to the* Ghost]. Avaunt, and quit my sight! Let the earth
   hide thee.
Thy bones are marrowless; thy blood is cold;
95 Thou hast no speculation in those eyes
Which thou dost glare with.

Lady Macbeth.   Think of this, good peers,
But as a thing of custom. 'Tis no other;
Only it spoils the pleasure of the time.

Macbeth [*to the* Ghost]. What man dare, I dare.
100 Approach thou like the rugged Russian bear,
The armed rhinoceros, or th' Hyrcan tiger;
Take any shape but that, and my firm nerves
Shall never tremble. Or be alive again
And dare me to the desert with thy sword.
105 If trembling I inhabit then, protest me
The baby of a girl. Hence, horrible shadow!
Unreal mock'ry, hence!

[Ghost *exits.*]

               Why, so, being gone,
I am a man again.—Pray you sit still.

Lady Macbeth. You have displaced the mirth, broke the good
   meeting

ANALYZE DRAMA

Annotate: Mark words that reflect happiness and love in lines 87–92.

Analyze: What is ironic about these expressions, given what Macbeth has done and what he is seeing?

93–96 avaunt: go away. Macbeth tells Banquo that he is only a ghost, with unreal bones, cold blood, and no consciousness (**speculation**).

99–104 Macbeth would be willing to face Banquo in any other form, even his living self.

105–106 If trembling ... girl: If I still tremble, call me a girl's doll.

The Tragedy of Macbeth, Act III, Scene 4   443

ANALYZE DRAMA

Have a student read aloud lines 87–92. Then call on others to describe the scene, or what they would imagine they would see if they were in the audience at a performance of the play. (*There's a great hall, lit with candles. Lords and ladies are seated at large tables filled with food and drink. Everyone is talking and laughing until Macbeth makes his toast.*) Reread the toast itself before students answer the question. Remind students that **irony** is a contrast between appearance and reality—here, what Macbeth says and what he is really thinking. (**Answer:** *It is ironic that Macbeth is wishing all his worthy friends love, joy, and health because he is hallucinating that his good friend, who he has just had murdered, is haunting and accusing him. His words are in stark contrast with what he has done and now is experiencing.*)

WHEN STUDENTS STRUGGLE . . .

Analyze Dramatic Irony Have small groups use the following instructions to analyze the dramatic irony in Scene 4:

- Review lines 60–122 and pay close attention to the stage directions.
- Underline words Macbeth speaks that would confuse his guests.
- Circle words that Lady Macbeth speaks to excuse Macbeth's behavior.
- Discuss how the guests perceive Macbeth.

 For additional support, go to the **Reading Studio** and assign the following LEVEL UP **Level Up Tutorial: Irony.**

ENGLISH LEARNER SUPPORT

Summarize the Drama Guide students to summarize Act III, Scene 4, using the following supports with students at varying proficiency levels:

- Ask students who is in Act III, Scene 4. Have students point to the speaker tags in this scene and copy the names into a simplified version of the chart below. **SUBSTANTIAL**

- Have partners work together to ask and answer Where? Who? What? questions about Act III, Scene 4, and add their responses to a chart like the one below. **MODERATE/LIGHT**

Act III, Scene 4	
Where?	The hall in the palace
Who?	Macbeth, Lady Macbeth, Ross, Lennox, Lords, Attendants, Ghost, Murderer
What?	Macbeth learns that Banquo is dead and Fleance escaped. Banquo's ghost enters the hall and sits in Macbeth's place. Lennox asks Macbeth to sit. Macbeth starts talking to the Ghost, whom no one else can see. Lady Macbeth tries to explain his behavior to the guests but finally asks everyone to leave.

ANALYZE CHARACTER AND THEME

Remind students that a playwright develops a **theme,** or a message about life or human nature, throughout the course of a drama. Readers make inferences about the developments of a theme based on details found in the text. Have students reread lines 134–144 and find text evidence that shows Macbeth has gone too far in his quest for power. Discuss the theme that this evidence develops. (**Answers will vary:** *Students should provide a statement about life or human nature that has to do with ambition; ambition has driven Macbeth to the point of no return.*)

NOTICE & NOTE

110 admired: astonishing.

110–116 Macbeth is bewildered by his wife's calm, which makes him seem a stranger to himself (**strange even to the disposition that I owe**): she has all the courage, while he is white (**blanched**) with fear.

119 Stand . . . going: Don't worry about the proper formalities of leaving.

122–126 Macbeth fears that Banquo's murder (**it**) will be revenged by his own murder. Stones, trees, or talking birds (**maggot pies and choughs and rooks**) may reveal the hidden knowledge (**augurs**) of his guilt.

128–129 How say'st . . . bidding: What do you think of Macduff's refusal to come?

131–132 Macbeth has paid (**fee'd**) household servants to spy on every noble, including Macduff.

133 betimes: early.

ANALYZE CHARACTER AND THEME

Annotate: Reread lines 134–144 and mark words that indicate Macbeth has gone too far in his quest for power.

Evaluate: What theme is being developed in this scene?

142–144 His vision of the ghost (**strange and self-abuse**) is only the result of a beginner's fear (**initiate fear**), to be cured with practice (**hard use**).

110 With most admired disorder.

Macbeth.   Can such things be
And overcome us like a summer's cloud,
Without our special wonder? You make me strange
Even to the disposition that I owe,
When now I think you can behold such sights
115 And keep the natural ruby of your cheeks
When mine is blanched with fear.

Ross.   What sights, my lord?

Lady Macbeth. I pray you speak not. He grows worse and worse.
Question enrages him. At once, good night.
Stand not upon the order of your going,
120 But go at once.

Lennox.   Good night, and better health
Attend his Majesty.

Lady Macbeth.   A kind good night to all.

[*Lords and all but* Macbeth *and* Lady Macbeth *exit.*]

Macbeth. It will have blood, they say; blood will have blood.
Stones have been known to move, and trees to speak;
Augurs and understood relations have
125 By maggot pies and choughs and rooks brought forth
The secret'st man of blood.—What is the night?

Lady Macbeth. Almost at odds with morning, which is which.

Macbeth. How say'st thou that Macduff denies his person
At our great bidding?

Lady Macbeth.   Did you send to him, sir?

130 **Macbeth.** I hear it by the way; but I will send.
There's not a one of them but in his house
I keep a servant fee'd. I will tomorrow
(And betimes I will) to the Weïrd Sisters.
More shall they speak, for now I am bent to know
135 By the worst means the worst. For mine own good,
All causes shall give way. I am in blood
Stepped in so far that, should I wade no more,
Returning were as tedious as go o'er.
Strange things I have in head, that will to hand,
140 Which must be acted ere they may be scanned.

Lady Macbeth. You lack the season of all natures, sleep.

Macbeth. Come, we'll to sleep. My strange and self-abuse
Is the initiate fear that wants hard use.
We are yet but young in deed.

[*They exit.*]

ENGLISH LEARNER SUPPORT

Using Side Notes Students may struggle with heavily glossed passages, such as lines 121–144 on page 444. Review the side notes as a class. Then, read short sections of the text aloud. Have students listen carefully and then summarize to a partner what they have heard. As students explain what they think is taking place, discuss their responses and help them correct any misunderstandings. Finally, ask students how they would describe Macbeth at this point. (*Macbeth seems worried and somewhat paranoid—perhaps even crazy. He fears that Macduff is plotting against him, so he has paid servants to be spies in Macduff's house. Macbeth has become less moral. He plans to talk to the witches.*) **ALL LEVELS**

Scene 5 *A heath.*

[*Thunder. Enter the three* Witches, *meeting* Hecate.]

First Witch. Why, how now, Hecate? You look angerly.

Hecate. Have I not reason, beldams as you are,
Saucy and overbold, how did you dare
To trade and traffic with Macbeth
5 In riddles and affairs of death,
And I, the mistress of your charms,
The close contriver of all harms,
Was never called to bear my part
Or show the glory of our art?
10 And which is worse, all you have done
Hath been but for a wayward son,
Spiteful and wrathful, who, as others do,
Loves for his own ends, not for you.
But make amends now. Get you gone,
15 And at the pit of Acheron
Meet me i' th' morning. Thither he
Will come to know his destiny.
Your vessels and your spells provide,
Your charms and everything beside.
20 I am for th' air. This night I'll spend
Unto a dismal and a fatal end.
Great business must be wrought ere noon.
Upon the corner of the moon
There hangs a vap'rous drop profound.
25 I'll catch it ere it come to ground,
And that, distilled by magic sleights,
Shall raise such artificial sprites
As by the strength of their illusion
Shall draw him on to his confusion.
30 He shall spurn fate, scorn death, and bear
His hopes 'bove wisdom, grace, and fear.
And you all know, security
Is mortals' chiefest enemy.

[*Music and a song*]

Hark! I am called. My little spirit, see,
35 Sits in a foggy cloud and stays for me.

[Hecate *exits.*]

[*Sing within "Come away, come away," etc.*]

First Witch. Come, let's make haste. She'll soon be back again.

[*They exit.*]

2 beldams: hags.

13 loves . . . you: cares only about his own goals, not about you.

15 Acheron: a river in hell, according to Greek mythology.

20–21 This . . . end: Tonight I'm working for a disastrous (**dismal**) and fatal end for Macbeth.

23–29 Hecate will obtain a magical drop from the moon, treat it with secret art, and so create spirits (**artificial sprites**) that will lead Macbeth to his destruction (**confusion**).

34–35 Hecate has a demon helper (**my little spirit**), to which she is raised by pulley to "the heavens" of the stage.

The Tragedy of Macbeth, Act III, Scene 5 445

ENGLISH LEARNER SUPPORT

Summarize the Drama Explain that in Greek myth, Hecate was a goddess who ruled over magic and spells. Point out that in Shakespeare's play, she is the source of the witches' magic ("the mistress of [their] charms"). Then guide students to summarize Act III, Scene 5, using the following supports with students at varying proficiency levels:

- Ask students who is in Act III, Scene 5. Have students point to the speaker tags in this scene and copy the names into a simplified version of the chart below. **SUBSTANTIAL**

- Have partners work together to ask and answer Where? Who? What? questions about Act III, Scene 5, and add their responses to a chart like the one below. **MODERATE/LIGHT**

Act III, Scene 5	
Where?	*A heath (open field)*
Who?	*Hecate, the witches*
What?	*Hecate scolds the witches. She tells them that they should have come to her before they spoke to Macbeth. Then she tells them that she will prepare a terrible way to destroy Macbeth.*

CLOSE READ SCREENCAST

Modeled Discussion In their eBook, have students view the Close Read Screencast, in which readers discuss and annotate Scene 5, lines 23–33.

ENGLISH LEARNER SUPPORT

Summarize the Drama Guide students to summarize Act III, Scene 6, using the following supports with students at varying proficiency levels:

• Ask students who is in Act III, Scene 6. Have students point to the speaker tags in this scene and copy the names into a simplified version of the chart below. **SUBSTANTIAL**

• Have partners work together to ask and answer Where? Who? What? questions about Act III, Scene 6, and add their responses to a chart like the one below. **MODERATE/LIGHT**

Act III, Scene 6	
Where?	Macbeth's palace at Forres
Who?	Lennox, a Lord
What?	Lennox still believes that Malcolm and Donalbain killed Duncan. He also believes that Fleance killed Banquo. Lennox says that Macbeth is angry with Macduff, who has gone to get the support of the King of England.

NOTICE & NOTE

1–3 Lennox and the other lord have shared suspicions of Macbeth.

6–7 Fleeing the scene of the crime must make Fleance guilty of his father's murder.

8–10 Everyone agrees on the horror of Duncan's murder by his sons.

12 pious: holy.

21 from broad words: because of his frank talk.

24 bestows himself: is staying

25 Macbeth keeps Malcolm from his rightful throne.

27 Edward: Edward the Confessor, king of England from 1042 to 1066, a man known for his virtue and religion.

28–29 that ... respect: Despite his bad fortune, Malcolm is treated respectfully by Edward.

29–37 Macduff wants the king to persuade the people of Northumberland and their earl, Siward, to join Malcolm's cause.

Scene 6 *The palace at Forres.*

[*Enter* Lennox *and another* Lord.]

Lennox. My former speeches have but hit your thoughts,
Which can interpret farther. Only I say
Things have been strangely borne. The gracious Duncan
Was pitied of Macbeth; marry, he was dead.
5 And the right valiant Banquo walked too late,
Whom you may say, if 't please you, Fleance killed,
For Fleance fled. Men must not walk too late.
Who cannot want the thought how monstrous
It was for Malcolm and for Donalbain
10 To kill their gracious father? Damnèd fact,
How it did grieve Macbeth! Did he not straight
In pious rage the two delinquents tear
That were the slaves of drink and thralls of sleep?
Was not that nobly done? Ay, and wisely, too,
15 For 'twould have angered any heart alive
To hear the men deny 't. So that I say
He has borne all things well. And I do think
That had he Duncan's sons under his key
(As, an 't please heaven, he shall not) they should find
20 What 'twere to kill a father. So should Fleance.
But peace. For from broad words, and 'cause he failed
His presence at the tyrant's feast, I hear
Macduff lives in disgrace. Sir, can you tell
Where he bestows himself?

Lord.   The son of Duncan
25 (From whom this tyrant holds the due of birth)
Lives in the English court and is received
Of the most pious Edward with such grace
That the malevolence of fortune nothing
Takes from his high respect. Thither Macduff
30 Is gone to pray the holy king upon his aid
To wake Northumberland and warlike Siward
That, by the help of these (with Him above
To ratify the work), we may again
Give to our tables meat, sleep to our nights,
35 Free from our feasts and banquets bloody knives,
Do faithful homage, and receive free honors,
All which we pine for now. And this report
Hath so exasperate the King that he
Prepares for some attempt of war.

Lennox.   Sent he to Macduff?

WHEN STUDENTS STRUGGLE . . .

Summarize to Check Understanding Summarizing a complex text can help students monitor their comprehension and predict plot events. Guide students to use the dialogue in Act III, Scene 6, to recall the main events of Act III. Then show students how to use a timeline or a sequence chart to list events in order. Also display a web diagram to group important events around main characters. Then have students choose an organizer to summarize events in Act III on their own.

 For additional support, go to the **Reading Studio** and assign the following Level Up Tutorial: **Summarizing.**

40 **Lord.** He did, and with an absolute "Sir, not I,"
The cloudy messenger turns me his back
And hums, as who should say, "You'll rue the time
That clogs me with this answer."

    Lennox.   And that well might
Advise him to a caution t' hold what distance
45 His wisdom can provide. Some holy angel
Fly to the court of England and unfold
His message ere he come, that a swift blessing
May soon return to this our suffering country
Under a hand accursed.

    Lord.   I'll send my prayers with him.

[*They exit.*]

40–43 The messenger, fearing Macbeth's anger, was unhappy (**cloudy**) with Macduff's refusal to cooperate. Because Macduff burdens (**clogs**) him with bad news, he will not hurry back.

CHECK YOUR UNDERSTANDING

Answer these questions before moving on to the **Analyze the Text** section on the following page.

1 How does Macbeth attempt to solve a problem in Act III?

  A He tries to get past his guilt for Duncan's murder by admitting what he has done.

  B He attempts to have Banquo and Fleance killed to end a line of future kings.

  C He returns to visit the witches a second time because the prophecy is not working.

  D He resolves to have all of his opponents murdered because he feels insecure in his power.

2 How does Macbeth's guilt become apparent at the banquet?

  F Lady Macbeth must speak for him.

  G He feels ill and has to leave early.

  H He sees the ghost of Banquo.

  J He confesses his crimes to the gathering.

3 At the end of Act III, Macduff has traveled to England to —

  A hide in safety as he fears for his life

  B find Malcolm and return him to Scotland

  C pursue the men he believes murdered Duncan

  D ask the king for help in dealing with Macbeth

The Tragedy of Macbeth, Act III   447

CHECK YOUR UNDERSTANDING

Have students answer the questions independently.

Answers:

1. *B*

2. *H*

3. *D*

If they answer any questions incorrectly, have them reread the text to confirm their understanding. Then they may proceed to ANALYZE THE TEXT on page 448.

ENGLISH LEARNER SUPPORT

Oral Assessment Use the following questions to assess students' comprehension and speaking skills. Ask students to respond in short, complete sentences.

1. *Macbeth tries to have ___ and ___ killed.* (*Macbeth tries to have Banquo and Fleance killed.*)

2. *At the banquet, Macbeth sees the ghost of ___.* (*At the banquet, Macbeth sees the ghost of Banquo.*)

3. *Does Macduff want help from the king of England?* (*Yes. Macduff wants help from the king of England.*)
   SUBSTANTIAL/MODERATE

ANALYZE THE TEXT

Possible answers:

1. **DOK 2:** *Macbeth feels threatened because the prophecy states that Banquo's sons will be kings. His hiring of the murderers may reflect his aversion to murdering his allies, or it may simply reflect his heightened status.*

2. **DOK 4:** *Lady Macbeth wants to get on with their lives as king and queen, but Macbeth is filled with regret. A lack of trust seems to have entered the relationship: Macbeth will not tell Lady Macbeth that he plans to have Banquo and Fleance killed, but he expects her to be pleased once it is done.*

3. **DOK 3:** *The witches' prophecy may indeed come true. Fleance survives and is available to succeed Macbeth as King of Scotland.*

4. **DOK 4:** *Banquo's ghost represents Macbeth's guilt and fear. Lady Macbeth remains calm but is becoming angry with Macbeth; she publicly supports her husband but privately bullies and cajoles him to be strong.*

5. **DOK 3:** *Macbeth realizes that he has done horrible things and feels trapped because he is in too deep to turn back now. His earlier actions were driven by ambition. Now, they seem driven by self-preservation.*

CREATE AND DISCUSS

Tell students to identify the scene number as well as the lines of dialogue. Then have them complete the activity. *(Strong examples of dramatic irony include Macbeth's friendliness toward Banquo in Scene 1, Fleance's escape in Scene 3, and Macbeth and Lady Macbeth's attempts to appear as gracious hosts at the banquet in Scene 4.)*

 RESPOND

ANALYZE THE TEXT

Support your responses with evidence from the text. ☰ NOTEBOOK

1. **Infer** Reread lines 47–56 in Scene 1. Why does Macbeth fear Banquo and feel threatened by his "being"? What is suggested about Macbeth's character through his action of hiring murderers to carry out his plan?

2. **Analyze** Review Scene 2. How has Duncan's murder affected the relationship between Macbeth and Lady Macbeth? Cite evidence from the text to support your ideas.

3. **Draw Conclusions** What does Fleance's escape suggest about the witches' prophecy?

4. **Analyze** What does Banquo's ghost in Scene 4 represent? Explain how the presence of the ghost affects Lady Macbeth's behavior even though she cannot see it.

5. **Compare** Review lines 135–140 in Scene 4. What does Macbeth realize, and in what way does this speech reveal a change in Macbeth's attitude from how he has felt in the past about his deeds?

CREATE AND DISCUSS

Share an Analysis How does dramatic irony intensify the impact of Act III?

❏ With a partner, identify the strongest instances of dramatic irony in Act III. Complete the chart below with details from those instances. Discuss how these instances affect the audience's understanding of Macbeth's character.

LINES	WHAT CHARACTERS DO OR SAY	WHAT THE AUDIENCE KNOWS

❏ Form a group with other students, and present your ideas about the impact of dramatic irony on the audience's understanding of Macbeth's character. Listen to their ideas, and arrive at a common analysis.

Go the **Speaking and Listening Studio** for more on conducting a group discussion.

SETTING A PURPOSE

As you read, refer to your character diagram and add any new information you learn in Act IV about the characters and their relationships.

ACT IV

Scene 1 *A cave. In the middle, a boiling cauldron.*

[*Thunder. Enter the three* Witches.]

First Witch. Thrice the brinded cat hath mewed.

Second Witch. Thrice, and once the hedge-pig whined.

Third Witch. Harpier cries "'Tis time, 'tis time!"

First Witch. Round about the cauldron go;
5 In the poisoned entrails throw.
Toad, that under cold stone
Days and nights has thirty-one
Sweltered venom sleeping got,
Boil thou first i' th' charmed pot.

[*The* Witches *circle the cauldron.*]

10 **All.** Double, double toil and trouble;
Fire burn, and cauldron bubble.

Second Witch. Fillet of a fenny snake
In the cauldron boil and bake.
Eye of newt and toe of frog,
15 Wool of bat and tongue of dog,
Adder's fork and blindworm's sting,
Lizard's leg and howlet's wing,
For a charm of powerful trouble,
Like a hell-broth boil and bubble.

20 **All.** Double, double toil and trouble;
Fire burn, and cauldron bubble.

Third Witch. Scale of dragon, tooth of wolf,
Witch's mummy, maw and gulf
Of the ravined salt-sea shark,
25 Root of hemlock digged i' th' dark,
Liver of blaspheming Jew,
Gall of goat and slips of yew
Slivered in the moon's eclipse,
Nose of Turk and Tartar's lips,
30 Finger of birth-strangled babe

1–3 Magical signals and the call of the Third Witch's attending demon (**harpier**) tell the Witches to begin.

4–34 The Witches are stirring up a magical stew to bring trouble to humanity. Their recipe includes intestines (**entrails, chaudron**), a slice (**fillet**) of snake, eye of salamander (**newt**), snake tongue (**adder's fork**), a lizard (**blindworm**), a baby owl's (**howlet's**) wing, a shark's stomach and gullet (**maw and gulf**), the finger of a baby strangled by a prostitute (**drab**), and other gruesome ingredients. They stir their brew until it is thick and slimy (**slab**).

SETTING A PURPOSE

Direct students to use the Setting a Purpose prompt to focus their reading. Remind them to keep adding to their character diagrams.

EL ENGLISH LEARNER SUPPORT

Develop Vocabulary Explain to students that they don't need to understand every word of this scene (or any scene) to understand the main events that happen in the play. Briefly introduce these terms:

cauldron	a large pot on a fire
potion	a magic mixture
round about. . . go	walk around
poison	something that will cause sickness or death
entrails	intestines and other internal organs
venom	poison
charmed pot	pot with a spell (witches' magic) on it
toil	hard work

Read aloud lines 1–38 in Scene 1 as students follow along. Ask: What are the witches doing? (*They are making a potion. They are walking around a cauldron.*) What is the mood of this scene; that is, how does this scene make you feel? (*It is dark, scary, exciting, and suspenseful.*) Ask students to predict what will happen when Macbeth comes. (*The witches may tell him more prophecies. Hecate may cast a spell on him.*)

MODERATE

WHEN STUDENTS STRUGGLE . . .

Read Aloud Tell students that they will work in groups to read lines 1–38 aloud. Each group will say the lines of one character only. Assign groups the roles of First Witch, Second Witch, and Third Witch. Have each group review their own lines as well as lines marked All. Circulate around the room and provide support as necessary. Allow ample time for groups to practice speaking. Then present a readers' theater as a class, with each group speaking its assigned lines and all groups speaking the lines marked All.

 For additional support, go to the **Reading Studio** and assign the following **Level Up Tutorial: Rhyme.**

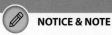

NOTICE & NOTE

Ditch-delivered by a drab,
Make the gruel thick and slab.
Add thereto a tiger's chaudron
For th' ingredience of our cauldron.

35 **All.** Double, double toil and trouble;
Fire burn, and cauldron bubble.

Second Witch. Cool it with a baboon's blood.
Then the charm is firm and good.

[*Enter* Hecate *and the other three* Witches.]

Hecate. O, well done! I commend your pains,
40 And everyone shall share i' th' gains.
And now about the cauldron sing
Like elves and fairies in a ring,
Enchanting all that you put in.

[*Music and a song: "Black Spirits," etc.* Hecate *exits.*]

Second Witch. By the pricking of my thumbs,
45 Something wicked this way comes.
Open, locks,
Whoever knocks.

[*Enter* Macbeth.]

Macbeth. How now, you secret, black, and midnight hags?
What is 't you do?

All.   A deed without a name.

50–61 Macbeth calls upon (**conjure**) the Witches in the name of their dark magic (**that which you profess**). Though they unleash winds to topple churches and make foaming (**yeasty**) waves to destroy (**confound**) ships, though they flatten wheat (**corn**) fields, destroy buildings, and reduce nature's order to chaos by mixing all seeds (**germens**) together, he demands an answer to his question.

50 **Macbeth.** I conjure you by that which you profess
(Howe'er you come to know it), answer me.
Though you untie the winds and let them fight
Against the churches, though the yeasty waves
Confound and swallow navigation up,
55 Though bladed corn be lodged and trees blown down,
Though castles topple on their warders' heads,
Though palaces and pyramids do slope
Their heads to their foundations, though the treasure
Of nature's germens tumble all together
60 Even till destruction sicken, answer me
To what I ask you.

First Witch.   Speak.

Second Witch.   Demand.

Third Witch.   We'll answer.

First Witch. Say if th' hadst rather hear it from our mouths
Or from our masters'.

63 masters: the demons whom the Witches serve.

Macbeth.   Call 'em. Let me see 'em.

WHEN STUDENTS STRUGGLE . . .

Confirm Understanding   Read aloud lines 50–61 and the related side note. Discuss with students how Macbeth demands to know more from the witches. Then have students review lines 68–124 and take notes on each apparition and what it foretells. Tell students to organize their notes in a chart such as this one:

Lines	Apparition	Notes
71–72	*First: an Armed Head*	*"Beware Macduff! / Beware the Thane of Fife"*
79–81	*Second: a Bloody Child*	*"none of woman born / Shall harm Macbeth"*

 For additional support, go to the **Reading Studio** and assign the following LEVEL **Level Up Tutorial: Symbols and Allegories.**

Universal Arts and Polish Cultural Institute perform *Macbeth* on stilts, Edinburgh Fringe Festival 2007, Edinburgh, Scotland.

TEACH

First Witch. Pour in sow's blood that hath eaten
65 Her nine farrow; grease that's sweaten
From the murderers' gibbet throw
Into the flame.

All.   Come high or low;
Thyself and office deftly show.

[*Thunder. First Apparition, an Armed Head.*]

Macbeth. Tell me, thou unknown power—

First Witch.   He knows thy thought.
70 Hear his speech but say thou naught.

First Apparition. Macbeth! Macbeth! Macbeth! Beware Macduff!
Beware the Thane of Fife! Dismiss me. Enough.

[*He descends.*]

Macbeth. Whate'er thou art, for thy good caution, thanks.
Thou hast harped my fear aright. But one word more—

75 **First Witch.** He will not be commanded. Here's another
More potent than the first.

[*Thunder. Second Apparition, a Bloody Child.*]

Second Apparition. Macbeth! Macbeth! Macbeth!—

Macbeth. Had I three ears, I'd hear thee.

Second Apparition. Be bloody, bold, and resolute. Laugh to scorn
80 The power of man, for none of woman born
Shall harm Macbeth.

[*He descends.*]

65–66 farrow: newborn pigs;
grease . . . gibbet: grease from a gallows where murderers were hung.

[Stage Direction] Each of the three apparitions holds a clue to Macbeth's future.

74 harped: guessed.

ANALYZE CHARACTER AND THEME

Annotate: Mark what is foretold in lines 79–81.

Predict: Consider what you know about the Witches. Can Macbeth trust this prediction? How might he act in response to it?

The Tragedy of Macbeth, Act IV, Scene 1   451

✎ **ANALYZE CHARACTER AND THEME**

Have a student read lines 79–81 aloud. Ask students to paraphrase what the Second Apparition seems to foretell for Macbeth. (*Macbeth won't be injured or killed by another person.*) After students have marked the prediction, discuss other ways that Macbeth could die if he isn't harmed by someone "of woman born." (*He could die of natural causes, or have an accident, or be killed by an animal.*) Ask students if they think that Macbeth should be worried—and, if so, why. Then ask them to share their predictions. (**Answer:** *The witches' earlier predictions for Macbeth have come true, but the result has not been positive. Macbeth should understand that this prediction is likely to be true but not good. If he were wise, he would be cautious, but he is hungry for power. If he thinks that he cannot be killed, he may stop worrying, or he may become even bolder in his actions.*)

TO CHALLENGE STUDENTS . . .

Analyze Character and Theme   Remind students that Shakespeare uses powerful imagery to shape characterization and support themes. Have students analyze and interpret Macbeth's speech in lines 50–61. Ask students to identify the images in this speech and then explain what Macbeth's speech reveals about him and about the lengths to which he will go in order to satisfy his ambition. Have students write a paragraph explaining how this scene illustrates the relationship between characterization and theme. Work with them to create a format for sharing their responses.

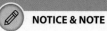

ENGLISH LEARNER SUPPORT

Make Inferences Read aloud the stage directions immediately before line 112 in Scene 1 and the side note that explains them. Then read aloud Macbeth's response to the vision in lines 112–124. Direct students to the side notes for those lines as well. Have groups of mixed proficiency review the lines and the side notes. Then have students use these sentence starters to interpret Macbeth's vision.

Macbeth sees. . . .

All eight kings. . . .

This means that Banquo's descendants. . . .

ALL LEVELS

---

84 The murder of Macduff will give Macbeth a guarantee (**bond**) of his fate and put his fears to rest.

87 issue: child.
88–89 the round and top: the crown.

90–94 The third apparition tells Macbeth to take courage. He cannot be defeated unless Birnam Wood travels the 12-mile distance to Dunsinane Hill, where his castle is located.

95 impress: force into service.
96 bodements: prophecies.
97–100 Macbeth boasts that he will never again be troubled by ghosts (**rebellious dead**) and that he will live out his expected life span (**lease of nature**). He believes he will die (**pay his breath**) by natural causes (**mortal custom**).

[Stage Direction]
A show . . . : Macbeth next sees eight kings, the last carrying a mirror (**glass**). According to legend, Fleance escaped to England, where he founded the Stuart family, to which King James belonged.

Macbeth. Then live, Macduff; what need I fear of thee?
But yet I'll make assurance double sure
And take a bond of fate. Thou shalt not live,
85 That I may tell pale-hearted fear it lies,
And sleep in spite of thunder.

[*Thunder. Third Apparition, a Child Crowned, with a tree in his hand.*]

                    What is this
That rises like the issue of a king
And wears upon his baby brow the round
And top of sovereignty?

All.   Listen, but speak not to 't.

90 **Third Apparition.** Be lion-mettled, proud, and take no care
Who chafes, who frets, or where conspirers are.
Macbeth shall never vanquished be until
Great Birnam Wood to high Dunsinane Hill
Shall come against him.   [*He descends.*]

Macbeth.   That will never be.
95 Who can impress the forest, bid the tree
Unfix his earthbound root? Sweet bodements, good!
Rebellious dead, rise never till the wood
Of Birnam rise, and our high-placed Macbeth
Shall live the lease of nature, pay his breath
100 To time and mortal custom. Yet my heart
Throbs to know one thing. Tell, if your art
Can tell so much: shall Banquo's issue ever
Reign in this kingdom?

All.   Seek to know no more.

Macbeth. I will be satisfied. Deny me this,
105 And an eternal curse fall on you! Let me know!

                    [*Cauldron sinks. Hautboys.*]
Why sinks that cauldron? And what noise is this?

First Witch. Show.

Second Witch. Show.

Third Witch. Show.

110 **All.** Show his eyes, and grieve his heart.
Come like shadows; so depart.

[*A show of eight kings, the eighth king with a glass in his hand, and* Banquo *last.*]

Macbeth. Thou art too like the spirit of Banquo. Down!
Thy crown does sear mine eyeballs. And thy hair,

WHEN STUDENTS STRUGGLE . . .

Analyze Dialogue Read aloud lines 82–86, emphasizing the shift that occurs between lines 82 and 83. Ask students to explain Macbeth's contradictory comments. (*In line 82, Macbeth says that he has nothing to fear from Macduff, but he changes his mind in lines 83–86, and decides to kill Macduff.*) Discuss what these lines reveal about Macbeth. (*They reveal that he will do anything to hold onto the throne.*)

 For additional support, go to the **Reading Studio** and assign the following ▤ **Level Up Tutorial: Character Motivation.**

Thou other gold-bound brow, is like the first.

115 A third is like the former.—Filthy hags,
Why do you show me this?—A fourth? Start, eyes!
What, will the line stretch out to th' crack of doom?
Another yet? A seventh? I'll see no more.
And yet the eighth appears who bears a glass

120 Which shows me many more, and some I see
That twofold balls and treble scepters carry.
Horrible sight! Now I see 'tis true,
For the blood-boltered Banquo smiles upon me
And points at them for his.

[*The* Apparitions *disappear.*]
What, is this so?

125 **First Witch.** Ay, sir, all this is so. But why
Stands Macbeth thus amazedly?
Come, sisters, cheer we up his sprites
And show the best of our delights.
I'll charm the air to give a sound

130 While you perform your antic round,
That this great king may kindly say
Our duties did his welcome pay.

[*Music. The* Witches *dance and vanish.*]

Macbeth. Where are they? Gone? Let this pernicious hour
Stand aye accursèd in the calendar!—

135 Come in, without there.

[*Enter* Lennox.]

Lennox.   What's your Grace's will?

Macbeth. Saw you the Weïrd Sisters?

Lennox.   No, my lord.

Macbeth. Came they not by you?

Lennox.   No, indeed, my lord.

Macbeth. Infected be the air whereon they ride,
And damned all those that trust them! I did hear

140 The galloping of horse. Who was 't came by?

Lennox. 'Tis two or three, my lord, that bring you word
Macduff is fled to England.

Macbeth.   Fled to England?

Lennox. Ay, my good lord.

Macbeth [*aside*]. Time, thou anticipat'st my dread exploits.

145 The flighty purpose never is o'ertook
Unless the deed go with it. From this moment

NOTICE & NOTE

112–124 All eight kings look like Banquo. The mirror shows a future with many more Banquo look-alikes as kings. The twofold balls and treble scepters foretell the union of Scotland and England in 1603, the year that James became king of both realms. Banquo, his hair matted (**boltered**) with blood, claims all the kings as his descendants.

133 pernicious: evil.

134 aye: always.

135 After the Witches vanish, Macbeth hears noises outside the cave and calls out.

The Tragedy of Macbeth, Act IV, Scene 1   453

TEACH

ENGLISH LEARNER SUPPORT

Summarize the Drama Guide students to summarize Act IV, Scene 1, using the following supports with students at varying proficiency levels:

- Ask students who is in Act IV, Scene 1. Have students point to the speaker tags in this scene and copy the names into a simplified version of the chart below. **SUBSTANTIAL**

- Have partners work together to ask and answer Where? Who? What? questions about Act IV, Scene 1, and add their responses to a chart like the one below. **MODERATE/LIGHT**

Act IV, Scene 1	
Where?	A cave
Who?	the Witches, Hecate, Macbeth, Three Apparitions, Lennox
What?	The witches are boiling a potion and casting spells. Macbeth arrives, wanting to learn more from them. Three Apparitions foretell his future. One tells him to beware of Macduff, but the others make Macbeth think that he cannot be killed. He asks the witches about Banquo and they show him more apparitions: eight kings and Banquo. Macbeth understands that Banquo's descendants will be kings.

TO CHALLENGE STUDENTS . . .

Analyze Verbal Irony Define **verbal irony** as a contrast between what is said and what is meant. Then direct students to lines 138–139. Have students write a paragraph defending whether they think that Macbeth is aware enough to recognize the verbal irony in his statement that all who trust the witches are damned. Ask students to defend their positions by citing evidence (words or actions) from the play. You may wish to have students share their thoughts in a brief, informal debate.

The Tragedy of Macbeth, Act IV, Scene 1   **453**

ENGLISH LEARNER SUPPORT

Paraphrase Read aloud Scene 1, lines 141–156, and the accompanying side notes. Then return to lines 150–153. Remind students that while Shakespeare inverted many lines, modern English follows a subject-verb-object sentence order. Also remind students that Shakespeare used an apostrophe (') to take the place of letters in words. Guide students to restate lines 150–153 in simple modern sentences:

I will surprise the castle of Macduff.

I will attack Fife.

I will kill ("give to the edge of the sword") Macduff's wife, his children, and everyone in his family.

LIGHT

NOTICE & NOTE

144–156 Frustrated in his desire to kill Macduff, Macbeth blames his own hesitation, which gave his enemy time to flee. He concludes that one's plans (**flighty purpose**) are never achieved (**o'ertook**) unless carried out at once. From now on, Macbeth promises, he will act immediately on his impulses (**firstlings of my heart**) and complete (**crown**) his thoughts with acts. He will surprise Macduff's castle at Fife and kill his wife and children.

3–4 Macduff's wife is worried that others will think her husband a traitor because his fears made him flee the country (**our fears do make us traitors**), though he was guilty of no wrongdoing.

9 wants the natural touch: lacks the instinct to protect his family.

14 coz: cousin (a term used for any close relation).

15 school: control; **for:** as for.

17 fits o' th' season: disorders of the present time.

18–22 Ross laments the cruelty of the times that made Macduff flee. Fears make people believe (**hold**) rumors, though they do not know what to fear and drift aimlessly like ships tossed by a tempest.

The very firstlings of my heart shall be
The firstlings of my hand. And even now,
To crown my thoughts with acts, be it thought and done:
150 The castle of Macduff I will surprise,
Seize upon Fife, give to th' edge o' th' sword
His wife, his babes, and all unfortunate souls
That trace him in his line. No boasting like a fool;
This deed I'll do before this purpose cool.
155 But no more sights!—Where are these gentlemen?
Come bring me where they are.

[*They exit.*]

Scene 2 *Macduff's castle at Fife.*

[*Enter* Lady Macduff, *her* Son, *and* Ross.]

Lady Macduff. What had he done to make him fly the land?

Ross. You must have patience, madam.

Lady Macduff.   He had none.
His flight was madness. When our actions do not,
Our fears do make us traitors.

Ross.   You know not
5 Whether it was his wisdom or his fear.

Lady Macduff. Wisdom? To leave his wife, to leave his babes,
His mansion and his titles in a place
From whence himself does fly? He loves us not;
He wants the natural touch; for the poor wren
10 (The most diminutive of birds) will fight,
Her young ones in her nest, against the owl.
All is the fear, and nothing is the love,
As little is the wisdom, where the flight
So runs against all reason.

Ross.   My dearest coz,
15 I pray you school yourself. But for your husband,
He is noble, wise, judicious, and best knows
The fits o' th' season. I dare not speak much further;
But cruel are the times when we are traitors
And do not know ourselves; when we hold rumor
20 From what we fear, yet know not what we fear,
But float upon a wild and violent sea
Each way and move—I take my leave of you.
Shall not be long but I'll be here again.
Things at the worst will cease or else climb upward
25 To what they were before.—My pretty cousin,
Blessing upon you.

Lady Macduff and children, The Conservatory of Theatre and Dance, Southeast Missouri State University, 2014.

Lady Macduff. Fathered he is, and yet he's fatherless.

Ross. I am so much a fool, should I stay longer
It would be my disgrace and your discomfort.
30 I take my leave at once.   [*Ross exits.*]

Lady Macduff.   Sirrah, your father's dead.
And what will you do now? How will you live?

Son. As birds do, mother.

Lady Macduff.   What, with worms and flies?

Son. With what I get, I mean; and so do they.

Lady Macduff. Poor bird, thou'dst never fear the net nor lime,
35 The pitfall nor the gin.

Son. Why should I, mother? Poor birds they are not set for.
My father is not dead, for all your saying.

Lady Macduff. Yes, he is dead. How wilt thou do for a father?

Son. Nay, how will you do for a husband?

28–30 Moved by pity for Macduff's family, Ross is near tears (**my disgrace**). He will leave before he embarrasses himself.

32–35 The spirited son refuses to be defeated by their bleak situation. He will live as birds do, taking whatever comes his way. His mother responds in kind, calling attention to devices used to catch birds: nets, sticky birdlime (**lime**), snares (**pitfall**), and traps (**gin**).

The Tragedy of Macbeth, Act IV, Scene 2   455

ENGLISH LEARNER SUPPORT

Confirm Understanding As students follow along in their books, read aloud the stage directions and lines 1–4 in Scene 2, pausing to paraphrase every sentence or two and consulting the side notes. Explain that in Shakespeare's time, the word *fly* was used to mean "leave quickly." Explain that a *traitor* is someone who betrays another person, or breaks that person's trust. Then ask: Does Lady Macduff understand why her husband left Scotland? *(no)*

Read aloud Lady Macduff's speech in lines 6–8. Then ask: Why is Lady Macduff angry with her husband? *(She is angry that he left his family in danger.)*

SUBSTANTIAL/MODERATE

CLOSE READ SCREENCAST

Modeled Discussion In their eBook, have students view the Close Read Screencast, in which readers discuss and annotate Scene 2, lines 30–41.

TOUGH QUESTIONS

Remind students that the Tough Questions a character asks can reveal a glimpse of that character's **internal conflict**. Tell students that in Lady Macduff's soliloquy, we learn her inner thoughts, feelings, and plans. Have students skim the passage, looking for question marks. Point out that *Whither should I fly?* means "Where should I run to?" (**Answer:** *Lady Macduff understands both the hopelessness of her situation and the injustice of the world. These are rhetorical questions with no real answers.*)

■ English Learner Support

Paraphrase and Read Aloud Assign pairs or groups the roles of Lady Macduff, the Messenger, and the Murderer in Scene 2, lines 61–81. (Take the role of the Son yourself.) Have groups read their assigned lines and paraphrase them in modern language, referring to the side notes and using a dictionary to help with key words. Ask each group to choose one person who will read their rewritten dialogue aloud. Then have all the groups deliver their dialogue for lines 61–81.
MODERATE/LIGHT

40–43 Lady Macduff and her son affectionately joke about her ability to find a new husband. She expresses admiration for his intelligence (**with wit enough**).

54–60 Her son points out that traitors outnumber honest men in this troubled time. The mother's terms of affection, **monkey** and **prattler** (childish talker), suggest that his playfulness has won her over.

61–69 The messenger, who knows Lady Macduff is an honorable person (**in your state of honor I am perfect**), delivers a polite but desperate warning, urging her to flee immediately. While he apologizes for scaring her, he warns that she faces a deadly (**fell**) cruelty, one dangerously close (**too nigh**).

TOUGH QUESTIONS

Notice & Note: Mark the questions Lady Macduff asks herself in lines 69–75.

Infer: What do these questions reveal about Lady Macduff's view of the world? Can these questions be answered?

40 **Lady Macduff.** Why, I can buy me twenty at any market.

Son. Then you'll buy 'em to sell again.

Lady Macduff. Thou speak'st with all thy wit,
And yet, i' faith, with wit enough for thee.

Son. Was my father a traitor, mother?

45 **Lady Macduff.** Ay, that he was.

Son. What is a traitor?

Lady Macduff. Why, one that swears and lies.

Son. And be all traitors that do so?

Lady Macduff. Every one that does so is a traitor and must be hanged.

50 **Son.** And must they all be hanged that swear and lie?

Lady Macduff. Every one.

Son. Who must hang them?

Lady Macduff. Why, the honest men.

Son. Then the liars and swearers are fools, for there are liars and
55 swearers enough to beat the honest men and hang up them.

Lady Macduff. Now God help thee, poor monkey! But how wilt thou do for a father?

Son. If he were dead, you'd weep for him. If you would not, it were a good sign that I should quickly have a new father.

60 **Lady Macduff.** Poor prattler, how thou talk'st!

[*Enter a* Messenger.]

Messenger. Bless you, fair dame. I am not to you known,
Though in your state of honor I am perfect.
I doubt some danger does approach you nearly.
If you will take a homely man's advice,
65 Be not found here. Hence with your little ones!
To fright you thus methinks I am too savage;
To do worse to you were fell cruelty,
Which is too nigh your person. Heaven preserve you!
I dare abide no longer. [Messenger *exits*.]

Lady Macduff. Whither should I fly?
70 I have done no harm. But I remember now
I am in this earthly world, where to do harm
Is often laudable, to do good sometime
Accounted dangerous folly. Why then, alas,
Do I put up that womanly defense
75 To say I have done no harm?

WHEN STUDENTS STRUGGLE . . .

Analyze Characters Students may better understand Shakespeare's development of characters in Scene 2 by reading aloud. Have students read one character's speech at a time and paraphrase the ideas expressed by the character. Conclude by asking students what they learn about the key characters in this scene.

- Lady Macduff (*She is angry with her cowardly husband and fears for the safety of her children and herself.*)
- Ross (*He defends Macduff's courage and honor, and tries to protect Lady Macduff by not revealing anything for which she could be implicated.*)

 For additional support, go to the **Reading Studio** and assign the following 🔼 **Level Up Tutorial: Methods of Characterization.**

[*Enter* Murderers.]

                              What are these faces?

Murderer. Where is your husband?

Lady Macduff. I hope in no place so unsanctified
Where such as thou mayst find him.

Murderer.   He's a traitor.

Son. Thou liest, thou shag-eared villain!

Murderer.   What, you egg!

[*Stabbing him*]

80 Young fry of treachery!

Son.   He has killed me, mother.
Run away, I pray you,

[Lady Macduff *exits, crying "Murder!" followed by the* Murderers
bearing the Son's *body.*]

Scene 3 *England. Before King Edward's palace.*

[*Enter* Malcolm *and* Macduff.]

Malcolm. Let us seek out some desolate shade and there
Weep our sad bosoms empty.

Macduff.   Let us rather
Hold fast the mortal sword and, like good men,
Bestride our downfall'n birthdom. Each new morn
5 New widows howl, new orphans cry, new sorrows
Strike heaven on the face, that it resounds
As if it felt with Scotland, and yelled out
Like syllable of dolor.

Malcolm.   What I believe, I'll wail;
What know, believe; and what I can redress,
10 As I shall find the time to friend, I will.
What you have spoke, it may be so, perchance.
This tyrant, whose sole name blisters our tongues,
Was once thought honest. You have loved him well.
He hath not touched you yet. I am young, but something
15 You may deserve of him through me, and wisdom
To offer up a weak, poor, innocent lamb
T' appease an angry god.

Macduff. I am not treacherous.

Malcolm.   But Macbeth is.
A good and virtuous nature may recoil

77 **unsanctified:** unholy.

79 **shag-eared:** longhaired.

80 **young fry:** small fish.

1–8 Macduff advises that they grab a deadly (**mortal**) sword and defend their homeland (**birthdom**). The anguished cries of Macbeth's victims strike heaven and make the skies echo with cries of sorrow (**syllable of dolor**).

8–15 Malcolm will strike back only if the time is right (**as I shall find the time to friend**). Macduff may be sincere, but he may be deceiving Malcolm to gain a reward from Macbeth (**something you may deserve of him through me**).

18–24 Even a good person may fall (**recoil**) into wickedness because of a king's command (**imperial charge**). Suspicions cannot change (**transpose**) the nature (**that which you are**) of an innocent person. Virtue cannot be damaged even by those like Lucifer (**the brightest angel**), who can disguise themselves as virtuous (**wear the brows of grace**).

The Tragedy of Macbeth, Act IV, Scene 3   457

TEACH

ⓔ ENGLISH LEARNER SUPPORT

Compare and Contrast Review with students the murders that Macbeth has caused so far in the play. Have pairs of students list their notes in a chart like this.

Duncan	*Macbeth wasn't sure if he should kill the king. His wife told him that he should. He felt very guilty and could not look at the king's dead body.*
Banquo	*Macbeth met twice with murderers. He lied to them about Banquo. He told them to kill Banquo and his son Fleance. They killed Banquo, but Fleance escaped. Macbeth felt guilty and saw Banquo's ghost at the banquet.*
Lady Macduff and her son	*Macbeth had murderers kill Macduff's family. They were all innocent and not a danger to Macbeth.*

Once partners have completed their charts, ask them to use the words *and*, *also*, and *but* to form sentences about similarities and differences in the three crimes. Tell students to explain how the crimes show that Macbeth has changed.

MODERATE/LIGHT

ENGLISH LEARNER SUPPORT

Develop Vocabulary to Describe Characters Explain that at the beginning of Scene 3, Malcolm tests Macduff to find out whether he is honest and loyal. Malcolm lies and tells Macduff that he himself has many vices (faults, or bad qualities). Macduff becomes very upset. He tells Malcolm that his father, King Duncan, and his mother were very good, so he can't be loyal to a king who has vices. That's how Malcolm discovers that Macduff is a man of virtue and someone he can trust.

Work with students to create lists of virtues and vices mentioned in the play. You may wish to include both adjective forms and noun forms and model how to use them to create sentences such as these:

Duncan was a <u>just</u> king.

Macduff proved his <u>loyalty</u> to Malcolm.

<u>Greed</u> has changed Macbeth.

He has become <u>dishonorable</u>.

Virtues: Good qualities	
loyal	loyalty
just	justice
truthful	truth
honorable	honor

Vices: Bad qualities	
greedy	greed
unfair	injustice
impatient	impatience
dishonorable	dishonor

MODERATE

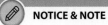

20 In an imperial charge. But I shall crave your pardon.
    That which you are, my thoughts cannot transpose.
    Angels are bright still, though the brightest fell.
    Though all things foul would wear the brows of grace,
    Yet grace must still look so.

Macduff.   I have lost my hopes.

25 **Malcolm.** Perchance even there where I did find my doubts.
    Why in that rawness left you wife and child,
    Those precious motives, those strong knots of love,
    Without leave-taking? I pray you,
    Let not my jealousies be your dishonors,
30 But mine own safeties. You may be rightly just,
    Whatever I shall think.

Macduff.   Bleed, bleed, poor country!
    Great tyranny, lay thou thy basis sure,
    For goodness dare not check thee. Wear thou thy wrongs;
    The title is affeered.—Fare thee well, lord.
35 I would not be the villain that thou think'st
    For the whole space that's in the tyrant's grasp,
    And the rich East to boot.

Malcolm.   Be not offended.
    I speak not as in absolute fear of you.
    I think our country sinks beneath the yoke.
40 It weeps, it bleeds, and each new day a gash
    Is added to her wounds. I think withal
    There would be hands uplifted in my right;
    And here from gracious England have I offer
    Of goodly thousands. But, for all this,
45 When I shall tread upon the tyrant's head
    Or wear it on my sword, yet my poor country
    Shall have more vices than it had before,
    More suffer, and more sundry ways than ever,
    By him that shall succeed.

Macduff.   What should he be?

50 **Malcolm.** It is myself I mean, in whom I know
    All the particulars of vice so grafted
    That, when they shall be opened, black Macbeth
    Will seem as pure as snow, and the poor state
    Esteem him as a lamb, being compared
55 With my confineless harms.

Macduff.   Not in the legions
    Of horrid hell can come a devil more damned
    In evils to top Macbeth.

26 rawness: vulnerability.

29 jealousies: suspicions.

34 affeered: confirmed.

46–49 yet my . . . succeed: To test Macduff's honor and loyalty, Malcolm begins a lengthy description of his own fictitious vices.

50–55 Malcolm says that his own vices are so plentiful and deeply planted (**grafted**) that Macbeth will seem innocent by comparison.

WHEN STUDENTS STRUGGLE . . .

Develop Vocabulary to Build Understanding Some students may be confused by the dialogue between Malcolm and Macduff. Have students read Scene 3 through line 139, using the side notes for clarification. Then have groups of students work together to answer these questions:

- How does Malcolm feel at the beginning of Scene 3? What words in lines 1–2 show that he feels this way?
- What does Macduff want at the beginning of Scene 3? What clues in lines 2–8 show that he wants this?

- Does Malcolm trust Macduff? (Review lines 8–24.)
- How does Malcolm test Macduff? (Review lines 46–100.)
- Why does Macduff cry out, "O Scotland, Scotland!" (See line 101.)
- How does Macduff show that he can be trusted? (Review lines 102–114.)

 For additional support, go to the **Reading Studio** and assign the following **Level Up Tutorial: Reading for Details.**

Malcolm.   I grant him bloody,
Luxurious, avaricious, false, deceitful,
Sudden, malicious, smacking of every sin
60 That has a name. But there's no bottom, none,
In my voluptuousness. Your wives, your daughters,
Your matrons, and your maids could not fill up
The cistern of my lust, and my desire
All continent impediments would o'erbear
65 That did oppose my will. Better Macbeth
Than such an one to reign.

Macduff.   Boundless intemperance
In nature is a tyranny. It hath been
Th' untimely emptying of the happy throne
And fall of many kings. But fear not yet
70 To take upon you what is yours. You may
Convey your pleasures in a spacious plenty
And yet seem cold—the time you may so hoodwink.
We have willing dames enough. There cannot be
That vulture in you to devour so many
75 As will to greatness dedicate themselves,
Finding it so inclined.

Malcolm.   With this there grows
In my most ill-composed affection such
A stanchless avarice that, were I king,
I should cut off the nobles for their lands,
80 Desire his jewels, and this other's house;
And my more-having would be as a sauce
To make me hunger more, that I should forge
Quarrels unjust against the good and loyal,
Destroying them for wealth.

Macduff.   This avarice
85 Sticks deeper, grows with more pernicious root
Than summer-seeming lust, and it hath been
The sword of our slain kings. Yet do not fear.
Scotland hath foisons to fill up your will
Of your mere own. All these are portable,
90 With other graces weighed.

Malcolm. But I have none. The king-becoming graces,
As justice, verity, temp'rance, stableness,
Bounty, perseverance, mercy, lowliness,
Devotion, patience, courage, fortitude,
95 I have no relish of them but abound
In the division of each several crime,
Acting it many ways. Nay, had I power, I should
Pour the sweet milk of concord into hell,

58 luxurious: lustful.

61 voluptuousness: lust.

63 cistern: large storage tank.

63–65 His lust is so great that it would overpower (**o'erbear**) all restraining obstacles (**continent impediments**).

66–76 Macduff describes uncontrolled desire (**boundless intemperance**) as a tyrant of human nature that has caused the early (**untimely**) downfall of many kings.

76–78 Malcolm adds insatiable greed (**stanchless avarice**) to the list of evils in his disposition (**affection**).

84–90 Macduff recognizes that greed is a deeper-rooted problem than lust, which passes as quickly as the summer (**summer-seeming**). But the king's property alone (**of your mere own**) offers plenty (**foisons**) to satisfy his desire. Malcolm's vices can be tolerated (**are portable**).

91–95 Malcolm lists the kingly virtues he lacks: truthfulness (**verity**), consistency (**stableness**), generosity (**bounty**), humility (**lowliness**), and religious devotion.

The Tragedy of Macbeth, Act IV, Scene 3   459

(EL) ENGLISH LEARNER SUPPORT

Simplify Sentences Explain to students that sentences—even long ones with difficult vocabulary—usually can be simplified so that they are easier to understand. Simplify Macduff's statement in Scene 3, lines 84–87, by formatting them as you would a normal sentence as shown here:

"This avarice sticks deeper, grows with more pernicious root than summer-seeming lust, and it hath been the sword of our slain kings."

Draw a box around the word *and*. Point out that *and* is a clue that there may be two parts to this long sentence. Guide students to circle a subject and underline one or more verbs in the first part of the sentence (before *and*). (*Subject: This avarice; verbs: sticks, grows*) Explain that *avarice* is greed, or always wanting more wealth and power. Then guide students to circle a subject and underline one or more verbs in the second part of the sentence. (*Subject: it; verb: hath been*). Ask: What does *it* refer back to in the first part of the sentence? (*avarice*).

Point out that locating *and* helped students divide the long sentence into two parts. Ask students to paraphrase the two parts of the sentence into two shorter sentences and explain the metaphors. (*Greed is stronger than lust, which is temporary. Kings have been killed because of greed.*)
LIGHT

TO CHALLENGE STUDENTS . . .

Analyze Character Have students write a character analysis of Malcolm, drawing on details in Scene 3 to support their position. Students might begin by noting Malcolm's character traits and evidence of those traits in a web diagram. Then have students use that information to write their analysis. Invite students to meet in small groups to compare their completed diagrams and analyses.

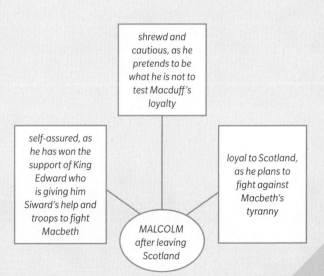

shrewd and cautious, as he pretends to be what he is not to test Macduff's loyalty

self-assured, as he has won the support of King Edward who is giving him Siward's help and troops to fight Macbeth

loyal to Scotland, as he plans to fight against Macbeth's tyranny

MALCOLM after leaving Scotland

Uproar the universal peace, confound
100 All unity on earth.

   Macduff.   O Scotland, Scotland!

   Malcolm. If such a one be fit to govern, speak.
   I am as I have spoken.

   Macduff.   Fit to govern?
   No, not to live.—O nation miserable,
   With an untitled tyrant bloody-sceptered,
105 When shalt thou see thy wholesome days again,
   Since that the truest issue of thy throne
   By his own interdiction stands accursed
   And does blaspheme his breed?—Thy royal father
   Was a most sainted king. The queen that bore thee,
110 Oft'ner upon her knees than on her feet,
   Died every day she lived. Fare thee well.
   These evils thou repeat'st upon thyself
   Have banished me from Scotland.—O my breast,
   Thy hope ends here!

102–114 Macduff can see no relief for Scotland's suffering under a tyrant who has no right to the throne (**untitled**). The rightful heir (**truest issue**), Malcolm, bans himself from the throne (**by his own interdiction**) because of his evil. Malcolm's vices slander his parents (**blaspheme his breed**)—his saintly father and his mother who renounced the world (**died every day**) for her religion.

APPLYING ACADEMIC VOCABULARY

❑ **comprise** ❑ **incidence** ☑ **predominant** ❑ **priority** ❑ **ultimate**

Write and Discuss Have students turn to a partner to discuss the following questions. Guide students to use the academic vocabulary word *predominant* in their responses. Ask volunteers to share their responses with the class.

- What are the **predominant** traits in Malcolm's true character?
- Think about the **predominant** characteristics of a good ruler. Does Malcolm possess these characteristics?

Malcolm.   Macduff, this noble passion,
115 Child of integrity, hath from my soul
     Wiped the black scruples, reconciled my thoughts
     To thy good truth and honor. Devilish Macbeth
     By many of these trains hath sought to win me
     Into his power, and modest wisdom plucks me
120 From overcredulous haste. But God above
     Deal between thee and me, for even now
     I put myself to thy direction and
     Unspeak mine own detraction, here abjure
     The taints and blames I laid upon myself
125 For strangers to my nature. I am yet
     Unknown to woman, never was forsworn,
     Scarcely have coveted what was mine own,
     At no time broke my faith, would not betray
     The devil to his fellow, and delight
130 No less in truth than life. My first false speaking
     Was this upon myself. What I am truly
     Is thine and my poor country's to command—
     Whither indeed, before thy here-approach,

114–125 Macduff has finally convinced Malcolm of his honesty. Malcolm explains that his caution (**modest wisdom**) resulted from his fear of Macbeth's tricks. He takes back his accusations against himself (**unspeak mine own detraction**) and renounces (**abjure**) the evils he previously claimed.

WHEN STUDENTS STRUGGLE . . .

Work as a Group Students can help each other to understand characters' complex speeches. Have students work with a partner or in small groups to identify and read aloud a speech that they are having trouble understanding. Offer the following reading tips:

- Read difficult passages slowly and clearly.
- Use the punctuation as guides for pausing (commas) and stopping (periods).
- Read with meaning to communicate your understanding to listeners.
- After reading, ask and answer questions to clarify ideas.
- Refer to the side notes for help with paraphrasing unfamiliar language.

 For additional support, go to the **Reading Studio** and assign the following 〔LEVEL UP〕 **Level Up Tutorial: Paraphrasing.**

ENGLISH LEARNER SUPPORT

Summarize the Drama Guide students to summarize Act IV, Scene 2 and Scene 3, using the following supports with students at varying proficiency levels:

- Ask students who is in Act IV, Scene 2 and Scene 3. Have students point to the speaker tags in these scenes and copy the names into simplified versions of the charts below. **SUBSTANTIAL**

- Have partners work together to ask and answer Where? Who? What? questions about Act IV, Scenes 2–3, and add their responses to charts like the ones below. **MODERATE/LIGHT**

Act IV, Scene 2	
Where?	Macduff's castle at Fife
Who?	Lady Macduff, her son, Ross, a Messenger, Murderers
What?	Ross tries to comfort his cousin, Lady Macduff. Lady Macduff tells her son that his father was a traitor because he left them alone. A messenger warns Lady Macduff that she should run away. Murderers arrive and kill Macduff's son and wife.

Act IV, Scene 3	
Where?	Outside King Edward's palace in England
Who?	Malcolm, Macduff, Ross
What?	Malcolm tests Macduff to see if he can trust him. Macduff proves himself to be noble and trustworthy. Malcolm tells Macduff that he has an army of 10,000 troops ready to do battle with Macbeth. Ross arrives with the news that Macduff's family has been killed.

NOTICE & NOTE

133–137 Malcolm already has an army, 10,000 troops belonging to old Siward, the earl of Northumberland. Now that Macduff is an ally, he hopes the battle's result will match the justice of their cause (**warranted quarrel**).

141–159 Edward the Confessor, king of England, could reportedly heal the disease of scrofula (**the evil**) by his saintly touch. The doctor describes people who cannot be helped by medicine's best efforts (**the great assay of art**) waiting for the touch of the king's hand. Edward has cured many victims of this disease. Each time, he hangs a gold coin around their neck and offers prayers, a healing ritual that he will teach to his royal descendants (**succeeding royalty**).

162–163 Good God . . . strangers: May God remove Macbeth, who is the cause (**means**) of our being strangers.

Old Siward with ten thousand warlike men,
135 Already at a point, was setting forth.
Now we'll together, and the chance of goodness
Be like our warranted quarrel. Why are you silent?

Macduff. Such welcome and unwelcome things at once
'Tis hard to reconcile.

[*Enter a Doctor.*]

140 **Malcolm.** Well, more anon.—Comes the King forth, I pray you?

Doctor. Ay, sir. There are a crew of wretched souls
That stay his cure. Their malady convinces
The great assay of art, but at his touch
(Such sanctity hath heaven given his hand)
145 They presently amend.

Malcolm.   I thank you, doctor.

[Doctor *exits*.]

Macduff. What's the disease he means?

Malcolm.   'Tis called the evil:
A most miraculous work in this good king,
Which often since my here-remain in England
I have seen him do. How he solicits heaven
150 Himself best knows, but strangely visited people
All swoll'n and ulcerous, pitiful to the eye,
The mere despair of surgery, he cures,
Hanging a golden stamp about their necks
Put on with holy prayers; and, 'tis spoken,
155 To the succeeding royalty he leaves
The healing benediction. With this strange virtue,
He hath a heavenly gift of prophecy,
And sundry blessings hang about his throne
That speak him full of grace.

[*Enter* Ross.]

Macduff.   See who comes here.

160 **Malcolm.** My countryman, but yet I know him not.

Macduff. My ever-gentle cousin, welcome hither.

Malcolm. I know him now.—Good God betimes remove
The means that makes us strangers!

Ross.   Sir, amen.

Macduff. Stands Scotland where it did?

Ross.   Alas, poor country,
165 Almost afraid to know itself. It cannot

Be called our mother, but our grave, where nothing
But who knows nothing is once seen to smile;
Where sighs and groans and shrieks that rent the air
Are made, not marked; where violent sorrow seems
170 A modern ecstasy. The dead man's knell
Is there scarce asked for who, and good men's lives
Expire before the flowers in their caps,
Dying or ere they sicken.

Macduff. O relation too nice and yet too true!

175 **Malcolm.** What's the newest grief?

Ross. That of an hour's age doth hiss the speaker.
Each minute teems a new one.

Macduff.   How does my wife?

Ross. Why, well.

Macduff.   And all my children?

Ross.   Well too.

Macduff. The tyrant has not battered at their peace?

180 **Ross.** No, they were well at peace when I did leave 'em.

Macduff. Be not a niggard of your speech. How goes 't?

Ross. When I came hither to transport the tidings
Which I have heavily borne, there ran a rumor
Of many worthy fellows that were out;
185 Which was to my belief witnessed the rather
For that I saw the tyrant's power afoot.
Now is the time of help. Your eye in Scotland
Would create soldiers, make our women fight
To doff their dire distresses.

Malcolm.   Be 't their comfort
190 We are coming thither. Gracious England hath
Lent us good Siward and ten thousand men;
An older and a better soldier none
That Christendom gives out.

Ross.   Would I could answer
This comfort with the like. But I have words
195 That would be howled out in the desert air,
Where hearing should not latch them.

Macduff.   What concern they—
The general cause, or is it a fee-grief
Due to some single breast?

Ross.   No mind that's honest

174 relation too nice: news that is too accurate.

176–177 If the news is more than an hour old, listeners hiss at the speaker for being outdated; every minute gives birth to a new grief.

ANALYZE DRAMA
Annotate: Mark lines that Ross speaks that relate to Macduff's family in lines 177–200.

Analyze: How does dramatic irony create tension in this scene?

180 well at peace: Ross knows about the murder of Macduff's wife and children, but the news is too terrible to report.

182–189 Ross mentions the rumors of nobles who are rebelling (**out**) against Macbeth. Ross believes the rumors because he saw Macbeth's troops on the march (**tyrant's power afoot**). The presence (**eye**) of Malcolm and Macduff in Scotland would help raise soldiers and remove (**doff**) Macbeth's evil (**dire distresses**).

195 would: should.
196 latch: catch.

197 fee-grief: private sorrow.

198–199 No mind . . . woe: Every honorable (**honest**) person shares in this sorrow.

The Tragedy of Macbeth, Act IV, Scene 3   463

ANALYZE DRAMA

Call on volunteers to summarize the events leading up to the murder of Lady Macduff and her son. (*Her cousin Ross visited her; she talked with her son; a messenger came to warn her to flee; then the murderers arrived and killed her and her son.*) Point out that although Lady Macduff was alive when Ross left the castle at Fife, she was killed shortly afterward. Ask students whether it is likely that Ross learned of Lady Macduff's murder—and, if so, why he might not tell Macduff right away. (*He probably doesn't know how to break the terrible news to Macduff; he may feel guilty that he didn't do anything to stop the murders.*) (**Answer:** *The dramatic irony lies in the fact that the audience knows that Macduff's family has been murdered, but Macduff does not. Ross's delay in revealing that news increases the audience's anticipation of how Macduff will react when he learns the truth.*)

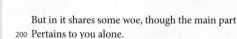
ENGLISH LEARNER SUPPORT

Read and Paraphrase Display and read aloud lines 231–232 from Act IV, Scene 3:

"Be this the whetstone of your sword. Let grief

Convert to anger. Blunt not the heart; enrage it."

Point out that Shakespeare is using the whetstone as a metaphor—he is comparing a whetstone to something. Read the side note definition of *whetstone*. Ask students if they have watched anyone sharpen a knife on a stone. Explain that by rubbing the edge of the knife's blade against the stone, the blade gets sharper. Ask students how Macduff could use his grief, or sadness, like a whetstone. *(Macduff can use his sadness to make his anger strong and sharp, like a blade. Then he will be more powerful in his fight against Macbeth, who is responsible for killing Macduff's family.)*

MODERATE/LIGHT

But in it shares some woe, though the main part
200 Pertains to you alone.

Macduff. If it be mine,
Keep it not from me. Quickly let me have it.

Ross. Let not your ears despise my tongue forever,
Which shall possess them with the heaviest sound
That ever yet they heard.

Macduff. Hum! I guess at it.

205 **Ross.** Your castle is surprised, your wife and babes
Savagely slaughtered. To relate the manner
Were on the quarry of these murdered deer
To add the death of you.

206–208 Ross won't add to Macduff's sorrow by telling him how his family was killed. He compares Macduff's dear ones to the piled bodies of killed deer (**quarry**).

Malcolm. Merciful heaven!
What, man, ne'er pull your hat upon your brows.
210 Give sorrow words. The grief that does not speak
Whispers the o'erfraught heart and bids it break.

210–211 The grief . . . break: Silence will only push an overburdened heart to the breaking point.

Macduff. My children too?

Ross. Wife, children, servants, all that could be found.

Macduff. And I must be from thence? My wife killed too?

215 **Ross.** I have said.

Malcolm. Be comforted.
Let's make us med'cines of our great revenge
To cure this deadly grief.

Macduff. He has no children. All my pretty ones?
220 Did you say "all"? O hell-kite! All?
What, all my pretty chickens and their dam
At one fell swoop?

219–222 He has no children: possibly a reference to Macbeth, who has no children to be killed for revenge. Macduff compares Macbeth to a bird of prey (**hell-kite**) who kills defenseless chickens and their mother.

Malcolm. Dispute it like a man.

Macduff. I shall do so,
But I must also feel it as a man.
225 I cannot but remember such things were
That were most precious to me. Did heaven look on
And would not take their part? Sinful Macduff,
They were all struck for thee! Naught that I am,
Not for their own demerits, but for mine,
230 Fell slaughter on their souls. Heaven rest them now.

228 naught: nothing.

Malcolm. Be this the whetstone of your sword. Let grief
Convert to anger. Blunt not the heart; enrage it.

231 whetstone: grindstone used for sharpening.

Macduff. O, I could play the woman with mine eyes
And braggart with my tongue! But, gentle heavens,

WHEN STUDENTS STRUGGLE . . .

Analyze Dialogue Some students may have difficulty inferring the feelings of Ross, Macduff, and Malcolm from the dialogue in lines 204–235. Have students work in groups of three, each student taking the role of one of the characters to read those lines aloud.

- Direct students to read through the dialogue for understanding, stopping to discuss the best way to read each character's lines using vocal tone, emphasis, and pacing.

- Have groups read through the dialogue again, incorporating the tone, emphasis, and pacing agreed on earlier.

- Ask groups to discuss the feelings that each character's dialogue conveys.

 For additional support, go to the **Reading Studio** and assign the following **Level Up Tutorial: Reading for Details.**

235 Cut short all intermission! Front to front
     Bring thou this fiend of Scotland and myself.
     Within my sword's length set him. If he scape,
     Heaven forgive him too.

Malcolm.   This tune goes manly.
     Come, go we to the King. Our power is ready;
240 Our lack is nothing but our leave. Macbeth
     Is ripe for shaking, and the powers above
     Put on their instruments. Receive what cheer you may.
     The night is long that never finds the day.

     [*They exit.*]

239–243 Our troops are ready to attack, needing only the king's permission (**our lack is nothing but our leave**). Like a ripe fruit, Macbeth is ready to fall, and heavenly powers are preparing to assist us.

NOTICE & NOTE

CHECK YOUR UNDERSTANDING

Answer these questions before moving on to the **Analyze the Text** section on the following page.

1 What does Macbeth learn from his visit to the Witches in Act IV?

  A That he can trust Macduff

  B How to conjure spirits for himself

  C That Banquo's line can no longer rule Scotland

  D That he will rule until the forest marches to his castle

2 Why does Macbeth decide to have Macduff's family killed?

  F He has resolved to act without hesitation and is angry at Macduff.

  G The Apparitions convince Macbeth that Macduff will kill him.

  H Macbeth hopes to make an example of Macduff to ensure others' loyalty.

  J Macduff has convinced everyone that Macbeth is unfit for the throne.

3 What advice does Malcolm give Macduff?

  A That he should be relieved that he was not at home when the murderers arrived

  B That he must admit defeat and never return to Scotland

  C To take all the time he needs to mourn his wife and children

  D To turn his strong emotions to the positive goal of eliminating Macbeth

TEACH

CHECK YOUR UNDERSTANDING

Have students answer the questions independently.

Answers:

  1. *D*

  2. *F*

  3. *D*

If they answer any questions incorrectly, have them reread the text to confirm their understanding. Then they may proceed to ANALYZE THE TEXT on page 466.

ENGLISH LEARNER SUPPORT

Oral Assessment Use the following questions to assess students' comprehension and speaking skills. Ask students to respond in short, complete sentences.

  1. Does the apparition warn Macbeth about Macduff? (*Yes. The apparition warns Macbeth to beware Macduff.*)

  2. Does the apparition tell Macbeth that Banquo's heirs will rule Scotland? (*Yes. The apparition tells Macbeth that Banquo's heirs will rule Scotland.*)

  3. Whose family does Macbeth have killed? (*Macbeth has Macduff's family killed.*)

  SUBSTANTIAL/MODERATE

ANALYZE THE TEXT

Possible answers:

1. **DOK 4:** *Macbeth manages to convince himself from the prophecies that he is safe. However, despite the second apparition's assurance (or warning) that "none of woman born" will hurt Macbeth, he decides to kill Macduff just for peace of mind. The audience knows that the witches intend to increase trouble from the line "Double, double, toil and trouble," so the audience sees the prophecies as trickery.*

2. **DOK 2:** *The messenger has come to warn Lady Macduff to give her a chance to escape. Lady Macbeth, who has become plagued with guilt over her role in the murder of Duncan, and possibly having knowledge of her husband's plan, may have sent the messenger.*

3. **DOK 3:** *Previously, Macbeth killed grown men who were his enemies, not defenseless women and children who pose no threat to him, so Macduff had no reason to worry about his family.*

4. **DOK 2:** *Shakespeare has built up interest and sympathy for Macduff's son earlier in the scene, so by showing the son defending his father's honor and being murdered onstage, Shakespeare increases the audience's emotions and awareness that Macbeth is now murdering innocent people for no purpose. Seeing the murder onstage is much more effective than hearing it occurring offstage.*

5. **DOK 4:** *Macduff asks why heaven did not do anything to save his innocent family from death. It is a question with no clear answer. One theme this statement suggests is that bad things happen to good people for no clear reason.*

CREATE AND DISCUSS

Discuss some ways to reach consensus. Point out that one way to begin is for everyone in the group to express his or her ideas as a note-taker records ideas on the board. If there's a majority view, then the group can start there and discuss ways of accommodating minority opinions so that everyone is included. If there are a number of minority views but no clear majority, then group members should work to find common ground. After groups reach consensus, poll students to find out whether they would prefer sharing ideas in a panel format or in a debate. *(Students will have varying opinions, for varying reasons, but should support them with evidence from the text and from their own experience.)*

 **RESPOND**

ANALYZE THE TEXT

Support your responses with evidence from the text. 📓 NOTEBOOK

1. **Analyze** How does Macbeth interpret the prophecies pronounced by the first three apparitions? Explain how knowledge of the witches' intent affects the audience's perception of these prophecies.

2. **Infer** What is the purpose of the appearance and speech of the messenger in Scene 2? Who might have sent this messenger?

3. **Draw Conclusions** Lady Macduff and Malcolm both question Macduff's motives for fleeing Scotland. Think about the crimes Macbeth has already committed. Why might the nature of these crimes have led Macduff to believe his family would be safe at his castle?

4. **Infer** Why might Shakespeare have decided to show the murder of Lady Macduff's son on stage? Explain how watching this scene rather than hearing about the event occurring offstage might affect the audience's view of Macbeth.

5. **Notice & Note** Consider Macduff's anguished question about his family in Scene 3: "Did heaven look on / And would not take their part?" How does the answer to this **Tough Question** point toward a possible theme of the play?

CREATE AND DISCUSS

Participate in a Debate Some directors omit much of the scene in which Malcolm tests Macduff. What would be lost or gained by omitting this part of the play?

Go to the **Speaking and Listening Studio** for help with group discussions.

❑ With a group, come to a consensus on the significance of that part of Scene 3. Create an outline that includes reasons and evidence to support your opinion.

Opinion
Reasons
Evidence

❑ Present your argument in the form of a panel discussion or debate. Have other groups present their opposing arguments.

❑ Ask listening classmates to evaluate which argument is most compelling and why.

SETTING A PURPOSE

As you read, pay attention to how the prophecies pronounced by the apparitions are fulfilled. Think about the characters affected by the prophecies. Revisit your character diagram as needed to recall the relationships between characters.

ACT V

Scene 1 *Macbeth's castle at Dunsinane.*

[*Enter a* Doctor of Physic *and a* Waiting Gentlewoman.]

Doctor. I have two nights watched with you but can perceive no truth in your report. When was it she last walked?

Gentlewoman. Since his Majesty went into the field, I have seen her rise from her bed, throw her nightgown upon her, unlock her closet, take forth paper, fold it, write upon' t, read it, afterwards seal it, and again return to bed; yet all this while in a most fast sleep.

Doctor. A great perturbation in nature, to receive at once the benefit of sleep and do the effects of watching. In this slumb'ry agitation, besides her walking and other actual performances, what at any time have you heard her say?

Gentlewoman. That, sir, which I will not report after her.

Doctor. You may to me, and 'tis most meet you should.

Gentlewoman. Neither to you nor anyone, having no witness to confirm my speech.

[*Enter* Lady Macbeth *with a taper.*]

Lo you, here she comes. This is her very guise and, upon my life, fast asleep. Observe her; stand close.

Doctor. How came she by that light?

Gentlewoman. Why, it stood by her. She has light by her continually. 'Tis her command.

Doctor. You see her eyes are open.

Gentlewoman. Ay, but their sense are shut.

Doctor. What is it she does now? Look how she rubs her hands.

Gentlewoman. It is an accustomed action with her to seem thus washing her hands. I have known her continue in this a quarter of an hour.

Lady Macbeth. Yet here's a spot.

Doctor. Hark, she speaks. I will set down what comes from her,

---

(Line numbers: 5, 10, 15, 20, 25)

3 went into the field: went to battle.

8–9 A great . . . of watching: To behave as though awake (**watching**) while sleeping is a sign of a greatly troubled nature.

13 meet: appropriate.

16 guise: usual manner.
17 stand close: hide yourself.

18 that light: her candle.

ANALYZE CHARACTER AND THEME

Annotate: Mark phrases in lines 23–37 that tell what Lady Macbeth is doing.

Analyze: What possible theme of the play might her actions support?

TEACH

SETTING A PURPOSE

Direct students to use the Setting a Purpose prompt to focus their reading. Remind them to keep adding to their character diagrams as the play reaches its conclusion.

ANALYZE CHARACTER AND THEME

Remind students that one way to determine theme is to examine how events that happen over the course of a play change the characters. Tell students to keep in mind earlier events and compare Lady Macbeth's present actions to those earlier in the play to observe how her character may or may not have changed. As students mark phrases in lines 23–37, ask them to consider the many references to blood and attempting to be cleansed. Call on volunteers to share their ideas about a theme that Lady Macbeth's actions may support. (**Answer:** *Lady Macbeth's actions suggest a theme that could be stated as, "Evil deeds cannot be erased."*)

WHEN STUDENTS STRUGGLE . . .

Analyze Characterization To help students analyze the character of Lady Macbeth, have them complete a character chart such as this one:

Words and Actions	What They Mean
She walks in her sleep.	Her guilt will not leave her in peace.
She rubs her hands.	She is trying to cleanse herself of guilt, which she perceives as blood on her hands.

 For additional support, go to the **Reading Studio** and assign the following Level Up Tutorial: **Characters and Conflict.**

ENGLISH LEARNER SUPPORT

Paraphrase Read aloud the doctor's speech in lines 61–69. Then work with students to paraphrase lines 61–64.

Shakespeare	Paraphrase
Foul whisp'rings are abroad.	People are talking about evil things.
Unnatural deeds Do breed unnatural troubles.	Bad acts cause more bad problems.
Infected minds To their deaf pillows will discharge their secrets	Guilty people tell their secrets in their sleep.
More needs she the divine than the physician.	Lady Macbeth needs God's help, not a doctor's.

ALL LEVELS

ENGLISH LEARNER SUPPORT

Role-play to Enrich Understanding Have students work in groups to role-play Scene 1. Ask students to assume the roles of Lady Macbeth, the Doctor, and the Gentlewoman. Tell students that they can use their own words, as well as those of Shakespeare, to retell the scene. After students have performed their role-play, invite them to ask questions or make constructive comments about groups' performances.

ALL LEVELS

to satisfy my remembrance the more strongly.

30 **Lady Macbeth.** Out, damned spot, out, I say! One. Two. Why then, 'tis time to do 't. Hell is murky. Fie, my lord, fie, a soldier and afeard? What need we fear who knows it, when none can call our power to account? Yet who would have thought the old man to have had so much blood in him?

35 **Doctor.** Do you mark that?

Lady Macbeth. The Thane of Fife had a wife. Where is she now? What, will these hands ne'er be clean? No more o' that, my lord, no more o' that. You mar all with this starting.

36–38 Lady Macbeth shows guilt about Macduff's wife. Then she addresses her husband, as if he were having another ghostly fit (**starting**).

Doctor. Go to, go to. You have known what you should not.

40 **Gentlewoman.** She has spoke what she should not, I am sure of that. Heaven knows what she has known.

Lady Macbeth. Here's the smell of the blood still. All the perfumes of Arabia will not sweeten this little hand. O, O, O!

44 sorely charged: heavily burdened.

45–46 The gentlewoman says that she would not want Lady Macbeth's heavy heart in exchange for being queen.

Doctor. What a sigh is there! The heart is sorely charged.

45 **Gentlewoman.** I would not have such a heart in my bosom for the dignity of the whole body.

Doctor. Well, well, well.

Gentlewoman. Pray God it be, sir.

49 practice: skill.

Doctor. This disease is beyond my practice. Yet I have known
50 those which have walked in their sleep, who have died holily in their beds.

Lady Macbeth. Wash your hands. Put on your nightgown. Look not so pale. I tell you yet again, Banquo's buried; he cannot come out on 's grave.

54 on 's: of his.

55 **Doctor.** Even so?

Lady Macbeth. To bed, to bed. There's knocking at the gate. Come, come, come, come. Give me your hand. What's done cannot be undone. To bed, to bed, to bed.

[Lady Macbeth *exits.*]

Doctor. Will she go now to bed?

60 **Gentlewoman.** Directly.

61 Foul whisp'rings are abroad: Rumors of evil deeds are circulating.

64 She needs a priest more than a doctor.

66 annoyance: injury. The doctor may be worried about the possibility of Lady Macbeth's committing suicide.

Doctor. Foul whisp'rings are abroad. Unnatural deeds
Do breed unnatural troubles. Infected minds
To their deaf pillows will discharge their secrets.
More needs she the divine than the physician.
65 God, God forgive us all. Look after her.
Remove from her the means of all annoyance
And still keep eyes upon her. So good night.

WHEN STUDENTS STRUGGLE . . .

Trace Character Development Have students locate passages that parallel lines from earlier in the play to help them analyze the development of Lady Macbeth's character. Ask pairs of students to do the following: Underline a sentence in Act V to compare with Lady Macbeth's words in Act II, Scene 2, lines 53–55: "If he do bleed, I'll gild the faces of the grooms withal, for it must seem their guilt." Then circle a sentence in Act V to compare with Macbeth's words in Act II, Scene 2, lines 58–61: "Will all great Neptune's ocean wash this blood clean from my hand?" Have students discuss how Lady Macbeth has changed over the course of the play.

For additional support, go to the **Reading Studio** and assign the following Level Up Tutorial: **Making Inferences About Characters.**

Russian soprano Anna Netrebko as Lady Macbeth in Verdi's 'Macbeth' at the Metropolitan Opera House, Lincoln Center, New York, 2014.

68 mated: astonished.

My mind she has mated, and amazed my sight.
I think but dare not speak.

Gentlewoman. Good night, good doctor.

[*They exit.*]

Scene 2 *The country near Dunsinane.*

[*Drum and Colors. Enter* Menteith, Caithness, Angus, Lennox, *and* Soldiers.]

Menteith. The English power is near, led on by Malcolm,
His uncle Siward, and the good Macduff.
Revenges burn in them, for their dear causes
Would to the bleeding and the grim alarm
5 Excite the mortified man.

3–5 for their dear . . . man: The cause of Malcolm and Macduff is so deeply felt that a dead (**mortified**) man would respond to their call to arms (**alarm**).

Angus. Near Birnam Wood
Shall we well meet them. That way are they coming.

Caithness. Who knows if Donalbain be with his brother?

Lennox. For certain, sir, he is not. I have a file
Of all the gentry. There is Siward's son
10 And many unrough youths that even now
Protest their first of manhood.

10–11 many . . . manhood: many soldiers who are too young to grow beards (**unrough**).

Menteith. What does the tyrant?

Caithness. Great Dunsinane he strongly fortifies.
Some say he's mad; others that lesser hate him
Do call it valiant fury. But for certain
15 He cannot buckle his distempered cause
Within the belt of rule.

15–16 Like a man so swollen with disease (**distempered**) that he cannot buckle his belt, Macbeth cannot control his evil actions.

Angus. Now does he feel
His secret murders sticking on his hands.

The Tragedy of Macbeth, Act V, Scene 2 469

ENGLISH LEARNER SUPPORT

Discuss Visuals Give students a few moments to examine the photograph on page 469 and to think about the events of Act V, Scene 1. Briefly discuss discuss the following questions:

- How can you tell that this photograph depicts Lady Macbeth at this point in the play, not earlier? (*Earlier, she was ambitious and composed. At this point, however, she is mad with guilt—the very look we see on the singer's face in the photograph.*)

- Based on what you know about what happens in Act V, Scene 1, what do you think the singer is singing about? (*She probably is singing about trying to clean the blood from her hands.*)

- How does this image help us understand what has happened to Lady Macbeth? (*She no longer looks royal or powerful. She looks untidy and out of control. Her guilt has made her insane.*)

If enough students speak the same primary language, allow them to work together to translate the questions into that language and to translate the responses into English. **ALL LEVELS**

WHEN STUDENTS STRUGGLE . . .

Connect Events Explain that students can recall important dialogue from earlier in a play to help them understand new information. Have students skim the first part of Scene 2. Ask them to identify where Menteith and the other noblemen in this scene are going to meet up with the English soldiers to march against Macbeth. (*near Birnam Wood*) Ask students why this setting is important. (*In Act IV, Scene 1, an apparition told Macbeth that he would never be conquered until Great Birnam Wood came to Dunsinane Hill. Macbeth has now* fortified himself inside Dunsinane. Whatever happens next will prove whether this prophecy, too, will come true.)

 For additional support, go to the **Reading Studio** and assign the following **Level Up Tutorial: Methods of Characterization.**

NOTICE & NOTE

 ENGLISH LEARNER SUPPORT

Discuss Figurative Language Ask students to read Angus's speech in Scene 2, lines 16–22. Discuss first what Angus means when he says, "Those he commands move only in command / Nothing in love." (*Macbeth's subjects follow his commands only because he is their king, not because they have any affection or respect for him.*) Then point out the word *like* in line 21. Explain that this is not *like* as in "to enjoy"; rather, this *like* signals a comparison. If possible, put on, or have a student put on, an overly large jacket or coat to provide a visual explanation of the simile. Then discuss the meaning of the simile—namely, that the comparison of a giant to a dwarfish thief makes clear Angus's belief that Macbeth does not have the character traits that would make him a fitting king. **MODERATE**

---

18 Every minute, revolts against Macbeth shame him for his treachery (**faith-breach**).

22–25 Macbeth's nerves, troubled by guilt, (**pestered senses**) have made him jumpy.

25–29 They give their loyalty to the only help (**med'cine**) for the sick country (**weal**). They are willing to sacrifice their last drop of blood to cleanse (**purge**) Scotland.

29–31 Lennox compares Malcolm to a flower that needs the blood of patriots to water (**dew**) it and drown out weeds like Macbeth.

1 Macbeth wants no more news of thanes who have gone to Malcolm's side.

2–10 Macbeth will not be infected (**taint**) with fear, because the witches (**spirits**), who know all human events (**mortal consequences**), have convinced him that he is invincible. He mocks the self-indulgent English (**English epicures**), then swears that he will never lack confidence.

11 loon: stupid rascal.

12 goose-look: look of fear.

14–17 Macbeth suggests that the servant cut his face so that blood will hide his cowardice. He repeatedly insults the servant, calling him a coward (**lily-livered**) and a clown (**patch**) and making fun of his white complexion (**linen cheeks, whey-face**).

Now minutely revolts upbraid his faith-breach.
Those he commands move only in command,
20 Nothing in love. Now does he feel his title
Hang loose about him, like a giant's robe
Upon a dwarfish thief.

Menteith.   Who, then, shall blame
His pestered senses to recoil and start
When all that is within him does condemn
25 Itself for being there?

Caithness.   Well, march we on
To give obedience where 'tis truly owed.
Meet we the med'cine of the sickly weal,
And with him pour we in our country's purge
Each drop of us.

Lennox.   Or so much as it needs
30 To dew the sovereign flower and drown the weeds.
Make we our march towards Birnam.

[*They exit marching.*]

Scene 3 *Dunsinane. A room in the castle.*

[*Enter* Macbeth, *the* Doctor, *and* Attendants.]

Macbeth. Bring me no more reports. Let them fly all.
Till Birnam Wood remove to Dunsinane
I cannot taint with fear. What's the boy Malcolm?
Was he not born of woman? The spirits that know
5 All mortal consequences have pronounced me thus:
"Fear not, Macbeth. No man that's born of woman
Shall e'er have power upon thee." Then fly, false thanes,
And mingle with the English epicures.
The mind I sway by and the heart I bear
10 Shall never sag with doubt nor shake with fear.

[*Enter* Servant.]

The devil damn thee black, thou cream-faced loon!
Where got'st thou that goose-look?

Servant. There is ten thousand—

Macbeth.   Geese, villain?

Servant.   Soldiers, sir.

Macbeth. Go prick thy face and over-red thy fear,
15 Thou lily-livered boy. What soldiers, patch?
Death of thy soul! Those linen cheeks of thine
Are counselors to fear. What soldiers, whey-face?

WHEN STUDENTS STRUGGLE . . .

Trace Changes in Character After students read lines 1–18 of Scene 3, discuss how Macbeth acts in this scene compared with his earlier behavior. Have students consider his level of confidence and previous interactions with Lady Macbeth with the way in which he treats the servant now. Then ask students to use a chart like the one shown to record what Macbeth thinks, says, and does. Students can use a similar chart to note details from other parts of the play and then compare them to trace how Macbeth changes from scene to scene.

Macbeth Thinks	Macbeth Says	Macbeth Does
Because a forest should not literally be able to travel to a castle and because Malcolm was "born of woman," Macbeth does not think he can be defeated.	*His mind and heart will never have doubt or fear.*	*He insults the servant, calling him a "cream-faced loon" and a "lily-livered boy"*

 For additional support, go to the **Reading Studio** and assign the following **Level Up Tutorial: Methods of Characterization.**

Servant. The English force, so please you.

Macbeth. Take thy face hence.

[Servant *exits.*]

                    Seyton!—I am sick at heart

20 When I behold—Seyton, I say!—This push
    Will cheer me ever or disseat me now.
    I have lived long enough. My way of life
    Is fall'n into the sere, the yellow leaf,
    And that which should accompany old age,
25 As honor, love, obedience, troops of friends,
    I must not look to have, but in their stead
    Curses, not loud but deep, mouth-honor, breath
    Which the poor heart would fain deny and dare not.—
    Seyton!

[*Enter* Seyton.]

30 **Seyton.** What's your gracious pleasure?

Macbeth.   What news more?

Seyton. All is confirmed, my lord, which was reported.

Macbeth. I'll fight till from my bones my flesh be hacked.
Give me my armor.

Seyton.   'Tis not needed yet.

Macbeth. I'll put it on.

35 Send out more horses. Skirr the country round.
    Hang those that talk of fear. Give me mine armor.—
    How does your patient, doctor?

Doctor.   Not so sick, my lord,
As she is troubled with thick-coming fancies
That keep her from her rest.

Macbeth.   Cure her of that.
40 Canst thou not minister to a mind diseased,
    Pluck from the memory a rooted sorrow,
    Raze out the written troubles of the brain,
    And with some sweet oblivious antidote
    Cleanse the stuffed bosom of that perilous stuff
45 Which weighs upon the heart?

Doctor.   Therein the patient
Must minister to himself.

Macbeth. Throw physic to the dogs, I'll none of it.—
Come, put mine armor on. Give me my staff.

[Attendants *begin to arm him.*]

Seyton, send out.—Doctor, the thanes fly from me.—

20–28 This push . . . dare not: The upcoming battle will either make Macbeth secure (**cheer me ever**) or dethrone (**disseat**) him. He bitterly compares his life to a withered (**sere**) leaf. He cannot look forward to old age with friends and honor, but only to curses and empty flattery (**mouth-honor, breath**) from those too timid (**the poor heart**) to tell the truth.

35 skirr: scour

47–54 Macbeth has lost his faith in the ability of medicine (**physic**) to help his wife. He says that if the doctor could diagnose Scotland's disease (**cast . . . land**) and cure it, Macbeth would never stop praising him.

(EL) ENGLISH LEARNER SUPPORT

Summarize the Drama Guide students to summarize Act V, Scene 1 and Scene 2, using the following supports with students at varying proficiency levels:

- Ask students who is in Act V, Scene 1 and Scene 2. Have students point to the speaker tags in these scenes and copy the names into a simplified version of the chart below. **SUBSTANTIAL**

- Have partners work together to ask and answer Where? Who? What? questions about Act V, Scenes 1–2, and add their responses to a chart like the one below. **MODERATE/LIGHT**

Act V, Scene 1	
Where?	*Macbeth's castle*
Who?	*Lady Macbeth, a Doctor, a Waiting Gentlewoman*
What?	*The doctor and a gentlewoman watch as Lady Macbeth wanders about, as if in a trance. She thinks that her hands are bloody and cannot be made clean again.*

Act V, Scene 2	
Where?	*The countryside near Dunsinane*
Who?	*Mentieth, Caithness, Angus, Lennox, Soldiers*
What?	*Plans are made to march against Macbeth and make Malcolm king.*

ANALYZE DRAMA

Ask students to recall what the Third Apparition said about when Macbeth would be vanquished, or defeated. (*The apparition said that Macbeth wouldn't be vanquished until Great Birnam Wood came to Macbeth's castle on Dunsinane Hill.*) Then have students reread lines 3–7 once more before answering the question. (**Answer:** *If the soldiers shield themselves from view with tree branches, it will appear that the forest is moving toward Macbeth's castle.*)

EL ENGLISH LEARNER SUPPORT

Paraphrase Read aloud the stage directions at the beginning of Scene 4 and have students identify the setting. (*the country near Birnam Wood*) Explain that in this context, *the country near* means "the countryside or land nearby"—not "a different country," such as England.

Remind students that *a wood* means a forest or an area with a lot of trees. Explain that the clue to this meaning is the word *a*. **SUBSTANTIAL**

NOTICE & NOTE

54 Pull 't off: Macbeth is referring to a piece of armor.

56 scour: purge; **them:** the English.

58–60 Macbeth leaves for battle, telling Seyton to bring the armor.

ANALYZE DRAMA
Annotate: Mark dialogue in lines 3–7 that reveals how Malcolm plans to attack Macbeth's castle.

Infer: How does this plan fulfill the prophecy Macbeth was given?

10 setting down: siege.

10–14 Malcolm says that men of all ranks (**both more and less**) have abandoned Macbeth. Only weak men forced into service remain with him.

14–16 Macduff warns against overconfidence and advises that they focus on fighting.

---

50 Come, sir, dispatch.—If thou couldst, doctor, cast
    The water of my land, find her disease,
    And purge it to a sound and pristine health,
    I would applaud thee to the very echo
    That should applaud again.—Pull 't off, I say.—
55 What rhubarb, senna, or what purgative drug
    Would scour these English hence? Hear'st thou of them?

Doctor. Ay, my good lord. Your royal preparation
Makes us hear something.

Macbeth.   Bring it after me.—
I will not be afraid of death and bane
60 Till Birnam Forest come to Dunsinane.

Doctor. [*aside*]. Were I from Dunsinane away and clear,
Profit again should hardly draw me here.

[*They exit.*]

Scene 4 *The country near Birnam Wood.*

[*Drum and Colors. Enter* Malcolm, Siward, Macduff, Siward's son, Menteith, Caithness, Angus, *and* Soldiers, *marching.*]

Malcolm. Cousins, I hope the days are near at hand
That chambers will be safe.

Menteith.   We doubt it nothing.

Siward. What wood is this before us?

Menteith.   The wood of Birnam.

Malcolm. Let every soldier hew him down a bough
5 And bear 't before him. Thereby shall we shadow
The numbers of our host and make discovery
Err in report of us.

Soldiers.   It shall be done.

Siward. We learn no other but the confident tyrant
Keeps still in Dunsinane and will endure
10 Our setting down before 't.

Malcolm.   'Tis his main hope;
For, where there is advantage to be given,
Both more and less have given him the revolt,
And none serve with him but constrainèd things
Whose hearts are absent too.

Macduff.   Let our just censures
15 Attend the true event, and put we on
Industrious soldiership.

TO CHALLENGE STUDENTS . . .

Map the Climax Have pairs of students look up the location of Birnam Wood and Dunsinane Hill on a map of Scotland and then create their own map, labeling it with characters' locations at the beginning of Scene 4. As students read Scene 4, have them annotate their maps by bulleting key events. Once the maps are created, have partners take turns describing them. For example, they might say: *This is a forest called Birnam Wood. Malcolm's soldiers are nearby, preparing to attack Macbeth's castle. Malcolm tells the soldiers to cut branches from the forest. If they hold the branches in front of them, Macbeth won't be able to tell how many soldiers there are.* Ask students to keep adding notes to their maps as they read the rest of Act V (Scenes 5–8).

Siward.   The time approaches
That will with due decision make us know
What we shall say we have and what we owe.
Thoughts speculative their unsure hopes relate,
20 But certain issue strokes must arbitrate;
Towards which, advance the war.

[*They exit marching.*]

Scene 5 *Dunsinane. Within the castle.*

[*Enter Macbeth, Seyton, and Soldiers, with Drum and Colors.*]

Macbeth. Hang out our banners on the outward walls.
The cry is still "They come!" Our castle's strength
Will laugh a siege to scorn. Here let them lie
Till famine and the ague eat them up.
5 Were they not forced with those that should be ours,
We might have met them dareful, beard to beard,
And beat them backward home.

[*A cry within of women.*]

                        What is that noise?

Seyton. It is the cry of women, my good lord. [*He exits.*]

Macbeth. I have almost forgot the taste of fears.
10 The time has been my senses would have cooled
To hear a night-shriek, and my fell of hair
Would at a dismal treatise rouse and stir
As life were in 't. I have supped full with horrors.
Direness, familiar to my slaughterous thoughts,
15 Cannot once start me.

[*Enter Seyton.*]

                        Wherefore was that cry?

Seyton. The Queen, my lord, is dead.

Macbeth. She should have died hereafter.
There would have been a time for such a word.
Tomorrow and tomorrow and tomorrow
20 Creeps in this petty pace from day to day
To the last syllable of recorded time,
And all our yesterdays have lighted fools
The way to dusty death. Out, out, brief candle!
Life's but a walking shadow, a poor player
25 That struts and frets his hour upon the stage
And then is heard no more. It is a tale
Told by an idiot, full of sound and fury,
Signifying nothing.

The Tragedy of Macbeth, Act V, Scene 5   473

16–21 Siward says that the approaching battle will decide whether their claims will match what they actually possess (**owe**). Now, their hopes and expectations are guesswork (**thoughts speculative**); only fighting (**strokes**) can settle (**arbitrate**) the issue.

4 ague: fever.

5–7 Macbeth complains that the attackers have been reinforced (**forced**) by deserters (**those that should be ours**), which has forced him to wait at Dunsinane instead of seeking victory on the battlefield.

9–15 There was a time when a scream in the night would have frozen Macbeth in fear and a terrifying tale (**dismal treatise**) would have made the hair on his skin (**fell of hair**) stand on end. But since he has fed on horror (**direness**), it cannot stir (**start**) him anymore.

17–18 Macbeth wishes that his wife had died later (**hereafter**), when he would have had time to mourn her.

▶ **AHA MOMENT**

Notice & Note: Mark words in lines 17–28 that reveal Macbeth's state of mind.

Infer: What has Lady Macbeth's death made Macbeth realize?

ENGLISH LEARNER SUPPORT

Summarize the Drama Guide students to summarize Act V, Scene 3 and Scene 4, using the following supports with students at varying proficiency levels:

- Ask students who is in Act V, Scene 3 and Scene 4. Have students point to the speaker tags in these scenes and copy the names into a simplified version of the chart below. **SUBSTANTIAL**
- Have partners work together to ask and answer Where? Who? What? questions about Act V, Scenes 3–4, and add their responses to a chart like the one below. **MODERATE/LIGHT**

Act V, Scene 3	
Where?	A room in Macbeth's castle
Who?	Macbeth, a Doctor, Servants, Seyton
What?	Macbeth learns of the English soldiers force and of Lady Macbeth's condition. He wishes that the doctor could heal Scotland, and he vows to fight to the death.

Act V, Scene 4	
Where?	The countryside near Birnam Wood
Who?	Malcolm and the English forces and their leaders
What?	Malcolm orders the troops to cut branches from the forest to hide themselves as they approach Macbeth's castle.

▶ **AHA MOMENT**

Remind students that a character's sudden realization can reveal a change in that **character** or signal an important development in the **plot.** Have partners compare their annotations and make an inference from the words they identified. Then call on students to share their inferences with the whole class. (**Answer:** *Macbeth realizes that his power is meaningless and that the kind of life he leads is short and empty.*)

 For **listening support** for students at varying proficiency levels, see the **Text X-Ray** on page 394C.

CLOSE READ SCREENCAST

Have students pair up to do an independent close read of lines 9–18. Students can record their answers on the Close Read Practice PDF.

 Close Read Practice PDF

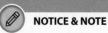 **NOTICE & NOTE**

Summarize the Drama Guide students to summarize Act V, Scene 5, using the following supports with students at varying proficiency levels:

- Ask students who is in Act V, Scene 5. Have students point to the speaker tags in these scenes and copy the names into a simplified version of the chart below. **SUBSTANTIAL**

- Have partners work together to ask and answer Where? Who? What? questions about Act V, Scene 5, and add their responses to a chart like the one below. **MODERATE/LIGHT**

Act V, Scene 5	
Where?	Macbeth's castle
Who?	Macbeth, Seyton, Soldiers, a Messenger
What?	As Macbeth prepares to fight, he learns that Lady Macbeth has died. He speaks briefly of the meaninglessness of life. Then a messenger arrives with news that Birnam Wood (Malcolm's forces, hidden behind tree branches) is approaching. Macbeth remembers the prophecy and goes out to face his enemy, even if it means his death.

38–52 The messenger's news has dampened Macbeth's determination (**resolution**); Macbeth begins to fear that the Witches have tricked him (**to doubt th' equivocation of the fiend**). His fear that the messenger tells the truth (**avouches**) makes him decide to confront the enemy instead of staying in his castle. Weary of life, he nevertheless decides to face death and ruin (**wrack**) with his armor (**harness**) on.

1–6 Malcolm commands the troops to put down their branches (**leafy screens**) and gives the battle instructions.

7 power: forces.

[*Enter a* Messenger.]

Thou com'st to use thy tongue: thy story quickly.

30 **Messenger.** Gracious my lord,
I should report that which I say I saw,
But know not how to do 't.

Macbeth.   Well, say, sir.

Messenger. As I did stand my watch upon the hill,
I looked toward Birnam, and anon methought
35 The wood began to move.

Macbeth.   Liar and slave!

Messenger. Let me endure your wrath, if 't be not so.
Within this three mile may you see it coming.
I say, a moving grove.

Macbeth.   If thou speak'st false,
Upon the next tree shalt thou hang alive
40 Till famine cling thee. If thy speech be sooth,
I care not if thou dost for me as much.—
I pull in resolution and begin
To doubt th' equivocation of the fiend,
That lies like truth. "Fear not till Birnam Wood
45 Do come to Dunsinane," and now a wood
Comes toward Dunsinane. —Arm, arm, and out!—
If this which he avouches does appear,
There is nor flying hence nor tarrying here.
I 'gin to be aweary of the sun
50 And wish th' estate o' th' world were now undone.—
Ring the alarum bell! —Blow wind, come wrack,
At least we'll die with harness on our back.

[*They exit.*]

Scene 6 *Dunsinane. Before the castle.*

[*Drum and Colors. Enter* Malcolm, Siward, Macduff, *and their army, with boughs.*]

Malcolm. Now near enough. Your leafy screens throw down
And show like those you are. —You, worthy uncle,
Shall with my cousin, your right noble son,
Lead our first battle. Worthy Macduff and we
5 Shall take upon 's what else remains to do,
According to our order.

Siward.   Fare you well.
Do we but find the tyrant's power tonight,
Let us be beaten if we cannot fight.

WHEN STUDENTS STRUGGLE . . .

Analyze Character Point out to students that examining how a character responds in a crisis can reveal insights into his or her personality and state of mind. Discuss Macbeth's attitude in Scene 5 toward the upcoming fight, helping students locate details from the text to explain why he feels this way. (In lines 33–35, Macbeth hears that the wood of Birnam is moving toward his castle. At first he responds with angry denial, but then he returns to his earlier hopeless state of mind in which he said that life is meaningless. Macbeth says in line 49 that he has grown weary of the sun, or of life. Growing weary of life and thinking it means nothing shows that Macbeth is becoming aware of the fact that his evil actions have ruined his life. There is nothing left for him to do but die, as he states in line 52.)

 For additional support, go to the **Reading Studio** and assign the following **Level Up Tutorial: Characters and Conflict.**

Macduff. Make all our trumpets speak; give them all breath,
10 Those clamorous harbingers of blood and death.

[*They exit. Alarums continued.*]

Scene 7 *Another part of the battlefield.*

[*Enter Macbeth.*]

Macbeth. They have tied me to a stake. I cannot fly,
But, bear-like, I must fight the course. What's he
That was not born of woman? Such a one
Am I to fear, or none.

[*Enter Young Siward.*]

5 **Young Siward.** What is thy name?

Macbeth.   Thou'lt be afraid to hear it.

Young Siward. No, though thou call'st thyself a hotter name
Than any is in hell.

Macbeth.   My name's Macbeth.

Young Siward. The devil himself could not pronounce a title
More hateful to mine ear.

10 harbingers: announcers.

1–4 Macbeth compares himself to a bear tied to a post (a reference to the sport of bearbaiting, in which a bear was tied to a stake and attacked by dogs).

Chinese bass Haojiang Tian performs Verdi's opera 'Macbeth' at the Hong Kong Cultural Centre, 2003.

The Tragedy of Macbeth, Act V, Scene 7   475

 ENGLISH LEARNER SUPPORT

Analyze Archaic Verbs   Have mixed language-ability groups work together to make a list of verbs in Scene 7, lines 1–28 that end in *-est* or *-st* and follow the subject word *thou*—for example, *call'st* (line 6), *liest* (line 10), *speak'st* (line 11), and *wast* (line 12). Then have the groups work together to use context clues and their knowledge of modern verb tenses to figure out the modern way to say the same verb. Finally, have students reread each line from the play using *you* and the modern form of the verb to make sure they understand the meaning of each sentence. **ALL LEVELS**

TEACH

(EL) ENGLISH LEARNER SUPPORT

Summarize the Drama Guide students to summarize Act V, Scene 6 and Scene 7, using the following supports with students at varying proficiency levels:

- Ask students who is in Act V, Scene 6 and Scene 7. Have students point to the speaker tags in these scenes and copy the names into a simplified version of the chart below. **SUBSTANTIAL**

- Have partners work together to ask and answer Where? Who? What? questions about Act V, Scenes 6–7, and add their responses to a chart like the one below. **MODERATE/LIGHT**

Act V, Scene 6	
Where?	*Outside Macbeth's castle*
Who?	*Malcolm and the English forces and their leaders*
What?	*Malcolm tells his troops to set aside their branches and to prepare to fight.*

Act V, Scene 7	
Where?	*Another part of the battlefield*
Who?	*Macbeth, young Siward, Macduff, Siward, Malcolm*
What?	*Macbeth is confronted by the son of Siward. They fight; Macbeth kills him and leaves. Macduff arrives, searching for Macbeth and vowing to kill him. The English forces capture Macbeth's castle.*

 NOTICE & NOTE

Macbeth. No, nor more fearful.

10 **Young Siward.** Thou liest, abhorrèd tyrant. With my sword
I'll prove the lie thou speak'st.

[*They fight, and* Young Siward *is slain.*]

Macbeth. Thou wast born of woman.
But swords I smile at, weapons laugh to scorn,
Brandished by man that's of a woman born. [*He exits.*]
[*Alarums. Enter* Macduff.]

Macduff. That way the noise is. Tyrant, show thy face!
15 If thou beest slain, and with no stroke of mine,
My wife and children's ghosts will haunt me still.
I cannot strike at wretched kerns, whose arms
Are hired to bear their staves. Either thou, Macbeth,
Or else my sword with an unbattered edge
20 I sheathe again undeeded. There thou shouldst be;
By this great clatter, one of greatest note
Seems bruited. Let me find him, Fortune,
And more I beg not.

[*He exits. Alarums.*]

[*Enter* Malcolm *and* Siward.]

Siward. This way, my lord. The castle's gently rendered.
25 The tyrant's people on both sides do fight,
The noble thanes do bravely in the war,
The day almost itself professes yours,
And little is to do.

Malcolm. We have met with foes
That strike beside us.

Siward. Enter, sir, the castle.

[*He exits. Alarum.*]

Scene 8 *Another part of the battlefield.*

[*Enter* Macbeth.]

Macbeth. Why should I play the Roman fool and die
On mine own sword? Whiles I see lives, the gashes
Do better upon them.

[*Enter* Macduff.]

Macduff. Turn, hellhound, turn!

Macbeth. Of all men else I have avoided thee.
5 But get thee back. My soul is too much charged
With blood of thine already.

Side notes

14–20 Macduff hopes to find Macbeth before someone else has the chance to kill him. Macduff does not want to fight the miserable hired soldiers (**kerns**), who are armed only with spears (**staves**). If he can't fight Macbeth, Macduff will leave his sword unused (**undeeded**).

22 bruited: rumored or heard.

24 gently rendered: surrendered without a fight.

27 You have almost won the day.

28–29 During the battle many of Macbeth's men deserted to Malcolm's army.

1–3 Macbeth refuses to commit suicide in the style of a defeated Roman general.

4–6 Macbeth does not want to fight Macduff, having already killed so many members of Macduff's family.

WHEN STUDENTS STRUGGLE . . .

Analyze Character Remind students that readers need to keep in mind a character's earlier dialogue to help them understand the significance of the actions taking place in the current scene. Discuss how Macbeth's attitude toward fighting changes over the course of this scene with Young Siward, and why. (*Before fighting, in lines 2–4, Macbeth recalls the third prophecy—that he cannot be killed by anyone except one not born of woman. After killing Young Siward, Macbeth grows in confidence and laughs at weapons carried by anyone born from a woman because he thinks that this prophecy protects him from harm.*)

 For additional support, go to the **Reading Studio** and assign the following [LEVEL] **Level Up Tutorial: Character Traits.**

Macduff.   I have no words;
My voice is in my sword, thou bloodier villain
Than terms can give thee out.

[*Fight. Alarum.*]

Macbeth.   Thou losest labor.
As easy mayst thou the intrenchant air
10 With thy keen sword impress as make me bleed.
Let fall thy blade on vulnerable crests;
I bear a charmèd life, which must not yield
To one of woman born.

Macduff.   Despair thy charm,
And let the angel whom thou still hast served
15 Tell thee Macduff was from his mother's womb
Untimely ripped.

Macbeth. Accursèd be that tongue that tells me so,
For it hath cowed my better part of man!
And be these juggling fiends no more believed
20 That palter with us in a double sense,
That keep the word of promise to our ear
And break it to our hope. I'll not fight with thee.

Macduff. Then yield thee, coward,
And live to be the show and gaze o' th' time.
25 We'll have thee, as our rarer monsters are,
Painted upon a pole, and underwrit
"Here may you see the tyrant."

Macbeth.   I will not yield
To kiss the ground before young Malcolm's feet
And to be baited with the rabble's curse.
30 Though Birnam Wood be come to Dunsinane
And thou opposed, being of no woman born,
Yet I will try the last. Before my body
I throw my warlike shield. Lay on, Macduff,
And damned be him that first cries "Hold! Enough!"

[*They exit fighting. Alarums.*]
[*They enter fighting, and* Macbeth *is slain.* Macduff *exits
carrying off Macbeth's body. Retreat and flourish. Enter, with
Drum and Colors,* Malcolm, Siward, Ross, Thanes, *and* Soldiers.]

35 **Malcolm.** I would the friends we miss were safe arrived.

Siward. Some must go off; and yet by these I see
So great a day as this is cheaply bought.

Malcolm. Macduff is missing, and your noble son.

Ross. Your son, my lord, has paid a soldier's debt.
40 He only lived but till he was a man,

8–13: Macbeth says that Macduff is wasting his effort. Trying to wound Macbeth is as useless as trying to wound the invulnerable (**intrenchant**) air. Macduff should strike at the helmets (**crests**) of more vulnerable foes.

15–16 Macduff . . . untimely ripped: Macduff was a premature baby delivered by cesarean section, an operation that removes the child directly from the mother's womb.

18 cowed: made fearful.

19–22 The cheating witches (**juggling fiends**) have tricked him (**palter with us**) with words that have double meanings.

23–27 Macduff tells Macbeth to surrender and become a public spectacle (**the show and gaze o' th' time**), with his picture displayed (**painted upon a pole**) as if he were in a circus sideshow.

[Stage Direction] **Retreat . . . :** The first trumpet call (**retreat**) signals the battle's end. The next one (**flourish**) announces Malcolm's entrance.

36–37 Though some must die (**go off**) in battle, Siward can see that their side does not have many casualties.

The Tragedy of Macbeth, Act V, Scene 8   477

WHEN STUDENTS STRUGGLE . . .

Analyze Characterization Explain to students that the audience can take final stock of Macbeth's character by examining how he interacts with Macduff in lines 1–14 and why Macbeth makes the decisions he does before his death. Discuss character traits that Macbeth shows in this final scene and guide students to cite evidence from the text to support their ideas. (*Even after all of his evil deeds, and even though he wants to fight instead of commit suicide [lines 1–2], Macbeth shows some remorse and goodness by refusing to fight Macduff at* first. *His reason [lines 4–6] is that his conscience is already stained with enough blood from Macduff's family for having murdered his wife and children, so he does not want more Macduff blood on his hands. At the same time, Macbeth shows arrogance as he tells Macduff [lines 12–13] that he believes he possesses a charmed life and will win if they fight.*)

 For additional support, go to the **Reading Studio** and assign the following [LEVEL UP] **Level Up Tutorial: Methods of Characterization.**

ENGLISH LEARNER SUPPORT

Clarify Pronoun Uses Guide students to clarify what subject a pronoun refers to in order to help them understand Ross's dialogue in lines 44–46. Ask: What is the cause of sorrow that Ross refers to? *(the death of Siward's son)* What does the pronoun *It* refer to? *(the sorrow caused by young Siward's death)* What does Ross mean by these words of comfort? *(Ross knows that Siward loved his son dearly and that his son's worth was too great to be measured. Thus, if Siward's sorrow matches his son's worth, Siward's sorrow will never end.)*

MODERATE

The which no sooner had his prowess confirmed
In the unshrinking station where he fought,
But like a man he died.

Siward. Then he is dead?

Ross. Ay, and brought off the field. Your cause of sorrow
45 Must not be measured by his worth, for then
It hath no end.

Siward. Had he his hurts before?

Ross. Ay, on the front.

Siward. Why then, God's soldier be he!
Had I as many sons as I have hairs,
I would not wish them to a fairer death;
50 And so his knell is knolled.

Malcolm. He's worth more sorrow, and that I'll spend for him.

Siward. He's worth no more.
They say he parted well and paid his score,
And so, God be with him. Here comes newer comfort.

[*Enter* Macduff *with* Macbeth's *head.*]

55 **Macduff.** Hail, King! for so thou art. Behold where stands
Th' usurper's cursèd head. The time is free.
I see thee compassed with thy kingdom's pearl,
That speak my salutation in their minds,
Whose voices I desire aloud with mine.
60 Hail, King of Scotland!

All. Hail, King of Scotland!

[*Flourish.*]

Malcolm. We shall not spend a large expense of time
Before we reckon with your several loves
And make us even with you. My thanes and kinsmen,
Henceforth be earls, the first that ever Scotland
65 In such an honor named. What's more to do,
Which would be planted newly with the time,
As calling home our exiled friends abroad
That fled the snares of watchful tyranny,
Producing forth the cruel ministers
70 Of this dead butcher and his fiend-like queen
(Who, as 'tis thought, by self and violent hands,
Took off her life)—this, and what needful else

46 hurts before: wounds in the front of his body, which indicate he died facing his enemy.

50 knell is knolled: Young Siward's death bell has already rung.

[Stage Direction] Macduff is probably carrying Macbeth's head on a pole.

56–57 The time . . . pearl: Macduff declares that the age (**time**) is now freed from tyranny. He sees Malcolm surrounded by Scotland's noblest men (**thy kingdom's pearl**).

61–76 Malcolm promises that he will quickly reward his nobles according to the devotion (**several loves**) they have shown. He gives the thanes new titles (**henceforth be earls**) and declares his intention, as a sign of the new age (**planted newly with the time**), to welcome back the exiles who fled Macbeth's tyranny and his cruel agents (**ministers**).

TO CHALLENGE STUDENTS . . .

Analyze Characterization Ask students to examine how Macbeth faces death and compare his character in Scene 8 to characterizations earlier in the play, such as the description of him in Act I, Scene 2. Have students consider what traits have stayed the same throughout the play. *(Macbeth has always been a brave fighter—the Captain in Act I, Scene 2, describes him in line 16 as brave—and it was his prowess on the battlefield that first won him a title from Duncan. Therefore, it is no surprise that he chooses to die fighting Macduff. At the same time, Macbeth has always been proud and has grown increasingly arrogant, so it is no surprise that he refuses to bow to Malcolm. Furthermore, in Act I, Macbeth disdains Fortune [Scene 2, line 17] and makes his own luck through the strength of his fighting. Over the course of the play, however, he comes to listen closely to the prophecies of the witches and rely on them to direct his future instead of relying on his own values and beliefs.)*

That calls upon us, by the grace of grace,
We will perform in measure, time, and place.
75 So thanks to all at once and to each one,
Whom we invite to see us crowned at Scone.

[*Flourish. All exit.*]

CHECK YOUR UNDERSTANDING

Answer these questions before moving on to the **Analyze the Text** section on the following page.

1 What happens to Lady Macbeth in Act V?

A She briefly experiences horrible nightmares.

B Overcome by guilt, she goes insane and dies.

C Although she begins sleepwalking, she is happy.

D She becomes fearful of germs and darkness.

2 In scene 3, Macbeth complains that he can only look forward to —

F a quiet death

G having grandchildren

H ruling Scotland

J empty flattery

3 How does Macbeth's rule end?

A Overwhelming guilt and grief cause him to give up the throne.

B He flees when he imagines that the forest is moving.

C Macduff kills him on the battlefield to avenge his family.

D His own soldiers turn on him and he is taken prisoner.

The Tragedy of Macbeth, Act V   479

 ENGLISH LEARNER SUPPORT

Oral Assessment Use the following questions to assess students' comprehension and speaking skills. Ask students to respond in short, complete sentences.

1. *In Act V, Lady Macbeth ___. (In Act V, Lady Macbeth goes insane and dies.)*

2. *Malcolm has the soldiers carry ___ to hide themselves as they come near Macbeth's castle. (Malcolm has the soldiers carry tree branches to hide themselves.)*

3. Who kills Macbeth? *(Macduff kills Macbeth.)* **SUBSTANTIAL/MODERATE**

 ENGLISH LEARNER SUPPORT

Summarize the Drama Guide students to summarize Act V, Scene 8, using the following supports with students at varying proficiency levels:

- Ask students who is in Act V, Scene 8. Have students point to the speaker tags in this scene and copy the names into a simplified version of the chart below. **SUBSTANTIAL**

- Have partners work together to ask and answer Where? Who? What? questions about Act V, Scene 8, and add their responses to a chart like the one below. **MODERATE/LIGHT**

Act V, Scene 8	
Where?	*Another part of the battlefield*
Who?	*Macbeth, Macduff, Malcolm, and the English forces and their leaders*
What?	*Macbeth finally faces Macduff. Macduff reveals that he was born by Caesarean section; thus, he was not "of woman born." Macbeth does not want to fight Macduff, but he fights rather than surrender. Macduff kills him and leaves with his body. The English forces arrive, and Siward learns of his son's noble death. Macduff returns, carrying Macbeth's head. Malcolm, now king, vows to restore Scotland.*

CHECK YOUR UNDERSTANDING

Have students answer the questions independently.

Answers:

1. *B*

2. *F*

3. *C*

If they answer any questions incorrectly, have them reread the text to confirm their understanding. Then they may proceed to ANALYZE THE TEXT on page 480.

APPLY

ANALYZE THE TEXT

Possible answers:

1. **DOK 4:** *The witches manipulate events. In Act III, Scene 5, Hecate chastises them for giving Macbeth information without her involvement, and she herself plans to confuse him with spirits and destroy him.*

2. **DOK 3:** *Macbeth's self-confidence helps him to be a great general. He is also devoted to his wife. Once he hears prophecies about becoming king, however, his courage and his marital devotion both contribute to his downfall. (Students should cite representative passages to support their responses.)*

3. **DOK 2:** *Birnam Wood marches on Dunsinane in the form of soldiers concealing their numbers with tree branches. Furthermore, Macbeth is killed by Macduff, who was delivered by Caesarean section rather than being "of woman born."*

4. **DOK 4:** *Responses will vary. Students may say that the play shows that the ends do not justify the means or that nothing good is worth doing evil to gain.*

5. **DOK 4:** *In Act II, Scene 2, lines 44–48, the image of blood was related to guilt. Darkness was associated with evil actions, such as the murders of Duncan and Banquo. Sleep is a peaceful time interrupted by nightmares and terrible acts. In Act II, Scene 2, lines 33–41, Macbeth imagines that he hears a voice cry out that Macbeth murders peaceful sleep. In Act V, as she sleepwalks and relives her guilt, Lady Macbeth has commanded that there be a light by her at all times (Scene 1, lines 19–20), as if to keep darkness at bay. Her deterioration redeems her somewhat because she, unlike her husband, seems to recognize that they have done something so terrible that nothing could wash away their guilt.*

RESEARCH

Suggest that students review notes that they took while reading or discussing the play. After students have recorded their questions and answers, allow time for sharing their responses. Discuss questions that seem to come up repeatedly.

Connect Have students look for examples in current or historical events as well as in books, movies, and TV shows. Encourage groups to decide why they think people are misled and how people can identify misleading information.

 RESPOND

ANALYZE THE TEXT

Support your responses with evidence from the text. 　NOTEBOOK

1. **Analyze** The Witches are sometimes seen as representing fate, or destiny. Do they merely reveal what will happen, or do they manipulate events? Explain your ideas.

2. **Cite Evidence** In what ways do Macbeth's strengths contribute to his downfall? Cite examples from the entire play to support your ideas.

3. **Interpret** In what ways are the Witches' prophecies revealed to be true in Act V?

4. **Evaluate** One scholar says that if we don't see ourselves in Macbeth, we misunderstand either the play or ourselves. In what way might this play be an allegory, or a lesson that we can apply to our own lives?

5. **Notice & Note** Explain how Lady Macbeth's actions in Act V, Scene 1, draw meaning from the repeated images of blood, darkness, and sleep that have run through the play. Does her deterioration redeem her character in the eyes of the audience? Why or why not?

RESEARCH TIP
Publishers of Shakespeare's plays often have additional information about each play on their websites. Some biography websites can also provide insight into Shakespeare's writings. Be sure to check the validity of the information and use websites that can be trusted.

RESEARCH

When you finish reading a Shakespearian tragedy, sometimes you are left with more questions than answers. What do you wonder about after reading this play? Conduct research to explore the question of your choice about Macbeth. In the chart, record your question and the answers you find.

QUESTION	POSSIBLE ANSWERS
Responses will vary. For example, students may wish to further explore connections between the play and Scotland's history.	

Connect In Scene 8, Macbeth says that it is impossible to kill him. He says this because the Witches told him that no man born of a woman can slay him. With a small group, discuss the ways in which people are misled by what other people tell them about dangers they may face.

 ## LEARNING MINDSET

Problem Solving Remind students that it is common to have to confront problems in order to achieve a goal, especially when that goal involves learning something new. (In *Macbeth*, for example, the "something new" might be Shakespeare's language.) Emphasize that whenever students solve a problem, they achieve not only a resolution to the issue at hand but also a sharpening of skills that will make them more effective problem-solvers in the future. Point out that although people often have unique ways of solving problems, there are some general techniques that can help—for example, asking for help and patiently trying different solutions instead of giving up if one does not work. Encourage students to share problem-solving techniques with the class that have worked for them.

CREATE AND DISCUSS

Document Information Take a look back at your character diagram, and complete it using evidence from Act V.

❏ Add events from Act V, including the ultimate fate of the play's major characters.

❏ Review your previous entries in the diagram, revising as needed to enhance or confirm your understanding.

❏ Add visual cues such as drawings or symbols to sum up the roles or outcomes of characters as you choose.

Discuss with a Small Group Have a discussion about the drama's relationships and events based on the character diagram you created.

❏ In your group, share your completed character diagrams, noting evidence for your ideas as needed.

❏ Work together to create a timeline of key events. Reach a group consensus on the layout and content of your group's timeline.

❏ Share your group's timeline with the class, explaining your choices.

 Go to the **Speaking and Listening Studio** for help with having a group discussion.

RESPOND TO THE ESSENTIAL QUESTION

 What are the sources of true power?

Gather Information Review your annotations and notes on *The Tragedy of Macbeth*. Then, add relevant information to your Response Log. As you determine which information to include, think about:

• the ways that power can corrupt people
• the ways in which power can be positive
• how people without power respond to those in power

At the end of the unit, use your notes to help you write a literary analysis.

UNIT 6
RESPONSE LOG

ACADEMIC VOCABULARY
As you write and discuss what you learned from the play, be sure to use the Academic Vocabulary words. Check off each of the words that you use.

❏ comprise
❏ incidence
❏ predominant
❏ priority
❏ ultimate

CREATE AND DISCUSS

Document Information Remind students that the outcomes of some characters' fates took place before Act V and that that information, too, should be included. Urge students to consider how events in this act shed light upon various characters. Point out that the visual cues students use in their diagrams will help them access information quickly in the discussion activity that follows. As students consider characters' roles or outcomes, have them also think about how the characters' fates point to themes of the play.

 For **writing support** for students at varying proficiency levels, see the **Text X-Ray** on page 394D.

Discuss with a Small Group Arrange groups so that each group includes students at various proficiencies. Choose group leaders who have a good grasp of the play, who will keep discussion going, and who will make sure that all group members have chances to participate. Provide time and materials for the creation of the timelines (though if you have access to computers, you may wish to have groups create timelines in an electronic format, possibly even making the timelines interactive). Work with groups to create a format for sharing the completed timelines.

For **speaking support** for students at varying proficiency levels, see the **Text X-Ray** on page 394D.

RESPOND TO THE ESSENTIAL QUESTION

Allow time for students to add details from *The Tragedy of Macbeth* to their Unit 6 Response Logs.

 ENGLISH LEARNER SUPPORT

Develop Vocabulary Through Discussion As students share ideas from their character diagrams, urge them to use precise language. Display the following to help guide students' discussions and elicit vocabulary growth:

• Many words could be used to describe Macbeth. Let's make a list of them and then put them in an order that matches Macbeth's behavior from the beginning to the end of the play.

• Why might you call Lady Macbeth "cruel"? What other words could you use to describe her?

• When you say that Banquo was a good friend to Macbeth, what do you mean?

• Malcolm flees Scotland when his father is murdered. Is he a coward? How does he behave when away from his homeland?

ALL LEVELS

VOCABULARY STRATEGY:
Archaic Language

Encourage students to try a variety of methods for determining the meaning of Shakespeare's archaic language. Invite volunteers to describe techniques that they have found effective. You may wish to use the final sentence of the first paragraph to demonstrate the first two bulleted strategies shown in the student edition:

- Display the following sentence from the student edition: "In addition, many of the archaic words Shakespeare uses, such as *thee* and *hath*, fell out of fashion centuries ago, so their meaning is not always easy to understand." Then work together as a class to figure out what *archaic* and *centuries* mean in this context.

- To determine the meaning of *archaic,* consider the context clue "fell out of fashion centuries ago."

- To help determine the meaning of *centuries,* consider the fact that the Latin root *cent* means "one hundred."

Practice and Apply Answers will vary, but consider the following:

1. Students should mark *thou, couldst,* and *thee,* along with other words that are unfamiliar to them.

2. Sample rewording: *Doctor, if you could determine the cause of her [my country's] illness and restore her to health, I would celebrate your success until it echoes endlessly.*

3. Students may bracket [find her disease] for *cast* and [to a sound and pristine health] for *purge.*

 RESPOND

VOCABULARY STRATEGY:
Archaic Language

Archaic language includes old words and phrases that are not commonly used in modern speech. Although Shakespeare's works brought to the English language a multitude of new words that people still use today, his poetic sentence structures are different from what we hear every day. In addition, many of the archaic words Shakespeare uses, such as *thee* and *hath,* fell out of fashion centuries ago, so their meanings are not always easy to understand.

To untangle a sentence, find the **subject** (who or what the sentence is about) and the **predicate** (what the subject is or does). Then you can separate out any other clauses in the sentence and consider the function of each one.

When you come across an unfamiliar word, use these strategies:

- Search the surrounding dialogue for helpful context clues.

- Try to break down the word into base or root words, suffixes, and prefixes and figure out the meaning from these parts.

- Use a dictionary to look up the definition of any unfamiliar words.

- Use the word in a sentence of your own to explore its meaning.

Practice and Apply Use the steps listed below to paraphrase what Macbeth asks of the Doctor in Act V, Scene 3:

> . . . If thou couldst, doctor, cast
> The water of my land, find her disease,
> And purge it to a sound and pristine health,
> I would applaud thee to the very echo
> That should applaud again. . . .

1. Mark archaic words and any other words with unclear meanings.

2. Reword as much of the speech as you can in today's English, maintaining a logical order of ideas. Leave a space in your rewording for any words whose meanings are still unclear.

3. In your reworded speech, bracket your best guesses from context at the meanings of the archaic words, or consult a dictionary.

ENGLISH LEARNER SUPPORT

Vocabulary Strategy Work with a small group of students as they complete the Practice and Apply activity. Help beginning students sound out any unfamiliar words in the Practice and Apply passage and practice pronouncing them. Speakers of Spanish may need extra help with the final consonant clusters in words such as *couldst.* Have more proficient students use a dictionary to look up the definition of unfamiliar words, such as *cast, disease, purge, pristine,* and *applaud.* Model how to use the context clue "to a sound and pristine health" to check which dictionary definition of *purge* fits the meaning of this passage. Assist the most proficient English learners with the rewording task. **ALL LEVELS**

LANGUAGE CONVENTIONS:
Inverted Sentence Structure

A key aspect of Shakespeare's style is his use of **inverted sentence structure.** In an inverted sentence, the normal word order is reversed. Some examples of inverted structure include:

• all or part of the predicate comes before the subject (*There go I.*)

• a subject comes between a helping verb and a main verb (*Had they known.*)

• a direct object precedes a verb (*Her triumph I celebrated.*)

• a prepositional phrase comes before the noun or verb it modifies (*Within the castle he waits.*)

Shakespeare includes many of these inverted sentence structures in his play. Read these lines from *The Tragedy of Macbeth*:

> **Come, go we to the King.** (Act IV, Scene 3, line 239)

> **The castle of Macduff I will surprise.** (Act IV, Scene 1, line 150)

Notice that in the first example the verb *go* precedes the subject *we*. In the second example, the direct object *the castle* and its modifier *of Macduff* appear before both the subject *I* and the verb phrase *will surprise*. Shakespeare could have written the lines this way:

> **Come, we go to the King.**

> **I will surprise the castle of Macduff.**

His use of inverted structures creates a poetic effect. Writers also use inverted sentence structures to add variety or to emphasize a word or an idea.

Practice and Apply On your own, identify the part that is inverted in each sentence below. Rewrite each sentence without the inversion. Then, working with a partner, write five original sentences on topics of your choice that use the same inverted structures found in Shakespeare's sentences.

1. O, full of scorpions is my mind, dear wife! (Act III, Scene 2, line 35)

_____

2. I'll fight till from my bones my flesh be hacked. (Act V, Scene 3, line 32)

_____

3. Retire we to our chamber. (Act II, Scene 2, line 64)

_____

4. For them the gracious Duncan have I murdered. (Act III, Scene 1, line 65)

_____

5. Then comes my fit again. (Act III, Scene 4, line 21)

_____

LANGUAGE CONVENTIONS:
Inverted Sentence Structure

If students have trouble untangling the syntax and meaning of sentences with an inverted sentence structure, suggest that they label the parts of the sentence (*S* for subject, *V* for verb, *O* for object) before trying to reorder them in a more conventional way. Also, suggest that students read the sentences aloud to listen to the way the sentences sound and see how they might be reorganized to sound clearer.

Answers:

1. *Oh, dear wife, my mind is full of scorpions!*

2. *I'll fight until my flesh is hacked from my bones.*

3. *We retire to our chamber.*

4. *I have murdered the gracious Duncan for them.*

5. *Then my fit comes again.*

Students' original sentences will vary but should use inverted structures similar to those shown in Shakespeare's sentences.

from MACBETH

Film by Rupert Goold

GENRE ELEMENTS
FILM

Tell students that the **film** they are going to watch is an excerpt from an adaption of Shakespeare's classic stage play *Macbeth*. In adapting a play or other work such as a novel for film, a director faces many challenges and opportunities. He or she must have a vision for the film and make choices to fulfill that vision. For example, a director may choose to alter actors' lines, stage directions, settings, and other elements. The director also uses filmmaking techniques and special effects to convey a particular tone and mood (atmosphere or feeling). In this lesson, students will analyze the choices the director Robert Goold made in interpreting the play and bringing it to life using the medium of film.

LEARNING OBJECTIVES

- Analyze a key scene from a Shakespearean drama in two different media.
- Understand how a director uses the elements of set, film shots, and special effects in adapting a Shakespearean drama.
- Conduct research on other film or TV adaptations of *Macbeth*.
- Write a one-paragraph analysis of a film clip, using understanding of setting and sets, film shots and angles, and special effects.
- Present an argument expressing an evaluation of a film's effectiveness, citing relevant evidence from both the film and the play.
- **Language** Explain the impact of the modern setting on the tone and mood of the film.

TEXT COMPLEXITY

Quantitative Measures	Macbeth	Lexile: N/A
Qualitative Measures	**Ideas Presented** Multiple levels of meaning presented.	
	Structures Used Adapted from the original print source.	
	Language Used Complex sentence structure and archaic unfamiliar language.	
	Knowledge Required Somewhat unfamiliar perspective.	

Online **Ed**

RESOURCES

- Unit 6 Response Log
- Writing Studio: Writing an Analysis
- Speaking and Listening Studio: Delivering an Argument
- ✓ *Macbeth* (film version) Selection Test

SUMMARIES

English

In this clip, based on Act I, Scene 3, of Shakespeare's play *Macbeth*, Macbeth and Banquo enter an abandoned warehouse and encounter three Witches, who deliver prophecies to the two men. Macbeth and Banquo express confusion and disbelief at the presence and words of the Witches, who then suddenly disappear. Ross and Angus arrive and announce that Macbeth is to become Thane of Cawdor. Macbeth and Banquo again react with confusion and disbelief, for one of the Witches' prophecies seems to have come true.

Spanish

En este fragmento, basado en el Acto I, Escena 3, de la obra de Shakespeare, *Macbeth*, Macbeth y Banquo entran a un almacén abandonado donde encuentran tres brujas, quienes dicen sus profecías a los dos hombres. Macbeth y Banquo expresan su confusión e incredulidad sobre la presencia y las palabras de las brujas, quienes súbitamente desaparecen. Ross y Angus llegan y anuncian que Macbeth va a convertirse en Thane de Cawdor. Macbeth y Banquo reaccionan nuevamente con confusión e incredulidad porque una profecía de las brujas parece haberse hecho realidad.

SMALL-GROUP OPTIONS

Have students work in small groups to read and discuss the selection.

Think-Pair-Share

- After viewing the clip from *Macbeth*, pose a question to the class—for example, How did the film's presentation of this scene compare with what you imagined when you read the text?
- Ask students to consider the question individually and to jot down a response.
- Have students meet with partners and collaborate on a shared response.
- Optional: Student pairs may consult with other pairs to reach a new consensus.
- Call upon pairs or larger groups to share and compare their responses in a whole-class discussion.

Focus on Details

- After students have viewed the clip from *Macbeth* at least once, have them break into small groups.
- Assign each group a detail to focus on the next time they view the film clip (music, acting, costumes and makeup, camera work, scenery, sound effects, special effects).
- As students watch the clip again, have them take notes on their assigned detail and the way in which it affects the film clip as a whole.
- Afterward, have students discuss their observations within the group and form a summary statement. Then, have each group share its findings with the class.

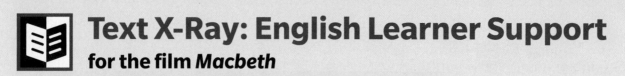

Text X-Ray: English Learner Support
for the film *Macbeth*

Use the Text X-Ray and the supports and scaffolds in the Teacher's Edition to help guide students at different proficiency levels through the selection.

INTRODUCE THE SELECTION
DISCUSS TONE AND MOOD

In this lesson, students will need to be able to discuss how film techniques are used in conjunction with Shakespeare's words to convey meaning. As a group, discuss the following terms:

- *tone:* the director's attitude toward the film (for example, serious or humorous)
- *mood:* the feeling or atmosphere that the filmmaker creates for the viewer through the audio and visual elements of the film

Ask students to describe the mood of a film they have seen and explain what effects created it, such as music, lighting, or sound. Have them speculate about the tone the effects suggested. Then ask students to restate the meanings of *tone* and *mood* in their own words and write the meanings in their notebooks. Encourage them to use these terms and others as they analyze the clip from the film *Macbeth*.

CULTURAL REFERENCES

The following words or phrases in the film may be unfamiliar to students:

- *chappy:* cracked, rough
- *fantastical:* unreal, imaginary
- *corporal:* physical, bodily
- *trifles:* trivial gifts
- *selfsame:* identical, exactly the same
- *hereafter:* from now on
- *insane root:* a poison or herb that could alter one's perceptions and behavior or cause insanity when consumed
- *borrowed robes:* in Macbeth's words and eyes, the underserved title of Thane of Cawdor

LISTENING

Identify Sound Effects

Draw students' attention to the role of voice, music, and sound used in the film clip. In particular, have students review these elements as they prepare for the Deliver an Argument activity on Student Edition page 487.

After viewing the clip, play it again with volume muted and then again with sound enabled. Then, use the following supports with students at varying proficiency levels:

- Have students hold up green cards (yes) and red cards (no) in response to questions related to the sounds used in the film clip. Ask questions such as these: Did you notice any sounds that seemed louder than others? *(yes)* Was there any music in the film? *(yes)* **SUBSTANTIAL**
- Supply students with a numbered sheet of paper to record the types of sounds they hear, in order, throughout the film clip. **MODERATE**
- Ask students to volunteer the different types of sounds they heard in the film. Then ask them to describe the mood these sounds evoked. **LIGHT**

SPEAKING

Explain the Film's Mood and Tone

As students prepare for the Deliver an Argument activity on Student Edition page 487, work with them to analyze how the modern setting, costumes, and specific images shape the mood and reflect the tone of the film.

Have small groups of mixed proficiency levels reread Act I, Scene 3, of Macbeth. Then, use the following supports with students at varying proficiency levels:

- Provide a word bank of "feeling" words. Pause the film at key points and have students choose words that describe how they feel about what they are viewing. Have them repeat words they understand. **SUBSTANTIAL**
- Discuss as a whole group the following questions about the scene: What feelings did you have as you viewed the film? How did the sound [or music] influence your feelings? The setting? **MODERATE**
- Have partners discuss these questions: How did the setting affect the film's mood? What effect did the costumes have? What do you think the filmmaker's tone toward the film was? How did the film's elements express this tone? **LIGHT**

READING

Paraphrase for Understanding

As students set a purpose for viewing the film clip, remind them that Shakespearean language can be challenging. Point out that this adaptation does not use the exact text of *Macbeth*.

Have students follow along in their text (Act I, Scene 3) as they view the film clip. Then, use the following supports with students at varying proficiency levels:

- Pause the film at key points and have students point out the stage directions in the written version of the play. **SUBSTANTIAL**
- Pause the film at key points and work as a whole group to paraphrase some of the key dialogue, such as lines spoken by the Witches or Macbeth. **MODERATE**
- Have partners view the film on their own and pause at key points that they determine and then paraphrase the dialogue. Then, have partners share some of their paraphrases with the whole group to confirm understanding. **LIGHT**

WRITING

Write an Analysis

Work with students to clarify and support the writing assignment on Student Edition page 487.

Use the following supports with students at varying proficiency levels:

- Create a word bank of terms students can use to describe the setting, camera shots and angles, and special effects used in the clip they researched. **SUBSTANTIAL**
- Provide sentence stems to help students organize their writing and introduce key details. For example: *In my opinion, the setting helped to ____. The director used special effects in order to ____. I think this adaptation was/was not successful because ____.* **MODERATE**
- Have students create their own word bank of terms to describe film elements. Invite students to use at least three of them in their analysis. **LIGHT**

Connect to the ESSENTIAL QUESTION

In this scene from the film *Macbeth*, Macbeth and Banquo encounter the Witches. Ask students to consider how the film portrays the supernatural powers of the Witches and their hold over the two men. Remind students that the Witches' prophecies relate to Macbeth's becoming king, which is a traditional source of absolute power.

QUICK START

Students regularly view different interpretations of classics through film, videos on the Internet, and television. Have students read the Quick Start question and invite them to share their experiences with the class. If students are having trouble thinking of adaptations, brainstorm as a class to name some examples. Then explain that this lesson explores the choices a director made when interpreting Shakespeare's *Macbeth*.

ANALYZE MEDIA REPRESENTATIONS

Have students read Act I, Scene 3, of *Macbeth* in preparation for watching the film clip. Tell students to keep Shakespeare's language in mind as they watch this contemporary version of the classic play. Point out that the choices a director makes about the setting and sets, film shots and angles, and special effects can drastically influence a production. Have students cite examples of how each of these aspects affected how the scene from Shakespeare's *Macbeth* was represented in this film clip.

■ English Learner Support

Internalize Vocabulary Provide students with a word bank of terms they can use to discuss the setting and sets, film shots and angles, and special effects.
SUBSTANTIAL/MODERATE

ANALYZE & APPLY

MEDIA

from

MACBETH

Film by **Rupert Goold**

 ESSENTIAL QUESTION:

What are the sources of true power?

QUICK START

Have you ever watched a film adaptation of a classic play or story? Discuss your experiences with the class.

GENRE ELEMENTS: FILM

- intended to be viewed by a wide, public audience
- tells a story visually, using actors on sets or locations
- develops from screenplays with actors' lines and direction
- includes planned camera shots and angles to evoke a mood

ANALYZE MEDIA REPRESENTATIONS

The Witches in *Macbeth* not only serve a crucial role in driving the plot, they also establish the tone of the entire play from their first appearance. Every director who stages the scene in which the Witches deliver their first prophecy to Macbeth brings a unique approach to it. This approach comprises a mix of Shakespeare's words, the mood the director wants to invoke, and the special effects that will create the strongest impact.

Consider what this production emphasizes in the scene as well as what it omits from the original play. Also consider how the director uses the medium of film in concert with Shakespeare's words. Note your responses in the chart.

SETTING / SETS	How does the modern setting affect the tone and theme of the scene?
FILM SHOTS AND ANGLES	What is the effect of multiple cuts and shots from various angles?
SPECIAL EFFECTS	How does the director use special effects to capture the Witches' supernatural powers?

BACKGROUND

In 2010, the BBC (British Broadcasting Corporation) broadcast a new version of Shakespeare's Scottish play starring Patrick Stewart in the title role. Director **Rupert Goold** *(b. 1972) modernized the play's setting to place it in a twentieth-century military dictatorship while retaining Shakespeare's powerful language. Goold has directed numerous stage versions of Shakespeare's plays. This production won a Peabody Award and aired in the United States on PBS's Great Performances.*

SETTING A PURPOSE

As you view the film, consider how the modern setting creates a certain mood or tone. Write down any questions you have during viewing. NOTEBOOK

To view the video, log in online and select **"from MACBETH"** from the unit menu.

As needed, pause the video to make notes about what impresses you or about ideas you might want to talk about later. Replay or rewind to clarify anything you do not understand.

from Macbeth (film version)   485

TEACH

BACKGROUND

Have students read the Background information. Remind students that a director makes many choices when adapting a work for the screen. While some viewers prefer a more traditional approach to a classic work such as *Macbeth*, others find modern adaptations such as this one more appealing and accessible to a wider audience.

SETTING A PURPOSE

Direct students to use the Setting a Purpose prompt to focus their viewing and listening.

For **reading support** for students at varying proficiency levels, see the **Text X-Ray** on page 484D.

WHEN STUDENTS STRUGGLE . . .

Analyze Media Have students view the film excerpt with partners. After they have watched it one time to get an overall "feel" for the scene, ask them to watch it again while taking notes. To help guide their notetaking, have students reread the questions presented in the chart on page 484. Model how to pause to take notes and clarify understanding. Afterward, invite partners to compare notes.

ANALYZE MEDIA

Possible answers:

1. **DOK 4:** *The scene is staged in a grim, rundown, abandoned warehouse. Costuming the Witches as nurses is especially effective because nurses are supposed to be caring; the contrast makes them even more chilling. These aspects set a bleak and ominous tone.*

2. **DOK 3:** *Omitted from the scene are all or part of lines 39, 40, 60, 61, 72, 90–100, 111–115, 117, 129, 135, 142, 144–146, and 151–153. A few words are changed as well: for example, Macbeth says "my father" instead of "Sinel," which might not otherwise make sense to modern viewers. Some of the omitted text wouldn't make sense in the modern warehouse setting (e.g., "Upon this blasted heath") or with the character's appearance ("doth unfix my hair"). Other omitted lines speed the pace, which increases tension.*

3. **DOK 4:** *The way the Witches say the word "Hail" sounds more like a curse than praise, which helps viewers see why Macbeth finds their words disturbing. Patrick Stewart's portrayal of Macbeth makes the rhythm and meaning of Shakespeare's words more conversational and therefore easier to understand.*

4. **DOK 3:** *The elevator in which Macbeth and Banquo arrive makes their happening upon the Witches more logical; it also adds to the strangeness of the Witches' vanishing. Flashlights allow the setting to be dark and foreboding. The photo op when Ross pins the medal of the Thane of Cawdor on Macbeth adds humor. Overall, the modern costumes make it easier to relate to all of the characters and situations.*

5. **DOK 4:** *The audio of the Witches' chant is distorted to make it more otherworldly. Actors in Shakespeare's time could only have used strange voices. Also, the Witches vanish, which would have been done using a trapdoor in Shakespeare's time.*

RESEARCH

Remind students to consider sets and setting, film shots and angles, special effects, actors' characterizations, and other elements as they evaluate the clip. Explain that the ethical use of the Internet also means downloading a movie only if it has been bought or rented from a legitimate site. Similarly, students should only watch clips online that are available on legitimate sites.

Connect Encourage students to use domain-specific vocabulary as they discuss their impressions with the group.

 RESPOND

ANALYZE MEDIA

Support your responses with evidence from the text. NOTEBOOK

1. **Analyze** How do the choices made by director Rupert Goold help develop a particular tone? Cite specific images and staging to support your answer.

2. **Compare** Which passages of Shakespeare's original text are omitted from this production of the scene? Explain how leaving out these lines affects the pacing and theme of the scene.

3. **Evaluate** How do the actors' use of emphasis and expression add meaning to this scene and help clarify your understanding? Cite specific lines.

4. **Cite Evidence** How does the twentieth-century resetting of the play's action affect your understanding of the scene? Cite specific details about costumes, setting, and other modern aspects of the production to support your answer.

5. **Analyze** What special effects are used in this scene? How might these effects have been achieved in a stage production of Shakespeare's time?

RESEARCH

RESEARCH TIP
Downloading movies illegally is copyright infringement and is not an ethical use of the Internet. Usually, clips of movies are available to watch online. You may want to begin your research on films and television with the Internet Movie Database (IMDb) website.

Shakespeare's most well-known plays have been adapted for film and television many times. Research other film or television adaptations of *Macbeth,* and if possible, view a clip from one of the adaptations. How is the clip similar to the clip from Rupert Goold's version? How is it different? What atmosphere, or feeling, is conveyed in the clip? Record what you learn in the chart.

MACBETH ADAPTATION:		
SIMILARITIES	DIFFERENCES	ATMOSPHERE/FEELING
Responses will vary. Students should use precise language in their responses and cite specific examples from both clips.		

Connect In film adaptations of plays, the camera shots and angles have a significant effect on the presentation of the story that a play in a theater cannot achieve. With a small group, discuss how the camera work of a film adaptation enhances or detracts from your enjoyment and understanding of the play.

EL ENGLISH LEARNER SUPPORT

Demonstrate Comprehension After students have viewed the film clip, ask questions to clarify their understanding of the scene. For example: Who are the two men who descend in the elevator? *(Macbeth and Banquo)* Replay the video as needed to reinforce understanding. Encourage students to follow along with the dialogue in their books if they have difficulty understanding the actors' accents. **SUBSTANTIAL**

CREATE AND PRESENT

Write an Analysis Write a one-paragraph analysis of the clip you researched, using the information from your chart.

- ❏ Introduce the clip of the adaptation you found and cite its director, writer(s), and clip source.

- ❏ Explain the setting and how it affects the mood and tone of the film. Discuss the camera shots and angles and their effects as well.

- ❏ End your analysis with a critique of the clip. Is it a successful adaptation? Give details to support your ideas.

Deliver an Argument How effective was this modern resetting of *Macbeth* in expressing key themes of Shakespeare's play? Develop your thesis in a short speech, using domain-specific vocabulary.

- ❏ Review the clip from *Macbeth,* making notes about themes that emerge through the modern setting. Cite specific details from the film that support your ideas.

- ❏ Compare the themes you noted to major themes of the play.

- ❏ Draft a statement expressing your overall evaluation of the modern production's effectiveness.

- ❏ Present your evaluation in a short speech in which you support your claim with specific, relevant evidence from both the film and the play.

RESPOND TO THE ESSENTIAL QUESTION

 What are the sources of true power?

Gather Information Review your notes on the film clip from *Macbeth.* Then, add relevant information to your Response Log. As you determine what information to include, think about:

- themes of the play that are suggested in the film clip
- reasons for changing the setting of the play to a modern one
- the atmosphere and mood the setting evokes

At the end of the unit, use your notes to write a literary analysis.

Go to the **Writing Studio** for more on writing an analysis.

Go to the **Speaking and Listening Studio** for help with delivering an argument.

ACADEMIC VOCABULARY
As you write and discuss what you learned from the film, be sure to use the Academic Vocabulary words. Check off each of the words that you use.

- ❏ **comprise**
- ❏ **incidence**
- ❏ **predominant**
- ❏ **priority**
- ❏ **ultimate**

CREATE AND PRESENT

Write an Analysis Have students review their notes from the Research activity. When students are finished writing, invite them to share their paragraph with a partner.

 For **writing support** for students at varying proficiency levels, see the **Text X-Ray** on page 484D.

Deliver an Argument Explain to students that their speeches should include a precise claim about whether the theme in the film clip is different from the themes of the play. Remind them to include specific, relevant examples from both the clip and the play to support their claim.

For **listening and speaking support** for students at varying proficiency levels, see the **Text X-Ray** on pages 484C– 484D.

RESPOND TO THE ESSENTIAL QUESTION

Allow time for students to add details from the excerpt from *Macbeth* to their Unit 6 Response Logs.

TO CHALLENGE STUDENTS . . .

Use Media Challenge students to use digital media to enhance their argument. Explain that when using digital media, they need to think about the purpose of their presentation and which element—or elements—would be most effective toward that purpose. Deciding when and how to include digital media in a presentation is an important part of the planning process. Students can use media they create—for example, digital photographs, posters, pictures they make and then digitize, recordings of sounds or music, or videos—or they can search online for existing material. Explain that if they use material created by someone else, they must credit the original source.

THE MACBETH MURDER MYSTERY

Short Story by James Thurber

GENRE ELEMENTS
SATIRE

Explain that this story is a **satire,** which means the author mocks common beliefs, social conventions, or institutions using humor, irony, and exaggeration. The goal of satire is to ridicule a vice or folly in society so that it may be improved. This may be achieved through gentle wit or bitter sarcasm, which will vary depending on the writer's attitude toward the topic they seek to mock. Readers may find themselves laughing at an exaggerated flaw within themselves and be mindful of their behavior in the future, feel ashamed of themselves, or be outraged at the social institution brought to light by the writer.

LEARNING OBJECTIVES

- Analyze satire.
- Analyze the author's use of genre and language and make connections between texts.
- Conduct research, locating relevant sources.
- Write a narrative using characteristics of genre.
- Participate in a group discussion and work collaboratively to draw conclusions.
- Identify and infer the meaning of idioms using context clues.
- Write an explanatory paragraph using correct pronoun-antecedent agreement.
- **Language** Discuss with a partner the elements of genre in the story using the key term *conventions*.

TEXT COMPLEXITY

Quantitative Measures	The Macbeth Murder Mystery	Lexile: 580L
Qualitative Measures	**Levels of Meaning/Purpose** Multiple levels of meaning.	
	Structure Simple, linear chronology; one consistent point of view.	
	Language Conventionality and Clarity Some unfamiliar language and sentence structure.	
	Knowledge Demands Some literary knowledge useful.	

RESOURCES

- Unit 6 Response Log
- Selection Audio
- Reading Studio: Notice & Note
- Level Up Tutorial: Reading for Details
- Writing Studio: Writing Narratives
- Speaking and Listening Studio: Participating in Collaborative Discussions
- Grammar Studio: Module 5: Lesson 8: Pronoun Agreement
- "The Macbeth Murder Mystery" Selection Test

SUMMARIES

English

Two travelers on vacation in the English lake country, an American woman and a presumably English man, meet. The American woman complains that she had accidentally purchased *Macbeth* when she had intended to buy a detective story. She says that she still read *Macbeth,* but she surprises the narrator by saying that she read it as a murder mystery. She then presents her "solution": Macduff committed the murders, not Macbeth. The narrator rereads *Macbeth* and comes up with an even more farfetched theory as to who was the murderer. The story ends with the narrator planning to read and "solve" *Hamlet* next.

Spanish

Dos viajeros de vacaciones en los lagos de Inglaterra, una americana y un supuesto inglés, se conocen. La americana se queja de que ha comprado *Macbeth* por accidente cuando pensaba comprar una novela detectivesca. Describe que leyó Macbeth, pero sorprende al narrador al decir que leyó la obra como una historia de misterio. Luego, presenta su "solución": Macduff cometió los asesinatos, no Macbeth. El narrador relee *Macbeth* y se le ocurre una teoría incluso más improbable sobre quién era el asesino. La historia termina con el narrador planeando leer y "resolver" *Hamlet*.

SMALL-GROUP OPTIONS

Have students work in small groups to read and discuss the selection.

Think-Pair-Share

- After students have read and analyzed "The Macbeth Murder Mystery," pose this question: What does the narrator mean when he says he will "solve" *Hamlet*?
- Have students think about the question individually and take notes.
- Then have pairs discuss their ideas about the question.
- Finally, ask pairs to share their responses with the class.
- Repeat with a new question or topic.

Numbered Heads Together

- After students have read and analyzed "The Macbeth Murder Mystery," pose this question: What do you think Thurber is satirizing in this story?
- Have students form groups of four and number themselves one to four within each group.
- Ask students to discuss their responses to the question within each group.
- Then, call a number from one to four. Have each student with that number respond for their group.
- Repeat with a new question or topic.

Text X-Ray: English Learner Support
for "The Macbeth Murder Mystery"

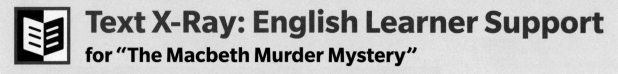

Use the Text X-Ray and the supports and scaffolds in the Teacher's Edition to help guide students at different proficiency levels through the selection.

INTRODUCE THE SELECTION
DISCUSS GENRE: MURDER MYSTERY

In this lesson, students will need to know about the purpose of satire. Explain that the purpose of a satire is to expose wrongdoing or show the foolishness of a society's practices or beliefs. Ask them what they know about the structure of murder mysteries. Guide them to understand the following elements of the genre:

- **Setting:** It is often a big house in the country or a remote area.
- **Plot:** A murder occurs at the beginning of the story and is followed by others. The character solving the case identifies clues that readers can also use to help them figure out the mystery.
- **Character:** The murderer is someone who appears throughout the story, usually the person that readers least suspect.

Explain that Thurber develops his satire by having his characters view *Macbeth* as a murder mystery instead of literature. Discuss why this is funny.

CULTURAL REFERENCES

The following words or phrases may be unfamiliar to students:

- *English lake country* (paragraph 1): a vacation destination
- *comfy* (paragraph 1): short for "comfortable"
- *a book for high-school students* (paragraph 1): implies a book people only read when required
- *rabbity* (paragraph 1): from English rhyming slang, meaning "talkative"
- *cut in* (paragraph 2): interrupt
- *mixed up* (paragraph 2): involved
- *got him* (paragraph 3): realized Macduff was the killer
- *off-hand* (paragraph 3): with no prior preparation, improvised
- *the rap* (paragraph 4): the blame for a crime
- *second sight* (paragraph 4): ability to see with eyes closed

LISTENING

Understand Main Ideas and Important Details

Have students make inferences about their initial impressions of the characters. Explain that to help the reader understand the characters, Thurber provides clues about their personalities.

Have students listen as you read aloud paragraph 1. Then, use the following supports with students at varying proficiency levels:

- Read part of paragraph 1, beginning with "All the others . . ." and ending with ". . . it was Shakespeare." Ask: Did the American woman want to buy Shakespeare's *Macbeth*? *(no)* **SUBSTANTIAL**
- Guide students in making inferences about the characters. Ask: How would you describe the American woman's personality? The narrator's personality? *(The American woman is careless and picky. The narrator is polite.)* **MODERATE**
- Have pairs list clues that reveal the characters' personalities. *(The American woman is unobservant; she buys a book without "looking at it carefully." The narrator murmurs "sympathetically" and tries to pacify her.)* **LIGHT**

SPEAKING

Discuss Conventions of Genre

Review the Background note on Student Edition page 491. Explain that Thurber uses conventions of the different genres to make his story funny.

Use the following supports with students at varying proficiency levels:

- Provide the sentence frames: *A murder mystery often begins with a _____. A _____ solves the crime by looking for _____.* Then provide terms to fill in the blanks *(murder, detective, clues)*. Have students practice saying the sentences aloud. **SUBSTANTIAL**
  Guide students in discussing the conventions of murder mysteries, using the sentence frame: *One convention of the murder mystery genre is that it often begins with a _____.* **MODERATE**
- Have pairs discuss why the American woman and narrator claim Shakespeare uses conventions of murder mystery stories in *Macbeth*. Have them use the term *conventions* in their responses. Ask pairs to share ideas with the class. **LIGHT**

READING

Make Connections Between Texts

Explain that murder mysteries include minor details that turn out to be important clues. Readers put the clues together and guess who the culprit is. Remind them that Shakespeare used details, images, and symbols to convey meaning.

Work with students to reread paragraph 4. Use the following supports with students at varying proficiency levels:

- Read aloud from "Macbeth was shielding somebody!" to "She was acting guilty to shield Macbeth." Ask students to complete this sentence frame: *The woman says people who sleepwalk never _____.* **SUBSTANTIAL**
- Echo read the paragraph with students, pausing to paraphrase as necessary. Then have pairs summarize the American woman's explanation for Macbeth and Lady Macbeth's suspicious behavior. **MODERATE**
- Have pairs reread paragraph 4, recall the sleepwalking scene in *Macbeth*, and evaluate how the American woman interprets it. *(If reading a murder mystery, her deduction makes sense, but Macbeth is a dramatic tragedy).* **LIGHT**

WRITING

Write a Narrative

Review with students the writing assignment on Student Edition page 497. Explain that to transform the genre of a story, they first need to identify the elements of both genres.

Use the following supports with students at varying proficiency levels:

- Have students work in pairs, using a familiar fable or fairy tale in the language they are most comfortable with. Help them work collaboratively to rewrite the story in English using sound/letter relationships to spell English words, or to retell the story in labeled pictures. **SUBSTANTIAL**
- Guide students in identifying elements of different genres by giving them a menu of genres and their characteristics. **MODERATE**
- Before rewriting their stories, have students create a Venn diagram of characteristics of both genres. Have them plan what to change in their revisions. **LIGHT**

Connect to the
ESSENTIAL QUESTION

"The Macbeth Murder Mystery" satirizes the genre of the murder mystery, in which sleuthing abilities and revealing hidden narratives are the source of the main character's power. The American woman in this story lauds fictional detectives who, according to convention, retell events as they actually happened in the resolutions of their stories; she does the same with the plot of *Macbeth*, reshaping the narrative by supposedly "solving" it on her own and imagining herself more intelligent than Shakespeare. The narrator then offers another, more absurd solution. The story concludes with him presented as the more powerful sleuth.

ANALYZE & APPLY

THE MACBETH MURDER MYSTERY

Short Story by **James Thurber**

ESSENTIAL QUESTION:

What are the sources of true power?

 LEARNING MINDSET

Persistence   Explain to students that it's normal to feel frustrated when reading a text in an unfamiliar genre. Even strong readers often have trouble completely understanding the complex points of satire the first time they read it. Tell students to take a break if they get frustrated, and then reread any parts they struggled with in "The Macbeth Murder Mystery." As they do, prompt them to consider what James Thurber wants his readers to think of his characters, and why. Remind students that sticking with a challenging task is a useful skill to develop, both for school and career.

QUICK START

Have you ever read or watched a murder mystery? Were you able to guess who the murderer was before it was revealed at the end? With a partner, discuss the plot of the story and any clues that helped you to solve the crime.

ANALYZE SATIRE

Satire is a literary work that ridicules a vice or folly found in society. Satirists use humor in their works to cause people to change how they think or what their priorities are. Satire can change society by forcing readers to see an idea, behavior, or custom in a critical light.

In "The Macbeth Murder Mystery," James Thurber draws upon Shakespeare's *Macbeth* to create a satire. Readers will be familiar with the references to *Macbeth*, but the unexpected way Thurber's characters transform the tragedy into a formulaic British murder mystery allows him to comment on how people approach literature. As you read, consider these questions:

- To which elements of Shakespeare's play does Thurber refer in his story?
- How are the play's elements transformed in the short story?
- What effect do these changes have on the characters? on the reader?
- What issue does Thurber ridicule in his story?

MAKE CONNECTIONS

The works of William Shakespeare have influenced many authors over the centuries. Shakespeare's plays contain insights on human nature that are timeless. For example, his tragedy *Macbeth* is known for themes of uncontrolled ambition, betrayal, and corrupting power, themes shared by many literary works. *Macbeth* is a serious drama. "The Macbeth Murder Mystery," however, is a humorous short story. James Thurber's short story relies upon his readers' knowledge of *Macbeth* to find humor in "rewriting" Shakespeare as if it were a British murder mystery. As you read, note the connections between elements of the three different genres.

ELEMENT	SERIOUS DRAMA	BRITISH MURDER MYSTERY	HUMOROUS SHORT STORY / SATIRE
Setting			
Plot			
Characters			
Purpose / Theme			

> **GENRE ELEMENTS: SATIRE**
> - mocks common beliefs, social conventions, or institutions
> - may be gentle and witty, slightly abrasive, or bitter and critical
> - often uses humor, irony, and exaggeration to make a point
> - written with the goal of improving society

TEACH

QUICK START

Have students read the Quick Start prompt and ask them what sorts of clues give away the murderer and what may lead them to the wrong conclusion, resulting in a twist at the ending. After students discuss with their partners, ask volunteers to share the plots and clues with the class.

ANALYZE SATIRE

Discuss the purpose of satire *(makes a point; seeks to improve society)* and how it meets this purpose *(mocks beliefs and institutions; tone can vary from gentle to bitter)*. Then review the list of questions with students and encourage them to add their own questions to the list as they read. Suggest that students use these questions to help analyze and annotate Thurber's satire.

MAKE CONNECTIONS

Tell students that comparing conventions of each genre will make it easier for them to understand and explain how Thurber's characters transform *Macbeth* into a formulaic British murder mystery and allow him to satirize how some people approach literature.

To help students understand how to use the chart, brainstorm to complete entries under the Serious Drama heading, using *Macbeth* as a guide. For example, ask students to describe the setting *(castles in medieval Scotland)*, summarize the plot *(Macbeth receives prophecy, acts in murderous ways, is defeated in the end)*, identify characters *(noblemen, kings, queens, witches)*, and recognize themes *(uncontrolled ambition, betrayal, corrupting power)*.

TEACH

CRITICAL VOCABULARY

Have students read each sentence before deciding which word belongs in each. Remind students to look at the context clues in the rest of the sentences to match the exact meaning of the word with the meaning of the sentence.

Answers:

1. *secluded*

2. *sacrilegious*

3. *cryptically*

4. *decisively*

5. *contention*

■ English Learner Support

Use Cognates Tell students a few of the Critical Vocabulary words have Spanish cognates: (*decisively/decisivamente, sacrilegious/sacrílego, cryptically/crípticamente*). Explain that there is also a false cognate, as the meaning of *contention* as it is used in this selection translates more closely to *aseveración.* **ALL LEVELS**

LANGUAGE CONVENTIONS

Review the information about pronoun-antecedent agreement. Point out the importance of being able to follow the pronouns in the story, which refer to multiple characters in *Macbeth.*

Read aloud the example, using pace and intonation to emphasize the dialogue. Discuss what using the pronoun *it* adds to this exchange. (*The pronoun makes it sound realistic and conversational and keeps the dialogue from being repetitive.*)

ANNOTATION MODEL

Remind students of the annotation ideas in Make Connections on page 489, which suggest noting the connections between elements of the three different genres. Point out that they should also use their annotations to comment on how Thurber creates satire through these connections, as shown in the model notes.

CRITICAL VOCABULARY

decisively   sacrilegious   secluded   contention   cryptically

To see how many Critical Vocabulary words you already know, use them to complete the sentences.

1. The famous detective hid from the press at a _____ location.

2. A _____ act might offend members of certain religious groups.

3. Speaking _____ keeps others from knowing what you are saying.

4. The astronaut acted _____ and closed the hatch without hesitation.

5. It was the lawyer's _____ that the murderer knew the victim.

LANGUAGE CONVENTIONS

Pronoun-Antecedent Agreement A **pronoun** is a word used in place of a noun or another pronoun. The word to which the pronoun refers is its **antecedent**. Writers use pronouns to avoid repetition and for variety. Here is an example of an antecedent and pronoun pair in the story you will read:

"Tell me," I said. "Did you read (Macbeth)?" "I had to read it," she said.

In this example, the noun "*Macbeth*" is the antecedent of the pronoun "it." As you read, determine the antecedent for each pronoun to help you understand the story's fast-paced dialogue.

ANNOTATION MODEL   NOTICE & NOTE

As you read, note how the author creates satire and makes connections. You can also mark evidence that supports your own ideas. Here are one reader's notes about connections in the story between Shakespeare and detective fiction:

"It was a stupid mistake to make," said the American woman I had met at my hotel in the English lake country, "but it was on the counter with the <u>other Penguin books</u>—the <u>little sixpenny ones,</u> you know, with the <u>paper covers</u>—and I supposed of course it was a <u>detective story</u>. All the others were detective stories. I'd read all the others, so I bought this one [without really looking at it carefully.] You can imagine how mad I was when I found out it was <u>Shakespeare.</u>"

connection between detective books and Shakespeare

not very observant for someone who likes detective stories

490   Unit 6

BACKGROUND

English murder mysteries follow a predictable framework and typically contain these elements that help readers predict the conclusion: a dead body; an intelligent detective; an isolated setting; a group of suspects; clues, some of which are misleading; a surprise twist; a capture; and an explanation of how the crime was committed.

James Thurber *(1894–1961) was an American humorist. His observational humor appeared in hundreds of essays, short stories, fables, and drawings and has been adapted for stage, film, and television. The Thurber Prize for American Humor was created in his honor. More information is available at www.ThurberHouse.org.*

THE MACBETH MURDER MYSTERY

Short Story by James Thurber

SETTING A PURPOSE

As you read, compare what you know about the plot and characters of Macbeth with the American woman's retelling of the story. What basic facts does she get right?

1   "It was a stupid mistake to make," said the American woman I had met at my hotel in the English lake country, "but it was on the counter with the other Penguin books—the little sixpenny[1] ones, you know, with the paper covers—and I supposed of course it was a detective story. All the others were detective stories. I'd read all the others, so I bought this one without really looking at it carefully. You can imagine how mad I was when I found out it was Shakespeare." I murmured something sympathetically. "I don't see why the Penguin-books people had to get out Shakespeare's plays in the same size and everything as the detective stories," went on my companion. "I think they have different-colored jackets," I said. "Well, I didn't

_____
[1] **sixpenny:** a former British monetary unit that is equal to six pennies.

The Macbeth Murder Mystery   **491**

NOTICE & NOTE

You can use the side margins to notice and note signposts in the text.

ANALYZE SATIRE

Annotate: Mark the reason for the American woman's anger in paragraph 1.

Analyze: Why is this reason humorous?

BACKGROUND

Have students read the Background and information about the author. Then explain how Thurber's idea to have a character uniquely interpret some key events in *Macbeth* allows the author to examine the tragedy as if it were an English murder mystery. Point out to students that Shakespearean tragedies and murder mysteries do have some things in common. In a classic English murder mystery, everyday life is interrupted by a death in a community and order is restored once the detective solves the case and catches the murderer. In Shakespearean tragedies, such as *Macbeth* and *Hamlet*, a hero's downfall causes chaos in a setting and the truth about his or her actions must be revealed before order can be restored.

 For **speaking support** for students at varying proficiency levels, see the **Text X-Ray** on page 488D.

SETTING A PURPOSE

Direct students to use the Setting a Purpose prompt to focus their reading.

ANALYZE SATIRE

Remind students that satirists use humor to ridicule a vice or folly found in society. Discuss students' first impressions of the American woman and how those impressions were formed. Emphasize the importance of keeping in mind what students already know about the play *Macbeth*, especially the characters and plot, when analyzing the story. (**Answer:** *Shakespeare is considered one of the greatest writers of all time, so it's funny that she's upset that she has Macbeth instead of a detective story.*)

 For **listening support** for students at varying proficiency levels, see the **Text X-Ray** on page 488C.

TO CHALLENGE STUDENTS . . .

Discuss Characters in Satire After they have read the story, have students discuss and compare how the American woman and the narrator each think about and interpret the works of Shakespeare. Ask them to consider questions such as how much background knowledge each character has about Shakespeare's works, how people have historically read and studied them, how each character feels about Shakespeare's works at the beginning of the story, and how each feels about his works at the end. To conclude, have students focus on the sections in which each character presents his or her "solution" of *Macbeth*.

TEACH

MAKE CONNECTIONS

Read aloud the dialogue in paragraph 2, beginning with the question, "Did you read `Macbeth'?" As you read, use pace and intonation to convey the woman's critical opinion of Shakespeare and the narrator's surprised reaction to what she is saying. To guide students' understanding of the woman as a satiric character, prompt them to analyze what she considers "smart." (**Answer:** *To her, a "smart" author would never give away who was guilty and spoil the book; it's humorous because Shakespeare did give it away, but he intended to.*)

■ English Learner Support

Comprehend Genre Remind students of the table for comparing genres on page 489. Have students work in pairs to evaluate and note which genre the narrator and the American woman fit into. Students with less proficiency in English may need a graphic organizer with elements of each genre listed clearly, with images used to support understanding and memorization. Ask volunteers to share their responses. **ALL LEVELS**

NOTICE & NOTE

decisively
(dĭ-sī´sĭv-lē) *adv.* in a firm and resolute manner.

MAKE CONNECTIONS
Annotate: Mark details that reveal the American woman's critical perspective of Shakespeare in paragraph 2.

Analyze: What is funny about this description?

notice that," she said. "Anyway, I got real comfy in bed that night and all ready to read a good mystery story and here I had 'The Tragedy of Macbeth'—a book for high-school students. Like 'Ivanhoe.'" "Or 'Lorna Doone,'"[2] I said. "Exactly," said the American lady. "And I was just crazy for a good Agatha Christie, or something. Hercule Poirot[3] is my favorite detective." "Is he the rabbity one?" I asked. "Oh, no," said my crime-fiction expert. "He's the Belgian one. You're thinking of Mr. Pinkerton, the one that helps Inspector Bull.[4] He's good, too."

2   Over her second cup of tea my companion began to tell the plot of a detective story that had fooled her completely—it seems it was the old family doctor all the time. But I cut in on her. "Tell me," I said. "Did you read 'Macbeth'?" "I had to read it," she said. "There wasn't a scrap of anything else to read in the whole room." "Did you like it?" I asked. "No, I did not," she said, **decisively**. "In the first place, I don't think for a moment that Macbeth did it." I looked at her blankly. "Did what?" I asked. "I don't think for a moment that he killed the King," she said. "I don't think the Macbeth woman was mixed up in it, either. You suspect them the most, of course, but those are the ones that are never guilty—or shouldn't be, anyway." "I'm afraid," I began, "that I—" "But don't you see?" said the American lady. "It would spoil everything if you could figure out right away who did it. Shakespeare was too smart for that. I've read that people never have figured out 'Hamlet,' so it isn't likely Shakespeare would have made 'Macbeth' as simple as it seems." I thought this over while I filled my pipe. "Who do you suspect?" I asked, suddenly. "Macduff," she said, promptly. "Good God!" I whispered, softly.

3   "Oh, Macduff did it, all right," said the murder specialist. "Hercule Poirot would have got him easily." "How did you figure it out?" I demanded. "Well," she said, "I didn't right away. At first I suspected Banquo. And then, of course, he was the second person killed. That was good right in there, that part. The person you suspect of the first murder should always be the second victim." "Is that so?" I murmured. "Oh, yes," said my informant. "They have to keep surprising you. Well after the second murder I didn't know who the killer was for a while." "How about Malcolm and Donalbain, the King's sons?" I asked. "As I remember it, they fled right after the first murder. That looks suspicious." "Too suspicious," said the American lady. "Much too suspicious. When they flee, they're never guilty. You can count on that." "I believe," I said, "I'll have a brandy," and I

---

[2] **Ivanhoe . . . Lorna Doone:** historical romance novels set in England and written in the 1800s by Sir Walter Scott and Richard Doddridge Blackmore, respectively.

[3] **Agatha Christie . . . Hercule Poirot:** Agatha Christie is a British author of crime novels, short stories, and plays; Hercule Poirot is a Belgian detective character who appears in many of her works.

[4] **Mr. Pinkerton . . . Inspector Bull:** series characters in American David Frome's (pseudonym for Zenith Jones Brown) mystery novels.

CRITICAL VOCABULARY

decisively: The American woman asserts strongly that she did not like *Macbeth*.

ASK STUDENTS to discuss how speaking decisively fits in with the rest of what they know about the woman's character. (*Once she makes a judgment or decision, she is very sure that she is right. She is equally decisive about her other ideas about how to figure out what "really happened" in* Macbeth.)

IMPROVE READING FLUENCY

Targeted Passage Have students work with partners to read paragraphs 2–3. First, use paragraph 1 to model how to read dialogue. Have students follow along in their books as you read the text with appropriate phrasing and intonation, emphasizing the differences in the way the two characters speak. Then, have partners each take a role and read both paragraphs (2–3). Encourage students to provide feedback and support for pronouncing multisyllabic words, reading with respect for punctuation, and conveying the personality of the character. Remind students that when they are reading aloud for an audience they should pace their reading so the audience has time to understand what is being read.

 Go to the **Reading Studio** for additional support in developing fluency.

summoned the waiter. My companion leaned toward me, her eyes bright, her teacup quivering. "Do you know who discovered Duncan's body?" she demanded. I said I was sorry, but I had forgotten. "Macduff discovers it," she said, slipping into the historical present. "Then he comes running downstairs and shouts, 'Confusion has broke open the Lord's anointed temple' and '**Sacrilegious** murder has made his masterpiece' and on and on like that." The good lady tapped me on the knee. "All that stuff was rehearsed," she said. "You wouldn't say a lot of stuff like that, off-hand, would you—if you had found a body?" She fixed me with a glittering eye. "I—" I began. "You're right!" she said. "You wouldn't! Unless you had practiced it in advance. 'My God, there's a body in here!' is what an innocent man would say." She sat back with a confident glare.

4   I thought for a while. "But what do you make of the Third Murderer?" I asked. "You know, the Third Murderer has puzzled 'Macbeth' scholars for three hundred years." "That's because they never thought of Macduff," said the American lady. "It was Macduff, I'm certain. You couldn't have one of the victims murdered by two ordinary thugs—the murderer always has to be somebody important." "But what about the banquet scene?" I asked, after a moment. "How do you account for Macbeth's guilty actions there, when Banquo's ghost came in and sat in his chair?" The lady leaned forward and tapped me on the knee again. "There wasn't any ghost," she said. "A big, strong man like that doesn't go around seeing ghosts—especially in a brightly lighted banquet hall with dozens of people around. Macbeth was shielding somebody!" "Who was he shielding?" I asked. "Mrs. Macbeth, of course," she said. "He thought she did it and he was going to take the rap himself. The husband always does that when the wife is suspected." "But what," I demanded, "about the sleepwalking scene, then?" "The same thing, only the other way around," said my companion. "That time she was shielding him. She wasn't asleep at all. Do you remember where it says, 'Enter Lady Macbeth with a taper'?" "Yes," I said. "Well, people who walk in their sleep never carry lights!" said my fellow-traveler. "They have second sight. Did you ever hear of a sleepwalker carrying a light?" "No," I said, "I never did." "Well, then, she wasn't asleep. She was acting guilty to shield Macbeth." "I think," I said, "I'll have another brandy," and I called the waiter. When he brought it, I drank it rapidly and rose to go. "I believe," I said, "that you have got hold of something. Would you lend me that 'Macbeth'? I'd like to look it over tonight. I don't feel, somehow, as if I'd ever really read it." "I'll get it for you," she said. "But you'll find that I am right."

sacrilegious
(săk-rə-lĭj´əs) *adj.*
grossly irreverent toward what is sacred.

LANGUAGE CONVENTIONS
Annotate: Mark pronouns in the part of paragraph 4 from "Macbeth was shielding somebody!" through "They have second sight."

Interpret: What are the antecedents of these pronouns? Do some pronouns lack antecedents?

LANGUAGE CONVENTIONS

Review the information about pronouns and antecedents. Explain that Thurber has purposefully used a lot of pronouns in this section to add variety, avoid repetition, quicken the pace of the story, and show the American woman's excitement about her theory. Have them focus on the informal, conversational tone this helps create. (**Answer:** *"I" and "my" refer to the narrator or the American woman, depending on who is talking; "he," "himself," and "him" refer to Macbeth; "she" refers to Lady Macbeth when it appears inside quotation marks and the American woman when it does not; "it" first refers to the murder and then to the text of the play; and "They" refers to sleepwalkers. Both "it" instances lack antecedents.*)

■ English Learner Support

Identify Antecedents Support students' ability to follow the pronouns in this section by stopping and asking students to reread it, marking all the pronouns. Have students turn to a partner and sort the pronouns into categories of singular/plural and subjective/objective. Collect responses to check understanding, then have students work in pairs to identify the antecedents of the pronouns. Remind speakers of Spanish and Arabic that personal pronouns should not restate the subject, as in "Macbeth he killed the king." Remind speakers of Spanish and Vietnamese that subjective and objective personal pronouns take different forms, as in *he/him.*

SUBSTANTIAL/MODERATE

For **reading support** for students at varying proficiency levels, see the **Text X-Ray** on page 488D.

WHEN STUDENTS STRUGGLE . . .

Make Connections Students must remember and understand the original text of *Macbeth* in order to recognize how the American woman is mistakenly interpreting the play. As needed, have students return to the play and reread the portions to which the American woman refers to refresh their memories of the dialogue and actions of the characters. Then have small groups take notes comparing what actually happens in the play (and the significance of each event) with the way the American woman is interpreting each event.

 For additional support, go to the **Reading Studio** and assign the following Level Up Tutorial: **Reading for Details.**

CRITICAL VOCABULARY

sacrilegious: Macduff describes the murder of King Duncan as a violation against something sacred or holy.

ASK STUDENTS to explain why Macduff might consider the murder of a king to be sacrilegious. (*Macduff refers to King Duncan as the Lord's anointed temple, which means that God chose this man to be king. Therefore, killing God's chosen ruler would mean violating something sacred.*)

ANALYZE SATIRE

Guide students to consider whose perspective is more absurd: the American woman's or the narrator's. Point out how the woman is focused on a problem that is not presented in the play—who really killed King Duncan—and evaluating the characters as suspects. Then, the narrator gets caught up in this same way of looking at the play, taking it to an even further extreme conclusion. (**Answer**: *At first the American woman's ideas seemed ridiculous to the narrator, but now his ideas are even more far-fetched than hers. Thurber's point is that illogical ideas have a way of infecting people's thinking.*)

CRITICAL VOCABULARY

secluded: The narrator escorts the American woman to a private spot where he can tell her his theory.

ASK STUDENTS to explain why the narrator wants to hold their conversation in a secluded spot. (*He doesn't want other people to overhear their conversation, which goes along with the air of secrecy that usually accompanies the solving of a mystery.*)

contention: The narrator makes a strong assertion that the "old Man" who enters in Act II, Scene 4, is "old Mr. Macbeth."

ASK STUDENTS to describe how the narrator supports his contention. (*The narrator offers what seems to be sound evidence on which to base his idea: Lady Macbeth's father's motive for murdering Duncan was to make his daughter queen.*)

cryptically: The narrator doesn't want to reveal outright who he suspects "did it" in *Hamlet*.

ASK STUDENTS to explain why looking cryptically at the American woman at this point is a good choice of words on Thurber's part. (*The narrator is aware of the plot points of* Hamlet, *so for him to give a cryptic look when stating that he suspects that everybody "did it" is ironic and humorous. It shows that he will enjoy reading* Hamlet *as if it were a murder mystery.*)

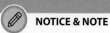 **NOTICE & NOTE**

secluded
(sĭ-klōō´dĭd) *adj.*
hidden from view.

ANALYZE SATIRE
Annotate: Mark accusations the narrator makes in paragraph 5.

Evaluate: How have the roles of the narrator and the American woman reversed? What point does Thurber make with this reversal?

contention
(kən-tĕn´shən) *n.*
an assertion put forward in argument.

cryptically
(krĭp´tĭk-lē) *adv.*
in a secretive or mysterious manner.

5 I read the play over carefully that night, and the next morning, after breakfast, I sought out the American woman. She was on the putting green, and I came up behind her silently and took her arm. She gave an exclamation. "Could I see you alone?" I asked, in a low voice. She nodded cautiously and followed me to a **secluded** spot. "You've found out something?" she breathed. "I've found out," I said triumphantly, "the name of the murderer!" "You mean it wasn't Macduff?" she said. "Macduff is as innocent of those murders," I said, "as Macbeth and the Macbeth woman." I opened the copy of the play, which I had with me, and turned to Act II, Scene 2. "Here," I said, "you will see where Lady Macbeth says, 'I laid their daggers ready. He could not miss 'em. Had he not resembled my father as he slept, I had done it.' Do you see?" "No," said the American woman, bluntly, "I don't." "But it's simple!" I exclaimed. "I wonder I didn't see it years ago. The reason Duncan resembled Lady Macbeth's father as he slept is that it actually was her father!" "Good God!" breathed my companion, softly. "Lady Macbeth's father killed the King," I said, "and hearing someone coming, thrust the body under the bed and crawled into the bed himself." "But," said the lady, "you can't have a murderer who only appears in the story once. You can't have that." "I know that," I said, and I turned to Act II, Scene 4. "It says here, 'Enter Ross with an old Man.' Now, that old man is never identified and it is my **contention** that he was old Mr. Macbeth, whose ambition it was to make his daughter Queen. There you have your motive." "But even then," cried the American lady, "he's still a minor character!" "Not," I said, gleefully, "when you realize that he was also one of the weird sisters in disguise!" "You mean one of the three witches?" "Precisely," I said. "Listen to this speech of the old man's. 'On Tuesday last, a falcon towering in her pride of place, was by a mousing owl hawk'd at and kill'd.' Who does that sound like?" "It sounds like the way the three witches talk," said my companion, reluctantly. "Precisely!" I said again. "Well," said the American woman, "maybe you're right, but—" "I'm sure I am," I said. "And do you know what I'm going to do now?" "No," she said. "What?" "Buy a copy of 'Hamlet,'" I said, "and solve that!" My companion's eyes brightened. "Then," she said, "you don't think Hamlet did it?" "I am," I said, "absolutely positive he didn't." "But who," she demanded, "do you suspect?" I looked at her **cryptically**. "Everybody," I said, and disappeared into a small grove of trees as silently as I had come.

APPLYING ACADEMIC VOCABULARY

☑ **comprise** ☐ **incidence** ☑ **predominant** ☐ **priority** ☑ **ultimate**

Write and Discuss Have students turn to a partner and discuss the following questions. Guide students to include the academic vocabulary words *comprise*, *predominant*, and *ultimate* in their responses.

- What is the narrator's **ultimate** conclusion on the identity of the murderer in *Macbeth*?
- What are the **predominant** points that **comprise** the narrator's theory?

CHECK YOUR UNDERSTANDING

Answer these questions before moving on to the **Analyze the Text** section on the following page.

1 What problem does the American woman have at the beginning of the story?

   A She has accidentally bought *Macbeth* but wants to read a mystery.

   B She is having trouble solving the crimes committed in *Macbeth*.

   C She is unable to convince the narrator that her theory is correct.

   D She can't recall which detective is which from the books she has read.

2 When the American woman reads *Macbeth,* she —

   F enjoys it so much that she tries to convince strangers to read it

   G sets it aside as soon as she can buy something different

   H comes to a new appreciation of Shakespeare

   J looks for clues that don't exist as if it's a mystery

3 What point does Thurber make in this story?

   A That Americans enjoy mysteries more than they enjoy Shakespeare

   B That *Macbeth* is far more complicated than traditionally thought

   C That people will stick with their views regardless of the facts

   D That vacations are for relaxation, not for academic reading

CHECK YOUR UNDERSTANDING

Have students answer the questions independently.

Answers:

1. *A*

2. *J*

3. *C*

If they answer any questions incorrectly, have them reread the text to confirm their understanding. Then they may proceed to ANALYZE THE TEXT on page 496.

ENGLISH LEARNER SUPPORT

Oral Assessment Provide students with the following sentence frames to assess their comprehension and speaking skills. Ask students to complete each sentence using a word or short phrase.

1. At the beginning of the story, the American woman explains that she bought _____ by mistake, but she wanted to read _____. (Macbeth; a mystery or detective story)

2. The woman reads Macbeth and concludes that _____ killed the king. (Macduff)

3. The narrator tells the woman that he believes _____ killed the king. (Lady Macbeth's father) **ALL LEVELS**

APPLY

ANALYZE THE TEXT

Possible answers:

1. **DOK 4:** *Thurber could be ridiculing people who view life through a narrow viewpoint. He also shows that ridiculous conspiracies can spread easily. Thurber makes the point that knowing conventions of different genres of literature lets readers understand different levels of meaning.*

2. **DOK 3:** *She explains that Malcolm and Donalbain fled, and guilty people never flee in murder mysteries. She thinks Macbeth and Lady Macbeth are innocent because characters the reader suspects the most are never guilty. She understands the text as a mystery novel but not as a Shakespearean tragedy.*

3. **DOK 2:** *She applies the rules of a formulaic murder mystery to the play, concluding that Macbeth was too obvious as the murderer; the ghost of Banquo wasn't believable, but his death was; Lady Macbeth must have been pretending to be guilty; and Macduff was obviously guilty because his words were rehearsed. The American woman's belief that her interpretation is right leads the narrator to doubt his own interpretation, which is ironic. The informed person is led down the path of disbelief by the incorrect assertions of the uninformed person.*

4. **DOK 4:** *The narrator speculates that Lady Macbeth's father is a character in the play and that he killed Duncan. The father then hid Duncan's body under the bed and crawled into the bed himself. The narrator adds that the father's motive was to make Lady Macbeth queen. Finally, the narrator asserts that Lady Macbeth's father also was one of the witches.*

5. **DOK 4:** *The American woman's misreading of the play is funny because she keeps interpreting the text differently than expected. Another layer of humor is brought in when the narrator gets drawn into "solving" the play. His actions contradict his previous behavior and what the reader expects. The reader can laugh at the images of him giving cryptic looks and hiding.*

RESEARCH

Provide students with guidance on finding and selecting well-supported, formally published opinions rather than inadequately supported opinions on personal websites.

Connect Guide students to understand that the narrator might prefer adaptations that are more traditional, while the American woman would probably be critical of such adaptations.

 RESPOND

ANALYZE THE TEXT

Support your responses with evidence from the text. ▤ NOTEBOOK

1. **Analyze** Writers use satire to ridicule follies or foolish ideas commonly held in a society. What does Thurber ridicule in his satire? What point does he make regarding the expectations of reading different types of literature?

2. **Draw Conclusions** The American woman explains why some characters in the play are not guilty of murder. What reasons does she provide to prove that Malcolm, Donalbain, Macbeth, and Lady Macbeth are innocent? Does she have an understanding of Shakespeare's play? Explain your answer.

3. **Cause/Effect** At the end of paragraph 4, the narrator says of Shakespeare's play, "I don't feel, somehow, as if I'd ever really read it." Describe the American woman's critical perspective of *Macbeth* and why it makes the narrator feel this way.

4. **Connect** In the last paragraph, the narrator presents his solution to Macbeth's murder mystery. How does his version of Duncan's murder differ from Shakespeare's? Explain how the characters are recast and the events of the play are changed.

5. **Analyze** Thurber is known for his humor and wit. How does he convey humor in this story? Cite details from the text to support your response.

RESEARCH

Macbeth has been performed countless times in many countries and languages around the world. Conduct research to find a review or analysis of any version of the play. Record main and supporting ideas as well as the reviewer's point of view or critical perspective in the chart.

RESEARCH TIP
Sometimes opinions you uncover in your research may present opposing points of view. Both sides can support their opinions with evidence. Think critically about the evidence and the context of the evidence to understand which position is better supported. Also consider factors that lead two people to have opposing opinions about the same literary work or performance.

VERSION / REVIEWER	MAIN IDEAS	SUPPORTING IDEAS	POINT OF VIEW
Students' responses will vary based on the review or analysis they find.			

Connect What review do you think the story's narrator would write of the version of *Macbeth* your source reviewed? What kind of review do you think the American woman would write?

⚙ LEARNING MINDSET

Problem Solving If students get stuck when trying to respond to the Analyze the Text questions, help them by asking them to apply problem-solving strategies as they work through the questions, such as revisiting the skills at the beginning of the selection or breaking down the question into separate parts. Encourage students to ask classmates for ideas about a learning strategy that worked for them when they got stuck or struggled to answer a challenging question.

CREATE AND DISCUSS

Write a Narrative In this story, characters misinterpret a dramatic tragedy as a murder mystery. How does the understanding of literary genres shape the interpretation of a story? Can characteristics of one genre be applied to another for a different interpretation? Explore these ideas by transforming one type of story into another.

❏ With a partner, choose a familiar fable or fairy tale. Note the elements that make the story you chose a fable or fairy tale.

❏ Think about the conflict or characters in the story. In what different genre might the conflict or characters appear? List the elements of the new genre. Genres you might consider include romance, science fiction, mystery, and comedy.

❏ Rewrite your story so that it maintains the same events but contains the characteristics of the new genre. For example, a fairy tale can be rewritten as a science fiction story by eliminating the magical elements and by changing the setting.

❏ Exchange your story with another pair and try to identify the fairy tale or fable your classmates used as their source.

Discuss Perspectives In a small group, share your findings about the review or analysis of a version of *Macbeth* that you researched.

❏ Identify the version of the play that was reviewed and discuss the reviewer's opinion of the play.

❏ Draw conclusions about reviewers' opinions based on your discussion. For example, did reviewers prefer traditional versions of *Macbeth* or fresh takes on the story?

❏ Write a summary of your group discussion.

RESPOND TO THE ESSENTIAL QUESTION

? What are the sources of true power?

Gather Information Review your annotations and notes on "The Macbeth Murder Mystery." Then, add relevant information to your Response Log. As you determine which information to include, think about:

- how Macbeth uses his power
- how interpretation and perspective can alter understanding
- how confidence can convince others that a baseless idea is a good idea

At the end of the unit, use your notes to help you write a literary analysis.

Go to the **Writing Studio** for more on writing a narrative.

Go to the **Speaking and Listening Studio** for help with having a group discussion.

ACADEMIC VOCABULARY
As you write and discuss what you learned from the satire, be sure to use the Academic Vocabulary words. Check off each of the words that you use.

❏ **comprise**
❏ **incidence**
❏ **predominant**
❏ **priority**
❏ **ultimate**

CREATE AND DISCUSS

Write a Narrative Before pairing students, discuss the conventions of different genres. Have students name stories from specific genres and chart elements found in each. *(For example, fairy tales typically include heroes and villains, magical creatures or supernatural elements, and a moral.)* Have partners choose a familiar story to reinterpret. Have them identify the genre and chart the conventions of the story they will rewrite. Remind them to refer to their charts while rewriting.

Discuss Perspectives Remind students that when they do not understand a comment made by another group member, they should ask questions to clarify meaning. The process of asking and answering questions respectfully can help everyone understand an issue more clearly and can lead to new insights about the reviewers' preferences. The summary should include the main points made by group members about the different versions of the play and the reviewers' opinions.

For **writing support** for students at varying proficiency levels, see the **Text X-Ray** on page 488D.

RESPOND TO THE ESSENTIAL QUESTION

Allow time for students to add details from "The Macbeth Murder Mystery" to their Unit 6 Response Logs.

 ## ENGLISH LEARNER SUPPORT

Discuss Perspectives Provide students with a graphic organizer to note the version of the play and the reviewers' opinions. Ask them to record the main ideas of each review as they listen to each other. Encourage them to ask clarifying questions when they do not understand what a group member has said. **ALL LEVELS**

CRITICAL VOCABULARY

Explanations will vary but should cite words listed:

1. *contention*

2. *cryptically*

3. *decisively*

4. *sacrilegious*

5. *secluded*

VOCABULARY STRATEGY:
Idioms

Review the definition of **idioms.** Point out that students can use context clues, or information in the sentence and surrounding sentences, to help figure out an idiom's meaning. Read aloud the following sentence from paragraph 1: "And I was just crazy for a good Agatha Christie, or something." Ask students to identify the idiom. *(crazy for)* Then guide students to look for context clues and develop a definition for the idiom. *(very enthusiastic about)* Ask volunteers to share their definition with the class.

Practice and Apply Encourage students to go back to the paragraphs cited in the questions if they need more context to infer the meaning of an idiom.

1. *I interrupted*

2. *involved in it*

3. *stared at me*

4. *take the blame*

RESPOND

CRITICAL VOCABULARY

Practice and Apply Explain which Critical Vocabulary word is most closely associated with each idea or situation.

1. Which word is associated with a disagreement? Why?

   _____

2. Which word is associated with a mysterious note? Why?

   _____

3. Which word is associated with a judge's ruling? Why?

   _____

4. Which word is associated with an angry, irreverent comment? Why?

   _____

5. Which word is associated with a secret hideout? Why?

   _____

VOCABULARY STRATEGY:
Idioms

Idioms are expressions whose meanings differ from the literal meanings of their words. Often in satire, authors will use idioms because they are colorful or humorous. In "The Macbeth Murder Mystery," the characters' informal way of speaking and use of idioms contrast with the archaic lines from Shakespeare quoted in the story.

Practice and Apply Read these idioms from the selection. Use context clues to define each phrase. Check your answers by substituting your definition in the idiom's place in the original sentence.

1. "I cut in on her" (paragraph 2)

   _____

2. "mixed up in it" (paragraph 2)

   _____

3. "fixed me" (paragraph 3)

   _____

4. "take the rap" (paragraph 4)

   _____

ENGLISH LEARNER SUPPORT

Pronounce Vocabulary Each of the Critical Vocabulary words contain sounds which present transfer issues from Spanish. Some present transfer issues from Vietnamese. Use the following supports for students at varying proficiency levels:

• Project or write each word on the board. Read aloud the words a few times each, pointing to individual syllables of the word as they are pronounced. Have students practice saying the word to each other. **SUBSTANTIAL/MODERATE**

• After completing the Practice and Apply activity, have students work in pairs to read aloud and discuss their responses with each other. Encourage them to provide feedback on their pronunciation and discuss any responses on which they disagreed. **LIGHT**

LANGUAGE CONVENTIONS:
Pronoun-Antecedent Agreement

A **pronoun** replaces a noun that has already been used (or sometimes another pronoun) to avoid repetition. The word the pronoun replaces is called its **antecedent.** Pronouns must agree with their antecedents in number. Here is an example from the story.

> "Hercule Poirot is my favorite detective." "Is he the rabbity one?" I asked.

The pronoun "he" is singular to match its antecedent, "Hercule Poirot." Use singular pronouns for singular antecedents. Use plural pronouns for plural antecedents.

SINGULAR PRONOUNS	PLURAL PRONOUNS
I, me	we, us
you	you
he, she, it, him, her	they, them

When you are reading a short story with dialogue, it is helpful to follow the pronouns and determine each pronoun's antecedent. A pronoun is vague when its antecedent is unclear.

In "The Macbeth Murder Mystery," the author presents conversations in which pronouns refer both to characters in the story and multiple characters in the play.

> "Do you remember where it says, 'Enter Lady Macbeth with a taper'?" "Yes," I said. "Well, people who walk in their sleep never carry lights!" said my fellow-traveler. "They have second sight. Did you ever hear of a sleepwalker carrying a light?" "No," I said, "I never did." "Well, then, she wasn't asleep."

The antecedent for "she" is found in the first sentence: "Lady Macbeth." However, if you are not following dialogue closely, you might think "she" refers to the American woman: "my fellow-traveler." The author intentionally uses vague pronouns to convey the idea of an intense and realistic face-to-face conversation.

Practice and Apply Write a short paragraph reviewing "The Macbeth Murder Mystery" using pronouns and clear antecedents, checking to make sure they agree in number. Your paragraph should explain your opinion about the story with supporting evidence. When you have finished, share your paragraph with a partner. Have your partner identify the antecedent of each pronoun and note any vague pronouns for you to correct.

Go to the **Grammar Studio** for more on pronouns and antecedents.

LANGUAGE CONVENTIONS:
Pronoun-Antecedent Agreement

Review the information about pronouns with students. Explain that Thurber purposefully used pronouns almost exclusively for the characters in *Macbeth*, to emphasize that these characters are the focus of the conversation between the narrator and the American woman. When students use pronouns in their own writing, they should ask themselves whether they have used the correct form of the pronoun or need to clarify antecedents.

Practice and Apply Have partners read each other's reviews and discuss whether pronouns are used correctly and effectively in their sentences. Students should make corrections as needed. (*Responses will vary but should use pronouns that agree in number with clear antecedents.*)

 ## ENGLISH LEARNER SUPPORT

Use Pronouns Correctly Use the following supports with students at varying proficiency levels:

- Have students search paragraph 5 of the selection for sentences that include pronouns and copy a few in their notebook. Have them draw lines connecting each pronoun to its antecedent and identify any pronouns with missing antecedents. **SUBSTANTIAL**

- Have students work with partners to write their reviews of the story. Then have them meet with another pair to compare their use of pronouns and edit if necessary. **MODERATE**

- After students write their reviews, have them explain to a partner where they have used pronouns, whether they are singular or plural. Have them identify the antecedent to each pronoun. **LIGHT**

from MANGA SHAKESPEARE: MACBETH

Graphic Novel by Robert Deas and Richard Appignanesi

MENTOR TEXT

SHAKESPEARE AND SAMURAI (AND ROBOT NINJAS?)

Book Review by Caitlin Perry

> This review serves as a **mentor text,** a model for students to follow when they come to the Unit 6 Writing Task: Write a Literary Analysis.

GENRE ELEMENTS
GRAPHIC NOVEL

Tell students that a graphic novel is a type of book that tells a story through a series of images that are divided into frames or panels. Most graphic novels also include text in the form of dialogue, thought bubbles, and boxes with bits of narration.

BOOK REVIEW

Explain that book reviews, like movie reviews, are written in order to evaluate a work and communicate to others whether or not they should read (or watch) it. Point out that a book review recaps just enough of the work for readers to get a sense of what the book is about. The writer then presents an opinion and provides evidence from the work to back it up.

LEARNING OBJECTIVES

- Analyze visual elements of a text.
- Analyze evidence.
- Compare texts across genres.
- Deliver a pitch.
- Identify the roots and meanings of words.
- Write and present an argument.
- **Language** Use transition words in a persuasive pitch.

TEXT COMPLEXITY

Quantitative Measures	Manga Shakespeare: Macbeth	Lexile: N/A
	Shakespeare and Samurai (and Robot Ninjas?)	Lexile: 1480L
Qualitative Measures	**Ideas Presented** Multiple levels of meaning in Selection 1; literal meanings in Selection 2.	
	Structures Used Implicit themes and relationships between images and narration in Selection 1.	
	Language Used Many Tier I and Tier II words; archaic language and complex sentence structures.	
	Knowledge Required Basic knowledge of the Shakespeare play *Macbeth* and of comics or manga.	

Online 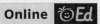 Ed

RESOURCES

- Unit 6 Response Log
- 🔊 Selection Audio
- 📖 Reading Studio:
  Notice & Note
- 📱 Level Up Tutorials, listed at point of use
- 🖥 Writing Studio:
  Using Textual Evidence
- 💬 Speaking and Listening Studio:
  Delivering Your Presentation
- ⚙ Vocabulary Studio:
  Word Roots
- ❗ Grammar Studio: Module 12:
  Lesson 6: Dashes and Parentheses
- ✓ from *Manga Shakespeare: Macbeth* / "Shakespeare and Samurai (and Robot Ninjas?)" Selection Test

SUMMARIES

English

This excerpt from *Manga Shakespeare: Macbeth* relates the events from Act I, Scene 3, of the original play. Fresh from battle, Banquo and Macbeth encounter the weird sisters and learn their prophecies. Ross and Angus arrive with news that the title of Thane of Cawdor has been granted to Macbeth, thereby fulfilling one of the witches' prophecies.

In "Shakespeare and Samurai (and Robot Ninjas?)," the reviewer points out that while she admires many of the visual elements of *Manga Shakespeare: Macbeth,* she objects to the sporadic use of technology. She feels that the story would have been better if set in feudal Japan.

Spanish

Este pasaje de *Manga Shakespeare: Macbeth* relata los eventos del Acto I, Escena 3, de la obra original. Luego de la batalla, Banquo y Macbeth encuentran a las hermanas misteriosas y escuchan sus profecías. Ross y Angus llegan con la noticia de que el título de Thane de Cawdor se le ha otorgado a Macbeth, de ese modo, cumpliendo una de las profecías de las brujas.

En "Shakespeare y el samurái (¿y robots ninja?)", el crítico señala que aunque admira muchos de los elementos visuales de *Manga Shakespeare: Macbeth*, se opone a los usos esporádicos de tecnología. Siente que la historia habría sido mejor si hubiese estado basada en el Japón feudal.

👥 SMALL-GROUP OPTIONS

Have students work in small groups to view, read, and discuss the two selections.

Think-Pair-Share

- After students have read the excerpt from *Manga Shakespeare*: *Macbeth,* pose this question: "If you were going to create your own manga for *Macbeth,* what changes would you make to the setting, characters, or other elements, without changing the plot?"
- Have students consider and take notes about the question individually.
- Then, have pairs discuss their ideas about the question.
- Finally, ask pairs to share their responses with the class.

Triple-Entry Journal

- Have students divide a page into three columns and label the columns "Quotes from the Book Review," "My Notes," and "My Partner's Notes."
- In the first column, instruct students to record passages from "Shakespeare and Samurai (and Robot Ninjas?)" that they found interesting, important, or confusing.
- In the middle column, instruct them to write their own reactions, interpretations, or questions.
- Then, ask partners to exchange journals. In the third column, have them write responses either to the quotations from the text or their partner's notes.

Text X-Ray: English Learner Support

for *Manga Shakespeare*: *Macbeth* and "Shakespeare and Samurai (and Robot Ninjas?)"

Use the Text X-Ray and the supports and scaffolds in the Teacher's Edition to help guide students at different proficiency levels through the two selections.

INTRODUCE THE SELECTIONS
DISCUSS GRAPHIC NOVELS

In this lesson, students will need to be able to discuss elements of a graphic novel. Display a graphic novel and provide the following explanations:

- A *graphic novel* is a narrative conveyed with images and minimal text. A *manga* is a Japanese style of graphic novel.
- Pages in a manga are divided into *frames*, or boxes.
- Frames have *dialogue bubbles*—circles with words that characters say. They also may have *thought bubbles*—circles with words that show what characters are thinking.
- Illustrations show *facial expressions*—looks on characters' faces—and *body language*—how characters' bodies suggest what characters are feeling (happy, confused, angry, and so on).

Encourage students to ask clarifying questions and to take notes to use as a reference when they read the selections.

CULTURAL REFERENCES

The following words or phrases may be unfamiliar to students:

- *adaptation* (paragraph 1): a piece of writing that has been made into a new form (for example, by changing the genre or altering elements such as setting and characters)
- *samurai* (paragraph 2): a member of a powerful group of Japanese fighters of long ago
- *futuristic technology* (paragraph 2): technology (such as tools and weapons) that people imagine may exist in the future
- *artistry* (paragraph 3): creative skill of an artist
- *worth a try* (paragraph 3): a descriptive phrase meant to suggest that something is worthwhile

LISTENING

Understand Main Ideas and Key Details

Direct students to Student Edition pages 512–513. Tell students that you will give directions and ask them some questions about the manga so that they can show their listening comprehension.

Use the following supports with students at varying proficiency levels:

- Provide instructions to check students' comprehension. Tell students to look at the top of page 512 and circle the picture of Ross. Point out that Ross has his arms in the air. *(Students should circle Ross in the top frame.)* Give other similar instructions. **SUBSTANTIAL**
- Tell students to look at the top of page 512. Note that Ross is wearing a helmet and Angus has a scar over his eye. Ask: Which character greets Macbeth with his arms raised in the air? *(Ross)* **MODERATE**
- Tell students that on page 512, Ross says to Macbeth, "He bade me call thee Thane of Cawdor, for it is thine." Explain that Macbeth doubts that he deserves that title because he knows that the Thane of Cawdor still lives. Ask: What does Macbeth doubt, and why? *(He doubts that he is truly the Thane of Cawdor; he knows that the Thane of Cawdor is still alive and does not yet know about his treason.)* **LIGHT**

SPEAKING

Use Transitions to Signal Ideas

Read the Deliver a Pitch activity on Student Edition page 521. Explain that using transitions such as *first, second,* and *finally* or *most of all* (to show order of importance, not chronology) will help signal each supporting point.

Use the following supports with students at varying proficiency levels:

- List three reasons why a graphic novel of *Macbeth* is a good idea, incorporating an appropriate transition to introduce each one. After each reason, pause to have students repeat it aloud. **SUBSTANTIAL**
- Have partners draft a pitch together. After they have come up with their pitch and reasons, guide students to add transitions such as *first* and *second*. Then have students take turns delivering their pitch. **MODERATE**
- Have partners draft a pitch together. After they have come up with a draft, guide students to add transitions such as *the first reason* and *the second reason*. Then have students take turns delivering their pitches to their group and respond to questions. **LIGHT**

READING

Read and Paraphrase or Summarize

Have students reread a passage from the manga text or Perry's book review and paraphrase or summarize its main idea and details.

Use the following supports with students at varying proficiency levels:

- Model reading aloud the first page of manga text. Have students follow along with an index finger or pointer. Pause periodically to see whether students have been able to track your progress. Then read the text again. Ask: Whose thumb is the sister holding? *(the pilot's)* Ask: Where was he flying toward? *(He was flying homeward.)* Discuss the meaning of "homeward." *(toward home)* **SUBSTANTIAL**
- Read aloud paragraph 1 from the review, pausing to paraphrase after each sentence. Then ask: How well does Caitlin Perry like Macbeth? *(She likes it a little.)* **MODERATE**
- Have pairs reread the first paragraph of Perry's review and take turns paraphrasing each sentence. **LIGHT**

WRITING

Use Comparing and Contrasting Words

Read the Write a Comparison assignment on Student Edition page 521. Tell students that words and phrases such as *both, also, but,* and *however* are good words to use to compare and contrast two things.

Use the following supports with students at varying proficiency levels:

- Develop and display a bank of words that are useful for comparing and contrasting. Then guide students to use these in simple sentence frames: _____ the Witches in the play and the Witches in the manga look mean. The Witches in the play were _____, [but/however] the Witches in the manga were_____. **SUBSTANTIAL**
- List these connectors on the board: *also, and . . . too, both . . . and, but,* and *however*. Elicit descriptions of the Witches in *Macbeth* and the manga and guide students to write comparing sentences using connectors. **MODERATE**
- Have pairs of students work together to write sentences that compare and contrast the Witches in *Macbeth* and the manga. Have students use the connectors *also, and . . . too, both . . . and, but,* and *however*. **LIGHT**

GRAPHIC NOVEL

from
MANGA SHAKESPEARE: MACBETH

by **Robert Deas and Richard Appignanesi**
pages 503–517

? Connect to the
ESSENTIAL QUESTION

As students have been learning in this unit, Macbeth's tragic story warns of the dangers that can befall those who seek power at any cost. If the setting of Shakespeare's play is changed—drastically so—will its ideas change as well? For example, should power be won, or earned? What are the sources of true power? How does the desire for power drive personal ambition? In this lesson, students will have the chance to consider those questions again by looking at Macbeth from another perspective.

COMPARE ACROSS GENRES

Point out that the first selection is an excerpt from the graphic novel *Manga Shakespeare: Macbeth* and that the second selection is a book review of that same graphic novel. Tell students that as they read the graphic novel, or manga, they should form their own opinions about how effective they think the adaptation is; that way, when they read the book review, they will be prepared to compare their own opinions with those expressed by the reviewer.

COMPARE ACROSS GENRES

The next two selections are different genres, or types of writing. One text, a book review, has been written in direct response to the other, a graphic novel. As you read, consider whether you agree with the opinions about the graphic novel that are expressed in the review.

 ESSENTIAL QUESTION:

What are the sources of true power?

BOOK REVIEW

SHAKESPEARE AND SAMURAI (AND ROBOT NINJAS?)

by **Caitlin Perry**
pages 518–519

⚙ LEARNING MINDSET

Persistence The first selection includes some of the original language from the Shakespeare play; thus, students may find it somewhat challenging to read. The second selection requires students to recall details from the first selection. Model positive self-talk that students can use if they get discouraged: "If I'm reading but I don't think that I'm 'getting it,' then there are several things I can do. I can take a break and try again a bit later. Or, I can try reading the text aloud to see if it makes more sense that way. Or, I can ask someone for help. I'll be persistent. I know that if I keep trying, I'll understand more."

QUICK START

Think about a book, TV show, or movie you have read or watched recently. What did you think about it? Think about *why* you hold that opinion. Can you provide details that back up your opinion? Tell a partner what you thought of the work and give examples of details that helped you form that opinion.

ANALYZE VISUAL ELEMENTS

A **graphic novel** is a book that tells a story through images and text that are laid out like a comic book. Pages of a graphic novel contain frames, which are boxes containing illustrations of events, actions, and reactions. Speech and thought bubbles often contain the characters' dialogue, and sometimes additional text on the edges of the frames provides narration. The visual elements of a graphic novel add depth, movement, drama, emotion, and meaning to the reader's experience. As you read the excerpt from *Manga Shakespeare: Macbeth,* use the chart below to record how different elements of graphic novels are reflected in the text.

GENRE ELEMENTS: GRAPHIC NOVEL

- contains images, often accompanied by text, in individual frames or panels
- tells a narrative through images and text
- makes use of dialogue, characters' expressions, and onomatopoeia

GRAPHIC NOVEL ELEMENT	HOW ELEMENT IS REFLECTED IN THE TEXT
Visual background details establish setting	*We can see that the characters are in a mountainous region, and some kind of plane or spaceship has crashed. In the final frame, we see the ruins of a city.*
Characters' appearance, body language, and expressions reveal their traits	*Macbeth and Banquo have confused expressions as they shrug at each other, showing that they find the witches and their prophesy puzzling.*
Dialogue drives the action	*The witches explain the prophesy to Macbeth and Banquo. They find out that part of the prophesy has come true when Angus delivers news.*
Styles of fonts reveal characters' intonation and expression	*Placing the words "SPEAK, I CHARGE YOU" in all capital letters, larger than the rest of the type, shows Macbeth's angry impatience.*

ANALYZE EVIDENCE

In an opinion piece such as a book review, the author tells what he or she thinks about a work of art. To explain these opinions, the author gives reasons. A **reason** tells why an opinion or claim is valid. **Evidence** provides specific examples that illustrate a reason. For example, in a review of a production of *The Tragedy of Macbeth,* an author might express her opinion that a high school audience would enjoy the production. Her reason for the opinion might be, "*Macbeth* addresses the importance of balancing your ambitions and your morals, a theme young people can relate to."

As you read "Shakespeare and Samurai (and Robot Ninjas?)," look for the reasons and evidence the author provides to support her opinions.

GENRE ELEMENTS: BOOK REVIEW

- provides a short summary of the work being reviewed
- includes the opinions of the reviewer, based on text evidence
- usually recommends or discourages the audience from reading or watching the work

QUICK START

Have students take a minute to jot down their opinions and several details from the work before exchanging ideas with a partner.

ANALYZE VISUAL ELEMENTS

Review each of the visual elements commonly used in **graphic novels.** Make sure students understand that visual elements include text as well as illustrations. Ask students familiar with comics or graphic novels to elaborate on the explanations provided in the table or to provide examples. As students read the excerpt from *Manga Shakespeare: Macbeth,* remind them to use the chart to make note of how each element is used in that text.

ANALYZE EVIDENCE

Review the information about supporting an opinion with **reasons** and about illustrating reasons with **evidence.** Invite volunteers to share the opinions and examples they came up with in the Quick Start activity. Ask why the writer of a book review would want to provide reasons and evidence. *(The writer would want to provide reasons to explain why a particular opinion is valid, and evidence to convince readers that each reason is true, in order to encourage people to read the book or discourage them from doing so.)*

ENGLISH LEARNER SUPPORT

Analyze Visual Elements Display a graphic novel and use it to reinforce key terms such as *visual elements, frames, speech and thought bubbles,* and *dialogue.* Then use pantomime to solidify students' understanding of the terms *body language* and *facial expressions.* Confirm students' understanding by pointing to something in the graphic novel and asking "What is this?" or "Is this a frame?" or "Is this a thought bubble or a speech bubble?"
SUBSTANTIAL/MODERATE

CRITICAL VOCABULARY

Encourage students to read all the sentences before deciding which word best completes each one. Remind students to look for context clues that suggest which word to use in each sentence.

Answers:

1. *daunting*

2. *enraptured*

3. *sporadic*

■ **English Learner Support**

Use Cognates Tell students that one of the Critical Vocabulary words has a Spanish cognate: *sporadic/esporádico*. **ALL LEVELS**

LANGUAGE CONVENTIONS

Review the information about **parentheses.** Read the example, using appropriate pauses and emphasis to indicate the **parenthetical phrase.** Discuss the value of including the parenthetical information. Point out that writers may use them for various reasons—for example, to provide helpful information (such as definitions or examples) or to provide colorful details that give readers a sense of the author's voice.

 ANNOTATION MODEL

Review the Annotation Model. Point out the evidence that the reviewer includes in her book review and connect it to the graphic novel. Remind students to annotate visual elements they notice in the manga that could serve as evidence in support of the book reviewer's opinion.

◎ **GET READY**

CRITICAL VOCABULARY

sporadic   enraptured   daunting

To preview Critical Vocabulary, use the words to complete the sentences.

1. If the large project is too _____, break it up into smaller pieces.

2. I enjoyed the concert. From the first chord, I was _____.

3. I am only a(n) _____ spectator; I don't go to every game.

LANGUAGE CONVENTIONS

Parentheses add or clarify information in a sentence. Usually, parentheses enclose information that is less important than the main part of a sentence. The text within parentheses is called a **parenthetical phrase** or **parenthetical expression**. Read the example below.

My problem lay in the sudden use of the technology, from telescoping binoculars and very basic motorbikes, to holographic messages and (admittedly my favorite part of the book) teleporting robot ninjas.

As you read the book review, notice how the reviewer uses parentheses to set apart less-important information within sentences.

ANNOTATION MODEL   **NOTICE & NOTE**

Look at the frame below from the graphic novel *Manga Shakespeare: Macbeth* and read the lines from the review. Notice how the reviewer uses evidence to support her opinion.

However, I found the artistry to be impressive, with randomly delightful tidbits of <u>hilarious facial expressions</u> (though not perhaps fitting with everyone's idea of the characters) and beautifully created weird sisters and spirit dragons.

502   Unit 6

EL **ENGLISH LEARNER SUPPORT**

Develop Vocabulary Review the terms *manga*, *book review*, and *evidence*. Explain that in a book review of a manga, evidence will be an example from the manga—either from the text or from the artwork. Then read aloud the Annotation Model. Paraphrase the text and explain any unfamiliar terms. Say, "Point to the hilarious, or funny, facial expressions in the manga." Explain that the facial expressions are evidence, or examples, of how good or interesting the artwork is. Have students locate the phrase "hilarious facial expressions" in the excerpt from the book review. Point out that this is evidence that supports the idea that the manga's artistry is impressive. **ALL LEVELS**

BACKGROUND

Manga *are Japanese comics that follow a style developed in the late 19th century. Characteristics of manga include expressive dialogue bubbles, lines that indicate movement and speed, and multiple flashbacks within the story. Today, manga has a growing global audience. Traditionally, manga comics are produced in black-and-white editions, and stories are often serialized, with new chapters published in separate editions. Genres are as varied as in other storytelling media, ranging from action and adventure to love stories to true historical events.*

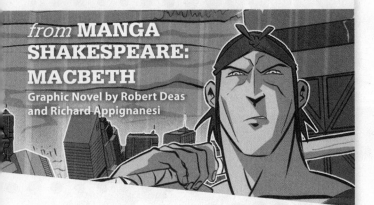

from **MANGA SHAKESPEARE: MACBETH**

Graphic Novel by Robert Deas and Richard Appignanesi

The purpose of the Manga Shakespeare *series is to bring Shakespeare's stories to a new audience by not only telling them through a different medium but also changing their context. With the help of Shakespeare scholars, a team of manga authors and artists have put new spins on classic stories. For example,* The Tragedy of Romeo and Juliet *moves to the streets of modern-day Tokyo, where Romeo is a rock star. And* Macbeth *combines a post-nuclear, futuristic setting with samurai—military leaders who rose to power in Japan between the twelfth and nineteenth centuries.*

Canadian writer and editor **Richard Appignanesi** *founded the* Manga Shakespeare *series with the hope that the adaptations would help educate readers about Shakespeare's stories. British artist* **Robert Deas,** *who has studied the manga style extensively, worked with Appignanesi to bring the* Macbeth *edition of the series to life.*

PREPARE TO COMPARE

As you read, notice which elements the graphic novelists used from Shakespeare's original play. Also notice where the authors had fun with new ideas. Ask yourself whether the manga version of the scene effectively conveys the events, ideas, and themes of Macbeth.

Notice & Note

You can use the side margins to notice and note signposts in the text.

TEACH

BACKGROUND

Have students read the Background note. Point out that one purpose of the *Manga Shakespeare* series is to bring Shakespeare's stories to a new audience. Ask students how the series' creators changed the stories to appeal to a modern audience. *(They are telling the stories through a different medium—the manga books—and they're changing the context, or setting.)* Ask students whether they would be more interested in reading manga than reading an original Shakespeare play. Then ask why the series' creators might care about keeping the stories of Shakespeare alive. *(The stories are still powerful and entertaining enough to appeal to modern audiences; they teach universal themes; they connect us to the history of the English language.)* Explain that the *Manga Shakespeare Macbeth* excerpt corresponds to the action in Act I, Scene 3, of the original play.

PREPARE TO COMPARE

Direct students to use the Prepare to Compare prompt to focus their reading.

WHEN STUDENTS STRUGGLE . . .

Review the Plot Before students start reading, they may find it helpful to review what they have learned previously about the plot of *Macbeth*. Point out that the action in this excerpt begins at the point when the three witches (the "weird sisters") appear to Macbeth and Banquo. Invite volunteers to recall what will happen when Macbeth and Banquo meet these characters. *(The weird sisters will give three prophecies.)* Ask students what happens after Macbeth and Banquo talk to the weird sisters. *(They learn that the Thane of Cawdor is dead. They go to greet King Duncan.)*

 For additional support, go to the **Reading Studio** and assign the following **Level Up Tutorial: Plot: Sequence of Events.**

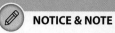
🗨️ ENGLISH LEARNER SUPPORT

Develop Vocabulary and Retell Stories Lead students on a walk-through of pages 504–505. Have students name things and describe actions in each of the frames. Read the dialogue aloud, paraphrasing it. Then guide intermediate and advanced students to write the dialogue in modern English. Paraphrase archaic language such as "hast thou" and "doth."

ALL LEVELS

ORIGINAL	MODERN PARAPHRASE
Where hast thou been, sister?	Where have you been, sister?
Sister, where thou?	Sister, where were you?
Here I have a pilot's thumb, wrecked as homeward he did come.	This is a pilot's thumb. He crashed as he was flying home.

🗨️ ENGLISH LEARNER SUPPORT

Reinforce Directionality in Reading Students—especially speakers of Arabic—may need some support tracking the text through the manga. To reinforce directionality, display pages 504–505 from the manga. Model how students should track the story from the topmost frame on the left to the bottommost frame on the right. Have pairs of students flip through the pages of the manga, sweeping their index fingers left to right and top to bottom across each page.
SUBSTANTIAL

ANALYZE VISUAL ELEMENTS

Annotate: Take notes about how the first two pages of this excerpt are similar to the original *Macbeth* and how they are different.

Analyze: How do the images place Shakespeare's words in a different context?

from Manga Shakespeare: Macbeth   505

✎ ANALYZE VISUAL ELEMENTS

Have students review their notes and then share their ideas. (**Annotate:** *Students may note the following: the characters are the same, but the settings are very different; some of the language is similar, but the graphic novel uses very few words; plot events are the same—Macbeth and Banquo meet the witches.* **Answer:** *The setting is not feudal Scotland, as an aircraft has crashed. The story has shifted context to a world that has modern technology but that appears to have been ruined.*)

🔵EL ENGLISH LEARNER SUPPORT

Develop Vocabulary and Retell Stories Have pairs of students begin a chart that they can use to summarize the graphic novel. **MODERATE/LIGHT**

Pages	Setting	Characters	Events
504–505	Someplace in the country. There is a storm and a fire. A plane crashed there.	Three sisters—the weird sisters—are floating in the air.	One sister says that she has been killing swine (pigs). She shows her sisters a thumb. It is from a pilot who was flying his plane home. The sisters hear Macbeth coming.

WHEN STUDENTS STRUGGLE...

Use a Graphic Organizer Work with a small group of students. Guide them to create a Venn diagram comparing the first two pages of the manga to Shakespeare's play about Macbeth. Instruct them to focus on setting, characters, plot, and language.

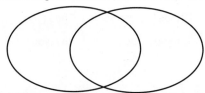

ENGLISH LEARNER SUPPORT

Develop Vocabulary to Build Understanding

Read aloud the dialogue on pages 506–507. Then guide students to write the dialogue in modern English.

MODERATE/LIGHT

ORIGINAL	MODERN PARAPHRASE
So foul and fair a day I have not seen.	I haven't seen a day like this—a day both bad [because of warriors lost in battle] and good [because Macbeth's side won].
What are these, so withered and so wild in their attire, that look not like inhabitants of the Earth?	What are these beings in front of us? They look so old and strange. They don't look human.
Why do you start and seem to fear things that do sound so fair?	Why do you look so surprised? Why do you seem afraid of things that sound good?
If you can look into the seeds of time, speak then to me who neither beg nor fear your favours nor your hate.	If you can look into the future, then speak to me. I won't beg, and I'm not afraid of you.

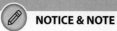

 ENGLISH LEARNER SUPPORT

Create a Glossary Have students create a glossary of terms they can refer to as they read the manga. (If they created one when they read the play *Macbeth*, urge them to refer to it as needed.) You might begin with the following:

doth (does)	hath (has)	thee (you/to you)	thou (you)
hast (have)	shalt (will)	thine (yours)	thy (your)

SUBSTANTIAL/MODERATE

ANALYZE VISUAL
ELEMENTS

Annotate: Write down details
you notice about how the artist
has chosen to portray Banquo.

Analyze: How do Banquo's
appearance and facial
expressions contribute to his
characterization?

from Manga Shakespeare: Macbeth   507

ANALYZE VISUAL ELEMENTS

Have students review pages 506–507 and answer the
question about Banquo's appearance. Ask students what
they think of how the artist chose to depict him. Ask them
if it matches the way they pictured him when they read the
play. (**Annotate:** *Students may note details such as his eye
patch, hairdo, facial hair, cigar, and angry expression.* **Answer:**
*Banquo's appearance—his clothing, hair, the way he's smoking
a cigar—and his facial expressions make him look rough and
tough. His aggressive nature is shown in his confrontation with
one of the witches.*)

■ English Learner Support

Analyze Visual Elements   Read aloud the instructions
under Annotate and Analyze. Explain that *portray* means
"to show in drawing or in writing." For example, if an artist
portrays Banquo a certain way, he draws Banquo to look and
act a certain way. If a writer portrays a character a certain
way, the writer uses words to show what a character is like.
Display these questions:

How does Banquo look?

What is Banquo wearing?

What is Banquo doing?

Have pairs take turns asking and answering the
questions.   **MODERATE/LIGHT**

APPLYING ACADEMIC VOCABULARY

❑ **comprise**   ❑ **incidence**   ☑ **predominant**   ❑ **priority**   ☑ **ultimate**

Write and Discuss   Have students turn to a partner to discuss the following questions based
on the story thus far. Guide students to include the academic vocabulary words *predominant*
and *ultimate* in their responses. Ask volunteers to share their responses with the class.

- Which of the sisters' predictions do you think is **predominant** in Macbeth's mind?
  Why?
- What would need to happen in order to enable Macbeth to achieve that **ultimate** goal?

TEACH

ANALYZE VISUAL ELEMENTS

Have students look closely at the image that forms the background for the three inset panels on this page. Then have them compare their notes to those of a partner. (**Annotate:** *Students may note that Macbeth and Banquo are looking at each other.* **Answer:** *The artist probably drew Banquo and Macbeth this way to show that they are confused over the prophecies that they both have received. They do not know how these prophecies can come true, so they are not sure if they can believe them.*)

■ English Learner Support

Develop Vocabulary to Build Understanding Remind students that the term *body language* refers to the way that peoples' bodies communicate what they are feeling. Point out how Banquo is standing with his arms apart and slightly raised. Explain that English speakers use nonverbal cues like these to communicate the ideas "I don't know!" or "I'm confused!"

Pantomime various examples of body language and have students interpret how you are feeling. (For example, if you cross your arms and frown, they might say, "You're angry!") Briefly discuss situations in which students might expect to see each example of body language used. **SUBSTANTIAL/MODERATE**

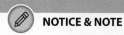

ANALYZE VISUAL ELEMENTS

Annotate: Write notes about Macbeth's and Banquo's expressions and body language at the bottom of this page.

Infer: Why might the artist have chosen to draw the characters this way?

508   Unit 6

WHEN STUDENTS STRUGGLE...

Paraphrase and Predict Work with a group of students to paraphrase the paradoxical prophecies about Banquo. Have students predict what it will mean for Banquo, based on what they already know.

Lesser than Macbeth and greater.	*He won't hold as high a rank, but he will have a greater life.*
Not so happy, yet much happier.	*He won't be as happy as Macbeth will be, but he will be happy longer.*

Thou shalt get kings, though thou be none.	*Your descendants will be kings, but you won't be a king yourself.*

 For additional support, go to the **Reading Studio** and assign the following LEVEL **Level Up Tutorials: Paraphrasing** and **Making Predictions.**

ANALYZE VISUAL ELEMENTS

Annotate: Mark the speech bubble in the last frame of the page.

Evaluate: How would a playwright instruct an actor to deliver this line in the way that the manga artist depicts it visually?

from Manga Shakespeare: Macbeth   509

✏ ANALYZE VISUAL ELEMENTS

Ask students to paraphrase the dialogue in the bottom two frames. *(In the middle frame, Macbeth is saying, "The possibility that I will become king is unbelievable." "Speak, I charge you" means "I demand you speak!")* Ask students how the lettering in the bottom speech bubble differs from the lettering of the speech bubbles above it. *(The lettering is much larger.)* Ask students why that might be. *(Macbeth is shouting. He is impatient, angry, or both.)* (**Answer:** *A playwright would write stage directions to indicate that Macbeth yells at the weird sisters—such as "(shouting angrily)".)*

■ English Learner Support

Analyze Visual Elements   Read aloud the instructions under Annotate and Evaluate. Explain that to depict something visually means to draw it. (Point out that the word *depict* is similar to the word *portray*.) Next, break down the Evaluate question: Who is in the bottom frame, or picture? *(Macbeth)* Does he look happy, or angry? *(angry)* How do you know? *(his face)* Look at the words he says. Are they bigger or smaller than the words above? *(bigger)* How do you think those words sound? *(loud, angry)* Explain that the sentence "Speak, I charge you" means "I order you to speak." **SUBSTANTIAL/MODERATE**

EL ENGLISH LEARNER SUPPORT

Develop Vocabulary   Direct students to the bottom frame on this page and tell them that Macbeth is shouting angrily. Write *angrily* on the board. List other adverbs, such as *deeply, meanly,* and *aggressively.* Explain the meaning of each adverb. Then guide students to use the adverbs to discuss characters' actions in the story thus far—for example: Are the witches frowning meanly? Macbeth is thinking deeply. How aggressively Banquo is talking to that witch! **SUBSTANTIAL/MODERATE**

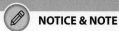

Develop Vocabulary to Build Understanding

Review what happens in the frames on this page. Point out that *whither* in the middle frame means "where," so the entire question means "Where did they go?" Next, draw students' attention to the metaphor "takes the reason prisoner." Remind students that a metaphor compares two things in a creative way. Ask students what would make reason, or sense, seem like a prisoner. *(If reason were locked up or couldn't be used, it would be like a prisoner.)* Then ask students to paraphrase what Banquo is asking or wondering about in the bottom frame. *("Have we eaten something that has made us imagine things that aren't real?")*

MODERATE/LIGHT

ANALYZE VISUAL ELEMENTS

Annotate: Write brief descriptions of Macbeth's and Banquo's expressions here.

Analyze: How do these characters' facial expressions add meaning to their dialogue?

from Manga Shakespeare: Macbeth   511

ANALYZE VISUAL ELEMENTS

Have partners discuss the characters' expressions and compare their annotations. (**Annotate:** *Students may note that in the top frame, Macbeth and Banquo appear to be grinning or smirking. Banquo is either squinting or winking. In the bottom frame, they are both scowling angrily.* **Answer:** *In the top frame, the two men look as if they are joking or speaking sarcastically. They probably are mocking what the witches have told them because they don't believe that the prophecy could possibly come true. In the bottom frame, they are ready to attack whomever they hear coming.*)

■ English Learner Support

Analyze Visual Elements   Read aloud the Analyze question. Review the term *facial expression*. Model some facial expressions and identify the related emotion—for example, frowning *(angry)* and smiling *(happy)*. Point to the frame at the top of the page. Ask whether Macbeth and Banquo look as if they are serious or joking. *(It may not be clear to all students, but some probably will recognize that they are joking.)* Ask students to describe Macbeth's and Banquo's expressions in the top and bottom frames. *(Top frame: They are grinning. Bottom frame: They are frowning. They are showing their teeth.)* Then guide students to write those descriptions. **SUBSTANTIAL/MODERATE**

ENGLISH LEARNER SUPPORT

Develop Vocabulary to Build Understanding

Point to the bottom frame on this page. List *surprised* and several synonyms on the board. *(amazed, shocked, startled, stunned)* Explain each one, pantomiming the degree of surprise. Have students say the words, write them, and possibly draw faces to reinforce meaning. Then display this sentence frame: _____ looks _____. Have students use the frame to describe the facial expressions of Banquo and Macbeth. (**Possible answer:** *Banquo looks shocked. Macbeth looks stunned.*)

MODERATE/LIGHT

WHEN STUDENTS STRUGGLE...

Understand Language Structures Work with a small group. Read aloud the dialogue on this page and then help students to paraphrase the dialogue using modern language. Direct students to the bottom frame and have students describe Banquo's and Macbeth's facial expressions. *(They both look shocked, especially Macbeth.)* Ask students what Banquo means when he asks, "Can the devil speak true?" *(He thinks that the three witches are evil and that they follow the devil. He wonders whether they spoke the truth because he assumes that the devil would lie.)* Then ask students why Banquo asks that. *(The representative of the king calls Macbeth "Thane of Cawdor." That Macbeth would receive that title was one of the witches' prophecies.)*

ANALYZE VISUAL
ELEMENTS

Annotate: Mark the illustration
of Angus's memory.

Analyze: How does the
illustration add to what Angus
is saying about his memory?

from Manga Shakespeare: Macbeth 513

✏ ANALYZE VISUAL ELEMENTS

Remind students that the king's men are Angus and Ross. Point out that in the graphic novel, Angus is depicted as having a scar over his left eye and Ross is shown wearing a Japanese coat of armor and a helmet. (***Answer:** In the center frame, Angus tells Macbeth that the Thane of Cawdor is still alive but that he deserves to lose his life. The image shown to the right in the same frame shows the Thane of Cawdor being captured—Angus may be remembering this because he and Ross captured the traitor themselves. The image suggests that the thane will soon be killed as punishment for treason.*)

Some students may be challenged by the language in the bottom dialogue bubble. Read the dialogue aloud. Explain that treason is a crime against the king or the government and that a capital crime is a crime punishable by death. So "treasons capital" means that people plotted against the king (so their actions, as a group, are called *treasons*) and for that reason they must die.

■ English Learner Support

Analyze Visual Elements Help speakers of Vietnamese and other Asian languages with tense markers. Ask students to point to the memory in the second panel. Make clear that Angus (on the left, speaking) is remembering what happened. Introduce the phrases *committed treason, was captured,* and *will be punished.* Offer these sentence starters to help students retell what happened:

> *The Thane of Cawdor.* . . . (*committed treason against the king*)
>
> *Ross and I.* . . . (*captured him*)
>
> *The king.* . . . (*took away his title*)
>
> *The former Thane of Cawdor will be.* . . . (*executed as punishment for his crime*)
>
> **MODERATE/LIGHT**

 For **listening support** for students at varying proficiency levels, see the **Text X-Ray** on page 500C.

TO CHALLENGE STUDENTS . . .

Critique Visual Elements Invite students to interpret and critique the illustration of the mask or face guard in the center frame and the bottom frame. Have students write a paragraph on why the artist included it, what it might symbolize, and whether or not they feel that it is an effective visual element.

ENGLISH LEARNER SUPPORT

Develop Vocabulary to Build Understanding
Read aloud the dialogue on this page. Paraphrase Banquo's dialogue in the bottom frame. *(Often, dark forces try to trick us and cause bad problems.)* Ask students what instruments of darkness, or dark forces, Banquo is talking about. *(the weird sisters, or witches)* Then have students use these sentence frames to summarize this page:

> *Macbeth thinks that _____ because _____.* (the witches' prophecy to Banquo will come true; the first part of his own prophecy has come true)
>
> *Macbeth looks _____ compared to Banquo.* (confident)
>
> *Banquo tells Macbeth that _____.* (evil beings often tell us what is true because they know that the truth ultimately will harm us)
>
> *Banquo seems _____, but Macbeth does not.* (worried)

MODERATE/LIGHT

WHEN STUDENTS STRUGGLE...

Understand Language Structures Have students read aloud the dialogue on pages 514–515. Point out Banquo's statement at the bottom of page 514. Ask them what he might be thinking. *(He is worried. He doesn't trust the witches.)* Remind students that **foreshadowing** occurs when a character says something or when something happens to suggest that something else (often something bad) will happen in the future. Ask students what Banquo's words might foreshadow. *(Something bad might happen to him and Macbeth as a result of the prophecy.)* Then ask pairs of students to work together to write a summary of these pages.

 For additional support, go to the **Reading Studio** and assign the following Level Up Tutorial: **Suspense and Foreshadowing.**

TO CHALLENGE STUDENTS . . .

Analyze Dialogue Have pairs of students memorize the lines on pages 514–515. Instruct them to take turns assuming the roles of Banquo and Macbeth and acting out their dialogue and Macbeth's aside. Then, have them improvise the same dialogue using modern language and mannerisms. Afterward, ask students to draw on their experience to critique the importance of the dialogue on pages 514–515.

EL ENGLISH LEARNER SUPPORT

Read and Paraphrase Read aloud the dialogue on pages 516–517. Paraphrase and explain the dialogue after reading each bubble. Then direct students back to the top of page 516. Coach students to use key words and expressions to retell what is happening in each frame on pages 516–517.

MODERATE/LIGHT

ANALYZE VISUAL ELEMENTS

Annotate: Mark details in the illustrations on this page and the previous one that give you a sense of setting.

Evaluate: How does the illustrator use different perspectives in the frames on these pages? What is the effect of the different perspectives?

from Manga Shakespeare: Macbeth   517

ANALYZE VISUAL ELEMENTS

Discuss the details in the illustrations on these last two pages. Have students describe the buildings. Ask them to describe the landscape. Point out that it's unclear whether the canyon is a natural formation (the result of an earthquake, for example) or the result of a war. Then have students share their responses to the Analyze Visual Elements activity. (**Answer:** *So far, most of the frames showed close-up details of the characters as they interacted. In this final frame, the perspective pulls back, and we get a sense of the landscape they are in. We see that they are among ruined buildings—buildings that look as if they were destroyed in a war.*)

ENGLISH LEARNER SUPPORT

Summarize Reading Working with a small group, guide students to flip back through the graphic novel and summarize the key dialogue and events they read about. Explain that when students summarize events from a story, they often use present-tense verbs instead of past tense. (Example: *As the scene begins, the weird sisters gather and talk. Soon, Macbeth and Banquo arrive and challenge the sisters. . . .*) Guide students to use the proper verb forms and subject-verb agreement as they retell this excerpt from the graphic novel.

LIGHT

BACKGROUND

Have students read the Background note. Explain that since Perry's review covers the entire graphic novel *Manga Shakespeare: Macbeth*, she includes a few references to things other than what students have just seen in the excerpt (for example, the "teleporting robot ninjas").

PREPARE TO COMPARE

Direct students to use the Prepare to Compare prompt to focus their reading.

 For **reading support** for students at varying proficiency levels, see the **Text X-Ray** on page 500D.

LANGUAGE CONVENTIONS

Have volunteers read aloud each sentence that contains a **parenthetical expression,** using appropriate pauses and emphasis to indicate how the information is set off by **parentheses.** (**Answer:** *The information may help clarify Perry's meaning; it reveals her personality and helps readers make a personal connection with her, while creating a fun, lighthearted tone.*)

■ English Learner Support

Use Language Conventions Display these simplified versions of sentences from paragraph 2:

> I thought the Japanese samurai twist was interesting (even though *Macbeth* was a Scottish play).

> I didn't like the sudden use of technology, such as telescoping binoculars, motorbikes, holographic messages and (my favorite part of the book) teleporting robot ninjas.

> Although I loved some of the changes to the story (mostly the ninjas), I was unhappy that the technology wasn't used more often.

Read aloud each sentence and explain any unfamiliar terms. Then invite volunteers to create a parenthetical expression that they could add to paragraph 2 and to explain its purpose. **MODERATE/LIGHT**

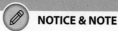 **NOTICE & NOTE**

BACKGROUND
Author **Caitlin Perry** wrote this book review for publication on a blog. Perry herself writes fantasy and paranormal romance novels. She has published two books, The Walker in the Dark and The Cursed Prophecy.

PREPARE TO COMPARE
As you read, prepare to defend or challenge the author's claims, marking relevant text evidence to support your ideas.

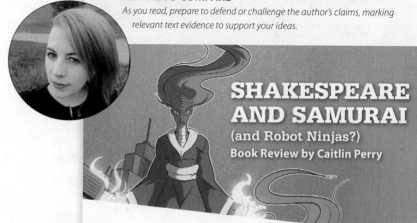

SHAKESPEARE AND SAMURAI
(and Robot Ninjas?)
Book Review by Caitlin Perry

Notice & Note

You can use the side margins to notice and note signposts in the text.

LANGUAGE CONVENTIONS
Annotate: Mark the parenthetical phrases in paragraph 2.

Connect: How does the information enclosed in parentheses add to the meaning and tone of the review?

1   I should start by saying that, while I don't dislike the "Scottish play", it is also not in my most beloved of Shakespeare's works. So when I give the Manga Shakespeare version of *Macbeth* a middling rating it is not a direct response to either the illustrations done by Robert Deas or the adaptation of the text as done by Richard Appignanesi. However, that is not to say that I was one hundred percent swayed by this adaptation either.

2   Initially I found the feudal-esque[1] Japanese samurai twist to be interesting (assuming you could ignore that it was intended to be a Scottish play, which I had no problem with). Jumping in head first, ready to see what delightful adaptations awaited me, I was met by a confusing but still interesting post-apocalyptic[2] world that combined feudal Japan with modern and futuristic technology alike, all in a world that had clearly been blown up quite a bit. My problem lay in the sudden use of the technology, from telescoping binoculars and very basic motorbikes, to holographic[3] messages and (admittedly my favorite part of the book) teleporting robot ninjas. However, as much as I loved some of these changes (mostly the ninjas), I became frustrated by how infrequently this technology was used, especially in a

---

[1] **feudal-esque** (fyōōd-l-ĕsk´): resembling the feudal system, a social system involving nobility who held lands given by a monarch.
[2] **post-apocalyptic** (pōst-ə-pŏk-ə-lĭp´tĭk): referring to an era after the destruction of the world.
[3] **holographic** (hō-lə-gra´fĭk): produced with three-dimensional images formed by light beams from a laser.

IMPROVE READING FLUENCY

Targeted Passage Use paired reading to help students read paragraph 2 with appropriate phrasing, intonation, and expression. Read the paragraph aloud to students, modeling how to use punctuation as a guide to phrasing and intonation. Next, have partners take turns reading each sentence in the paragraph. Then have partners read the entire paragraph again—first one student, then the other. Each time, the partner who is listening should follow along and provide coaching as appropriate.

 Go to the **Reading Studio** for additional support in developing fluency.

world that was both at war and had a murder to deal with. Obviously they couldn't have changed much of that without altering the whole story of *Macbeth*, but for that reason I feel like the story could have done without this **sporadic** technology. Perhaps sticking to a post-apocalyptic feudal Japan feel alone, with a heavier reliance on samurai history, would have been enough. That is, in truth, what I had been expecting when I'd picked it up, and I found the technology, while occasionally intriguing, to be quite jolting.

3 However, I found the artistry to be impressive, with randomly delightful tidbits of hilarious facial expressions (though not perhaps fitting with everyone's idea of the characters) and beautifully created weird sisters and spirit dragons. I also believe that this visual medium for Shakespeare would be a great way to get those less inclined toward literature to become interested in literature, and luckily the series offers a variety of the Bard's plays in various tellings based on Japanese history and culture. And despite not being overly **enraptured** with the work itself, I was impressed enough to want to read these other works, especially those that I hold higher in my personal esteem. Definitely worth a try for anyone with an interest in graphic novels as a genre, especially if they already have a love of Shakespeare's plays or would like to have but find the texts themselves **daunting**.

sporadic
(spə-răd´ĭk) *adj.* happening occasionally and at random.

ANALYZE EVIDENCE

Annotate: Mark evidence that the author gives in paragraph 3 to support her opinion about the book.

Analyze: What did Perry dislike about the book? How persuasive is the evidence she provides?

enraptured
(ĕn-răp´chərd) *adj.* filled with delight.

daunting
(dônt´ing) *adj.* seemingly impossible.

CHECK YOUR UNDERSTANDING

Answer these questions before moving on to the **Analyze the Text** section.

1 What is Perry's overall reaction to *Manga Shakespeare: Macbeth*?

  A It's fantastic!

  B It's OK.

  C It's pretty bad.

  D She didn't read it.

2 What aspect of the graphic novel bothered Perry?

  F The use of Shakespeare's language

  G The feudal Japanese setting

  H The sporadic use of technology

  J The characters' expressions

3 Which of these disclaimers does Perry give?

  A She has never read manga.

  B Her copy of the book was incomplete.

  C She is mostly unfamiliar with samurai culture.

  D *Macbeth* is not her favorite of Shakespeare's plays.

Shakespeare and Samurai (and Robot Ninjas?) 519

ANALYZE EVIDENCE

You may want to point out that the author gives the book "a middling rating" in paragraph 1. Her evidence lies in paragraph 2. Still, with the possible exception of the parenthetical comment in the first sentence of paragraph 3, most of what she says in that final paragraph is positive—that is, reasons why she thinks some readers might want to try the book. (**Answer:** *She is rather disappointed in the work overall, but she makes a persuasive argument for experiencing Shakespeare in the graphic novel format.*)

CHECK YOUR UNDERSTANDING

Have students answer the questions independently.

Answers:

  1. *B* 2. *H* 3. *D*

If they answer any questions incorrectly, have them reread the text to confirm their understanding. Then they may proceed to ANALYZE THE TEXT on page 520.

CRITICAL VOCABULARY

sporadic: The references to technology were random.

ASK STUDENTS to name a kind of weather that can be sporadic. (*rain showers, cloudy days*)

enraptured: Perry wishes she could have liked the book a lot.

ASK STUDENTS to name things that might enrapture children. (*movies, toys*)

daunting: Many readers find Shakespeare's language hard to read.

ASK STUDENTS why the graphic novel is less daunting to read than the original play. (*The novel uses fewer words, modern language, and helpful visuals.*)

 ENGLISH LEARNER SUPPORT

Oral Assessment Use the following questions to assess students' comprehension and speaking skills. Ask students to respond in short, complete sentences.

  1. Does Perry think the graphic novel is great? (*No. She thinks that it's okay but not great.*)

  2. What didn't Perry like about the use of technology? (*She didn't like that it was used so sporadically.*)

  3. Is *Macbeth* Perry's favorite Shakespeare play? (*No. It's not her favorite play by Shakespeare.*) **SUBSTANTIAL/MODERATE**

ANALYZE THE TEXTS

Possible answers:

1. **DOK 4:** *The artist draws the setting as a ruined landscape of destroyed buildings and jutting mountains. This suggests that the book will have a grim tone.*

2. **DOK 4:** *The authors have left out some of the lengthy speeches in favor of statements in which the characters learn information from one another (such as the prophecy and the information about the Thane of Cawdor). Other information is conveyed through the images.*

3. **DOK 3:** *The disclaimer may suggest that the author could be open to changing up the text, as it might make her appreciate the play more. It also alerts readers to look for opinion statements about the basic plot of* Macbeth, *for she read the graphic novel already knowing that she doesn't like* Macbeth *that much.*

4. **DOK 2:** *It adds humor to the title; it seems to be asking, "Really? Robot ninjas?" This reflects Perry's opinion that the technology added to the story is unnecessary.*

5. **DOK 2:** *After explaining her reservations about the book in paragraph 2, she starts paragraph 3 with the word* however. *She uses adjectives like* impressive, hilarious, *and* beautifully created *to describe elements of the book. Her final sentence, a limited recommendation, starts with "Definitely worth a try."*

RESEARCH

Discuss the Research task and the Research Tip. Instruct students to keep their research simple and to focus only on those items in the left-hand column of the chart. Then have students conduct their research and record their notes in the chart, either independently or with a partner.

Extend Briefly review the features of a blog post with students before having them begin writing. These features include the following:

- builds a relationship with readers by being engaging, conversational, and sharing personal stories
- is relevant to its readers
- provides information its readers will find useful
- asks for feedback and then responds to it (*Explain that while students won't be able to respond to feedback in their posts, they can still ask for it.*)
- uses text features to make content easy to absorb
- usually conveys a complete thought in 500–1000 words

 RESPOND

ANALYZE THE TEXTS

Support your responses with evidence from the text. ▤ NOTEBOOK

1. **Analyze** How does the manga artist use the setting to establish a tone for the graphic novel?

2. **Analyze** The authors of the manga used much of Shakespeare's original language, but the play has been abridged, or shortened. How have the authors selected portions of the text to propel the story?

3. **Evaluate** In her review, Perry provides a disclaimer in the first sentence. How do you think this disclaimer should affect the way readers evaluate her opinion?

4. **Interpret** What is the effect of the parenthetical phrase in the title of the book review?

5. **Infer** In contrast to the first two paragraphs, what language does Perry use in the third paragraph to show that, despite her reservations, she recommends the book?

RESEARCH

RESEARCH TIP
Samurai have appeared widely in pop-culture genres such as action movies. During your research on samurai, you might come across sources that have inaccurate information based on fictional representations of feudal Japan. Look for credible sources such as university or museum websites.

The authors of the graphic novel researched the role of samurai in feudal Japan, though they present elements of the culture with a twist. Since the samurai of the manga dwell in a post-apocalyptic world, they are similar to historical samurai in only some ways. Skim resources for characteristics of feudal Japan and complete the chart. Think about how well the manga fits the original story line of *The Tragedy of Macbeth*.

FEUDAL JAPAN	
Time Period	*12th to 19th centuries*
Social Hierarchy	*Powerful families called daimyos and warlords called* shogun *controlled different lands. Warriors called* samurai *supported them. Peasants worked the land for them.*
Clothing	*Men and women wore kimonos. Samurai often wore a split skirt that allowed them to ride horses.*
Role of Samurai	*The military class; supported the daimyos; loyal to the* shogun *instead of the emperor (Mikado). Followed a code of honor called* bushido *("the way of the warrior").*

Extend Write a blog post that explains whether your evaluation of the graphic novel stayed the same as a result of your research or if you made adjustments when evidence warranted.

⚙ **LEARNING MINDSET**

Problem Solving Remind students that encountering problems while working is a common experience—an experience that can be resolved with some extra effort and determination. Encourage students to look for the reason they are having trouble with a particular question or activity and then to consider various problem-solving strategies (including trying other approaches and asking for help). Most of all, encourage them not to give up!

CREATE AND DISCUSS

Write a Comparison Think about how the manga artist chose to portray the Witches of *The Tragedy of Macbeth*. Write a comparison about the effects of the Witches in the play and in the manga.

❑ Review Act I, Scene 3, of *Macbeth*. Think about the historical and cultural setting of the play: Scotland in medieval Europe. How do you visualize the Witches in this setting? How would you describe their effect on the scene and on the audience?

❑ Now, look back to see how the manga artist has drawn the Witches. What words would you use to describe them? How do they fit the setting of the manga? What effect do these images have on the reader?

❑ Write a paragraph comparing the two portrayals of the Witches. Then, using the play and the manga as evidence, write a paragraph generalizing how the historical and cultural setting of a work of fiction affects the text's plot, theme, and characters.

Deliver a Pitch *The Tragedy of Macbeth* has been adapted to many different media, such as movies and manga. What kind of media adaptation of the play would you like to see? Deliver a pitch—a persuasive presentation to someone who can fund a project.

❑ Look back at Perry's review and choose one of her points to incorporate into your idea. Then write a short pitch that persuades someone to fund your adaptation. Anticipate questions that the potential funders might ask you and prepare answers to those questions.

❑ Present your pitch to your group and answer their questions about your idea. After other group members deliver their pitches, ask them to clarify anything you don't understand about their ideas.

RESPOND TO THE ESSENTIAL QUESTION

 What are the sources of true power?

Gather Information Review your annotations and notes on the excerpt from *Manga Shakespeare: Macbeth* and "Shakespeare and Samurai (and Robot Ninjas?)" and highlight those that help answer the Essential Question. Then, add relevant details to your Response Log.

At the end of the unit, you will use your notes to write a literary analysis.

UNIT 6
RESPONSE LOG

from Manga Shakespeare: Macbeth / Shakespeare and Samurai (and Robot Ninjas?) 521

 RESPOND

 Go to the **Writing Studio** for more on using textual evidence.

 Go to the **Speaking and Listening Studio** for help with delivering a speech.

ACADEMIC VOCABULARY

As you write and discuss what you learned from the graphic novel and the book review, be sure to use the Academic Vocabulary words. Check off each of the words that you use.

❑ comprise
❑ incidence
❑ predominant
❑ priority
❑ ultimate

CREATE AND DISCUSS

Write a Comparison Review the steps of the writing activity. Explain that students will write two paragraphs. The first will compare the portrayal of the Witches in the play *Macbeth* with their portrayal in *Manga Shakespeare: Macbeth*. The second will explain how the historical and cultural setting of a work affects the work's plot, theme, and characters. Emphasize that the paragraphs should read as one unified piece of writing rather than two separate paragraphs. Students might link the second paragraph to the first by introducing that second paragraph with sentences such as these: "These differences in the portrayals of the Witches are a natural result of the differences in each version's setting. A work's historical and cultural setting usually affects its characters as well as its plot and theme."

For **writing support** for students at varying proficiency levels, see the **Text X-Ray** on page 500D.

Deliver a Pitch To help students get started, lead students in brainstorming some different types of media adaptations, such as movies, musicals, TV shows, podcasts, video blogs, and songs. Next, briefly review what makes a good pitch: a concise opinion statement, clear and compelling reasons, and a powerful call to action. Have volunteers provide some example questions that potential funders might ask. Then have students prepare their pitches and present them in groups.

For **speaking support** for students at varying proficiency levels, see the **Text X-Ray** on page 500D.

RESPOND TO THE ESSENTIAL QUESTION

Allow time for students to add details from the excerpt from *Manga Shakespeare: Macbeth* and from "Shakespeare and Samurai (and Robot Ninjas?)" to their Unit 6 Response Logs.

EL **ENGLISH LEARNER SUPPORT**

Write a Comparison Use the following supports with students at varying proficiency levels:

- Help students write sentences comparing the Witches in *Macbeth* and the manga by guiding them to complete the following sentence frames: *The Witches are _____ in both the manga and the play. However, in the manga the Witches are _____, while in the play the Witches are _____.* **SUBSTANTIAL**

- Have partners orally compare the Witches in *Macbeth* and the manga. Then have them write two sentences comparing them. **MODERATE**

- Have students share their paragraphs with a peer editor and exchange feedback. **LIGHT**

© Houghton Mifflin Harcourt Publishing Company

CRITICAL VOCABULARY

Possible answers:

1. *If you were sporadic about brushing your teeth, you might experience tooth decay.*

2. *I was enraptured by a set of books set in a future society because I felt the stories led me into a magical world.*

3. *I would tell the person with the daunting task to break it up into manageable steps.*

VOCABULARY STRATEGY:
Word Roots

Answers will vary. Possible sentences are shown.

1. *tele: at a distance*

   *In the science fiction movie, characters **teleported** from one location to another.*

   *I use my **telephone** to call my grandmother, who lives far away.*

   ***Television** lets us see what is going on all over the world.*

   port: to carry

   *I wanted a **portable** gaming system so that I could play games wherever I was.*

   *Public **transportation** is great because it can carry many people at once.*

   *Large ships carry the **exports** to different countries.*

2. *graph: to write*

   *I want to study **graphic** arts like illustration and typography when I am in college.*

   *I'm writing a **biography** about the life of Benjamin Franklin.*

   *We waited by the stage door, hoping to get the singer's **autograph** after the concert.*

3. *cent: portion of one hundred*

   *I got nine out of ten questions correct, giving me a score of ninety **percent**.*

   *Our town was founded in 1808, so we celebrated its **bicentennial** in 2008.*

   *The twentieth **century** was a time of dramatic changes.*

 RESPOND

WORD BANK
sporadic
enraptured
daunting

 Go to the **Vocabulary Studio** for more on word roots.

CRITICAL VOCABULARY

Practice and Apply Use your knowledge of the Critical Vocabulary words to respond to each question.

1. Name something that becomes a problem if you are **sporadic** about doing it. What might happen?

   _____

2. Describe a time when you were **enraptured** by a song, book, or other work of art. Why did you feel that way about it?

   _____

3. What advice would you give someone facing a **daunting** task?

   _____

VOCABULARY STRATEGY:
Word Roots

A word's **etymology** is its origin and historical development. Many English words are derived from the Latin, Greek, and Anglo-Saxon (Old English) languages. For example, the Critical Vocabulary word *enraptured* contains the Latin root *rapt*, which means "carried away." You can see how this relates to the meaning of *enraptured*, as something that delights you and carries your mind away as you experience it. Understanding a word's etymology helps you grasp its meaning. In addition, knowing the meanings of roots will help you define other words with similar roots.

Practice and Apply Follow these steps to complete the activity:

1. Use a dictionary to look up the etymology of each word in the chart, and write the meaning of its root or roots.

2. Identify two additional words that contain the same root.

3. Write three sentences for each root, one using the word that appears in the selection and two others using the additional words you identified.

WORD	ROOT OR ROOTS
teleport:	*tele, port:*
graphic:	*graph:*
percent:	*cent:*

EL **ENGLISH LEARNER SUPPORT**

Vocabulary Strategy Point out that many words in English with Greek and Latin roots also have cognates in languages such as Spanish, French, and Italian. List Spanish cognates for *teleport*, *graphic*, and *percent*. (*teleportación, gráfico,* and *por ciento*) Then have Spanish speakers work together to list other English/Spanish cognate pairs that have the same roots (for example, *transportation/transporte, biography/biografía, centennial/centenario*). Remind students to use what they know about Spanish or other languages to help them develop word awareness in English. **ALL LEVELS**

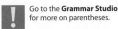
LANGUAGE CONVENTIONS
Parentheses

Parentheses allow a writer to add or clarify information in a sentence. Usually, parentheses enclose nonessential information; if you remove the text within the parentheses, the sentence keeps its overall meaning.

Text enclosed by parentheses is called a **parenthetical phrase** or **parenthetical expression.** Parenthetical expressions can also be set apart with commas or dashes.

Think about the title of the review: "Shakespeare and Samurai (and Robot Ninjas?)." The parenthetical phrase isn't necessary to communicate the topic of the text. It adds a bit of humor, however, as it draws attention to something the reviewer found surprising.

Look at the following sentence from the book review:

> However, I found the artistry to be impressive, with randomly delightful tidbits of hilarious facial expressions (though not perhaps fitting with everyone's idea of the characters) and beautifully created weird sisters and spirit dragons.

The author's main point would remain intact even if she removed the parenthetical phrase. But the parenthetical phrase gives additional information that she thinks might be useful to the reader.

Practice and Apply Write a brief review stating your opinion of the excerpt you read from *Manga Shakespeare: Macbeth*. Include two parenthetical phrases in your review. Share your review with a partner and discuss what the parenthetical expressions add to your writing.

Go to the **Grammar Studio** for more on parentheses.

LANGUAGE CONVENTIONS:
Parentheses

Review the information about parentheses. Ask students to compare the title "Shakespeare and Samurai (and Robot Ninjas?)" with "Shakespeare and Samurai." Ask them what the parenthetical phrase adds to the actual title of the review *(It adds a layer of meaning, and it also reveals the author's voice. It gives readers a hint of the style that she will use to write the review.)*

Practice and Apply As students write their reviews, circulate and check to ensure that they are adding parenthetical phrases correctly. Then have partners share their reviews.

 ENGLISH LEARNER SUPPORT

Use Parentheses Provide scaffolded instruction and practice in using parentheses:

- Display this sentence: I liked the manga. Then model adding a parenthetical phrase: I liked the manga *(even if it was hard to read)*.
  SUBSTANTIAL

- Introduce *especially* and *even if*. Then have students complete the following frame twice, using first *especially* and then *even if* to begin their parenthetical expression: *I liked the* _____ *(*_____*)*.
  MODERATE

- Have students write a short paragraph about what they liked or didn't like about the manga. Ask them to include at least three parenthetical phrases. **LIGHT**

COMPARE ACROSS GENRES

Point out that reviewers will often analyze story elements such as setting, characters, and plot in their review. Since Perry was reviewing a graphic novel, she also considered various visual elements. Instruct students to look back over the excerpt from *Manga Shakespeare: Macbeth* and Perry's review of it to complete their charts. When students have finished working on their charts, have partners compare their results.

ANALYZE THE TEXTS

Possible answers:

1. **DOK 4:** *Perry gives examples of the kind of artistry she found impressive, such as the characters' facial expressions, the weird sisters, and the spirit dragons. She describes these elements with positive words such as "hilarious" and "beautiful."*

2. **DOK 3:** *Perry would have set the play in feudal Japan and left out the post-apocalyptic angle. This would take care of her frustration with the sporadic use of modern and futuristic technology. Students may think that this change would make the story simpler, as moving it to Japan is a big enough change to explore.*

3. **DOK 2:** *She might be frustrated by the airplane: it's a piece of modern technology that appears in the background, but then not much else happens with it. Perry says that she didn't enjoy sudden and sporadic appearances of technology in this book.*

4. **DOK 4:** *She thinks that placing a familiar text in a different medium and context is a great way to get some readers interested in literature, especially Shakespeare's work. Changing up a classic text draws more people's interest, as they are less likely to dismiss it as irrelevant to their lives. Younger readers who might have trouble with texts like Shakespeare's plays can also enjoy the stories when supported with the illustrations in a graphic novel.*

 RESPOND

from MANGA
SHAKESPEARE: MACBETH
Graphic Novel by Robert Deas
and Richard Appignansi

SHAKESPEARE AND
SAMURAI
(AND ROBOT NINJAS?)
Book Review by Caitlin Perry

Collaborate & Compare

COMPARE ACROSS GENRES

How would you defend or challenge Perry's overall opinion of the scene from *Manga Shakespeare: Macbeth*? Based on the excerpt that you read from the graphic novel, do you agree or disagree with her review? To better understand her analysis of the book, revisit the chart you used to record graphic novel elements while reading. Does Perry address any of these elements? If so, what is her assessment of how the authors of the manga handled them? Use a chart like the one below to describe Perry's analysis of the manga. Note that she may not have addressed all of these characteristics.

GRAPHIC NOVEL ELEMENT	PERRY'S ASSESSMENT OF THE ELEMENT
Visual background details establish setting	*Perry is excited about the setting. She finds it "interesting" but also "confusing."*
Characters' appearance, body language, and expressions reveal their traits	*Perry is impressed with the characters' "hilarious facial expressions."*
Dialogue drives the action	*Perry does not address this.*
Font styles reflect characters' intonation and expression	*Perry does not address this.*

ANALYZE THE TEXTS

Discuss these questions in your group.

1. **Analyze** What evidence does Perry give for her positive feelings toward the excerpt from *Manga Shakespeare: Macbeth*? How does she present this evidence to portray it in a positive light?

2. **Evaluate** How would Perry have changed the graphic novel? Why do you think this change would change her opinion? What would you think of this change?

3. **Infer** What do you think Perry would say about the airplane in the first frame of the graphic novel?

4. **Connect** What does Perry think of similar work, in which a familiar text is explored in a different medium and context? What do you think are benefits of these kinds of works?

EL ENGLISH LEARNER SUPPORT

Ask Questions Use the following questions to help students compare the selections.

1. What did Perry like best about *Manga Shakespeare: Macbeth*?

2. What did Perry not like about the graphic novel?

3. Do you agree with Perry, or do you disagree? Why? **ALL LEVELS**

COMPARE AND PRESENT

Now, you can deliver an argument agreeing or disagreeing with Perry's assessment of the manga version of *The Tragedy of Macbeth*.

1. **Plan Your Argument** Review Perry's assessment of the book. Now, think about how you would respond to her opinion. Answer the following questions:

What do I think of the change in setting?	
What details in the graphic novel do I find interesting? Which ones would I change?	
Do I think that a graphic novel is an effective medium for a Shakespeare play?	
Would I recommend this book to others? Why or why not?	

Write your argument about whether or not you agree with Perry and why. You may find that you agree with some points but not others. Be sure to use evidence from both the graphic novel and the book review to support your argument.

2. **Present and Evaluate** Present your argument to your class or a small group. Be sure to do the following:

❑ Speak clearly and make eye contact with your listeners.

❑ Provide relevant evidence from both sources. If possible, show or project specific frames from the graphic novel as you discuss them.

❑ As your group members present their arguments, briefly note what you think about their point of view, reasoning, rhetoric, and use of evidence from the texts. Also, write down words and phrases from their arguments that you found particularly persuasive.

❑ After everyone has had a turn, discuss as a group, pointing out elements in others' arguments that you found effective.

Go to the **Speaking and Listening Studio** for help with delivering an argument.

COMPARE AND PRESENT

Point out that students have been comparing the two selections just by reading Perry's review. They also have probably been thinking, "She's right about that" or "I disagree" at points during that review. The task now is for students to put their thoughts into writing and then to share their thoughts in an oral presentation.

1. **Plan Your Argument** Make sure that students understand the questions that will guide their writing. As students plan their argument, have them refer to the manga, the book review, the visual elements charts they completed as they read the manga, and the charts they completed with notes from Perry's review. Circulate as they write to provide support as they develop their arguments. Check to make sure that they have included evidence from both the manga and the book review.

2. **Present and Evaluate** Before students present to their groups, review some tips for an oral presentation. Remind students that they can refer to their written arguments but that they also should look up and make eye contact with group members. Model how to do this. Then have students take turns presenting to their groups, with listeners taking notes about each presentation. After everyone has presented, have groups compare the arguments, especially regarding points in which the presenters disagree.

TO CHALLENGE STUDENTS...

Create an Alternate Format Allow groups to present their arguments in a way that goes beyond having each group member read his or her argument to the rest of the group. Here are just two of the many possibilities:

• Groups might hold a panel discussion, inviting comments from group members on Perry's review, point by point.

• Groups might create an infographic entitled "We Agree/Disagree with Perry's Review" and list quotations from students' written arguments.

Whatever format groups choose, have them prepare a self-evaluation of their work.

INDEPENDENT READING

READER'S CHOICE

Setting a Purpose Have students review their Unit 6 Response Log and think about what they've already learned about the sources of true power. As they choose their Independent Reading selections, encourage them to consider what more they want to know.

NOTICE & NOTE

Explain that some selections may contain multiple signposts; others may contain only one. And the same type of signpost can occur many times in the same text.

 INDEPENDENT READING

 ESSENTIAL QUESTION:

What are the sources of true power?

Reader's Choice

Setting a Purpose Select one or more of these options from your eBook to continue your exploration of the Essential Question.

- Read the descriptions to see which text grabs your interest.
- Think about which genres you enjoy reading.

Notice & Note

In this unit, you practiced noticing and noting these signposts: **Aha Moment, Again and Again,** and **Tough Questions.** As you read independently, these signposts and others will aid your understanding. Below are the anchor questions to ask when you read literature and nonfiction.

Reading Literature: Stories, Poems, and Plays		
Signpost	**Anchor Question**	**Lesson**
Contrasts and Contradictions	Why did the character act that way?	p. 145
Aha Moment	How might this change things?	p. 394
Tough Questions	What does this make me wonder about?	p. 2
Words of the Wiser	What's the lesson for the character?	p. 3
Again and Again	Why might the author keep bringing this up?	p. 145
Memory Moment	Why is this memory important?	p. 3

Reading Nonfiction: Essays, Articles, and Arguments		
Signpost	**Anchor Question**	**Lesson**
Big Questions	What surprised me? What did the author think I already knew? What challenged, changed, or confirmed what I already knew?	p. 220 p. 319 p. 74
Contrasts and Contradictions	What is the difference, and why does it matter?	p. 318
Extreme or Absolute Language	Why did the author use this language?	p. 221
Numbers and Stats	Why did the author use these numbers or amounts?	p. 75
Quoted Words	Why was this person quoted or cited, and what did this add?	p. 221
Word Gaps	Do I know this word from someplace else? Does it seem like technical talk for this topic? Do clues in the sentence help me understand the word?	p. 75

Develop Fluency Have students select a text and give them strategies to understand the content when they are reading independently or with support.

- Read a passage aloud while students follow along. Have them raise their hands to indicate that a word or phrase is unfamiliar. Explain or act out the meaning. Review and explain the passage, telling students that asking questions can help them comprehend. **SUBSTANTIAL**
- Have students work in pairs. Have each student read a passage from his or her selected text aloud with the partner following along. Then have

students read the passages silently to themselves. Ask them to collaborate on summarizing the meaning of each passage. **MODERATE**

- Have each student read the same passage silently. Have them discuss strategies for staying on task or for enhancing comprehension of the text. **LIGHT**

 Go to the **Reading Studio** for additional support in developing fluency.

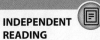

You can preview these texts in Unit 6 of your eBook.

Then, check off the text or texts that you select to read on your own.

HISTORY

from *Holinshed's Chronicles*
Raphael Holinshed

Was the historical Macbeth just as power-hungry as the character in Shakespeare's play?

ARGUMENT

Why Read Shakespeare?
Michael Mack

Hint: The answer isn't just because it's good for you. Find out how the Bard applies to today.

POEM

Ozymandias
Percy Bysshe Shelley

A renowned poet considers what the lasting legacy of a powerful leader might be.

DRAMA

***Julius Caesar*, Act III, Scene 2**
William Shakespeare

What kind of power did Caesar really want? And what kind of friend was Brutus, really? Mark Antony has his say.

Collaborate and Share Discuss with a partner what you learned from at least one of your independent readings.

- Give a brief synopsis or summary of the text.
- Describe any signposts that you noticed in the text and explain what they revealed to you.
- Describe what you most enjoyed or found most challenging about the text. Give specific examples.
- Decide whether you would recommend the text to others. Why or why not?

Go to the **Reading Studio** for more resources on **Notice & Note.**

INDEPENDENT READING

MATCHING STUDENTS TO TEXTS

Use the following information to guide students in choosing their texts.

from **Holinshed's Chronicles**   Lexile: 1630L
   Genre: history
   Overall Rating: Challenging

Why Read Shakespeare?   Lexile: 980L
   Genre: argument
   Overall Rating: Accessible

Ozymandias
   Genre: poem
   Overall Rating: Challenging

***Julius Caesar*, Act III, Scene 2**
   Genre: drama
   Overall Rating: Challenging

Collaborate and Share To assess how well students read the selections, walk around the room and listen to their conversations. Encourage students to be focused and specific in their comments.

 for Assessment

- Independent Reading Selection Tests

 Encourage students to visit the **Reading Studio** to download a handy bookmark of **NOTICE & NOTE** signposts.

WHEN STUDENT STRUGGLE . . .

Keep a Reading Log As students read their selected texts, have them keep a reading log for each selection to note signposts and their thoughts about them. Use their logs to assess how well they are noticing and reflecting on elements of their texts.

Reading Log for (title)		
Location	**Signpost I Noticed**	**My Notes About It**

UNIT 6 Task

• WRITE A LITERARY ANALYSIS

MENTOR TEXT

SHAKESPEARE AND SAMURAI (and Robot Ninjas?)

Book Review by Caitlin Perry

LEARNING OBJECTIVES

Writing Task

- Write a literary analysis about one of Macbeth's universal traits.
- Use a graphic to organize ideas and evidence.
- Develop a focused, structured draft of a literary analysis.
- Use the Mentor Text as a model for writing.
- Revise drafts for use of transitions and vivid details and to incorporate feedback from peers.
- Edit drafts to incorporate standard English conventions.
- Use a rubric to evaluate writing.
- Publish writing to share it with an audience.
- **Language** Identify the correct spelling of homophones, easily confused words, and compound words.

Assign the Writing Task in **Ed.**

Online

RESOURCES

- Unit 6 Response Log
- Reading Studio: Notice & Note
- Writing Studio: Writing Informative Texts; Writing as a Process
- Grammar Studio: Module 13: Spelling

Language X-Ray: English Learner Support

Use the instruction below and the supports and scaffolds in the Teacher's Edition to help you guide students at different proficiency levels.

INTRODUCE THE WRITING TASK

Explain that the writer of a **literary analysis** starts with an idea that relates to one or more works of literature. This is the controlling idea or thesis statement. The writer then collects details from the literature that support this idea.

Review the writing prompt on page 528 with students. Rephrase it as a question: How does one trait of Macbeth's represent something that's true of all people? Work with students to brainstorm words that

describe Macbeth's traits, such as *ambition, courage,* and *guilt.* Point out that any of these words could be used to complete the thesis statement in the chart on page 529.

Tell students that they have probably already noted many details they can use in their literary analysis essays. Once they have chosen a trait to focus on, they can review their notes and their Response Logs for ideas and details that support their thesis.

WRITING

Use Supporting Evidence

Tell students that they will practice using evidence to support key ideas in their literary analyses. Review the different types of evidence that might be used.

Use the following supports with students at varying proficiency levels:

- Refer students to Act 1, Scene 1, lines 16–18. Have them circle words and details that give evidence that Macbeth has courage. **SUBSTANTIAL**
- Ask students to review the mentor text and locate a sentence or phrase they might use in the introduction to their literary analysis. **MODERATE**
- Have students think of an event or response that occurs in all the versions of Macbeth's story. Ask pairs to write a summary statement that will grab readers' attention. **LIGHT**

SPEAKING AND LISTENING

Discuss Ideas for a Thesis

Tell students that they will discuss ideas about what all people have in common. They will use their ideas to develop the thesis of their literary analysis. Remind them that a thesis is the main point they want to make.

Use the following supports with students at varying proficiency levels:

- Provide these sentence frames: *Most people are ____ to others. People who commit crimes may feel ____.* Guide students to complete them. **SUBSTANTIAL**
- Read aloud paragraph 1 of the mentor text. Have students raise their hands when they hear the thesis statement. Write it on the board and have partners rephrase it. **MODERATE**
- Read aloud the following statement: *Anybody faced with danger needs to be brave.* Ask: Is this true? Could this be a good thesis statement? What examples might support it? **LIGHT**

WRITING

WRITE A LITERARY ANALYSIS

Have a volunteer read the introductory paragraph; then discuss the writing task with students. Encourage them to refer to the notes they recorded in the Unit 6 Response Log before they begin planning and writing a draft. Explain that the Response Log will contain a variety of ideas that may be useful as they plan their literary analyses. Emphasize that the goal of the writing task is to trace one aspect of Macbeth's character across multiple texts and to discuss how it represents a universal human trait.

USE THE MENTOR TEXT

Explain to students that their literary analysis will share some similarities with "Shakespeare and Samurai (and Robot Ninjas?)" by Caitlin Perry. Like Perry's book review, their essay will have an engaging introduction that includes an interesting observation, detail, or quotation as well as a clear thesis statement. The body of their essay will develop the thesis with text details, and the conclusion may synthesize ideas to generate a fresh insight. An important distinction is that while Perry's review focuses on one work, students' analyses must include details from more than one work.

WRITING PROMPT

Discuss the prompt with students. Encourage them to ask questions about any part of the assignment they do not completely understand. Review the checklist of key points that students should consider as they write their essays.

 WRITING TASK

 Go to the **Writing Studio** for help writing a literary analysis.

Write a Literary Analysis

This unit focuses on human ambition and our eternal quest for power. What makes the character of Macbeth remarkable is that he's not a monster; he begins as someone we can empathize with, which makes his fall all the more shocking. Review the texts in this unit, including Shakespeare's *The Tragedy of Macbeth*. Then write a literary analysis that explains how one aspect of Macbeth's character represents a universal human trait. For an example of a well-written literary analysis you can use as a mentor text, look at the review "Shakespeare and Samurai (and Robot Ninjas?)."

As you write your analysis, you will want to look at the notes you made in your Response Log after reading the texts in this unit.

Writing Prompt

Read the information in the box below.

This is the topic or context for your literary analysis.

> **Human ambition is timeless, and its fruits are fleeting.**

Think carefully about the following question.

This is the Essential Question for the unit. How would you answer this question, based on the texts in this unit?

> **What are the sources of true power?**

To find a topic for your essay, think about an aspect of Macbeth's character that is a universal human trait.

Write a literary analysis using multiple texts to explain how one aspect of Macbeth's character represents a universal human trait.

An effective literary analysis—

Review these points as you write and again when you finish. Make any needed changes.

- ❑ includes a clear thesis about the universality of one of Macbeth's key personality traits
- ❑ engages readers with an interesting observation, quotation, or detail
- ❑ organizes central ideas in a logically structured body that clearly develops the thesis
- ❑ uses precise word choice, domain-specific vocabulary, and logical transitions to clarify and connect ideas
- ❑ includes evidence from the texts to illustrate central ideas
- ❑ concludes by summing up central ideas in a way that follows logically from the body of the literary analysis

---

⚙ LEARNING MINDSET

Asking for Help Explain to students that just about everyone gets stuck when trying a new or challenging task. A useful strategy to employ in these situations is to ask an experienced person for suggestions or advice. Discuss a range of possible sources of help, such a teacher, a classmate, an older sibling, and a parent or guardian. Emphasize that students should not think that asking for help is a sign of failure. Explain that, in fact, it is a tried-and-true learning technique and one that creates a good model for others with the same or similar questions.

① Plan

To begin planning your analysis, review *The Tragedy of Macbeth* and other texts in the unit. First, take notes on Macbeth's character traits. He is often used as an example of unbridled ambition, but that is only one of the aspects of his character that leads to his undoing. Look at the character of Macbeth from the perspective of psychological accuracy as well as from the perspective of effective drama. Then ask yourself, "Which of his traits are revealed in other texts in this unit and in people today?" Write a thesis statement that answers the question, "What trait of Macbeth's is a universal human trait?" Choose examples from two other texts and from life that provide strong support for your thesis.

Use the graphic organizer to write down important details, examples, and relevant quotations from all of your chosen sources that support your thesis.

LITERARY ANALYSIS: MACBETH

Thesis:
Macbeth's _____ is a universal human trait.

Supporting Details, Examples, and Quotations

Text One: *Macbeth*	Text Two:	Text Three:	Life

Background Reading Review the notes you have taken in your Response Log after reading the texts in this unit. These texts provide background reading that will help you think about what you want to say in your literary analysis.

Go to **Writing as a Process: Planning and Drafting** for help planning your literary analysis.

Notice & Note

From Reading to Writing

As you plan your literary analysis, apply what you've learned about signposts to your own writing. Think about how you can incorporate **Contrasts and Contradictions** into your analysis.

Go to the **Reading Studio** for more resources on **Notice & Note**.

Use the notes from your Response Log as you plan your literary analysis.

UNIT 6
RESPONSE LOG

Essential Question:
What are the sources of true power?

The Tragedy of Macbeth	
from Macbeth film version	
The Macbeth Murder Mystery	
from Manga Shakespeare Macbeth	
Shakespeare and Samurai (and Robot Ninjas?)	

Write a Literary Analysis **529**

WHEN STUDENTS STRUGGLE . . .

Small Group Brainstorming If students are struggling to come up with ideas for their literary analyses, organize them into small groups. Have one student serve as group secretary. Then have students go in turn, quickly naming a characteristic they associate with Macbeth's personality (for example, his ambition, his bravery, his brutality, his tyranny, and his impulsive actions). Emphasize that students should consider Macbeth's character as it is displayed in multiple texts. After several rounds, have the secretary read the responses. Students should then discuss which characteristics they think are most important.

 For additional support, go to the **Reading Studio** and assign the following [LEVEL] **Level Up Tutorial: Character Traits.**

---

① PLAN

Read the introductory text. Then, review some types of support—details, examples, and quotations—students should consider as they explore their theses.

Suggest that students brainstorm some characteristics of Macbeth's personality that are touched upon in the selections. Then have them scan the texts for details, examples, and quotations that support each characteristic. Examples from life can be general, or from students' experiences. If necessary, model questions for thought: What does Macbeth think about Duncan and other members of the royal court? How would you describe Macbeth's attitude toward nature and the supernatural world? Why do you think Lady Macbeth has so much influence over Macbeth's actions?

■ English Learner Support

Understand Academic Language Review the headings in the planning chart and discuss some examples to guide students before they begin working independently.

Emphasize that the introductory paragraph of their literary analysis must state the topic in a concise thesis statement, or controlling idea. Note that the sentence frame in the planning chart can serve as the basis for their thesis statement. Review the structure of the chart, modeling where comments from each text or from life should be recorded. Use the chart to reinforce directionality with speakers of Arabic.

ALL LEVELS

 For **speaking and listening support** for students at varying proficiency levels, see the **Language X-Ray** on page 528B.

▶ NOTICE & NOTE

From Reading to Writing Discuss the focus of the **Contrasts and Contradictions** signpost, in which the writer points out a contrast between two situations, facts, or ideas. Emphasize that words and phrases such as "on the one hand," "however," and "another viewpoint" often signal Contrasts and Contradictions.

Background Reading As students plan their literary analyses, encourage them to review the notes in their Response Log for Unit 6. Suggest that they look back at the unit's selections to identify specific details to support their thesis statements.

WRITING

Organize Your Ideas Emphasize the importance of organizing their ideas before students begin drafting their literary analyses. Explain that students can choose from a variety of organizational patterns, such as cause and effect, chronological, classification, and order of importance. Briefly describe each of these patterns. However students choose to organize their essays, remind them that their ideas should flow logically throughout; each paragraph should provide examples and evidence supporting the thesis statement.

Point out the hierarchy diagram, and tell students they may use this diagram to outline their essays. Alternatively, they may use a more conventional outline. Provide the following sample outline based on the chart.

I. Introduction: Thesis Statement and Interesting Quotation or Detail

II. Body Paragraph 1: Idea or Example/Evidence from Texts

III. Body Paragraph 2: Idea or Example/Evidence from Texts

IV. Conclusion: Restate or Synthesize the Thesis Statement

Explain to students that they can prepare more detailed outlines of each body paragraph by developing a topic sentence and listing evidence from the selections they have chosen.

 For **reading support** for students at varying proficiency levels, see the **Language X-ray** on page 528B.

② DEVELOP A DRAFT

Remind students that an outline is only a first step in the writing process and that they should feel free to change their plans if new ideas come to them during the drafting stage.

■ English Learner Support

Analyze the Literature Use the following supports with students at varying proficiency levels:

- Help students complete the thesis statement in the planning chart on page 529 with a universal trait of Macbeth's. Then have them complete this sentence frame: *Everyone shows _____ sometimes.*
  SUBSTANTIAL/MODERATE

- Form small groups of students who require direct support in drafting their literary analyses. Work together to write a literary analysis that responds to the writing prompt. Begin by focusing on drafting a thesis statement that reflects the writing task and will serve as a guidepost for their analysis.
  SUBSTANTIAL/MODERATE

 **WRITING TASK**

 Go to **Writing Informative Texts: Organizing Ideas** for more help.

Organize Your Ideas After you have examined your chosen texts, organize your ideas. Write a clear thesis statement about how a particular aspect of Macbeth's character represents a universal human trait. Search for an interesting quotation or detail to introduce your thesis statement.

❏ Decide which organizational pattern you will use to develop your essay. Present your key ideas and specific details, examples, and commentary in a logical order that flows smoothly from one thought to the next.

❏ Use your chosen organizational pattern to sort the evidence you have gathered. A hierarchy diagram like the one below can help you plan the body of your essay. Your diagram may need more ideas or evidence.

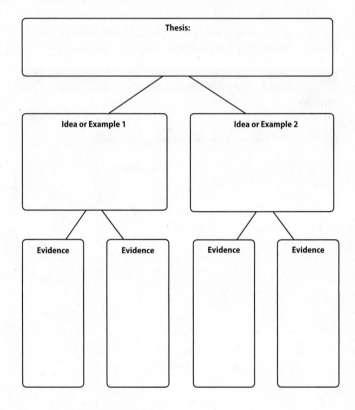

You might prefer to draft your essay online.

② Develop a Draft

Write a draft of your literary analysis, using information from your graphic organizer. Remember that a literary analysis requires formal language and a respectful tone. As you write, remember to analyze the text from the critical perspectives of both psychological accuracy and effective drama.

TO CHALLENGE STUDENTS . . .

Create Graphic Organizers Encourage students to develop their own graphic organizers or ways to list and prioritize their ideas. Discuss the fact that their planning devices are personal and should reflect their personal thoughts about the subject. Emphasize that graphic organizers are most helpful if they include a place to record the thesis statement of the essay, the essay's main ideas, and the key evidence that supports each main idea. Encourage students to research graphic organizers online to spark their creativity.

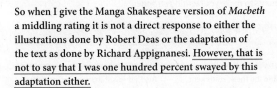

WRITING

Use the Mentor Text

Author's Craft

A clear, effective thesis statement is crucial when you write a literary analysis. Imprecise wording in a thesis statement can confuse the reader. Look at this example of an effective thesis statement from Caitlin Perry's "Shakespeare and Samurai (and Robot Ninjas?)."

> So when I give the Manga Shakespeare version of *Macbeth* a middling rating it is not a direct response to either the illustrations done by Robert Deas or the adaptation of the text as done by Richard Appignanesi. However, that is not to say that I was one hundred percent swayed by this adaptation either.

The author's thesis uses simple, clear language to state that she does not entirely like the Manga Shakespeare adaptation of Macbeth.

Apply What You've Learned State your thesis clearly, in one sentence, near the beginning of your literary analysis.

Genre Characteristics

It is also important to be able to support your thesis statement with examples from the text you are analyzing. Here, Perry cites specific examples of what she did not think worked in Manga Shakespeare's *Macbeth*.

> My problem lay in the sudden use of the technology, from telescoping binoculars and very basic motorbikes, to holographic messages and (admittedly my favorite part of the book) teleporting robot ninjas.

The examples provide clear, specific support for the author's thesis statement.

Apply What You've Learned Choose specific examples from the text or texts you're analyzing to support your thesis.

WHY THIS MENTOR TEXT?

"Shakespeare and Samurai (and Robot Ninjas?)" provides a good example of literary analysis. Use the instruction below to model how a concise, effective thesis statement makes the main point of a literary analysis clear to readers and how evidence from the text can be used effectively to support the essay's thesis statement.

USE THE MENTOR TEXT

Author's Craft Have a volunteer read aloud the introduction to this section and the example from the mentor text. Ask: Which aspect of Manga Shakespeare's *Macbeth* does Perry mention in the lead-up to her thesis statement? *(the illustrations and the adaptation of the text)* Does Perry's thesis statement indicate that she completely dislikes the adaptation? *(no)* Based on her thesis statement, what is Perry's general evaluation of the text? *(She does not give it her overwhelming approval.)*

Genre Characteristics Discuss the introductory text. Ask a volunteer to read aloud the example from "Shakespeare and Samurai (and Robot Ninjas?)." Ask: What major criticism do all of Perry's examples reflect? *(an overuse of technological devices)* How does Perry feel about the teleporting robot ninjas used in the adaptation? *(She likes them but thinks they are part of the problem created by too much technology.)*

ENGLISH LEARNER SUPPORT

Use the Mentor Text Use the following supports with students at varying proficiency levels:

- Read aloud the first sentence under Genre Characteristics. Provide students with sentence frames to think about supporting a thesis statement: *A thesis statement tells a main _____. One way to support a thesis statement is with _____. Another is to use _____.* **SUBSTANTIAL**

- Read the excerpt from the introduction aloud, and invite students to ask about any words or phrases that are unclear. Ask students if this text makes them want to read more, and why. **MODERATE**

- Have students work independently to write a brief introduction that uses an interesting detail or effective quotation. Have students share their paragraphs with partners or group members and ask for peer feedback. **LIGHT**

③ REVISE

Have students determine how they can improve their drafts by reading and discussing the revision suggestions.

On Your Own   Read aloud the introductory text and discuss the techniques described. Ask volunteers to suggest other phrases they might use to introduce an idea or quotation from a text.

With a Partner   Review the questions, tips, and revision techniques presented in the Revision Guide.

Have students work with peer reviewers to evaluate their drafts. Use the following questions as a guide for peer review:

- Does the introduction to the literary analysis grab the reader's attention with an engaging detail, example, or quotation?
- Do the body paragraphs provide a variety of detailed evidence from the selections being analyzed?
- Is there a more logical and effective way to organize the ideas presented in the essay?
- Are the connections, or transitions, between ideas clear?
- Does the conclusion encourage readers to think further about the thesis statement?

Encourage students to carefully evaluate their reviewers' comments as they further develop their literary analyses.

 **WRITING TASK**

③ Revise

 Go to **Writing Informative Texts: Precise Language and Vocabulary** for help revising your literary analysis.

On Your Own   After you write your draft, you will use the process of revision to turn that draft into a well-crafted literary analysis.

Introduce examples and quotations smoothly in your analysis. You might use a phrase such as "According to many experts…." Or you could use a dependent clause such as "As Gloria Perez points out…." The important thing is to use your own words as part of any sentence that includes an example or quotation from another text. The Revision Guide will help you focus on specific elements to make your writing stronger.

REVISION GUIDE

Ask Yourself	Tips	Revision Techniques
1. Does the introduction engage readers and state a clear thesis?	**Underline** the thesis statement and **mark** an engaging idea in the introduction.	**Add** a thesis statement and add an interesting example or detail from one of the texts you are analyzing.
2. Are ideas organized logically and linked with transitions?	**Note** the idea explored in each paragraph. **Underline** transitional words and phrases.	**Reorder** evidence to center each paragraph around one idea. **Add** transitions to link ideas.
3. Does text evidence support the ideas in each paragraph?	**Mark** text evidence in each paragraph.	**Add** evidence from more than one text to each paragraph.
4. Are quotations smoothly integrated into the analysis?	**Mark** quotations that support ideas. **Underline** the introductory text for each quotation.	**Add** phrases or dependent clauses to introduce quotations.
5. Does the conclusion effectively summarize ideas?	**Underline** the restated thesis or summary of ideas in the conclusion.	**Add** a restatement of the thesis or summary of the essay's ideas.
6. Is the style appropriately formal, including domain-specific vocabulary?	**Note** slang or informal word choices. **Mark** terms specific to literary analysis.	**Replace** informal language. **Revise** to include literary, psychological, or academic language as appropriate.

ACADEMIC VOCABULARY
As you conduct your peer review, try to use these words.

❑ comprise
❑ incidence
❑ predominant
❑ priority
❑ ultimate

With a Partner   After you have revised your analysis based on the Revision Guide, do a peer review by exchanging papers with a partner. Apply the guide to each other's essays. Explain how you think your partner could better accomplish his or her purpose in writing and share your specific suggestions for revision. Look for language that is too casual or conversational and for misspellings, either of which will make readers take the analysis less seriously.

 ## ENGLISH LEARNER SUPPORT

Write Effective Body Paragraphs   Discuss the importance of body paragraphs to the development of a well-crafted literary analysis. Discuss the following points with students.

- The body paragraphs of a literary analysis develop the thesis statement.
- There are different types of development used in body paragraphs:

  Summary—provides a brief statement of some key idea or event that relates to the thesis

  Paraphrase—expresses what a writer or speaker says, but in different words

  Specific details—should be carefully chosen and well connected to the thesis

  Direct quotation—the exact words from a text set off in quotation marks

  MODERATE/LIGHT

4 Edit

After you have worked on the organization, development, and flow of ideas in your literary analysis, you can look carefully at the finer points of your draft. Edit for the proper use of standard English conventions and be sure to correct any misspellings or grammatical errors.

Language Conventions

Correct Spelling Take the time to check the spelling in your literary analysis, for two reasons:

> **!** Go to **Spelling** in the **Grammar Studio** to learn more.

- **Misspellings** make your essays, articles, and reports more difficult to read. If you want a reader to pay attention to what you have to say, you should make it as easy as possible for them to read and understand your ideas.

- **Correct spelling** is an important part of meeting academic writing standards. Writing that does not meet academic standards will hurt your performance evaluations and prevent you from getting the credit you should have for otherwise good work.

Here are three types of spelling errors that you should avoid and that your computer's spell-check program will not catch for you.

ERROR	EXAMPLE
Homophone Confusion	When the Witches make **there** first prediction, Macbeth does not know whether to believe them. **Solution:** Replace *there* with *their*.
Easily Confused Words	Costume designers love designing the **Whiches'** costumes for Macbeth. **Solution:** Replace *Whiches'* with *Witches'*.
Incorrectly Divided Compounds	The Witches' predictions are a remarkably effective use of **fore shadowing**. **Solution:** Replace *fore shadowing* with *foreshadowing*.

5 Publish

Finalize your literary analysis, and choose a way to share it with your audience. Consider these options:

- Present your literary analysis as a speech to the class.
- Post your literary analysis as a blog on a classroom or school website.

4 EDIT

Explain to students that after they have revised their literary analysis, the final step before they share it with others is to remove errors in grammar and spelling.

LANGUAGE CONVENTIONS

Correct Spelling Review the three types of spelling errors discussed in this section. Remind students that the purpose of correct spelling is to make the writer's ideas clear to the reader and to prevent readers from being distracted from the intended meaning.

Have volunteers examine the chart and identify the three types of errors listed in the left column. Explain that the word *homophone* means "same sound." Homophones are two or more words that have the same pronunciation but different meanings or spellings. Have volunteers read the example sentence. Ask: Can you think of another word that is also a homophone for *there/their*? *(they're)* Can you think of other examples of common homophones? *(Possible responses: to/two/too, your/you're, for/four)*

Continue discussing the remaining two categories in the chart: Easily Confused Words and Incorrectly Divided Compounds. Write examples on the board. Have students record commonly misspelled words organized by type of error in their handbooks for future reference. Encourage them to add to the list as they come across new examples.

5 PUBLISH

Discuss the suggested publishing options. If students decide to present their literary analysis as a speech, have them refer to guidelines for making presentations in previous units. If students post their literary analyses as blog posts on a school website, encourage other students to read the blogs and post meaningful comments and helpful suggestions.

 ENGLISH LEARNER SUPPORT

Use Correct Spelling Use the following supports with students at varying proficiency levels:

- Read aloud sentences that include homophones. For example: Those <u>four</u> gifts are <u>for</u> the child. Have students identify the homophones, and then show them the correct spelling of each word. **SUBSTANTIAL**

- Have partners skim the mentor text or other unit selections for examples of words that are easily confused. Have students use each in an original spoken sentence. **MODERATE**

- Have students work in small groups to identify examples of closed compounds *(boxcar)*, open compounds *(living room)*, and hyphenated compounds *(brother-in-law)*. After each student reads an example aloud, have others identify the compound word and then correctly spell its plural form. **LIGHT**

WRITING

USE THE SCORING GUIDE

Allow students time to read the scoring guide. Encourage them to ask questions about any ideas, sentences, phrases, or words they find unclear. Tell partners to exchange their final literary analyses and score them using the guidelines. Have each student reviewer write a paragraph explaining the reason for the score he or she awarded in each category.

 **WRITING TASK**

Use the scoring guide to evaluate your literary analysis.

	Organization/Progression	Development of Ideas	Use of Language and Conventions
4	• The organization is effective and appropriate to the purpose. • All ideas are focused on the topic specified in the prompt. • Transitions clearly show the relationship among ideas.	• The introduction catches the reader's attention and clearly states the thesis. • The body of the analysis develops key ideas in a clear and logical way. • The ideas are well supported by examples and details from literary texts and from life. • The conclusion presents a thought-provoking statement about the topic.	• Language and word choice is purposeful and precise. • The style is appropriately formal. • Phrases and dependent clauses are used consistently to smoothly embed quotations in the text. • Spelling, capitalization, and punctuation are correct. • Grammar and usage are correct.
3	• The organization is, for the most part, effective and appropriate to the purpose. • Most ideas are focused on the topic specified in the prompt. • Transitions generally clarify the relationship among ideas.	• The introduction could be more engaging. The thesis is stated. • The body of the essay develops key ideas in a fairly logical way. • The ideas are supported by examples and details from the literary texts and from life. • The conclusion presents a statement about the topic.	• Language is for the most part specific and clear. • The style is mostly formal. • Phrases and dependent clauses introduce most quotations. • Some spelling, capitalization, and punctuation errors are present. • Some grammar and usage errors occur.
2	• The organization is evident but is not always appropriate to the purpose. • Only some ideas are focused on the topic specified in the prompt. • More transitions are needed to show relationships among ideas.	• The introduction is not engaging. A vague thesis is stated. • The analysis shares one or more key ideas but does not develop them in a logical way. • Ideas are supported by few examples and details from the literary texts and/or from life. • The conclusion merely restates the thesis.	• Language is somewhat vague and unclear. • The style is often informal. • Phrases and dependent clauses occasionally introduce quotations and examples. • Several errors in spelling, capitalization, and punctuation occur. • Grammar and usage are often incorrect, but the writer's ideas are still clear.
1	• The organization is not appropriate to the purpose. • Ideas are not focused on the topic specified in the prompt. • No transitions are used, making the essay difficult to understand.	• The introduction and thesis are missing or confusing. • The analysis does not logically develop ideas that support the thesis statement. • Ideas presented are not supported by evidence. • The conclusion is missing or illogical.	• Language is vague and style is too informal. • Quotations, if present, are not introduced. • Many spelling, capitalization, and punctuation errors interfere with reading. • Many grammatical and usage errors make it difficult to understand the writer's ideas.

WRITING TASK SCORING GUIDE: LITERARY ANALYSIS

534   Unit 6

Reflect on the Unit

In this writing task, you wrote about your own experience in the light of ideas and insights from the readings in this unit. Now is a good time to reflect on what you have learned.

Reflect on the Essential Question

- What are the sources of true power? How has your answer to this question changed since you first considered it when you started this unit?

- What are some examples from the texts you've read that show the sources of true power?

Reflect on Your Reading

- Which selections were the most interesting or surprising to you?

- From which selection did you learn the most about the nature of power and ambition?

Reflect on the Writing Task

- What difficulties did you encounter while working on your literary analysis? How might you avoid them next time?

- What part of the literary analysis was the easiest and what part was the hardest to write? Why?

- What improvements did you make to your literary analysis as you were revising?

UNIT 6 SELECTIONS

- *The Tragedy of Macbeth*
- from *Macbeth* (film version)
- "The Macbeth Murder Mystery"
- from *Manga Shakespeare: Macbeth*
- "Shakespeare and Samurai (and Robot Ninjas?)"

REFLECT ON THE UNIT

Have students reflect independently on the questions. Tell them to think about each question and write their responses. Then have students form small groups to discuss their responses. During these discussions, move about the classroom and note questions that seem to produce the liveliest conversations. Use these questions as the basis for a whole-class discussion that wraps up the unit.

LEARNING MINDSET

Self-Reflection Point out that self-reflection can be a valuable tool for improving one's skills and for developing a learning mindset that embraces growth. Note that self-reflection can help students understand where they may have made errors and how they can avoid them in the future. Encourage students to think about what learning strategies worked well for them and how they might apply them to future situations. Emphasize that everyone faces difficult challenges at times, but that building on one's abilities to overcome those problems will lead them toward greater successes in the future.

HMH

(into) **Literature**

Student Resources

 HMH *Into Literature* **Studios**
For more instruction and practice,
visit the HMH *Into Literature* Studios.

 Reading Studio

 Writing Studio

 Speaking & Listening Studio

 Grammar Studio

 Vocabulary Studio

UNIT 1
RESPONSE LOG

Use this Response Log to record your ideas about how each of the texts in Unit 1 relates to or comments on the **Essential Question**.

? **Essential Question:**
How do we engage with others while staying true to ourselves?

What, of This Goldfish, Would You Wish?	
By Any Other Name	
Without Title	
from Texas v. Johnson Majority Opinion	
American Flag Stands for Tolerance	

UNIT 2
RESPONSE LOG

Use this Response Log to record your ideas about how each of the texts in Unit 2 relates to or comments on the **Essential Question**.

 Essential Question:
How does our point of view shape what we think we know?

Coming to Our Senses	
The Night Face Up	
Mirror	
The World as 100 People	
A Contribution to Statistics	

UNIT 3
RESPONSE LOG

Use this Response Log to record your ideas about how each of the texts in Unit 3 relates to or comments on the **Essential Question**.

? **Essential Question:**
What effect do we have on nature, and how does nature affect us?

My Life as a Bat	
Joyas Voladoras	
Find Your Park	
The Seventh Man	
Carry	

UNIT 4
RESPONSE LOG

Use this Response Log to record your ideas about how each of the texts in Unit 4 relates to or comments on the **Essential Question**.

? **Essential Question:**
What do we need in order to feel free?

Letter from Birmingham Jail	
Elsewhere	
The Hawk Can Soar	
The Briefcase	
from Letter to Viceroy, Lord Irwin	
from Gandhi: The Rise to Fame	

UNIT 5
RESPONSE LOG

Use this Response Log to record your ideas about how each of the texts in Unit 5 relates to or comments on the **Essential Question**.

? **Essential Question:**
How do changes around us reveal who we are?

from Total Eclipse	
from The Fever	
A Sound of Thunder	
5 P.M., Tuesday, August 23, 2005	
from Rivers and Tides	
Sonnets to Orpheus, Part Two, XII	

UNIT 6
RESPONSE LOG

? **Essential Question:**
What are the sources of true power?

The Tragedy of Macbeth	
from Macbeth (film version)	
The Macbeth Murder Mystery	
from Manga Shakespeare: Macbeth	
Shakespeare and Samurai (and Robot Ninjas?)	

Using a Glossary

A glossary is an alphabetical list of vocabulary words. Use a glossary just as you would a dictionary—to determine the meanings, parts of speech, pronunciation, and syllabification of words. (Some technical, foreign, and more obscure words in this book are defined for you in the footnotes that accompany many of the selections.)

Many words in the English language have more than one meaning. This glossary gives the meanings that apply to the words as they are used in the selections in this book.

The following abbreviations are used to identify parts of speech of words:

adj. adjective   *adv.* adverb   *n.* noun   *v.* verb

Each word's pronunciation is given in parentheses. A guide to the pronunciation symbols appears in the Pronunciation Key below. The stress marks in the Pronunciation Key are used to indicate the force given to each syllable in a word. They can also help you determine where words are divided into syllables.

For more information about the words in this glossary or for information about words not listed here, consult a dictionary.

Pronunciation Key

Symbol	Examples	Symbol	Examples	Symbol	Examples
ă	pat	m	mum	ûr	urge, term, firm, word, heard
ā	pay	n	no, sudden* (sud´n)	v	valve
ä	father	ng	thing	w	with
âr	care	ŏ	pot	y	yes
b	bib	ō	toe	z	zebra, xylem
ch	church	ô	caught, paw	zh	vision, pleasure, garage
d	deed, milled	oi	noise	ə	about, item, edible, gallop, circus
ĕ	pet	ŏŏ	took	ər	butter
ē	bee	ōō	boot		
f	fife, phase, rough	ŏŏr	lure		
g	gag	ôr	core		
h	hat	ou	out	**Sounds in Foreign Words**	
hw	which	p	pop	KH	*German* ich, ach; *Scottish* loch
ĭ	pit	r	roar	N	*French,* bon (bôn)
ī	pie, by	s	sauce	œ	*French* feu, œuf; *German* schön
îr	pier	sh	ship, dish	ü	*French* tu; *German* über
j	judge	t	tight, stopped		
k	kick, cat, pique	th	thin		
l	lid, needle* (nēd´l)	*th*	this		
		ŭ	cut		

*In English the consonants *l* and *n* often constitute complete syllables by themselves.

Stress Marks

The relative emphasis with which the syllables of a word or phrase are spoken, called stress, is indicated in three different ways. The strongest, or primary, stress is marked with a bold mark (´). An intermediate, or secondary, level of stress is marked with a similar but lighter mark (´). The weakest stress is unmarked. Words of one syllable show no stress mark.

© Houghton Mifflin Harcourt Publishing Company

GLOSSARY OF ACADEMIC VOCABULARY

abstract (ăb-străkt´) *adj.* apart from physical existence; theoretical rather than concrete.

advocate (ăd´və-kāt) *v.* to argue for or plead in favor of.

comprehensive (kŏm-prĭ-hĕn´sĭv) *adj.* complete or of sufficient scope to include all aspects.

comprise (kəm-prīz´) *v.* to consist or be made up of.

differentiate (dĭf-ə-rĕn´shē-āt) *v.* to distinguish or demonstrate the individual qualities of.

discrete (dĭ-skrēt´) *adj.* made up of separate or distinct things or parts.

discriminate (dĭ-skrĭm´ə-nāt) *v.* to note clear differences; to separate into categories.

diverse (dĭ-vûrs´) *adj.* made up of elements that are different from each other.

domain (dō-mān´) *n.* a sphere of activity.

enhance (ĕn-hăns´) *v.* to make better, or add to the value or effectiveness.

equivalent (ĭ-kwĭv´ə-lənt) *adj.* equal to or similar.

evoke (ĭ-vōk´) *v.* to draw forth or produce.

evolve (ĭ-vŏlv´) *v.* to change or develop gradually over time.

explicit (ĭk-splĭs´ĭt) *adj.* clearly stated or expressed.

facilitate (fə-sĭl´ĭ-tāt) *v.* to make something easier.

incentive (ĭn-sĕn´tĭv) *n.* an inducement or motivation to do something.

incidence (ĭn´sĭ-dəns) *n.* the occurrence or frequency of something.

incorporate (ĭn-kôr´pə-rāt) *v.* to absorb or make part of a whole.

infer (ĭn-fûr´) *v.* to deduce from evidence or reason.

inhibit (ĭn-hĭb´ĭt) *v.* to hold back or prevent from acting.

innovate (ĭn´ə-vāt) *v.* to change or develop through new or original methods, processes, or ideas.

intervene (ĭn-tər-vēn´) *v.* to come between two things, persons, or events.

mode (mōd) *n.* a way or means for expressing or doing something.

orient (ôr´ē-ənt) *v.* to place or align in relation to something else.

perspective (pər-spĕk´tĭv) *n.* a viewpoint from a particular position; an outlook or standpoint.

predominant (prĭ-dŏm´ə-nənt) *adj.* having influence or importance.

priority (prī-ôr´ĭ-tē) *n.* something that is more important or considered more important than another thing.

rational (răsh´ə-nəl) *adj.* based on logic or sound reasoning.

subordinate (sə-bôr´dn-ĭt) *adj.* belonging to a lower class or rank.

ultimate (ŭl´tə-mĭt) *adj.* concluding a process or progression; final.

GLOSSARY OF CRITICAL VOCABULARY

acuity (ə-kyōō´ĭ-tē) *n.* critical perceptiveness; awareness.

anomalous (ə-nŏm´ə-ləs) *adj.* unusual; different from the norm.

atrophy (ăt´rə-fē) *v.* to deteriorate due to disease, injury, or lack of use.

beleaguered (bĭ-lē´gərd) *adj.* troubled with many problems.

beneficent (bə-nĕf´ĭ-sənt) *adj.* beneficial; producing good.

cognizant (kŏg´nĭ-zənt) *adj.* aware or conscious of.

complacency (kəm-plā´sən-sē) *n.* contented self-satisfaction.

compulsion (kəm-pŭl´shən) *n.* forced obligation.

consecrate (kŏn´sĭ-krāt) *v.* to make or define as sacred.

consensus (kən-sĕn´səs) *n.* agreement.

contemptuous (kən-tĕmp´chŏŏ-əs) *adj.* scornful.

contention (kən-tən´shən) *n.* an assertion put forward in argument.

cryptically (krĭp´tĭk-lē) *adv.* in a secretive or mysterious manner.

daunting (dônt´ĭng) *adj.* seemingly impossible.

decisively (dĭ-sī´sĭv-lē) *adv.* in a firm and resolute manner.

delirium (dĭ-lîr´ē-əm) *n.* a state of mental confusion.

denizen (dĕn´ĭ-zən) *n.* a resident.

dogma (dôg´mə) *n.* principles or beliefs that an authority insists are true.

enraptured (ĕn-răp´chərd) *adj.* filled with delight.

entranced (ĕn-trănsd´) *v.* filled with wonder and delight.

equidistant (ē-kwĭ-dĭs´tənt) *adj.* at equal distance from.

expendable (ĭk-spĕn´də-bəl) *adj.* worth sacrificing to gain an objective.

felled (fĕld) *v.* knocked down.

flagrantly (flā´grənt-lē) *adv.* in a blatantly or conspicuously offensive manner.

flail (flāl) *v.* to thrash or wave about wildly.

fluent (flōō´ənt) *adj.* able to express oneself clearly and easily.

frail (frāl) *adj.* physically weak.

harrowed (hăr´ōd) *adj.* greatly distressed.

havoc (hăv´ək) *n.* destructive disorder or chaos.

GLOSSARY OF CRITICAL VOCABULARY

hue (hyo͞o) *n.* a color, shade, or tint.

humility (hyo͞o-mĭl´ĭ-tē) *n.* modesty; lack of superiority over others.

icon (ī´kŏn) *n.* symbol of deeply held values.

implicit (ĭm-plĭs´ĭt) *adj.* understood, but not expressed.

incendiary (ĭn-sĕn´dē-ĕr-ē) *adj.* intended to cause fire; flammable.

iniquitous (ĭ-nĭk´wĭ-təs) *adj.* wicked, evil.

insidious (ĭn-sĭd´ē-əs) *adj.* spreading harmfully in a subtle way.

insular (ĭn´sə-lər) *adj.* narrow-minded or detached from others.

interlude (ĭn´tər-lo͞od) *n.* a time of rest between two tasks.

intrinsic (ĭn-trĭn´zĭk,-sĭk) *adj.* of or relating to the essential nature of a thing.

inversion (ĭn-vûr´zhən) *n.* reversal or upside-down placement.

irrefutable (ĭ-rĕf´yə-tə-bəl) *adj.* impossible to disprove; unquestionable.

lucid (lo͞o´sĭd) *adj.* thinking rationally and clearly.

malevolence (mə-lĕv´ə-ləns) *n.* the quality of having a harmful influence.

manifest (măn´ə-fĕst) *v.* to show or reveal.

moratorium (môr-ə-tôr´ē-əm) *n.* a temporary suspension or agreed-upon delay.

mores (môr´āz) *n.* established customs and conventions.

occult (ə-kŭlt´) *adj.* mysterious or hidden.

paradox (păr´ə-dŏks) *n.* something that has or seems to have contradictory qualities.

peremptory (pə-rĕmp´tə-rē) *adj.* imperative; required; not able to be denied.

permeate (pûr´mē-āt) *v.* to spread through an area.

poignant (poin´yənt) *adj.* emotionally moving or stimulating.

precarious (prĭ-kâr´ē-əs) *adj.* dangerously insecure.

precipitate (prĭ-sĭp´ĭ-tāt) *v.* to cause something to happen rapidly or unexpectedly.

premonition (prĕm-ə-nĭsh´ən) *n.* an unproven feeling that something specific will happen.

propensity (prə-pĕn´sĭ-tē) *n.* a tendency to behave in a certain way.

provocation (prŏv-ə-kā´shən) *n.* an action intended to elicit an angered response.

reaffirmation (rē-ăf-ər-mā´shən) *n.* the act of verifying or endorsing again.

recede (rĭ-sēd´) *v.* to move back or away from something.

reconciliation (rĕk-ən-sĭl-ē-ā´shən) *n.* the act of coming to an agreement.

resilience (rĭ-zĭl´yəns) *n.* ability to return to a normal state after a change or an injury.

retaliate (rĭ-tăl´ē-āt) *v.* to respond in kind to having been acted upon, often with harmful intent.

sacrilegious (săk-rə-lĭj´əs) *adj.* grossly irreverent toward what is sacred.

sanctity (săngk´tĭ-tē) *n.* sacredness or ultimate importance.

saturate (săch´ə-rāt) *v.* to soak with liquid to the point where nothing more can be absorbed.

secluded (sĭ-klōō´dĭd) *adj.* hidden from view.

sedately (sĭ-dāt´lē) *adv.* in a calm and dignified manner.

sentiment (sĕn´tə-mənt) *n.* the emotion behind something.

sociable (sō´shə-bəl) *adj.* able to enjoy the company of others.

solace (sŏl´ĭs) *n.* source of relief and comfort.

sporadic (spə-răd´ĭk) *adj.* happening occasionally and at random.

stimuli (stĭm´yə-lī) *n.* things that cause a response or reaction.

subliminal (sŭb-lĭm´ə-nəl) *adj.* below the level of awareness.

subtle (sŭt´l) *adj.* so slight as to be difficult to detect or describe.

subtleties (sŭt´l-tēz) *n.* fine details or nuances.

taut (tôt) *adj.* pulled tight; tense.

tepid (tĕp´id) *adj.* neither hot nor cold; lukewarm.

transcend (trăn-sĕnd´) *v.* to go beyond or rise above.

translucent (trăns-lōō´sənt) *adj.* semitransparent; indistinct.

transpire (trăn-spīr´) *v.* to happen or occur.

unadulterated (ŭn-ə-dŭl´tə-rā-tĭd) *adj.* pure and untainted.

undulate (ŭn´jə-lāt) *v.* to move in waves.

unpalatable (ŭn-păl´ə-tə-bəl) *adj.* unpleasant or unacceptable.

vestige (vĕs´tĭj) *n.* a visible trace of something that once existed.

virulence (vîr´yə-ləns) *n.* the quality of aggressively causing disease.

wane (wān) *v.* to gradually decrease in size or intensity.

wizened (wĭz´ənd) *adj.* shrunken and wrinkled.

Index of Skills

Key

Teacher's Edition subject entries and page references are printed in **boldface** type. Subject entries and page references that apply to both the Student Edition and Teacher's Edition appear in lightface type.

A

Absolute Language. *See* Extreme or Absolute Language (Notice & Note)

Academic Vocabulary, 1, 73, 143, 219, 317, 393

accuracy, of sources, 38, 172, 328, 340

active voice, 286, 295

affixes, 342

Again and Again (Notice & Note), 96, 145, 152, 183, 288, 395, 406, 422

agreement
    pronoun-antecedent, 490, 499
    subject-verb, 334, 339, 343

Aha Moment (Notice & Note), 100, 354, 394, 408, 473

allusions, 266
    classical, 350
    historical, 326, 328, 350
    literary, 261

American Psychological Association (APA), 387

analysis, writing, 103, 155, 255, 293, 371, 418, 487

analyze, 14, 28, 38, 46, 56, 60, 102, 112, 126, 154, 166, 192, 202, 244, 254, 264, 280, 292, 360, 370, 378, 418, 432, 448, 466, 480, 496, 520, 524
    accounts, 302
    archetypes, 5, 11
    argument, 228, 231, 238, 241, 242, 287
    audience, 60
    author's purpose, 19, 23, 27
    character, 271, 275, 276, 277, 278
    character and theme, 425, 467
    development of ideas, 77, 80, 82, 84
    diction and syntax, 259, 261, 262
    drama, 413, 420, 443, 463
    evidence, 519
    figurative language, 108, 110
    free verse, 198, 200
    historical context, 19, 22, 25
    language, 147, 150, 151
    literary devices, 5, 8, 121, 124
    literary nonfiction, 325
    media, 172, 300, 486
    media techniques and purposes, 170
    motif, 251
    motives, 116, 117
    plot, 175, 178, 180, 190
    plot structure, 91, 94, 95, 96, 98, 356
    poetic structure, 252
    purpose, 60

purpose and audience, 337
rhetoric, 51, 53, 288
satire, 491
setting, 33, 35, 356
speaker, 107, 109
structure, 122, 123, 147, 149, 153, 159, 162, 252
style, 159, 162, 327
symbols, 175, 181, 186, 187, 190, 197, 200
text structure, 260, 335
theme, 103, 175, 181, 186, 187, 190, 197, 200, 272
tone, 77, 79
visual elements, 505, 507, 511, 513

analytic writing, 103, 155, 255, 293, 371, 418, 487

Analyze the Text
    analyze, 14, 28, 38, 46, 56, 60, 102, 112, 126, 154, 166, 192, 202, 244, 254, 264, 280, 292, 360, 370, 378, 418, 432, 448, 466, 480, 496, 520, 524
    cause/effect, 496
    cite evidence, 28, 46, 264, 280, 292, 340, 370, 432, 480
    compare, 46, 60, 86, 102, 128, 154, 166, 204, 328, 378, 448
    connect, 46, 60, 204, 380, 496, 524
    contrast, 128, 380
    critique, 264, 328
    draw conclusions, 14, 112, 126, 244, 254, 280, 292, 360, 370, 418, 448, 466, 496
    evaluate, 14, 38, 56, 60, 86, 102, 126, 128, 154, 166, 192, 204, 254, 264, 292, 340, 480, 520, 524
    identify, 38, 86, 340, 378
    infer, 14, 28, 38, 46, 56, 102, 112, 126, 192, 264, 340, 360, 370, 378, 380, 418, 432, 448, 466, 520, 524
    interpret, 28, 38, 154, 166, 192, 202, 254, 280, 328, 370, 480, 520
    Notice & Note, 14, 56, 86, 102, 126, 154, 166, 192, 244, 292, 328, 340, 360, 418, 432, 466, 480
    summarize, 86, 202, 244, 280, 328, 378, 432
    synthesize, 112, 128, 360, 380

Anchor Questions (Notice & Note), 2, 3, 221, 318, 319, 394, 395

annotate, 41. *See also* Annotation Model

Annotation Model, 6, 20, 34, 42, 52, 78, 92, 108, 116, 122, 148, 160, 176, 198, 224, 250, 258, 270, 286, 322, 334, 346, 366, 400, 490, 502

antithesis, 51, 223, 230, 285, 288, 397

antonyms, 362

appeals, 51, 223, 285

Applying Academic Vocabulary, 10, 21, 53, 81, 96, 149, 164, 182, 200, 229, 261, 272, 288, 329, 337, 350, 381, 430, 441, 460, 494, 507

archaic language, 482

archetypes, 5, 11

argumentative texts. *See* arguments

arguments,
    analyzing, 223, 285
    delivering, 313–314, 487, 525
    evaluating, 51
    writing, 306–312

asides, 396, 399

audience, 60, 313, 333

author's craft, 67, 135, 211, 309, 387, 531

author's purpose, 19, 23, 27, 333, 340

B

bias, 46, 56, 244

Big Questions (Notice & Note), 74, 83, 220, 233, 319, 326, 336

blank verse, 396

book reviews, 501

brainstorming, 65, 129, 133

brochure, 341

C

capitalization, 311

cause/effect, 351, 496
    transitions, 346, 351, 363, 432

central ideas, 77, 159, 166, 373

character, 11, 14, 102, 269, 271, 404, 480

character and theme, 399, 404, 425

character development, 269, 422, 448

character foils, 399

charts, 14, 28, 102, 112, 202, 250, 297
    podcast planning, 139
    in research, 244, 264, 280, 292, 300, 328, 340, 360, 480, 486, 496, 520
    for writing, 65, 133, 385

Check Your Understanding, 13, 27, 37, 45, 55, 85, 101, 111, 119, 125, 153, 165, 191, 201, 243, 253, 263, 279, 291, 327, 339, 359, 369, 377, 417, 431, 447, 465, 479, 495, 519

chronological order, 67, 192, 302

citations, of research sources, 102, 112, 254, 280, 387, 389

cite evidence, 28, 46, 172, 202, 264, 280, 292, 370, 432, 480, 486

claims, 41, 51, 195, 223, 285, 287

clauses
    adjective, 137
    adverb, 137
    dependent, 49, 92, 97, 137, 176, 181, 195
    independent, 49, 92, 97, 137, 176, 181, 195, 283

climax, 134, 147

Close Read Screencasts, 7, 43, 54, 79, 150, 225, 231, 413, 427, 445, 456, 473

Collaborate & Compare, 60, 128, 204, 302, 380, 524

Collaborate and Share, 207, 305

colons, 148, 157
    dashes instead of, 52

commas, 42, 45, 195
    dashes instead of, 52
    to set off phrases and clauses, 49

comma splice, 105, 137

commentary, 67, 302

compare, 46, 60, 86, 102, 109, 123, 128, 154, 166, 204, 299, 328, 347, 378, 448, 491
    accounts, 302
    across genres, 299, 372, 380, 500, 524
    arguments, 40, 60
    and debate, 303
    details, 114, 120
    media, 299, 486
    rhetoric, 288
    rhetorical devices, 230
    texts, 128, 204, 491, 503, 518
    themes, 174, 196, 199, 376, 380

comparisons, writing, 47, 329, 521

complex sentences, 92, 105, 137, 176, 195

concessions, 51, 223

conclusions,
    in an argument, 51, 223
    drawing. *See* draw conclusions
    in an essay, 77, 333
    in writing, 103, 155, 386

conflict, 15, 134, 418

conjunctions, 195

connect, 21, 46, 60, 204, 251, 380, 489, 496, 524
    in research, 86, 172, 264, 360, 480, 486, 496

INDEX OF TITLES AND AUTHORS

ACKNOWLEDGMENTS

ACKNOWLEDGMENTS

Quote by Barbara Jordan from "All Together Now" from *Sesame Street Parents Magazine,* September 1994. Text copyright © 1994 by Barbara Jordan. Reprinted by permission of the Sesame Workshop. All Rights Reserved.

"The Seventh Man" from *Blind Willow Sleeping Woman* by Haruki Murakami. Text copyright © 2006 by Haruki Murakami. Reprinted by permission of ICM Partners.

"Shakespeare and Samurai (and Robot Ninjas?) - A Review of Manga Macbeth" by Caitlin Perry. Text copyright © 2013 by Caitlin Perry. Reprinted by permission of Caitlin Perry.

"Sonnets to Orpheus, Part Two, XII" from *In Praise of Mortality* by Rainer Maria Rilke, translated by Anita Barrows and Joanna Macy. Text copyright © 1996 by Anita Barrows and Joanna Macy. Reprinted by permission of the translators.

"A Sound of Thunder" by Ray Bradbury from *Collier's*, June 20, 1952. Text copyright © by the Crowell Collier Publishing Company, renewed © 1980 by Ray Bradbury. Reprinted by permission of Don Congdon Associates, Inc. Photocopying, printing and other reproduction rights are strictly reserved.

Excerpt from "Total Eclipse" from *Teaching a Stone to Talk*: *Expeditions and Encounters* by Annie Dillard. Text copyright © 1982 by Annie Dillard. Reprinted by permission of HarperCollins Publishers and Massie & McQuilkin as agents for the author.

"What, of This Goldfish, Would You Wish?" from *Suddenly, A Knock on the Door* by Etgar Keret, translated by Miriam Shlesinger, Sondra Silverston and Nathan Englander. Translation copyright © 2012 by Etgar Keret. CAUTION: Users are warned that this work is protected under copyright laws and downloading is strictly prohibited. The right to reproduce or transfer work via any medium must be secured with Farrar, Straus and Giroux. Reprinted by permission of Farrar, Straus and Giroux, Random House Australia Pty. Ltd, and the Random House Group Limited.

"Without Title" from *Iron Woman* by Diane Glancy. Text copyright © 1990 by Diane Glancy. Reprinted by permission of The Permissions Company on behalf of New Rivers Press.

"The World as 100 People" by Jack Hagley. Text copyright © 2014 by Jack Hagley. Reprinted by permission of Jack Hagley.